# Encyclopedia of Networking, Electronic Edition

Tom Sheldon

Osborne **McGraw-Hill**

Berkeley   New York   St. Louis   San Francisco
Auckland   Bogotà   Hamburg   London   Madrid
Mexico City   Milan   Montreal   New Delhi   Panama City
Paris   São Paulo   Singapore   Sydney
Tokyo   Toronto

**Osborne/McGraw-Hill**
2600 Tenth Street
Berkeley, California 94710
U.S.A.

For information on translations or book distributors outside the U.S.A., or to arrange bulk purchase discounts for sales promotions, premiums, or fund-raisers, please contact Osborne/**McGraw-Hill** at the above address.

### Encyclopedia of Networking, Electronic Edition

1234567890 DOC DOC 901987654321098

ISBN 0-07-882333-1 PPBK          ISBN 0-07-882350-1 HRDBK

**Publisher**
  Brandon A. Nordin

**Editor-in-Chief**
  Scott Rogers

**Acquisitions Editor**
  Wendy Rinaldi

**Project Editor**
  Emily Rader

**Editorial Assistant**
  Ann Sellers

**Technical Editor**
  Terè Parnell

**Copy Editor**
  Dennis Weaver

**Proofreader**
  Karen Mead

**Indexer**
  Dan Logan

**Computer Designer**
  Jani Beckwith

**Illustrators**
  Sue Albert
  Leslee Bassin
  Arlette Crosland
  Lance Ravella

**Cover Design**
  Regan Honda

To my readers. I know you are busy.

To Becky. I'm finally home from the battle, ready to cast off the warrior.

## About the Author . . .

Tom Sheldon is no stranger to the computer industry.
Since the late 1970s, he has worked as a computer
programmer, consultant, and network administrator.
He has been designing and building networks since
the invention of Ethernet. Tom has written 30 books,
and his articles have appeared in *PC World Magazine,
PC Magazine, BYTE* magazine, and *Windows NT
Magazine.* He runs a computer and software testing
laboratory where he does research for Microsoft,
Novell, and other companies. In addition, Tom is
familiar to thousands of computer users who have
learned by watching his best-selling educational
videotapes. Tom lives with his family on the Big Sur
coast of California. He enjoys mountain biking,
kayaking, and golfing.

# Contents

# Acknowledgments

The author usually holds the most complete picture of a book in progress, but readers will be happy to know that this book passed across the desk of Emily Rader during its production phase. Her concern for quality matched my own, and she became so familiar with the content that she made recommendations about cross references, related entries, and Web sites. Given the production schedules of publishers, this book could not have made it through the system without her meticulous tracking of details and minutiae. Thanks, Emily!

Thanks also to Wendy Rinaldi, my editor and coach for seeing me through this project. Also thanks to everyone at McGraw-Hill, including editorial assistant Ann Sellers, typesetter Jani Beckwith, and illustrators Leslee Bassin and Lance Ravella, for their hard work on the line drawings in the book. Finally, thanks to Dan Logan for contributing important research.

# Introduction

Life on this planet has grown, as a whole, toward higher levels of complexity. Over billions of years, neural structures and "sensing" organs have become more and more elaborate. One could say that consciousness has grown from this (or is consciousness driving it?). Our own neural systems have developed over millions of years as we "awakened" to the world around us. Now we are very busy creating a global communications network that looks a lot to me like an extension of our neural system. It potentially links everybody on the planet, and it extends our ability to communicate and to "sense" the world. For example, you can connect to a weather station in Antarctica or view traffic conditions from cameras pointed at city intersections.

*"If you look as if you were on another planet and you saw the proliferation of networks, Internet and Intranet, you would see a fantastic project that the human race has undertaken. It is like one gigantic project, and it dwarfs the building of the cathedrals and the pyramids."*

—Alvin Toffler

As this book was going to press, a device was released that transmits information through your body. When you touch another person, the device sends electronic information about you through your finger to the other person's device. It's an on-contact electronic calling card. In another report, scientists had wired some brain cells to microchips! What's next?

Networks and the Internet are no longer the exclusive interest of information systems managers and the technically advantaged. Web protocols have made information systems available to everyone. People tap into multimedia information and contribute their own knowledge. They participate in chat forums, exchange messages in discussion groups, post Web pages, contribute to information warehouses, use collaborative applications, and videoconference with one another. We are creating a globally accessible information warehouse.

This book helps you understand networks and global communication systems by providing succinct executive-style briefings of important network technology. Here are 1,200 pages of concise information including Web site addresses that lead you to information so you can continue your research.

This is not a dictionary, so you won't find an entry for every industry protocol, product, or technology. The publisher did not allocate enough pages! However, you'll find many terms and concepts are discussed within the text, and you can use the extensive index to help you find those discussions.

You can also check our Web site (http://www.tec-ref.com) for new terms, updates, Web links, and breaking news. Be sure to check the site on a regular basis for the latest information.

*Get the latest terms, updates, Web links, and breaking news at our Web site: http://www.tec-ref.com*

## About the Internet Links

By including Web links in this book, we risked publishing information that may go quickly out of date. The Web is constantly changing, and Web site managers often reorganize their sites or move them to other locations on the Internet. The alternative was to leave out the Web sites, but better to have a few bad links than none at all. Here are some tips to help you recover from "Web site not found" messages:

- Most of the sites I have selected are actually lists of links that lead you to related Web sites. That way you have a number of alternative choices in the first place. Web developers usually put author names or titles on their Web documents. I include those names in my listings so you can use the search engines described below to search for documents that have moved.

- Web site developers often rearrange their sites, impairing the Web addresses. That does not mean the document is no longer accessible. Try going to the home page of a site to access a main menu, a search engine, or a site map to find the document. For example, if the address

    http://www.networkcompany.com/whitepapers/ATMpaper.html

    produces a "document not found" message, you could try opening the home page by typing just the domain name for the Web site (in this case, you would type **http://www.networkcompany.com**).

- You can also try the "back-out" method. In the example above, you could back out one step by deleting "ATMpaper.html" and reenter the Web site. Doing so may display a list of documents in the "whitepapers" directory.

- When all else fails, refer to "Search Engines" in this book. There you will find the many search sites on the Web where you can search for documents via keywords. The Web document titles found in this book provide enough keywords to help you search for lost documents. Learn to use advanced search features. At the AltaVista Web site, you can use parameters such as *url:* and *title:* to locate specific types of information. For example, typing **url:unix** will list sites in which the word "unix" is in the Web site address. (Many Web site administrators will often include information about a topic in a directory with a related name.) Typing **title:UNIX** will list Web pages with "UNIX" in the document title. Of course, you can combine these parameters in various ways to refine your search.

One other point: if you are trying to find technical information about Internet standards, refer to "RFC (Request for Comment)" in this book. It describes how to find and search for Internet technical documents.

*NOTE:* *Refer to Appendix A for a listing of Web sites for vendors, service providers, standards groups, associations, and organizations. Also note that Appendix A on the CD-ROM included with this book contains a more extensive listing of vendor Web sites organized in alphabetical order as well as by product type.*

## Major Topics, Including References to other Topics

An encyclopedia does not provide the flow of a tutorial, which starts you off with introductory concepts and leads into more complex topics. However, you can refer to the following topics for major concepts as well as technology overviews. These topics recommend other, related topics that are important to read. Also, don't forget to refer to the "Related Entries" sections, which appear at the end of most topics throughout the book, for a list of entries that are related (and sometimes indirectly related) to the subject at hand.

Asynchronous Communications
Backbone Networks
Cellular Communication Systems
Circuit-Switching Services
Client/Server Computing
Collaborative Computing
Communication Services
Component Software Technology
Connection Technologies
Cryptography
Database Connectivity
Data Communication Concepts
DBMS (Database Management System)
Distributed Applications
Distributed Computer Networks
Distributed Object Computing
Document Management
Electronic Commerce
Enterprise Networks
File Systems
Groupware
High-Speed Networking
Hubs/Concentrators/MAUs
Information Publishing
Internet
Internet Backbone
Internet Organizations and Committees

IP over ATM
IP Switching
LAN (Local Area Network)
Middleware and Messaging
Mobile Computing
Multimedia
Network Concepts
Network Design and Construction
Network Management
Object Technologies
Packet and Cell Switching
Protocol Concepts
QoS (Quality of Service)
Remote Access
Security
Standards Groups, Associations, and Organizations
Storage Systems
Switched Networks
VLAN (Virtual LAN)
Voice/Data Networks
WAN (Wide Area Network)
Web Middleware and Database Connectivity
Web Technologies and Concepts
Wireless Communications

# Alphabetical
# Reference of
# Terms

## 10Base-*x*/100Base-*x* LANs

The IEEE has defined a family of Ethernet LANs (local area networks) that have a range of transmission speeds and media types. These LANs include the following:

- **10Base-T**   10 Mbits/sec over copper twisted-pair cable

- **10Base-F**   10 Mbits/sec over optical fiber cable

- **100Base-T (Fast Ethernet)**   100 Mbits/sec over a variety of cable types

**RELATED ENTRIES**   Ethernet; IEEE (Institute of Electrical and Electronic Engineers)

## 100VG-AnyLAN

Ethernet has proven to be a versatile networking standard. The 10Base-2 standard and the 10Base-T twisted-pair standard are installed at thousands of sites. Ethernet is well tested and well understood. Twisted-pair wiring technology brings the cost of installation down and simplifies cabling procedures by taking advantage of structured cabling techniques. Now, high-speed Ethernet (100 Mbits/sec as opposed to the traditional 10 Mbits/sec) standards are available, such as 100VG-AnyLAN (voice grade) and Fast Ethernet (100Base-T), that provide exceptional LAN performance for the backbone or all the way to the desktop. These higher speed standards are necessary as multimedia, real-time video, and imaging applications, which demand higher throughput, become available.

*NOTE: Although this discussion centers around Ethernet, compatibility for the token ring was later added to the 100VG-AnyLAN standard.*

The 100VG-AnyLAN standard is based on technology originally developed by AT&T and Hewlett-Packard. It is under the direction of the IEEE 802.12 committee. The standard was designed to use four-wire twisted-pair cable like that pictured in Figure 1. Category 3 (voice grade), category 4, or category 5 (UTP, or unshielded twisted-pair) cable can be used. Support for 2-pair UTP, 2-pair STP (shielded twisted-pair), and fiber-optic cabling is also in the works. 100VG-AnyLAN also uses the *demand priority* medium access method that replaces the CSMA/CD (carrier sense multiple access/collision detection) method used in existing Ethernet networks. Demand priority centralized access methods to a hub.

Because 100VG-AnyLAN is similar to 10Base-T in topology, adapters and other components share many of the same features. The star topology and structured cabling system approach are retained, as is the frame format of existing Ethernet. This allows 100VG-AnyLAN to connect to existing Ethernet and token ring networks via a simple bridge. According to Hewlett-Packard, the Ethernet frame format, not CSMA/CD, is the component that defines interoperability and compatibility between different Ethernet standards.

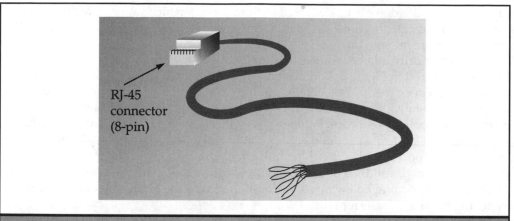

**Figure 1.** *Ethernet 100VG-AnyLAN quartet signaling uses all four wire pairs for signaling*

## 100VG-AnyLAN Specifications

100VG-AnyLAN is designed to use the same cable already installed at many existing 10Base-T installations. Because this cable is rated as voice grade, a quartet signaling method was used to assure reliable 100-Mbit/sec transmissions over the line. While 10Base-T uses two pairs in the cable—one to transmit and one to receive—100VG-AnyLAN uses all four of the wire pairs.

The quartet signaling method uses the same frequencies as 10Base-T, but transmits 25 MHz signals on each of the wire pairs in the cable. An encoding scheme called 5B6B replaces the Manchester encoding used in 10Base-T. The lower signal frequencies in 100VG-AnyLAN, split across the wires, keep radiofrequency emissions within required standards and allow use of voice-grade cable. In contrast, the 10Base-T standard transmits a 20 MHz signal split over two wire pairs.

Demand priority is the new access method in 100VG-AnyLAN that replaces the CSMA/CD method used in existing Ethernet standards. With demand priority, workstations can receive at the same time they transmit. This is possible through the use of the four pairs of wires in the twisted-pair bundle and the use of quartet signaling.

In the demand priority scheme, the hub arbitrates when and how workstations get access to the network. Efficiency is improved with the hub approach because contention is basically eliminated. When a station wants to transmit a frame, it contacts the hub. The hub operates using a "round-robin" polling mode in which it looks at each port one after the other, looking for a station that wants to transmit, and then grants that station (or stations) permission to transmit a single frame. A primary advantage of 100VG-AnyLAN is that it has an isochronous mode that allows prioritization of real-time traffic such as audio and video. By prioritizing this type of traffic, audio and video can be delivered without delays which cause distortion. The station must indicate that it has a high-priority transmission, and the hub will grant it appropriate transmission time.

Demand priority takes advantage of the structured wire design and hub-centric approach pictured in Figure 2. This design is similar to the Ethernet 10Base-T approach; however, the 100VG-AnyLAN hub controls access to the network. In a hierarchical scheme like that pictured, every port on every hub is included in the "round-robin" polling sequence. Polling starts with the first port on the root hub, then the second port, and so on. If another hub is attached to, say, port 3, the polling continues with port 1 on the branching hub, then port 2, and so on until all the ports have been scanned, and then polling continues with port 4 on the root hub. If a station attached to a branching hub wants to transmit, it signals the branching hub, then the branching hub signals the root hub.

If two workstations request the same priority at the same time, both are serviced by alternating between the two. This transmission method is superior to the CSMA/CD access method used in existing Ethernet LANs. In CSMA/CD, workstations compete for access to the cable on their own rather then under the direction of a central hub. Contention occurs when two or more workstations attempt access at the same time. Each workstation backs off and waits for a period of time before attempting access again. This reduces performance and causes more contention because workstations may still need to compete for access to the cable if the LAN is highly populated and overloaded.

An added advantage of the demand priority method is that transmissions sent through the hub are not broadcast to all other workstations, as is the case with standard Ethernet. This reduces the chances that transmissions will be monitored by eavesdroppers and ensures privacy.

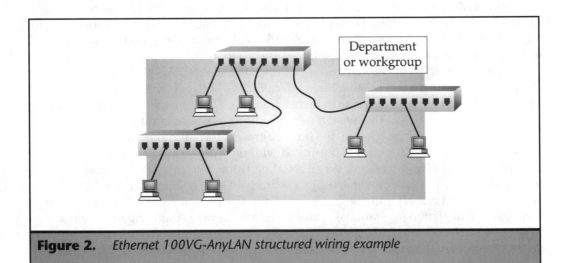

**Figure 2.**    *Ethernet 100VG-AnyLAN structured wiring example*

**RELATED ENTRIES**   Data Communication Concepts; Ethernet; Fast Ethernet; Gigabit Ethernet; Iso-Ethernet; Network Concepts; Network Design and Construction; TIA/EIA Structured Cabling Standards; *and* Transmission Media, Methods, and Equipment

**INFORMATION ON THE INTERNET**

| | |
|---|---|
| Ocampa Technologies' 100VG page | http://www.100vg.com |
| The Unofficial 100VG AnyLan Web FAQ | http://www.io.com/~richardr/vg |
| University of New Hampshire Research Computing Center | http://www.iol.unh.edu/consortiums/vganylan |
| Yahoo!'s Ethernet links page | http://www.yahoo.com/Computers_and_Internet/Communications_and_Networking/LANs/Ethernet |
| Charles Spurgeon's Ethernet page | http://www.ots.utexas.edu/ethernet |

## 31xx/32xx/37xx Devices, IBM

The following devices and systems are part of IBM's SNA (Systems Network Architecture):

- **3172**   A PC-based LAN gateway device that can provide Ethernet, token ring, token bus, and FDDI (Fiber Distributed Data Interface) links to IBM SNA systems. With appropriate software, TCP/IP (Transmission Control Protocol/Internet Protocol), OSI (Open Systems Interconnection), DECNET, and MAP (Manufacturing Automation Protocol) environments are supported. It can also be a mainframe connector/extender, but not if it is used as a gateway.

- **3174**   An IBM cluster controller (called the Establishment controller) that provides a concentration point for 3270 terminals via an SDLC or S/370 channel link. It also provides attachments points for LANs.

- **3270**   IBM terminals that implement IBM 3270 data streams. Other terminals that support 3270 data streams include the 3178, the 3179, the 3278, the 3279, and the 3290.

- **3274**   The predecessor to the 3174.

- **3705/3720**   IBM devices that link cluster controllers at remote sites to an IBM host.

- **3725/3745**   FEPs (front-end processors) that run the IBM NCP (Network Control Program), which communicates with programs running in PUs (physical units). FEPs connect to IBM 3270 hosts. See "Front-End Processor."

## 802 Standards, IEEE

*See* IEEE (Institute of Electrical and Electronic Engineers).

# Access Control

Access controls limit user access to resources on computers and networks. A logon routine that requires a password is the best example. Users are assigned accounts on systems and must supply the name of that account, along with a password to access it. Most modern local networks implement a single logon feature in which the user logs on once to access resources anywhere on the network. The users are authenticated by a security server and carry special IDs that verify who they are to other systems.

The logon "event" has the greatest potential for compromising security on your systems. Users must make sure that no one sees them type in their passwords. Obviously, anyone who obtains a password for an account can access a computer system with all the rights and privileges of that account. A leak of the administrator account password is a serious problem. Two-factor authentication schemes in which users enter a password as well as an access code generated by a "smart card" device are recommended for higher levels of security. See "Authentication and Authorization" for more information.

When creating passwords, never use real words. Mix up characters to create passwords like "Qp&yTx." That's extremely difficult to guess or even crack, but also easy to forget. A more effective method is to create a phrase and use the first letter of each word as the password. For example, the password "Mbiot4oJ" is derived from "My birthday is on the 4th of July."

Access controls can also include station and time restrictions. For example, a user might be restricted from logging on to any systems that are outside of their work area or from logging on to any system after normal work hours. This prevents users from accessing systems in areas where they don't belong during off-hours when they could perform illegal activities like downloading the customer database and carrying it out the door.

Not all systems are tightly secured, nor do they need to be. You can access most servers on the Web without logging in. Likewise, many internal systems are freely available for employee access. A *guest* account, which allows anyone to have access without a password, is usually activated on such systems; however, it can be a security risk if it is not properly configured. Guest accounts should only be given for access to specific directories and the rights/permissions should be read-only in most cases.

Auditing is a part of the access control process. An auditing system can track when specific users log on and what resources they access. A typical auditing system can be configured to track specific events, such as access to sensitive files or activities that are performed by administrators. See "Auditing" for more information.

Access controls are also essential when corporate networks are connected to the Internet. So-called *screening routers* and *firewalls* are necessary to block unwanted traffic and prevent outside users from accessing internal systems where they could corrupt or steal information.

**RELATED ENTRIES**   Access Rights; Authentication and Authorization; Directory Services; Logons and Logon Accounts; Rights and Permissions; Security; *and* Users and Groups

## Access Method, Network

*See* MAC (Medium Access Control); Medium Access Control Methods.

## Access Rights

Access rights are the "keys" that define a user's ability to access resources on a network. They are usually assigned by network administrators, supervisors, or department managers, depending on the management structure. Access rights control the following:

- The time the user can log in or the specific computers the user can operate.

- The resources the user can access, such as printers, fax machines, communication services, and an administrator's or subadministrator's right to manage resources.

- The ability to access directories and files. Typical access rights or permissions include *no permission, execute-only, write-only, write/execute, read-only, read/execute, read/write*, and *read/write/execute*.

Users who have rights to access files, directories, or objects are usually called *trustees* of those files, directories, or objects.

Microsoft Windows NT defines both *rights* and *permissions*:

- **Rights**   Rights control the actions a user can perform on the system, such as logging on from the network, managing printers, or backing up files.

- **Permissions**   Permissions give users access to directories, files, and resources such as printers. Permissions include the ability to read, write (change), execute, and delete files, among others. There are also share permissions, which give users the ability to access shared files over the network.

**RELATED ENTRIES**   Novell NetWare File System; Rights and Permissions; UNIX File System; Windows NT File System; *and* Windows NT Permissions

## Access Server

An access server provides communication services for remote dial-up users. It either controls a pool of external modems or is a modular and scaleable platform that supports plug-in modem boards. The former is usually implemented when only a few remote users need to dial in. The latter is often implemented by organizations with a large mobile work force or even ISPs (Internet service providers) that provide dial-up access to the Internet. These high-end modular access servers support hundreds of modems and are built with multibus backplanes to provide high performance. A typical modular device might also provide LAN ports and T-1 connections for wide area networking. Some vendors of high-end access servers are listed here:

- 3Com Corporation's Access Builder (http://www.3com.com)
- Ascend Communications Corporation Max TNT (http://www.ascend.com)
- Bay Networks' System 5000 (http://www.baynetworks.com)
- Shiva Corporation's LanRover Access Switch (http://www.shiva.com)
- U.S. Robotics' Total Control Enterprise Network Hub (http://www.usrx.com)

## Access Server Example

Ascend's MAX TNT is a multiprotocol WAN access switch that is designed for use by large organizations or Internet service providers. The scope of this device is pictured in Figure A-1. Note that it provides connections for analog, ISDN, leased T1, and frame relay.

The MAX TNT implements a backplane architecture that can be scaled by adding modular cards. This modular approach allows the system to be used in a variety of installations and for a variety of bandwidth requirements. The hybrid backplane implements three distinct buses: Cell, TDM, and packet. Up to 672 digital modem, ISDN, or 56/64 Kbit/sec frame relay sessions can run simultaneously. A single MAX TNT (called a *shelf*) supports up to 16 modules and redundant, load-balancing power supplies. Up to three shelves can be interconnected to provide redundancy and fault tolerance for central office applications. Add-in modules may be installed to digital modem module, ISDN, switched digital, frame rRelay, T-1, Fractional T-1, and E-1 frame relay.

Each digital modem module supports 48 V.34 digital modems to provide analog and cellular connections at rates up to 33.6 Kbits/sec. The 48-port digital modem (DM48) occupies two expansion slots on the MAX TNT. Remote users with a modem and an analog or cellular line can dial in to the MAX TNT over channelized T1, ISDN PRI, or channelized T3 access lines.

## Account, User

User accounts are fundamental to the security of information systems. Most network operating systems such as Windows NT, NetWare, and others require that most users have an account in order to access a system or network. If a person is not assigned a specific account, access is often allowed through a guest account or with an anonymous user account. For example, you can access Web sites on the Internet by accessing anonymous user accounts at the site that do not require a logon name or password.

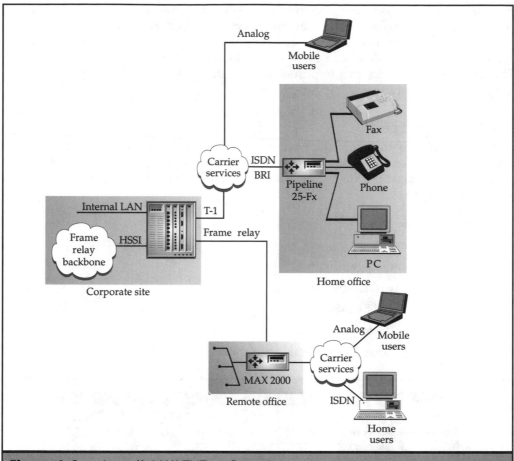

**Figure A-1.**   *Ascend's MAX TNT configuration*

A network user account holds information such as username, password, and restrictions to the network. Network administrators control user access by either changing values in individual user accounts or by setting global controls for all users or groups of users. For example, an account may be temporarily disabled if a user is on vacation in order to avoid illegal access. Accounts can also have time limits, as in the case of a temporary employee. An account can also restrict a user to logging in only during a specific time period (8:00 A.M. to 5:00 P.M.) or on a specific machine.

An account may also hold general information, such as the address of the user's workstation or the user's phone number or department name. In a directory services system like NDS (Novell Directory Services), user accounts appear as objects in the directory tree. Other users can scan through the directory tree, select a user, and view information about that user unless security restrictions prevent such access.

Information about users and user accounts can be seen in Figure A-2. This is the dialog box you see if you select a user in the NDS tree. Note the button on the right, which provides access to other information about the account such as login restrictions, password restrictions, and login scripts.

## Accounting Services

Accounting services are provided by some network operating systems to track the usage of resources and the users who access those resources. Accounting systems also provide network asset tracking. Typical network resources tracked by accounting systems are listed here:

- Files accessed
- Disk space used
- User logons and logoffs
- Messages transferred by users
- Bytes transferred by users
- Applications started
- Access to resources like printers and databases

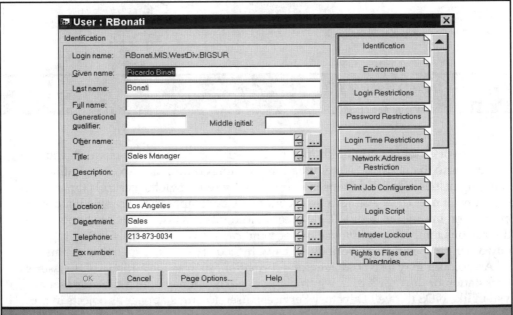

**Figure A-2.**    *User account information in NetWare*

In most cases, it is possible for the administrator or supervisor of a network or server to set limits on the amount of time a user can access the system, the amount of disk space a user can use, and the resources a user can access. Users can be granted a certain amount of time or access to resources, which gets used up as the user accesses the resources. The user can then request or purchase additional time or resources. The values are tracked in the user's account. The accounting system in NetWare can track and charge users for blocks read and written to disk, connect time, or service requests.

**RELATED ENTRY**    Auditing

## Acknowledgments

An acknowledgment is a confirmation of receipt. When data is transmitted between two systems, the recipient can acknowledge that it received the data. Acknowledgments compensate for unreliable networks. However, acknowledgments can reduce performance on a network. If every packet sent requires an acknowledgment, then up to half of the network's throughput is used to confirm receipt of information.

Modern networks such a LANs and WANs are considered highly reliable. There is little need to acknowledge every packet, so acknowledgments are used for groups of packets or not at all. Unreliable networks still exist, however—especially if you are building WANs in third-world countries or using wireless devices to transmit data. Acknowledgments were traditionally handled in the data link layer. This is extremely wasteful of bandwidth, but often there is little choice. X.25 packet-switching networks use this technique. The alternative is to acknowledge higher up in the protocol stack and remove error checking from the network so it can transmit bits as fast as it can. Transport layer services such as TCP provide reliability services in the TCP/IP protocol suite.

**RELATED ENTRIES**    Connection Establishment; Connection-Oriented and Connectionless Services; Data Communication Concepts; Flow-Control Mechanisms; NAK (Negative Acknowledgment); *and* Transport Protocols and Services

## ACL (Access Control List)

An ACL is a list or table belonging to a file or object that contains information about the users, processes, or objects that can access the file or object. ACLs are usually attached to file system directories and other objects and specify user access permissions like read, write, delete, and so on. In object-oriented systems, objects that represent resources like file servers and printers have ACLs. An ACL can define the access rights/permissions for many different users. Typically, the owner of a directory or file can change the ACLs. This is usually the system supervisor/administrator when a system is first installed. Typically, users can also change ACLs in their home directories.

ACLs are implemented in Novell NetWare, UNIX, Microsoft Windows NT, and other operating systems to control access to network resources.

■ In the Novell NetWare environment where NDS (Novell Directory Services) is implemented, ACLs are associated with every object in the NDS directory tree. The ACL stores a list of rights for each trustee (users or entities) that can access the object.

■ In the NFS (Network File System), which is implemented in most versions of the UNIX environment, ACLs include the name of a user or group along with the rights granted to that user or group. Rights include lookup, insert, delete, and administer (which allows ACL modification). Three additional rights define access to files in the directory: read, write, and lock.

■ In the Windows NT environment, everything is an object and every object has an ACL. The ACL contains a list of users, groups, and other entities that have permission to access an object, along with the permissions.

The Windows NT environment provides a good example of how ACLs are implemented. At logon, the user supplies credentials (username, password, domain name), and those credentials are checked in the user account database. If the credentials are authentic, an access token is created to identify the user for all subsequent requests for resources. The access token contains the user's SID (security identifier), group IDs, and user rights. When a user attempts to access some resource like a file, the type of access requested is compared to the ACL. The user's SID is obtained from the token and matched up with entries for the same SID in the ACL. If the user's requested access matches the permissions allowed for the SID in the ACL, the user is granted access.

**RELATED ENTRIES**    Access Control; Authentication and Authorization; Rights and Permissions; *and* Security

## Acrobat

Acrobat is a product from Adobe Systems Incorporated that strives to be a universal document formatter and viewer. Documents can be created with various typefaces and font sizes, layouts, and graphical information; and then sent to anyone that has an Acrobat reader. Many documents available on the Internet and Web are available for download as Acrobat documents.

Acrobat is designed to assist companies in distributing their documents over the Internet, on disk and CD-ROM, or via electronic mail messages. Adobe also recommends Acrobat for long-term archiving of documents.

■ The Acrobat toolset is used to create Acrobat documents. It costs under $300 and is available for Windows, Macintosh, and UNIX platforms. The toolset includes tools for converting files created in other applications into the Adobe PDF (Portable Document Format). All subsequent files have the PDF filename extension.

- Acrobat readers are free and available at the Adobe (http://www.adobe.com) site or at most sites that provide Acrobat files for downloading.

**RELATED ENTRY**    Information Publishing

## Active Documents

An active document is a document that has links to programs or other information sources. The link may display information in the document that is continually updated, only updated when the document is loaded, or updated when the user requests it.

On the World Wide Web, active documents refer to Web pages that are dynamically updated. Note that Web pages may be either static or dynamic. A static page does not change except when the Webmaster makes changes to it. Everyone who accesses the page sees the same information. Dynamic Web pages, on the other hand, are created "on the fly" based on information the user typed into a form or on other information such as the current time, date, and other information. For example, you may enter stock symbols into a form, then get a personalized Web page back from the server that details the current value of your stock holdings.

**RELATED ENTRIES**    Component Software Technology; Compound Documents; Information Publishing; *and* Web Technologies and Concepts

## Active Platform, Microsoft

Microsoft's Active Platform is a set of client and server development technologies for building component-based applications. It is based on HTML, open scripting, and component architectures. The Active Platform consists of three primary components:

- **Active Client**   Active Client runs ActiveX components on a variety of computer platforms, including Windows, Macintosh, and UNIX. It is Microsoft's answer to the Java Virtual Engine. Active Client content will run on any operating system that hosts the Active Client and in any browser that supports Active Client technologies.

- **Active Server**   Microsoft's Active Server runs on Windows NT Server with Microsoft IIS (Internet Information Server). It helps developers build component-based server applications. Active Server includes Active Server Pages, MTS (Microsoft Transaction Server), and MSMQ (Microsoft Message Queuing). Active Server Pages are HTML pages that perform server-side automation.

- **ActiveX**   ActiveX is the glue that ties the client and server components together in the same computer or across intranets or the Internet. It defines how to build software components called ActiveX controls that can talk to one another using the COM (Component Object Model) and DCOM (Distributed Component Object Model) architecture. See "ActiveX" for more information.

Active Platform can be compared to Netscape's ONE. The primary difference is that Active Platform uses a language-independent component model while ONE is built around Netscape's proprietary JavaScript language. With ONE, users must purchase a copy of Navigator to run components. See "Distributed Object Computing" for additional information. Developers interested in this technology should visit the Active Group at http://www.activex.org on the Web.

## Active Desktop

Active Desktop is Microsoft's strategy to integrate Web browser technologies directly into the Windows desktop. Also part of the plan is to integrate the PC97 home entertainment specification into the operating system. With such an operating system, launching a separate Web browser is no longer necessary because the desktop is basically the browser interface. A similar strategy from Netscape, called Constellation, integrates a universal graphical user interface and a browser that is designed to be resident in a server. This technology is based on Live Sites.

## Active Directory, Microsoft

Directory services provide a way to locate users and resources throughout a distributed computing system that spans an entire enterprise. You can think of a directory service as white pages for the organization, except that each entry in the directory services database also holds information about the person or resource the entry represents. Network administrators typically access the directory to manage users and resources. Regular users get limited access to the directory so they can locate resources or people in the organization. The most important thing about directory services is that they centralize information about network resources.

Microsoft's Windows NT Directory Services provides the Active Directory API, which is a set of COM objects for manipulating and querying multiple directory services. It provides the best of X.500 and DNS, according to Microsoft. With Windows NT Directory Services, an organization can integrate the directory services that it may have already deployed. In addition, it addresses different application-specific directories, such as Lotus Notes, cc:Mail, and Microsoft Mail. Internet mail names and HTTP URL names (Web browser addresses) are also supported.

The Active Directory API provides a single, consistent, open set of interfaces for managing and using multiple directories. To help integrate these directories, Microsoft developed ODSI (Open Directory Services Interface), which is a set of WOSA (Windows Open System Architecture) application programming interfaces for developing applications that interoperate with different directories services.

Active Directory components are also available for Windows NT, Novell NetWare 3.x and 4.x, and other directory services that support the LDAP (Lightweight Directory Access Protocol). In fact, LDAP is the primary protocol for Active Directory. However, DAP (Directory Access Protocol), DSP (Directory System Protocol), and DISP (Directory Information Sharing Protocol) are also supported.

For more information about Microsoft directory services, refer to "Windows NT Directory Services."

# ActiveX

ActiveX is Microsoft's component technology, formerly known as COM (Component Object Model). ActiveX provides a framework for building software components that can communicate with one another. A related technology called DCOM (Distributed COM) is what allows ActiveX components to communicate across networks and the Internet.

Microsoft promotes ActiveX technology as a tool for building dynamic and active Web pages and distributed object applications. When a user visits an ActiveX Web site, ActiveX controls are downloaded to the user's browser, where they remain in case the user visits the site again. ActiveX controls may display a moving object or banner, or they may provide a sophisticated program that calculates amortization schedules or financial information. Further, ActiveX controls may provide components that give clients direct access to data servers using protocols that are more sophisticated and efficient than the Web's HTTP (Hypertext Transfer Protocol). See "Distributed Object Computing" for more information.

## How ActiveX Works

In the ActiveX scheme of things, a user's Web browser (or active desktop) is considered a container that can hold ActiveX controls. ActiveX controls are the interactive objects that developers create and distribute to users over the Internet or intranets. As mentioned, when a user visits an ActiveX Web site, the components associated with a specific Web page are downloaded to the user and remain on the user's system for later use.

For the Web site developer, ActiveX controls provide a way to easily manage and update Web content and client systems. Sophisticated applications in the form of many ActiveX components can be put up at the site for users to download. Initially, it may take some time for the user to download all the components, but updates and upgrades are easy because only specific components need to be copied to the user's computer.

Another advantage of ActiveX Controls is that they can work closely with the user interface of the target operating system, especially Windows systems, since ActiveX is based on COM technology that has been a traditional part of Windows. Microsoft's Active Platform technology is extending this high-level interoperability to other operating systems, including Macintosh and UNIX. With Active Scripting, ActiveX Controls and/or Java applets can be integrated and controlled from the server or browser. With ActiveX Server Framework, Web servers can provide security and access back-end databases to provide information from the database to users.

## Security Issues

In the Java environment, downloadable Java applets run in a Java VM (Virtual Machine) on the user's computer. For security reasons, the Java applet does not interact with the native operating system. It runs safely in the VM, where it can't access the memory of other applications on the user's computer or execute instructions that might cause damage to data on disk (although such features can be enabled at the user's discretion). While this prevents Java applets from doing harm to a system, it also limits what can be done with Java. According to a Microsoft paper mentioned at the end of this section, "In Java, you get no right mouse button. No QuickTime. No Sound. No printing. No DirectX. Layout options are North, South, East, and West. In short, there is no way on earth you can create a competitive Macintosh, Windows, or even Solaris application. But in many cases developers will want to trade off rich functionality to support multiple platforms, and for these scenarios Java is a great solution." In the meantime, it is now possible to let Java applets work outside of the VM in special cases (i.e., in-house applications).

Because ActiveX Controls work closely with the operating system, they pose a security risk, but Microsoft has countered this problem with its Authenticode code-signing security scheme. Authenticode provides a way for users to know that a component is from a reliable source. It is the equivalent of shrink-wrapping packages. Digital signature technology and public-key schemes can verify the authenticity of the code and assure you that it has not been tampered with in transit. A similar technology is available for Java called JAR (Java Archive Format). Both Authenticode and JAR are proprietary, so the World Wide Web Consortium (http://www.w3.org) has stepped in to bridge such proprietary methods with its DSig (Digital Signature Initiative), which provides digital signing and authentication for both Java applets and ActiveX Controls. It supports encryption standards such as PCKS#7 and X.509v3. (A very informative paper about standards is "Frequently Asked Questions About Today's Cryptography" at http://www.rsa.com.) The initiative is designed to allow independent software testing centers to verify that code is authentic and bug/virus-free.

## More Information

While Java and ActiveX compete in the market, there is a considerable amount of support for running both in the same environments, so you don't need to choose one over the other. Java applets can link to ActiveX controls, which in turn provides a link to higher level operating system functions. Cross-platform ActiveX support has been developed for Macintosh by Metrowerks (http://www.metrowerks.com) and for the UNIX environment by Bristol Technologies (http://www.bristol.com) and Mainsoft (http://www.mainsoft.com).

To promote ActiveX as a standard, in October 1996, Microsoft turned control of ActiveX over to The Open Group, which formed a subgroup called "The Active Group" to specifically manage the evolution of ActiveX technologies. It also provides development, branding, testing, and licensing services.

**RELATED ENTRIES**   Client/Server Computing; COM (Component Object Model); Component Software Technology; Compound Documents; DCOM (Distributed Component Object Model); Distributed Object Computing; Java; Middleware and Messaging; *and* Object Technologies

**INFORMATION ON THE INTERNET**

| The Active Group | http://www.activex.org |
|---|---|
| Techweb | http://www.techweb.com/tools/developers |
| The Open Group | http://www.rdg.opengroup.org |

## Adapter

An adapter is an add-in board that expands the capabilities of a computer system. In the network environment, a NIC (network interface card) is the typical adapter that provides connections to Ethernet, token ring, or other types of networks.

**RELATED ENTRY**    NIC (Network Interface Card)

## ADC (Analog-to-Digital Conversion)

ADC, or *digitizing*, converts analog waveforms to digital representations that can be processed and stored in computers. The analog wave is *sampled*, or read, hundreds or thousands of times per second to determine the position and value of analog waves. Digital music requires extremely high sampling rates (44,100 samples/sec), but voice sampling is usually acceptable at 11,000 samples/sec or higher. There is also a factor that determines the precision of the captured signal—the more bits used to record the value of the sampled signal, the higher its resolution and the better it sounds when played back. However, the more bits used, the more disk space required for storage or bandwidth for transmission. For example, one minute of sampling at 44.1 kHz using 16 bits per sample (the compact disc specification) requires 5.292MB of disk space.

The telephone companies convert analog voice calls to digital at their central offices (there is one in your neighborhood) for transmission across trunk lines to other central offices or to long-distance systems. Voice converted to digital requires a 64-Kbit/sec channel, which is the rate used worldwide for transmitting digital voice.

Analog-to-digital converters are used in a variety of information-processing applications. Information collected from analog phenomena such as sound, light, temperature, and pressure can be digitized and made available for digital processing. A *codec* (coder/decoder) is the device that transforms the analog signals to digital signals. The process involves sampling, quantizing, and digitizing. The amplitude of a signal is measured at various intervals. The tighter these intervals, the more accurate the recording. Figure A-3 illustrates how a wave is sampled 16 times per second, which implies a sampling rate of 16 Hz. While sampling at this rate is impractical for voice or music, it illustrates how each sample records a different amplitude value for the sound. Generally, a rate of 8,000 samples per second or higher using 8 bits per sample is adequate for voice-quality signals. *Quantizing* is the process of replacing the sampled value with the nearest value within the range of the device and the sampling rate. Digitizing completes the process.

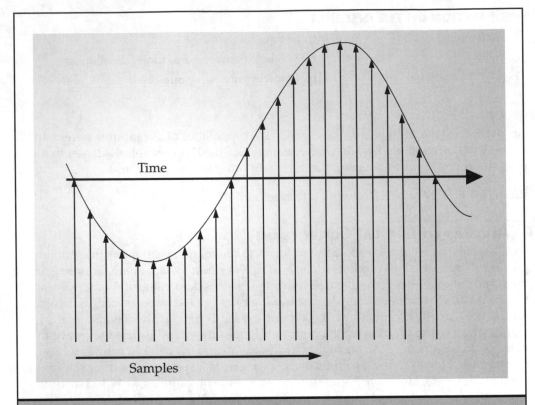

**Figure A-3.**    *Analog-to-digital conversion*

Scanners are devices that record the differences in dark and light areas in photographs and convert them to digital values. The picture becomes a matrix of dots, and each dot is represented in memory as a color or gray-scale value that can be displayed on a screen or transmitted to another device. Fax machines have built-in scanners.

**RELATED ENTRY**    ADPCM (Adaptive Differential Pulse Code Modulation)

# ADCCP (Advanced Data Communications Control Procedure)

ADCCP is a data link layer protocol that places data on a network and ensures proper delivery to a destination. ADCCP is basically an ANSI modification of IBM's SDLC (Synchronous Data Link Control) protocol. It is the ANSI (American National Standards Institute) X3.66 standard. The ISO then modified ADCCP into HDLC (High-level Data Link Control) and the CCITT (now ITU) modified HDLC for its

LAPB (Link Access Procedure Balanced) protocol. The other protocols are described in this book under appropriate headings.

## Addresses, Electronic Mail

Electronic mail systems have specific addressing schemes that identify users and resources on the network. These addressing schemes identify the area or domain where a user or resource exists and the specific node within the area or domain.

The Internet, a global network of users, employs a hierarchical naming scheme as part of its DNS (Domain Name System). An address for a user attached to a local area network or a network attached to the organization's e-mail hub might be the following, which addresses John Doe (jdoe) at the library, University of California, Berkeley. The last portion, "edu," is an Internet-type code indicating an educational institution.

jdoe@library.berkeley.edu

Many networks provide directory services, many of which follow the X.500 set of standards for naming services. Users can access these directory services to determine the address of a user or resource anywhere on the network. In most cases, addressing a message to another person in the organization is a simple matter of scanning through the directory tree to locate the division and department where the user works.

The X.400 specifications are a set of e-mail communications standards developed by the CCITT (now called the ITU).

**RELATED ENTRIES**    Directory Services; DNS (Domain Name System); Electronic Mail; X.400 Message Handling System; *and* X.500 Directory Services

## Addresses, Network

There are two types of network addresses, depending on whether you are talking about a LAN or an interconnected set of LANs (an internetwork). The two type of addresses are as follows:

- A hardwired NIC (network interface card) address that is associated with a computer attached to a specific LAN. This address is usually called the MAC address because it is defined in the medium access control sublayer of the data link layer in the OSI protocol stack.

- A higher-level internetwork address like that used in the TCP/IP protocol suite to identify individual stations attached to subnetworks of an internetwork.

When you send a message on the local network, the MAC address of the destination on that network is used. For Ethernet and token ring network adapters, unique addresses are assigned at the factory. ARCNET networks have user-definable addresses. For example, the address of an Ethernet and token ring network adapter consists of a 6-byte address, half of which is a special number identifying the board's manufacturer. The last half of the address is a unique number for the board, assigned at the factory. This strategy virtually guarantees that no two Ethernet or token ring network interface cards will ever have the same address and prevents conflicts.

NIC addressing does not work on internetworks such as the Internet or an intranet. You must use an address that identifies a network segment and a node on that segment. Initially, a packet is sent to a router on the source network segment, which then identifies a path to the destination network segment and forwards the packet. When the packet reaches the LAN to which the destination machine is attached, the router then uses the MAC address to forward the message to the computer on that LAN. Note that the MAC address is not used during transit across the internetwork.

**RELATED ENTRIES**    Data Link Layer, OSI Model; MAC (Medium Access Control); Network Concepts; NIC (Network Interface Card); *and* TCP/IP (Transmission Control Protocol/Internet Protocol)

## Administrator Account

An administrator is a person that usually has the highest level of control on a server or network. In this case, we are talking not about the job title "administrator" but an actual user account that exists on a network. In the NetWare and Windows NT environments, a person typically becomes an administrator by installing the first server on a network and specifying the password to use for the administrator account. He or she then controls access to all system resources and information.

In older versions of NetWare, a person that installed a server became the *supervisor* for that server only, with unlimited rights to manage that server. In versions of NetWare that implement NDS (Novell Directory Services), the management structure for administrators has been expanded. The administrator account manages NDS and all the servers, users, and resources tracked by it. The administrative user can assign other people as subadministrators for part of the directory tree, if necessary, to enable distributed management.

In the traditional Windows NT environment, a person becomes administrator by installing the first server in a domain. That server becomes the PDC (primary domain controller) for the domain and other servers become BDCs (backup domain controllers). The administrator can manage all the servers in the domain. Of course, other domains can be created, but they can have their own administrators. The new Windows NT Directory Services is built on a hierarchical directory tree, as is NDS. In this environment, a single administrator can manage the entire tree or separate managers can be assigned to manage specific parts of the tree.

An administrator has many tasks. He or she may install new servers, create and manage user accounts, manage security, install new applications, manage data backup, monitor performance, and perform troubleshooting.

All administrative users should have a separate logon account that they use to access the network when performing nonadministrative tasks. Administrator-level access should not be taken lightly. If the administrator's workstation is left unattended, an intruder could walk up to it and potentially gain unrestricted access to the entire internetwork. For security reasons, administrative accounts should be prevented from logging in over the network. Then, if a logon name and password is obtained illegally by someone, they cannot use the information to log on to the network from a remote location where their activities would be unmonitored.

The system administrator's password is the master key to the system. Write it down and place it in a locked safe or give it to a trusted person of authority for safekeeping. Another suggestion is to create a two- or three-word password and then give a portion of the password to two or three people in the company. This "fail-safe" approach ensures that others can gain administrative access to the server should something happen to the administrator. To gain access, they must do so together.

In NetWare, a separate auditor account exists that can monitor the activities of the administrator. This is a good idea. When the system is first installed, an administrator enables auditing and creates the auditor account. Once the auditor is given control of the account, he or she can change the password to ensure that the administrator can no longer access it. The auditor can track the activities of the administrator but not perform any other tasks that the administrator can perform.

**RELATED ENTRIES**    Auditing; Network Management; Rights and Permissions; *and* Users and Groups

## ADPCM (Adaptive Differential Pulse Code Modulation)

ADPCM is a more efficient version of the digitizing method called PCM (pulse code modulation). It converts analog signals to digital data and is used to transmit analog voice over digital channels. Organizations that establish digital lines between remote sites can transmit both voice and data over these lines by digitizing the voice signals before transmitting. ADPCM uses a lower bit rate than normal PCM, which permits more voice channels to be transmitted over a typical digital line. The difference between samples is used and the coding scale can be dynamically changed to compensate for amplitude and frequency variations.

**RELATED ENTRIES**    ADC (Analog-to-Digital Conversion); Multiplexing; *and* Transmission Media, Methods, and Equipment

## ADSL (Asymmetrical Digital Subscriber Line)

The telephone system in the United States is largely digital, even though most telephones are analog devices. The so-called "last mile" is the local loop of wire that stretches from most homes to the telephone company's central office, which is usually located nearby. This local loop is copper twisted-pair wire that has been in place for years and is adequate for voice, but not for high-speed digital transmissions. However, new technologies that use line-encoding have appeared to provide very high data transmission rates over the local loop, including ADSL.

**RELATED ENTRY**    DSL (Digital Subscriber Line)

## Advertising

Advertising is a technique used by a server to announce on the network that it has services available. Advertising was traditionally used in the NetWare environment, although that has changed recently. In NetWare, the SAP (Service Advertising Protocol) broadcasts information about available services on the network that other network devices can listen to. A server sends out SAP messages every 60 seconds. A server also sends out SAP messages to inform other devices that it is closing down. Workstations use SAP to find services they need on the network. For example, a workstation can send a SAP message to a local router to obtain the address of a node on another network.

SAP is a legacy protocol that has been used in almost all versions of NetWare. However, excessive SAP messages can sap network throughput. In NetWare 4, NDS (Novell Directory Services) helps reduce the need for SAP because the NDS database can be consulted for service locations. Still, SAP is still used on NetWare 4.x networks because many network devices require it.

## AFP (AppleTalk Filing Protocol)

AFP is the file protocol in the Macintosh environment that lets users access files on other systems. AFP uses AppleTalk for communication between systems. It passes user commands down the AppleTalk protocol stack to lower layer protocols that handle establishing connections and monitoring data flow between systems. AFP itself resides in the presentation and application layers of the AppleTalk protocol stack. It has the following features:

- AFP sets up an environment for a user in which it appears as if files on a remote file server are available locally.

- Access to server files is handled using the same procedures as access to local files, except that a user must initially establish a connection to the remote file server.

- AFP provides security features that can restrict user access to files.

AppleShare is Apple's client and server software that allows Mac OS (operating system) users to access shared files and printers. It is based on AFP. Macintosh users access AppleShare servers through AppleShare Client software. Note that starting with the Macintosh System 7 OS, Macintosh users were able to share files on their own systems with other users.

Apple's new Open Transport software is designed to replace existing AppleTalk stacks with a new enhanced AppleTalk as well as a TCP/IP protocol stack. With this support, AFP will be transportable across AppleTalk and TCP/IP networks, and will also be able to operate with HTTP, FTP, and Internet mail protocols.

**RELATED ENTRIES**    Apple Computer; Apple Open Transport Protocol; AppleShare; *and* AppleTalk

## AFS (Andrew File System)

AFS was developed by the ITC (Information Technology Center) at Carnegie Mellon University; its current development and marketing is in the hands of Transarc Corporation. A version of AFS called the DFS (Distributed File System) is a component in the Open Software Foundation's DCE (Distributed Computing Environment). AFS is architecturally similar to the NFS (Network File System). Basically, AFS/DFS provide a way to join dissimilar server and client machines into a global shared information system.

AFS is specifically designed to provide reliable file services in large distributed environments. It creates manageable distributed environments with a structure based on cells. A cell is a collection of file servers and client systems within an autonomous area that is managed by a specific authority. It typically represents the computing resources of an organization. Users can easily share information with other users within the cell. They can also share information with users in other cells, depending on access rights granted by the authorities in those cells.

A major objective of AFS/DFS is to make the way users retrieve information the same from any location, allowing users to collaborate and share information. It removes the barriers that separate the file systems of each different network operating system.

AFS/DFS provide the following features:

- A *file server process* responds to client workstation requests for file services, maintains the directory structure, monitors file and directory status information, and verifies user access.

- A *BOS (basic overseer)* server process runs in a BOS-designated server. It monitors and manages processes running other servers and can restart server processes without human assistance.

- A *volume server process* handles file system operations related to volumes, such as volume create, move, replicate, backup, and restore.

- Replication automatically locates replicas of information across multiple locations. Replication can take place while users remain online.

- Optimized performance is provided by buffering commonly accessed files on local drives with the guarantee that the information in the files is up to date. This helps avoid network bottlenecks.

- Files can be moved around to different systems to adjust loads on servers. A *VL (volume location)* server process provides location transparency for volumes, so if volumes are moved, users can access them without the knowledge that they have moved.

■ Security mechanisms for controlling access to information according to users and groups. Uses encrypted login mechanisms and flexible access control lists for directories and files. The authentication system is based on Kerberos.

■ Management of clients and server machines can be done from any point, allowing smaller numbers of administrators to manage more systems. A system monitoring tool provides a view of system loads and alerts administrators of potential problems.

■ Support for building scaleable Web servers.

■ Cluster-computing in DFS allows administrators to run processor-intensive jobs across a network with portions of the processing task running on different computers.

■ Clustering in DFS also allows files to be stored on a collection of smaller, lower-cost machines as opposed to one big server.

DFS competes with Sun Microsystems' NFS (Network File System) in some environments. Transarc developed the following comparisons between DFS and NFS:

■ **File access**   In DFS, the filename is independent of the file's physical location. NFS filenames must be addressed by referencing physical file locations.

■ **Performance**   DFS uses client data caching to reduce network load. NFS does not.

■ **Replication**   DFS supports replication, NFS does not.

■ **Availability**   With DFS, files are available during system maintenance. This is not true with NFS.

■ **Security**   DFS supports encrypted login and data transmission. NFS does not.

■ **Access control**   DFS supports access control lists for user and group accounts. NFS does not.

**RELATED ENTRIES**   DCE (Distributed Computing Environment), The Open Group; Distributed File Systems; *and* NFS (Network File System)

### INFORMATION ON THE INTERNET

AFS and DFS information                    http://www.transarc.com

## Agent, Internet

Internet agents are software entities that are designed to intelligently seek out information on the Internet or on intranets. They are similar to Web search engines except that they are designed to find information specific to a user's request and deliver it in a form that is similar to a newspaper. A typical agent is directed to find specific types of information. It then begins searching public and private networks (where authorized) and returns its results to the user. Agents may operate during off-hours to take advantage of low-traffic periods.

An agent product from Autonomy Systems called AgentWare uses fuzzy logic techniques to search out information. The package also includes a utility that creates custom "newspapers" for the owner based on information searches. For more information, send Internet e-mail to autonomy@stjohns.co.uk.

Search engines such as DEC's AltaVista (http://www.altavista.digital.com) can provide Internet searching through literally millions of Web documents that DEC has already indexed. See "Search Engines."

## Agent, Network Management

In general, an *agent* is a background process that performs an action when an event occurs. In the realm of networking, an agent is part of a network management system that resides in workstations or other network devices (called *managed elements*) and collects information to report back to a management system about those devices. The management system runs at a central location, but in a distributed management system, management subsystems may reside at various points in the network to collect local information that is periodically collected by the main management system. Note that a client-server relationship exists between the agent and the management system, but the term "agent" is often used for management systems to avoid confusion.

In the SNMP (Simple Network Management Protocol) system, which provides a tool for tracking workstations and compiling information about them, agents are called *network agents*. As shown in Figure A-4, agents reside in devices on the network and monitor activities on those devices. For example, an agent in a router can monitor packet transmissions, error conditions, and connections. The agents then make this information available to NMSs (network management stations). The NMS is the controlling device that gathers information from network agents, stores it in an MIB (management information base) on disk, and presents it to network administrators or supervisors for evaluation. Statistical information can show how the network is reacting to its current load and provide a way to detect potential problems.

**RELATED ENTRY**   Network Management

## AIX (Advanced Interactive Executive)

*See* IBM AIX (Advanced Interactive Executive).

## ALOHA

ALOHA is a system for coordinating and arbitrating access to some shared communication channel. It was developed in the 1970s at the University of Hawaii.

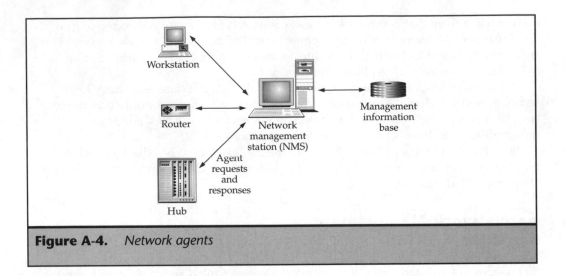

**Figure A-4.** *Network agents*

The original system used terrestrial radio broadcasting, but the system has been implemented in satellite communication systems.

A medium access method is supposed to prevent two or more systems from transmitting at the same time on a shared medium. There must be some method for handling so-called "collisions." In the ALOHA system, a system transmits whenever data is available to send. If another system transmits at the same time, a collision occurs and the frames that were transmitted are lost. However, a system can listen to broadcasts on the medium, even its own, and determine if the frames were transmitted.

This technique is simple and elegant, but another method called slotted ALOHA was devised in 1972 to double the capacity. In the slotted scheme, distinct time slots are created in which systems can transmit a single frame. One system emits a signal at the start of each slot to let all other systems know when the slot is available. By aligning frames on slots, overlaps in the transmissions are reduced. However, systems must wait a fraction of a second for the beginning of a time slot before they can transmit. Also, data may be lost if stations contend for the same slot. However, tests have shown that slotted ALOHA has a performance advantage.

## Alpha Microprocessors, DEC

The DEC Alpha implements a 64-bit RISC (Reduced Instruction Set Computer) architecture microprocessor designed for use in high-powered desktop systems and servers. It runs a variety of operating systems, including VAX VMS, Digital UNIX, and Windows NT. The architecture is designed, according to Digital, to "last well into the 21st century." The 64-bit design allows addressing of up to four billion times more information than is possible with 32-bit systems. Digital's Alpha architecture avoids bias toward any particular operating system or programming language.

The Digital Semiconductor 21164 Alpha is a high-performance implementation of the Digital Alpha architecture that supports multiple operating systems, including Microsoft Windows NT, Digital UNIX, and OpenVMS. The chip can issue four instructions every clock cycle. It has an integrated instruction cache, data cache, and second-level cache, along with a high-performance interface to access main memory, data buses, and an optional board-level cache. The chip is available in various models to match different operating systems with operating frequencies in the 300 MHz to 500 MHz range. The Alpha 21064A microprocessor is very similar to the 21164, but implements dual instruction issues and operates at either 200, 233, 275, or 300 MHz.

**RELATED ENTRIES**   DEC (Digital Equipment Corporation); RISC (Reduced Instruction Set Computer)

## AltaVista

AltaVista is Digital Equipment Corpoation's Internet search engine. AltaVista's Web site is located at http://www.altavista.digital.com. For more information, see "Search Engines."

## AM (Amplitude Modulation)

A technique for modulating the amplitude of a carrier signal based on another signal, usually an audio frequency.

## Amaya Web Client

Amaya is a both a Web browser and an authoring tool that was designed for testing purposes. It allows Web developers to experiment and demonstrate new Web protocols and standards. Amaya was first conceived in 1994 as a way to evaluate structured editing and authoring for Web documents. The product is supported by and available at the World Wide Web Consortium Web site listed at the end of this section. Source code for UNIX platforms is available to the public at the site and PC/Windows source code is in the works.

Amaya's primary features include WYSIWYG editing, which integrates editing and browsing. Developers can edit documents that appear as they will in a user's browser. Structure editing is also available so developers can see the hierarchy of document elements and their attributes. The HTML 3.2 specification is supported, including tables, forms, divisions, client side image maps, and other features. Amaya also supports cascading style sheets, the latest version of HTTP, the PUT method for writing documents on remote servers, and graphics support including pixmaps, GIF, JPEG, and PNG.

**RELATED ENTRIES**   Internet; Web Technologies and Concepts

**INFORMATION ON THE INTERNET**

World Wide Web Consortium           http://www.w3.com

## AMPS (Advanced Mobile Phone Service)

Cellular systems provide wireless telephone and data services to mobile users within a specific area (which is often pictured as a hexagonal cell). Transmitter / receiver towers (called base stations) are typically located on buildings or hilltops, and anyone within the cell can send or receive transmissions. Cellular systems differ from older radio-telephone systems in that they provide more communication channels for users. This is done by limiting frequencies to *cells*. Each cell is assigned a set of frequencies, and no adjoining cells have the same frequencies. While adjoining cells never use the same frequency, cells elsewhere in the grid might do so. But the transmission power of each cell is limited to the specific area it covers.

Cellular systems are perfect for building phone systems in developing countries where cabling a telephone infrastructure may be too expensive or difficult. It is far easier to bypass such traditional systems for cellular systems. It is not uncommon to see more portable cellular phones in third-world countries than in the developed countries.

AMPS (Advanced Mobile Phone Service) is the most established cellular voice communication system in the United States. The first system was developed by Bell Labs and deployed in 1982. AMPS is an analog that operates in the 800 MHz range and uses frequency-division multiplexing. To provide packet-switching services that benefit mobile computer users, the CDPD (Cellular Digital Packet Data) standard is being added to the system in most markets.

As an aside, note that CDPD may be only a temporary fix to prolong the life of AMPS. Fully digital cellular systems are popular in Europe and other foreign countries and are starting to appear in U.S. markets. These systems perform packet-switching and provide the best service for mobile computer users and users of other digital electronic devices. GSM (Global System for Mobile Communications) is a digital cellular system on which emerging applications such as PCS (Personal Communications Services) are based. However, AMPS is well-established all over the U.S., and CDPD is available as well in most of those areas.

As mentioned, AMPS broadcasts signals limited to a specific frequency within each cell. In some areas, a single cell may be adequate, but in metropolitan areas, it is usually necessary to create a honeycomb of smaller cells. Since towers transmit in roughly circular patters that may vary due to elevation or lack of obstructions, there may be some overlap of signals between cells. Therefore, no adjoining cells can ever use the same frequency. However, the same frequency can be used by another cell elsewhere in the general area, as long as there is a buffer zone of at least one cell. This is called *reusing transmission frequencies*.

In densely populated areas such as downtown metropolitan areas, one or more large cells may be subdivided into smaller cells while outlying cells retain their original size. The advantage of this subdivision is that individual cells can be subdivided to fit the usage patterns in the metropolitan area. In some cases, a cell may be as small as a single block or building. Using smaller cells also reduces power requirements and ultimately leads to smaller devices.

## Operation and Management

The entire cellular system consists of a switching office, the base stations and antennae at cell sites, and the mobile transceivers owned by users. The switching office provides call routing and long-distance connections. Within each metropolitan area, there are 832 receive channels and 832 send channels. Thus, there are 832 channel pairs. The Federal Communications Commission licenses cellular communication systems and has allocated half of these channel pairs to the LEC (local exchange carrier) and the other half to independent service providers normally selected by lottery.

Of the available channels, some are used by the base station to manage the system (control channels) while others are used to send ring signals to mobile users. The remaining channels are available for voice and data transmissions. When a user turns a phone on, its phone number and serial number are broadcast within the local cell. The base station picks up these signals and informs the switching office that the particular device is located within its area. This information is recorded by the switching office for future reference. An actual call takes place when the user enters a phone number and hits the Send button. The cellular system selects a channel for the user to use during the duration of the call.

As users travel, they may move from one cell to another, necessitating a *hand-off* and the selection of a new channel. While in the vicinity of a cell, mobile phone users are under the control of the transmitter/receiver in that cell. A hand-off takes place when the base station in one cell transfers control for a user's call to a base station in another cell. When a base station begins to lose a user's signal, it notifies base stations in all the surrounding cells that the user may be moving into their cells. As the user moves into a new cell, the base station in that cell takes over the call. The frequency of the call is changed to a frequency used in the new cell during the transition. This is because adjoining cells cannot use the same frequencies.

**RELATED ENTRIES**    CDPD (Cellular Digital Packet Data); Cellular Communication Systems; GSM (Global System for Mobile Communications); Mobile Computing; PCS (Personal Communications Services); *and* Wireless Communications

**INFORMATION ON THE INTERNET**

| | |
|---|---|
| CDPD Web site | http://www.cdpd.com |
| World of Wireless Communications | http://www.wow-com.com |

## Analog Signals

Analog values are continuously variable voltages or waves that can represent an infinite number of values within the range of the device that is producing, measuring, or recording the signals. Contrast this with digital signals, which use discrete high and low voltage levels to represent the 1s and 0s of the digital transmission. In data communications, analog signals are used to transmit information over the telephone system or over radio transmission systems (such as satellite links). A modem converts digital data to analog signals. Alternatively, analog signals can be converted to digital information using a codec (coder/decoder). This process is called digitizing. Phones that connect to digital communication links use codecs to convert analog voice signals to digital signals. The phone company digitizes voice transmissions between its central offices and long distance sites. In fact, the only remaining analog portion of the phone system is the twisted-pair wire that runs between homes and the telephone companies' central offices, which are usually buildings in the local neighborhood.

**RELATED ENTRIES** ADC (Analog-to-Digital Conversion); Data Communication Concepts; Signals; *and* Transmission Media, Methods, and Equipment

## Analog Transmission Systems

There are analog transmission systems and digital transmission systems. To transmit data, it must be encoded into a signal, then transmitted across a communication system. In an analog transmission system, signals propagate through the medium as continuously varying electromagnetic waves. In a digital system, signals propagate through the medium as discrete voltage pulses (i.e., a positive voltage represents binary 1 and a negative voltage represents binary 0).

The medium for an analog transmission may be twisted-pair cable, coaxial cable, fiber-optic cable, the atmosphere, or space. A technique called modulation is used to combine an input signal (the data) onto a carrier signal. The carrier signal is a specific frequency. Consider what happens when you tune in a radio station. You select a specific frequency. The radio then extracts (demodulates) the signal that has been added by the radio station to the frequency you tuned in to. There are two primary modulation techniques: amplitude modulation, which varies the amplitude (height) of the carrier signal; and frequency modulation, which modulates the frequency of the carrier. Refer to "Modulation Techniques" for more information.

The most common analog transmissions systems are the local loop portion of the telephone system and wireless systems such as cellular phone systems, terrestrial microwave systems, and satellite systems. The frequency ranges of these systems are listed here:

| | |
|---|---|
| 300 to 3,000 kHz (kilohertz) | AM radio |
| 3 to 30 MHz(megahertz) | Short-wave and CB radio |
| 30 to 300 MHz | VHF television and FM radio |
| 300-3,000 MHz | UHF television and terrestrial microwave |
| 3 to 30 GHz (gigahertz) | Terrestrial and satellite microwave |
| 30 GHz and above | CIA, UFO, and alien transmissions |

Microwave systems are highly directional and can be focused for point-to-point transmissions. These systems are widely used for long-distance telephone communications. An organization may also build its own microwave system to create point-to-point links across metropolitan areas. Satellite systems provide the same features at much wider distances.

**RELATED ENTRIES**    Analog Signals; Communication Services; Data Communication Concepts; Electromagnetic Spectrum; Modulation Techniques; Satellite Communication Systems; Signals; Terrestrial Microwave; *and* Transmission Media, Methods, and Equipment

## Anonymous (Guest) Access

Many computer systems and network servers provide what is called anonymous or guest access. An account is set up with the name anonymous or guest, which do not require a password. Multiple users can log in to the account at the same time and it often does not require a password, although users are sometimes asked to type a username. The anonymous/guest account user usually has very restricted access to the system and is often only allowed to access special public files. Such accounts are used on FTP (File Transfer Protocol) and Web servers on the Internet (and intranets). The accounts are also used for kiosk information systems in public areas or in organizations that make computers available to employees that need to look up information such as pension fund data or archival data.

**RELATED ENTRIES**    Account, User; Administrator Account; *and* Users and Groups

## ANSI (American National Standards Institute)

ANSI is an organization that defines coding standards and signaling schemes in the United States and represents the United States in the ISO (International Organization for Standardization) and within the ITU (International Telecommunications Union). ANSI was a founding member of the ISO and plays an active role in its governance. It is one of five permanent members to the governing ISO Council. ANSI promotes the use of U.S. standards internationally, advocates U.S. policy and technical positions in international and regional standards organizations, and encourages the adoption of international standards as national standards where these meet the needs of the user community.

According to ANSI, "it does not itself develop ANSs (American National Standards); rather it facilitates development by establishing consensus among qualified groups. The Institute ensures that its guiding principles—consensus, due process and openness—are followed by the more than 175 distinct entities currently accredited by the Federation." The U.S. standards are presented to international standards organizations by ANSI, where they may be adopted as a whole or in part as international standards. Volunteers from industry and government carry out much of the technical work, so the success of ANSI's work largely depends on the amount of participation by U.S. industry and U.S. government.

**RELATED ENTRIES**    IEEE (Institute of Electrical and Electronic Engineers); ISO (International Organization for Standardization); *and* Standards Groups, Associations, and Organizations

**INFORMATION ON THE INTERNET**

American National Standards Institute          http://www.ansi.org

## Antivirus Software

*See* Virus and Antivirus Issues.

## AnyNet, IBM

AnyNet is a family of access node and gateway products that help you integrate IBM SNA, TCP/IP, IPX, and NetBIOS networks with products on IBM AIX/6000, MVX/ESA, OS/2, OS/400, and the Microsoft Windows platform. The AnyNet family is based on MPTN (Multiprotocol Transport Networking) architecture, an X/Open standard. AnyNet basically makes it easier to build multiprotocol networks in IBM environments and eliminates the need to build parallel networks that provide interconnections between computing devices.

**RELATED ENTRIES**    IBM (International Business Machines); IBM Open Blueprint; MPTN (Multiprotocol Transport Networking); *and* SNA (Systems Network Architecture)

## API (Application Programming Interface)

APIs are the language and messaging formats that define how programs interact with an operating system, with functions in other programs, with communication systems, or with hardware drivers. For example, an operating system provides a set of standard APIs that programmers can use to perform common tasks such as accepting user input, writing information to the screen, or managing files. The APIs in Microsoft Windows are quite sophisticated because they allow programs to build programs that easily access features such as pull-down menus, icons, scroll bars, and more. In the network environment, APIs are available that interface network services for delivering data across communication systems. In database management systems, APIs bind the user applications with the data management system.

APIs are often called *hooks*. Programmers see APIs as routines they can use to quickly build programs for specific systems. A *cross-platform API* provides an interface for building applications or products that work across multiple operating systems or platforms.

There are three types of APIs for communications in a network or Internet environment. These are the *conversation, RPC (remote procedure call),* and *message* APIs. IBM's APPC (Advanced Program-to-Program Communications) model is conversational. RPC models have been developed by Sun Microsystems, by the OSF (Open Software Foundation), and by Microsoft for its Windows environment. Messaging models include IBM MQSeries and MSMQ (Microsoft Message Queuing).

For example, MSMQ is a store-and-forward service that enables applications running at different times to communicate across networks and systems that may be temporarily offline. Applications send messages to MSMQ, and MSMQ uses *queues of messages* to ensure that the messages eventually reach their destination. MSMQ provides guaranteed message delivery, efficient routing, security, and priority-based messaging.

**RELATED ENTRIES**    Database Connectivity; DCE (Distributed Computing Environment), The Open Group; Middleware and Messaging; RPC (Remote Procedure Call); Sockets API; *and* WinSock

# APPC (Advanced Program-to-Program Communications)

APPC, along with APPN (Advanced Peer-to-Peer Networking) and CPI-C (Common Programming Interface for Communications), are networking technologies that are available on many different IBM and non-IBM computing platforms. APPC, also known as LU 6.2, is software that enables high-speed communications between programs on different computers, from portables and workstations to midrange and host computers over SNA, Ethernet, X.25, token ring, and other network topologies. APPC software is available for many different systems, either as part of the operating system or as a separate software package. It is an open and published communications protocol.

APPC represented a major strategy change for IBM when it was introduced. It demonstrated a shift in network control away from the centralized host systems to the systems that were attached to the network. Systems running LU 6.2 sessions do not need the services of a host system when establishing sessions.

LU 6.2 was developed to allow computers on the network with their own processing power to set up their own sessions. In the older hierarchical approach, terminals attached to host computers relied completely on the host to set up and maintain sessions. LU 6.2 provides peer-to-peer communications between systems other than hosts and allows those systems to run distributed applications like file sharing and remote access. The entire range of IBM platforms is supported by LU 6.2, including LANs, desktop systems, and mainframes.

LU 6.2 relies on SNA (Systems Network Architecture) Type 2.1 nodes. Type 2.1 nodes are different than other SNA nodes in that they run CP (Control Point) software that allows them to engage in peer-to-peer connections with other Type 2.1 nodes. This arrangement became increasingly important as LANs were installed in IBM SNA environments. While the LAN provided a connection from a network node to a connected host, those LAN nodes could also use LU 6.2 to communicate directly with other LAN nodes rather than go through the host.

Applications using the LU 6.2 protocols are called *TPs (transaction programs)*. Examples of TPs are IBM DDM (Distributed Data Management), which provides file sharing and database sharing among systems that implement DDM and DIA (Document Interchange Architecture), which is a document exchange standard that defines searching, browsing, printing, and the distribution of documents.

A TP opens a session, performs data transfers, and closes. A TP performs a "unit of work" on a channel that interconnects IBM systems. The sessions are designed to be short-lived because some systems cannot perform other tasks until they complete the transactions. A transaction is like a conversation, and a TP can hold multiple conversations with multiple systems. Each conversation has a name and buffers for sending and receiving data, along with a code that is returned to indicate success or failure of the transaction. The parameters are simple, so code can be portable among systems.

Programs use LU 6.2 services through an interface called the LU 6.2 Protocol Boundary or through the CPI-C (Common Programming Interface for Communications). CPI-C is the current preferred method. CPI provides a common environment for the execution of programs on different IBM platforms, and the C version provides the LU 6.2 communication interface. Recently, IBM has implemented CPI-C in its Open Blueprint, which supports TCP/IP.

**RELATED ENTRIES** APPN (Advanced Peer-to-Peer Networking); IBM (International Business Machines); SAA (Systems Application Architecture); *and* SNA (Systems Network Architecture)

### INFORMATION ON THE INTERNET

| | |
|---|---|
| IBM APPN information | http://www.networking.ibm.com/app/aiwinfo/aiwintro.htm |
| General IBM information | http://www.raleigh.ibm.com |
| IBM networking information | ftp://networking.raleigh.ibm.com |

# Apple Computer

Apple Computer is the manufacturer of the Macintosh line of computers and developed the AppleTalk networking system that works over LocalTalk, EtherTalk, TokenTalk, and FDDITalk networks. Apple is involved extensively in networking and distributed management. Its products are widespread and can be used as nodes on almost every available network operating system and topology. Its Macintosh System 7 and Mac OS operating systems are in use on Macintosh systems everywhere. In addition, Macintosh users have relied on the AppleTalk networking protocols and AppleShare servers for all their networking needs.

Apple's next generation operating system is called Rhapsody and is due out in late 1997 or early 1998. Rhapsody will implement Internet and multimedia capabilities with a new advanced Mac look and feel. Rhapsody will also incorporate Java support by integrating Java Libraries and a Java VM (Virtual Machine). Rhapsody will also deliver preemptive multitasking, protected memory, and symmetrical multiprocessing capabilities.

The recent merger of Apple and NeXT will produce an interface that has the best features of the Mac OS and the NeXT interface technology, as well as new APIs from which to develop new classes of software products. These APIs are based on NeXT Software Inc.'s OPENSTEP development environment.

A Mac OS compatibility environment is also included. This environment is a complete native implementation of the Mac OS hosted on Rhapsody's infrastructure. The entire Mac OS will be ported to Rhapsody rather than implementing a software *emulation* layer.

The core operating system is based on the Mach kernel, which provides a high-performance I/O (input/output) architecture, file system, messaging and scheduling between applications, and networking.

**RELATED ENTRIES**    AppleShare; AppleTalk; Mach Kernel; *and* Mac OS

**INFORMATION ON THE INTERNET**

| | |
|---|---|
| General information | http://www.apple.com |
| Macintosh operating systems information | http://www.macos.apple.com |
| Apple products | http://products.info.apple.com |
| Developer information | http://devworld.apple.com |
| Apple OpenDoc information | http://www.opendoc.apple.com |
| Apple's unique new Web-based interface | http://www.cyberdoc.apple.com |

## Apple Open Transport Protocol

Apple Open Transport is Apple's solution for transport-independent networking for the Mac OS. Transport-independence is designed to free network developers and users from any need to know about the underlying network. Open Transport brings together the technologies to support transport-independent applications. It provides a consistent set of network services across multiple protocols including AppleTalk and TCP/IP. It also provides a name-to-network address mapping service so users can access resources using familiar names rather than cryptic network addresses. New implementations of Mac OS protocol stacks that replace existing AppleTalk and TCP/IP implementations have been released, including support for PPP (Point-to-Point Protocol), NetWare NCP and IPX, Windows 95 and Windows NT (SMB/TCP/NetBIOS), DECnet, and LAT.

Note that Apple is no longer doing development work on its traditional AppleTalk protocol stack. Instead, it has moved all development to Open Transport. Likewise, MacTCP (the TCP/IP protocol stack in early releases of Mac OS) was pushed aside in favor of Open Transport. Apple is also moving Mac OS networking services such as AppleEvents, FileSharing, electronic mail, and AppleShare to Open Transport.

As of this writing, Apple has a strategy in place that includes the release of new operating systems and enhanced versions of Open Transport. A multihoming feature is planned to allow a server to have multiple TCP/IP addresses for the same network interface card. This is useful for Web servers that need to represent several different Web sites or provide firewall protection.

**RELATED ENTRIES**   Apple Computer; AppleTalk; TCP/IP (Transmission Control Protocol/Internet Protocol); *and* Transport Protocols and Services

**INFORMATION ON THE INTERNET**

General Mac OS and Open Transport    http://www.macos.apple.com
information

# AppleShare

AppleShare is a file sharing solution built on the AppleTalk protocols by Apple Computer. AppleShare provides a range of functions and features, including:

■ File and printer sharing services. It allows sharing of folders, entire disks, and CD-ROMs.

■ Operates concurrently in the same system with print services, administrative services, and electronic mail services.

■ Provides queue services for up to five network printers.

■ Provides security in the form of password access and file or folder locking. The network administrator can set various password features, such as aging, and also set time limits on user accounts.

■ Provides network administrators with accounting information, such as when users logged on and what resources they accessed.

■ Can be combined with System 7 to provide an optimized file server environment that takes advantage of System 7's multitasking features so administrators can install and run multiple network services such as electronic mail and management software.

## Access Control

Network administrators can control access to AppleShare resources through user accounts that require a password logon. The password aging feature requires users to enter new passwords periodically. A history of recent passwords can be kept to prevent users from using a recent password. AppleShare can lock the account after a specified number of failures to prevent intruders from attempting to gain access by trying different passwords.

Administrators can control the number of users that can access the server at any one time to prevent performance degradation. For the same reason, administrators can restrict the number of users starting a particular program. When the number of concurrent logons is restricted, users attempting to log on after the maximum value is reached see a message that the server is unavailable. Administrators can also log off any user at any time.

Access privileges let users view or change the files on the AppleShare server. Administrators can set access privileges for any folder on a volume, while users can set privileges for the folder they own. By setting the privileges listed here, owners or administrators can share files with other users:

- **See folders**   This privilege lets other users see, but not change, the folders contained within a volume or within another folder.

- **See files**   This privilege lets other users see the files within a volume or folder, but not change them. However, users can copy the files to their own system and change them there.

- **Make changes**   With this privilege, users can change folders and their contents. This includes adding and removing information in a folder. It also includes moving, renaming, or deleting the folder. If a folder has this privilege only, it is a drop box and anything placed in it cannot be removed.

Administrators have unlimited rights and can override privileges set by users. If a folder is created without privileges, the folder is assigned the privileges of the folder in which it resides. The privileges of a folder change when the folder is moved into another folder. The new privileges assigned to it are called *inherited privileges*. However, explicit privileges can be assigned to override inherited privileges—they travel with the folder.

Accounting functions let administrators collect data about user accounts and use that data to monitor system usage and security. Administrators can also use the information to validate the need for new equipment in their budgetary requests. An Admin program provides a log of drives and available space, users and groups they belong to, and a list of file names and folders along with the owner names, access privileges, and locked status.

## FutureShare

FutureShare is the latest incarnation of AppleShare. It lets you share files over the Internet in the same way you can share them over internal networks. FutureShare basically turns an AppleShare server into an Internet server and allows clients to access it with FTP, Web browsers, and traditional AppleTalk services. As of this writing, FutureShare was the product code name. The Internet server (FTP and Web) software components use the same security and administrative features as the file server. A POP3 and SMTP mail server are also part of the plan, along with a plan to support the emerging IMAP protocol. Also included is a new print server. The software is designed to run on a server, not on desktop Macintosh systems.

A list of related Web sites is listed under "Apple Computer."

**RELATED ENTRIES**   AFP (AppleTalk Filing Protocol); Apple Computer; AppleTalk; File Sharing; File Systems; LocalTalk; *and* Network Concepts

## AppleTalk

AppleTalk has been the networking protocol for the Macintosh nearly as long as the Macintosh has been around. It provides a way for individual users to share files and is the basis for dedicated AppleShare servers. It also supports printer sharing and remote access. As of this writing, however, AppleTalk is starting to show its age and Apple was already announcing products that were designed to shift Apple network users into the world of the Internet and TCP/IP networks. While Apple will continue to support AppleTalk networking in future operating systems, the new direction is Apple Open Transport, which supports not only AppleTalk but TCP/IP and, eventually, other protocols such as IPX. On the server side, Apple is also upgrading its long-standing AppleShare server software to a new Internet-enabled product called FutureShare, as discussed under "AppleShare." See also "Apple Open Transport Protocol."

Still, AppleTalk is suitable for workgroups of Macintosh users who don't need sophisticated networks that need to support hundreds of users. In addition, it is installed in many organizations and probably will not go away soon.

AppleTalk is the architecture that defines a set of protocols used by devices to communicate over the network. Originally, AppleTalk was designed to use the LocalTalk cabling system, but AppleTalk now supports Ethernet and token ring topologies. AppleTalk was also designed for small local workgroups, and so its performance is not adequate for large LANs and WANs, although some improvements have been made for WAN connections.

## AppleTalk Operation and Protocol Stack

Devices attached to AppleTalk networks dynamically assign themselves an address when first attached. The address is randomly selected from a range of allowable addresses. The address is then broadcast out over the network as a check to see if another device is already using the address. A device stores its selected address for use the next time it is turned on. Node addresses are mapped to names that make the network easier to access by humans. These names appear in the Macintosh graphic interface.

*Zones* provide internetworking in AppleTalk. They are logical areas that primarily exist to make access to resources easier for users. Zones may extend across multiple networks, and routers separate them. Basically, zones make it easier for users to find services. Users see only local resources rather than everything on the network, but they can still access internetwork resources if necessary.

The AppleTalk protocol stack is pictured in Figure A-5. Like most other protocol suites, AppleTalk exists as protocol modules in various layers of a protocol stack. The lower layers deal with framing and transmission of bits, the middle layer deals with packaging and addressing information and maintaining sessions between computers, and the top layers define application protocols and how programs can use the underlying network services.

**RELATED ENTRIES**    AFP (AppleTalk Filing Protocol); Apple Computer; AppleShare; LocalTalk; *and* Network Concepts

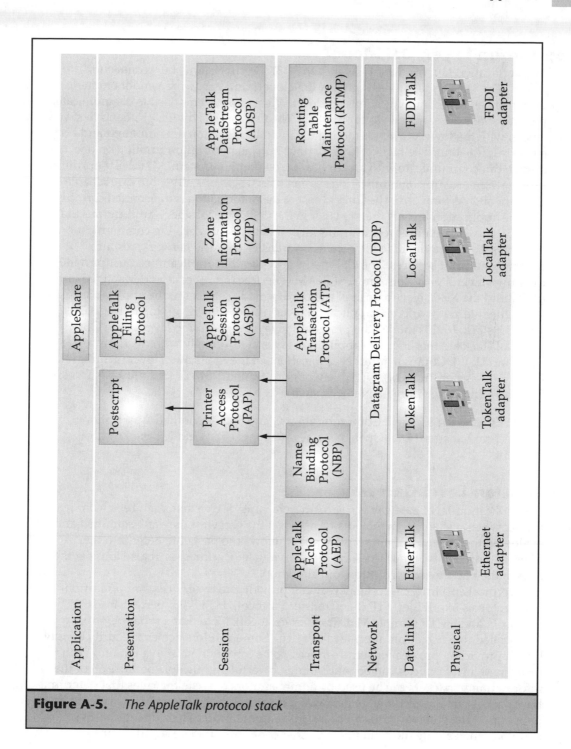

**Figure A-5.** *The AppleTalk protocol stack*

## Application Layer, OSI Model

The application layer is the top layer of the OSI (Open Systems Interconnection) model. The OSI model guides software developers and hardware vendors in the design of network communications products. When two systems need to communicate, they must use the same network protocols. The OSI models divide protocols in seven layers, with the lowest layer defining the physical connection of equipment and electrical signaling. The highest layer defines how an application running on one system can communicate with an application on another system. Middle layers define protocols that set up communication sessions, keep sessions alive, provide reliable delivery, and perform error checking to ensure that information is transmitted correctly.

The application layer is the top layer in the OSI protocol stack. Applications that provide network features reside at this layer and access underlying communication protocols. Examples include file access and transfer over the network, resource sharing, and print services. The OSI model specifies that applications must provide their own layer 7 protocols. The OSI FTAM (File Transfer, Access, and Management) utility and the X.400 electronic mail standard provide services at the application layer.

In the Internet world, the application layer resides directly on top of the TCP/IP protocol stack. In this model, the presentation layer and session layer of the OSI protocol stack are missing. The application layer talks directly with the transport layer (TCP and UDP). Common Internet applications in the application layer include Telnet, FTP (File Transfer Protocol), NFS (Network File System), SMTP (Simple Mail Transport Protocol), and DNS (Domain Name System).

**RELATED ENTRIES**    Data Communication Concepts; Distributed Applications; Layered Architecture; OSI (Open Systems Interconnection) Model; *and* Protocol Concepts

## Application-Level Gateway

An application-level gateway is a security screening device that analyzes incoming traffic. When packets from the outside arrive at the gateway, they are examined and evaluated to determine if the security policy allows the packet to enter into the internal network. Not only does the server evaluate IP addresses, it also looks at the data in the packets for corruption and alteration.

A typical application-level gateway can provide proxy services for applications and protocols like Telnet, FTP (File Transfer Protocol), HTTP (Hypertext Transfer Protocol), and SMTP (Simple Mail Transfer Protocol). Note that a separate proxy must be installed for each application-level service. (Some vendors achieve security simply by not providing proxies for some services, so be careful in your evaluation.) With proxies, security policies can be much more powerful and flexible because all of the information in packets can be used by administrators to write the rules that determine how packets are handled by the gateway. It is easy to audit just about everything that happens on the gateway. You can also strip computer names to hide internal systems, and you can evaluate the contents of packets for appropriateness and security.

**RELATED ENTRY**    Firewall

## Application Server

An application server is a server that runs programs in a network environment. The applications may be network versions of commercial, off-the-shelf software that allow multiple users to access and run the program. This avoids loading the program on each user's computer and allows central updates to take place on the server. Custom built or off-the-shelf client-server applications may run on application servers as well. A client-server application distributes processing between the client and the server, with the server handling file and data access and the client handling presentation and user input. A database server is also an application server, but is optimized for disk I/O (input/output) and may include attached servers that contain replicas of the data for fault tolerance.

**RELATED ENTRIES**    Client/Server Computing; Distributed Applications; *and* Servers

## Applications, Network

*See* Distributed Applications.

## APPN (Advanced Peer-to-Peer Networking)

APPN was introduced by IBM in 1985 and integrated into SNA (Systems Network Architecture). It provides peer-to-peer networking services similar to but not quite the same as TCP/IP. One of the main reasons IBM introduced APPN was to provide client/server computing services to users who might have moved to TCP/IP or other services. APPN is basically link-layer independent. It can run over token ring, Ethernet, FDDI (Fiber Distributed Data Interface), frame relay, ISDN (Integrated Services Digital Network), X.25, SDLC (Synchronous Data Link Control), and ultra high-speed networks such as B-ISDN and ATM.

APPN is based on the concept that computers on the network have enough processing power of their own to handle session management and routing. APPN moves various services from central control (such as that provided by a host mainframe computer) to decentralized control points that operate in a peer-to-peer relationship. In the old SNA model, a mainframe was required to control sessions. In the APPN model, user stations set up and maintain their own sessions.

APPN is part of IBM's revision to SNA and is often called the "new SNA." APPN is still tightly integrated with SNA, and it uses the SNA LU 6.2 protocol that is formally marketed as APPC (Advanced Program-to-Program Communications). In addition, APPN implements a newer application interface, the CPI-C (Common Programming Interface for Communications). APPN is compared to OSI and TCP/IP in Figure A-6.

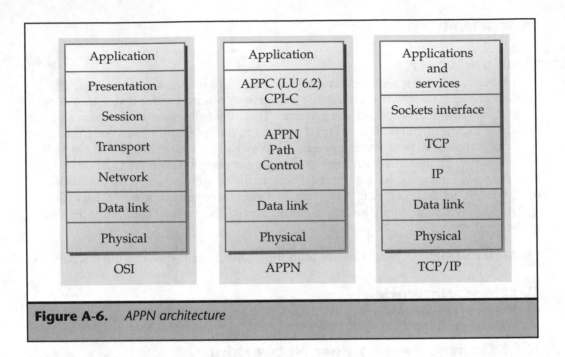

**Figure A-6.** *APPN architecture*

- **APPC** Introduced in the early 1980s, APPC is also called LU 6.2. It is the application interface for APPN. By providing a way for applications on separate systems to communicate without involving a host system, APPC forged the way for APPN. It provided the shift away from centralized mainframe control and allowed programmable devices like computers to control their own sessions.

- **CPI-C** CPI is a set of APIs that provide a common environment for the execution of programs on different IBM platforms. Recently, IBM has implemented CPI-C in its Networking Blueprint and included support for OSI and TCP/IP protocols.

APPN provides routing services for APPC sessions. The routing environment consists of the following hierarchy as pictured in Figure A-7:

- **ENs (end nodes)** An EN is a computer with its own operating system. It transmits information about itself and any locally attached resources to adjacent NNs (network nodes) when it logs in to the network. The NN then holds this information and provides it to other nodes on the APPN network. This reduces the need to search every EN when establishing sessions. IBM mainframe and midrange computers as well as AIX or UNIX systems and desktop computers running OS/2 are end nodes. These larger systems can also be network nodes, as discussed next.

- **NNs (network nodes)**  An NN is a routing node that moves traffic between end nodes. NNs exchange routing information about the topology of the network with other NNs as changes occur. To conserve network bandwidth, only information about recent changes is exchanged, rather than entire routing tables. NNs also locate resources and store the resource information for later use. Thus, NNs serve as distributed depositories for information about the network. This caching feature "improves with age" as more routes are added to the list, reducing the number of required route searches. IBM AS/400 minicomputers, IBM 6611 routers, and 3174 terminal controllers are devices that can serve as NNs.

- **CNN (composite network node)**  A CNN provides seamless communications between an SNA subarea and APPN. The subarea network, which may contain a VTAM (Virtual Telecommunication Access Method) node and any number of NCP (Network Control Program) nodes, emulates an NN. Note that VTAM provides users with access to network resources and information, and NCP is the control program that runs in an IBM FEP (front-end processor) such as an IBM 3745.

- **LENs (low-entry nodes)**  A LEN can participate in a session with another LEN node on the network, but it requires the services of a network node to do so. This network node can be part of a local area network or directly connected to the LEN. PCs running DOS are examples of LEN nodes because they don't have the capability of operating as end nodes. OS/2, on the other hand, has full end-node capabilities.

- **BN (border node) and EBN (extended border node)**  Subdivision of an APPN network is possible if a network broadcast becomes excessive. Division of the network isolates a broadcast to specific subnetworks. The BN or EBN routes information among subnetworks.

APPN NNs dynamically locate resources on the network and store the routing information locally. In older SNA networks, network elements were defined in a VTAM table stored in a mainframe. In contrast, APPN networks can configure themselves using route discovery methods. Network nodes work together to establish a path through a network so two end stations can set up a communication session. Each node contains a routing table used to establish the pathway for the link. One potential problem with APPN is that the selected path remains fixed for the duration of the session. If a node fails along the path, the session is not rerouted and fails as well. IBM fixed this with HPR (High-Performance Routing), which was introduced in late 1994. You can refer to "HPR (High-Performance Routing)" for more information.

Applications establish sessions with other destination nodes on the network by accessing logical unit software interfaces that correspond roughly to OSI session layer protocols. These high-level interfaces provide names for software entities that reside in ENs and NNs on the network. Note that applications go through LUs (logical units) to establish sessions, not directly to APPN. Basically, an LU in one station uses APPN

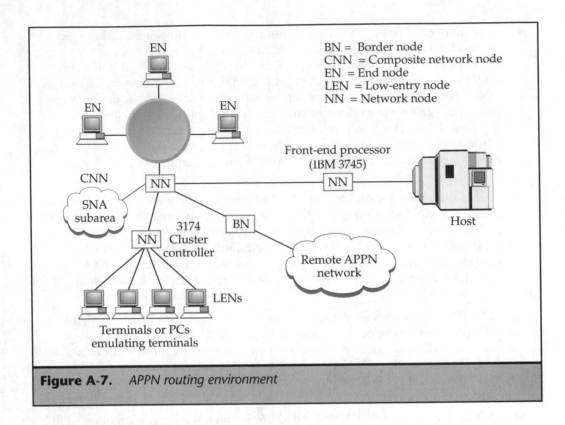

**Figure A-7.** *APPN routing environment*

services to locate a destination LU and set up a session. Think of LU sessions as pipes transmitting data across the network from one application to another. Multiple applications can access a single LU, or applications can access multiple LUs.

## The Future

The future of APPN is in question. TCP/IP networks have proliferated in many organizations. However, SNA protocols are not routable and APPN and TCP/IP do not mix. So network designers have a problem. They can build two networks or look for a solution that takes advantage of the internetworking features of TCP/IP to transport SNA traffic throughout the enterprise. A vendor consortium called the APPN Implementers Workshop is working to integrate TCP/IP and APPN. A protocol called DLSw (Data Link Switching) is based on its standards. It provides a way to move SNA traffic over TCP/IP networks by encapsulating the traffic into TCP/IP packets. The IETF (Internet Engineering Task Force) has also been working on DLSw.

Basically, DLSw provides a way for routers to route "unroutable" SNA traffic (and NetBIOS sessions) across an internetwork. The technique is to link the two SNA or NetBIOS systems with a pair of DLSw routers. The routers then take all traffic that is destined for the other SNA system, encapsulate it, and send it across the internetwork.

An even more intriguing solution is the World Wide Web model of Web browsers and servers. Many organizations are building intranets that take advantage of Web technologies to give users of any operating system access to information on internal servers. Web technology can also provide a way to get at mainframe data as well. New methods for accessing SNA systems using Web browsers over TCP/IP networks are emerging, such as Cisco Systems' IOS/390 TCP/IP intranet software. IOS is Cisco's Internetwork Operating System.

Browser-based access is especially attractive to remote and mobile users who make temporary connections into the corporate network. The best way for them to do that is through a single Web-based interface that gives them access to all the corporate information systems.

In general, SNA traffic on enterprise networks and on WANs will no doubt decrease significantly over the next few years as new methods for accessing traditional IBM systems take hold.

**RELATED ENTRIES**   APPC (Advanced Program-to-Program Communications); DLSw (Data Link Switching); HPR (High-Performance Routing), IBM; SAA (Systems Application Architecture); *and* SNA (Systems Network Architecture)

## Archiving of Data
*See* Data Protection.

## ARCNET

The ARCNET (Attached Resource Computing Network) is a baseband, token-passing network system that offers flexible star and bus topologies at a low price. Transmission speeds are 2.5 Mbits/sec. ARCNET uses a token-passing protocol on a token bus network topology. ARCNET is showing its age and is no longer sold by major vendors. However, ARCNET networks still exist in many small offices.

A typical ARCNET configuration is shown in Figure A-8. Although ARCNET is generally considered to have a slow throughput, it does support cable lengths of up to 610 meters when using active hubs. It is suitable for office environments that use text-based applications and where users don't often access the file server.

ARCNET connections are made to *active* and *passive* hubs. An active hub is a network relay that conditions and amplifies the signal strength. Most active hubs have eight ports to which workstations, passive hubs, or additional active hubs can be attached.

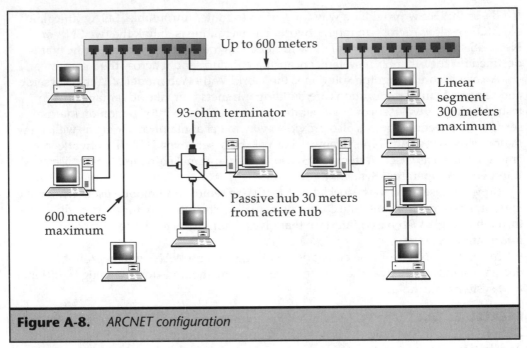

**Figure A-8.** *ARCNET configuration*

A passive hub is a four-port connector with BNC jacks, as shown here:

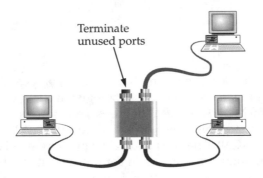

ARCNET uses 93-ohm RG-62 A/U coaxial cable, although twisted-pair and fiber-optic cable can also be used. Fiber-optic cable is used for backbones between active hubs and for outside runs.

## ARDIS (Advanced National Radio Data Service)

ARDIS is a nationwide radio data communication service that enables field workers, using handheld devices, to access centralized host computer applications. ARDIS coverage is available in almost any location in 400+ metropolitan areas in the United

States, Puerto Rico, and the U.S. Virgin Islands. Portable, handheld data terminals and similar devices with RF (radio frequency) modems can access the ARDIS system and communicate with home office systems. In 1993, service applications made up 80 percent of ARDIS's customer activity. Field technicians can use portable data terminals in their vehicles and at commercial and residential customer sites to access dispatch and diagnostic information as well as service call, service history, and parts availability data.

Competing services include cellular services such as GTE Mobilnet and similar offerings from the RBOCs (regional Bell operating companies). Another threat comes from wireless network services such as PCS (Personal Communications Services) and CDPD (Cellular Digital Packet Data).

ARDIS is a communications system developed by a partnership between IBM and Motorola, but it is now owned by Motorola. It was originally used by 15,000 IBM field engineers. IBM's Netview system and the Codex 9800 network management system are integrated so the health of the ARDIS network can be managed, all the way from the radio transmitter component on a remote rooftop to the modem attached to a host computer.

ARDIS provides a nationwide radio data communication service in which more than 1,250 radio base stations are deployed. They are typically co-located with their antennae on the tops of multistory buildings or on towers. They incorporate a 40W transmitter and operate in the 800 MHz band of frequencies. Depending on the antenna height and surrounding terrain, each site provides a coverage radius of 15 to 20 miles. Multiple sites providing overlapping coverage are deployed throughout a typical metropolitan area in order to provide wide area coverage and to penetrate buildings. The user has seamless access to the network while traveling because all the base stations operate at the same frequency.

Base stations are connected to one of more than 30 radio network controllers located at various points across the United States via dedicated leased lines. Each controller is responsible for the radio communications in one or more metropolitan areas. Each controller holds registration information for terminals that are authorized to communicate on the network. The controllers also hold last-known-location information for terminals for message forwarding.

There are three network hubs, located in Chicago, Los Angeles, and Lexington. These hubs serve as the point of access to ARDIS for customer host applications. They also perform message routing, network management, and accounting/billing functions. The hubs are interconnected via dedicated leased lines with alternate communication paths for redundancy. Lexington is the primary operation center, but a duplicate center is maintained in Chicago for backup. Customers can connect to ARDIS either through dedicated leased lines to one of the hubs or through a VAN (value added network).

ARDIS has been implemented in a number of new ways in recent years. Microsoft has put support for ARDIS into its new operating systems for handheld devices and provides support for it in Microsoft Exchange Server and other Microsoft BackOffice products.

**RELATED ENTRIES**   Mobile Computing; Wireless Communications

**INFORMATION ON THE INTERNET**

ARDIS                                    http://www.ardis.com

# ARIS (Aggregate Route-based IP Switching)

As you probably know, IP datagrams are normally routed through an IP network. Routing is an activity that takes place in the network layer (layer 3) relative to the OSI protocol stack. At each router along a path to a destination, a decision must be made about which way to send the packet. This adds considerable overhead. To overcome this overhead, various strategies have been proposed for switching packets through such networks. ARIS is a protocol that establishes switched paths through networks that act as virtual circuits, moving packets through the network without the need to make routing decisions at every step along the way.

ARIS and other IP switching schemes employ *label routing* or *tagging* techniques, which provide a way to add information to packets that can be used to guide those packets through VCs (virtual circuits). The technique can provide service levels if necessary by tagging some packets with higher priority than others. It is also viewed by many vendors as the best way to combine switching and routing.

ARIS is IBM's scheme for switching IP datagrams. It is normally associated with ATM networks, but ARIS can be extended to work with other switching technologies. This topic discusses ATM. ARIS and other IP switching technologies take advantage of ISRs (interswitch routers), switches that have been modified to provide IP routing support, or seen another way, routers that have been augmented to support ATM switching and virtual circuit capabilities.

An ISR can be viewed as an entry point into the ATM switching environment. It has a routing table, but the next route in the table can refer to a switched path VC through the network. The VC leads to an ISR on the other side of the network, which connects to the destination system. Datagrams can be transmitted directly through the VC without any delays associated with routing. Note that *virtual circuit* is used loosely to mean a switched path across any network that employs switching technology.

What ARIS does is set up a virtual circuit through a network based on the forwarding paths already established by routers that use routing protocols such as OSPF (Open Shortest Path First) and BGP (Border Gateway Protocol). IP datagrams are then switched through the network following these paths. No routing is done by any device along the VC. Instead, the datagrams are "tagged" with a label that is read by intermediate switches along the way, identified with a particular destination network, and sent along the appropriate circuit to that destination.

The aggregation features provide a way to allow two or more computers on one side of an ATM network to send their datagrams through the same VC that has already been established on a network on the other side of the ATM network. Thus, new VCs don't need to be made, and network resources are optimized.

At the time of this writing, IBM was submitting ARIS to the IETF (Internet Engineering Task Force) for consideration as the standard protocol in the MPLS (Multiprotocol Label Switching) standard. Another important standard is Cisco's Tag Switching standard, which is being considered by the IETF as well.

There is currently a lot of development work in the area of running multiple protocols over switched networks. The IETF Web site has the most up-to-date information on this protocol.

**RELATED ENTRIES**    IP over ATM; IP Switching; Routing Protocols and Algorithms; *and* Switched Networks

### INFORMATION ON THE INTERNET

| | |
|---|---|
| IETF (Internet Engineering Task Force) | http://www.ietf.org |
| IBM site for ARIS information | ftp://ftp.raleigh.ibm.com/nswww/ipsw |

## ARP (Address Resolution Protocol)

On TCP/IP networks, the ARP protocol is used to match up an IP (Internet Protocol) address with a MAC (medium access control) address. An *IP address* is a high-level internetwork address that identifies a specific computer on a subnetwork of interconnected networks. A *MAC address* is the hardwired address of a NIC (network interface card). MAC addresses are only used to forward frames between computers attached to the same network. They cannot be used to send frames to computers on other networks that are interconnected by routers. IP addressing must be used to forward frames across router boundaries (assuming TCP/IP networks).

ARP is used in all cases where one node on a TCP/IP network needs to know the MAC address of another node on the same network or on an internetwork. Basically, ARP lets a computer ask the question "will the computer with the IP address w.x.y.z send me its MAC address." This ARP message is broadcast on the local network so all nodes hear it but only the node that has the IP address in question responds. The address resolution process is shown here:

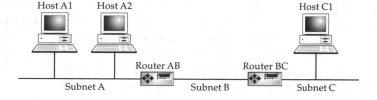

Three subnetworks (A, B, and C) are connected by Router AB and Router BC. Hosts A1 and A2 are on network A and Host C1 is on network C. Subnet B is an interconnecting LAN or a WAN. Assume Host A1 wants to transmit to Host A2. It knows the IP address of Host 2, but must have a hardware address to transmit on the network. To get the address, it creates an ARP request and "broadcasts" the frame on the network. All the other hosts on the network receive the broadcast, but only Host A2 (which owns the address in question) prepares an ARP response that contains its MAC address and sends it directly back to Host A1. The response is saved in a cache by Host A1 for future use.

If Host A1 wants to transmit to Host C1, Router AB must get involved. ARP is used to discover the MAC address of Router AB, and all frames for transmission to Host C1 are then sent to Router AB's MAC address. Router AB then forwards packets to Router BC. Presumably Router BC already used ARP to determine the MAC address of Host C1. It simply forwards the packets in frames addressed to Host C1 on the network.

To make ARP efficient, each computer caches IP-to-MAC address mappings to eliminate repetitive ARP broadcast requests. Most operating systems age ARP entries in the cache if they are not used for some time. Entries are made to the ARP cache on a first response basis.

Adding a permanent ARP entry can be useful to decrease the number of ARP broadcasts for frequently accessed hosts. Creating permanent ARP cache entries can speed performance to heavily used IP resources such as local servers and the default gateway. However, if the entries are invalid or the network interface card in the local server or default gateway changes, the permanent entry remains unless updated by an ARP from the server or default gateway. You can check for invalid ARP mappings with the PING command. It will display the message "Request timed out" if there is an invalid mapping.

**RELATED ENTRIES**    Internet; Internetworking; IP (Internet Protocol); MAC (Medium Access Control); Routing Protocols and Algorithms; *and* TCP/IP (Transmission Control Protocol/Internet Protocol)

# ARPANET (Advanced Research Projects Agency Network)

ARPANET was a packet-switching network developed in the early 1970s. ARPANET was funded by ARPA (Advanced Research Projects Agency), which later became DARPA (Defense Advanced Research Projects Agency). The ARPANET network linked defense facilities, government research laboratories, and university sites. It evolved into the backbone of the Internet, and the term ARPANET was officially retired in 1990. However, MILNET (military network) was spun off from ARPANET in 1983. In addition, ARPANET spurred the development of TCP/IP, one of the most important protocol suites available today. TCP/IP (Transmission Control Protocol/Internet Protocol) is a set of communications procedures and standards that provide a basis for interconnecting dissimilar computers.

DARPA was interested in interlinking the many different computer systems that were spread out across the country as part of the nation's research and development effort. DARPA's goal was to create a set of nonproprietary communications protocols that would make it easy to connect many different computers together. Much of the original work was done at the Massachusetts Institute of Technology and with the help of companies such as BBN (Bolt, Beranek, and Newman, Inc.). In 1980, the first TCP/IP modules were installed.

One of the most important aspects of TCP/IP's development was the program of testing and certifying carried out by the government to ensure that developers met published TCP/IP standards, which were (and still are) available to the public free of licensing arrangements. This ensured that developers did not alter the standard to fit their own needs and possibly cause confusion in the rest of the TCP/IP community. Today, the use of TCP/IP protocols virtually assures interconnection (and in some cases, interoperability) among systems that use it for communications.

**RELATED ENTRIES**    DARPA (Defense Advanced Research Projects Agency); Internet; Internet Organizations and Committees; *and* TCP/IP (Transmission Control Protocol/Internet Protocol)

## AS/400, IBM

*See* IBM AS/400.

## Associations

*See* Standards Groups, Associations, and Organizations.

## Asymmetrical Multiprocessing

Computer systems with multiple processors can utilize the processors in one of two ways. In *asymmetrical* multiprocessing, each CPU (central processing unit) is dedicated to a specific function, such as network interface card I/O (input/output), or file operations. In *symmetrical* multiprocessing, which is generally agreed to be superior to asymmetrical multiprocessing (but harder to implement), any CPU can handle any task if it is available to do so. Depending on the operating system and/or applications, tasks can be split up and simultaneously handled by multiple processors. Microsoft Windows NT and other new-generation operating systems perform symmetrical multiprocessing.

**RELATED ENTRY**    Multiprocessing

## Asynchronous Communications

Asynchronous communications is the transmission of data between two devices that are not synchronized with one another using a clocking mechanism or other technique. Basically, the sender can transmit data at any time and the receiver must be ready to accept information when it comes in. In contrast, a synchronous transmission is a precisely timed stream of bits in which the start of a character is located by using a clocking mechanism.

In the mainframe/terminal environment, where asynchronous and synchronous transmissions are used abundantly, an asynchronous transmission is used to transmit characters from a terminal in which the user presses keys periodically. The receiving system knows to wait for the next key press, even though that may take a relatively large amount of time. In contrast, synchronous transmissions are used as data links between large systems that transfer large amounts of information on a regular basis. The protocol is optimized to take advantage of slow links over public telephone systems, so extraneous bits are removed from the transmissions and clocks are used to separate characters.

In asynchronous communications, a character is coded as a string of bits and separated by a "start-of-character" bit and "stop" bit. A parity bit is sometimes used for error detection and correction. The start-stop mode of transmission means that transmission starts over again for each new character, which eliminates any timing discrepancies that may have occurred during the last transmission. When discrepancies do occur, error-detection and correction mechanisms can request a retransmission.

Asynchronous transmissions can take place between two nearby computers by connecting a null-modem cable between the asynchronous communications ports of each computer. If computers are at distant locations, a modem is required on each end to convert computer digital signals for transmission over analog phone lines. Asynchronous transmission can take place at speeds up to 56 Kbits/sec over normal switched (dial-up) or leased telephone lines.

A channel is a single communication path between two communicating devices that is created by physical connections or by multiplexing techniques. A circuit is an actual physical connection that provides a communication channel. The dial-up phone system provides circuits for channel communication between two systems. A *simplex* circuit is a unidirectional transmission path that transmits signals in one direction. A *half-duplex* circuit is a bidirectional transmission path that provides transmission in both directions, but only one direction at a time. A *full-duplex* circuit is a bidirectional transmission path that can transmit both ways at the same time.

## Error-Correction Methods

All transmission media are susceptible to interference and problems introduced by the medium itself, such as current resistance and signal attenuation. Outside interference may be introduced by background noise, atmospheric radiation, machinery, or even faulty equipment. As transmission rates increase, the number of bits affected by disturbances increases because there are more bits involved in the time frame of the disturbance. To correct these problems, error-detection and error-correction methods are used.

In parity checking, the numbers of 1s in groups must always be the same, either even or odd, to indicate that a group of bits was transmitted without error. Checking on a per-character basis is called VRC (vertical redundancy checking). Checking on a block-by-block basis is called LRC (longitudinal redundancy checking). Both systems must agree on the parity method before transmission begins. There is even parity (number of 1s must be even), odd parity (number of 1s must be odd), space parity (parity bit is always 0), and mark parity (parity bit is always 1).

Newer modems provide advanced error-checking and error-correcting methods that are much more practical and efficient than those just discussed.

## Interface Standards

The connections used for asynchronous communications are defined in the physical layer of the OSI reference model. This layer defines specifications related to connector types, pin-outs, and electrical signaling. Standards such as RS-232, RS-449, CCITT V.24, and others define these interfaces for various requirements.

Various standards are defined to ensure that connected devices can communicate with one another. The EIA (Electronic Industries Association) has set standards for transmitting asynchronous information across copper wires between computer devices. The EIA RS-232-C standard defines such things as the physical connections, signal voltages and timing, error checking, and other features. The standard defines serial transmissions of bitstreams across a single wire. In contrast, a parallel transmission involves sending multiple bits simultaneously across multiple wires in the same cable, similar to a multilane freeway.

The EIA RS-232-C standard supports transmissions over short distances. For example, you use it to connect a computer to a modem. If the cable length becomes too long, the electrical current weakens and the receiver may not be able to read it. The recommended maximum length of an RS-232 cable is 50 feet with a maximum signaling rate of 20 Kbits/sec (see "Serial Communication and Interfaces" for more details). To connect in-house systems over longer distances, set up a LAN. To connect with systems outside your own building, use a modem and the telephone system or other services provided by local and long-distance carriers (see "Communication Services").

**RELATED ENTRIES**    Data Link Protocols; Error Detection and Correction; Flow-Control Mechanisms; Framing in Data Transmissions; Modems; Modulation Techniques; Serial Communication and Interfaces; *and* Synchronous Communications

## AT&T (American Telephone and Telegraph)

AT&T is the outcome of Alexander Graham Bell's phone company. The company grew so large that the federal government had to regulate it. In 1913, the Department of Justice brought an antitrust suit against AT&T that resulted in the Kingsbury Commitment. It forced AT&T to divest itself of Western Union and allow independent carriers to use the long-distance network it had established. In 1956, the Justice Department limited AT&T to providing only regulated services to customers and, in 1968, ruled that customers could attach non-AT&T equipment to the public telephone network.

The 1969 MCI Decision allowed MCI and other carriers to compete with AT&T for long-distance communications. From 1982 to 1984, the Justice Department finalized its antitrust suit by forcing AT&T to break up and reform into seven regional holding companies called RBOCs (regional Bell operating companies), or "baby Bells." A manufacturing, research, and long-distance operation called AT&T Corporation was allowed to continue operation.

The RBOCs provide their services within specific geographic areas called LATAs (local access and transport areas). A LATA basically separates local and long-distance telephone markets. A LEC (local exchange carrier) has a franchise within a LATA (intraLATA) to provide services. A LEC may be an RBOC or an independent telephone company.

InterLATA telecommunication refers to services provided between LATAs by IXCs (interexchange carriers) such as AT&T, MCI, US Sprint, and others. RBOCs must provide all interexchange carriers with equal access to their LATA facilities. Users can therefore choose which interexchange carrier they want to use. That carrier then provides switching services between LATAs.

Until early 1996, RBOC and AT&T services were regulated and prices were fixed for services. For example, tariffs that controlled interLATA service rates could not be changed without approval from the federal government. IntraLATA tariffs were controlled at the state level. The Telecommunications Reform Act of 1996 changed that. The FCC (Federal Communications Commission) dissolved the 62 year-old tariff system for long-distance carriers and opened the pricing system up to negotiable contracts. The RBOC's tariffing system is still in place. Note also that long-distance companies like AT&T can compete in local areas and RBOCs can provide long-distance services, but the outcome of this ruling may take some time to see. There has been some hesitation by one side to jump into the market of the other. Many administrators want end-to-end data services from a single carrier, but for now AT&T is more likely to resell services it obtains from the RBOCs when building such networks.

ATM (Asynchronous Transfer Mode) is the key to AT&T's communication system, which provides various types and speeds of access and trunk interfaces so service providers can build the "gigabit" data highways for future networking systems. AT&T has also set up one of the fastest wide area networks in the nation. It uses ATM technology over a 500-mile, fiber-optic network that runs at 622 Mbits/sec between the University of Wisconsin at Madison and the University of Illinois at Urbana-Champaign. This new network is an enhancement of a previous experimental network that will test the ability to transmit complex imaging, multimedia, and supercomputer information.

**RELATED ENTRIES**   Carrier Services; RBOCs (Regional Bell Operating Companies); *and* Telecommunications and Telephone Systems

### INFORMATION ON THE INTERNET

| | |
|---|---|
| AT&T Corporation | http://www.att.com |
| AT&T Wireless Data division | http://www.airdata.com |

## ATDM (Asynchronous Time Division Multiplexing)

*See* Multiplexing.

## ATM (Asynchronous Transfer Mode)

ATM is a high-speed network technology that is designed for both LAN and WAN use. It is a connection-oriented switching technology, meaning that a dedicated circuit is set up between two end systems before a communication session can begin.

Information is transported in cells through a switching fabric. A cell is a fixed-size packet of information, as opposed to a frame, which is a variable-length packet of information. This differentiation between fixed and variable length is crucial to what ATM offers. Picture a busy intersection. A semi tractor-trailer is attempting to negotiate a tight turn. All the rest of the traffic in the intersection is held up while this happens. Now picture the same intersection where all the vehicles are sports cars. In the latter case, traffic flows smoothly, and even predictably, because there are no delays caused by big trucks.

ATM cells negotiate ATM switches with the same efficiency, providing several benefits:

- Cell switching is efficient and fast. The switch does not need to make allowances for variable lengths. It can easily clock the flow of cells.

- With fixed-size cells, traffic flow is predictable. You can accurately time the flow of cells because there are no variable-length cells that would throw such a calculation off.

- Because traffic is predictable, it is possible to guarantee that time-sensitive information will arrive on time, given that the network has enough capacity to carry it.

- ATM includes *QoS (quality of service)* features that let customers prioritize certain types of traffic, such as voice and video that must arrive on time, to ensure that less important traffic does not preempt real-time traffic.

ATM was originally defined by the telephone companies and has been heavily promoted by them as an end-to-end networking technology, as well as a voice technology. In this respect, ATM is both a LAN and WAN technology that can potentially allow customers to replace their separate voice and data networks with a single network to handle both voice and data, as well as other multimedia content such as video.

In the early 1990s, ATM was widely considered the most likely to succeed as an all-pervasive network technology. New companies were formed to develop and market ATM switches and adapters for public and private use. But ATM has been a long time in coming. Many of its features are still being ironed out. In particular, customers and vendors are still trying to figure out how to meld existing LAN technology into ATM networks (for example, see "IP over ATM"). In the meantime, Gigabit Ethernet (1,000 Mbits/sec) has emerged as a likely competitor to ATM. It offers high capacity and compatibility with existing Ethernet networks.

Still, ATM is probably the best technology if your organization has mixed traffic such as data, voice, video, and other multimedia. For data-only traffic in existing Ethernet environments, Gigabit Ethernet is a good choice, but only if you don't expect to integrate data and multimedia in the future.

Keep in mind that it is becoming more and more practical to build premises cabling systems that handle both voice and data. ATM is the clear choice because it has QoS built in. It is a scalable technology that operates from 25 Mbits/sec to 2.46 Gbits/sec, it easily integrates with carrier networks, and it supports integration with any existing technology (with appropriate adaptations).

ATM's scalability is important to growing companies. As the business grows, ATM does not constrain that growth. More bandwidth can be added to accommodate increased data and voice circuit requirements. In the next few years, multimedia applications such as videophone and videoconferencing over networks will become commonplace. Organizations that do not provide such services will not remain competitive. Consider that only 10 years ago, many organizations were still largely using typewriters.

Communication is the key to competitiveness and applications such as e-mail, document sharing, groupware, discussion groups, workflow software, and other applications are surely essential to help people communicate. As the use for these applications grows, so will the need for more bandwidth. ATM is the one technology that can continue to scale up to meet those demands.

## Building ATM Networks

ATM networks can be classed as private and public. Private ATM is the ATM network within an organization, while public ATM is a wide area networking service sold by carriers. As an organization implements ATM, the dividing line between public and private ATM shifts. For example, Figure A-9 illustrates the phases of ATM use. In the first phase, illustrated at the top, a customer uses a carrier's ATM network for wide area links. Notice that data frame and voice traffic from the customer site are delivered to the carrier's ATM switch. In this case, the carrier converts frames to ATM cells.

In phase 2, as illustrated at the bottom of Figure A-9, the customer obtains a private ATM switch and performs all frame-to-cell conversion. The ATM switch also provides a backbone for the data network.

Most organizations will build private ATM networks in phases to accommodate their existing frame-based networks. Figure A-10 illustrates the initial phase and subsequent phase or phases. On the left, an ATM switch is installed as a backbone, possibly to replace an existing FDDI (Fiber Distributed Data Interface) or Fast Ethernet backbone. Routers connect each of the existing networks into this backbone.

In the next phase, switching devices are added at various levels in the network hierarchy. Also, servers are moved to the backbone where they are more accessible to users. Note that cell switching is brought closer to the end user in this phase. At some

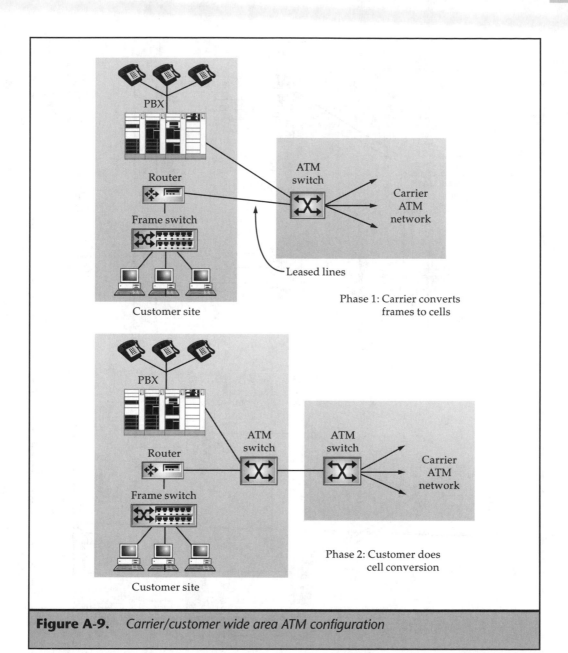

**Figure A-9.**    *Carrier/customer wide area ATM configuration*

point (probably in the distant future), cell switching may be brought all the way to the desktop, but current investment in shared LAN technologies will probably stall this development for some time. Refer to "Network Design and Construction" for more information on building structured networks.

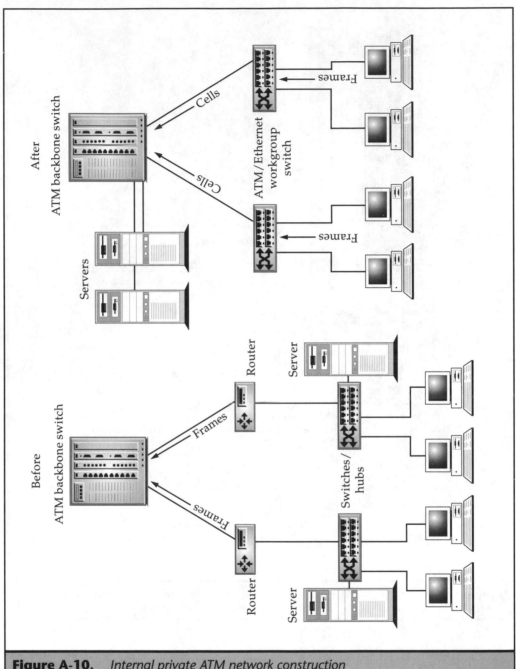

**Figure A-10.** *Internal private ATM network construction*

Fitting ATM into existing networks is not easy. Shared LANs use broadcast, while ATM uses point-to-point connections. LANs are connectionless, while ATM is connection-oriented. A number of proposals, drafts, and standards have been written to help ATM work with existing network technology. This is covered later in this topic under "Internetworking with ATM."

## How ATM Works

ATM was originally defined as part of the B-ISDN (Broadband-Integrated Services Digital Network) standard. B-ISDN is a public digital telecommunications network standard that is designed to offer high-end multimedia, television, CD-quality music, data networking, and other services to business and home users. ATM is the underlying network technology that makes B-ISDN possible. The ATM reference model is shown in Figure A-11 and described here:

■ The physical layer defines the electrical or physical interface, line speeds, and other physical characteristics. ATM is independent of any specific transmission medium.

■ The ATM layer defines the cell format, how cells are transported, and how congestion is handled. It also defines virtual circuit creation and termination.

■ The ATM adaptation layer defines the process of converting information from upper layers into ATM cells. In the networking environment, it provides an interface for converting frames into cells for Ethernet, token ring, and other network standards.

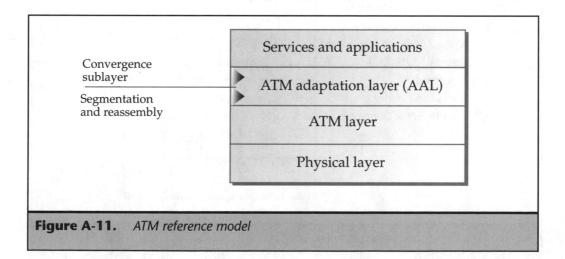

**Figure A-11.**   *ATM reference model*

## The Physical Layer

The physical layer of ATM does not define any one specific medium. LANs were designed for coaxial or twisted-pair cable and have rigid specifications that define the exact bandwidth. The specifications were established to match the electrical components available at the time of design. ATM supports many different media, including existing media used by other communications systems.

Industry experts are endorsing SONET (Synchronous Optical Network) as the ATM physical transport media for both LAN and WAN applications. The ATM Forum is recommending FDDI (100 Mbits/sec), Fibre Channel (155 Mbits/sec), OC3 SONET (155 Mbits/sec), and T3 (45 Mbits/sec) as the physical interfaces for ATM. Currently, most carriers are providing T3 links to their ATM networks.

## The ATM Layer

The ATM layer defines the structure of the ATM cell. It also defines virtual channel and path routing, as well as error control.

There are two forms of the ATM cell header. One is the UNI (User Network Interface), which is used in cells sent by users, and the other is the NNI (Network-to-Network Interface), which is sent by switches to other switches. The UNI cell is

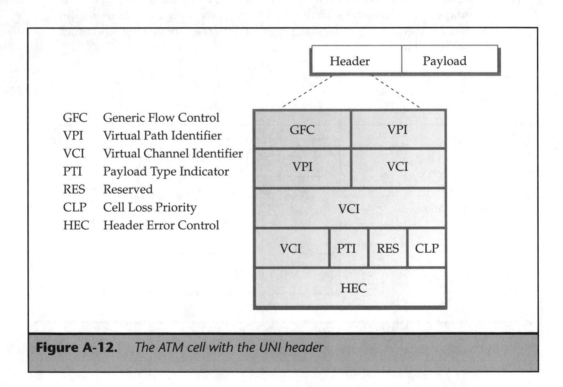

| GFC | Generic Flow Control |
| VPI | Virtual Path Identifier |
| VCI | Virtual Channel Identifier |
| PTI | Payload Type Indicator |
| RES | Reserved |
| CLP | Cell Loss Priority |
| HEC | Header Error Control |

**Figure A-12.**   *The ATM cell with the UNI header*

pictured in Figure A-12. The NNI cell does not have the GFC (Generic Flow Control) field.

The cell is 53 bytes in length: 48 bytes for payload and 5 bytes for header information. Note that header information is almost 10 percent of the cell, which adds up to extensive overhead on long transmissions. ATM cells are packets of information that contain *payload* (data) and header information that contain channel and path information to direct the cell to its destination. The information held by each field in the header is explained here:

- **GFC (Generic Flow Control)**  This field is still undefined in the UNI cell header and is not even in the NNI cell header.

- **VPI (Virtual Path Identifier)**  Identifies virtual paths between users or between users and networks.

- **VCI (Virtual Channel Identifier)**  Identifies virtual channels between users or between users and networks.

- **PTI (Payload Type Indicator)**  Indicates the type of information in the payload area, such as user, network, or management information.

- **CLP (Cell Loss Priority)**  Defines how to drop certain cells if network congestion occurs. The field holds priority values, with 0 indicating a cell of the highest value.

- **HEC (Header Error Control)**  Provides information for error detection and correction of single bit errors.

## AAL (ATM Adaptation Layer)

AAL converges packets from upper layers into ATM cells. For example, in the case of a 1K packet, AAL would segment it into 21 fragments and place each fragment into a cell for transport.

AAL has several service types and classes of operation to accommodate different types of traffic. The service classes categorize applications based on how bits are transmitted, the required bandwidth, and the types of connections required. Figure A-13 illustrates the different types and classes of service.

- **Type 1**  A connection-oriented CBR (constant bit rate) service with timing for audio and video applications. It is similar to T1 or T3 and provides a variety of data rates.

- **Type 2**  A connection-oriented VBR (variable bit rate) service for real-time applications where minor loss is acceptable, and for non-real-time VBR, such as transaction processing.

- **Type 3/4**  An ABR (available bit rate) service for non-time-critical applications such as LAN internetworking and LAN emulation. A base level of service is guaranteed, and extra bandwidth is available for traffic spikes if the network capacity is not filled.

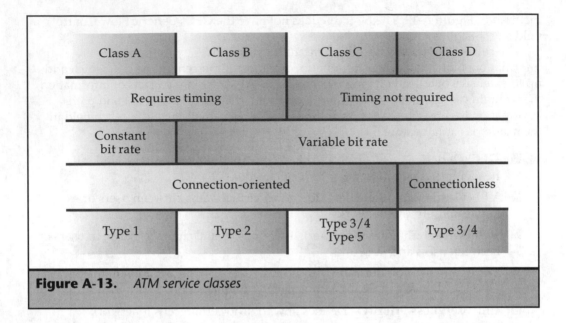

**Figure A-13.** *ATM service classes*

■ **Type 5** A UBR (unspecified bit rate) service that provides spare bandwidth to noncritical services such as file transfers.

QoS (quality of service) can be negotiated with carriers when contracting for services. Keep in mind that circuits can be obtained to transmit in both directions between sites, and those circuits might have different data rates and QoS.

The first parameters for circuit negotiation have to do with the cell delivery rate. There is a maximum data rate that the circuit should carry, an average rate over a period of time, and a minimum rate. Then, there are negotiable parameters such as the level of acceptable cell loss and delay. Finally, there are negotiable parameters related to the number of cell errors.

There are also parameters related to the following:

■ **Admission control** For switched circuits, this is the ability to control a circuit based on the class of the user. When the network is busy, higher class users are given circuit priority, but pay for that status.

■ **Resource reservation** This is simply the ability to reserve a level of service in advance. For example, you could reserve bandwidth for a videoconference to take place at a particular time.

■ **Congestion control**  This control involves congested networks where cells are being dropped. Basically, stations sending low-priority traffic are asked to back off so higher priority (real-time) traffic can get through.

Contract negotiation is an art. Readers should check the Web sites listed at the end of this section for more information on contract negotiation and service provider information.

## Virtual Circuits

As mentioned, ATM is a connection-oriented technology, meaning that it sets up virtual circuits over which end systems communicate. Cells can be quickly forwarded through the circuit, with little processing required by intermediate devices along the path. The terminology for virtual circuits is as follows and is pictured in Figure A-14:

■ **VC (virtual channel)**  Logical connections between end stations

■ **VP (virtual path)**  A bundle of VCs

Think of a VP as a cable that contains a bundle of wires. The cable connects two points, and wires within the cable provide individual circuits between the two points. The advantage of this method is that connections sharing the same path through the network are grouped together and take advantage of the same management actions. If a VP is already set up, adding a new VC is easy since the work of defining paths through the network is already done. Only the end points need to be established. In addition, if a VP changes to avoid congestion or a downed switch, all the VCs (potentially over 65,000) within the VP change with it.

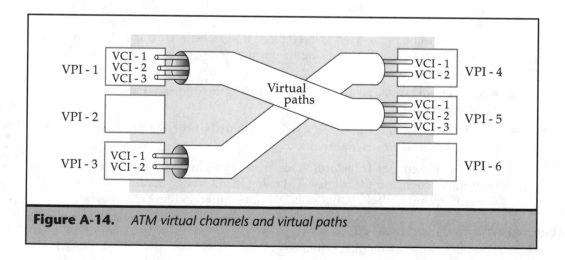

**Figure A-14.**    *ATM virtual channels and virtual paths*

In an ATM cell header, a VPI (Virtual Path Identifier) identifies a link formed by a virtual path and a VCI (Virtual Channel Identifier) identifies a channel within a virtual path. The VPI and VCI are identified and correspond to termination points at ATM switches. For example, in Figure A-14, a virtual path connects VPI-1 and VPI-5. Within this path are three virtual channels. Note that VPIs identify the equivalent of a port specific to the network, while channels within virtual paths are identified relative to that path.

ATM supports both PVCs (permanent virtual circuits) and SVCs (switched virtual circuits). PVCs are always available and SVCs require a setup every time they are used. Multicast channels are also supported, so a single sender can establish a circuit to multiple receivers.

Setting up VCs requires that each switch along the path determine whether it has enough capacity to handle the circuit. If voice and video transmission are required, then enough capacity must be set aside to guarantee the flow and arrival of this time-critical information. Basically, the switch must make sure that all its VCs do not overwhelm its capacity.

Switches contract with one another to build the VCs, and no data is transmitted until the VC is completely established across the network. Of course, setting up VCs is relatively time-consuming, so many switches are rated according to their call setup time. A typical switch can set up 100 to 200 VCs per second. This is usually not an issue in the local environment, but is an issue for the carriers.

## ATM Interfacing

There are a number of ways of connecting ATM networks, as illustrated in Figure A-15. Each of the interfaces shown in the figure is described here:

■ **UNI (User Network Interface)**   Defines the connection between user equipment and ATM equipment. When connected to an ATM WAN, the UNI is the leased line link between the customer site and the carrier access point. It may be a T1 line or an ATM FUNI (Frame UNI). The latter transmits frames to the ATM network, where they are then converted to cells by the carrier. FUNI can reduce hardware costs.

■ **NNI (Network-to-Network Interface)**   This is the interface between ATM devices.

■ **ICI (Intercarrier Interface)**   This is the interface between the ATM connection points of different carrier networks.

■ **DXI (Data Exchange Interface)**   This provides an interface for legacy equipment such as routers into ATM using HDLC (High-level Data Link Control) framing. Packets, not cells, are transmitted to the ATM interface.

## Internetworking with ATM

Most of the above discussion relates to using carrier ATM networks to build WANs, but ATM can also be used to build private networks. An internal LAN can be built

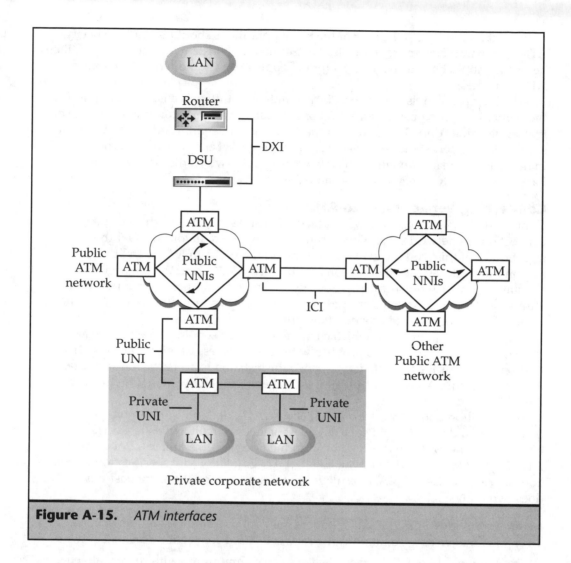

**Figure A-15.** *ATM interfaces*

entirely with ATM by installing ATM NICs in workstations and connecting those workstations to an ATM switch. However, all-ATM networks are rare. The more common scenario is to connect frame networks such as Ethernet to an ATM backbone or build a switched network as shown on the right in Figure A-10.

To get a feel for this topic, digress for a minute to the old phone system. In the early days, one had to call an operator to get a phone connection. Today, anybody can dial anybody else without operator assistance. This is the goal of ATM—to allow a user to connect with any other user over a local or wide area ATM network. The important feature is that the user or the user applications should be able to specify the ATM QoS parameter. In other words, if a user needs a constant bit rate for video, then he or she should be able to request it (or the application should request it) from the ATM network.

The only problem is that current LAN emulation strategies tend to hide ATM from the higher layer protocols and applications running in a user's computer. Because of this, applications don't have a way to specify QoS, but vendors and the ATM Forum are developing new strategies to allow it. Keep this goal of end-to-end ATM connectivity in mind as you read through the next few paragraphs, which discuss the steps that have been taken to integrate LANs and ATM.

### Connecting Legacy LANs to ATM

Connecting legacy LANs to ATM is difficult. One reason is that traditional LANs are connectionless networks and ATM is connection oriented. If you consider the significance of this, you can get to the essence of the problem. When an Ethernet station transmits, all the other stations on the network can hear the message, but only the station to which the message is addressed responds. But if the network is built with an ATM switch, stations can potentially connect to one another over ATM virtual circuits instead of a shared broadcast medium.

How does a station know which circuit to use when sending a message to another station? IP networks solve this problem with ARP (Address Resolution Protocol). A host sends a message to all stations asking which station has a particular IP address. A MAC (Medium Access Control) address is then returned by the station that owns the address.

This method doesn't work on ATM because ATM does not support broadcast. A station would need to send such a request on every circuit, which is a waste of bandwidth. The problem is solved by introducing a way to emulate a LAN across ATM. The ATM Forum defined the LANE (LAN Emulation) 1.0 specification in 1995. You can refer to "LANE (LAN Emulation)," for more information, but basically LANE does two things:

- It provides a protocol-independent method for frame-based, connectionless LAN devices to communicate over a cell-based connection-oriented network.

- It defines how LAN-attached clients can communicate with servers attached to an ATM network without changing application software.

To solve the problem of matching IP addresses to circuits, LANE defines a *LES* (*LAN emulation server*), which maintains a table that matches IP addresses with ATM circuits. The IETF (Internet Engineering Task Force) also adopted this model to some extent and called the LES server the ATMARP (ATM Address Resolution Protocol) server.

Still another problem is that Ethernet networks use broadcast and multicast (sending to all or selected stations, respectively) to perform a variety of operations. If you are going to connect Ethernet and ATM together, you need to support these operations. In this case, a *BUS (broadcast/unknown server)* is introduced. It maintains a connection to every station and can perform the broadcast or multicast operations.

LANE does not provide a total solution for getting end-to-end ATM connectivity. Once legacy LAN clients are connected to this ATM backbone, they still need a way to specify ATM's QoS. As mentioned, LANE tends to hide applications from ATM so existing Ethernet and token ring clients can run unchanged. However, applications see only the frame-based LAN and have no way of talking to the ATM network so they can specify the QoS levels available in ATM. The ATM Forum is working to fix this problem with LANE version 2.0. See "LANE (LAN Emulation)" for more details. In the meantime, solutions such as 3Com's PACE (priority access control enabled) can extend QoS to the desktop. See also "IP over ATM."

Another solution, called Cells in Frames, defines how to emulate ATM all the way to the desktop by carrying cells in frames. See "CIF (Cells in Frames)" for more information.

Still another solution is to put ATM support in the APIs used by programmers to develop applications. The WinSock Group has added QoS to the Windows API, and X/Open is enhancing the UNIX API set. Upgrades will be available in the form of installable drivers. Basically, a QoS-compliant application will be able to pass a request for a virtual circuit with a specific type of service, bandwidth, and delay characteristics down to an ATM driver that will in turn signal the ATM network to set up the virtual circuit.

## Building Virtual Networking

ATM can provide the basis for building virtual networks. Basically, a virtual network is a network that exists logically on top of the physical internetwork. Suppose a new corporate structure calls for relocating members of the marketing department into special task groups that include people from other departments. A marketing person working with Team X gets physically relocated to a special facility, where he or she works with other Team X members from other departments such as engineering and design.

Even though the marketing people are now physically located throughout the organization, they still need to work as a group and share common resources. With virtual networking, you can create a *logical network* for the marketing people on top of the physical network. This logical network is called a *VLAN (virtual LAN)*.

An administrator creates a VLAN by grouping the workstations together, no matter where they exist on the network. All the users on the same VLAN share the same subnetwork address. When a user in a VLAN broadcasts a message, all the users in the VLAN hear the message, even though their computers are attached at a variety of physical locations on the network.

### Routing over VLANs

When users in one VLAN need to communicate with users in another VLAN, routing is necessary to establish a path between the VLANs. One technique for doing this is the ATM Forum's MPOA (Multiprotocol over ATM), a specification that defines layer-3 routing over ATM. Basically, MPOA moves routing to a special server. The approach works like this:

■ To transmit packets between stations in the same VLAN, an MLS (multilayer switch) requests a virtual circuit from the ATM connection manager. The packets are then switched at layer 2.

■ To transmit packets between stations on different VLANs, a routing path is required, which involves layer 3 functionality. In this case, a separate device, called a *route server*, first creates a logical path through the network. Then, the ATM connection manager converts the path into a virtual circuit. Data can then be transmitted on the circuit.

The route server approach has some problems, however. The path creation process is done separately from the ATM connection manager, so the route server may not know the best path currently available on the network, In addition, separate route paths are calculated for each different protocol (IP, SNA, IPX, etc.).

An alternative approach is called I-PNNI (Integrated Private Network-to-Network Interface). PNNI is an ATM standard for creating QoS paths between ATM switches. I-PNNI extends PNNI to provide integrated routing. All the switching and routing devices on the network that are I-PNNI–compatible can share information in order to calculate the best path through the network for end-to-end connections. I-PNNI provides a way for routers and switching devices at the edge of an ATM network to propagate routing information across the ATM network.

IP switching is a technique that was first developed by Ipsilon in the form of IFMP (Ipsilon Flow Management Protocol), but now there are several different proposals on the market. The switches are ATM-based, but the strategy for setting up VCs is simplified. Basically, a switch starts out routing packets but can detect packet flows, for which it sets up a VC with another switch as appropriate. That switch then creates a VC with the next switch, if necessary, and so on.

The advantage of this technique is that VCs are set up on the fly and taken down after a period of nonuse. The constraints of preestablishing a VC all the way through before transmission are removed. In addition, some traffic is simply routed. The strength of this technique lies in the ability to rapidly sense a flow. IFMP only works with IP. Other vendor proposals are discussed under "IP Switching." In all cases, traditional ATM setup and signaling is bypassed to obtain speed and support for legacy systems.

## ATM Alternatives

ATM has been a long time in coming, and several movements are underway that bypass parts of the standard in the interest of support for legacy protocols and networks. In addition, Gigabit Ethernet is becoming available as this book goes to press.

Gigabit Ethernet offers existing Ethernet users the ability to improve backbone speeds (up to 1,000 Mbits/sec) and maintain compatibility with existing Ethernet networks. Gigabit Ethernet proponents are counting on increased capacity to make up for the lack of QoS in Ethernet. With high speed, delivering voice and video in a frame environment becomes possible, as long as the backbone does not become overloaded.

Several vendors have concentrated on improving their routers. Bay Networks and Cisco have multiport router devices in which each port has its own processor for routing traffic at rates up to 100,000 packets per second. That brings the total packet processing power of such devices to over 1 million packets per second.

Cisco's NetFlow algorithms identify long or recurring packet flows between source and destination and establish connection-oriented sessions for those flows. Instead of looking at the complete header of every packet, which takes a lot of processing time, only the first packet is read, and the packet flow is established from the information in that packet. Of course, not all information exchanges constitute a flow of packets that is substantial enough to set up a flow session.

**RELATED ENTRIES**    Cell Relay; Gigabit Ethernet; IMA (Inverse Multiplexing over ATM); IP over ATM; IP Switching; LANE (LAN Emulation); Network Concepts; Network Design and Construction; Prioritization of Network Traffic; QoS (Quality of Service); Routing Protocols and Algorithms; Switched Networks; Virtual Circuit; *and* VLAN (Virtual LAN)

### INFORMATION ON THE INTERNET

| | |
|---|---|
| ATM (documentation, sites, people, vendors, research groups) | http://www.cs.tamu.edu/research/realtime/atm.html |
| The ATM Forum | http://www.atmforum.com |
| Telecom Information Resources (has a large list of related sites) | http://www.spp.umich.edu/telecom/technical-info.html |

## Attenuation

Attenuation is signal loss, measured in decibels, of a signal transmission over distance. The opposite of attenuation is amplification. On network cables, attenuation is the degradation of the digital signal or a loss of amplitude of an electric signal. Repeaters are used to regenerate signals by amplifying them but not changing their information content in any way. With a repeater, a network can be extended beyond its normal range.

**RELATED ENTRIES**    Data Communication Concepts; Signals; *and* Transmission Media, Methods, and Equipment

## Attributes

Attributes define user access to files and directories and the properties of files and directories. A common attribute is "Archive Needed," which indicates that a file has been modified and needs to be included in the next backup. This attribute is then turned off when the file is backed up, but is set on again if a user changes the file. Read-only attributes found on most network operating systems prevent users from changing the contents of files or deleting them.

NetWare 4.x has some interesting attributes. DI (Delete Inhibit) prevents a user from deleting a file or directory. IM (Immediate Compress) causes a file, or the files in a directory to be compressed as soon as possible. DC (Don't Compress) prevents a file, or the files, in a directory from being automatically compressed.

Objects within object-oriented filing systems, databases, and programming languages have attributes called *properties*. If an object is compared to a record within a database, its properties are like the fields within a record that hold values.

## Auditing

Auditing is the collection and monitoring of events on servers and networks for the purpose of tracking security violations and to keep track of how systems are used. A network auditing system logs details of what users are doing on the network so that malicious or unintended activities can be tracked. When auditing is in place, vast amounts of information may be recorded and even archived for future reference. Some audit systems provide event alarms to warn administrators when certain levels or conditions are met.

NetWare 4.x provides a good example of an auditing system. A person called the *auditor* is designated to track events on the network. The events fall into two categories: *volume tracking* and *container tracking*. Each auditing category can have a distinct password, so, for example, the auditor who tracks volume events cannot track container events if they don't have the container password. However, one auditor can track all events if necessary.

One of the primary users to track with the auditing system is the network administrator, who basically has unlimited rights to the system. An auditor can keep administrators "honest" by passively tracking and monitoring all their activities. Initially, the network administrator creates a special auditor account, usually as directed by higher level management. The auditor then logs in to the account and immediately changes the password, effectively blocking all access to the account, even by the network administrator.

The auditor can then set up auditing features, view audit logs, and work in designated audit directories. A record is kept for every activity that is designated for tracking. Events that can be tracked are listed here:

- Directory creation and deletion
- Creating, opening, closing, deleting, renaming, writing, and salvaging files
- Modifying directory entries
- Queue activities
- Server events, such as changing the date and time, downing the server, and mounting or dismounting volumes
- User events, such as logon, logoff, connection termination, space restrictions, granting of trustee rights, and disabling of accounts
- Directory Services events, such as changes in passwords, security, and logon restrictions

■ Activities of a specific user, such as a supervisor or network administrator

Auditing records can be viewed using special filters to produce reports that show specific activities. Filters can be applied to show specific date and time ranges, specified events, file and directory events, or user events.

The Windows NT Auditing system lets you track events that occur on individual servers related to security policies, system events, and application events. There are two types of auditing that you can track with the auditing tools included in Windows NT. The first is user account auditing, which tracks security events and logs them in the server's security log. The second is file system auditing, which tracks file system events. For example, to set up auditing in Windows NT, you open the dialog box pictured next. Note that you can track the success and/or failure of an event. For example, you might want to always track logon failures.

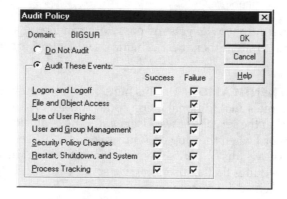

The **syslog** facility exists in the UNIX operating system to create audit trails. It is necessary to protect the audit records from alteration or destruction. They can, for example, be copied to another system that is accessible only by administrators or an auditor.

Administrators should be on the lookout for a large number of failed logon attempts or logins that take place at odd hours, which usually indicate that an intruder is attempting to access the system.

**RELATED ENTRIES**   Logons and Logon Accounts; Security

## Authentication and Authorization

Authentication is required on secure systems to ensure that the person who is logging in is who they say they are. Once individuals are logged in, they are authorized to access various resources based on the rights and privileges assigned to their user accounts or the objects they access. Authentication is also required for message exchange to verify that a particular message has not been fabricated or altered in transit. Authorization determines what users can do once they are authenticated.

There are various levels of authentication, depending on how involved you want to get in validating a user. In the simplest scheme, the user supplies a username (so a server can reference a user account) and a password (so the server can know that the person logging in must be the owner of that account). Of course, this scheme breaks down under a number of circumstances:

- Someone might unknowingly release their password (for example, by writing it on a Post-it note near their desk, perhaps).

- A password could be discovered because it is too simple (such as the name of the user's dog, for example).

- A password is sent across a network in plain text (unencrypted) and is monitored by someone.

In all these cases, someone who gets the password can log on as the user. Two methods are available to strengthen these schemes: two-factor authentication and certificates.

**TWO-FACTOR AUTHENTICATION**    In this method, a token device such as a *smart card* is used that generates an additional logon code. This logon code is synchronized in time with a code that the server knows. Users enter the code along with their username and password when they log on. Thus two items are required to log on: something the user knows (his or her password) and something the user has (the token). This scheme requires that all users carry a smart card (or software equivalent) and is usually implemented for remote users.

**CERTIFICATES**    If you require secure logon to Internet servers or other public servers, the certificate scheme is appropriate. A certificate is basically a digital ID that is guaranteed by a well-known certificate authority such as Verisign. It can prove that the person on the other end of a connection is who they say they are. This scheme uses public-key encryption and provides a way for a user to provide you with his or her public key so that sessions can be encrypted or secure transactions can take place. The details of certificates are quite elaborate, but they make interesting reading. Refer to "Certificates and Certification Systems" and "Public-Key Cryptography" for more details.

**RELATED ENTRIES**    Access Control; ACL (Access Control List); Certificates and Certification Systems; Challenge/Response Protocol; Cryptography; Digital Signatures; Hacker; Logons and Logon Accounts; Passwords; PKI (Public-Key Infrastructure); Public-Key Cryptography; Rights and Permissions; Security; *and* Token-Based Authentication

## Authenticode, Microsoft

Microsoft's Authenticode is part of its larger Internet Security Framework. It attempts to solve one of the larger questions facing the software industry today: How can users trust code that is published on the Internet? It provides a way to sign code so users know that programs obtained from the Internet are legitimate, just as shrink wrap and sealed boxes imply that off-the-shelf packaged software is authentic. Authenticode provides

- Authenticity, so you know who published the code
- Integrity, so you know that code hasn't been tampered with since it was published
- A legitimate and safe way to exchange programs over the Internet

The basic procedure for signing code is for a publisher to get a certificate from a certification authority. The publisher then encrypts its certificates into the code with its private key to create a unique digital signature. The code can then be verified using functions that validate the digital signature, as discussed under "Certificates and Certification Systems." The functions indicate whether the code is valid or whether it is possibly fake or has been tampered with.

While Authenticode is a Microsoft initiative, Netscape and JavaSoft have developed their own code-signing technology called JAR (Java Archive Format). Still other vendors are developing their own technologies. The W3C (World Wide Web Consortium) at http://www.w3.org is attempting to consolidate these digital signing and certificate technologies into a single framework called the Digital Signature Initiative.

**RELATED ENTRIES**    Certificates and Certification Systems; Digital Signatures; *and* Security

## AWG (American Wire Gauge)

AWG is a measurement system for wire that specifies its thickness. As the thickness of the wire increases, the AWG number decreases. Some common cable conductor gauges are listed here:

- **RS-232 serial cable**   22 AWG and 24 AWG
- **Telephone cable**   22 AWG, 24 AWG, and 28 AWG
- **Coaxial thick Ethernet cable**   12 AWG
- **Coaxial thin Ethernet cable**   20 AWG

**RELATED ENTRY**    Transmission Media, Methods, and Equipment

## Baby Bells

The Baby Bells were the result of the restructuring agreement of AT&T in 1984. The agreement created 22 RBOCs (regional Bell operating companies).

**RELATED ENTRIES**   IXC (Interexchange Carrier); LEC (Local Exchange Carrier); *and* RBOCs (Regional Bell Operating Companies)

## Backbone Networks

The backbone is the most basic and predominant network topology. It is used to tie together diverse networks in the same building, in different buildings in a campus environment, or over wide areas. Backbones handle internetwork traffic. If the networks it ties together are departmental networks, then the backbone handles interdepartmental traffic. With the increasing use of Web technology, more traffic has been flowing across the backbone. Users click buttons on Web pages that call up documents on servers throughout the organization or on the Internet. This places more traffic on the backbone than ever before.

There are distributed backbones which tie together distinct LANs and there are collapsed backbones, which exist as wiring hubs and switches. The two topologies are illustrated in Figure B-1.

The distributed backbone on the left in Figure B-1 shows how the network (in this case, an FDDI ring) extends to each department or floor in a building. Each network is connected via a router to the backbone network. In the collapsed backbone shown on the right, a cable runs from each department (or floor) network to a central hub, usually located in a building wiring closet or possibly in the IS (information systems) department. The hub or switch becomes the backbone, moving traffic among the different networks.

The distributed backbone approach can retain its availability. If one of the routers fails, the rest of the network is not affected. However, a packet on one LAN must make a minimum of two router hops to reach another LAN.

In the collapsed backbone, routing is centralized, minimizing hops between LANs. If the departmental devices and the backbone device are switching hubs, then performance can increase dramatically because VLANs (virtual LANs) can be created between any two workstations, eliminating router hops altogether and in some cases, providing nonshared, collision-free circuits between workstations.

So far, our backbone has been limited to a single building. A backbone can link multiple networks in the campus environment or connect networks over wide area network links. These two approaches are pictured in Figure B-2.

The primary reason for a campus backbone is that it is impractical to use the collapsed backbone approach over an entire campus area. Running cable from each site back to a central site is costly, so the alternative is to install a single network such as an FDDI ring throughout the campus.

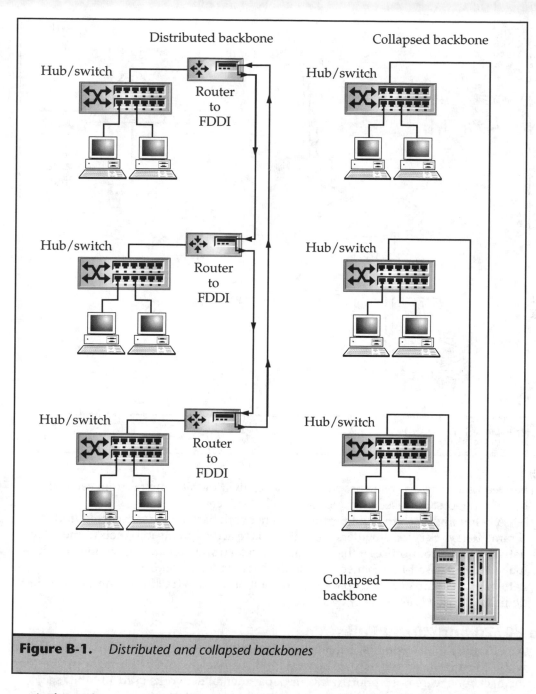

**Figure B-1.** *Distributed and collapsed backbones*

As for wide area networks, two approaches are possible. The private network approach is pictured on the right in Figure B-2. Dedicated leased lines are installed

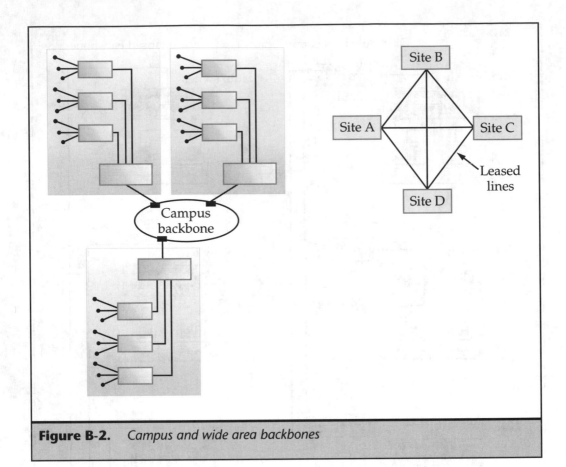

**Figure B-2.** *Campus and wide area backbones*

between each site—a costly proposition, especially if the sites are far from each other, because the cost of leased lines increases with distance.

A better approach to building wide area network backbones is discussed under "Frame Relay." Service providers most likely have access points into their frame relay networks near your offices if they are located in metropolitan areas. That means you make a short leased-line connection into the "frame relay" cloud, and the frame relay network takes care of routing packets to distant offices at a fraction of the cost of using dedicated leased lines.

## The 80/20 and 20/80 Rules

An old rule for backbones was that 80 percent of the traffic stayed in the department while 20 percent crossed the backbone. With this model, high data throughput rates on the backbone were not a priority. If your departmental networks used 10-Mbit/sec Ethernet, you could possibly get by with a 10-Mbit/sec Ethernet backbone or at most, a 100-Mbit/sec FDDI backbone for expanding traffic loads.

However, the 80/20 rule no longer applies for most networks. In fact, it is reversed to the point where backbone networks now handle a majority of the network traffic. This is due to a number of factors, including the following:

- Users are distributed throughout organizations and not located in a single department.

- Database servers and Web servers are centrally located, rather than departmentally located, so the majority of network traffic flows to the same place.

- Hierarchical networking schemes and centralized management naturally create a structure where traffic flows to a central hub or switch.

- Users access the Internet through firewall gateways, which means that all Internet traffic is funneled through the same location.

Because of these factors, the backbone has become the focus of a need for higher and higher data throughput capabilities. Added to that are increasing traffic loads put on the network by multimedia applications. Videoconferencing requires quality of service (QoS) guarantees, meaning that a certain part of the network bandwidth must be set aside to ensure that packets arrive on time. On top of this, many organizations want to integrate their voice telephone system into the network which will demand even more bandwidth.

A hierarchical wiring structure is a priority for being able to handle this type of data traffic. As pictured on the right in Figure B-1, this type of wiring provides a topology that keeps local traffic local (from station to station on the same hub/switch) and funnels traffic to the backbone only when necessary.

ATM (Asynchronous Transfer Mode) has been the most likely contender to satisfy the requirements for collapsed backbones. ATM hubs have high-performance switching matrices that can handle millions of packets per second. Also, ATM provides QoS guarantees for video and voice.

Another more recent contender is Gigabit Ethernet, which provides Gbit/sec (1,000-Mbit/sec) throughput on the backbone switch or between switches. It fits in well with existing Ethernet networks because the same frame format, medium access method, and other defining characteristics are retained. In many cases, a Gigabit Ethernet switch can replace an existing Fast Ethernet switch with little other modification to the network.

In general, switched-based building blocks are the components you need to build a high-speed hierarchical network that maintains high performance under big traffic loads. Refer to "Switched Networks," for more information on how to build these "new" networks.

In the wide area, a new approach is to build VPNs (virtual private networks) over the Internet. The strategy is simple: install encrypting routers at each site with connections to the Internet. The routers encrypt the data contents of packets but keep the network addresses readable so they can be routed across the Internet. This is a cheap way to build secure links between your remote sites; however, the Internet is subject to delays, as you probably well know.

**RELATED ENTRIES**    ATM (Asynchronous Transfer Mode); Frame Relay; Gigabit Ethernet; Network Design and Construction; Structured Cabling Standards; Switched Networks; VLAN (Virtual LAN); *and* VPN (Virtual Private Network)

## Back-End Systems

*Back-end systems* loosely refers to servers, superservers, midrange systems, and mainframes that provide services to users. They may be grouped together at a so-called *server farm*. In the client/server relationship, these systems are obviously servers. Client/server computing splits processing between a front-end system that runs on the client's workstation, and back-end systems. Typical back-end services include DBMSs (database management systems), messaging systems (for example, Lotus Notes and Microsoft Exchange), gateways to other systems such as IBM hosts, and network management systems.

Users interact with applications in front-end systems to make requests on back-end systems. The back-end systems then process the requests, searching and sorting data, serving up files, and providing other services. The back-end systems are close to the data they work on, so this arrangement uses the network efficiently.

Three-tier systems extend the client/server system by adding a middle system (such as a Web server) that performs some processing normally done by either the client or the server. A Web server accepts requests from clients, passes those requests to back-end systems, accepts the response, formats it into a Web page, and sends the Web page to the user. This system is scalable. If traffic increases, the Web server can distribute some of its workload to peer servers that are not as busy. More important, the middle tier in mission-critical business environments may hold the *business logic* (rules, procedures, and/or operational sequences) that is shared by all applications.

**RELATED ENTRIES**    Client/Server Computing; Multitiered Architectures; *and* Servers

## Backplane

Hubs and switches are the building blocks of structured networks. They are boxes built on a chassis that typically includes redundant power supplies and a modular plug-in board called the backplane. The backplane is like the motherboard of a personal computer but far superior in its architecture, at least on high-end hub/switch devices. Most hubs and switches today implement a shared-bus design, which is discussed here.

A shared bus on the backplane moves data among the modules and ports installed in the hub. On a simple hub, the bus is a simple repeater. On a sophisticated switching device, the bus typically implements high-speed TDM (time division multiplexing) to shuttle information among ports. The design of this bus is critical to the performance of the hub. With switching, the hub can provide a dedicated line between two ports.

A traditional hardware-based cross-bar switch is pictured in Figure B-3(a) to help illustrate how switches operate. It uses a point-to-point matrix that can provide a link between any input port and any output port. Circuitry on the switch establishes links as required. Note that input port 4 is connected with output port 5, and input port 7 is connected to output port 4.

The bus design using TDM is pictured in Figure B-3(b). A slot is reserved in a continuously repeating transmission on the bus for each port. When one port is linked to another, data from the input port moves into the slot changer, where the order of the slots is rearranged to match the current switching configuration. For example, to move frames on input port 6 to output port 4, the slot changer rearranges the slot order so that the number 6 slot is in the number 4 position on the output side. Bus architectures provide predictable performance because every port has a dedicated slot it can use. They are also easy to scale to much larger sizes. The bus speed can be increased to provide higher-performance inputs and outputs.

**RELATED ENTRIES**  Cell Relay; Hubs/Concentrators/MAUs; Matrix Switch; *and* Switched Networks

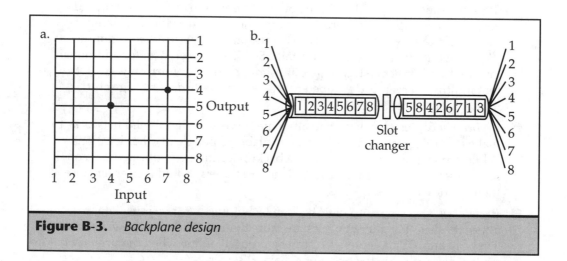

**Figure B-3.** *Backplane design*

# Backup and Data Archiving

It is essential to back up the data on servers and other systems throughout your network. That is obvious. This section describes a number of ways you can perform backups, including copying data to magnetic tape or optical disks, or by copying or replicating information to other systems. Before getting started, take note of the following terminology:

- A *backup* is a copy of online storage information that provides fault protection. An *archive* is a historical backup.

- An *online storage device* is a high-performance magnetic disk that stores information users access most often. *Nearline* and *offline storage devices* are slower, secondary storage devices that provide backup services or archiving services.

- *Hierarchical file systems* move little-used files or large image files from online storage to nearline storage systems such as optical disk, where they remain available to users. For more information, see "Storage Management Systems."

- *Tape backup systems* are the traditional backup medium while *optical disk systems* provide archiving and nearline storage requirements.

- *Real-time backups* take place at any time and must have a procedure for handling files that are opened by users. In most cases, the backup system tracks open files and returns to back them up later.

- *Disk Mirroring* is a real-time strategy that writes data to two or more disks at the same time. If one disk fails, the other continues to operate and provide access for users. *Server mirroring* provides the same functionality, except that an entire server is duplicated. This strategy allows users to continue accessing data if one of the servers fails. See "Fault Tolerance" for additional information. *Clustering* techniques are similar to server mirroring, except that multiple servers are grouped together to provide data storage and multisystem processing.

- *Replication* copies information to alternate servers on distributed networks to make that information more readily available to people in other locations. While replication is not necessarily a backup technique, replicated data on remote servers can be made available to local users should the server close to them go down.

- *Remote vaulting* is an automatic backup technique that transmits data to alternate sites. The alternate sites are more than just data storage warehouses. They are entire data centers that can be brought online when the primary data center goes offline in the event of a major disaster.

The traditional backup medium is magnetic tape. Tapes are relatively inexpensive, making it economical to devise an archiving scheme where you store tapes permanently at safe locations rather than reusing the tapes. This section first discusses backups in terms of magnetic tape, then looks at other backup devices. You can refer to "Storage Systems" for additional information.

Here are some points to keep in mind:

■ Back up data regularly or whenever you make major upgrades to software, directory structures, and configurations.

■ Even if disk mirroring, server mirroring, and replication are implemented, you still need an archival storage mechanism that can restore corrupted data. For example, in a mirrored setup, corrupted data is written to most disks or servers at the same time. To recover, you might need to go to the most recent offline backup set.

■ Perform incremental backups to the files that have changed since you last made a major backup. If the information on your server changes constantly, you'll need to back up constantly.

■ Store a duplicate backup set at an off-site location to protect the backups from local disasters such as fires, earthquakes, and floods.

■ Before you put your server into service, back it up, then try restoring the information to make sure everything works and that you are familiar with the process.

■ A backup system must have a way to deal with files that are open at the time of backup. Schedule all of your backups during hours when fewer files are likely to be open.

■ To minimize network traffic imposed by backups, attach backup systems to the systems that need to be backed up.

## Backup Operators

Backup operators are administrative personnel that handle backing up data. Keep in mind that they have full access to all your data. They can carry tapes off-site, and they have the rights/permissions to access all files on systems, giving them the opportunity to steal, corrupt, alter, or use the data for their own benefit.

Designate only trusted people as backup operators, and make sure their rights are limited to only those files and directories they need to back up. As an added precaution, you should make sure that an auditing system tracks and logs all activities of the backup operator.

## Types of Backup

There are three types of backup: *normal*, *incremental*, and *differential*. The type of backup you choose depends on how many tapes you use, how often you want to back up, whether you are archiving tapes at a permanent storage location, and whether you rotate copies of your tapes off-site.

**NORMAL BACKUP**   A normal backup copies all the files selected for backup to a backup device and marks the files with a flag to indicate that they have been backed up. This method is the easiest to use and understand, because the most recent tape has the most recent backup. However, you'll need more tapes and more time for backup since all the selected files are backed up.

**INCREMENTAL BACKUP**   Incremental backup backs up only files that have been created or changed since the last normal or incremental backup. Files are marked with an archive flag so that they don't get backed up in the next backup unless they have been changed. This method requires that you create a normal backup set on a regular basis. If you need to restore from backup, you first restore the normal backup, then restore each incremental backup in order.

**DIFFERENTIAL BACKUP**   With differential backup, you back up only files that were created or changed since the last normal (or incremental) backup. This method does not mark files with an archive flag to indicate that they have been backed up; consequently, they are included in a normal backup. If you implement this method, you should still create a normal backup on a regular basis. If you need to restore, first restore the normal backup, then restore the last differential backup tape.

The above backup procedures assume that files are being backed up one at a time. This is called a *file-by-file backup*. While such backups are usually slow, they allow the backup operator to back up individual files as they change between backup. An alternative method is the *image backup*, which basically streams all the information on a disk without regard for the file structure to the backup medium. The advantage of this method is speed, but the entire volume must be backed up at the same time and the restore must usually be done on a disk that is physically the same as the original.

Stac Electronics (http://www.stac.com) has a product that bridges the gap between file-by-file and image backup. File-by-file systems are slow because each file must be opened, copied, then closed. Stac's Replica product uses a special technique to quickly copy volumes without the need to open and close every file. This provides backup speeds similar to image backups, but the disk is not copied sector by sector, so there is no need to use a similar storage device in the event of a restore.

## Tape Rotation Methods

The number of backups you perform depends on the number of copies you want to keep, whether you want to keep on-site and off-site copies, and the age of the last backup (hours, days, weeks). You should consider a backup rotation method, which keeps incremental copies of backup data available.

The backup rotation method discussed here stores current and older data on a set of media that you can store in other locations, thus reducing the risk of losing your only backup set. If you have a five-day work week, you need 20 tapes. Increase the number of tapes if you have six- or seven-day work weeks. Here are the key points of this rotation method:

- Four tapes are labeled Monday, Tuesday, Wednesday, and Thursday. Use these tapes for incremental or differential backup.

- Four tapes are labeled Week 1, Week 2, Week 3, and Week 4. Create a complete backup to these tapes every Friday.

- Twelve tapes are labeled for each month of the year; back up to these tapes at the end of each month. These tapes are stored off-site.

To create a duplicate backup set that you can carry to an off-site location, double the number of tapes.

 *NOTE:  This is only one example of a rotation method. You may need to alter this technique to fit your own needs.*

With any backup system, you need to run a restoration test to ensure that your backup and restore procedures work. You might want to set aside spare servers and then run restoration tests using these servers on a regular basis. Before dismissing the concept of spare servers as an unjustifiable expense, consider how much a downed server could cost you in dollars and in customer dissatisfaction.

## Backup Management Systems

Automated backup systems include dedicated backup servers that can automatically back up data to magnetic disk, jukebox tape libraries, and jukebox optical disk systems. They may provide hierarchical storage management functions as well. A typical automated system will run 24 hours a day and provide backup services for a number of clients (clients in this case are file and application servers that use the backup services). For example, ARCserve from Cheyenne Software (http://www.cheyenne.com) runs on Novell NetWare servers and provides support for NetWare, Windows NT, SCO UNIX, SCO UnixWare, SUN systems, IBM/AIX, HP/UX, and SGI IRIX. It provides centralized backup administration, data compression, security, and a number of other features specific to the clients it supports. The Arback and Boole & Babbage products also support remote vaulting. A list of vendors that make backup products is presented at the end of this section, under "Information on the Internet." Others can be found in Appendix A.

There are many problems with tape backup. Files may have changed since the last backup and these changes will be lost in the event of a restore. Also, the administrator is faced with creating and tracking incremental or differential backups. Tape backup is also slow. Because of these problems, many backup products now take advantage of server mirroring techniques and magnetic disk storage. To overcome the problem of file corruption being written to mirrored systems simultaneously, additional backup servers are included in the arrangement that retain data without new changes for a period of time.

Figure B-4 shows a hierarchical backup system. Note that mirrored servers provide reliable real-time backup for the current state of all files. The backup server may back up files on the mirrored servers every day, every hour, or at other defined intervals. Files on the backup server move to offline optical disk storage and eventually to tape storage, which is carried off-site. In the event that corrupted information is written to the mirrored servers, users can fall back to the backup server. If corrupted files are not detected and are written to the backup server, the most recent good file can be obtained from the optical disk or tape archives. This system can be totally automated and run continuously so that the most recent uncorrupted copy of a file can be traced back through the backup server to the archive, as necessary.

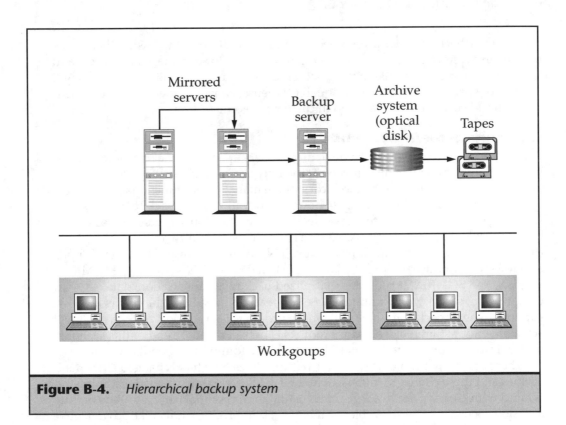

**Figure B-4.**   *Hierarchical backup system*

**RELATED ENTRIES**   Clustering; Data Migration; Data Protection; Disaster Recovery; Fault Management; Fault Tolerance; Mirroring; Power and Grounding Problems and Solutions; Replication; Storage Management Systems; *and* Storage Systems

### INFORMATION ON THE INTERNET

| | |
|---|---|
| Boole & Babbage, Inc. | http://www.boole.com |
| Cheyenne Software | http://www.cheyenne.com |
| CommVault Systems, Inc. | http://www.commvault.com |
| Computer Associates International, Inc. | http://www.cai.com |
| Dantz Development Corp. | http://www.dantz.com |
| EMASS, Inc. | http://www.emass.com |
| EMC Corporation | http://www.emc.com |
| Legato Systems, Inc. | http://www.legato.com |
| MTI Technology Corp. | http://www.mti.com |
| NCE Storage Solutions | http://www.ncegroup.com |
| NovaStor Corp. | http://www.novastor.com |
| Novell, Inc. | http://www.novell.com |
| Software Partners/32, Inc. | http://www.sp32.com |

## BACP (Bandwidth Allocation Control Protocol)

BACP is a proposed Internet protocol that helps users manage a combination of dial-up links, usually over ISDN (Integrated Services Digital Network) connections. BACP provides what is called *dial on demand* (or *bandwidth on demand)*, a technique for providing additional bandwidth as needed by combining two or more circuits into a single circuit with a higher data throughput rate. The technique is useful for accommodating bursts in traffic, videoconferencing, backup sessions, and other requirements.

Basic rate ISDN consists of two digital circuits for home or business use. The circuits can be used for two separate phone calls, a phone call and a computer connection, or two separate computer connections. Each circuit provides a data rate of 64 Kbits/sec. In addition, the circuits can be combined into a single 128-Kbit/sec channel. You use dial on demand to automatically combine channels when data traffic increases beyond the capacity of a single channel. One advantage of dialing on demand with ISDN is that calls are usually charged on a per-call basis. When the demand falls back, the second line is automatically disconnected to save phone charges.

BACP will work in conjunction with the IETF (Internet Engineering Task Force)'s PPP Multilink (Point-to-Point Protocol Multilink). BACP extends PPP Multilink by providing a way for different vendors' equipment to negotiate for additional bandwidth. Routers exchange BACP messages to negotiate link requirements for providing extra bandwidth or to take lines down when extra bandwidth is no longer needed.

The BACP specification was under evaluation by the IETF at the time of this writing.

**RELATED ENTRIES**    Bandwidth on Demand; Bandwidth Reservation; Bonding; Circuit-Switching Services; DDR (Dial-on-Demand Routing); Inverse Multiplexing; ISDN (Integrated Services Digital Network); Load Balancing; *and* PPP Multilink

**INFORMATION ON THE INTERNET**

Ascend Communications, Inc. has information    http://www.ascend.com
on BACP, along with its own related protocol
called MP+ (Multilink Protocol+)

# Balun

Balun is a contraction of *bal*anced/*un*balanced. Transmission lines can be balanced or unbalanced. A *balanced* line is typically a twisted-pair or twinax cable that contains two conductors. An *unbalanced* line is typically a coaxial cable. In a balanced line, both wires are connected to the generator (sender) and receiver and each of the wires has an equal current, but the currents are in opposite directions. In an unbalanced line, current flows through the signal conductor and returns on the ground.

A balun provides a way to join these two different types of cables when connecting terminals to IBM hosts. Network installers who want to convert from coaxial to twisted-pair cable for a particular cable run can do so by installing balun transformers. A balun is required on each side of the twisted-pair run.

# Bandwidth

Bandwidth is a measure of the difference between the highest and lowest frequencies available in a communication channel. The range of frequencies is specified in hertz (cycles per second). For example, the analog signals for telephone communication occupy the voice frequency range of 400 to 3,400 Hz. Thus, the voice bandwidth, or passband, is approximately 3,000 Hz wide, as pictured in Figure B-5. Bandwidth is often used to refer to the throughput of a system, but it is only indirectly related to throughput. *Data rate* or *capacity* is a better way to refer to the amount of data that can pass through a system.

The capacity of a data channel is a measure of its transmission rate, usually measured in bits per second. The higher the bandwidth, the higher the transmission rate. That is because it is easier to encode data into a high-bandwidth signal and because higher frequencies simply transmit signal changes at a faster rate. For simplicity, look at Figure B-6. The bit rate is directly proportional to the frequency of the signal. Voice-grade telephone lines have a cutoff frequency at around 3,400 Hz. At that frequency, it is very difficult to send binary signals at data rates higher than 38.4

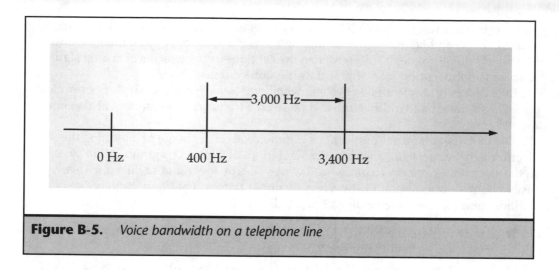

**Figure B-5.**   *Voice bandwidth on a telephone line*

Kbits/sec without using special techniques. In this case, the capacity of the channel is 38.4 Kbits/sec.

Note that in a purely digital transmission where signals are transmitted as discrete high and low voltages, it is more appropriate to talk about the frequency of the signal changes rather than bandwidth. That is why processors and data buses are rated in

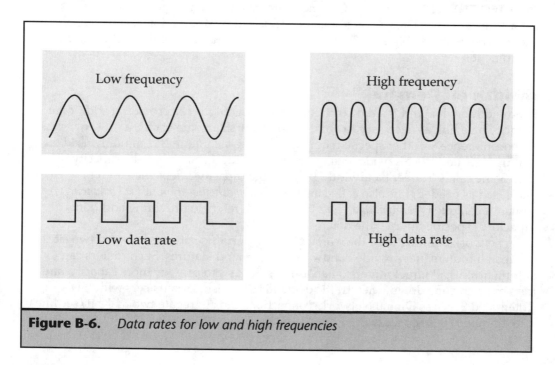

**Figure B-6.**   *Data rates for low and high frequencies*

megahertz. For example, the PCI bus has a rate of 66 MHz. If you can imagine turning a flashlight on and off at a rate of 66 million times per second, you can imagine how this purely digital signal is different than the continuous waveforms of analog signals used on telephones and many other transmission systems.

Every physical transmission system, whether it is copper cable, air, or fiber-optic cable, has a finite bandwidth. Note that noise on a transmission system will also limit the data rate.

The FCC (Federal Communications Commission) is in charge of allocating the electromagnetic spectrum and thus the bandwidth of various communication systems. In the electromagnetic spectrum, sound waves occupy low ranges while microwaves, visible light, ultraviolet, and X-rays occupy upper ranges. The bandwidth occupied by various communication technologies is listed here:

- Bandwidths in the 500 to 929 MHz range are allocated to television and radio broadcast, as well as transportation radio (taxis, for example).

- The bandwidth from 932 to 1,999 MHz is allocated to planes and ships.

- Spread-spectrum radio used for security and paging systems occupies 902 to 928 MHz.

- Wireless mobile communications is allocated to the 930 to 931 MHz and 2,000 to 2,400 MHz (2 to 2.4 GHz) ranges.

**RELATED ENTRIES**    Capacity; Channel; Circuit; Data Communication Concepts; Data Transfer Rates; Delay; Electromagnetic Spectrum; Modulation Techniques; PPS (Packets per Second); Signals; Throughput; *and* Transmission Media, Methods, and Equipment

## Bandwidth on Demand

Bandwidth on demand is a data communication technique for providing additional capacity on a link as necessary to accommodate bursts in data traffic, a videoconference, or other special requirements. The technique is commonly used on dial-up lines and WANs (wide area networks) to temporarily boost the capacity of a link. Some call it "rubber bandwidth" because the capacity can be increased or decreased as needed. It is also called *dynamic bandwidth allocation* or *load balancing*. A similar technique is *bandwidth on time-of-day* which refers to providing additional capacity at specific times of the day.

A network administrator that cannot be sure of traffic patterns between two sites can install routers that provide bandwidth-on-demand features. Such routers can automatically call target routers on an as-needed basis to provide more capacity, and then bring the line down when traffic demands diminish. Home users with ISDN (Integrated Services Digital Network) connections can aggregate two 64-Kbit/sec lines into a single 128-Kbit/sec line.

Bandwidth on demand is both economical and practical. It makes sense to use a switched line and only pay for services as they are needed, rather than lease an expensive dedicated line that may go underused part of the time. Networks such as frame relay can automatically provide more capacity without the need to add additional lines, but the capacity is limited by the size of the trunk that connects a customer to the frame relay network.

*Inverse multiplexing* is typically used to combine individually dialed lines into a single, higher-speed channel. Data is divided over the lines at one end and recombined at the other end. Both ends of the connection must use the same inverse multiplexing and demultiplexing techniques. A typical dial-on-demand connection happens like this: a router on one end makes a normal connection, and then queries the router at the other end for additional connection information. When traffic loads are heavy, the additional connections are made to accommodate the traffic requirements.

The Ascend Pipeline 75 remote access device determines when to add or subtract channels as follows: A specified time period is used as the basis for calculating ALU (average line utilization). The ALU is then compared to a target percentage threshold. When the ALU exceeds the threshold for a specified period of time, the Pipeline 75 attempts to add channels. When the ALU falls below the threshold for a specified period of time, it then removes the channels.

## Telephone Company Offerings

The telephone companies and other providers offer bandwidth on demand as part of their service offerings. Both ISDN and frame relay provide the services and have the potential to replace expensive dedicated leased lines such as T1 lines. As mentioned, basic rate ISDN has two 64-Kbit/sec B channels that can be combined into a single 128-Kbit/sec channel using bandwidth-on-demand techniques. See "BACP (Bandwidth Allocation Control Protocol)." For corporate users, AT&T provides worldwide switched digital services over an ISDN backbone that provides bandwidth on demand in increments of 64 Kbits/sec up to T1 rates (1.544 Mbits/sec).

A common telephone company offering called *Multirate ISDN* is not necessarily automatic. It requires that you call the phone company in advance of needing the bandwidth and "demand" the extra bandwidth. This service is often used for videoconferencing and is not appropriate for the unpredictable bandwidth requirements of LAN traffic.

An alternative method is called *bonding*. Instead of calling the phone company to have multiple lines combined, customers bind multiple lines that are connected into routers or inverse multiplexing devices. Once again, bonding takes place when the call is set up. There is no dynamic allocation, so this technique is best suited for videoconferencing and not the dynamic requirements of LANs.

An option for handling LAN traffic is PPP Multilink (Point-to-Point Protocol Multilink), an IETF recommendation. This protocol dynamically allocates bandwidth as needed and is supported in most vendors' routers. PPP Multilink is well suited for traffic bursts and overflows caused by backup sessions, conferences, large file transfers, or start-of-day traffic spikes. The protocol supports many different types of connections, including ISDN, frame relay, and analog lines; and it operates in software, making it more efficient for on-the-fly allocation of lines. BACP (Bandwidth Allocation Control Protocol) is an extension to the protocol that defines a way for devices from different vendors to negotiate bandwidth.

**RELATED ENTRIES**    Bandwidth on Demand; Bandwidth Reservation; Bonding; Circuit-Switching Services; DDR (Dial-on-Demand Routing); Frame Relay; Inverse Multiplexing; ISDN (Integrated Services Digital Network); Load Balancing; PPP Multilink; *and* WAN (Wide Area Network)

## Bandwidth Reservation

Bandwidth reservation is a way of reserving bandwidth on a channel for special transmissions, usually time-sensitive transmissions such as real-time voice and videoconferencing. On private networks, bandwidth reservation is a matter of setting aside bandwidth for specific data transmissions such as a videoconference. On WANs (wide area networks) or Internet connections, bandwidth reservations must be established by contacting the service provider and reserving bandwidth in advance. Bandwidth reservation can provide a guaranteed level of service, however, governing the bandwidth can be a problem. On public networks, bandwidth reservation carries an extra charge.

Bandwidth reservation is a built-in feature of cell-based ATM (Asynchronous Transfer Mode) networks. The fixed size of the ATM cell (53 bytes) makes it easy to move traffic through switches at predictable rates. Imagine an intersection in which all cars are exactly the same size. Traffic flows smoothly. Now picture the same intersection in which semi-trailer trucks are negotiating turns. The normal flow of traffic gets held up. It is hard to predict how long it will take a single vehicle to get through. Variable-length frames like those used in Ethernet are like the semi trucks. They produce unpredictable traffic flows that are unsuitable for real-time traffic like video. Interestingly, Gigabit Ethernet (Ethernet at 1,000 Mbits/sec) attempts to get around this problem using fat data pipes.

On ATM networks, cells can be allocated to a specific transmission, such as a videoconference, in advance. Think of the traffic moving across a connection as a train with many boxcars. To guarantee delivery, every other boxcar (or every third boxcar) is allocated to the video transmission. All other traffic contends for the remaining cells.

Bandwidth reservation is also described as *quality of service* (*QoS*) or *prioritization*. With QoS, different qualities of traffic can be designated, with some traffic getting more bandwidth than others, depending on the category assignment.

A protocol called RSVP (Resource Reservation Protocol) was in the draft stages at the IETF at the time of this writing. RSVP provides bandwidth reservation on the Internet and a way to bill users who need more bandwidth for special requirements.

**RELATED ENTRIES** ATM (Asynchronous Transfer Mode); Cell Relay; Prioritization of Network Traffic; QoS (Quality of Service); RSVP (Resource Reservation Protocol); *and* RTP (Real-time Transport Protocol)

## Banyan VINES

Banyan VINES is a networking operating system with a UNIX kernel that allows users of popular PC desktop operating systems such as DOS, OS/2, Windows, and those for Macintosh systems to share information and resources with each other and with host computing systems. VINES first appeared in the 1980s. It provides full UNIX NFS (Network File System) support in its core services and TCP/IP for transport. It also includes Banyan's StreetTalk Directory Services, possibly the most popular component of the operating system. In fact, Banyan has marketed StreetTalk on other platforms, including Windows NT Server.

In recent years, VINES has not been able to keep market share and its future remains in doubt, especially as other, more powerful network operating systems, such as Novell NetWare and Windows NT, with their own directory services, are pushed to market with much more enthusiasm and dollars by their vendors. Banyan has been branching into other areas. Its Coordinate.com division provides products based on the Banyan StreetTalk Directory and BeyondMail messaging technologies.

## VINES Features

Like other networks, VINES is built around servers that provide services to client workstations. It is designed to help organizations build fully distributed computing environments around a suite of enterprise network services, including security, messaging, administration, host connectivity, and wide area network communication.

VINES provides enterprise network services that are not server-centric, but services-centric. Users on Banyan networks access and view resources logically, without needing to know where resources are physically located. Users see the entire network and need only log on once.

Banyan StreetTalk allows VINES users to quickly find and access all resources, regardless of where they reside in the enterprise. StreetTalk's unique use of attributes keeps naming simple while maintaining useful descriptive information about the properties of every resource on the network. An enhanced graphical administration tool makes it easier to explore and manage resources across the enterprise. And a powerful directory assistance service speeds the search of StreetTalk directories throughout the networked environment.

Banyan's StreetTalk Directory service is designed to integrate and manage a growing variety of heterogeneous environments including Banyan networks, Windows NT, UNIX, and NetWare. StreetTalk extends peer-to-peer client workgroups to encompass every user and resource on the network. StreetTalk integrates with all VINES core services so that network services and applications always know a user's physical location and security privileges. Users can log on from any location and their network environment remains the same. In addition, users log on to the network, not to an individual server.

StreetTalk Directory Assistance provides distributed directory services. It collects information about network-wide services and places the information in databases that users can search when looking for other users or services on the network. The data includes information about users, printers, files, and gateways. Administrator-defined attributes are preconfigured with the standard attribute types defined in the X.500 specification.

With the *Intelligent Messaging* option, Banyan's robust messaging backbone, VINES supports a wide range of messaging capabilities. These include messaging-enabled workflow applications that streamline communications, reduce cycle time for business processes, and improve productivity.

Through its distributed management architecture, VINES establishes a framework for highly scalable, standards-based SNMP (Simple Network Management Protocol) management, allowing administrators to cost effectively manage the network from any point.

The product has a number of other features or options, including support for a wide range of peripherals (CD-ROM drives, fax gateways, and network printers), network management and analysis applications for monitoring the network, software distribution and metering, mini/mainframe connectivity applications, terminal emulation packages, and security/backup/restore applications.

VINES runs on an Intel-based processor system and supports Ethernet, token ring, or FDDI (Fiber Distributed Data Interface) network adapters. It support popular clients including DOS, OS/2, Windows, and Macintosh. The package comes on CD-ROM with licenses for 100, 250, 500, and 1,000 users.

**INFORMATION ON THE INTERNET**

Banyan Systems, Inc.          http://www.banyan.com

## Baseband Network

Baseband is a transmission method in which direct current pulses are applied directly to the cable to transmit digital signals. The discrete signal consist of either high- or low-voltage pulses that represent binary 1s and 0s or that that hold binary information in encoded form. (For more information, see "Signals.") A baseband network is usually limited to a local area. Ethernet is a shared baseband network on which many stations transmit signals, but only one at a time.

Compare baseband to broadband transmission, in which radio signals from multiple channels are modulated onto separate "carrier" frequencies, and in which the bandwidth is subdivided into separate communication channels, each of which occupies a specific frequency range. Broadband transmission distances can be very large.

The direct-current signals placed on a baseband transmission system have a tendency to degrade over distance due to resistance, capacitance, and other factors. In addition, outside interference from electrical fields generated by motors, fluorescent lights, and other electrical devices can further corrupt the signal. The higher the data transmission rate, the more susceptible the signal is to degradation. For this reason, networking standards such as Ethernet specify cable types, cable shielding, cable distances, transmission rates, and other details that are known to work and provide relatively error-free service in most environments.

**RELATED ENTRIES**   Broadband Transmission; Ethernet; Signals; *and* Transmission Media, Methods, and Equipment

## Bastion Host

A bastion host is a security firewall the protects an internal network from attacks that come from external networks such as the Internet. The bastion host is the main point of contact to the outside and so is the most vulnerable system. For more information, see "Firewall."

## Baud

Baud is a measure of signal changes per second in a device such as a modem. It represents the number of times the state of a communication line changes per second. The name comes from the Frenchman Baudot, who developed an encoding scheme for the French telegraph system in 1877.

Baud is rarely used to refer to modem speeds because it does not have a relationship to the number of bits transferred per second on high-speed modems. If a modem transferred 1 bit for every signal change, then its bits-per-second rate and baud rate would be the same. However, encoding techniques are employed to make 1 baud or signal change represent 2 or more bits. Two bits per baud is known as dibit encoding and 3 bits per baud is known as tribit encoding.

**RELATED ENTRIES**   Analog Signals; Data Communication Concepts; Modems; Modulation Techniques; Signals; *and* Transmission Media, Methods, and Equipment

## BBN (Bolt, Beranek, and Newman)

This company received the first contract to build what became the ARPANET (the forerunner of the Internet) in July 1968. The contract's purpose was to construct a network for sharing resources that used existing telephone circuits and switching nodes. The contract specified that protocols and procedures were to be implemented as well. The original plan was to connect dissimilar and geographically dispersed mainframe computers so that attached terminals could access resources on any of the connected computers. BBN and a group of university-based researchers and graduate students eventually worked out many of the details of the network, but BBN was responsible for developing the core packet-switching technology that eventually became TCP/IP, the networking protocol for the Internet.

Today, BBN is a major Internet service provider that builds and maintains networks throughout the world for government and commercial customers. It offers products for creating secure Internet infrastructures, electronic commerce systems, and other advanced technologies. Its BBN Planet service offerings include high-speed, dedicated and dial-up Internet access, managed Internet security, World Wide Web site creation and hosting, custom Internet application consulting, and systems integration.

**RELATED ENTRY**    Internet

**INFORMATION ON THE INTERNET**

BBN Corporation                http://www.bbn.com

# Beans

*See* the "JavaBeans" subheading under "Java."

# Bellcore

Bellcore was established on January 1, 1984 to provide engineering, administrative, and other services to the telecommunications companies of Ameritech, Bell Atlantic, BellSouth, NYNEX, Pacific Telesis, SBC Communications, and US WEST. Today, Bellcore operates globally to provide communications software, engineering, and telecommunications consulting services. It is a leader in the creation and development of technologies such as ADSL (Asymmetrical Digital Subscriber Line), ATM (Asynchronous Transfer Mode), ISDN (Integrated Services Digital Network), frame relay, PCS (Personal Communications Services), SMDS (Switched Multimegabit Data Service), SONET (Synchronous Optical Network), and video on demand.

**INFORMATION ON THE INTERNET**

Bellcore                http://www.bellcore.com

# Bellman-Ford Distance-Vector Routing Algorithm

The Bellman-Ford distance-vector routing algorithm is used by routers on internetworks to exchange routing information about the current status of the network and how to route packets to their destination. The algorithm basically merges routing information provided by different routers into lookup tables. It is well defined and used on a number of popular networks. It also provides reasonable performance on small- to medium-sized networks, but on larger networks, the algorithm is slow at calculating updates to the network topology. In some cases, looping occurs in which a packet goes through the same node more than once. In general, most distance-vector routing algorithms are not suitable for larger networks that have thousands of nodes or if the network configuration changes often. In the latter case, the routing algorithm must be able to dynamically update the routing tables quickly to accommodate changes. A more efficient routing protocol is OSPF (Open Shortest Path First).

**RELATED ENTRIES**    OSPF (Open Shortest Path First) Protocol; Routing Protocols and Algorithms

## Bell Modem Standards

The Bell standards were the first methods used to control the communication process between two modems. The first of these standards was Bell 103, which paved the way for today's complex and efficient modem standards, such as V.32bis and V.42bis. While AT&T largely controlled the standardization of the original modem standards, the CCITT (Consultative Committee for International Telephony and Telegraphy), established as part of the United Nations' ITU (International Telecommunication Union), controls most standardization today. The Bell standards are summarized here:

- **Bell 103**   Supports 300-baud full-duplex asynchronous modem transmissions
- **Bell 113A and 113D**   A originates calls, and D answers calls
- **Bell 201B**   Supports synchronous 2,400-bit/sec full-duplex transmissions
- **Bell 202**   Supports asynchronous 1,800-bit/sec full-duplex transmissions
- **Bell 208**   Supports synchronous 4,800-bit/sec transmissions
- **Bell 209**   Supports synchronous 9,600-bit/sec full-duplex transmissions
- **Bell 212A**   Supports 1,200-bit/sec full-duplex transmissions (equivalent CCITT V.22 standard)

Many other standards have been developed since these initial standards, such as the CCITT "V dot" series standards. Microcom, a modem and communications software vendor, developed several standards on its own that have also come into widespread use or been integrated into ITU standards.

**RELATED ENTRIES**    Asynchronous Communications; CCITT (Consultative Committee for International Telephony and Telegraphy); Data Communication Concepts; MNP (Microcom Networking Protocol); Modems; Modulation Techniques; *and* Synchronous Communications

## Bell Operating Companies

*See* AT&T (American Telephone and Telegraph); Carrier Services; Communication Services; *and* RBOCs (Regional Bell Operating Companies).

## Best-Effort Delivery

At the lowest layers of the communication protocol stack are physical networks and data link protocols that define how bits are transmitted between two systems. This is pictured in Figure B-7. At this level, the communication system can only provide best-effort delivery service because the underlying network is unpredictable. A glitch on the line may cause a lost frame. The data link layer can provide guaranteed delivery services, such as an acknowledgment of receipt, but modern networks have so few errors that implementing such services at the data link level is considered an inefficient use of bandwidth.

Moving up the protocol stack to the network layer, we find datagram delivery services such as IP (Internet Protocol). IP is a best-effort service because it delivers datagrams across a network with no guarantee that those packets will arrive on time, arrive in order, or arrive at all. Datagram services are connectionless services because no prior agreement is made between the sender and receiver to watch over or manage the delivery of datagrams.

The opposite of a best-effort delivery service is a connection-oriented service. Such services are provided by protocols in the transport layer and sometimes the data link layer. TCP (Transmission Control Protocol), for example, is a connection-oriented service that sets up a virtual circuit or session between a sender and receiver to

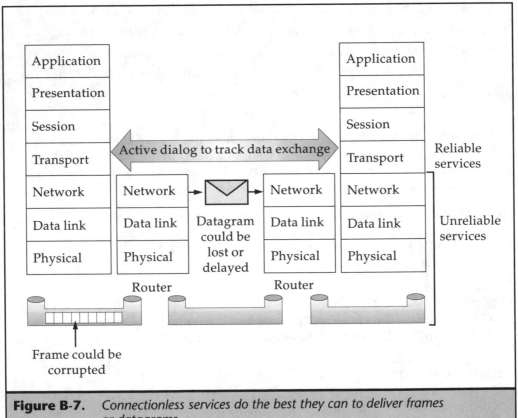

**Figure B-7.**   *Connectionless services do the best they can to deliver frames or datagrams*

manage data transmissions. TCP uses IP to deliver packets, but if IP fails to deliver a packet, TCP provides the necessary services to resend the packet. It puts sequence numbers in packets so the destination knows if a packet is missing.

**RELATED ENTRIES**    Data Communication Concepts; Datagrams and Datagram Services; Data Link Protocols; Framing in Data Transmissions; IP (Internet Protocol); Network Concepts; Packet; Protocol Concepts; *and* Transport Protocols and Services

## BGP (Border Gateway Protocol)

BGP is an Internet exterior gateway routing protocol for use with TCP/IP. It accumulates information about the reachability of neighbors from packets as they traverse the network. Route attributes such as the cost or security of a path are also added. BGP reduces the bandwidth required to exchange routing information because the information is exchanged incrementally rather than by sending the entire database.

**RELATED ENTRY**    Routing Protocols and Algorithms

## Bindery

The bindery is a database file in the NetWare network operating systems for versions previous to NetWare 3.x. It holds security, accounting, and name management information for the server on which NetWare is installed. Because NetWare servers that use binderies still exist in many environments, newer versions of NetWare provide bindery emulation to support them. NDS (Novell Directory Services) replaced the bindery in later versions of NetWare, although the bindery is still supported.

Every Pre-NetWare 3.x server maintains its own bindery. The bindery contains *object* records. Objects are server entities, such as users, groups, and the server name. Objects have attributes, called *properties*, such as passwords, account restrictions, account balances, group membership, and so on. Properties have values, which are kept in a separate but related file.

For more information about the NetWare network operating system, see "Novell NetWare."

## B-ISDN (Broadband ISDN)

B-ISDN is an effort by the telephone companies to develop a single integrated digital network that can be used for voice, video, and data communications. Much of the existing telephone system consists of the old circuit-switching equipment that is based on Alexander Graham Bell's original operator-controlled switching system, although far more automatic. In addition, the phone companies have call management systems and newer data services in place such as frame relay. B-ISDN can provide all these services in an integrated framework that scales up to very high data rates. B-ISDN is a CCITT (now referred to as the ITU) recommendation that defines data, voice, and video transmission operating in the megabit-to-gigabit range.

As shown in Figure B-8, the underlying transfer mode for implementing B-ISDN is cell switching. Refer to "ATM (Asynchronous Transfer Mode)" and "Cell Relay" for more information. In the carrier networks, ATM cells are delivered across a physical network called SONET (Synchronous Optical Network), which now makes up the trunk topology for most of the phone system in the United States. A similar standard used elsewhere in the world is called SDH (Synchronous Digital Hierarchy). SDH is a CCITT recommendation.

SONET is the physical transport backbone of B-ISDN. It is a fiber-optic–based networking standard that defines a hierarchy of transmission rates and data framing formats. It is used as a transmission medium to interconnect carrier-switching offices worldwide, and so forms the structure of current and future global communications. B-ISDN, FDDI (Fiber Distributed Data Interface), and SMDS can be transported on SONET networks. SONET is now used as the medium between carrier-switching offices and many customer premises sites. SONET transmission rates start at 51.4 Mbits/sec and increase in 52-Mbit/sec building blocks. Speeds up to 50 Gbits/sec are possible.

ATM is the switching technology for B-ISDN and provides B-ISDN users access to the SONET fiber-optic network. Information received at the ATM layer is placed in fixed-length cells, addressed, and transmitted over the SONET network. ATM provides very high-speed switching of these packets between the links attached to the SONET network. ATM takes full advantage of the transmission speeds available on fiber-optic cable.

**RELATED ENTRIES**    ATM (Asynchronous Transfer Mode); ISDN (Integrated Services Digital Network); NADH (North American Digital Hierarchy); SDH (Synchronous Digital Hierarchy); SONET (Synchronous Optical Network); *and* WAN (Wide Area Network)

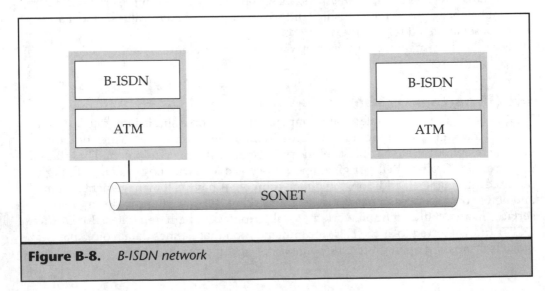

**Figure B-8.**    *B-ISDN network*

## BISYNC (Binary Synchronous Communications)

BISYNC is a character-, or byte-oriented, form of communication developed by IBM in the 1960s. It was originally designed for batch transmissions between the IBM S/360 mainframe family and IBM 2780 and 3780 terminals. It supports online and RJE (remote job entry) terminals in the CICS/VSE (Customer Information Control System/Virtual Storage Extended) environment.

BISYNC provides the rules for the transmission of binary-coded data between a terminal and a host computer's BISYNC port. While BISYNC is a half-duplex protocol, it will synchronize in both directions on a full-duplex channel. BISYNC supports both point-to-point (over leased or dial-up lines) and multipoint transmissions. Each message must be acknowledged, adding to its overhead.

BISYNC is character-oriented, meaning that groups of bits (bytes) are the main elements of transmission, rather than a stream of bits. The BISYNC frame is shown here:

| SYNC | SOH | Header | STX | Text | EOT | CRC |
|------|-----|--------|-----|------|-----|-----|

It starts with two sync characters that the receiver and transmitter use for synchronizing. This is followed by an SOH (start of header) command, and then the header. Following this are the STX (start of text) command and the text. Finally, an EOT (end of text) command and a CRC (cyclic redundancy check) end the frame. The CRC provides error detection and correction.

Most of the bisynchronous protocols, of which there are many, provide only half-duplex transmission and require an acknowledgment for every block of transmitted data. Some do provide full-duplex transmission and bit-oriented operation. BISYNC has largely been replaced by the more powerful SDLC (Synchronous Data Link Control) protocol.

**RELATED ENTRIES**    Asynchronous Communications; Bit-Oriented Protocol, Byte-Oriented Protocol; Data Communication Concepts; SDLC (Synchronous Data Link Control); *and* Synchronous Communications

## Bit-Oriented Protocol

In any communication session between devices, control codes are used to control another device or provide information about the status of the session. Byte- or character-oriented protocols use full bytes (8 bits) to represent established control codes such as those defined by ASCII (American Standard Code for Information Interchange). Thus a character-oriented protocol can only be used with its native character set because that character set has the specific control characters. In contrast, bit-oriented protocols rely on individual bits for control information and are a preferred method for transmitting data. Most data link protocols like those used for local area networks are bit oriented.

In a bit-oriented transmission, data is transmitted as a steady stream of bits. Before actual data transmission begins, special *sync* characters are transmitted by the sender so the receiver can synchronize itself with the bit stream. This bit pattern is usually in the form of a specially coded 8-bit string. IBM's SDLC (Synchronous Data Link Control) protocol is bit-oriented. The sync character is the bit string 01111110, and this is followed by an 8-bit address, an 8-bit control field, and the data. Once the receiving system receives these start frames, it begins reading eight bits at a time (a byte) from the bit stream until an error check and an ending flag appear.

IBM's SDLC and HDLC (High-level Data Link Control) are bit-oriented protocols that control synchronous communication. HDLC is used in X.25 packet-switching networks; SDLC is a subset of HDLC.

**RELATED ENTRIES**    Asynchronous Communications; Byte-Oriented Protocol; Data Communication Concepts; LAP (Link Access Procedure); SDLC (Synchronous Data Link Control); *and* Synchronous Communications

## Block Suballocation

This Novell NetWare operating system feature maximizes disk space. If there are any partially used disk blocks (usually a block is 8K in size), NetWare divides them into 512-byte suballocation blocks for the storage of small files or fragments of files.

**RELATED ENTRIES**    Novell NetWare File System; Volume and Partition Management

## Block Transmission

When an application such as FTP (File Transfer Protocol) needs to send a file from one computer to another, it can select from several transmission modes. A concern with any long data transmission is that the transmission might be interrupted or part of the transmission might be corrupted. The selected mode can assist in recovery and throughput.

Block-mode transmissions divide data into multiple blocks and treat each block as a record. Each record has a *count field*, a *data*, and an *end of record* marker. The data is sent one block at a time. If the transmission fails, it can be resumed starting at the last record sent.

The other transmission modes are *stream* and *compressed*. In stream mode, data is passed down to the lower-level transport protocol, which handles segmenting the data for transfer. TCP (Transmission Control Protocol) is a stream-oriented protocol that fragments incoming byte streams into messages that can be reliably transmitted across a connection-oriented link to a destination system.

**RELATED ENTRIES**    Data Communication Concepts; Data Link Protocols

# BNC Connector

BNC connectors are used to connect, extend, or terminate coaxial cable networks such as Ethernet and ARCNET. There are various connectors, such as the BNC T-connector, the BNC barrel connector, and the BNC terminator, as pictured in Figure B-9.

The BNC connector attaches directly to the cable. It has a center pin that is soldered onto the center wire of the cable and an outer casing to which the shielding ground wire is attached. BNC connectors are pushed onto the ends of T-connectors, then the outer housing is twisted to lock it into place.

The BNC T-connector provides the cable attachment to the network interface card. Cables branch from either side of the T to the next stations up or down in the trunk cable.

The BNC terminator has a resistor to terminate the coaxial cable. Each end of the coaxial cable trunk requires a terminator, and one end requires a ground lead, as shown in the illustration.

The BNC barrel connector is used to join two cable segments.

**RELATED ENTRIES**    Ethernet; Transmission Media, Methods, and Equipment

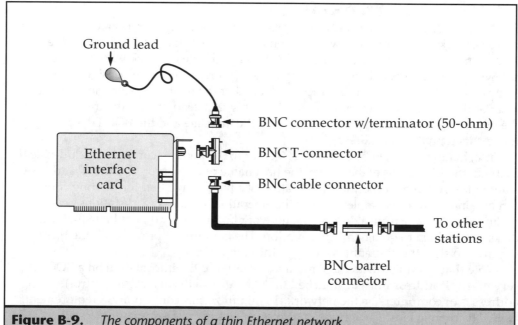

**Figure B-9.**    *The components of a thin Ethernet network*

# Bonding

Bonding is a technique of combining data channels to form a higher-capacity data channel. Bonding provides a way to obtain bandwidth on demand without contacting the phone company. You typically use it to obtain more capacity before a high data-rate session such as a videoconferencing session. A router that supports bonding will dial and/or connect one or more extra transmission lines and combine them into a single channel. After the videoconference, you terminate the bound channels. The purpose of bonding (and bandwidth on demand) is to obtain more capacity without obtaining an expensive dedicated line that might go underused most of the time.

Note that bonding takes place when the call is set up. The phone company can also perform bonding within its own system for customers. In addition, most new routers support PPP Multilink (Point-to-Point Protocol Multilink), which provides automatic bandwidth on demand at any time and is more appropriate for bursty and unpredictable local area network traffic.

In the ISDN (Integrated Services Digital Network) environment, bonding refers to combining the two 64-Kbit/sec B channels to create a higher-capacity 128-Kbit/sec channel.

**RELATED ENTRIES**     Bandwidth on Demand; Bandwidth Reservation; Circuit-Switching Services; DDR (Dial-on-Demand Routing); Inverse Multiplexing; ISDN (Integrated Services Digital Network); Load Balancing; *and* PPP Multilink

# BOOTP (Bootstrap Protocol)

BOOTP is an Internet protocol that can provide network configuration information to diskless workstations or other workstations if necessary on a local network. When a workstation boots, it broadcasts a BOOTP message on the network. A BOOTP server receives this message, obtains the configuration information for the designated computer, and returns it to the computer. Note that the booting system does not have an IP address when it sends out a BOOTP message. Instead, the hardware address of the NIC (network interface card) is placed in the message and the BOOTP server returns its reply to this address.

Information returned by the BOOTP server to the booting computer includes its IP address, the IP address of the server, the host name of the server, and the IP address of a default router. It also specifies the location of a boot image that the booting computer can obtain in order to complete its startup operation. Diskless workstations need to obtain a boot image from a disk on the network because they do not have their own disks from which to obtain this information. The boot image provides all the files required to start the operating system on the computer.

Note that administrators must manually configure the information on a BOOTP server. An IP address must be matched to the MAC (Medium Access Control) addresses of computers on the network. To minimize this configuration requirement, DHCP (Dynamic Host Configuration Protocol) was developed to automatically allocate IP addresses to clients.

**RELATED ENTRIES**    Bootstrapping; DHCP (Dynamic Host Configuration Protocol)

## Bootstrapping

When a computer is first started, a bootstrapping routine (on ROM) provides it with enough logic to obtain startup programs from a permanent storage device. The built-in ROM routines are small; there is just enough code to direct the system to a disk where it can begin to load the much larger operating system files. But what if the computer is a diskless workstation (a computer with no local storage device)?

In the case of a diskless workstation, boot information is typically obtained from a network server. The diskless workstation has a special ROM inserted on its NIC (network interface card) that directs it to contact a specific computer on the network. This computer then has a program that sends a startup disk image to the diskless workstation so it can boot. All subsequent disk access is performed on network servers.

Network computers need quite a bit of information to get started, including a network address and the location of important services. In the TCP/IP environment, a system needs an IP address, a default router address, a subnet mask, a DNS (Domain Name System) server address, and some other parameters, depending on the environment. However, creating a startup configuration file for every diskless workstation on a network can be a daunting task, especially if the information changes often, as it might for mobile users. A number of protocols have been developed to dynamically assign IP addresses as will be discussed in a moment.

TCP/IP includes a protocol called RARP (Reverse Address Resolution Protocol) that allows a computer to obtain an IP address from a server. When a diskless TCP/IP workstation is booted on a network, it broadcasts a RARP request packet on the local network. This address packet is broadcast on the network for all to receive because the workstation does not know the IP address of the server that can supply it with an address. It includes its own physical network address (the MAC address) in the request so the server will know where to return a reply. The server that receives the request looks in a table and matches the MAC address with an IP address, then returns the IP address to the diskless workstation.

Another protocol called BOOTP (Bootstrap Protocol) provides a way for a server to supply even more configuration information to a workstation at boot time. For more information, see "BOOTP (Bootstrap Protocol)." Another similar protocol is DHCP (Dynamic Host Configuration Protocol), which can provide automatic and dynamic IP address allocation for some or all of the workstations on a network. For more information, see "DHCP (Dynamic Host Configuration Protocol)."

## Breakout Box

*See* Testing and Diagnostic Equipment and Techniques.

## BRI (Basic Rate Interface)

BRI is the minimal service obtainable for ISDN (Integrated Services Digital Network). ISDN is a digital phone service that is meant to replace the traditional analog phone system.

BRI consists of two 64-Kbit/sec B channels and one 16-Kbit/sec D channel. Each B channel can carry a single digitized voice call or be used as a data channel. The B channels can also be combined to form a single 128-Kbit/sec data channel. The D channel is used for call establishment and other signaling.

**RELATED ENTRIES**   B-ISDN (Broadband ISDN); Bonding; *and* ISDN (Integrated Services Digital Network)

## Bridges and Bridging

A bridge is a LAN connection device with two or more ports that forwards frames from one LAN segment to another. Figure B-10 illustrates a two-port bridge. A bridge is one step up from a repeater in the hierarchy of network connection devices. In addition to being able to extend a single LAN to greater distances, it provides a frame-forwarding service between the LANs it connects. Each LAN is distinct from the others electrically, but the bridged LANs become part of the same broadcast domain (assuming Ethernet). Frames from one LAN are automatically forwarded across a bridge to a connected LAN, but filtering can be employed to selectively forward frames.

Bridges operate in "promiscuous" mode, which means they listen to all traffic on all connected segments. The bridge forwards frames to attached LAN segments if the frames are addressed to stations on that LAN segment.

So far, this is not much different than using a repeater, except that bridges forward frames based on their MAC (Medium Access Control) addresses, which are the hardware-level addresses of NICs (network interface cards). Part of this filtering is to

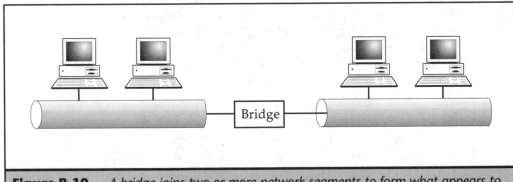

**Figure B-10.**   *A bridge joins two or more network segments to form what appears to be a single LAN*

block collisions occurring in one LAN segment from affecting other LAN segments. Thus, bridges can prevent problems in one segment from affecting another. Bridges also join networks over different types of links, such as dial-up links, fiber-optic links, and even satellite links. Repeaters are simple wire-connection devices.

You can segment a network and rejoin it with a bridge, then use filtering to control traffic flow. Separating segments reduces the chances that errors or disruptions in one segment will affect another segment. A bridge can also extend the physical distance limitation of a network like a repeater, with the added benefit of traffic filtering.

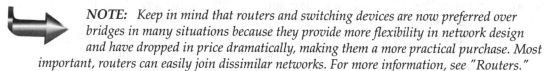

*NOTE: Keep in mind that routers and switching devices are now preferred over bridges in many situations because they provide more flexibility in network design and have dropped in price dramatically, making them a more practical purchase. Most important, routers can easily join dissimilar networks. For more information, see "Routers."*

## Types of Bridges

There are generally three types of bridges: *local*, *remote link*, and *translation*. A local bridge provides connection ports for two or more LANs, and is used to interconnect LAN segments within the same building or area as shown on the bottom in Figure B-11. Remote link bridges have ports for analog or digital telecommunication links to connect networks at other locations, as shown on the top in Figure B-11. Connections

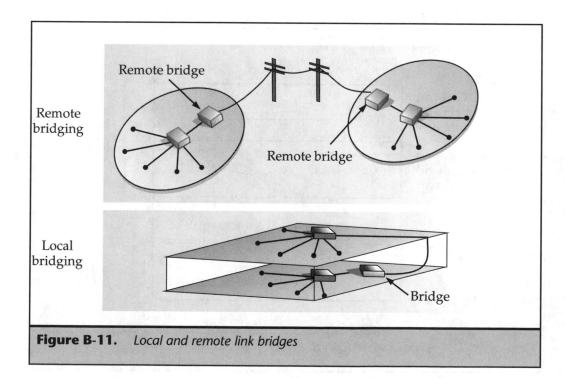

**Figure B-11.** *Local and remote link bridges*

between remote bridges are made over analog lines using modems or over digital leased lines.

For remote links, the choice of dedicated or dial-up lines depends on the traffic. In some cases, the only traffic traveling between sites is electronic mail, file updates, backups, and similar information. A dial-on-demand link is often appropriate for this type of traffic—connections are made only when necessary, thus reducing call charges. A dedicated line may be best on links where users constantly communicate between two sites and traffic is heavy and consistent. Private bridges using radio communications or fiber-optic links are common in campus environments to link LANs in different buildings.

A translation bridge can be used to connect different types of LANs by resolving the differences between frame layout, transmission speed, and control codes. However, routers are usually more suitable for this task.

## Bridge Functionality

Bridging takes place in the data link layer relative to the OSI protocol model as shown in Figure B-12. Ethernet, token ring, and FDDI (Fiber Distributed Data Interface) are examples of networks that conform to IEEE 802 standards for MAC-level bridging. The data link layer is subdivided into the upper LLC (Logical Link Control) sublayer and the lower MAC sublayer. The modular MAC sublayer handles different types of

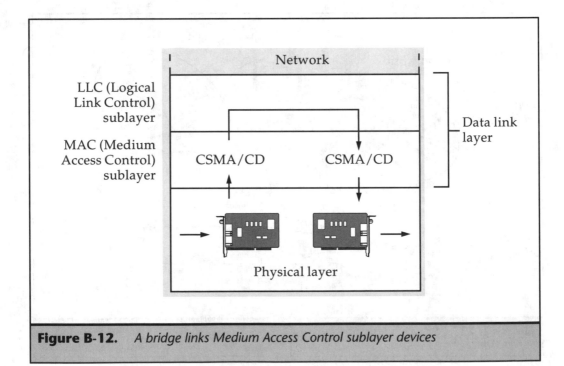

**Figure B-12.** *A bridge links Medium Access Control sublayer devices*

medium access methods and the upper layer acts as a sort of "switchboard" to move frames among the network modules in the MAC sublayer.

Bridges provide the following functions:

- **Frame forwarding** As mentioned, a bridge will forward frames to another network if they are addressed for a device on that network.

- **Loop resolution** Large-bridged LANs may have loops that could cause frames to travel continuously. Most bridges can detect such looping frames and intercept them.

- **Learning techniques** Bridges build address tables that describe routes by either examining traffic flow or obtaining information from "explorer frames" that have learned about the network topology during their travels. The first method is called *transparent bridging*, and the second is called *source routing*.

Early bridges required that network managers hand-enter the address tables. This was a tedious task, and the tables had to be periodically updated if a workstation or user moved to another location. Today's advanced bridges can learn the address of other stations on the network using techniques discussed here. Note that transparent bridges are often called learning bridges, and they use the spanning tree algorithm, which is the IEEE 802.1 standard.

## Transparent Bridging

Transparent bridges automatically set about learning the topology of the network environment as soon as they are installed and powered up. When a frame from a new source arrives at a port, the bridge makes an entry in its table that associates the frame's source address with the port on which it arrived. A typical table for two LAN segments is shown in Figure B-13. Note that the source address of a frame is associated with a port. Arriving packets are forwarded by the bridge based on the entries it has in its table. The bridging table is constantly updated with new source addresses and updates as the network changes.

A discovery process is initiated if an address is not found in the table. A frame is sent to all LAN segments except the one from which the frame originated. Eventually, the destination sends a response back to the bridge and the bridge makes an entry in its table that associates the address with the port on which it received the response. Given time, a bridge will learn the address of every node on the network.

The number of interconnected network segments is an issue in the learning process. If a bridge only connects two network segments, it is relatively easy to build a table that defines which stations are on one side and which are on the other. However, the bridge must first learn the address of each connected network by forwarding packets from one side of the bridge to the other and listening for a response from the destination.

How do you interconnect multiple LAN segments? The network at the top in Figure B-14 must transmit packets from the left segment through the middle segment to reach the right segment. This can cause excess traffic and performance problems in

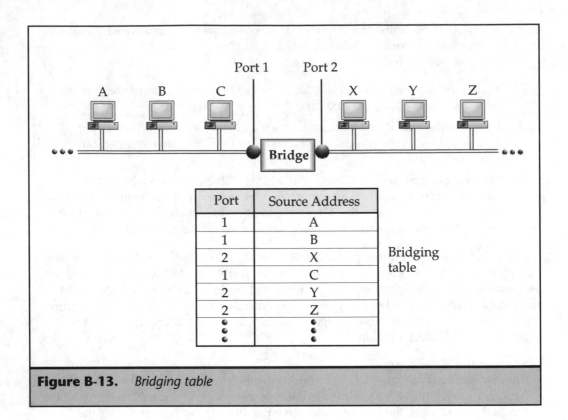

**Figure B-13.** *Bridging table*

the middle segment; however, only two bridges are required. An alternate method is to attach a bridge to each LAN segment and connect the bridges to a backbone network such as an FDDI ring, as shown at the bottom in Figure B-14. This eliminates the need to transmit frames through one segment to reach another segment, except for the backbone, which is installed specifically for shuttling frames between networks.

On large interconnected networks, multiple bridge paths that can form a closed loop may be created inadvertently and cause packets to circle endlessly, reducing performance or crippling the network. In the worst case, *broadcast storms* occur when new packets are endlessly generated to correct the problem. But multiple paths are necessary to provide fault tolerance, as shown in Figure B-15. If the link between LAN A and LAN B goes down, an alternate link is still available indirectly through LAN C. The STA (spanning tree algorithm) provides a way to create multiple paths while preventing loops. However, STA does this by blocking one path until it is needed. An alternate strategy, called *load sharing,* solves this problem somewhat, as discussed below under "Load-Sharing Bridges."

### The Spanning Tree Algorithm

Spanning tree bridges detect and break circular traffic patterns by disabling certain links in Ethernet networks. The IEEE 801.2-D STP (Spanning Tree Protocol) inhibits

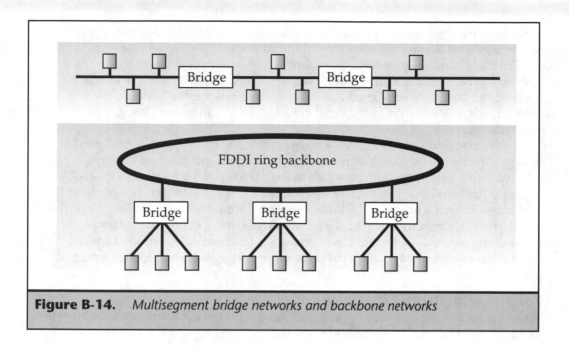

**Figure B-14.** *Multisegment bridge networks and backbone networks*

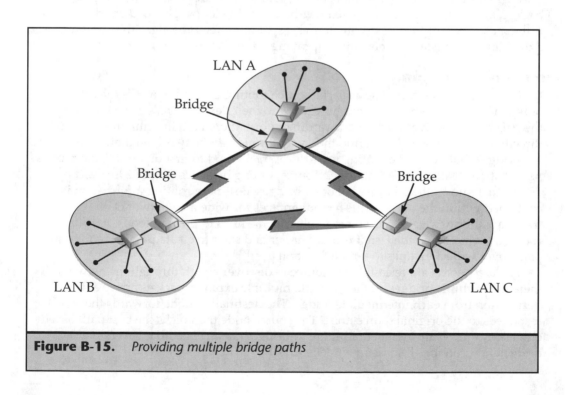

**Figure B-15.** *Providing multiple bridge paths*

loops in redundant bridges by maintaining the secondary bridge as a backup. If the first bridge goes down, the secondary bridge takes over.

The algorithm assigns unique *identifiers* to each bridge. A *priority value* is also assigned to each bridge. Each port on every bridge is assigned a unique *identifier*. Each bridge port is then assigned a *path cost* that assigns a value to ports. The network administrator can change cost values manually to assign preferences for a particular port.

As the algorithm proceeds, a root bridge is selected from the set of bridges. The bridge with the lowest identifier is selected as the root. Once the root bridge is selected, other bridges determine which of their ports provides access to the root bridge at the least cost. This port becomes the *root port* of the bridge. If ports have the same costs, then the one with the least number of bridge-to-bridge hops is used. The last step is to determine which bridges and bridge ports will provide a pathway through the network to the root based on the least path cost. This process enables some ports to ensure forwarding paths for some bridges and disables other ports to prevent loops.

### Load-Sharing Bridges

When bridges use leased lines to span wide areas, it is not economically feasible in the minds of most network managers to block the line and only use it for a backup. Some bridge manufacturers provide load-sharing bridges that are capable of using the backup link to share the network load without causing loops. The load-sharing bridge is the most efficient form of bridge. It uses a spanning tree-type algorithm, and it uses a dual link to transfer packets, thus improving internetwork performance.

## Source Route Bridging

IBM Token Ring networks use a special source routing method that tells the bridge not only where packets should go but how to get to their destination. In source routing, the packets themselves hold the forwarding information. Path information is placed directly in packets so they can find their way through the network on their own.

Bridges that do source routing use a *discovery* method to first determine the route a packet should take to a destination. A source routing bridge is simply a forwarding device that knows the addresses of other bridges. Best-path routing information is contained within the packet. This has advantages for wide area networks. In transparent bridging, it is necessary to block some links to prevent loops. In source routing, loops are avoided, so it is much easier and safer to create parallel redundant paths over wide area links to remote locations.

*Explorer packets* are released by a source to discover a path through the network. If there are multiple bridges on the network, multiple explorer packets arrive at the destination from each intermediate bridge. The destination node forwards these responses to the original source node. The source node then picks the best path based on factors such as the number of bridge-to-bridge hops. This path is saved by the bridge and used for all subsequent deliveries.

## FDDI Backbone Bridges

The FDDI (Fiber Distributed Data Interface) network standard has been used extensively as a backbone medium for a building or campus environment. Many vendors provide FDDI bridges for linking Ethernet and/or token ring networks. More recently, the Fast Ethernet standard has become more popular for building Ethernet backbones because it is Ethernet; in other words, the frame format and medium access method are the same. A version that supports fiber-optic cable over long distances is also available.

When bridging Ethernet or token ring networks onto an FDDI backbone, the frame must be repackaged for transport over the network. This is done in one of two ways:

■ **Encapsulation**  This method simply places an FDDI envelope around the Ethernet frame and sends it across the backbone network as a packet. When the packet reaches the bridge for the destination network, it is unpackaged and sent to the destination. Encapsulation is normally implemented in most Ethernet_to_FDDI bridges. This method assumes that nodes on the Ethernet will never need to communicate with nodes attached directly to the FDDI LAN, except for other bridges that are attached to Ethernet networks. Encapsulation makes the frames unusable until they are unpackaged at the receiving bridge.

■ **Translation**  A translation bridge converts Ethernet packets to FDDI packets. There are potential problems with translation, as discussed earlier, but it does allow nodes on the Ethernet network to communicate with nodes on the FDDI network. If FDDI is used simply as a backbone, encapsulation is preferable to translation.

## Remote Bridging Techniques

There are a number of connection methods for remote bridges. The topic "Data Transfer Rates" defines rates for common network applications and activities that can help you determine transmission requirements. The most important consideration is that filtering is even more important on dial-up or leased lines because of the limited bandwidth of the lines.

The dial-up modem and asynchronous link are adequate for occasional low-volume internetwork traffic. For heavier traffic, dedicated analog lines or digital lines are necessary. A CSU/DSU (channel service unit/data service unit) links the bridge to the digital line, as shown in Figure B-16. If you plan to mix voice and data, you'll need a multiplexor.

**RELATED ENTRIES**  Campus Network; Circuit-Switching Services; Communication Services; Network Concepts; Routers; *and* WAN (Wide Area Network)

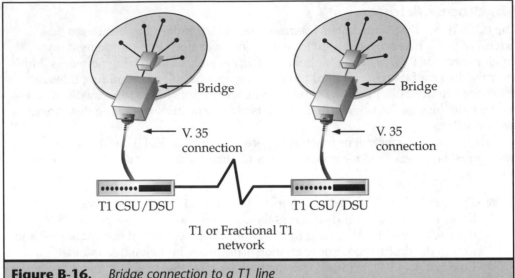

**Figure B-16.** *Bridge connection to a T1 line*

## Broadband Transmission

A broadband transmission is an analog transmission with a wide range of frequencies. The term is used in two contexts. Broadband networking refers to networks that have very high transmission rates. Data rate is related to higher-frequency ranges. Broadband networks can transmit in the multimegabit and gigabit range.

Broadband networks also refers to networks that allow multiple transmissions at the same time on different frequencies. Compare this to baseband networks such as Ethernet in which only one transmission is allowed on the medium. Broadband networks can span larger distances than baseband networks.

## Broadcast

In radio communication, a broadcast is a one-to-many signal transmission. *Transmitters* broadcast signals to *receivers.* In Ethernet networks, stations broadcast packet transmissions on a shared medium. Other stations listen to these broadcasts but receive only frames addressed to them. This broadcast network metaphor is the opposite of a point-to-point network in which transmissions take place between two systems over a circuit that is only used by the end systems. Multicasting is a limited form of broadcasting in which transmissions are targeted to a select group of stations on a network.

## Broadcast Addressing

Broadcast addressing refers to the ability to address a broadcast message to all stations on a network. In the Ethernet environment, stations access a shared medium and transmit frames on it. Each frame is normally addressed to a particular destination computer, and while all other stations on the network can listen to the broadcast, only the station with the destination address bothers to receive it. A broadcast message is addressed to all stations on the network. Technically, the destination address consists of all 1 bits and a frame containing all 1s in the destination field is received by all stations on the network.

## Broadcast Domain

A broadcast domain is an Ethernet local area network segment in which transmissions can be heard by every station attached to the network. If two network segments are joined by a repeater or bridge, a larger broadcast domain is created because the devices relay the broadcasted frames to all connected segments. However, if a router is used to join LAN segments, each segment retains its independent network status. Routers only forward frames that are specifically addressed to devices on other networks.

Note that VLAN (virtual LAN) technology can create "virtual" broadcast domains. A network built with switching devices can treat each workstation as an independent entity, and groups of these workstations can be joined into a virtual broadcast domain, no matter where they are attached to the physical network.

**RELATED ENTRIES**    Bridges and Bridging; Broadcast Networking; Ethernet; Switched Networks; *and* VLAN (Virtual LAN)

## Broadcast Networking

Broadcast networking occurs on shared networks such as Ethernet where multiple nodes are attached to the same LAN segment. It is a one-to-many method of transmitting information. Any device attached to the network can listen to traffic generated by other nodes. If network segments are interconnected with repeaters or bridges, the broadcast domain is extended into the attached segments.

In contrast, a *point-to-point* link is an unshared connection between two systems. On a point-to-point link, there is no contention for the cable because it connects only the sender and receiver, not a number of shared devices. Likewise, a mesh network is a collection of point-to-point links. Some of the links may provide alternate pathways through the mesh network on which to transmit information.

A transmission on a broadcast network consists of frames that include the MAC (Medium Access Control) address of the destination node. This is the hardwired address on network interface cards. Each node listens to traffic on the network and reads the destination address in the frames. If a node receives a frame that has its own node address, it accepts the frame. Other nodes ignore the frame. There is also a *broadcast address* that is used to address frames to every node on the network.

Before a node can transmit on a shared broadcast network, it must first gain access to the medium. Various strategies are used to ensure that no two nodes gain access and transmit at the same time. The CSMA/CD (carrier sense multiple access/collision detection) method provides a way to arbitrate access to a shared medium. Since a broadcast network implies a shared network, there must be some way to limit the amount of time that a single node can broadcast. One method is to allocate a limited amount of time. Another method is to have a central control unit allocate time based on the priority requirements of each transmission, as in the 100VG-AnyLAN demand priority access method. These techniques are discussed under "MAC (Medium Access Control)."

A limited form of broadcasting is called *multicasting*. In this scheme, broadcasts are sent to a limited group of systems on the network. Even though the broadcast is targeted to multiple systems, only one broadcast is needed, rather than a separate broadcast to each destination.

**RELATED ENTRIES**    Bridges and Bridging; Broadcast Domain; Data Communication Concepts; Ethernet; MAC (Medium Access Control); Multicasting; Network Concepts; *and* Point-to-Point Communications

## Broadcast News Technology

Broadcast news technology, also called *push,* is the latest trend on the Web for delivering information to users. Instead of starting up a Web browser and venturing out into the global information system to search for things that interest you, push technologies deliver information directly to you. The metaphor is this: your desktop is a receiver much like a television or radio. You subscribe to Web servers that broadcast information (continuously or intermittently). Broadcast information appears in a window or icon on your desktop and is dynamically updated as necessary. For example, stock quotes may appear as a continuously moving banner along the bottom of your screen while the latest news headlines from CNN appear in a window at the top. You can also customize what you receive, so sites like *USA Today* can deliver the latest news soccer scores or news about the political situation in China.

The best example of this model is the PointCast (http://www.pointcast.com) system. PointCast provides free software that loads on top of the desktop and allows users to pick from up to 23 channels. Other developers include BackWeb Technologies (http://www.backweb.com), Data Channel Corp. (http://www.datachannel.com), Intermind (http://www.intermind.com), Marimba (http://www.marimba.com), and Wayfarer Communications (http://www.wayfarer.com).

Microsoft's new Windows operating system includes the broadcast news technology from PointCast, while Netscape is building its own system.

While the term *broadcast news* (and *newsfeed services*) may more correctly identify this technology, not all information pushed to your desktop is news. The industry has rallied around the term "push," so coverage of this technology is covered under the heading "Push." In addition, the technology is not just for the Internet. It can be used on intranets to broadcast information to select users. It can also used to automatically update software components as discussed under "Distributed Object Computing."

**RELATED ENTRIES**   Component Software Technology; Distributed Object Computing; Marimba Castanet; MBone (Multicast Backbone); Multicasting; NNTP (Network News Transport Protocol); PointCast; *and* Push

## Broadcast Storm

A broadcast storm occurs when a host system responds to a packet that is continuously circulating on the network or attempts to respond to a system that never replies. Typically, request or response packets are continuously generated to correct the situation, often making matters worse. As the number of packets on the network increases, congestion occurs that can reduce network performance or cripple it.

**RELATED ENTRY**   Bridges and Bridging

## Brouter (Bridge/Router)

A brouter is a hybrid device that represents the merging of bridge and router technology. Brouters can bridge multiple protocols and provide routing for some of those protocols. In this sense, a brouter is a device that forwards packets between networks at the network layer and the data link layer in the OSI protocol stack.

**RELATED ENTRIES**   Bridges and Bridging; Router

## Burst and Bursty Traffic

A burst is a continuous transfer of data without interruption from one device to another. Microprocessors such as the Intel x86 allow burst-mode block transfers of data to memory and onboard caches. Computer buses provide burst-mode transfers in which an adapter can control the bus to send multiple blocks of data.

On a multiplexed data communication channel that normally merges and transfers data from several sources, burst mode provides a way to dedicate the entire channel for the transmission of data from one source. Normally, a timeslot is dedicated for each device that needs to transmit. Statistical multiplexing can handle bursts from one source.

**RELATED ENTRIES**   Bandwidth on Demand; Bonding; *and* Multiplexing

## Burst Mode

Burst-mode technology was added to NetWare in early 1993 to enhance NetWare's native IPX (Internetwork Packet Exchange) protocol for use over wide area links. Burst mode lets a workstation make one request for a file. The server then responds with a continuous stream of packets without the need for an acknowledgment, thus improving throughput. A single acknowledge response is sent after the burst of packets has been received. Burst mode greatly reduces the amount of traffic on the network and is essential for improving performance over wide area links.

Burst mode improves performance in the following environments:

■ LAN (local area network) segments that typically transmit large files

■ WAN (wide area network) with slower (9,600 baud or less) asynchronous links

■ Internetworks linked with bridges and routers

■ WANs using X.25 packet switching or T1 and satellite links

The size of the burst mode packets is negotiated between the workstation and server. Slow machines like older PCs don't benefit from burst mode because they cannot transfer information over their own bus fast enough to keep up with burst mode. You'll need to disable burst mode in these machines if the network has problems or the workstation loses packets.

**RELATED ENTRIES**   Novell NetWare; Novell NetWare Protocols

## Bus Topology

The layout of a network's cable system and the methods that workstations use to access and transmit data on the cable are part of the topology of a network. A bus topology network consists of a single cable trunk that connects one workstation to the next in a daisy-chain configuration, as shown in Figure B-17. In an actual installation, the cable snakes its way through a building from office to office. All nodes share the same medium, and only one node can broadcast messages at a time. While bus

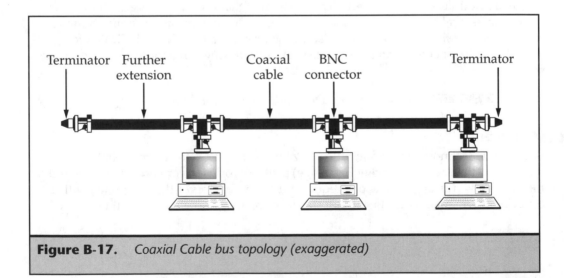

**Figure B-17.**   *Coaxial Cable bus topology (exaggerated)*

topologies are easy to install because they conform well to office layouts, a break in the trunk cable will disable the entire network.

The most common bus topology network is Ethernet. Coaxial cable has been its primary transmission media, although twisted-pair wire is now used in most new installations. Twisted-pair Ethernet (10Base-T) is a star-configured bus topology. The bus itself is collapsed into a small box called a *concentrator*. Wires branch out to workstations from the connection in a star configuration as shown in Figure B-18.

**RELATED ENTRIES**    Ethernet; Network Design and Construction; Token Ring Network; *and* Topology

## Byte-Oriented Protocol

In any communication session between devices, control codes are used to control another device or provide information about the status of the session. Byte-, or character-oriented, protocols use full bytes to represent established control codes such as those defined by the ASCII (American Standard Code for Information Interchange) scheme. In contrast, bit-oriented protocols rely on individual bits for control codes.

Byte-oriented protocols transmit data as strings of characters. The transmission method is asynchronous. Each character is separated by a start bit and a stop bit, and no timing mechanism is needed. Asynchronous protocols used with most modems and IBM's BISYNC (Binary Synchronous Communications) protocol are byte-oriented protocols.

**RELATED ENTRIES**    Asynchronous Communications; Bit-Oriented Protocol; *and* Modems

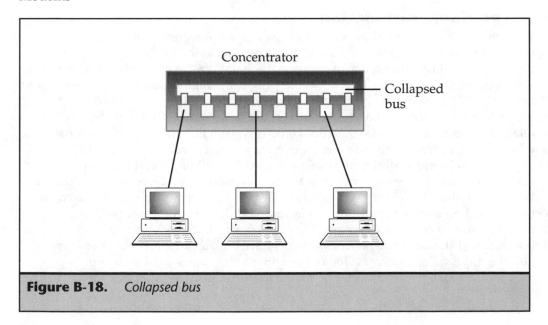

**Figure B-18.**    *Collapsed bus*

## C2 Security Rating

The NSA (National Security Agency) has outlined the requirements for secure products in a document titled "Trusted Computer System Evaluation Criteria" (TCSEC). TCSEC is more commonly called "The Orange Book." This document defines access control methods for computer systems that computer vendors can follow to comply with Department of Defense security standards. Secure networking is defined in the "Red Book," which is titled "Trusted Network Interpretation."

The C2 rating refers to a set of security policies that define how a secure system operates. It is one level in a range of seven for DOD computer system security. C2 requires that users be logged in and tracked during their session, that resources have owners, that objects (files, systems resources) be protected from other processes that might use or corrupt them, that events be audited, and that systems be protected from tampering. C2 compliance relates to stand-alone system security, rather than network security. Technically, a C2-compliant workstation cannot be hooked into a network. However, following C2 can help you implement more secure systems.

The NSA's B-level security scheme defines classified objects and a MAC (medium access control) system in which objects have a security level defined independently from the owner's discretion. A user who receives a file marked "secret" cannot give other users permission to view the file unless they have a "secret" clearance.

For information on operating-system security/certification specifications, contact the NCSC (National Computer Security Conference) at (202) 783-3238 or visit their Web site at http://www.ncsc.com.

**RELATED ENTRY**    Security

## Cable and Cable Installation

Current trends in cable and cable installation favor the integration of multimedia (voice and video) and data on the same infrastructure. In the 1970s, departmental LANs were build with a variety of cable media. Today, the trend is to build structured wiring systems that connect the entire enterprise using high-capacity backbone networks. ATM (Asynchronous Transfer Mode) is specifically designed to deliver real-time media such as voice and video over the same network that transfers data. A relative newcomer for backbone technologies is Gigabit Ethernet, which is compatible with existing Ethernet networks and relies on raw speed to compete with ATM.

In the 1970s and 1980s, coaxial cable was used for building a vast majority of networks. In the late 1980s, a trend toward data-capable twisted-pair wiring emerged. While twisted-pair wire has cable distance limitations, hubs provided a way to create hierarchical networks that support workgroup and department networks that branched from a central cable center. This hierarchical design has become an international standard and network vendors have built an array of equipment for building high-speed networks. Today, switching technologies combined with high-speed backbones hubs form the core of most company networks.

The TIA (Telecommunications Industry Association) and the EIA (Electronic Industries Association) have developed an international telecommunications wiring standard called the TIA/EIA-568 that defines how to design, build, and manage a structured wiring system. Note that the standard is also called the EIA/TIA-568 in some references. The following specifications are included in the standard:

- **TIA/EIA-568-A**  Defines a standard for building cable systems for commercial buildings that support data networks, voice, and video.

- **TIA/EIA-569**  A standard that defines how to build the pathways and spaces for telecommunication media.

- **TIA/EIA-606**  Defines the design guidelines for managing a telecommunication infrastructure.

- **TIA/EIA-607**  Defines grounding and bonding requirements for telecommunication cabling and equipment.

The primary discussion of these standards are defined under "TIA/EIA Structured Cabling Standards." Other references are given below.

**RELATED ENTRIES**    Backbone Networks; Data Communication Concepts; Network Concepts; Network Design and Construction; Testing and Diagnostic Equipment and Techniques; TIA/EIA Structured Cabling Standards; *and* Transmission Media, Methods, and Equipment

## Cable (CATV) Data Networks and Modems

The television cable industry is in a rush to bring broadband data services to home and business users by taking advantage of the CATV cable system that is already in place and wired into nearly every home in the country. Such a system would provide Internet surfers with access to the Web at speeds from 3 to 10 Mbits/sec. While the concept is good, at this writing, at least three organizations were working on cable modem standards, and there was some doubt whether the cable companies would actually upgrade their infrastructure for use as a massive data system. If standards are not put in place in the next few years, other technologies such as the phone company's DSL (Digital Subscriber Line) may overtake cable.

### Equipment and Architecture

Cable connections require a cable "modem" to connect a computer to the CATV network. Some vendors are designing internal modems, but others are designing modems that have Ethernet 10BaseT connectors so computers can be connected in the style of a network. 3COM, AT&T, General Instruments, Hewlett-Packard, Hughes, IBM, Intel, Motorola, Panasonic, Scientific-Atlanta, Toshiba, and Cox are just a few of the companies involved in the cable modem business.

Once connected, users have a continuous connection to the Internet through the cable company's broadband network. The system has a downstream data rate (from network to computer) and an upstream data rate (from computer to Internet). The downstream data rate can be as high as 36 Mbits/sec, but the cable industry states that 3 to 10 Mbits/sec is probably more realistic. The upstream data rate can be up to 10 Mbits/sec, but cable modem vendors are opting for 200 Kbits/sec to 2 Mbits/sec on this channel. The difference in these channels rates should not be a concern since most upstream traffic is light while downstream traffic from the Internet is heavy.

A typical cable modem must receive downstream data that has been modulated onto a 6 MHz channel that is adjacent to the TV signal. Several modulation techniques are possible, but the most efficient can produce a data rate of up to 36 Mbits/sec. Transmitting on the upstream channel is more difficult because it is noisy and subject to signals and interference from a variety of sources. To overcome these problems, a modulation technique called QPSK (Quadrature Phase-Shift Keying) is used, but it runs slow and so upstream data transfers will not be as high as downstream transfers. Once again, this is usually not a problem since most Internet activity involves downstream data.

The structure of the cable system is pictured in Figure C-1. It consists of the head end, the trunk cable, the distribution (or feeder) cable into neighborhoods, the drop cable to the home and in-house wiring, and the terminal equipment (consumer electronics).

The cable head end office receives signals from a variety of sources, and these signals are retransmitted over the trunk cable and neighborhood distribution cables to homes, businesses, and schools. The cable head end office has equipment to receive terrestrial and space-based transmissions from sources around the world. It can also provide high-capacity connections to the Internet.

Cable providers are working to provide a number of services to their users, including audio and video servers that can serve up music and movies. A big player is @Home, which is a cable-specific ISP (Internet service provider). It is providing cable modem infrastructure and national broadband content to cable companies throughout the United States. Proxy servers are used at the cable offices to cache information from Web sites that customers access most often. You can visit their Web page at http://www.home.net. Cable companies such as Cox Communications will deploy @Home Network as part of their interactive content for homes and workplaces. Cox is an equity partner in At Home Corporation, along with Comcast Corporation and Tele-Communications.

Keep in mind that the existing cable system does not support the broadband services that cable vendors have in mind. A high-capacity cable network upgrade is required in the form of HFC (hybrid fiber-coax) all the way to subscribers. Whether cable companies will actually do this upgrade is a question. Whether they have the money to do it is another question. Perhaps a better choice for Internet users would be direct broadcast satellite or wireless cable systems that use terrestrial microwave and don't require a massive infrastructure upgrade.

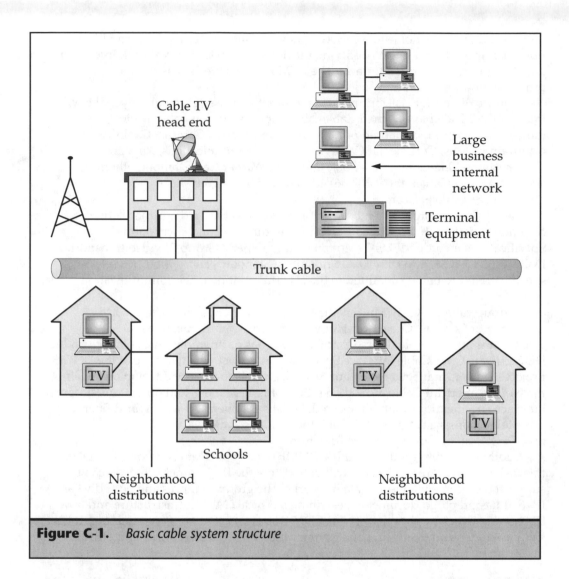

**Figure C-1.** *Basic cable system structure*

## Standards Development

As mentioned, there are many proposed cable modem standards. The IEEE 802.14 Cable TV Working Group is defining the physical layer and MAC (Medium Access Control) layer protocol specifications for HFC. The architecture as defined includes a hybrid fiber/coaxial cable plant with an 80-kilometer radius. The group hopes to have its specification available by late 1997.

More information about IEEE 802.14 is available at http://walkingdog.com/catv or at http://isdn.ncsl.nist.gov/misc/hsnt/prj_macprot.html. The ATM Forum Residential Broadband (RBB) Working Group is defining an end-to-end ATM system both to and from the home to a variety of devices, such as set-top boxes and PCs. Emphasis is on defining and specifying the home UNI (User-to-Network Interface) and ANI (access network interface). The ATM Forum's Web site is http://www.atmforum.com.

A group of vendors is working to make sure that the equipment they make will interoperate. They have formed CableLabs (Cable Television Laboratories), an industry consortium composed of cable operators such as Comcast Cable Communications, Continental Cablevision, Cox Communications, Rogers Cablesystems, Tele-Communications, and Time Warner Cable, among others. You can contact CableLabs at 303-661-9100 or visit their Web site at http://www.cablelabs.com.

CableLabs has already created specifications for cable modems that define common signaling, transport, compression, modulation, and encryption. Specifications include MPEG-2 (Motion Picture Experts Group-2) video transport, Dolby Audio AC-3, and DES (Data Encryption Standard) encryption. These specifications are being submitted to the ITU (International Telecommunication Union).

A group called MCNS (Multimedia Cable Network System Partners) Ltd., consisting of Comcast Cable Communications, Cox Communications, Tele-Communications, and Time Warner Cable, has partnered with CableLabs on the DOCIS (Data Over Cable Interface Specification) project. The objective of the DOCIS project, which is managed by Arthur D. Little, Inc., is to rapidly develop on behalf of the North American Cable Industry a set of communications and operations support interface specifications for high-speed data delivery over two-way hybrid fiber/coax cable televisions systems. Additional information is available at http://ww.cablemodem.com/mcnsfaq.htm.

Another working group called IPCDN (IP over Cable Data Network) has taken on this task, which more specifically will define how the IP (Internet Protocol) can be supported on cable television data networks. The group is addressing both IPv4 and IPv6. It has prepared documents describing a typical CATV infrastructure and how an IP-based network might use it. The IPCDN Web site is at http://www.ietf.org. It has technical details on symmetric and asymmetric CATV data networks and other useful information.

**RELATED ENTRIES**    Internet; Internet Connections; ISPs (Internet Service Providers); *and* Web Technologies and Concepts

### INFORMATION ON THE INTERNET

| | |
|---|---|
| Cable modems site | http://www.cablemodems.com |
| Cox Communications, Inc. | http://www.cox.com |
| @Home site | http://www.home.net |
| Doug Lawlor's High Bandwidth page with Cable modem links | http://www.specialty.com/hiband/cable.html |

# Cache

A *cache* is a block of memory that holds frequently used data or data that is waiting for another process to use it. When a process needs information, it first checks the cache. If the information is already in the cache, performance is improved. If the information is not in the cache, it is retrieved from alternate storage and placed in the cache where it might be accessed again. There are several types of caches and applications that use caches:

- **Processor cache**   A processor cache is a block of memory that is part of the processor itself and has very fast access.

- **Disk cache**   A disk cache is located in a computer's RAM memory. It holds blocks of information from disk rather than whole files.

- **Client/server cache**   In a client/server system, large chunks of data are "shipped" to a cache in the client workstation. Data must be synchronized between the client and server to ensure consistency.

- **Remote cache**   Remote users benefit from cached information since it reduces information exchanges across slow links.

- **Distributed directory caching**   Some distributed file systems cache directory information in users' workstations to improve access.

- **Intermediate server cache**   In a distributed client/server environment, information may be cached from a back-end server to a workgroup server to improve access for local users who access the same information.

- **Web server/proxy server cache**   Web servers cache often-accessed pages to improve access for Internet users. A proxy server caches information for internal users who visit the Internet. The proxy server is situated at the Internet gateway, and it handles all Internet requests for users. It also caches pages that have been accessed for others to use.

In some distributed file systems (such as the Andrew File System), client workstations maintain a cache on a local hard disk (rather than in RAM memory) for information requested from servers. This cache can become quite large, which introduces consistency problems. There are two methods that help overcome this problem. One model has the client constantly checking with the server to see if information has changed, but this adds a great deal of overhead. Another model uses a *call-back* approach, in which the server informs clients when information they have in their cache is changed by someone else.

**RELATED ENTRIES**    Client/Server Computing; Distributed File Systems; Firewall; Proxy Server; Servers; Storage Systems; *and* Web Technologies and Concepts

## Call Setup

Call setup describes the establishment of a VC (virtual circuit) in a connection-oriented network environment. For example, ATM (Asynchronous Transfer Mode) networks are connection oriented. When a client needs to connect with another device, at least one VC is established to send data to that device. In a LANE (LAN Emulation) environment, additional VCs may be required for full duplex mode and overhead. To set up a VC, an ATM client sends out a request to establish a connection with another device. It takes time (approximately 100 milliseconds) to set up the circuit. This is called the call setup time, and it will vary depending on the hardware in use. On busy networks, call setup time can play an important factor in overall performance. Also, should a switch go down, many call setups will be necessary when the switch comes back online.

**RELATED ENTRIES**   ATM (Asynchronous Transfer Mode); Circuit; Circuit-Switching Services; *and* Virtual Circuit

## Campus Network

While the term campus network obviously refers to networks that exist on university campuses, it also refers to networks in local geographic areas, such as business parks, administrative centers, government centers, research centers, and medical centers. Usually the cabling and other transmission media are privately owned and managed. Underground fiber optic cable and/or microwave transmission systems may be used to link distant buildings.

Only a few years ago, campus backbone networks provided basic information sharing between the different departments or offices on campus that maintained their own LANs. Today, the trend is to consolidate voice, video, and data on the same network. ATM (Asynchronous Transfer Mode) is the best candidate for building such networks because it provides the quality-of-service requirements needed to deliver constant bit-rate traffic like live video and voice.

**RELATED ENTRIES**   ATM (Asynchronous Transfer Mode); Backbone Networks; FDDI (Fiber Distributed Data Interface); Fiber-Optic Cable; Network Concepts; Network Design and Construction; TIA/EIA Structured Cabling Standards; *and* Transmission Media, Methods, and Equipment

## Capacity

Capacity is the throughput rate of a transmission medium, usually measured in bits per second. See "Throughput."

## Carrier Services

The term *carrier* is commonly used to refer to the local or long-distance telecommunication service providers that offer a range of data communication services. Refer to "Communication Service Providers" and "Communication Services."

## Carrier Signal

A carrier signal is a specific frequency in a communication channel that is modulated to carry information. Carrier signals are commonly used in AM, FM, and other radio transmissions to differentiate the signals of each transmitting station. When you turn the dial of a radio, you are selecting a carrier frequency. The radio then amplifies the signal carried on the selected frequency. In AM (amplitude modulation), modulation changes the strength or amplitude of the carrier signal. In FM (frequency modulation), the frequency of the carrier signal is modulated.

**RELATED ENTRIES** Analog Signals; Analog Transmission Systems; Data Communication Concepts; Modulation Techniques; *and* Signals

## Castanet, Marimba

*See* Marimba Castanet.

## CCITT (Consultative Committee for International Telephony and Telegraphy)

The CCITT is part of the ITU (International Telecommunication Union), which has a history that stretches back to 1865. In that year, 20 countries agreed to standardize telegraph networks. The ITU was set up as part of the agreement to work on subsequent amendments. In subsequent years, the ITU got involved with telephony regulation, wireless radiocommunications, and sound broadcasting. In 1927, the Union was involved in allocating frequency bands for radio services, including fixed radio, mobile radio (maritime and aeronautical), broadcasting, and amateur/experimental radio. Formerly called the International Telegraph Union, in 1934, the union changed its name to the International Telecommunication Union to more properly define its role in all forms of communication, including wire, radio, optical, and electromagnetic systems.

After World War II, the ITU became a special agency of the United Nations and moved its headquarters to Geneva. Also at this time, it made mandatory the Table of Frequency Allocations, which allocates frequency bands for each radio service. This table is meant to avoid interference between aircraft and ground communications, car telephones, maritime communications, radio stations, and spacecraft communications.

Then, in 1956, two separate ITU committees, the CCIF (Consultative Committee for International Telephony) and the CCIT (Consultative Committee for International Telegraphy) were joined to create the CCITT (Consultative Committee for International Telephony and Telegraphy) to more effectively manage the telephone and telegraph communications.

In 1993, the ITU went through a reorganization and the French name was changed to simply ITU-T, which refers to the ITU's Telecommunications Standardization Sector. Two other main sectors formed at this time were the ITU-R (Radiocommunications Sector) and the ITU-D (Development Sector).

Even though the ITU-T now creates recommendations and standards, the CCITT recommendations are still mentioned quite frequently.

**RELATED ENTRIES**    ITU (International Telecommunication Union); Standards Groups, Associations, and Organizations

## CDDI (Copper Distributed Data Interface)

CDDI is a version of FDDI (Fiber Distributed Data Interface) designed to run on shielded and unshielded twisted-pair cable. It is currently a standard that was developed separately by Cabletron and Crescendo, who combined their technology work and received ANSI standards approval in 1993. A typical CDDI network consists of concentrators with a number of ports for the connection of workstations. Because CDDI has limited cable distances, a CDDI concentrator can connect to an FDDI ring as a subnetwork.

**RELATED ENTRY**    FDDI (Fiber Distributed Data Interface)

## CDE (Common Desktop Environment)

The CDE is a user interface for UNIX environments that was developed as a cooperative effort by members of The Open Group (http://www.opengroup.org). CDE is meant to provide a user interface that helps UNIX systems compete with Windows NT. It also provides a common programming environment for developing off-the-shelf software that works across different vendors' versions of the operating system.

CDE was first introduced in 1995 as a graphical user interface that provided a consistent user interface to both users and system administrators. The CDE interface is designed to make operating systems less complex for users who need powerful desktop platforms to get their work done. At the same time, CDE provides system administrators with a higher level of control of desktop environments in client/server and distributed computing environments.

The latest release of the software provides a standard application presentation environment for multiple distributed platforms. It integrates the Motif 2.0 graphical user interface, the X Window system, and CDE. CDE incorporates Motif 2.0 user interface objects (widgets) spin box, combo box, container, and notebook. This latest release has graphical desktop development tools, 64-bit support, SGML online help and documentation, multilanguage support, and programming enhancements.

The source code is available for evaluation at $5,000 and full-distribution source code is available for $40,000. You can contact Open Group Direct, at 1-800-268-5245, or send e-mail to direct@opengroup.org.

**RELATED ENTRIES**   The Open Group; UNIX; *and* X Window

## CDMA (Code Division Multiple Access)

CDMA is a digital cellular standard that uses wideband spread spectrum techniques for signal transmission, as opposed to narrowband channel techniques used in conventional analog systems. It combines both digital voice and data into a single wireless communication network and can provide customers with digital voice services, voice mail, caller ID, and text messaging. CDMA was approved as a digital multiple access technique for cellular telephony by the TIA (Telecommunications Industry Association) in 1993. It is also called IS-95.

In general, a cellular telephone system is a multiple access system. In the traditional analog cellular system, multiple users can make simultaneous calls over a number of radio channels. The radio spectrum allocated to the cellular system is divided into a range of channels, depending on the service in use.

For example, the traditional AMPS (Advanced Mobile Phone Service) analog cellular system, first deployed in 1982, uses FDMA (Frequency Division Multiple Access). With this technique, channels are defined as frequencies within an allocated range, and each band is 30 kHz wide. In contrast, NAMPS (Narrowband AMPS) has 10 kHz channels. Each channel supports one conversation.

In contrast to CDMA, new digital cellular systems use a different channel allocation technique called TDMA (Time Division Multiple Access). With TDMA, a band is subdivided into "time slots," and each slot is allocated to a channel. In other words, if a band is divided into three time-division channels, every third slot is allocated to carry information for a user whether or not there is information to transmit. There are three TDMA standards, described here for comparative reference:

- **North American Digital Cellular (also know as IS-54)**   This system works with AMPS and divides the 30 kHz bands into three time-division channels.

- **GSM (Global System for Mobile Communications)**   GSM frequency bands are 200 kHz wide and are divided into eight time-division channels.

- **PDC (Personal Digital Cellular)**   PDC frequency bands are 25 kHz wide and are divided into three time-division channels.

CDMA uses spread spectrum technologies. Spread spectrum is a transmission technique that spreads the information contained in a transmission over a very large bandwidth. The technique has been used for years by the military because the signal is hard to detect and difficult to jam.

Technically, a 9,600-bit/sec CDMA call is spread out to a rate of about 1.23 Mbits/sec. Spreading involves applying a code to data bits that specifically identifies the information belonging to a particular call (user) in the current cell (generally, the area reachable by the local transceiver station). While this adds much overhead to a call, the bandwidth of the system is wide enough to handle it.

Note that the data bits for all users in the cell are simultaneously transmitted across the wide bandwidth of the system. A user's device picks up the signals and then discards all the coded bits except those specifically targeted to it. It then strips off the code and restores the transmission to its original 9,600-bit/sec data stream.

Stations within the CDMA system differentiate themselves from one another by using a pseudorandom code that is generated with the help of the GPS (Global Positioning System). Each station transmits a version of the same code, but each code is offset in time relative to other stations. GPS ensures that the codes are synchronized.

CDMA advocates promote the security and privacy that spread spectrum can provide. Eavesdroppers have trouble picking up the signal because it is spread out and requires knowledge of a code to separate one call from another. In contrast, the AMPS system and TDMA systems concentrate channels into a narrow band that is easy to monitor with radio receivers.

In early 1997, Sprint began financing a national PCS (Personal Communications Services) network with its cable partners TCI, Cox, and Comcast. They formed a group called Sprint Spectrum, with the goal of developing a future wireless telecommunication system. Another CDMA player is PrimeCo Personal Communications L.P. (http://www.primeco.com), which recently established PCS services in a number of U.S. cities. The company is an alliance that includes members such as AirTouch Communications, Bell Atlantic, NINEX, and US West Media Group. GTE is also involved in CDMA deployment.

Vendors supporting the standard claim that CDMA can provide 20 to 40 times the capacity of analog cellular systems. It competes with TDMA technology such as the early D-AMPS system and the GSM standard that is used throughout Europe. However, of the two systems, TDMA appears to be superior in actual usage. A recent deployment in the Washington D.C. area by APC (American Personal Communications) has been extremely successful at delivering good service. In contrast, CDMA installations have been plagued by interference and poor quality. One of the reasons for this is that CDMA systems trade off voice quality for capacity. While early designs called for digitizing voice at 13 Kbits/sec, working systems use a rate of 8 Kbits/sec.

An industry consortium called CDG (CDMA Development Group) develops products and services for CDMA and works to promote its adoption around the world. The CDG is composed of telecommunication service providers and manufacturers who are pushing for interoperability standards among related equipment vendors.

**RELATED ENTRIES**   AMPS (Advanced Mobile Phone Service); CDPD (Cellular Digital Packet Data); Cellular Communication Systems;  GSM (Global System for

Mobile Communications); Mobile Computing; PCS (Personal Communications Services); *and* Wireless Communications

**INFORMATION ON THE INTERNET**

CDG (CDMA Development Group)   http://www.cdg.org

Cellular Network Perspective, Inc.   http://www.cadvision.com/cnp-wireless
(wireless publications and links)

# CDPD (Cellular Digital Packet Data)

**C**

CDPD is a specification that defines how to package data and carry it over existing analog cellular radio systems. It was designed to go on top of AMPS (Advanced Mobile Phone Service), the analog cellular system that was first put into service in 1982. CDPD is based on IBM CellPlan II technology.

CDPD provides some interesting benefits over the older AMPS method. For one thing, it provides more error control and security through encryption. In addition, CDPD handles the type of bursty traffic that is common with network-connected users, such as short exchanges of information like electronic mail or database queries. Users are billed in subminute billing units to accommodate short data bursts.

CDPD uses idle channels on the analog cellular system to transmit digital data. Capacity on the channel is made available for data transmissions when voices switch from cell to cell or when calls are set up and terminated. For example, a time interval of 10 seconds must elapse after a voice call is terminated before another voice call can be set up.

The 30 kHz channels used in AMPS can provide a data rate of 19.2 Kbits/sec, but overhead reduces this to a more realistic rate of 9,600 bits/sec. Data is divided up into 274-bit units, compressed and encrypted, and placed into blocks that total 420 bits after overhead is added. These blocks are then divided into seven 60-bit microblocks, which are then transmitted over the network. A single channel is used for transmitting data, so mobile devices must sort through the blocks and pull out only those blocks meant for it. Multiple channels are used for transmitting data from mobile devices to the base station. Mobile devices contend for these channels.

CDPD is defined by a consortium of cellular carriers and computer companies, including eight of the nine RBOCs (regional Bell operating companies), McCaw Cellular Communications, Contel Cellular, and GTE Mobilnet. The consortium published its first specifications in July 1993 that define how network providers and equipment manufacturers should design and build products and services for the cellular networks. A number of computer manufacturers are creating CDPD-enabled portable devices, often called PDAs (personal digital assistants).

McCaw Cellular Communications has developed a wireless internetworking system called MDBS (Mobile Database Station) in conjunction with IBM, GTE Mobile Communications, and some of the RBOCs. Developers of mobile computing devices are also involved. MDBS includes accounting services, authentication, and control software provided by Inet, X.400 and X.500 message-handling services from Retix, and fault-tolerant systems provided by Tandem Computer.

Additional trends and services related to CDPD include the following:

■ The CDPD Forum is a consortium that provides information about CDPD. Visit http://www.cdpd.org.

■ The AT&T PocketNet cellular phone lets you access Web pages and has its own IP address and Internet-based e-mail box. More information is available at http://www.airdata.com.

■ Embedded browser software is available for many devices from Unwired Planet. Visit their Web site at http://www.uplanet.com.

■ Motorola's AirMobile Software lets cellular users access cc:Mail on corporate mail servers. Visit http://www.mot.com, for more information.

■ Many cellular phone manufacturers are offering phones with built-in CDPD modems. At the Motorola site mentioned above, you can find information on the Personal Messenger Wireless PC Card modems for portable computers.

**RELATED ENTRIES**    AMPS (Advanced Mobile Phone Service); Cellular Communication Systems; GSM (Global System for Mobile Communications); Mobile Computing; PCS (Personal Communications Services); and Wireless Communications

## CD-ROM (Compact Disc, Read-Only Memory)

*See* Storage Systems.

## Cell

A cell is a fixed-length packet of data as opposed to a variable-length frame of data. Cells are the basic unit of data transport in ATM (Asynchronous Transfer Mode), while frames are the basic unit of data transport in local area networks and frame relay networks. ATM cells are 53 bytes in length while frames vary in size and may be up to 8,000 bytes in length. The 53-byte ATM cell consists of 48 bytes of data and 5 bytes of header information.

**RELATED ENTRIES**    ATM (Asynchronous Transfer Mode); Cell Relay

## Cell Relay

Cell relay is the basis of ATM (Asynchronous Transfer Mode). Information is transmitted in a fixed-size envelope called a cell. Cell relay is really cell switching, but the term *relay* caught on because it is analogous to frame relay.

The concept of switching cells is the gist of this discussion. A cell is a fixed-size (53 bytes) data packet. Fixed-size cells can be switched at very high speed. Picture a busy intersection. If a long semi-trailer truck negotiates the intersection, other traffic gets held up and it adds unpredictability to the rate at which vehicles can pass through the intersection. If all the vehicles are the same size, you can closely estimate the number of cars that will get through on a green light. If a truck periodically negotiates the intersection, such estimates are impossible. Likewise, if switches in your network handle variable length frames, you can't accurately predict when a frame going into the network will come out the other side. Steady and predictable traffic flow is essential to running voice and video traffic over networks, and that is why cell relay is important. You can set aside cell slots in the traffic flow to guarantee that real-time information will arrive on time.

Cell relay combined with fast switches and fiber-optic cable are at the core of high-performance, scaleable networks. ATM implements cell relay to provide data throughput rates in the multimegabit and multigigabit-per-second range.

An important characteristic of ATM is that it is connection oriented. An initial cell is released to set up a connection through the network, then all subsequent cells follow the same path. Packets arrive in order at the destination by following this path. ATM trades off error checking and acknowledgment features for raw speed. If packets are lost, higher-layer protocols in end systems must manage retransmissions.

A cell switch is pictured in Figure C-2. Note that it contains the same number of inputs and outputs on either side of a switching fabric. This switch can provide a temporary dedicated path from any input port to any output port.

Assume a cell needs to get from input port D to output port B. The path through the switch forms a circuit called, for example, 110. Each bit in this number indicates the direction the cell should take at each individual switching element. At the first switch, the left-most 1 indicates that the cell should go "up." At the second switch, the middle 1 bit indicates that the cell should once again go up. At the third switch, the right-most 0 indicates that the cell should go "down," where it arrives at the correct destination port.

Public data network providers like AT&T are busy installing ATM cell-switching devices with SONET (Synchronous Optical Network) interfaces that operate in the multigigabit range. Switches may have hundreds or thousands of ports or be arranged in arrays to handle thousands of circuits.

**RELATED ENTRIES**    ATM (Asynchronous Transfer Mode); Hubs/Concentrators/ MAUs; Packet and Cell Switching; Switched Networks; *and* Virtual Circuit

## Cellular Communication Systems

Cellular radiotelephone systems in the United States began in 1983 and have grown rapidly ever since. The systems were largely analog until the early 1990s, when the first digital systems were put in place. There are many benefits to digital systems, and a number of standards have been introduced. The abundance of standards in the digital market along with continued advances in analog services has slowed the move to fully digital systems. Still, there are benefits in all-digital systems, and the latest

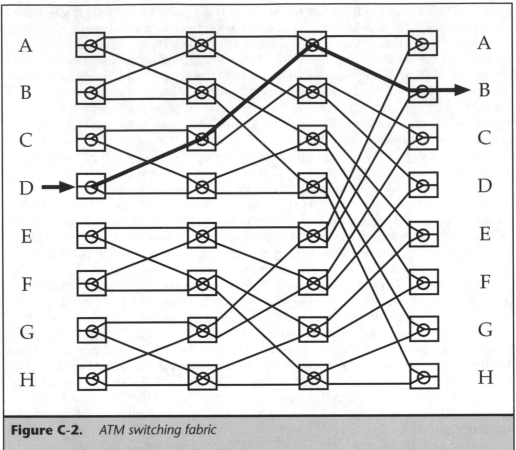

**Figure C-2.** *ATM switching fabric*

trend is to build a global system that allows cellular phone users to make calls anywhere in the world with a single device and a single phone number.

Cellular phone systems consist of mobile units, base stations, and switches. A cellular phone is different from a regular phone in that it has a transceiver (transmitter/receiver). The transmitter sends radio signals to an antenna at a base station, and the receiver receives radio signals from the base station antenna.

A base station is a stationary antenna located within the middle of a cell-shaped transmit and receive area. The cells have a limited geographic area that may cover an entire town or a segment of a large metropolitan area, as shown in Figure C-3. A typical cell is 20 kilometers across but can vary in size.

Cellular systems in large metropolitan areas may be overused, so cells are made smaller to service more customers. Adjoining cells have their own tower and cannot use similar operating frequencies. However, stations that are separated by at least one

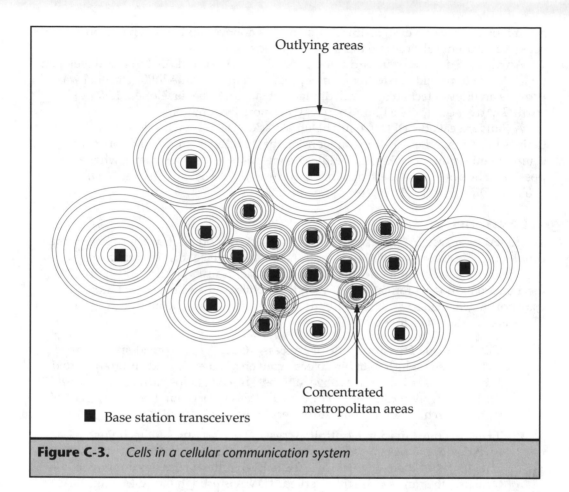

**Figure C-3.** *Cells in a cellular communication system*

cell may reuse frequencies, and this provides expansion of the system. The technique is referred to as *frequency reuse*.

As a mobile user travels from one cell to another, there is a hand-off from one base station to another. This hand-off requires a certain amount of time and allocation of a new frequency in the new cell. It can produce a discontinuity in the call, which might disrupt data transmissions.

## Analog Systems

The first cellular system in the United States, AMPS (Advanced Mobile Phone Service), was built in 1983. It is a fully analog system (i.e., voice is not digitized for transmission) that uses FDMA (Frequency Division Multiple Access) techniques for creating user communication channels. A channel consists of a specific frequency within the bandwidth of frequencies allocated to the system. An AMPS system consists of up to 818 channel pairs (transmit and receive). The transmitter in each cell has relatively low power so its transmission does not overlap too much into adjacent cells. No adjacent cells can use the same frequencies.

An advanced AMPS standard called NAMPS (Narrowband AMPS) was developed by Motorola to provide up to three times greater capacity than AMPS. The goal was to provide an interim technology until digital systems could be developed. Refer to "AMPS (Advanced Mobile Phone Service)" for more information.

A standard called CDPD (Cellular Digital Packet Data) was developed in 1993 that defines how to handle data transmissions on the AMPS system. CDPD's primary claim to fame is that it makes use of idle channels and sends data frames whenever possible. The system make efficient use of the existing AMPS system. See "CDPD (Cellular Digital Packet Data)" for more information.

## Digital Systems

The first digital systems were set up in 1993 by McCaw and Southwestern Bell. Some providers have chosen to wait for standards to settle and feel that current analog systems provide superior performance. Digital systems use a specific transport mechanism to move information between the mobile user and the base station. The transport mechanisms in this case are the channel allocation schemes for digital radio. There are two schemes in use:

- **CDMA (Code Division Multiple Access)**  CDMA uses spread-spectrum techniques in which data bits in each conversation are coded and transmitted simultaneously with other conversations. The code helps each receiver access the bits that are meant for it. The coded data is spread out in a very wideband signal, which is hard for eavesdroppers to listen in on.

- **TDMA (Time Division Multiple Access)**  This is a time-slot technique where each device on the network is given a specific time slot in which to transmit. The time allocation for a device is fixed. Even if the device has nothing to transmit, the time slot is still reserved. TDMA is used in the GSM (Global System for Mobile Communications) system. It implements eight time-division channels in 200 kHz wide carriers. A carrier is a "slice" of the available spectrum. GSM is the basis for PCS (Personal Communications Services), an emerging set of services that may transform the wireless landscape. See "GSM (Global System for Mobile Communications)" for more information.

## Emerging Standards

The PCS (Personal Communications Services) and the Iridium system being deployed by Motorola and a consortium of global users will change the way people communicate. Both systems are designed for wireless use.

PCS (also called PCN, or Personal Communications Network, outside the United States) is a personalized communication system that assigns an individual one phone number. Note that the individual has the phone number, not a device. This phone number works no matter where the user travels to on the planet. PCS is fully digital and has some unique features. It implements 50- to 100-meter wide microcells with low transmission rates, making equipment very inexpensive. The U.S. government has already auctioned off licenses for the service. One drawback is that some of the frequencies are already allocated to other services, which must apparently move out to make room for PCS. The investment and the changes required to get the system going may be too high to make it practical in the near future. Refer to "PCS (Personal Communications Services)" for more information.

Another system is Iridium. When established in 1998, it will provide wireless telephone services by using low-orbit satellites and connections into the existing telephone system. Users can travel anywhere in the world, and their handset will provide the system with information about their location. The Iridium system consists of 66 satellites, weighing approximately 689 kilograms (1,500 pounds), that will be launched into low-earth orbit at an altitude of 420 nautical miles. The satellite project tightly focused beams over the ground to create a cellular-like system. Refer to "Iridium System" for more information.

**RELATED ENTRIES**  AMPS (Advanced Mobile Phone Service); CDPD (Cellular Digital Packet Data); GSM (Global System for Mobile Communications); Mobile Computing; PCS (Personal Communications Services); *and* Wireless Communications

**INFORMATION ON THE INTERNET**

| | |
|---|---|
| International Trade Administration's cellular site | http://www.ita.doc.gov/industry/tai/telecom/cellular.html |
| CTIA (Cellular Telecommunications Industry Association) site | http://www.wow-com.com |
| Cellular Network Perspective, Inc. (wireless publications) | http://www.cadvision.com/cnp-wireless |

## Central Office

*See* CO (Central Office).

## Centrex (Central Exchange)

Centrex is a form of PBX (private branch exchange) that is handled by equipment located at the local exchange carrier's central office. A PBX is a telephone circuit-switching device that services a number of telecommunication devices. It is usually privately owned by an organization and connected into the telephone network. The PBX can switch calls among internal callers or calls with the LEC (local exchange carrier). With Centrex, the job of a PBX is basically moved to the LEC and handled by the LEC-owned equipment rather than equipment owned by a private organization.

**RELATED ENTRY**   PBX (Private Branch Exchange)

# CERN

CERN is the French acronym for the European Laboratory for Particle Physics, which is located in Geneva, Switzerland. CERN gained importance with regard to networking and the Internet because it is where Tim Berners-Lee and associates created the communication protocols that brought about the World Wide Web. The protocols allowed users with browsers to access information on Web servers. This work was extended in 1993 when the NCSA (National Center for Superconducting Applications) released the graphically oriented Mosaic Web browser. Marc Andreessen, now head of Netscape, was responsible for that work.

# CERN Proxy Services

A proxy server is a caching and security device. The CERN proxy services are a set of protocols recognized around the world as a standard for implementing proxy services on intranets and the Internet. The protocols operate on TCP/IP networks in conjunction with the HTTP (Hypertext Transfer Protocol).

A proxy server runs as software on a computer and acts on behalf of a client to make requests outside the client's network. For example, when an internal user attempts to access the Internet, the proxy server intercepts the request and makes the request itself. The internal user never makes a direct request to an outside system. Likewise, when the Internet server returns a response, it is intercepted by the proxy server and transferred to the user. The proxy server can filter all incoming packets and discard any that are not related to an internal request. This prevents hackers from attacking internal systems.

The proxy server can be viewed as a gateway between two networks, usually a private internal network and the Internet. With the proliferation of internal intranets, a proxy server may be used to control internal traffic.

CERN's proxy server grew over time as it added application-aware proxy support for its HTTP servers (Web servers). The WWW community made its own contributions over time, and today the proxy services are well established. For example, Microsoft and Novell implement the CERN proxy services in their own proxy server implementations.

**RELATED ENTRIES**   Firewall; Internet; Proxy Server; *and* Web Technologies and Concepts

# CERT (Computer Emergency Response Team)

CERT is an Internet security advisory group that tracks security breaches and publishes advisory reports about them.

### INFORMATION ON THE INTERNET

CERT                http://www.cert.org

# Certificates and Certification Systems

In the words of Ron Rivest, one of the cofounders of RSA Data Security (http://www.rsa.com), "digital certificates are your Internet calling card." A digital certificate is something that can prove who you are on the Internet or on internal networks. It is a *personal digital ID* or *digital signature* that can be used for authentication or to ensure that a message is from who you think it is from and has not been altered during transit.

A certificate can verify the authenticity of a user who is logging on to a secure server. Likewise, a Web server can have a certificate to prove its authenticity to users who access it. Such users must be assured that a site is not being spoofed by malicious people who want to collect credit card numbers and personal information or distribute bogus and virus-infected copies of popular programs. Certificates can even be used in place of credit card numbers for online buying transactions. The SET (Secure Electronic Transaction) scheme developed by major credit card companies is designed to hide credit card numbers from merchants by substituting the card number with a digital certificate. See "SET (Secure Electronic Transaction)" for more details.

The risk of *message forgery* is perhaps a more important reason to use a digital signature. In a recent sexual harassment case, it was found that an employee forged messages from her boss, but this falsification was only found after the courts had awarded her $100,000. Message forgery can also occur on the Internet if someone wants to smear another person or an organization. Another side of this is *message repudiation*—that is, the author of a message denies having sent it.

Certificates are issued by a *CA* (*certificate authority*), which is a trusted organization that verifies the credentials of people and puts its stamp of approval on those credentials. A CA is often called a "trusted authority," but there is more involved than the CA's good name and how well you trust them. The whole certification process uses known and reliable computerized security mechanisms based on public key cryptography. An understanding of public key cryptography is important to understanding how certificates work. You can refer to "Public-Key Cryptography" for details.

Basically, the scheme creates two linked but separate keys for each user. One is held privately and one is made available publicly. If someone wants to send you an encrypted message, they obtain a copy of your public key to encrypt the message before sending it. When you receive the message, you decrypt it with your private key. Your private key is the only key that can decrypt a message that has been encrypted with your public key. The scheme is simple, elegant, and secure. Public keys can be given to anyone, while private keys are held by their owners.

Now suppose you want to send a message to a friend, but your friend needs some assurance that the message indeed came from you. For this trick, you can reverse the above steps. Basically, you encrypt the message with *your* private key, not the recipient's public key. Your friend then decrypts the message with *your* public key. Since your public key is the only key that can do this, your friend knows the message came from you (at least in theory).

So far, we have two uses for the public key cryptography scheme:

- **Private message**   Sender encrypts with the recipient's public key. Recipient encrypts with recipient's private key.

- **Signed message**   Sender encrypts with sender's private key. Recipient encrypts with sender's public key.

Now suppose you want to hide a signed message in transit. That's simple. First create a signed message, then create a private message out of the signed message. When your friend receives this message, she first decrypts it with her private key, then decrypts it again with your public key. The last step proves the message is from you. Note that the steps involved in creating a signed message are often a little more involved. This is discussed in more detail under "Digital Signatures."

All of the above examples assume that the public key is trusted. If you give a friend your public key in person, then your friend will trust it. But how can a merchant on the Internet or a business partner be sure that your public key is authentic? What if someone forges a message from you, then forges a public key to open that message? The recipient may not know the message and the key are fake and accept the contents of the message. Obviously, some secure and verifiable method is needed to distribute public keys, and this is where certificate authorities come into the picture.

The simplest definition of a certificate is that it is a "container" that holds your public key and possibly some information about you. This container is then "signed" by a trusted CA using its private key. Basically, the CA approves the certificate and encrypts its contents. The certificate can then be used for online business transactions or for secure logon to servers. The system accepting the certificate can obtain a copy of the CA's public key and verify that the certificate is authentic.

But this assumes the CA is trusted. Would you trust a certificate that has been issued by an organization in a third-world country or by a local bank? To solve this problem, a hierarchy of trust is being set up in the United States. Local certificate authorities are authorized by states, which in turn are authorized by national CAs. At the time of this writing, several states were drafting legislation to regulate certification authorities and allow digital signatures to replace handwritten signatures. The reason for legislation is to provide auditing and ensure levels of security. Most states will be requiring that CAs obtain a license to operate.

Verisign (http://www.verisign.com) is a well-known certificate authority. You can visit its Web site for a complete description of the procedures the company uses to issue and manage certificates. Verisign's class 1 certificate, which you can obtain for free, contains only a user's name and e-mail address. Higher-level certificates may contain more personal information. In fact, companies can work with Verisign to create custom containers with specific information fields.

To get a certificate from Verisign, you go through a process of establishing your credentials in much the same way you apply for a credit card. The first step in the process is to generate your public and private keys. Web browsers, electronic mail servers, and operating systems like Windows 95 have facilities for generating these keys. Once the keys are created, you package the public key with required information about yourself or your company and send it to the CA. The Verisign site or other CA Web sites have full instructions for completing this process. If everything checks out, you are issued a certificate.

## Internal Certification Systems

Public CAs such as Verisign offer a valuable service, but many organizations may have a need to issue their own certificates for internal use. As mentioned, certificates can be used to verify users during a server logon process. They are also important in verifying electronic mail messages from other users in the organization, and they provide a way to verify document flows in groupware and business-related workflow software. For example, a budget director may authorize a million-dollar equipment purchase by digitally signing a document. This document moves through the computerized workflow system to a purchasing agent. The purchasing agent can know that the document is authentic because of the attached certificate.

Many organizations will prefer to manage their own certificate issuance based on their own policies and certificate requirements. To fill this need, a number of vendors offer in-house certificate servers, including Certificate Server from Netscape (http://www.netscape.com), Sentry CA from Xcert Software (http://www.xcert.com), and e-Lock from Frontier Technologies (http://www.frontiertech.com). In particular, Netscape's product is fully compatible with public-key infrastructures.

**RELATED ENTRIES**    Authentication and Authorization; Cryptography; Digital Signatures; Electronic Commerce; PKI (Public-Key Infrastructure); Public-Key Cryptography; Security; SET (Secure Electronic Transaction); *and* Token-Based Authentication

### INFORMATION ON THE INTERNET

| | |
|---|---|
| CommerceNet | http://www.commerce.net |
| U.S. Postal Service | http://www.usps.gov |
| GTE-CyberTrust | http://www.cybertrust.gtc.com |
| VeriSign, Inc. | http://www.verisign.com |
| World Wide Web Consortium | http://www.w3.org |

# CGI (Common Gateway Interface)

CGI is a server extension that extends the capabilities of Web servers. You write server extensions to make your Web site more active and interesting. Instead of delivering a stale static page, CGI (and other server extensions) provides a way for Web clients to request information from Web servers. The user fills out a form that is submitted to the server, and the server responds with dynamic information obtained by processing the information on the form. The Web server may interact with a back-end database server or get the information from another source.

The CGI interface is the protocol that provides a two-way interface between Web clients and Web servers and the CGI script is the set of commands that determines what happens when they communicate. CGI was invented to extend the HTTP protocol.

CGI defines the control tags and fields specifiers to be placed in HTML documents, environment variables in memory where the server places information used by scripts, and the flow of information between client, server, and script.

The steps that Web site developers follow to use CGI are to first create the HTML (Hypertext Markup Language) form and add the tags that define the input boxes, drop-down list boxes, and buttons that appear on forms to collect input from users. Next, a CGI script is written to accept the input that the end user types on the HTML form and do something with it, like make a query to a back-end database.

For more information on gateways, forms, and CGI, refer to specific books on Web server design. Many books include disks that contain sample programs for collecting common information from Web clients.

**RELATED ENTRIES**   HTML (Hypertext Markup Language); HTTP (Hypertext Transfer Protocol); Web Middleware and Database Connectivity; *and* Web Technologies and Concepts

## INFORMATION ON THE INTERNET

CyberWeb Software CGI page      http://www.stars.com/Vlib/Providers/CGI.html

# Challenge/Response Protocol

A challenge/response is a security mechanism for verifying the identity of a user or system that is attempting to make a connection to a secure system. When a user contacts a server, the server responds with a *challenge* (also called a *nonce*). The user then takes this challenge and uses it to perform a cryptographic operation that produces some result that is sent back to the server. The server then performs a similar operation, and if it comes up with the same results, it knows the user must be authentic.

The specifics of the routine are described here and pictured in Figure C-4.

1. The client makes a logon request to the server.
2. The server responds with a challenge (nonce) to the client.
3. The client combines the user name with the nonce and encrypts this combination using the user's password as the key.
4. The results of this operation are returned to the server.
5. The server performs the same operation as described in step 3.
6. The server compares its results with the results returned from the client.
7. If they match, the client is considered authentic.

**C**

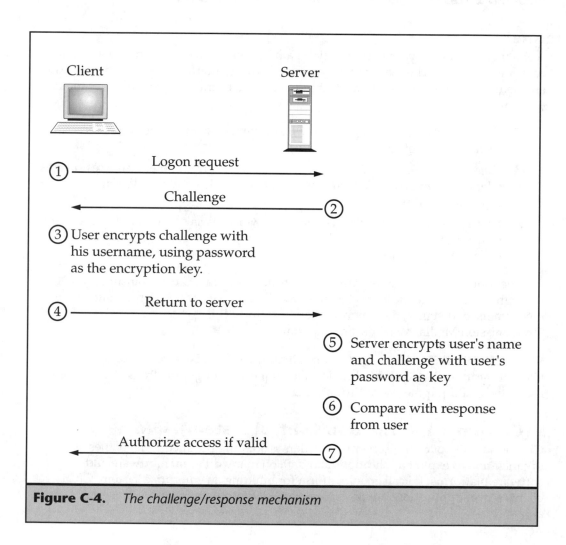

**Figure C-4.** *The challenge/response mechanism*

This sequence assumes that both the server and the user have some secret piece of information that is shared in common (i.e., the user's password). It also assumes they use the same encryption method.

Note that this technique doesn't require that the user send a password "over the wire" (either encrypted or unencrypted) to the server. The password is used as the key for the encryption, so if both client and server encrypt the same information with the same key, they should come up with the same results. Another important feature is that the server can issue a different challenge at every logon, so if a hacker does manage to capture any session information, that information cannot be used to spoof some future session.

**RELATED ENTRIES**    Authentication and Authorization; Security

# Channel

A channel is essentially a communication path between two or more devices. In a computer system, a channel provides an input/output interface between the processor and some peripheral device. In telecommunication, a channel may take one of the following forms:

- *One channel* carried on a physical wire or wireless medium between two systems (also referred to as a circuit).

- *Time-division multiplexed channels,* in which signals from several sources such as telephones and computers are merged into a single stream of data and separated by intervals of time

- *Frequency-division multiplexed channels,* in which signals from many sources are transmitted over a single cable by modulating each signal on a carrier at different frequencies

The topic "Throughput" discusses the rate at which data can be transmitted through a channel. In addition, channels have limited bandwidth depending on the medium used, distance, distortion, and other factors. This is discussed under "Transmission Media, Methods, and Equipment."

**RELATED ENTRIES**    Capacity; Circuit; Circuit-Switching Services; Data Communication Concepts; Modulation Techniques; Throughput; Transmission Media, Methods, and Equipment; *and* Virtual Circuit

# CICS (Customer Information Control System), IBM

CICS is a family of client/server transaction-processing products that enables an organization to exploit applications and data on many different hardware and software platforms. It is an open platform for building an enterprise system. CICS client/server applications are portable across IBM and many non-IBM systems, interoperable across LANs and WANs, scaleable up to thousands of users, and manageable from a single point of control. CICS is normally found in large online networks and provides application compatibility with platforms such as IBM's AIX, MVS, OS/2, OS/400, and VSE, as well as non-IBM environments such as Windows NT, HP, Digital, and Sun.

**RELATED ENTRIES**    IBM (International Business Machines); Transaction Processing

## CIDR (Classless Interdomain Routing)

One of the problems with the explosion of the Internet is that IP (Internet Protocol) addresses are becoming scarce. CIDR is an interim solution to the address problem. It was first implemented in the early 1990s. While the Internet Protocol's 32-bit address space can in theory provide up to two billion addresses, a class system was implemented that makes inefficient use of the addresses. The class system was put into place in the early days of the Internet when no one conceived of the Internet as being as large as it is today.

Basically, the class system was developed to provide a range and variety of network addresses and to give different organizations a choice of IP addressing schemes to fit their internal requirements. There are 126 class A networks with 16 million hosts each, 16,384 class B networks with 65,536 hosts each, and over 2 million class C networks with 254 hosts each. The class A networks are already assigned, and most organizations are too large for class C networks. Subsequently, all the class B networks are taken because they fit the profile of most companies and organizations. Even so, many host addresses go unused by organizations that have class B address. This is where IP addresses are wasted by the class system.

Now consider that every IP address is split in two. One part of the address designates the network and the other part designates a host on that network. If only class A addressing schemes were used, there would only be 126 networks in the routing scheme and each router would only need to keep track of the location of these networks. However, class C networks are rapidly being assigned, creating a Internet with millions of networks. This is an incredible amount of networks for routers to keep track of. In addition, routers exchange routing information tables. If these tables are large, they can tie up network bandwidth and are susceptible to errors in transmission.

CIDR, as defined in RFC 1519, provides some relief from the addressing problem. The basic idea is to assign blocks of class C addresses to a site based on the number of host addresses that site needs. This prevents wasted addresses as has occurred with class B addressing. In addition, the class C address space is divided into four world zones (Europe, North America, Central and South America, and Asia and the Pacific). Each zone is assigned 32 million addresses. This latter scheme helps routers dispense with large routing tables. If a datagram arrives at a American router with an Asian address, it is simply forwarded to an Asian gateway.

**RELATED ENTRIES**    IP (Internet Protocol); Routing Protocols and Algorithms; *and* TCP/IP (Transmission Control Protocol/Internet Protocol)

# CIF (Cells in Frames)

CIF defines a way to carry ATM (Asynchronous Transfer Mode) traffic on a network segment that uses frames, such as Ethernet. ATM uses cells as its basic unit for moving data across the underlying medium. All cells are small 53-byte units that allow high-speed switching, while frames are large and may be variable in size. With CIF, existing legacy LANs can participate in ATM networks without the need to upgrade NICs (network interface cards) in end systems with ATM NICs.

CIF was developed by the Cells in Frames Alliance, a consortium of network hardware and software vendors, Internet service providers, and others. Much of the work has been done by Scott Brim of Cornell, who chairs the alliance. Information about CIF is available at the CIF Web site (http://www.cif.cornell.edu). Its goals allow network administrators to design all-ATM networks using existing LAN hardware, develop and publish standard protocols that define how ATM cells are carried in LAN frames, provide ATM QoS (Quality of Service) features that can be controlled by users, and provide a system that can transport data, voice, and video throughout an enterprise network.

In essence, an Ethernet or token ring NIC in a workstation can appear to be an ATM NIC. CIF defines how cells and other information are arranged in the Ethernet frames. Up to 48 ATM cells can be placed inside Ethernet frames.

One of the reasons for moving to ATM is to provide traffic prioritization and other QoS features throughout the enterprise. In fact, Cornell University is in the process of replacing its PBX (private branch exchange ) systems with a phone system that runs over its network. The benefits of cells (as opposed to frames) for data delivery are discussed further under "Cell Relay" and "Packet and Cell Switching."

CIF allows an ATM-compliant application to run on a LAN framing protocol and still use the QoS features of ATM. For example, ATM can provide a higher level of service to real-time video or audio, ensuring that such transmissions reach their destinations without delays that can cause distortion. Of course, this means that other types of traffic might be delayed, but if that traffic is e-mail and other nonpriority traffic, then delays are probably not a problem.

Note that CIF requires a replacement of existing Ethernet or token-ring hubs and switches for ATM switches that run CIF software. Madge Networks is developing products based on CIF and that provide various levels of prioritization for network traffic. However, Madge and other vendors that support CIF stress that CIF is a transition solution that can help organizations move to ATM while taking advantage of existing legacy LANs. Full end-to-end ATM is necessary to create high-performance enterprisewide ATM networks.

The following "Related Entries" list gives some of the other topics in this book that are related to or contrast with CIF. You can refer to these topics for comparative information.

**RELATED ENTRIES**    Cell Relay; Gigabit Ethernet; IP over ATM; IP Switching; LANE (LAN Emulation); Network Design and Construction; PACE (Priority Access Control Enabled); Prioritization of Network Traffic; QoS (Quality of Service); RSVP (Resource Reservation Protocol); Switched Networks; Tag Switching; Virtual Circuit; *and* VLAN (Virtual LAN)

## CIFS (Common Internet File System)

CIFS is a new file system supported by Microsoft and other vendors such as Data General, Digital Equipment Corp., Intel Corporation, Intergraph, Network Appliance Inc., and SCO. It is an extension of Microsoft's existing SMB (Server Message Blocks) file-sharing protocol and allows individuals and organizations to run file systems over the Internet. In the past, most Internet file exchanges have been one-way transfers. CIFS goes beyond this by allowing groups of users to work together and share documents over the Internet in the same way they share documents when running peer networking services on Windows clients. Users can collaborate over the Internet by defining shared folders and files on systems that are connected to the Internet. CIFS has been submitted by Microsoft to the IETF (Internet Engineering Task Force) as a proposed Internet standard. Here are some of its important features:

- CIFS uses the same multiuser read and write operations, locking, and file-sharing semantics that are used on most networks.

- It runs over TCP/IP and uses the Internet's global DNS (Domain Name System).

- It supports multiple clients accessing and updating the same file without conflicts over the Internet.

- CIFS supports fault tolerance and can automatically restore connections and reopen files that were open prior to interruption.

- CIFS is "tuned" to provide optimal performance over dial-up links.

- Users refer to remote file systems with an easy-to-use file-naming scheme.

- CIFS is also widely available on UNIX, VMS, and other platforms.

CIFS is basically an enhanced version of Microsoft's open, cross-platform SMB (Server Message Blocks) protocol, the native file-sharing protocol in the Windows 95, Windows NT, and OS/2 operating systems. CIFS complements standard Web protocols such as HTTP (Hypertext Transfer Protocol) by providing a more sophisticated file-sharing protocol. Users do not need to rely solely on their Web browsers to access Internet information, because with CIFS most existing applications can access that data directly by using the standard Open and Save dialog boxes that users are already familiar with.

The security features in CIFS include support both for anonymous transfers and for secure, authenticated access to named files. File and directory security policies are easy to administer, and use the same paradigm as share-level and user-level security policies in Windows environments. Most major operating system and application developers support CIFS.

CIFS competes with Sun Microsystem's Web NFS, a distributed file system that Sun is attempting to integrate directly into Web browsers and other clients. Netscape is embedding Web NFS into Navigator. See "NFS (Network File System)" for more information.

**RELATED ENTRIES**   DFS (Distributed File System), Microsoft; File Sharing; File Systems; Internet; NFS (Network File System); SMB (Server Message Blocks); Web Technologies and Concepts; *and* Windows NT File System

**INFORMATION ON THE INTERNET**

| | |
|---|---|
| CIFS specification in Microsoft Word format | http://www.microsoft.com/workshop/prog/cifs |
| CIFS specification as a text file | ftp://ietf.cnri.reston.va.us/internet-drafts/draft-heizer-cifs-v1-spec-00.txt |

## CIR (Committed Information Rate)

Frame relay is a popular choice for building wide area networks. It transports frames of information through a connectionless packet-switched-like network. However, service providers do market frame relay as a connection-oriented network by selling PVCs (permanent virtual circuits). (SVCs, or switched virtual circuits, have only recently been made available). In buying a PVC, you specify the two end points of a connection, and the provider supplies you with a guaranteed data rate between those end points. The data rate you choose based on your requirements is called the CIR (committed information rate). CIR is the minimum throughput rate that you negotiate with a service provider, and the provider will usually attempt to guarantee that data rate. However, some service providers "overbook" the capacity of their networks, which can cause delays when traffic is heavy. Delays can be a serious problem with some network traffic, such as SNA (Systems Network Architecture). Dedicated leased lines may be the only solution in such cases.

It is important to set the CIR high enough to prevent dropped packets. A frame relay network will drop packets when the CIR is reached, meaning that the packets must be resent. This generates additional traffic, including the frames required to negotiate a retransmission.

Most service providers have a burst rate that lets you exceed the CIR rate to accommodate spikes in traffic, but only if the network itself is not overburdened. Note that frame relay is like a leased line in that the service provider maintains the entire frame relay network except for the equipment you purchase to connect into it. The service provider maintains all the facilities. Also, frame relay is usually charged per frame or as a flat rate, but there is usually no distance charge as there is with dedicated leased lines. Other switched network services such as ATM follow a similar pricing model.

**RELATED ENTRIES**    ATM (Asynchronous Transfer Mode); Communication Services; Frame Relay; Leased Line; Packet and Cell Switching; Switched Telephone Services; *and* WAN (Wide Area Network)

## Circuit

In the world of computer networking, the term *circuit* is used in many different contexts. A circuit is basically a link between two devices. A voice telephone call is a dedicated circuit between two people. In a LAN, the physical wire may be shared by many different workstations, but when two stations are communicating with one another, the physical wire appears as a circuit between them.

Virtual circuits are common in WANs and internal networks that use ATM backbones. Basically, a virtual circuit appears to the end systems as a dedicated wire for transmitting information across a communication system. However, the underlying communication system may be cell, frame, or packet switched. The underlying network may be a mesh network on which a dedicated path through the network has been created. This path appears as a circuit.

Telephone companies offer circuit-switched services and packet-switched services. A circuit-switched service is one in which you make a call to another location to transmit voice or data. A packet-switched service is more like an any-to-any connection, in which packets from one site can be routed to many different destination sites over a packet-switched network. Put another way, there are connection-oriented services that appear as circuits and connectionless services, which are often called datagram delivery services because they emulate a postal system in their deliver context.

**RELATED ENTRIES**    Bandwidth; Capacity; Channel; Circuit-Switching Services; Connection-Oriented and Connectionless Services; Data Communication Concepts; Modulation Techniques; Multiplexing; Point-to-Point Communications; Throughput; Transmission Media, Methods, and Equipment; *and* Virtual Circuit

## Circuit Relay Firewall

A circuit relay firewall is a type of security firewall (proxy server) that provides a controlled network connection between internal and external systems. A virtual circuit exists between the internal client and the proxy server. Internet requests go through this circuit to the proxy server, and the proxy server delivers those requests to the Internet after changing the IP address. External users only see the IP address of the proxy server. Responses are then received by the proxy server and sent back through the circuit to the client. While traffic is allowed through, external systems never see the internal systems. This type of connection is often used to connect "trusted" internal users to the Internet.

**RELATED ENTRY**    Firewall

## Circuit-Switched Cellular System

The existing analog cellular telephone network is a circuit-switched cellular system. When you make a call, you get a dedicated frequency for transmitting and another dedicated frequency for receiving. These basically act like hardwired dedicated circuits between caller and callee. Data can be transmitted over this link by using a cellular modem in the same way that modems are used to transport data over conventional phone lines. The main point is that there is no packetizing of information as is done on CDPD-enabled cellular networks or on digital cellular services.

**RELATED ENTRIES**   AMPS (Advanced Mobile Phone Service); CDPD (Cellular Digital Packet Data); Cellular Communication Systems; GSM (Global System for Mobile Communications); Mobile Computing; PCS (Personal Communications Services); *and* Wireless Communications

## Circuit-Switching Services

Circuit switching, as opposed to packet switching, sets up a dedicated communication channel between two end systems. Voice calls on telephone networks are an example. For a home or office connection, a circuit starts out on a pair of twisted wires from the caller's location to a telephone switching center in the local area. If the connection is between two phones in the same area, the local switch completes the circuit. This is pictured as connection A1-A2 in Figure C-5. If the connection is between phones in two different

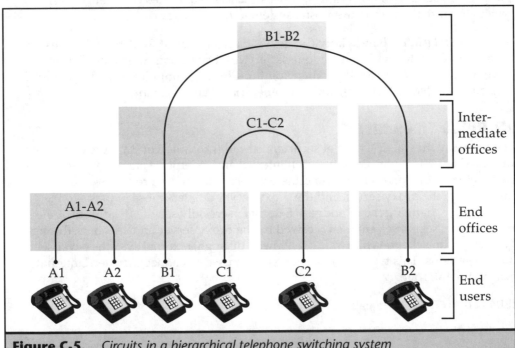

**Figure C-5.**   *Circuits in a hierarchical telephone switching system*

areas, a circuit is set up through an intermediate exchange as shown by circuit C1-C2. Long-distance circuits are made through a remote switching office as shown by circuit B1-B2.

The difference between dedicated and switched circuits is that a dedicated circuit is always connected, and a switched circuit can be set up and disconnected at any time, reducing connect charges. The difference between circuit- and packet-switching services is pictured in Figure C-6.

Switched circuits can supplement a dedicated line. For example, an appropriate bridge or router may use a dial-on-demand protocol to automatically dial a switched line if the traffic on the dedicated line exceeds its capabilities. Refer to "DDR (Dial-on-Demand Routing)" for more information. Switched circuits are also used to perform

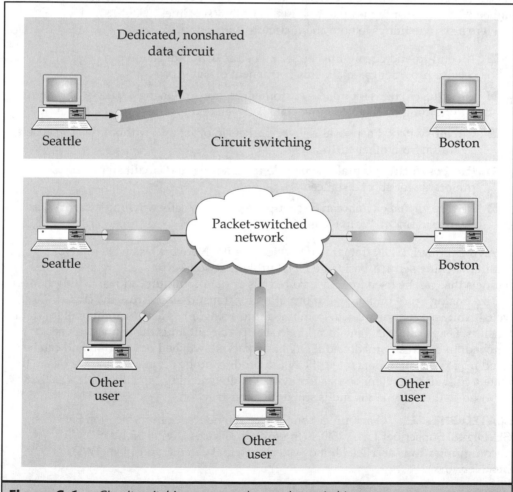

**Figure C-6.**    *Circuit switching compared to packet switching*

occasional data transfers between remote offices. A switched circuit might connect every 15 minutes to transfer the latest batch of electronic mail.

In a packet-switching network, data is divided into packets and transmitted across a network that is shared by other customers. The packets are interleaved with packets from other sources. This uses the network more efficiently and reduces usage charges, but packet-switched networks are subject to delays if another customer overloads the network with too much traffic. The phone companies have developed high-speed switching networks that implement ATM (Asynchronous Transfer Mode) to solve this problem. ATM uses fixed-size cells and high-speed switching to improve service.

Note in Figure C-6 that dedicated circuits are used to access a packet-switched network. These circuits are usually local leased lines or circuit-switched connections that funnel packets from a customer's site into the packet-switched network. They may be ISDN lines or high-capacity T-1 (1.544-Mbit/sec) lines.

Here are some things to note about circuit-switched services:

- An end-to-end circuit must be set up before communication can begin. The service provider can make this permanent or dial-up.

- Once the circuit is set up, the customer can transmit using a variety of bit rates and framing methods to move data between end systems.

- Circuit-switched networks deliver packets in order and without delays caused by traffic from other customers.

- Packet switching is preferable for long distances, and circuit switching is preferable for short distances.

- Private virtual circuits can be set up over packet/cell-switching networks, as described under "Virtual Circuit."

As mentioned, ISDN (Integrated Services Digital Network) is an example of a circuit-switching service. Basic rate ISDN provides two 64-Kbit/sec circuit-switched channels that can be used for either voice calls or data communications. ISDN phones digitize analog voice into digital information for transmission across the circuit. The two 64-Kbit/sec channels can be combined into a single 128-Kbit/sec channel for data transfers. Users can "dial" any location to set up a circuit, thus the connection is switched. In contrast, broadband ISDN has a packet-switched orientation and can be scaled up to very high data rates. ISDN is a product of the phone company's desire to create a fully digital telephone system with circuit-switching capabilities. It was first proposed in the early 1980s and is still under construction.

**RELATED ENTRIES**   Communication Service Providers; Communication Services; DSL (Digital Subscriber Line); ISDN (Integrated Services Digital Network); Telecommunications and Telephone Systems; Virtual Circuit; and WAN (Wide Area Network)

# Circuit, Virtual

*See* Virtual Circuit.

## CISC (Complex Instruction Set Computer)

The microprocessor is the basic processing component of desktop computer systems and at the heart of every microprocessor is circuitry that performs instructions. Instructions consist of various steps that complete a task, such as moving a value into a register or adding values. The instructions are called the microprocessor's microcode. Each manufacturer's microprocessors have different sets of microcode. Manufacturers are free to make the microcode as simple or as complex as they want. The richer the instruction set, the easier it is to write programs for the microprocessor. However, the richer the microcode set, the slower the performance. This tradeoff differentiates the two categories of microprocessors:

- CISC (Complex Instruction Set Computer) designs include a rich set of microcode that simplifies the creation of programs that run on the processor.

- RISC (Reduced Instruction Set Computer) designs, as the name implies, have a reduced set of instructions that improves the efficiency of the processor but requires more complex external programs.

RISC designs are based on work performed at IBM by John Cocke, who found that about 20 percent of a computer's instructions did about 80 percent of the work. Thus, RISC-designed systems are generally faster than CISC systems. His 80/20 rule spawned the development of RISC architecture.

Most desktop microprocessor designs such as the Intel and Motorola chips are CISC designs. Workstation processors such as the MIPS (million instructions per second) chips, the DEC Alpha, and the IBM RS family of chips use RISC architectures. Current and future processor designs seem to favor RISC over CISC.

**RELATED ENTRY**   RISC (Reduced Instruction Set Computer)

## Cisco Systems

Cisco Systems is a global provider of internetwork hardware and software solutions for corporate intranets and the global Internet. It is not a stretch to say that Cisco equipment is part of the network infrastructure for the vast majority of corporations in the United States and around the world. According to the company, over 80 percent of the backbone routers for the Internet are from Cisco routers.

The company was founded in late 1984 by a small group of computer scientists from Stanford University. It shipped its first product in 1986. Since then, Cisco has grown steadily. The company went public in February of 1990. In 1997, Cisco reported over $5 billion in annual revenues. As a testament to the strength of the network industry in general, $1 invested with the company in 1990 is now worth ore than $100.

Cisco is most famous for its line of routers and switches, but its IOS (Internetwork Operating System) is becoming an important industry routing standard that other vendors are incorporating into their own products.

**INFORMATION ON THE INTERNET**

Cisco Systems, Inc.          http://www.cisco.com

## Class of Service

*See* ATM (Asynchronous Transfer Mode); Prioritization of Network Traffic; *and* QoS (Quality of Service).

## Client

A client may be either a device or a user on a network that takes advantage of the services offered by a server. Client is often used in a loose way to refer to a computer on the network. It also refers to a user that is running the client side of a client/server application.

**RELATED ENTRIES**    Client/Server Computing; Node; *and* Users and Groups;

## Client/Server Computing

This section is about client/server computing, which defines an architecture for designing programs that distribute their processing load between a client computer and a server computer. Client/server computing is a direct outcome of the trend in the late 1980s and early 1990s that placed powerful computers on desktops that were interconnected with LANs. It was a model designed to replace the mainframe computing model in which all the processing was done by a centralized system.

With the rise of the Internet, the client/server computing model has evolved from a two-way relationship to a multitier relationship in which clients communicate with a Web server, which in turn queries back-end data systems. The Web server then returns the results of the queries back to the client. In addition, a new distributed object architecture is emerging in which Java applets and ActiveX controls are downloaded and run on the client.

Change on the Web is relentless, and as this book was being written, the traditional Web browser/Web server model was under attack for its inability to provide an environment for running sophisticated applications. The existing Web protocols are useful for displaying information, but are not sufficient for traditional applications that require a long-term client/server connection.

The new model is truly distributed. Applications are broken up into component parts (objects) that run as services on different computers, depending on where data is located or where systems are managed. Services such as application logic, information retrieval, transaction monitoring, data presentation, and management may each run on different computers on the network. The network provides a communication infrastructure on which these components communicate to provide the end user with an experience of working with a seamless application. This new model even sidesteps Web protocols such as HTTP and HTML in some cases, bypassing Web servers and setting up direct links between clients and core servers over intranets or the Internet.

See "CORBA (Common Object Request Broker Architecture)," "DCOM (Distributed Component Object Model)," and ORB (Object Request Broker)" for more information about this new model.

## The Client/Server Model

Client/server computing is all about applications that take advantage of networks. A server process running in some system waits for a request from a client. The request may be for a file or to process a sophisticated transaction that takes place over multiple servers.

 *NOTE: The term "server" is used here to refer to both the computer and the server software running in the computer. Traditionally, server has referred to software, but in the PC world, server has come to mean both hardware and software.*

Servers provide services to many clients, so they must be powerful systems to maintain performance. In some cases, the server does most of the work. In other cases, the client and server (or multiple servers) share the work.

A normal client/server environment consists of clients accessing servers. In the three-tier model, most of the processing is removed from the client and placed on a middle-tier system (not the server). In a business environment, the middle-tier system may hold all the "business logic" for an organization. Business logic includes the rules, procedures, and operational sequences that provide services to data-processing systems. By consolidating business logic on a shared system, all the rules are grouped onto a single server where they are easier to manage and where applications can more easily access them.

Concurrent execution provides a way for a server program to "spawn" a thread of execution for each request that arrives. A thread completes its tasks, and any results are returned to the client if necessary. Multiple threads may run simultaneously while new threads start and running threads end.

A "dialog" takes place in both directions between client and server. A typical session can get quite "chatty," adding traffic to the network that can be a problem over low-speed WAN links.

Here are some of the advantages in the client/server model:

- Client/server computing helps organizations downsize from mainframes and minicomputers to networks that provide an enterprisewide data communication platform.

- Multiple systems can get involved in parallel processing, in which they cooperate in the completion of a processing task.

- Data is stored close to servers that work on that data, minimizing the amount of information sent over the network.

- A large percentage of information is cached once into the server's memory rather than the memory of every workstation that needs it.

■ Network traffic is reduced because the server only gives the client the information requested, not large blocks of information that the workstation must process.

■ Large server systems can offload applications that are better handled by personal workstations.

■ Data is safe and secure in one location. Data warehousing provides a way to make specific data available at intermediate workgroup servers while maintaining control of the data.

■ With centralized data, administrators can apply security controls to restrict data access and use tracking mechanisms to monitor data access.

## Client/Server Configurations

Client/server defines a relationship between a user's workstation (the front-end client) and a back-end file server, print server, communication server, fax server, or other type of system that provides services. The client is an intelligent system that performs its own processing. The client typically runs GUIs (graphical user interfaces) like Windows 95 (and now Web browsers), and client/server application developers take advantage of this fact to build applications that have sophisticated user interfaces.

There are several possible client/server configurations. In Figure C-7, several clients access a single server. This is the usual configuration of a small LAN. Figure C-8 is a distributed database model in which clients access data located on several servers. These servers can coordinate with one another to provide data updates and multiprocessing for back-end tasks.

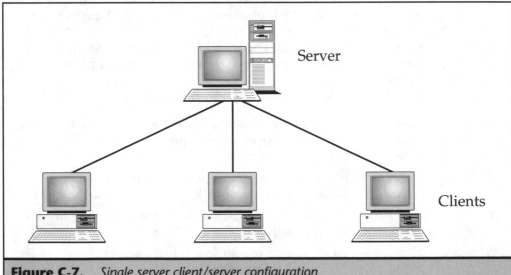

**Figure C-7.**   *Single server client/server configuration*

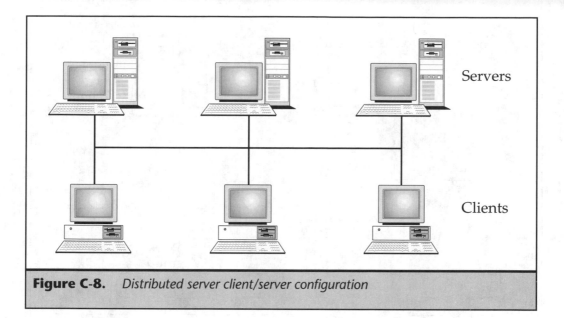

**Figure C-8.** *Distributed server client/server configuration*

A more elaborate model is shown on the left in Figure C-9, in which a database is copied (replicated) to a remote system so that users at the remote site can access data at their local site rather than over a WAN link. The two servers periodically synchronize with each other to ensure that users are working with the latest information. On the right in Figure C-9, vast amounts of data for the enterprise are stored in a data "warehouse." Workgroups don't normally access the warehouse data directly, although that is possible. Instead, a staging system caches commonly accessed data or makes queries to the back-end system for clients. This latter scheme helps reduce traffic, assuming that users in the same group are on the same LAN (or virtual LAN) and access the same staging system. For more on this topic, see "Information Warehouse."

These discussions have assumed that the client is software-compatible with the server, but this is not always the case. An enterprise network is usually a conglomeration of LANs and applications from different departments. A variety of clients also exist. Middleware helps meld these heterogeneous components together as shown in Figure C-10 so that developers can hide the differences between applications and provide connections for a variety of clients.

There are many types of middleware to fit different environments. There is middleware that hides the differences in databases and middleware that provides transaction processing to ensure that multiple servers coordinate their activities. Middleware also provides a communication system in the form of a messaging system or a direct real-time link between client and server. For more information on middleware, see "Middleware and Messaging."

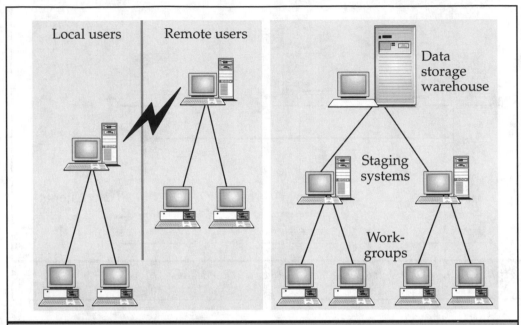

**Figure C-9.** *Database replication and data warehousing in the client/server environment*

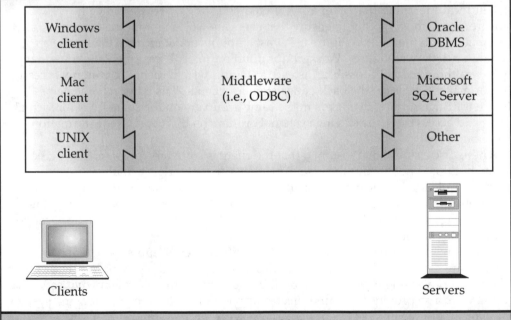

**Figure C-10.** *Middleware is the glue that melds heterogeneous environments*

## Client/Server Applications

The distributed database is usually the core server application in a client/server environment. With multiple users accessing the same database, a number of problems must be dealt with. Consider the following:

- Some clients only need to read data, while others must read and write data.

- When several users are manipulating the same data, does one user's write operation take precedence over another's, or does the last write have precedence?

- If two users are accessing the same data and one writes changes, should the other user's data also be updated?

Most client/server applications handle these problems, but distributing linked data over many servers throughout the enterprise can pose some interesting logistics problems. Real-time access to the same data by multiple users must be dealt with. In addition, a database may be replicated from the home office to a branch office. The replicated database must be kept synchronized with the home office. There are also issues about where remote users write data (in the replicated database or the home database).

Locking mechanisms can prevent a user from accessing a block of records until another user is finished making changes, but these solutions introduce their own problems. For example, in a time-sensitive environment, waiting for another user to free up a block of records is impractical. These are problems that must be dealt with. Interleaved updates can help the server keep track of changes on an ongoing basis.

Another concern is handling simultaneous writes to multiple databases, as happens in critical business transactions. What happens if a server crashes during a write operation? The crashed server must be updated when it is brought back online. In addition, any incomplete transactions must be rolled back, not just on the crashed server, but on all servers that received the transaction to maintain synchronization. Transaction-processing mechanisms for doing this are discussed under "Transaction Processing."

**RELATED ENTRIES** Component Software Technology; CORBA (Common Object Request Broker Architecture); Database Server; Data Warehousing; Distributed Applications; Distributed Database; Distributed Object Computing; Middleware and Messaging; Multitiered Architectures; Object Technologies; ORB (Object Request Broker); Transaction Processing; *and* Web Middleware and Database Connectivity

## Client/Server LAN Protocols

Client/server LAN protocols are used in network operating systems in which a workstation, acting as a client, makes requests for services from a back-end server. Protocols are optimized for workgroups, and 802.x access methods are Microsoft's SMB (Server Message Blocks), AppleTalk, and Novell's NCP

(NetWare Core Protocol). The TCP/IP protocol suite is well suited to enterprise-wide client/server computing.

## CLNP (Connectionless Network Protocol)

CLNP is the equivalent of the IP (Internet Protocol) for OSI networks, with the primary difference being the size of the address. CLNP's address size is 20 bytes, as compared to IP's 4 bytes, so it is much more appropriate for addressing on networks the size of the Internet. However, the OSI protocols have not gained worldwide acceptance and do not appear to be viable for anything other than a reference model at this writing. CLNP exists in the network layer of the OSI protocol stack. As the name implies, it provides connectionless datagram services over OSI networks.

## Cluster Addressing

Cluster addressing is a new feature with Internet Protocol version 6. It provides a way to send an IP datagram to a cluster of computers that are basically at the same location and offering similar services. For example, a provider of some Internet service might install multiple Web servers to handle a large number of requests from Internet clients. All the computers in the cluster are assigned the same address. IPv6 will route datagrams to computers in the cluster that are available to process the packets.

## Cluster Controllers, IBM

A cluster controller is an IBM-manufactured or compatible device used to channel-attach 3270 terminals to a host system. A cluster controller may also communicate with a host via a SDLC (Synchronous Data Link Control) link, or a bisynchronous link to a host-attached communication controller. There are channel-attached cluster controllers and link-attached cluster controllers:

- **Channel-attached cluster controller** These controllers are directly attached to the multiplexor channel of the host system. Model numbers for this type of cluster controller end in A (SNA [Systems Network Architecture] controller) or D (non-SNA controller), such as IBM 3274 Model 41D.

- **Link-attached cluster controller** These controllers are connected to communication controllers. The communication controller is then attached to a channel of the mainframe. The link between the cluster controller and the communication controller is either a modem for analog circuits or CSUs/DSUs (channel service units/data service units) for digital circuits. Model numbers for this type of controller end in C, such as IBM 3274 Model 41C.

SNA cluster controllers are called PU (physical unit) Type 2 devices, and terminals attached to the cluster controller are called LU (logical unit) Type 2 devices. A printer device attached to a PU Type 2 is either an LU Type 1 or LU Type 3, depending on the printer type.

The 3274 series cluster controllers are actually the older series IBM cluster controllers. New models are the IBM 3174 series. The new models provide advanced features like IBM Token Ring attachment interfaces, management, and monitoring. Also note that SNA gateways such as Microsoft SNA gateway provide network connections to IBM systems and can replace cluster controllers in many cases.

**RELATED ENTRIES**   Communication Controller; IBM (International Business Machines); IBM Mainframe Environment; *and* SNA (Systems Network Architecture)

# Clustering

Clustering is a fault-tolerant server technology that provides availability and scalability. It groups servers and shared resources into a single system that can provide immunity from faults. Improved performance is a byproduct of such a system. Clients interact with clusters of servers as if they are a single system. Should one of the servers fail in the cluster, the other servers can take over its load.

A simple clustering solution is pictured on the left in Figure C-11. In this case, two servers share the same hard disks. A cluster may also consist of more than two servers, as shown on the right in Figure C-11. The latter is often established to provide additional performance. In fact, a multicluster system is designed to allow scaling as well as fault tolerance. Additional servers are added to the cluster as the processing needs increase.

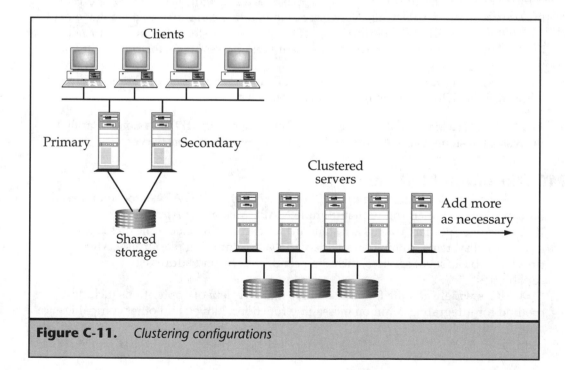

**Figure C-11.**   *Clustering configurations*

Clustering technology can provide better performance than large symmetric multiprocessing servers because multiple systems provide better I/O (input/output) for a large number of network clients. Other clustering features and benefits are outlined here:

- **Failover**   This is the term used to describe how other servers take over the load of a failed server.

- **Fault resilience**   The ability to provide uninterrupted service. Obviously, this depends on the number of servers, disk arrays, backup power supplies, and quality of equipment.

- **Multiport disk access**   Each system in the cluster has access to the same RAID (redundant arrays of inexpensive disks) system. RAID systems have their own built in fault tolerance.

- **Scalability**   The ability to scale the system up to handle more clients on an as-needed basis.

Major vendors have announced clustering technologies, including Microsoft with its Wolfpack technology; IBM, which is working on its clustering technology, code-named Phoenix; and SunSoft with its strategy, called Full Moon. Microsoft has also worked with DEC on its clustering technology.

Both clients and network administrators view clusters of servers as a single server. A file system distributed over a cluster appears as a single file system even if one of the servers in the clusters fails. Network administrators can run a single management application to monitor the performance of the cluster. Cluster software also provides load balancing among the processors to ensure that processing is distributed in a way that optimizes the system.

If clusters are used as Web sites, a virtual IP addressing scheme is implemented in which a single URL points to the entire cluster of servers.

**RELATED ENTRIES**   Fault Management; Fault Tolerance; MPP (Massively Parallel Processor) Systems; NUMA (Non-Uniform Memory Access); *and* Servers

## CMC (Common Mail Calls)

CMC is a cross-platform messaging API released by the X.400 API Association based on work done by Microsoft with its Simple MAPI (Messaging Application Programming Interface). X.400 is a standard for exchanging electronic messages among mail systems running on a wide variety of computing platforms. CMC provides a basic set of services, including send, receive, and address lookup capabilities.

CMC is widely accepted, which ensures that a variety of applications include a method for integrating common messaging functions. Novell and other companies are supporting CMC as follows:

- The Novell Global Message Handling Service includes CMC support.
- Microsoft includes CMC in Windows.
- Lotus and the VIM committee include CMC in the VIM standard and the VIM Simple Mail Interface calls.

**RELATED ENTRIES**    Electronic Mail; MAPI (Messaging Application Programming Interface; VIM (Vendor Independent Messaging); *and* X.400 Message Handling System

## CMIP (Common Management Information Protocol)

CMIP is an OSI model that defines how to create a common network management system. While both CMIP and the Internet SNMP (Simple Network Management Protocol) define network management standards, CMIP is richer in functionality. However, CMIP acceptance has been slow, and few CMIP products exist. Additionally, some of the supporting components have not been standardized. In contrast, SNMP is common, primarily because it is an Internet design that has been well tested. In addition, it is easy to implement.

Some of the telephone companies are using CMIP for public network management, and CMIP is included, along with SNMP, in the Open Software Foundation DME (Distributed Management Environment).

**RELATED ENTRIES**    DMI (Desktop Management Interface); Network Management; *and* SNMP (Simple Network Management Protocol)

## CMIS (Common Management Information Service)

CMIS provides a way to share management information in the CMIP (Common Management Information Protocol) environment.

## CO (Central Office)

A CO is part of the telephone network in your area. It is a building where the phone lines in your home or office terminate and connect to a much large switching system. The stretch of cable is often called the local loop and is in most cases the last remaining part of the telephone network that uses analog voice signaling. The maximum distance of a CO-to-home/office cable is about 5 kilometers. From the CO, transmissions are largely digital over fiber-optic cables or microwave transmission systems.

**RELATED ENTRIES**    Carrier Services; Circuit-Switching Services; Communication Service Providers; Communication Services; *and* Telecommunications and Telephone Systems

## Coaxial Cable Media

Coaxial cable consists of a solid copper core surrounded by an insulator, a combination shield and ground wire, and an outer protective jacket, as pictured in Figure C-12. The primary types of coaxial cable used for networking are listed here:

- **RG-58A/U**   50-ohm cable used in Ethernet 10Base2 (Thinnet)
- **RG-59/U**   CATV cable (75 ohm)
- **RG-62/U**   93-ohm cable used in ARCNET and to connect IBM 3270 terminals

Coaxial cable can be cabled over longer distances (186 meters for 10Base2 Ethernet) than twisted-pair cable (about 100 meters), but because twisted-pair now offers higher data rates and is easier and cheaper to install, it is now favored over coaxial cable. The shielding on coaxial cable makes it less susceptible to interference from outside sources. Still, new categories of twisted-pair wire now allow data rates to surpass that available on coaxial cable. Coaxial cable requires termination at each end of the cable and a single ground connection. In long runs, there is a possibility that secondary grounds can form on the cable, causing noise problems and the potential for electric shock.

While coaxial cable is the traditional media for Ethernet and ARCNET networks, twisted-pair and fiber-optic cable are more common today. New structured wiring system standards call for data-grade twisted-pair cable wire that transmits at 100 Mbits/sec, ten times the speed of coaxial cable. Coaxial cable is most likely a dead-end cabling scheme for large office environments.

**RELATED ENTRIES**   Cable and Cable Installation; Transmission Media, Methods, and Equipment

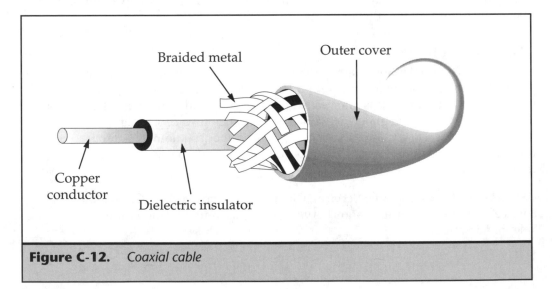

**Figure C-12.**   *Coaxial cable*

# Collaborative Computing

Collaborative computing allows users to work together on documents and projects, usually in real time, by taking advantage of underlying network communication systems. Whole new categories of software have been developed for collaborative computing, and many existing applications now include features that let people work together over networks. Here are some examples:

- Application suites such as Microsoft Office and Exchange, Lotus Notes, and Novell Groupwise that provide messaging, scheduling, document coauthoring, rules-based message management, workflow routing, and discussion groups.

- Videoconferencing applications that allow users to collaborate over local networks, private WANs, or over the Internet. See "Videoconferencing and Desktop Video" for more information.

- Internet collaboration tools that provide virtual meetings, group discussions, chat rooms, whiteboards, document exchange, workflow routing, and many other features. Multicasting is an enabling technology for groupware and collaborative work on the Internet that reduces bandwidth requirements. A single packet can be addressed to a group, rather than having to send a packet to each member of the group. See "Multicasting" for more details.

A good example of collaborative applications designed for Internet use are Microsoft's NetMeeting and NetShow. NetMeeting allows intranet and Internet users to collaborate with applications over the Internet while NetShow lets users set up audio and graphic (nonvideo) conferences. These products are described below as examples of the type of collaborative applications available in the intranet/Internet environment. More information about the products is available at http://www.microsoft.com.

## NetMeeting

NetMeeting uses Internet phone voice communications and conferencing standards to provide multiuser applications and data sharing over intranets or the Internet. Two or more users can work together and collaborate in real time using application sharing, whiteboard, and chat functionality. NetMeeting is included in Microsoft's Internet Explorer.

NetMeeting can be used for common collaborative activities such as virtual meetings. It can also be used for customer service applications, telecommuting, distance learning, and technical support. The product is based on ITU (International Telecommunication Union) standards, so it is compatible with other products based on the same standards. Some of NetMeeting's built in features are listed here.

**INTERNET PHONE**   Provides point-to-point audio conferencing over the Internet. A sound card with attached microphone and speaker is required.

**ULS (USER LOCATION SERVICE) DIRECTORY**    Locates users who are currently running NetMeeting so you can participate in a conference. Internet service providers can implement their own ULS server to establish a community of NetMeeting users.

**MULTIPOINT DATA CONFERENCING**    Provides a multipoint link among people who require virtual meetings. Users can share applications, exchange information through a shared clipboard, transfer files, use a shared whiteboard, and use text-based chat features.

**APPLICATION SHARING**    Allows a user to share an application running on his computer with other people in a conference. Works with most Windows-based programs. As one user works with a program, other people in the conference see the actions of that user. Users may take turns editing or controlling the application.

**SHARED CLIPBOARD**    Allows users to easily exchange information by using familiar cut, copy, and paste operations.

**FILE TRANSFER**    Lets you transfer a file to another person by simply choosing a person in the conference and specifying a file. File transfers occur in the background as the meeting progresses.

**WHITEBOARD**    Provides a common drawing surface that is shared by all users in a conference. Users can sketch pictures, draw diagrams, or paste in graphics from other applications and make changes as necessary for all to see.

**CHAT**    Provides real-time text-based messaging among members of a conference.

## NetShow

NetShow is basically a low-bandwidth alternative to videoconferencing. It provides live multicast audio, file transfer and on-demand streamed audio, illustrated audio, and video. It is also a development platform on which software developers can create add-on products. According to Microsoft, NetShow provides "complete information-sharing solutions, spanning the spectrum from one-to-one, fully interactive meetings to broadly distributed, one-way, live, or stored presentations."

NetShow takes advantage of important Internet and network communication technologies to minimize traffic while providing useful tools for multiuser collaboration.

IP multicasting is used to distribute identical information to many users at the same time. This avoids the need to send the same information to each user separately and dramatically reduces network traffic. Routers on the network must be multicast-enabled to take advantage of these features.

NetShow also uses streaming technology, which allows users to see or hear information as it arrives, rather than wait for it to be completely transferred.

## Other Products

A number of other companies are working on collaborative products that do many of the same things as NetMeeting and NetShow. Netscape Conference and SuiteSpot are similar products. SuiteSpot integrates up to ten collaborative applications into a single package. Additional information is available at http://www.netscape.com.

Netscape Collabra Server, which is included in its SuiteSpot enterprise suite of applications lets people work together over intranets or over the Internet. Companies can create discussion forums and open those forums to partners and customers. Collabra Server employs a standards-based NNTP (Network News Transport Protocol) and it allows discussions to be opened to any NNTP-compliant client on the Internet. In addition, discussions can be secured and encrypted.

Another interesting product is one called CyberHub from Blaxxun Interactive (http://www.blaxxun.com). It provides a high-end virtual meeting environment that uses 3-D graphics and VRML (Virtual Reality Modeling Language).

**RELATED ENTRIES**    Compound Documents; Document Management; Electronic Mail; Groupware; IBM Network Computing Framework; Information Publishing; Lotus Notes; Microsoft BackOffice; Microsoft Exchange Server; Netscape SuiteSpot; Videoconferencing and Desktop Video; *and* Workflow Management

## COM (Common Object Model)

COM (Common Object Model), not to be confused with COM (Component Object Model), is a superset of the OLE (Object Linking and Embedding) component object model. Microsoft and DEC defined COM to provide cross-platform interoperability, and the companies are working with HP, Sun, and IBM to provide COM on HP-UX, SunOS, IBM AIX, OpenVMS, Ultrix, and OSF/1. With distributed COM, developers will be able to build solutions that use components across platforms over a network.

Basically, COM is a combination of the Component Object Model plus OLE that can be used on non-Windows platforms. RPCs (remote procedure calls) are the underlying communication infrastructure.

**RELATED ENTRY**    COM (Component Object Model)

## COM (Component Object Model)

COM (Component Object Model) is a Microsoft specification that defines the interaction between objects in the Windows environment. DCOM (Distributed Component Object Model) is the network version of COM that allows objects running in different computers attached to a network to interact. Microsoft describes DCOM as "COM with a long wire." COM and DCOM are the core technologies of ActiveX, Microsoft's component model for intranets and the Internet.

OLE (Object Linking and Embedding) is a set of Microsoft-defined, object-based services that are based on COM. OLE enables interoperability among objects within the same computer that are written by different companies in any different programming language. OLE allows components, created by different vendors, to be combined together to form a single application. Almost all of Microsoft's applications are based on this model. During the installation process, you can choose which components to install. Installing only the components that are needed reduces the applications memory and resource requirements.

**RELATED ENTRIES**   ActiveX; Compound Documents; CORBA (Common Object Request Broker Architecture); DCOM (Distributed Component Object Model); Distributed Object Computing; Java; Object Technologies; *and* OLE (Object Linking and Embedding)

## Commercial Building Wiring Standard

*See* TIA/EIA Structured Cabling Standards.

## Committed Information Rate

*See* CIR (Committed Information Rate).

## Common Carrier

Common carriers are companies in the United States that provide public communication services.

**RELATED ENTRY**   Communication Service Providers

## Communication

*See* Data Communication Concepts.

## Communication Controller

A communication controller manages data input and output to a host computer or computer network. The units may be complex front-end mainframe interfaces or simpler devices such as multiplexors, bridges, and routers. The devices convert parallel computer data to serial data for transmission over communication lines and perform all the necessary control functions, error checking, and synchronization. The most recent devices perform data compression, route selection, and security functions, and collect management information. Some examples are listed here:

- Terminal servers provide a way to connect large numbers of terminals to host systems. The terminals connect into a single box that has a connection to the host over a network or remote link.

- Front-end processors provide the connection of terminals and networks to host systems.

■ Multiplexors merge the data streams from a number of devices into a single line for transmission over long distances using various media.

■ Repeaters, bridges, and routers are used to interconnect local area networks.

In the IBM mainframe environment, a communication controller is an IBM 3705, IBM 3720, IBM 3725, or IBM 3745. These devices provide a way to link cluster controllers at remote sites to an IBM host. There are two possible connection methods. In the first, the cluster controller at the remote site is connected via a telecommunication link to the communication controller at the main site, which is itself connected to the host. In the second method, the communication controller is at the remote site and provides a connection point for multiple cluster controllers. The communication controller then manages the flow of information from these cluster controllers over a telecommunication link to a communication controller at the main site, which is itself connected to the host.

The communication controller is often called a front-end processor because it is a separate device from the host system that handles all communication with external devices such as terminals. This frees the host computer from being continuously interrupted by external devices and allows it to process applications more efficiently. Communication controllers establish communication sessions, manage and control the flow of data, poll cluster controllers to see if they have data to transmit, buffer incoming and outgoing data, perform error control, and provide routing functions to get data to its destination.

A communication controller is really a computer in itself with a bus, memory, and CPU (central processing unit). It also contains the adapter to connect with the host channel and interface units that connect with the cluster controllers. The CPU manages the flow of information between the channel adapter and the interface units. The various models of communication controllers, depending on the model, support different line speeds, increasing numbers of connections, token ring interfaces, and fault tolerance.

**RELATED ENTRIES**   IBM Mainframe Environment; SNA (Systems Network Architecture)

## Communication Protocol

A communication protocol provides the rules and procedures that enable two or more devices to communicate over a medium and to establish sessions that manage the exchange of information.

**RELATED ENTRY**   Protocol Concepts

## Communication Server

A communication server is a dedicated system that provides communication services for users on a network who need to transfer files or access information on systems or networks at remote locations over telecommunication links. The communication server provides communication channels for one or more users simultaneously, depending on the software and the hardware capabilities. Communication servers may provide one or more of the following functions:

- **Gateway functions**  These provide users with connections to host computers by translating between data formats, communication protocols, and cable signals.

- **Modems**  Communication servers provide banks of modems that internal users access for dial-out sessions or remote users access for dial-in sessions.

- **Access services**  These enable remote users to dial into the network from their homes or other remote locations and obtain "remote node" or "remote control" access. With the remote node method, all processing takes place at the remote workstation. With the remote control method, the user connects to a dedicated workstation on the LAN, and all processing takes place at the LAN-attached dedicated workstation.

- **Bridge and router functions**  A communication server with these features maintains a dedicated or dial-up (intermittent) link with remote LANs and automatically transfer data packets between the LANs as necessary

- **Electronic mail servers**  These automatically connect with other LANs or electronic "post offices" to pick up and deliver e-mail. The systems may call at timed intervals or whenever there is enough outgoing mail to make the call worthwhile.

## Communication Server Example: NetWare Connect 2

NetWare Connect 2 is a server-based remote communication platform that enables remote clients to dial in and access resources on internal NetWare networks. Internal users can also dial out to access other users, the Internet, information services, and bulletin boards. You can find additional information about this product at http://www.novell.com.

A design goal for Connect 2 was to consolidate communication resources and services on a single platform. The software runs as a NLM (NetWare Loadable Module) and takes advantage of NDS (Novell Directory Services). The software has enhanced management, monitoring, and security features. It can handle up to 128 sessions on a single server.

Administrators can use a Windows-based monitoring console to view access profiles and usage patterns so managers can analyze and manage traffic patterns. An account package lets administrators bill users, if necessary. Various levels of security can be set, including several authentication models.

Connect 2 supports asynchronous communication, ISDN (Integrated Services Digital Network), and X.25 connections. A typical Connect 2 configuration is pictured in Figure C-13.

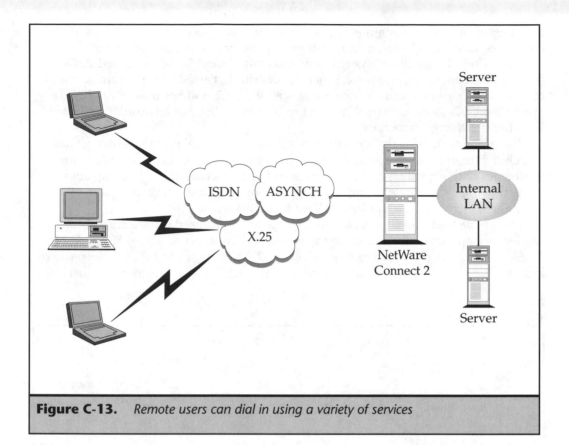

**Figure C-13.** *Remote users can dial in using a variety of services*

Connect 2 supports both remote node and remote control connections. Remote node users can dial in and access network services and information with a point-to-point protocol connection that transports IP or IPX (Internetwork Packet Exchange) traffic over the link. A high-speed connection is recommended for this type of connection. Remote control users can dial in using most popular third-party remote control software. Connect 2 operates as a host and handles all the processing for the remote user. Only screen updates, keystrokes, and mouse movements travel across the remote link. This method uses the link efficiently, but the Connect 2 server must be a powerful system to host the session of many users.

**RELATED ENTRIES**    Mobile Computing; Modems; Servers; *and* WAN (Wide Area Network)

# Communication Service Providers

Communication service providers or carriers provide telephone and data communication services in the local and long-distance environment. Carriers own and operate switching systems, transmission facilities such as guided media (copper wire and fiber-optic cable) or unguided media (radio waves) spectrum, as well as facilities for maintenance equipment, billing systems, and other internal components.

Until 1996, the telephone system consisted of the "baby" Bells, also called RBOCs (regional Bell operating companies) such as Ameritech, Pacific Bell, and others. It also consisted of long-distance providers such as AT&T, MCI, and Sprint. The RBOCs are also called LECs (local exchange carriers) and the long-distance companies are called IXCs (interexchange carriers).

Today, the regulation that kept the long-distance and local providers distinct has been lifted to promote competition. The current trend seems to favor long-distance companies with providing end-to-end data and voice services for large companies while the RBOCs continue to manage the local loop. Both are trying to get into other businesses, including satellite, cable TV, and wireless services.

LECs have traditionally operated within specific franchised service areas (basically service monopolies) called a LATA (local access and transport area). See Figure C-14. LATAs were defined during the split-up of AT&T. The border of a LATA defines where local service ends and long-distance service begins. LECs are not restricted to just one

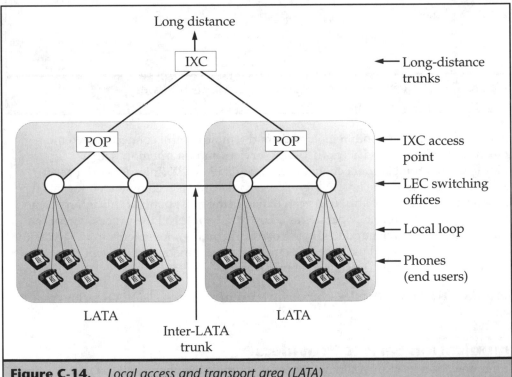

**Figure C-14.** *Local access and transport area (LATA)*

LATA. Pacific Bell, for example, operates franchises in all the California LATA areas, and these are connected with inter-LATA trunks.

IXCs connect into local services at a POP (point of presence). Even under new regulations, the LECs are required to keep these lines of communication open to promote fairness and competition. The IXCs use terrestrial and satellite microwave systems or optical cable to connect their sites over long distances.

The Telecommunications Act of 1996 required that all local markets be opened up so that long-distance carriers could compete in the local area. Likewise, the RBOCs were allowed to establish long-distance services.

For more information about the structure of the telephone system itself, refer to "Telecommunications and Telephone Systems." A list of telecommunications companies and their Web site addresses are listed under "Telecommunications Companies" in Appendix A. See also "Communication Services" (next) and "WAN (Wide Area Network)."

# Communication Services

Organizations build wide area enterprise networks to link remote users and create LAN-to-LAN links that allow users in one geographic area to use resources on LANs in other areas. A variety of carrier services are available to create these links:

- **Circuit switching (analog)**  Provides dial-up lines with relatively low throughput for point-to-point connections. This type of service is best for occasional traffic between two points, such as a single-user connection or file transfer.

- **Circuit switching (digital)**  Provides temporary connections between two points with rapid setup times. This type of service is preferred for periodic connections between a number of different points where speeds higher than dial-up lines is required.

- **Dedicated line**  Provides a permanent connection between two points on a leased, month-to-month basis, usually with an initial setup charge. These lines are suitable for handling constant traffic between two sites.

- **Packet switching**  Provides the most flexible service for companies that need to connect with many different sites. A packet-switched network provides simultaneous connections to many points and bandwidth on demand in most cases.

Managers must evaluate the volume of network traffic and its destination to determine the type of services to use. The following table lists the transmission requirements for various types of activities. If traffic is light, dial-up services are sufficient. For continuous traffic between two points, dedicated lines or high data rate switching services such as frame relay and ATM (Asynchronous Transfer Mode) are recommended.

| Application | Rate |
| --- | --- |
| Personal communications | 300 to 9,600 bits/sec or higher |
| E-mail transmissions | 2,400 to 9,600 bits/sec or higher |
| Remote control programs | 9,600 bits/sec to 56 Kbits/sec |
| Database text query | Up to 1 Mbit/sec |
| Digital audio | 1 to 2 Mbits/sec |
| Access images | 1 to 8 Mbits/sec |
| Compressed video | 2 to 10 Mbits/sec |
| Medical transmissions | Up to 50 Mbits/sec |
| Document imaging | 10 to 100 Mbits/sec |
| Scientific imaging | Up to 1 Gbit/sec |
| Full-motion video (uncompress) | 1 to 2 Gbits/sec |

Switching can be done on the customer's site (private networking) or by the carrier (public networking). If the customer does switching, appropriate equipment is installed and the customer sets up dedicated lines between all the points that require connections. This private networking strategy gets more expensive as distance between sites grows. If the carrier provides switching, the customer funnels all its traffic to the carrier, which then routes the traffic to various destinations. This is how frame relay is handled.

If you decide to install dedicated leased lines between two geographically remote locations, you might have to deal with a number of carriers, including the local exchange carrier at the local site, a long-distance carrier, and the local exchange carrier at a remote site.

The following sections describe services available from the local and long-distance carriers. For additional information about the services provided by specific providers, refer to the Web sites of the companies listed in Appendix A under "Telecommunications Companies." For information about building WANs over the Internet, refer to "VPN (Virtual Private Network)."

## Traditional Analog Lines

Traditional analog voice lines provide a convenient and relatively inexpensive way to set up point-to-point links between computers and remote LANs. Specialized modems are now available that operate as high as 56 Kbits/sec (in one direction over appropriate lines). The two types of connections over the analog telephone network are described next. See also "Leased Line" and "Modems" for more information.

**DIAL-UP LINES**   Connections are made only when needed for file transfers, e-mail connections, and remote users sessions.

**PERMANENT LEASED LINES**    These analog lines provide the same data rates as dial-up lines, except that customers contract with the carrier to keep the lines available for immediate use when necessary.

## Circuit-Switched Services

A circuit-switched service provides a temporary dedicated point-to-point circuit for data transmission through a carrier's switching systems (see "Circuit-Switching Services"). Customers can contract for various types of services, depending on their anticipated bandwidth needs. Each of the services discussed in the following paragraphs are covered in more detail under separate headings.

**SWITCHED-56 SERVICES**    Switched-56 is a digital switched service that operates at 56 Kbits/sec. A special Switched-56 *data set* device interfaces between the carrier's wire pairs and the customer's internal device (usually a router). Switched-56 services were originally intended to provide an alternate backup route for higher-speed leased lines such as T1. If a leased line failed, a Switched-56 line would quickly establish an alternate connection. Switched-56 can still be used in this way, but it is also used to handle peaks in traffic, fax transmissions, backup sessions, bulk e-mail transfers, and LAN-to-LAN connections. Rates are calculated by the minute in most cases.

**DIGITAL 800 SERVICES**    This is a carrier offering that expands on Switched-56. Basically, it provides toll-free (800 number) digital switched services. Inverse multiplexing can be used to combine multiple circuits into a wide-bandwidth circuit as network traffic increases.

**ISDN (INTEGRATED SERVICES DIGITAL NETWORK)**    ISDN is a circuit-switched service that provides three channels for voice or data transmissions. Two of the channels provide 64-Kbit/sec data or voice, and a third provides signaling to control the channels. ISDN is offered in selected areas. See "ISDN (Integrated Services Digital Network)" for more details.

## Dedicated Digital Services

Digital circuits can provide data transmission speeds up to 45 Mbits/sec. Currently, digital lines are made possible by "conditioning" normal lines with special equipment to handle higher data rates. The lines are leased from the telephone company and installed between two points (point to point) to provide dedicated, full-time service. You'll need bridges or routers to connect LANs to digital lines. Voice and data multiplexors are also required if you plan to mix both voice and data channels.

The traditional digital line service is the *T1 channel*, which provides transmission rates of 1.544 Mbits/sec. T1 lines can carry both voice and data, so they are often used to provide voice telephone connections between an organization's remote sites. The lines are fractional, meaning that they can be leased as subchannels. T1 can be divided into 24 channels of 64-Kbit/sec bandwidth each, which is the bandwidth needed for a digitized voice call. Alternatively, a T3 line can provide the equivalent of 28 T1 lines for users who need a lot of bandwidth. See "T1/T3."

**EMERGING SERVICES**    DSL (Digital Subscriber Line) services are emerging that use the existing twisted-pair copper wire in the local loop to provide data rates of up to 60 Mbits/sec. Interestingly, the closer an end user is to the telephone company's switching office, the faster the data rate. In the past, these rates were not possible because the carrier's switching equipment was only designed to handle a narrow bandwidth for voice. But carriers see DSL as a way to provide bandwidth-hungry Internet users with all the speed they need. The equipment will typically require a PC with an Ethernet card and a DSL modem. The service is dedicated, not dial-up, so the typical configuration is to run a line from the customer's site to an ISP (Internet service provider). From there, customer data is packet-switched to appropriate destinations. Both voice and data can be transported using this scheme, so voice calls over the Internet products should become more popular as these schemes are put into place. There are many levels of service, and these are discussed further under "DSL (Digital Subscriber Line)."

## Packet-Switching Services

A packet-switched network transports data (or digitized voice) over a mesh of interconnected circuits. The term *packet* is used loosely here because the carriers deliver data in either frames (i.e., frame relay) or cells (i.e., ATM, Asynchronous Transfer Mode). Here, *packet* refers to a generic block of information that is transmitted through the mesh from one point to another. The important point about a switched service is that it provides any-to-any connections, as shown in Figure C-15.

The carriers prefer to preprogram VCs (virtual circuits) through their networks and lease them. You specify the locations where you want to send data (i.e., your remote branch offices) and the carrier programs the routers at each of the junctions to immediately switch the packets along an appropriate path.

Note that a circuit of appropriate bandwidth is required between the customer site and the carrier's access point into the switched network. This circuit might be a dial-up line or a dedicated circuit. However, because the distance between the customer and the access point is small, charges are minimal when compared to running a dedicated circuit end to end since such circuits carry distance charges. Organizations can use these services to create virtual data networks over wide areas that connect all of their remote sites.

**X.25**    X.25 is a standard, well-tested, protocol that has been a workhorse packet-switching service since 1976. It is suitable for light loads and was commonly used to provide remote terminal connections to mainframe systems. X.25 packet-switched networks are not suitable for most LAN-to-LAN traffic because they are slow

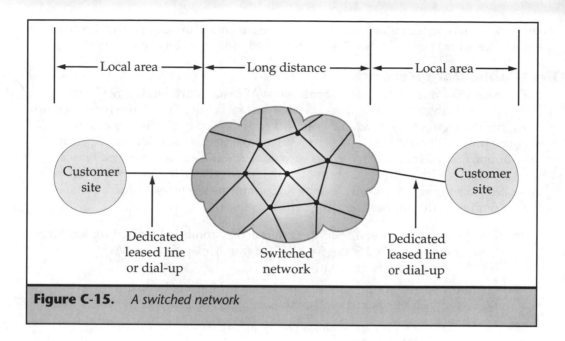

**Figure C-15.**  *A switched network*

and because a large portion of the bandwidth is used for error checking. This error checking was important in the days of low-quality analog telephone lines, but today's high-quality fiber-optic circuits do not usually need these controls. See "X.25" for more information.

**FRAME RELAY**    Frame relay provides services similar to X.25, but is faster and more efficient. Frame relay assumes that the telecommunication network is relatively error-free and does not require the extensive error-checking and packet acknowledgment features of X.25. Frame relay is an excellent choice for organizations that need any-to-any connections on an as-needed basis. See "Frame Relay" for more details.

**CELL SWITCHING**    Cell-switching networks, namely ATM, provide "fast-packet" switching services that can transmit data at megabit- and potentially gigabit-per-second rates. Carriers have already made a major switch to ATM switching and are now moving the services into local areas. The goal is to eventually use ATM all the way up to the customer premises. See "ATM (Asynchronous Transfer Mode)" and "Cell Relay" for more details.

**SMDS (SWITCHED MULTIMEGABIT DATA SERVICE)**    SMDS is cell-based service provided by the RBOCs (regional Bell operating companies) in selected areas. SMDS uses ATM switching and provides services such as usage-based billing and network management. The service will eventually grow from MAN (metropolitan area network) use to wide area network use and take advantage of SONET (Synchronous Optical Network) networks. See "SMDS (Switched Multimegabit Data Service)."

## PDNs (Public Data Networks)

PDN providers (called value added carriers or VACs) have created data networks that they make available to organizations at leased-line rates (monthly charge) or at dial-up rates (per-use charge). A typical PDN network forms a web of global connections between the PDN's switching equipment. Circuits consist of the PDN's own private lines or lines leased from major carriers such as AT&T. Dial-up or dedicated lines are used to connect with a PDN at access points that are available in most metropolitan areas. Services provided typically include X.25, frame relay, and even ATM. Some of the major PDNs offering these services are listed here:

- CompuServe Information Services offers access points in hundreds of locations throughout the United States for X.25 and frame relay services. Visit http://www.compuserve.com.

- GE Information Services provides packet-switching and high-speed services, as well as asynchronous and synchronous services. Visit http://www.geis.com.

- Infonet Services Corp. provides an array of international services. Visit http://www.infonet.com.

Using a PDN saves you the trouble of contracting for the lines and setting up your own switching equipment. The service provider handles any problems with the network itself and can guarantee data delivery through a vast mesh of switched lines.

## Other Services

There are a variety of other services that network managers can choose for wide area connections or other types of network activity. These are listed here.

**INTERNET CONNECTIVITY**    The Internet provides access to a wide range of information services, electronic mail services, and connectivity services. With the popularity of the Internet and Web, ISPs (Internet service providers) are everywhere. Refer to "VPN (Virtual Private Network)" for more information.

**WIRELESS SERVICES**    Wireless communication consists of either local area services or wide area services. Local area services involve wireless communication between workstations that are in a fixed position within an office. Wide area services involve mobile workstations that communicate using technologies such as packet radio, cellular networks, and satellite stations. See "Cellular Communication Systems" for more details.

**INFORMATION ON THE INTERNET**

| | |
|---|---|
| World Wide Web virtual library telecommunication links | http://www.analysys.com/vlib |
| Telecom Information Resources on the Internet | http://www.spp.umich.edu/telecom |
| PTC Telecom Resources Links | http://alex.ptc.org/links |
| Computer and Communication hot links | http://www.cmpcmm.com/cc/standards.html |
| The ITU's list of Web sites | http://info.itu.ch/special/web-sites.html |

## Communicator, Netscape

Communicator is Netscape's (http://www.netscape.com) newest client software suite for browsing the Web and intranets and for communicating and collaborating with others. It includes Netscape Navigator 4.0 and a suite of other components, including a messaging system, collaboration software, conferencing software, calendaring/scheduling software, IBM host access software, and Constellation, a cross-platform Internet desktop.

Constellation allows users to receive "netcasted" information (see "Push") from Web or intranet sites and manipulate it in a number of ways. Users can access their desktop from anywhere on the network because personal information is stored centrally, rather than in one specific workstation.

Netscape's next-generation Communicator client suite is code-named Mercury. It further expands the technologies in Communicator to include a dynamic rendering engine and personal assistants that can search out, track, and filter information for users.

**RELATED ENTRY**   Netscape

## Component Software Technology

Component software technology breaks large and complex applications into smaller software modules called *components* or *objects*. (In the Java environment, objects are called *applets*). By breaking applications into components, complex software is simplified. Each component is like a building block that performs a specific task and has an interface that lets developers combine it with other components to build applications. Some other advantages are listed here:

- If the application needs updating, it is only necessary to upgrade the component in question.
- New components can be added at any time to expand the functionality of the program.

- Users need only install the components they need, not every component that makes up an application.

- Individual components can be sold on the commercial market to provide functions that developers need to build applications or that users need to expand programs they already use.

- Software deployment is simplified using commercial techniques, as described above, or by deploying software over networks using distributed object technologies such as ORBs (object request brokers).

- Software development time is reduced because existing components can be reused to build new applications.

- Using standard interfaces and programming languages like ActiveX and Java, components from different developers and vendors can be combined.

- Maintenance costs are reduced because individual components can be upgraded without having to change the entire application.

Component software is revolutionizing the Web. Components can be downloaded from Web sites to expand the functionality of Web browsers or provide a user with a whole new interface for accessing information at a Web site. Java applets and ActiveX components are available for download all over the Web. The simplest applet or components might provide a spinning logo or rolling text banner. Complex components can be combined to create complete applications.

For example, most financial sites have a portfolio management utility, which you can download to run in your Web browser. The component stays on your computer and goes into action every time you visit the financial site by downloading the latest information about the holdings in your portfolio. If the software needs updating, the Web site managers simply post new components at the site. The next time you visit, the components are downloaded automatically.

Marimba's Castanet is a good example of a technology called *broadcasting* that lets users tune into sites on the Web as if they were tuning in a radio or TV broadcast. Information updates at the sites are automatically delivered to users that are tuned into the site. See "Marimba Castanet" for more information. Also see "Broadcast News Technology" and "Push."

## Component Models

The component-based software model consists of the components themselves, *containers*, which are the shells where objects are assembled, and scripting, which allows developers to write the directives that make components interact. The primary containers are ActiveX and JavaBeans. Scripting languages are ActiveX Script and JavaScript. When a component is put in a container, it must register and publish its interfaces so that other components know about it and know how to interact with it.

Components are usually deployed in distributed computing environments. For example, components that read sensor information in remote computers may report this information at various intervals to a central monitoring system. The way these components communicate in object environments is through ORBs (object request brokers). The most common ORB is used in CORBA (Common Object Request Broker Architecture). CORBA is cross platform and allows components written for different operating systems and environments to work together.

Component technology enables multitiered environments in which applications are broken up into different services that run on different computers. Services such as application logic, information retrieval, transaction monitoring, data presentation, and management may run on different computers that communicate with one another to provide end users with a seamless application interface.

To run sophisticated applications and transactions over networks, there is a need to register components and coordinate their activities so that critical transactions can take place. For example, if data is being written to multiple databases at different locations, a transaction monitor is needed to make sure that all those writes take place. Otherwise, they must all be rolled back. A funds transfer is a good example. If money is withdrawn from one account but fails to be deposited in another due to a communication glitch, you'll want to make sure that the original withdrawal is rolled back, otherwise you'll end up with no money in any account!

Microsoft has developed the Microsoft Transaction Server to coordinate the interaction of components and ensure that transactions are implemented safely. Microsoft Transaction Server provides transaction processing and monitoring along with message queuing and other traditional features normally found on high-end transactions systems. Because it provides these features in an object-based environment, it is essentially a transaction-based object request broker. Refer to "Microsoft Transaction Server" for more information.

The following list provides definitions of related entries in this book that talk about component technology.

- **Distributed Object Computing**  Technologies for distributing objects over networks.

- **Object Technologies**  Technologies for development with objects.

- **Compound Documents**  Methods for storing objects in documents that act like containers.

- **ORB (Object Request Broker)**  A common messaging system that allows objects distributed throughout a network to communicate.

- **DCOM (Distributed Component Object Model)**  An ORB-like facility that allows components (primarily Windows components) to communicate across networks.

- **CORBA (Common Object Request Broker Architecture)**  An industry standard ORB that competes with Microsoft's DCOM.

- **ActiveX**  Distributed object technology defined by Microsoft but now in the open environment. ActiveX is a container in the component object scheme.

■ **Java** A programming language defined by Sun Microsystems that is revolutionizing the Internet. Also described under Java is JavaBeans, a platform-neutral, component-based software model for building and using dynamic Java components.

■ **Netscape ONE Development Environment** A network-centric application development environment based on open Internet standards.

**RELATED ENTRIES** ActiveX; COM (Component Object Model); Compound Documents; DCOM (Distributed Component Object Model); Distributed Object Computing; Java; Middleware and Messaging; Netscape ONE Development Environment; Object Technologies; OMA (Object Management Architecture); Oracle NCA (Network Computing Architecture); ORB (Object Request Broker); Sun Microsystems Solaris NEO; *and* Web Technologies and Concepts

**INFORMATION ON THE INTERNET**

| | |
|---|---|
| OMG (Object Management Group) | http://www.omg.org |
| ComponentWare Consortium | http://www.componentware.com |
| JavaSoft | http://www.javasoft.com |
| Marimba, Inc. | http://www.marimba.com |
| Microsoft Corporation | http://www.microsoft.com |
| The Active Group | http://www.activex.org |

# Compound Documents

A compound document is like a container that holds text, graphics, and multimedia video and sound objects. Microsoft Windows and the Macintosh use this technology. Users can create documents with a word processor, spreadsheet program, or other program and embed or link objects in the documents. A Web page is a compound document. It can hold text and individual objects like pictures, sounds, videos, Java applets, and ActiveX controls. An electronic mail message with an attachment such as a graphic is also a compound document.

The original purpose of compound documents was to provide a single place where users could create a document that contained all the elements related to that document. When you save a compound document, you save all the text and objects under the same filename even though objects remain as separate files for editing or inclusion in other documents.

An active document contains objects or components that are manually or automatically updated from a source called the server. For example, if a compound document contains a link to a graphic image that has been updated by someone else, the graphic in the compound document is updated the next time it is opened. This concept has been extended to the Internet and the Web. Java and ActiveX are now the primary tools for creating active documents that contain applets and components that perform a variety of actions or tasks.

One of the advantages of this technology is that the document signals the source when it needs to have its objects updated. This frees the server from having to continuously provide updates when it may be unnecessary. When an active document is opened, that is when updates can occur, but if necessary, an active document can be continuously updated. This is the case where information is updated in real time and the server broadcasts information on a continuous basis. See "Push" for more information on this technology.

The new model is the *component container*. As mentioned earlier, a Web browser is a container that can hold ActiveX and JavaBeans components (objects). In both cases, scripting languages are available to provide functionality between objects that are added to containers.

**RELATED ENTRIES**    ActiveX; COM (Component Object Model); Component Software Technology; CORBA (Common Object Request Broker Architecture); DCOM (Distributed Component Object Model); Information Publishing; Java; *and* Object Technologies

## Compression Techniques

There is a lot of interest in compression as more organizations have a need to transmit voice, video, and data across in-house networks and the Internet. Data compression squeezes data so it requires less disk space for storage and less bandwidth on a data transmission channel. Most compression schemes take advantage of the fact that data contains a lot of repetition. They replace repeating information with a symbol or code that represents the information in less space. A symbol dictionary is used for data-to-symbol conversion.

Some compression schemes work at the character level while others work at the bit level. For example, a repeating sequence of underscore or asterisk characters is replaced with a symbol sequence. Bit-level compression locates repeating patterns of bits, and converts them to symbols. In some cases, long stretches of "nothing" are removed. For example, a voice conversation contains a lot of silence, and graphic images may contain large blocks of white space.

Compression has become critical in the move to combine voice and data networks. MICOM (http://www.micom.com), for example, has developed compression techniques that reduce the data requirements for a voice channel down to 8 Kbits/sec. This is a significant improvement over noncompressed voice (64 Kbits/sec) and older compression techniques yielding 32 Kbits/sec.

Compression is also important for new collaborative applications such as videoconferencing, where the amount of data and the amount of available bandwidth must be carefully juggled.

Data warehousing is another area where data compression is important. A data warehouse stores vast quantities of information and then stages often-accessed data on an intermediate system. Data warehousing systems compress files for long-term storage and uncompress the files if they need to be brought back online.

The most basic compression techniques are described here:

- **Null compression**  Replaces a series of blank spaces with a compression code, followed by a value that represents the number of spaces.

- **Run-length compression**  Expands on the null compression technique by compressing any series of four or more repeating characters. The characters are replaced with a compression code, one of the characters, and a value that represents the number of characters to repeat. Some synchronous data transmissions can be compressed by as much as 98 percent using this scheme.

- **Keyword encoding**  Creates a table with values that represent common sets of characters. Frequently occurring words like for and the or character pairs like sh or th are represented with tokens used to store or transmit the characters.

- **Adaptive Huffman Coding and Lempel-Ziv algorithms**  These compression techniques dynamically update a symbol dictionary as new, and recurring patterns appear in data that is being compressed. In the case of a data transmission, the dictionary is passed to a receiving system so it knows how to decode the characters.

Because compression algorithms are software-based, overhead exists that can cause problems in real-time environments. The use of high-performance systems to perform the actual compression of files is helpful. Another consideration is that compression removes portability from files unless the decompression software is shipped with the files.

Note that some files are already compressed to begin with and don't benefit from any further external compression techniques. Some graphics file formats, such as TIFF (tagged image file format), include compression.

## Storage System Compression

Before discussing compression algorithms for file storage, you should understand that file compression is different from disk encoding, which is commonly employed by disk drives to pack more digital 1s and 0s onto the physical surface of a disk. File compression squeezes the characters and bit strings in a file down to a smaller size and takes place in software before the file information ever gets to the write head of the hard drive. Modern hard drives that use encoding simply accept the stream of 1s and 0s from the CPU and pack them into a much smaller space than is possible if encoding is not used. Disk encoding is discussed briefly here, followed by a more expanded discussion of file compression.

A magnetic recording system such as a hard drive records information by changing a magnetic field over the disk surface. A change in the field between two possible states is called a *flux transition*. In simple terms, a flux transition can represent a digital 1, and the absence of a transition can represent a digital 0. Encoding provides a way to represent more digital information per flux transition. MFM (modified frequency modulation) stores digital 1s as a flux transition and 0s as the absence of a flux transition. Encoding techniques include the following:

- **RLL (run length limited)**  Represents bit patterns as codes, which can be stored with fewer changes in magnetic flux, improving on MFM storage capabilities by 50 percent.

- **ARLL (advanced run length limited)**  Doubles the density of MFM recording by converting patterns into codes that can be stored in flux transitions that are four times as dense.

Because disk encoding is automatically handled by the disk drive at the hardware level, it is of no further importance to this discussion. When you purchase a disk drive, it has a certain capacity that is obtained using an encoding scheme.

## File Compression Techniques

File compression is handled in several ways. Various utilities are available that let you compress files one at a time or as a group. Groups of files can be compressed into a single file that is much easier to send to another user. A decompression utility unpacks the files. A popular shareware utility called PKZIP (http://www.pkware.com) is used almost exclusively to compress files. A Windows version is available at http://www.winzip.com.

Most operating systems, including DOS, NetWare, Windows NT, and others, now include compression software. In the case of NetWare 4.x, you can enable automatic compression for specific files, or all files that reside on a volume or in a specific directory. Special file attributes can be set to flag the files you want the system to automatically compress when not in use. Be careful when enabling automatic compression systems. Some applications may not work properly with files in a compressed state.

Two important concepts in file compression are lossless and lossy:

- **Lossless compression**  A lossless compression system assumes you want to get everything back from a file that you have compressed. Every bit in the file is critical, so the compression algorithm meticulously compresses and uncompresses the file.

- **Lossy compression**  A lossy system assumes that some loss of information during compression and uncompression is acceptable. Many high-definition graphics files contain information that will not be missed if it is dropped during the compression cycle. For example, if you scan a color picture at high resolution, but your display is not capable of displaying that resolution, you can use a lossy compression scheme, since you won't miss the details. Sound and video files are also appropriate for lossy compression, since loss of some information produces subtle changes that may not be detectable when played back.

**C**

While no information is lost in lossless compression, compression ratios usually only achieve a 2:1 compression. Lossy compression can provide compression ratios of 100:1 to 200:1, depending on the type of information being compressed. Voice and video information compresses well because it usually contains a lot of redundant information.

## Graphics, Video, and Voice Compression

Most multimedia images can use lossy compression techniques as discussed in the preceding section. In video compression, each frame is an array of pixels that must be reduced by removing redundant information. Video compression is usually done with special integrated circuits, rather than with software, which operates too slowly. Standard video is normally about 30 frames/sec, but some studies have found that 16 frames/sec is acceptable to many viewers, so methods that remove frames can provide another form of compression.

Several compression standards for handling multimedia information are described here:

■ **JPEG (Joint Photographic Experts Group) compression** JPEG uses a generic algorithm to compress still images. The three-dimensional color and coordinate image information is first translated into a format that is more responsive to compression. Color information is also encoded, and some is discarded if a system is incapable of using it. Values are user-selectable, depending on the amount of image degradation that can be tolerated. Once these initial settings are made, the file is compressed using either lossless or lossy compression techniques. JPEG was not designed to handle video, but it does so to some extent by compressing frames and reducing the frame size and rate.

■ **Fractal compression** In the fractal compression technique developed by Iterated Systems (http://www.iterated.com), images are broken into smaller and smaller tiles as the compression engine (a dedicated board) searches for matching patterns in the image using a mathematical transformation that manipulates tiles in various ways. Repetitive patterns are saved to reconstruct the original, and unmatched data that is considered unimportant is discarded. The amount of time the process runs is user-selectable and determines the amount of compression applied to the data.

■ **AVI (Audio-Video Interleave)** AVI was developed by Microsoft as a way to store motion video on CD-ROM discs. Software decompression is used to read the information. The technique combines lossless techniques and a special compression algorithm that is fast but not effective. AVI images have a reduced number of frames per second, which produces an unpleasing image. However, the technique is acceptable for some applications.

■ **DVI (Digital Video Interactive)** DVI is an Intel-developed motion video compression scheme that is considered a de facto standard. Like AVI, it is primarily used in CD-ROM applications and has been successful in bringing video to the desktop in that format.

■ **Indeo video** Indeo video is a digital video recording format and compression software technology that can reduce video files from five to ten times their uncompressed size. For example, Indeo can reduce a 50-megabyte file to about 9 megabytes. Indeo is included with products like Microsoft Video for Windows, the OS/2 operating system, and Apple QuickTime for Macintosh and Windows. Playback is optimized for the type of hardware available so frame rate is increased on faster systems. Recording is optimized with the Intel i750 Video Processor because video is compressed as it is received rather than being first stored, then compressed. Multiple compression techniques are used, including lossy and lossless techniques.

■ **MPEG (Motion Picture Experts Group)** MPEG is developing several video compression standards that define formatting, data rates, and compression techniques for international use. The MPEG-1 specification defines video and audio and how to access full-motion video from disk at 1.5 to 2 Mbits/sec. MPEG-2 strives to provide full-motion video quality that surpasses NTSC, PAL, and SECAM broadcast systems.

Other compression methods are on the way, and many existing methods are being revised. ITU committees are working on standards for video phones and videoconferencing over ISDN (Integrated Services Digital Network) and other services.

## Compression for Data Communication

Compression provides a way to improve throughput on wide area links. In the case where you need to make a decision as to whether a link requires an inexpensive dial-up line connected by modems or a more expensive dedicated connection, a modem that has data compression features might provide the added throughput you need to decide on the cheaper solution.

If full-time connections are required, data compression can help you get the most out of those connections, as well. However, there are limitations. Performing data compression automatically at the connection point to the wide area network is impractical if the transmission speed is above 64 Kbits/sec, because compression cannot keep up with the line speed. An alternative is to manually compress files to reduce their size before they are sent using a compression utility like PKZIP. The resulting compressed file is transmitted, and the recipient unpacks the file on receipt.

Modem manufacturers have used many of the data-compression techniques mentioned earlier, but the Lempel-Ziv technique has become popular with the acceptance of the CCITT V.42 bis data-compression standard and its incorporation in most modems. In some cases, using software-based compression is preferred. For example, Microsoft recommends turning off hardware compression on the modem and using its own software compression for RAS (Remote Access Server) dial-up connections. It claims its RAS data compression can be two to four times as efficient as modem compression.

In the Lempel-Ziv data-compression algorithm, all single character strings occupy the table. As new strings appear, a tree structure is created, similar to Figure C-16, which shows the "T" branch of the tree. Note that a three-character word can be deduced by following any branch of the tree. Each branch of the tree is identified by a code word, and the code word is sent in any transmissions. If a new string appears, nodes are added to an appropriate branch of the tree and a new code word is generated to represent it.

There are other methods of compression, such as the MNP (Microcom Networking Protocol) Class 5 and Class 7 series, but the V.42 standard has taken off in recent years as the compression method used by most modem vendors.

A proposed standard called CCP (Compression Control Protocol) provides a way for two linked systems to negotiate the type of data compression over a PPP (Point-to-Point Protocol) connection. Many vendors have incorporated CCP into their products, such as ISDN (Integrated Services Digital Network) devices. Stac Inc.'s LZS compression algorithm is the one most commonly used.

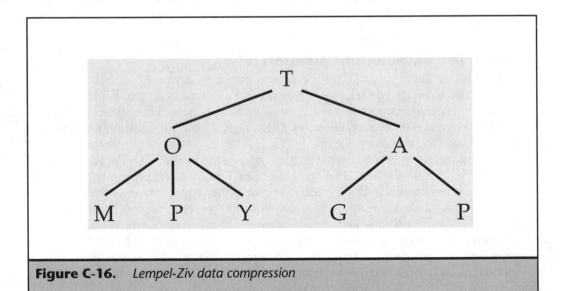

**Figure C-16.** *Lempel-Ziv data compression*

In the case of ISDN connections, Stac compression can be used on both B channels (normally 65 Kbits/sec each) to gain a peak throughput of up to 512 Kbits/sec. Note that such speeds require a serial port that implements the 16650 serial interface chip.

## Concentrator Devices

A concentrator is a device that provides a central connection point for the connection of terminal, computer, or communication devices. It can be a central point where cables converge. Technically, a concentrator merges a certain number of incoming lines with a number of outgoing lines, or provides a central communication link for a number of devices. Various types of concentration equipment, most of which originated in the mainframe world, are covered next.

**CONCENTRATORS**   In the mainframe environment, a concentrator can merge the lines from a number of terminals and provides a link to another concentrator in a hierarchical arrangement, or links directly to the front-end processor of a host computer. Data from the low-speed terminal lines is transferred over a high-speed line using a multiplexing method or a contention method. In the multiplexing method, a terminal gets a fixed time slot in the multiplexed stream. In the contention method, each low-speed line gets full access to the high-speed line for a brief period. See "IBM Mainframe Environment."

**FRONT-END PROCESSORS**   A front-end processor is similar to the concentrator just described in function, but it is usually a dedicated computer in its own right that performs concentration functions at higher speeds and supports more attached devices. See "IBM Mainframe Environment."

**LAN CONCENTRATORS**   In the LAN environment, concentrators have grown from simple wire management facilities to hub devices that provide "collapsed backbone," bridging, and routing functions. A collapsed backbone is equivalent to shrinking a bus cable system like Thinwire coaxial Ethernet down to the size of a small box. A separate wire of inexpensive twisted-pair wire then runs to each workstation. See "Ethernet" and "Hubs/Concentrators/MAUs."

**PORT-SHARING AND SELECTOR UNITS**   Port-sharing units provide a way for multiple terminals at a remote site to share a modem connection to a computer or host system. The device fits in between the terminals and the modem.

**MULTIPLEXORS**   The original design of a multiplexor was based on a need to reduce the cost of data transmissions for terminal devices that needed to communicate with a host device over a telecommunication link. A multiplexor is a device that merges the data from multiple terminals into one line and then ships the merged data over the link, where it is demultiplexed at the other end. Multiplexing cost-justifies the leasing of a high-speed digital line such as T1. See "Multiplexing" for more details.

## Conditioning

A conditioned line is a normal telephone line that has been amplified and attenuation-equalized to reduce transmission problems caused by noise, phase jitters, and distortion. Telephone companies provide line conditioning upon request, and it is often necessary to improve transmission performance when communicating at higher rates, such as 19,200 bits/sec. Leased digital lines such as T1 and T3 lines are conditioned.

## Configuration Management

Configuration management covers a wide range of network administration topics. It is often referred to as a practice for software development, but this topic is about network management.

As the size of networks grows, configuration management software, along with other centrally located management software (security, accounting, and performance tracking, for example) are becoming more important. It becomes impossible for network managers to perform these functions on-site due to travel time and expenses. Automating the procedures to take advantage of the network that is already in place is what configuration management is all about.

In its simplest form, configuration management has to do with storing information about devices on the network such as bridges, routers, workstations, servers, and other equipment. Administrators can refer to this information when changing configurations or to determine the cause of some failure. The database can hold important infrastructure information, such as physical connections and dependencies. In advanced systems, changes made to a central database automatically affect network devices. For example, changing a subnetwork number updates all the appropriate devices connected to that subnetwork.

Configuration management also deals with issues like password management, printing configurations, and user or group management. It also may provide software installation, updates, and reconfiguration from a single location. Version numbers and licensing can be tracked and updated.

On the hardware side, configuration management provides a way to configure systems once new hardware is installed and to report this information to dependent systems. Information such as serial numbers, settings, and version information are reported back to the management database. Once the management system knows where hardware is located, it can automatically update drivers and driver updates.

**RELATED ENTRIES**   Distributed Management; DMI (Desktop Management Interface); DMTF (Desktop Management Task Force); *and* Network Management

# Congestion

Like congestion of LA freeways, network congestion is due to excess traffic on a network. When congestion occurs, packets may be lost or dropped. Recovering from these losses and retransmitting data causes even more congestion.

## Congestion Control

TCP (Transmission Control Protocol) networks have an automatic mechanism to control the flow of data when networks become congested. Doing so helps reduce packet loss and the need to retransmit those packets. One aspect of the mechanism helps the sender detect possible congestion and throttle back its transmissions. Here's how it works: When a system sends data, it waits for the receiver to acknowledge the data. The acknowledgment must arrive within a certain time period. If not, the sender retransmits the data. The wait period can vary depending on whether data is being transmitted on a LAN or over a satellite link.

Setting a specific wait period is not always a good idea since the network may consists of subnetworks that have different delivery times or congestion problems. TCP uses a scheme called adaptive retransmission to continuously measure round-trip delays and adapt itself to changing conditions. The time between sending data and receiving an acknowledgment is recorded and an estimate of the expected response time is continually updated. This allows TCP to adjust to network condition and throttle back if traffic peaks on the network.

In some cases, an acknowledgment may never arrive back from the destination. In this case, TCP sends a single block of data and waits for the response. If a response arrives, it doubles the transmission and waits for the next response. If that response arrives, it continues to increase its transmission rate until a balance is once again achieved.

## Hardware Solutions

A typical solution to congestion problems is to spend more money. Common hardware solutions are to split up shared networks using bridges and routers or to improve the data rate by installing faster network equipment. Congestion is common on WAN links and Internet connections, where the data rate is usually much less than it is on the local network. A bottleneck occurs at the point of entry into the WAN or Internet.

Backbone networks can also be a point of congestion since they handle traffic among all the subnetworks of an organization. In most cases, a high-speed gigabit-per-second backbone hub is the solution. Many implement high-speed ATM (Asynchronous Transfer Mode) but Gigabit Ethernet is getting attention because it is compatible with the existing Ethernet standards, which make up most of the LANs used in the world. Refer to "ATM (Asynchronous Transfer Mode)," "Backbone Networks," "Gigabit Ethernet," and "Hubs/Concentrators/MAUs" for additional information.

Congestion is a major problem for real-time traffic such as audio and video. Many organizations are planning to use their internal data networks (and the Internet) for voice calls. This is possible due to higher-speed networks and takes advantage of a single cable infrastructure instead of one for voice and one for data. At the same time, videoconferencing is becoming more popular. But voice and video cannot tolerate delays on the network. To guarantee delivery of voice and video, QoS (quality of service) options are being implemented into networks so administrators can specify exactly which traffic should have priority over other traffic. Refer to "QoS (Quality of Service)." RSVP (Resource Reservation Protocol) is another method for guaranteeing delivery of real-time information.

**RELATED ENTRIES**    Connection Establishment; Data Communication Concepts; Data Link Protocols; Flow-Control Mechanisms; Handshake Procedures; Prioritization of Network Traffic; QoS (Quality of Service); RSVP (Resource Reservation Protocol); TCP/IP (Transmission Control Protocol/Internet Protocol); Throughput; *and* Transport Protocols and Services

## Connection Establishment

How does one computer on a network connect with another computer? The procedure on TCP/IP networks appears simple but involves a number of underlying processes and parameters. In a typical client/server environment, both the client and server use the underlying transport and network protocols to handle data transmissions. A place to deliver data must be obtained in the form of a computer's IP address and the port number in that computer associated with the process that should receive the data.

The socket API is an interface that lets application programmers design applications that interface with underlying TCP/IP protocols. It consists of procedures that are used to establish communications between clients and servers. A socket is like the end of a communication link. A socket is created in order to transfer information, and each socket is identified by a descriptive address called a port number. A server establishes sockets in order to provide services to clients. Each socket then waits for a client to connect with it.

A three-way handshake is used to make the actual connection. It involves sending three packets (called segments in the TCP layer) across the network. To start, the client uses a sockets procedure called CONNECT, which creates a TCP segment that includes the server's IP address and the port number of the desired service. Two bits are set in this segment to indicate that this is a connection request. The SYN bit is set on and the ACK bit is set off. When the server receives this segment, it checks to make sure that the specified port is available and, if so, returns an acknowledgment segment back to the client. The client then acknowledges that it received the acknowledgment, and data transmission begins.

**RELATED ENTRIES**    Acknowledgments; Congestion; Data Communication Concepts; Data Link Protocols; Handshake Procedures; TCP/IP (Transmission Control Protocol/Internet Protocol); Throughput; *and* Transport Protocols and Services

# Connection-Oriented and Connectionless Services

Two distinct techniques are used on networks to transfer data: the connection-oriented method and the connectionless method. Each has its own philosophy, advantages, and disadvantages.

- **Connection-oriented**  Requires a session connection (analogous to a phone call) be established before any data can be sent. This method is often called a *reliable* network service. It can guarantee that data will arrive in the same order. Connection-oriented services set up virtual links between end systems through a network as shown in Figure C-17. Note that the packet on the left is assigned the virtual circuit number 01. As it moves through the network, routers quickly send it through virtual circuit 01.

- **Connectionless**  Does not require a session connection between sender and receiver. The sender simply starts sending packets (called datagrams) to the destination. This service does not have the reliability of the connection-oriented method, but it is useful for periodic burst transfers.

These methods may be implemented in the data link layers of the protocol stack and/or in the transport layers of the protocol stack, depending on the physical connections in place and the services required by the systems that are communicating. TCP (Transmission Control Protocol) is a connection-oriented transport protocol, while IP (Internet Protocol) is a connectionless network protocol.

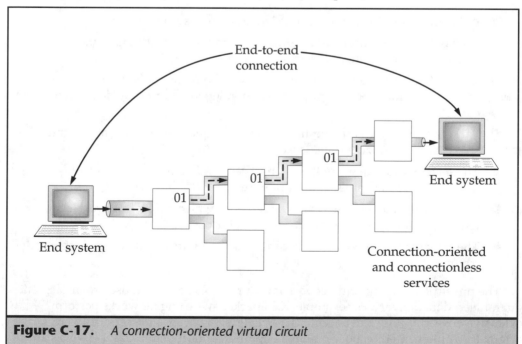

**Figure C-17.**    *A connection-oriented virtual circuit*

## CONNECTION-ORIENTED SERVICE FEATURES

■ These features require that a connection be established before data can be transferred. Some setup time is involved.

■ The connection that is established is called a virtual path or virtual circuit.

■ Routers along the circuit don't need to make routing decisions because the direction of flow has already been established.

■ Packets (segments in TCP) have less overhead and more data because the header only needs the circuit number, not the IP address.

■ These features use acknowledgments so higher-layer protocols are guaranteed that data will be delivered to the destination.

■ They are good for long, steady transmissions as opposed to short bursts of traffic.

■ Because a connection-oriented service guarantees data delivery, upper layer applications can communicate with one another over a network without any need to know about or monitor the activities of the underlying networks.

■ Connection-oriented features are implemented by carrier services because they provide easy billing and better allocation of network bandwidth.

## CONNECTIONLESS TRANSPORT SERVICE FEATURES

■ A datagram service analogous to a letter delivery systems.

■ Each datagram packet must be addressed individually, adding to the overhead, which means less data is delivered per packet.

■ A store-and-forward process moves packets from one router to the next, and each router along the way must make an independent routing decision for each packet.

■ Packets may arrive at the destination out of sequence. The destination must spend time organizing such packets.

■ There is no setup time involved. A host can send data immediately without the need to go through a session setup process.

■ These features do not use acknowledgments, which reduces network traffic but requires that higher-layer protocols check for packet delivery.

■ These features are good for traffic that is sent in bursts, rather than long steady traffic patterns.

The physical, data link, and network layer protocols have been used to implement guaranteed data delivery. For example, X.25 packet-switching networks perform extensive error checking and packet acknowledgment because the services were originally implemented on poor-quality telephone connections. Today, networks are more reliable. It is generally believed that the underlying network should do what it does best, which is deliver data bits as quickly as possible. Therefore, connection-oriented services are now primarily handled in the transport layer. This allows lower-layer networks to be optimized for speed.

LANs provide connectionless services. A computer attached to a network can start transmitting frames as soon as it has access to the network. It does not need to set up a connection with the destination system ahead of time. However, this activity takes place at the data link and network level. A computer may still use transport-level TCP to set up a connection-oriented session when necessary.

The Internet is one big connectionless packet network in which all packet deliveries are handled by connectionless IP. However, TCP adds connection-oriented services on top of IP. Basically, TCP segments are inserted into IP datagrams for delivery across the network. TCP provides all the upper level connection-oriented session requirements to ensure that data is delivered properly.

A WAN service that uses the connection-oriented model is frame relay. The service provider sets up permanent virtual connections through the network as required or requested by the customer. Connection-oriented SVCs (switched virtual circuits) are also possible, but many carriers do not offer them at this point. ATM is another networking technology that uses the connection-oriented approach.

Generally, network application developers decide which type of service their applications will use. For example, a management application that monitors remote systems for relatively long periods should use connection-oriented services.

**RELATED ENTRIES**    Acknowledgments; Circuit-Switching Services; Connection Establishment; Data Communication Concepts; Flow-Control Mechanisms; Handshake Procedures; Network Concepts; Sequencing of Packets; Sliding-Window Flow Control; TCP (Transmission Control Protocol); Transport Protocols and Services; *and* Virtual Circuit

## Connection Technologies

There are a number of technologies available for connecting devices together in networks or in a simple data-sharing arrangement. Some of these technologies are listed here and covered in more detail under the appropriate headings.

- **ATM (Asynchronous Transfer Mode)**   A high-speed cell-based backbone network technology used by the carriers and in private network environments.

- **Ethernet**   A traditional shared-access local area network with a data rate of 10 Mbits/sec.

- **Fast Ethernet**   Ethernet at 100 Mbits/sec over Category 5 unshielded twisted-pair cable.

- **100VG-AnyLAN**   Another 100-Mbit/sec Ethernet standard that uses a priority access method.

■ **Gigabit Ethernet** A gigabit-speed connection method that requires fiber-optic cabling, although copper cabling may become part of the spec in the future.

■ **LocalTalk** An Apple networking standard. Has low data rates.

■ **Token Ring** An IBM-developed ring network topology that operates at 4 Mbits/sec or 16 Mbits/sec.

■ **FDDI** A traditional 100-Mbit/sec networking technology. Typically used for backbones and to interconnect servers. Costly to deploy to the desktop.

■ **Wireless** There are a variety of wireless networking and mobile user standards. For more information, refer to "Wireless Communications."

The following standards are peripheral interfaces that can also provide some level of networking service.

■ **Fibre Channel** A peripheral connection standard that acts like a shared network. It supports data transfer rates in the 100-Mbit/sec to 4-Gbit/sec range. It has been available for a number of years, but is just taking hold.

■ **Firewire** An Apple and Texas Instruments specification for connecting peripherals and real-time, full-motion video applications. It has data transfer rates of 100 Mbits/sec to 400 Mbits/sec.

■ **SCSI (Small Computer System Interface)** A pervasive disk and peripheral connection standard with data rates up to 40 Mbits/sec.

■ **SSA (Serial Storage Architecture)** An IBM serial peripheral connection specification that has data transfer rates of 80 Mbits/sec. IBM is the only vendor using this standard and even it is moving to Fibre Channel.

## Container Objects

Container objects are part of a directory services structure such as NetWare Directory Services, a feature in Novell NetWare 4.x. Container objects hold other objects, including other containers, and so form branches in a hierarchical directory tree used to organize the user accounts and resources of an organization. Container objects usually represent the divisions or departments of a company and contain the user accounts and resources belonging to the division or department. The managers or supervisors of the department have special management rights to the containers, which automatically give them rights to manage the objects within the container.

**RELATED ENTRIES**    Directory Services; X.500 Directory Services

## Containers, Component and Object

A container is a document or an application in which objects and components can be placed. A Web browser is an example of a container. It displays HTML (Hypertext Markup Language) pages that contain text and objects. Objects can be pictures, sounds, videos, Java applets, and ActiveX controls.

**RELATED ENTRIES**    ActiveX; COM (Component Object Model); Component Software Technology; Compound Documents; Java; *and* Object Technologies

## Contention

Contention occurs on shared-media networks in which multiple workstations vie to have access to the medium. Contention is most often associated with CSMA (carrier sense multiple access) networks such as Ethernet. Contention occurs when two or more devices attempt to use the channel at the same time. When contention does occur, all stations wait for a random amount of time, then attempt access again. If many stations are competing for the cable, the situation becomes worse because the wait time reduces performance in addition to the need for workstations to continually attempt to access the cable.

**RELATED ENTRIES**    CSMA/CD (Carrier Sense Multiple Access/Collision Detection); Ethernet

## Cooperative Processing

Cooperative processing occurs in distributed computing systems in which two or more computers share the processing of a program or computational task. Cooperative processing requires sophisticated programs that can share workloads, data files, and memory contents over the network while maintaining synchronization, security, and accuracy of information.

The platform that enables cooperative processing is a distributed, client/server system in which systems can communicate with one another. The process is easiest to implement in an environment that uses common communication protocols and compatible processing platforms and peripheral devices. With the emergence of the RPC (remote procedure call), which can invoke procedures on other machines, cooperative processing is becoming more of a reality, even in heterogeneous environments.

**RELATED ENTRIES**    Client/Server Computing; Component Software Technology; CORBA (Common Object Request Broker Architecture); DCOM (Distributed Component Object Model); *and* Distributed Object Computing

# CORBA (Common Object Request Broker Architecture)

CORBA is a distributed object technology defined by the OMG (Object Management Group) in its OMA (Object Management Architecture) specification. The architecture has also been adopted by The Open Group.

What is distributed object technology? A simple model is the Web and the relationship between Web browser and server. A Web browser is like a container that can hold text and objects. When a user connects with a Web server, objects such as text, graphics, Java applets, and ActiveX controls are downloaded into the Web browser. The contents of the Web browser become a *compound document*.

However, the traditional Web protocols such as HTTP (Hypertext Transfer Protocol) and HTML (Hypertext Markup Language) are best for Web publishing, not running mission-critical applications over the Web that require transaction monitoring. HTTP fails at providing an adequate environment for running complex client/server applications over the Web because it does not provide *state management*. That is, after a client request is satisfied, any connection that existed is removed. If a user clicks a button on the Web page just received, a whole new connection is set up.

Client/server applications, on the other hand, rely on state management so critical operations can be completed safely. Critical operations must be monitored to ensure their completion. For example, a funds transfer between two accounts must ensure that after the money is withdrawn from one account, it is deposited in another. If the deposit doesn't take place due to a communication glitch, the withdrawal must be rolled back.

Many vendors have accomplished this high level of transaction processing over the Internet by using proprietary communication protocols between clients and servers. The usual operation goes like this:

- A user with a Web browser contacts a Web server.

- The Web server downloads some necessary client/server interface components.

- The new components allow the client to make direct calls to back-end data systems, bypassing HTTP and HTML.

In this case, the Web browser is more like an Internet program launcher that gets out of the way once the user has appropriate objects to connect directly with data servers.

The same procedures can take place on in-house networks as well. Unlike the Web, where a server contacts a single Web server, a sophisticated client/server application may need to contact multiple servers in different locations. Often, the location of these servers may not be known. What is needed is a system that can coordinate communication among objects running in different systems on networks and track transactions to make sure that operations are completed. The system must also help the user locate the components that are needed to get the operation done.

Enter CORBA. CORBA is based on the OMG's Object Management Architecture, as discussed next.

## OMA (Object Management Architecture)

The OMG developed the OMA architectural model as a vision of what a distributed environment should look like. CORBA follows this model. It consists of system-level and application-level components as pictured in Figure C-18. The components are described here:

- **The ORB (Object Request Broker)**  Manages communication among objects. It provides mechanisms for finding objects on a network that can satisfy a client request for services. It also prepares the target object to accept the request (there may be a difference in implementation).

- **Object Services**  Supplements the ORB by providing services to any objects, such as security services and transaction-processing services.

- **Application Interface**  Is on the end-user side of the model. It provides an interface for specific applications that are usually not shared by other objects, such as a word processing or spreadsheet program.

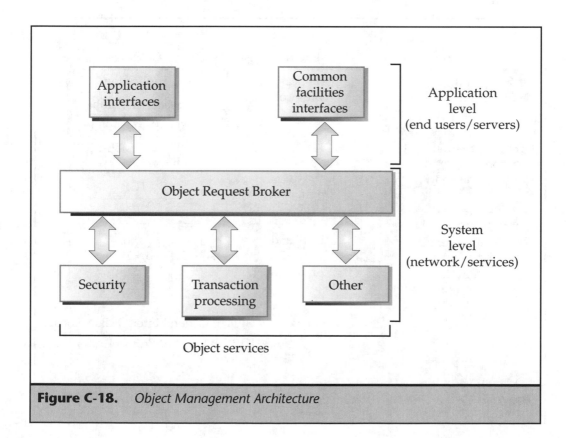

**Figure C-18.**   *Object Management Architecture*

■ **Common Facilities**  Is also an end-user interface. It supports applications that many applications can access and share, such as a spelling checker, a charting utility, or a sorting routine.

Note that the ORB is often described as a "bus" that interconnects all objects. However, the ORB is really just a set of interfaces that interact with one another to provide object-to-object communications. The underlying network and the processes associated with object interfacing are hidden from the user, who sees only what appears to be a single application, even though the system may be interacting with objects on a remote multiplatform system.

## CORBA Architecture

The initial task of the OMG was to create a standard architecture for developing object-oriented applications that would run across a diversity of multivendor products and operating environments. CORBA is the outcome of its work.

Figure C-19 illustrates where CORBA fits relative to the OSI and TCP/IP protocol stacks. The top layers of CORBA provide the object interfaces into the GIOP (General Inter-ORB Protocol) or ESIOP (Environment-Specific Inter-ORB Protocol) layer.

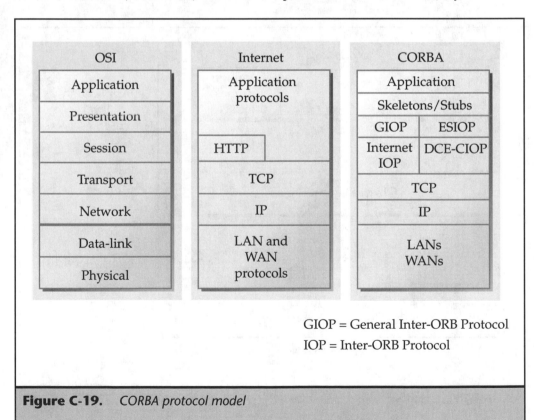

**Figure C-19.**  *CORBA protocol model*

Under GIOP is the IIOP (Internet Inter-ORB Protocol) layer, which provides an interface to network topologies. So far, CORBA has been mapped to TCP/IP as shown through IIOP (Internet Inter-ORB Protocol), but it could be mapped to other transport protocols such as IPX, OSI, and SNA. Note that IIOP connects directly to TCP and can replace HTTP in most implementations.

ESIOP accommodates interfaces that might have special requirements. Currently, DCE (Distributed Computing Environment) is supported with DCE-CIOP (DCE Common Inter-ORB Protocol), which binds DCE to TCP.

Note that IIOP may upstage HTTP as a client/server protocol on the Web. It provides services that are much better at handling mission-critical business applications over the Internet. Netscape is including IIOP in its browsers. Soon, you will type **iiop://www.*website*.com** instead of **http://www.*website*.com** to access Web sites that provide more than just information publishing. Sites that use IIOP will be implementing CORBA to provide communication between objects on your computer and objects on remote computers. Refer to "IIOP (Internet Inter-ORB Protocol)" for more information on this protocol.

## CORBA Object Interface and Operation

As mentioned, the ORB is often seen as a bus connecting a client with objects that provide services. This can be seen in Figure C-20. The interface is well defined and is specified by the OMG's *IDL (Interface Definition Language)*. IDL describes a consistent object interface.

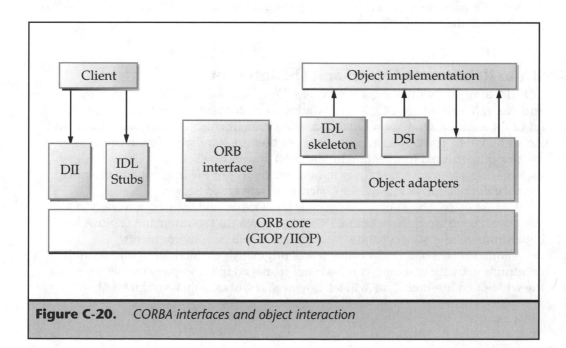

**Figure C-20.** *CORBA interfaces and object interaction*

Objects written to conform with IDL are essentially portable. IDL provides programming language independence and allows developers to create CORBA components using a language of choice. Objects created with IDL have a specific behavior that can be exploited by other CORBA-compatible objects, no matter how the object was created.

A client communicates with another object (called the *object implementation*) by passing requests through the ORB. The target object receives the request from the ORB. The object implementation is code and data.

To make a request, the client can access three different interfaces. Some system functions require that the client directly access the ORB interface. Two other interfaces are accessed depending on the nature of the target object:

- The IDL Stubs interface is used when IDL is required to translate between different client and server implementations. In this case, the server-side IDL skeleton is involved in the connection.

- The DII (Dynamic Invocation Interface) interface allows inter-ORB interoperability. A client dynamically issues a request without requiring a specific IDL interface-specific stub. In this case, the server-side DSI (Dynamic Skeleton Interface) is involved in the connection.

Finally, the OA (Object Adapter) helps the ORB to link object implementations with the ORB. The OA may provide support for special implementations such as an object-oriented database.

More detailed information for developers and programmers is available at the Web sites listed at the end of this section.

## CORBA in Relation to DCOM and the Internet

CORBA competes with Microsoft's DCOM (Distributed Component Object Model) and ActiveX technology. DCOM is a Windows-based object technology. It is not based on CORBA. It is a single-vendor solution; however, Microsoft has turned DCOM and ActiveX over to The Open Group to promote them as standard. More recently, Microsoft has turned its attention to Microsoft Transaction Server, which is designed to support object transactions over in-house networks or the Internet and provides connectivity to legacy systems. See "Microsoft Transaction Server."

Because of existing support, developer knowledge, and the pervasiveness of Windows clients, some believe that DCOM is a preferred solution, but CORBA has better multivendor support and is best for heterogeneous environments.

Another aspect of CORBA is that it was originally designed for tightly controlled enterprise network environments and well-managed intercompany connections, not the wide-open Internet. Time will tell how well it works in this environment.

## CORBA Systems

A number of vendors have defined CORBA-compliant ORBs:

| | |
|---|---|
| Digital Equipment ObjectBroker | http://www.digital.com |
| Expersoft PowerBroker | http://www.expersoft.com |
| Hewlett-Packard ORB Plus | http://www.hp.com |
| IBM Component Broker Connector (CBConnector) | http://www.software.ibm.com |
| IONA Orbix | http://www.iona.com |
| Netscape ONE | http://developer.netscape.com/library/one |
| Solaris NEO | http://www.sun.com/solaris/neo |
| Visigenic VisiBroker | http://www.visigenic.com |

**RELATED ENTRIES**    Component Software Technology; Compound Documents; DCOM (Distributed Component Object Model); Distributed Object Computing; IBM Network Computing Framework; IIOP (Internet Inter-ORB Protocol); Java; Middleware and Messaging; Netscape ONE Development Environment; Object Technologies; OMA (Object Management Architecture); ORB (Object Request Broker); Sun Microsystems Solaris NEO; *and* UNO (Universal Networked Object)

**INFORMATION ON THE INTERNET**

| | |
|---|---|
| Alan Pope's Excellent On-Line CORBA tutorial | http://www.qds.com/people/apope |
| OMG (Object Management Group) | http://www.omg.org |
| CORBA documentation | http://www.omg.org/corba/corbiiop.htm |
| CORBA information and references | http://www.acl.lanl.gov/CORBA |

## CPE (Customer Premises Equipment)

CPE is the privately owned telecommunication equipment at an organization's site that is attached to the telecommunication network. CPE equipment includes PBXs (private branch exchanges), telephones, key systems, facsimile products, modems, voice processing equipment, and video communication equipment.

Previous to 1996, carriers were not allowed to be involved in the manufacturing, marketing, and sales of this equipment, but to promote competition, Congress opened up the telecommunication markets. Now companies like AT&T can provide one-source solutions for wide area networks by providing customers with on-site equipment and long-distance services.

**RELATED ENTRIES**    PBX (Private Branch Exchange); Telecommunications and Telephone Systems; *and* Voice/Data Networks

# CPI-C (Common Programming Interface for Communications), IBM

CPI-C is a platform-independent API that interfaces to a common set of APPC (Advanced Program-to-Program Communications) verbs. It is simple and straightforward, and is portable across all platforms that support CPI-C. CPI-C is designed to provide a common environment for the execution of applications across IBM platforms, such as IBM MVS (Multiple Virtual Storage), VS (Virtual Storage), OS/400, and OS/2-based systems.

CPI-C provides an interface to LU 6.2 (logical unit 6.2) services. LU 6.2 is the technical name for IBM APPC. LU 6.2 was developed to allow computers in IBM environments to set up their own communication sessions, rather than rely on a host computer to do so. LU 6.2 provides peer-to-peer communications between systems other than hosts, and allows those systems to run distributed applications such as file sharing and remote access. LU 6.2 supports the entire range of IBM platforms, including local area networks, desktop systems, and mainframes.

CPI-C is the current preferred method for interfacing to LU 6.2. An older interface called the LU 6.2 Protocol Boundary also exists. IBM provides mapping to TCP/IP. IBM has also worked out a way to interface Java applets and CPI-C.

IBM also submitted CPI-C to the X/Open organization (now The Open Group), which adopted it as a standard for developing client/server transaction-processing applications. IBM guides The Open Group in its implementation of CPI-C and supports features such as full-duplex communications between CPI-C applications so programs can send and receive data at the same time. Multivendor distributed directory services are also supported, including X.500 and the directory services in The Open Group's DCE (Distributed Computing Environment). These services let applications locate users and resources without the need to know physical location information.

**RELATED ENTRIES**    AnyNet, IBM; APPC (Advanced Program-to-Program Communications); APPN (Advanced Peer-to-Peer Networking); DCE (Distributed Computing Environment), The Open Group; IBM (International Business Machines); IBM AIX (Advanced Interactive Executive); *and* IBM AS/400

**INFORMATION ON THE INTERNET**

| | |
|---|---|
| IBM software | http://software.ibm.com |
| IBM products | http://www.ibm.com/Products |

# Cryptography

Cryptography is concerned with keeping information, usually sensitive information, private. Information is *encrypted* to make it private and *decrypted* to restore it to human-readable form.

Encryption is performed using an *algorithm,* which is usually well known. The algorithm takes some input, which is called the *plaintext,* and converts it to *ciphertext.* A key is applied to the algorithm that affects the ciphertext output. A different key used on the same plaintext will produce different ciphertext. Because algorithms are well known, the strength of encryption relies on the key and its length.

One of the most well-known encryption algorithms is the U.S. government-endorsed DES (Data Encryption Standard). It uses a 56-bit key and an algorithm that scrambles and obscures a message by running it through multiple iterations or rounds of an obfuscation algorithm. This process is pictured in Figure C-21 and is greatly simplified in the following description. It helps to visualize this process as threads being woven together and the key providing a color change during each iteration.

1. The plaintext is divided into 64-bit blocks. Each block is worked independently through 16 iterations of the algorithm.

2. At the same time, the 56-bit key is divided in half. In each iteration, the bits in each half are shifted to the left to change the key values (like changing the color to be applied to the thread).

3. A 64-bit block is divided in half (now we have two threads) and the right half is combined with the two key halves created in step 2 (this is like coloring one of the threads).

4. The results of step 3 are converted again using some specific techniques (too complex to discuss here), then the results are combined with the left half of the 64-bit block (like weaving in another thread).

5. The results of the above steps become the new right half. Now the next iteration for the same 64-bit block is ready to start. The right half from the previous iteration is brought down to become the new left half (the thread to be colored). Also, the left and right halves of the key are bit-shifted left and combined to create a new key (like changing the color).

6. The process repeats again using the new left half and new right half for 15 more iterations. This produces the first 64-bit block of ciphertext.

The next 64-bit block is processed using the same procedure.

One of the interesting things about this process is that the algorithm is well known, so anyone who is trying to break your DES-encrypted ciphertext will have the algorithm to work with. This is true of most encryption schemes, so the strength of the system is in the size of the key used and how well the algorithm does its job. However, the 56-bit key size of DES is now considered insecure. In fact, it was broken by a group of computers linked over the Internet as this book was being written. More-advanced encryption schemes such as IDEA (discussed under "Types of Ciphers," next) have been developed.

**C**

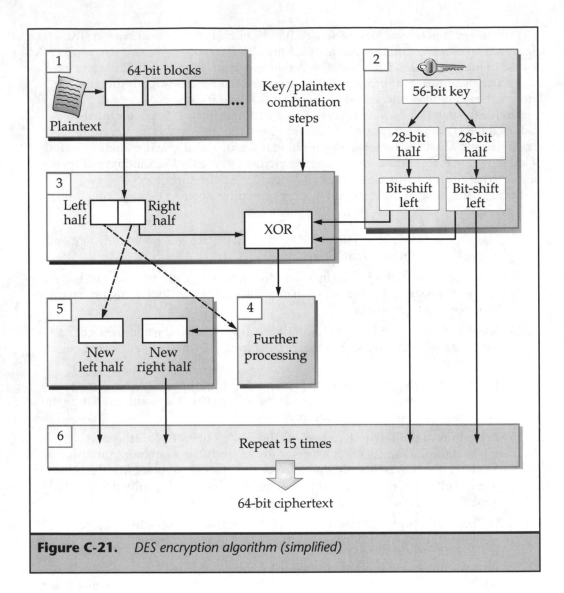

**Figure C-21.** *DES encryption algorithm (simplified)*

## Types of Ciphers

DES is a *block cipher* because it takes the plaintext and divides it up into blocks that are processed individually in multiple rounds (iterations). There are also *stream ciphers* that work on streams of raw bits and are much faster.

In addition, there are symmetrical (single-key) and asymmetrical (two-key) ciphers. Symmetric schemes are also called *private-key* or *secret-key* encryption schemes.

A single key is used for both encrypt and decrypt messages. If you send a decrypted message to someone, you must get them a copy of the key. This is a problem in some environments, especially if you don't know the recipient and need to transport or transmit the key using untrusted people or channels. How can you be sure the key has not been compromised? Asymmetric schemes solve this problem, as discussed in a moment.

DES is a symmetrical (single-key) cryptographic scheme. However, DES has shown its age, as mentioned previously. A replacement is IDEA (International Data Encryption Algorithm), a block-oriented secret-key encryption algorithm developed by the Swiss Federal Institute of Technology. It uses a 128-bit key compared to DES's 56-bit key, and so its resulting ciphertext is substantially more secure. IDEA is generally considered a better choice than DES, and the algorithm is publicly available, easy to implement, and exportable. As of this writing, there have been no successful attacks against IDEA.

Asymmetrical *public-key cryptography* is an alternative to the private-key DES and IDEA schemes. In this scheme, everybody gets a set of keys. One key, called the public key, is made freely available. The other, called the private key, is held secretly. Sending encrypted messages to someone is simple. You obtain a copy of their public key, either directly from the person or from a public-key server, and use it to encrypt the message. This message can only be decrypted with the recipient's private key. The private key is never made publicly available.

The public-key scheme is revolutionizing computer security by providing ways to enable electronic commerce, authenticate users, validate and timestamp documents and programs, exchange secure electronic messages, and more. Refer to "Public-Key Cryptography," for more details.

There is another important encryption scheme called the *one-way function*. With this scheme, there is often no intention of ever deciphering the text. Encrypting with a one-way function is easy and takes little computer processing power. Reversing the encryption is considered impossible. Why encrypt something that never gets decrypted?

Suppose you want to send a business partner a message and provide some proof that the message contents have not been altered in transit. The first step is to encrypt the message with a one-way function to produce a *hash* (also called a message digest). The hash represents the original document as a unique set of numbers. You then send the document to your business partner, encrypting it with his or her public key. Upon receipt, he or she runs the same one-way function on the contents of the document. The resulting hash should be the same as the one you sent. If not, the document is suspect.

One-way functions are also used to store passwords. Actually, the technique doesn't store the password, but its hash, and that is why it is secure. When a user logs on, a hash of the password is created and compared to the hash in the password file. If they compare, the user is considered authentic. Refer to "Challenge/Response Protocol" for more details on this technique.

## Cryptanalysis

*Cryptanalysis* has to do with analyzing a cryptosystem. A person analyzes a system to verify its integrity. An *attacker* also analyzes a system to find its weaknesses. Cryptanalysts are often paid for what they do. Attackers do what they do to gain illegal access to documents and systems.

How are systems broken? Successful attacks usually take place under optimal conditions, i.e., using million dollar computer systems that are run by expert cryptanalysts (such as people at the National Security Agency) or by coordinating many interconnected network computers.

One method is called the *brute force attack*. This method was used to break DES. Every possible key is tried in an attempt to decrypt the ciphertext. Often, a dictionary of common passwords (freely available on the Internet) is used. This type of attack is often successful if weak passwords are used. A weak password is a common name, words out of the dictionary, and common abbreviations. Brute force attacks are difficult if long keys are used and if the keys consist of mixed numbers and characters in a nonsense pattern. It is estimated that a 100-bit key could take millions to billions of years to break. However, a weakness in a system might reduce the number of keys that need to be tried, thus making an attack feasible.

Another possibility is that the cryptanalyst knows something about what is inside an encrypted message and has the algorithm used to create the ciphertext. In this case, the cryptanalyst can analyze the original plaintext, the algorithm, and the resulting ciphertext to find some pattern or weakness in the system. Message content is often not hard to figure out. Documents created in popular word processors often have hidden formatting codes and header information. Invoices or other business documents have a company's name and address. The names of persons or systems may be repeated throughout a document.

The cryptanalyst might even find a way to get some text inserted into a sensitive document before it is encrypted, then use the techniques described above to look for the message in the ciphertext. There are also some special techniques, called differential cryptanalysis, in which an interactive and iterative process works through many rounds and uses the results of previous rounds to break ciphertext.

One of the best sources of information on cryptography is RSA Security System (now part of Security Dynamics) cryptography FAQ (Frequently Asked Questions). You can find it at the site listed under "Information on the Internet," at the end of this section.

**RELATED ENTRIES**    Authentication and Authorization; Digital Signatures; PKI (Public-Key Infrastructure); Public-Key Cryptography; Security; *and* SET (Secure Electronic Transaction)

**INFORMATION ON THE INTERNET**

| | |
|---|---|
| RSA's Crypto FAQ | http://www.rsa.com/PUBS |
| Ron Rivest's Links (possibly the most complete set of links on the Web) | http://theory.lcs.mit.edu/~rivest/crypto-security.html |
| Peter Gutmann's Security and Encryption-related Resources and Links | http://www.cs.auckland.ac.nz/~pgut001/links.html |
| Terry Ritter's Cyphers by Ritter page | http://www.io.com/~ritter |
| The Computer Virus Help Desk (has a good archive of encryption software and information) | http://iw1.indyweb.net/~cvhd/crypto.html |

# CSMA/CD (Carrier Sense Multiple Access/Collision Detection)

CSMA is a network access method used on shared network topologies such as Ethernet to control access to the network. Devices attached to the network cable listen (carrier sense) before transmitting. If the channel is in use, devices wait before transmitting. MA (multiple access) indicates that many devices can connect to and share the same network. All devices have equal access to use the network when it is clear. Even though devices attempt to sense whether the network is in use, there is a good chance that two stations will attempt to access it at the same time. On large networks, the transmission time between one end of the cable and another is enough that one station may access the cable even though another already has just accessed it. There are two methods for avoiding these so-called collisions, listed next.

CD (collision detection) defines what happens when two devices sense a clear channel, then attempt to transmit at the same time. A collision occurs, and both devices stop transmission, wait for a random amount of time, then retransmit. This is the technique used to access the IEEE 802.3 Ethernet network channel. This method handles collisions as they occur, but if the bus is constantly busy, collisions can occur so often that performance drops drastically. It is estimated that network traffic must be less than 40 percent of the bus capacity for the network to operate efficiently. If distances are long, time lags occur that may result in inappropriate carrier sensing, and hence collisions.

> **NOTE:** Another CSMA method is CSMA/CA (carrier sense multiple access/collision avoidance), in which collisions are avoided because each node signals its intent to transmit before actually doing so. This method is not popular because it requires excessive overhead that reduces performance.

**RELATED ENTRIES**   Ethernet; IEEE (Institute of Electrical and Electronic Engineers); MAC (Medium Access Control); *and* Medium Access Control Methods

## CSU/DSU (Channel Service Unit/Data Service Unit)

CSUs (channel service units) and DSUs (data service units) are actually two separate devices, but they are used in conjunction and often combined into the same box. The devices are part of the hardware you need to connect computer equipment to digital transmission lines, as shown in Figure C-22.

**CHANNEL SERVICE UNIT**   This inexpensive device connects with the digital communication line and provides a termination for the digital signal. The CSU provides various loop-back tests on the line and keeps the line connected if the other communication equipment attached to it fails.

**DATA SERVICE UNIT**   This device, sometimes called a digital service unit, is the hardware component you need to transmit digital data over the hardware channel. The device converts signals from bridges, routers, and multiplexors into the bipolar digital signals used by the digital lines. Multiplexors mix voice signals and data on the same line.

## CTI (Computer-Telephony Integration)

CTI is all about integrating telephones and computers. It is also about carrying voice conversations over in-house computer networks. These two areas are slightly different, but are merging as organizations install high-speed networks that can carry both voice and data.

The other part of CTI is the integration of telephony services into desktop computers, servers, PBX devices, and other computer-related equipment. Novell created TSAPI (Telephony Services API) and Microsoft created TAPI (Telephony API) for just this purpose. TSAPI was enhanced in 1996 by a vendor consortium called Versit, which includes IBM, Siemens, and Apple Computer as its members.

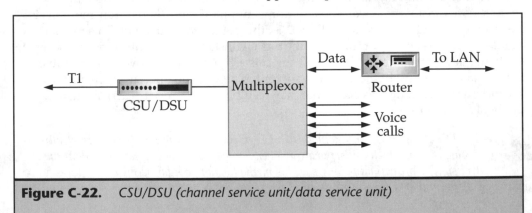

**Figure C-22.**   *CSU/DSU (channel service unit/data service unit)*

Note, however, that these protocols do not combine voice and data networking. They allow a computer to manipulate telephone devices that are connected to telephone lines. In some cases, telephony devices might be connected over a network, but the signals that cross the network are for control. They are not voice signals.

Applications can use TSAPI or TAPI to interact with devices like phones, PBXs, and modems. Windows 95 uses TAPI in a number of built-in applications to interact with modems. For example, a phone dialer program lets you enter names and phone numbers in a notepad that can be selected and dialed at any time. Windows can do a number of other things as well using TAPI, like answer incoming phone calls and faxes, forward calls, and provide voice mail. A fax application is included that receives incoming faxes and displays them in a graphical interface where they can be manipulated as if working in a drawing program.

IVR (Interactive Voice Response) is a CTI application. It is the front-end computerized "operator" that guides you through button-pushing options when you call a company (i.e., "press 1 for sales, press 2 for service"). Putting this on computers has simplified setup for administrators because an easy-to-use interface makes it easy to program selections and add or change messages. It is even possible to have messages change automatically based on programmed times or dates.

*Universal in-boxes* are another aspect of CTI. It can provide services such as voice mail, faxing, and e-mail on a companywide basis. Information is stored on disk and is accessible to users who dial into the server from their phone or access it from their workstation. In the latter case, voice messages travel across the network to the recipient's computer where they are played back, so this is similar to voice networking. However, stored messages are not real-time voice, so there is no concern about having enough network bandwidth to ensure real-time delivery. This is one of the biggest concerns with integrating voice over networks. The voice calls are live, and if enough bandwidth is not available, the conversation becomes garbled.

## Voice Networking

Currently, most organizations have separate cables for telephone and data services, but with new high-data-rate cabling and network technologies, and the ability to compress a voice telephone conversation to 8 Kbits/sec, there is little reason not to integrate these two services on the same network.

The telephone networks long ago set aside 64 Kbits/sec of digital bandwidth to transmit a voice call across their backbone networks. If you want to hook into the telephone company with something other than a few standard telephone lines, you lease services in chunks of 64 Kbits/sec. A T1 line, which many organizations use to connect voice and data with remote sites, consists of 24 64-Kbit/sec channels.

So, 64 Kbits/sec is the basic rate you'll need to set aside on an internal network to carry a single voice call. By using compression technology from MICOM (http://www.micom.com), you can bring this rate down to 8 Kbits/sec, making voice networking a reality on high-data-rate cabling systems.

See "Voice/Data Networks" for more information about integrating voice onto existing networks.

**RELATED ENTRIES**   PBX (Private Branch Exchange); TAPI (Telephony API); Telephony; Voice/Data Networks; Voice over ATM; *and* VoIP (Voice over IP)

### INFORMATION ON THE INTERNET

| | |
|---|---|
| IBM and Genesys CTI Web page | http://www.ctinet.co.uk |
| NetPhone's CT Library | http://www.netphone.com/ctlibrar.htm |
| Flatiron Publishing's Computer Telephony site | http://www.computertelephony.com |
| Computer Telephony Magazine | http://www.computertelephony.com/ct/ct_home.html |
| Computer Telephony paper on CT | http://www.computertelephony.com/ct_white.htm |

## CU-SeeMe

CU-SeeMe is a relatively inexpensive videoconferencing solution from White Pines Software (http://www.cu-seeme.com). It allows people to set up conferences over the Internet or other TCP/IP networks using inexpensive hardware. CU-SeeMe is the software behind a number of videoconferencing systems. It provides full-color video, audio, chat window, and white board communications. The system works adequately over 28.8-Kbit/sec modems although ISDN (Integrated Services Digital Network) links provide better service. The software is designed for use in instructions, business communications, or personal use.

CU-SeeMe uses a unique protocol developed specifically for TCP/IP networks and the Internet to manage, receive, and rebroadcast video and audio data. Special software-only algorithms reduce the amount of data to transmit over the wire and allow the system to work quite well over dial-up lines. CU-SeeMe is compatible with video codec and audio standards on both Windows and Macintosh systems.

## Customer Premises Equipment

*See* CPE (Customer Premises Equipment).

## Cyclic Redundancy Check

*See* Error Detection and Correction.

# Daemon

Pronounced "demon," it is a background process or program on UNIX systems. Once started, daemons usually run on their own without any further need of input from an operator. A system administrator may need to set initial startup parameters and change those parameters occasionally.

# DARPA (Defense Advanced Research Projects Agency)

In 1972, ARPA (Advanced Research Projects Agency) became DARPA (Defense Advanced Research Projects Agency. DARPA is an extension of the Department of Defense assigned to fund basic research. DARPA funded most of the basic research for the TCP/IP (Transmission Control Protocol/Internet Protocol) protocol suite and the Internet in the early 1970s.

**RELATED ENTRIES**    Internet; Internet Backbone; Internet Organizations and Committees; NII (National Information Infrastructure); Standards Groups, Associations, and Organizations; *and* TCP/IP (Transmission Control Protocol/ Internet Protocol)

# Database

*See* Database Connectivity; DBMS (Database Management System); Distributed Database; *and* Web Middleware and Database Connectivity.

# Database Connectivity

An organization that has consolidated its departmental networks into an enterprise network usually finds itself with a variety of autonomous DBMSs (database management systems) that are structured on different models. Most are probably relational databases, but some may be object oriented or hierarchical. All may be from different vendors, and all may have incompatible interfaces.

In the early days of DBMSs, programmers spent a lot of time writing programs that allowed people to access data in a specific way on database systems. But users needed a better way to get at data, so query languages were developed that let users make requests directly to the database using commands (called statements) that were supposed to mimic spoken language. In the mid-1970s, IBM developed a query tool called SQL (Structured Query Language) that eventually became the recognized industry standard for database access. See "SQL (Structured Query Language)" for more information about SQL.

It is usually the case that a client has a need to connect with many different back-end systems that may be from different vendors. In addition, clients need to access back-end data using common desktop applications such as Microsoft Access and Excel or Lotus 1-2-3. Given this, an interface is required that can transform client requests to match the target DBMS and that can provide a "universal" interface for any client application. This "middleware" layer must deal with a number of problems:

**D**

- While SQL is a standard, each DBMS may implement SQL in a different way.

- RDBMSs (relational DBMSs) often use different techniques for describing how information is stored in the database. This is often called metadata or the "data catalog."

- Nearly every DBMS on the market uses different methods to transfer data and communicate information between the client and server, such as alerts, requests for data, and status information.

- DBMSs typically use different IPC (interprocess communication) mechanisms to transport the messages just described. Some DBMSs use named pipes, some use TCP/IP sockets, and some use other methods.

- Databases may reside on network servers that are connected with different network protocols, including TCP/IP, IPX/SPX (Internet Packet Exchange/Sequenced Packet Exchange), and NetBEUI (NetBIOS Extended User Interface).

**ODBC (OPEN DATABASE CONNECTIVITY)**    ODBC provides a common interface to provide connectivity among heterogeneous databases. ODBC makes it easy to create database client and server applications that are interoperable. It hides the differences among systems and defines methods that allow applications to access multiple different DBMS systems through a single programming interface. With ODBC, client applications do not need to know what kind of database is being accessed, whether a database is local or remote, or what communication method is used to connect with the database. ODBC only requires that SQL be used to access the database. For more information about ODBC, refer to "ODBC (Open Database Connectivity), Microsoft."

**MICROSOFT OLE DB**    OLE DB is a set of Microsoft data access interfaces that provides universal data integration over an enterprise's network regardless of the data type. These interfaces allow data sources to share their data through common interfaces without having to implement database functionality not native to the data store. OLE DB is a freely published specification designed with industrywide participation. Information is available at http://www.microsoft.com/oledb. Refer to "OLE DB" for more information.

**RELATED ENTRIES**    Client/Server Computing; Data Warehousing; DBMS (Database Management System); Distributed Database; Distributed Object Computing; DRDA (Distributed Relational Database Architecture); Enterprise Networks; IBM Host Connectivity; Middleware and Messaging; ODBC (Open Database Connectivity), Microsoft; Replication; SQL (Structured Query Language); Transaction Processing; *and* Web Middleware and Database Connectivity

**INFORMATION ON THE INTERNET**    Refer to "DBMS (Database Management System)" for a complete list of Internet sites.

## Database Server

A database server is a computer attached to a network that runs a client/server DBMS (database management system). Workstations, acting as clients, can send requests to the server over the network. The server then responds. Client workstations handle the presentation of data and interact with users while the server performs the workhorse operations such as sorting, indexing, and delivering data to users.

A database server is a central depository for information that many users access. In fact, most of the database architectures and query languages (such as Structured Query Language, or SQL) used to access the DBMS on a database server have roots in the mainframe world. However, LAN-based database servers use client/server models in which the processing load is divided between the back-end database server and the front-end client. This model takes advantages of the processing power of both client and server computers.

The hardware components of a database server are typically high-performance systems running multiple Pentium processors or RISC-based designs from IBM and Sun Microsystems. Superserver systems with special proprietary high-speed busses and multiple processors are available from Tricord Systems, Parallan Computers, and NetFrame.

New approaches to client/server computing in distributed environments take advantage of data on multiple servers at multiple locations. There are client/server relationships and server-server relationships. In the server-server relationship, networks of servers can appear as a single system to users.

**RELATED ENTRIES**    Client/Server Computing; Data Warehousing; DBMS (Database Management System); Distributed Database; *and* Servers

## Data Communication Concepts

Data communications is all about transmitting information from one device to another. All the controls and procedures for communicating information are handled by communication protocols. At the most basic level, information is converted into signals that can be transmitted across a guided (copper or fiber-optic cable) or unguided (radio transmission) medium. At the highest level, users interact with applications. In between is software that defines and controls how applications take advantage of the underlying network.

This section outlines data communication technologies and makes reference to other sections in this book. If you are interested in a specific aspect of data communications, you can refer to the related topics listed at the end of each subsection for more information.

### Communication Protocols

Any discussion of data communications must begin with a discussion of protocols. Communication protocols are the rules and procedures that networked systems use to communicate on a transmission medium.

Communication protocols are responsible for establishing and maintaining communication *sessions*. Two computers engage in a session to coordinate the transfer of data. Sessions are *connection-oriented*. In contrast, a *connectionless* transmission occurs when data is sent to a device without the sender first establishing contact with the receiver. The Internet is a connectionless system. Connection-oriented and connectionless sessions are discussed under "Connection-Oriented and Connectionless Services."

Communication protocols can be compared to the diplomatic protocols used by foreign embassies. Diplomats of various rank handle different types of negotiations. They communicate with peer diplomats in other embassies. Likewise, communication protocols have a layered structure in which protocols at one layer in the transmitting system communicate with protocols in the same peer layer of the receiving system. A simplified diagram is pictured in Figure D-1. Note the top layer is a high-level, network-enabled application where users make requests for network services. This layer talks with its peer layer in the computer it is communicating with. The messages sent by this layer travel down the protocol stack, across the wire and up through the protocol stack to the destination.

The top layer is where applications interact with the network and is called the application layer protocol. The middle protocol layer, generically called the *transport layer* in this case, is responsible for keeping the communication session alive and running and for coordinating the transfer of information. It also provides "services" to the upper application layer. The lower layer defines connections to the physical transmission medium and the signaling techniques used on the medium. Note that the physical layer might provide modem connections, network connections, or even connections to satellites.

For later reference, you should know that data passes through the protocol stack in blocks. For example, a file transfer might be broken up into any number of pieces, then transmitted one piece at a time. If one of the pieces is lost, it can be re-sent without needing to retransmit the entire file. Technically, pieces of data passing through the protocol stack are called *PDUs (protocol data units)*. This is discussed further under "Protocol Concepts."

In more general terms, people talk about *packets* of data moving from one system to another. Another term you will encounter is *frames*, which has to do with dividing serial streams of data into manageable blocks for transmission as discussed later in this topic under the subheading "Framing in Data Transmissions."

The reason for layering the protocol stacks is simple. Protocols are published as worldwide standards so that one vendor can create network hardware or software that will work with another vendor's hardware or software. A developer references a particular part of the protocol stack that is appropriate for the product being developed.

Long ago, the ISO (International Organization for Standardization) developed the seven-layer OSI (Open Systems Interconnection) model. This model was supposed to have provided a framework for integrating data processing systems everywhere. However, to date it has only served as a very useful model for discussing how other

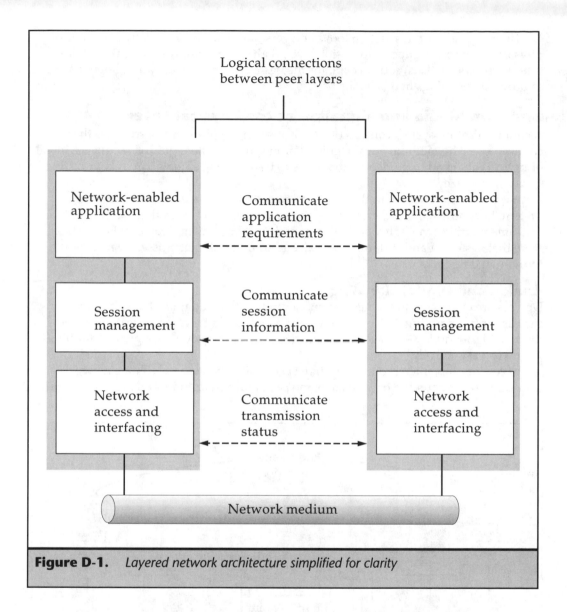

**Figure D-1.** *Layered network architecture simplified for clarity*

more popular protocols operate and work together. References are made to the layers of this model throughout this text, so you may want to refer to "OSI (Open Systems Interconnection) Model" for more information.

The Internet protocols, including TCP/IP, are now commonly used throughout the world. Only a few years ago, a number of other protocols were vying for this top spot, including the OSI protocols. Other network protocol suites include Novell's IPX/SPX, AppleTalk, and IBM SNA.

The remainder of this section looks at layers of the protocol stack from the bottom physical layer to the upper application layer, with an emphasis on TCP/IP and other Internet protocols. Each section explains the basic terminology only and refers you to appropriate headings in this book.

## Transmission Media and Signaling at the Physical Layer

A communication system consists of a transmission medium and the devices that connect to it. The medium may be guided or unguided, where guided media is a metal or optical cable and unguided media refers to transmitting signals through air or the vacuum of space.

A communication system that connects two devices is said to be a *point-to-point* system. In contrast, a *shared* system connects a number of devices that can transmit on the same medium, but only one at a time. Both systems are illustrated in Figure D-2. Note that system A and system Z have an end-to-end link that crosses over several individual data links.

### Analog and Digital Signaling

Devices are connected to a transmission medium with an adapter that generates signals for transmitting data over some medium. For digital communication systems, discrete high- and low-voltage values are generated to provide the signaling for binary 1s and 0s, respectively.

In contrast, an analog communication system like the voice telephone network transmits continuous analog signals that vary in amplitude and frequency over time.

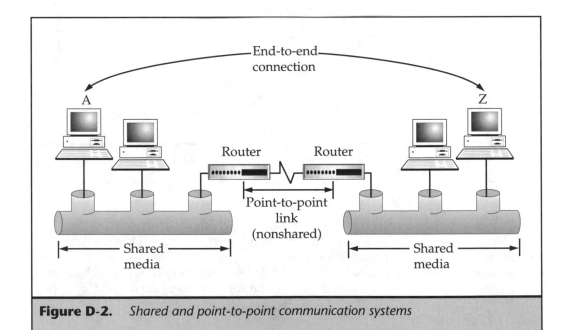

**Figure D-2.** *Shared and point-to-point communication systems*

The frequency of these sine wave signals is measures in cycles per second, or Hz (hertz). As you'll see, the frequency of the signals plays a role in the amount of data that can be transmitted without distortion over an analog telephone line. The *bandwidth* of a system refers to its data-carrying capacity.

A modem (modulator/demodulator) is a device that can be used to transmit digital signals over analog transmission lines. A modem is required at both ends of a transmission to modulate, then demodulate the signal. As shown in Figure D-3, the transmitting modem converts a digital signal into an analog signal and the receiving modem converts the signal back to discrete digital signals.

There are a number of factors that limit the data rate (bandwidth) of a transmission system. One is the frequency allowed on the channel. It may be limited for a number of reasons, including government restrictions or the specifications of the transmission system. The telephone system has bandwidth limitations due to its use as a voice communication system. When transmitting digital data over analog systems, the higher the frequency, the higher the data rate. Figure D-4 illustrates why this is so. In A, the frequency is low, so it is more difficult to transpose the discrete digital signal on the analog transmission. Note that the discrete signal is poorly represented, and this will result in distortion at the receiving end. In B, the bandwidth is much higher and more capable of representing the discrete digital signal without distortion.

## Data Encoding

In its simplest form, digital data is transmitted as high- or low-voltage pulses. In a one-to-one relationship, a binary 0 may be transmitted as a zero-voltage level, and a binary 1 may be transmitted as +5V voltage level. However, special encoding schemes are used to more efficiently transmit signals. In these encoding schemes, 1s are not always represented by a high voltage and 0s by a low voltage (or vice versa). Instead, a change in polarity may reverse the scheme at any time, depending on the bit value. This is explained next.

A scheme called Manchester encoding is used on Ethernet LANs. Its most important feature is that it provides a way for sender and receiver to synchronize and track the exact location of bits in a transmission without the need for a clocking mechanism. Note in Figure D-5 that a bit transition always takes place in the middle of transmitting a single bit. This transition serves as a built-in clocking mechanism that

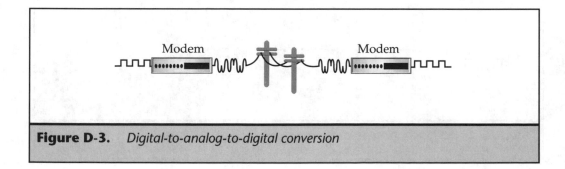

**Figure D-3.**    *Digital-to-analog-to-digital conversion*

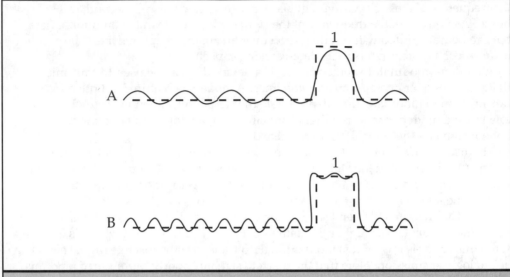

**Figure D-4.** *Representing discrete digital signals on analog transmissions*

the receiver can track. This also divides each bit period into two intervals in which bits are represented as follows:

- A binary 1 is represented by the first interval set high and the second interval set low.

- A binary 0 is represented by the first interval set low and the second interval set high.

Note that Manchester encoding is not the most efficient of the encoding schemes, but it is easy to implement and is used on many LANs today. This topic is covered further under "Modems" and "Signals."

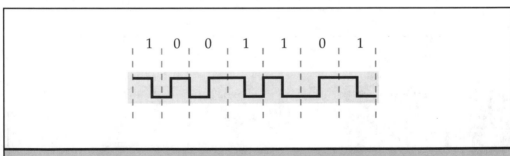

**Figure D-5.** *Manchester encoding*

## Synchronous and Asynchronous Transmissions

Not all transmissions are a steady flow of characters. A transmission that consists of many starts and stops is an asynchronous transmission. Assume you are back in the 1960s, sitting at a dumb terminal connected to a mainframe computer. As you type, each character is transmitted to the computer over an asynchronous link. You pause and the transmission pauses. Because the systems operate in asynchronous mode, the receiver is not expecting a steady stream of bits. It waits for further transmission at any time and does not assume that the link has been disrupted when transmissions stop.

In contrast, a *synchronous transmission* is characterized by a long string of bits in which each character in the string is demarcated with a timing signal. Both types of transmissions are commonly used to connect computer systems over telephone lines or other channels. The choice of one over the other depends on the installation. In fact, modems that provide asynchronous operation for users may switch to synchronous mode for extended transmissions. See "Asynchronous Communications" and "Synchronous Communications."

## Serial Interfaces

A standard interface is required to connect communication devices like modems to computers. The most common interface for modems is the EIA-232 standard, which was originally called RS-232. In this scheme, computers or other similar devices are called DTE (data terminal equipment) and devices like modems are called DCE (data circuit-terminating equipment). The interface connector has 25 pins that are wired through to the opposite connector. Each pin represents a channel on which data is transferred or a specific control signal is sent. For example, pin 4 is the *request to send* line and the DTE uses it to signal that it wants to transmit. Pin 5 is the *clear to send* line and the DCE uses it to indicate that it is ready to receive. See "Serial Communication and Interfaces" for more information about this subject.

## Transmission Media

There are a variety of transmission media including copper cable, fiber-optic cable, and unguided wireless techniques. Each has transmission characteristics that restrict data transmission rates. Some of these restrictions are imposed by the designers of the communication systems on which the cable are used, based on various factors such as a need to reduce signal emanation. Other restrictions are based on signal loss over distance or even curvature of the earth in the case of ground-based microwave transmissions systems. Designers of communication systems take all of these factors into consideration when designing network systems such as Ethernet, token ring, FDDI (Fiber Distributed Data Interface), and others. Therefore, networks should be assembled within the standard specifications to avoid problems.

Computer data can be transmitted over RFs (radio frequencies) in cases where wires are impractical. These RF transmissions take place between a transmitter and a receiver within a single room or across town. RF networks provide unique solutions for campus and business park environments where links are required across roads,

**D**

rivers, and physical space (in general, where it is not practical to run a cable). Terrestrial microwave systems are commonly seen on the top of buildings and towers everywhere. The telephone companies have built networks of microwave transmitters and receivers for the telephone network.

Satellite communication systems provide another solution for long-distance communication. See "Microwave Communications," "Satellite Communication Systems," and "Wireless Communications" for more details. Cable characteristics, impairments, and other factors related to transmission media are covered further under "Transmission Media, Methods, and Equipment." See also "Network Design and Construction."

### The Telephone System

The telephone system has always been an integral part of data communications. If an organization needs 24-hour connections to remote sites, it can lease dedicated digital transmission lines from the telephone company or other service providers or it can take advantage of packet-switched networks. These options are discussed further under "Telecommunications and Telephone Systems" and "WAN (Wide Area Network)." An emerging trend is to build VPNs (virtual private networks) over the Internet. This saves much of the cost of leasing long-distance lines. Refer to "VPN (Virtual Private Network)" for more details.

## Data Link Protocols

Now the discussion moves up the protocol stack above the hardware level. The next layer up is commonly referred to as the *data link layer*. The primary purpose of the data link layer is to manage the flow of bits between systems that are connected to a transmission medium. It is helpful to think of water flowing through a hose. Once transmission starts, the physical network sends raw bits through the hose to the receiver. Interference and electrical problems can disturb an electrical transmission, just like a kink in a hose can disrupt the flow of water. Also, the "bit buckets" on the receiving end may fill up quickly and overflow before the receiving system can process the data.

The data link layer can provide a mechanism for controlling the transmission of bits across the physical layer. If necessary, it can detect and correct errors in transmission and tell the sending system to slow down or stop sending data until the receiving system catches up. On the other hand, performing all these tasks in the data link layer can reduce performance, so many networks only rely on the data link layer for fast data transmission. Higher-level protocols in the transport layer handle error detection and recovery.

### Framing

Framing provides a controlled method for transmitting bits across a physical medium and provides error control and data retransmission in the event of an error. It is helpful to think of a freight train. A block of bits is put into each frame and delivered to the destination. A checksum is appended so the frame can be checked for corruption. If a frame is corrupted or lost, only that frame needs to be re-sent, rather than the entire set of data.

Frames have a specific structure, depending on the data link protocol in use. The frame structure for a popular data link protocol called HDLC (High-level Data Link Control) is pictured in Figure D-6. Note that the information field is where data is placed, and it is variable in length. An entire packet of information may be placed into the information field. The beginning flag field indicates the start of the frame. The address field holds the address of the destination, and the control field describes whether the information field holds data, commands, or responses. The FCS field contains error-detection coding.

### Error Detection and Control

The data link layer is also responsible for error detection and control. One error control method is to detect errors and then request a retransmission. This method is easy to implement, but if errors are high, it affects network performance. Another method is for the receiver to detect an error and then rebuild the frame. This latter method requires that enough additional information be sent with the frame so the receiver can rebuild it if an error is detected. This method is used when retransmissions are impractical, such as a transmission to a space probe. These techniques are discussed further under "Error Detection and Correction."

### Flow Control

Finally, we get to flow control. As mentioned earlier, if a data transmission is like water flowing through a hose, some control is needed to prevent the bucket at the other end from overflowing. In this analogy, the bucket is the data buffer that the receiver uses to hold data until it can be processed. The buffers on some NICs (network interface cards) are large enough to hold an entire transmission until the processor can get to it. When buffers overflow, frames are usually dropped, so it is useful for the receiver to have some way to tell the sender to slow down or stop sending frames. See "Acknowledgments" and "Flow-Control Mechanisms" for more information.

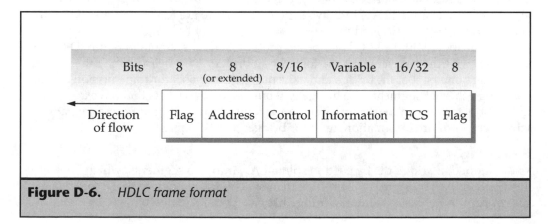

**Figure D-6.**   *HDLC frame format*

## Network Access and Logical Link Control for Shared LANs

Access methods are necessary on networks that are shared by multiple devices. Only one device can transmit on the network at a time, so a medium access control method is needed to provide arbitration.

In the local area network environments defined by the IEEE, medium access protocols reside in a sublayer of the data link layer called the MAC (Medium Access Control) sublayer. The MAC sublayer sits below the LLC sublayer, which provides the data link control for any installed MAC drivers below it. The subdivision of the layers can be seen in Figure D-7.

The MAC sublayer supports a variety of different network types, each of which has a specific way of arbitrating access to the network. Three different access methods are described here.

- **Carrier sense methods**  With this technique, devices listen on the network for transmissions and wait until the line is free before transmitting their own data. If two stations attempt to transmit at the same time, both devices back off and wait a random amount of time before retransmitting.

- **Token access methods**  A token ring network forms a logical ring on which each transmission travels around the ring from station to station. Only a station that has possession of a special *token* can transmit.

- **Reservation methods**  In this scheme, every transmitting device has a specific slot of time or frequency allotted to it. A device can choose to place data in the slot for transmission. This technique can waste bandwidth if a device has nothing to transmit.

Refer to "Data Link Protocols," MAC (Medium Access Control)," and "Medium Access Control Methods" for more information.

### Bridging

A bridge is a device that connects two network segments. In this discussion, the segments are IEEE 802.x LANs. A bridge can extend the distance of a LAN and can be used to split a shared LAN into two segments so there are fewer stations trying to share each segment of the medium.

Bridges operate in the LLC layer of the protocol stack, as shown in Figure D-8. Note that two Ethernet networks are joined by a bridge. A frame from the Ethernet LAN enters one port of the bridge and exits out the other port for transmission on the adjoining Ethernet segment. The bridge will only forward packets that have a destination address on the destination segment, thus minimizing unnecessary packet deliveries. For more information, refer to "Bridges and Bridging."

### Switching

As mentioned, a bridge can be used to split a LAN into two segments, which effectively makes two smaller shared segments. A switch is a device that expands on this concept. Whereas a traditional bridge has two ports to join two LAN segments, a

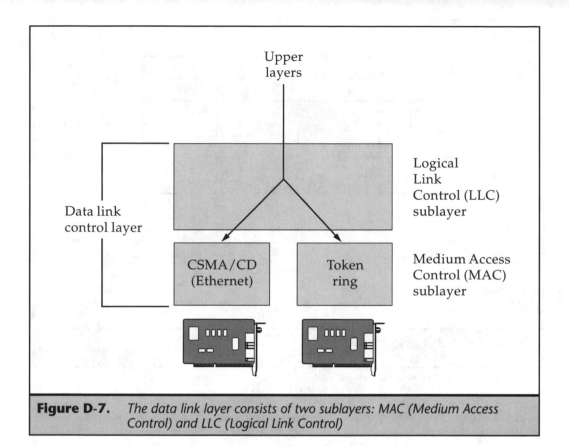

**Figure D-7.** *The data link layer consists of two sublayers: MAC (Medium Access Control) and LLC (Logical Link Control)*

switch has an array of ports for joining more than two segments. As shown in Figure D-9, a hub is usually attached to a port. Then, only the workstations on that hub contend for access to the LAN segment. If a workstation needs to transmit to a workstation on another port, the switch will quickly set up a temporary connection between the ports so that all the workstations attached to the two ports share what is essentially a dedicated network segment. For example, in Figure D-9, the switch could join segment A/B/C to G/H/I.

The purpose of switching is to boost LAN performance by reducing the number of workstations on each LAN segment. The switch itself moves frames between ports at very high speeds so it does not introduce any delay to the network. The best performance is achieved with one workstation per port so that there is no contention at all when that workstation wants to transmit. The switch sets up a port connection between the sender and receiver for the duration of the transmission.

Note that a switch operates in the data link layer relative to the OSI protocol. The industry refers to this as *Layer 2 switching*. The technique of dividing LANs is often called *microsegmentation* because a network can be split into smaller and

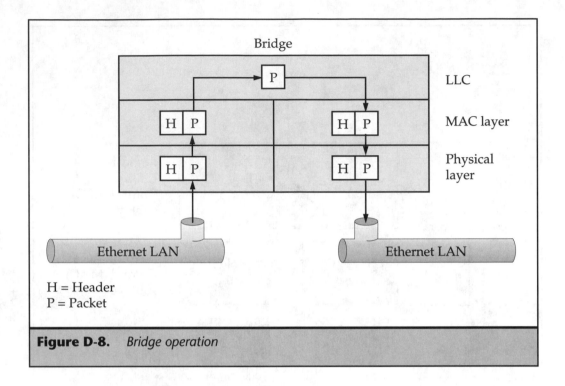

**Figure D-8.** *Bridge operation*

smaller segments up to the point where a single port segment may be dedicated to a single computer.

Most switching devices provide a way to configure VLANs (virtual LANs) as well. With a traditional hub, all the connected workstations are part of the same LAN segment. In a VLAN-capable network, workstations can be configured to belong to one or more logical LANs. For example, if the hubs in Figure D-9 are replaced with VLAN-capable switches, workstations A and D could be configured into a VLAN, and workstations B, E, and H could be configured into another VLAN. Broadcasts from A are heard by D, and broadcasts from B are heard by E and H. Refer to "VLAN (Virtual LAN)" for more details.

## Routing, Internetworking, and the Network Layer

Only a few years ago, bridges were essential devices in corporate networks. Today, routers are more often selected because they provide a better way to connect the individual networks an organization may have installed over the years.

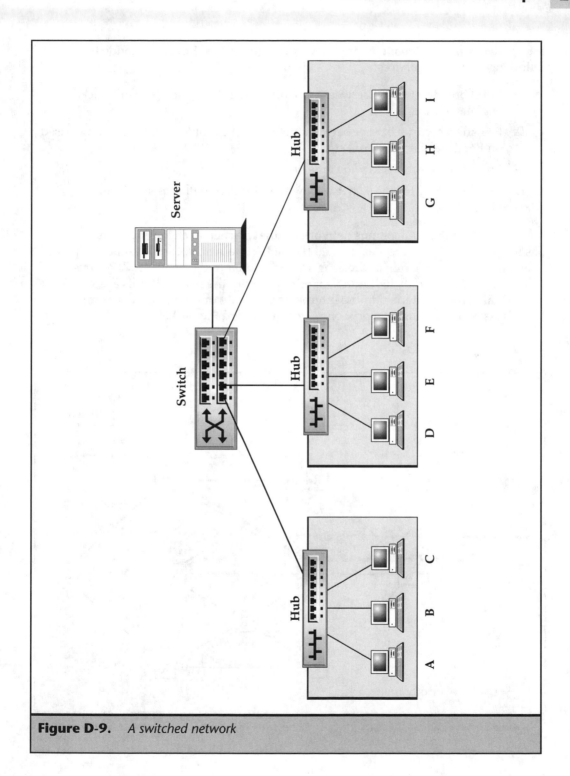

**Figure D-9.** *A switched network*

Internetworking is all about joining networks with routers. Routers provide the following important services:

- Limit broadcast traffic between networks and intelligently forward packets between networks
- Provide a security barrier between networks (i.e., routers can filter traffic based on IP address, application, etc.)
- Provide connections to wide area networks
- Provide a way to build a network with redundant paths, as shown in Figure D-10

Routers join the autonomous networks of the Internet. Each individual network has its own network address as defined by the IP (Internet Protocol). What IP offers is a higher-level internetwork addressing scheme similar to the way U.S. ZIP codes provide a way to identify individual cities throughout the nation. In this analogy, each individual network attached to the Internet is like a city or town. Routers examine the IP address and determine the port on which to forward the packet.

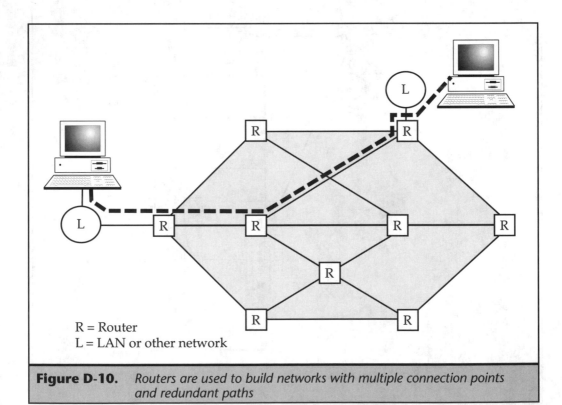

R = Router
L = LAN or other network

**Figure D-10.** *Routers are used to build networks with multiple connection points and redundant paths*

To understand the role of routers, it may be useful to consider how the Internet joins the autonomous networks of organizations throughout the globe. The TCP/IP addressing scheme is an important part of the Internet because it provides a way to assign a unique address to all the networks and hosts attached to it. Keep in mind that individual networks already have a MAC layer addressing scheme that identifies individual nodes on that network. IP identifies individual networks in an internetwork.

See "Internetworking," "Packet and Cell Switching," "Routers," "Routing Protocols and Algorithms," and "WAN (Wide Area Network)."

## Transport Layer Services

The transport layer provides a unique service. It allows two systems to set up a "conversational" session with one another so they can reliably exchange data. The session achieves reliability because the transport layer processes in each system exchange messages about the status of the session. Figure D-11 illustrates how a transport layer session is a logical end-to-end connection that spans intermediate devices like routers. The two peer transport layers appear to be talking to one another.

The network layer IP protocol is a connectionless service while the transport layer provides reliable connection-oriented services, in some cases over highly unreliable networks. For example, if a network link temporarily fails, a connection-oriented

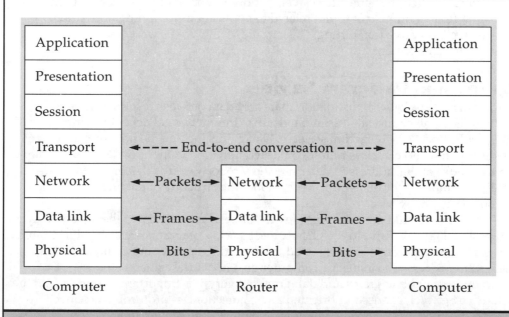

**Figure D-11.**    *The transport layer can engage in end-to-end "conversations" across internetworks*

session does not immediately give up the connection, but attempts to keep it alive until the underlying link is reestablished or until a time-out occurs. Once the session is reestablished, data transmission continues from where it was interrupted. A connection-oriented session is actively monitored and dynamically managed to ensure proper delivery of data. While connection-oriented virtual circuits take time to set up, they are appropriate for lengthy "conversations" and data transmissions.

In contrast, connectionless services like IP send datagrams to recipient systems without first notifying them.The recipient is expected to accept the datagrams and handle them as appropriate. If datagrams are lost, the recipient must detect that a packet is missing and request a retransmission from the sender. Interestingly, the Internet is based on IP, an unreliable protocol, but TCP adds reliability to the Internet.

For more information on the procedures and processes implemented in the transport layer, refer to "Transport Protocols and Services."

## The Application Layer

Applications that run at the highest level of the protocol stack are not really involved in communications, but they do use communication services and so have appropriate features and user interfaces that take advantage of the underlying network. Network file-sharing services like NCP (NetWare Core Protocol), NFS (Network File System) in the UNIX environment, or SMB (Server Message Blocks) in the Windows environment are specifically designed to use network services so that users can share files over networks. These systems are designed to work with most underlying networks.

Having reached the application layer, our discussion of network concepts ends. You can refer to a number of topics related to applications for more information, such as "Collaborative Computing," "Electronic Mail," "Groupware," and "Workflow Management."

## Datagrams and Datagram Services

Datagrams are packets of information that carry data between a source and a destination using connectionless methods. IPX (Internetwork Packet Exchange) and IP (Internet Protocol) are datagram services. Datagrams include the network address of the destination and can cross router-connected network boundaries. Each router along the way looks at this address to determine how to forward the datagram. Refer to "IP (Internet Protocol)" for more information about the structure of datagrams and their use on specific networks.

Datagrams should not be confused with frames. Frames exist in the data link layer and physical layer relative to the OSI protocol stack. Datagrams are encapsulated into frames. While datagrams are addressed to a specific computer on an internetwork, frames are addressed to a specific computer on a network segment.

To understand datagrams and datagram delivery, it is important to understand the difference between connection-oriented and connectionless protocols. A connection-oriented protocol basically sets up a session between the sender and receiver and can create a virtual circuit (data pipe) for streaming data across a network. Connectionless protocols like IP are ideal for bursty data transmissions like those common on LANs. It is not necessary to set up a session in advance. Routers along the way may make routing decisions about the path a datagram should take to reach its destination, based on traffic conditions or downed lines. Because of this, data may arrive out of sequence, be delayed, or get lost.

Higher-layer protocols add reliability services to underlying networks that may be unreliable. IP and IPX are considered best-effort delivery mechanisms that cannot guarantee delivery. The connection-oriented TCP (Transmission Control Protocol) adds reliability to the underlying connectionless IP (Internet Protocol).

**RELATED ENTRIES**    Data Communication Concepts; Data Link Protocols; Encapsulation; Fragmentation of Frames and Packets; IP (Internet Protocol); Novell NetWare Protocols; Packet and Cell Switching; *and* Protocol Concepts

## Data Link Layer, OSI Model

In the OSI (Open Systems Interconnection) model, the data link layer sits just above the physical layer. Therefore, it defines the protocols that directly interact with the physical components of the link, such as the network adapters and cable. It frames data and controls the flow of information across the link. Originally, data link protocols were designed for point-to-point links, and this is still the primary way that communication is handled, although shared LANs such as Ethernet require additional medium access control protocols to arbitrate access to the shared medium.

**RELATED ENTRIES**    Data Link Protocols; OSI (Open Systems Interconnection) Model; *and* Protocol Concepts

## Data Link Protocols

Often called Layer 2 protocols, data link protocols exist in the protocol layer just above the physical layer relative to the OSI protocol model. Data link protocols directly control physical layer communication. Because there are many different ways to connect devices, there are many different data link protocols. For example, two devices may be connected over a shared LAN, and thus the data link protocol will need to arbitrate access to the network. Ethernet and token ring are examples of shared data link protocols. The PPP (Point-to-Point Protocol) that many people use to connect to the Internet via a dial-up modem is an example of a data link protocol over a nonshared link.

Because the link between two systems is point to point (even while transmitting on shared media), the bits are always delivered from sender to receiver in order. Basically, a data link is a wire between two points. Packet-switched networks are made up of numerous point-to-point links that employ data link protocols between each link.

The purpose of the data link protocol is to provide the following:

- **Session setup and termination for connection-oriented transmissions**
  Session control messages are used by end systems to exchange status information about the session.

- **Addressing on a multipoint medium such as a LAN**   A computer's address is usually the hardwired address of the NIC (network interface card).

- **Framing**   Data is broken up into discrete units that can be transmitted as independent units. Errors can be detected within each unit and if detected, only that frame need be retransmitted.

- **Error detection**   Determines if a frame has been delivered accurately. A checksum is calculated on a frame by the sender and the receiver must perform the same calculation and come up with the same checksum. If not, the frame is considered corrupted and must be retransmitted.

- **Flow control**   A technique that prevents the sender from sending more information than the receiver can handle at any one time. A stop-and-wait flow control acknowledges every frame. Alternatively, sliding-window flow controls allow the sender to dynamically adjust the number of frames it can send without acknowledgments and is very efficient.

Like the higher-level transport protocol, data link protocols can provide connection-oriented services in addition to a connectionless service. In the former, the sender and receiver establish a session with one another prior to transmitting data. All the frames are numbered and the receiver acknowledges receipt of frames. Lost or corrupted frames are retransmitted. Thus the service provides a reliable and guaranteed service.

Some network designers feel that providing reliable services in the data link layer is unnecessary and that the data link layer should simply provide high-speed bit transmission without all acknowledgments. This connectionless type of service cannot guarantee that data will be delivered. Instead, transport layer protocols provide these reliability services. In the TCP/IP protocol suite, TCP provides connection-oriented services for the network service in use.

The choice between using a connection-oriented or connectionless channel depends on the underlying service. If the service is wireless and prone to a lot of lost frames, then data link layer acknowledgment is preferable. However, much of the bandwidth will be taken up by acknowledgments. Connection-oriented data link protocols are usually unnecessary on reliable networks.

## Common Data Link Protocols

The most common data link level protocols are listed here with a short description. You will find more information about each protocol under appropriate headings in this book.

- **HDLC (High-level Data Link Control)** This protocol is based on the SDLC (Synchronous Data Link Control) protocol originally developed by IBM, which was part of IBM's SNA (Systems Network Architecture). A number of other protocols are available that use the same formats and procedures as HDLC.

- **LLC (Logical Link Control)** The IEEE (Institute of Electrical and Electronic Engineers) defines this protocol in its 802.x family of network standards.

- **LAP (Link Access Procedure)** There are three main LAP protocols. LAPB (LAP Balanced) is a protocol that provides point-to-point connections on X.25 packet-switched networks. LAPD (LAP for D Channel) provides the data link control over the D channel of an ISDN (Integrated Services Digital Network) connection. LAPF (LAP for Frame-Mode Bearer Services) provides the data link for frame relay networks.

- **SLIP (Serial Line Interface Protocol)** SLIP is a data link control facility for transmitting IP packets, usually between an ISP (Internet service provider) and a home user over a dial-up link. SLIP has some limitations, including a lack of any error-detection and correction mechanisms. It is up to higher-layer protocols to perform these checks.

- **PPP (Point-to-Point Protocol)** PPP provides the same functionality as SLIP (i.e., it is commonly used for Internet connections over dial-up lines), but it is a more robust protocol that can transport not only IP, but other types of packets.

## LAN Data Link Controls

The IEEE (Institute of Electrical and Electronic Engineers) has split the data link layer for LANs into two sublayers, called the MAC (Medium Access Control) sublayer and the LLC (Logical Link Control) sublayer, as shown in Figure D-12. The lower MAC layer defines the media access method, which can be either CSMA/CD (carrier sense multiple access/collision detection), token ring, or another IEEE physical interface. The LLC sublayer provides a way for the network layer to communicate with one of these protocols.

## High-Speed Data Link Protocols

Frame relay is considered a high-speed data link networking facility. It uses LAPF (Link Access Procedure for Frame-Mode Bearer Services). See "Frame Relay" for more information. ATM (Asynchronous Transfer Mode) is a cell-based data service that does not have any ties with traditional frame-based data link services like HDLC (High-level Data Link Control). See "ATM (Asynchronous Transfer Mode)" for more information.

**RELATED ENTRIES** Connection-Oriented and Connectionless Services; Data Communication Concepts; Encapsulation; Framing in Data Transmissions; LLC (Logical Link Control); MAC (Medium Access Control); Medium Access Control

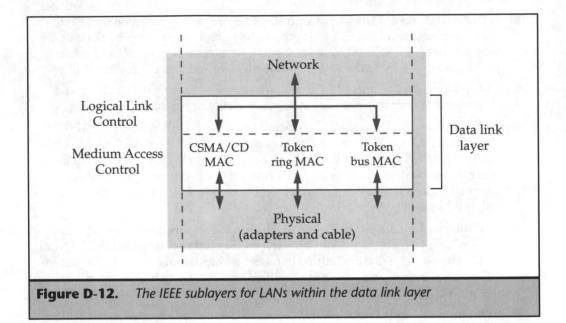

**Figure D-12.** *The IEEE sublayers for LANs within the data link layer*

Methods; OSI (Open Systems Interconnection) Model; Protocol Concepts; *and* Serial Communication and Interfaces

# Data Management

Data management is concerned with the distribution of data to users and the protection of that data from loss such as fire, theft, or unauthorized access. Data management includes these areas:

- **Archiving**   Copying files that are no longer needed to archival storage. See "Data Protection."

- **Backup**   Backing up current files for protection. See "Backup and Data Archiving" and "Data Protection."

- **Data migration**   Similar to archiving, but provides a way for users to quickly access files that have been archived. See "Data Migration" and "Storage Management Systems."

- **Data warehousing**   Data warehousing uses data summarization techniques to make large volumes of data available in a form that is easily accessible to data clients. See "Data Warehousing."

- **DBMS (database management system)**   A database is a file that contains records with information in fields. A DBMS is a complete package that provides a query language and provides access to the data. See "DBMS (Database Management System)."

■ **Distributed and replicated data**   Distributed data is stored on multiple servers across a network. The data is usually in the form of a database that is automatically replicated (copied) to other locations where it is easily accessible by users at those locations. See "Distributed Database" and "Replication."

■ **Security**   User access rights, directory rights, and file rights all deal with restricting user access to specific files, directories, and servers. See "Security."

# Data Migration

Data migration is an archiving process that moves little-used or unused files to a secondary storage system, such as magnetic tape or optical disk. The files are typically imaged documents or historical information that needs to be readily accessible at any time in the future. Migration works in conjunction with backup strategies, and regular backups are still required. Migration (and de-migration) is a process that moves files off valuable high-speed magnetic disk space and onto secondary, high-volume media, primarily optical disk. Files remain available offline, but are accessible to users over the network.

**RELATED ENTRIES**   Imaging; Optical Libraries; *and* Storage Management Systems

# Data Protection

Besides people, data is the most important asset to most organizations. Everything else can be replaced. If systems are destroyed, you can replace hardware in a day, but you can't bring your network back up and running if you don't have proper data backups. In addition, if your company is like most, even a day of downtime is intolerable, and thousands or millions of dollars could be lost while a system is not operating. In addition to protecting current data, many organizations must store data on a permanent basis for legal reasons. For example, a company that works with hazardous substances needs to keep accurate records of its activities. The following sections outline some measures for protecting systems and data.

**PROTECT AGAINST THEFT**   You must protect systems from theft, not only because the equipment is valuable, but because the downtime it takes to replace the servers can cost many times more than the equipment. Consider the amount of time you would need to replace servers and restore backups. You can bolt computers down; lock up servers in data centers; staff your facilities 24 hours a day; and ensure that all personnel are trustworthy, competent, and know the security procedures.

**PROTECT AGAINST FIRE AND NATURAL DISASTERS**   Place equipment in rooms that have fire protection systems. Protect equipment from natural disasters such as earthquakes and floods. You might need to reinforce or elevate the server area and develop plans so users can access server data in case there is a disaster. Gas-powered generators can supply power to servers and workstations when electricity is cut off.

**CENTRALIZE OR DISTRIBUTE MANAGEMENT** There are advantages to both centralized management and distributed management. To centralize management, move network resources—servers, hubs, switches, routers, and even printers—to central locations where trained staff can manage the systems in secure and protected areas. However, doing so puts you at risk of catastrophes such as earthquakes and fires. An alternative is to distribute network resources and automatically replicate data to remote sites on a regular basis. Use high-speed data links between the sites.

**USE FAULT TOLERANCE TECHNIQUES** Network operating systems should provide fault tolerance techniques such as disk mirroring and disk duplexing for quick recovery from disk failures. Clustering techniques provide fault tolerance for entire servers by duplexing an entire data system over one or more servers. Entire data centers can be duplicated. If one center goes down due to a natural disaster, the other can immediately replace it.

**KEEP ADEQUATE BACKUPS** Ensure that data is properly backed up. Implement a backup plan that rotates backup to off-site storage. Use data migration techniques to keep some data available on near-line storage devices (see "Data Migration").

**USE DISKLESS WORKSTATIONS OR NCs (NETWORK COMPUTERS)** Diskless workstations and NCs don't have disk drives, so users can't download valuable company data or upload information that might contain viruses or clutter the server's disk.

**PROTECT AGAINST INTRUDERS** Intruders can use various methods to gain access to a network. You can prevent intruders from accessing a LAN by ensuring that users protect their passwords, log off when they step away from their system, and aren't lax about security. Most network operating systems provide features that restrict the station that users log on at and the time they log on. You can also add time restrictions to prevent access before or after normal working hours. See "Hacker" for related information.

**ADMINISTER ACCESS RIGHTS** Logon restrictions and directory or file access rights are important techniques that administrators and supervisors have to protect data against malicious or accidental loss or corruption by users. Users should never be given more rights than they need in program and data directories. Most users don't need more than the right to read in a program directory. Anything more opens program files to corruption, overwrites, and virus attack.

**TRAIN USERS** Train users to properly log on and log off of the network and to protect their passwords. If they need to leave their computers unattended, make sure they log off or know how to activate a password-protected screen saver that locks the computer (but maintains logon) while they are gone. Set options in user accounts that force users to change their passwords at a predetermined interval, prevent them from reusing recent passwords, or require them to use passwords that haven't been used before.

**TRACK USERS** Keep track of users. Have department administrators inform you of users who have left the company or changed roles so that you can remove or alter their user accounts appropriately. Audit trails created by an auditing system can help you track users who disrupt the network either accidentally or on purpose.

**RELATED ENTRIES** Access Control; Authentication and Authorization; Backup and Data Archiving; Clustering; Data Migration; Data Warehousing; Disaster Recovery; Fault Management; Fault Tolerance; Power and Grounding Problems and Solutions; Replication; Rights and Permissions; Security; Storage Management Systems; Storage Systems; *and* Virus and Antivirus Issues

# Data Striping

Data striping is a technique used in RAID (redundant arrays of inexpensive disks) systems to write data evenly across a series of disk drives. Striping divides data over two or more drives, as shown by the simplified example in Figure D-13. Data striping can occur at the bit level or sector level. A sector is a block of data. Striping improves throughput and provides a form of redundancy that protects against the failure of one disk in the array.

This protection comes from a technique that encodes the scattered data to a *parity drive*. Should one drive fail, the parity drive provides the information to fill in the missing bits from the lost drive and rebuild the data. The strategy assumes that it is unlikely that two drives will fail at the same time. RAID systems usually have a hot replacement feature that lets you immediately replace a drive without bringing the system down. Once the replacement drive is installed, the system starts rebuilding the

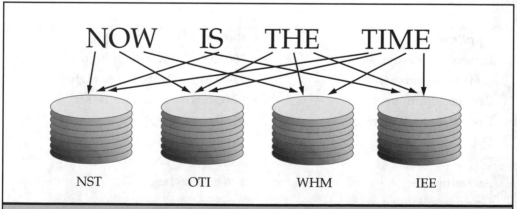

**Figure D-13.** *Data striping distributes data over two or more drives*

data on the replaced drive using the parity information on the parity drive. The operating system can continue to provide user access to the drive array during the rebuilding operation.

**RELATED ENTRY**    RAID (Redundant Arrays of Inexpensive Disks)

## Data Switch

A device that links terminals, computers, and other computing devices to host computers. It is basically a concentrator device that provides a way for a large number of devices to share a limited number of ports.

**RELATED ENTRIES**    Cluster Controllers, IBM; Concentrator Devices; Ethernet; *and* Hubs/Concentrators/MAUs

## Data Transfer Rates

Data transfer rates are a measure of the amount of digital information that can be transmitted through a channel per second. Data transfer rates are also referred to as *throughput* rates. A number of factors determine data transfer rates, including bandwidth of the line, transmission impairments, distance, media type, and so on. These are discussed under "Transmission Media, Methods, and Equipment."

The *bit rate* of a channel is the bits-per-second transfer rate that the channel supports. A 10-Mbit/sec Ethernet cable provides 10 times the data rate of a line rated at 1 Mbit/sec. Telecommunication systems and networks such as Ethernet have specific bit rates defined by standards to ensure that communication systems do not exceed the capacity of the specified equipment.

The bandwidth requirements of various applications are listed here. The rates are shown in bits/sec (bits per second), Kbits/sec (thousands of bits per second), Mbits/sec (millions of bits per second), and even Gbits/sec (billions of bits per second).

| Application | Rate |
|---|---|
| Personal communications | 300 to 9,600 bits/sec or higher |
| E-mail transmissions | 2,400 to 9,600 bits/sec or higher |
| Remote control programs | 9,600 bits/sec to 56 Kbits/sec |
| Digitized voice phone call | 64,000 bits/sec |
| Database text query | Up to 1 Mbit/sec |
| Digital audio | 1 to 2 Mbits/sec |
| Access images | 1 to 8 Mbits/sec |
| Compressed video | 2 to 10 Mbits/sec |
| Medical transmissions | Up to 50 Mbits/sec |

| Application | Rate |
|---|---|
| Document imaging | 10 to 100 Mbits/sec |
| Scientific imaging | Up to 1 Gbit/sec |
| Full-motion video | 1 to 2 Gbits/sec |

The transmission rates of various communication media are listed here. Compression techniques can boost data rates in many cases. For example, modem rates have been boosted above 1 Mbit/sec in some controlled environments, although these rates are not possible using existing serial ports on most computers.

| Type | Rate |
|---|---|
| Dial-up modem connection | 1,200 to 56,000 bits/sec |
| Serial port file transfers | 2,000 bits/sec |
| Fractional T1 digital WAN link | 64,000 bits/sec |
| Parallel port | 300,000 bits/sec |
| T1 digital WAN link | 1.544 Mbits/sec |
| ARCNET LANs | 2.5 or 20 Mbits/sec |
| Token ring LANs | 4 or 16 Mbits/sec |
| Ethernet LANs | 10 or 100 Mbits/sec |
| T3 digital WAN link | 44.184 Mbits/sec |
| HSSI (High-Speed Serial Interface) | 52 Mbits/sec |
| FDDI (Fiber Distributed Data Interface) | 100 Mbits/sec |
| Fibre Channel | 1 Gbit/sec |
| Gigabit Ethernet | 1 Gbit/sec |
| SONET (Synchronous Optical Network) | 51.9 Mbits/sec to 2.5 Gbits/sec |
| Potential future SONET | 13.2 Gbits/sec |

**RELATED ENTRIES**    Bandwidth; Bandwidth on Demand; Bandwidth Reservation; Capacity; Channel; Circuit; Data Communication Concepts; Delay; Electromagnetic Spectrum; PPS (Packets per Second); Signals; Throughput; *and* Transmission Media, Methods, and Equipment

## Data Transmission Equipment

Data transmission equipment is any equipment that transmits data from one system to another. This is such a wide category that it is covered under the following specific categories:

Bridges and Bridging
Cable (CATV) Data Networks and Modems
Cabling (see "Transmission Media, Methods, and Equipment")
CSU/DSU (Channel Service Unit/Data Service Unit)
Ethernet
Hubs/Concentrators/MAUs
Matrix Switch
Modems
Multiplexing
NIC (Network Interface Card)
PBX (Private Branch Exchange)
Repeater
Routers
Switched Networks
Token Ring Network

**RELATED ENTRIES**   Communication Services; Connection Technologies; Data
Communication Concepts; Internetworking; LAN (Local Area Network); Network
Concepts; Network Design and Construction; WAN (Wide Area Network); *and*
Wireless Communications

## Data Warehousing

Every day, organizations capture data that is essentially unavailable for use because
there is no way to conveniently access, manipulate, and present it. Billions of bytes of
data are "locked up" on computer systems throughout an organization. *Data
warehousing* defines strategies for making this data more accessible.

Industry analysts and system vendors long ago recognized that there are two types
of information systems:

■ **Operational systems**   These are the systems that handle day-to-day processes
such as accounting, order entry, and inventory management. These are the
systems that keep a business running.

■ **Informational systems**   These are systems that people use to analyze data,
make business management decisions, and plan for the future. These systems
are often referred to as executive management systems.

The important difference between the two systems for the purposes of this
discussion is that operational systems deal with a specific set of data, such as the
inventory, while information systems are concerned with extracting useful
information from a variety of related information sources. Informational systems
access and use data from the following information sources:

- **Legacy data systems** The storehouse of data that an organization has collected over many years. Systems include older mainframe or minicomputer systems that run specific applications that are not easily accessible from more modern PC-based applications.

- **External data systems** These are systems outside the organization, such as the Web servers or subscription data services that provide a range of information (demographic data, economic trend data, product data, etc.).

- **Operational data systems** As described earlier, operational data is the day-to-day data collected by and generated by accounting and other business systems.

A data warehouse can be thought of as a *three-tier system* in which a middle system provides usable data in a secure way to end users. On either side of this middle system are the end users and the back-end data stores. The data warehouse is typically made up of the following components, which are illustrated in Figure D-14:

- **Data mart or staging systems** This is the place where selected data from back-end systems is stored for access by clients. The data is usually cleaned up and manipulated in a variety of ways before it is stored on the staging systems, as discussed later. A data warehouse may consist of many staging systems (one for each department).

- **Front-end client** These are the end users who access data using PC-based applications such as Microsoft Access and Excel, Lotus 1-2-3, SAS, and other data management applications. These front-end tools provide sophisticated methods for displaying and analyzing data.

- **Middleware** This is a layer of software that hides the differences between data management systems and allows clients to easily access those systems. Staging systems may use a common data access language such as SQL (Structured Query Language) to access data on legacy and operational systems. ODBC (Open Database Connectivity) provides a common middleware interface between clients and most back-end systems. See "Database Connectivity," "ODBC (Open Database Connectivity), Microsoft," and "SQL (Structured Query Language)" for more information.

- **Messaging systems** The data warehouse typically consists of multiple back-end systems and multiple clients. A message system is a delivery system that transports requests and responses throughout the data system. The messaging system uses the underlying network protocols and facilities to deliver information to end users.

By looking at Figure D-14, you can see that clients have access to data stored on the staging systems, although direct access to legacy, operational, or external systems

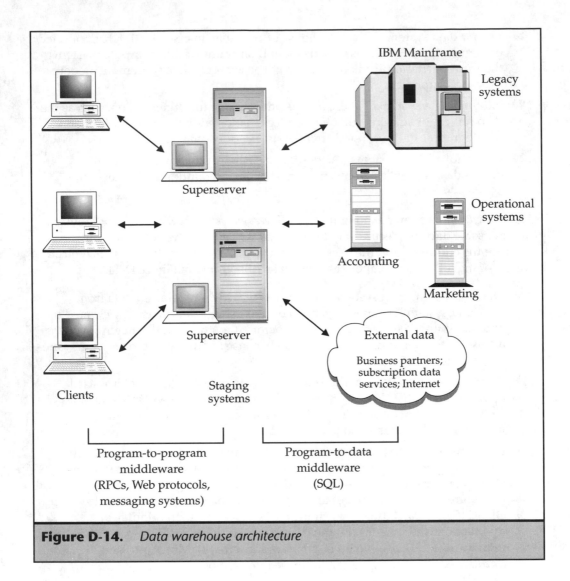

**Figure D-14.** *Data warehouse architecture*

is also possible. However, the staging approach provides a number of benefits, including security and client access to data that is tightly controlled by data analysts or data managers.

A *metadata store* is a system that holds information about the location and structure of data in the data warehouse. It allows end users to access data anywhere without having to know the exact location of the data, and it stores information about how that data is structured and the statements or commands that are required to access it.

## About Information in the Data Warehouse

The data warehouse can be thought of as a system that holds summary information from legacy, operational, or external data sources. Staging systems store only the latest information for read-only purposes. All data updates take place on operational systems, not on the staging system.

According to Prism Solutions (http://www.prismsolutions.com), there are different levels of summarization and detail in the data warehouse, as shown in Figure D-15 and explained here:

- Older detail data is historical or legacy data.

- Current detail data (typically operational data) is the most recent data. It is voluminous and requires extensive summarization to make it easily accessible.

- Lightly summarized data is data that has been distilled from the current detail data by a database analyst or some other process.

- Highly summarized data is compact and easily accessible by end users within specific departments.

It is assumed that data stored on legacy, operational, or external systems is encoded, structured, and stored in a number of different ways, and that over the years, database designers have used their own conventions in building database structures. Therefore, the way that information is stored in one database is largely inconsistent with the way related information is stored in other databases.

When data is transferred to the staging systems, it must be "preprocessed" either by the database analysts or by applications specifically designed for the task. Processing involves extracting, cleaning, combining, altering, and manipulating data into new sets of data that are more relevant to end users. It may also include extensive integrity checking to ensure that end users access accurate and timely data.

A key feature of this process is to integrate data using common naming conventions and consistent attributes, coding, and structure. For example, date information from different databases may be in a variety of formats (Julian, yymmdd, mmddyy, etc.), but may be reformatted and stored in Julian format only on the staging system.

As mentioned, each department in a company may have its own staging system for lightly or highly summarized data. A database analyst usually handles the task of summarizing and extracting data from back-end systems and making it accessible to users. D2K, Inc. (http://www.d2k.com) calls these analysts "farmers," presumably because they work to extract data stored at the "server farm." The data farmer may use OLAP (online analytical processing) and "data mining" tools that help them correlate information and discover interesting and meaningful relationships in the data.

**D**

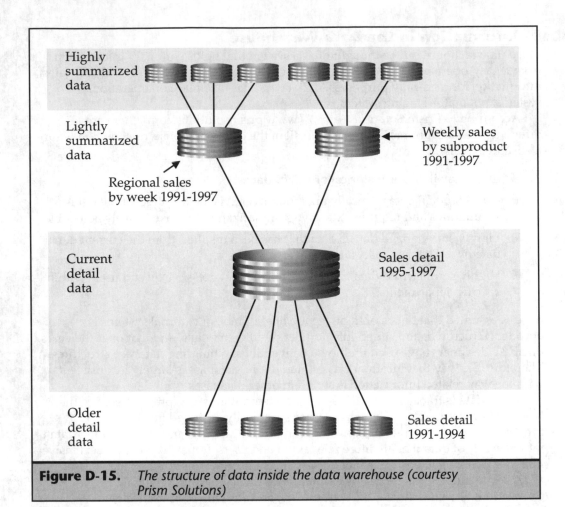

Highly summarized data

Lightly summarized data

Regional sales by week 1991-1997

Weekly sales by subproduct 1991-1997

Current detail data

Sales detail 1995-1997

Older detail data

Sales detail 1991-1994

**Figure D-15.**    *The structure of data inside the data warehouse (courtesy Prism Solutions)*

New and emerging software to support the data warehousing concept can replace EISs (executive information systems) and DSSs (decision support systems). These early systems did not benefit from the constant updating of data that can take place in a data warehouse and were limited in use to only a few decision makers.

The IDWA (International Data Warehousing Association) has identified a new type of data warehouse called the "operational data warehouse." This warehouse offers dynamic access to back-end data that has been identified at the front-end system. The example it uses is a bank that has been called upon to identify all the assets of a particular company. The bank extracts relevant data from many different systems. The court then orders that all accounts be frozen. This is a problem if all the accounts are stored on many different legacy systems. Bank employees will need to close each account individually. With an operational data warehouse, all the accounts can be closed using the same software that was used to pull up the account information in the first place.

## Planning and Building a Data Warehouse

An organization that decides to build a data warehouse faces the daunting task of making information available to users that is timely, accurate, and useful. There are many stories of misguided attempts to build data warehouses that end up providing inaccurate or inadequate information. Still, there is often no choice but to build a data warehouse. The alternative is to leave valuable data locked up on legacy systems.

The process of building a data warehouse should start with carefully planned strategy and a prototype. Before expensive hardware is purchased, developers should work closely with users to determine exactly what information is required on staging systems and how it will be used. This can often be done by building small systems that grow into full production systems.

Vendors have developed special systems for data warehousing. IBM has its Information Warehouse system as described under "Information Warehouse." Parallel database systems are emerging that improve access to database systems. New data visualization tools are emerging that help people see relevant information in the data available to them. Pyramid Technology (http://www.pyramid.com) has developed parallel processing systems specifically designed for this purpose.

The Web interface is perhaps the most important new aspect in data warehousing. A number of vendors, including D2K Inc., are developing applications that deliver warehoused data to Web browsers. Push technologies are used to automatically provide subscribed users with the latest view of the data they are interested in. With Web technologies, it is only necessary to format data for display in a Web browser. Then users on any system, using any Web browser, can display the information.

Readers should check the Web sites listed under "Information on the Internet" at the end of this section for more information. There are many Web sites and white papers available on the topic from individuals and vendors. There are also many vendors products that simplify the whole process.

**RELATED ENTRIES**    Client/Server Computing; Database Connectivity; DBMS (Database Management System); Distributed Database; Middleware and Messaging; Multitiered Architectures; ODBC (Open Database Connectivity), Microsoft; SQL (Structured Query Language); Transaction Processing; *and* Web Middleware and Database Connectivity

**INFORMATION ON THE INTERNET**    Refer to "DBMS (Database Management System)" for a complete list of database-related Internet sites.

| The Data Warehousing Institute | http://www.dw-institute.com |
| The International Data Warehousing Association | http://www.idwa.org |
| Larry Greenfield's Data Warehousing Information Center (be sure to see the "White Papers" section) | http://pwp.starnetinc.com/larryg |

## DB2, IBM

DB2 is a relational DBMS (database management system) from IBM. It first appeared on IBM mainframes and has had a long life of service. Today, DB2 is IBM's most important database system and is available on all of its major platforms. It uses SQL (Structured Query Language).

The latest incarnation of DB2 is DB2 Universal Database, a scaleable, multimedia Web-enabled database that runs on Intel and UNIX platforms, as well as a variety of SMP (symmetrical multiprocessing) and MPP (massively parallel processing) environments. The product also supports Java and JDBC (Java Database Connectivity). It can also handle distributed multimedia data warehousing and includes database tools, World Wide Web connectivity, and multimedia object-relational support.

### INFORMATION ON THE INTERNET

| IBM's Software site | http://www.software.ibm.com |

## DBMS (Database Management System)

A DBMS is a software program that typically operates on a database server or mainframe system to manage data, accept queries from users, and respond to those queries. A typical DBMS has the following features:

- Provides a way to structure data as records, tables, or objects
- Accepts data input from operators and stores that data for later retrieval
- Provides query languages for searching, sorting, reporting, and other "decision support" activities that help users correlate and make sense of collected data
- Provides multiuser access to data, along with security features that prevent some users from viewing and/or changing certain types of information
- Provides data integrity features that prevent more than one user from accessing and changing the same information simultaneously
- Provides a data dictionary that describes the structure of the database, related files, and record information

Most DBMS systems are client/server-based and operate over networks. The DBMS is an engine that runs on a powerful server with a high-performance channel to a large data store. The DBMS accepts requests from clients that may require sorting and extracting data. Once the server has processed the request, it returns the information to the client.

There are diverse collections of back-end database systems and methods for accessing those systems. In addition, there are a variety of clients. Database middleware products are designed to provide a middle layer of software that hides the differences among databases. ODBC (Open Database Connectivity), originally designed by Microsoft, is now the de facto standard middleware product in the industry. See "Database Connectivity" for more information.

The common language for accessing most database systems is SQL (Structured Query Language), which is discussed under the heading, "SQL (Structured Query Language)."

Most databases are operational databases, meaning that data going into the database is used in real time to support the ongoing activities of a business. An accounting system is an example. An OLAP (online analytical processing) system is used to analyze data in these database systems to find trends or make business decisions. A *data warehouse* is a large-scale OLAP system that is specifically designed to extract, summarize, combine, clean up, and process information from a number of data sources such as the operational databases, legacy (historical) databases, and online subscription databases for the purpose of analysis. See "Data Warehousing" for more information.

## Types of DBMS Systems

A simple database is a collection of records that contain fields of information. A simple name and address database is basically a *flat-file database*, since all the information can be stored in one file. Flat-file databases are usually inadequate for business applications. Instead, relational and/or object-oriented database systems are required as described here.

### RDBMS (Relational Database Management System)

An RDBMS is a system that stores data in multiple databases called tables. The tables can be related and combined in a number of ways to correlate and view data. A typical database for an accounting system might contain hundreds of tables that can potentially produce thousands of relationships. A common element, such as a customer number, may link information across the databases. A query for a particular customer may pull the customer's address from one database, an account balance from another, and some historical purchasing information from another.

The RDBMS is currently the most popular type of database. However, there is a growing need to store more than text and numbers. Object-oriented DBMSs (as discussed next) can store many different data types, including images, audio, and video, but many organizations are not ready to move away from their RDBMS investment.

Most RDBMS vendors now provide hybrid RDBMS systems that provide storage for multimedia types. These systems are called object-relational databases or, more recently, *universal databases*. There are two possible approaches to extending RDBMS systems to support objects:

- Separate data management and data processing tasks into different processes. Oracle and Sybase use this approach. The Oracle technique is to provide plug-in software "cartridges" that run as separate processes in the server. This approach has performance problems.

- Integrate data management and data processing tasks into the DBMS engine, as IBM and Informix have done. This approach provides tight integration of processes in the server, but could make the server unstable.

An alternative approach is provided by Microsoft with its OLE DB standard, which may provide a better way to integrate databases than the universal server approaches outlined above. OLE DB is a set of Microsoft data access interfaces that provides universal data integration over an enterprise's network regardless of the data type. These interfaces allow data sources to share their data through common interfaces without having to implement database functionality not native to the data store. See "Database Connectivity" and "OLE DB" for more information.

Refer to the following Web sites for extensive product information and additional information on database systems in general.

| | |
|---|---|
| IBM Corporation | http://www.software.ibm.com |
| Informix Software, Inc. | http://www.informix.com |
| Oracle Corporation | http://www.oracle.com |
| Microsoft OLE DB information | http://www.microsoft.com/oledb |
| Sybase, Inc. | http://www.sybase.com |

## OODBMS (Object-Oriented Database Management System)

An object database is designed to handle a variety of different data types, including documents, images, audio, and video. But a true OODBMS goes beyond this. It also stores methods, which include properties and procedures that are associated directly with objects in the database. In addition, new object types can be created as necessary to define any type of information.

The relational database program is used in an environment where procedures are designed into programs and data goes into the database. The program then works on the data in the database. In a true object-oriented database, procedures and data go together.

An OODBMS consists of a model of all the data in the database. The database contains many different data types that can be defined in advance or at any time. Each data type can be assigned meaning that is relevant to the object it represents. There can be a class such as "person" and subclasses of that class such as "doctor," "lawyer," and "accountant." If a change is made to a class, the change is made to all objects in that class. Each class can have specific procedures associated with it, so programming and data manipulation are not separate. See "Object Technologies."

The following vendors provide object-oriented database systems and have extensive information available at their site to continue your research.

| | |
|---|---|
| Objectivity, Inc.'s Objectivity/DB site | http://www.objectivity.com |
| Object Design, Inc.'s ObjectStore site | http://www.odi.com |
| Versant Object Technology Corp.'s Versant ODBMS site | http://www.versant.com |

**RELATED ENTRIES**    Client/Server Computing; Database Connectivity; Distributed Database; Middleware and Messaging; Multitiered Architectures; ODBC (Open Database Connectivity), Microsoft; SQL (Structured Query Language); Transaction Processing; *and* Web Middleware and Database Connectivity

## INFORMATION ON THE INTERNET

| | |
|---|---|
| Data Management Association | http://www.dama.org |
| DBMS Magazine | http://www.dbmsmag.com |
| DBMS Magazine links page | http://www.dbmsmag.com/resource.html |
| Database Magazine | http://www.onlineinc.com/database |
| Object Magazine (has extensive links) | http://www.sigs.com/omo |
| Objectivity, Inc.'s list of database links | http://www.objectivity.com/ObjectDatabase/outsrefs.html |
| The Very Large Data Bases (VLDB) Endowment, Inc. | http://www.vldb.org |
| Database Systems Laboratory, Department of Computer Science, University of Massachusetts, Amherst (extensive links) | http://www-ccs.cs.umass.edu/db.html |
| The Stanford University Database Group | http://www-db.stanford.edu |

| | |
|---|---|
| Association for Computing Machinery's Special Interest Group on Management of Data | http://bunny.cs.uiuc.edu |
| UCB DBMS Research Group links (includes extensive vendor list) | ftp://s2k-ftp.cs.berkeley.edu/pub/postgres/otherdbms.html |

## DCE (Data Circuit-terminating Equipment)

DCE equipment is typically a modem or other type of communication device. The DCE sits between the DTE (data terminal equipment) and a transmission circuit such as a phone line. Originally, the DTE was a dumb terminal or printer, but today it is a computer, or a bridge or router that interconnects local area networks. In an IBM mainframe environment, a communication controller and a link-attached cluster controller are examples of DTEs.

A DCE provides a connection for the DTE into a communication network and back again. In addition, it terminates and provides clocking for a circuit. When analog telephone lines are the communication media, the DCE is a modem. When the lines are digital, the DCE is a CSU/DSU (channel service unit/data service unit).

DTE and DCE interfaces are defined by the physical layer in the OSI (Open Systems Interconnection) model. The most common standards for DTE/DCE devices are EIA (Electronic Industries Association) RS-232-C and RS-232-D. Outside the United States, these standards are the same as the V.24 standard of the CCITT. Other DTE/DCE standards include the EIA RS-366-A, as well as the CCITT X.20, X.21, and V.35 standards. The later standards are used for high-speed communication over telephone lines.

DTE and DCE devices send and receive data on separate wires that terminate at a 25-pin connector. It is useful to know that DTE devices transmit on pin connector 2 and receive on pin 3. DCE devices are just the opposite—pin 3 transmits and pin 2 receives.

## DCE (Distributed Computing Environment), The Open Group

DCE is the product of the OSF (Open Software Foundation), which merged with X/Open Company Ltd. in February 1996 to form The Open Group. OSF was originally founded in 1988 to research and develop distributed computing environments. X/Open was founded in 1984 to provide compliance to open systems specifications. The Open Group's mission is to enable customer choice in the implementation of multivendor information systems. The Open Group's Web site is located at http://www.opengroup.org.

DCE is a suite of "enabling" software services that allow organizations to distribute processing and data across the enterprise. It hides the difference between multivendor products, technologies, and standards. Thus, DCE provides an independence from operating systems and networks. No specific network protocol is specified, so the underlying network can use IP (Internet Protocol), IPX (Internetwork Packet Exchange), or SNA (Systems Network Architecture).

Its open development environment allows developers to easily create applications that integrate key software services for distributed applications while insulating developers from the complexities of the underlying network and its transport mechanisms. Users gain single log-in, access to legacy data, reliability, file replication, and availability. In the last few years, DCE has become critical in the areas of security, distributed objects, and Internet/intranet computing.

The Open Group makes DCE source code available to vendors, who then incorporate it into their products. It also provides specifications for use by developers and a test suite used to validate conformance to the DCE standard.

The DCE architecture is shown in Figure D-16. It is a layered model that integrates a set of technologies described in the remainder of this section. At the bottom are the most basic services (such as operating systems) and at the top are applications. The services provided by DCE are designed to mask the complexity of multivendor network environments and let information flow easily to where it is needed.

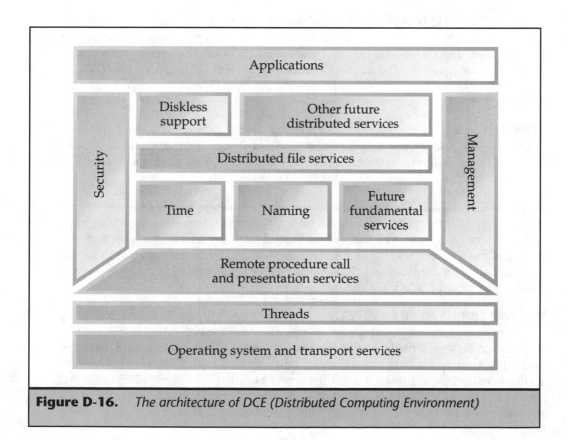

**Figure D-16.** *The architecture of DCE (Distributed Computing Environment)*

The DCE services are grouped into two categories: development tools and data-sharing services. The development tools help software developers create end-user services needed for distributed computing. They include RPCs (remote procedure calls), directory services, time services, security services, and threads services. Data-sharing services provide end users with capabilities built upon the development tools to easily access information. They include distributed file system and diskless workstation support.

**RPCs (REMOTE PROCEDURE CALLS)**   RPCs are tools for creating client/server applications that can run procedures on other computers attached to a network. RPCs let clients interact with multiple servers and allow servers to handle multiple clients simultaneously.

**THREADS SERVICE**   The threads service provides portability features that support concurrent processing, allowing an application to perform many actions simultaneously. While one thread executes a remote procedure call, another thread can process user input. The threads service is suited to dealing with multiple clients in client/server-based applications.

**DDS (DISTRIBUTED DIRECTORY SERVICES)**   DDS provides a single naming model throughout the distributed environment so users can identify resources such as servers, files, disks, and print queues by name and without the need to know their location in the network. The X.500 global naming system is integrated into DCE's directory service. LDAP (Lightweight Directory Access Protocol) is also being integrated into DCE's directory service.

**TIME SERVICES**   Time services lets applications schedule activities and determine event sequences and duration. The distributed time services keep track of time in networks and determine the accuracy associated with each clock used to synchronize time.

**SECURITY SERVICE**   In a distributed environment where activities span multiple hosts with multiple operating systems, authentication and authorization require an independent security service that can be trusted by many hosts. DCE's security service provides the network with three conventional services: authentication, authorization, and user account management. These facilities are made available through a secure means of communication that ensures both integrity and privacy.

**DFS (DISTRIBUTED FILE SYSTEM)**   The DFS is an optional information-sharing component that makes global file access possible over the network. It provides a uniform name space, file location transparency, and performs across long distances and with large numbers of users. Files and directories are replicated invisibly on multiple machines to protect against file server failure. DFS is derived from the AFS (Andrew File System), and it is built on the components discussed above. DFS interoperates with the NFS (Network File System) from Sun Microsystems.

## Enhancements

The latest version of DCE provides a variety of improvements in manageability, fault tolerance, performance, and scalability. Security features include support for public keys and Kerberos Version 5. The most critical enhancements are improvements in security for the Internet as well as for intranet environments. The Open Group developed the Secure Enterprise Web technology to allow off-the-shelf browsers and servers to interact with DCE naming and security services.

DCE is a key component in the implementation of distributed object-oriented technologies. According to The Open Group, DCE meets the requirements for use in the CORBA specification as an ESIOP (Environment-Specific Inter-ORB Protocol), and unlike the GIOP (General Inter-ORB Protocol), is available, tested, and used today. For more information about component techniques, refer to "Distributed Object Computing."

**RELATED ENTRIES**    Directory Services; Distributed Database; Distributed File Systems; Distributed Object Computing; Enterprise Networks; *and* RPC (Remote Procedure Call)

**INFORMATION ON THE INTERNET**

The Open Group                http://www.opengroup.org

# DCOM (Distributed Component Object Model)

DCOM is a Microsoft object model that goes back as far as DDE (Dynamic Data Exchange), which was a messaging system used to exchange information among Windows programs. DDE evolved into OLE (Object Linking and Embedding), a method of embedding links to objects within programs and documents. This gave rise to COM, which became the basis for all object binding and eventually DCOM and ActiveX (which is essentially COM enabled for the Internet). DCOM is COM extended over the network. Microsoft describes DCOM as "COM with a long wire."

The idea behind component technology is to break large and complex applications into smaller software modules that are easier to develop, modify, and upgrade. By breaking applications into parts, a modification or upgrade affects only specific components, not the entire program. Application logic, information retrieval, transaction monitoring, data presentation, and management may run on different computers that communicate with one another to provide end users with a seamless application interface.

 *NOTE: For more information about component technology, see "Component Software Technology" and "Distributed Object Computing."*

Microsoft's DCOM takes all the qualities of COM and extends it over a network. DCOM works with TCP/IP, the Java language, and HTTP (Hypertext Transfer Protocol). It provides the underlying binding elements for extending components across networks. It is designed to run on Windows 95, Windows NT, Macintosh, UNIX, and legacy operating systems.

Microsoft openly licenses DCOM technology. In October of 1996, Microsoft turned control of ActiveX technology, which is built on DCOM, over to The Open Group, an industry consortium that manages open software development. DCOM is also part of The Open Group's DCE (Distributed Computing Environment) technology. Information is available at http://www.activex.org.

Microsoft is also working with Internet standards bodies, including the IETF (Internet Engineering Task Force) and the W3C (World Wide Web Consortium), to make DCOM viable on the Internet. Software AG (http://www.sagus.com) has done extensive work with DCOM and has ported it to the Sun Solaris operating system.

DCOM is also language neutral, meaning that components can be written in a variety of languages. The Web browser is the most common "container" for running components. Users download components at the sites they visit. The components may be stored permanently on the user's system for later use or may go into the cache, where they may be deleted after a period of nonuse.

To extend its component model to a model that supports sophisticated applications, Microsoft has integrated DCOM into its ActiveX Server, a series of technology services that speed deployment of component-based applications across the Internet and corporate intranets. The ActiveX Server Framework services are described under "Active Platform, Microsoft."

While components written to the COM specification use DCOM to communicate over networks, there is a need to register components and coordinate their activities when critical transactions are taking place. Microsoft Transaction Server coordinates the interaction of components and ensures that transactions are implemented safely. It provides transaction processing and monitoring along with message queuing and other traditional features normally found on high-end transaction systems. Because it provides these features in an object-based environment, it is essentially a transaction-based *object request broker*. Refer to "Microsoft Transaction Server" for more information.

**RELATED ENTRIES**   Active Platform, Microsoft; ActiveX; COM (Component Object Model); Component Software Technology; Compound Documents; Distributed Object Computing; Java; Microsoft Transaction Server; Object Technologies; OLE (Object Linking and Embedding); ORB (Object Request Broker); *and* RPC (Remote Procedure Call)

**INFORMATION ON THE INTERNET**

| | |
|---|---|
| Microsoft's DCOM site | http://www.microsoft.com/intdev/prog-gen/dcom.htm |
| Software AG Americas, Inc. | http://www.sagus.com |
| The Active Group | http://www.activex.org |

# DDE (Dynamic Data Exchange)

DDE is an interprocess mechanism for exchanging messages between processes running in a computer. It is implemented in Microsoft Windows products. Successor technologies include OLE (Object Linking and Embedding), COM (Component Object Model), and DCOM (Distributed COM).

**RELATED ENTRIES**    COM (Component Object Model); Component Software Technology; DCOM (Distributed Component Object Model); Object Technologies; *and* OLE (Object Linking and Embedding)

# DDP (Datagram Delivery Protocol)

DDP is a routing protocol developed by Apple Computer for its AppleTalk networks.

**RELATED ENTRY**    AppleTalk

**D**

# DDR (Dial-on-Demand Routing)

DDR provides a way to link two sites over a public network and provide needed bandwidth by setting up additional lines as required. DDR is a feature of routers from Cisco and other vendors. It allows the router to establish a circuit-switched analog or digital connection to a remote location. Switched connections can provide alternate routes to back up primary communications lines that might fail. Switched lines are also used to handle peaks in traffic, fax transmissions, backup sessions, bulk e-mail transfers, and LAN-to-LAN connections.

A Cisco router running the DDR utility issues a dial-up command to the connected DCE (data circuit-terminating equipment) when it receives packets destined for remote networks. The network administrator can designate which packets can initiate a dial-on-demand sequence. Cisco routers use the CCITT V.25 bis protocol to initiate calls on automatic calling devices. DDR provides an alternative to leased lines, assuming your network can handle the brief pause that occurs while the dial-on-demand connection is made. Managers who need to decide between leased lines or traditional dial-up lines may choose dial-up lines when this feature is available.

**RELATED ENTRIES**    Bandwidth on Demand; Bandwidth Reservation; Bonding; Circuit-Switching Services; Inverse Multiplexing; Load Balancing; PPP Multilink; *and* Routers

# DEC (Digital Equipment Corporation)

Digital Equipment Corporation, usually called DEC, was founded in 1957 in Maynard, Massachusetts by Kenneth Olsen. The company initially sold a set of computer systems for scientists and engineers and soon began competing with IBM in the business environment. DEC is best known for its minicomputer systems, which provided departments within companies with their own affordable computers so those departments didn't need to rely on a single, all-powerful information systems department. This trend of making computer power more accessible to people continued in the 1980s with the development of personal computers, but that's a story that DEC does not play into as much as IBM and Apple Computer do.

In 1959, DEC announced the PDP (Programmed Data Processor), an 18-bit computer with a relatively inexpensive price tag of $120,000 and a very innovative idea—a built-in CRT. This model evolved into the PDP-8 minicomputer and other PDP systems with 12-, 18-, and 32-bit architectures. The most popular PDP system is the 16-bit PDP-11, but the VAX (Virtual Address Extension) 32-bit family of computers, first introduced in 1977, makes up the current DEC minicomputer line.

VAX systems were manufactured in a range of sizes, from desktop systems to large-scale multiprocessing mainframes that service thousands of users. The VAX systems use the VMS (Virtual Memory System) operating system, a multiuser, multitasking, operating system that provides virtual memory capabilities. VAX systems will also run software written for PDP systems.

With the introduction of the VAX, DEC also announced its DECnet networking product. DECnet is built around DNA (Digital Network Architecture) and provides a way for multiple computers to link and share resources. DECnet was originally designed for parallel interfaces that connected nearby systems within about 30 feet of one another. In 1980, DEC, Xerox, and Intel announced Ethernet as a way to interconnect computer systems. The protocol layers of DECnet, which later influenced the OSI protocol stack, worked well in implementing the signaling and access scheme for nodes attached to Ethernet.

Today, DEC's minicomputer systems run either VMS or ULTRIX, which is a version of UNIX. DEC's line of Alpha processors is used in desktop and server systems and runs a variety of operating systems, including Windows NT.

**RELATED ENTRIES**   Alpha Microprocessors, DEC; DECnet; *and* OpenVMS

## INFORMATION ON THE INTERNET

| | |
|---|---|
| Digital Equipment Corporation | http://www.digital.com |
| DEC's Network site | http://www.networks.digital.com |
| DEC's Software site | http://www.software.digital.com |
| Open VMS information | http://openvms.digital.com |
| Digital UNIX information | http://www.unix.digital.com |
| Digital AltaVista information | http://altavist.software.digital.com |
| Ongoing research at DEC | http://www.research.digital.com |

## DECnet

DECnet is Digital Equipment Corporation's name for the set of hardware and software products that implement the DNA (Digital Network Architecture). DECnet defines communication networks over Ethernet local area networks, FDDI (Fiber Distributed Data Interface) metropolitan area networks, and wide area networks that use private or public data transmission facilities. It can use TCP/IP and OSI protocols, as well as Digital's DECnet protocols.

DECnet was first announced in 1977 along with the introduction of the DEC VAX 11/780. It was originally designed for parallel interfaces that connected nearby systems (within 30 feet). In 1980, Digital, Xerox, and Intel announced Ethernet as a way to interconnect computer systems. The protocol layers of DECnet (which later influenced the OSI protocol stack) worked well in implementing the signaling and access scheme for nodes attached to Ethernet. Digital makes a number of Ethernet products; they are described under "DEC (Digital Equipment Corporation)."

In 1991, DEC announced ADVANTAGE-NETWORKS, a strategy that adds support for other protocols, such as TCP/IP, and the ability to build multiprotocol backbones that can transport DECnet, TCP/IP, and other protocol data.

**RELATED ENTRY**    DEC (Digital Equipment Corporation)

## Dedicated Circuits

A dedicated circuit is a data-communication pathway between two communicating systems. The circuit may exist as a physical cable between two systems or may exist logically within a multiplexed or switched system. Dedicated circuits, created across a telephone network, are usually leased on a contract basis, requiring modems at each end. Leased lines are permanent point-to-point connections that are usually billed based on the distance and throughput of the line. A dedicated circuit is either a voice-grade analog line or a digital line such as a T1-type service that provides transmission speeds up to 1.544 Mbits/sec or a T3 line at 45 Mbits/sec.

A dedicated circuit can also exist logically (as a virtual circuit) in switching networks such as X.25, frame relay, and ATM networks. A path with a guaranteed bandwidth is predefined through the network by the service provider. Charges are based on packets sent, so the overall cost is lower than leased lines.

Network administrators evaluating the use of these lines must weigh the cost of a leased line based on the amount of traffic that will traverse it and whether an uninterrupted connection must be maintained at all times. If traffic is light, or peaks during parts of the day, a dial-up line may be appropriate. A dial-up line may also supplement a dedicated circuit. Dial-up lines are appropriate for occasional transmissions such as e-mail. Dedicated lines are best when traffic is constant and service is required on an immediate basis.

In contrast, ISDN (Integrated Services Digital Network) provides nondedicated circuit capabilities and allows users to dial any other site. The emerging DSL (Digital Subscriber Line) services offer similar capabilities at higher data rates.

**RELATED ENTRIES**    Capacity; Channel; Circuit-Switching Services; Communication Service Providers; Communication Services; Leased Line; Multiplexing; Point-to-Point Communications; T1/T3; Telecommunications and Telephone Systems; Throughput; Transmission Media, Methods, and Equipment; Virtual Circuit; VPN (Virtual Private Network); *and* WAN (Wide Area Network)

# Dedicated Server

A dedicated server is a computer system that is used exclusively to provide services to network users. In contrast, a nondedicated server is set up in environments with light network loads in which local users run processes and applications on a system that is running the server process. Peer-to-peer operating systems like Microsoft Windows can operate in this way. Each workstation can share its resources with other network users while allowing the local user to access those resources as well.

Dedicated servers are recommended in busy network environments. When a server is dedicated, there is little chance that users or applications will disturb the network operating system or slow down its performance. For example, a user might run an application that locks up the system. Other users cannot access the system until it is rebooted, and worse, may lose open files that are stored on the server.

The decision to run a computer in dedicated or nondedicated mode is not much of an issue with the drastic price drops in computer hardware. It is best to purchase servers for dedicated use and let users share resources on their personal computers for occasional use, not as full-time file-sharing systems. Another reason for using dedicated servers is so you can secure them in a locked closet or data center with other shared network equipment.

**RELATED ENTRIES**    Network Operating Systems; Servers

# Delay

Delay is a measure of the amount of time it takes for a bit of data to travel across a transmission line. Delay may be caused by properties of the transmission medium, or it may be caused by bottlenecks in the data delivery process. The former is known as propagation delay while the latter is referred to as the throughput of a system, which is a measure of all the factors in a communication system that determine the actual data transfer rate between two systems.

## Propagation Delays

A transmission medium such as copper wire has a much higher propagation delay than fiber-optic wire, and this delay increases with distance. A typical LAN has a delay that is measured in milliseconds. This is a large amount of time when compared to the speed of most processors. A typical computer can execute thousands of instructions in the time it takes a message to traverse a LAN link. Delay is a primary reason for limiting the maximum length of a cable on a shared LAN.

Assume a computer at one end of the cable puts a signal on the cable. At the other end of a cable, another computer puts a signal on the cable as well because, due to propagation delay, it has not detected that the other computer has already put a signal on the cable. A collision occurs that must be corrected, and this causes throughput delays on the network. If distances are long, time lags occur that may result in inappropriate carrier sensing, and thus increased collisions.

## Throughput Delays

The throughput of a system is determined by a number of factors, including the packet processing speed of routers along the path, the number of devices and networks between two systems, and the specified bit rate of the medium (i.e., 10Base-T Ethernet delivers 10 Mbits/sec while a modem link delivers approximately 28 Kbits/sec). The latter is determined by the designers of the network based on propagation delay, among other things.

Throughput on a shared LAN is also determined by the number of computers on the system and how often they vie for access to the network. Shared Ethernet networks will experience increased collisions as more and more users attempt to transmit. If the bus is constantly busy, collisions can occur so often that performance drops drastically. It is estimated that network traffic must be less than 40 percent of the bus capacity for the network to operate efficiently.

A queuing delay will also affect throughput. Assume several users on a LAN attempt to transmit across a slow WAN link. Traffic will back up on the LAN link to the point where packets might be dropped. Dropped packets cause even more delay because they must be reprocessed.

Switching delays occur in devices likes hubs, bridges, and routers that need to receive an entire packet before making a forwarding or routing decision. The better the equipment, the faster these decisions are made. Thus, bridges and routers are often rated based on packets/sec processing capabilities.

**RELATED ENTRIES**    Bandwidth; Capacity; Channel; Circuit; Data Communication Concepts; Data Transfer Rates; Electromagnetic Spectrum; PPS (Packets per Second); Signals; Throughput; *and* Transmission Media, Methods, and Equipment

## Demand Priority Access Method

Demand priority is an access method designed for use with the 100-Mbit/sec Ethernet standard called 100VG-AnyLAN. Demand priority takes advantage of structured wiring systems and a hub-centric approach to network design. Unlike hubs in Ethernet 10Base-T, the 100VG-AnyLAN hubs control access to the network, eliminating the need for workstations to sense for a carrier signal as is done with standard Ethernet's CSMA/CD (carrier sense multiple access/collision detection).

As shown on the right in Figure D-17, when a workstation using demand priority needs to transmit, it sends a request to the hub. If the network is not busy, the workstation gets permission to transmit. All transmissions are directed through the hub, which provides rapid switching to the destination node. Transmissions are between sender and receiver only, eliminating the ability of one node to listen to another node's transmissions. In contrast, CSMA/CD network transmissions are broadcast over the entire network.

If multiple requests for transmission arrive at the hub, the highest priority is serviced first. If two workstations request the same priority at the same time, both are serviced by alternating between the two. This transmission method is superior to CSMA/CD, in which workstations compete for access to the cable on their own as shown on the left in Figure D-17. Contention occurs when two or more workstations attempt access at the same time. Each workstation backs off and waits for a period of time before attempting access again. This reduces performance and causes more contention because workstations still need to compete for access to the cable.

It is possible to designate priority service for time-sensitive local area network traffic, particularly real-time video. In this way, the video is delivered on time before other traffic. If the network does not have enough bandwidth to deliver the video, packets are dropped and the image appears jerky to the viewer.

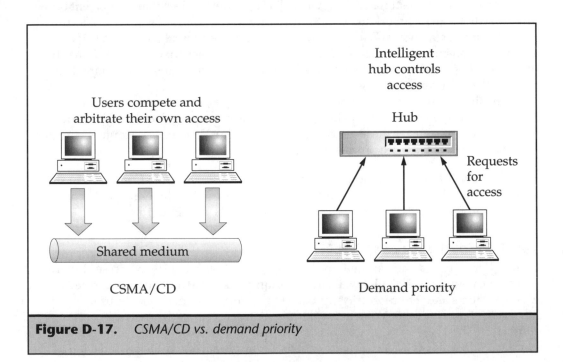

**Figure D-17.** *CSMA/CD vs. demand priority*

**RELATED ENTRIES**   100VG-AnyLAN; Ethernet; Medium Access Control Methods; *and* Network Concepts

## Demodulation

Demodulation is the reverse modulation process. When a signal is modulated, it is added to a carrier signal so that the receiving station can "tune in" to the carrier signal and receive the signal that was modulated onto the carrier. For example, when you tune in an AM radio station, your radio demodulates the radio broadcast from the carrier signal that you dialed into.

In computer communication, a sending modem (modulator/demodulator) modulates a digital signal into an analog wave for transmission over a voice telephone line. A modem at the receiving end demodulates the signal back into digital information.

**RELATED ENTRIES**   Modems; Modulation Techniques

## DES (Data Encryption Standard)

DES is a private-key symmetrical cryptosystem, meaning that both sender and receiver must know the same key. This method is also called secret-key or symmetrical cryptography. The problem with this scheme is that sender and receiver must safely exchange the key. An alternative scheme is public-key cryptography. In this scheme, each person gets a pair of keys, one to hold privately and one to make public. A sender encrypts a message with the receiver's public key and that message can only be decrypted with the receiver's private key. The freely available public key solves the key exchange problem.

DES was developed by IBM in the 1970s. It was adopted by the National Bureau of Standards, which is now called the NIST (National Institute of Standards and Technology). DES became an official U.S. government standard for data encryption in 1977. NIST extended DES as a government standard until 1999. However, NIST has indicated that it may not extend that status past 1999.

DES has been exposed to many years of evaluation and "attack" and is considered safe. Only in June of 1997 was DES successfully attacked by a coordinated effort involving many computers connected over the Internet, but even the attackers stated that they still considered DES safe for many applications.

DES is a private-key cryptographic technique that uses an algorithm to encrypt data in 64-bit blocks using a 56-bit key. The encryption algorithm is explained further under "Cryptography." The 56-bit key provides quadrillions of possible key combinations. In addition, every block in the data stream is encoded using a different variation of the key, which reduces the chance that a coding scheme might be revealed over a lengthy transmission.

**D**

**RELATED ENTRIES**   Authentication and Authorization; Certificates and Certification Systems; Cryptography; Digital Signatures; Private-Key Cryptography; Public-Key Cryptography; *and* Security

**INFORMATION ON THE INTERNET**

| | |
|---|---|
| Serge Hallyn's DES page | http://www.cs.wm.edu/~hallyn/des |
| Greg Sterijevski's DES page | http://raphael.math.uic.edu/~jeremy/crypt/contrib/stj.html |
| Raewyn Michele Smith's DES page | http://snoopy.falkor.gen.nz/~rae/DES.html |
| David Buttler's DES page | http://www2.andrews.edu/~buttler/des_project.html |
| RSA Laboratories | http://www.rsa.com/rsalabs/newfaq |
| Ron Rivest's Links (possibly the most complete set of security links on the Web) | http://theory.lcs.mit.edu/~rivest/crypto-security.html |
| Peter Gutmann's Security and Encryption-related Resources and Links | http://www.cs.auckland.ac.nz/~pgut001/links.html |
| Terry Ritter's Cyphers by Ritter page | http://www.io.com/~ritter |

## Desktop Management

*See* Network Management.

## DFS (Distributed File System), Microsoft

Microsoft DFS is designed to make it easier to access files on networks. It provides a way to unite files on different computers under a single name space. To the user, files appear as if they are in one location rather than on separate computers. A hierarchical tree provides a view of these files, and users can "drill down" through the tree to find just the information they are looking for.

The user does not need to know or care about the physical location of the file, only where it is located in the hierarchical view. That means that users no longer search for files by opening file servers and disk drives and looking through a separate directory structure on each. Instead, users look through a logical directory that places shared information in a place that makes more sense to users and administrators alike. With DFS, an administrator does up-front work to logically organize information, so users don't have trouble finding it later on.

Some of the benefits of DFS are outlined here:

- Users can access information with DFS's hierarchical view of network resources. Administrators can create custom views to make file access easier for users.

- Volumes consist of individual shares and those shares can be at many different locations. A share can be taken offline without affecting the rest of the volume.

- To ensure that critical data is always available, administrators can set up alternate locations for accessing data by simply including the alternate locations under the same logical DFS name. If one of the locations goes down, the other location is automatically selected.

- Response time can be improved by load-balancing the system. Often-accessed files can be stored in multiple locations and the system will automatically distributed requests across the drives to balance traffic during peak usage periods.

- Users don't need to know about the physical location of files. Administrators can physically move files to other drives, but to the user the files still appear under the same location in the hierarchical tree.

- Client access to shares is cached to improve performance. The first time a user accesses a published directory, the information is cached and used for future references.

- DFS simplifies enterprise backups. Since a DFS tree can be built to cover an entire enterprise, the backup software can back up this single "tree," no matter how many servers/shares are part of the tree. The tree can include Microsoft Windows desktops as well.

- Graphical administration tool makes it easy to configure volumes, DFS links, and remote DFS roots.

DFS fits into an organization's Internet and intranet strategy. The Web page of individual departments or even users can be included within the directory tree. DFS can also hold HTML links so if linked pages are moved to a different physical location, all links pointing to the pages will not have to be reconfigured.

## DFS Volumes

A DFS volume starts out by being hosted by a specific computer. There may be many individual DFS volumes available on a network, and each will have its own distinct name. Windows NT 4.0 (or greater) servers are currently the only systems that can host DFS volumes. An organization might have a master DFS volume that contains *links* to other DFS volumes at the department or division level. Another volume might tie together shares that are common in each department, such as public documents.

In the DFS volume name shown here, the hosting computer name is \ \ *Server_Name*:

\ \ *Server_Name* \ *DFS_Share_Name* \ *path* \ *name*

Like a local file system, a DFS volume has a root that is its starting point. This is represented by *DFS_Share_Name*. The reference to *path* \ *file* can be any valid pathname.

Figure D-18 illustrates how links work. Three departments—Marketing, Engineering, and Research—have set up their own name spaces to fit their own needs. The corporate DFS volume links into specific parts of these shares as needed to provide corporate users with information from other locations in the organization. When a link is accessed, the junction between two different DFS volumes is crossed and the server that provides the DFS root changes. This is transparent to the user, however.

### INFORMATION ON THE INTERNET

Microsoft's NT Server site          http:/ /www.microsoft.com/ntserver

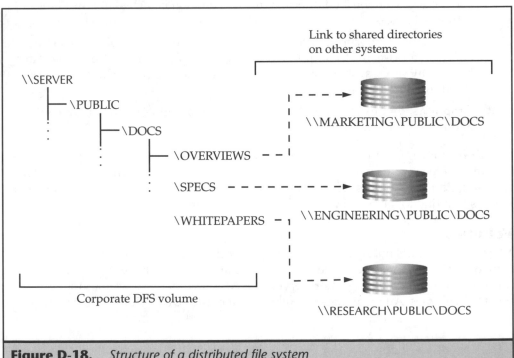

**Figure D-18.** *Structure of a distributed file system*

## DFS (Distributed File System), The Open Group

DFS is a version of the AFS (Andrew File System) that is included with The Open Group's DCE (Distributed Computing Environment). Transarc is responsible for DFS. Its Web site is listed under "Information on the Internet" at the end of this section.

**RELATED ENTRIES**    AFS (Andrew File System); DCE (Distributed Computing Environment), The Open Group; *and* Distributed File Systems

**INFORMATION ON THE INTERNET**

Transarc Corporation                    http://www.transarc.com

## DHCP (Dynamic Host Configuration Protocol)

**D**

DHCP is designed to help reduce configuration time for TCP/IP networks by automatically assigning IP addresses to clients when they log on. DHCP centralizes IP address management on central computers that run the DHCP server program.

Although you can manually assign permanent IP addresses to any computer on your network, DHCP provides a way to automatically assign addresses. In order to have a client get its IP address from a DHCP server, you configure the client to "obtain its address automatically from a host server." This option appears in the TCP/IP configuration area of most clients' operating systems. Once these options are set, the client "leases" an IP address from the DHCP server every time it boots.

At least one DHCP server must exist on a network. Once the DHCP server software is installed, you create a DHCP scope, which is a pool of IP addresses that the server manages. When clients log on, they request an IP address from the server, and the server provides an IP address from its pool of available addresses.

DHCP is a boon to network administrators. It relieves configuration problems that are inherent with manual configurations. Review this chart to see how DHCP alleviates problems:

**Without DHCP**

In manual configuration, you must assign an address at every workstation on the network. Users will need to call you for an IP address since you don't want to depend on them to configure their own IP addresses.

Configuring a large number of addresses may lead to errors that are difficult to track down and may cause errors in communication on the network.

**With DHCP**

The DHCP server automatically leases IP addresses to users when they log on. You only need to specify the scope of addresses that can be leased at the server. You are no longer burdened by calls from users who need an IP address, or worse, the need to go on-site and configure the address.

DHCP automatically manages IP addresses and eliminates errors that might disrupt communication. It automatically reassigns unused addresses.

### Without DHCP

You'll eventually run out of IP addresses for a subnet of the network or for the entire network if you don't carefully manage the assigned addresses.

You must change the IP address in a workstation if it moves to another subnet.

Mobile users that move from one location to another will need to change the IP addresses of their computers if they connect with a different subnet of the network.

### With DHCP

DHCP leases addresses for a period of time, which means that addresses are made available to assign to other systems. You are less likely to run out of available addresses.

DHCP automatically assigns an IP address that is appropriate for the subnetwork to which the workstation attaches.

As above, DHCP automatically assigns IP addresses to mobile users at the subnet where they attach. Mobile computing becomes more of a reality as management headaches are reduced.

## The Leasing Sequence

DHCP is an Internet protocol that has its roots in the *bootstrap protocol*, or BOOTP, which is used to configure diskless workstations. DHCP takes advantage of the messaging protocol and configuration techniques that are already defined for BOOTP, including the ability to assign IP addresses. This similarity also allows existing routers that relay BOOTP messages between subnets to relay DHCP messages as well. Because of this, a single DHCP server can handle IP addressing for multiple subnets.

The process of acquiring an IP address is described here:

- ■ **Step 1** The client workstation boots and initializes with a "null IP address" that lets it communicate with the DHCP server using TCP/IP. It prepares a message that contains its MAC address (for example, the hardwired address of its Ethernet adapter) and its computer name. The message may also contain a previous IP address that it has leased from a DHCP server. The client "broadcasts" the message on the network and continues to send the message until it receives a response from the server.

- ■ **Step 2** Any DHCP server can receive the message and prepare to lease the client an IP address. If a server has a valid configuration for the client, it prepares an "offer" message, which contains the client MAC address, the IP address that the server is offering to lease, a subnet mask, the IP address of the server, and the time length of the lease. The offered address is marked as "reserved." DHCP servers broadcast offer messages over the network.

- ■ **Step 3** When the client receives the offer messages and accepts one of the IP addresses, the client broadcasts a message to confirm which DHCP server it has accepted as an IP address from.

■ **Step 4** Finally, the DHCP server confirms the whole arrangement with the client.

Note that clients initially broadcast IP address requests on the network, which means that any DHCP server can receive the message. Therefore, more than one DHCP server might attempt to lease the client an IP address by sending it offers. The client only accepts one offer, then broadcasts the confirmation message on the network. Since the message is broadcast, all DHCP servers can receive it. The message contains the IP address of the DHCP server that leased the IP address it will use, so other DHCP servers retract their offer to lease an IP address and return the IP address to the address pool to be assigned to other clients.

**RELATED ENTRIES**    Internet; Intranets and Extranets; IP (Internet Protocol); TCP (Transmission Control Protocol); *and* TCP/IP (Transmission Control Protocol/Internet Protocol)

**D**

### INFORMATION ON THE INTERNET

| | |
|---|---|
| IETF Dynamic Host Configuration Working Group with drafts and RFC links | http://www.ietf.org/html.charters/dhc-charter.html |
| Ralph Droms' DHCP page (links to pertinent IETF drafts and RFCs) | http://www.bucknell.edu/~droms/dhcp |
| John Wobus's DHCP FAQ | http://web.syr.edu/~jmwobus/comfaqs/dhcp.faq.html |

## Diagnostic Testing Equipment

*See* Testing and Diagnostic Equipment and Techniques.

## Dial-up Line

A dial-up line is a connection or circuit between two sites through a switched telephone network (i.e., the telephone network). In the data communication world, a dial-up line forms a link between two distant computers or local area networks. Features that are important in data communication are listed here:

■ Dial-up lines provide any-to-any connections. The originating site can call any other site, unlike dedicated lines that connect two sites.

■ Modems are required on both ends of a dial-up line.

■ A call setup and disconnect sequence is required for dial-up lines.

- Dial-up lines are inexpensive and charges are incurred only during connection time and are based on distance. They are useful for occasional file transfers, e-mail transmissions, anad backup links.

- The transmission rate is typically 28,800 bits/sec with the V.34 standard and the use of compression, but higher rates (up to 56 Kbits/sec) are available for download speeds.

**RELATED ENTRIES**   Circuit-Switching Services; Communication Service Providers; Communication Services; Leased Line; Modems; Point-to-Point Communications; Telecommunications and Telephone Systems; *and* WAN (Wide Area Network)

# Digital Signatures

Digital signatures are based on public-key encryption techniques in which people have a pair of keys, one public and one private. The private key is never given out while the public key is made freely available. To send a private message to someone, you encrypt the message with the recipient's public key. The recipient then decrypts the message with his or her private key. A digital signature works in the opposite direction. In the most basic usage, the sender uses his or her private key to encrypt a message. The receiver then uses the sender's public key to open the message. These two strategies are pictured in Figure D-19. However, for true security, additional steps are needed as discussed in this section.

Digital signatures are the equivalent of a handwritten signature, but also much more. When properly implemented, they provide a high level of authenticity for electronic messages. As message exchange and electronic commerce on the Internet grows, so will the need for digital signatures. Electronic messages are susceptible to alteration and may be forged. The purpose of digital signatures is to provide assurances that messages are not forged, have not been altered, and were sent at the time defined in the message.

## The Signing Process

Here's an example of how the process works. Bob is going to the horse races and Alice wants Bob to place $300 on Rock-n-Roll, the horse. Alice and Bob have digital encryption software loaded on their computers, so Alice sends Bob a message to bet on the horse. Of course, Bob will wonder about the authenticity of the message and want to make sure that Alice doesn't disavow having sent it if the horse loses. The message must be digitally signed before Bob will accept it and go to the races.

### Step 1: Digest

Alice puts her digital message software to work on securing her message. Electronic mail and messaging programs like Microsoft Exchange include all the appropriate software for handling digital signatures. The software will warn users when messages may be corrupted or altered as described in the following sections.

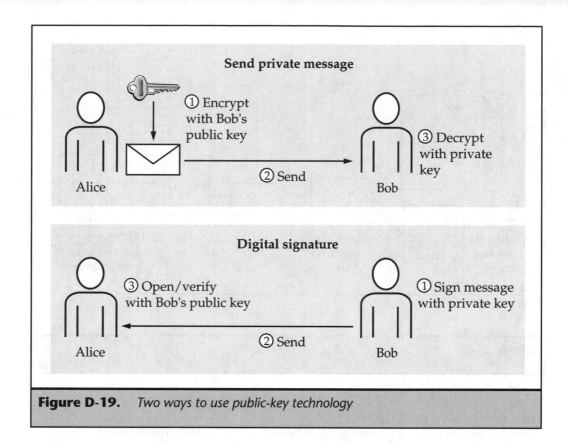

**Figure D-19.** *Two ways to use public-key technology*

First, a *message digest* (also sometimes called a hash) must be created as shown in Figure D-20. A message digest is a long string of numbers that is calculated by using the text of the message as the basis for the calculation. A one-way encryption algorithm is applied to create this digest.

Now Alice encrypts the digest with her private key to create a digital signature. When Bob receives the message, he calculates the same one-way function on the message, then compares his resulting message digest with the one sent with the message by Alice. If they compare, Bob knows the message is authentic.

### Step 2: Close and Send
Once Alice has produced a message digest, she is ready to package and send it to Bob. Alice now encrypts the digest and the message with her private key, thus digitally signing the document. This is sent to Bob. If Bob does not have Alice's public key, Alice can also send a copy of her digital certificate, which contains her public key (as discussed in the next section).

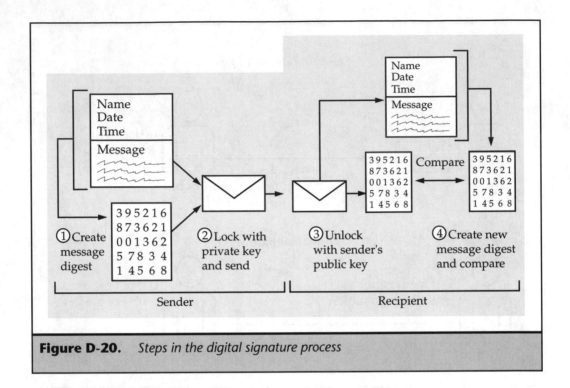

**Figure D-20.** *Steps in the digital signature process*

## Step 3: Receive and Open

Once Bob receives the message, the digital message software on his computer uses Alice's public key (which he may pull out of Alice's digital certificate) to decrypt the message, revealing the message digest.

Bob now uses the same one-way function that Alice used to calculate a message digest on the contents of the message. If this new message digest is the same as the message digest that Alice put in the message, then Bob knows that the message is authentic, that it has not been compromised, and that Alice cannot disavow or repudiate it at a later time (i.e., in a court of law).

All of the above assumes that the public key is trusted. If you give a friend your public key in person, your friend will trust it. But how can a merchant on the Internet or a business partner be sure that your public key is authentic? Certificates provide a solution, as discussed under "Certificates and Certification Systems."

Over the last few years, product vendors and companies wishing to do business on the Internet have been working overtime to come up with digital signature standards that can be put into software and used on public networks. Legislation has been proposed, and some states are licensing and regulating companies that provide certificate authority services. Two initiatives having to do with digital signatures are

DSig (Digital Signature Initiative) and PKI (public-key infrastructure). See "PKI (Public-Key Infrastructure)" for a discussion of the latter.

## Digital Signature Initiative

The World Wide Web Consortium's DSig (Digital Signature Initiative) is designed to develop trust on the Internet. DSig is a response to requests by vendors such as Microsoft, JavaSoft, and IBM to develop an interoperable infrastructure for digital signatures and code signing. These vendors had already introduced incompatible code-signing schemes. Microsoft had its Authenticode, JavaSoft had its JAR (Java Archive), and IBM had its Cryptolopes. But these competing standards are not interoperable. The DSig project is working to develop digital signature interoperability. This is done with digital signatures, identity certificates, packing lists, and content label technologies.

There are two mechanisms at the core of the project:

- Provide signature labels that allow a user or organization that signs an object to make statements about the object. These statements are called assertions and/or endorsements.

- Provide trust management systems that allow end users to verify the creator of downloadable code and what it does by interpreting statements made by the signers of the objects.

For example, a digital signature may hold machine-readable code that makes assertions and endorsements. An example assertion might be "this Microsoft code was designed to run on Windows NT." Another party can make assertions about the code as well, such as "Code x from Microsoft will run with our software." The DSig Signature Label design team is still formulating the specifications and language for assertions and endorsements. The mechanism for doing this will be built into browsers and take place automatically when a user downloads code.

**RELATED ENTRIES**    Certificates and Certification Systems; Kerberos Authentication; PKI (Public-Key Infrastructure); Public-Key Cryptography; Security; *and* SET (Secure Electronic Transaction)

### INFORMATION ON THE INTERNET

| | |
|---|---|
| Cylink Corporation | http://www.cylink.com |
| Cylink's Digital Signature paper | http://www.cylink.com/products/security/digsig |
| Law-on-Line Digital Certificate tutorial | http://lawonline.jp.pima.gov/interim/digsig1.HTM |
| OnWatch's security links page | http://www.public-key.com/sec.html |

| RSA Data Security, Inc. | http://www.rsa.com |
| VeriSign, Inc. | http://www.verisign.com |
| W3C's general security information | http://www.w3.org/pub/WWW/Security |
| W3C's digital signature information | http://www.w3.org/pub/WWW/Security/DSig/Overview.html |

## Digitizing

Digitizing is the process of converting any kind of information to digital information (1s and 0s). An analog signal such as a voice telephone conversation is converted to digital for transmission across a digital link. Sound is digitized for storage in computers or on CD-ROMs. Pictures are digitized with scanners so they can be displayed on computer screens and stored on disk.

**RELATED ENTRIES**    ADC (Analog-to-Digital Conversion); Imaging

## Dijkstra Routing Protocol Algorithm

The Dijkstra routing algorithm enables routers to find a pathway through a mesh of network connections based on the path with the least cost. The algorithm runs through a series of calculations that eventually develops the cost of pathways to nodes and the pathway that has the least cost.

**RELATED ENTRIES**    Link State Routing; Routing Protocols and Algorithms

## Directory Attributes and Management

This section explains directory attributes and management for popular network operating systems, namely Novell NetWare, Windows NT, and UNIX.

There are local file systems and shared or network file systems. Most operating systems today allow files to be shared over a network with other users, so these systems can be called network file systems. However, the level of control over who can access files is much greater with sophisticated network operating systems like Novell NetWare and Windows NT.

A client operating system like Windows 95 has simple access controls for hiding files or for making them read-only. However, these controls are usually designed to protect files from accidental erasure. Another user could easily walk up to such a system, change the access controls, and alter or copy a file. Windows 95 has a logon feature, but its primary purpose is to collect the name of the current user and display a custom desktop for that user rather than protect files on the hard drive of the system.

More sophisticated operating systems like Windows NT have strict logon requirements. No users can access files on the disk unless they are properly logged on, and then they can only access files to which they have permissions. A Windows NT Workstation computer allows several different people to log on under their own user names and work with their own custom desktop and files. No user can see another user's files unless they have been shared by the user. A system administrator controls access to the entire system. If the system is attached to a network, network users can be given access to files on the system. This is the case with Windows NT Server and Novell NetWare 4.x, both dedicated server operating systems.

## Organizing Directories

You can organize directory structures to simplify user access, to provide a more consistent data structure, and to simplify management. Whenever possible, separate document files from program files and organize the structure in a way that makes backup easier. Normally, data files require a more intensive backup cycle than programs since the files in the program directory do not change often. Figure D-21 shows a rudimentary example of a directory structure for a small-office server. Note that applications are stored in the tree under the Applications directory and documents are stored in the tree under the Docs directory. Other directories such as

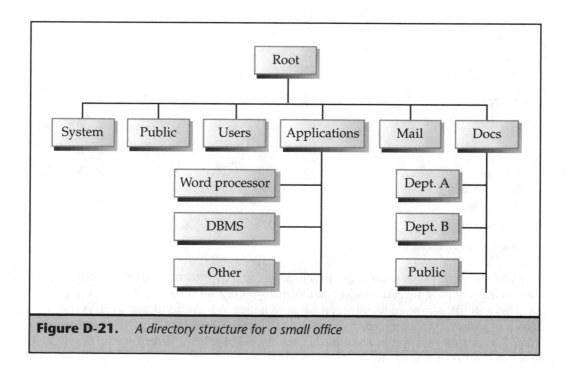

**Figure D-21.** *A directory structure for a small office*

Public may hold Web-based HTML files that users access with their Web browsers. Public may also be where users place files they want to exchange with other network users.

Most network operating systems will create a directory called Users, under which a personal directory is created for each user account. Users typically have full rights to their own directories, which means they can create new branching subdirectories and share files or directories with other users. For example, some users might create their own HTML Web pages for others to access. The user creates a directory and sets the rights/permissions on the directory so that everyone else in the organization can open the files. Rights and permissions are discussed next.

## Security and Access Rights and Permissions

Network operating systems have access rights (called *permissions* in Windows) that grant users specific rights in directories. For example, the Read right allows a user to open but not change a file, while the Write right lets the user change the file. Every network operating system has a specific set of rights/permissions, as shown in the following table. Note that some operating systems such as Windows NTFS (NT File System) clearly provide more security options at the directory level than other operating systems.

| Permission | MS-DOS | NTFS | NetWare | UNIX | OS/2 | MVS | OS/400 | VAX | VM |
|---|---|---|---|---|---|---|---|---|---|
| No Access | | X | X | X | | X | X | X | X |
| List | | X | X | | | | | X | |
| Read | | X | X | X | | X | X | X | X |
| Add & Read | | X | X | | | | X | | |
| Change (Write) | X | X | X | X | X | X | X | X | X |
| Delete | | X | X | | | X | X | X | X |
| Execute | | X | X | X | | X | X | X | |
| Change Permissions | | X | X | | | X | X | X | X |
| Take Ownership | | X | | * | | | | | |

*Available in some versions

When a right/permission is granted to a user in a directory, the user typically *inherits* the same right/permission in subdirectories of that directory. Inherited rights are a boon to directory administration because a user or a group of users can be given access to a whole directory tree in one step. However, administrators/supervisors can "block" inherited rights to prevent users from access to specific directories in a tree or to set custom rights as appropriate.

The fact that rights carry down through the directory tree is of great importance in the planning of directory structures. You should create directory structures that take advantage of the way that rights are set at specific branches of the tree.

Here are some common settings for access to a directory:

■ An administrator can create a subadministrative user at branches in the directory tree by granting that user a full set of rights, including the ability to change the rights/permissions of other users.

■ In order for users to open files in a directory, the Read right is usually sufficient, although List (File Scan) may also be required to display a listing of the files in a directory.

■ If users need to open and change files in a directory, a set of rights that includes List, Read, Add & Read, and Change (Write) are necessary. Delete can also be set if appropriate.

■ If users need to run programs, Read and Execute is required.

Of course, these rights/permissions differ with each operating system. The descriptions above are general and you should refer to information related to each operating system for more information.

Network operating systems typically provide mechanisms for limiting the amount of disk storage space that users have available. Implement this feature to prevent users from filling the drive with unnecessary programs, utilities, files, and other information.

**RELATED ENTRIES**   Access Rights; ACL (Access Control List); File Systems; *and* Rights and Permissions

## Directory Services

A directory service is to a network what white pages are to the telephone system. At the same time, directory services can emulate the yellow pages as well, providing users with an easy way to look up available services. Large organizations everywhere are in desperate need of directory services. Likewise, a universal directory service will be critical on the Internet and for public service networks such as America Online and others.

Common distributed networks have resources and users at many locations. If a user needs to send a message to a person or access a service at a remote site, directory services can help the user locate the user or service. Names are placed in database lists and made available to users. The way the directory services user interface is implemented makes the system either simple and intuitive or complex. Some examples follow:

■ **Graphical user interface**  In this approach, users may see a graphical directory tree of the organization. Branches in the tree represent divisions, departments, or workgroups. Users can "drill down" through the tree to locate people and resources. NDS (Novell Directory Services) uses this approach, as shown in Figure D-22.

- **Address book**  Users may access address books that hold the list of users and resources in their department or other departments they often contact or connect with.

- **Search method**  Users can query the directory services interface to find resources that have a particular class of services, or users with specific roles, such as "trainer" or manager. For example, a user could request a list of servers that provide information on a particular topic.

- **Search agents**  On large networks such as the Internet, special agents can search the network, looking for resources that match specific search criteria.

A typical directory service is organized into a hierarchical tree as shown in Figure D-22. The primary object for organizing the tree is the *OU* (*organizational unit*) object. An OU is a container that contains other objects—usually other OUs or *leaf objects*. Leaf objects are not containers; they are representations of real objects such as servers and printers or users. Note in Figure D-22 that CambriaCorp is a container that holds the DivEast container and DivWest containers. Containers in the tree can be expanded and collapsed to view the leaf objects in them. The DivWest container is expanded and contains leaf objects such as printers, users accounts, and servers. An administrator

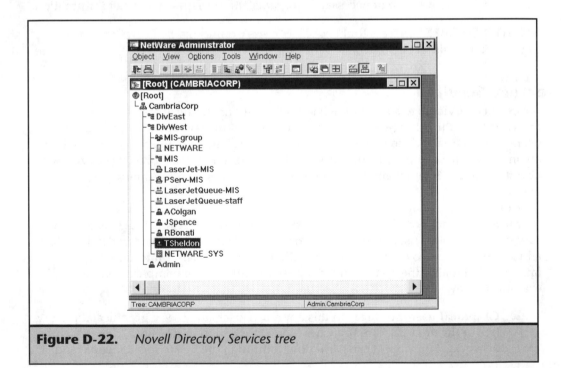

**Figure D-22.**    *Novell Directory Services tree*

can select an object to manage, or a user can select an object to use it or view information about it.

Some typical users of a directory service include people and applications. For example, a white pages server accepts queries from people about other people and their mailing addresses. A Web catalog server accepts text search queries from people and produces relevant document URLs. A security server accepts queries from applications about the access rights of users and other security information. A name server accepts queries from people or applications about information related to accessing network resources like servers and printers.

Almost every major distributed network operating system vendor now has or is implementing a *directory service*. The CCITT X.500 directory services standard provides the model that vendors have been following to build proprietary directory services. However, X.500 has not been fully adopted. Vendors have been locked into their traditional protocols, and X.500 is based on OSI. However, most vendors are now targeting LDAP (Lightweight Directory Access Protocol), an IETF standard directory service that has its roots in X.500 but runs on the TCP/IP protocol instead of the OSI protocol.

## Replication and Partitioning

Because directory services are essential to locating services on the network, they must be available at all times. Directory service information is typically stored in a directory database that can be partitioned and replicated to other locations. This benefits users at remote locations who can access the database locally rather than over wide area network links. Replication also ensures that a copy of the database is available should one of the directory service systems go down.

Partitioning is useful for large databases and provides a way to store parts of the database on different computers. The database is typically partitioned according to geographic locations for wide area networks. For example, a company's Chicago division stores the Chicago partition of the database on its own local server while a master copy of the entire database is stored and maintained at the central corporate office.

Replicating and partitioning a database introduces synchronization problems. Changes made in one database must be made as soon as possible in replicas. Fortunately, a database that provides a list of services for users' convenience can tolerate a few seconds' delay in getting its updates, unlike other types of distributed databases, such as online transaction processing systems.

## Security Issues

Most of the discussion above has assumed that a company maintains a directory service of internal users and resources. This would be an intracompany directory service. However, the X.500 goal is to make all users on global networks accessible using directory services. The Internet is an example of an international system in which millions of users can exchange electronic mail, and users can search for services that might be available on Internet-connected networks. The DNS (Domain Name

System) provides a way to locate servers and organizations on the Internet by specifying a unique name (i.e., http://www.whitehouse.gov), but it does not go far enough. A global directory service is necessary if we want to be able to locate anyone anywhere.

However, many organizations are not ready to expose their internal employee and resource lists to outsiders. Why would an organization want to make its employee list available to headhunters in the high-technology arena? Why would they open themselves up to a potential flood of electronic junk mail? Time will tell. For now, intercompany directory services and the X.500 standard have limited acceptance due to these questions.

Another aspect of directory service security is the ability of the service to authenticate users and grant them access to the directory. Most vendors are implementing X.509 public-key encryption standards, which can provide single logon to a variety of network services after users have checked in with the directory. A unique session ID is created to track users during their online sessions. In addition, an encrypted channel can also be implemented to prevent hackers from making sense out of information that crosses the line.

## Metadirectories

Metadirectories is the term used for products that integrate information from multiple directory services. The purpose of metadirectories, and the reason why many organizations are implementing them, is to integrate disparate directory service information into a single location or registry. These directories range from address books and e-mail information to network operating systems' user account databases, in addition to the dedicated naming services described above. In the past, an organization that implemented many different types of directories had to manually enter changes as users joined or left the company or changed job positions. Metadirectories can help synchronize this information.

## Available Services

This section describes some of the directory services and related protocols of importance to network administrators.

**X.500 DIRECTORY SERVICES**    X.500 directory services are a family of standards developed as an OSI standard by ISO and the CCITT (now referred to as ITU). X.500 was one of the first standards for providing white pages directory services, but it remains a largely unused standard because the TCP/IP protocol suite became the industry's de facto network protocol instead of the OSI protocols. See "X.500 Directory Services" for more information.

**LDAP (LIGHTWEIGHT DIRECTORY ACCESS PROTOCOL)**    LDAP is a subset of the X.500 naming standard. Its primary claim to fame is that is runs on TCP/IP networks and reduces the amount of network traffic exchanged between a client and an X.500 directory database. LDAP is now a widely accepted directory service and is discussed further under "LDAP (Lightweight Directory Access Protocol)."

**BANYAN STREETTALK**    StreetTalk is the directory service originally built into the Banyan VINES network operating system but now available to run on other operating systems. It is designed to integrate Banyan enterprise networks, SCO UNIX, Novell NetWare, and Windows networks. Refer to "Banyan VINES" for additional information.

**DCE DIRECTORY SERVICES, THE OPEN GROUP**    The Open Group's DCE (Distributed Computing Environment) includes its own directory services that are integrated with other DCE components as described under "DCE (Distributed Computing Environment), The Open Group." LDAP clients are now supported in DCE.

**NETSCAPE DIRECTORY SERVICES**    Netscape's Directory Server is designed to be a central place for adding, modifying, and removing user information. It can organize and distribute the information throughout a series of servers on an organization's intranet. The services can be integrated with Netscape's SuiteSpot to provide structured information and group information for the entire suite of applications. Directory Server implements advanced LDAP support and tools for writing directory-enabled apps. It also includes enhancements for continuous operation and heterogeneous replication between LDAP servers. See "Netscape" for more details.

**NDS (NOVELL DIRECTORY SERVICES)**    NDS is a feature in NetWare 4.x that implements a distributed directory service similar to the X.500 specification. Novell has adapted NDS for use on Windows NT and UNIX platforms. See "NDS (Novell Directory Services)" for more information.

**WINDOWS NT SERVER DIRECTORY SERVICES**    Microsoft's directory services runs on Windows NT Server 4.0 or greater and combines features of the Internet's DNS locator service and X.500 naming. LDAP is the core protocol for the service. LDAP allows Microsoft's directory service to work across operating system boundaries and integrate multiple name spaces, thus allowing administrators to manage other vendors' directory services. Refer to "Windows NT Directory Services" for more information.

# Disaster Recovery

Disasters are occurrences that disrupt data communications and a user's access to data. A simple server or communication link failure is a disaster to a company that relies on that server to provide life-saving information or business transaction information. Fires, earthquakes, storms, and theft are all disasters that network managers must prepare for. There are a number of ways to protect data as summarized here:

*D*

■ **Backups** Backing up data is a necessary requirement. Backups must be brought to an off-site location, but the backups must be protected from theft or loss during their transit. *Replication* of data to other sites over WAN links is another option.

■ **Disk mirroring and duplexing** Mirroring and duplexing provide protection against disk failure in servers. With mirroring, data is written to two disks at once. If one disk goes down, the other takes over until the disk is replaced. With duplexing, the disk drive adapter (channel) is duplicated as well to further protect against hardware failure.

■ **Mirrored servers** In this strategy, an entire server is duplicated to protect against the failure of any component. Data is written to both systems simultaneously, and they are interconnected with fast data links to ensure synchronization. If the servers are located in different geographic areas, protection from local disasters such as fire and earthquakes is also facilitated.

■ **Duplicate data centers** Some organizations running mission-critical applications duplicate their entire data center to an off-site location to provide recovery from local disasters.

■ **Distributed computing** In a distributed computing environment, data resources such as user databases or directory services are stored on multiple servers in different locations. Information is replicated from a master server and kept synchronized over time. Users can access data locally rather than over WAN connections. Should a server fail, a replication server can take its place.

■ **Transaction monitoring** A transaction is an update to a record in a database. Transaction monitoring (also called online transaction processing, or OLTP, if it takes place in real time) protects data from corruption if a communication link or system fails during the writing of a transaction. When the system is brought back up, incomplete transactions are backed out. If the database is distributed and writes take place in several locations, any of the links or servers could fail. Two-phase commit procedures ensure that writes are either properly committed in all locations or backed off in all locations.

A communication link keeps services and data at remote sites available. If those services and data are critical to operations, then backup links are required. A backup link can be a line that is always available and in use or a line that is switched into use when another fails. The type of service used depends on the level of service required should a main link fail. Most carriers provide packages that include automatic line failure recovery. The types of available lines are listed here. There are several scenarios:

■ Remote sites are connected with two or more lines that take different paths through the communication grid. Should one line fail, the other can take up the slack until the failed line is restored.

- You can install a backup line with a dial-on-demand router that connects the line should the master line fail. You can also use this line to handle extra traffic should the main line become overloaded.

- Rely on the service provider to provide line backup.

**RELATED ENTRIES**   Backup and Data Archiving; Clustering; Data Migration; Data Protection; Fault Management; Fault Tolerance; Power and Grounding Problems and Solutions; Replication; Security; Storage Management Systems; *and* Storage Systems

## Disk Arrays

*See* RAID (Redundant Arrays of Inexpensive Disks).

## Diskless Workstation

A diskless workstation is an inexpensive computer without a floppy or hard disk drive. It provides a user with network access at a reasonable price, and offers data security because the user can't download data to floppy disks and carry it off-site. Diskless workstations are a consideration for use by temporary employees or installation in unsupervised areas.

When using diskless workstations, you'll need a network interface card that supports the use of a remote boot PROM (programmable read-only memory) chip. Most interface cards have this option, but it's a good idea to make sure. Remote boot PROMs cost about $50 and are added to cards as an option. The PROM allows the workstation to boot from a boot file located on the network server, which means that cards that use PROMs immediately connect with the network cable and server when you turn them on.

**RELATED ENTRIES**   BOOTP (Bootstrap Protocol); Bootstrapping; NC (Network Computer) Devices; *and* NetPC

## Disk Partitioning and Volume Management

*See* Volume and Partition Management.

## Disk Storage Systems

*See* Storage Systems.

## Distributed Applications

Distributed applications are the reason for building enterprise networks. They operate between systems to allow users to run programs and access resources on multiple systems at the same time. A distributed application is divided into two parts—the front-end client and the back-end server. This is the client/server model, which has the objective of dividing the processing load among clients and servers.

Distributed applications take on a whole new meaning with intranets and the Internet. Web browsers provide a universal client for accessing applications and resources on local and remote systems either within the organization or outside. The so-called three-tier architecture for distributed applications puts reusable component software in the middle, between clients and back-end server systems. Components help users interact with any system by hiding the differences between them and by providing unique functions. On the Internet and the intranet, Java and ActiveX provide these component functions.

Application suites like Microsoft BackOffice and Office 95, Netscape's SuiteSpot, and Novell's GroupWise are designed for distributed networks. But distributed applications are not limited to client use. Management applications are designed to take advantage of distributed computing. The SNMP (Simple Network Management Protocol) provides a way to collect information from remote systems and report it back to an administrative workstation.

Refer to "Client/Server Computing" for more information.

## The Component Approach

The component approach breaks up complex programs into smaller components that are easier to manage, deploy, and update. The model provides a better way to distribute and update applications, especially on the Internet. If applications are built as discrete components, then changes and updates can be made only to the components that need them. Updating clients is easier because you only need to send them the updated components.

Components also make building business solutions easier because components can be reused if necessary. Developers can build components with the idea of reusing them in other applications. Microsoft's COM (Component Object Model) and technologies such as CORBA are designed to provide standard interfaces and technologies for distributing and integrating components.

A common three-tier model is pictured in Figure D-23. This model consists of the standard client on the left and back-end server services on the right. In the middle are components that provide services, business rules, transaction management, and other logic.

The client tier interacts with the components and the components interact with the data services tier. The data-services tier is commonly made up of any database management system or storage system that provides data in any format on platforms that range from PC servers to mainframe systems. The whole system can be expanded at any time by upgrading the client, adding or updating new components, or adding new data to the data-services tier.

Components are basically business logic put into objects. The components have a standard interface so that they can be combined like building blocks into complex business solutions. Since components are generally designed to be reusable, a

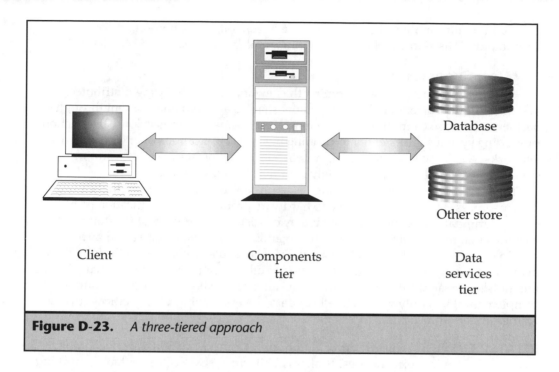

**Figure D-23.** *A three-tiered approach*

component may appear in many different applications. For example, Microsoft's spelling checker is a component that appears in all of its Office products. See also "Component Software Technology" and "Object Technologies."

## Distributed Application Models

There are several models for creating distributed applications and providing a way for client, server, and components to communicate:

- **RPC (remote procedure call)** A session-oriented communication protocol between computers connected across networks. RPCs are generally used for real-time, connection-oriented activities.

- **Messaging services** Messaging services (usually called MOM, or message-oriented middleware) provide a way to exchange information between applications and components using queues and store-and-forward messaging. It is not appropriate for real-time communications.

- **ORB (object-request broker)** An ORB (object request broker) handles the plumbing that allows objects to communicate over a network. For example, an object running on a client sends a message to an object running on the server by sending a message from its ORB interface (called a stub) to the server's ORB interface.

For more information about middleware in general, see "Component Software Technology," "Distributed Object Computing," and "Middleware and Messaging."

## Transaction Processing

The Internet and intranets are becoming the new models for building distributed systems. But the current model of document sharing and dynamic content through back-end database connections is not enough for businesses transactions. Transaction processing systems are essential to running business applications over distributed networks. A transactions processing system allows businesses to run accounting systems and order entry systems safely over distributed systems.

The purpose of a transaction system is to protect data from damage that can occur if an in-process transaction fails due to hardware problems, communication problems, or user termination. A business system may consist of data servers at far-flung locations that must contain the same information. If an inventory is stored over multiple servers to make data more available to local users, changes to the inventory in one location must be immediately posted to other locations. If a glitch occurs during the transaction, all the changes made so far must be backed out. No transaction is complete until it is fully written to all the data servers involved. This topic is covered further under "Transaction Processing."

**RELATED ENTRIES**    Client/Server Computing; Component Software Technology; CORBA (Common Object Request Broker Architecture); DCE (Distributed Computing Environment), The Open Group; DCOM (Distributed Component Object Model); Directory Services; Distributed Computer Networks; Distributed Database; Distributed File Systems; Distributed Object Computing; Information Warehouse; Middleware and Messaging; Multitiered Architectures; Object Technologies; SQL (Structured Query Language); Transaction Processing; *and* Web Middleware and Database Connectivity

## Distributed Computer Networks

A distributed computing system is an evolutionary growth from centralized computer systems and client/server computer systems, as shown in Figure D-24. Distributed computing is basically client/server computing on a wide scale. Data is not located in one server, but in many servers, and these servers might be at geographically diverse areas, connected by WAN links into enterprise networks that join the many formerly autonomous computer systems in workgroups, departments, branches, and divisions of an organization.

Networks built with Web technologies (i.e., intranets and the Internet) are distributed computer networks. Back-end database systems may be connected to these Web servers to provide dynamic information. Web technologies add a new dimension to distributed computing. Web browsers are universal clients that can connect with Web servers, no matter what computer platform or operating system is in use. A new

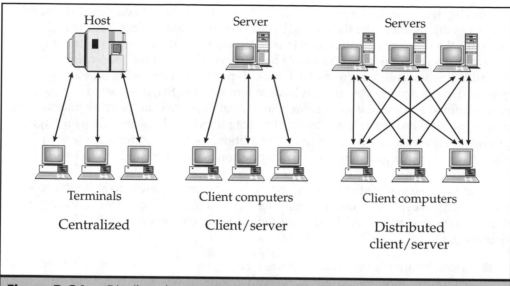

**Figure D-24.** *Distributed computing has evolved from centralized and client/server computing*

trend is to build intranets in which all data is centralized on clustered servers that can handle the requests of many, many users at the same time. In fact, mainframe systems are coming back because organizations need powerful central processing systems. This trend may appear to be in contrast to distributed computing, but in fact many organizations use both approaches.

Distributed computing systems have advantages and disadvantages:

■ The distributed computing model supports access to data already located at diverse sites.

■ Databases are replicated to other locations (i.e., mirrored sites) so that users at those locations can access data locally, rather than use an expensive WAN link to access centralized data at corporate headquarters.

■ Distributing data provides protection from local disasters. If one site goes down, users can still access data at other sites.

■ Distributing data requires complex replication and synchronization over LAN or WAN links that requires more management and supervision. Some managers may feel a loss of security or control in such a system.

■ The evolutionary trend is toward distributed systems built with TCP/IP protocols and Web technologies or operating systems and middleware applications that promote distributed computing. The task is to make the transition as painless as possible.

The client/server model provides the architecture required to deploy distributed systems as discussed under the heading "Client/Server Computing." Figure D-25 illustrates the many ways computers in a distributed, client/server environment can access one another. The mainframe may hold legacy data, or it may serve as a centralized data warehouse (or both). It makes specific data available on staging systems that are accessed by users at local or remote sites. Staging systems and local servers offload some of the work from primary data systems and provide information for specific workgroups or tasks. Users at remote sites can also access data on staging systems or servers located at their sites. In addition, users can communicate with other users to exchange e-mail and form workgroups. For more details, refer to "Data Warehousing."

As mentioned, a distributed computing environment is similar to a client/server environment, except that there are many servers and many clients who access any one of those servers at any time. The distributed environment needs the following components:

- The network *platform* that supports a variety of multivendor products and communication protocols necessary to link those systems. Alternatively, TCP/IP can be a protocol that unites systems due to its wide acceptance.

- Application interfaces that let users make requests to servers using real-time connection-oriented methods or message-passing systems that deliver responses on a more relaxed schedule.

- A *directory naming service* that keeps track of resources and information and where they are located.

- A *time service* to synchronize events among servers that hold related information.

- DBMSs (database management systems) that support advanced features such as *partitioning* and *replication* to provide the distribution of data and ensure the availability, reliability, and protection of that data. See "Distributed Applications" and "Distributed Database" for more information on this subject.

- A *distributed file system* that operates in a peer-to-peer mode to allow users working at workstations to act as both clients and servers. Servers mount or publish directories that client machines can access. Once a server system is accessed, its directories appear to the client as if they are local drives. Refer to "Distributed File Systems" for more information.

- Security features such as authentication and authorization, as well as trust relationships between systems so users can access multiple servers and databases without the need to prove their identity every time they access a remote resource.

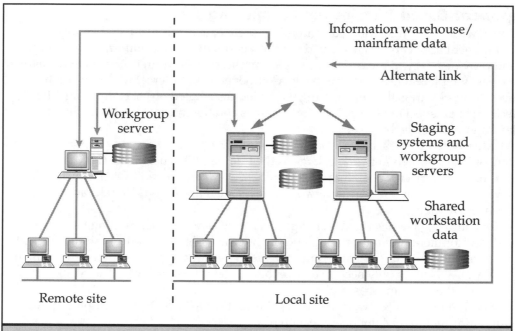

Workgroup server

Information warehouse/ mainframe data

Alternate link

Staging systems and workgroup servers

Shared workstation data

Remote site

Local site

**Figure D-25.**   *Access methods in a distributed computing environment*

## Security in Distributed Environments

Once you've distributed data, adequate security procedures such as authentication, authorization, and encryption must be used. It is assumed that some users will need to access systems at remote sites or that database replication is necessary, and that this will occur over public data networks. Therefore, consider the following security measures. See "Cryptography," "Digital Signatures," and "Security" for more details on these topics.

- **Authentication**   Provides verification of users during an initial logon and a secure way for one server to trust that another server has properly identified a user so users only need to log on once.

- **Authorization**   Provides a way to grant users access to remote resources based on their role or level of authority.

- **Digital signatures and certificates**   Provide enhanced authentication for logon and for message verification.

- **Encryption**   Protects transmitted data from eavesdroppers.

## Component-Based Distributed Computing

The newest trend in distributed computing is to create component applications. Component applications are created with object-oriented programming techniques and provide a way to break down complex applications into small components that are easily replaceable and upgradeable. Components can interact with one another over networks, thus the new paradigm is called distributed object computing. The technique is especially compelling for intranets and the Internet, and is the basis for Java and ActiveX technologies.

Microsoft's view is that component technology is the only way to support access to data on a distributed network as large as the Internet. It is pushing its COM (Component Object Model) technology and DCOM (Distributed COM), which defines how components interact over networks. Developers use ActiveX to take advantage of these technologies.

In contrast, Java has rapidly emerged as a very serious programming language and development tool for intranets and the Internet. The Java model is simple—clients run a Java VM (Virtual Machine) and downloadable Java applets (components) run in the VM. Developers only need to ensure that applets run in the VM. The type of computer the VM runs in is irrelevant.

See "Component Software Technology" and "Distributed Object Computing" for more information on component technology.

**RELATED ENTRIES**    Client/Server Computing; DCE (Distributed Computing Environment), The Open Group; DCOM (Distributed Component Object Model); Directory Services; Distributed Applications; Distributed Database; Distributed File Systems; Distributed Object Computing; Enterprise Networks; Information Warehouse; Middleware and Messaging; Multitiered Architectures; *and* Web Middleware and Database Connectivity

## Distributed Database

A distributed computing system consists of data located at multiple sites. Users should be able to access that data without regard to its location. After all, users are interested in results, not in the details of the computer network. General guidelines for developing distributed database systems are listed here and were originally outlined by Chris J. Date, one of the designers of relational database systems:

- *Local autonomy* allows each site to maintain an independent nature so data and resources can be secured, protected, and managed by local authorities.

- *Noncentralization* eliminates central data sites that represent a single point of failure.

- *Continuous operation* provides services to users, even during backup.

- *Transparency* hides the location of the data from users so they don't need to be concerned where that data is or how to get to it.

- *Fragmentation* (partitioning) provides a way to split the database and store it at multiple sites.

- *Replication* provides a way to copy multiple fragments of the database to multiple sites.

- *Distributed query processing* provides a way for users to query remote sites using the best path to the site and the best resources to satisfy the query.

- *Distributed transaction processing* provides a way to ensure that writes to multiple databases are correctly written on all databases, or backed out if a failure occurs anywhere.

- *Hardware independence* implies support for multivendor computer systems and platforms.

- *Operating system independence* implies support for a number of operating systems.

- *Network independence* implies support for multiple network topologies and communication protocols.

- *DBMS independence* allows users to access any database management system from their client application. See "Database Connectivity."

Once data is distributed, transaction processing, fragmentation, and replication techniques are put in place to ensure the reliability, availability, and protection of data, as described in the following paragraphs.

In heterogeneous environments, database connections between clients and servers is not always easy. There may be a variety of back-end data systems and a variety of client systems in use. Many connectivity options are now available to help bridge the gap between these systems, as discussed under "Database Connectivity" and "Web Middleware and Database Connectivity."

When data is distributed over many database servers, various protection mechanisms are required to ensure that data is properly written to all databases. For example, consider a customer account balance that is updated at three separate remote databases. If a connection to any database fails during the transaction write phase, the databases will be out of synchronization. Transaction processing solves this problem by monitoring the changes that must occur to all the databases involved. If any one of the writes fails, the transaction monitor backs them all out to ensure data integrity. See "Transaction Processing" for more details.

*Partitioning* is a method of splitting a database into related blocks of information and *replication* is the process of copying those blocks to other locations. A master database is still maintained at one site, and a partition is a portion of that database that is replicated to another site. Partitioning and replication are used for the following reasons:

- To make specific data more readily available to users at other sites

■ To protect the data by duplicating it

■ To provide alternate sources for the data should primary or secondary sites fail

Object-oriented systems provide a unique solution for storing data and creating applications in enterprise environments. *Objects* are abstractions of real-world entities such as people in a customer database, invoices in an accounting system, or printers and servers in a network directory services database. See "Object Technologies" for more information.

**RELATED ENTRIES**    Client/Server Computing; Database Connectivity; Data Warehousing; DBMS (Database Management System); Distributed Object Computing; Enterprise Networks; IBM Host Connectivity; Middleware and Messaging; Object Technologies; ODBC (Open Database Connectivity), Microsoft; Replication; SQL (Structured Query Language); Transaction Processing; *and* Web Middleware and Database Connectivity

**INFORMATION ON THE INTERNET**    Refer to "DBMS (Database Management System)" for a complete list of database-related Internet sites.

## Distributed File Systems

Distributed file systems are designed around the client/server model. A typical network might consist of several servers that many different users can access. In addition, peer-to-peer features allow some systems to act as both clients and servers. For example, a user can "publish" a directory, which allows other clients to access it. Once accessed, the directories appear to the client as if they are local drives.

The definition of a distributed file system depends on your point of view. In the recent past, a file system was considered distributed if clients could access files on any server across the network (i.e., in other departments). However, this model required users to keep track of the contents of servers and distinguish among them. Today, most network operating systems provide advanced features like directory services and replication to make access more transparent.

Novell NetWare provides an example of the transition between the old distributed file server model and the distributed file system model. Early versions of the operating system allowed users to access files on any server attached to the network. With the introduction of NDS (Novell Directory Services), administrators could create a hierarchical view that let users see dispersed servers under a single branch of the directory tree. The point is that users don't need to search out servers, they just look in the directory tree under a branch of the tree that is appropriate for the systems or data they are looking for.

Some of the most common network file systems are described here:

■ **AFS (Andrew File System)**    AFS is architecturally similar to NFS. AFS was developed by the Information Technology Center at Carnegie Mellon

University, but its current development and marketing is in the hands of Transarc Corporation, which is made up of former ITC staff. AFS has some enhancements that NFS does not. See "AFS (Andrew File System)" for more details or visit Transarc's Web site at http://www.transarc.com.

■ **DFS (Distributed File System), DCE** DFS is a version of AFS. It serves as the file system component in the DCE (Distributed Computing Environment). See "DCE (Distributed Computing Environment), The Open Group" for more details, or contact Transarc's Web site at http://www.transarc.com.

■ **DFS (Distributed File System), Microsoft** Windows NT 4.0 includes Microsoft's new hierarchical distributed file system. Windows NT DFS is a true distributed file system that lets administrators create custom hierarchical trees that group file resources from anywhere in the organization. See "DFS (Distributed File System), Microsoft." for more details, or visit Microsoft's Web site at http://www.microsoft.com.

■ **NCP (NetWare Core Protocol)** NCP is NetWare's proprietary set of service protocols that the operating system follows to accept and respond to service requests from clients and other servers. It includes services for file access, file locking, security, resource tracking, and other network-related features. See "NCP (NetWare Core Protocol)" for more details, or contact Novell's Web site at http://www.novell.com.

■ **NFS (Network File System)** NFS was originally created by Sun Microsystems, Inc. as a file-sharing system for TCP/IP networks. NFS is running on millions of systems, ranging from mainframes to personal computers. See "NFS (Network File System)" for more details, or visit SunSoft's Web site at http://www.sun.com/solaris/networking/nfs-spec.html.

■ **SMB (Server Message Blocks)** SMB is Microsoft's traditional shared file system that runs on Windows 3.x, Windows 95, and Windows NT platforms. Third-party versions of this protocol are also available, such as Samba. See "SMB (Server Message Blocks)" for more details, or visit Microsoft's Web site at http://www.microsoft.com.

Several additional file protocols have been developed for the Web. Traditionally, when a Web client connects with a Web server, a Web page is downloaded to the user's computer. This may require a series of connections and reconnections until the document is completely downloaded. The first connection downloads text and subsequent connections download graphics and other page elements. New Web-based distributed file systems are designed to download all the related files with a single connection, thus improving performance. The two competing Web file systems are

■ **SunSoft's WebNFS** Implements all the features of NFS and is optimized to run over the Internet or intranets. Also provides a way to implement file security

*D*

mechanisms over the Web. See "NFS (Network File System)" for more details, or visit SunSoft's Web site at http://www.sun.com/webnfs/webnfs.html.

■ **Microsoft's CIFS (Common Internet File System)** CIFS is an extension of Microsoft's SMB (Server Message Blocks) file protocol. Like WebNFS, it is optimized to run over the Internet or intranets and implements file-level security mechanisms. See "CIFS (Common Internet File System)" for more details, or visit Microsoft's Web site at http://www.microsoft.com.

## Distributed File System Features

A distributed file system should provide clients with access to files no matter where they are located. The traditional model consists of many servers, but users may have trouble finding files on those servers. Directory services allow administrators to group files and file storage systems in a hierarchical tree under branches that make sense to people. For example, an administrator could create a branch of the tree called White Papers, then create links to all the directories on all the servers in the organization that contain white papers. Novell's NDS (Novell Directory Services) and Microsoft's DFS provide these features.

A distributed file system should also provide replication. If users throughout the organization require access to files on a particular server, it makes sense to replicate those files to a server that is closer to the user, especially if they are at very remote offices. Replication can also minimize traffic by distributing the load to other servers. A distributed file system should be able to allocate a file request to a server in a replicated set that is most available to handle the request.

A distributed file system should also implement single sign-on so users do not need to enter a password every time they access a file on a connected or replicated system. One additional feature is encryption. If a user is going to access a sensitive file from a secure server, the transmission of the file should be encrypted, especially if the file is being transmitted over the Internet.

A common problem with any shared file system is that multiple users need to access the same file at the same time. Concurrency controls are required to arbitrate multiuser access to files. These controls take the following forms:

■ **Read-only sharing** Any client can access a file, but not change it. This is simple to implement.

■ **Controlled writes** In this method, multiple users can open a file, but only one user can write changes. The changes written by that user may not appear on the screens of other users who had the file open.

■ **Concurrent writes** This method allows multiple users to both read and write a file simultaneously. It requires a tremendous amount of monitoring by the operating system to prevent overwrites and ensure that users see the latest information. Processing requirements and network traffic may make this method unacceptable in many environments, even if implemented properly.

Shared file systems differ in the way they handle concurrent writes. When a client requests a file (or database records) from a server, the file is placed in a cache at the client's workstation. If another client requests the same file, it is also placed in a cache at that client's workstation. As both clients make changes to the file, technically, three versions of the file exist (one at each client and one at the server). There are two methods for maintaining synchronization among the versions:

- **Stateless systems** In stateless systems, the server does not keep information about what files its clients are caching. Therefore, clients must periodically check with the server to see if other clients have changed the file they are caching. This causes excess LAN traffic in large environments, but is usually a satisfactory method for small LANs. NFS is a stateless system.

- **Callback systems** In this method, the server retains information about what its clients are doing and the files they are caching. The server uses a *callback promise* technique to inform clients when another client has changed a file. This method eliminates a lot of network traffic. AFS (and DFS in OSF DCE) are callback systems. As clients change files, other clients holding copies of the files are called back and notified of changes.

There are performance advantages to stateless operations, but AFS retains some of these advantages by making sure that it does not become flooded with callback promises. It does this by discarding callbacks after a certain amount of time. Clients check the expiration time in callback promises to ensure that they are current. Another interesting feature of the callback promise is that it provides a guarantee to a client that a file is current. In other words, if a cached file has a callback promise, the client knows the file must be current unless the server has called to indicate the file changed at the server.

**RELATED ENTRIES**   AFS (Andrew File System); CIFS (Common Internet File System); Client/Server Computing; DCE (Distributed Computing Environment), The Open Group; DFS (Distributed File System), Microsoft; DFS (Distributed File System), The Open Group; Directory Services; Distributed Applications; Distributed Computer Networks; Distributed Database; File Systems; Network Operating Systems; NFS (Network File System); Novell NetWare File System; SMB (Server Message Blocks); *and* UNIX File System

# Distributed Management

As distributed systems grow, central control is often lost. Administrators need a way to manage hardware, software, users, updates, configurations, and security. In addition, there are synchronization problems related to making changes to interdependent systems. Differences in operating systems, hardware, or protocols complicate this.

A distributed management system lets administrators do the following:

■ Manage users and their workstation configurations

■ Manage software distribution, updates, and licensing

■ Manage hardware monitoring, maintenance, and inventory functions

In addition, a management system needs to provide a method for collecting data about the network and reporting it back to managers.

Distributed network management systems can take advantage of the network platform to spread management functions around the network, rather than centralize them in a single data center. Administrators may still run a management system from a single location, but management agents located around the network collect information and report it back to the management system. Information that was impossible to obtain in the past due to time and travel restrictions becomes available to managers. Troubleshooting and preventive maintenance is simplified. Alarms can warn of impending problems.

**RELATED ENTRY**   Electronic Software Distribution and Licensing

## Distributed Object Computing

Distributed object computing provides a way to create reusable code, usually called *objects* or *components*, and a way to distribute those objects to different computers and let them talk to each other over the network using a standard interface. The location of the objects is not important—distributed objects may communicate over local networks, WANs, or the Internet.

So, what are objects? Objects are typically small pieces of program code that perform some very specific task. An entire application can be built by combining objects. Many people consider objects to be "black boxes." The contents of the box (code and/or data) is unimportant. What is important is the functionality provided on the outside of the box. An object is analogous to a box with buttons (input) that produce some output depending on how they are pushed.

Every object is a stand-alone piece of code that can be combined with other objects. Therefore, the object's interface must be standardized so different objects can be combined and can communicate.

The idea is to use objects like building blocks to create full-featured applications. In the network environment, some of those objects run on the user's computer and some run on application servers or other computers. If the application needs updating, only the object that needs updating is changed. Users may obtain these updates automatically when they log onto a server. If a user needs additional functionality, other objects may be downloaded to add that functionality. All of this can take place over internal networks or over the Internet.

Two important object technologies are Java and ActiveX. Both are common on the Internet and are also being implemented on corporate intranets.

The industry is pushing for a standard distributed object model that will conceivably allow objects everywhere to communicate. This is explored further in the following section.

## Distributed Object Environments

Distributed object technologies can be used in-house, between business partners over private networks, or over the public Internet. In the first case, applications developed for in-house use may reside on multiple servers in multiple departments. Some objects are used everywhere throughout the organization. These objects may form the core structure of an organization-wide data processing system. On top of this structure, individual departments or groups can create their own objects to add the enhancements they need. Because objects with a common interface are used, adding new objects or updating existing objects is easy.

If multiple companies are involved in business-to-business relationships over private networks (or the Internet), object technologies can be used to integrate business processes. All that is necessary is a standard object interface that lets each company access common data or objects.

The Internet provides a good example of how object technology can be used. One example is upgrading Web browsers. For example, a VRML (Virtual Reality Modeling Language) component can be added so a user can access a Web site that presents 3-D worlds. This is an example of an object that expands the functionality of a program, but many objects users might download from the Web are quite simple, such as a rotating logo.

Some objects are temporary like the logo just mentioned. They are downloaded and held in the Web server's cache for a while. If the user visits the site again, the logo is pulled up from the cache instead of being downloaded from the site. Some objects are more permanent, like a stock portfolio management utility that gets downloaded when you visit a financial site.

The component-based software model consists of the *components* themselves, *containers*, which are the shells where objects are assembled and run, and *scripting*, which allows developers to write the directives that make components interact. The primary containers are ActiveX and JavaBeans. Scripting languages are ActiveX Script and JavaScript.

You can think of the Web browser as a container that holds objects you collect on the Internet and that provides a place to run those objects. The object adds functionality to the Web browser, and the Web browser provides an environment where the objects can run.

What kind of problems are encountered with distributing applications across networks? In a stand-alone system, components run as a unit in the memory space of the same computer. If a problem occurs, the components can easily communicate that problem with one another. But if components are running on different computers, they need a way to communicate the results of their work or problems that have occurred. A failure in one of the components can be a serious problem with some applications.

**D**

A transaction monitor is essential for running business transactions in a distributed computing environment. Microsoft Transaction Server is an example of a transaction server for distributed object environments. See "Transaction Processing" for more information.

## Object Request Brokers

An ORB (object request broker) handles the plumbing that allows objects to communicate over a network. For example, an object running on a client sends a message to an object running on the server by sending a message from its ORB interface (called a stub) to the server's ORB interface.

CORBA (Common Object Request Broker Architecture) is at the heart of most vendors' object request brokers. CORBA is defined and controlled by the OMG (Object Management Group) at http://www.omg.org. Web sites for some available ORBs that take advantage of CORBA are listed here:

| | |
|---|---|
| DEC's ObjectBroker site | http://www.digital.com |
| Expersoft's PowerBroker site | http://www.expersoft.com |
| Hewlett-Packard's ORB Plus site | http://www.hp.com |
| IONA Orbix's site | http://www.iona.com |
| Visigenic's VisiBroker site | http://www.visigenic.com |

Competing technologies are Microsoft's COM (Component Object Model) and DCOM (Distributed COM). DCOM is the version of COM that works over networks and is the basis of Microsoft's ActiveX technology. Microsoft turned the development of DCOM over to The Open Group (http://www.opengroup.org) to help promote the technology as an industry standard. Information is available at http://www.activex.org.

Both CORBA and DCOM have been under development for years. Although DCOM itself was introduced in late 1996, it has its roots in COM, which is part of Windows. CORBA is basically for all non-Windows environments, and while its acceptance has been slow, interest has surged recently because of its potential for use on the Internet and in the intranet environment. Netscape has implemented CORBA into its Web browsers, and a new technology called "ORBlets" provides a way to let Java applets communicate with CORBA-compliant objects.

DCOM's strength is its roots in the Windows environment, the fact that thousands of programmers are already familiar with the technology, and that many existing applications can take advantage of it with little or no change.

Separate from DCOM and CORBA, Sun Microsystems is developing RMI (Remote Message Invocation), a mechanism that lets Java objects communicate over networks using the same methods used to communicate locally. RMI can be used between Java clients and Java servers.

**RELATED ENTRIES**   ActiveX; COM (Component Object Model); Component Software Technology; Compound Documents; CORBA (Common Object Request Broker Architecture); DCOM (Distributed Component Object Model); IBM Network Computing Framework; Java; Middleware and Messaging; Netscape ONE Development Environment; Object Technologies; OMA (Object Management Architecture); Oracle NCA (Network Computing Architecture); ORB (Object Request Broker); RMI (Remote Message Invocation); *and* Sun Microsystems Solaris NEO

### INFORMATION ON THE INTERNET

| | |
|---|---|
| ComponentWare Consortium, Inc. | http://www.componentware.com |
| Microsoft Corporation | http://www.microsoft.com |
| Netscape Communications Corp. | http://www.netscape.com |
| OMG (Object Management Group) | http://www.omg.org |
| The Open Group | http://www.opengroup.org |
| The Open Group's ActiveX site | http://www.activex.org |
| Software AG Americas, Inc. | http://www.sagus.com |
| Sun Microsystems' Solaris NEO site | http://www.sun.com/solaris/neo |

*D*

## Distributed Processing

There are two definitions of distributed processing, and both are related. First, distributed processing relates to client/server computing, in which an application is divided into a client portion and a server portion. The client runs on a user's computer and handles things like screen display, graphical user interface features, and user input. The server runs on a back-end system and handles requests from multiple clients. It also has direct access to data stored on disk and processes disk information for clients.

The second definition relates to performing complex processing tasks over multiple systems. The processors and memory space in multiple computers are put to work on a task, each getting a part of the task to process. A central computer manages and monitors the process. Networks tie the system together. In some cases, hundreds of computers connected by the Internet have been used to work on a single task. In one case, students used multiple Internet computers and brute force techniques to break an encryption scheme.

**RELATED ENTRIES**   Client/Server Computing; Component Software Technology; DCE (Distributed Computing Environment), The Open Group; Distributed Applications; Distributed Computer Networks; Distributed Database; Distributed File Systems; *and* Distributed Object Computing

# DLSw (Data Link Switching)

DLSw is a standard for tunneling or encapsulating IBM SNA (Systems Network Architecture) and NetBIOS applications across IP (Internet Protocol) networks. The protocol is the result of a need to integrate SNA and non-SNA networks, rather than deploy two separate networks or use a variety of proprietary schemes to tunnel SNA data over non-SNA networks.

Many organizations have built SNA backbone networks that are separate from their router-based internetworks. One reason is that router-based networks have grown at the department level, while SNA networks were built to support organization-wide, mission-critical applications such as transaction processing and business-related applications. SNA is a nonroutable protocol, so it is difficult to run SNA over corporate internetworks.

As it became clear that building two separate networks was a waste of resources, organizations began looking at methods for combining SNA and non-SNA protocols on the same network. Various tunneling schemes were tried, but eventually IBM and other vendors agreed to extend IBM's Data Link Switching specification to work over IP networks. The work was sponsored by the AIW (APPN Implementers Workshop) and submitted to the IETF (Internet Engineering Task Force), where it eventually became the DLSw specification.

DLSw works over DLSw-capable routers, which provide a link over an IP network, as shown in Figure D-26. Note that LANs carrying IBM LLC2 (Logical Link Control, Type 2) frames are connected to an IP network by way of the data link switch multiprotocol routers. The data link switches encapsulate the LLC2 frames in a TCP segment and transport them across the IP connection.

The gist of this is that the DLSw device captures an SNA or NetBIOS session that must cross the IP link, and then terminates the session, encapsulates the frames, and

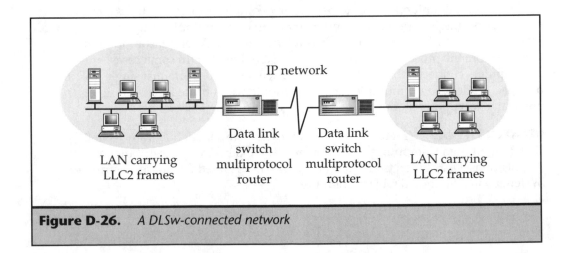

**Figure D-26.**    *A DLSw-connected network*

transports the frames across the link. At the other end of the session, it resumes by making a connection to the appropriate end system.

Major vendors now support DLSw, including IBM, Cisco, Bay Networks, 3Com, and other network router vendors. Some related Web addresses are given at the end of this section (see the heading, "Information on the Internet") to help you find more information on DLSw and DLSw products.

Note that current trends favor extending TCP/IP all the way up to the SNA devices. Web technologies are providing a new way to get at corporate data, even data stored on mainframe systems. IBM and other vendors promote technology that provides SNA access via Web browsers. Cisco (http://www.cisco.com), for example, has its IOS/390 TCP/IP intranet software that provides access to mainframes.

Browser-based access is especially attractive to remote and mobile users who make temporary connections to the corporate network. The best way for them to do that is through a single Web-based interface that gives them access to all the corporate information systems. As TCP/IP-based intranets grow, there will be less SNA traffic to deal with on the corporate network.

**RELATED ENTRIES**    APPN (Advanced Peer-to-Peer Networking); IBM Host Connectivity; IBM Mainframe Environment; IBM Network Computing Framework; IBM Open Blueprint; MPTN (Multiprotocol Transport Networking); SNA (Systems Network Architecture); *and* TCP/IP (Transmission Control Protocol/Internet Protocol)

### INFORMATION ON THE INTERNET

| | |
|---|---|
| AIW (APPN Implementers Workshop) | http://www.networking.ibm.com/app/aiwhome.htm |
| IETF Data Link Switching Working Group | http://www.ietf.org/html.charters/dlswmib-charter.html |
| ACC's DLSw white papers | http://www.acc.com/internet/technology/whitepapers/DLSw.html |
| Bay Network's DLSw white paper | http://www.baynetworks.com/Products/Routers/Protocols/IBM/dlsw.html |
| Cisco Systems' DLSw white paper | http://202.96.59.10/warp/public/614/2.html |

# DME (Distributed Management Environment)

The Open Software Foundation (OSF)'s DME provides a foundation for managing computer systems and networks in the enterprise environment. (OSF is now part of The Open Group.) It is independent of any operating system and supports most network and system management standards.

OSF is the organization that put together the DCE (Distributed Computing Environment), a platform for integrating mixed-vendor systems and for developing distributed applications that work in the environment. DME is the management component that helps administrators manage and maintain the components of a DCE network.

DME has two main components: application services and a framework. Application components provide system management functions such as automatic software updates, license management, and printing services. The framework provides the building blocks for developing management applications. The DME architecture is based on an object model in which all information and operations are classified into objects. The object-oriented approach encourages an open modular system in which developers and vendors can create their own functionality. Components can be mixed and matched as needed. Object services include a management request broker that provides communication among components, an object server that maintains objects for short-term tasks, an event notification system, and a management data repository for storing data contained in managed objects on disk.

### INFORMATION ON THE INTERNET

The Open Group          http://www.opengroup.org

# DMI (Desktop Management Interface)

The DMI is a programming and reporting standard for managing desktop workstations. It was defined by the DMTF (Desktop Management Task Force), which is a consortium of industry vendors including Digital Equipment Corporation, Hewlett-Packard, Intel, Microsoft, and other companies.

The DMI is an API that provides network managers with information about workstations on the network. The primary objective is to reduce network managers' workloads by providing them with vital workstation information and assisting them with configuration and updating tasks. Managers can view information and carry out management tasks from their office, saving time and even eliminating travel in some cases.

The DMI defines how manufacturers of hardware products such as network interface cards or networking software can integrate "agents" into their products that collect information and report back to a management utility. Manufacturers don't need to worry about which protocols and operating systems end users will run with their management products. This is all handled by management software. The DMI is open to any management application or protocol, and all applications that adopt the DMI can call the same interface. IBM-compatible PCs, Macintosh, and UNIX systems are part of the DMI plan. DMI can be implemented in peripheral components as well, such as printers, modems, and storage devices.

Automation is the primary advantage of DMI. DMI-compatible agents perform tasks in the background and compile information that a normal network manager would never have time to gather using manual methods. This information can provide vital information required for network troubleshooting or to monitor changing conditions on the network. Potential problems may become evident through this process.

Local area network administrators can determine the following through the DMI interface:

- Basic information such as the processor type, available memory, and disk space information
- Hardware and software components installed in network systems
- How components are configured
- How well the components are working
- Whether the components are due for an upgrade

This information can help managers quickly resolve problems and provide upgrades.

## DMI Architecture

The DMI provides a common method for issuing requests and commands called the MI (Management Interface). Management systems that are DMI-compliant use this interface to access management information. The CI (Component Interface) allows products to be managed by applications calling the DMI. The CI lets product manufacturers define the level of management needed for their products.

One component defined in the DMI is the MIFF (management information format file). The MIFF is a text file that collects information about systems and makes it available to management programs. Vendors provide MIFFs with their DMI-compliant products.

**RELATED ENTRIES**    DMTF (Desktop Management Task Force); Network Management

**INFORMATION ON THE INTERNET**

DMTF                    http://www.dmtf.org

Adrian Pell's DMTF      http://www-uk.hpl.hp.com/people/arp/dmtf/sdk.htm
page

## DMTF (Desktop Management Task Force)

The DMTF was founded in 1992 by a group of vendors including Digital Equipment Corporation, Hewlett-Packard, IBM, Intel, Microsoft, and Novell. The goal of the DMTF is to deliver enabling technologies for a new generation of personal computer systems and products. With the DMI (Desktop Management Interface), it has developed a common management framework for PCs that will help vendors bring products to market that can easily be managed. See "DMI (Desktop Management Interface)."

In 1996, the DMTF began work on developing an object-oriented common information model for management data. The same year, it announced a way to remotely access DMI information.

The DMTF Steering Committee includes the following companies: Compaq, Dell, Digital Equipment, Hewlett-Packard, IBM, Intel, Microsoft, NEC, Novell, Santa Cruz Operation, SunSoft, and Symantec.

**INFORMATION ON THE INTERNET**

DMTF                            http://www.dmtf.org

# DNS (Domain Name System)

On the Internet, networks are connected to routers that are organized hierarchically as shown in Figure D-27. A packet might be sent to a router at the very top of the hierarchy in order to find a path to its destination. Every router along the way knows about the networks that are connected to it and if a packet can't be sent along one of those paths, the router just sends it up to the next highest router in the hierarchy.

Closely related to this routing hierarchy is the DNS (Domain Name System), which links names to IP addresses. When you access Web sites on the Internet, you can type the IP address of the site or the DNS name. Since few people have any desire to keep track of IP addresses, DNS is considered a very valuable service. It helps people refer to Internet sites by name.

DNS servers are strategically located on the Internet to convert domain names to IP addresses. Your own Internet service provider may do this conversion or connect to a specific DNS server that does. When you type a domain name in a Web browser, a query is sent to the primary DNS server defined in your Web browser's configuration dialog box. The DNS server converts the name you specified to an IP address and returns this address to your system. From then on, the IP address is used in all subsequent communications.

The naming system is hierarchical in structure, as Figure D-28 shows. The tree has a topmost root level and major divisions called *domains* branch from the root. Not all the domains are shown, including those for other countries. The top-level domains are listed here. Your local service provider is probably part of the *.net* domain, while your company is probably part of the *.com* domain.

| | |
|---|---|
| COM | commercial |
| EDU | education |
| GOV | government |
| ORG | organizational |
| NET | networks |
| INT | International treaty organizations |
| MIL | U.S. military organizations |

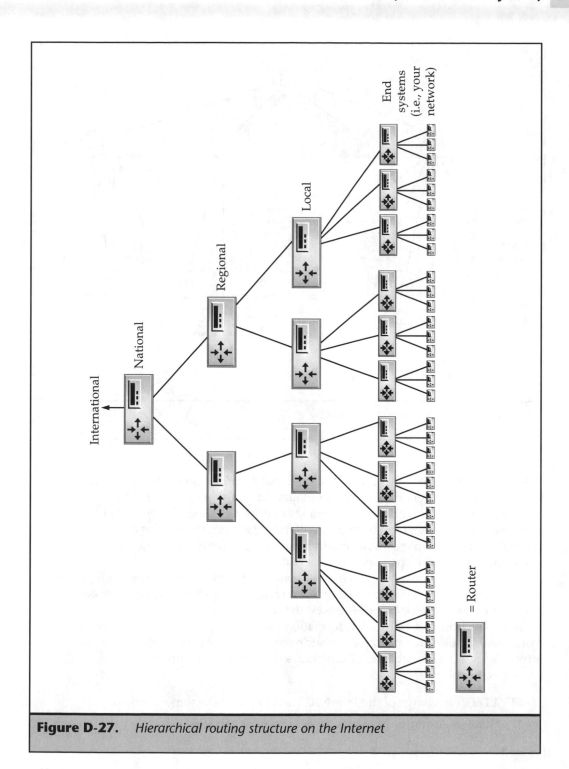

**Figure D-27.**    *Hierarchical routing structure on the Internet*

D

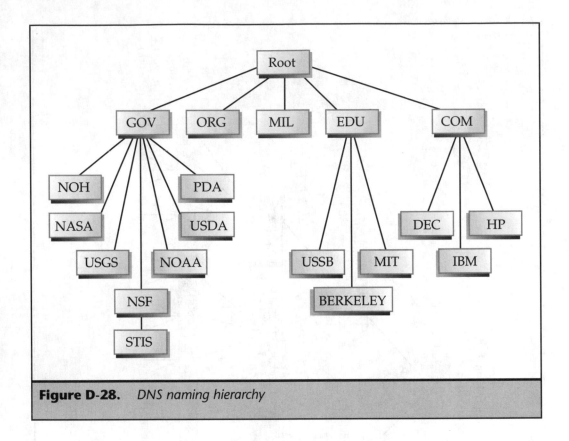

**Figure D-28.** *DNS naming hierarchy*

In February of 1997, the IAHC (International Ad Hoc Committee) announced seven new gTLDs (generic top-level domains), in addition to the existing ones (.com, .net, and .org), under which Internet names may be registered. The new fields are .firm (businesses or firms), .store (businesses offering goods), .arts (culture and entertainment), .rec (recreational entertainment), .info (information services), and .nom (for individual or personal nomenclature).

DNS address information is stored at many locations on the Internet, not just at one central depository. These sites "reflect one another" so that similar users can obtain information from the DNS server closest to them.

InterNIC (Internet Network Information Center) assigns all Internet domain names and ensures that no names or addresses are duplicated. Its Web site is at http://www.internic.net. InterNIC includes the following companies, which have specific roles:

■ **AT&T** In charge of the InterNIC Directory and Database Services
■ **General Atomics** Manages the information services

■ **NSI (Network Solutions, Inc.)**   Network integrator that manages Registration Services

When an organization applies for a domain name, it chooses a name that includes one of the domain names listed above. If you want to contact someone within a domain by electronic mail, you simply append that person's e-mail name to their domain name, separated by an at sign (@). For example, to contact the president, you would address e-mail to the following address:

president@whitehouse.gov

The only way you can register domain names is with NSI. You can go through an Internet service provider, but they basically charge you a fee for registering your domain name with the InterNIC. As new domains are registered, administrators of DNS servers around the world must add the new names and create pointers for them. This task has become increasingly more complex in recent years. Domain names are hot commodities and people or organizations want to register names that exemplify their products or services. For example, Proctor and Gamble recently registered a whole batch of domain names, including badbreath.com, dandruff.com, and underarms.com.

Registrations are made on a first-come, first-serve basis, but a name that infringes on a registered trademark will be rescinded by NSI if the trademark holder contests the name. NSI has had numerous requests to increase the number of top-level domains. Some proposed examples are .mall (online shopping), .ask (assistance and information), .med (medical), .inc, and .media.

**RELATED ENTRIES**   Internet; Internet Backbone; *and* Internet Connections

**INFORMATION ON THE INTERNET**

| | |
|---|---|
| IETF Domain Name System Security (dnssec) Working Group | http://www.ietf.org/html.charters/dnssec-charter.html |
| Internet Domain Name System site | http://www.itu.ch/intreg/dns.html |
| DNS information (DNS Resources Directory) | http://www.is.co.za/andras/computer/dnsrd |
| DNS-related Internet draft proposals | visit http://www.dns.net/dnsrd/docs/id.html |

# Document Management

Document management is the storing, categorizing, and retrieval of documents, spreadsheets, graphs, and imaged (scanned) documents. Each document has an index-card-like record that holds information such as the author, document description, creation date, and type of application used. Such documents usually are targeted for archiving on less expensive tape or optical disk where they remain available for future access if necessary.

Document management is often referred to as EDM (electronic document management). In the case of a law firm, document management tracks all activities occurring with a document, such as the number of keystrokes, revisions, and printings, so clients can be charged for the services.

## AIIM (Association for Information and Image Management International)

AIIM is a 9,000-member organization that manages document imaging and interoperability standards. It is also the umbrella organization for the DMA (Document Management Alliance) and the ODMA (Open Document Management API). AIIM is accredited by the ANSI (American National Standards Institute). The organization's Web site is at http://www.aiim.org.

DMA is a task force of AIIM that is concerned with ensuring that document management applications, services, and repositories are interoperable. DMA has developed a document management framework that defines programming interfaces and services for document management systems. For example, a *query service* allows users to search multiple repositories anywhere on the network and a *library service* provides version and access control to reduce the risk of users working on outdated documents.

The ODMA specification is a platform-independent API (application programming interface) and platform-specific registration and binding specification. It runs on Windows, Macintosh, and other platforms and is supported by major vendors including Novell, Saros, Documentum, Interleaf, and FileNet. There is also an ODMA Extension for Workflow. Additional information can be found at the AIIM Web site mentioned above.

According to AIIM, documents hold the "intellectual assets of organizations, the knowledge and expertise of its people, and the information and data they have compiled. These valuable assets must be managed and protected. Everything a company knows about itself, its products and services, its customers, and the business environment in which it exists are stored in documents."

Modern electronic documents contain multimedia information, including graphics, voice clips, and video clips. Physical documents may be scanned, indexed, and stored on computer for quick access. Imaged and archived documents can be retrieved in a matter of seconds. Optical character recognition is used to "read" documents and turn them into computer text files. Once stored, the document can be duplicated indefinitely. Parts of the document can be cut and pasted into other documents.

Document management becomes essential as network users begin to take advantage of these technologies. According to AIIM, a document management system should do the following:

- Manage documents that are distributed and stored in repositories throughout an organization

- Provide services such as storing, tracking, versioning, indexing, and searching for documents

- Manage document revisions and "audit trails" to track where a document has been

- Make information available both inside and outside the organization

- Make it easier to access any kind of documents over computer networks

- Perform document imaging and forms processing

- Provide workflow and groupware technologies for transaction-oriented and collaborative document management

## Web-Based Document Management Products

Most vendors of document management software and systems have made the move to Web technologies. Web servers and HTML (Hypertext Markup Language) provide an example of a document management system. Documents are stored in the HTML format, which is readable by any Web browser. Web browsers provide a universal interface to documents on any Web server. Because HTML documents support hyperlinking, users can quickly move between document references. HTML documents also hold objects such as buttons or icons that automatically launch program code or database queries, or execute ActiveX controls and Java applets. Two examples are given here:

- **Information Dimensions' BASIS Document Manager**  This system provides control, management, retrieval, and navigation of document collections. It includes complete library services, full-text retrieval, document control, document delivery, security, and authentication. Documents, their attributes, and their structure are stored in BASISplus, an extended relational database optimized specifically for document objects. Supported document types include SGML, HTML, tagged text, word processing documents, and bibliographic records. Information Dimensions can be reached at http://www.idi.oclc.org.

- **IntraNet Solutions' Intra.doc!**  The Intra.doc! Management System helps companies automatically maintain an internal or external Web site containing volumes of documents, such as product literature, policies and procedures,

**D**

price pages, and other essential information. Intranet Solutions can be reached at http://www.intranetsol.com.

**RELATED ENTRIES**    Backup and Data Archiving; Compound Documents; EDI (Electronic Data Interchange); Groupware; Imaging; Information Publishing; Storage Management Systems; *and* Workflow Management

**INFORMATION ON THE INTERNET**

| | |
|---|---|
| AIIM International | http://www.aiim.org |
| Document Management Industries Association | http://www.dmia.com |
| FORM Magazine online | http://www.formmag.com |
| Document management links at FORM Magazine | http://www.formmag.com/links.html |

## Domains in Windows NT

Windows NT Server domains are collections of computers and computer users that are managed by a central authority. Domains may span departments, divisions, and/or workgroups, as well as other types of computer groups. You implement domains to make groups of computers more manageable and to apply a security policy to specific areas of your network. In addition, domains logically split large networks into groups of resources that make it easy for users to find those resources.

A *distributed network* is one in which networks in different divisions, departments, or workgroups, all with different data sources, have been linked together to provide an enterprise-wide information system, as pictured in Figure D-29. Domains provide a way to maintain a single directory of users in large distributed-network environments. Because a domain is an administrative entity that encompasses a collection of computers, those computers might be next to each other or separated by some distance.

In a Windows NT domain environment, network users have user accounts that are maintained on a Windows NT Server *domain controller* in a *directory database*. Each domain has a PDC (primary domain controller) and may have one or more BDCs (backup domain controllers) as well. The directory database holds all the accounts and security information for a domain. It is replicated (copied) to other domain controllers in the domain for backup reasons and to make it more readily available to people in different geographic locations. Replication is automatic among domain controllers.

In the domain environment, there is almost always a need for users in one domain to access resources in another domain. To allow cross-domain activities, domain administrators set up *trust relationships*.

If an organization has only one domain, trust relationships are not required, but in large organizations many domains may exist, requiring trust relationships to allow information exchange. A single administrator can manage all the domains, or each domain can be managed separately with its own tight security.

D

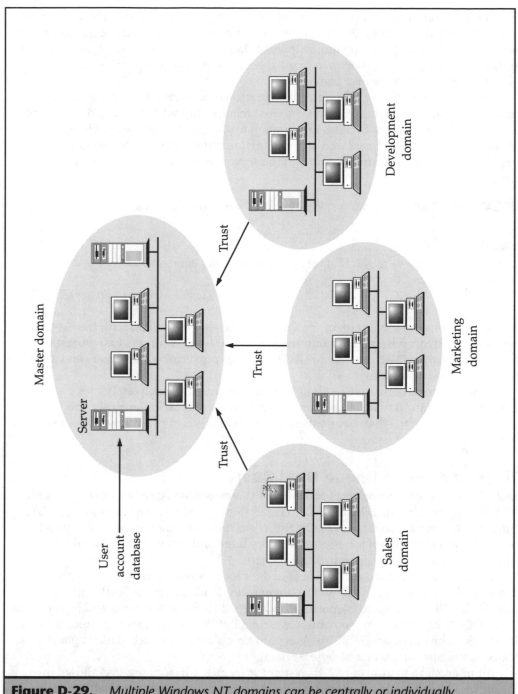

**Figure D-29.** *Multiple Windows NT domains can be centrally or individually managed*

There are one-way and two-way trust relationships. In a one-way relationship, one domain trusts the users in the other domain to use its resources, but not the other way around. In a two-way trust relationship, each domain trusts the other. Of course, after setting up trusts, the next step is to grant specific users and groups in one domain access to resources in another domain.

The best way to think of this is at the department level. For example, users in the accounting department often need a trust relationship with the sales department so that they can access daily sales information for accounting purposes. However, users in the sales department don't need a trust relationship with the accounting department, because the information on the servers in accounting is none of their business.

**RELATED ENTRIES**    Windows; Windows NT Directory Services

## Downsizing

*Downsizing: An excuse to get rid of your highly paid senior employees and put in a workforce of "temps."*

—*Upside Magazine*, Foster City, CA

In the computer environment, downsizing has been associated with the process of replacing minicomputers and mainframes with LAN-based servers and workstations, typically associated with a move to UNIX boxes or powerful superservers and a shift to client/server computing.

Many organizations have too much of an investment to completely move away from mainframe and minicomputer systems, or have special engineering and scientific applications that require their use, or find it is cost prohibitive to redesign for network systems.

## DQDB (Distributed Queue Dual Bus)

DQDB is the access technology for the MAN (Metropolitan Area Network) standard, which is defined by the IEEE 802.6 committee. Since MAN is an 802.x standard like Ethernet, token ring, and token bus, it fits in well with common local area network technology, but the MAN is designed for very large and fast networks based on fiber-optic cables that span up to 50 kilometers.

The LAN access standards are designed for local networks that have relatively limited cable lengths and that tend to become overloaded as more workstations are added. The MAN standard is specifically designed for large networks and heavy loads.

A DQDB network is implemented as a ring, but the ring is not connected. Instead, it acts like a bus network. It fills the bus with time slots into which stations place data. Cells on the bus can carry a 44-byte payload.

An interesting feature of DQDB systems is its dual-bus topology. As shown in Figure D-30, each station is attached to each bus. One bus generates upstream cells

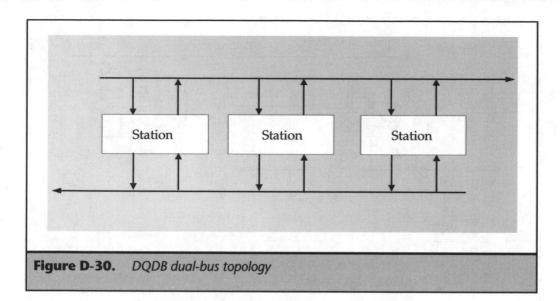

**Figure D-30.**   *DQDB dual-bus topology*

and the other bus generates downstream cells. When a station wants to transmit, it chooses the bus that will send data in the direction of the destination.

**RELATED ENTRY**   MAN (Metropolitan Area Network)

# DRDA (Distributed Relational Database Architecture)

DRDA is an IBM standard for accessing database information across IBM platforms that follows SQL standards. It is a key component in IBM's Information Warehouse framework, which defines large back-end servers that clients can access through smaller, workgroup-based intermediate servers. DRDA has the following capabilities:

- Defines protocols for providing interfaces between clients and back-end databases
- Provides a framework for interconnecting IBM's DB2, DBM, SQL/DS, and SQL/400 database systems
- Supports multivendor database systems
- Supports transaction (unit of work) processing over distributed databases

In DRDA, clients are called ARs (application requesters) and back-end servers are called ASs (application servers). A protocol called the ASP (Application Support Protocol) interfaces the ARs with the ASs. The whole process operates on SNA networks, but OSI and TCP/IP support is planned. An additional protocol, called the DSP (Database Support Protocol), lets an AS act as an AR to another server. In this

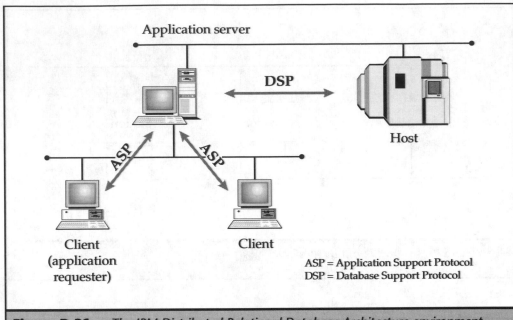

Application server

DSP

Host

ASP

ASP

Client
(application
requester)

Client

ASP = Application Support Protocol
DSP = Database Support Protocol

**Figure D-31.** *The IBM Distributed Relational Database Architecture environment*

way, servers can talk to servers and forward requests from client ARs, as shown in Figure D-31. The initial protocol supports one SQL statement to one database, but future versions will support multiple statements to one or more databases.

DRDA is one of the foundations for building client/server computing in IBM environments. The others are APPN (Advanced Peer-to-Peer Networking) and DDM (Distributed Data Management). Through the Information Warehouse and DRDA, IBM plans to keep its mainframes as central components in the enterprise—as storage platforms for all types of information, including multimedia.

**RELATED ENTRIES**    APPN (Advanced Peer-to-Peer Networking); Database Connectivity; Distributed Database; *and* Information Warehouse

**INFORMATION ON THE INTERNET**

IBM's DRDA site                              http://www.software.ibm.com/data/drda.html

The International DB2 Users Group    http://www.idug.org

## DSL (Digital Subscriber Line)

DSL technologies can dramatically improve the bandwidth of the existing analog phone system. It can provide data throughput of up to 52 Mbits/sec over limited distances. At this writing, DSL is still taking shape and vendors are hyping its capabilities. By 1998, we will know what DSL can really deliver.

As mentioned, DSL enhances the data capacity of the existing twisted-pair wire that runs between the local telephone company switching offices and most homes and offices. The bandwidth of this wire is limited to approximately 3,000 Hz due to its use as a voice telephone system. While the wire itself can handle higher frequencies, the telephone switching equipment is designed to cut off signals above 4,000 Hz to filter noise off the voice line. Obviously, the phone companies have not been anxious to upgrade their switching equipment to obtain more bandwidth, at least not until the Internet came along.

Now, everybody is searching for ways to get more bandwidth to improve access to the Web. DSL has been the next greatest thing, but many will remember the promises of ISDN (Integrated Services Digital Network), which has only recently become widespread after 12 years of hype. The cable TV companies are also offering high-speed access (using 10-Mbit/sec Ethernet) over their existing cable systems. This will produce competition that either cuts into the phone company offerings or spurs the phone company to offer DSL service much faster than it took them to offer convenient ISDN services.

There are actually seven types of DSL service, ranging in speeds from 16 Kbits/sec to 52 Mbits/sec. The services are either symmetrical (traffic flows at the same speed in both directions), or asymmetrical (the downstream capacity is higher than the upstream capacity). Asymmetrical services are suitable for Internet users because more information is usually downloaded than uploaded. For example, a simple button click can start an extended download that includes graphics and text.

Keep in mind that as data rates increase, the carrying distance decreases. That means that users who are beyond a certain distance from the telephone company's central office may not be able to obtain the higher speeds. For example, the highest-speed service requires that customers be within 1,000 feet of the central office. Not too many homes qualify for that service, but businesses in downtown areas might.

DSL connections are point-to-point dedicated circuits, meaning that they are always connected. There is no dial-up. There is also no switching, which means that the line is a direct connection into the carrier's frame relay, ATM (Asynchronous Transfer Mode), or Internet-connect system. A DSL modem is required at the customer site and the carrier must have supporting equipment to provide the service. There are two conflicting modulation techniques, so users must make sure that the modems they purchase are compatible with their carrier. Many carriers are offering package deals that include the appropriate modem.

As of this writing, pricing is still up in the air for DSL services. Since the line is always on, you would think the RBOCs (regional Bell operating companies) would price the services high, but recent quotes for services that offer the same throughput as a T1 line were under $150 per month. That may seem high to home users, but it is a good price for telecommuters and home office users. Users also need to factor in the price of modems, which are in the $500 to $1,000 range.

Note that T1 service is not suitable for home use for a number of reasons. One is that it causes cross talk among cable pairs in the 50-pair cable that the telephone company runs into residential areas. That means that only one T1 circuit can be used per 50-pair cable. The line-coding technique in T1 also wastes bandwidth, and repeaters are required at 2-kilometer intervals. The DSL services solve these problems and provide potentially higher throughput.

> **NOTE:** *The different versions of DSL described next are often collectively referred to as* xDSL.

■ **HDSL (High-bit-rate Digital Subscriber Line)**  HDSL is the most common and mature of the DSL services. It provides T1 data rates of 1.544 Mbits/sec over lines that are up to 3.6 kilometers (12,000 feet) in length. Generally, HDSL is a T1 service that requires no repeaters but does use two lines. Voice telephone services cannot operate on the same lines. It is not intended for home users, but is instead intended for the telephone company's own feeder lines, interexchange connections, Internet servers, and private data networks.

■ **SDSL (Symmetrical Digital Subscriber Line)**  SDSL is a symmetrical, bidirectional DSL service that is basically the same as HDSL but operates on one twisted-pair wire. It can provide data rates up to the T1 rate of 1.544 Mbits/sec, and it operates above the voice frequency, so voice and data can be carried on the same wire.

■ **ADSL (Asymmetrical Digital Subscriber Line)**  ADSL is the most likely service to succeed as a high-speed service for the local loop. It is an asymmetrical technology, meaning that the downstream data rate is much higher than the upstream data rate. As mentioned, this works well for a typical Internet session in which more information is downloaded from Web servers than is uploaded. ADSL operates in a frequency range that is above the frequency range of voice services, so the two systems can operate over the same cable. The downstream rates and distances of ADSL are listed here. Upstream speeds range from 16 Kbits/sec to 640 Kbits/sec.

| Downstream Rate | Downstream Distance |
|---|---|
| 1.544 Mbits/sec | 5.5 km (18,000 ft.) |
| 2.048 Mbits/sec | 4.8 km (16,000 ft.) |
| 6.312 Mbits/sec | 3.6 km (12,000 ft.) |
| 8.448 Mbits/sec | 2.7 km (9,000 ft.) |

■ **VDSL (Very high bit rate Digital Subscriber Line)**  VDSL is basically ADSL at much higher data rates. It is asymmetrical and thus has a higher downstream rate than upstream rate. The service can be used on the same wire as the voice telephone network and ISDN. The upstream rates are from 1.6 Mbits/sec to 2.3 Mbits/sec. The upstream rates and distances are listed in the following table:

| Upstream Rate | Upstream Distance |
|---|---|
| 12.96 Mbits/sec | 1.4 km (4,500 ft.) |
| 25.82 Mbits/sec | 0.9 km (3,000 ft.) |
| 51.84 Mbits/sec | 0.3 km (1,000 ft.) |

■ **RADSL (Rate-Adaptive Digital Subscriber Line)**   This service is also similar to ADSL, but it has a rate-adaptive feature that will adjust the transmission speed to match the quality of the line and the length of the line. A line-polling technique is used to establish a connection speed when the line is first established.

ADSL is getting the most attention as an Internet access service. It has been ratified as an ANSI (American National Standards Institute) standard. Carriers and Internet service providers are trying to shake off the bad press about ISDN installation and are going all out to ensure that ADSL is easy to set up. Customers only need a TCP/IP-compatible system with an Ethernet adapter and an ADSL modem to obtain Internet access. They are leasing modems as part of the service, although modems are also available in the $500 to $1,000 range.

For office connections, the ADSL line can carry ATM traffic directly into the carrier's ATM switching systems. IP packets can be put in ATM cells, which are then transported across the ADSL line. Arial Corporation (http://www.arial.com) has developed an ATM adapter for workstations that allows direct connection to an ADSL without a modem.

Two competing line-encoding (modulation) schemes are currently used for ADSL. One technique is DMT (discrete multitone), which has been established as an ANSI standard. The other, called CAP (carrierless amplitude and phase), is advocated by numerous vendors. With DMT, the phone line spectrum is divided into 256 4-kHz channels. Each channel avoids some of the noise and interference problems of a wide-spectrum signal. CAP uses a single channel and a modulation technique called QAM (quadrature amplitude modulation) similar to that used in V.34 (28.8 Kbits/sec) modems. When you purchase ADSL modems, make sure that devices that you intend to connect to support the same encoding techniques.

ADSL modems that use DMT use frequency division multiplexing to create three separate channels, as shown in Figure D-32. Note the voice telephone channel, the low-speed upstream channel, and the high-speed downstream channel. Filtering is used to isolate the voice circuit from the ADSL channels and provides guaranteed uninterrupted phone service over the line. It also separates data services from voice services at the central office, thus reducing congestion in the telephone system.

**RELATED ENTRIES**   Carrier Services; Circuit; Circuit-Switching Services; Communication Services; Data Link Protocols; ISDN (Integrated Services Digital Network); PSTN (Public-Switched Telephone Network); T1/T3; Telecommunications and Telephone Systems; *and* WAN (Wide Area Network)

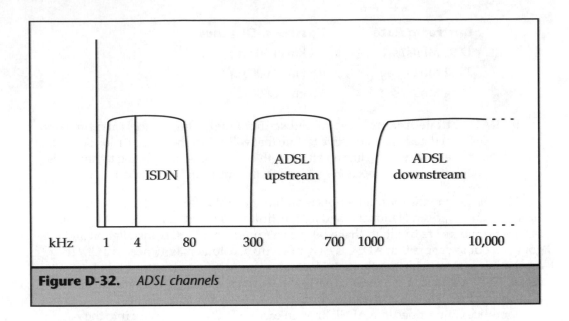

**Figure D-32.** *ADSL channels*

**INFORMATION ON THE INTERNET**

| | |
|---|---|
| The ADSL Forum | http://www.adsl.com |
| DSL news | http://www.telechoice.com/xdslnewz |
| NIST's High Speed Network Technologies site | http://www.hsnt.nist.gov |
| Doug Lawlor's High Bandwidth page | http://www.specialty.com/hiband |

## DSOM (Distributed System Object Model)

DSOM is IBM's extension to SOM (System Object Model) that allows objects to communicate across platforms in distributed computing environments. SOM is an object-oriented technology that specifies an interface to enable object classes created in different environments to interoperate. SOM is implemented in the IBM OS/2 WorkPlace Shell as the mechanism for providing onscreen object icons. It also provides the tools for developers to create such icons. DSOM is the network version that provides cross-platform interoperability.

While SOM and DSOM provide low-level languages to developers of object-oriented applications, its VisualAge product provides object-oriented tools for creating graphical interface applications without any knowledge of the programming language.

**RELATED ENTRIES** Component Software Technology; Object Technologies; *and* ORB (Object Request Broker)

## DSU/CSU (Data Service Unit/Channel Service Unit)

A DSU (data service unit) is a communication device that connects a company's telephone premises equipment to digital communication lines, such as a T1. A CSU (channel service unit) provides line termination and signal regeneration. The DSU and the CSU are often combined in one device and connected to a channel bank, which provides analog-to-digital conversion and multiplexing of voice transmissions.

## DSVD (Digital Simultaneous Voice and Data)

A feature of modems that allows voice and data signals over the same link. DSVD is a proposed Internet standard. When two DSVD-capable modems are communicating, users can voice chat while collaborating on a project or playing a game.

### INFORMATION ON THE INTERNET

DSP Group's DSVD site          http://www.dspg.com/dsvd.htm

## DS-x (Digital Signal Level x)

Digital signal refers to the rate and format of digital telecommunication circuits. DS is related to the T designations, but DS refers to signal rates and formatting while the T designations are usually applied to equipment. There are various DS levels, starting with DS-0, a 64-Kbit/sec line that accommodates one voice telephone call (after analog-to-digital conversion). The DS levels are outlined here:

| DS Level | T-Carrier Equivalent | Speed | Number of 64-Kbit/sec Channels |
|----------|----------------------|-------|-------------------------------|
| DS0 | Fractional T1 | 64 Kbits/sec | 1 |
| DS1 | T1 | 1.544 Mbits/sec | 24 |
| DS3 | T3 | 44.736 Mbits/sec | 672 |

This DS signal hierarchy is part of the NADH (North American Digital Hierarchy). Eventually, SONET (Synchronous Optical Network) will replace NADH. SDH (Synchronous Digital Hierarchy) is the European equivalent of SONET.

**RELATED ENTRIES**    NADH (North American Digital Hierarchy); SONET (Synchronous Optical Network); T1/T3; *and* Telecommunications and Telephone Systems

## DTE (Data Terminal Equipment)

A DTE is the source or destination of data in a communication connection connected to DCE (data circuit-terminating equipment), which in turn is connected to the communication channel, as shown in Figure D-33. Dumb terminals were originally classified as DTEs, but computers also fall into this category. A DCE is a modem if the circuit is an analog voice line, or a DSU/CSU if the line is digital.

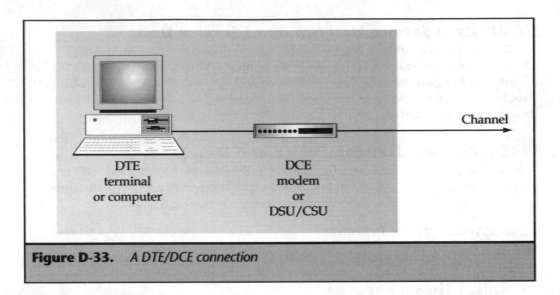

**Figure D-33.** *A DTE/DCE connection*

## Duplexed Systems

A duplexed system provides data protection in the form of mirroring, in which data is simultaneously written in two places at once. Mirroring implies that two disks are present, but attached to one disk channel (adapter card). Duplexing implies that each disk is attached to its own adapter card, which adds another level of protection. The entire server can also be duplexed so users are never without a server should one server go down. Duplexed servers are attached with high-speed interfaces (fiber) and can be placed in separate locations to protect them from local disasters.

**RELATED ENTRY**    Mirroring

## DVA (Distance-Vector Algorithm) Routing Protocol

The Bellman-Ford algorithm is used to calculate routes for transmitting packets through networks with multiple paths to a destination. Routing decisions are based on the least number of "hops" to a destination. Tables are built by routers and exchanged with other routers, which use the routing information to construct a map of the network.

**RELATED ENTRY**    Routing Protocols and Algorithms

## Dynamic Routing

Dynamic routing is a process in which routers automatically adjust to changes in network topology or traffic. The opposite is static routing, in which the router manager enters the routes manually. Dynamic routing is used in all modern routers, but some amount of programming is still available for customizing routes if necessary.

**RELATED ENTRY**    Routing Protocols and Algorithms

# E-1/E-3 European Digital Hierarchy

The "E" standards are the European equivalent to the "T" standards in the NADH (North American Digital Hierarchy). The basic channel in both systems is the 64-Kbit/sec channel that supports one voice call. The following table describes the circuits in the hierarchy:

| Circuit Name | Data Rate | Number of 64-Kbit/sec Channels |
|---|---|---|
| E1 | 2.048-Mbit/sec circuit | 30 voice channels, 2 control and synchronization channels |
| E3 | 34.368-Mbit/sec circuit | Equivalent to 16 E1 circuits |
| E4 | 139.26-Mbit/sec circuit | Equivalent to 4 E3 circuits |
| E5 | 565.148-Mbit/sec | Equivalent to 4 E4 circuits |

Note that the E1 circuits carry more channels that T1 circuits (24 channels), so repeaters are required every 6,000 feet when copper wire is used. The SDH (Synchronous Digital Hierarchy) optical cable standards are replacing these standards, and the SONET (Synchronous Optical Network) standards are replacing the NADH standards. SONET and SDH are very similar, which will allow telecommunication companies to build interconnected global networks with ease. The differences in E1 and T1 do not provide seamless integration, and this makes it difficult to build global networks.

**RELATED ENTRIES**    Multiplexing; NADH (North American Digital Hierarchy); SONET (Synchronous Optical Network); T1/T3; Telecommunications and Telephone Systems; *and* WAN (Wide Area Network)

**INFORMATION ON THE INTERNET**

| | |
|---|---|
| Prof. Jeffrey MacKie-Mason's Telecom page | http://www.spp.umich.edu/telecom |
| Telecom Digest | http://massis.lcs.mit.edu/telecom-archives |
| Hilary Bailey's Telecoms Virtual Library | http://www.analysys.com/vlib |
| Computer and Communication hot links | http://www.cmpcmm.com/cc/standards.html |

# Edge Devices

Edge devices are routers or switches that typically provide entry points into ATM switching networks. Edge devices are used when connecting legacy Ethernet and token ring LANs to the ATM network in a configuration where the ATM network serves as a bridge between a LAN on one edge of the network and a LAN on another edge of the network.

Virtual circuits extend over the ATM network from one edge device to another. A workstation on one LAN can then send messages through ATM virtual circuits to a LAN and workstation connected to another edge device. An edge device may have routing tables that are referred to when mapping layer 3 routes to layer 2 virtual circuits. There are a number of initiatives and standards for mapping legacy LANs onto ATM. You'll find additional information under the topics referenced below under "Related Entries."

In the MPOA (Multiprotocol over ATM) environment, edge devices are LAN switches with ATM connections that provide both layer 3 routing and layer 2 forwarding. The edge devices share routing functions with a special route server. The route server calculates routes through the ATM network, and then provides route information to edge devices. Edge devices then use that information to forward packets. Together, the edge devices and the route server provide *distributed routing* functions.

**RELATED ENTRIES**    ATM (Asynchronous Transfer Mode); IP over ATM; IP Switching; LANE (LAN Emulation); MPOA (Multiprotocol over ATM); Network Concepts; Network Design and Construction; Routing Protocols and Algorithms; Switched Networks; Virtual Circuit; *and* VLAN (Virtual LAN)

# EDI (Electronic Data Interchange)

EDI is the electronic exchange of structured business data such as purchase orders, invoices, and shipping notices, typically between one organization and another. The relationship is usually between a vendor and customer. For example, EDI provides a way for a customer's computer to place orders for goods with a vendor's computers, based on reorder levels. The EDI system coordinates the deliveries and generates the invoices.

EDI has the potential to reduce costs, reduce workforce requirements, and most important, reduce retyping errors. With EDI, computer data already entered by one organization is made available to a business partner. EDI is typically handled using store-and-forward technologies similar to e-mail. A third party such as GEIS (General Electric Information Service) often serves as a "middleman" to help organizations establish business relationships and handle business transactions.

Typical business activities that can be handled by EDI include distribution, finance and accounting, health care, manufacturing, purchasing, retail, tax form filing, transport, and shipping.

Early EDI packages used rather simple standard forms that forced companies to design their in-house documents around these generic forms. Newer EDI systems allow companies to create custom systems using simple programming or authoring tools. In addition, it is not necessary for trading partners to have identical business systems or systems that generate compatible documents. EDI translation software converts the sender's proprietary document formats into standard formats. Similar software converts the standard formats back into the proprietary document standards used by the receiving trading partner.

There are two approaches to implementing EDI. Many large organizations acquire or build their own proprietary systems, often in association with their business partners. If a business partner is small, it may have little choice but to adopt the proprietary system of its much large business associate. The other approach is to work with a VAN (value added network) provider, which provides EDI transaction services, security, document interchange assistance, standard message formats, communication protocols, and communication parameters for EDI. Most VANs also provide a network on which to transmit information.

EDI is just beginning to move into the Internet. Premenos Corporation (http://www.premenos.com) offers an EDI product that works over the Internet. Most EDI experts agree that the current use of proprietary systems and VANs will give way to Internet technologies. The Internet can help reduce the cost of doing EDI, although security and reliability are areas of concern.

## Standards

EDI standards activities in the United States are handled by DISA (Data Interchange Standards Association, Inc.). The Web site for DISA contains a treasure trove of information about EDI and EDI-related organizations.

X.12 is a U.S. standard that defines many different types of documents, including air shipments, student loan applications, injury and illness reports, and shipment and billing notices. A full list can be found under the X.25 heading at Premenos. The ANSI (American National Standards Institute) assigned responsibility for development of EDI standards to the ASC (Accredited Standards Committee) X.12 organization in 1979. X.12 has roots with work done in the shipping industry by the TDCC (Transportation Data Coordinating Committee) and work done in the food distribution industry by the UCC (Uniform Code Council).

X.12 ensures that documents are compatible among computing platforms. Documents mimic standard business forms with ASCII data in a standard data file format that is structured with records and fields. A document sent from, for example, a PC-based EDI system can be read by a mainframe-based EDI system because the text and data separators follow a standard format. The electronic documents are sent using a *store-and-forward* process similar to electronic mail systems. In this way, daily transactions can accumulate and be transferred to host systems during evening hours to reduce costs.

UN/EDIFACT (United Nations/Electronic Data Interchange for Administration Commerce and Transport) is an international EDI standard. EDI INT is the EDI Internet standard, which Netscape is actively using in its Internet products such as CrossCommerce (see "Electronic Commerce").

## EDI and the Internet

As the Internet grows, companies are finding that implementing EDI over it is more cost effective than building private systems or going through value-added network providers. The Internet is already in place as a business-to-business communication system. The startup costs are cheaper and, in most cases, the organization is already connected to the Internet. This makes it easier for more businesses to join the electronic commerce web, especially those who previously could not afford the expense of EDI. Companies can now conduct business with other companies in cases where only EDI-type business transactions were possible in the past.

## Open-EDI

The ISO (International Organization for Standardization) and IEC (International Electrical Committee) are developing EDI standards for the Internet under a joint committee called Open-EDI. The goal of Open-EDI is to allow businesses to establish trading arrangements over the Internet upon first contact, assuming trust systems are in place.

Open-EDI uses the Internet as the electronic platform for information and transaction exchange. Standards are being developed that will reduce or eliminate the need to translate and convert business transactions. The Internet helps reduce setup and equipment costs and allows more organizations to participate in a system where business transaction methods have been standardized. The open nature of the Internet promotes business opportunities. For example, an organization can e-mail its request for bids over the Internet to potential bidders and quickly create and change relationships with business partners.

Organizations like CommerceNet are actively involved in designing new procurement techniques and providing services that can help businesses connect with one another and do business together electronically.

## Internet Hurdles and Solutions

The current EDI structure is expanding to accommodate the Internet, but this expansion requires a way for organizations that have not previously established electronic business relationships to translate among systems and electronic forms. There are gateway services that perform translations. For example, there are services for translating between the Internet's SMTP (Simple Mail Transfer Protocol) mail protocol and other mail protocols such as X.400, and there are translation services for converting between EDI and non-EDI standards. As exchange formats become standardized, this should become less of a problem.

There are also a number of electronic business service providers that offer value-added services such as business yellow pages, vendor databases, parts listings, catalog services, and technical information services. The place to check for this type of information is CommerceNet. Its goal is to develop and maintain conventions for representing this type of business information so that more organizations can participate directly in electronic transaction environments.

CommerceNet is working with a number of EDI vendors and VeriSign to provide secure EDI transactions. Verisign is providing digital authentication services through its Get-rEDI Digital ID Center, a Web-based enrollment site. Parties involved in electronic transactions are verified and authenticated through VeriSign Digital IDs to ensure the integrity of messages. The CommerceNet initiative is testing the exchange of EDI documents over SMTP (Simple Mail Transport Protocol) using MIME (Multipurpose Internet Mail Extension). It is also testing the use of S/MIME (Secure Multipurpose Internet Mail Extension). Final testing will involve testing receipt requests and signed and unsigned receipts.

One company that is developing extranet technologies is CrossRoute Software, at http://www.crossroute.com. The company is developing solutions for what it calls business-to-business electronic commerce. Netscape is developing similar business-to-business software.

Refer to "Electronic Commerce" for more information on CommerceNet and Internet-related business transactions.

## OBI (Open Buying on the Internet)

OBI is a protocol designed by American Express and SupplyWorks for executing real-time business transactions on the Web. Microsoft, Netscape, Oracle, Open Market, and a number of other companies back the specification. The goal is to reduce costs, improve the overall buying/paying process, and increase service levels to end users using Internet technology. OBI will achieve some of the same results as EDI. The EDI X12-850 document standard is used for structuring and sending electronic documents. Digital certificates are required for this type of transaction so companies receiving business document can prove their authenticity.

To get more information about OBI, send electronic mail to the OBI Consortium, at OBI@supplyworks.com.

**RELATED ENTRIES**    Certificates and Certification Systems; Digital Signatures; Electronic Commerce; Electronic Mail; Extranet; Groupware; Intranets and Extranets; IPSec (IP Security); OBI (Open Buying on the Internet); Security; SET (Secure Electronic Transaction); S/WAN (Secure WAN); VPN (Virtual Private Network); Web Technologies and Concepts; *and* Workflow Management

### INFORMATION ON THE INTERNET

| | |
|---|---|
| DISA (Data Interchange Standards Association, Inc.) | http://www.disa.org |
| CommerceNet | http://www.commerce.net |
| The Computer Information Centre (check the EDI section for extensive links) | http://www.compinfo.co.uk |
| NAFTAnet EDI page | http://www.nafta.net/ecedi.htm |
| Electronic Commerce World Institute EDI road map | http://www.ecworld.org/Resource_Center/Agora/Roadmap/content.html |
| IETF EDI-Internet Integration (ediint) charter | http://www.ietf.org/html.charters/ediint-charter.html |
| Premenos Corporation | http://www.premenos.com |

| | |
|---|---|
| VeriSign, Inc. | http://www.verisign.com |
| Sterling Commerce, Inc. | http://www.sterling.gentran.com |
| GEIS (General Electric Information Services) | http://www.geis.com |
| Actra Business Systems | http://www.actracorp.com |
| AT&T Corporation | http://www.att.com |
| DEC's EDI Infocenter | http://www.digital.com/info/edi/edi-lit.html |
| Jim Smith's EDI Web site links | http://penny.ibmpcug.co.uk/~jws |

## EDM (Electronic Document Management)

*See* Document Management.

## EGPs (Exterior Gateway Protocols)

The Internet and TCP/IP networks in general are divided into autonomous systems, which are collections of hosts and routers that typically use the same routing protocol and are administered by a single authority. Autonomous systems are considered domains. An autonomous system might be a collection of interconnected routers administered by a university or a company. There are two categories of protocols to handle traffic within these domains and outside the domains. While *interior routing protocols* are used within a domain, *exterior routing protocols* provide a way for two neighboring routers located at the edges of their respective domains to exchange messages and information.

EGPs are exterior routing protocols. The term gateway is the older term for router in the Internet lexicon. The usual protocol within autonomous systems is the OSPF (Open Shortest Path First) protocol. The BGP (Border Gateway Protocol) is an exterior gateway protocol used between autonomous systems.

**RELATED ENTRIES**    BGP (Border Gateway Protocol); Internet Backbone; *and* Routing Protocols and Algorithms

## EIA (Electronic Industries Association)

Founded in 1924, the EIA is a U.S. organization of electronics manufacturers. The EIA has published a number of standards related to telecommunication and computer communication, and works closely with other associates such as ANSI (American National Standards Institute) and the ITU (International Telecommunication Union). The EIA Web site is at http://www.eia.org.

The primary EIA standards for telecommunication define the serial interface between modems and computers. These interfaces are described under "Serial Communication and Interfaces."

In the area of structured cabling for networks, the EIA has recently joined with the TIA (Telecommunications Industry Association) to create the Commercial Building Telecommunications Wiring Standards (TIA/EIA 568 and 569), which define hierarchical wiring systems in campus environments using data-grade twisted-pair wire. These standards provide a wiring structure that building designers can use to facilitate high-speed data communication equipment without the need to know in advance what that equipment will be.

## EIA/TIA Structured Cabling Standards

*See* TIA/EIA Structured Cabling Standards.

## Electromagnetic Interference

*See* EMI (Electromagnetic Interference).

**E**

## Electromagnetic Spectrum

Energy is transmitted in three ways: electromagnetic radiation, conduction, and convection (heat transfer). Because electromagnetic waves do not necessarily need a material medium for transmission, they are used for a wide range of communication, including communication over a material media such as copper and fiber-optic wire, as well as through air and the vacuum of space.

Electron movement causes electromagnetic radiation. The frequency is the number of oscillations per second of the resulting wave, also called Hz (hertz). The wavelength is the distance between crests in the wave. The higher the frequency, the shorter the wavelength. As shown in Figure E-1, the highest frequencies in the gamma ray spectrum have the shortest wavelengths.

Information can be carried on electromagnetic waves by modulating either the wave's amplitude, frequency, or phase. The higher the frequency, the higher the data rate. For example, many wireless LAN products operate in the 2.4 GHz band at a data rate of 1 Mbit/sec to 2 Mbits/sec. In 1997, the U.S. FCC (Federal Communications Commission) opened up 300 MHz of bandwidth in the 5 GHz range, providing a potential data rate of 10 Mbits/sec for wireless LANs. However, this range is currently limited to LAN use because it has limited range, even with increased power outputs.

Specific parts of the spectrum are allocated for various types of communication, as shown in Figure E-1. A receiving device then "tunes" itself to the designated frequency and extracts the modulated signal. The spectrum is allocated by governments and international organizations. In the United States, the FCC allocates bandwidth and sells it at auctions to companies that want to operate communication services in various markets. For example, AT&T owns rights to the 10 MHz radio spectrum band in 93 percent of the United States. It may use this spectrum to deploy a wireless telephone system in major markets, bypassing the need to deploy a wired system or work with local providers that have existing wired systems.

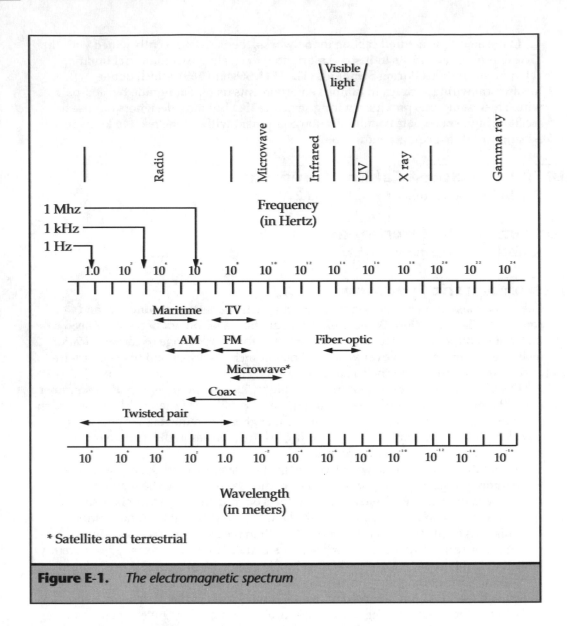

**Figure E-1.** *The electromagnetic spectrum*

# Electronic Commerce

Electronic commerce has come to be associated with the buying and selling of goods on the Internet. It involves some method of securing transactions, authorizing payments, and moving money between accounts. Electronic commerce may also involve business-to-business transactions, expanding on the older EDI (Electronic

Data Interchange) techniques of exchanging purchase orders, invoices, and other documents in electronic form.

EDI and other forms of business transactions have been taking place over public and private networks for some time. The financial system literally runs over the telecommunication network. Banks and bank branches execute transactions and move money this way on a regular basis. Credit card transactions are approved over dial-up or dedicated lines. Millions of stock market transactions take place every day using electronic means.

What is different with the Internet is that these transactions take place over public networks between buyers and sellers who may not have had any previous business relationship. The element of trust is missing and must be established in some way, as described here.

## Electronic Commerce Information

A number of companies are involved in setting standards and developing products for electronic commerce. Relevant companies and Web sites are mentioned throughout this topic.

By far the best place to find information about doing business on the Internet is at the CommerceNet site (http://www.commerce.net). Another useful site for electronic commerce information is Open Market (http://www.openmarket.com).

The goal of CommerceNet is to make electronic commerce over the Internet a reality. Backed by sponsors such as Apple Computer, Bank of America, Dunn & Bradstreet, IBM, Intel, Pacific Bell, and Wells Fargo, CommerceNet was started in 1994 as a place where businesses with similar needs could pool their resources. From CommerceNet you can order Internet business starter kits that help you build and maintain Web sites.

CommerceNet focuses on connectivity, data transfer, secure transactions, data transfer, payment services, marketing, collaboration techniques and tools, computer-aided logistics support, public policy, electronic directories and catalogs, Internet EDI, and network services. Indeed, these are the critical areas that anyone involved in doing business on the Internet must focus their attention on.

CommerceNet has been instrumental in the development of Internet security tools and financial transaction techniques. In fact, vendors of popular Web browsers are installing transaction security features in their browsers that are based on work done by CommerceNet and its members. CommerceNet was instrumental in the development of S-HTTP (Secure Hypertext Transfer Protocol), a secure version of HTTP that allows clients and servers to exchange encrypted information.

According to CommerceNet, electronic commerce will take hold once users have easy access to high-bandwidth connections, easy access to information and resources, encryption and security, and financial exchange mechanisms that make buying on the Internet easy. For the most part, these are now in place and users are gaining more trust in buying on the Internet.

## Electronic Commerce Security

There is a lot of apprehension about lack of security on the Internet. It took people a long time just to get used to bank ATMs. Security on public networks is provided by using cryptographic techniques. There are many works in progress that are meant to set security standards for electronic commerce.

To transact business, companies must have the means to conduct safe, private, and reliable transactions. To get to that level, the four cornerstones of secure electronic transactions must be present:

- The ability to prevent unauthorized monitoring of data transmissions

- A way to prevent the content of messages from being altered after they are sent and/or a way to prove that they have been altered

- The ability to determine whether a transmission is from an authentic source or from someone or something masquerading as that source

- A way to prevent a sender from denying (repudiating) that they sent a message (such as a buy order) or that they received and read a message

Cryptographic systems provide a way to transmit information across an untrusted communication system without disclosing the content of the information to someone monitoring the line. Cryptographic systems provide confidentiality and can also provide proof that a transmission has or has not been altered.

More information on the specifics of public-key cryptography can be found under "Certificates and Certification Systems," "Digital Signatures," "Private-Key Cryptography," "Public-Key Cryptography," and "Security."

## Security Services and Payment Systems

Security services provide a range of services and protocols for electronic commerce, including private communications, authentication, security in business transactions, electronic cash management, password-based authentication, and access controls. The following sections describe some of the technologies.

### Secure Channel Services

People who engage in business transactions over the Internet need secure connections. A secure channel service can provide this level of security. SSL (Secure Sockets Layer) is a transport-level protocol developed by Netscape that provides channel security. With SSL, the client and the server use a handshaking technique to agree on the level of security they want to use during a session. Authentication takes place over a security channel, and all information transmitted during the sessions is encrypted. The protocol authenticates the client, then exchanges a master key which is used to encrypt subsequent data exchanges. Both SSL and PCT (private communication technology) are under scrutiny in the IETF-TLS (Transport Layer Security) group. The charter for this group is at http://www.ietf.org/html.charters/tls-charter.html.

PCT is an alternative to SSL that was developed by Microsoft and Visa International. It provides many of the same functions as SSL but uses different keys for authentication and encryption.

S-HTTP (Secure Hypertext Transfer Protocol) goes a step further by providing a way to attach digital signatures to Web pages, thus verifying to users that the pages are indeed from the intended source. It is useful in workflow and document routing applications where documents must be signed and verified using digital signatures.

## Payment Protocols

The SET (Secure Electronic Transaction) protocol was developed by Microsoft, IBM, Netscape, GTE, Visa, and MasterCard so merchants could automatically and safely collect and process payments from Internet clients. Additional information on SET is available at the following Web sites:

| | |
|---|---|
| Visa International | http://www.visa.com |
| MasterCard International | http://www.mastercard.com |
| American Express Company | http://www.americanexpress.com |

SET secures credit card transactions by authenticating cardholders, merchants, and banks and by preserving the confidentiality of payment data. SET requires digital signatures to verify that the customer, the merchant, and the bank are legitimate. It also uses multiparty messages that prevent credit card numbers from ending up in the wrong hands. Microsoft uses SET in its Merchant Services product (discussed later in this topic under "Microsoft Merchant Services") as illustrated in Figure E-2.

There is a negotiation layer on top of SET and other payment protocols. The definition of this layer is the task of the JEPI (Joint Electronic Payment Initiative), a project managed by the W3C (World Wide Web Consortium) and CommerceNet. Information about JEPI is available at http://www.w3.org/pub/WWW/Payments.

The JEPI project explores the technology required to provide a negotiation layer over multiple payment methods, protocols, and transports. Examples of payment methods include credit cards, debit cards, electronic cash, micropayments, and electronic checks. Payment protocols (for example, SET) define the message format and sequence required to complete the payment transaction.

JEPI defines how to extend HTTP in a way that allows automatic selection of payment protocols. For example, a simple client/server exchange might go as follows. The server says "I support MasterCard and Visa." The client says "I have Visa." From this exchange, the two can negotiate a payment method.

Two protocols emerged from JEPI: PEP (Protocol Extensions Protocol) and UPP (Universal Payment Preamble). PEP sits on top of HTTP and UPP is a negotiations protocol that identifies appropriate payment methods. Both protocols automate payment negotiations.

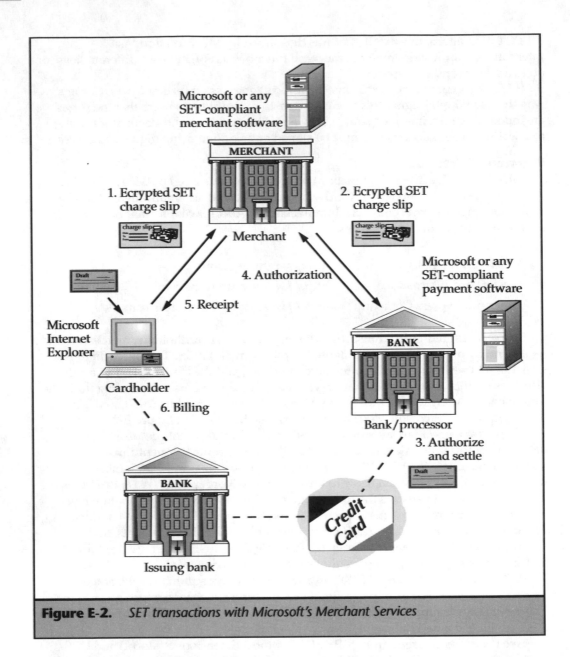

**Figure E-2.** *SET transactions with Microsoft's Merchant Services*

## Code-Signing Schemes

Code signing solves one of the larger questions facing the software industry today: How can users trust program code that is published on the Internet? Code signing provides a way to verify to users that programs obtained from the Internet are legitimate, just as shrink wrap and sealed boxes imply that off-the-shelf packaged software is authentic. Code signing provides

- Authenticity, so you know who published the code
- Integrity, so you know code has not been tampered with since it was published
- A legitimate and safe way to exchange programs over the Internet

Code signing schemes include Microsoft's Authenticode, JavaSoft's JAR (Java Archive), and IBM's Cryptolopes. The W3C (World Wide Web Consortium) is attempting to integrate these schemes into its Digital Signature Initiative. You can read more information about these technologies and the Digital Signature Initiative at http://www.w3.org/pub/WWW/Security/DSig/DsigProj.html.

## Electronic Cash

Electronic cash is a scheme that makes purchasing easier over the Internet. One method is for electronic cash companies to sell "Web dollars" that purchasers can use when they visit Web sites. Web sites accept these Web dollars as if they are coupons. Another analogy is that they are the online electronic version of American Express Travelers Cheques. Companies involved in this business are listed here. Note that these companies are also involved in other forms of Internet money transactions, which you can learn about by visiting their Web sites.

| | |
|---|---|
| CyberCash, Inc. | http://www.cybercash.com |
| DigiCash, Inc. | http://www.digicash.com |
| First Virtual Holdings, Inc. | http://www.fv.com |
| Mondex International | http://www.mondex.com |

### Wallets

A wallet is an electronic cash component that resides on the user's computer or another hardware device such as a smartcard. It stores personal security information such as private keys, credit card numbers, and certificates; can be moved from place to place so users can work at different computers; and has its access controlled by policies.

The PFX (Personal Information Exchange) is a Microsoft protocol that enables users to transfer sensitive information from one environment or platform to another. For example, a user may have information such as certificates and keys stored on a PC in her office, but she also needs to securely transfer this information to her Macintosh at home. With this protocol, a user can securely export personal information from one computer system to another. Visit http://www.microsoft.com for information about PFX.

### Cybercash

CyberCash uses the wallet concept. A consumer selects items to buy, and the merchant presents him or her with an invoice and a request for payment. The consumer can then have the CyberCash Wallet pay for the purchase by simply clicking the Pay button. From there, encrypted messages are exchanged between the merchant server, the consumer, and the CyberCash server, as well as the conventional credit card networks, to transfer funds appropriately.

CyberCash's Digital NewsStand is a technology that lets digital publishers allow access to visitors who are willing to pay for the content they want to see. People who want to purchase content use CyberCoins. A CyberCoin is designed to imitate a real coin that you would insert into a newspaper stand to release the door and get a paper.

### First Virtual

First Virtual's Internet Payment System operates with ordinary e-mail. A VirtualPIN (an alias for a credit card) is used to make purchases. Credit card numbers are never transmitted over the Internet. Every purchase is confirmed by a return e-mail.

To become a buyer using First Virtual's system, you must have an Internet e-mail address and a valid Visa or MasterCard. You also must complete an application and receive your VirtualPIN. Your credit card is registered with First Virtual over the telephone, not over the Internet.

To buy, you give your VirtualPIN to a seller instead of a credit card number. First Virtual will then send you an e-mail to confirm the purchase, and you reply to the e-mail with a "yes" to confirm the sale or a "no" to cancel it. If you confirm the sale, your credit card is charged by First Virtual, completely off the Internet.

### Micropayments

Because electronic transactions are so easy and inexpensive, Internet businesses feel that it's reasonable to charge a penny, or even less than a penny, every time someone accesses information at a site. This is called making *micropayments*.

Publishers need to have an incentive for putting content up, and that incentive is profit; but if they charge too much, people won't access their systems. Micropayments produce a profit as long as enough people buy content. Messages like "access will require a charge of .25" will become common on the Web. The alternative is to just give things away and sell advertising space.

## Electronic Commerce Solution Providers

This section describes three electronic commerce solutions, ranging from EDI-like business-to-business software to electronic online Internet storefronts. Software from Open Market, CrossRoute, Netscape, and Microsoft is highlighted.

### Open Market

Open Market is a public Internet software company founded in 1994. It develops, markets, licenses, and supports software products that "allow its customers to engage in business-to-consumer and business-to-business electronic commerce on the Internet." Its current lineup of software is designed to provide secure electronic commerce. The products are described here. For additional information, visit Open Market's Web site at http://www.openmarket.com.

- **OM-Transact** A commerce application that enables companies to offer secure payment, complete order management, and online customer service.

- **OM-Axcess** An access management and reporting solution for centrally managing and authenticating end users. It provides a way of building authentication, authorization, and session tracking into Web-based applications and content.

- **OM-SecureLink** Works with OM-Transact and OM-Axcess applications to provide a way to turn existing Web content into a commerce-enabled site.

## CrossRoute

CrossRoute Software (http://www.crossroute.com) has developed software that automates business-to-business transactions and processes. It is cross-business workflow software. The software uses intelligent components from which customers can create transaction processes and define custom rules for controlling those processes. Businesses can exchange standard EDI format documents or custom format documents. A single integrated application automates business processes between companies using the Internet or private networks.

Other features include

- Workflow features, such as document routing and the ability to initiate processes based on events.

- Based on Java and uses any ODBC-compliant database to store process information.

- Business connections can be made over the Internet, private networks, dial-up connections, and e-mail.

- Set security policies, including privacy, authentication, data integrity, and nonrepudiation options. Uses public-key cryptography.

- Simulation and monitoring tools for preproduction testing and in-process monitoring and auditing.

Visit the CrossRoute Web site listed above for more details on this product.

## Actra CrossCommerce from Netscape

Actra CrossCommerce is an electronic commerce solution from Netscape that provides EDI-like business-to-business transactions over the Internet and/or online Internet storefronts. Transaction processing allows advanced purchase and supplier management, electronic payments, online catalogs, registry, dynamic page management, authentication, and billing.

CrossCommerce implements open standards such as EDI INT (provides a way to use existing EDI technology over the Internet), X12 and EDIFACT (EDI-structured document standards). CrossCommerce also support CORBA and IIOP (Internet

Inter-ORB Protocol), which provide distributed component technology. See "Component Software Technology" and "EDI (Electronic Data Interchange)" for more information.

CrossCommerce components are described here:

- **Xpert** An administrative interface for building cross-business relationships, document workflow, and user privileges.

- **OrderXpert Seller** A tool for establishing a sales site that includes a transaction and order processing system, encrypted payments, membership system, access control system, order fulfillment, and order status capability for buyers.

- **OrderXpert Buyer** A tool for building an internal procurement system. It complements OrderXpert Seller as an internal procurement system.

- **Merchant Xpert** A business-to-consumer sales system for creating online stores.

- **Publishing Xpert** A transaction-based content publishing system that provides a way to collect customer interests, demographics, and site usage.

For additional information, visit Netscape's Web site at http://www.netscape.com.

## Microsoft Merchant Services

Microsoft's Merchant Services is a set of technologies for building and operating an electronic retailing system. It helps alleviate some of the difficulties of building and operating an electronic retail site. It provides consistent software formats and interoperability so merchants can integrate their services with suppliers, and it provides a secure and reliable shopping experience for customers that can be convenient as well as fun. Merchant Services is pictured in Figure E-2.

One of the primary goals of Merchant Services is to let merchants quickly create their own online store operation and focus on merchandising rather than concentrating on developing their own in-house solution. Components include a shopping interface called Internet Shopper, an order-capturing system, a processing and routing system, and merchandising tools. Internet Shopper downloads to users' Web browsers when they visit the merchant site. It provides a consistent interface while shopping.

As online shoppers browse for things to buy, they can put items in a shopping basket. When they are ready to buy, they authorize payment from their wallet, which holds credit information. Customers enter credit card information once, when they first use their card. The information is password protected, so the next time they use a service, they enter only their password to authorize payments. Other aspects of Internet Shopper include

- It stores credit card information on the local system in a secure way and encrypts order information before transmitting it.

- It calculates shipping, handling, sales tax, and totals online, and credit information is authenticated at the same time.

- An address book stores shipping and billing addresses so customers don't need to do a lot of retyping.

- Customers can place items in a shopping basket and defer purchases until later.

- Internet Shopper stores a history of online shopping for later referral. Customer tracking numbers are also maintained for this purpose.

The server components of Merchant Services handle order processing, financial transactions, and the creation of Web pages from information pulled from product databases. An online store consists of a collection of HTML (Hypertext Markup Language) pages that customers browse through when connected to the store. This browsing is designed to mimic walking around a real store with a shopping basket.

Additional information about Merchant Services can be found on Microsoft's Web site at http://www.microsoft.com.

## OBI (Open Buying on the Internet)

OBI is a protocol designed by American Express and SupplyWorks for executing real-time business transactions on the Web. Microsoft, Netscape, Oracle, Open Market, and a number of other companies back the specification. The goal is to reduce costs, improve the overall buying/paying process, and increase service levels to end users using Internet technology. OBI will achieve some of the same results as EDI. The EDI X12-850 document standard is used for structuring and sending electronic documents. Digital certificates are required for this type of transaction so companies receiving business documents can prove their authenticity.

To get more information about OBI, send electronic mail to the OBI Consortium, at OBI@supplyworks.com.

## Developing Trust

New technologies and tools have been developed to make Internet electronic commerce secure. The technologies just need acceptance. The industry has been working to develop the methodologies that will make public acceptance more widespread.

Security has increased overall on the Internet. Companies that connect electronic commerce systems to the Internet have been concerned about the security of their internal networks. In some cases, internal networks should be disconnected from external networks, but firewall technology has vastly improved to provide a way to keep intruders out while letting real customers in.

The EFF (Electronic Frontier Foundation) and CommerceNet are working to overcome some of the issues people have with trust on the Internet. The partners have implemented eTRUST, an initiative that is meant to establish more consumer trust and confidence in electronic transactions. The purpose of the initiative is to build a log system that consumers will associate with trust and to make the eTRUST brand known worldwide.

A Commercial Guidelines and Auditing Standards committee was formed to oversee privacy issues and develop guidelines for an accreditation program. Its members include Coopers & Lybrand, Firefly Network, KPMG, and Test Drive. Online companies can use the program to gain consumer trust. A third-party auditing and monitoring program is part of the scheme. Companies that meet eTRUST privacy and security guidelines will be able to display eTRUST logos on their Web pages.

The Electronic Frontier Foundation Web site is at http://www.eff.org. CommerceNet's Web site is at http://www.commerce.net.

**RELATED ENTRIES**   Authenticode, Microsoft; Certificates and Certification Systems; Digital Signatures; EDI (Electronic Data Interchange); Electronic Mail; Extranet; Groupware; Intranets and Extranets; IPSec (IP Security); Security; SET (Secure Electronic Transaction); S/WAN (Secure WAN); VPN (Virtual Private Network); Web Technologies and Concepts; *and* Workflow Management

**INFORMATION ON THE INTERNET**

| | |
|---|---|
| CommerceNet | http://www.commerce.net |
| Electronic Commerce World Institute | http://www.ecworld.org |
| W3C (World Wide Web Consortium) | http://www.w3.org |
| EFF (Electronic Frontier Foundation) | http://www.eff.org |
| Open Market, Inc. | http://www.openmarket.com |
| The Computer Information Centre (check the electronic commerce section for extensive links) | http://www.compinfo.co.uk |
| DISA (Data Interchange Standards Association, Inc.) | http://www.disa.org |
| Premenos Corporation | http://www.premenos.com |

# Electronic Frontier Foundation

According to the EFF (Electronic Frontier Foundation) Web site, EFF is a nonprofit civil liberties organization working in the public interest to protect privacy, free expression, and access to public resources and information online, as well as to promote responsibility in new media. It is also dedicated to finding ways to resolve information-age-related conflicts.

The foundation is located in San Francisco, and their Web site is at http://www.eff.org.

# Electronic Mail

Electronic mail (e-mail) is probably the most common application used on networks. Indeed, the growth of enterprise networks is often based on getting everyone in the organization connected just so they can share e-mail. Messaging systems are becoming an important tool for program development in distributed environments. Many collaborative applications are built upon electronic messaging systems.

There are many different e-mail systems in use on networks, mainframe systems, and public networks. The Internet's message standard is SMTP (Simple Mail Transfer Protocol), which has become a de facto standard. The growth of the Internet and intranets has promoted its acceptance almost everywhere. In addition, Netscape integrated SMTP-compatible e-mail services into its Navigator Web browser in 1996, and Microsoft quickly followed. As a result, almost every Web user has an SMTP mail client available for their use.

Legacy mail systems still abound, and most administrators need to provide interoperability among them. These systems include IBM PROFS (Professional Office System) and SNADS (SNA Distributed Services), which are used in the IBM mainframe environment. VAXmail or All-In-1 are used in the DEC environment.

In addition, numerous e-mail systems have been available in the desktop networking environment. A single organization might have numerous e-mail systems that were implemented in the days when departments or workgroups maintained their own LANs. As the organization was interconnected, e-mail gateway systems were often employed to translate messages among the different systems. The CCITT X.400 Message Handling System was supposed to provide a system for exchanging messages among a wide variety of messaging platforms, but it has not caught on.

Today, most network administrators prefer to use a single mail standard, and that is the Internet SMTP protocol. Vendors are also integrating the standard into their proprietary systems. Because of its pervasiveness, the Internet mail standard is covered in this section.

## Electronic Mail Features

An electronic mail system for an enterprise network consists of the following components, which are illustrated in Figure E-3.

- A front-end application called a *UA* (*user agent*) that provides facilities for creating, addressing, sending, receiving, and forwarding messages. Other features include the ability to attach files and other information to messages and the ability to manage a personal address book.

- A back-end *MTA* (*message transfer agent*) that transfers messages from the UA and delivers them to mail servers. A message might need to move between a number of mail servers before it reaches its destination.

- Mail servers that run MTAs and provide temporary message stores.

**E**

■ A directory service that maintains a database of users and services on the network. Users can access the service to locate a user and his or her e-mail address.

Additional features in some e-mail systems include the ability to secure messages with encryption or add a digital signature to prove the authenticity of messages and prevent alterations. The ability to send and receive facsimiles is another feature included with many systems.

## Electronic Mail Standards

The following is a list of major electronic mail standards that are in use today. Some standards, such as X.400 have been around for a long time but have not been widely accepted. Others, such as the Internet mail standards, are in widespread use.

**X.400** The CCITT X.400 MHS standard defines an electronic system for exchanging messages among store-and-forward mail systems running on a wide variety of platforms. In ISO terminology, X.400 is called the MOTIS (Message-Oriented Text Interchange System). It outlines the protocols, procedures, components, terminology, and testing methods required to build interoperable e-mail systems. X.400 is based on a distributed client/server model. Refer to "X.400 Message Handling System" for more information.

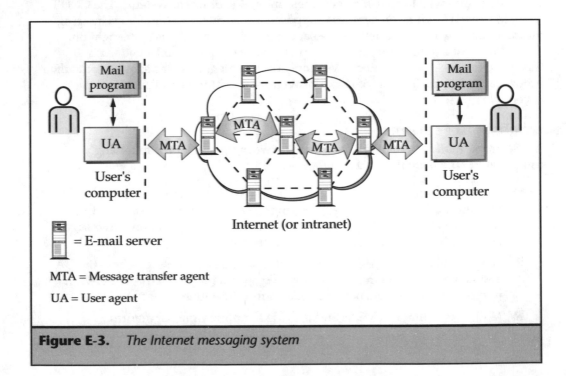

**Figure E-3.** *The Internet messaging system*

**SMTP (SIMPLE MAIL TRANSFER PROTOCOL)**   SMTP is the message-exchange standard for the Internet. It is familiar to most people by its addressing technique—the username@company.com format. SMTP provides the very important function of moving messages from one e-mail server to another. SMTP is designed for TCP/IP networks and uses the IP addressing scheme. It works in conjunction with POP (Post Office Protocol), a mail server, to receive and send mail. POP receives mail and holds it in a user's post office mailbox, while SMTP provides message transport services. See "SMTP (Simple Mail Transfer Protocol)" for more information.

**MIME (MULTIPURPOSE INTERNET MAIL EXTENSION) AND S/MIME (SECURE MIME)**   SMTP can only handle messages that contain 7-bit ASCII text. MIME provides a way to insert 8-bit binary data into messages. This type of data is usually multimedia such as graphics and sound, but new encoding schemes can be defined at any time. The data is "attached" to the message in a format that is compatible with the SMTP message format. Lines are added to the header of the message to indicate the presence and structure of MIME information. S/MIME is a de facto standard for securing mail messages that can replace PGP (Pretty Good Privacy) and PEM (Privacy-Enhanced Mail). See "MIME (Multipurpose Internet Mail Extension)" for more information.

**POP (POST OFFICE PROTOCOL)**   POP is an Internet mail server protocol that provides an incoming message storage system. It works in conjunction with the SMTP to provide a message system for the Internet and intranets. SMTP provides message transport services. Many e-mail systems will be described as POP3 compatible. See "POP (Post Office Protocol)" for more information.

**IMAP4 (INTERNET MAIL ACCESS PROTOCOL 4)**   IMAP is considered the successor to POP. It is a store-and-forward mail server protocol that goes a step beyond POP. IMAP lets users access a mail box on the mail server, as opposed to having mail delivered directly to the inbox in their SMTP-compatible client software. IMAP4 is the latest version of IMAP and provides better mail server management capabilities. For example, administrators can manage folders from a remote location (i.e., over a WAN link). Mailboxes can also be replicated to benefit mobile users. See "IMAP (Internet Mail Access Protocol)" for more information.

**LDAP (LIGHTWEIGHT DIRECTORY ACCESS PROTOCOL)**   LDAP is a directory services protocol that goes beyond simple e-mail address books by providing a way for e-mail clients to browse directories of users on any LDAP-compliant messaging server. LDAP has basically taken the industry by storm. Almost every vendor of directory services products is integrating LDAP support into their products. See "LDAP (Lightweight Directory Access Protocol)" for more information.

**MAPI (MESSAGING APPLICATION PROGRAMMING INTERFACE)**   MAPI is a set of interfaces that helps developers integrate support for a variety of e-mail systems into their applications. MAPI has become widely accepted in the industry. Today, most messaging systems provide support for MAPI. See "MAPI (Messaging Application Programming Interface)" for more information.

## How Internet Mail Works

In the old days, e-mail was designed to run on mainframes, and since everyone accessed the same system with their terminal, there was no need to transfer mail to other computer systems. Eventually there was a need to do this, and the SMTP protocol was defined in 1982 for delivering mail over the growing internet.

The Internet mail system must send and receive messages from potentially millions of different computers on thousands of different networks. The SMTP protocol is the protocol that defines the format of messages and how they are processed and delivered. A mail program running on a user's computer follows these standards and presents an interface to the user for reading, creating, and deleting messages. When a user creates a message, the UA background process submits the messages for deliver to the MTA. The MTA then performs the task of moving the message to the destination. Mail servers must run continually in order to transfer messages at any time.

MTAs communicate with other MTAs on the Internet because the messaging infrastructure consists of many mail servers through which messages pass, as shown in Figure E-3. Messages are routed through the infrastructure from one mail server to the next until the messages reach their destination. The following describes the message transfer path:

1. Sender types message at mail interface connected to UA.

2. UA submits message to local MTA.

3. MTA to MTA to MTA (and so on to destination MTA).

4. Destination MTA sends message to UA.

5. Recipient reads message.

The final message server in the chain provides a mailbox for the user and holds messages until the user asks for them. This is the purposes of a POP server.

SMTP was designed to move messages between mail servers relatively quickly, and this works well on local area networks. But an intermediate storage system is needed. On dial-up lines and WANs, as well as on the Internet, time-out problems can occur if a message can't be completely delivered within a certain period of time. The Post Office Protocol solves the time-out problem by temporarily storing messages so an SMTP transfer can be completed before the time-out occurs. Clients (typically remote dial-up users) connect with the POP server to access their e-mail. The clients must use a mail application that has built-in POP client software in order to access mail from a POP server.

If a message is destined for a recipient on the Internet, the mail server contacts a DNS (Domain Name System) server and has the recipient's e-mail server address converted to an appropriate IP address. The message is then sent by the MTAs. As with all packets on the Internet, the message may be forwarded through several intermediate servers until it reaches the destination.

Historically, the most common MTA has been a daemon called *sendmail*. However, sendmail is hard to administer and is a known security problem. A number of sendmail replacements exist, especially in the DOS and Windows environment where entirely new programs had to be developed to work with the traditionally UNIX-based mail system. An MTA called post.office is available from Software.com (http://www.software.com).

As mentioned, users do not interact directly with MTAs, but instead go through a mail interface that is connected to the UA. Many different UAs are available, either from vendors or as free public software. A program called *mail* is the most pervasive user agent in the UNIX environment because it comes with most UNIX systems. Other common user agents in the UNIX environment are Elm and Pine, both of which have simple interfaces and are easy for beginners to use. Still others are MH (Message Handler) and Mush (Mail User's Shell). In the PC environment, a free product called Pegasus works like Novell's MHS (Message Handling Service). Pine is usually recommended, and the Web site address for downloading it is given at the end of this topic.

## Other Aspects of Internet Mail Protocols

There are several other features of the SMTP protocol. To ensure reliable delivery, the UA on a sender's computer keeps a copy of a message until the receiving computer has stored the message. A server may also reject messages from some sources or prevent a particular system from receiving messages.

Messages can also be addressed to multiple users. If the users are all at the same location (i.e., have mailboxes at the same server), then a single message is sent to the server, which in turn sends copies to all the recipients listed in the message. This technique is used by groupware and collaborative software packages to send messages to members of a workgroup.

With regard to POP, messages are usually deleted on the server after the client retrieves them. This has been a source of frustration to many users, especially mobile users. Many mobile devices are small computers with limited or no storage. With current systems, once a user reads a message from his or her mailbox, the message is lost unless he can store it locally. IMAP4 will solve this problem by providing a way to create a hierarchy of folders for message storage at the mail server.

Mailing list programs are programs that distribute messages to large numbers of recipients by taking advantage of the Internet mail protocols. A manager can create a mailing list and have all messages submitted to the listserver automatically forwarded to the names on the list. LISTSERV is the name of a mailing list product sold by L-Soft International, Inc., that has its roots in the original mailing list server product created by Eric Thomas in 1986. A public package called Majordomo is also available. See "Mailing List Programs" for more information.

### The Internet Mail Consortium

The IMC (Internet Mail Consortium) is an international organization that promotes electronic mail and electronic mail standards on the Internet. The goals of the IMC include greatly expanding the role of mail on the Internet into areas such as commerce and entertainment, advancing new Internet mail technologies, and making it easier for all Internet users, particularly novices, to get the most out of this versatile communications medium. IMC's Web site is listed at the end of this topic.

## E-mail Systems and Products

A typical enterprise might have a variety of SMTP clients already running and exchanging mail with little problem. For example, PC users might run Eudora while UNIX users might run Pine. The users are happy because they are getting reliable message exchange. In addition, most Web browsers now include mail clients that use Internet mail protocols, so mail clients are essentially everywhere.

Most vendors of proprietary e-mail systems have already integrated Internet protocols into their systems. Most proprietary systems offer features that Internet mail systems have not traditionally provided. Their proprietary nature makes it easy for the vendor to add features that will enhance the salability of the product. But this also locks the customer into proprietary transport mechanisms and message formats. While customers may have a strong need for these custom features, they also have a need to connect with the Internet and exchange messages on a global scale.

As shown in Figure E-4, a vendor might need to supply an e-mail gateway that allows users to access Internet mail. The gateways provide relay and translation services between the proprietary e-mail system and the Internet e-mail system.

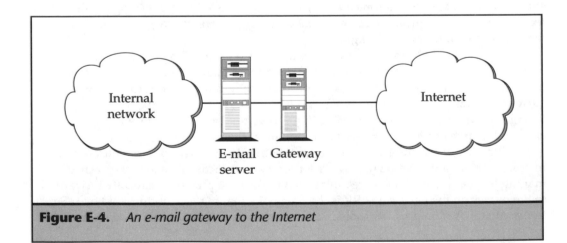

**Figure E-4.**   *An e-mail gateway to the Internet*

However, with the proliferation of the Internet, most administrators feel this approach is unsuitable and that Internet protocols should form the basis of messaging throughout their organizations. Because of this, existing e-mail vendors have scrambled to convert their systems as new vendors quickly appeared to provide customers with just what they needed. Software.com introduced products that are built entirely on Internet protocols or new protocols that improve on those protocols.

Many of the new mail systems that support Internet protocols also offer some of the features that have been provided in high-end proprietary mail systems, such as:

- Mail server replication that protects the system and makes messages more readily available to users at other locations in the company

- Server-bound mail boxes that let users keep messages in a central location for later referral

- Directory services to make it easier for people to locate e-mail addresses

- Public folders that serve as repositories for shared messages, forms, documents, applications, and other information

- Discussion databases and chat rooms that let people actively post and exchange messages on an ongoing basis, using the message thread approach

- Support for remote users that dial directly into the mail server

- The ability to build applications such as groupware and workflow products that take advantage of the services provided in the messaging server

Microsoft Exchange is a good example of a messaging product that provides an expanded set of features and support for a range of industry standards. Refer to "Microsoft Exchange Server" for more details. Lotus Notes and Novell GroupWise are other examples of this type of platform.

Here is a list of e-mail products and their vendors' Web sites:

| | |
|---|---|
| Attachmate's Emissary | http://www.attachmate.com |
| Banyan's Beyond Mail | http://www.banyan.com |
| Baranof Software's MailCheck | http://www.baranof.com |
| Control Data Systems' Mail*Hub | http://www.cdc.com |
| Fujitsu's TeamWare Messaging | http://www.fujitsu.com |
| Galacticom's Worldgroup | http://www.gcomm.com |
| LAN-ACES' Office-Logic | http://www.lan-aces.com |
| Lotus Notes | http://www.lotus.com |
| Microsoft Exchange Server | http://www.microsoft.com |
| Novell's GroupWise | http://www.novell.com |
| Software.com | http://www.software.com |

*E*

**ELECTRONIC MAIL AND MIME RFCs ON THE INTERNET**   MIME is defined in a number of different Internet RFCs, including RFC 822 (the original Internet mail definition), RFC 1049, RFC 1154, RFC 1521, RFC 1522, RFC 2045, RFC 2046, RFC 2047, RFC 2048, and RFC 2049. You can view these RFCs by entering the following address in your Web browser, replacing the italic placeholders with the number of the RFC you want to view: http://www.internic.net/rfc/rfc*nnnn*.txt.

**RELATED ENTRIES**   Groupware; IMAP (Internet Mail Access Protocol); Information Publishing; Lotus Notes; Mailing List Programs; Microsoft Exchange Server; MIME (Multipurpose Internet Mail Extension); POP (Post Office Protocol); SMTP (Simple Mail Transfer Protocol); *and* Workflow Management

**INFORMATION ON THE INTERNET**

| | |
|---|---|
| Internet Mail Consortium | http://www.imc.org |
| Electronic Messaging Association | http://www.ema.org |
| The IMAP Connection | http://www.imap.org |
| IMAP Information Center | http://www.washington.edu/imap |
| The Carnegie Mellon Enterprise Electronic Mail Project | http://andrew2.andrew.cmu.edu/cyrus/cyrus |
| Yahoo!'s Electronic Mail links page | http://www.yahoo.com/Computers_and_Internet/Communications_and_Networking/Electronic_Mail |
| Douglas W. Sauder's MIME Information Page | http://www.fwb.gulf.net/~dwsauder/mime.html |
| Pine—a Program for Internet News & Email (free) | http://www.washington.edu/pine/index.html |

## Electronic Software Distribution and Licensing

Software distribution and the licensing of that software is a big problem on large networks. Without an automated method for installing and updating programs, utilities, and drivers, network managers or their assistants must spend time manually updating workstations on the network. This involves travel time and expense in many cases. A typical organization may have thousands of workstations at diverse sites, some requiring more than one day's travel. It makes sense to rely on management software to handle these tasks whenever possible.

ESD (electronic software distribution) and ESL (electronic software licensing) are now recognized as critical to the proper management of large networks. ESD provides automatic software updating, and ESL provides automatic tracking of software usage to ensure that an organization stays within its software licensing requirements.

Licensing packages are used to ensure that a company is operating within its legal boundaries for software usage. A licensing package typically holds keys that allow users to access software applications. Each key is a license that has been purchased from the software vendor. The licensing program delivers keys to users who request the use of an application. When the keys are gone, other users can't access applications until a key frees up or more keys are added. Licensing programs usually include controls that prevent unauthorized users from accessing programs or prevent users from holding a key for too long.

## Software Distribution and Management Programs

Software distribution programs for in-house use ideally copy software to workstations, install the software, configure it, and provide periodic updates when necessary. The programs can look at system configurations and update the configurations if necessary.

Much of the work in software distribution and management programs is being handled by the DMTF (Desktop Management Task Force) and is defined in DMTF's DMI (Desktop Management Interface). Part of the DMI is an agent that collects information about network workstations and other nodes and places the information in a file called the MIFF (management information format file). MIFFs provide information required to install and configure an application for a specific machine, such as its type of video, printer, and memory configuration.

The latest trend is to use Internet and Web technologies for software distribution on in-house platforms. Push technologies are often employed to automatically distribute software to users, as opposed to pull technologies in which users choose to update on their own. See "Push" for more information on push technologies.

Novell NAL (NetWare Application Launcher) is a software distribution utility included in NetWare Client, IntranetWare, or you can obtain it for free by accessing Novell's Web site, at http://www.novel.com. NAL enables administrators to install and manage applications on Windows-based workstations across networks. It uses NDS (Novell Directory Services) as a central repository for all application information.

Microsoft Windows NT includes ESD functions in the BackOffice SMS (System Management Server) module. It distributes and installs software on desktops and servers at both local and remote sites. Administrators can time the installation events, set who can access shared software on servers, configure desktop settings, schedule commands on specific PCs, and perform a number of other tasks from the SMS console.

Other ESD packages includes the following:

■ **LANDesk Management Suite from Intel**   This package works with NetWare servers and includes software distribution and inventory functions. Visit http://www.intel.com.

*E*

■ **SiteExpress from McAfee Associates** A PC-based distribution package that includes an inventory application. It distributes software to Windows and OS/2 clients. Visit http://www.mcafee.com.

■ **Xfer from Platinum Technology** A UNIX-based package that can distribute software to UNIX, Windows, and OS/2 clients. Visit http://www.platinum.com.

# EMBARC (Electronic Mail Broadcasts to a Roaming Computer)

EMBARC is a provider of one-way beeper and pager communication services. It was first launched in 1992, into 112 markets in the United States and Canada. It competes with SkyTel and provides messaging capabilities as high as 30,000 characters, compared to the SkyTel limit of 240. EMBARC also allows users to send messages to a number of users at the same time. This is useful for updating information on several remote machines. EMBARC users can also get news from various sources, such as *USA Today*.

# EMI (Electromagnetic Interference)

EMI is waves of energy that emanate from electrical devices and cables. The waves may interfere with the proper operation of nearby devices or the proper transmission of signals in nearby cabling systems. Electromechanical devices emit low frequency waves, while computer chips and other integrated circuit emit high-frequency waves. If the emissions have sufficient energy and are close enough to another device, they will interfere with that device. U.S. and international regulatory agencies provide standards that ensure that devices do not exceed certain emission levels. The FCC (Federal Communication Commission) regulates emissions in the United States.

# Emulated LAN

*See* IP over ATM; LANE (LAN Emulation); MPOA (Multiprotocol over ATM); Switched Networks; Virtual Circuit; *and* VLAN (Virtual LAN).

# Encapsulation

Encapsulation is a method of packaging information into packets. In the TCP/IP protocol suite, the network layer encapsulates TCP segments from the transport layer into IP datagrams. The data link layer then encapsulates IP datagrams into the frames defined by the physical network.

Encapsulation also takes the form of *tunneling*, which is a way of inserting one type of packet into another type for delivery across a network. The encapsulated packet "piggybacks" a ride on the packet of the native protocol's network. While this adds overhead, it provides a way to send packets from one network to another over an intermediate network that uses a different protocol.

For example, in a technique called *IP tunneling,* it's possible to encapsulate NetWare IPX (Internetwork Packet Exchange) packets into IP packets and transmit them over the TCP/IP network as shown in Figure E-5. Another example is the ability to encapsulate SNA (Systems Network Architecture) or NetBIOS packets into IP packets. Routers are used to interconnect the different networks and encapsulate the packets. At the receiving end, the packet is unencapsulated and travels on to its destination on that network. See "Tunnels" and "VPN (Virtual Private Network)" for more information.

Public data network providers such as AT&T use encapsulation to transport data packets over ATM cell-switching devices with SONET (Synchronous Optical Network) interfaces. In SMDS (Switched Multimegabit Data Services), a packet structure is defined on top of a cell-switching structure. A customer's data packets are encapsulated in SMDS packets, then placed into cells to take advantage of the greater speed of cell switching.

Encapsulation also provides a way to use FDDI (Fiber Distributed Data Interface) as a backbone for a local or campus-wide network. For example, an Ethernet frame is placed inside an FDDI frame and sent across the FDDI backbone. When the packet reaches the bridge attached to the destination network, it is unpackaged and sent to the destination. Encapsulation is normally implemented in most Ethernet-to-FDDI bridges.

## Encapsulation Protocols

Some common encapsulation protocols are described next. These protocols are often supported by routers and other types of network connection devices available from a variety of network vendors. Encapsulation is widely used, and related topics are listed under "Related Entries" at the end of this topic.

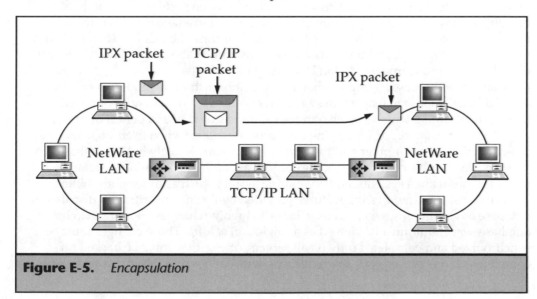

**Figure E-5.**    *Encapsulation*

**PPP**    PPP (Point-to-Point Protocol) is a protocol for transporting a variety of network protocol information over a dial-up link. Internet users often use PPP to obtain a TCP/IP connection between their computer and an ISP (Internet service provider). Many commercially available routers and bridges also use the protocol. TCP/IP protocol packets are encapsulated inside the PPP frames and transported across the link. IPX, NetBEUI, SNA, and other protocols are also supported. See "PPP (Point-to-Point Protocol)" for more details.

**PPP MULTILINK**    PPP Multilink is an inverse-multiplexing standard. It provides a way to combine several dial-up lines to form a single aggregate channel. Other protocols are then encapsulated using the same methods as PPP. MPP (Multichannel PPP) is an Ascend extension that provides dynamic bandwidth allocation, allowing the data rate of the line to be increased as needed by making additional dial-up connections. See "PPP Multilink" for more information.

**FRAME-RELAY ENCAPSULATION**    Many routers take advantage of encapsulation on frame relay. With this method, protocol packets are encapsulated into frame relay frames and transmitted across a frame relay PVC (permanent virtual circuit).

**RELATED ENTRIES**    IPSec (IP Security); PPP (Point-to-Point Protocol); PPP Multilink; PPTP (Point-to-Point Tunneling Protocol); Routers; Security; S/WAN (Secure WAN); Tunnels; VPN (Virtual Private Network); *and* WAN (Wide Area Network)

## Encina, Transarc

Encina is a product from Transarc Corporation for building and operating distributed OLTP (online transaction processing) applications in open system environments. It combines many of the concepts from conventional mainframe-based transaction processing systems such as IBM's CICS (Customer Information Control System) with research on distributed and transactional systems done at the Massachusetts Institute of Technology and Carnegie-Mellon University in the 1980s.

Transaction processing implies that a transaction, such as the updating of a bank account in a database management system, is executed immediately, as opposed to batch processing, in which a batch of transactions is stored over a period of time, then executed later. Transaction processing can occur in *real time* when users are connected directly online to a computer and the results appear immediately in the database. The most common transaction processing examples are airline reservation systems, banking transactions systems, and accounting systems such as order-entry billing.

The transaction-monitoring features provided by Encina are critical in distributed database environments, where transactions can involve changes on more than one database server but must be viewed as a single *unit of work*. Those changes must be synchronized and completed fully on all servers, or else they must be backed off completely. If one server goes down during a write, any writes made on other systems during the transactions must be backed off. See "Transaction Processing" for more details.

In early 1996, Transarc released DE-Light, which allows Web browsers to connect into DCE networks and take advantage of transaction processing. In the past, this was difficult to do because of the application overhead required in the client. DE-Light reduces the amount of code required in the client by moving it to an intermediate system that executes the transactions for the client. The client merely calls the transactions and receives the results.

Transarc is now a subsidiary of IBM.

**RELATED ENTRY**     Transaction Processing

**INFORMATION ON THE INTERNET**

Transarc Corporation          http://www.transarc.com

# Encryption

*See* Cryptography.

# End System

End systems are the hosts in TCP/IP networks, but more specifically, end systems are the computers at either side of a communication session. This latter explanation is most relevant when discussing transmissions between systems that may take place across any number of networks and involve any number of routing devices. In this case, many intermediate systems provide communication links, but the two end systems assume that they are communicating directly with one another.

A connection-oriented session is a session between two end systems over a mesh network in which a virtual circuit is established through the network. End systems are the computers at either end of the virtual circuit.

An end system can also be described as the system where a circuit originates and is terminated.

# Enterprise Networks

During the 1980s and early 1990s, organizations began to install local area networks to connect computers in departments and workgroups. Department-level managers usually made decisions about what type of computers and networks they wanted to install.

Eventually, organizations saw benefits in building enterprise networks that would let people throughout the organization exchange e-mail and work together using collaborative software. An enterprise network would connect all the isolated departmental or workgroup networks into an intracompany network with the potential of allowing all computer users in a company to access any data or computing resource. It would provide interoperability among autonomous and heterogeneous systems and have the eventual goal of reducing the number of communication protocols in use. Toward this goal, industry organizations were formed to create open standards, and vendors developed their own strategies.

The latest trend is to build so-called *intranets* using TCP/IP protocols and Web technologies. While intranet technologies have emerged only recently, they take a different approach to consolidating networks than the traditional enterprise computing strategy. In some respects, the intranet model has achieved better results at less cost and with fewer configuration problems than the traditional enterprise model.

## The Traditional Enterprise Network

An enterprise network is both local and wide area in scope. It integrates all the systems within an organization, whether they are DOS-based computers, Apple Macintoshes, UNIX workstations, minicomputers, or mainframes.

Many people thought that a network should be a "plug-and-play" platform for connecting all sorts of devices, as shown in Figure E-6. In this platform scenario, no user or group is an island. All systems can potentially communicate with all other systems while maintaining reasonable performance, security, and reliability.

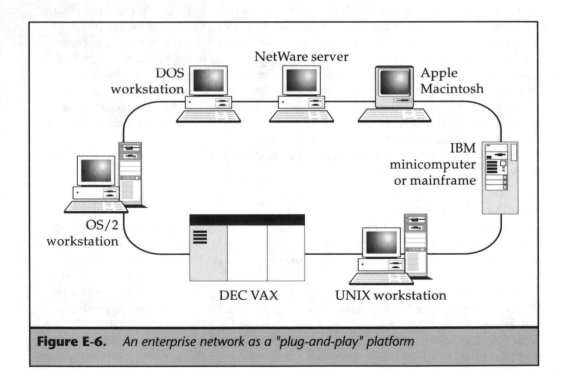

**Figure E-6.**    *An enterprise network as a "plug-and-play" platform*

The trick to making these "blue sky" objectives work is to follow one of two scenarios:

- Create a network platform with underlying standards that allows multivendor hardware and software products to work together.
- Create operating systems and applications that support multiple standards.

Over the last few years, both strategies were implemented. Operating system vendors included support for almost every network protocol. Driver support was added to allow clients to access resources on almost any other operating system. It is not uncommon to find a network that simultaneously uses IPX (Internetwork Packet Exchange), TCP/IP, and SNA (Systems Network Architecture) protocols to allow communication with a variety of systems.

However, this strategy has limitations. Just because a Windows NT system supports TCP/IP does not mean that a UNIX station can seamlessly access resources on that system. A higher level of interoperability is necessary, and this is where the enterprise strategies began to show their shortcomings. One solution was to develop client/server computing and middleware strategies that could hide the difference between systems. Here is a sampling of some of the vendor strategies or industry consortium strategies for integrating systems:

- **Microsoft's WOSA (Windows Open Services Architecture)**   A strategy to build middleware directly into its operating systems so that information flows more easily throughout the enterprise. WOSA includes ODBC (Open Database Connectivity), a standard database interface.

- **The Open Group's DCE (Distributed Computing Environment)**   A set of *enabling* software that hides the difference between multivendor products, technologies, and standards by providing tools for the development and maintenance of distributed applications.

- **SAG (SQL Access Group) and the X/Open Group**   Consortiums of database vendors that are enforcing SQL (Structured Query Language) standards for accessing databases across multivendor systems. Both groups are now part of The Open Group.

- **DRDA (Distributed Relational Database Architecture)**   An IBM standard for accessing database information across IBM platforms that follows SQL standards.

- **OMG (Object Management Group)**   An organization that is providing standards for implementing cross-platform, object-oriented environments. CORBA (Common Object Request Broker Architecture) is part of OMG's OMA (Object Management Architecture).

**E**

## The New Enterprise Computing Model

The so-called *enterprise computing strategy* began to take root as more and more organizations adopted TCP/IP. TCP/IP makes internetworking easy. However, a typical enterprise network has a diversity of operating systems, applications, and data formats that restrict the free flow of information. People wanted to collaborate without the need for translating, reformatting, and recompiling their programs and data.

In 1994, people started to notice that the Web was providing the heterogeneous environment that people wanted all along, and that it was practically free. You could use a single interface (the Web browser) to access information on any system running Web server software. In fact, when you access a server on the Web, the server's operating system and hardware platform are unimportant. In this respect, Web browsers are like universal client interfaces.

By the end of 1995, it was clear to many in the industry that at least until something better came along, setting up internal Web servers might be a good way to disseminate information throughout an organization. After all, almost everybody accessing the Internet had a Web browser. Why not use it to access information on back-end database systems and IBM mainframe computer systems?

This new *intranet* strategy really brought a lot of things into focus. Why write several different versions of a program to access database servers and mainframe systems when you can write one Web-based application that Macintosh, PC, and UNIX users can access with a Web browser? Web development tools benefit developers, Web site administrators, and users. They merge traditional programming languages and document processing (markup) languages, making it much easier to develop applications with custom user interfaces.

Getting information off database servers and legacy systems is easier because you only need to write a link between the Web server and the back-end system. Users access the Web server and the Web server accesses back-end systems. This is often called a multitiered approach. Java applets, ActiveX, and component software technology take advantage of this model.

So intranets are the new enterprise network. This technology has grown without control, for our benefit in most cases. In fact, I sometimes wonder whether we are getting too locked into this technology. At some point, its deficiencies will start to pop up and make themselves known. We will then search for new technologies to overcome those deficiencies, just as the enterprise network was supposed to overcome the confusion caused by the proliferation of departmental LANs.

**RELATED ENTRIES**    Client/Server Computing; Component Software Technology; CORBA (Common Object Request Broker Architecture); Database Connectivity; Data Warehousing; DCE (Distributed Computing Environment), The Open Group; Directory Services; Distributed Computer Networks; Distributed Database;

Distributed File Systems; Distributed Object Computing; Intranets and Extranets; Java; Middleware and Messaging; Multitiered Architectures; Network Concepts; ODBC (Open Database Connectivity), Microsoft; OLE DB; Web Middleware and Database Connectivity; *and* Web Technologies and Concepts

## Error Detection and Correction

Data processing and transmission systems use a variety of techniques to detect and correct errors that occur, usually for any of the following reasons:

- Electrostatic interference from nearby machines or circuits
- Attenuation of the signal caused by a resistance to current in a cable
- Distortion due to inductance and capacitance
- Loss in transmission due to leakage
- Impulses from static in the atmosphere

It is estimated that an error occurs for every 1 in 200,000 bits. While most LAN technologies and optical cable networks reduce errors considerably, wireless networks and WAN links have high error rates.

There are two solutions to this problem:

- **Error correction strategy**  Send enough additional information to correct problems at the destination. This is called FEC (forward error correction).
- **Error detection strategy**  Send only enough extra information to detect an error, then request a retransmission from the source. This is called ARQ (automatic repeat request).

ARQ is usually preferred because it requires fewer bits for transmission, but if many errors do occur, such as in wireless mobile communications, retransmission may occupy a large part of the bandwidth. FEC is used when retransmission is not practical or possible. Sending program data to an interplanetary spacecraft comes to mind.

The "additional information" sent in either case is called *redundant bits*. These bits provide enough addition information to determine what a corrupted block of data should really be (as in FEC) or to determine if the block is corrupted (as in ARQ). FEC requires that more bits be sent with each transmission and does not use the transmission line efficiently (although you might consider it efficient if a lot of errors are occurring). Because ARQ is used most often, it is discussed next.

ARQ strategies allow a receiving device to detect errors in transmissions and request a retransmission from the sender. Two ARQ strategies are outlined next:

**PARITY CHECK**    This is the simplest error-detection mechanism. A parity bit is appended to a block of data, normally at the end of a 7-bit ASCII (American Standard Code for Information Interchange) character. Two techniques—even parity or odd parity—are available and which method is used is up to the user. In even parity, a parity bit is selected so that the character has an even number of 1s. In odd parity, the parity bit is selected so that the character has an odd number of 1s. So, for example, if even parity is selected and a computer receives a character with an odd number of 1s, it assumes an error and asks for a retransmission. This method easily breaks down. If two bits change, an error is undetectable by the receiver.

**CRC (CYCLIC REDUNDANCY CHECKSUM)**    The CRC method operates on blocks of data called frames. Basically, the sender appends a bit sequence to every frame called the FCS (frame check sequence). The resulting frame is exactly divisible by a predetermined number. The receiving computer divides the frame by the predetermined number. If there is a remainder, the frame is considered corrupted and a retransmission is requested. This method is commonly used in many forms of communication. It provides a high level of error-detection with speed and ease of use.

**RELATED ENTRIES**    Asynchronous Communications; Flow-Control Mechanisms; Handshake Procedures; *and* Serial Communication and Interfaces

# ESA (Enterprise System Architecture), IBM

*See* SAA (Systems Application Architecture).

# ESCON (Enterprise System Connections)

ESCON is a set of IBM products and services that provides a dynamically connected environment within an enterprise. ESCON provides direct channel-to-channel connections between mainframe systems over fiber-optic links at distances up to 60 kilometers (36 miles). It also provides a way for communication controllers and other devices to share a single channel to a mainframe.

**RELATED ENTRIES**    Cluster Controllers, IBM; IBM Mainframe Environment

# ES-IS (End System-to-Intermediate System) Routing

ES-IS routing is an OSI (Open Systems Interconnection) method for routing within autonomous domains. A *domain* is a set of networks administered by a single company or organization. Access into a domain is controlled by security measures put in place by the administrators of the domain. A typical network consists of a group of user computers, called *end systems,* within a department or workgroup. These subnetworks are connected to backbone networks via routers. ES-IS routing takes place only between the end systems and the routers or intermediate systems. Other types of routing are used across domains.

**RELATED ENTRY**    Routing Protocols and Algorithms

## Ethernet

The Ethernet networking system was created at Xerox's Palo Alto Research Center in 1970 by Dr. Robert Metcalfe. The system was jointly developed as a standard in 1980 by Digital Equipment Corporation, Intel, and Xerox. This standard became known as DIX Ethernet in reference to the developers' names. The IEEE (Institute of Electrical and Electronic Engineers) 802.3 standard defines a similar, but slightly different, network that uses an alternate frame format. (The *frame* is the structure and encoding of a transmitted bit stream across a link.) Because the IEEE 802.3 standard has been widely adopted and because it was adopted as an ISO (International Organization for Standardization) worldwide standard, it is discussed here.

Note that the industry has adopted the name Ethernet to refer to all forms of the shared CSMA/CD (carrier sense multiple access/collision detection) networking scheme. The actual name for most implementations today is IEEE 802.3, but the name Ethernet has become so pervasive that it is hard to find a vendor or publication that does not refer to IEEE 802.3 as Ethernet. Ethernet 802.3 is often used to clarify this point.

There are a number of adaptations to the IEEE 802.3 Ethernet standard, including adaptations with data rates of 10 Mbits/sec and 100 Mbits/sec over coaxial cable, twisted-pair cable, and fiber-optic cable. Currently, the twisted-pair variety of Ethernet is the most popular. The latest version of Ethernet, *Gigabit Ethernet,* has a data rate of 1 Gbit/sec.

The following list describes the different varieties of Ethernet. Note that the first number in the name refers to the speed in Mbits/sec, and the last number refers to the meters per segment (multiplied by 100). *Base* stands for baseband and *Broad* stands for broadband. Note that a description of cabling types can be found under the heading "Transmission Media, Methods, and Equipment."

- **10Base-5**    *Thicknet* coaxial cable with maximum segment lengths of 500 meters; uses baseband transmission methods.

- **10Base-2**    *Thinnet* coaxial cable (RG-58 A/U) with maximum segment lengths of about 185 meters; uses baseband transmission methods.

- **10Base-T**    Twisted-pair cable with maximum segment lengths of 100 meters.

- **10Base-F**    Supports fiber-optic cable backbones of up to 4 kilometers with transmission at 10 Mbits/sec. The TIA/EIA (Telecommunications Industry Association/Electronic Industries Association) has approved this cable for cross-connects between campus buildings in its Commercial Building Wiring Standard.

- **100Base-TX**    *Fast Ethernet* (100 Mbits/sec) over two pairs of Category 5 UTP (unshielded twisted-pair) or Category 1 shielded twisted-pair cable.

*E*

- **100Base-T4** *Fast Ethernet* (100 Mbits/sec) over four pairs of Category 3, 4, or 5 UTP wiring.

- **100Base-FX** Fast Ethernet (100 Mbits/sec) over fiber-optic cable.

- **100VG-AnyLAN** A *Fast Ethernet* standard that supports 100-Mbit/sec throughput and uses a *demand priority access method* instead of CSMA/CD over hierarchical twisted-pair wiring configurations.

Because 10Base-2, 10Base-T, and 100Base-T are the most popular topologies, only they are discussed in this section in detail. Because 100VG-AnyLAN is not an Ethernet 802.3 standard, it is discussed under its own heading.

## General Ethernet Features

The topology of Ethernet 802.3 networks, with the exception of those that implement the new 100VG-AnyLAN standard, is a linear bus with a CSMA/CD access method. In coaxial cable Ethernet implementations, workstations are connected in a daisy-chain fashion by attaching segments of cable between each station as shown on the left in Figure E-7. The segments form a single, large cable system called the *trunk*. The twisted-pair version of Ethernet (10Base-T and 100Base-T) is configured as a star topology in which the cable to each station branches from a central wiring hub, as shown on the right in Figure E-7.

Note that the cable layouts (physical topology) in Figure E-7 are quite different. However, in both cases, a single Ethernet signal is carried to all stations at once. In other words, the entire network operates as a single *logical* communication channel, in which transmissions from one computer are "broadcast" to all other computers.

A repeater is a device that can extend an Ethernet LAN by amplifying and retiming the signals. A repeater simply extends the broadcast domain of the network.

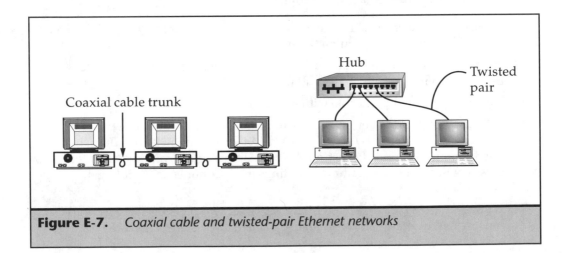

**Figure E-7.**  *Coaxial cable and twisted-pair Ethernet networks*

It does not create two separate networks. There are limitations to the number of repeaters that can be used, due to propagation delays. You cannot create a network that is so large that a station at one end cannot detect when a station at the other end has just begun to transmit. Both stations would end up using the cable at the same time.

The rules and restrictions for building Ethernet networks must be adhered to in order to prevent signal timing problems, loops, and potential network lockouts. Each adaptation of Ethernet has its own specifications for cable lengths, maximum number of stations, and other factors.

## Medium Access Controls

An Ethernet LAN is shared by all the stations attached to it. The CSMA/CD access control method is used to arbitrate how stations access the shared medium. With carrier-sensing access methods, workstations sense whether the cable is in use and transmit only if it is not in use. However, collisions do occur if two stations happen to transmit at the same time. A collision detection mechanism provides arbitration if two stations happen to transmit at the same time. The CSMA/CD collision detection mechanism senses collisions, and both workstations back off for a random period of time and then try transmitting again later.

The CSMA/CD method is efficient when network traffic is light. As traffic increases, more collisions occur. Stations back off and retransmit again, but if the network is still busy, this process continues and escalates, causing a performance drop and a perceived slowdown to the users. One solution is to reduce the number of workstations on each LAN segment by using segmentation techniques, as discussed later in this topic under "Hubs, Switches, and Segmentation."

The collision problem is one factor that imposes a limit on the trunk length of an Ethernet segment. The maximum distance is 2,500 meters (2.5 miles). Trunks beyond this limit are subject to signal propagation delays that can cause a failure in the collision detection mechanism. A station at one end of the cable may not sense the access of another if the cable is too long. A failure to detect multiple access causes data corruption and can lock the LAN segment.

## Frame Formats

An Ethernet frame format defines the layout for packaging data and control information into frames and transmitting it over a network. It defines the position of headers and control bits, and the position and size of the data. Figure E-8 shows the frame for the original Ethernet_II at the top and the IEEE 802.3 frame at the bottom. Important fields in the frames are described here.

- **Preamble** This field marks the start of a frame. It always contains the bit pattern 10101010. Interestingly, this pattern produces a clocking signal that appears as a 10 MHz square wave for 5.6 microseconds to the receiver.

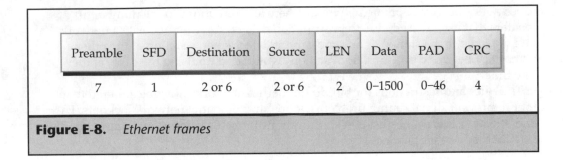

**Figure E-8.** *Ethernet frames*

- **SFD (start frame delimiter)** This field indicates the actual start of the frame itself and always contains the bit pattern 10101011.

- **Destination and Source** These fields hold the address of where the frame came from and where it is supposed to go.

- **Length (LEN) of data field** This field indicates the length of the data portion of the frame.

- **CRC (cyclic redundancy checksum)** This field holds a value calculated on the packet by the sender. The receiver performs the same calculation to see if it comes up with the same CRC value. If not, the frame is considered corrupted and must be retransmitted.

## Addressing and Operation

All Ethernet NICs (network interface cards) come with a preassigned 48-bit network address. This address is made up of a 24-bit number that identifies the vendor of the card and a 24-bit number assigned by the vendor to identify the card, like a serial number. When the NIC is installed into a computer and the computer is attached to a network, the address on the NIC serves as the network address for the computer. No two network cards ever have the same NIC address, so Ethernet address configuration is a no-brainer for administrators. This NIC address becomes what is commonly known as the physical address or the MAC (Medium Access Control) address.

A sending computer puts the NIC address of the recipient computer in the frame that it is sending that computer. When the computer gets access to the network, it broadcasts the frame, and all other stations on the same network segment read the address in the frame to determine if it is addressed to them. When a station finds a frame that is addressed to it, it reads the entire frame into its buffer.

A special multicast address is also used to send a message to all stations attached to the network. This "broadcast" address is 48 bits wide and is filled with all 1s. A multicasting technique is also available in which a frame can contain an address that multiple stations will receive as a group.

So far, this discussion has focused on sending frames on a local network, i.e., a network within the same broadcast domain. In this case, the MAC address is used. But what if the network is attached to another network via a router and you want to transmit to a computer on the other network? In this case, a higher-level addressing scheme is required. TCP/IP and IPX/SPX (Internetwork Packet Exchange/Sequenced Packet Exchange) are common internetworking protocols.

TCP/IP internetworks consist of subnetworks connected by routers as shown in Figure E-9. A subnetwork for the purposes of this Ethernet discussion is an Ethernet broadcast domain. Every computer on a TCP/IP network has two addresses: a MAC address that is only used within the subnetwork and an IP address that identifies the computer on the internetwork. In this configuration, two computers on the same subnetwork send each other messages by using the MAC address. In contrast, two computers on different subnetworks need to know each other's IP address to transmit messages.

Referring to Figure E-9, note that the subnetwork on the left has the IP address 100.20.10.x, and the subnetwork on the right has IP address 100.20.11.x. You can replace the x with a value to represent each node on the subnetwork. Assume that node 100.20.10.1 (called *sender* from here on) wants to send a message to node 100.20.11.1 (called *destination*). Here is the procedure:

1. *Sender* broadcasts a request on its own local network that it wants to send a message to *destination*.

2. The router knows *destination's* address, so it returns a message to *sender* containing its own MAC address. Basically, the router is saying to *sender* "send your message to me because I know how to get it to *destination*."

3. *Sender* builds a message with the MAC address of the router and *destination's* IP address.

4. When the router receives this message, it recognizes *destination's* IP address and repackages the message as a frame to be delivered on network 100.20.11.0 with a header that contains *destination's* MAC address.

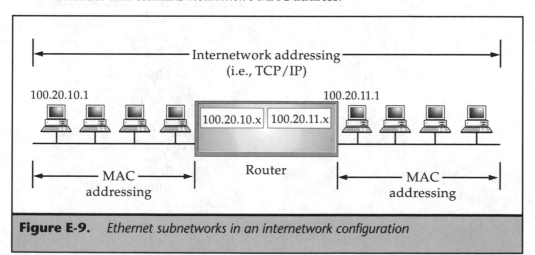

**Figure E-9.** *Ethernet subnetworks in an internetwork configuration*

The important point is that once a message arrives at a router that is attached to the destination computer's subnetwork, the IP address is no longer used. Instead, the MAC address is used to forward the message in an Ethernet frame over the local Ethernet subnetwork to the destination.

## Hubs, Switches, and Segmentation

As mentioned earlier, Ethernet networks can be built with coaxial cables in a bus topology or with twisted-pair cables using a star topology. In the latter case, hubs provide a central place from which cables branch to the network stations. This wiring scheme prevents breaks in any one wire from bringing down the whole network and promotes structured cabling methods.

A simple hub is basically a repeater. All the stations attached to it participate in the same broadcast domain. Similar repeater hubs can be attached to create a hierarchical wiring scheme as shown on the left in Figure E-10. This scheme creates a larger LAN that extends the broadcast domains and adds more stations.

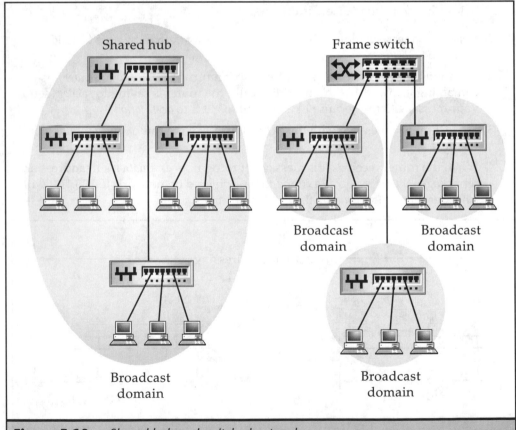

**Figure E-10.** *Shared hub and switched network*

The problem with adding more stations to a broadcast domain is that it increases the number of users that need to transmit on the LAN. This increases contention for the network and causes collisions that further degrade the performance of the network. A more practical approach is to split networks into smaller broadcast domains, Each segment is now a separate broadcast domain with fewer stations than before, so there is less contention. Routers move packets among networks as necessary. However, routers are expensive, so this approach is not really cost effective.

Enter the *switching hub* (also called a frame switch or LAN switch). Switching hubs are multiport devices in which each port operates like a separate LAN with its own broadcast domain. You can put a single station on each port for the highest performance, or you can attach repeater hubs that provide connections for a number of stations. This configuration is shown on the right in Figure E-10. Now, all the stations attached to a single port contend for only the network to which they are attached. If a station needs to transmit to a station attached to another port, the switch handles the forwarding of frames by setting up a temporary line connection between the two. This is similar to bridging.

Almost every vendor of network devices has pursued this approach and expanded on it with new backbone technologies that implement high-speed ATM (Asynchronous Transfer Mode) or Gigabit Ethernet networking. The structure of these new networks is pictured in Figure E-11. Note that the backbone must be fast because it moves frame/packets among all the network segments in the organization.

This topic is covered further under "Switched Networks." Related topics are "ATM (Asynchronous Transfer Mode)," "Gigabit Ethernet," and "TIA/EIA Structured Cabling Standards."

## Ethernet 10Base-2 (Thinnet)

Ethernet 10Base-2 is the coaxial cable version of Ethernet that was widely installed in the 1980s. Ethernet 10Base-5 was popular earlier on, but the Thinnet coaxial cable was physically easier to handle and cheaper than Thicknet Ethernet cable, although the maximum trunk length is less than is possible with Thicknet Ethernet. Figure E-12 illustrates a thin Ethernet network, and Figure E-13 illustrates the components of the wiring system.

The components of a 10Base-2 network are described in the next sections.

- **Network interface board**  Most Ethernet boards support either thick or thin Ethernet cabling. The board should have a BNC-type connector attached to the back and might also have a thick Ethernet connector. The trunk cable attaches to a BNC T-connector, which is then attached to a male BNC connector on the back of the board. You must use a remote-boot PROM (programmable read-only memory) if the card is installed in a diskless workstation.

- **Repeater**  A repeater is an optional device used to join two Ethernet trunks and to strengthen the signals between them. A message transmitted on a LAN must pass through no more than two repeaters before either reaching its destination or passing through a LAN bridge.

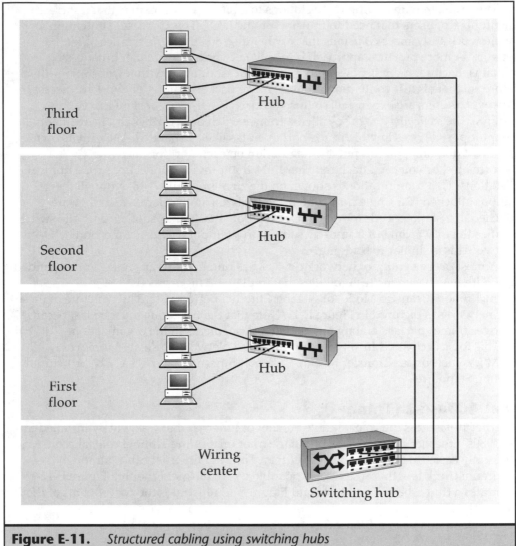

**Figure E-11.** *Structured cabling using switching hubs*

■ **Thin Ethernet cable** The cabling used for thin Ethernet is a 50-ohm 0.2-inch-diameter RG-58 A/U or RG-58 C/U coaxial cable. Thin Ethernet cable is available from many vendors who have precut standard lengths ready to ship with attached connectors. Bulk cable can also be purchased, but you'll need to cut the cable and mount BNC connectors on the ends. Note that cable is available as fire-safe plenum cable, nonplenum interior cable, underground-rated cable, and aerial-rated cable.

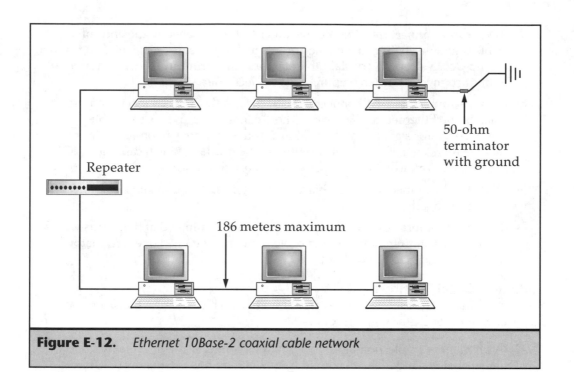

**Figure E-12.** *Ethernet 10Base-2 coaxial cable network*

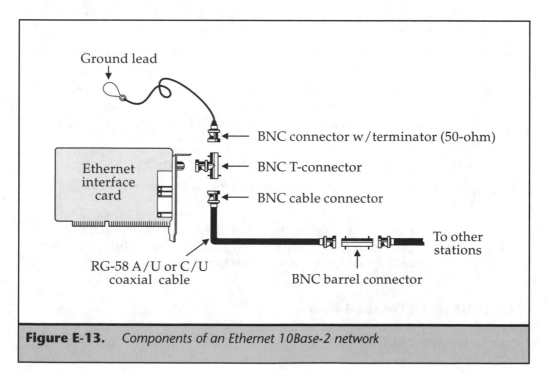

**Figure E-13.** *Components of an Ethernet 10Base-2 network*

E

- **BNC cable connectors** BNC connectors must be attached to the ends of all cable segments. BNC cable-connector kits include a center pin, a housing, and a clamp-down sleeve. A coaxial cable stripping and crimping tool is required to mount connectors. It can be purchased at electronics stores.

- **BNC T-connectors** A T-connector is attached to the BNC connector on the back of the Ethernet interface card. The T-connector provides two cable connections for signal-in and signal-out. You will need a T-connector for each workstation, even if it is the last station in the trunk, in which case the BNC terminator is attached to the open end of the T-connector.

- **BNC barrel connectors** BNC barrel connectors are used to join two cable segments together.

- **BNC terminators** Each cable segment must be terminated at both ends with a 50-ohm BNC terminator. For each cable segment, you need one terminator with a ground and one without.

### 10Base-2 Specifications

You must abide by the following rules and limitations when wiring Ethernet networks with RG-58 A/U or RG-58 C/U coaxial cable:

- A segment is a collection of up to 30 stations connected with cable in a daisy-chain fashion. The maximum segment length is 186 meters (607 feet).

- A trunk is a collection of up to 5 segments, connected together with repeaters. The maximum network trunk length is 910 meters (3,035 feet).

- When segments are joined to trunks with repeaters, the repeater counts as a station, allowing only 29 additional stations.

- On a trunk that consists of five segments, stations are allowed on only three of the segments. The others are used for distance.

- No piece of cable interconnecting two stations may be shorter than 0.5 meters (1.64 feet) in length.

- T-connectors are used to connect the network interface card to the cable.

- A terminator must be placed at each end of a trunk, and one end must be grounded.

Note that once the cable and T-connectors are configured into a segment, the T-connector can be removed from and reattached to a station without bringing down the network. However, if the cable itself is disconnected from a T-connector, the network will stop working.

## Ethernet 10Base-T (Twisted-Pair)

10Base-T provides the advantages of 10Base-2 Ethernet without the limitations and cost of coaxial cable. In addition, a star, or distributed, topology allows for clusters of workstations in departments or other areas. It is easy to build hierarchical wiring systems with this system. Even though cable segment distances are shorter, the hierarchical topology provides a cabling scheme that makes up for this deficiency.

A basic 10Base-T network is shown in Figure E-14. Workstations are attached to a central hub, or concentrator, that acts as a repeater. When a signal from a workstation arrives, the hub broadcasts it on all output lines. You can attach hubs to other hubs in a hierarchical configuration. Workstations are attached to the hub with a UTP (unshielded twisted-pair) cable that cannot exceed 100 meters (328 feet).

10Base-T connections use Category 3 cabling as shown in Figure E-15. Two pairs of wires are used—one pair for receiving data and the other for transmitting data. The transmit wires connect to pins 1 and 2, and the receive wires connect to pins 3 and 6, as shown in Figure E-15. The twists in each pair must be maintained all the way up to the connection point. Higher grades of cable can be used, such as Category 5. This provides for future growth into faster transmission technologies such as 100Base-T.

Figure E-16 illustrates a small-office wiring configuration. Note that the hub in the wiring closet connects to a coaxial or fiber-optic backbone that interconnects other departments within a building. A 50-wire telephone jumper cable connects the concentrator to a telephone punchdown block. Twisted-pair cable then runs from the punchdown block to wall faceplates near workstations. At the workstation, a cable is

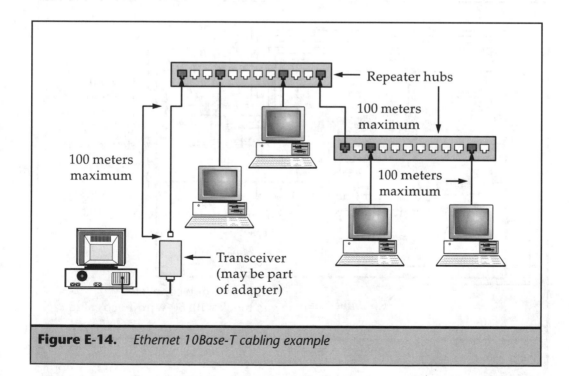

**Figure E-14.** *Ethernet 10Base-T cabling example*

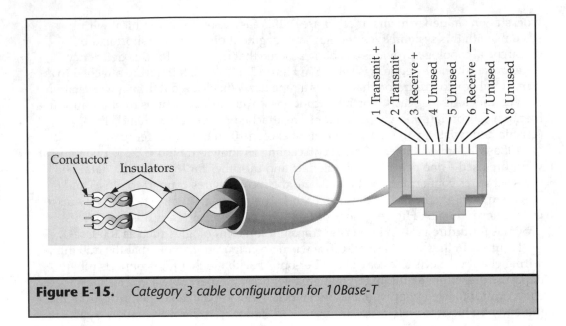

**Figure E-15.**   *Category 3 cable configuration for 10Base-T*

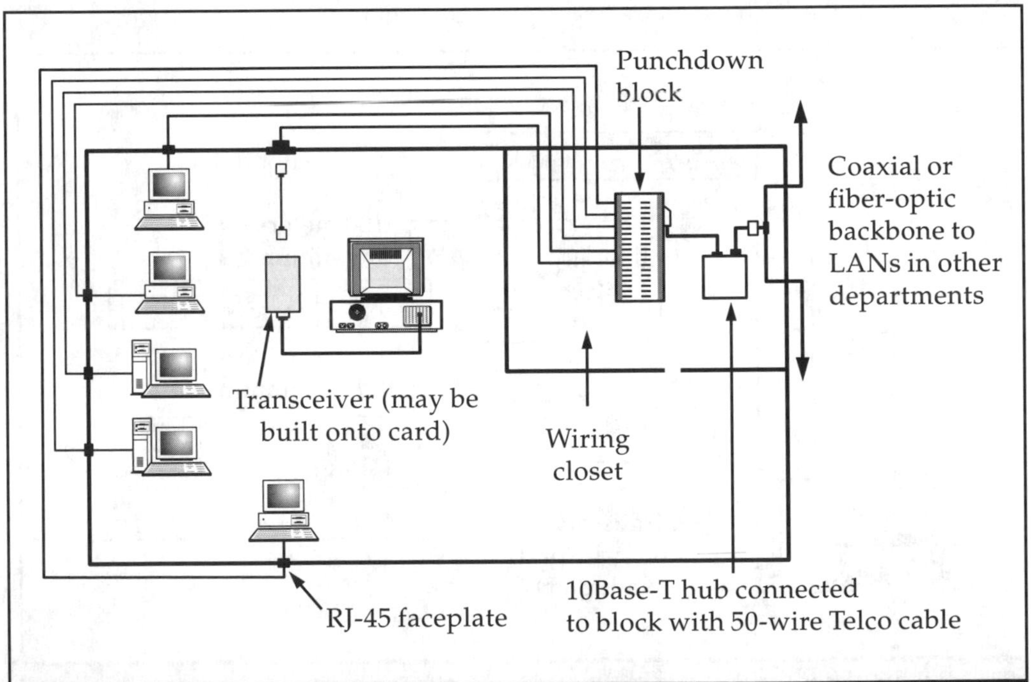

**Figure E-16.**   *Ethernet 10Base-T wiring closet configuration*

strung from the faceplate to a transceiver, which then connects to the workstation. Note that the Ethernet specification recommends a maximum of 90 meters from wiring closet to faceplate. The remaining 10 meters should be sufficient for the faceplate-to-station cable. This cable must be the same Category 3 or greater twisted-pair variety and not the cables used to connect telephones.

The components described in the following sections are typically part of a 10Base-T network. Keep in mind that a system doesn't always require all of these components.

- **Network interface card** An Ethernet card with a 10Base-T RJ-45 connector is required. Add a remote-boot PROM if you install the card in a diskless workstation.

- **Hub** The hub (also called a concentrator) often has up to 12 ports. One of the ports can be used to attach to other hubs. Advanced devices may have high-speed ports for connection to fiber-optic backbones.

- **Twisted-pair cable** 10Base-T uses twisted-pair cable with RJ-45 connectors that can be up to 100 meters long. You can purchase bulk cable and connectors to make custom cables. You'll need an RJ crimp tool if you are installing the cable yourself.

- **Punchdown block connector cable** If existing telephone cable is to be used, a 50-pin Telco cable that connects the concentrator directly to a telephone punchdown block simplifies the installation. Check with your hub vendor.

- **Wall plate** A wall plate is a connector with an RJ plug. If a phone connection is also required, dual plates can be purchased.

## 10Base-T Specifications

The 10Base-T specifications are listed here. Note that some of these specifications are flexible, depending on the vendor. An entire connection from wall plate to hub is pictured in Figure E-17.

- Use Category 3, 4, or 5 unshielded twisted-pair cable.

- Use RJ-45 jacks at the end of cables. Pins 1 and 2 are "transmit" and pins 3 and 6 are "receive." Each pair is crossed over so that the transmitter at one end connects to a receiver at the other end.

- The distance from a station to a hub cannot exceed 100 meters (328 feet).

- Up to 12 hubs can be attached to a central hub to expand the number of network stations.

- Hubs can be attached to coaxial or fiber-optic backbones to become part of larger Ethernet networks.

- Up to 1,024 stations are possible on a network without using bridges.

**E**

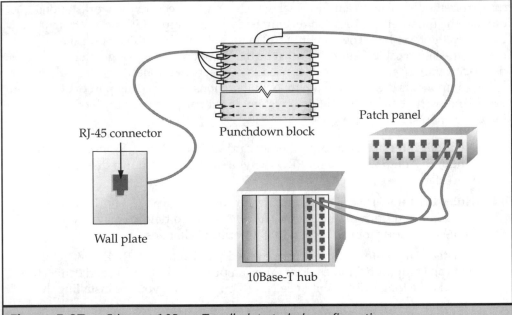

**Figure E-17.** *Ethernet 10Base-T wall-plate-to-hub configuration*

## Ethernet 100Base-T (Fast Ethernet)

During the development of Fast Ethernet, two groups had different ideas about how to implement it. One group wanted to keep the CSMA/CD medium access method and retain some compatibility with existing Ethernet standards. This group referred to their specification as *Fast Ethernet*. The other group wanted to create a new access scheme called *demand priority*. This demand priority group eventually developed 100VG-AnyLAN (IEEE 802.12).

For information about the IEEE 802.12 specification, refer to "100VG-AnyLAN." Fast Ethernet falls under the original IEEE 802.3 specifications. For information, refer to "Fast Ethernet."

## Additional Information

Ethernet equipment is available from a variety of vendors. Check the following sources online for additional information. You can also order informative catalogs from these vendors.

| | |
|---|---|
| Black Box Corporation (412) 746-5500 | http://www.blackbox.com |
| Andrews Worldwide Communications (800) 255-1479 | http://www.andrews.com |
| Allied Electronics, Inc. (800) 433-5700 | http://www.allied.avnet.com |

**RELATED ENTRIES**   100VG-AnyLAN; ATM (Asynchronous Transfer Mode); Backbone Networks; CSMA/CD (Carrier Sense Multiple Access/Collision Detection); Data Communication Concepts; Fast Ethernet; Gigabit Ethernet; Iso-Ethernet; LANE (LAN Emulation); Network Concepts; Network Design and Construction; Point-to-Point Communications; Switched Networks; Testing and Diagnostic Equipment and Techniques; Throughput; TIA/EIA Structured Cabling Standards; Transmission Media, Methods, and Equipment; *and* Wireless Communications

### INFORMATION ON THE INTERNET

| | |
|---|---|
| Yahoo!'s Ethernet links page | http://www.yahoo.com/Computers_and_Internet/Communications_and_Networking/LANs/Ethernet |
| Charles Spurgeon's Ethernet page | http://www.ots.utexas.edu/ethernet |
| NetSuite's Ethernet Technical Reference Summary | http://www.netsuite.com/ts/tr/ethernet.htm |
| Cisco Systems' Ethernet information page | http://www.cisco.com/univercd/data/doc/cintrnet/ito/55771.htm |
| Nathan Muller's Ethernet document | http://iquest.com/~nmuller/ether1.shtml |
| H. Gilbert's Ethernet document | http://pclt.cis.yale.edu/pclt/comm/ether.htm |

## EtherTalk

EtherTalk is an implementation of the IEEE (Institute of Electrical and Electronic Engineers) 802.3 Ethernet standard for Apple Macintosh computers. EtherTalk adapters provided by Apple include media adapters for thin coaxial cable, twisted-pair cable, and fiber-optic cable. The cards are called the Ethernet NuBus (NB) card for Macintosh IIs or the Ethernet LC card for Macintosh LCs. An external adapter is also available for non-NuBus systems. It attaches to the SCSI (Small Computer System Interface) port.

**RELATED ENTRIES**   AppleTalk; Ethernet

## Exterior Routing

Interconnected networks such as the Internet consist of autonomous systems that are connected to one another with gateway systems (routers). Routers within an autonomous system are called interior routers, and routers that interconnect autonomous systems are called exterior routers. Interior routing is handled by IRPs (interior routing protocols), and exterior routing is handled by ERPs (exterior routing protocols).

**RELATED ENTRY**   Routing Protocols and Algorithms

## Extranet

The term extranet is an outgrowth of intranet, a term that describes internal networks that are built with Internet technologies such as TCP/IP and Web protocols such as HTTP (Hypertext Transfer Protocol). Independent organizations that need to connect their networks together to engage in business transactions or other exchanges can do so by using the same Internet and Web technologies—thus the term extranet. Extranets are cross-business connections built with private leased lines or secure Internet connections that allow people and businesses to engage in secure business relationships.

Note that extranet is not an official term. It probably first appeared in a computer publication and was quickly embraced by the rest of the industry because it so aptly describes the business-to-business connection.

Perhaps the best example of extranet technology comes from Netscape. The company has fully committed itself to the Internet protocols and builds all its applications to take advantage of Web technologies. It designs for all major operating system platforms and so provides products that companies can use to build enterprise-wide networks.

Netscape's extranet standards depend on firewalls, certificate authorities, metadirectories (a store for information from multiple directory services), software distribution standards, and data exchange formats.

According to Netscape, a new type of software has emerged (which it calls crossware) that allows on-demand applications to run across networks and operating systems. These applications are based entirely on open Internet standards like HTML (Hypertext Markup Language), Java, and JavaScript. It is these technologies that allow companies to build extranets that help them communicate with business partners, suppliers, and customers.

Netscape's extranet strategy involves the following standards and protocols. This strategy clearly outlines the technologies required to build extranets and points out that they are much more than simple communication links between businesses.

- **LDAP (Lightweight Directory Access Protocol)**   Allows companies to exchange directory information, something that is analogous to exchanging internal phone books.

- **X.509 v3 digital certificates**   Provides security with digital signatures and authentication between parties, content, or devices on a network including secure servers, firewalls, e-mail, and payment systems.

- **S/MIME**   Provides secure message transmission.

- **vCards**   Provides a way to exchange personal contact information.

- **Signed objects**   Provides verification that software applications and Java applets are authentic and safe to run.

■ **EDI INT** This is a set of recommendations and guidelines for executing EDI (Electronic Data Interchange) over the Internet.

## Setting Up an Extranet

Setting up an extranet requires a lot of coordination between the partners involved. Both partners must set up firewalls to protect their own internal systems while letting appropriate traffic flow through. The firewalls essentially "duel" with one another. The links between firewalls are secure encrypted tunnels.

However, extranets usually involve allowing a whole company or workgroups at that company to access databases and proprietary information like engineering drawings or customer lists. Beyond access to databases, partners may need to be involved interactively using collaborative applications like bulletin boards, chat groups, messaging, and workflow applications.

Business partners should agree on how users are defined, as well as how to define their access levels, the type of software they use, and so on. For example, two partners may agree to standardize on Netscape's SuiteSpot application suite because it is so well adapted to intranet and extranet environments.

An extranet may be defined by simply granting users in the partner company access privileges to programs or data on your own systems. This is not much different than allowing your own mobile users to access corporate data and has many of the same security implications.

The following elements are recommended when setting up an extranet:

■ **Proxy server** To control how internal users access your partner's systems and the Internet. See "Proxy Server."

■ **Firewall** To control Internet connections. See "Firewall."

■ **Authentication** To validate users that are trying to access your system. Certificates, token-based systems, and challenge-response techniques can be used. See "Authentication and Authorization."

■ **Encryption** To hide transmissions on public networks, you need encryption. Tunneling is one technique. It puts up a secure virtual private network between partners, on which all transmissions can take place. See "Security" for a description of encryption techniques.

Your ISP gets involved in the relationship as well.

**RELATED ENTRIES** Certificates and Certification Systems; Digital Signatures; EDI (Electronic Data Interchange); Electronic Commerce; Electronic Mail; Groupware; Intranets and Extranets; IPSec (IP Security); Security; SET (Secure Electronic Transaction); S/WAN (Secure WAN); VPN (Virtual Private Network); Web Technologies and Concepts; *and* Workflow Management

*E*

## Fast Ethernet

Fast Ethernet is traditional CSMA/CD (carrier sense multiple access/collision detection) at 100 Mbits/sec over twisted-pair wire. The original Ethernet data rate was 10 Mbits/sec. During the early development of Fast Ethernet, two different groups worked out standards proposals and both were finally approved, but under different IEEE (Institute of Electrical and Electronic Engineers) committees. One standard, originally developed by Grand Junction Networks, 3Com, Intel, and other vendors became IEEE 802.3 Fast Ethernet.

The other proposal became know as 100VG-AnyLAN, which is now governed by the IEEE 802.12 committee. Is uses the "demand priority" medium access method instead of CSMA/CD. This section is about Fast Ethernet, which is also referred to as 100Base-T. The IEEE 802.12 standard is covered under the heading "100VG-AnyLAN."

Refer to "Ethernet" for a general discussion of the Ethernet standard, medium access methods, and other IEEE 802.3 features.

## New Features

100Base-T takes advantage of the scalability of CSMA/CD hierarchical networking. It is designed after the 10Base-T standard and can be built into hierarchical networking topologies like that shown in Figure F-1. This type of configuration is compatible with structured wiring strategies as discussed under "TIA/EIA Structured Cabling Standards."

The primary concern of 100Base-T developers was to preserve the CSMA/CD medium access method of 802.3 Ethernet while boosting the data rate. In addition, the developers kept the frame format. Because of this, 100Base-T fits in well with existing Ethernet installations. In most cases, an organization can use the same twisted-pair cabling systems it installed for 10Base-T networks. Both networks can coexist as well. A 100Base-T compatible hub simply needs to perform speed matching when exchanging frames. An auto-negotiate feature allows devices to detect the speed of incoming transmissions and adjust appropriately.

Fast Ethernet supports three media types:

■ **100Base-TX**   Uses two pairs of data-grade twisted-pair wire with a maximum distance of 100 meters between hub and workstation.

■ **100Base-T4**   Implements four pairs of telephone-grade wire with a maximum distance of 100 meters between hub and workstation.

■ **100Base-FX**   Uses optical cable and allows up to 2-kilometer cabling distances. Ideal for backbone use.

The twisted-pair versions of the standard can support full duplex modes to provide even higher performance. If a workstation is directly attached to a switch (which can provide a nonshared link) and no other workstations are sharing that link, collision detection and loopback functions can be disabled. This is usually more practical on backbones rather than client/server links, however.

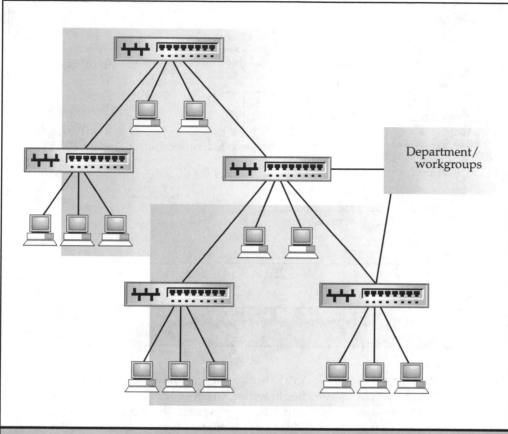

Department/
workgroups

**Figure F-1.** *Ethernet 100Base-T supports hierarchical topologies*

Depending on the type of cable already installed, some sites may be able to connect new 100Base-T systems directly into existing cables. New NICs (network interface cards) are required in workstations and new hubs are required in wiring closets.

Distance limitations in the twisted-pair versions of 100Base-T are more limited than the original 10Base-T to ensure proper timing for data transmissions at higher speeds. In 10Base-T, distance limitations had more to do with signal loss.

The maximum distance between two end systems for a 100Base-T twisted-pair broadcast/collision domain segment is approximately 200 to 250 meters (depending on the hardware and configuration, so check with your vendor). At the same time, the maximum distance between a hub and an end system is 100 meters. This is shown in Figure F-2. To take advantage of the maximum network diameter, you can connect two hubs together. While these distances may seem restrictive compared to 10-Mbit/sec

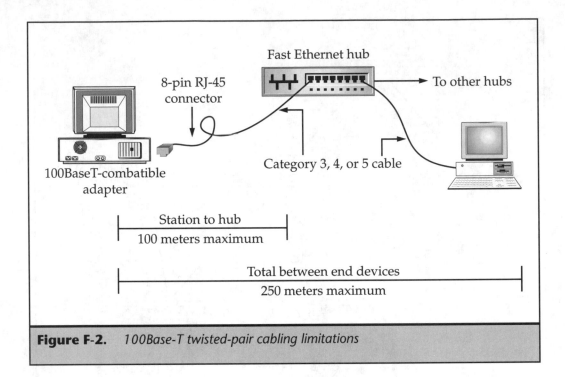

**Figure F-2.** *100Base-T twisted-pair cabling limitations*

Ethernet, consider that most networks are now built with collapsed backbones and hierarchical wiring that places switches in wiring closets very near end systems.

If faceplates are used, the maximum cable length from the hub to the faceplate should be 90 meters or less. This leaves at least 10 meters of cable to connect the workstation to the faceplate.

## 100Base-TX

This version works with two pairs of UTP (unshielded twisted-pair) or STP (shielded twisted-pair). Transmission takes place on one pair of wires and collision detection takes place on the other pair of wires. Two types of cable can be used with this specification: Category 5 UTP and IBM's Type 1 STP. Category 5 cable has four pairs of wire. Since only two of the pairs are used, the other two are available for other uses or future expansion. However, it is not recommended that another *high-speed* network be used on the pairs.

Category 5 cable has very stringent installation requirements. All the components in the cabling system must be Category 5-compliant, including connectors, patch panels, punchdown blocks, and hubs/switches. The twists in the cable must be maintained all the way up to within ½ inch of a connector. The twists in the cable help maintain proper signaling, especially at high data rates.

A link segment is the connection between a workstation and a hub. The maximum link segment distance is 100 meters, but if faceplates are used, the specification recommends not exceeding 90 meters from hub to faceplate. This allows 10 meters for the faceplate-to-station connection.

There are two types of hubs in the 100Base-TX scheme: class I and class II. Both hubs are repeaters, but class I hubs provide a way to repeat signals to devices that use different signaling techniques (100Base-TX, 100Base-FX, and 100Base-T4), while class II hubs require that all the connected devices use the 100Base-TX signaling technique. Basically, a class I hub does a signal translation, if necessary, when repeating those signals between hubs. A class II hub is strictly a repeater that sends all incoming signals to all other ports without translation.

## 100Base-T4

The cabling requirement for 100Base-T4 is four pairs of wire, which means you can use Category 3, Category 4, and Category 5 UTP cabling. Category 3 wiring has been extremely popular, and many sites are already prepared to run 100Base-T4. All four wires are used in a half-duplex signaling scheme. Three pairs are used to either transmit or receive data and the other pair is used for collision detection. Spreading the 100-Mbit/sec signal over three pairs reduces the frequency of the cable and allows the use of the higher-speed signaling on lower-grade cable. Basically, 33.33 Mbits/sec is transmitted over each of the three pairs. Another trick is also required to reduce the frequency, and that is to use a special three-level encoding scheme (as opposed to two-level in other media) to reduce the clock rate to 25 MHz.

Higher-grade cable such as Category 5 is recommended for future expansion, but Category 3 cable can be used if it is already installed. Like 100Base-TX, the 100Base-T4 specification has a maximum hub-to-station cable length of 100 meters and an end-to-end maximum of 250 meters. 100Base-T4 also uses the same repeater classing scheme as 100Base-TX. Class I hubs allow mixed 100Base-T networks, and class II hubs allow only one scheme (refer to the description in the previous section). All eight wires of the cable are used.

## 100Base-FX

100Base-FX is the fiber-optic cable implementation of the Fast Ethernet standard. It is ideal for backbone use because cable distances can be as high as 2 kilometers. Fiber-optic cable is not prone to interference, and it does not emit a signal, so it is more secure (especially for wiring across public areas). In addition, fiber-optic cable can scale up to higher transmission rates for future expansion.

100Base-FX requires a cable with two strands of 62.5/125-micron fiber. One of the fibers is used for signal transmission while the other is used to receive and detect collisions. 100Base-FX also uses the same repeater classing scheme as 100Base-TX. Class I hubs allow mixed 100Base-T networks and class II hubs allow only one scheme (refer to the description in the previous section).

**RELATED ENTRIES**    100VG-AnyLAN; Backbone Networks; CSMA/CD (Carrier Sense Multiple Access/Collision Detection); Data Communication Concepts; Gigabit Ethernet; Iso-Ethernet; Network Concepts; Network Design and Construction;

F

Switched Networks; Testing and Diagnostic Equipment and Techniques; Throughput; TIA/EIA Structured Cabling Standards; *and* Transmission Media, Methods, and Equipment

### INFORMATION ON THE INTERNET

| | |
|---|---|
| Fast Ethernet Consortium | http://www.iol.unh.edu/consortiums/fe/index.html |
| Dan Kegel's Fast Ethernet Page | http://alumni.caltech.edu/~dank/fe |
| 3Com's Networking Solutions Center | http://www.3com.com/nsc |
| Asante's Fast Ethernet Primer | http://www.asante.com/Products/fast_ethernet_primer/page1.html |
| Fast Ethernet Alliance paper | http://iquest.com/~nmuller/fast.html |

## Fast IP

Fast IP (Internet Protocol) is 3Com Corporation's answer to expanding network services. In a paper on the subject called "Fast IP: The Foundation for 3D Networking," available at the 3Com Web site (given later), John Hart discusses 3Com's move to 3D networking. In two-dimensional networks, according to the paper, network evolved "by adding bandwidth—the speed dimension—and by expanding connectivity—the distance dimension." The third dimension, according to the paper is *policy management*.

Policy management is similar to quality of service. Most legacy networks don't have it. The result is that all stations on a shared network wait to transmit while another station completes its transmission. Policy management can provide a way to give some types of traffic, such as real-time video, priority over other, less important traffic, such as an e-mail transmission.

A variety of techniques exist for providing policies, including techniques that add flow control to hubs and other wiring devices. 3Com feels that policies should be set at the source—at the desktop and server. The idea is to let a workstation or server request a level of priority, then tag the associated frames as appropriate. When the transmission is complete, the device signals the completion so wiring closets and data center devices can free up associated resources.

The high-speed switching scheme is pictured in Figure F-3. This example assumes that two IP subnets exist in separate buildings and the buildings are interconnected via a data center switch. The data center switch also connects with the wiring closet switches on each floor. Normal layer 2 switching is used within each building, but the interbuilding connection requires a routed layer 3 path. This is provided by the data center switch. However, if the end systems can establish a Fast IP connection between end systems, then layer 2 switching is used; otherwise, the layer 3 connection is retained.

Competing schemes include IP Switching from Ipsilon Corporation and Tag Switching from Cisco. In IP Switching schemes, high-volume traffic is detected by an IP switch controller at the core of the network and an end-to-end virtual circuit is created without involving the end devices. The Tag Switching scheme is designed for

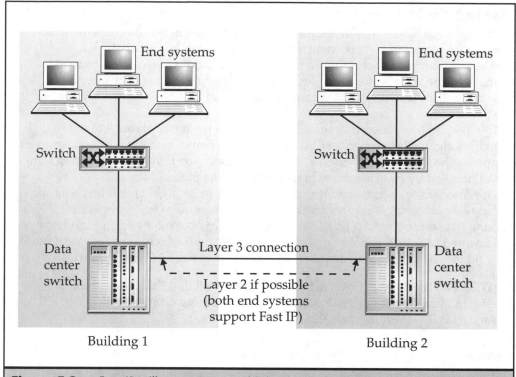

**Figure F-3.**    *Fast IP will attempt to establish a layer 2 connection over a normally routed path, if possible*

WANs. It optimizes virtual circuits over WANs by aggregating traffic over WAN circuits as much as possible.

**RELATED ENTRIES**    ATM (Asynchronous Transfer Mode); Cell Relay; IP over ATM; IP Switching; ISA (Integrated Services Architecture); Prioritization of Network Traffic; QoS (Quality of Service); RSVP (Resource Reservation Protocol); *and* RTP (Real-time Transport Protocol)

**INFORMATION ON THE INTERNET**

Fast IP paper at 3Com site                    http://www.3com.com/FastIP

## Fast IR (Infrared) Protocol

Fast IR is a product of the IrDA (Infrared Data Association). It is the 4-Mbit/sec extension to the IrDA Serial Infrared Data Link Standard that provides high-speed wireless data transmission between any IrDA-compliant device. Refer to "Infrared Technologies" and "IrDA (Infrared Data Association)" for more details.

## Fast Packet Switching

Fast packet switching is a common industry term that refers to data transmissions through high-speed mesh-type switching networks. A mesh network transfers information (in frame, packet, or cell form) through various network paths to a destination. The term is often used by carriers to describe their service offering for frame relay, ATM (Asynchronous Transfer Mode), and SMDS (Switched Multimegabit Data Service).

The "fast" in fast packet technologies comes from the fact that much of the error-checking, packet sequencing, and acknowledgment services have been removed to improve the speed of the network. These error detection and recovery services are instead handled by end systems at higher layers in the protocol stack.

Most modern telecommunication facilities are built on highly reliable media such as fiber-optic cable, are inherently reliable, and do not require extensive error checking. The error checking in X.25 (essentially a slow packet-switching service) was implemented to accommodate unreliable telephone lines, which were prevalent when the standard was implemented and which are still prevalent in some countries.

**RELATED ENTRIES**    ATM (Asynchronous Transfer Mode); Cell Relay; Frame Relay; Framing in Data Transmissions; Packet and Cell Switching; SMDS (Switched Multimegabit Data Service); *and* X.25

## Fault Management

Fault management is the ability to locate faults, determine their cause, and make corrections. It also includes implementing fault-tolerant hardware systems and fault-tolerant procedures, as discussed under "Fault Tolerance." Fault managment is concerned with keeping systems available for users, and involves the following:

- Continuous monitoring and the collection of statistics on workstations, traffic conditions, and usage so potential faults can be forecast and avoided

- Setting threshold conditions that can warn you with alarms of conditions on the network that may cause failures

- Setting alarms that warn of performance degradation on servers, routers, and wide area network links

- Setting alarms that warn of resource usage problems, such as a server that is almost out of disk space

- The ability to remotely control workstations and other devices

- The ability to perform some or all of the above tasks from a single management location, which may be extremely remote from some sites

Fault management requires certain procedures, personnel, and equipment to handle alarm conditions, as listed here:

- Using pager devices to warn staff members who are not at the office
- Testing equipment such as protocol analyzers
- Preparing an inventory of spare parts
- Writing procedures that unskilled users can follow, if necessary
- Ensuring proper documentation of all systems

Management software and management protocols are available to handle some of these tasks, although software and equipment for centralized control of large networks is still an immature technology. Some companies outsource these tasks. See "Network Management" for more information.

**RELATED ENTRIES**    Backup and Data Archiving; Clustering; Data Migration; Data Protection; Disaster Recovery; Fault Tolerance; Mirroring; Power and Grounding Problems and Solutions; Replication; Security; Storage Management Systems; Storage Systems; UPS (Uninterruptible Power Supply); *and* Virus and Antivirus Issues

## Fault Tolerance

*F*

Fault tolerance is a method for providing redundancy in hardware systems to protect against downtime that would occur if a system failed. In some environments, a company can lose thousands or millions of dollars when data systems are not available. Implementing fault-tolerant systems protects against this loss. Fault-tolerant techniques are described next.

**DISK-LEVEL PROTECTION**    The following features are implemented at the disk level in most network operating systems:

- Most network operating systems now create multiple copies of the file tables that keep track of files and their locations on disk. One copy of the table stored elsewhere on the disk provides a backup in case the other is corrupted.

- Features such as Novell NetWare's *hot fix* will automatically detect bad blocks on a disk and move data from those areas to a new area on the disk to prevent potential loss of data.

**TRANSACTION-MONITORING SYSTEMS**    *Transaction monitors* can ensure that incomplete disk writes are backed off the disk. This occurs if a system or communication link fails while information is being written to the disk. In distributed environments, a transaction can involve more than one system and database. If these databases are at different remote locations, any of the communication links or systems may fail during the write. It is the job of the transaction monitor to track the write events and either commit or back them off. See "Transaction Processing."

**DISK MIRRORING AND DUPLEXING**    *Disk mirroring* and *duplexing* are features that write data to two disks simultaneously. The disks can share the same controller, or each disk can be attached to its own controller. The latter method is called duplexing. See "Mirroring."

**RAID SYSTEMS**    *RAID (redundant arrays of inexpensive disks)* systems are devices with multiple disks that appear as one disk to the operating system. If one disk in the array fails, the rest can still operate because a separate disk provides parity information that can supply the missing data. See "RAID (Redundant Arrays of Inexpensive Disks)."

**FAULT-TOLERANT DUPLEXED SERVERS**    Data is simultaneously written to two entirely different computer systems that are usually in separate locations to protect against natural disasters such as earthquakes and floods. High-speed, proprietary, fiber-optic connections are required between the server to keep them synchronized. NetWare SFT Level III is for an example of this type of system.

**CLUSTERING**    Clustering is a fault-tolerant server technology that is more scaleable than are duplexed server technologies. It allows many servers to be grouped and to share their resources as if they were a single system. The scalability of clustering solutions allows more servers to be added as the load increases. The systems can provide immunity from faults and improve overall data access performance. Servers in the cluster share the same hard disks. If a server in the cluster fails, another server can take over its workload. See "Clustering."

**REDUNDANT COMMUNICATION CHANNELS**    When communication between systems is critical and there is a chance the communication link could be severed, it's a good idea to create a redundant link. That link should follow a different path between systems to avoid the same problems that took out the first line (such as a backhoe or storm). Redundant backbones within a building or redundant wide area connections are part of this recommendation.

**REDUNDANT COMPONENTS**    Backup power supplies are critical components for servers, and they may also be appropriate for communication devices if you want to keep communication channels open. It may also be necessary to duplicate other components, such as the power units in servers. Some systems support hot swapping, which lets you replace parts while a system is running.

**MANAGEMENT SYSTEMS**    Centralized management systems can provide network troubleshooting and monitoring. "Agents" can gather statistics about systems and warn of impending problems. See "Network Management."

## Fax Servers

Fax servers are computers with fax devices that manage incoming and outgoing faxes. Users at workstations can avoid lines at the office fax machine by simply sending faxes from their desktop to the fax server. Because the fax server is shared by many users, it reduces the need to install many individual fax devices throughout a company. Most fax servers also provide inbound services, which route incoming faxes to users on a network. Fax servers can keep log files of faxing activities for later scrutiny and manage the fax address books for a company.

Users equipped with personal computers can generate faxes in a number of ways. For example, text documents can be sent as faxes. Most word processors also allow graphic images to be inserted into those documents and the images are converted to fax graphics. In fact, almost any document created on a Windows systems can be faxed.

Companies can also set up fax information services. Users on the network or users dialing in can select from lists of documents by pressing buttons on their phone or choosing from a menu on their computer. The information is then faxed to them by the fax server.

A fax server will usually require quite a few telephone lines to handle the incoming and outgoing faxing requirements of an organization. Some of the companies mentioned in the next section, "Fax Products," provide boards that can handle multiple lines. Some boards support T1 lines, which provide 24 voice/fax channels over a direct link to the phone company. Check with the vendors listed in the next section, for more information.

Faxing out is relatively easy compared to handling incoming faxes. There are a number of ways to handle inbound faxes. One method is to print the faxes directly at the fax server, then have someone distribute the faxes to recipients. This method is inefficient and has no privacy. Another method is to have someone at the fax computer route received faxes from the fax server across the network to recipients. Once again, this tends to be inefficient and has no privacy. Clearly, automated methods are the best.

One automated method is to have senders enter special codes after phone numbers to direct faxes to specific recipients, but this puts too much reliance on the sender. Another method is called DID (Direct Inward Dialing), and it relies on the phone company to create a virtual fax phone number for each recipient in your organization but routes all incoming faxes over a single line to your fax server. The fax server then routes the faxes to the recipient's fax phone number. DID requires compatible fax boards, which can be more costly, but the price for the service from the phone company is relatively cheap.

## Fax Products

Advanced fax boards designed specifically for server use are essential to any fax server. One reason that advanced products are necessary for high-volume use is that they offload processing from the computer CPU (central processing unit), handling functions such as fax conversion and compression. The following companies provide fax equipment that is suitable for fax servers:

| | |
|---|---|
| Brooktrout Technology, Inc. | http://www.brooktrout.com |
| Dialogic Corp. | http://www.dialogic.com |

F

| | |
|---|---|
| WildCard Technologies, Inc. | http://www.puredata.com |
| Castelle | http://www.castelle.com |
| The Bristol Group, Ltd. | http://www.bg.com |
| SoftLinx, Inc. | http://www.softlinx.com |

**RELATED ENTRIES**   Access Server; Communication Services; Modems; PBX (Private Branch Exchange); *and* Servers

## FDDI (Fiber Distributed Data Interface)

FDDI is a high-speed networking technology developed by the ANSI (American National Standards Institute) X3T9.5 committee. It was originally designed for fiber-optic cable but also now supports copper cable over much shorter distances. The standard is commonly used in the LAN and campus environment. FDDI has a data rate of 100 Mbits/sec and uses a redundant dual-ring topology that supports 500 nodes over a maximum distance of 100 kilometers (60 miles). Such distances also qualify FDDI for use as a MAN (metropolitan area network).

The dual counter-rotating rings offer redundancy (fault tolerance). If a link fails or the cable is cut, the ring reconfigures itself, as shown on the right in Figure F-4, and the network continues operating. Each station contains relays that join the rings in case of a break or bypass the station in case it is having problems.

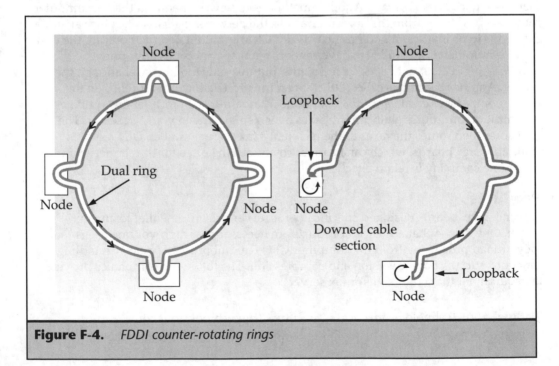

**Figure F-4.**   *FDDI counter-rotating rings*

FDDI has been used extensively as a network backbone topology. LAN segments attach to the backbone, along with minicomputers, mainframes, and other systems. Small networks that consist of a few LAN segments will probably benefit more from a coaxial Ethernet backbone. Large networks with many LAN segments and heavy traffic produced by high-performance workstations, graphics file transfers, or other internetwork traffic will benefit from FDDI.

Note that high-speed Ethernet such as Fast Ethernet and 100VG-AnyLAN can provide the same functionality as FDDI, but the distance limitations do not make them suitable for backbones that need to span large geographic areas.

## FDDI Configuration

As mentioned, the maximum ring length is 100 km. In addition, the maximum distance between adjacent stations is 2 km. The topology is what is called a physical ring of trees, but logically, the entire network forms a ring. The two FDDI rings are known as the primary ring and the secondary ring. Both may be used as a transmission path or one may be set aside for use as a backup in the event of a break in the primary ring.

Note in Figure F-5 that you can trace the route of the primary ring through each device. In this illustration, the secondary ring is basically in standby mode and is capable of reforming the ring should any link in the network be broken.

There are three types of devices that can attach to the ring:

- **DAS (dual attached station)**   Connected to both rings, such as a critical server and other pieces of equipment
- **DAC (dual attached concentrator)**   Connected to both rings and provides a connection point for stations
- **SAS (single attached station)**   Attached to the primary ring via a concentrator

A dual attached device can bridge the ring if it is cut at some point. Single attached devices cannot do this bridging, but they are cheaper. If a computer attached to an FDDI concentrator fails, the concentrator ensures the ring is maintained, not the FDDI adapter in the computer.

Because FDDI implements a logical ring in a physical star, you can build hierarchical networks as shown in Figure F-6. Most end systems will be connected to hubs or switches that have an FDDI backbone connector.

FDDI operates over single-mode and multimode fiber-optic cable as well as STP (shielded twisted-pair) and UTP (unshielded twisted-pair) copper cable. The latter standards are part of the CDDI (Copper Distributed Data Interface), which is limited to 100 meters.

## FDDI Operation and Access Method

FDDI uses a token-passing access method. A token frame is passed around the network from station to station; if a station needs to transmit, it acquires the token.

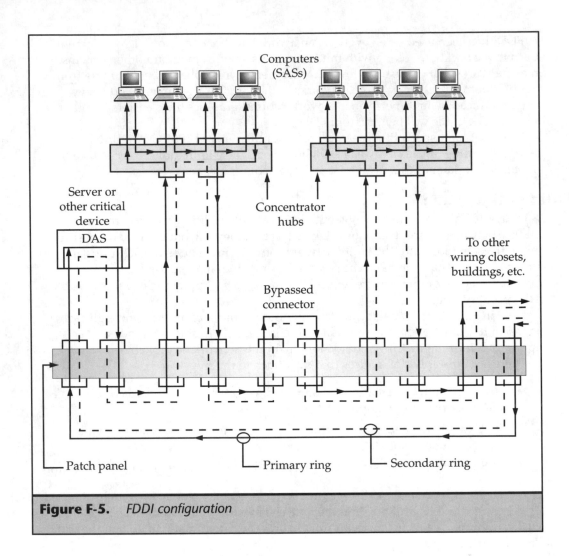

**Figure F-5.** *FDDI configuration*

The station then transmits a frame and removes it from the network after it makes a full loop. A regulation mechanism is used to prevent one station from holding the token for too long. The FDDI frame size is 1,500 bytes.

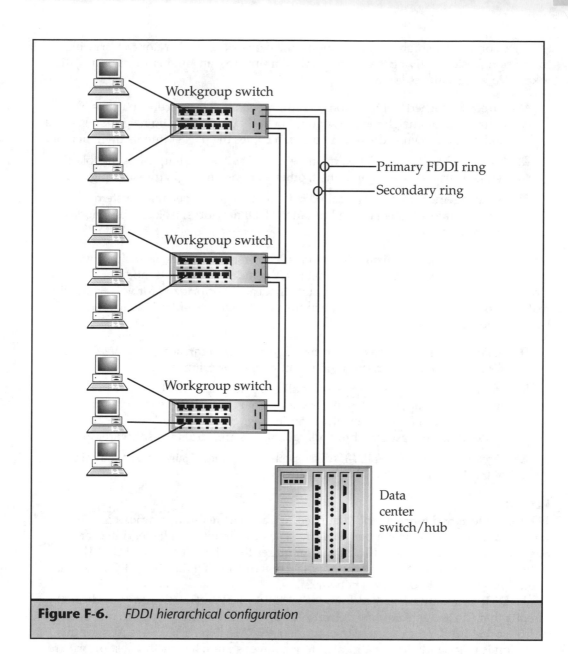

**Figure F-6.** *FDDI hierarchical configuration*

Workgroup switch

Workgroup switch

Workgroup switch

Primary FDDI ring

Secondary ring

Data center switch/hub

To accommodate high-volume stations, the network administrator can prioritize the station, basically giving it a longer period of time to transmit before releasing the token. Note the features listed here:

■ Directly attached FDDI stations act like repeaters. They receive packets from their upstream neighbor and send them to their downstream neighbor. When a node sees its own address in a packet, it copies the packet into its own memory.

■ Multiple frames can exist on the network. If a station relinquishes the token while its frames are still in transit, other stations can begin transmitting.

■ A management mechanism called station management enables system administrators to manage and monitor FDDI networks, isolate faulty nodes, and route traffic.

FDDI now has three transmission modes. The first two modes, asynchronous and synchronous, are available in the original FDDI standard. The third mode, circuit-based, can provide dedicated circuits that can be prioritized for voice and other real-time traffic. This mode is available in the new FDDI-II standard, which requires new adapter cards.

■ *Asynchronous ring mode* is token-based. Any station can access the network by acquiring the token. In this mode, traffic is not prioritized.

■ *Synchronous token-passing ring mode* allows prioritization. FDDI cards with synchronous capabilities give network managers the ability to set aside part of the bandwidth for time-sensitive traffic. Asynchronous workstations then contend for the rest. Synchronous capabilities are added via software upgrades.

■ *Circuit-based mode in FDDI-II* (discussed next) creates 16 individual circuits out of the 100-Mbit/sec FDDI bandwidth.

## FDDI-II

FDDI-II is designed for networks that need to transport real-time traffic. It is FDDI modified to support synchronous data such as voice circuits and ISDN (Integrated Services Digital Network) traffic. FDDI-II requires that all nodes on the FDDI-II network use FDDI-II; otherwise the network reverts to FDDI. Existing FDDI stations should be attached to their own networks.

FDDI-II uses multiplexing techniques to divide the bandwidth into 16 dedicated circuits that can provide on-time delivery for prioritized traffic. These circuits operate at from 6.144 Mbits/sec each to a maximum of 99.072 Mbits/sec. The reason for this variation is that bandwidth is allocated to whatever station has the highest priority for it. Each of these channels can be subdivided further to produce a total of 96 separate 64-Kbit/sec circuits.

These channels can support asynchronous or isochronous traffic. Regular time slots in the ring are allocated for the transmission of data. Prioritized stations use the number of slots they need to deliver their data on time. If slots go unused, they are reallocated immediately to other stations that can use them.

FDDI-II has not become a widespread networking technology because it is incompatible with the existing FDDI design. Another reason is that 100-Mbit/sec Ethernet and ATM (Asynchronous Transfer Mode) have provided better solutions in most cases.

### CDDI (Copper Distributed Data Interface)

CDDI is an alternative cabling technology that follows the FDDI standard. It uses UTP copper wire. It was originally proposed by IBM, DEC, Cabletron Systems, Crescendo Communications, and others. The ANSI TP-PMD (Twisted-Pair-Physical Medium Dependent) standard defines an FDDI network that runs over Category 5 data-grade cable and IBM Type 1 STP cable. It provides the features of normal FDDI, except for a difference in the distance of the cable. UTP supports 100 meters (330 feet) between nodes while fiber supports 2 kilometers between nodes.

For more information about FDDI, visit the Web sites of the major network vendors listed in Appendix A. Most vendors are actively marketing FDDI because many organizations have refused to make the upgrade to faster ATM technologies.

**RELATED ENTRIES**    Backbone Networks; Data Communication Concepts; Network Concepts; Network Design and Construction; Throughput; TIA/EIA Structured Cabling Standards; *and* Transmission Media, Methods, and Equipment

### INFORMATION ON THE INTERNET

| | |
|---|---|
| FDDI Consortium | http://www.iol.unh.edu/consortiums/fddi/index.html |
| NetSuite's FDDI Information page | http://www.netsuite.com/ts/tr/fddi.htm |
| ANSI X3T12 (FDDI) Home Page | http://sholeh.nswc.navy.mil/x3t12 |

# Fiber-Optic Cable

Fiber-optic cable employs photons for the transmission of digital signals. A fiber-optic cable consists of a strand of pure glass a little larger than a human hair. Photons pass through the glass with negligible resistance. The glass is so clear that, according to Michael Coden of Codenoll Technologies Corporation (a major fiber vendor), "a 3-mile-thick fiber-optic window would give you the same view as a 1/8-inch-thick plate glass window." The optic core of fiber-optic cable is pure silicon dioxide. It makes for good tricks. You can wrap it around yourself, then shine a light in one end and see that light on the other end. Copper cable, on the other hand, is subject to problems with attenuation, capacitance, and crosstalk.

Fiber-optic cable is resistant to electromagnetic interference and generates no radiation of its own. This last point is important in locations where high levels of

*F*

security must be maintained. Copper wire radiates energy that can be monitored. In contrast, taps in fiber-optic cable are easily detected. Fiber-optic cable also extends to much longer distances than copper cable.

Information is transmitted through fiber-optic cable by pulsing laser light. The electronic 1s and 0s of computers are converted to optically coded 1s and 0s. A light-emitting diode on one end of the cable then flashes those signals down the cable. At the other end, a simple photodetector collects the light and converts it back to electrical signals for transmission over copper cable networks.

## Cable Construction

Figure F-7 illustrates the fiber-optic cable structure. The core is the transparent glass (or plastic) component of the cable. Light shines through it from one end to the other. The cladding, which is a glass sheath that surrounds the core, is a key component. Like a mirror, it reflects light back into the core. As light passes through the cable, its rays bounce off the cladding in different ways as shown in Figure F-8.

A "dopant" is added to the core to actually make it less pure than the cladding. This changes the way the core transmits light. Because the cladding has different light properties than the core, it tends to keep the light within the core. Because of these properties, fiber-optic cable can be bent around corners and can be extended over distances of up to 100 miles.

A typical laser transmitter can be pulsed billions of times per second. In addition, a single strand of glass can carry light in a number of wavelengths (colors), meaning

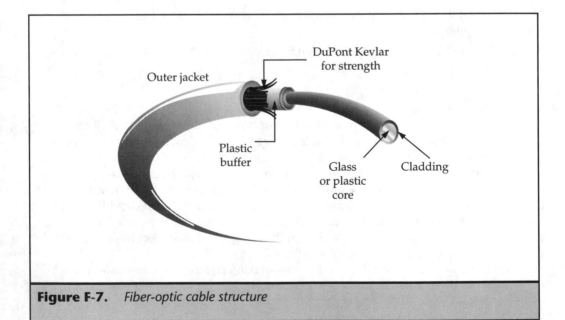

**Figure F-7.**  *Fiber-optic cable structure*

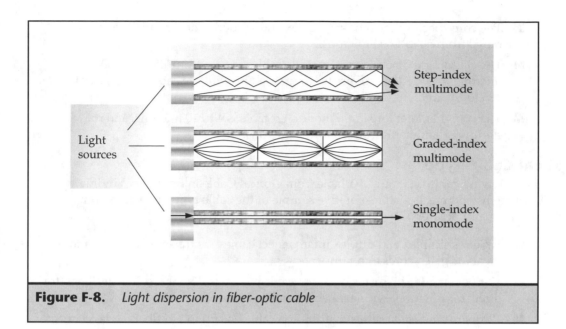

**Figure F-8.** *Light dispersion in fiber-optic cable*

F

that the data-carrying capacity of fiber-optic cable is potentially thousands of times greater than copper cable.

The types of fiber-optic cable are listed here:

- *Plastic cable,* which works only over a few meters, is inexpensive and works with inexpensive components.

- *Plastic-coated silica cable* offers better performance than plastic cable at a little more cost.

- *Single-index monomode fiber cable* is used to span extremely long distances. The core is small and provides high bandwidth at long distances. Lasers are used to generate the light signal for single-mode cable. This cable is the most expensive and hardest to handle, but it has the highest bandwidths and distance ratings.

- *Step-index multimode cable* has a relatively large diameter core with high dispersion characteristics. The cable is designed for the LAN environment and light is typically generated with a LED (light-emitting diode).

- *Graded-index multimode cable* has multiple layers of glass that contain dispersions enough to provide increases in cable distances.

Cable specifications list the core and cladding diameters as fractional numbers. For example, the minimum recommended cable type for FDDI (Fiber Distributed Data Interface) is 62.5/125 micron multimode fiber-optic cable. That means the core is 62.5 microns and the core with surrounding cladding is a total of 125 microns.

- The core specifications for step-index and graded-index multimode cables range from 50 to 1,000 microns.

- The cladding diameter for step mode cables ranges from 125 to 1,050 microns. The cladding diameter for graded multimode cable ranges from 125 to 140 microns.

- The core diameter for single-mode step cable is 4 to 10 microns, and the cladding diameter is from 75 to 125 microns.

## Optical Cable Types

The following cable types are available from Optical Cable in Roanoke, Virginia. They are listed here as a representative sample of the cable types available from various manufacturers.

- A-Series simplex and duplex interconnect cables are flexible, resilient, and ideal for patch cords and jumpers.

- 12-fiber standard B-series breakout cable has up to 156 fibers. It is designed for direct terminations with connectors in local area networks.

- 12-fiber standard D-series distribution cable has up to 156 fibers. It is compact in design and ideal for longer trunking distances. The cable is designed for direct termination with connectors within patch panels.

- 36-fiber DB-series subgrouping cable has up to 1,000 fibers. It is designed for high fiber count packaging with easy direct termination. Plenum-rated (firesafe) cable is also available.

- 12-fiber D-series S-type plenum cable has 12 fibers and is designed for plenum areas.

- 4-fiber standard B-series plenum breakout cable has up to 102 fibers and is designed for plenum areas.

- D-series distribution armored cable has 156 fibers and is designed to be "rodent-proof" in direct-burial environments.

- M-series aerial cable has up to 48 fibers and a stainless steel or all-dielectric messenger or self-supporting round cable for outside plant aerial installations.

**RELATED ENTRIES**  Backbone Networks; Data Communication Concepts; Network Concepts; Network Design and Construction; Testing and Diagnostic Equipment and Techniques; TIA/EIA Structured Cabling Standards; *and* Transmission Media, Methods, and Equipment

**INFORMATION ON THE INTERNET**

| | |
|---|---|
| Yahoo!'s Fiber Optics links page | http://www.yahoo.com/Business_and_Economy/ Companies/Computers/Hardware/Components/ Cables_and_Connectors/Fiber_Optics |

| Corning Optical Fiber Information Center | http://www.corningfiber.com |
| The Fiber Optic Marketplace | http://www.fiberoptic.com |
| Optical Cable Corporation | http://www.occfiber.com |

## Fibre Channel

Fibre Channel is a campus-wide interconnection standard that is designed primarily to interconnect peripherals, mass storage systems such as RAID (redundant arrays of inexpensive disks) devices, imaging and archiving systems, mainframes, engineering workstations, and other high-speed devices. Fibre Channel has features of a network, but it is not a network in the traditional sense. Instead, it is a high-speed channel that uses fiber-optic cable to interconnect computing devices in a relatively local environment, such as a laboratory or a campus environment, as shown in Figure F-9. The speed of Fibre Channel is its most distinguishing feature: it provides bandwidth in the range of 100 Mbits/sec to 800 Mbits/sec over a variety of cable types, including multimode fiber, coaxial cable, and shielded twisted-pair wire. Another distinguishing feature is that it is a switched technology.

The ANSI (American National Standards Institute) X3T9 committee developed the Fibre Channel Interconnect standard.

Fibre Channel is a good choice for connecting two or more parallel processing computers together or for attaching mass storage devices to a superserver. However, Fibre Channel can also be used to build networks with a number of user workstations.

### Where Fibre Channel Fits In

Existing network technologies such as Ethernet suffer from limited transmission speeds. These networks frame data for transport over a shared medium using connectionless methods. This strategy is not ideal for communication between high-speed workstations and peripheral devices. For example, a research laboratory may have a few workstations that need to connect with peripheral devices, superservers, minicomputers, mainframes, and supercomputers. It is not practical to use LAN technology such as Ethernet in this environment because the throughput would be far below the processing power and throughput of the computer equipment.

The Fibre Channel interface dedicates circuits for transferring data while allowing other devices to access the channel when it is free. If multiple sessions must run simultaneously, that is possible too. There are three possible connection types with Fibre Channel:

- *Point-to-point device connections* for high transfer rates over greater distances. An example would be a direct connection between a RAID disk system and a superserver. Notice that this point-to-point connection can occur over a network that other users share, but the cable is unavailable until the communication session is complete.

■ *Cluster (workgroup) connections* for high-speed workstations.

■ *Switched connections* for supporting Ethernet, FDDI, and token ring networks that allow multiple, simultaneous point-to-point connections between workstations.

The Fibre Channel interface supports variable-length transmissions, which means it can transmit large blocks of data without dividing them into smaller packets. The

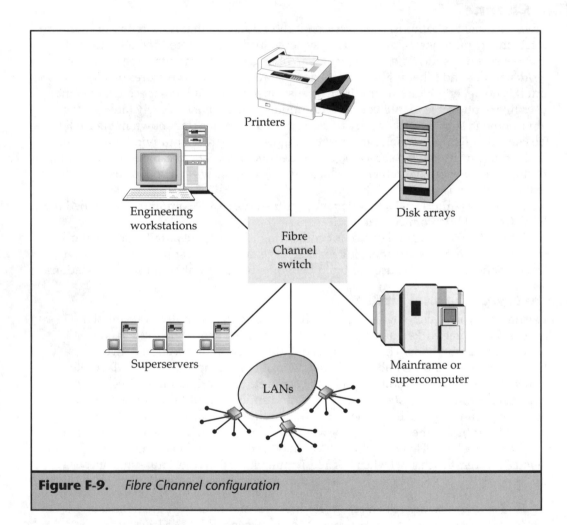

**Figure F-9.**   *Fibre Channel configuration*

following network topologies can be used with Fibre Channel. Frames or cells are encapsulated inside Fibre Channel frames.

ATM (Asynchronous Transfer Mode)
FDDI (Fiber Distributed Data Interface)
HIPPI (High-Performance Parallel Interface)
IPI (Intelligent Peripheral Interface)
LANs (local area networks) such as Ethernet and token ring
SCSI (Small Computer System Interface)

Fibre Channel transports data coming from devices by simply reading the buffer information, packaging it, and sending it across the fabric. *Fabric* refers to the crossbar switching architecture employed by the Fibre Channel switch. Underlying data formats, packet structures, or frame types are not important in the switching scheme. Fibre Channel overcomes device restrictions, as well. Consider the SCSI interface. You can normally connect up to 8 or 16 devices to a SCSI adapter. With Fibre Channel switching, you could connect millions of devices.

As mentioned, Fibre Channel can establish dedicated, point-to-point connections between devices. These connections are like circuits, and multiple high-bandwidth circuits can exist simultaneously. The circuits are bidirectional and can provide 100 MB/sec (or greater) of transmission speed in both directions. When a device wishes to transmit over a switching device or network, it simply attempts to get a dedicated circuit to that device.

Fibre Channel is similar to ATM and competes with it. But Fibre Channel makes a better peripheral connection technology, while ATM is better for network backbones, in the WAN environment, or for teleconferencing applications. Latency (delay) is another thing to consider. Fibre Channel uses frame sizes that are 2KB in size. Only about 1.5 percent of this frame is used for header information. On the other hand, ATM cells are 53 bytes long, and 10 percent is used for header information. What this means is that Fibre Channel will transfer more data than ATM under comparable conditions. However, ATM's fixed cell size provides predictable throughput, which is critical for live audio and video.

Network administrators should consider the possibility of using Fibre Channel in local environments for high-bandwidth users and devices, and ATM as the network backbone and WAN interconnect. The Web sites listed at the end of this section provide additional information on Fibre Channel usage. Fibre Channel is also used in some clustering configurations.

**RELATED ENTRIES**     ATM (Asynchronous Transfer Mode); Backbone Networks; Cell Relay; Clustering; Data Communication Concepts; Hubs/Concentrators/MAUs;

*F*

Network Concepts; Network Design and Construction; Packet and Cell Switching; Switched Networks; Throughput; TIA/EIA Structured Cabling Standards; *and* Transmission Media, Methods, and Equipment

### INFORMATION ON THE INTERNET

| | |
|---|---|
| CERN Fibre Channel home page | http://www.cern.ch/HSI/fcs/fcs.html |
| FCA (Fibre Channel Association) | http://amdahl.com/ext/CARP/FCA/FCA.html |
| Fibre Channel Consortium | http://www.iol.unh.edu/consortiums/fc/index.html |
| Fibre Channel FAQ | http://www.symbios.com/fclc/frame_fclc-faqr1.html |

## File and Directory Rights and Permissions

*See* Novell NetWare File System; UNIX File System; *and* Windows NT File System.

## File Server

*See* Servers.

## File Sharing

File sharing is a feature that allows users of network-connected computers to make files on their own systems available to other users or to access shared files on other systems. While desktop operating systems like Windows 95 provide file sharing, such peer-to-peer systems provide limited security. Dedicated server operating systems like NetWare and Windows NT are required, which provide more advanced security attributes and require user logon and authentication before any type of file access.

For example, Windows 95's simple security system allows a user to set the security level to read-only, read/write or "depends on password." So, for example, the password FOO is used to access files for read-only, and the password BAR is used to access and change files. In either case, the user sharing the files gives the same password to any user that needs to access the files. Obviously, this security is lax since the passwords may be freely distributed by anyone that gets a copy.

Windows NT, NetWare, and other more advanced network operating systems require each user to have an account. Users log on and are authenticated for access to servers on the network. Users must have the right credentials in order to access files, and then they are restricted by the rights and permissions that have been assigned to their account for files. For example, Joe may have read-only access to a file while Mary has read/write access.

**RELATED ENTRIES**    Access Rights; File Systems; Novell NetWare File System; Rights and Permissions; UNIX File System; *and* Windows NT File System

# File Systems

A file system provides persistent storage of information. The file system interfaces with disk drives and provides a system for organizing the way information is stored in the tracks and clusters of the drives. Users interface with the file system by working with files and directories, both of which can have various attributes such as read-only, read/write, execute, and so on.

A local file system may allow users to only access local disk drives. However, most operating systems also allow users to access disk drives located on other network computers and to share or "publish" directories on their own systems. These network-aware operating systems require a higher level of security since unknown users may access the files over the network. Therefore, more advanced network operating systems like Windows NT and NetWare provide special attributes to access files. In high-security environments, remote users will almost always require a user account and must be properly authenticated before they can access a file.

Most file systems today use the hierarchical directory structure in which a directory tree is built from a root directory. Directories are like containers that can hold other directories (subdirectories) or files. A directory is a parent to its subdirectories (the child directories). Directories have attributes that are usually "inherited" by all the files and subdirectories of the directory; however, attributes can be changed for individual files and directories in most cases.

Common file systems are briefly described here. Some of these file systems are discussed elsewhere in this book, as noted.

- **FAT (file allocation table)**   The IBM/Microsoft DOS-based file system that is also used by Windows, although Windows NT supports NTFS (New Technology File System). FAT divides hard disks into one or more partitions that become drive letters, such as C:, D:, and so on. Disks are formatted into sectors and sectors are grouped into clusters of from 4 to 32 sectors at the user's discretion. A FAT entry describes the location of files or parts of those files on the disk.

- **FAT32**   Windows 95 (release 2) provides this update to FAT that allows for a default cluster size as small as 4K, as well as support for hard disk sizes in excess of 2GB.

- **HPFS (High-Performance File System)**   This file system was first introduced with OS/2 when Microsoft was working on the project with IBM. A design goal was to have HPFS allocate as much of a file in contiguous sectors as possible to increase speed.

- **NTFS (New Technology File System)**   NTFS is the file system for Windows NT. It builds on the features of FAT and HPFS and adds new features or changes. While Windows NT still supports FAT, NTFS is recommended because it provides advanced security features and better performance, especially for server operations. See "Windows NT File System" for more information.

*F*

- **NetWare UFS (Universal File System)** UFS is the file system for NetWare, which is strictly a network server operating system. All of its features are enhanced to provide high performance to multiple users. It includes such features as elevator seeking, background writes, overlapped seeks, Turbo FAT, file compression, and block suballocation. See "Novell NetWare File System" for details.

- **UNIX File System** The UNIX file system is based on the hierarchical directory tree structure like the file systems mentioned above. The original file system was not specifically designed for remote file sharing, but these features were added later with NFS (Network File System), RFS (Remote File System), and AFS (Andrew File System). These network file systems are covered under their own headings. See "UNIX File System."

As mentioned above, there are file-sharing systems as well, but these systems take advantage of the underlying file systems that run on individual computers. For example, NFS is a file-sharing system that takes advantage of existing UNIX file systems. Likewise, Microsoft's SMB (Server Message Blocks) takes advantage of FAT and NTFS, as does the new CIFS (Common Internet File System). Microsoft's new DFS (Distributed File System) is covered under "DFS (Distributed File System), Microsoft" and "Distributed File Systems."

**RELATED ENTRIES** AFP (AppleTalk Filing Protocol); AFS (Andrew File System); AppleShare; CIFS (Common Internet File System); Compression Techniques; DFS (Distributed File System), Microsoft; DFS (Distributed File System), The Open Group; Directory Attributes and Management; Distributed File Systems; Information Warehouse; Network Operating Systems; NFS (Network File System); Novell NetWare File System; Rights and Permissions; SMB (Server Message Blocks); Storage Management Systems; Storage Systems; UNIX File System; Volume and Partition Management; *and* Windows NT File System

## File Systems, Distributed

*See* DFS (Distributed File System), Microsoft; Distributed File Systems.

## Finger

Finger is a UNIX and Internet-related command that can be used to find out if a user is logged on. The command may display information about the user, depending on the operating system and security policies in place. The command requires the user ID or name of a user. For example, you could type **finger tsheldon@ntresearch.com** to see if I am working at my Web site.

# Firewall

A *firewall* puts up a barrier that controls the flow of traffic between networks, typically between a corporate network and the Internet but also between divisional networks or intercompany networks.

Discussions about protecting networks usually focus on threats from the Internet, but internal users are also a threat. Indeed, surveys indicate that most unauthorized activities are perpetrated by internal users. In addition, organizations that connect with business partners over private networks create a potential avenue for attack. Users on the business partner's network may take advantage of the intercompany link to steal valuable information.

 **NOTE:** *This discussion concentrates on TCP/IP networks.*

## Defensive Strategies

Firewalls are often described in terms of perimeter defense systems, with a so-called "choke point" through which all internal and external traffic is controlled. The usual metaphor is the medieval castle and its perimeter defense systems, as pictured in Figure F-10. The moats and walls provide the perimeter defense, while the gatehouses and drawbridges provide "choke points" through which everyone must travel to enter or leave the castle. You can monitor and block access at these choke points.

Internet-connected private networks are often portrayed as being under threat by storming hordes of attackers. To protect internal data systems, a defensive system is recommended that includes the equivalent of trip wires, moats, boiling oil, and other strategies to repel the hordes. But while the storming horde analogy might be appropriate in some cases, the real threat is often the stealthy spy who slips over walls in the dark of night and scales every barrier undetected to reach his target of attack.

If a firewall is like a castle, how far do you let legitimate users into it, and what do you allow them to do once inside? Obviously, any firewall needs to provide some way of allowing legitimate users and blocking unauthorized users.

In medieval times, local townspeople and traders were usually allowed to enter the market yard of the castle with relative ease so they could deliver or pick up goods. At night, the gates were closed and goods were brought into the castle—usually after close inspection. While just about anybody could enter the market yard, only trusted people and people with special credentials were allowed into the inner perimeters of the castle. Within these walls was the *keep,* a heavily fortified structure that provided the last defense against attackers. Likewise, your public Web and FTP servers are situated in the "market yard," where they connect to the Internet to provide public access. Beyond these systems is your private network that must be protected with firewalls.

F

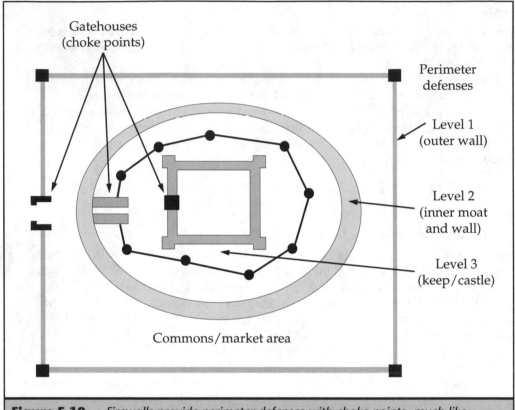

Gatehouses
(choke points)

Perimeter
defenses

Level 1
(outer wall)

Level 2
(inner moat
and wall)

Level 3
(keep/castle)

Commons/market area

**Figure F-10.**   *Firewalls provide perimeter defenses with choke points, much like medieval castles*

Interestingly, the castle proved quite capable of withstanding attacks until the cannon came along. In the 16th century, Essex and Cromwell overran many castles in Ireland with little artillery. They simply blew the parapets off the top of castle walls to make them indefensible, then scaled the walls. What similar weapons will our network defenses face?

Like a castle's multiple perimeter defenses, you can install multiple firewall devices to keep wily hackers out of your networks. Trip-wire devices can warn you when the spies and assassins are vaulting the moats and scaling the walls. This is where inexpensive screening routers used in conjunction with your firewall can help, as discussed in a moment.

### Strip Searches and Proxy Services

In times of peace, the rulers of a castle would meet with local townspeople, tradesmen, and dignitaries from other areas. Any direct meeting with the king or queen was usually preceded by a strip search. But if the political situation was tense, the ruler might prefer to avoid direct contact with visitors. In this case, the protocol was for all visitors to meet with the agent of the king or queen, who would then relay messages between parties. The agent provided proxy services.

Firewalls have been designed around these two approaches. A *packet-filtering firewall* uses the strip-search method. Packets are first checked and then either dropped or allowed to enter based on various rules and specified criteria. A *proxy service* acts as an agent for a user who needs to access a system on the other side of the firewall. A third method, called *stateful inspection*, is also used. This method would be analogous to a gatekeeper remembering some defining characteristics of anyone leaving the castle and only allowing people back in with those characteristics.

## Classifying Firewalls

Any device that controls network traffic for security reasons can be called a firewall, and in fact the term "firewall" is used in a generic way. However, there are three major types of firewalls that use different strategies for protecting network resources. The most basic firewall devices are built on routers and work in the lower layers of the network protocol stack. They provide packet filtering and are often called *screening routers*. High-end *proxy server gateways* operate at the upper levels of the protocol stack. The third type of firewall uses stateful inspection techniques.

Routers are often used in conjunction with gateways to build a multitiered defense system, although many commercial firewall products may provide all the functionality you need.

Figure F-11 and Figure F-12 illustrate the differences between screening routers and proxy servers, both of which are described in the next few sections.

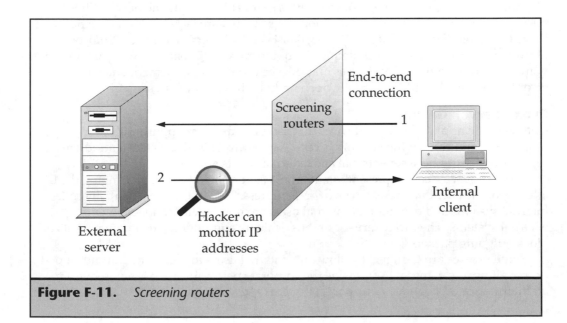

**Figure F-11.** *Screening routers*

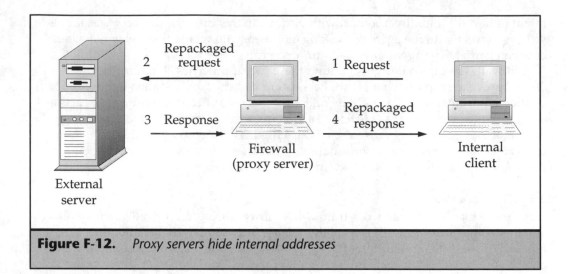

**Figure F-12.** *Proxy servers hide internal addresses*

### Screening Router (Packet Filters)

Screening routers can look at information related to the hardwired address of a computer, its IP address (network layer), and even the types of connections (transport layer), and then filter packets based on that information. A screening router may be a stand-alone routing device or a computer that contains two network interface cards (dual-homed system). The router connects two networks and performs packet filtering to control traffic between the networks.

Administrators program the device with a set of rules that define how to filter a packet. For example, you can usually block packets that are targeted for a specific service such as FTP (File Transfer Protocol) or HTTP (Hypertext Transfer Protocol). However, the rules that you can define for routers may not be sufficient to protect your network resources. Those rules may also be difficult to implement and error-prone, which could potentially open up holes in your defenses.

### Proxy Server Gateways

Gateways are application-level devices that can provide more opportunities for monitoring and controlling network access. A gateway firewall acts like a middleman, relaying messages between internal and external clients and services.

A proxy service can "represent" an internal user on the Internet by changing the IP address of the client in packets to its own IP address. This technique essentially hides internal systems and ensures that internal users are not directly connecting with external systems. The proxy server can thus evaluate and filter all incoming packets or block outgoing packets.

Some proxies are designed to allow only internal users to access the Internet and do not allow any external users inside the corporate network. Because any request to an Internet server generates a response, the proxy server must allow traffic back in, but it does this by only allowing traffic that is a response to in internal request. Other types of proxy servers provide secure relay services in either direction.

A proxy server can also provide a caching service for internal users. It stores information about sites that can be used by internal users who need to access information from those sites. The "Dilbert analogy" is appropriate here. Every morning, hundreds of people in an organization access the Dilbert Web site to see the latest cartoon. Upon the first access, the proxy server stores the cartoon in its cache. All subsequent requests for the cartoon are then filled from the cache.

There are two types of proxy servers: circuit-level gateways and application-level gateways, as explained here.

**CIRCUIT-LEVEL GATEWAY**    This type of proxy server provides a controlled network connection between internal and external systems. A virtual circuit exists between the internal client and the proxy server. Internet requests go through this circuit to the proxy server, and the proxy server delivers those requests to the Internet after changing the IP address. External users only see the IP address of the proxy server. Responses are then received by the proxy server and sent back through the circuit to the client. While traffic is allowed through, external systems never see the internal systems. This type of connection is often used to connect "trusted" internal users to the Internet.

**APPLICATION-LEVEL GATEWAY**    An application-level proxy server provides all the basic proxy features and also provides extensive packet analysis. When packets from the outside arrive at the gateway, they are examined and evaluated to determine if the security policy allows the packet to enter into the internal network. Not only does the server evaluate IP addresses, it also looks at the data in the packets to stop hackers from hiding information in the packets.

As shown in Figure F-13, a typical application-level gateway can provide proxy services for applications and protocols like Telnet, FTP (file transfers), HTTP (Web services), and SMTP (e-mail). Note that a virtual "air gap" exists in the firewall between the inside and outside networks and that proxies bridge this gap by working as agents for internal or external users. A separate proxy must be installed for each application-level service.

With proxies, security policies can be much more powerful and flexible because all of the information in packets can be used by administrators to write the rules that determine how packets are handled by the gateway. It is easy to audit just about everything that happens on the gateway. You can also strip computer names to hide internal systems, and you can evaluate the contents of packets for appropriateness and security. Appropriateness is an interesting option. You might set up a filter that discards any e-mail messages that contain "dirty" words.

## Stateful Inspection Techniques

One of the problems with proxies is that they must evaluate a lot of information in a lot of packets. In addition, you need to install a separate proxy for each application

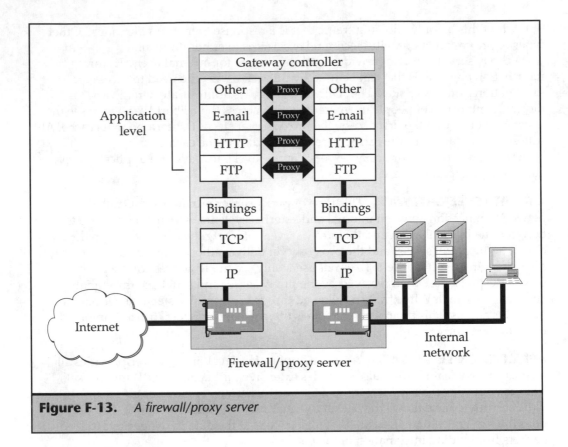

**Figure F-13.**   *A firewall/proxy server*

you want to support. This affects performance and increases costs. With stateful inspection, bit patterns of the packets are compared to packets that are already known to be trusted.

For example, if you access some outside service, the proxy server remembers things about your original request, like the port number and source and destination addresses. This "remembering" is called *saving the state*. When the outside system responds to your request, the firewall server compares the received packets with the saved state to determine if they are allowed in.

## High-End Firewalls

A router-based Internet connection allows point-to-point connections between clients on internal networks and Internet servers. Because such connections are generally considered unsafe, network administrators have been turning to high-end gateway firewalls.

*Application-level gateways* provide proxies that control access through the firewall in a unique way. They fully understand the protocols of the applications that are allowed to interoperate through the gateway and fully manage both inbound and outbound traffic at a level that is not possible with screening routers.

Readers who want to explore firewall concepts and architecture in more detail should refer to the following books. These books and their authors are the usual sources of reference for firewalls and Internet security.

- *Firewalls and Internet Security: Repelling the Wily Hacker.* William R. Cheswick and Steven M. Bellovin. Addison-Wesley, Reading, MA, 1994.

- *Building Internet Firewalls.* D. Brent Chapman and Elizabeth D. Zwicky. O'Reilly & Associates, Sebastopol, CA, 1995.

According to Cheswick and Bellovin, "an application-level gateway represents the opposite extreme in firewall design. Rather than using a general-purpose mechanism to allow many different kinds of traffic to flow, special-purpose code can be used for each desired application. Although this seems wasteful, it is likely to be far more secure than any of the alternatives. One need not worry about interactions among different sets of filter rules, nor about holes in thousands of hosts offering nominally secure services to the outside. Only a chosen few programs need to be scrutinized."

The FTP service provides a good example of how an application-level proxy server can provide advanced filtering. The application-level server can allow users from the outside to access an FTP server, but it will look in each packet and block any packets with the PUT command for specific users. This prevents just anyone from writing files to the server.

Another important feature of application-level servers is authentication. You can allow only specific users through the firewall on the basis of their credentials. Doing this is useful for trusted mobile users or people from affiliated organizations who need to access specific systems on your networks.

Also keep in mind that firewalls can hide your internal network addresses from the Internet. This lets you implement any internal IP addressing scheme without the need to register with Internet authorities. This feature is increasingly important as registered IP addresses become scarce.

## Firewall Implementations

The Cheswick/Bellovin and Chapman/Zwicky books mentioned above provide the material that most firewall vendors use when describing their firewall implementations. This section outlines the basic architectures that are described in Chapter 4 of Chapman and Zwicky's *Building Internet Firewalls*.

Note that these texts refer to the firewall as the *bastion host*. According to Chapman and Zwicky, a bastion host is "a computer system that must be highly secured because it is vulnerable to attack, usually because it is exposed to the Internet and is a main point of contact for users of internal networks. It gets its name from the highly fortified projections on the outer walls of medieval castles."

Of course, a firewall installation must consist of several devices, including the packet-filtering routers, discussed previously. Often these routers are used for *perimeter defense,* providing the first wall that attackers must scale in order to reach the bastion host. They may also be used for other lines of defense inside the network, as you'll see.

### Dual-Homed System

The dual-homed system is a computer that includes at least two network interface cards, as pictured in Figure F-14. Windows NT supports this configuration, and you can enable or disable routing between the cards, depending on your requirements. Routing is disabled between the network interface cards in the dual-homed system so that the application-level software can control how traffic is handled between networks.

There is one other use for this type of configuration. Assume that the dual-homed host runs an HTTP Web service. If routing is disabled, then the host on either network can still access the Web services, but packets cannot be exchanged between the networks. For example, if several departments in an organization need to share the same Web server but you don't want to create a routable link between the departments, you could use this configuration.

### Screening Host Architecture

In this scenario, pictured in Figure F-15, the screening router only allows Internet users to connect with a specific system on the internal network—the application-level gateway (bastion host). The gateway then provides inbound and outbound controls.

The packet-filtering router does a lot of work in this configuration. Not only does it direct packets to a designated internal system, it may also allow internal systems to open connections to Internet systems or disallow these connections. You set these options based on your security requirements. Chapman and Zwicky note that this architecture may be risky because it allows packets to move from the Internet to the

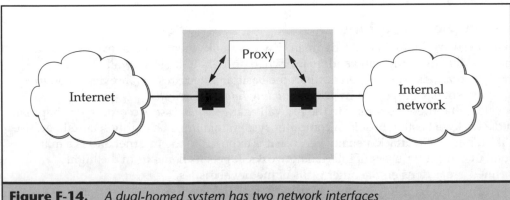

**Figure F-14.** *A dual-homed system has two network interfaces*

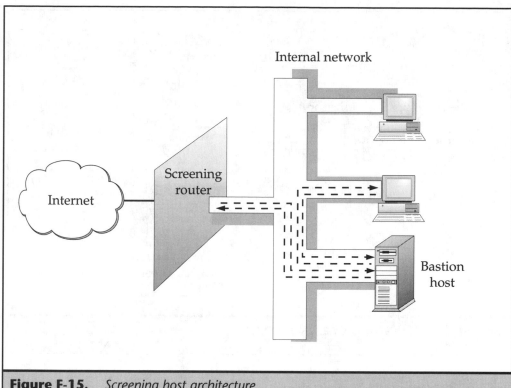

**Figure F-15.** *Screening host architecture*

internal network, unlike the dual-homed architecture, which blocks all packet
movement from the external network to the internal network.

### Screened Subnet Architecture

This architecture, pictured in Figure F-16, is similar to the screening host architecture
described in the previous section, except that an extra layer of security is added
by putting up a perimeter network that further separates the internal network from
the Internet.

A reason for doing this is to protect the internal network if the bastion host
succumbs to an attack. Since the bastion host is basically connected to the Internet,
hackers will target it. According to Chapman and Zwicky, "by isolating the bastion
host on a perimeter network, you can reduce the impact of a break-in on the
bastion host. It is no longer an instantaneous jackpot: it gives an intruder some
access, but not all."

### Variations

Chapman and Zwicky offer some variations on the designs described in the previous
section, along with some warnings. For example, they mention that using multiple

F

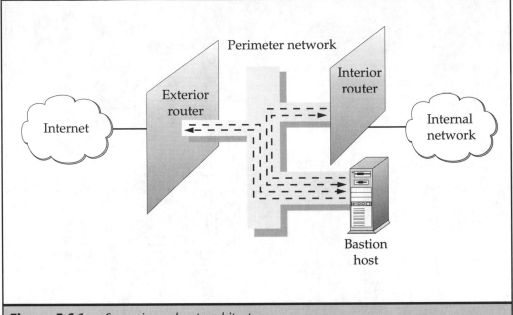

**Figure F-16.** *Screening subnet architecture*

bastion hosts attached to the perimeter network is OK. You might run different services in each of these hosts, such as HTTP Web services, e-mail services, or an external DNS (Domain Name System). Of course, each system must be hardened against attacks.

Another option is to combine the interior and exterior routers (see Figure F-16) if you use a router that has more than two ports, although this configuration is vulnerable if the single router is attacked. You can also merge the bastion host and the exterior router (as in Figure F-16). However, do not merge the bastion host and the interior router.

If multiple interior routers are used, a situation could occur in which the internal router decides that the fastest way to another internal system is via the perimeter network, thus exposing internal network packets on the perimeter network.

For more information about these configurations and others, refer to the previously mentioned books.

## SOCKS

SOCKS is an IETF (Internet Engineering Task Force) standard that defines how to develop proxy mechanisms that control traffic between networks. SOCKS essentially defines how to implement firewalls. A SOCKS server is installed between the internal and external networks (the Internet). It allows internal users to access the external network but blocks all attempts by external users to access the internal network. In this way, it provides one-way firewall services.

One of the key elements of SOCKS is the ability to "fool" the internal client and the external server into believing that they are talking directly to one another. In fact, the client talks to the SOCKS server and the SOCKS server talks to the target server on the external network.

The three important operations performed by SOCKS are

■ Providing a way for clients to request an outside connection from a proxy server. This request contains the address of the target server and other pertinent information.

■ Setting up a circuit between the client and the proxy server. Once the circuit is in place, the client thinks that it is directly accessing the Internet.

■ Relaying data between the outside and inside network.

A new version of SOCKS (version 5) that was finalized in 1996 includes interesting features such as authentication, the ability to go through multiple firewalls, improved security policies, and more flexible filtering methods. Refer to "SOCKS" for more information.

## Commercial Firewalls

As mentioned, firewalls that provide circuit-level proxy services, application-level proxy services, and stateful inspection techniques are available. If you need to allow some access to internal systems, then you'll need to look beyond screening routers to application-level gateways and other high-end firewall products, although routers might still be included in your defensive system. There are a number of important features to look for in such products, as follows.

**ADDRESS TRANSLATION/PRIVACY**   Prevents internal network addresses from appearing on the Internet. The firewall itself appears to be the originator of all traffic as it makes the Internet available to internal users.

**ALARMS/ALERTS**   Warns administrators when an attacker is attempting to breach the system. Threshold settings must be available and properly tuned to warn of attacks without triggering unnecessary alarms. Notification of attacks should be done with real-time messages, pagers, electronic mail, and other means.

**LOGS AND REPORTS**   Provides valuable information that helps you evaluate and detect potential security problems.

**TRANSPARENCY**   Allows internal users to access the Internet without facing hurdles or delays that make access difficult.

**VIRUS CHECKING**   Checks for viruses and looks for Trojan Horse executable programs (available in some commercial firewall products). However, this feature can affect performance and is not yet widely available.

Some firewalls provide interesting and advanced features. For example, the Sidewinder, from Secure Computing (http://www.sctc.com), will spoof potential intruders into thinking that they have broken into a secure area. It basically detects the attack and takes it over, leading the attacker along using a "hall of mirrors" approach. If the attacker believes that he or she has entered a part of the system that may provide further access, the attacker's activities can be tracked and possibly be traced.

If you can keep a hacker involved online for some time, you might be able to track the hacker down. For example, you could use the finger command to trace a hacker or set up a large "decoy" file that requires a long time to transmit, and then track the file transfer backwards over Internet connections to the hacker's site.

### Firewall References

There are an incredible number of resources on the Internet to help you learn more about firewalls and research available products. You can obtain a document called the "Firewall Product Matrix" from the CSI (Computer Security Institute) at http://www.gocsi.com or by calling (415) 905-2626. The CSI site also has an extensive list of Web sites you can visit.

The NCSA (National Computer Security Association) is an independent organization that is concerned with computer security issues. It shares knowledge about security, disseminates information, and certifies security products such as firewalls. The NCSA Web site is at http://www.ncsa.com.

Great Circle Associates, run by Brent Chapman, author of the aforementioned book *Building Internet Firewalls* (see reference in earlier heading, "High-End Firewalls"), has a Web site with firewall information. It also includes a link for getting on the *Firewalls mailing list,* which is hosted by Great Circle. You can visit the Web site at http://www.greatcircle.com.

**RELATED ENTRIES**    Access Control; Access Rights; ACL (Access Control List); Authentication and Authorization; C2 Security Rating; Certificates and Certification Systems; Challenge/Response Protocol; Digital Signatures; Internet Connections; IPSec (IP Security); PKI (Public-Key Infrastructure); PPTP (Point-to-Point Tunneling Protocol); Proxy Server; Public-Key Cryptography; Rights and Permissions; Security; SOCKS; S/WAN (Secure WAN); Virtual Dial-up Services; *and* VPN (Virtual Private Network)

### INFORMATION ON THE INTERNET

| | |
|---|---|
| The Rotherwick Firewall Resource (close to 1,000 links) | http://www.zeuros.co.uk/firewall |
| Trusted Information Systems, Inc. | http://www.tis.com |
| Great Circle Associates, Inc. | http://www.greatcircle.com |
| Great Circle firewall mailing list | http://www.greatcircle.com/firewalls |
| Firewall Product Overview | http://www.access.digex.net/~bdboyle/firewall.vendor.html |

# Firewire

Firewire is a peripheral connection technology developed by Apple Computer and Texas Instruments. The high-speed interface is suitable for real-time, full-motion video applications. Its high-speed bus supports data transfer rates of 100 Mbits/sec to 400 Mbits/sec, and the designers are working toward a 1-Gbit/sec data transfer rate. Officially, Firewire is IEEE P1394.

Firewire is an asynchronous technology that also supports real-time isochronous (time-dependent) data traffic such as full-motion video transfers. Firewire peripherals are daisy-chained from a controller port on a device such as a PC. This daisy-chaining allows all the devices to be connected to a single port. Devices can be connected without shutting down the rest of the system. Some of the devices you might connect using Firewire include consumer electronic equipment like digital audio and video players and recorders, as well as computer peripherals like optical disks and high-performance disk drives.

Firewire has many similarities to the SCSI (Small Computer System Interface) peripheral interface commonly used to connect hard drives to computers. However, Firewire has a much higher data rate and uses different cabling technology. Up to 63 devices can be connected to a single bus using twisted-pair cabling. Unlike SCSI, Firewire devices do not need to be connected in a line and terminated at the end. There is also no need to assign addresses to devices.

Firewire protocols include commands for controlling devices on the bus, including commands for starting and stopping devices like video recorders and players. Firewire will be a boon in the video production field because it provides a fast interface for not only controlling video devices but for streaming audio/video data to hard disks with little, if any, loss in quality.

A product that competes with Firewire is USB (Universal Serial Bus), discussed elsewhere in this book.

**RELATED ENTRIES**    Connection Technologies; Fibre Channel; SCSI (Small Computer System Interface); Throughput; *and* Transmission Media, Methods, and Equipment

### INFORMATION ON THE INTERNET

| | |
|---|---|
| 1394 Trade Association | http://firewire.org |
| Texas Instruments' IEEE 1394 page | http://www.ti.com/sc/docs/msp/1394/1394.htm |
| Skipstone (Adaptec) IEEE 1394 papers | http://www.skipstone.com/paper.html |

# Flow-Control Mechanisms

Flow-control mechanisms are designed to control the flow of data between sender and receiver so that the receiver's buffers do not overflow. If overflow occurs, frames or packets will be lost. Flow controls are used in the data link layer to control flow on point-to-point links and in the transport layer to control end-to-end flow on a routed network.

The data link layer protocols include SDLC (Synchronous Data Link Control), HDLC (High-level Data Link Control); LAPB (Link Access Procedure Balanced), which is used by many networks; SLIP (Serial Line Interface Protocol); and PPP (Point-to-Point Protocol). The latter two are typically used for point-to-point links on the Internet. Transport layer protocols include TCP (Transmission Control Protocol) and Novell SPX (Sequenced Packet Exchange). When discussing data link layer protocols, the unit of transmission is the frame. In the transport layer, the unit of transmission is called a *segment* for TCP and is called a TPDU (Transport Protocol Data Unit) in OSI (Open Systems Interconnection) terminology. At any rate, this discussion refers to units of transmitted information as packets.

Flow controls are necessary because senders and receivers are often unmatched in capacity and processing power. A receiver might not be able to process packets at the same speed as the sender, so its buffers quickly back up and packets get dropped.

## Stop-and-Wait Flow Control

The simplest flow control is called *stop and wait*. It uses ACKs (acknowledgments). First, the sender transmits a frame to the destination. The destination then returns an acknowledgment frame to the receiver, indicating that it is ready to receive data. The source always waits for the acknowledgment frame before transmitting another frame. This technique will usually not cause any overflows at the destination, but if the destination does need to pause before receiving more data, it simply holds up sending the acknowledgment.

This technique is useful if information can be sent in just a few frames. On some networks, the frame size is large enough that some transmissions can be sent in a single frame. However, this method is inefficient for long transmissions that require many frames. The overhead of sending acknowledgments for each frame adds too much traffic to the network.

In addition, smaller frames are preferred on some networks, which means there are more frames and thus more acknowledgments. A smaller frame translates to a smaller block of data that is affected by a communication glitch. If a large frame is used and a frame is lost due to a glitch, then more information must be retransmitted.

## Sliding-Window Flow Control

The purpose of the sliding-window flow control is to efficiently use the network bandwidth that is wasted in the stop-and-wait technique when the sender waits for an acknowledgment. The sliding-window technique basically lets the sender transmit multiple frames at a time to utilize the transmission channel as much as possible. At the same time, the flow-control technique provides a way for the receiver to indicate to the sender that its buffers are getting full.

You can understand the sliding-window technique as a conversation between sender and receiver. The sender starts out by saying, "I will send you x number of frames before you need to send me an acknowledgment." If the receiver starts to overflow, it says, "Scale back your transmission because I'm overflowing." The advantage of this dynamic process is that the channel can be better optimized.

The procedure works like this. Assume a server is transmitting to a client. Also, every frame is tagged with a sequence number so the order of frames can be tracked. The client keeps track of the frames that it can receive and the server keeps track of the frames that it can send. This tracking is done in a window that is constantly updated as the frames are sent and received—thus the sliding window.

1. The send window is set to 3 by mutual agreement or as a preset parameter.

2. The client allocates buffers for three frames.

3. The server sends three frames and waits for an acknowledgment. It also updates its sliding window to indicate that frames 4, 5, and 6 are to be transmitted next.

4. The client sends an acknowledgment that contains the sequence number of the next frame it expects (i.e., frame 4) and updates its sliding window to indicate that frames 4, 5, and 6 are expected next.

5. The server receives the acknowledgment and the process continues with step 3 above.

An adaptive sliding window will try to determine the best window size for the network, boosting the number of frames transmitted if necessary. However, the window should not get too large; otherwise, the receiver will get overloaded and start to drop frames. If that occurs, it sends an RNR (Receive-Not-Ready) message to the sender that acknowledges the frames it has received but that also indicates it cannot receive additional packets until further notification.

**RELATED ENTRIES**   Acknowledgments; Connection Establishment; Connection-Oriented and Connectionless Services; Data Communication Concepts; Data Link Protocols; NAK (Negative Acknowledgment); TCP (Transmission Control Protocol); *and* Transport Protocols and Services

# Forwarding

Forwarding is the process used by a bridge, switch, or router to move a frame or packet from an input to an appropriate output port. Bridges and switches forward frames while routers forward datagrams (packets).

A bridge references a table that contains information about where to send a frame based on the MAC (Medium Access Control) level destination address in the frame. This table associates MAC addresses with a port that leads to a particular network segment that the destination is attached to. Bridges use learning techniques to build such tables, but they can also be manually built.

Normally, the forwarding process is really a *store-and-forward* process, meaning that a frame must be fully received in memory by the bridge before it is forwarded.

However, cut-through techniques are often used to boost performance. With cut-through, the address is pulled from the frame header even before the frame is fully received and matched up to a port, then immediately forwarded through the port.

Switches and routers use similar forwarding techniques. A router references a routing table to determine the next hop in a router-connected network on which to forward a packet. If the router is directly connected to the network segment to which the destination is attached, then the packet is forwarded to that network and the MAC address of the destination is used to get the packet to that destination.

**RELATED ENTRIES**   Bridges and Bridging; Data Communication Concepts; Framing in Data Transmissions; Network Concepts; Packet and Cell Switching; Routers; Routing Protocols and Algorithms; *and* Switched Networks

## Fractional T1/Fractional T3

A fractional T1 line is a subchannel of a full T1 line that is sold by telephone companies and other providers at a lower price. There are 24 fractional T1 lines in a full T1 line and each has a bandwidth of 64 Kbits/sec, which is just enough bandwidth to handle one digitized voice call. There are 28 T1 channels in a T3 line. Users can purchase one or more fractional lines without the need to purchase the full line and can add additional fractional lines at any time.

**RELATED ENTRIES**   Multiplexing; NADH (North American Digital Hierarchy); *and* T1/T3

## Fragmentation of Frames and Packets

Fragmentation is a process that occurs at many places in the communication process. It basically involves breaking a block of data up into smaller pieces so the data can be *encapsulated* into a PDU (protocol data unit), datagram, or frame. At the receiving end, the fragmented pieces must be reassembled. Fragmentation takes place in layered protocol stacks and in heterogeneous network environments.

In protocol stacks, data moves down from the application layer to the physical layer. A large file must be fragmented in order to fit into packets, and eventually frames, at the data link layer. When the destination receives these fragments, they are reassembled and handed to the application layer on that system.

In the TCP/IP protocol suite, TCP segments defined in the transport layer can be no bigger than IP datagrams minus the IP header. The maximum size of an IP datagram is 65,535 bytes minus the header. Few LANs have frame sizes that will accommodate this datagram size. For example, Ethernet frames are 1,500 bytes and FDDI (Fiber Distributed Data Interface) frames are 4,500 bytes. Therefore, IP datagrams are fragmented and encapsulated into frames as shown in Figure F-17. Note that the maximum amount of data that a frame will hold is known as its *MTU* (*maximum transmission unit*).

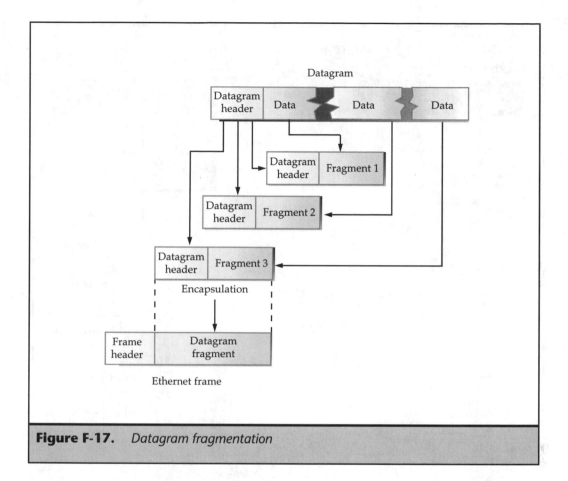

**Figure F-17.** *Datagram fragmentation*

Most corporate networks are interconnected networks that may consist of many different network segments. For example, an internetwork may consist of Ethernet and token ring LANs that are interconnected with an FDDI backbone. All of these networks use different frame sizes. If the frame size on one network is larger than the frame size on another network, then the frames must be fragmented, encapsulated into the smaller frames, transmitted across the network, and reassembled at the destination as shown in Figure F-18.

Note that routers perform the fragmentation process on internetworks. When a datagram arrives at a router for transport across another network that has a smaller frame size, the datagram is fragmented and encapsulated into outgoing frames. Those fragments may go to still another router, but routers do not normally reassemble fragments, even if they will all fit into a single frame on the next segment. The reason for this is that fragments may travel different paths through a routed network. The

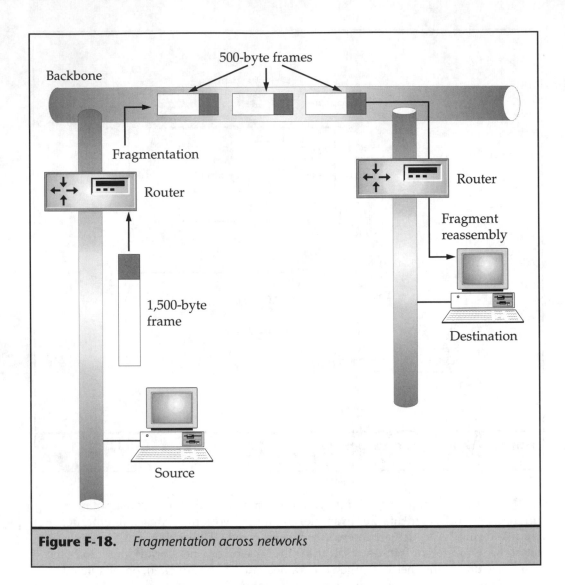

**Figure F-18.**    *Fragmentation across networks*

same router may not receive all the fragments. Only the destination will eventually receive all the fragments, so it is responsible for reassembly.

As shown in Figure F-17, the original header for a datagram is copied into each fragment. This provides each fragment with the destination address just like the original datagram. The router then modifies bits in those headers as appropriate. The bits provide fragmentation and reassembly information to the destination. The MF (More Fragments) bit indicates that the information in a frame is part of fragmented data set. A Fragment Offset field includes a sequence number to indicate where the fragment belongs in the original datagram.

## Frame Relay

Frame relay is a metropolitan and wide area networking solution that implements a form of packet-switching technology. It routes frames of information from source to destination over a switching network owned by a carrier such as Sprint, MCI, AT&T, or one of the RBOCs (regional Bell operating companies).

Frame relay is an outgrowth of work done on ISDN (Integrated Services Digital Network). Basically, frame relay is the packet-switching component of ISDN that is now sold as a separate service. While ISDN is primarily a circuit-based service, frame relay was designed into the service to provide short-duration communication links between router-connected devices.

To get an idea of what frame relay is and how it is useful, picture a corporate network with branch office in different cities. You need to interconnect these offices with both data links and voice lines. Data traffic between sites is relatively continuous during the day, so one option is to set up dedicated leased lines among the offices. However, to interconnect every site in an efficient way, you'll need to set up a leased line configuration like that pictured on the left in Figure F-19.

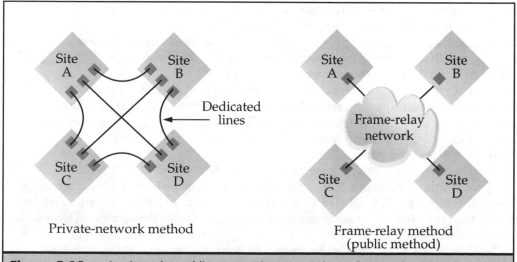

Private-network method

Frame-relay method
(public method)

**Figure F-19.**   *A private leased line network compared to a frame-relay virtual private network*

Now consider the frame-relay solution. As shown on the right in Figure F-19, you can build a virtual private network through the carrier's packet-switched network and instead of leasing a dedicated line that runs all the way to your remote sites, you lease a "short" dedicated line that runs from your site to the carrier's frame-relay access point, which may be as close as a few blocks. The carrier programs virtual circuits into the network between your sites and charges you for a specific level of service called the *CIR (committed information rate)*, which can range from 56 Kbits/sec all the way up to T3 speeds (44.736 Mbits/sec). The CIR is the negotiated rate, but if you go over it, additional charges apply.

Frame relay is widely deployed. Recently, voice over frame relay has become a hot option. Companies such as MICOM Communications (http://www.micom.com) have enhanced voice compression, making it more feasible to transport it over frame relay. Combining voice and data on the same network links to remote offices can be very economical.

Until recently, you went to one service provide for all your frame-relay needs. The long-distance carriers have dominated this market because they can provide the best connectivity over a wider geographic area. Still, you usually had to contact more than one service provider to build a private network frame relay, and there were no guarantees that those providers would work together to give you the best service. Today, intercarrier frame relay is easier to implement.

## Frame-Relay Operation and Features

Frame relay is based on the packet-switching metaphor but operates in the lower level 2 data link layer. Carriers predominantly sell the service as connection-oriented virtual circuits between two sites, although switched circuits that provide any-to-any connections are becoming available. In the frame-relay world, frames are "relayed" through switching devices in the network. When you link your sites with frame relay, you basically create a *virtual private network,* or *VPN.*

As mentioned, a leased line between your site and the carrier's frame-relay access point is usually essential, although switched-circuit ISDN is also a possibility. Figure F-20 shows the details of this connection.

A FRAD (frame relay access device) is a router-type device that customers install at their site. It connects over the access line to an edge switch on the carrier's frame-relay network. The network appears as a cloud in Figure F-20, with many edge devices at different locations. The access line must be of sufficient capacity to handle the bandwidth expected by the customer.

Data packets arrive from the customer's network at the FRAD. The FRAD encapsulates the packets into frames (which may be variable in length) and sends the frames through a predefined virtual circuit that gets them to their destination. At the destination, the internal packet is removed and routed on the destination network to the end system.

Note that a FRAD is similar to a router but does not require routing protocols because it does not need to participate in the location of a routing path or make

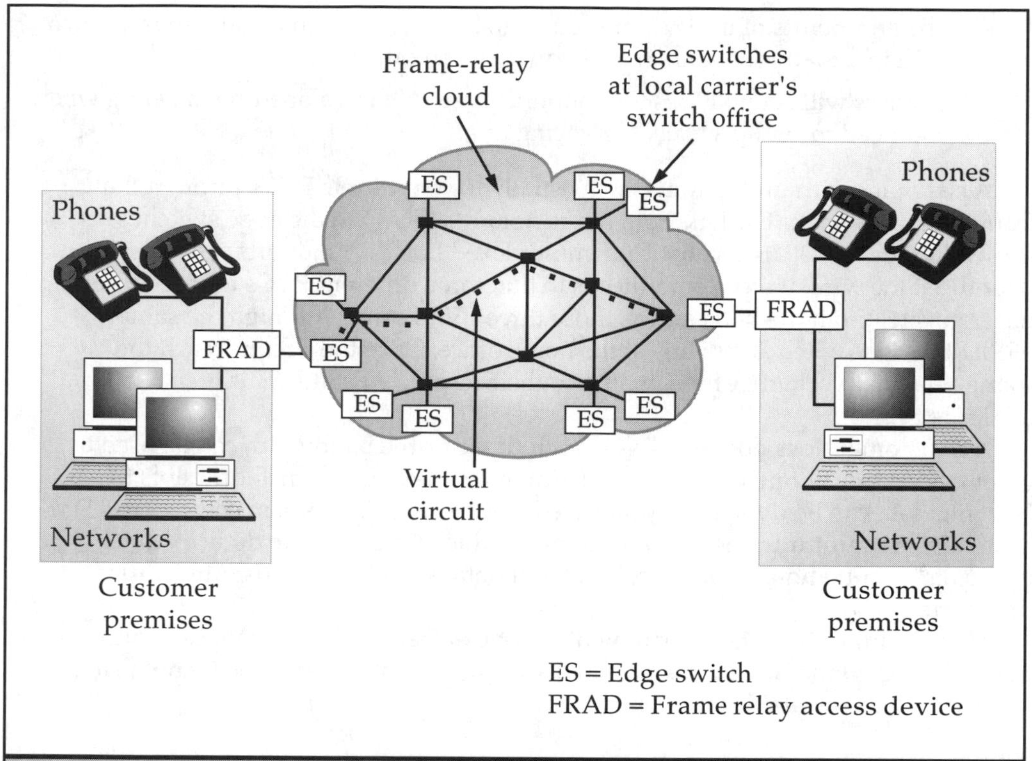

**Figure F-20.** *Details of the customer premises-to-carrier connection*

routing decisions about where packets should go. Instead, a FRAD simply connects to a frame-relay network and forwards traffic into and out of that network.

## PVCs (Permanent Virtual Circuits)

Carriers establish *virtual circuits* for customers through the frame-relay cloud. A virtual circuit starts at one FRAD and ends at another FRAD. It is essentially a private line with a data capacity that is agreed upon in advance by the customer and the carrier. The agreed upon capacity is called the CIR (committed information rate). PVCs have the following features:

- A PVC is a logical point-to-point circuit between customer sites.
- PVCs are low-delay circuits because routing decisions do not need to be made along the way.
- Permanent means that the circuit is preprogrammed by the carrier as a path through the network. It does not need to be set up or torn down for each session.

■ The end points of the PVC are constant, but a carrier can usually reprogram a PVC in a matter of hours (i.e., if you move an office).

■ Carriers will set up PVCs for temporary use, such as a one-time meeting where you need to set up a teleconferencing link.

A customer with multiple sites will usually have multiple PVCs through the frame-relay network. The link from the customer's FRAD to the edge switches, as shown in Figure F-20, is a statistically multiplexed line that supports multiple circuits over the same wire. If a customer needs to buy three different PVCs to reach three different sites from the home office, those three PVCs can go through the same FRAD-to-edge switch access line at the home office. Once the circuits reach the frame-relay network, they branch off into their respective paths. This is shown in Figure F-21.

If a customer does not use a PVC to full capacity, the bandwidth can be used by other customers. Frame relay uses statistical multiplexing in which timeslots for carrying data can be dynamically allocated to other users. This is in contrast to TDM (time division multiplexing; i.e., a T1 line), in which time slots are dedicated to a particular circuit and cannot be reallocated if data is not being transmitted on that circuit.

The dynamic allocation of bandwidth is one of frame relay's strongest features. Bandwidth is cooperatively shared by customers. When one customer is not using bandwidth, it is available for others to use.

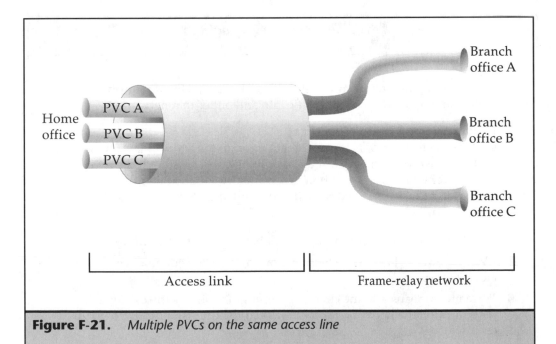

**Figure F-21.**   *Multiple PVCs on the same access line*

## CIR (Committed Information Rate) and Bursts

When customers buy a PVC, they specify a capacity in the form of the CIR (committed information rate). The CIR is basically a guarantee from the carrier that it will always have that bandwidth available. If the data rate is not available, customers are often given credits at a specified rate toward future service. All of these items are negotiated when the circuit is purchased.

The network dynamically allocates bandwidth up to the CIR to the PVCs as needed, and then may allocate additional bandwidth for bursts in traffic, depending on what was negotiated with the customer. Unlike a leased line that has a fixed capacity that can never be exceeded, frame-relay PVCs can be stretched as needed. This is like borrowing bandwidth from elsewhere in the network to fill a temporary need.

The bandwidth that is available for "borrowing" is bandwidth that is not in use on the network. Usually, there is no charge up to a certain rate. It might even be bandwidth on another of the customer's PVCs that is unused. There is a maximum burst rate, called the CBIR (committed burst information rate). Data can burst up to this rate and still get through the network, but bursts higher than the CBIR are likely to be dropped by the carrier in favor of other traffic if the network gets busy. This relationship is pictured in Figure F-22.

Ultimately, the access line between the customer and the network does determine the high-end data rate, but customers may choose to lease a line that has a data rate higher than the highest burst rate.

**F**

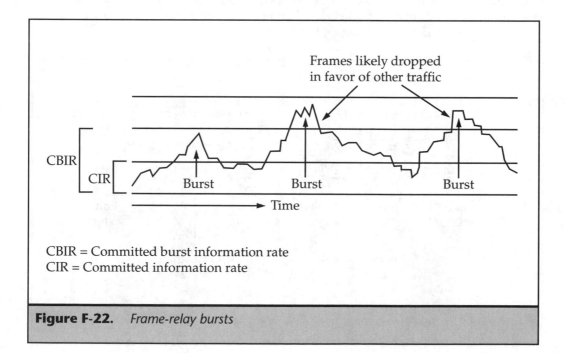

CBIR = Committed burst information rate
CIR = Committed information rate

**Figure F-22.** *Frame-relay bursts*

## Error Detection and Recovery

Frame relay is usually compared to X.25, an older packet-switching technology that has been widely implemented throughout the world. X. 25 was used in the mainframe environment to connect dumb terminals to mainframes over remote links. While X.25 has a relatively low data rate, it worked well for terminal communications.

X.25 was specifically designed for error-prone communication systems and provides extensive error checking at the data link level to guarantee packet delivery. X.25 is still used in many countries where the telecommunication system is inadequate. Today, most networks are extremely reliable. There is little need for the network to do error checking because few errors occur, so error checking has been shifted to end systems, which usually have the capacity to handle the few errors that do occur.

Frame relay takes advantage of reliable networks by reducing the error-checking overhead that was inherent in X.25. As seen in Figure F-23, the X.25 network on the left requires that an acknowledgment be returned to a sending node at every step along the transmission path. Transmitting a single frame through this network is a 12-step process!

Frame relay, on the other hand, eliminates excessive traffic by requiring only end systems to acknowledge receipt, as shown on the right in Figure F-23. This takes only six steps.

Also note that frame relay checks for errors in frames and discards the frames if they are corrupted. This is the only real error control that takes place. The network does nothing to warn that a packet was dropped or to request a new packet. The end systems must detect missing packets and handle retransmissions on their own. Frame-relay networks are basically optimized for speed.

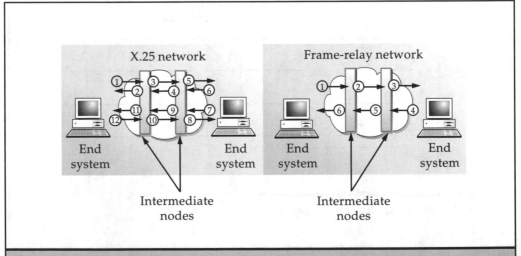

**Figure F-23.** *Acknowledgments in X.25 and frame relay*

## Frame-Relay Operation and Specifications

The frame format for frame relay contains special fields that hold control information for establishing and releasing connections. The frame is pictured in Figure F-24, and the fields are described here.

**FLAG**    The flag field holds the "Start of frame" marker.

**LINK INFO**    This field holds the logical connection address and control fields as described here:

- **DLCI (data link connection identifier)**  An address that identifies logical connections
- **C/R**  Command / Response bit related to congestion control
- **EA (extended address)**  Used to extend the header field to support DLCI addresses of more than 10 bits
- **FECN (forward explicit congestion notification)**  Warns receivers about network congestion
- **BECN (backward explicit congestion notification)**  Warns senders about network congestion
- **DE (discard eligibility)**  Indicates whether frames can be discarded if the network is congested

**DATA**    Control information or encapsulated data goes in this field.

**FCS (FRAME CHECK SEQUENCE)**    FCS is a checksum used for error detection.

**FLAG**    This flag field holds the "End of frame" marker.

Multiplexing efficiently interleaves data from multiple sources at the customer site on a single line to the frame-relay network. Frame relay is a modification to HDLC (High-level Data Link Control), so it is available as an upgrade in some bridges and routers.

### Connection Setup and Release

The following discussion concentrates on PVCs (permanent virtual circuits) rather than SVCs (switched virtual circuits) since they are most common. A PVC is set up at the time of registration by a carrier and exists until the carrier takes it down. It provides an immediate connection that does not require dialing or any sort of connection establishment phase. SVCs are more complicated in this respect because the customer equipment must be able to set up and take down connections as necessary.

For each PVC, the carrier gives you a specific DLCI (data link connection identifier) number that you program into the FRAD. Once the FRADs on either end of the connection are set up and programmed with the DLCI, they can communicate

*F*

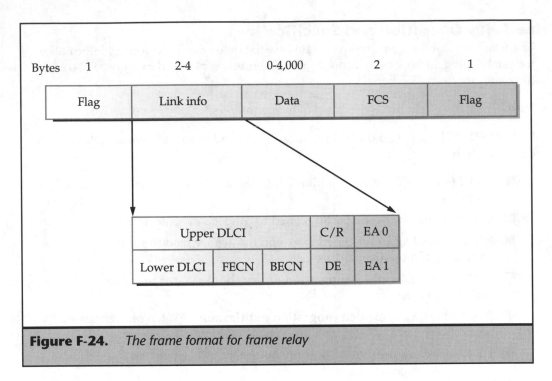

**Figure F-24.**   *The frame format for frame relay*

immediately. Thus, the DLCI identifies a preestablished portion of a PVC through the frame-relay network.

Of course, a single FRAD can be programmed to support multiple DLCIs, each of which provides a link to any location in the frame-relay network. Note that frames carry the DLCI number, which is a path number, rather than the address of the destination. However, the DLCI leads to that destination. Note that DLCIs are only significant locally—as a frame traverses the network, the DLCI changes for each data link (hop) taken through the network.

A management protocol called LMI (Local Management Interface) provides information about the status of PVC-to-network access devices. It defines management frames for monitoring the integrity of a link and whether a link is active or inactive.

There are two levels of operation in the frame-relay network. The first is a control level that sets up and terminates virtual circuits. For a PVC, the carrier uses this interface. The LAPD (Link Access Procedure for D Channel) protocol is used to provide control-level signaling on a separate channel, much like is done in ISDN. Control signals are communicated through the channel to set up and terminate virtual calls. The second is the user interface on which actual data is transferred between end systems. The LAPF (Link Access Procedure for Frame-Mode Bearer Services) protocol is used to provide frame delimiting, multiplexing and demultiplexing, frame inspection (for length), error detection, and congestion control.

### Congestion Control

The frame-relay network manages congestion by setting bits in frames that warn end devices that there is congestion on the network. A bit called FECN (forward explicit congestion notification) is set to notify a receiving system of congestion and a bit called BECN (backward explicit congestion notification) is set to notify sending devices of congestion. In the latter case, the sending device will temporarily slow down or stop transmissions.

The most interesting control is the DE (discard eligibility) bit. If a frame-relay device is transmitting on a PVC above the CIR for a certain period of time, the DE bit is set in frames to indicate that it can be discarded if the network becomes more congested.

## SVCs (Switched Virtual Circuits)

SVCs were added to the frame-relay standard after the initial design work although switched circuits were always intended. Only recently have carriers begun to offer SVCs for customer use. Customer premises equipment is now available to support SVCs as well. SVCs offer several benefits over PVCs, the most important being any-to-any connectivity. An organization can use frame-relay SVCs to set up temporary connections to remote sites, business partners, or data center backup/replication servers. An SVC is also useful for applications such as teleconferencing and, of course, voice calls.

PVCs have not provided the kind of convenience that customers would like for some of the applications mentioned above. For example, to set up a teleconference over frame relay, the customer must call the carrier in advance and have a PVC established. This process may take hours or days, depending on the carrier. With SVCs, setting up such links is as simple as making a phone call.

Voice calls over frame relay are becoming more of a reality as discussed in the next section. Currently, the voice calls an organization makes on its frame-relay connections are usually to its own remote sites. With SVCs, this restriction would change and allow customers to make calls to any other site. If voice over frame relay becomes popular for in-house use, it could drive carriers to implement SVCs on a bigger scale.

Another thing that may promote better support for frame-relay SVCs is greater use of Internet-based VPNs (virtual private networks), which are encrypted tunnels through the Internet. Today, such tunnels are not appropriate for on-time delivery of information because the Internet is subject to traffic problems and delays, but as network throughput increases, Internet VPNs will compete with many services offered by the carriers.

## Voice over Frame Relay

Frame relay can help you fully consolidate voice, data, and fax into a single network. In the past, voice quality was poor because of delay problems and the quality of compression equipment. In 1997, voice over frame relay may become more of a reality as companies like MICOM Communications bring their products to market. MICOM's

*F*

ClearVoice compression allows customers to compress voice while retaining a high level of quality and network bandwidth.

The current standard for voice compression is the ITU (International Telecommunication Union) G.729 algorithm, which can provide toll-quality voice and uses only 8 Kbits/sec of bandwidth per voice channel. Compare this to the traditional voice compression standard G.724, which compresses to 32 Kbits/sec.

The added benefit of voice over frame relay is that all calls are included in the price of the link and might be considered free to some manager's way of thinking. If numerous calls are made by employees to remote sites, there may be considerable savings in moving those calls to the frame-relay network. It is estimated that a majority of frame-relay networks go underused (but the management software described next can help you optimize your lines). Voice-over-frame-relay routers are available from MICOM Communications Corp. (http://www.micom.com) and RAD Data Communications (http://www.rad.com).

MICOM products also provide a way to multiplex voice, data, and other traffic (such as SNA traffic) over a single PVC, rather than setting up a different PVC for every traffic type. Numerous white papers on voice over frame relay can be found at the MICOM Web site.

## Managing Frame Relay

Third-party management tools can help you manage a frame-relay network and track throughput. Because frame relay itself provides no delivery guarantees, obtaining information about the number of lost packets is critical to evaluating the performance you are getting from your frame-relay connections. A carrier might have created a PVC through an overburdened part of the network, and without adequate packet delivery information, you might not be able to access the problem. A management tool can provide you with the information you need to demand better service.

Management packages like Network Health - Frame Relay from Concord Communications (http://www.concord.com) can help access the requirements for WAN services. The software shows bandwidth utilization in relation to the CIR, provides modeling for optional CIR and burst relationships, and helps managers identify needed service-level upgrades or downgrades. In particular, the product identifies the CIR you need and demonstrates in charts and graphs how much burst or excess bandwidth is appropriate, taking the normal guesswork out of such activities. The product can also help administrators move bandwidth from busy circuits to circuits that can handle the bandwidth. A typical chart produced by Network Health is pictured in Figure F-25.

## Ordering Frame-Relay Services

Most carriers now offer frame-relay services, as do the PDN (public data network) providers such as CompuServe. Each carrier has a specific number of places where customers can link into the network, called *points of presence*. Access to these points is through the LEC (local exchange carrier) or other service providers. Refer to

| Rank | Prior Rank | Name | Speed | Volume (MB) | Volume Baseline | Average Bandwidth | Peak Bandwidth | Average Health Index | Peak Health Index |
|------|-----------|------|-------|-------------|-----------------|-------------------|----------------|---------------------|-------------------|
| 1 | 3 | Boston to NY | 64K | 342.2 | 93.8% | 48.8% | 251.8% | 1.1 | 8.0 |
| 2 | 4 | NY CRP | 227K | 233.9 | 33.4% | 9.5% | 146.2% | 0.1 | 8.0 |
| 3 | 5 | NY 22 | 64K | 233.6 | 33.1% | 33.6% | 215.6% | 0.3 | 8.0 |
| 4 | 1 | Boston to Chicago | 64K | 224.7 | 31.0% | 32.8% | 313.2% | 0.2 | 8.0 |
| 5 | 2 | Boston to Washington | 64K | 223.0 | 30.9% | 32.3% | 131.2% | 0.1 | 8.0 |
| 6 | 7 | Boston to Toronto | 64K | 203.8 | 98.1% | 43.4% | 332.1% | 1.2 | 8.0 |
| 7 | 6 | Boston to SF | 64K | 159.9 | 49.8% | 23.9% | 166.8% | 0.2 | 8.0 |
| 8 | 10 | NY to Boston | 64K | 93.1 | 29.4% | 13.4% | 216.0% | 0.2 | 8.0 |
| 9 | 8 | Chicago to Boston | 64K | 77.2 | 10.0% | 11.2% | 144.2% | 0.1 | 8.0 |
| 10 | 9 | D.C. to Boston | 64K | 70.2 | 18.6% | 10.1% | 60.5% | 0.0 | 0.0 |

**Figure F-25.**    *Frame-relay circuit activities as charted by Network Health - Frame Relay*

*F*

"Telecommunications Companies" in Appendix A for a list of telecommunication providers.

Here are some things to consider when evaluating frame-relay services or putting together requests for proposals:

- Are switched service offerings available for any-to-any connections? Are Internet virtual circuits available? Are voice services available?

- What kind of service guarantees are available and how are they available (in the form of credits)? What are the fees for additional offerings such as disaster recovery services and equipment management?

- What kind of access is available into the frame-relay network? This access will depend on the distance from your site to the frame-relay access point, but it often involves a major portion of the cost to implement the service (approximately 50 percent in many cases).

- What are the paths of the PVCs through the network? Ask to see a map so you can determine if they pass through potentially congested areas.

- Establish a CIR (committed information rate) for your needs and obtain a level of commitment from the carrier for providing services over that rate.

- Is usage-based billing available in which you are charged for the amount of traffic sent, usually above a low monthly fee? A maximum charge rate is usually set as well.

- Can you obtain usage and performance information from the carrier that will help you optimize your use of the network?

- What type of management facilities are available for monitoring and managing connections from your own site? Is SNMP (Simple Network Management Protocol) supported?

**RELATED ENTRIES**    Communication Services; Data Communication Concepts; Network Concepts; Packet and Cell Switching; Switched Networks; Virtual Circuit; Voice over Frame Relay; WAN (Wide Area Network); *and* X.25

### INFORMATION ON THE INTERNET

| | |
|---|---|
| Frame Relay Forum | http://www.frforum.com |
| Motorola Frame Relay Resources page (very extensive) | http://www.mot.com/MIMS/ISG/tech/frame-relay/resources.html |
| High Bandwidth Frame Relay page | http://www.specialty.com/hiband/frame_index.html |
| Network World's Frame Relay Pricing page | http://www.nww.com/pricing.html |

## Frame Switch

A frame switch is like a multiport bridge in which each port can support a single computer or a multiport hub. The switch sets up a temporary link between any two ports on the fly so that end systems on those ports can exchange data. When the two ports are connected, they essentially become a single network segment. The network segment acts as a single broadcast/collision domain in which frames are broadcast over the entire segment. If only one workstation is attached per switch port, then a dedicated network is set up for the two stations attached at either end of the connection, and those stations get to transmit without contention using the entire bandwidth of the network. Frame switches are also known as LAN switches and can be used to build hierarchical structured networks.

As frames enter a frame switch, the switch looks at the MAC (Medium Access Control) address in the frame, then sets up a connection to the port on which the computer with that address is connected. Once the transmission is complete, the port connection is disabled. Frame switches consist of high-speed switching fabrics in the form of ASICs (application-specific integrated circuits). These circuits are extremely fast compared to traditional routers which use memory to store and forward frames.

The most important feature is that the frame switch divides the LAN into multiple LAN segments in which each segment has the full bandwidth of the network topology in use. If only one station is attached to a port, it gets this full bandwidth without any contention from other stations. Because not every computer requires full bandwidth, multiport hubs are often attached to switch ports so that multiple users can share the bandwidth. Even though this reverts back to shared segments, there are fewer workstations sharing the segment and contending for its bandwidth than in a conventional shared network in which all stations share the same network. At the same time, the switch can ensure that any station can obtain a connection to any other station on the LAN.

**RELATED ENTRIES**    Bridges and Bridging; Data Communication Concepts; Data Link Protocols; Ethernet; Frame Relay; Framing in Data Transmissions; Gigabit Ethernet; Matrix Switch; Medium Access Control Methods; Packet; Packet and Cell Switching; Protocol Concepts; *and* Switched Networks

## Framing in Data Transmissions

A point-to-point connection between two computers or devices consists of a wire in which data is transmitted as a stream of bits. The bits are converted to a series of electromagnetic pulses that the receiver must interpret. In the simplest model, the sender can simply transmit all the bits as a continuous stream, but the receiver needs a way to interpret where a group of bits (that represents a character or control code) begins and ends.

Framing is the technique of grouping data bits. The actual framing takes place in the data link layer, and the data link layer passes these frames to the physical layer for transmission. Each frame is treated as an individual entity that is checked for errors.

The advantage of using frames is that data is broken up into recoverable chunks that can easily be checked for corruption. A glitch in the line during the transmission of a frame will corrupt the frame, but the receiver only needs to discard that frame and request another. The entire transmission is not lost. Detecting and correcting errors is discussed under "Error Detection and Correction."

A basic asynchronous transmission like a modem connection transmits one character at a time. In this case, the characters are framed and consist of 8 bits to represent the character, a start bit, and a stop bit (or bits). The start and stop bits differentiate one frame from the next. A more complex byte-oriented strategy involves sending multiple characters in a single frame that begins with a start character (byte) and an end character (byte). Frames on network interfaces are more complex still. An Ethernet frame (IEEE 802.3), pictured in Figure F-26, can hold up to 1,500 bytes of data.

Note in Figure F-26 that the frame includes header and trailer bytes along with the encapsulated data. The information in the header adds overhead in the form of additional data that must be transmitted, but the information is essential, especially on shared networks where frames must be addressed to a specific system on the network.

Data at higher layers in the protocol stack is handled in *packets*, which is a generic term that refers to blocks of information that are handled in a communication session.

*F*

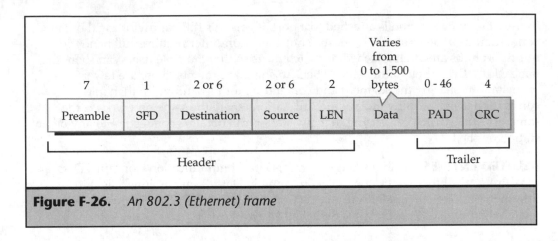

**Figure F-26.** *An 802.3 (Ethernet) frame*

Figure F-27 illustrates how data from the application layer is handled in the TCP/IP protocol suite. TCP adds its own header information in the transport layer to form a packet called a segment. In the network layer, the IP adds a header to create a datagram. Finally, the datagram is passed to the data link layer, where it is fragmented and placed in frames as defined by the network topology in use.

While frames are defined on the physical transmission medium, higher level protocols put information into packets. This may seem confusing, but remember that packets are built in software while frames are built for transmission over physical media. Recall that the underlying LAN might be Ethernet, token ring, or some other topology. Both Ethernet and token ring define their own frame sizes. In fact, if you are building a network operating system, you don't really need to know what type of framing the underlying hardware uses. You can just put information to be transferred into software packets and the underlying network will put the packet into a frame for transmission across the medium. This process is discussed further under "Protocol Concepts."

Note that frames are used to transmit data across a particular data link. An internetwork consists of multiple data link segments, as pictured in Figure F-28. Each data link segment may use a different frame format, so the routers that link the segments remove the packet information from frames, look inside the packet to determine address and routing information, then reframe the packet for delivery on the next network segment. It is usually the case that one network segment's frame size is smaller than another, in which case the data must be fragmented to fit into the new frame size. This is discussed under "Fragmentation of Frames and Packets." If data is fragmented, the final destination system is responsible for reassembling it, not routers along the way, so once data is fragmented, it travels that way all the way to the destination.

**RELATED ENTRIES**    Acknowledgments; Circuit-Switching Services; Connection Establishment; Data Communication Concepts; Flow-Control Mechanisms;

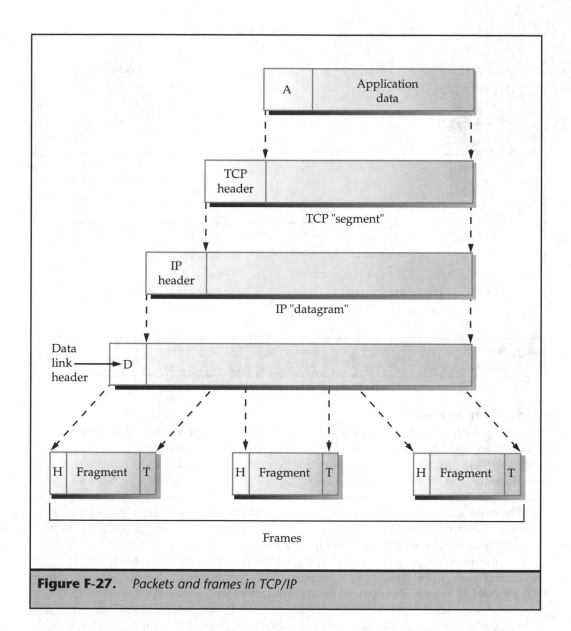

**Figure F-27.** *Packets and frames in TCP/IP*

Fragmentation of Frames and Packets; Frame Switch; Handshake Procedures; NAK (Negative Acknowledgment); Network Concepts; Packet; Packet and Cell Switching; Sequencing of Packets; Sliding-Window Flow Control; TCP (Transmission Control Protocol); Transport Protocols and Services; *and* Virtual Circuit

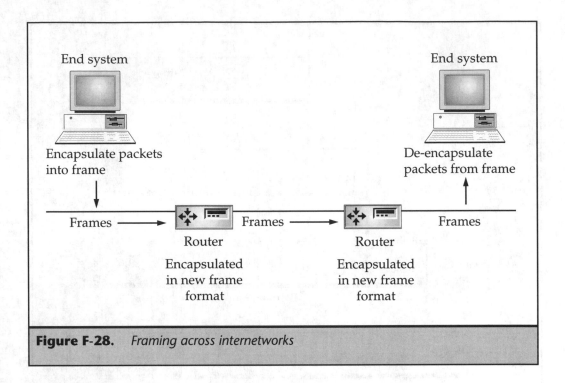

**Figure F-28.** *Framing across internetworks*

## Front-End Processor

A *front-end processor,* or *FEP,* is a dedicated computer that controls communication between an IBM host computer and the terminals that communicate with it. The IBM 3725 and 3745 are front-end processors that run the NCP (Network Control Program), which communicates with programs running in PUs (physical units). FEPs connect to IBM 3270 hosts.

The primary function of the front-end processor, or communication controllers as they are commonly called, is to free up the host computer to run applications. In this way, the host is not continually interrupted by the external devices.

Communication controllers establish sessions, manage communication links, detect and correct errors, and provide concentration points for cluster controllers. The older model 3705 provides up to 352 communication lines at line speeds up to 230.4 Kbits/sec and can attach to eight hosts. Newer models, such as the IBM 3745, provide full-duplex communication lines and dual processors for standby service and backup, as well as IBM Token Ring Network support. IBM 3745 also supports IBM SNA (Systems Network Architecture) networks and public packet-switched networks (with appropriate software).

**RELATED ENTRIES**   Communication Controller; IBM Mainframe Environment; *and* SNA (Systems Network Architecture)

## Front-End System

In a client/server environment, the front-end system is typically a computer on the network that a person uses to access data stored on a back-end server system.

**RELATED ENTRIES**    Client/Server Computing; Distributed Computer Networks

## FTAM (File Transfer Access and Management)

FTAM is an OSI standard that provides file transfer services between client (initiator) and server (responder) systems in an open environment. It also provides access to files and management of files on diverse systems. In these respects, it strives to be a universal file system. An interesting feature of FTAM is that it is implemented in all seven layers of the OSI protocol stack.

FTAM is designed to help users access files on diverse systems that use compatible FTAM implementations. It is similar to FTP (File Transfer Protocol) and NFS (Network File System), both of which operate in the TCP/IP environment. Users can manipulate files down to the record level, which is how FTAM stores files. In this respect, FTAM has some relational database features. For example, users can lock files or lock individual records.

FTAM is a system in which connection-oriented information about the user and the session is maintained by a server until the session is taken down. In a stateless system, such as NFS, requests are made independently of one another in a connectionless manner. There are advantages to stateless operation. If the server crashes, the request simply goes away and the client makes another request. This simplifies recovery after the crash. In a stateful system, both systems must be aware that one or the other has crashed so they can restore the states and prevent data corruption.

Files are transferred between systems by first establishing a connection-oriented session. The FTAM client contacts the FTAM server and requests a session. Once the session is established, file transfer can take place. FTAM uses the concept of a *virtual filestore*, which provides a common view of files. The FTAM file system hides the differences between different vendor systems. FTAM specifies document types as files with straight binary information or text files in which each line is terminated with a carriage return. Data is interpreted as records and FTAM provides the virtual filestore capabilities that store record-oriented structured files.

So far, FTAM, like other OSI protocols, has not caught on as a useful system for transferring files between different vendor systems in the LAN environment. Many of the implementations so far have failed to interoperate with one another. FTAM has worked well as a way to bring mainframe information systems into distributed environments.

**RELATED ENTRIES**    Client/Server Computing; Distributed File Systems; File Systems; Network Operating Systems; *and* OSI (Open Systems Interconnection) Model

*F*

# FTP (File Transfer Protocol)

FTP is an Internet file transfer service that operates on the Internet and over TCP/IP networks. FTP is basically a client/server protocol in which a system running the FTP server accepts commands from a system running an FTP client. The service allows users to send commands to the server for uploading and downloading files. FTP operates among heterogeneous systems and allows users on one system to interact with another type of system without regard for the operating systems in place.

FTP clients run an interactive, command-driven, text-based interface. The basic steps a client goes through to interact with an FTP server are described here:

1. Start the FTP command interface.

2. Type **?** to get command help.

3. Use the **open** command to specify the IP address or domain name of the FTP server to access.

4. Log in (at public sites, type **anonymous** as your login name).

5. Use the **dir** or **ls** command to list files on the FTP server.

6. Use the **cd** command to switch directories.

7. Use the **get** command to download files or the **put** command to upload files.

8. Type **close** to close the current session (and **open** to access a different server).

9. Type **quit** to end the program.

In most cases, these steps represent most of what you will do when interacting with an FTP server. As mentioned, you can type **?** to see a complete list of commands, and there are many. Many FTP sites use minimal file access security because they provide files to the public. These sites are called *anonymous FTP* sites. As mentioned in step 4 above, you simply type **anonymous** as your login name, then type your e-mail address (or anything really) as your password.

FTP works across many different files systems, so users must be aware that file types on FTP servers may not be compatible with their systems. Text (txt) files are generally viewable by all, and new universal files types like Adobe's PDF (Portable Document Format) make this less of a problem. One other thing: type **binary** before downloading graphics files or executables; type **ascii** before downloading text files.

The FTP client actually handles much of the command processing. It first interprets the user's commands and then sends a request to the FTP server using the FTP protocol.

Commands and data are sent across two different connections. When you start FTP and connect with an FTP server, a connection is opened to that server that remains open (is persistent) until you type the **close** command. When you request a file transfer, the file's data is transferred across a different connection, and that connection is taken down when the file transfer completes. Thus, a typical FTP session may have several open connections at the same time if multiple files are being transferred. Using this scheme to separate control and data means that that control connection can be used while data is transferred.

**RELATED ENTRIES**   File Systems; Internet; *and* TCP/IP (Transmission Control Protocol/Internet Protocol)

## Full-Duplex Transmissions

A full-duplex transmission is a data transmission between two computers in which data can flow in both directions at the same time. Two separate channels are required for full duplex, either two separate wire pairs or two multiplexed channels. In contrast, a half-duplex connection allows data to flow in only one direction at a time.

A typical serial connection (RS-232) between a computer and some other device like a modem or printer is pictured in Figure F-29. Note that this is the minimal wire configuration and that the transmit and receive lines share the ground wire. An RS-232 cable will typically consist of additional wire for transmitting control signals.

## FutureShare, Apple

*See* AppleShare.

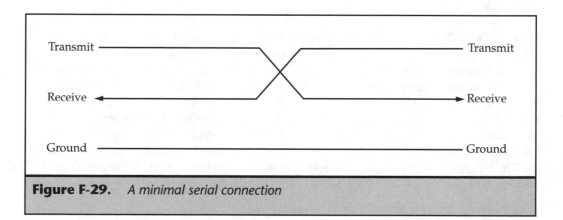

**Figure F-29.**   *A minimal serial connection*

# Gateway

A gateway is a computer system or other device that acts as a translator between two systems that do not use the same communication protocols, data formatting structures, languages, and/or architecture. Unlike a bridge, which simply passes information between two systems without conversion, a gateway repackages information or changes its syntax to match the destination system. A gateway may also provide filtering and security functions, as in the case of a proxy server and/or firewalls. Note that most gateways operate at the application layer relative to the OSI protocol model, which is the topmost layer. Some examples of gateways are described in the following sections.

**IBM HOST GATEWAYS**    An IBM host gateway allows workstations attached to LANs to connect with IBM mainframe systems. With the earliest gateways, workstations on the LAN appear as 3270 terminals to the IBM host. A PC's keyboard is mapped to the 3270 keyboard format. It was also possible to switch between the 3270 session and a normal stand-alone computer session by pressing ALT+ESC or another appropriate key sequence. More sophisticated gateway functions allow PCs connected to the gateway to transfer files to and from the host, or to run client/server applications that let PCs access back-end database services on the host system. IBM's APPN (Advanced Peer-to-Peer Networking) provides peer-to-peer networking services in the IBM environment, so gateways became less of an issue. In other words, the IBM host simply becomes part of the network. Today, the trend is to extend TCP/IP networks all the way up to the mainframe system, which also support TCP/IP. Thus, all the systems use the same protocol and no gateway is required. Another trend is to provide mainframe connections through Web servers, where users running Web browsers connect with the Web server and make requests through it to the mainframe. This model is often called *three-tiered*.

**LAN GATEWAYS**    A LAN gateway provides a pathway for data to flow from one LAN to another with an intermediate LAN providing the connection. This intermediate LAN typically uses a different protocol, so data is converted for transport over it. A router might perform these services. For example, many routers provide both Ethernet and FDDI (Fiber Distributed Data Interface) connections. Packets moving from the Ethernet LAN to the FDDI LAN can be either translated (a gateway function) and delivered to a node on the FDDI LAN, or they can be routed to another Ethernet LAN attached to the FDDI LAN. This last option is a form of encapsulation, and the FDDI network serves as a backbone for the Ethernet LANs. There are also protocol gateways such as AppleTalk-to-TCP/IP, IPX-to-TCP/IP, and others.

**ELECTRONIC MAIL GATEWAYS**    Electronic mail gateways translate messages from one vendor's messaging application to another's so that users with different e-mail applications can share messages over a network. A typical e-mail gateway converts messages from a proprietary message format to the X.400 format.

**INTERNET GATEWAYS**   In the world of the Internet, what used to be called gateways are now called routers, and gateways now refer to systems that convert network or application protocols so users and applications on TCP/IP networks and non-TCP/IP networks can communicate. A gateway also refers to devices that translate between applications. A proxy server gateway is a form of firewall that allows internal network users to access the Internet while blocking Internet users from accessing the internal network. A full-featured firewall provides advanced screening, authentication, and proxy services to keep hackers and attackers from reaching vulnerable internal systems.

**RELATED ENTRIES**   Electronic Mail; Firewall; Internet; Proxy Server; Routing Protocols and Algorithms; *and* Servers

## Gateway-to-Gateway Protocol

This protocol is one of the first routing protocols developed for use on the Internet. It was similar to the Xerox Network System's RIP (Routing Information Protocol), but was found to be inadequate because it could not keep up with dynamic changes in the network. Eventually, the concept of autonomous systems (domains) was developed and IGPs (Interior Gateway Protocols) and EGPs (Exterior Gateway Protocols) were developed.

**RELATED ENTRY**   Routing Protocols and Algorithms

## Gigabit Ethernet

Gigabit Ethernet is a 1-Gbit/sec (1,000-Mbit/sec) extension of the IEEE 802.3 Ethernet networking standard. At the time of this writing, the IEEE (Institute of Electrical and Electronic Engineers) was ironing out the final details of Gigabit Ethernet. Its primary niche is large campus environments, where it can be used to tie together existing 10-Mbit/sec and 100-Mbit/sec Ethernet networks. Gigabit Ethernet can provide a replacement for 100-Mbit/sec FDDI (Fiber Distributed Data Interface) backbones, and it competes with ATM (Asynchronous Transfer Mode) technologies in the private network environment.

Gigabit Ethernet expands on the Ethernet networks that many organizations already have in place. It uses the existing CSMA/CD (carrier sense multiple access/collision detection) medium access protocol, the same frame format, and the same frame size. Most existing Ethernet equipment, including workstation components, does not need upgrading. An organization's large investment in Ethernet hubs, switches, and wiring plants can also be retained in most cases. In addition, management tools can be retained, although network analyzers will require updates to handle the higher speed.

Gigabit Ethernet competes with ATM as an ultra-high-speed backbone network choice. ATM is considered a better choice for networks that integrate data, voice, video, and other real-time traffic because it has built-in QoS (Quality of Service). ATM is also widely used in the carrier networks where Gigabit Ethernet is inappropriate. For internal private networks, many believe that Gigabit Ethernet will solve some of the inherent problems of Ethernet simply because it provides much more bandwidth. That may be the case in some environments but not in all. Additional features such as service guarantees will also help. RSVP (Resource Reservation Protocol) is an example.

Work is being done on Gigabit Ethernet by the IEEE 802.3z Task Group and the Gigabit Ethernet Alliance (discussed at the end of this section). The 802.3z Task Group completed a core set of proposals in late 1996. It is estimated that the standardization process will be complete by late 1997. Major vendors, such as Bay, Cabletron, Cisco, and 3Com, already have products in the works. To speed up standardization, it was decided early in the process to leverage the ANSI (American National Standards Institute) Fibre Channel standard, which implements high-speed data transmissions on fiber-optic cable.

The IEEE task force has initially defined the following specification, which it collectively calls 1000Base-X:

- **1000Base-LX**  Implements long-wavelength laser transmissions with links up to 550 meters over multimode fiber-optic cable and 3,000 meters over single-mode fiber-optic cable.

- **1000Base-SX**  Implements short-wavelength laser transmissions with links up to 300 meters over 62.5-micron multimode fiber-optic cable or 550 meters over 50-micron multimode fiber-optic cable.

- **1000Base-CX**  Designed for connecting devices over short distances (in the same wiring closet), this standard will use high data rate twisted-pair copper cable with a maximum distance of 25 meters.

- **1000Base-T**  This proposed standard allows Gigabit Ethernet transmissions over category 5 copper cable with a maximum distance of 100 meters.

Gigabit Ethernet supports full-duplex mode for switch-to-switch and switch-to-end-station connections and supports half-duplex mode on shared network connections that use repeaters and the CSMA/CD medium access method. In a full-duplexed switched environment, there is actually no need for collision detection (CSMA/CD) because a dedicated connection is set up between end stations, and each has its own private *data pipe* to transmit on. However, CSMA/CD was retained to maintain compatibility with existing Ethernet standards.

Figure G-1 illustrates the functional elements of Gigabit Ethernet based on prestandard information obtained from the Gigabit Ethernet Alliance. Note that the physical layer media includes fiber-optic cable and is based on Fibre Channel, a proven high-speed network technology discussed elsewhere in this book.

## Where to Apply the Technology

As mentioned, Gigabit Ethernet is designed for the campus or building environment as a high-bandwidth backbone and a way to connect routers, switches, hubs,

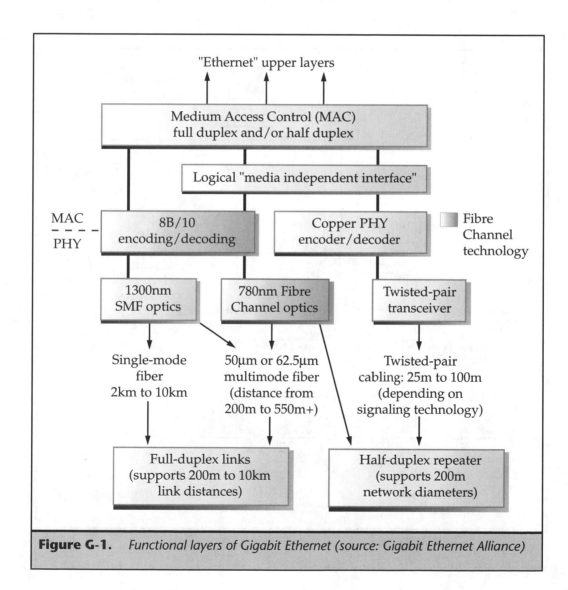

**Figure G-1.** *Functional layers of Gigabit Ethernet (source: Gigabit Ethernet Alliance)*

repeaters, and servers. The designers do not expect the technology to be deployed directly to desktop systems, although that is possible in the future. The Gigabit Ethernet Alliance has outlined several upgrade scenarios, as follows.

**FAST ETHERNET BACKBONE UPGRADE**    In this scenario, an existing Fast Ethernet backbone is upgraded to a Gigabit Ethernet backbone by replacing the core switch. This improves overall throughput among networks attached to the switch, which may run 100-Mbit/sec or 10-Mbit/sec Ethernet. Figure G-2 illustrates this scenario.

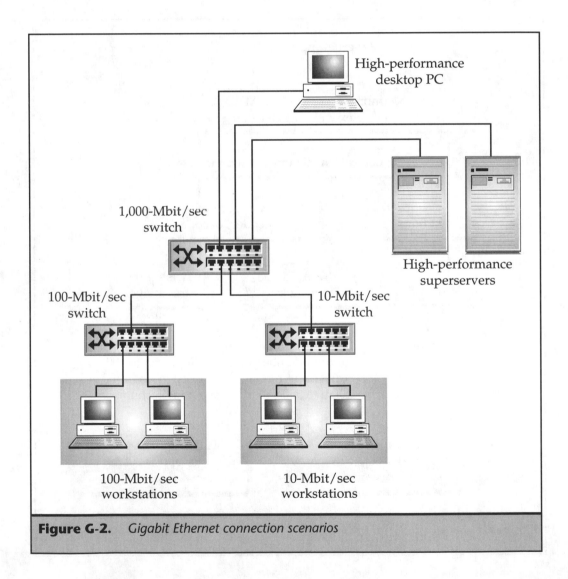

**Figure G-2.**    *Gigabit Ethernet connection scenarios*

**SWITCH-TO-SERVER LINKS**    In the scenario, the bandwidth to the server farm is increased by replacing the NICs (network interface cards) in the servers with Gigabit Ethernet NICs. This upgrade provides 1,000-Mbit/sec throughput to the servers. In Figure G-2, note that high-performance superservers are connected directly to the Gigabit Ethernet switch. Servers equipped with Gigabit Ethernet NICs must potentially handle over a million packets (and thus interrupts) per second. This is beyond the means of many servers, but a company called Alteon has developed a special NIC that offloads interrupt handling to help in this task. Basically, if the server is busy and cannot handle interrupts, the card buffers incoming packets and then hands them to the server using a single interrupt. Alteon's Web site is at http://www.alteon.com.

**GIGABIT ETHERNET TO THE DESKTOP**    In this scenario, a Gigabit Ethernet NIC is installed in a high-performance engineering or scientific workstation and connected directly to the Gigabit Ethernet network. Note the workstation attachment at the top in Figure G-2.

**SWITCH-TO-SWITCH LINKS**    In this scenario, Gigabit Ethernet switches are linked together using fiber-optic cable, as shown in Figure G-3. The links between the switches provide a high-performance backbone and promote a hierarchical network infrastructure.

**FDDI BACKBONE UPGRADE**    In this scenario, an FDDI backbone is upgraded to a Gigabit Ethernet backbone. This upgrade allows the organization to retain existing fiber-optic cabling but improve the aggregate bandwidth tenfold. It has much of the same characteristics as the network pictured in Figure G-3.

## The Gigabit Ethernet Alliance

The Gigabit Ethernet Alliance is an open forum that promotes industry cooperation in the development of Gigabit Ethernet. It fully supports and promotes the standards under development in the IEEE 802.3z working group. It is also involved in establishing and demonstrating product interoperability.

**RELATED ENTRIES**    ATM (Asynchronous Transfer Mode); Backbone Networks; Ethernet; Fast Ethernet; Fibre Channel; Network Concepts; Network Design and Construction; Switched Networks; Throughput; TIA/EIA Structured Cabling Standards; *and* VLAN (Virtual LAN)

### INFORMATION ON THE INTERNET

| | |
|---|---|
| Gigabit Ethernet Alliance | http://www.gigabit-ethernet.org |
| 3Com's Network Solutions Center (choose Gigabit Ethernet) | http://www.3com.com/nsc |
| Cisco Systems' Gigabit Ethernet page | http://www.cisco.com/warp/public/729/gigabit/index.html |

G

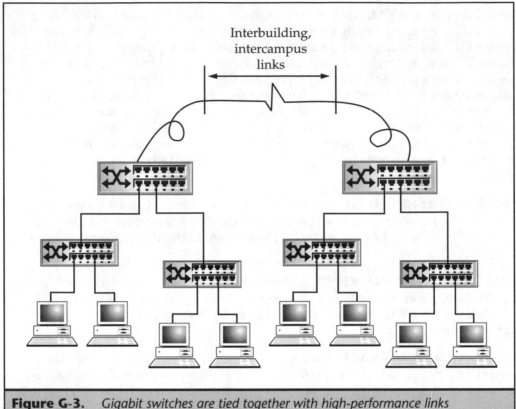

**Figure G-3.** *Gigabit switches are tied together with high-performance links*

## GII (Global Information Infrastructure)

The GII was proposed by Vice President Al Gore in a speech to the ITU (International Telecommunication Union) World Telecommunication Development Conference in Buenos Aires, Argentina. The speech took place in March of 1994. Gore also proposed the creation of a global digital library that would enable schools and libraries in every country to connect to the Internet. The GII is based on these five principles:

- Encourage private investment.
- Promote competition.
- Create a flexible regulatory framework to keep pace with technological and market changes.

- Provide open access to the network for all network providers.
- Ensure universal service.

The GII will facilitate the sharing of information over local, national, and regional networks and create a global information marketplace. It will be built as a cooperative effort among countries, with the goal of providing economic and social benefits to all participants. A key goal is to open up overseas markets and eliminate barriers caused by incompatible standards.

The U.S. contribution to the GII is the NII (National Information Infrastructure), which will link to the GII and provide Americans with access to the global community.

The GIIC (Global Information Infrastructure Commission) was formed to advance the concepts of a global information infrastructure. The commission was officially inaugurated in July, 1995, at a meeting hosted by The World Bank. It is an independent, nongovernmental organization that includes communication industry leaders from countries around the world.

**RELATED ENTRIES**    Internet; NII (National Information Infrastructure); NIST (National Institute of Standards and Technology); *and* NREN (National Research and Education Network)

**INFORMATION ON THE INTERNET**

| | |
|---|---|
| NII Web site | http://nii.nist.gov |
| GII page at NII Web site | http://nii.nist.gov/gii/whatgii.html |
| Global Information Infrastructure Commission | http://www.gii.org |
| ITU's GII page | http://www.itu.int/Sites/wwwfiles/tel_gii.html |

## Global Information Infrastructure

*See* GII (Global Information Infrastructure).

## Global Naming Services

A naming service is similar to a phone book or directory of users and services on a network. A global naming service is one that tracks users and services on an enterprise computing system, or even a network that spans the entire globe. The Internet Standards Committees are looking into the OSI (Open Systems Interconnection) X.500 global naming service as a way to provide lookup services for everyone attached to the network.

**RELATED ENTRY**    Directory Services

## GOSIP (Government OSI Profile)

GOSIP is (or was as of recently) a set of standards, adopted by governments, that specify the use of OSI (Open Systems Interconnection) standards in the procurement of computer equipment for agencies of a government. OSI sets standards for management functions, security features, and a range of other networking functions as defined by the ISO (International Organization for Standardization). OSI is very broad and strives to set standards on a global level, although it is unlikely that all the standards will be followed by any one organization or vendor. The United States, the United Kingdom, Canada, Japan, France, Germany, and Australia have implemented OSI procurement standards.

GOSIP was defined in the United States by the GOSIP FIPS (Federal Information Processing Standard), which was issued by the government in 1990 through the NIST (National Institute of Standards and Technology).

What really happened to GOSIP over the years was that it caused vendors to include OSI in their products. However, most vendors also retained or added TCP/IP and Internet standards. While GOSIP requires OSI for procurement, what people ended up using was TCP/IP. In 1994, NIST renamed GOSIP to POSIT (Profiles for Open Systems Internetworking Technologies). POSIT does not require OSI procurement. Instead, it recommends TCP/IP as outlined by the IETF (Internet Engineering Task Force) and the IAB (Internet Architecture Board), the parent of the IETF.

Basically, the U.S. Government has scrapped GOSIP and now prefers TCP/IP over OSI.

### INFORMATION ON THE INTERNET

Information on GOSIP, POSIT, and other related government computer standards

http://www.epm.ornl.gov/~sgb/GOSIP.html

## Grounding Problems

*See* Power and Grounding Problems and Solutions.

## Groups

Groups are collections of users or user accounts. You create groups to simplify the task of managing and defining rights for large numbers of users. It's also easier to send messages to groups than it is to send messages to each individual user within a group. Groups have names and can include users who work on similar projects, belong to the same department, or even belong to a club within the company. A user can belong to more than one group. For example, a user might belong to the *manager* or *administrator's* group, the *advisory* group, and the *golf* group.

You assign directory and file access rights (permissions in Windows NT) to groups in the same way you can assign those rights to users. However, it is much easier to assign the rights to groups, and then add users to the group. The user then gets all the rights and privileges of that group. Groups should be defined when planning a network and created before adding any users. Then, as you create new user accounts, you can add a user to a group. A user can be a member of more than one group.

Here are some examples of ways you could use groups:

- A word processing group with rights to run a word processing program and store files in its data directories.

- Electronic mail groups to simplify message addressing. For example, create a group called Managers, Employees, or Temporaries.

- A management group that has rights to create new user accounts.

- A backup group that has special access rights to back up directories.

Another interesting aspect of groups is that they provide a convenient way to change or remove the rights of a large number of users at the same time. You can delete an entire group, or you can remove users from a group. When users are removed from a group, they still retain an account on the system, but any rights they had with the group are no longer valid.

**RELATED ENTRIES**    Access Rights; File Systems; Rights and Permissions; *and* Users and Groups

**G**

## Groupware

Groupware is software that groups of people use together over computer networks and the Internet. It is based on the assumption that computer networks can help people increase their productivity by collaborating and sharing information. Electronic mail is a form of groupware. It lets users communicate with one another, coordinate activities, and easily share information. Electronic mail is the foundation and data transport system of many groupware applications.

Some example groupware applications are outlined here:

- A scheduling program that schedules a group of people into meetings after evaluating their current personal schedules.

- A network meeting application that allows users to hold meetings over the network. Attendees sit at their workstations and collaborate on a joint project by opening documents on the screen and working on those documents together.

- A videoconferencing application that works in conjunction with the network meeting applications described above so attendees can see one another and collaborate on computers at the same time.

Groupware also comes in the form of *bulletin board, interactive conferencing, threaded discussion,* and *chat room* applications. These applications provide a place to post messages that other users see and can respond to, either in real time or over a period of time. All dialogs can be archived for future reference and users can respond to them at any time. The archive provide a record of events, activities, problems, and solutions that can be referred to at any time.

Once groupware applications are in place and users begin to take advantage of them, traditional methods of communicating fall by the wayside. Meetings seem inconvenient due to travel and inefficient use of time. In fact, meetings become events that take place over days, and in which attendees make contributions at their convenience using electronic mail or the bulletin board system.

Here are some expectations and advantages of groupware:

- Groupware stimulates cooperation within an organization and helps people communicate and collaborate on joint projects.

- Groupware coordinates people and processes.

- Groupware helps define the flow of documents and then defines the work that must be done to complete a project.

- Groupware provides a unique way for users to share information by building it into structured, compound documents. The document becomes the central place where shared information is stored.

- Ideally, groupware should be able to help each person in a collaborative project perform his or her specific job in a more efficient way.

- Ideally, groupware simply defines ways of using existing applications to share information and help users collaborate, rather than being a special application from a single vendor.

One aspect of groupware is called workflow, which combines electronic messaging with document management and imaging. Accounting and procurement systems can use workflow management, for example. A document moves through various stages of processing by being sent to appropriate people who work on the documents, authorize the documents, and validate them. Part of this automated process is the use digital certificates so that a person receiving a document knows that it is has come from an authorized person. See "Workflow Management" for more information.

## Large-Scale Groupware

Three major vendors provide groupware packages that are all-encompassing collaborative computing products. Those vendors and their products are outlined here:

- **Lotus Notes and Domino**   Lotus Notes was one of the first full-featured messaging and groupware products. It was built for client/server operations and uses the concept of object stores in which information is stored on multiple replicated servers. Domino adds HTTP (Hypertext Transfer Protocol) services and transforms Notes into an Internet application server. Domino also adds security features such as encryption. For more information, see "Lotus Domino" and "Lotus Notes." Also visit Lotus's site at http://www.lotus.com.

- **Microsoft Exchange Server**   Microsoft Exchange Server provides many of the same features of Notes and Domino, including workgroup collaboration features, security, and more. See "Microsoft Exchange Server" for more information, or visit http://www.microsoft.com.

- **Netscape SuiteSpot**   Netscape SuiteSpot is a set of integrated server components that provide information publishing, messaging services, groupware services, directory services, security, and replication for organizational intranets. These products are built upon open Internet standards. See "Netscape" for more information, or visit their Web site at http://www.netscape.com.

As mentioned, Netscape's products are built on open Web standards, and this has advantages for organizations that are building internal intranets and connections with the Internet. Netscape's products are more flexible in that you can exchange parts you don't like for other parts. Many organizations that have an existing TCP/IP infrastructure and a lot of UNIX systems will obviously choose this product.

However, Netscape's products have only recently been introduced. In contrast, Lotus Notes is well established, and the company has made the product Internet compatible with Domino. Microsoft's Exchange Server is popular where Windows clients are used throughout the organization and integrates better than any other product with Windows NT, the fastest growing server platform.

## Web-Based Groupware

Web-based groupware (intranet software) is all the rage, and products are rapidly taking hold because they are generally inexpensive and take advantage of open Internet standards. Solutions like Notes and Exchange Server are seen as monolithic platforms that require large dollar expenditures and lock users into proprietary solutions. The Internet and corporate intranets provide an ideal platform for deploying groupware.

One of the advantages of Web-based groupware is that the Web is basically blind to the computer platform being used by end users. Groupware servers can provide information to Web browsers in the form of HTML (Hypertext Markup Language),

JavaScript, and component software. Web browsers have been designed for most computer platforms that can display this information.

Here are some of the features to look for in Web-based groupware:

- Support for the NNTP (Network News Transport Protocol) news readers, which can provide threaded discussions
- POP mail client access
- Support for directory services such as LDAP (Lightweight Directory Access Protocol)
- Support from programming interfaces like CGI (Common Gateway Interface), ISAPI (Internet Server API), Java, and ActiveX
- Replication of server-based information to other servers for backup purposes or to place replicated information closer to users at other locations
- Applications features such as calendaring, discussion groups, news services, newspaper creation, file sharing, document versioning, and workflow capabilities
- The use of security features to authenticate users and certify documents
- The ability to create and support teams of users

There are, of course, many other features to look for. Keep in mind that Web-based groupware has limitations. A Web browser cannot provide some of the features you may have gotten used to if you run Windows or the Macintosh operating system, like drag-and-drop, certain menuing features, and right-mouse button behavior (in Windows). Also, administrators interested in security and the stability of applications may be more interested in the high-end proprietary platforms discussed in the previous section.

**RELATED ENTRIES**    Collaborative Computing; Compound Documents; Document Management; Electronic Mail; Extranet; IBM Network Computing Framework; Imaging; Information Publishing; Intranets and Extranets; Lotus Notes; Microsoft BackOffice; Microsoft Exchange Server; Netscape SuiteSpot; Push; Videoconferencing and Desktop Video; Web Technologies and Concepts; *and* Workflow Management

**INFORMATION ON THE INTERNET**    The following groupware and workflow products provide proprietary and Internet-based open-standards support. Visit these Web sites for more information:

| | |
|---|---|
| AltaVista Forum, from DEC | http://www.dec.com |
| Ensemble, from FileNet | http://www.filenet.com |

| | |
|---|---|
| FirstClass 4, from SoftArc | http://www.softarc.com |
| GroupWise, from Novell | http://www.novell.com |
| InConcert, from InConcert | http://www.inconcert.com |
| LAVA, from LAVA Systems | http://www.lavasys.com/front.html |
| Notes and Domino, from Lotus | http://www.lotus.com |
| OpenMind Web, from Attachmate | http://www.attachmate.com |
| OPEN/workflow, from Eastman Software | http://www.eastmansoftware.com |
| PaperClip Workflow, from PaperClip Software | http://www.paperclip.com |
| RightSite, from Documentum | http://www.documentum.com |
| RouteOne, from Syrius Research | http://www.routeone.com |
| WebPower, from Arachnid Software | http://www.arachnid.com |
| WebShare Server, from Radnet | http://www.radnet.com |
| WorkMAN, from Reach Software | http://www.reachsoft.com |
| WorkPoint, from WorkPoint Systems | http://www.workpoint.com |

## GSM (Global System for Mobile Communications)

GSM is an all-digital cellular phone system, as opposed to a traditional analog cellular phone system such as AMPS (Advanced Mobile Phone Service). GSM is a European system that was designed from the ground up as a digital system. It does not provide any backward compatibility with previous systems and so is not constrained by the need to be compatible.

The original GSM system operates in the 900 MHz range as pictured in Figure G-4. As with other cellular systems, mobile users communicate with a base station in each cell by using separate uplink and downlink channels. The uplink frequencies start at 935.2 MHz and the downlink channels start at 890.2 kHz. All frequency channels are 200 kHz wide.

Each of the 124 frequencies in the uplink and downlink consists of frames that have eight separate slots on which voice or data can be transmitted. Each slot represents a user channel and is created by using time-division multiplexing. Active customers are assigned to an uplink and downlink frequency, then assigned one time slot in each frame sent on that frequency. For example, note slot 3 in Figure G-4, which is shaded. The customer on the left is transmitting in this slot on the 935.2 MHz frequency and receiving in this slot on the 890.2 kHz frequency.

Since there are eight slots per frame and 124 frequency channels, the system can theoretically support 992 users; however, some of these channels cannot be used if they conflict with a frequency currently being used in an adjacent cell.

Each time-division multiplexed frame in the uplink or downlink is 1,250 bits wide and holds eight 148-bit-wide slots. Each slot can hold 114 actual bits of data, with the

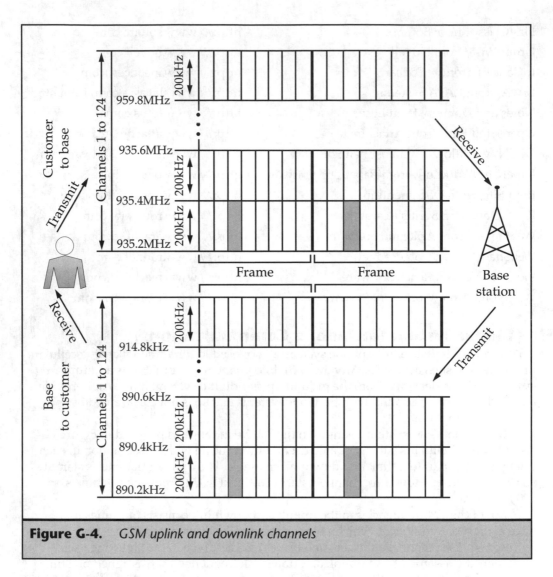

**Figure G-4.** *GSM uplink and downlink channels*

remainder used for header information and synchronization. In general, each channel can transmit one voice conversation or transmit data at a rate of 9,600 bits/sec.

The GSM standard has been expanded in many countries to the 1,800 MHz frequency band as well. This system, called DCS-1800 (Digital Communication System-1800), uses a smaller cell size, ideal for dense metropolitan areas. Smaller cell sizes translate to lower power requirements for portable devices and thus smaller batteries. PCS 1900 is a similar system designed to operate in the 1,900 MHz frequency band in North America.

**RELATED ENTRIES**   AMPS (Advanced Mobile Phone Service); Cellular Communication Systems

**INFORMATION ON THE INTERNET**

| | |
|---|---|
| GSM Online Web site | http://www.starvision.net/gsm |
| GSM Information Network | http://www.gin.nl/engindex.htm |
| GSM magazine | http://www.unik.no/~markus/mobitel.html |
| GSM World site | http://www.gsmworld.com |
| GSM information at Supercall Cellular | http://www.supercall.co.za/gsm |

# GSMP (General Switch Management Protocol)

GSMP is an Ipsilon protocol specification that is designed to control an ATM (Asynchronous Transfer Mode) switch. With GSMP, a controller can establish and release connections across the ATM switch, add and delete nodes on a point-to-multipoint connection, manage switch ports, request configuration information, and request statistics.

**RELATED ENTRY**   IP Switching

**INFORMATION ON THE INTERNET**

| | |
|---|---|
| Ipsilon Web site | http://www.ipsilon.com/protocols/rfc1987.txt |

# Guided Media

Guided media include metal wire (copper, aluminum, and so on) and fiber-optic cable. Cable is normally installed within buildings or through an underground conduit. Metal wires include twisted-pair wire and coaxial cable, with copper being the preferred core transmission material for networks. Fiber-optic cable is available with either single or multiple strands of plastic or glass fiber.

**RELATED ENTRY**   Transmission Media, Methods, and Equipment

## H.323

H.323 is a videoconferencing standard defined by the ITU (International Telecommunication Union). It supersedes the ITU H.320 standard. H.323 promotes multimedia videoconferencing from desktops over LANs, intranets, and the Internet.

**RELATED ENTRY**   Videoconferencing and Desktop Video

## Hacker

A hacker is a person that is knowledgeable enough about some computer system to be able to exploit that system in some way. This has both good and bad connotations. A hacker might work long hours to learn about a system, then come up with some way to make that system do something it wasn't designed to do. Unfortunately, the more modern definition of a hacker is someone that illegally breaks into a system.

Related to hacking is *cracking* (breaking encryption schemes), *spoofing* (masquerading as another user to gain access to a system), *sniffing* (listening to traffic on a network to gain useful information), and *phreaking* (illegally gaining access to phone lines). These activities are performed by internal malicious users and the underground community of pranksters, hardened criminals, industrial spies, and international terrorists who want to break into your systems for profit and pleasure. John O'Leary of the Computer Security Institute says that "the biggest problem with the hacker threat is that hacking is fun!"

It is believed that hundreds or even thousands of unemployed Eastern European computer experts have begun to attack systems around the world. They are especially skilled at break-ins. In 1994 a Russian hacker cracked Citicorp's electronic funds transfer system more than 40 times and managed to transfer millions of dollars into other accounts. He was eventually arrested, but Citicorp apparently never figured out how he broke into the systems. A large British bank has reportedly been paying ransom to a hacker that has proved on several occasions that he has the power to bring down their information system.

Bill Hancock is a security analyst who has been paid to break into companies and systems in order to find their weaknesses. His exploits are outlined in the April 1996 issue of *Network Security* magazine (http://www.elsevier.com/locate/netsec). In one case, he showed up at the computer room as a technician with network hardware in hand. Employees helped him into the communication closet where he was able to install phone taps. In another case, he walked into a company's branch office claiming to work for the corporate office. He asked for some space where he could get work done before a plane flight. They gave him a spare office that had a live network connection. He hooked a network analyzer into the connection and monitored traffic on the network. In another case, he created a fake user ID with a magnetic strip made of electrical tape. Then he waited for someone to enter a secure area and entered with them as they held the door.

Part of being a hacker, cracker, or spoofer is gaining information about a target company and its computer systems. A popular trend among hackers is to get a job as a janitor at the target site they intend to attack. While on-site, information can be collected to help in the attack, such as information stored on desktop computers or passwords left on sticky notes!

# Half-Duplex Transmission

A transmission that takes place in only one direction at a time is a half-duplex transmission. The transmission takes place over a single channel. Since there is only one channel, only one system can send and the other system must wait. In contrast, full duplex transmission can take place in two directions at the same time, usually on two separate wires or, as in radio transmissions, over two different frequencies. In a full duplex transmission, one transmission is the send channel and the other is the receive channel.

# Handshake Procedures

Handshaking is a procedure that establishes a link between systems. The procedure starts with a link setup phase and after data has been transmitted, ends with a link termination phase. Terminal and modem interfaces (such as RS 232) employ a data link that has a number of separate lines for transmitting data and control signals. This interfacing dates back to the days of dumb terminals and mainframe computers. When a terminal is switched on, for example, a line called *data terminal ready* is activated. The attached computer detects this signal on the data terminal ready line and activates its *clear to send* line. When the terminal sees this line active, data transmission can begin.

The above procedure is called a hardware handshake because it is done by activating specific control lines in the hardware interface. The terminal is "dumb" in that there is no built-in software that initiates a communication. The user simply turns the terminal on and the hardware interface lets the host system know that it is online by using the handshake routing.

Desktop computer systems run applications that access other systems on networks or across preestablished links. The upper-layer software uses lower-level protocols to contact another system and establish a communication session. In the TCP/IP environment, a *three-way handshake* procedure is used to start a communication session. A client initiates a session by sending a message to the server. Technically, a TCP segment (packet) is sent with the SYN flag set. The server returns an acknowledgment that it is ready to receive. The client then acknowledges this acknowledgment by sending a message back to the server. Data transmission can then begin.

A type of handshake procedure is used in a transaction-processing environment as well. Consider a situation where funds are to be transferred between two bank accounts. Money is removed from an account at one bank and moved into an account at another, but a glitch on a communication line may cause money to be removed from one account but not moved into the destination account. A *two-phase commit* procedure can prevent this problem. A separate transaction monitor first informs both systems

**H**

about the transaction. They acknowledge that they are ready to write the transaction. The monitor then tells them to commit the transaction, and one of the systems must acknowledge that they did indeed commit the transaction. If an acknowledgment is not received from any system during the procedure, the whole transaction is rolled back.

**RELATED ENTRIES**    Acknowledgments; Data Communication Concepts; Flow-Control Mechanisms; Transaction Processing ; *and* Transport Protocols and Services

# Hash Function

A hash function is an encryption mechanism that takes some plain text input and transforms it into a fixed-length encrypted output called a *message digest*. A hash function is used in digital signatures and for other uses as described in a moment. A primary characteristic of a hash function is that it is easy to compute the message digest but extremely difficult if not impossible to revert the message digest back to the original plain text.

The reason for using hash functions is to create a unique value that serves as a digital "fingerprint" of the original. For example, suppose you need to send the following message to your broker: "Buy 500 shares of ABC."

Before sending the message, you run it through a hash function to create a unique message digest. You send both the message and the hash value to your broker. Along the way, some trickster intercepts the message and changes the number of shares to 5,000. When your broker receives this message, he or she runs the same hash function on your message, which should produce a message digest that matches the one you sent in the message. However, since your original message was altered, the hash value your broker obtains is different and your broker considers the message fraudulent.

As mentioned, hash functions are used to digitally sign documents. Once the message digest is created, it can be encrypted together with the original message by using the recipient's public key. The results of this encryption can be safely transmitted. Only the recipient can open the message with his or her private key. One other feature of hash functions is that they produce message digests that are difficult to reverse. Thus, the message digest can be made public with little chance that anyone will be able to derive the original message from the message digest.

# HCSS (High-Capacity Storage System), NetWare

*See* Storage Management Systems.

# HDLC (High-level Data Link Control)

HDLC is a bit-oriented, link layer protocol for the transmission of data over synchronous networks and is defined by the ISO. HDLC is a superset of IBM's SDLC (Synchronous Data Link Control) protocol. SDLC was the successful follow-up to the

BISYNC communication protocol and was originally introduced with IBM SNA (Systems Network Architecture) products. Another name for the protocol is the ANSI (American National Standards Institute) standard called ADCCP (Advanced Data Communication Control Procedure), but HDLC is the widely accepted name for the protocol. There are some incompatibilities between SDLC and HDLC, depending on the vendor.

HDLC is bit-oriented, meaning that the data is monitored bit by bit. Transmissions consist of binary data without any special control codes. Information in the frame contains control and response commands, however. HDLC supports full-duplex transmission in which data is transmitted in two directions at the same time, resulting in higher throughput. HDLC is suitable for point-to-point and multipoint (multidrop or one-to-many) connections. Subsets of HDLC are used to provide signaling and control data links for X.25, ISDN, and frame relay networks.

When an HDLC session is established, one station, called the *primary station*, is designated to manage the flow of data. The other station (or stations) is designated as the *secondary station*. The primary station issues commands and the secondary stations issue responses. There are three possible connection methods, as shown in Figure H-1. The top two support either *point-to-point* connections between two systems or *multipoint* connections between a primary station and two or more secondary stations.

- The normal mode is unbalanced because the secondary station can only transmit when permitted to do so by the primary station.

- The asynchronous mode is also unbalanced, but the secondary station may initiate a transmission on its own.

- The asynchronous balanced mode is designed for point-to-point connections between two computers over a duplex line. Each station can send commands and responses over its own line and receive commands and responses on the duplexed line. This is the mode used to connect stations to X.25 packet-switched networks.

The HDLC frame defines the structure for delivering data and command/response messages between communicating systems. The frame is pictured in Figure H-2 and described here:

- The flag fields contain the bit sequence 01111110, which indicates the beginning and end of the HDLC frame. If any portion of the data in the frame contains more than five 1-bits, a *zero-bit insertion* technique inserts a zero bit to ensure that data is not mistaken for a flag.

- The address field generally contains the address of a secondary station. This field is normally 8 bits, but extended addressing is possible for multipoint connections that contain many different addresses. A broadcast address can also be inserted in the field to send messages to all stations in a multipoint connection.

■ The control field identifies the information contained in the frame as either data, commands, or responses. Commands are sent by the primary station, and responses are sent by the secondary station. The control information can acknowledge frames, request retransmission of frames, request a suspension of transmission, as well as other commands and responses.

A communication session starts by establishing connections between primary and secondary stations. The primary station transmits a special frame to either a single station or to multiple stations to initiate a setup procedure. The secondary stations respond with information that is used for error and flow control during the session. When everything is set up, data transmission begins, and when data transmission ends, the primary station sends a frame to initiate a disconnection of the session.

As mentioned, HDLC forms the basis for data link layer control in X.25 packet-switching networks. A subset of HDLC is LAPB (Link Access Procedure

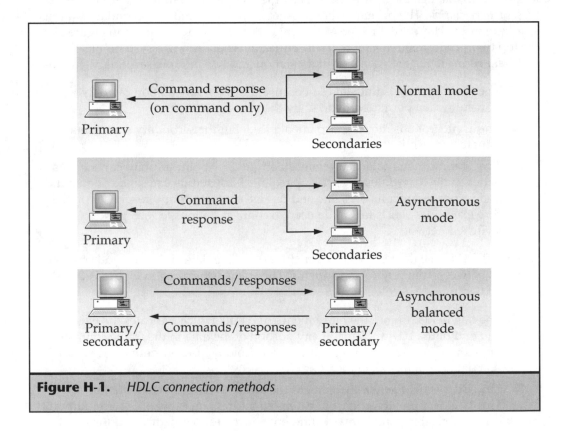

**Figure H-1.**   *HDLC connection methods*

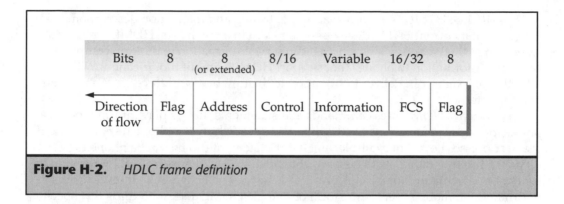

| Bits | 8 | 8 (or extended) | 8/16 | Variable | 16/32 | 8 |
|------|------|------|------|------|------|------|
| Direction of flow ← | Flag | Address | Control | Information | FCS | Flag |

**Figure H-2.** *HDLC frame definition*

Balanced), which is designed for point-to-point connections, so the address field is not necessary to identify the secondary stations. It provides the frame structure and error and flow control mechanisms for an asynchronous balanced-mode session. Another subset of HDLC is the LAPD (Link Access Procedure for D Channel) protocol associated with ISDN (Integrated Services Digital Network). The D channel is the signaling channel that controls the data flowing through the two B (bearer) channels. Think of the B channels as two separate phone lines and the D channel as the line that sets up the call.

**RELATED ENTRIES**    Data Communication Concepts; Data Link Protocols; ISDN (Integrated Services Digital Network); LAP (Link Access Procedure); SDLC (Synchronous Data Link Control); *and* Synchronous Communications

## HDML (Hand-held Device Markup Language)

HDML was developed by Unwired Planet, Inc. as a markup language for pocket-sized devices such as cellular phones and two-way pagers that conform to Internet standards and protocols. Unwired Planet creates technology for the growing mobile cellular market and Internet information publishing. It is creating a network- and device-independent software platform for accessing personal, corporate, and public information from pocket-sized cellular devices.

HDML is a complete and freely available language specification similar to HTML (Hypertext Markup Language) in concept but designed for developing applications and services for cellular devices. It is compatible with all Web servers, uses little memory, makes efficient use of wireless network transmissions, and supports integrated phone features like voice. In particular, HDML addresses pocket-sized devices, which are constrained to a few lines of display, a limited keypad, and little memory. HDML is like a wireless connection to the Internet.

*H*

HDML, like HTML, is an information publishing and interaction description language that current HTML developers can learn in a few hours. HDML is a natural extension of the Web. Any Web site that can serve information to desktop computers can serve information to phones that support HDML without modification. With HDML, companies can deliver information to their mobile workforce via Web servers and the Internet.

Like HTML, HDML uses commands and statements that display information on a phone, provide input options for the user, and specify how the phone responds when the user presses keys. For example, an HDML statement can instruct a phone to display a prompt and allow the user to enter text. HDML differs from HTML in that its fundamental structural unit is a deck of cards instead of a page. A Web server sends information to mobile users in the form of a single HDML deck with cards that specify a single interaction between the phone and the user. There are cards that display information, cards that prompt for input, and cards that display lists of options for the user to select.

Some example HDML code is shown here, and the resulting display on an HDML device is pictured in Figure H-3. HTML developers will be familiar with the coding.

```
<HDML VERSION=0.1>
  <CHOICE NAME=card1 KEY=cust>
    <ACTION TYPE="ACCEPT" LABEL="View" GOARGS=?mode=view>
    <ACTION TYPE="SOFT1" LABEL="Fax" GOARGS=?mode=fax>
    <LINE>Cust Status
    <CE VALUE=ord>Orders
    <CE VALUE=bal>Balance
  </CHOICE>
</HDML>
```

**INFORMATION ON THE INTERNET**

Unwired Planet, Inc.                    http://www.unwiredplanet.com

# HDSL (High-bit-rate Digital Subscriber Line)

HDSL is one of the DSL (Digital Subscriber Line) options that permits high-speed data transmissions over the existing copper-based lines that provide telephone service between most homes and the telephone companies' central offices.

**RELATED ENTRY**    DSL (Digital Subscriber Line)

# Heterogeneous Network Environments

Heterogeneous network environments consist of computer systems from different vendors that run different operating systems and communication protocols. An

**Figure H-3.** *A sample screen from an HDML device*

organization that consolidates its computer resources is usually faced with the task of integrating its heterogeneous systems. Typically, each department or division has defined its own network needs in terms of operating systems, LAN (local area network) topology, communication protocols, applications, e-mail systems, and other components.

The goal of an enterprise network is to get these diverse resources to interconnect and interoperate (at various levels) so that network users can share files and electronic mail with other users or access the data resources of the enterprise. In addition, an interoperable environment provides the basis for implementing groupware and workflow software applications.

The starting point for building enterprise networks is to tie everything together. Over the last few years, practical experience and the direction of the computer industry in general has shown that the TCP/IP protocol suite is the best choice for building internetworks. TCP/IP overlays existing LANs and their MAC addressing scheme with an internetwork addressing scheme that lets a user on one segment of the internetwork send messages to users on any other segment. TCP/IP masks the differences among LAN protocols, frame types, and addressing schemes.

A TCP/IP network is built with routers. A router is essential for connecting heterogeneous networks because it operates at the network layer protocol along with TCP/IP. Bridges cannot tie together different types of LANs. They can only be used if the frame structures, formats, and addressing schemes are the same between linked networks.

TCP/IP provides fragmentation at routers, which can solve the problem of differences between frame sizes on two different networks. For example, if a packet arrives at a router in a 2K frame and its next hop is over a network that uses 1K frames, the router can fragment the packet to fit the frame size of the next hop network.

Beyond the network level, high-level "middleware" products can hide the differences between applications and allow information exchange, messaging, and other cross-platform activities.

Another goal in uniting heterogeneous systems is to allow users to access back-end database systems and mainframes that were previously unavailable due to protocol and platform differences. The users' application may also present some difficulties in accessing the data, or the data may be in a format that can't be interpreted properly. A number of developments correct these problems. Microsoft's ODBC (Open Database Connectivity) is a standard for interfacing applications to back-end databases.

Up until about 1995, organizations were looking at complex middleware solutions and database access techniques to integrate their enterprise networks. The popularity of the Internet and the development of Web protocols changed all that. By 1996, most organizations were building or planning to build intranets, which are internal networks that take full advantage of Internet protocols and Web technology to tie together people and information resources.

The Web browser is seen as a *universal client* that provides a standard interface for accessing enterprise information It simplifies access to information and makes program development easier. All the old problems about making sure that different clients can access data on back-end systems went away. They were replaced with a three-tier model in which users connect with Web servers that in turn connect with back-end systems. The Web server gets the information users need, then sends it to them using industry-standard protocols and data-formatting techniques provided by Web protocols such as HTTP (Hypertext Transfer Protocol) and HTML (Hypertext Markup Language).

Even these traditional Web protocols are starting to show their age. They provide a standard way for users to access information in the form of text and graphics, but they are limited in their ability to let developers build sophisticated applications that work over intranets or the Internet. Java and ActiveX solve some of these problems but not all. If a Web browser or any application on a user's desktop is to run sophisticated applications, better delivery protocols are needed. Standards such as CORBA (Common Object Request Broker Architecture) promise to provide a standard interface for applications that will let any application talk to any other CORBA-compliant application anywhere in the world via the Internet.

**RELATED ENTRIES**    ActiveX; CORBA (Common Object Request Broker Architecture); DCOM (Distributed Component Object Model); Distributed Computer Networks; Distributed Database; Distributed File Systems; Distributed Object Computing; Enterprise Networks; Intranets and Extranets; Routing Protocols and Algorithms; TCP/IP (Transmission Control Protocol/Internet Protocol); *and* Web Technologies and Concepts

# Hierarchical Storage Management Systems

*See* Storage Management Systems.

## Hierarchical Wiring Schemes

A hierarchical wiring scheme uses a top-down structured approach to wiring that looks like a branch tree topology. A central hub or switch provides a connection point for hubs and switches in different buildings, departments, floors, and offices. In a multistory building, a central hub may connect to hubs on each floor, which in turn connect to hubs in specific areas on that floor, which in turn connect to workstations.

**RELATED ENTRIES**    TIA/EIA Structured Cabling Standards; Transmission Media, Methods, and Equipment

## High-Speed Networking

High-speed network designs are motivated by the limitations of existing network topologies. The basic concept has been to simply increase the data rate of the network. For example, 10-Mbit/sec Ethernet was improved tenfold with the standardization of Fast Ethernet (100 Mbits/sec). For technical reasons, increasing the data rate reduces the maximum station-to-station distance, so alternative schemes such as FDDI (Fiber Distributed Data Interface) are often employed as a backbone technology when long distance and high data rate are required, such as in campus environments. Fast Ethernet can fulfill backbone requirements as long as the network is usually within the confines of a single building.

The typical strategy is to connect servers to the backbone, where they can take advantage of the higher throughput. For example, a server connected to a 100-Mbit/sec backbone can simultaneously handle ten clients operating at 10 Mbits/sec with ease.

Pushing the bandwidth even further is Gigabit Ethernet, which operates at a data rate of 1,000 Mbits/sec. Its primary purpose is for use in the network backbone or as a replacement for existing 100-Mbit/sec switches.

Still, pumping up the bandwidth is not always a complete solution. While Gigabit Ethernet can improve backbone performance, local network traffic may still suffer from bottlenecks due to the shared nature of the LANs or the collisions caused under heavy traffic loads on Ethernet networks. Switching and virtual networking can provide a solution.

**RELATED ENTRIES**    ATM (Asynchronous Transfer Mode); Backbone Networks; Fast Ethernet; FDDI (Fiber Distributed Data Interface); Frame Relay; Gigabit Ethernet; Switched Networks; *and* VLAN (Virtual LAN)

**INFORMATION ON THE INTERNET**

| | |
|---|---|
| NIST's High Speed Networking Technologies page | http://www.hsnt.nist.gov |
| Doug Lawlor's High Bandwidth page | http://www.specialty.com/hiband |

*H*

# HiperLAN (High-Performance LAN)

HiperLAN is a high-speed wireless LAN standard under development by the ETSI (European Telecommunications Standards Institute). It operates at 5.2 GHz with data rates as high as 24 Mbits/sec. The standard will not use spread spectrum technology to achieve high data rates. It is scheduled for completion in 1997.

The standard uses a shared access method similar to CSMA/CD (carrier sense multiple access/collision detection), which is used in Ethernet. The allocated bandwidth from 5.2 to 5.35 GHz can be divided into five wireless LANs that operate in the same area. Each channel has a data rate of 24 Mbits/sec.

The HiperLAN standard was developed in Europe, but it now has an equivalent in North America. In January of 1997, the FCC (Federal Communications Commission) granted 300 MHz of spectrum at 5.15 to 5.35 GHz and 5.725 to 5.825 GHz for U-NII (Unlicensed National Information Infrastructure). The so-called "NII Band" radio service is available to any supplier of LAN equipment, without licensing or air time charges. It basically adds wireless networking to the NII and makes the radio spectrum available to schools, libraries, local communities, individuals, businesses, and institutions. Apple Computer has been a big backer of U-NII and has additional information at http://www.research.apple.com/research.

**RELATED ENTRIES**  NII (National Information Infrastructure); Wireless Communications

# HIPPI (High-Performance Parallel Interface)

HIPPI is an ANSI (American National Standards Institute) standard that grew out of work done at the LANL (Los Alamos National Laboratory). It has data transfer rates of 800 Mbits/sec or 1,600 Mbits/sec. The interface is point-to-point, meaning it forms a connection between two devices. It is also simplex, meaning it transmits data in one direction; however, two simplex channels can be set up to create a duplex channel. HIPPI can be used to connect peripheral devices or establish connections between processors or supercomputers.

The interface specification calls for a cable that has 50 copper twisted-pair wires. Data is transferred on 32 of the wires at 25 Mbits/sec each, providing a total throughput of 800 Mbits/sec. This supports 32-bit bus operations; a 64-bit bus operating at 1,600 Mbits/sec is possible using dual cables. The actual distance of transmission on copper cables is limited to 25 meters (82.5 feet); but if fiber-optic connections are used, distances can range from 300 meters to 10 kilometers.

While HIPPI can be used for point-to-point connections, a more common setup is to use a switch with from 8 to 32 ports. Each port has a specific address using a 24-bit addressing scheme. The switch sets up a point-to-point circuit between two different end systems. HIPPI is useful for direct connections to high-performance peripherals and supercomputers, but it is rarely used as a LAN (local area network), although that is possible.

There are request lines and connect lines used to establish connections, and parity-checking lines to ensure that data is transmitted correctly. A transmission sequence consists of bursts of data that form variable-length datagrams of 64K to 4.3GB of data. The data dumps into frame buffers, and these buffers can continue filling while information in the buffers is processed.

Fibre Channel is an alternative to HIPPI that provides longer cable distances and data transfer rates up to 800 Mbits/sec. Translation is possible between HIPPI and Fibre Channel, so they can be used in the same environment.

**RELATED ENTRIES**    Connection Technologies; Fibre Channel; High-Speed Networking; *and* Switched Networks

## HMMP (Hypermedia Management Protocol)

HMMP is part of the WBEM (Web-Based Enterprise Management) initiative, which sets standards for managing networks using browser software. Microsoft, Intel, Compaq, and Cisco Systems are a few of the companies that are participants in WBEM.

The goal of WBEM is to consolidate and unify data provided by existing management technologies. It does not replace existing technologies such as SNMP (Simple Network Management Protocol) but works with them and consolidates data. WBEM consists of the HMMS (Hypermedia Management Schema) object model for structuring data and HMMP, which provides a new communication protocol for transmitting management information over HTTP (Hypertext Transfer Protocol).

**RELATED ENTRY**    WBEM (Web-Based Enterprise Management)

## HMMS (Hypermedia Management Schema)

*See* WBEM (Web-Based Enterprise Management).

## Homogeneous Network Environments

Generally, a homogeneous network is a network of components from the same vendor or compatible equipment that all run under the same operating system or network operating system. Up until the mid-1980s, IBM and DEC could claim that many companies were using their products exclusively. But as the use of personal computers and local area networks grew, many different types of systems began to populate the desktop. Today, most managers balk at proprietary systems. There are few if any companies that have homogeneous networks. This is especially true as organizations interconnect department and workgroup networks.

**RELATED ENTRY**    Heterogeneous Network Environments

# Hop

In a packet-switched network that is connected by routers, such as TCP/IP networks and the Internet, a hop is a jump that a packet takes from one router to the next. Routers on connectionless networks do not keep complete information about how to reach all possible destinations on the network. If they did, the routing tables would be enormously large for networks like the Internet. Instead, routers know about the next router that will potentially get the packet to its destination. The router then forwards the packet over this hop.

Throughout this routing process, the destination for the packet remains constant. Each router reads the destination address in a packet, then looks in a *routing table* for the destination network (not a host address). The table indicates which output port the router should forward the packet on.

In Figure H-4, a packet arriving at an input port on a router is first stored in memory. The destination address is then looked up in the routing table to obtain the port number to forward the packet on. If a packet is destined for A, it is output on port 1. Likewise, a packet bound for D is also output on port 1, as indicated in the table. A is one hop away and D is two hops away.

The simplicity of this scheme in the TCP/IP environment is that destination addresses have two parts: a network address and a host address. When a packet is routed, only the network address is used, so routers only need to know about interconnected networks, not every host. When a packet reaches its destination

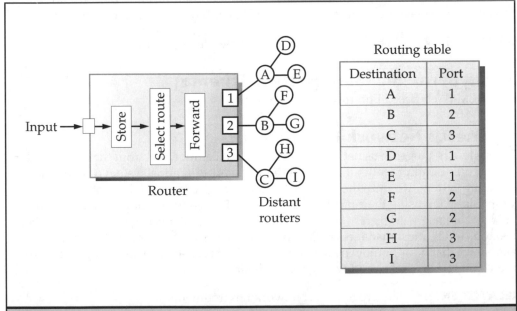

**Figure H-4.** *Routers forward packets in hops from one router to another*

network, frames are removed from the packet and transmitted on the network using native protocols (Ethernet, token ring, etc.) and the MAC address in the frames.

*Routing protocols* are used between routers as a way to update routers about the current state of the network. This allows the routers to know which port to forward packets on to reach their destination. In the Distance-Vector Algorithm (also called the Bellman-Ford algorithm), routing decisions are based on the least number of "hops" to a destination. RIP (Routing Information Protocol) was one of the first routing protocols to use DVA (Distance-Vector Algorithm). RIP limits the number of hops to 16 and drops packets that need to travel farther. New routing protocols have been devised that reduce network traffic, as discussed under "Routing Protocols and Algorithms."

**RELATED ENTRIES**    Data Communication Concepts; Encapsulation; Fragmentation of Frames and Packets; Framing in Data Transmissions; IP (Internet Protocol); Network Concepts; Routing Protocols and Algorithms; *and* TCP/IP (Transmission Control Protocol/Internet Protocol)

# Horizontal Wiring System

In a structured wiring system, the horizontal wiring is the cable that runs from a telecommunication wiring closet to workstations, printers, and other network peripherals, usually on one of the floors of a multistory building. In contrast, vertical wiring is the cable that stretches from the wiring closet on each floor to the main equipment room in the basement or first floor of the building. The vertical system is usually referred to as the backbone. Fiber-optic cable is usually used to handle the increased traffic loads of the backbone. The horizontal wiring system is usually wired with copper twisted-pair cable.

**RELATED ENTRY**    TIA/EIA Structured Cabling Standards

# Host

In the TCP/IP networking environment, a host is basically a node on the network that has an IP address and that usually runs applications. It contrasts to a router, which interconnects networks.

In a network environment where multiple LANs are connected together with a series of routers, a host is often referred to as the *end system* or *ES*. For example, if the accounting department is connected to the sales department with a router, then workstations in each department are referred to as *hosts* (or *end systems*), and the router is referred to as an *intermediate system*. There may be a number of intermediate systems that a communication message has to cross between one end system and another.

In the IBM environment, *host* is the term normally applied to mainframe computer systems. More appropriately, they are called *host processors*. These hosts include the IBM model 3090, IBM model 4381, or IBM model 9370. These mainframes usually run

**H**

the MVS (Multiple Virtual Storage) operating system, running as either XA (Extended Architecture) or ESA (Enterprise System Architecture). MVS is part of IBM's SAA (Systems Application Architecture). Refer to "IBM Mainframe Environment" for more details.

## Host Connectivity, IBM

*See* IBM Host Connectivity.

## HPR (High-Performance Routing), IBM

HPR is an internetworking protocol designed by IBM as an upgrade to its APPN (Advanced Peer-to-Peer Networking) protocol. It was originally referred to as APPN+, but is now officially referred to as APPN HPR or simply HPR. IBM designed the protocol to provide the same internetworking functionality as TCP/IP. HPR handles routing around failed nodes and avoids the packet overhead handled by network nodes to improve performance.

IBM released HPR in late 1996 to work with its aging APPN protocol. Some feel that it was released too late because many network managers would rather implement TCP/IP throughout, especially with its growing support for intranet technology. There is doubt that APPN itself will survive the TCP/IP, Internet, and Web technology tidal wave. Network managers can install DLSw (Data Link Switching) to provide a transport for SNA and APPN datagrams over an IP network. However, the latest trend seems to be to install TCP/IP throughout the entire network and all the way up to host systems.

HPR provides high-end routing features that its predecessor, ISR (Intermediate Session Routing), does not have. The primary difference between HPR and ISR is that HPR provides a connectionless service that can route around link failures, just like IP. HPR also provides better performance than ISR because it eliminates the need for intermediate routers along a path to get involved with detecting and recovering errors or managing the flow of data. Only the end systems perform these functions in HPR, thus eliminating excessive traffic and overhead.

Some see HPR as being useful in a move to building ATM networks. In particular, HPR has ATM-like QoS (quality of service) features that could possible be mapped to ATM. The AIW (APPN Implementers Workshop) Web site, listed at the end of this section, has more information on HPR.

**RELATED ENTRIES**    DLSw (Data Link Switching); IBM Mainframe Environment; IBM Open Blueprint; Routing Protocols and Algorithms; SNA (Systems Network Architecture); *and* TCP/IP (Transmission Control Protocol/Internet Protocol)

**INFORMATION ON THE INTERNET**

AIW (APPN                            http://www.networking.ibm.com/app/aiwhome.htm
Implementers Workshop)

## HSSI (High-Speed Serial Interface)

HSSI is a high-speed interface for connecting routers and multiplexors to high-speed communication services such as frame relay, SMDS, and ATM. HSSI has a synchronous data rate of up to 52 Mbits/sec. Many vendors now integrate this interface onto their router and multiplexor devices in place of serial interfaces such as V.35 and EIA-530 (EIA-422). Not only does it operate at much higher data rates, it also has superior flow control and additional loopback capability. The EIA-530 interface has a maximum bit rate to about 10 Mbits/sec over short distances, and V.35 is even slower. Information about this interface is available from WAN vendors. A list of these vendors is provided in Appendix A.

## HTML (Hypertext Markup Language)

HTML is the language used to create Web pages. Files are created using simple text with embedded codes. These files are stored on Web servers. When a Web client accesses a Web site, a default or *home* Web page in the HTML format is transmitted to the user. This page may contain links to other pages at the same site or at other Web sites.

Coding HTML files is so easy that you can create one right now on your computer using a simple text editor and a little knowledge of HTML coding. After creating and saving the file, open your Web browser and use the File/Open command to open the file you just created.

HTML documents have the filename extension "HTML" or "HTM." They can display images, sounds, and other multimedia objects. The objects are not actually stored in the document. Instead, an external reference to a picture or multimedia object is inserted in the text of the HTML document. When a user displays the HTML document in his or her Web browser, the external reference pulls up the file. Thus, an HTML page actually consists of the HTML file itself along with any additional references, graphics, and multimedia files. All of the these objects must be online and available to a user when the file is opened.

*Hypertext* is nonlinear text. It allows you to quickly switch to a reference or another source of information with the click of a button, then jump back and continue reading where you left off. A historical perspective on hypertext is given under "Hypermedia and Hypertext."

### A Very Short Introduction to HTML

This section gives a very brief introduction to HTML, not for the purposes of helping you learn the language but to merely understand its basic concepts. There are many good books available that fully explain HTML, such as *Beyond HTML* by Richard Karpinski (Berkeley, CA: Osborne/McGraw-Hill, 1996). There are also Web sites that provide tutorials; they are listed at the end of this topic under "Information on the Internet."

**H**

As mentioned, HTML documents are plain text documents that you can create in any word processor, although a number of development tools are available. Formatting instructions are embedded in a document with the rest of the text, so when you open the source code of a Web page, you see HTML code.

You can try this now. Open your Web browser and go to your favorite Web page on the Internet. After the page opens, choose Source (or Document Source) from the View menu of your browser. Figure H-5 shows the White House home page and Figure H-6 shows the source code for the page.

The HTML tags are all the funny items enclosed in angle brackets (< and >). There is an opening tag for a format or property change and sometimes a closing tag, which has a slash (/) in it. So to include a title, you start with <TITLE> and end with </TITLE>. Type this text in a text processor, changing any text you want, then open it with your Web browser:

```
<HTML>
<HEAD>
<TITLE>Your Company Name Home Page</TITLE>
</HEAD>
<BODY>
<H1>Welcome to Your Company Name</H1>
Put some introductory text here.
<B>Put boldfaced text between these tags anywhere in the text </B>
<I>Put italic text between these tags anywhere in the text</I>
Below is the start of a bulleted list
<UL>
<LI>This is the first bulleted item
<LI>This is the second bulleted item
<LI> This is the third bulleted item
</UL>
</BODY>
</HTML>
```

Of course, building HTML documents can get quite complex. You can add hyperlinks to other HTML documents that exist in the same directory, on other directories, or on other Web servers. This is all explained in any book that teaches HTML.

## HTML Developments and Extensions

Many companies and organizations are advancing the HTML standard. Microsoft and Netscape continue to improve HTML so they can provide more features in their Web browsers. The W3C (World Wide Web Consortium) tracks these improvements

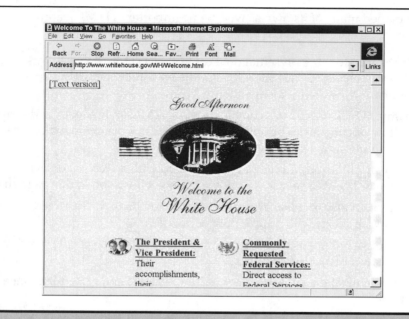

**Figure H-5.**    *The White House home page*

**Figure H-6.**    *Source code for the White House home page*

H

and has developed many of its own as well. Some important HTML features are outlined here:

- Style sheets add more presentational control for HTML. Both authors and readers can change a style sheet to alter the way information is displayed, without affecting device independence.

- Dynamic HTML describes a combination of HTML, style sheets, and scripts that allow documents to be animated. The W3C is working to make sure vendor solutions are interoperable.

- Scripts can call up additional pages associated with a Web page, such as a table of contents. The Web server does not need to get involved in this page change.

- Users can cut and paste on Web pages. An edited page can be saved on the original Web server with appropriate permissions.

- Absolute positioning is a feature that locks an object to a specific position on a page (instead of just left or right).

- Internationalization supports other writing systems and mixed-language documents.

- Access for people with disabilities is in the works. It will render HTML into Braille or use speech synthesis to convert HTML to voice.

- HTML Math can display intricate mathematical expressions and technical notations.

- HTML now includes support for tables with row and column information.

- Frames provide separate scrollable windows within a Web browser.

Microsoft and Netscape have both developed so-called "dynamic HTML" models that combine style sheets, scripts, and document animations. The W3C is working to ensure that these models are interoperable and scripting-language neutral. It has developed a Document Object Model platform that allows programs and scripts to dynamically access and update the content, structure, and style of documents, and further process that document with the results incorporated back into the presented page.

**RELATED ENTRIES**   HTTP (Hypertext Transfer Protocol); Information Publishing; Java; Push; TCP/IP (Transmission Control Protocol/Internet Protocol); *and* Web Technologies and Concepts

## INFORMATION ON THE INTERNET

| | |
|---|---|
| W3C (World Wide Web Consortium) | http://www.w3.org/pub/WWW/MarkUp |
| Central Oregon Community College | http://www.cocc.edu/Resources/HTML/ref.html |

National Center for            http://www.ncsa.uiuc.edu/General/Internet/WWW/
Supercomputing Application's   HTMLPrimer.html
Beginners Guide to HTML

Network Communication          http://ncdesign.kyushu-id.ac.jp/html/
Design's HTML                  html_design.html
Design Guide

## HTTP (Hypertext Transfer Protocol)

The World Wide Web is built on top of the Internet and uses the TCP/IP protocols to transport information between Web clients and Web servers. HTTP is the client/server protocol for the World Wide Web. It provides a way for a Web browser to access a Web server and request hypermedia documents created using HTML (Hypertext Markup Language). HTML documents can contain hyperlinks to other places in the same document, to other documents at the same Web site, or to documents at other Web sites. HTTP is responsible for processing those links and providing a client/server communication protocol in general.

According to RFC 1945, "the Hypertext Transfer Protocol (HTTP) is an application-level protocol with the lightness and speed necessary for distributed, collaborative, hypermedia information systems. It is a generic, stateless, object-oriented protocol which can be used for many tasks, such as name servers and distributed object management systems, through extension of its request methods (commands)."

When a client running a Web browser types a server name (or IP address) in the Address field of a browser, the browser locates the address on the network (either an internal intranet or the Internet, depending on the connection), and a connection is made to the designated Web server.

HTTP is the command and control protocol that sets up communication between a client and a server and passes commands between the two systems. HTML is the document formatting language.

As shown in Figure H-7, the client makes a request to the Web server, and the Web server sends HTML information back to the client. The client's Web browser properly formats and displays the HTML information from the server.

The HTTP protocol sets up the connection between the client and the server. The connection can be secured using the S-HTTP (Secure HTTP) protocol or some other protocol such as SSL (Secure Sockets Layer). Encrypted information is transmitted on a secure channel to prevent eavesdropping. Securing a session usually requires that the user or the Web site have a certificate that is issued by a CA (certificate authority), such as VeriSign (www.verisign.com). See "Certificates and Certification Systems" for more information on CAs.

The link process starts when you type the address of a Web site in your Web browser (or click a button). First, the IP address for this Web site is needed, so a lookup is performed at a DNS (Domain Name System) server that knows about the name and

**H**

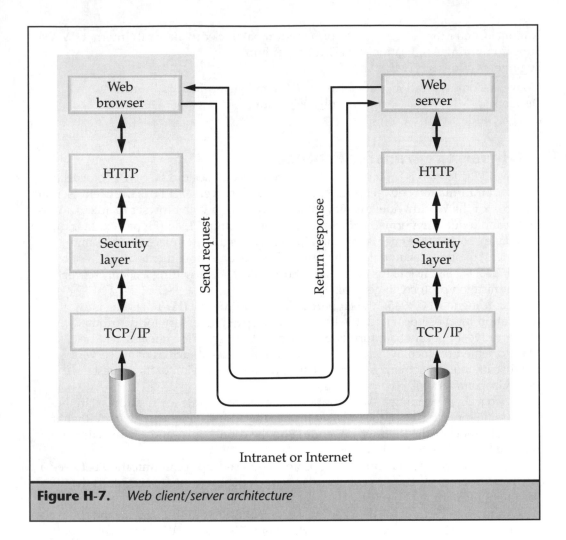

**Figure H-7.**    *Web client/server architecture*

its associated address. The corresponding address is returned to your Web browser, which then makes a direct connection to the Web server.

Web servers may provide any of the following to Web clients:

■ The version of HTTP in use

■ Status information about the request, such as whether the information was found

■ The MIME (Multipurpose Internet Mail Extension) type, which defines the media format (text, sound, pictures, video, and so on)

■ HTML-coded documents

To connect with a Web site, you type the URL (Uniform Resource Locator) for the site into the Address field of a Web browser. Here is an example of a URL that retrieves a document called info.html from the White House Web site:

www.whitehouse.gov/public/info.html

When you type this request, the Web browser first gets the IP address of the White House from a nearby DNS server, then it connects with the target server. The server responds to the client and the tail end of the URL (public/info.html) is processed. In this case, the info.html file in the public directory has been requested, so the Web server transfers the HTML-coded document to your Web browser. Your Web browser then displays the HTML information.

## HTTP 1.0

HTTP has been in use on the Web since 1990. The original version, called HTTP/0.9, provided basic raw data transfers across the Internet. Later, HTTP 1.0 was defined in RFC 1945. It improved on the original protocol by "allowing messages to be in the format of MIME-like messages, containing metainformation about the data transferred and modifiers on the request/response semantics." The text of RFC 1945 is available at the following Web site:

http://www.internic.net/rfc/rfc1945.txt

Unlike traditional client/server applications, a Web browser and server do not maintain a persistent link during the course of a user's browsing session. The text of the page is downloaded, and that is it. Every other object on the page is downloaded as a separate transmission. If a user clicks a link on the page, another transmission takes place.

## HTTP 1.1 and S-HTTP (Secure HTTP)

HTTP version 1.1 offers new features that add persistent connections and pipelining to make the connections between Web browsers and servers more efficient. With these features, servers can transmit multiple objects to a client over a single TCP connection using longer, more efficient packets. In addition, multiple objects can be sent during a single connection. Another important feature is cache management in the browser. Basically, a server page is compared against a page that a browser has in its cache. Only items that need updating are sent. Tests have shown that HTTP 1.1 provides approximately a 50 percent improvement in download times and reduces the number of packets traversing the Internet by more than 50 percent.

HTTP 1.1 includes more stringent requirements than HTTP 1.0 to ensure reliable implementations. The previous version was inconsistently implemented, causing interoperability problems. HTTP 1.1 is described in RFC 2068, which is available at

**H**

http://www.internic.net/rfc/rfc2068.txt

S-HTTP is a secure version of HTTP that is designed to coexist with HTTP and provide a variety of security mechanisms that can secure transactions between Web clients and servers. The existing HTTP transaction model is retained. It implements the PKCS-7 and other cryptographic messaging standards. Refer to "S-HTTP (Secure Hypertext Transfer Protocol)" for more information.

## HTTP and the Future

The deficiencies in the HTTP protocol make it difficult to run sophisticated, business applications over the Internet. Java and ActiveX have provided quite a lot of program functionality, but for critical business transactions, there is a need to maintain high levels of data integrity, reliability, and security. On in-house networks or non-Internet business-to-business networks, these are processes normally handled by transaction monitors, but getting such monitors to work over the Internet is a problem. See "Transaction Processing" for more details.

Some vendors have come up with middleware solutions that basically bypass HTTP. Initially, a user accesses a Web server via HTTP. Some initial components are downloaded to the user's system that provide the middleware functionality between the client and an application server over the Internet. Basically, after the Web server does its job of setting up the user, it gets out of the way. All further interaction is directly between the client and the application server through the middleware components.

BEA Software has developed an interesting middleware component called BEA Jolt that provides Web clients with direct access to BEA's TUXEDO transaction and messaging engine. You can obtain more information about TUXEDO at http://www.beasys.com.

Another area of interest related to how HTTP may change is OMG (Object Management Group)'s work on CORBA (Common Object Request Broker Architecture) and IIOP (Internet Inter-ORB Protocol). IIOP can provide an alternative to HTTP to support interoperability among objects on different systems over TCP/IP. Refer to "CORBA (Common Object Request Broker Architecture)" and "IIOP (Internet Inter-ORB Protocol)" for more information on these technologies.

**RELATED ENTRIES**    HTML (Hypertext Markup Language); Internet; TCP/IP (Transmission Control Protocol/Internet Protocol); *and* Web Technologies and Concepts

**INFORMATION ON THE INTERNET**

| | |
|---|---|
| World Wide Web Consortium | http://www.w3.org/hypertext/WWW/Protocols/Overview.html |
| IETF (Internet Engineering Task Force) | http://www.ietf.org/html.charters/http-charter.html |

# Hubs/Concentrators/MAUs

A hub is a central component in a LAN or an enterprise network, depending on how you define a hub. There are several types of hubs, including simple repeater hubs used with traditional twisted-pair Ethernet networks, workgroup hubs, and enterprise hubs. Also in this lexicon is the wiring concentrator for token ring networks. These hubs are pictured in Figure H-8 and described here:

- **Repeater hub**   A repeater hub is an Ethernet LAN device with multiple 10Base-T twisted-pair connection ports. Recall that Ethernet is a shared network topology. When one station transmits, all the other stations on the same network must hear the transmission. The repeater repeats, or *copies*, frames to each of the ports in the hub. Even though each workstation is attached to the workstation with its own cable, the repeater hub ensures that each station still hears all the broadcasts on that network.

- **Wiring concentrator**   A token-ring network concentrator, often called a multistation access unit, or MAU, is basically a ring network in a box. It provides a connection point for multiple workstations, as does the repeater hub.

- **Workgroup hub**   A workgroup hub provides a place to connect other hubs or workstations. It may be a repeater hub or a switching device. It may also have a modular design so that additional ports can be added as the need arises.

- **Enterprise hub**   The enterprise hub is a high-speed core device that provides a collapsed backbone. Workgroup hubs, located at different floors or locations in the organization, connect into the enterprise hub. Traffic for the entire enterprise may flow through the hub.

The following discussion assumes an Ethernet network. The hierarchical wiring scheme pictured in Figure H-8 follows the TIA/EIA 568 Commercial Building Wiring Standard, which you can read more about under "TIA/EIA Structured Cabling Standards." It is meant to keep local traffic local and allow internetwork traffic to flow through the workgroup hubs and enterprise hubs.

In Figure H-8, workstations attached to the same repeater hub can communicate among themselves because they are in the same broadcast domain. A cable connects these hubs to the workgroup hub to allow communication to the rest of the network. The workgroup hub may use switching and routing techniques to separate attached devices and provide internetwork capabilities. This hierarchical scheme ensures that the enterprise hub only handles traffic that needs to be transmitted across the networks directly connected to it.

*Intelligent hubs* include management features that let network administrators disable ports, monitor traffic, and perform troubleshooting.

**H**

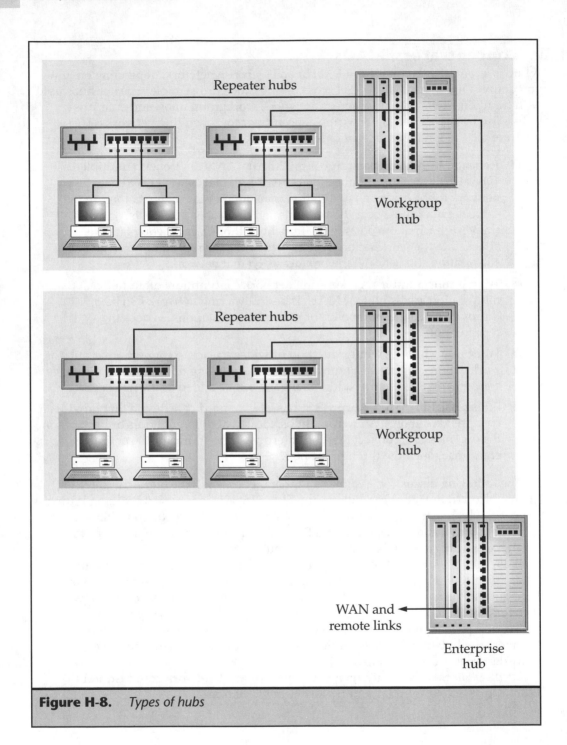

**Figure H-8.** *Types of hubs*

Hubs are also classified as *stand-alone*, *stackable*, and *modular*:

- A stand-alone hub is designed for a group of workstations at a specific location away from other groups. It will have a connector that provides interconnection to other hubs with long coaxial or fiber-optic cable.

- Stackable hubs are just like stand-alone hubs except that they are designed to be linked together in the same wiring closet. Once connected together, the hubs usually operate as a single hub and a single LAN. Alternatively, a manager may be able to create several LANs across the attached hubs and then link them with routers.

- Modular hubs are built on a chassis design that has card slots for multiple add-in boards. Add-in boards may be repeater hubs, token ring concentrators, switched hubs, routers, WAN links, or other modules.

Modular hubs are now the most popular design and are discussed next.

## Modular Hub Features

A modular hub chassis, illustrated in Figure H-9, provides a connection for multiple network cards, power supplies, and network management options.

The backplane of a hub is like the motherboard of a personal computer in concept, but usually far superior in design. It must have enough card slots to meet your future expansion needs and it must have backplane design that can scale up to your future performance requirements.

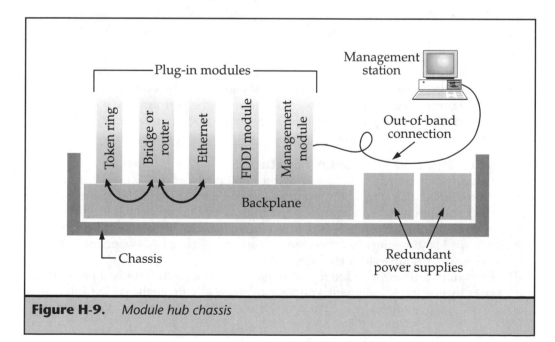

**Figure H-9.** *Module hub chassis*

This section will outline some of the traditional backplane designs, but you should refer to "Switched Networks" to learn about new high-performance switching hubs that can provide superior performance and a more practical network topology that accommodates future networking technologies.

While a bus on a hub can be compared to the bus on a computer motherboard, its requirements are quite different. Several designs are outlined here and pictured in Figure H-10. The idea is to provide network managers with a way to configure multiple LANs within the same hub. Note that some of these designs are not used much now that switching devices have taken the industry by storm.

- **Standard bus** A PCI (Peripheral Component Interconnect) bus like those used in personal computers is used in inexpensive devices. All modules become part of the same LAN.

- **Multiple bus** In this design, the backplane has several buses, each of which is dedicated to a specific LAN. An expansion card is plugged into one of the buses to join the LAN configured for that bus. A router may be installed to provide internetworking.

- **Segmented bus** In this design, the multibus design is divided into segments and joined with common connectors. The network administrator can create logical LAN segments by configuring any port to be part of a specific LAN. The network administrator uses manual configuration methods or a management interface to configure the logical LANs.

- **Multiplexed bus** A single bus is divided into multiple logical buses using multiplexing techniques. Each bus is a channel in the multiplexed stream. Like the segmented bus design, logical LANs can be configured over the physical network.

As hub technology and structured wiring become the accepted methods for connecting an enterprise, the need for high-speed backplanes becomes more important. High-performance RISC processors improve the performance of the backplane and provide the processing support for more nodes, integrated bridging, routing, and wide area networking.

### Port-Switching and Virtual LAN Features

Port switching is a relatively new feature in hubs that provides a way to reconfigure workstation connections quickly (for example, when a user switches departments). Consider what happens when a company reorganizes, or the company is highly workgroup oriented. Each user needs to join a different department or workgroup and each user's workstation must be connected into an appropriate LAN segment so he or she can access the resources located there.

Repeater hubs are hardwired to repeat signals only among the attached ports. To move a user to a new LAN segment, you have to physically move the cable from one repeater module to another. Also, if a repeater module has ten ports, but a department

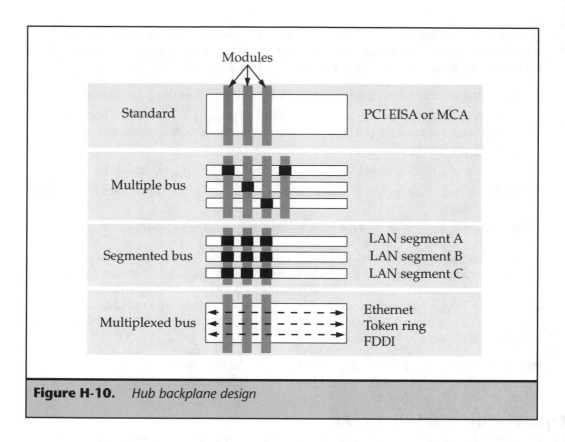

**Figure H-10.**    *Hub backplane design*

or workgroup only has five workstations, five of the ports go unused while another module might not have enough ports.

Hubs that use multiplexed bus designs support the creation of logical networks that overlay the physical network. Managers simply choose which ports are to be part of which LAN segment, thus creating VLANs (virtual LANs). VLANs support temporary workgroups with members at diverse locations. Each VLAN is its own broadcast and collision domain and users within the VLAN have access to the resources configured as part of the domain. Access to other VLANs requires routing devices. VLANs are covered in more detail under "VLAN (Virtual LAN)."

### Management Features

Management features are important. Information can be collected about packet flows and errors and used to tune and troubleshoot the hubs. Management information is stored in a MIB (management information base) where it can be collected by a management program running at a network administrator's workstation. Alarms can alert administrators when various thresholds are met that might pose problems.

SNMP (Simple Network Management Protocol) is the most common management protocol. It runs on TCP/IP networks, which use the protocol as a transport for getting information from the workstation MIB to the management computer. A graphical software application lets managers control each device and network node from a single management station. Common control features include the following:

- Automatically disconnect problem nodes that are disrupting the network.

- Provide a way to isolate ports for testing purposes. For example, a node might be sending excessive packets out on the network. You can isolate the node for diagnostic purposes.

- Connect and disconnect workstations based on the time or day of the week.

- Some hub vendors are providing protocol analysis tools as modules that fit into the hub.

- Off-site management of network components at remote locations.

Graphical user interfaces let you zoom in on specific LAN segments and display information about the nodes, bridges, or routers at those locations. You can also add or move users. Management software also provides a way to gather information about the network over a specific time period for analysis, or you can look at historical information for comparisons to current information. This can help you justify the need for new components or expansion modules.

**RELATED ENTRIES**    Bridges and Bridging; LAN (Local Area Network); Network Concepts; Routers; Switched Networks; *and* TIA/EIA Structured Cabling Standards

## Hypermedia and Hypertext

Hypermedia and hypertext is nonlinear information, presented to users in a way that lets them jump from one reference to another with the click of a button. Hypertext is basically text information and hypermedia is both text and multimedia (graphics, sound, video, animation, etc.) information. The difference is really a moot point since hypertext documents with hypermedia elements is now the predominant paradigm.

Hypermedia is all about hyperlinking: while browsing through a hypermedia document, you can select a link and quickly jump to a reference or another source of information, then jump back and continue reading where you left off. The concept is now very familiar. Vannevar Bush is usually noted as the first person to suggest using electronic technology to access cross-links and references. His ideas appeared in the August 1945 issue of *Atlantic Monthly*!

Ted Nelson actually coined the term *hypertext* back in 1965 and created a vision for a project called Xanadu that would actually implement hypertext on a Sun workstation. I heard Nelson speak about Xanadu in the early 1980s and how it would handle copyright laws and payments to authors for referenced works. I'm not sure if Ted Nelson was thinking about the Internet when he came up with these ideas in 1980.

At any rate, most people realize the potential of the Internet the first time they use a graphical Web browser.

On the Internet and the World Wide Web, hypermedia is used by Web servers to dish up text information, graphics, video, and sounds to users who visit the site using a Web browser. The most important feature is hyperlinking. With it, Web site authors can include the following kinds of links:

- **Links to other sections on the same document**  A common practice is to build a table of contents at the beginning of a Web document. When you click an item in the table, you will jump to a lower section in the document.

- **Links to other documents at the same Web site**  The link usually opens a document in a different directory.

- **Links to documents at other Web sites**  These require that the full URL to other Web sites be embedded in the HTML document.

One of the unifying concepts of the Internet is that all the documents stored on Web servers are created with the same document-formatting structure (at least in theory). The HTML language is based on some early work done by IBM, and takes into account the fact that most documents have similar features. For example, the title is usually a large bold font and the text is a smaller font with occasional underlined or italicized elements. In the late 1980s, IBM developed the GML (Generalized Markup Language) as a way to tag or mark these elements so that documents could be moved from one place to another and retain their formatting.

Consider the difference between documents created in Microsoft Word and WordPerfect. Each word processor uses a different system to code how text and paragraphs are formatted. You can't open a WordPerfect document in Microsoft Word without first converting it. But GML is designed to be a universal document language. It was even standardized by the International Standards Organization, which called it SGML (Standard Generalized Markup Language). Tim Berners-Lee derived the Hypertext Markup Language from SGML in 1990 when he put together the first proposals for the World Wide Web.

The other component that makes hypermedia work on the Web is HTTP (Hypertext Transfer Protocol). HTTP is the language that Web browsers and Web servers use to communicate. When a Web browser accesses a Web server, it requests a specific HTML page on that server. The server then responds by sending the page to the client using HTTP protocols.

**RELATED ENTRIES**    ActiveX; Broadcast News Technology; HTML (Hypertext Markup Language); HTTP (Hypertext Transfer Protocol); Information Publishing; Java; Push; TCP/IP (Transmission Control Protocol/Internet Protocol); *and* Web Technologies and Concepts

**H**

# IAB (Internet Architecture Board)

*See* Internet; Internet Organizations and Committees.

# IAHC (International Ad Hoc Committee)

*See* Internet; Internet Organizations and Committees.

# IANA (Internet Assigned Numbers Authority)

*See* Internet; Internet Organizations and Committees.

# IBM (International Business Machines)

IBM began operations in 1911 as the Computing-Tabulating-Recording Co. (CTR). In 1914, under the direction of Thomas J. Watson, CTR became IBM (International Business Machines). In 1953, IBM announced its first computer, the model 701, and shortly after, the model 650, which became its most popular model during the 1950s. The standard-setting computer for all modern IBM systems, the System/360, was introduced in 1964. An alternative line of computers, starting with the System/3, was introduced in 1970. The AS/400 is the current model in this series. For a discussion of IBM mainframe systems, see the heading "IBM Mainframe Environment."

During the late 1970s and 1980s, IBM pushed its SNA (Systems Network Architecture). SNA is a hierarchical networking strategy that provides a way for hardware and software products to interact with one another under the control of a program running in a central computer. SNA dominated the large system environment for years, but IBM also recognized the trend toward client/server computing and enterprise networks that link heterogeneous systems. IBM's traditional customers began shying away from proprietary systems. IBM has developed strategies that support client/server computing, application interoperability, multivendor product support, and the support of multiple communication protocols, including wide support for TCP/IP.

Some of the more important IBM technologies discussed in this book are listed here:

- **The Open Blueprint** IBM's architecture for building and deploying distributed applications.

- **NCF (Network Computing Framework)** A specialization of IBM's Open Blueprint focused on network computing and Internet and Web standards.

- **SNA (Systems Network Architecture)** IBM's traditional communication framework. APPN (discussed next) adds networking protocol support.

- **APPN (Advanced Peer-to-Peer Networking)** The underlying network communication and routing protocol that supports program-to-program communications.

Starting in 1996, many IBM sites using SNA systems and APPN began to see the possibility of moving to TCP/IP rather than using IBM networking schemes. In fact, IBM and other vendors like Cisco are developing hardware and software for integrating legacy systems into TCP/IP networks, not the other way around. These are discussed under "IBM Host Connectivity."

**RELATED ENTRIES**   AnyNet, IBM; APPC (Advanced Program-to-Program Communications); APPN (Advanced Peer-to-Peer Networking); CICS (Customer Information Control System), IBM; CPI-C (Common Programming Interface for Communications), IBM; Data Warehousing; DRDA (Distributed Relational Database Architecture); Enterprise Networks; HPR (High-Performance Routing), IBM; IBM AIX (Advanced Interactive Executive); IBM AS/400; IBM Host Connectivity; IBM Mainframe Environment; IBM Network Computing Framework; IBM Open Blueprint; IBM Operating Systems; MPTN (Multiprotocol Transport Networking); *and* SNA (Systems Network Architecture)

**INFORMATION ON THE INTERNET**

| | |
|---|---|
| IBM home page | http://www.ibm.com |
| IBM products | http://www.ibm.com/Products |
| IBM direct (ordering) | http://direct.boulder.ibm.com |
| IBM Java information | http://www.ibm.com/java |
| IBM software | http://www.software.ibm.com |
| IBM networking | http://www.networking.ibm.com |
| IBM servers | http://www.servergroup.hosting.ibm.com |
| IBM AS/400 | http://www.as400.ibm.com |
| IBM RS/6000 | http://www.rs6000.ibm.com |
| IBM Internet/intranet | http://www.internet.ibm.com |
| IBM security products | http://www.ibm.com/Security |

# IBM AIX (Advanced Interactive Executive)

AIX is IBM's UNIX operating system that runs on RS/6000 POWER, POWER2, or PowerPC systems. It is a 32-bit, multitasking, multiuser operating system and is suited for commercial client/server environments. IBM was seeking X/Open UNIX95 branding for AIX Version 4.2 at the time of this writing.

IBM AIX is built around the Carnegie Mellon University Mach operating system. Other functions such as file management are modular and layered on top of the microkernel. AIX implements the CDE (Common Desktop Environment) as its user interface. CDE provides an environment for running a majority of applications based on OSF/Motif. It also supports distributed, enterprise-wide computing.

In late 1996, IBM announced AIX Version 4.2, a version that includes support for Lotus Notes 4.5 and Domino, the Internet-enabled version of Notes. An electronic commerce product that resembles a browsable storefront is also included. Domino includes a component for load-balancing multiple servers called TCP Router.

**RELATED ENTRIES**    IBM (International Business Machines); IBM AS/400; IBM Host Connectivity; IBM Mainframe Environment; *and* IBM Operating Systems

### INFORMATION ON THE INTERNET

IBM's RS6000 Web site        http://www.rs6000.ibm.com

## IBM AS/400

The IBM AS/400 Advanced Series is a family of midrange business computers and server-capable systems. IBM calls the system a *superserver,* which fits the system's new role as a server on a network rather than as a central processing system.

Because the AS/400 traces its roots back to IBM's System 36 and System 38 midrange systems, a wealth of software applications has been maintained for the product (over 28,000 by IBM estimates). There are 17 AS/400 models, including a portable AS/400 and 64-bit models based on the PowerPC processors. At the time of this writing, IBM had shipped over 400,000 AS/400 systems.

IBM has an Internet/Web solution called Internet Connection for AS/400 (or WebConnection for OS/400) that converts an AS/400 into a Web server. A feature of the product called the AS/400 HTML Gateway converts AS/400 applications to HTML, which is accessible by any Web browser. The software also allows direct access to DB2/400 databases.

**RELATED ENTRIES**    APPN (Advanced Peer-to-Peer Networking); DLSw (Data Link Switching); IBM (International Business Machines); IBM Midrange Systems; Servers; *and* SNA (Systems Network Architecture)

### INFORMATION ON THE INTERNET

IBM AS/400 information                http://www.as400.ibm.com

IBM general networking information       http://www.networking.ibm.com

3Com Corporation information           http://www.3com.com

## IBM Host Connectivity

Organizations that implement IBM mainframe and IBM AS/400 hosts need a way to let users access data on those systems from their desktop systems. According to IDC (International Data Corporation), DB2 makes up roughly 70 percent of the relational databases in use today.

The most common PC-to-host connectivity configurations are outlined here:

- **Terminal emulation software** A PC is equipped with software that makes it look like an IBM 3270 or 5250 terminal.

- **File transfer** Files are copied to PCs where they can be edited using PC applications. This method is considered clunky and inefficient.

- **Program-to-program communication** IBM's APPC (Advanced Program-to-Program Communications) allows PC applications to work with an application on the host system using SNA protocols. This method requires custom applications on the PC.

- **Proxy Software** In this approach, a program running on the host itself accepts requests from PC clients, and then reformats and sends them to the host applications. For example, software from ShowCase Corporation (http://www.showcasecorp.com) uses a proxy that issues SQL (Structured Query Language) commands on behalf of clients to a DB2 database.

- **DRDA/ODBC Solutions** Microsoft's ODBC (Open Database Connectivity) technology and IBM's DRDA (Distributed Relational Database Architecture) provide direct links to host data. DRDA provides interoperability between DB2 and other relational databases. ODBC is a middleware interface that allows most clients to connect with most back-end databases. By installing ODBC-to-DRDA drivers on client systems, users can access data on IBM midrange and mainframe hosts at the record level and manipulate it as necessary with any ODBC-enabled application (i.e., Windows application). An SNA gateway is required such as Microsoft's SNA Server or Novell's NetWare for SAA. This configuration is pictured in Figure I-1.

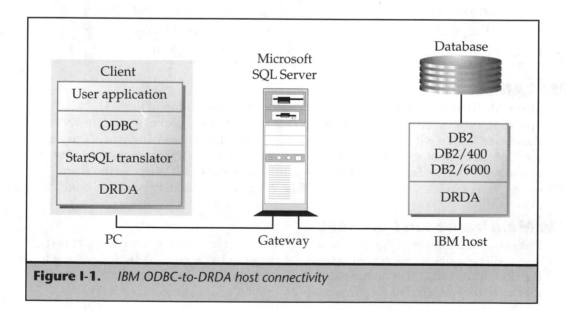

**Figure I-1.** *IBM ODBC-to-DRDA host connectivity*

Another aspect of host connectivity is to do away with the gateway. Many IBM sites using SNA systems and APPN began to see the possibility of moving to TCP/IP rather than using IBM's SNA-compatible networking schemes. MPTN (Multiprotocol Transport Networking) is an IBM networking architecture that enables integration of IBM hosts into TCP/IP network environments. NCF (Network Computing Framework) is a specialization of IBM's Open Blueprint focused on network computing and Internet standards. See "IBM Network Computing Framework."

**RELATED ENTRIES**    APPN (Advanced Peer-to-Peer Networking); Client/Server Computing; Database Connectivity; Data Warehousing; DBMS (Database Management System); Distributed Database; Distributed Object Computing; DRDA (Distributed Relational Database Architecture); IBM Mainframe Environment; IBM Network Computing Framework; IBM Open Blueprint; IBM Operating Systems; ODBC (Open Database Connectivity), Microsoft; SNA (Systems Network Architecture); SQL (Structured Query Language); *and* Web Middleware and Database Connectivity

**INFORMATION ON THE INTERNET**

| | |
|---|---|
| CiscoBlue intranet roadmap | http://www.cisco.com/warp/public/731/cblue/cblue_pa.htm |
| Attachmate Corporation | http://www.attachmate.com |
| Computer Associates International, Inc. | http://www.cai.com |
| IBM Java information | http://www.ibm.com/java |
| Microsoft Corporation | http://www.microsoft.com |
| Open Horizon, Inc. | http://www.openhorizon.com |
| Proginet Corporation | http://www.proginet.com |
| WRQ, Inc. | http://www.wrq.com |

# IBM LAN Server

IBM LAN Server is a network server system that operates on top of the OS/2 operating system. LAN Server is based on the LAN Manager server operating system developed jointly with Microsoft. Microsoft has since developed Windows NT using some of the technology developed in LAN Manager, such as the concept of security and administrative domains. In early 1996, IBM unveiled OS/2 Warp Server as an enhancement to LAN Server. Refer to "OS/2 Warp Server" for details on this product.

# IBM Mainframe Environment

In 1964, IBM announced the IBM System/360 series of mainframe computers, or *host systems*. The series was extremely popular during the 1960s. In 1970, IBM announced the IBM System/370. The architectural design allowed developers to create programs that were independent of the physical configuration of a particular computer installation. This concept stimulated the growth of commercial applications development. The System/370 architecture became System/370 Extended Architecture and eventually grew into ESA/390 (Enterprise Systems Architecture/390). The IBM Enterprise System/9000 (ES/9000) is a recent implementation of this architecture.

Today, IBM sells much smaller, but potentially more powerful "superservers" for network environments. Some follow the same architectural design as previous systems. Some run versions of the same operating system used on previous systems to maintain application compatibility. This section will discuss IBM's traditional mainframe environment. For new systems, refer to "IBM Servers."

In the traditional IBM host environment, communication takes place between terminals and host systems. Terminal are often called "dumb" devices because they have no processor of their own. The terminal for the S/3xx system was the IBM 327x model. When PCs came into use, hardware or software emulation was used to make the PC appear to be a 3270 terminal. A device called a *cluster controller* provides connections for a cluster of terminals and handles the input/output from the terminals to the host, as shown on the left in Figure I-2.

A remote cluster controller such as the IBM 3174 R serves as the connection point for multiple terminals at a remote site, and more than one can be used if necessary. It

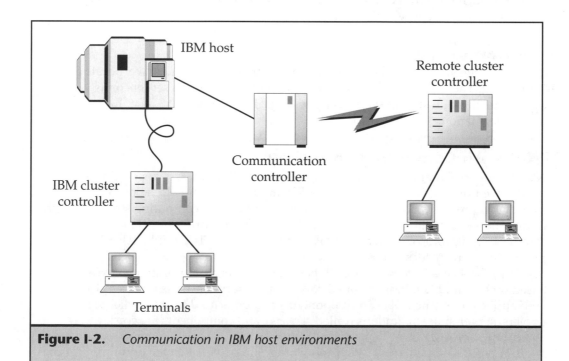

**Figure I-2.** *Communication in IBM host environments*

connects via telecommunication link to an IBM 37xx (3745, 3720, or other) series *communication controller* at the host computer site. Communication controllers are also referred to as *FEPs (front-end processors)* and attach directly to the host systems. NCP (Network Control Program) runs in the communication controller. This remote communications linking method is shown on the right in Figure I-2. Communication controllers now include LAN links. See "Cluster Controllers, IBM."

Nodes connected to hosts have a PU (physical unit) designation. PU Type 2 is for cluster controllers and PU Type 4 is for an FEP. Terminals attached to the cluster controller are called LU (logical unit) Type 2 devices. Printing devices are LU Type 1 or LU Type 3 devices.

An SNA gateway provides a connection point for a single network protocol into the SNA host. This removes SNA from the network environment and simplifies management. SNA gateways connect via high-speed channels to the host, replacing FEPs and cluster controllers. Switches make it possible to create multipoint connections into the host system.

Microsoft SNA Server is a gateway system that can provide connections into IBM mainframe and AS/400 computers for TCP/IP, IPX/SPX, Banyan VINES, and NetBEUI networks. Figure I-3 illustrates a typical configuration.

**RELATED ENTRIES**    APPN (Advanced Peer-to-Peer Networking); IBM (International Business Machines); IBM Open Blueprint; IBM Operating Systems; Mainframe; *and* SNA (Systems Network Architecture)

# IBM Midrange Systems

IBM midrange systems fill the gap between personal computing and corporate computing. They are typically designed for departmental use as servers or as computers that run specific vertical applications. Refer to "IBM AS/400" for more information.

# IBM Network Computing Framework

NCF (Network Computing Framework), pictured in Figure I-4, is a specialization of IBM's Open Blueprint focused on network computing. It is a melding of IBM's transaction processing and database support, collaborative computing strategies from Lotus, and systems management from Tivoli. The framework is based on Internet standards and protocols such as Java, HTTP, HTML, IIOP, TCP/IP, LDAP, SSL, and public-key security techniques.

Using NCF as a framework, developers can work in a programming environment based on Java and JavaBeans to build collaboration services, messaging services, and Web applications. The JavaBean component standard is used to create client-side applets, server-side applications (called *servlets*), and components to access enterprise services.

IBM has developed a set of Web and workgroup servers that are optimized for the Network Computing Framework, including Lotus Go (an entry-level server), Lotus

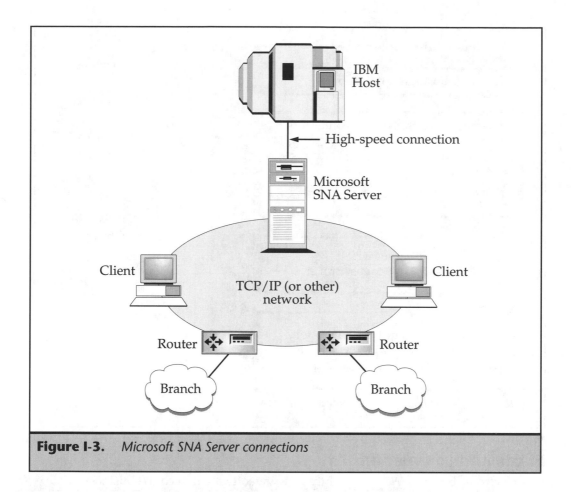

**Figure I-3.**    *Microsoft SNA Server connections*

Domino (a workflow and collaborative server solution), IBM DB2 Universal Database (Web-enabled object-relational database), and IBM Transaction Series (CICS and Encina transaction-monitoring server).

HTTP (Hypertext Transfer Protocol) and IIOP (Internet Inter-ORB Protocol), are used to link components. Components can be distributed across the intranet or Internet with IIOP acting as the glue that ties them together. Support for industry-standard IIOP and CORBA (Common Object Request Broker Architecture) allows NCF to interact with the ORBs (object request brokers) from HP, Sun, and others.

**RELATED ENTRIES**    CICS (Customer Information Control System), IBM; CORBA (Common Object Request Broker Architecture); Distributed Object Computing; Groupware; IBM Open Blueprint; IIOP (Internet Inter-ORB Protocol); Intranets and Extranets; Java; Transaction Processing; *and* Web Technologies and Concepts

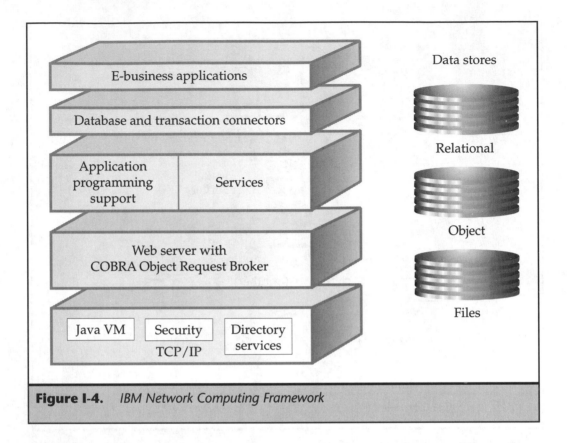

**Figure I-4.** *IBM Network Computing Framework*

**INFORMATION ON THE INTERNET**

IBM electronic business Web site    http://www.software.ibm.com/ebusiness

# IBM Open Blueprint

IBM's Open Blueprint is a standards-based architecture for building, deploying, and managing applications in a distributed environment that includes new applications running on computing platforms from different vendors. It includes the Internet and other open standards. The Open Blueprint architecture includes support for all major network and transport protocols. It also supports a wide range of distributed services and object management services, as well as major applications and collaborative/workgroup services such as transaction processing, workflow, collaborative computing, telephony, and others.

Open Blueprint combines formal and de facto standards along with new, innovative technologies. The goal is to provide a layer between end users and software developers that makes it easier to build and use client/server solutions on distributed systems.

Most existing IBM products running under OS/2, AIX, OS/400, OS/390, MVS, VM, or VSE already conform to Open Blueprint. Open Blueprint also supports Windows and NetWare environments, and new technologies such as objects, multimedia, and workflow. As new standards evolve, IBM plans to include them into Open Blueprint.

**RELATED ENTRIES**    IBM (International Business Machines); IBM Host Connectivity; IBM Mainframe Environment; IBM Network Computing Framework; IBM Operating Systems; *and* SNA (Systems Network Architecture)

**INFORMATION ON THE INTERNET**

IBM Open Blueprint Web site                   http://www.software.ibm.com/openblue

# IBM Operating Systems

IBM operating systems are for traditional mainframes, and new IBM servers are described here. Be sure to check the IBM Web page listed at the end of this section for additional information..

**AIX**    IBM's UNIX operating system runs a full range of applications on RS/6000 systems, including SMP (symmetrical multiprocessor) and PowerPC models. It is suited for commercial client/server environments and provides scalability, 32-bit multitasking, and multiuser functionality. See "IBM AIX (Advanced Interactive Executive)" and visit http://www.rs6000.ibm.com/software.

**OS/400**    OS/400 is the operating system for IBM AS/400 midrange systems. Facilities such as relational databases, communication and networking capabilities, online education, and more are fully integrated into the operating system and the machine. The user can communicate with all components of OS/400 using a single command language. A client/server environment and TCP/IP support are available. See "IBM AS/400" and visit http://as400.rochester.ibm.com/products/software/os400.htm.

**OS/2 WARP AND OS/2 WARP SERVER**    These are networked operating systems for desktop computers and servers, respectively. They provide Internet/intranet connectivity, systems management, ease of use, and support for Java technology. See "OS/2 Warp" and "OS/2 Warp Server" for more information, or visit IBM's OS/2 Warp Web site at http://www. software.ibm.com/os/warp.

**OS/390**    This operating system provides an enterprise-wide network computing server platform on IBM S/390 computer systems. OS/390 integrates fundamental MVS-based operating system components and communication functions. Besides the base OS and communications features, it includes Internet connection, security services, UNIX services, LAN services, object-oriented technology, DCE (Distributed

Computing Environment), multimedia support, and systems management services. Its UNIX support allows S/390 systems to run UNIX applications unchanged. OS/390 is Web-enabled and can take advantage of Internet, Lotus Domino, and Java-based applications. OS/390 is branded as an X/Open XPG4 UNIX system (also known as UNIX 95 Specification) and allows you to develop new UNIX-based applications or port existing applications from today's heterogeneous UNIX and multivendor environments. Visit http://www.s390.ibm.com/os390.

**MVS (MULTIPLE VIRTUAL STORAGE)**   This is the primary operating system, introduced in 1974, for IBM mainframes. It is batch-oriented and designed to manage large amounts of memory and disk space. MVS runs on IBM S/390 and ES/9000 series computers. Visit http://www.s390.ibm.com.

**VM/ESA (VIRTUAL MACHINE/ENTERPRISE SYSTEM ARCHITECTURE)**   VM (Virtual Machine) has long been recognized as a robust computing platform, spanning the entire IBM System/390 family. In fact, almost nine million people log on to a VM system every day. With its rich function and superior quality, VM/ESA is one of IBM's premier operating systems. Visit the VM home page at http://www.vm.ibm.com (or http://vmdev.gpl.ibm.com).

**VSE/ESA (VIRTUAL STORAGE EXTENDED/ENTERPRISE SYSTEM ARCHITECTURE)**   IBM VSE was originally called DOS (Disk Operating System), but because that acronym became so popular on the personal computer, the name VSE came into use. VSE is a multiuser, multitasking operating system that traditionally ran on IBM 43xx series computers, but now is available for other IBM systems. IBM's S/390 site has information about VSE/ESA. Visit http://www.s390.ibm.com.

**RELATED ENTRIES**   IBM (International Business Machines); IBM Mainframe Environment; *and* SNA (Systems Network Architecture)

**INFORMATION ON THE INTERNET**

IBM operating system Web site        http://www.software.ibm.com/os

# IBM SAA (Systems Application Architecture)

*See* SAA (Systems Application Architecture).

# IBM Servers

IBM supports multiple servers because, as it says, one size does not fit all needs. *PC Servers* use standard Intel processors and support multiple operating systems. The *AS/400 systems* are for customers that want to take advantage of the business applications available on that platform. The *RS/6000 platforms* offer power, scalability, and the ability to support a variety of operating systems. The *S/390* supports the traditional S/390 architecture.

**RELATED ENTRIES**    IBM (International Business Machines); IBM AIX (Advanced Interactive Executive); IBM AS/400; IBM Network Computing Framework; IBM Open Blueprint; *and* SNA (Systems Network Architecture)

**INFORMATION ON THE INTERNET**

| | |
|---|---|
| IBM Servers Web site (for an overview of IBM server products | http://www.servergroup.hosting.ibm.com |
| IBM PC servers | http://www.us.pc.ibm.com/server |
| IBM AS/400 systems | http://www.as400.ibm.com |
| IBM RS/6000 systems | http://www.rs6000.ibm.com |
| IBM S/390 systems | http://www.s390.ibm.com |

## IBM SNA (Systems Network Architecture)

*See* SNA (Systems Network Architecture).

## ICMP (Internet Control Message Protocol)

ICMP is an error-reporting protocol that works in concert with IP. If an error on the network occurs, such as a failure in one of the paths, IP sends an ICMP error message within an IP datagram. ICMP therefore requires IP as its transport mechanism. Routers send ICMP messages in response to datagrams that cannot be delivered. The router puts an ICMP message in an IP datagram and sends it back to the source of the datagram that could not be delivered.

The ping command uses ICMP as a probe to test whether a station is reachable. Ping packages an ICMP *echo request* message in a datagram and sends it to a selected destination. The user chooses the destination by specifying its IP address or name on the command line in a form such as:

    ping 100.50.25.1

When the destination receives the echo request message, it responds by sending an ICMP echo reply message. If a reply is not returned within a set time, ping resends the echo request several more times. If no reply arrives, ping indicates that the destination is unreachable. Another utility that uses ICMP is *traceroute*, which provides a list of all the routers along the path to a specified destination.

**RELATED ENTRIES**    IP (Internet Protocol); TCP/IP (Transmission Control Protocol/Internet Protocol)

## IDEA (International Data Encryption Algorithm)

IDEA is a block-oriented secret-key (single-key) encryption algorithm developed by the Swiss Federal Institute of Technology. It uses a 128-bit key compared to DES's

56-bit key and encrypts 64-bit blocks at a time. The algorithm is readily available and requires no licensing. It is implemented in PGP (Pretty Good Privacy), an encryption tool often used in e-mail programs.

IDEA is gaining worldwide acceptance and is considered a better choice than DES (Data Encryption Standard). The encryption rate is high, and it has been implemented on chips that encrypt at 177 Mbits/sec. The algorithm is considered suitable for electronic commerce and is exportable around the world.

**RELATED ENTRIES**    Authentication and Authorization; Certificates and Certification Systems; Cryptography; DES (Data Encryption Standard); Digital Signatures; PKI (Public-Key Infrastructure); Public-Key Cryptography; *and* Security

**INFORMATION ON THE INTERNET**

| | |
|---|---|
| Ascom (provides additional information about IDEA) | http://www.ascom.ch/Web/systec/security/page1.htm |

# IEEE (Institute of Electrical and Electronic Engineers)

The IEEE is a society based in the United States that develops, among other things, data communication standards. It consists of committees that are responsible for developing LAN drafts that are passed on to the ANSI (American National Standards Institute) for approval and standardization within the United States. The IEEE also forwards the drafts to the ISO (International Organization for Standardization).

The IEEE Computer Society is a diverse group of industry professionals with a common interest in advancing all communications technologies. The society sponsors publications, conferences, educational programs, local activities, and technical committees. Its Web page is at http://www.comsoc.org.

The IEEE 802 committees described next concentrate on the physical network interfaces such as network interface cards, bridges, routers, connectors, cables, and all the signaling and access methods associated with physical network connections.

**802.1 INTERNETWORK DEFINITION**    This working group defines the relationship between the IEEE 802 standards and other reference models. It focuses on LAN optimization of bridging/switching and cooperates with the IETF and ATM Forum. It is also working on VLAN (virtual LAN) standards.

**802.2 LOGICAL LINK CONTROL**    This working group defines the IEEE LLC (Logical Link Control) protocol, which provides a connection to lower-layer MAC (Medium Access Control) networks such as the IEEE 802 standards described here. See "Data Link Protocols," "LLC (Logical Link Control)," and "MAC (Medium Access Control)."

**802.3 CSMA/CD NETWORKS**   This working group defines how the CSMA/CD (carrier sense multiple access/collision detection) method operates over various media, such as coaxial cable, twisted-pair cable, and fiber-optic medium. See "Ethernet" and "Gigabit Ethernet."

**802.4 TOKEN BUS NETWORKS**   The Token Bus Working Group defines a broadband networking scheme that is used in the manufacturing industry. It is derived from the MAP (Manufacturing Automation Protocol). The network implements the token-passing method on a broadcast bus network. The standard is not widely implemented in the LAN environment.

**802.5 TOKEN RING NETWORKS**   The Token Ring Working Group defines the access protocols, cabling, and interfaces for token ring LANs made popular by IBM. See "Token Ring Network."

**802.6 MANs (METROPOLITAN AREA NETWORKS)**   The IEEE 802.6 MAN Working Group defines a high-speed protocol in which attached stations share a dual fiber-optic bus using an access method called DQDB (Distributed Queue Dual Bus). DQDB is the underlying access protocol for SMDS (Switched Multimegabit Data Service). See "DQDB (Distributed Queue Dual Bus)," "MAN (Metropolitan Area Network)," and "SMDS (Switched Multimegabit Data Service)."

**802.7 BROADBAND TECHNICAL ADVISORY GROUP**   This working group provides technical advice to other subcommittees on broadband networking techniques. It was inactive at this writing.

**802.8 FIBER-OPTIC TECHNICAL ADVISORY GROUP**   This working group provides advice to other subcommittees on fiber-optic networks as alternatives to existing copper-cable–based networks. Proposed standards are still under development at this writing.

**802.9 INTEGRATED DATA AND VOICE NETWORKS**   The IEEE 802.9 Working Group is working on the integration of voice, data, and video traffic to 802 LANs (basically ISDN and Ethernet on the same wire). The specification has been called IVD (Integrated Voice and Data), but is now commonly referred to as *isochronous Ethernet* or *iso-Ethernet*. See "ISDN (Integrated Services Digital Network)" and "Iso-Ethernet."

**802.10 NETWORK SECURITY TECHNICAL ADVISORY GROUP**   This working group is working on the definition of a standard security model that interoperates over a variety of networks and incorporates authentication and encryption methods. The group is also developing a mechanism that allows LAN traffic (frames) to carry an identifier that indicates which VLAN a frame belongs to. This would allow quick switching of information. Proposed standards are still under development.

**802.11 WIRELESS NETWORKING**   This working group is defining standards for wireless networks. It is working on the standardization of mediums such as spread-spectrum radio, narrowband radio, infrared, and transmission over power lines. See "Wireless Communications."

**802.12 DEMAND PRIORITY (100VG-ANYLAN)**   This working group is defining the 100 Mbit/sec Ethernet standard with the demand priority access method developed by Hewlett-Packard and other vendors. The access method uses a central hub to control access to the cable and support real-time delivery of multimedia information. See "100VG-AnyLAN."

**802.14 CABLE MODEMS**   This working group is chartered to create standards for data transport over traditional cable TV networks. The reference architecture specifies a hybrid fiber/coax plant with an 80 kilometer radius from the head end. The group is working on carrying Ethernet and ATM traffic. See "Cable (CATV) Data Networks and Modems" and "IP over Cable Data Network."

**RELATED ENTRIES**   Data Communication Concepts; Data Link Protocols; *and* Network Concepts

**INFORMATION ON THE INTERNET**

IEEE          http://www.ieee.org

# IESG (Internet Engineering Steering Group)

*See* Internet; Internet Organizations and Committees.

# IETF (Internet Engineering Task Force)

*See* Internet; Internet Organizations and Committees.

# IFMP (Ipsilon Flow Management Protocol)

IFMP is a protocol that communicates route information between switch controllers in an IP switching environment. IP switching provides a way to switch IP packets across virtual circuits rather than route them. See "Ipsilon IP Switching and "IP Switching" for a broader discussion of these topics.

# IGMP (Internet Group Management Protocol)

IGMP is an Internet protocol that hosts use to join or remove themselves from multicast groups. A multicast group is a select group of computers that can receive packets from a host that is transmitting multicast packets. Multicast packets are addressed with IP class D addresses. Hosts can have their normal class A, B, or C address along with one or more class D addresses. The Class D addresses indicate that they are part of a multicast group. This topic is covered under "Multicasting."

## IGPs (Interior Gateway Protocols)

The Internet is divided into domains, or autonomous systems. A *domain* is a collection of hosts and routers that use the same routing protocol and are administered by a single authority. IGPs route within a domain. The EGP (Exterior Gateway Protocol) provides a way for two neighboring routers located at the edges of their respective domains to exchange messages and information. On the Internet, IGP is used inside regions and EGP ties the regions together. Common IGPs include RIP (Routing Information Protocol) and OSPF (Open Shortest Path First).

**RELATED ENTRIES**   CIDR (Classless Interdomain Routing); Internet; *and* Routing Protocols and Algorithms

## IIOP (Internet Inter-ORB Protocol)

IIOP is part of the CORBA (Common Object Request Broker Architecture). It provides a way to allow CORBA-based object interaction over TCP/IP protocol networks, including the Internet. IIOP basically works in conjunction with or replaces HTTP (Hypertext Transfer Protocol), the primary protocol for Web browser/server interaction.

IIOP allows CORBA to be implemented into Web browsers and servers, and Netscape has included it in its Netscape browsers and Netscape SuiteSpot server software via VisiBroker for Java from Visigenics (http://www.visigenics.com).

IIOP provides a way for any CORBA-compliant system to communicate with any other CORBA-compliant system over the Internet. Figure I-5 illustrates how IIOP fits into the protocol stack. GIOP (General Inter-ORB Protocol) provides a general interface for connecting objects through IIOP into the network transport (TCP).

IIOP exposes application interfaces so that other applications can access those interfaces as available services. The services are available as known names, and an application accesses the services by referencing the name. Because object interfaces are exposed in a standard way, objects are interoperable. This feature allows developers to create collections of reusable services that can be used throughout internal networks or the Internet.

Netscape ONE (Open Network Environment) uses IIOP extensively to provide scalable and reusable services. IIOP is used to connect Netscape ONE clients, servers, and legacy applications on the internal network and the Internet. Initially, Web clients on the intranet or Internet connect with a Web server using HTTP. Java applets are downloaded from the server to the client and provide the functionality to make a direct IIOP connection to back-end systems, thus bypassing HTTP.

Netscape notes the following about IIOP:

"Just as HTML unlocked information within organizations by providing an open, platform-independent standard for exchanging content, IIOP unlocks the power of network applications by providing an open, platform-independent protocol for connecting network-centric applications. Through IIOP, corporations can gradually expose and interconnect their business processes and applications, not only behind the corporate firewall but also through the Extranet to electronic markets, consumers, and other companies."

**RELATED ENTRIES**    Component Software Technology; CORBA (Common Object Request Broker Architecture); Distributed Object Computing; Java; Object Technologies; OMG (Object Management Group); ORB (Object Request Broker); *and* UNO (Universal Networked Object)

**INFORMATION ON THE INTERNET**

| | |
|---|---|
| Netscape Communications Corp. | http://www.netscape.com |
| Object Management Group | http://www.omg.org |

## IMA (Inverse Multiplexing over ATM)

IMA is a specification defined by the ATM Forum (http://www.atmforum.com) that provides a way to combine an ATM cell stream over two or more T1 lines, thus allowing an organization to lease just the bandwidth it needs. When more than T1 and less than T3 is required, IMA provides a solution. It lets an organization purchase just the bandwidth it needs to transmit ATM cells across a carrier's network to its remote sites.

As shown in Figure I-6, IMA distributes traffic across multiple T1 circuits. The T1 lines act as a single circuit rather than multiple separate circuits. This optimizes

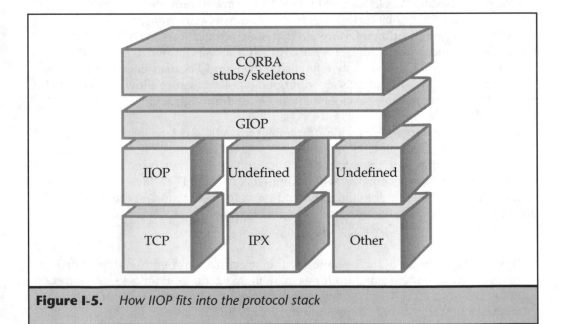

**Figure I-5.**    *How IIOP fits into the protocol stack*

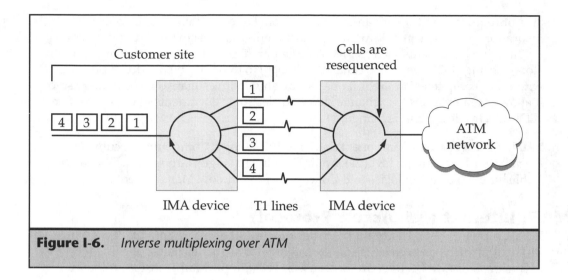

**Figure I-6.** *Inverse multiplexing over ATM*

bandwidth. For example, if separate ATM virtual connections were carried over separate T1 lines, some of the bandwidth on those lines might go unused. If each of the circuits only required 1 Mbits/sec of bandwidth rather than 1.544, the .544 Mbits/sec of bandwidth would go unused. IMA also allows bigger virtual connections. For example, if three T1 lines are aggregated, a virtual circuit can be as big as the three T1 lines combined.

A round-robin approach is used to distribute cells across the lines. Note in Figure I-6 that cell 1 is placed on line 1, cell 2 is placed on line 2, and so on. At the receiving end, the cells are recombined in their proper order to maintain ATM's quality-of-service characteristics.

**RELATED ENTRIES**  ATM (Asynchronous Transfer Mode); Inverse Multiplexing; Multiplexing; *and* T1/T3

# Imaging

Imaging is the process of capturing, storing, displaying, and printing graphical information. This process includes the capturing of paper documents for archival purposes. Imaging procedures involve the use of scanners to capture the image and optical disks to store the many megabytes of information the captured images contain. With the advent of high-speed local area networks, distributed computing, and relatively inexpensive capture and storage equipment, imaging has become a popular networking application.

Imaging systems available today allow users on a network to store and call up imaged documents from centralized image storage systems. The network provides easy access to these files so users don't need to make a trip to the back-office storage area or request the files from an off-site location. For example, a branch office of an insurance company can call up imaged documents that are stored at a central office.

Imaging documents such as invoices and purchase orders for processing and storage brings EDI (Electronic Data Interchange) to mind. If you are doing business with other companies on a regular basis, you should investigate this technology since it allows organizations to exchange standard electronic documents like invoices. See "EDI (Electronic Data Interchange)."

**RELATED ENTRIES**    Component Software Technology; Compound Documents; Document Management; EDI (Electronic Data Interchange); Groupware; Information Publishing; Web Technologies and Concepts; *and* Workflow Management

## IMAP (Internet Mail Access Protocol)

IMAP is an Internet protocol that expands on the of the features of POP (Post Office Protocol), which has been in use on the Internet for years. The latest version of IMAP is version 4, or IMAP4. Both protocols use SMTP (Simple Mail Transfer Protocol). SMTP is the transport mechanism that moves messages from one place to another.

IMAP4 is more flexible and has more functionality than POP, so it will eventually take hold. In addition, IMAP provides all the features of POP and can replace POP without disrupting the current mail system. It lets users store mail on the mail server, rather than always needing to download all new messages to their local machine. This is especially useful for mobile users who might be reading their mail at someone else's computer.

An Internet mail server must run SMTP and either POP or IMAP. SMTP receives incoming messages from any source without checking identities. POP or IMAP stores the messages in the appropriate recipient's mailbox. They also allow users to access their mailbox and retrieve messages. While accessing a mailbox, any outgoing messages are uploaded and forwarded as necessary.

Some important features available with IMAP that are not available in POP are described here:

- Users can selectively download from the server only the mail they want to read, or download only part of a message.

- Users can review the headers of messages in their mailbox and choose to only download messages that interest them.

- Users can build a hierarchical message store on the server for storing messages.

- IMAP includes support for address books and links to documents and USENET newsgroups.

- IMAP has strong authentication features. It supports Kerberos and other security protocols.

- Search commands are available that let users find messages based on their header, subject, or content information.

IMAP requires much larger and more powerful servers since users are storing information and executing complex commands at the server. Major vendors now support IMAP, and applications are coming online that have sophisticated collaborative features, groupware support, and workflow options, made possible by IMAPs feature set.

A list of e-mail vendors that support Internet protocols and provide cross-platform support can be found under "Electronic Mail." Also note that POP and IMAP are still evolving.

**RELATED ENTRIES**    Collaborative Computing; Electronic Mail; Groupware; Intranets and Extranets; Middleware and Messaging; POP (Post Office Protocol); SMTP (Simple Mail Transfer Protocol); *and* Workflow Management

**INFORMATION ON THE INTERNET**

| | |
|---|---|
| The IMAP Connection | http://www.imap.org |
| IMAP Information Center | http://www.washington.edu/imap |
| Electronic Messaging Association | http://www.ema.org |
| Internet Mail Consortium | http://www.imc.org |

## In-Band Signaling

With in-band signaling, control messages that provide connection management for phone calls, network sessions, and other types of communications are sent as signals on the same channel (wire) as the voice or data. For example, the tones heard when pressing buttons on a phone travel on the same wire as the voice signals. Out-of-band signaling, in contrast, transmits control signals on a separate line than the voice or data signal. The phone company uses out-of-band signaling for its trunk lines. ISDN (Integrated Services Digital Network) uses out-of-band signaling in the D Channel.

## Information Publishing

Information publishing in the context of this book is the publishing of information on computer networks. A Web server is a good example of an information publishing system. The Web browser is the container into which Web information is published. This section is about the standards and protocols used for information publishing and about future directions in information publishing.

By far, the most practical way to publish information is with Web technologies. The Internet and intranets provide the platform for disseminating information either internally or externally. End users can visit Web sites to obtain published information or have it automatically "pushed" to them using technologies described under "Broadcast News Technology," "Marimba Castanet," "PointCast," and "Push."

Publishing information is more than creating content. It is also about managing security, document flow, copyright, and other factors. Document management is a science unto itself. See "Document Management" for a discussion of services for storing, tracking, versioning, indexing, and searching for documents, as well as providing "audit trails" to track who has read and altered a document, if necessary. This is usually done on internal networks.

The Windows and Macintosh environments were important in developing the concept of *compound documents*. A compound document starts as a document created in an application like Microsoft Word, i.e., it starts as a text document. The document is viewed as a container that can hold objects such as graphics, voice clips, and video clips. These objects are either embedded or linked. An embedded object such as a picture travels with the document but can still be edited using an appropriate application. A linked object may be stored in another location. The document simply contains a link to the object at that location and may display it as well. For example, a document might contain a link to a picture or to some spreadsheet data. The advantage of links is that if the linked object is edited or updated, the contents of the compound document change as well.

Web page are compound documents that can hold text and individual objects like pictures, sounds, videos, Java applets, and ActiveX controls. An electronic mail message with an attachment such as a graphic is also a compound document. The original purpose of compound documents was to provide a single place where users could store all the elements related to a document and, if necessary, send the document to someone else.

## Document Interchange Standards

The exchange of computer information would be impossible without character formatting standards such as ASCII (American Standard Code for Information Interchange). ASCII identifies each letter of the alphabet with a 7-bit code and provides an extended character set using 8-bit codes. Almost every computer recognizes the ASCII code set, making file exchange possible without conversion in most cases. However, ASCII does not support document formatting, such as page layout, paragraph alignment, and font selections. Preserving document formats during file exchange is essential.

Document interchange standards attempt to provide universal document formatting. Users on different computer platforms should be able to exchange documents and retain formats even though the applications and operations are different. Document standards should at a minimum provide a way to describe the following document features in a language that is understood by any system that needs to open and display the document:

- Document *structure*, which defines segments of the document, such as headers and paragraphs
- Document *content*, which is arranged on pages in a particular *layout*

One way users can exchange documents is by using the same application from the same vendor across platforms. For example, users of Microsoft Word can exchange documents with users on any other platform where Word runs. Microsoft and other vendors have their own document standards for this purpose. However, this doesn't work on large networks like the Internet where people have their own preferences for applications. What is needed is a pervasive document standard. Some of the standards that have been developed are outlined here.

### EDI (Electronic Data Interchange)

EDI is a business-to-business electronic document exchange standard defined by ANSI (American National Standards Institute) that defines structures for business forms such as purchase orders, invoices, and shipping notices and provides a way for organizations to exchange those forms over communication links. See "EDI (Electronic Data Interchange)" and "Electronic Commerce" for more information.

### Acrobat, Adobe Systems Inc.

Adobe Systems' Acrobat provides portable document exchange capability that lets document recipients view a document as it was formatted. It is also widely used as a document interchange format on the Internet and on the Web. For information on Adobe Acrobat, see "Acrobat." Adobe's Web site is at http://www.adobe.com.

### MIME (Multipurpose Internet Mail Extension)

MIME is an Internet standard that provides a way to include different types of data, such as graphics, audio, video, and text in electronic mail messages. See "MIME (Multipurpose Internet Mail Extension)" for more information.

### SGML (Standard Generalized Markup Language)

SGML is a portable document language that defines the structure and content of a document. SGML documents contain attributes to define components like paragraphs and headers, thus making the documents hardware and software independent. Information in documents is translated to perform actions or formatting on other systems. See "SGML (Standard Generalized Markup Language)" for more information.

### HTML (Hypertext Markup Language)

HTML is the page description language for the Web. While related to SGML, it provides many advanced features. Documents written in HTML will display in a Web browser on any system. Many companies and organizations are advancing the HTML standard. Microsoft and Netscape keep improving HTML to provide more features in their Web browsers. The W3C is also improving the standard. Refer to "HTML (Hypertext Markup Language)" for more information.

**RELATED ENTRIES**    Component Software Technology; Compound Documents; Document Management; Groupware; Imaging; Web Technologies and Concepts; *and* Workflow Management

## Information Warehouse

An *information warehouse* is an entity that allows end users to quickly and easily access an organization's data in a consistent way. In the view of large system vendors like

IBM and Digital, the information warehouse recasts mainframe and midrange computer systems as the central repository for current and historical data, as well as predefined data sets, reports, and catalogs of data. This strategy protects high-end system technology and customers' investments. The information warehouse provides a central point where all data is collected and made available, repackaged, or redistributed to end users. This topic is covered further under "Data Warehousing."

IBM has an extensive set of products for building small "datamarts" for single workgroups or fully automated, enterprise-wide data warehouses. Some of the features outlined by IBM include

- Accessing a variety of data sources for populating your data warehouse
- Transforming the data into information using tools for cleansing, summarizing, and aggregating source data before placing it in the data warehouse
- Distributing the information to other locations as necessary
- Finding and understanding the information in the data warehouse and understanding exactly what the warehouse information means in business terms
- Displaying, analyzing, and discovering the information and using it for business decision making

**RELATED ENTRIES**     Database Connectivity; Data Warehousing; DBMS (Database Management System); Distributed Database; Enterprise Networks; IBM (International Business Machines); IBM Mainframe Environment; IBM Open Blueprint; OLAP (Online Analytical Processing); *and* SQL (Structured Query Language)

**INFORMATION ON THE INTERNET**

| | |
|---|---|
| IBM Information Warehouse Web site | http://www.software.ibm.com/data/warehouse |
| IBM Information Warehouse white papers | http://www.software.ibm.com/data/pubs/papers |

# Infrared Technologies

While most people are familiar with infrared as implemented in remote control devices, its use in computer communications is of considerable interest to the portable computing device industry. The IrDA (Infrared Data Association) has worked out infrared standards with transmission rates as high as 4 Mbits/sec. Devices that take advantage of IrDA standards include PCs, PC adapters, printers, notebook computers, PDAs, and certain LAN access devices.

The advantages of infrared are many. It provides incredible wireless convenience for portable device users, and the technology is inexpensive and reliable. Almost every portable device vendor is implementing IrDA standards, so many devices are interoperable. In addition, there are few international regulatory constraints, so vendors can ship IrDA-enabled products around the world.

Infrared connections can be used to send documents from portable computers to printers, to transmit data between other portable computers, to exchange information between computers and cellular phones and faxes, to connect with ATMs and other public machines, and to connect with home entertainment devices and control systems.

IrDA is responsible for the IrDA SIR (serial infrared) Data Link standards, the IrLAP (Link Access Protocol) specification, and IrLMP (Link Management Protocol). In October 1995, it extended SIR's data rate to 4 Mbits/sec with a standard called Fast IR. You can visit the IrDA Web site at http://www.irda.org. See "IrDA (Infrared Data Association)" for a brief description of IrDA.

## Infrared LANs

Infrared LANs are wireless networks. An infrared signal similar to the signal in a television remote control transmits signals between two stations. Workstations must be within line of sight of the infrared transmitter, which gives them some (but limited) mobility. Some infrared LANs operate by bouncing signals off of walls in a dispersed pattern. However, these LANs have limited distances.

**RELATED ENTRIES**    IrDA (Infrared Data Association); Mobile Computing; *and* Wireless Communications

## Inherited Rights

Network operating systems such as NetWare and Windows NT use the concept of *inherited rights* (permissions in Windows NT). Rights are the settings that a user has in a directory that determines what they can do in the directory (read files, change files, delete files, etc.). Inherited rights are the rights a user has in subdirectories that have "flowed down" from the parent directory. In NetWare 4.x, the concept of inheritance also works in container objects of NDS (Novell Directory Services).

If a user has Read, Write, and Create rights to a directory, that user has those same rights in its subdirectories unless the rights are specifically changed. When a supervisor *specifically changes* rights, it means that he or she blocks the rights from being inherited in the subdirectory for all users, for a group of users, or for a single user. An IRF (inherited rights filter) is used to block the normal flow of rights down the directory tree.

**RELATED ENTRIES**    Access Control; Access Rights; File Systems; Novell NetWare; Novell NetWare File System; Rights and Permissions; *and* Users and Groups

## Interface Connection

*See* Connection Technologies.

## Internet

The Internet is a global web of interconnected computer networks. It is a network of networks that link schools, libraries, businesses, hospitals, federal agencies, research institutes, and other entities into a single, large communication network that spans the globe. The underlying connections include the dial-up telephone network, satellite and ground-based microwave links, fiber-optic networks, and even the cable TV (CATV) network. The actual network cannot be mapped at any one time because new computers and networks are constantly joining the network and electronic pathways are constantly changing.

While the Internet was originally conceived as a communication network for researchers, today it is used by millions of people in business, in education, or for just plain communication. The thousands of interconnected networks that make up the Internet include millions of computers and users. It provides the basis for global electronic mail and information exchange via the Web (World Wide Web) and other services.

The Internet grew out of an earlier U.S. Department of Defense project, the ARPANET (Advanced Research Projects Agency Network), that was put into place in 1969 as a pioneering project to test packet-switching networks. ARPANET provided links between researchers and remote computer centers. In 1983, the military communication portion of ARPANET was split off into MILNET (Military Network), although cross-communication was still possible. ARPANET was officially dismantled in 1990. Its successor, Internet, continues to grow.

The Internet is based on TCP/IP (Transmission Control Protocol/Internet Protocol), an open internetwork communication protocol. TCP/IP networks consist of router-connected subnetworks that are located all over the world. Packet-switching techniques are used to move packets from one subnetwork to another.

No person, government, or entity owns or controls the Internet. The process of setting standards on the Internet is handled by organizations based on input from users. These organizations and the standards process are covered under "Internet Organizations and Committees."

Figure I-7 shows roughly how the Internet is structured. At the bottom, organizations and home users connect to local ISPs (Internet service providers). ISPs are in turn connected to regional networks with data pipes that are "fat" enough to handle all the traffic produced by the ISP's subscribers. The regional networks are connected to the U.S. backbone network, which has even bigger data pipes. The U.S. backbone is also connected internationally. Internet backbone is discussed fully under "Internet Backbone."

**NOTE:** *Anyone interested in the history of the Internet should visit the Internet Society's page at http://www.isoc.org/internet-history.*

**RELATED ENTRIES**    Internet Backbone; Internet Connections; Internet Organizations and Committees; Intranets and Extranets; IP (Internet Protocol); ISPs (Internet Service

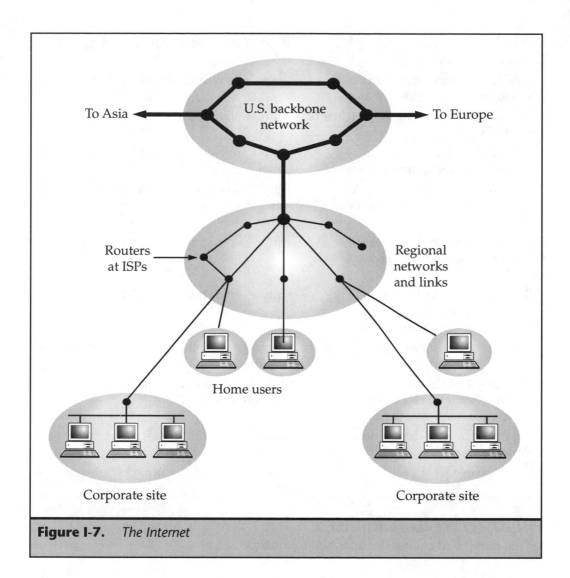

**Figure I-7.** *The Internet*

Providers); NII (National Information Infrastructure); Standards Groups, Associations, and Organizations; TCP (Transmission Control Protocol); TCP/IP (Transmission Control Protocol/Internet Protocol); *and* Web Technologies and Concepts

### INFORMATION ON THE INTERNET

| | |
|---|---|
| Internet Society | http://www.isoc.org |
| World Wide Web Consortium | http://www.w3.org/pub/WWW |
| IETF (Internet Engineering Task Force) | http://www.ietf.org |

| | |
|---|---|
| InterNIC Directory and Database Services | http://www.internic.net/ds/dspg01.html |
| InterNIC Directory of Directories (links to resources on the Internet) | http://www.internic.net/dod |
| U.S. National Information Infrastructure Virtual Library | http://nii.nist.gov |
| The InterNIC's search page for RFCs (requests for comment) | http://www.internic.net/ds/dspg1intdoc.html |
| All the RFCs, listed in order with author names and descriptions (a very long list) | http://www.cis.ohio-state.edu/htbin/rfc/rfc-index.html |
| FYI on Questions and Answers to Commonly asked "New Internet User" Questions | http://www.internic.net/rfc/rfc1206.txt |
| FYI on Questions and Answers to Commonly asked "Experienced Internet User" Questions | http://www.internic.net/rfc/rfc1207.txt |
| Yahoo!'s Internet links page | http://www.yahoo.com/Computers_and_Internet/Internet |
| Prof. Jeffrey MacKie-Mason's Telecom Information Resources on the Internet | http://www.spp.umich.edu/telecom/telecom-info.html |
| InternetSourceBook.com guide to Internet companies | http://www.internetsourcebook.com |
| Internet-related site listings | http://www.spp.umich.edu/telecom/technical-info.html |

## Internet Architecture Board

*See* Internet; Internet Organizations and Committees.

## Internet Backbone

The structure of the Internet backbone has changed radically over the years. Not only has the data rate increased, but the topology has changed extensively. This topic describes the Internet's backbone topology and how global, national, regional, and local ISPs (Internet service providers) fit into the picture.

As explained under the topic "Internet," the Internet began as the ARPANET in the late 1960s. That network grew through the 1970s with funding from the U.S. government, which provided an internetwork for the U.S. Department of Defense, government agencies, universities, and research organizations.

By 1985, the network was congested enough that the NSF (National Science Foundation) started evaluating new network designs. It built a network, called NSFNET, that connected six sites with 56-Kbit/sec lines. The TCP/IP protocol tied the network segments together and provided traffic routing through gateways (now called routers). NSFNET formed a core that other regional networks could connect into.

> **NOTE:** *An outline of the NSFNET history along with interesting maps and pictures is available at http://www.nlanr.net/INFRA/NSFNET.html.*

During the years from 1987 to 1990, the backbone was upgraded to T1 circuits, and management was passed over to Merit. NSF also realized that it could not fund NSFNET forever. In addition, many private organizations wanted to get involved and had the resources to support the network. In 1990, NSF began the process of commercializing the network. It helped Merit, IBM, and MCI form ANS (Advanced Network and Services), which took control of NSFNET and eventually upgraded the backbone to run at DS-3 (45 Mbits/sec).

By 1992, NSF had defined a new architecture that would supersede NSFNET. The new network was to consist of the following features and components:

- **vBNS (Very high speed Backbone Network Service)** A network that would provide 155 Mbits/sec of bandwidth to connect supercomputer centers, research facilities, and educational institutions. The network was meant for research and educational traffic.

- **NAP (network access point)** Four regional NAPs were required to provide a connection point and traffic exchange facility for regional networks and network service providers. A NAP provides either high-speed switching or shared LAN technology that allows multiple providers to exchange traffic.

- **NSP (network service provider)** NSPs are required to connect to three of the NAPs and provide connections for regional networks that support research and education.

- **Routing Arbiter** The Routing Arbiter provides master routing tables for all the routers connected to the NAPs and other Internet exchanges, thus eliminating the need for routers to exchange routing information with every other router.

In 1994, NSF awarded the contract for the vBNS to MCI, the Routing Arbiter contract to Merit (which was in partnership with the Information Science Institute at the University of Southern California), and the NAP contracts to MFS Communications in Washington D.C., Sprint in New York; Ameritech and Bellcore (now Lucent) in Chicago, and Pacific Bell and Bellcore in San Francisco.

The vBNS is described under "vBNS (Very high speed Backbone Network Service)." The remainder of this topic outlines the current structure of the Internet based on the NSF design and contracts issued in 1994.

## NAPs and MAEs

NAPs are *Internet exchange* points. ISPs connect into these exchange points to do two things: exchange traffic with other ISPs (called *peering*) or sell transit services to other ISPs. Transit services are used by smaller regional and local ISPs who need to send traffic across a national ISP's network. Internet exchanges provide layer 2 switching services which means that no routing takes place. However, ISPs connect their routers directly to the Internet exchanges. The general agreement among NAP users is that they exchange routing information and that traffic passing through the NAP is not filtered, examined, or tampered with.

While the four original NAPs were funded by the NSF, many other Internet exchanges have been built:

- **MAEs (metropolitan area exchanges)**  MAEs provide essentially the same function as NAPs, but without the funding of the NSF. Private companies built MAEs to fill the needs of the ever-expanding Internet.

- **LAP (local access point)**  Primarily developed by CRL Network Services (http://www.crl.net), LAPs are designed to route traffic that is destined for points in the same metropolitan area.

- **CIX (commercial Internet exchange)**  An Internet exchange service formed by a consortium of service providers. (CIX was the first to develop peering arrangements for ISPs). Check http://www.cix.org for more information.

MFS Communications maintains a number of MAEs, include MAE EAST in Washington D.C., which connects the major ISPs as well as European providers. In June of 1996, MAE EAST's FDDI switch was switching 380 Mbits/sec. MFS also maintains MAE WEST in California's Silicon Valley, as well as MAE CHICAGO, MAE DALLAS, MAE HOUSTON, MAE LOS ANGELES, AND MAE NEW YORK. A typical NFS MAE consists of a switching platform that is a combination of an Ethernet switch, an FDDI concentrator, and/or an FDDI switch. All the devices are linked with FDDI and provide ISPs with a choice of connection options.

Figure I-8 illustrates how the NAPs and MAEs provide traffic exchange points for the national ISPs. There are many national ISPs, four NAPs, and many MAEs. Note the dotted lines show typical connections between Web clients and servers. Not shown are the FIXs (Federal Internet exchanges) at the University of Maryland and NASA Ames Research Center (Mountain View, California) that provide the connection points for federal networks and some international traffic.

> *NOTE:  CERFnet has an interesting map of NAPs, and the ISPs connected into those NAPs are mapped at http://www.cerf.net/cerfnet/about/interconnects/orig-interconnects.html.*

LAPs similar to those operated by CRL Network Services are designed to avoid the problems of packets needing to travel outside of a metropolitan (or regional) area to a NAP, MAE, or other switching center, and then back into the same metropolitan area

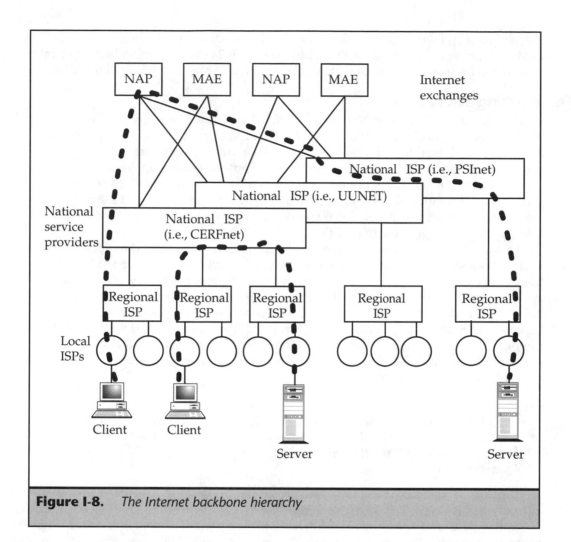

**Figure I-8.** *The Internet backbone hierarchy*

to reach their destination. CRL's LAPs allow regional customers to establish frame relay PVC (permanent virtual circuit) connections to all other LAP participants. The services are available in most major U.S. cities and help ease traffic problems on the Internet by keeping local traffic local. Reducing the number of hops reduces packet loss and corruption. The CRL LAPs are also connected into the NAPs and MAEs.

Another type of Internet exchange is offered by companies like Digital. Its *Digital IX*, located in Palo Alto, California, provides a combined switching and commercial data center. The IX provides ISPs and their customers with a mission-critical full-time operation, a full range of Internet services, and a choice of telecommunication carriers such as Pacific Bell and MFS Telecom. Service providers can put their production systems (i.e. server farms) at a major hub of the Internet and receive system management and administration services. The charges of reaching a hub over a dedicated line are eliminated, and ISPs benefit from 7x24 staffing, redundant electrical power, and high-speed links. Digital IX information is at http://www.ix.digital.com.

## The Routing Hierarchy

While NAPs and MAEs provide switching, they don't provide routing services. National ISPs connect their routers to the NAP and MAE switches. NAPs and MAEs are at the top of the routing hierarchy. Next down in this hierarchy are routers connected to regional ISPs. Still further down are routers connected to local ISPs.

Packets that are destined for networks across the country or around the planet probably go through a NAP or MAE, although in many cases, a national ISP may have a direct link to a remote destination network, thus avoiding the NAP or MAE. In other cases, packets may go through LAPs.

This hierarchy minimizes the amount of information that local and regional routers need to know about. For example, routers in local areas only need to keep track of networks that are in the local area. If one of these routers receives a packet for an unknown network, it forwards the packet to a higher-level router. That router may know what to do with the packet. If not, it will also forward the packet to the next higher-level router. This process may continue until the packet reaches the top-level routers connected to the NAPs and MAEs. As explained next, these routers theoretically know about all other networks connected to the Internet and are able to forward the packet appropriately.

**TIP:**  *You can trace the route a packet takes from your computer to a destination with the* traceroute *utility in UNIX or the* TRACERT *command in Windows. For example, type* **TRACERT www.whitehouse.gov** *to see a list of router hops to the White House.*

The Pacific Bell NAP in San Francisco is pictured in Figure I-9. This NAP is in an interim state as Pacific Bell upgrades from FDDI to ATM switching.

One of the defining features of NAP- and MAE-connected routers is that they keep track of other networks that are connected to the NAPs and MAEs so that packets can be routed anywhere on the Internet. Internet routers typically use the BGP (Border Gateway Protocol) to exchange routing information among themselves and thus learn about the networks connected to the NAPs and MAEs. Routers may also be programmed with routes by administrators.

The NSF sponsors the RA (Routing Arbiter) service, which builds a master routing table that includes all the networks on the Internet and provides a single place where ISP routers can obtain this information. Without the RA, the alternative would be for each router to query and obtain this information from all the other routers connected to a NAP or MAE. Still, not all ISPs choose to use the Routing Arbiter services. Instead, many ISPs have established agreements with one another to exchange routing information and network traffic, as discussed next.

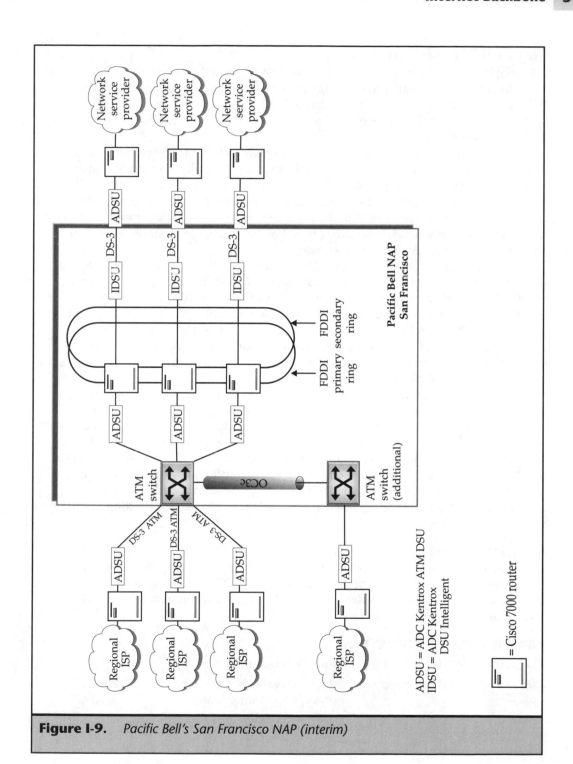

**Figure I-9.** *Pacific Bell's San Francisco NAP (interim)*

## Peering and Transit Agreements

ISPs that have routers connected to NAPs and MAEs establish what are called *peering agreements* with one another to exchange traffic. There is no requirement that the ISP establish peering agreements nor do the NAP and MAE authorities get involved in these agreements. The agreements are strictly between ISPs who want to exchange information.

Peering arrangements are normally set up between ISPs of the same size in cases where both can benefit from the other's infrastructure. Usually, no money changes hands because the data flow and infrastructure usage is equal between the two ISPs. However, smaller ISPs inevitably need to use the services of the larger ISPs, which creates an unbalanced relationship. Basically, the larger ISPs provide *transit services* by delivering packets across the national (or global) backbones to other networks, but the smaller ISPs cannot provide equal services.

In the past, many larger ISPs have allowed the smaller ISPs to use their national networks for free. But recently, this has changed. UUNET Technologies, one of the world's largest ISPs, announced in early 1997 that it would only peer with ISPs that can route traffic on a bilateral and equitable basis, and that it will no longer accept peering requests from ISPs whose infrastructures do not allow for the exchange of similar traffic levels. UUNET only plans to peer with ISPs that operate national networks with dedicated and diverse DS-3 (or faster) backbones with connections in at least four geographically diverse locations.

ISPs that connect into the NAPs and MAEs form bilateral or multilateral peering agreements with other NAP-attached networks by signing *MLPAs (multilateral peering agreements).* A typical peering agreement has the participants agree to exchange routes at the NAP. This involves the advertising of routes via BGP-4 (Border Gateway Protocol-4). Participants also agree to exchange traffic among the customers of all the MLPA-participating ISPs. ISPs are entitled to select routing paths of their choice among the MLPA-participating ISPs. In addition, ISPs can make additional peering agreements on their own, and participants usually agree to use the Routing Registry provided by the RA.

**RELATED ENTRIES**    Internet; Internet Connections; Internet Organizations and Committees; Intranets and Extranets; IP (Internet Protocol); ISPs (Internet Service Providers); NII (National Information Infrastructure); NSF (National Science Foundation) and NSFNET; Routers; Routing Protocols and Algorithms; *and* Web Technologies and Concepts

**INFORMATION ON THE INTERNET**

| | |
|---|---|
| The Routing Arbiter | http://www.ra.net |
| Pacific Bell's NAP information | http://www.pacbell.com/products/business/ fastrak/networking/nap |
| Ameritech's NAP information | http://www.aads.net/The_Chicago_NAP.html |

| | |
|---|---|
| MFS's MAE information | http://www.mfsdatanet.com/MAE/doc/mae-info.html |
| NSFNET information | http://www.nlanr.net/INFRA/NSFNET.html |
| Russ Haynal's ISP page | http://navigators.com/isp.html |
| Bill Manning's Exchange Point Information | http://www.isi.edu/div7/ra/NAPs |
| David Papp's Connectivity page (links to ISP, NAPs, MAE, etc.) | http://admin.oanet.com/connectivity.html |
| Gassman's Internet Service Provider Information Pages | http://www.spitbrook.destek.com/isp |
| MicroWeb Technology, Inc. (good links to other sites) | http://www.mtiweb.com/isp |
| Randall S. Benn's ISP Information page | http://www.clark.net/pub/rbenn/isp.html |
| G. Huston's ISP Peering paper | http://www.users.on.net/tomk/docs/settleme.htm |

## Internet Connections

Internet connections can be classified as connections for individual users or clients, and connections for servers. A typical client connection goes through an ISP (Internet service provider). You get an account, attach a modem to your computer, then dial into the ISP and log on. Once logged on, you can use a Web browser to access the Web. If you want to publish information on the Web, you need a Web server. There are two possible scenarios:

- **Web site hosting**   In this scheme, your Web pages are stored on the ISP's computer. You get a private link to a private directory on the server so you can copy and update Web pages. The ISP usually handles the paperwork to register your Web site and obtain a domain name of your choice. You can also go through the InterNIC (http://www.internic.com) on your own.

- **On-site servers**   In this scheme, the servers are set up at your site. You usually still work with an ISP (unless you become your own ISP). The ISP extends the Internet all the way to your servers. A router is needed to connect your site to the ISP.

ISPs are everywhere. They basically lease high-bandwidth lines that connect into the Internet, then sublease the bandwidth to Internet users and Web sites. See "ISPs (Internet Service Providers)" for more details.

The line into your Web site must have sufficient bandwidth to handle the traffic you expect. A dial-up connection at 28.8 Kbits/sec is only sufficient for a few visitors at a time and you need to leave the line on 24 hours a day. Higher-throughput links such as ISDN and T1 provide 128 Kbits/sec and 1.5 Mbits/sec, respectively. A T1 line can handle up to 100 users at once. See "Dedicated Circuits" for more information.

A typical configuration is pictured in Figure I-10. Starting on the left, the ISP has a big data pipe into the Internet, such as a T3 line (45 Mbits/sec). ISP customers connect into the ISP site with T1 lines or other appropriate links. The CSU/DSU (channel service unit/data service unit) connects the customer's router to the phone company's network. The router has a port for an Ethernet network. The Web servers and/or data servers are connected to the Ethernet network. A firewall/proxy server provides a security barrier between the internal network and the external network. Refer to "Firewall," "Proxy Server," and "Security" for more information about protecting internal networks.

**RELATED ENTRIES**    Circuit-Switching Services; Firewall; Internet; Internet Backbone; ISPs (Internet Service Providers); Proxy Server; Security; *and* Web Technologies and Concepts

# Internet Organizations and Committees

The Internet is a collection of autonomous and interconnected networks that implement open protocols and standards. The protocols and standards are defined by

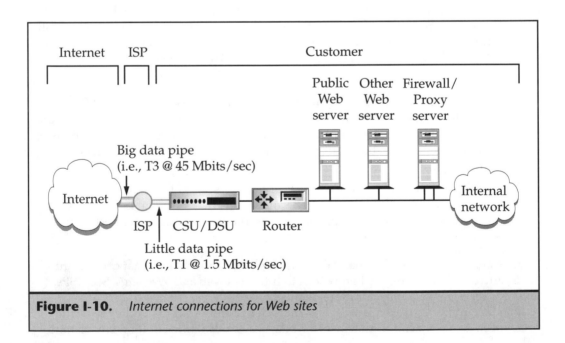

**Figure I-10.**    *Internet connections for Web sites*

organizations and committees after working their way through review and standardization processes.

No person, government, or entity owns or controls the Internet. Instead, a volunteer organization called ISOC (Internet Society) controls the future of the Internet. It appoints a technical advisory group called the IAB (Internet Architecture Board) to evaluate and set standards.

Input on standards can come from anybody—individuals, research groups, companies, and universities. An Internet draft is a preliminary document that authors use to describe their proposals and solicit comments. It may eventually become an RFC (request for comment), which is a formal document describing a new standard. Both Internet drafts and RFCs are submitted to the IESG (Internet Engineering Steering Group). RFCs are the official publications of the Internet and have been used since 1969 to describe and get comments about protocols, procedures, programs, and concepts.

In general, the best place to go for information about all the Internet organizations and committees and for a starting place for further links is the IETF Web site at http://www.ietf.org.

**ISOC (INTERNET SOCIETY)**    The ISOC is a nongovernmental international organization to promote global cooperation and coordination for the Internet and its internetworking technologies and applications. The ISOC approves appointments to the IAB from nominees submitted by the IETF nominating committee. The ISOC Web site is at http://www.isoc.org.

**IAB (INTERNET ARCHITECTURE BOARD)**    The IAB is a technical advisory group of the ISOC. Its responsibilities are to appoint new IETF chairs and IESG candidates, serve as an appeals board, manage editorial content and publication of RFCs, and provide services to the Internet Society. IAB's Web site is at http://www.iab.org/iab.

**IESG (INTERNET ENGINEERING STEERING GROUP)**    The IESG is chartered by the ISOC to provide technical management of IETF activities and the Internet standards process. The IESG Web site is at http://www.ietf.org/iesg.htm.

**IETF (INTERNET ENGINEERING TASK FORCE)**    The IETF is a large open international community of network designers, operators, vendors, and researchers concerned with the evolution of the Internet architecture and the smooth operation of the Internet. It provides technical and development services for the Internet and creates, tests, and implements Internet standards which are eventually approved and published by the ISOC. The actual technical work of the IETF is done in its working groups. The IETF Web site is at http://www.ietf.org.

**IRTF (INTERNET RESEARCH TASK FORCE)**    The purpose of the IRTF is to create research groups that focus on Internet protocols, applications, architecture, and technology. The groups are small and long term and are put together to promote the development of research collaboration and teamwork in exploring research issues. The IRTF Web site is at http://www.irtf.org.

**IAHC (INTERNATIONAL AD HOC COMMITTEE)**   The IAHC is an international multi-organization effort for specifying and implementing policies and procedures relating to DNS (Domain Name System) assignment procedures. The IAHC Web site is at http://www.iahc.org.

**IANA (INTERNET ASSIGNED NUMBERS AUTHORITY)**   The IANA acts as the clearinghouse to assign and coordinate the use of numerous Internet protocol parameters such as Internet addresses, domain names, protocol numbers, and more. The IANA Web site is at http://www.isi.edu/iana.

**INTERNIC (INTERNET NETWORK INFORMATION CENTER)**   The InterNIC is a cooperative activity of the NSF (National Science Foundation), AT&T, and Network Solutions, Inc. It provides domain name registration and IP network number assignment, a directory of directories, white page services and publicly accessible databases, and tools and resources for the Internet community. The InterNIC Web site is at http://www.internic.net.

**W3C (WORLD WIDE WEB CONSORTIUM)**   The W3C was founded in 1994 as an industry consortium to develop common protocols for the evolution of the World Wide Web. It maintains vendor neutrality and works with the global community to produce specifications and reference software that is made freely available throughout the world. The W3C Web site is at http://www.w3.org.

**FNC (FEDERAL NETWORKING COUNCIL)**   FNC membership consists of one representative from 17 U.S. federal agencies (for example, NASA, National Science Foundation, Dept. of Education, and Dept. of Commerce's NTIA) whose programs utilize interconnected Internet networks. The FNC Web site is at http://www.fnc.gov.

**INFORMATION ON THE INTERNET**

IETF (Internet Engineering Task Force)　　　　　http://www.ietf.org

# Internetworking

An internetwork is a set of subnetworks that are connected with routers. For private company networks, each subnetwork is usually a LAN. The Internet is one of the best examples of an internetwork. It consists of many interconnected subnetworks that are joined by routers to the much larger network.

An internetwork protocol such as TCP/IP or IPX is required to build an internetwork. Since TCP/IP is now the de facto standard for both internal networks (intranets) and the Internet, it is the protocol discussed here. Other network protocols such as NetBEUI only operate over a single LAN and there is no mechanism for addressing and sending packets to interconnected networks.

One of the most important features of an internetwork protocol such as IP (Internet Protocol) is an addressing scheme that identifies any subnetwork on the internetwork. An analogy can be drawn from the postal system. By placing a city and ZIP code on an envelope, you can send mail to anyone in the country. Without the city and ZIP code, you can send mail only to people in your own town. A non-internetwork protocol lacks the equivalent of the city and ZIP code addressing mechanism.

TCP/IP identifies each subnetwork on the Internet with a unique address and name. This addressing scheme is at a higher level than the addressing scheme used by each individual LAN. A workstation attached to a LAN is identified by the hardwired address on its NIC (network interface card). This same computer also has an IP address, which identifies it on the internetwork. The IP address is composed of two elements: the network address and the host address. Therefore, every subnetwork and every host on it can be identified. Refer to "IP (Internet Protocol)" for a more detailed discussion.

One of the issues with internetworks is how a packet is forwarded from one subnetwork to another. If only two subnetworks are connected with a router, it is trivial to get a packet from one subnetwork to the other. But if many subnetworks are "meshed" into a large internetwork (i.e., a campus network or the Internet), then packets must be forwarded through multiple routers. Some of the subnetworks provide a path for moving the packet from one router to another until it gets to the destination network.

Routing protocols provide the all-important mechanism of finding the most efficient path through a network. Routers exchange information about paths with one another and put this information in tables. When a packet arrives, the router then knows which router to forward the packet to so that it may reach its destination. Packets move through the network from one router to the next in a hop-by-hop fashion, with each router making a decision about where to send the packet next. Refer to "Routing Protocols and Algorithms" for more information.

**RELATED ENTRIES**   Data Communication Concepts; Datagrams and Datagram Services; IP (Internet Protocol); Network Concepts; Routers; *and* Routing Protocols and Algorithms

## InterNIC (Internet Network Information Center)

*See* Internet Organizations and Committees, or visit http://www.internic.net.

## Interoperability

Interoperability describes how different computer systems, networks, operating systems, and applications work together and share information. There are different levels of interoperability. Connecting two systems with a wire doesn't mean they will communicate. Attaching them to the same network and using the same network protocols provides network-level connections, but that still doesn't imply that users at those systems will be able to communicate. To be of benefit to users, systems must provide some level of interoperability all the way up to the application layer.

Interoperability is a networking issue. In the days of centralized mainframe systems, all the components attached to the system were specifically designed to work together. With networks, it is possible to attach different computer platforms running different operating systems and different applications. Actually, the network itself provides the first level of interoperability. For example, all the workstations attached to an Ethernet network can communicate with one another (at least at the network level).

However, early on, it was difficult for PC, UNIX, and Macintosh users to simply exchange files, even when connected to the same network. The file storage techniques, formats, and file transfer programs on these systems were different. Users often converted files to simple ASCII text and transmitted them to one another using modems, losing formatting and control codes in the process. Network servers solved the problem to some extent by providing a single place to store files. Most servers expanded to support a variety of clients, allowing them to store files in a single location for other clients to access.

The following outlines some of the steps taken toward interoperability:

- Standard file formats were developed to save formatting information and make it available to a variety of readers. See "Information Publishing."

- Application interoperability across platforms is achieved through client/server computing and Web technologies. See "Client/Server Computing," "Web Middleware and Database Connectivity," and "Web Technologies and Concepts."

- Middleware products provide a layer of functionality that allows developers to create applications that work across platforms. See "Database Connectivity," "Middleware and Messaging," and "ODBC (Open Database Connectivity), Microsoft" for more information.

- Component software and distributed object computing provide a new paradigm for developing interoperable applications using languages such as Java and ActiveX. See "Component Software Technology" and "Distributed Object Computing" for more information.

## Intranets and Extranets

An *intranet* is an internal network that implements Internet and Web technologies. An *extranet* is an intranet that has been extended outside the company to a business partner, with transmissions going over the Internet or across private lines.

# Intranets

An intranet runs the TCP/IP protocol and other Internet-related protocols, includes Web servers to publish information and provide access to back-end systems, supports Web browsers as a universal client interface, and supports Internet mail as the pervasive mail system.

Internet and Web technologies are cross-platform. Web browsers running on UNIX, Macintosh, and Windows clients can access the same internal Web servers with no modifications. The technology is well known and easy to learn and use. Interoperability is a plus because intranet products are based on the open architecture of the Internet. Other advantages include lowered user costs and quick development and deployment of systems or products.

Some examples of applications that are easily deployed on intranet platforms include

- Employee directory (phone number, personal interest, etc.) or personal Web pages for employees
- Collaborative applications such as calendaring/scheduling tools, group editing, and workflow software
- Electronic meeting tools such as chat rooms, voice and videoconferencing, and whiteboard applications
- Libraries for marketing, technical, and other types of information

Microsoft, Netscape, and other vendors have interesting products designed to take advantage of intranets. For example, two collaborative applications from Microsoft are NetMeeting and NetShow. NetMeeting allows intranet and Internet users to work together using the same applications over the network. NetShow lets users set up audio and graphic (nonvideo) conferences. See "Collaborative Computing" and "Groupware" for more information.

There are entire suites of products that provide intranet services on network-connected servers. Netscape's SuiteSpot, for example, includes a standard Web server, a mail server, a news server, a catalog server, a directory server, a certificate server, and a proxy server. Netscape also has a complete Web development environment called ONE (Open Network Environment). See "Netscape," "Netscape ONE Development Environment," and "Netscape SuiteSpot." Similar environments are discussed under "IBM Network Computing Framework," "Microsoft BackOffice," and "Novell IntranetWare."

Push technologies can distribute information to users without them specifically asking for it. This is useful for intranet environments where employees must be informed of events or have software distributed to their desktop. Marimba's Castanet is an interesting software and information distribution environment. PointCast is another. See "Marimba Castanet," "PointCast," and "Push."

*I*

Delivering real-time multimedia over intranets is becoming more common as network bandwidth increases. In addition, new compression technologies reduce the bandwidth requirements, making real-time delivery of live voice conversations and videoconferencing a reality. Refer to "Multimedia" for more details.

The emerging trend in the Internet/intranet environment is the use of component technologies. Applications are split into smaller components that can be easily distributed to users and updated as necessary. Object request brokers such as those defined with the CORBA (Common Object Request Broker Architecture) help keep objects coordinated across the network. Transaction-monitoring systems keep changes to objects and data in multiple locations safe and accurate. See "Component Software Technology," "Distributed Object Computing," and "Transaction Processing" for more information.

## Extranets

An extranet is basically an intranet linked up with some other organization's intranet. The link may cross the Internet or use private network links. In either case, two organizations have decided to share information and allow users to interact between the organizations. Trading partners often do this using traditional EDI (Electronic Data Interchange). With EDI, the format and structure of electronic documents such as invoices and purchase orders follows published standards so that document flows can occur among organizations. A supplier of parts is a trading partner with the buyer of those parts. EDI has been extended to Web technologies as well, either as traditional EDI or as completely new business-to-business technologies.

This topic is covered further under "Extranet." Also see "EDI (Electronic Data Interchange)," "Electronic Commerce," "Firewall," and "Proxy Server."

**RELATED ENTRIES**    Collaborative Computing; EDI (Electronic Data Interchange); Extranet; Groupware; Heterogeneous Network Environments; Network Design and Construction; Push; Tunnels; VPN (Virtual Private Network); *and* Web Technologies and Concepts

### INFORMATION ON THE INTERNET

| | |
|---|---|
| The Intranet Journal | http://www.intranetjournal.com |
| Innergy's Intranet Design Magazine | http://www.innergy.com/index.html |
| The Intranet Construction Site | http://www.intranet-build.com |
| Prof. Jeffrey MacKie-Mason's telecom intranet links | http://www.spp.umich.edu/telecom/intranet.html |
| Intranets Unleashed | http://www.intranetsu.com |
| Open Market, Inc. | http://www.openmarket.com |
| Open Text Corp. | http://www.opentext.com |
| Sun Microsystems, Inc. | http://www.sun.com |

# Inverse Multiplexing

An inverse multiplexor splits a data stream into two or more data streams for transmission over multiple channels, as shown in Figure I-11. At the receiving end, the data is recombined into a single stream. The links may be dial-up or permanent leased lines. The process is used to provide more bandwidth, avoid leasing a high-speed line that may go unused part of the time, or take advantage of several available low-speed lines. For example, a facility that transfers data at night might use two or more available phone lines to transfer a high-speed data stream to another facility. In this way, it is not necessary to lease a dedicated line or contract for a circuit-switched, high-speed line.

An important feature is the ability to set up the lines automatically when demand requires it, a feature referred to by various names including channel aggregation, dial on demand, bandwidth on demand, rubber bandwidth, and bonding. Windows 98 includes a modem aggregation feature to combine the throughput of multiple modem lines.

Home Internet users can now purchase inverse multiplexing modems that let them combine multiple telephone lines to improve throughput. U.S. Robotics recently introduced a router for home users that aggregates two telephone lines to provide throughput as high as 450 Kbits/sec using U.S. Robotics' (now part of 3Com) 56-Kbit/sec x2 technology and compression. Ramp Networks has a less expensive device that combines the throughput of up to three external modems to provide a data rate as high as 168 Kbits/sec. The latter solution lets users select an external modem of choice.

Ascend MP+ (Multichannel Protocol Plus) is an inverse multiplexing scheme developed and maintained by Ascend Communications. MP+ is a protocol extension to the Internet MP (Multichannel Protocol). The protocol defines how to manage a call setup, provide authentication, and determine which incoming calls are added to which existing inverse multiplexing session. MP+ is backward compatible with MP. It is meant to be used primarily with ISDN (Integrated Services Digital Network). The advantages of MP+ are described at Ascend's Web site.

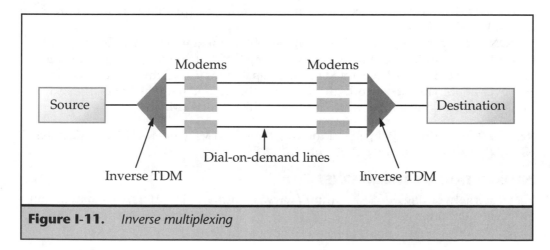

**Figure I-11.** *Inverse multiplexing*

A similar protocol called PPP Multilink is under development by the IETF. See "PPP Multilink" for more details.

**RELATED ENTRIES**    BACP (Bandwidth Allocation Control Protocol); Bandwidth on Demand; Bandwidth Reservation; Bonding; Circuit-Switching Services; DDR (Dial-on-Demand Routing); IMA (Inverse Multiplexing over ATM); ISDN (Integrated Services Digital Network); Load Balancing; Multiplexing; *and* PPP Multilink

### INFORMATION ON THE INTERNET

| | |
|---|---|
| 3Com Corp. (U.S. Robotics) | http://www.3com.com |
| Ramp Networks | http://www.rampnet.com |
| Ascend Communications, Inc. | http://www.ascend.com |

## ION (Internetworking over NBMA)

ION is an IETF working group focused on the creation of standards for running network layer protocols over NBMA (nonbroadcast multiple access) media such as ATM (Asynchronous Transfer Mode), frame relay,  and X.25. (In contrast, Ethernet is a broadcast multiple access medium.) One objective is to support all the network layer protocols (IPv4, IPv6, IPX, SNA, NetBIOS, AppleTalk, etc.)

ION is a combination of two previous working groups. It combines IPATM (IP over ATM) and ROLC (Routing over Large Clouds), both of which were working on similar technology. The new group will continue the work of the previous groups on NHRP (Next Hop Resolution Protocol), IPv4 over ATM, and IPv6 over ATM.

According to the ION charter, "the group will focus on protocols for encapsulation, multicasting, addressing, address resolution and neighbor discovery, interactions with and optimization of internetworking-layer routing protocols when run over NBMA subnetworks, and protocol-specific network management support, as appropriate. For ATM, the group will continue the transition from the LIS model in RFC 1577 (Classical IP over ATM) to the generalized NHRP model, which was previously managed by the IPATM Working Group."

ION is coordinating its activities with the ISSLL (Integrated Services over Specific Lower Layers) Working Group, which is defining QoS (quality of service) issues and the implementation of IP integrated services capabilities (RSVP, the service models, etc.) over nonbroadcast networks. ION is also coordinating with the IPNG (IP Next Generation) Working Group, which is defining IPv6 over ATM.

**RELATED ENTRIES**    IP (Internet Protocol); IP over ATM; IP over ATM, Classical; *and* NHRP (Next Hop Resolution Protocol)

### INFORMATION ON THE INTERNET

| | |
|---|---|
| ION (Internetworking over NBMA) charter | http://www.ietf.org/html.charters/ion-charter.html |

Com21 (Communication          http://www.com21.com/pages/ietf.html#B4
for the 21st Century) on IP
over ATM

## IOS (Internetwork Operating System), Cisco Systems

IOS is Cisco's internetwork operating system. Just as PCs have operating systems and LANs have network operating systems, IOS was designed as an operation system for internetworks. Cisco's goal was to create an operation system that could evolve as the network evolved. IOS supports change and migration through its ability to integrate all evolving classes of network platforms, including routers, ATM switches, LAN and WAN switches, file servers, intelligent hubs, personal computers, and other devices.

IOS spans the core network, workgroups, remote access, and IBM internetworking. It supports formal and de facto standard interfaces including major network protocols such as IP, IPX, NetBIOS, SNA, and AppleTalk. IOS provides important internetwork services, including routing services, WAN optimization services, management and security services, and scalability services.

### INFORMATION ON THE INTERNET

Cicso Systems, Inc.              http://www.cisco.com

## IP (Internet Protocol)

*NOTE:*  *This section covers the IP portion of the TCP/IP protocol suite. Refer to "TCP/IP (Transmission Control Protocol/Internet Protocol)" for a general overview.*

The IP (currently IP version 4, or IPv4), is the underlying protocol for routing packets on the Internet and other TCP/IP-based networks. This section discusses IP in general and unicast IP, which is host to host. *Multicast IP* is a one-to-many transmission scheme, and it is discussed under "IP Multicast."

IP is an internetwork protocol. It provides a communication system that works across linked networks. In an internetwork, the individual networks that are joined are called *subnetworks* or *subnets*. An internetwork is pictured in Figure I-12. A router joins two subnetworks (A and B) to create the internetwork (A/B).

Each subnetwork in this scheme can be different—i.e., one subnetwork can be Ethernet while another can be token ring. Therefore, each subnetwork has its own MAC (medium access control) methods for putting information into frames and addressing those frames for transmission to other nodes on the same network. However, these frames cannot be reliably sent to other networks because those other networks probably use different framing formats, access methods, and addressing schemes.

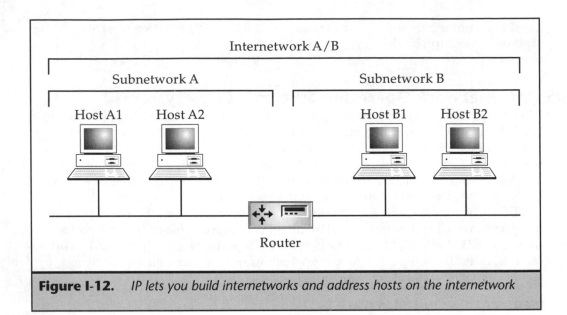

**Figure I-12.** *IP lets you build internetworks and address hosts on the internetwork*

IP provides a universal way of packaging information for delivery across network boundaries. Whereas frames are used to transmit information on subnetworks, IP datagrams are the "envelopes" for transmitting information across the internetwork. But datagrams do not replace frames. Frames are the only way to transmit across subnetworks. As datagrams cross a subnetwork, they "piggyback" a ride in the frames of that subnetwork. Upon arrival at a router, the datagrams are removed from the frames and repackaged into the frame type of the next network.

When a router extracts a datagram from a frame, it looks at the destination IP address and then makes a decision about where to route it. If the destination IP address matches a host on the next network, the datagram is put in a frame and addressed to that host. Otherwise, the datagram is put in a frame and addressed to the next router that will get the datagram to its destination. During this process, ARP (Address Resolution Protocol) is used to resolve IP addresses, if necessary.

This process is pictured in Figure I-13 and outlined here. For simplicity, the numeric IP addresses of networks, hosts, and routers are replaced with abbreviated letters (For example, the source resides on subnet A and is called A1, and router A/B connects subnets A and B.)

1. At the source (A1), a datagram is created with the IP address of the destination host (C1).

2. Software in A1 determines that the IP address is for a host on another subnetwork. Therefore, it must be sent to router A/B to reach that network. The software puts the datagram in a frame and inserts the MAC address of router A/B.

3. The frame arrives at router A/B on port A. The datagram is extracted and the IP address is inspected. The router determines that the destination can be reached through router B/C, so it puts the datagram in a frame type to match subnet B and attaches the MAC address of router B/C.

4. At router B/C, the frame arrives on port B. The datagram is extracted and the IP address is inspected. The router determines that the host is attached to subnet C, so it does a table lookup to resolve the IP address into a MAC address. The router then puts the datagram in a frame, attaches the MAC address of destination C1, and transmits the frame on the network.

5. Host C1 sees the frame on the network as being addressed to it, accepts the frame, and processes it.

Note that the path between the source and destination is not a straight-through circuit. The path is a series of individual data links first between the source and its local router, then router to router, then router to destination. These links are handled by data link protocols associated with the underlying networks.

Routers are responsible for determining the next hop that will get a packet to its destination, not the complete path to the destination. This is like getting directions—a person may point you in the right direction at an intersection. At the next intersection, another person points you in the right direction. Eventually, you get to where you wanted to go. In some cases, you might be pointed in a direction that avoids construction or congestion. On a large meshed network consisting of many possible

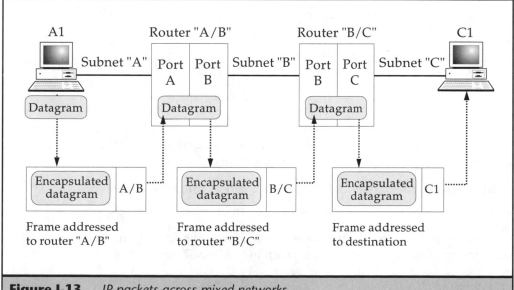

**Figure I-13.**    *IP packets across mixed networks*

paths, routers can do the same thing for packets, helping them to avoid downed or congested links.

Note that IP is a connectionless service, unlike the higher-level TCP protocol, which is connection oriented. IP does its best to deliver packets, but they may be dropped or lost. It is up to end systems to recover those packets and provide other service features such as flow control and packet sequencing by using TCP. See "TCP (Transmission Control Protocol)" for more details.

## IP Addressing and Host Names

There are three ways to identify a host computer system in a TCP/IP network environment: the physical address, the IP host address, or the domain name. The physical address is the MAC address that is hardwired into network interface cards. It is used for LAN addressing, not internetwork addressing. The IP host address identifies a specific host on an IP internetwork. The domain name provides an easily recognized name for a host on an IP internetwork. While humans use domain names, they are resolved into IP addresses by DNS (Domain Name System) for general addressing on IP internetworks.

In February of 1997, the IAHC (International Ad Hoc Committee) announced seven new gTLDs (generic top-level domains), in addition to the existing ones (.com, .net, and .org), under which Internet names may be registered. The new fields are as follows:

| | |
|---|---|
| .firm | Businesses or firms |
| .store | Businesses offering goods |
| .arts | Culture and entertainment |
| .rec | Recreational entertainment |
| .info | Information services |
| .web | Entities related to the Web |
| .nom | For individual or personal nomenclature |

An IP address is a numeric address that uniquely identifies a host system on an internetwork. The address is a 32-bit (4-byte) binary number (called the address space) that contains two important pieces of information:

- **Network identifier**   Indicates the network (a group of computers)
- **Host identifier**   Indicates a specific computer on the network.

An Internet address uses the dotted-decimal notation format similar to the following in which a period separates each byte of the 32-bit address:

192.100.10.5

When you connect to the Internet, you must obtain an IP address from the InterNIC (http://www.internic.net). The address you are assigned is just the network identifier portion. You are responsible for assigning host identifiers.

## IP Address Classes

The 32-bit IP address space is divided into two parts with the left part identifying a particular network and the right part identifying a host on a network. There are three ways to split the address—after the first byte, the second byte, or the third byte—as pictured in Figure I-14, forming class A, class B, and class C addresses. What is the significance of splitting the IP address in this way? First, it creates many millions of possible addresses out of the rather limited 32-bit address space. Basically, three addressing schemes are derived from the 32-bit scheme, but all can be used over the Internet. Second, the different classes support organizations of different sizes as will become clear. Refer to "CIDR (Classless Interdomain Routing)" for additional information. The IP address classes are described here:

- **Class A** The first bit set as 1 identifies class A. The next 7 bits define the network address, and the remaining 24 bits identify hosts. The 7-bit network address space allows 127 network addresses and the 24-bit host address space identifies 16,777,214 hosts per network.

- **Class B** The first 2 bits set as 10 identifies class B. The next 14 bits define the network address, and the remaining 16 bits identify hosts. This scheme defines 16,382 networks and 65,534 hosts per network.

- **Class C** The first 3 bits set as 110 identify class C. The next 21 bits define the network address, and the remaining 8 bits identify hosts. This scheme defines 2,097,150 networks and 254 hosts per network.

*NOTE: A class D scheme also exists for multicasting. The first 4 bits identify the class, and the remaining 28 bits refer to a group of hosts, all of which receive the same IP packet. Refer to "IP Multicast." A class E is also defined for future use.*

Unfortunately, most class A network schemes were assigned to U.S. government agencies and large companies early in the history of the Internet, so if you have a network with 16 million hosts, you're out of luck! The class B scheme provides for over 16,000 networks, but these addresses are also allocated. Only class C addresses are still available (as of this writing). Some organizations will find the 254-host limit a bit restrictive, but as discussed shortly, there are ways to get around this problem. Also note that IPv6 will alleviate some of these addressing problems, as discussed later.

When you configure a host or router with an IP address, a *subnet mask* must also be specified. The subnet mask basically serves as a sort of template to indicate which part of the address defines the network and which part defines the host. The subnet masks

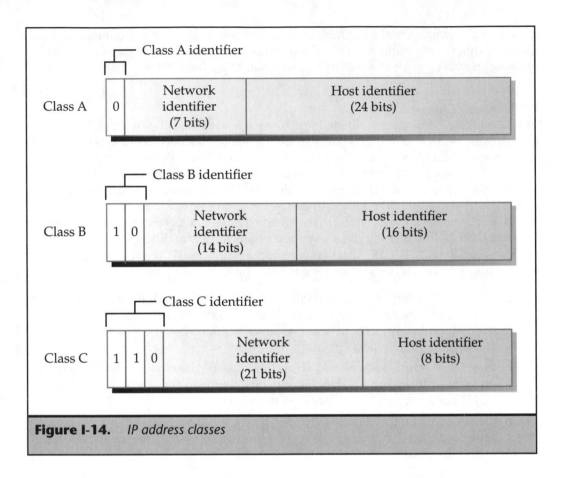

**Figure I-14.** *IP address classes*

for the different classes of networks are shown in the following table, along with the binary equivalent:

| Class | Subnet Mask (Decimal) | Subnet Mask (Binary) |
|---|---|---|
| Class A | 255.0.0.0 | 11111111 00000000 00000000 00000000 |
| Class B | 255.255.0.0 | 11111111 11111111 00000000 00000000 |
| Class C | 255.255.255.0 | 11111111 11111111 11111111 00000000 |

Binary 1s mask out the network address to reveal the host address. As an example, a class B address of 128.10.50.25 and a class B subnet mask of 255.255.0.0 are shown in the following table. If you put the subnet mask over the IP address, the 1s basically mask out the first two bytes and reveal the host address in the last two bytes. Routers are interested in the network address, so they reverse the process to extract the network portion of the IP address.

| Class B address | 128.10.50.25 | 10000000 00001010 00110010 00011001 |
| Class B subnet mask | 255.255.0.0 | 11111111 11111111 00000000 00000000 |

As mentioned previously, class C addresses restrict the number of hosts per network to 254. To get around this problem, a *subnetting* scheme was devised that basically divides the host portion of the address into two parts and uses some of the bits to identify subnetworks within your own network. However, there is a trade-off in doing this. If you use some of the bits in the host address to identify a subnet, then you reduce the number of bits that are available for host addressing. This is outlined in the following table. For example, if you split your network into two subnets, you can have 126 hosts per subnet. With 16 subnets, only 14 hosts are possible per subnet.

| Subnet Mask | Binary Value of Last Byte | Number of Subnetworks Allowed | Number of Hosts per Subnet |
| --- | --- | --- | --- |
| 255.255.255.128 | x.x.x.10000000 | 2 | 126 |
| 255.255.255.192 | x.x.x.11000000 | 4 | 62 |
| 255.255.255.224 | x.x.x.11100000 | 8 | 30 |
| 255.255.255.240 | x.x.x.11110000 | 16 | 14 |

For the technically inclined, note how the last byte in the subnet mask adds binary 1s to the mask in the second column. In the first case, decimal 128 adds binary 1 to the last byte of the mask. This single bit is the subnet address space, but only two values are possible—binary 0 and 1, so only two subnets are allowed. In the second case, decimal 192 adds two binary 1s to the last byte of the mask. With two bits, four subnets are possible—00, 01, 10, 11.

Alert readers might notice that the number of possible hosts is shy by two. This is because the first and last binary values are used for broadcasting and internal use.

## IP Datagram

The IP datagram header, pictured in Figure I-15, is the envelope in which data is transmitted. It is sometimes referred to as a packet, in general discussions. The datagram fields are described in the following list. Note that the maximum length of the datagram including header and data cannot exceed 65,535 bytes.

- **Version** The version number of the protocol.
- **IHL (Internet header length)** Length of the header.
- **Type of service** The various levels of speed and/or reliability.
- **Total length** The total length of the datagram.
- **Identification** If a datagram is fragmented, a value that identifies a fragment as belonging to a particular datagram.

*I*

- **Flags**   DF (Don't Fragment) or MF (More Fragments). An indication of whether or not this is not the last fragment.

- **Fragment offset**   Where the datagram fragment belongs in the set of fragments.

- **Time to live**   A counter that is decremented with every pass through a router. When 0, the datagram is discarded.

- **Protocol**   The transport layer process to receive the datagram.

- **Header checksum**   Error correction for the header.

- **Source address**   The IP address of the host sending the datagram.

- **Destination address**   The IP address of the host to receive the datagram.

- **Options/padding**   Optional information and filler to ensure the header is a multiple of 32 bits.

- **Data**   The user data (a variable field, not shown in the figure).

## IPv6 (Internet Protocol version 6)

IPv4 has served the Internet community well, but it has limited address space and is causing major problems as more and more hosts connect to the Internet. A solution was developed with the creation of CIDR (Classless Interdomain Routing), which

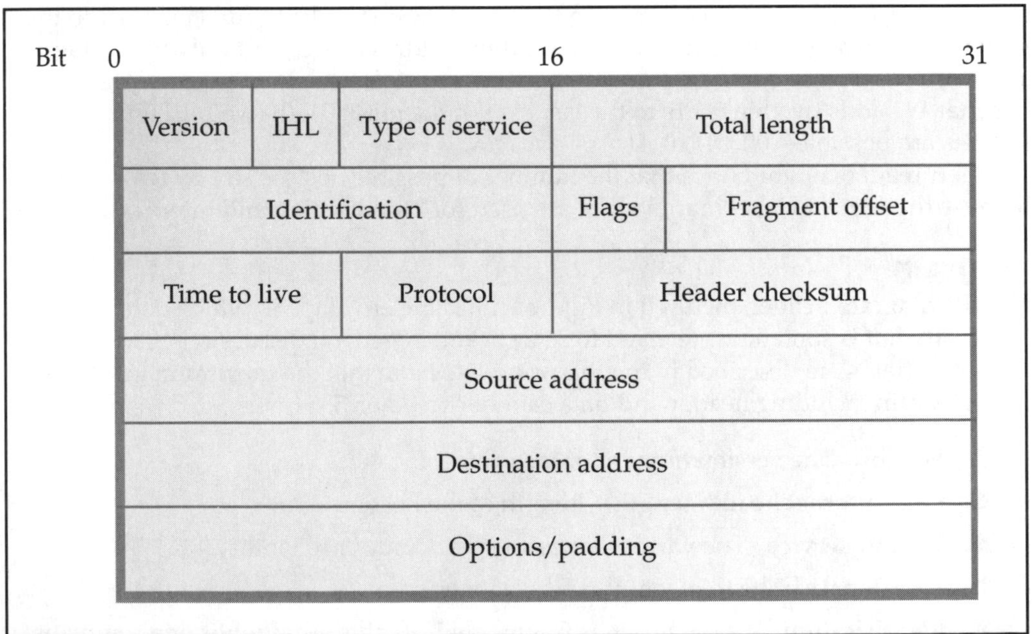

| Bit   0 | | | 16 | 31 |
|---|---|---|---|---|
| Version | IHL | Type of service | Total length | |
| Identification | | | Flags | Fragment offset |
| Time to live | | Protocol | Header checksum | |
| Source address | | | | |
| Destination address | | | | |
| Options/padding | | | | |

**Figure I-15.**   *IP datagram header*

allocated class C addresses as variable-size blocks. A block is a range of addresses (without excess addresses) appropriate for an organization's needs. This leaves addresses free for other users. Still, CIDR only buys time.

The IETF began working on an IP protocol update in 1990. What was eventually hammered out was IPv6, which supports all the other Internet protocols but is not backward-compatible with IPv4. IPv6 is outlined in RFC 1883 and RFC 1887, which are available at the IETF Web site (http://www.ietf.org).

The most important feature of IPv6 is its longer address space. It is 16 bytes long, compared to 16 bits for IPv4! That will provide enough addresses to assign an IP address to every person and every conceivable device on the planet. Imagine your home entertainment system has an IP address. From your office, you could send a command to have it record a television show. Imagine that every person has their own personal IP address, allowing anyone to communicate with you anywhere. GPS (Global Positioning System) is a satellite system that can locate any GPS transmitter on the planet. GPS devices can be assigned IP addresses so they are locatable through the Internet. Imagine you're waiting for a city bus that is equipped with such a device. You open your portable Web browser, locate the bus system's Web page, and then display a map of the bus route. The current location of the bus is shown via information provided by GPS. You can take this a step further. Imagine implanting such GPS devices in criminals on probation so you always know their whereabouts. You could even implant them in kids to track them in case of a kidnapping.

Another important feature of IPv6 is support for multimedia. Basically, source and destination can establish a path through the network that can provide guaranteed delivery of real-time audio and video.

An extension scheme is also included so that senders can add custom information into a datagram. This will allow flexible expansion of the design as new requirements appear.

There are many other changes in IPv6 when compared to IPv4. You can refer to the Web sites listed at the end of this section under, "Information on the Internet" for full details of this new protocol. Full implementation may take up to 10 years, so there may be some time before you need to consider all the aspects of this new protocol.

**RELATED ENTRIES**   CIDR (Classless Interdomain Routing); Data Communication Concepts; Datagrams and Datagram Services; Fragmentation of Frames and Packets; Framing in Data Transmissions; ICMP (Internet Control Message Protocol); Internet; Mobile IP; Packet; Protocol Concepts; Routing Protocols and Algorithms; *and* TCP/IP (Transmission Control Protocol/Internet Protocol)

## INFORMATION ON THE INTERNET

| | |
|---|---|
| IETF (Internet Engineering Task Force) | http://www.ietf.org |
| Internet-related site listings | http://www.spp.umich.edu/telecom/technical-info.html |

| Understanding IP Addressing by Chuck Semeria (3COM) | http://www.3com.com/nsc/501302s.html |
| NIST Project: IPv6 Technology | http://snad.ncsl.nist.gov//ant-proposals/proj-ipv6/proj-ipv6.html |
| IPv6 information | http://ganges.cs.tcd.ie/4ba2/ipng/index.html |
| | http://www-ks.rus.uni-stuttgart.de/atp/ipng/ipng-main.html |
| Connected: An Internet Encyclopedia (programmed instruction course, with pages on major Internet concepts, and RFCs) | http://www.freesoft.org/Connected |

# IPC (Interprocess Communication)

IPC is a set of techniques used by programs and processes running in multitasking operating systems or between networked computers. There are two types of IPCs. An LPC (local procedure call) is used in multitasking operating systems to allow concurrently running tasks to talk to one another. They can share memory spaces, synchronize tasks, and send messages to one another. An RPC (remote procedure call) is similar to the LPC but works over networks. RPCs provide the communication mechanism for a client to communicate its requests for service to a back-end server. If you think of a client/server application as a program that has been split between front-end and back-end systems, the RPC can be viewed as the component that reintegrates them over the network.

The normal interprocess communication mechanism in UNIX is the *pipe*, and the *socket* is the interprocess communication mechanism that works across networks. It became a part of UNIX when the TCP/IP protocol stack was integrated into Berkeley UNIX in the early 1980s. This was a project funded by DARPA.

**RELATED ENTRIES**    API (Application Programming Interface); Middleware and Messaging; MOM (Message-Oriented Middleware); Named Pipes; RPC (Remote Procedure Call); Sockets API; *and* WinSock

# IP Multicast

IP Multicast is an open Internet standard that allows a single host to distribute data to multiple recipients. IP Multicasting has the potential to turn the Internet into a mass-distribution channel for digital information on the same scale as broadcast television. An industry consortium called the IPMI (IP Multicast Initiative) is dedicated to this task. This topic is covered further under "MBone (Multicast Backbone)" and "Multicasting."

## I-PNNI (Integrated-Private Network-to-Network Interface)

I-PNNI is an emerging routing protocol that is based on the ATM Forum's PNNI standard that allows ATM switches to communicate with one another. I-PNNI includes additional features that support the use of IP on an ATM network that uses PNNI. To understand what I-PNNI does, it is helpful to understand the ATM Forum's MPOA (Multiprotocol over ATM) specification.

Briefly, MPOA is a multilayer switching protocol that combines layer 2 switching and layer 3 routing to gain improved performance. Edge devices obtain virtual circuit information by requesting it from a special route server. The route server performs routing calculations and responds with an appropriate virtual circuit. Packets are then switched along this circuit.

I-PNNI alters this approach as follows: Edge devices perform their own route calculations and exchange routing information with other edge devices. A route server is not required. The advantage of this approach is that all edge devices are peers that know the network topology and can exchange information about it with other peers. Also, route servers in the MPOA approach are additional devices that are prone to failure. However, I-PNNI edge devices are more expensive because they need the circuitry and software to perform routing calculations.

**RELATED ENTRIES**    ATM (Asynchronous Transfer Mode); ION (Internetworking over NBMA); IP over ATM; IP over ATM, Classical; IP Switching; MPOA (Multiprotocol over ATM); NHRP (Next Hop Resolution Protocol); *and* RSVP (Resource Reservation Protocol)

**INFORMATION ON THE INTERNET**

The ATM Forum        http://www.atmforum.com

## IP over ATM

IP over ATM in this context refers to general methods for running the IP network routing protocol over an ATM network. (Note that RFC 1577 described a specific protocol called Classical IP over ATM, which is discussed under "IP over ATM, Classical.") This section outlines the many techniques that have been devised to run IP over ATM and refer you to appropriate sections in this book where the techniques are covered.

First, what are the goals, benefits, concerns, and drawbacks of running IP over ATM? ATM has many benefits, including speed, scalability, and the ability to specify QoS (quality of service). However, it is different from IP in many ways:

- ATM is a connection-oriented scheme, while IP is connectionless. ATM sets up virtual circuits between endpoints, which has many benefits of its own. However, IP's success is attributed to its connectionless nature, which works well on heterogeneous interconnected networks.

■ IP is stateless, meaning that it is not necessary to set up individual connections. Stations can essentially send and forget. ATM will only transmit across virtual circuits. Combining IP with ATM requires merging IP routes into ATM virtual circuits.

■ At the same time, most network applications are session oriented, meaning that communication processes in two systems like to maintain a connection between one another. This connection is a good fit for ATM virtual circuits.

■ VLANs (virtual LANs) can be configured on top of ATM switching environments, but routers are needed to move traffic between VLANs. One technique is to set up a centralized *route server* where clients can obtain address resolution from a single server.

The goal of running IP over ATM is to find the best way to integrate IP and ATM while preserving the best features of connectionless IP and connection-oriented ATM. The newest strategies include a multilayer switching technique that determines if a particular transmission constitutes a long *flow* (long transmission), and then finds a layer 2 virtual circuit through which it transmits the remaining packets at high speed.

This technology is called by many names, including *layer 3 switching*, *multilayer switching*, *short-cut routing*, and *high-speed routing*. A lack of a naming convention, along with a variety of techniques from different vendors and standards bodies, has only made things more confusing. The technology was originally made popular by Ipsilon, with its IP Switching technology, so the name *IP switching* has stuck. However, IP is not the only protocol under consideration. Multilayer switching is probably a better name since it implies multiple protocols. At the time of this writing, vendors were still hammering out their IP switching strategies. Most of the activity related to switching with layer 3 intelligence is covered under "IP Switching."

## IP over ATM Developers

One of the first things that happens when exploring IP over ATM is confusion over the terminology, standards, and protocols. As mentioned, there are several techniques, some of which are built on others. It helps to separate out each of the IP over ATM strategies according to the groups that are developing them. These groups are outlined here and discussed further in the following sections:

■ **ATM Forum**  A consortium of vendors and users that recommends and develops ATM standards.

■ **IETF (Internet Engineering Task Force)**  This group has developed open Internet-compatible standards for running IP over ATM.

■ **Layer 3 Switching/Routing Advocates**  There are a number of vendor initiatives to take advantage of the intelligence in layer 3 protocols to add functionality to layer 2 switching.

## IP over ATM According to the ATM Forum

As mentioned, the ATM Forum is a vendor consortium that sets standards for ATM. It has come up with the following schemes for running IP (and other protocols) over ATM networks:

- **LANE (LAN Emulation)**  This specification was standardized by the ATM Forum in 1995 to address ways of connecting *legacy* LANs such as Ethernet and token ring to an ATM backbone network. LANE emulates a LAN across the ATM network. See "LANE (LAN Emulation)" for more details.

- **MPOA (Multiprotocol over ATM)**  The ATM Forum found that LANE did not scale well or take advantage of many of ATM's features. MPOA provides a way to route multiple network layer protocols over ATM switching networks. It allows network layer protocols to directly use virtual circuits to forward data and to access QoS (quality of service) features. MPOA uses an overlay model that maps IP addresses (and other network layer addresses such as IPX) to ATM addresses. See "MPOA (Multiprotocol over ATM)" for more details.

- **I-PNNI (Integrated-Private Network-to-Network Interface)**  I-PNNI is not really an IP over ATM specification. It is a protocol that can distribute routing information about ATM paths and address information throughout the network. I-PNNI is based on PNNI, an approved protocol that ATM switches use to communicate routing information. I-PNNI extends this capability to end systems.

## IP over ATM According to the IETF

The IETF has developed several schemes for IP over ATM. The first appeared in the early 1990s. Other schemes have emerged more recently. Note that many independent vendors have developed their own schemes due to lack of standards. Many have also submitted their schemes to the IETF for standardization. The IETF currently has a working group called ION (Internetworking over NBMA [nonbroadcast multiple access]) that is working to develop a new standard that integrates the best of these schemes with support for multiple network protocols (IP, IPX, etc.) over a variety of nonbroadcast media (ATM, frame relay, SMDS, and X.25). See "ION (Internetworking over NBMA)" for more details.

Current standards or works in progress are outlined here:

- **Classical IP over ATM**  This is defined in RFC 1577. In this scheme, the ATM network is treated like a LAN and the overlying IP network operates as it normally would over any other network such as Ethernet or token ring. See "IP over ATM, Classical" for more details.

- **NHRP (Next Hop Resolution Protocol)**  NHRP is a protocol that assists in the establishment of routes through switched networks. The ATM Forum's MPOA uses NHRP. See "NHRP (Next Hop Resolution Protocol)."

■ **RSVP (Resource Reservation Protocol)** IP hosts have traditionally had no way to request a particular QoS (quality of service). RSVP adds this support. See "RSVP (Resource Reservation Protocol)."

■ **IPv6** IP version 6 has a new addressing scheme and supports new and interesting features, such as flows of traffic. Refer to "IP (Internet Protocol)."

**RELATED ENTRIES** ATM (Asynchronous Transfer Mode); IP Switching

**INFORMATION ON THE INTERNET**

| | |
|---|---|
| The ATM Forum | http://www.atmforum.com |
| IETF (Internet Engineering Task Force) | http://www.ietf.com |
| Noritoshi Demizu's Multi Layer Routing page | http://www.csl.sony.co.jp/person/demizu/inet/mlr.html |

## IP over ATM, Classical

Classical IP over ATM, or *IP/ATM*, as it is sometimes called, is IETF specification RFC 1577, meaning that it is an official standard for implementing the IP (Internet Protocol) over ATM networks. The goals of running IP over ATM and the many ways of doing it are outlined under the preceding heading, "IP over ATM." This section covers specific aspects of IP/ATM. In contrast, the ATM Forum designed LANE (LAN Emulation) to do much the same thing.

For those interested in specifications and working groups, the original working group for IP/ATM was merged with the ROLC (Routing over Large Clouds) Working Group to form the new working group called ION (Internetworking over NBMA). Information about the new group is under the heading "ION (Internetworking over NBMA)."

One way to think of IP/ATM is as a data link layer LAN. For example, assume you replace an Ethernet adapter in a host with an ATM adapter. The Ethernet MAC protocols are replaced with ATM protocols, and the ATM adapter is assigned an IP address just as the Ethernet adapter was assigned an IP address. Outgoing IP datagrams are put into ATM cells instead of Ethernet frames. A VCI (virtual channel identifier) that identifies the "virtual wire" onto which the cells will be transmitted is placed in the header of each cell.

In this model, LANs use the ATM network as a high-speed backbone network. One issue, then, is how a router on one side of an ATM network addresses a router on the other side of an ATM network. For example, assume several LANs are connected via routers to ATM networks. A packet arrives at a router that is addressed to a host on another LAN across the ATM network. The router must know what the ATM address of the destination router is. It obtains this address by consulting an address resolution table, which is located in a special *address resolution server* as discussed in a moment. The table may indicate the PVC (permanent virtual circuit) to use on the ATM network to get to that router.

The model implements the concept of a *LIS (logical IP subnet)*, a closed logical IP subnetwork (such as a department or workgroup) consisting of a group of hosts and routers. Each LIS operates and communicates independently of other LISs on the same ATM network. Hosts communicate directly with other hosts on the same LIS but must go through a router to communicate with hosts on other LISs.

Each LIS includes a single ATMARP (ATM Address Resolution Protocol) server, which resolves IP to ATM addresses. When a host is turned on, it connects with the ATMARP server. The ATMARP server then requests the host's IP and ATM addresses, which are then stored in the ATMARP lookup table for future use. Hosts and routers contact the ATMARP server when they need to resolve IP addresses into ATM addresses.

There is some inefficiency in this configuration. If two LISs are on the same ATM network, a host on one LIS must go through a router to communicate with a host in the other LIS, even though the underlying ATM network is capable of setting up a direct VC between the hosts. This is by design and accounts for the term *classical* in the name of the model. The reason for this design is to retain the requirement that packets addressed to hosts in other subnets be sent to a default router. This is exactly how classical IP works.

As mentioned, this classical approach is inefficient and is generally not the best way to support IP over ATM. Routing becomes a bottleneck and virtual circuits that provide QoS (quality of service) between two nodes are not possible. LANE (LAN Emulation) or MPOA (Multiprotocol over ATM), discussed elsewhere in this book, provide better routing between subnets.

**RELATED ENTRIES**    ATM (Asynchronous Transfer Mode); ION (Internetworking over NBMA); IP over ATM; I-PNNI (Integrated-Private Network-to-Network Interface); IP Switching; NHRP (Next Hop Resolution Protocol); MPOA (Multiprotocol over ATM); *and* RSVP (Resource Reservation Protocol)

## INFORMATION ON THE INTERNET

| | |
|---|---|
| ION (Internetworking over NBMA) charter | http://www.ietf.org/html.charters/ion-charter.html |
| Classical IP and ARP over ATM Internet draft | ftp://ftp.ietf.org/internet-drafts/draft-ietf-ion-classic2-02.txt |
| George Marshall's paper on classical IP over ATM | http://www.data.com/Tutorials/Classical_IP_Over_ATM.html |
| Additional ATM and IP references listed by Prof. Jeffrey MacKie-Mason | http://www.spp.umich.edu/telecom/technical-info.html |
| Com21 (Communication for the 21st Century) on IP over ATM | http://www.com21.com/pages/ietf.html#B4 |

# IP over Cable Data Network

The IETF IPCDN (IP over Cable Data Network) Working Group has the goal of defining how IP (Internet Protocol) runs on top of Cable Television (CATV) data networks. The group is preparing information about how IP will utilize the CATV infrastructure, the service interface between IP and the CATV Data Network, and technical details related to the differences between symmetric and asymmetric CATV Data Networks.

IPCDN is also addressing issues such as multicast, broadcast, address mapping and resolution (for IPv4), neighbor discovery (for IPv6), network management, and the mappings of RSVP (Resource Reservation Protocol) service classes to lower-layer services.

Currently, the IEEE 802.14 Working Group is chartered to specify the physical layer and data link layer protocols for the CATV Data Network, but the group is not addressing how IPv4 and IPv6 will be mapped onto the network.

**RELATED ENTRY**   Cable (CATV) Data Networks and Modems

**INFORMATION ON THE INTERNET**

IETF IPCDN                 http://www.ietf.org/html.charters/ipcdn-charter.html
Working Group

# IP Routing

*See* Routing Protocols and Algorithms.

# IPSec (IP Security)

The IETF's IPSec Protocol Working Group is developing security protocols for creating VPNs (virtual private networks). A VPN is basically an *Internet tunnel* that provides privacy and authentication on public networks. Normally, a tunnel is used to transport a foreign protocol across a network by encapsulating it into the packets of the host network. A VPN extends this idea by also encrypting the packets for security reasons. The reason for using VPNs on the Internet is because of the Internet's inherent lack of physical security. With an Internet tunnel, all data is encrypted before crossing the Internet and decrypted at the receiving end.

The IPSec protocol provides cryptographic security services supporting a combination of authentication, integrity, access control, and confidentiality. These services are in the network layer of the protocol stack. The initial work focused on host-to-host security. This was followed with work on subnet-to-subnet and host-to-subnet topologies.

The work is based on ISAKMP (Internet Security Association and Key Management Protocol), which defines procedures and packet formats to establish, negotiate, modify, and delete security associations. A *security association* is a relationship between two or more entities (i.e., computers on different sides of the

Internet) that describes how the entities will utilize security services to communicate securely. This relationship is viewed as a *contract* between the entities because they both must agree on what their relationship will be.

ISAKMP is distinct from key exchange protocols in order to cleanly separate the details of security association management (and key management) from the details of key exchange. There may be many different key exchange protocols, each with different security properties.

The S/WAN Initiative was started in 1995 to provide an industry forum for interoperability and standardized implementation of IPSec for use in the commercial market. Information about S/WAN is available at RSA Data Security, Inc.'s S/WAN site, listed below under "Information on the Internet."

A similar initiative is L2TP (Layer 2 Tunneling Protocol), which combines Microsoft's PPTP (Point-to-Point Tunneling Protocol) and Cisco's L2F (Layer 2 Forwarding). While IPSec is specifically designed for IP, L2TP supports IP and other protocols.

**RELATED ENTRIES**    PPTP (Point-to-Point Tunneling Protocol); Routers; Security; S/WAN (Secure WAN); Tunneling; Virtual Dial-up Services; *and* VPN (Virtual Private Network)

**INFORMATION ON THE INTERNET**

| | |
|---|---|
| IETF IPSec charter | http://www.ietf.cnri.reston.va.us/html.charters/ipsec-charter.html |
| Security Architecture for IP (RFC 1825) | http://www.internic.net/rfc/rfc1825.txt |
| The IETF IP Security Working Group News | http://www.cs.arizona.edu/xkernel/www/ipsec/ipsec.html |
| RSA Data Security, Inc.'s S/WAN site | http://www.rsa.com/rsa/SWAN |
| ISAKMP (Internet Security Association and Key Management Protocol) draft | ftp://ftp.ietf.org/internet-drafts/draft-ietf-ipsec-isakmp-07.txt |

# Ipsilon IP Switching

Ipsilon pioneered IP switching, a technique that combines layer 2 switching techniques with layer 3 routing. Ipsilon refers to its own technology as IP Switching, but the term is now used generically. Basically, an IP switching device identifies a long flow of packets and switches the flow in layer 2 if possible, thus bypassing routers and improving throughput. However, Ipsilon's IP Switching discards the connection-oriented nature of ATM and integrates fast ATM hardware directly with IP, thus preserving the connectionless nature of IP.

To implement IP Switching, Ipsilon developed the *IP Switch*, which is pictured in Figure I-16. Ipsilon modifies an existing ATM switch by removing software in the control processor that performs signaling, routing, LAN Emulation, and address

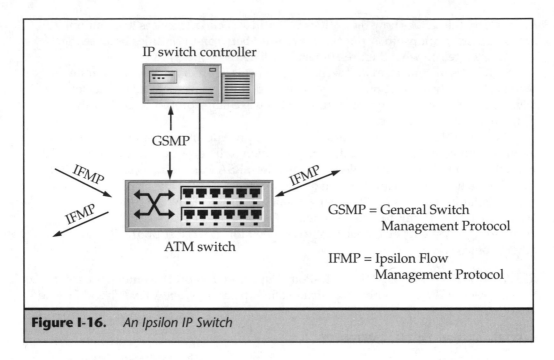

**Figure I-16.** *An Ipsilon IP Switch*

resolution. Then they load a simple, low-level control protocol called GSMP (General Switch Management Protocol). An IP switch control that communicates with the ATM switch via GSMP is attached. The switch controller is basically a high-speed IP router that can control an ATM switch.

The switch controller runs IFMP (Ipsilon Flow Management Protocol), which allows it to map IP flows with ATM virtual channels. It also includes flow classification software used to make decisions about whether a flow should be routed or switched.

Flows are identified based on field information in IP, TCP, and UDP headers. If two or more packets have identical field information, they constitute a flow. The first packet is always forwarded along the hop-by-hop layer 3 channel, but the switch controller makes a note of its contents. If another similar packet arrives, a flow may be underway and the switch controller may switch the packet at layer 2. Switch controllers then negotiate virtual circuits with upstream controllers.

In Figure I-17, a path is found through the switch controllers. The third switch controller detects a flow and requests a virtual circuit, which eliminates the second switch controller. At the next hop, a flow is again detected and another virtual circuit is set up to eliminate the third switch controller. Traffic now flows on a virtual circuit between the switch controllers on each end of the connection.

There is considerable discussion about Ipsilon's IP Switching technique. As mentioned, it bypasses traditional ATM signaling, OSI addressing, and other features and essentially gives the overlying IP layer direct control of the ATM hardware. QoS is supported by setting priorities based on the IP address or the port number used by an

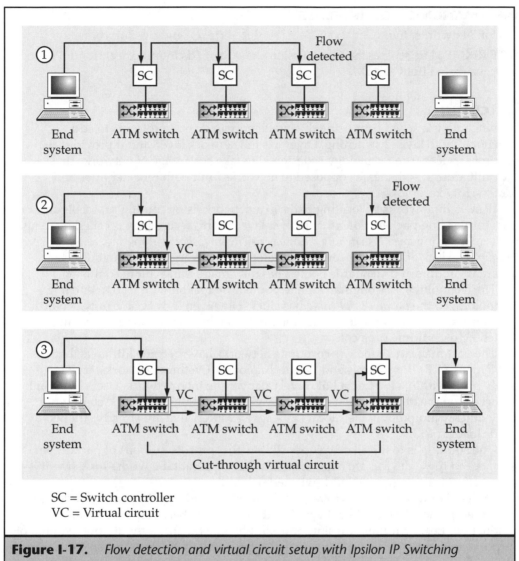

SC = Switch controller
VC = Virtual circuit

**Figure I-17.** *Flow detection and virtual circuit setup with Ipsilon IP Switching*

application. VLANs (Virtual LANs) are not supported. In addition, only IP is handled, although support for IPX will be available in the future. See "IP Switching" for a discussion of additional switching techniques.

**RELATED ENTRIES**    ATM (Asynchronous Transfer Mode); IP over ATM; IP Switching; MPOA (Multiprotocol over ATM); NHRP (Next Hop Resolution Protocol); *and* Tag Switching

**INFORMATION ON THE INTERNET**

Ipsilon Networks, Inc.                                  http://www.ipsilon.com

IETF RFC 1954 (discusses the transmission      ftp://ds.internic.net/rfc/rfc1954.txt
of flow labeled IP over ATM)

# IP Switching

IP switching is a scheme for using the intelligence in layer 3 protocols to add functionality to layer 2 switching. Layer 3 is the network layer, and it provides routing services. The technology is designed to take advantage of networks that are built around switches (as opposed to networks built with repeater hubs and routers, for example).

IP switching works by locating paths in a network using routing protocols and then forwarding packets along that path at layer 2. This technology is called by many names, including *layer 3 switching*, *multilayer switching*, *short-cut routing*, and *high-speed routing*. The lack of a naming convention, along with a variety of techniques from different vendors and standards bodies, has only made things more confusing.

The technology was originally made popular by Ipsilon with its IP Switching technology, so the name *IP switching* has stuck. However, IP is not the only protocol under consideration. Multilayer switching is probably a better name since it implies switching of multiple protocols.

The vast majority of today's corporate networks have become intranets that implement TCP/IP protocols and Web technologies. On these networks, traffic rarely stays within a local area but travels all over the internetwork. Users hyperlink to servers on the other side of a network by clicking buttons on their Web browser. They quickly jump out of their local LAN across routers that are already strained by traffic loads.

One solution is to install new super-routers that process millions of packets per second. But these devices are expensive and may represent the wrong investment if your network strategy is to build switched networks.

The goal of IP switching is to reduce the need to send a packet through a router (or routers) when a more direct Layer 2 path is available between a source and a destination. Legacy routers are slow and can't handle the throughput now required on corporate networks. IP switching techniques generally first determine a route through a network using layer 3 routing protocols. The route may be stored for later reference or used only once. Packets are then quickly sent through a layer 2 virtual circuit that bypasses the router.

One way to think about these schemes is to consider how you might find your way around in a big city. One method is to ask directions at each intersection, where someone points you to the next intersection where you again get directions. This is how traditional routing works. Packets move from one router to the next, with each router pointing the packet in the general direction of the destination. The process is relatively slow because routers must process each packet in turn.

IP switching could be compared to getting on a bus that takes you directly to your destination. The only thing is, you still need to know which bus will take you there. Initially, you must ask someone about the bus routes or look them up on a chart. This is analogous to initially finding a path to a destination. Some techniques establish virtual circuits in advance, then simply pick a circuit that will get a packet to its destination. Another technique is to discover paths on the fly.

Performance improvements are considerable. While routers typically handle 500,000 to 1 million packets per second, IP switching techniques can provide up to 10 times that amount.

Sounds great, except that over 20 vendors are implementing different IP switching techniques. At the time of this writing, many are still under development. Some vendors have joined forces. In addition, the IETF and IEEE are working out interoperability issues and coming up with standards. Several of the most important techniques are described in the next section. Most discussions of IP switching involve ATM switching backbones, but other switching environments also figure into the picture, such as Gigabit Ethernet.

## Switching Techniques

The following switching techniques provide a good sampling of what the industry has come up with to provide IP switching. Many specifications are in the early stages of development. Some may become less important than others. You can refer to appropriate sections in this book for a more detailed discussion of each technique.

In particular, refer to "MPLS (Multiprotocol Label Switching)" for more information about the IETF label-switching specifications, or visit the IETF's Web site on this topic at the address listed under "Information on the Internet" at the end of this section.

*NOTE: Noritoshi Demizu of Sony has created the Multi Layer Routing Web page to track the latest developments in this technology. The Web address is given at the end of this topic under "Information on the Internet."*

**IPSILON IP SWITCHING**    Ipsilon pioneered IP Switching, which identifies a long flow of packets and switches them in layer 2 if possible, thus bypassing routers and improving throughput. Ipsilon modifies an existing ATM switch by removing software in the control processor that performs normal ATM functions. It then attaches an IP switch controller that communicates with the ATM switch. Ipsilon's technique is appropriate for in-house LANs and campus networks. See "Ipsilon IP Switching."

**CISCO TAG SWITCHING**    Like IP Switching, Cisco's Tag Switching is both proprietary for Cisco and used generically to identify various tag switching schemes. It assigns tags (also called labels) to packets that switching nodes read and use to determine how the packet should be switched through the network. This scheme is designed for large networks and for use on the Internet. In fact, one of the reasons for tag switching is to reduce the size of the routing tables, which are becoming too large and unmanageable in routers on the Internet. See "Tag Switching."

**3COM FAST IP**    3Com's scheme focuses on traffic policy management, a prioritization and quality-of-service scheme. The FAST IP protocol's focus is on ensuring that the end system with priority data, such as real-time audio or video, get the bandwidth it needs to transmit the data. Workstations and servers tag frames as appropriate. The tag is then read by switches and if switching rather than routing can be performed, the frames are sent over a wire-speed circuit. Fast IP supports other protocols such as IPX and runs over switched environments other than ATM. Clients require special software since they set their own priorities. See "Fast IP."

**IBM ARIS (AGGREGATE ROUTE-BASED IP SWITCHING)**    ARIS, like Cisco's Tag Switching, attaches labels to packets that guide them through a switched network. IP switching is usually associated with ATM networks, but ARIS can be extended to work with other switching technologies. Edge devices are entry points into the ATM switching environment and have routing tables that are referred to when mapping layer 3 routes to layer 2 virtual circuits. Virtual circuits extend from an ISR on one edge of the network to an ISR on the other edge. Aggregation features provide a way to allow two or more computers on one side of an ATM network to send their datagrams through the same VC, thus reducing network traffic. See "ARIS (Aggregate Route-based IP Switching)."

**MPOA (MULTIPROTOCOL OVER ATM)**    MPOA is an ATM Forum specification for overlaying layer 3 network routing protocols like IP (Internet Protocol) over ATM. In this scheme, a source client first requests a route from a route server. The route server performs route calculation services and defines optimal routes through the network. An SVC (switched virtual circuit) is then established across subnet (VLAN) boundaries without any further need for routing services. An important feature is that routing functions are distributed between route servers and switches at the edge of the network. See "IP over ATM" and "MPOA (Multiprotocol over ATM)."

**RELATED ENTRIES**    ARIS (Aggregate Route-based IP Switching); ATM (Asynchronous Transfer Mode); ION (Internetworking over NBMA); I-PNNI (Integrated-Private Network-to-Network Interface); IP over ATM; IP over ATM, Classical; Ipsilon IP Switching; MPLS (Multiprotocol Label Switching); MPOA (Multiprotocol over ATM); NHRP (Next Hop Resolution Protocol); Switched Networks; Tag Switching; *and* VLAN (Virtual LAN)

**INFORMATION ON THE INTERNET**

| | |
|---|---|
| The ATM Forum | http://www.atmforum.com |
| IETF Multiprotocol Label Switching site | http://www.ietf.org/html.charters/mpls-charter.html |

| Noritoshi Demizu's Multi Layer Routing page | http://www.csl.sony.co.jp/person/demizu/inet/mlr.html |
| HTML versions of more than 50 major RFCs | http://www.freesoft.org/Connected/RFC |

## IPv6 (Internet Protocol version 6)

*See* IP (Internet Protocol).

## IPX/SPX (Internetwork Packet Exchange/Sequenced Packet Exchange)

*See* Novell NetWare Protocols.

## IRC (Internet Relay Chat)

IRC is group messaging system that allows two or more people at remote locations to hold a real-time conversation. The conversation takes place via typed messages, and the users must be connected to the same IRC server. IRC sites are known as "chat rooms." IRC is defined in RFC 1459, which describes IRC as a teleconferencing system. Clients connect to a central server where messages are delivered and picked up. Many IRC servers are interconnected over the Internet into an IRC network.

Recently, IRC has been enhanced by a number of vendors. For example, Microsoft NetMeeting is a collaborative application suite that provides multiuser applications and data sharing over intranets or the Internet. Two or more users can work together and collaborate in real time using application sharing, whiteboard, and an IRC-compatible chat feature called Microsoft Chat. NetMeeting is included in Microsoft's Internet Explorer.

Microsoft Chat has advanced features such as searching, which lets users easily locate chats of interest. A user can search chats by multiple attributes, including user alias, key word, chat channel size, or channel type. Multiple chat channels are supported, including public, invite-only, persistent, authenticated, and auditorium chat channels. Chat also supports Unicode and ANSI characters for international language support.

**RELATED ENTRIES** Mailing List Programs; NNTP (Network News Transport Protocol); *Push; and* USENET

**INFORMATION ON THE INTERNET**

| EFnet IRChelp site (everything about IRC) | http://deckard.mc.duke.edu |
| RFC 1459 | http://www.internic.net/rfc/rfc1459.txt |

*I*

IRC FAQ                           http://www.cis.ohio-state.edu/hypertext/faq/
                                  bngusenet/alt/irc/top.html

## IrDA (Infrared Data Association)

IrDA is a nonprofit organization made up of over 150 corporate members worldwide that is dedicated to creating standards for infrared communication links. It was established in 1993. According to the association's Web site, its charter is to "create an interoperable, low-cost, low-power, half-duplex, serial data interconnection standard that supports a walk-up, point-to-point user model that is adaptable to a wide range of applications and devices."

IrDA is responsible for the IrDA Serial Infrared Data Link Standard and other related protocols that you can read about under "Infrared Technologies."

### INFORMATION ON THE INTERNET

IrDA (for more information on       http://www.irda.org
infrared standards)

## Iridium System

The Iridium system is a satellite-based, wireless personal communication network designed to permit any type of telephone transmission—voice, data, fax, or paging—to reach its destination anywhere on earth. A constellation of 66 Iridium satellites will orbit above the earth at an altitude of 420 nautical miles and communicate directly with handheld Iridium subscriber equipment. The satellites function like extremely tall cellular towers.

To provide global communication coverage, each satellite has cross-links and can hand off calls to other satellites. Users can make and receive calls anywhere on the earth. Iridium gateways, located around the world, will interconnect the Iridium constellation to the public switched telephone network. The system employs a combination of FDMA/TDMA (frequency division multiple access/time division multiple access) signal multiplexing to make efficient use of limited spectrum. The L-band (1616–1626.5 MHz) serves as the link between the satellite and Iridium subscriber equipment. The Ka-band (19.4–19.6 GHz for downlinks; 29.1–29.3 GHz for uplinks) serves as the link between the satellite and the gateways and earth terminals.

### RELATED ENTRIES   Cellular Communication Systems; Mobile Computing; *and* Wireless Communications

### INFORMATION ON THE INTERNET

Iridium LLC                        http://www.iridium.com

# ISA (Integrated Services Architecture)

ISA is outlined in IETF RFC 1633. It proposes an extension to the Internet architecture and protocols to provide integrated services that would support real-time applications over the Internet. Real-time services do not work well on the Internet due to variable queuing delays and congestion losses. See http://www.internic.net/rfc/rfc1633.txt.

To resolve the problem, the RFC recommends that routers must be able to reserve resources for specific streams of packets called *flows*. A flow might consist of a video stream between a source and a destination or between one source and multiple destinations. However, having a router reserve resources may mean that some users get privilege, so policies and administrative control will be required. Authentication will be required of users that make requests of reservations and of packets that make such requests. An integrated services framework includes these components:

- A *packet scheduler* that manages the forwarding of packet streams.

- A *classifier* that maps incoming packets into some class so that packets in the same class can get the same treatment.

- An *admission control* component that decides whether a new flow gets the QoS (quality of service) requested. It also handles the authentication functions, as well as accounting and administrative reporting.

- The final component is a *reservation setup protocol* that creates and maintains flow in the hosts and in routers along the path of a flow. RSVP (Resource Reservation Protocol) is recommended.

The account feature handled by the admission control component is important. If users want to reserve bandwidth, they will need to pay for it. This implies a different payment structure for Internet access than the monthly service charges now used.

**RELATED ENTRIES**    IP over ATM; IP Switching; Prioritization of Network Traffic; QoS (Quality of Service); *and* Switched Networks

# ISDN (Integrated Services Digital Network)

ISDN is an all-digital, circuit-switched telephone system that was originally designed by the world's telephone companies and service providers as a replacement for the aging analog telephone system. It was originally proposed in 1984, with the goal of a complete switchover by the turn of the century. An all-digital system has many advantages, including reliability, scalability, and a good fit for data transmissions.

Switching to ISDN for data is a natural fit, but voice calls require a conversion to ISDN phones. Adapters are available to convert existing non-ISDN equipment. For businesses, ISDN can provide switched circuit connections that are more practical than analog modems and more cost effective than leased lines if the bandwidth requirements vary. ISDN supports bandwidth on demand, as discussed later.

There are three different ISDN implementations, as described here and pictured in Figure I-18:

■ **BRI (Basic Rate ISDN)**  The version of ISDN that is of most interest to consumers because it operates over the existing copper wire local loop to provide digital voice and data channels. BRI is sold as two channels of 64 Kbits/sec each (called the B channels) and one 16-Kbit/sec channel (called the D channel) used for signaling, such as call setup. The B channels can be used for either voice or data and combined to form a 128-Kbit/sec data channel.

■ **PRI (Primary Rate ISDN)**  Organizations with a need for ISDN at higher data rates (for network connections) get involved with PRI. It basically provides additional channels as required up to a total of 23 B channels and one 64-Kbit/sec D channel for a total bandwidth that is equivalent to T1 (1.544 Mbits/sec).

■ **B-ISDN (Broadband-ISDN)**  Starting in 1988, the CCITT began developing B-ISDN services with rates above 155 Mbits/sec in anticipation of future video and multimedia services. The B-ISDN architecture defines ATM (Asynchronous Transfer Mode) at roughly the data link layer and SONET (Synchronous Optical Network) at the physical layer. SONET is a fiber-optic network implemented primarily by the carriers on an international scale. The carriers use B-ISDN technology to connect their own systems. End users can take advantage of it through prior other high-data-rate links such as DSL. See "B-ISDN (Broadband ISDN)" for more details.

There is one outstanding difference between the BRI/PRI and B-ISDN. B-ISDN is an ATM-based cell-switching service. In contrast, BRI and PRI are circuit-switching services. However, B-ISDN can implement virtual circuits in its cell streams. A fully developed B-ISDN environment would implement ATM cell switching everywhere—in computers and networks at customer sites and in the carrier network. Many large corporations have the means to do this. Most will simply implement ATM backbone switches on their premises that connect directly into carrier ATM equipment.

The remainder of this section covers the consumer-oriented Basic Rate ISDN and Primary Rate ISDN. It is now widely available and many people are using it to build WANs or gain high-speed access to the Internet. There are competing methods that boost signals on the existing local loop, as described under "DSL (Digital Subscriber Line)," and there are new products for multiplexing analog modems, as described under "Inverse Multiplexing."

## ISDN Services and Connections

ISDN services can provide end-to-end digital connectivity for consumers. The services take advantage of existing local loop cables, but give consumers access to the ISDN

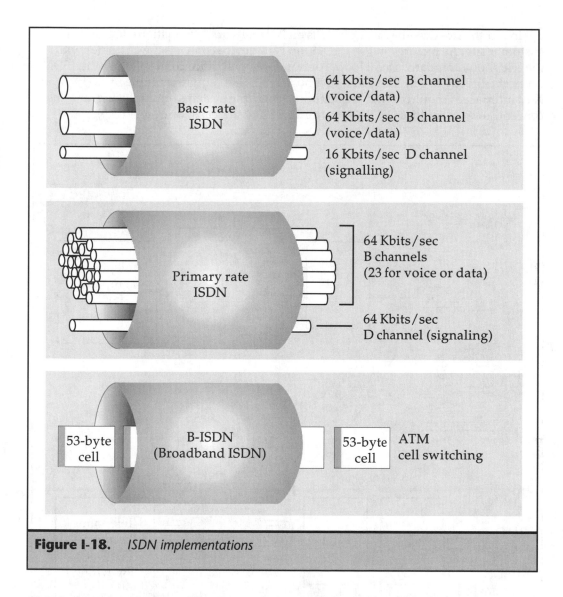

**Figure I-18.**  *ISDN implementations*

digital network created by the carriers. ISDN requires special ISDN phones that convert voice into digital data. This is the reverse of the older analog system in which modems were used to convert end-user digital data to analog data for transmission across the local loop.

The ISDN circuit supports multiple devices at the same time by implementing time division multiplexing. That means the bit stream is divided up into frames that can each carry data from a different device. The bits flow in a stream through the circuits and are extracted at the carrier end for delivery to a destination device.

In North America, the carrier installs an NT (network termination) device at the customer site. As pictured in Figure I-19, an NT1 device connects the customer with the telephone company's local loop. For home or small office connections (BRI), ISDN connects directly to the NT1. For larger businesses that require multiple lines (PRI), an NT2 interface is required. An NT2 supports switching systems, multiplexing, and the concentration of multiple ISDN lines from a PBX (voice calls) or from a LAN.

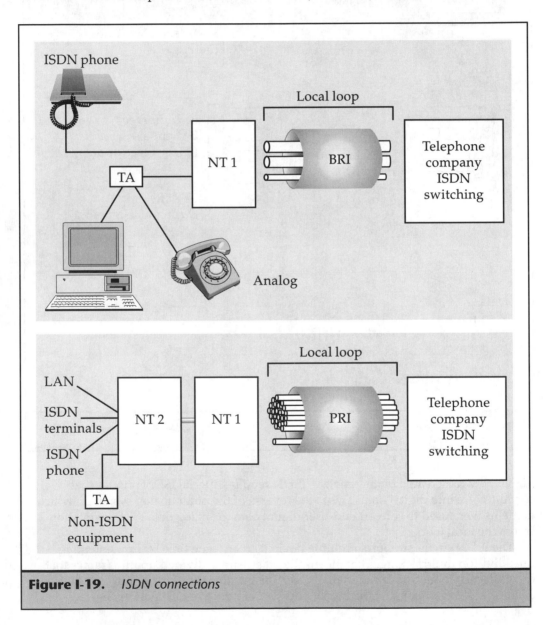

**Figure I-19.**   *ISDN connections*

The NT device provides a connection for TE (terminal equipment) and TA (terminal adapter) equipment to the local loop. TE devices are ISDN compatible, while TAs are devices that provide a connection point for non-ISDN equipment such as existing phones. A TA looks like a modem and usually has a jack for a telephone and a jack for a PC.

NT devices have a unique design that allows up to eight devices to connect with and be addressed by the NT device. Circuitry in the NT device allocates time for each device to access the line using a contention control scheme. Note that not all NT devices are the same. Some may have only two connectors, one for data equipment and one for a phone. Additional devices are then daisy-chained together.

## Bandwidth on Demand

As mentioned, ISDN supports *bandwidth on demand* to boost the transmission rates on a temporary basis. With appropriate equipment and software, ISDN equipment will connect additional lines as needed to handle surges in traffic or to handle the temporary needs of a videoconference. As discussed under "Bandwidth on Demand," additional circuits are aggregated to form a larger data pipe. This process can be automatic or programmed for specific times of the day. With switched circuits, you only pay for what you use, so circuits are taken down as soon as the demand subsides.

With BRI, both channels can be combined into a 128-Kbit/sec data link. With PRI, up to 23 channels can be combined as needed to provide a throughput rate up to 1,536 Mbits/sec (in the U.S.).

Protocols for aggregating lines are PPP Multilink (Point-to-Point Protocol Multilink) and BACP (Bandwidth Allocation Control Protocol), which are discussed under separate headings in this book. Both protocols define how to send datagrams over multiple aggregated lines. However, BACP works in conjunction with PPP Multilink to provide dynamic channel aggregation. Two peer systems negotiate with one another to change PPP Multilink bandwidth as needed.

## Signaling Channel Interface

The D channel is separated from the B channels and provides the signaling to set up calls. This signaling operates in the physical, data link, and network layers relative to the OSI protocol model. The protocols define message types that are exchanged between the customer equipment and the local exchange for setting up and maintaining services. The services provided by each protocol layer are described here:

■ The *physical layer* sets up a circuit-switched connection that provides 64-Kbit/sec transmission. Loopback testing and monitoring is also handled in this layer. This layer also supports a multidrop line for the connection of telephones, computers, and other equipment.

■ The *data link layer* uses the LAPD (Link Access Procedure for D Channel), which is related to HDLC (High-level Data Link Control). LAPD works across the D channel to provide control and signaling information. It provides frame relay and frame-switching services in which frames are routed through intermediate nodes. The data link layer relays frames by reading address information and forwarding frames appropriately along virtual paths to their destination. There may be several destinations. Devices operating at this level are digital PBXs (private branch exchanges) and computer bridging devices. This level would be used to set up a private network between two sites.

■ The *network layer* can provide packet-switching services similar to X.25. It can also provide circuit-switching and user-to-user connections. Messages generated in this layer are transported by data link layer protocols.

**RELATED ENTRIES**   BACP (Bandwidth Allocation Control Protocol); Bandwidth on Demand; B-ISDN (Broadband ISDN); Carrier Services; Circuit; Circuit-Switching Services; Communication Services; Data Link Protocols; DSL (Digital Subscriber Line); Inverse Multiplexing; Iso-Ethernet; PSTN (Public-Switched Telephone Network); Switched-56 Services; Telecommunications and Telephone Systems; *and* WAN (Wide Area Network)

**INFORMATION ON THE INTERNET**

| | |
|---|---|
| NIUF (North American ISDN Users' Forum) | http://www.niuf.nist.gov/misc/niuf.html |
| Yahoo!'s ISDN links page | http://www.yahoo.com/Computers_and_Internet/Communications_and_Networking/ISDN |
| Dan Kegel's ISDN Page with useful information and links | http://alumni.caltech.edu/~dank/isdn |
| Computer and Communication page (extensive links) | http://www.cmpcmm.com/cc/standards.html |
| Prof. Jeffrey MacKie-Mason's Telecom Information Resources page | http://www.spp.umich.edu/telecom/technical-info.html |
| Doug Lawlor's High Bandwidth ISDN page (extensive links) | http://www.specialty.com/hiband/isdn.html |

# ISO (International Organization for Standardization)

The ISO is a worldwide federation of national standards bodies with representatives from over 100 countries. It is a nongovernmental organization established in 1947 with a mission to promote the development of worldwide standards that promote the international exchange of goods and services and to develop cooperation in the spheres of intellectual, scientific, technological, and economic activity.

Of interest to readers of this book is the *OSI reference model*, which the ISO maintains. The OSI model is described under "OSI (Open Systems Interconnection) Model." It promotes open networking environments that let multivendor computer systems communicate with one another using protocols that have been accepted internationally by ISO members.

### INFORMATION ON THE INTERNET

ISO (International Organization for Standardization)          http://www.iso.ch

## ISOC (Internet Society)

*See* Internet; Internet Organizations and Committees.

## Isochronous Services

Isochronous (iso = same, chronous = time) network technologies are designed to deliver real-time voice and video over data networks. Isochronous is the opposite of asynchronous, which is non-real-time delivery of data.

The technology involves CTI (computer-telephony integration), multimedia, videoconferencing, and other technologies. Real-time delivery is critical for voice and live video to prevent detectable jitter and corruption. For example, without real-time delivery, the voice may not match the lip movements and may be unintelligible. In the past, data networks were not designed with real-time delivery in mind. The current trend is to build a single cabling system that supports data transmission, voice conversations, and videoconferencing. ATM (Asynchronous Transfer Mode) networks and iso-Ethernet are examples of networks that can do this. See these topics, for more information.

**RELATED ENTRIES**    ATM (Asynchronous Transfer Mode); CTI (Computer-Telephony Integration); Iso-Ethernet; Multimedia; QoS (Quality of Service); Telephony; Videoconferencing and Desktop Video; *and* Voice/Data Networks

## Iso-Ethernet

The iso-Ethernet standard (IEEE 802.9a) is a combination of Ethernet and ISDN (Integrated Services Digital Network) on the same cable. It basically provides the following services over one cable:

■ Standard 10-Mbit/sec Ethernet LAN connections over Category 3 or Category 5 UTP (unshielded twisted-pair) wire.

■ Up to 96 ISDN basic-rate B channels (64 Kbits/sec each) ISDN voice, video, or data service connections to internal or external users or systems. A 64-Kbit/sec ISDN channel is enough to carry a typical voice conversation. Voice channels can be combined or aggregated for higher-bandwidth requirements such as real-time video.

The ISDN channels replace the need for each workstation to have an ISDN adapter or an ISDN modem. Instead, users make ISDN connections over the iso-Ethernet LAN to a single hub, which itself is connected to the outside world. Of course, ISDN connections can also be made between workstations on the same network.

The iso-Ethernet network requires special hubs that control ISDN connections and channel aggregation. When a node needs a voice or higher-bandwidth connection (for video), it makes a request to the hub. This is not much different than making an ISDN call through the telephone company's ISDN network. The hub determines if the "call" is local or to an outside computer or phone. If the call is outside, it sets up a circuit on the wide area network to the phone company's ISDN switching system.

The only problem with iso-Ethernet is that it currently only supports 10-Mbit/sec Ethernet. So far, iso-Ethernet is considered just another "too little, too late" technology. However, the IEEE 802.9 committee is working on a 100-Mbit/sec version of the standard.

**RELATED ENTRIES**    CTI (Computer-Telephony Integration); Ethernet; ISDN (Integrated Services Digital Network); Multimedia; QoS (Quality of Service); TAPI (Telephony API); Telephony; Videoconferencing and Desktop Video; Voice/Data Networks; Voice over ATM; *and* VoIP (Voice over IP)

### INFORMATION ON THE INTERNET

| | |
|---|---|
| Dave Hawley's isoEthernet Page | http://members.aol.com/dhawley/isoenet.html |
| National Semiconductor's Web page promoting iso-Ethernet | http://www.natsemi.com/appinfo/isoethernet |
| Isochronous Network Communications Alliance | http://www.natsemi.com/appinfo/isoethernet/incalliance.html |

## ISPs (Internet Service Providers)

ISPs provide connections into the Internet for home users and businesses. There are local, regional, national, and global ISPs. In most cases, local ISPs connect into the regional ISPs, which in turn connect into national or global ISPs. However, its also possible to bypass this hierarchy and connect directly to Internet switching points. If you think of the Internet as a big data pipe with many smaller data pipes connected to

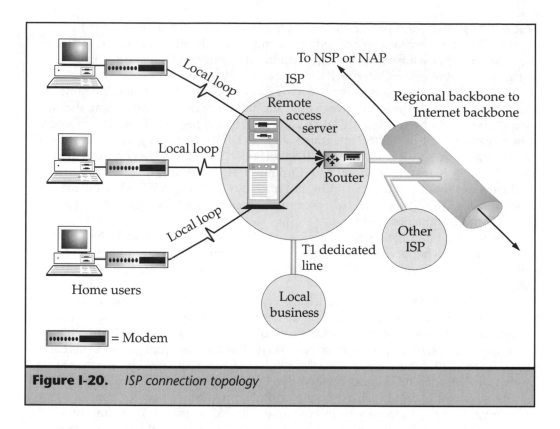

**Figure I-20.**    *ISP connection topology*

it, then you can think of local ISPs as the gatekeepers into the Internet. MCI, UUNET Technologies, PSINet, and Sprint are some of the larger ISPs that own their own national and global transmission facilities. It has been estimated that over 250 terabytes (trillion bytes) of information are transmitted over the Internet every month through these ISPs.

Common ISP connections are pictured in Figure I-20. Home users connect via modems over dial-up lines to an access server at the ISP. This data link usually runs the PPP (Point-to-Point Protocol), which encapsulates and delivers IP packets to the ISP's site. The ISP then forwards these through a router to the Internet. Business users may connect into the Internet over leased lines such as T1 lines (1.544 Mbits/sec) or T3 (45 Mbits/sec) lines, depending on the bandwidth requirements.

In all cases, traffic arriving at the ISP is shuttled directly into a pipe that connects to the Internet. This pipe may carry your ISP's traffic and the traffic of other ISPs into a NAP (network access point) traffic exchange facility such as those in San Francisco,

Chicago, New York, and Washington D.C. Other exchange sites are called MAEs (metropolitan area exchanges) and tend to be more local. In all cases, the exchange sites provide a place for ISPs to exchange traffic and routing information. This is discussed in detail under "Internet Backbone."

Home and business users only need to be concerned about their own "on ramp" to the Internet, which is the link between their site and the ISP. If the ISP is local, then an inexpensive local phone call or dedicated link is all that is needed. Typical connection options include dial-up, ISDN (Integrated Services Digital Network), T1 and fractional T1, and emerging services such as DSL (Digital Subscriber Line). These are outlined under "Circuit-Switching Services" and "Communication Services."

Businesses that want to set up Web sites may also go through ISPs. The ISP may either host the Web site on their own computers or provide all the connections for Web servers located at the business's site.

ISPs are also offering tunneling services that help companies set up VPNs (virtual private networks) between remote sites or virtual dial-up services for remote and mobile users. See "Tunnels" and "VPN (Virtual Private Network)" for more information.

Many ISPs would like to provide a higher quality of service by setting aside bandwidth for users, especially those requiring real-time voice and video service. One solution is RSVP (Resource Reservation Protocol), which can signal special handling all the way through the network from one end to the other. Internet users can signal special bandwidth requirements from their ISP if they are willing to pay for the extra bandwidth. See "RSVP (Resource Reservation Protocol)" for more information.

The cable companies are also becoming ISPs by providing a way for home users and companies to connect into the Internet over the CATV system. There are some advantages in this scheme, including always-on service and high-throughput rates. See "Cable (CATV) Data Networks and Modems."

**RELATED ENTRIES**    Circuit-Switching Services; Communication Services; Internet; Internet Backbone; Intranets and Extranets; VPN (Virtual Private Network); WAN (Wide Area Network); *and* Web Technologies and Concepts

## INFORMATION ON THE INTERNET

| | |
|---|---|
| InternetSourceBook.com guide to Internet companies | http://www.internetsourcebook.com |
| ISP Select | http://home.netscape.com/assist/isp_select |
| thedirectory (7,500 ISPs) | http://www.thedirectory.org |

| | |
|---|---|
| Telecom's Internet Service Providers Resources | http://www.spp.umich.edu/telecom/isp.html |
| David Papp's Connectivity page (links to ISP, NAPs, MAE, etc.) | http://admin.oanet.com/connectivity.html |
| Gassman's Internet Service Provider Information Pages | http://www.spitbrook.destek.com/isp |
| Adrian Bates's ISP page | http://www.vicnet.net.au/vicnet/help/isp.htm |
| MicroWeb Technology's ISP page | http://www.mtiweb.com/isp |

## ITU (International Telecommunication Union)

The ITU is an agency of the United Nations that coordinates the establishment and operation of global telecommunication networks and services. It includes governments and private sector organizations from around the world as its members. ITU activities include the coordination, development, regulation, and standardization of international telecommunications as well as the coordination of national policies. According to the ITU, its goals are "to foster and facilitate the global development of telecommunications for the universal benefit of mankind, through the rule of law, mutual consent and cooperative action."

*NOTE:* See "CCITT (Consultative Committee for International Telephony and Telegraphy)" for historical information on the ITU.

### INFORMATION ON THE INTERNET

| | |
|---|---|
| ITU (International Telecommunication Union) | http://www.itu.ch |

*I*

## IVD (Integrated Voice and Data)

IVD is the acronym for the movement to integrate voice and data over the internal network and do away with cumbersome PBX systems in many cases. IVD is possible on networks that provide QoS (quality of service) features in which the on-time delivery of voice traffic can be guaranteed. ATM networks can do this. Frame-based networks like Ethernet can also do it as long as the bandwidth is increased and protocol upgrades are made that add QoS services. See "QoS (Quality of Service)" for more details.

The goal of IVD supporters is to treat voice as any other application on the network. Doing so requires that desktop computers be upgraded with voice-processing hardware such as sound cards and telephone-like equipment (i.e., a microphone and speaker combination). New desktop PCs using Intel processors already include support for such devices and a connection port in the form of the USB (Universal Serial Bus).

There are advantages to running voice over the network infrastructure. The single cabling system can be installed and managed by the same group. In addition, PBX hardware, often proprietary and in need of updating, can be replaced. Integrating voice and data also can often justify the need to upgrade an overtaxed, data-only system.

**RELATED ENTRIES**   CTI (Computer-Telephony Integration); Ethernet; Iso-Ethernet; Multimedia; QoS (Quality of Service); TAPI (Telephony API); Telephony; Videoconferencing and Desktop Video; Voice/Data Networks; Voice over ATM; *and* VoIP (Voice over IP)

# IXC (Interexchange Carrier)

Before the breakup of AT&T in the U.S., long-distance calls were mostly handled by AT&T. After the breakup, the RBOCs (regional Bell operating companies) handled telephone services in regional areas and the IXCs handled long-distance services. AT&T became an IXC, along with new companies such as MCI and US Sprint. IXCs are also called IECs (interexchange carriers).

IXCs handle calls and other telecommunication services between LATAs (local access and transport areas). A LATA is associated with an area code, and calls between LATAs are considered long distance. A LEC (local exchange carrier) has a franchise within a LATA (intraLATA) to provide services. A LEC may be an RBOC or an ITC (independent telephone company). Appendix A lists IXCs under the heading "Telecommunications Companies."

As a result of the Telecommunications Reform Act of 1996, IXCs can offer services in local areas, and the LECs and RBOCs can offer long-distance services. Most of the IXCs are simply reselling services provided by the LECs, rather than building infrastructure. This allows the IXCs to offer end-to-end service to its customers.

**RELATED ENTRIES**   Communication Services; LATA (Local Access and Transport Area); LEC (Local Exchange Carrier); PSTN (Public-Switched Telephone Network); RBOCs (Regional Bell Operating Companies); Telecommunications and Telephone Systems; *and* WAN (Wide Area Network)

# Java

Java is a programming language and development environment created by Sun Microsystems. It took the computer industry by storm as a language for building downloadable Web components. From there, it grew into a sophisticated environment for building Internet and intranet business applications of all kinds.

Java programmers create Java applets, and Java applets run inside what is called a Java VM (Virtual Machine). Think of the VM as a software box where Java applications run. Only the VM must be designed to be compatible with any specific platform (i.e., Windows, UNIX, etc.). Once a VM is available, any Java applet will run inside the VM. This "universal" program model has developers scrambling to ensure that VMs are available for nearly every computer platform on the planet and to write Java applets that take advantage of them.

Java's architectural model is pictured in Figure J-1. At the top are Java applications that run on any platform. The blocks under this layer on the left represent how Java runs on existing PCs, Macintosh computers, and other systems that have their own operating systems. The blocks on the right show how Java is supported on so-called "thin" clients or *network computers* that are specifically designed to run Java on top of JavaOS, discussed in the next section.

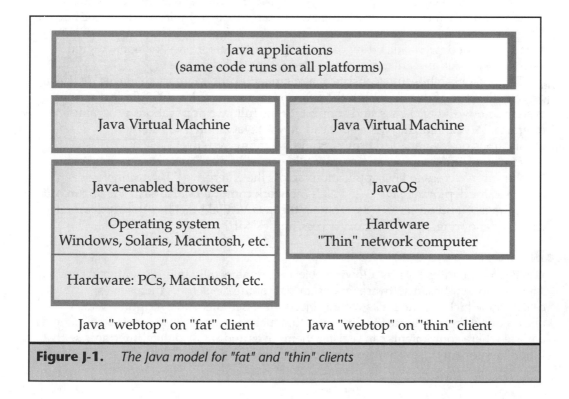

**Figure J-1.**    *The Java model for "fat" and "thin" clients*

Java is growing into a sophisticated development environment that is widely supported. Hundreds of companies are developing Java tools, libraries of code, and other enhancements to speed application development. Web browsers such as Netscape Navigator and Internet Explorer are Java-enabled and can run Java applications. Also, since Java is supported on multiple platforms, migration issues are simplified. Rapid application development and deployment are possible with Java's component model, and components can be reused to build other applications as described under "Component Software Technology."

Of course, Java has its downside. Applets are designed to run in the VM and are prevented from accessing external resources. This adds security, but also restricts functionality. Starting with Java 1.1, the VM's restrictions were relaxed to allow Java applets to access local resources, but anyone using this feature must ensure that the applets they run are safe. In addition, the Java specification has been undergoing continuous revision to handle enterprise-wide application development.

Still, Java is supported industrywide. The Java Fund is an industry consortium of vendors including IBM, Netscape, Oracle, and others that are working together on Java development. The Java Fund Web site is at http://www.kpcb.com/keiretsu/ JavaFund.html.

## JavaOS

JavaOS is a relatively small operating system that executes Java applications directly on hardware platforms. The operating system can be stored in flash ROM or be booted from the network. It is the smallest and fastest operating system for running Java on a broad range of devices, including computers, "smart" telephones, personal digital assistants, kiosks, and entertainment systems.

The JavaOS architecture consists of a microkernel and memory manager, device drivers, the Java Virtual Machine, the JavaOS Graphics and JavaOS Windowing systems, networking classes, and support for the full Java applications programming interface. Developers that write applications for JavaOS can also run those applications on Java-enabled browsers and operating systems.

HotJava Views is a user environment that according to Sun "provides intuitive 'push-button' access to Java applications across the enterprise." The technology is designed for deploying Java-based NCs (network computers). HotJava Views runs on top of JavaOS and on servers that contain the Java Virtual Machine. It includes mail client, calendaring, name directory access, and HTML browsing capabilities.

## JavaBeans

JavaBeans enhances Java by allowing objects to dynamically interact with one another. The component-based software model consists of the *components* themselves; *containers*, which are the shells where objects are assembled; and scripting, which allows developers to write the directives that make components interact. A container is a place where components can register themselves and publish their interfaces so that other components know how to interact with them.

JavaBeans is a complete component model that supports common component architecture features such as properties, events, methods, and persistence, as described here. Note that many supporters of OpenDoc have shifted their support to JavaBeans.

- **Interface publishing and discovery**   When a component is placed in a JavaBean container, these features register the object so it can be identified by other objects and publish its interfaces so other objects can use those interfaces.

- **Event handling**   Allows objects to communicate with messaging.

- **Persistence**   Provides a way to store information about an event or object for later use.

- **Layout control**   Provides controls for visual appearance and the layout of components inside a container.

- **Application builder controls**   Allows components to expose their properties and behaviors to development tools so developers can quickly build applications.

The *InfoBus* is a compact Java programming interface that allows cooperating applets or JavaBeans on a Web page or in a Java application to communicate data to one another. The InfoBus is a communication mechanism designed to run in a single client or a single server. It is not a network communication mechanism. CORBA (Common Object Request Broker Architecture) and RMI (Remote Method Invocation) are designed for network communications, as discussed later.

The InfoBus categorizes JavaBeans as "data providers" and "data consumers." Data providers access data from native stores such as DBMSs, spreadsheets, and flat files. The data is put on the InfoBus where it is retrieved by data consumers. This technique allows data consumers to operate independently of the data they use. For example, a JavaBean does not need to know SQL (Structured Query Language) to access data from a SQL database.

JavaBeans can be layered on top of existing component models, including Microsoft ActiveX and Netscape's LiveConnect (see "Netscape"). For security reasons, developers can control the behavior of components to a fine degree using rules that determine what resources a component can access. This allows untrusted applets to be combined with trusted applications.

## Java Distributed Network Environment

The usual configuration of a Java-enabled enterprise environment consists of Java-enabled clients with client data and components stored on a central file server or servers. This centralized model is easier to administer. As pictured in Figure J-1, the clients may be traditional desktop computers or NC (network computer) devices that are optimized to run the JavaOS.

This model uses standard Internet transport and network protocols (TCP/IP) and HTTP (Hypertext Transport Protocol). More sophisticated protocols can also be used so objects can communicate and interact over networks. This is usually done through ORBs (object request brokers).

**JAVA RMI (REMOTE METHOD INVOCATION)**    Java RMI provides communication across Java Virtual Machines running on a network. Java RMI is used to build distributed applications in Java for Java-only environments. Sun recommends using the CORBA IDL (Interface Definition Language) for application development in heterogeneous environments. CORBA IDL can connect a variety of non-Java components.

**JOE (JAVA OBJECTS EVERYWHERE)**    Joe is connection software that ties together Java applets running on client desktops with enterprise applications running on servers. Joe includes an ORB (object request broker) that connects Java applets to remote CORBA objects running on any machine across the Internet or intranet. The Joe ORB is automatically downloaded into Web browsers along with Java applets. Joe then establishes and manages connections between local Java objects and remote CORBA objects using the industry standard IIOP (Internet Inter-ORB Protocol). For more information, visit http://www.sun.com/solaris/neo/joe.

**ENTERPRISE JAVABEANS**    Enterprise JavaBeans is a programming interface specification for building Java component-based applications for distributed environments. Its primary feature is that it provides an object-oriented transaction environment. It enables access to existing transaction-processing systems. Enterprise JavaBeans extends JavaBeans and defines how communication among components maps into underlying protocols such as CORBA IIOP.

**JDBC (JAVA DATABASE CONNECTIVITY)**    JDBC allows Java applications to connect with back-end database systems. It provides uniform access methods to a variety of databases. JDBC is included with the Java Development Kit. A driver manager supports connection to many different databases by managing driver interfaces to those databases.

**RELATED ENTRIES**    ActiveX; Component Software Technology; CORBA (Common Object Request Broker Architecture); Distributed Object Computing; Netscape ONE Development Environment; ORB (Object Request Broker); RMI (Remote Method Invocation); Sun Microsystems Solaris NEO *and* Virtual Machine, Java

**INFORMATION ON THE INTERNET**

| | |
|---|---|
| Sun's Java site | http://www.sun.com/java |
| Sun's Java Source site | http://java.sun.com |
| Sun's Java Products site | http://www.javasoft.com/products |
| Java Resource list | http://www.sun.com/java/list.html |
| Sun's JavaBeans site | http://splash.javasoft.com/beans |
| Java Report Online (JRO) | http://www.sigs.com/jro |
| Java World Magazine | http://www.javaworld.com |

| Web Developer's Journal Java site | http://webdevelopersjournal.com/hubs/ javahub.html |
| Cup O' Joe Java Shop | http://www.cupojoe.com |
| Marty Hall's Java resources page | http://www.apl.jhu.edu/~hall/java |
| Yahoo!'s Java links page | http://www.yahoo.com/Computers_and_Internet/ Programming_Languages/Java |
| Carmen Pancerella's Java/ CORBA integration page | http://nittany.ca.sandia.gov:8001/java.corba.html |

## Jigsaw

Jigsaw is a full-blown HTTP server, written entirely in Java. It is designed to be portable (run on any machine running Java), extensible (extended by writing new resource objects), and efficient (minimizes file system accesses with caching). Information is available at the World Wide Web Consortium. The specific Web site is at http://www.w3.org/pub/WWW/Jigsaw.

## Joe, Sun Microsystems

*See* Java.

## Jukebox Optical Storage Devices

A *jukebox* is an optical disk device that can automatically load and unload optical disks and provide as much as 500 gigabytes of near-line information. The devices are often called *optical disk libraries, robotic drives,* or *autochangers.* Jukebox devices may have up to 50 slots for disks, and a picking device either traverses the slots, or the slots move to align with the picking device. The arrangement of the slots and picking devices affect performance, depending on the space between a disk and the picking device. Seek times are around 85 milliseconds and transfer rates are in the 700-Kbit/sec range.

Jukeboxes are used in high-capacity storage environments such as imaging, archiving, and HSM (hierarchical storage management). HSM is a strategy that moves little-used or unused files from fast magnetic storage to optical jukebox devices in a process called *migration.* If the files are needed, they are de-migrated back to magnetic disk. After a certain period of time or nonuse, the files on optical disk might be moved to magnetic tape archives for long-term storage.

**RELATED ENTRIES**    Backup and Data Archiving; Data Protection; Disaster Recovery; Fault Management; Fault Tolerance; Optical Libraries; *and* Storage Management Systems

**J**

## K56Flex

K56Flex is a modem technology from Rockwell Semiconductor Systems that is supported by Lucent technologies. It provides 56-Kbit/sec downstream and 40-Kbit/sec upstream data transfer rates. It competes with X2 from U.S. Robotics.

**RELATED ENTRY**   Modems

## Kerberos Authentication

Kerberos is security system developed at MIT for verifying the identities of users and devices in client/server network environments. It can encrypt network transmissions and provide password authentication services that grant clients access to servers. Kerberos is usually called a *trusted third-party authentication protocol*, meaning that it runs in a computer that is separate from any client or server. This computer is called the AS (authentication server). Normally, Kerberos is implemented as part of a complete security system because it does not provide a full set of security features on its own.

Kerberos was created by MIT's Project Athena, a test project for enterprise-wide computing that took place in the late 1980s. Kerberos is available for public use and is documented in Internet RFC 1510. The name comes from the three-headed dog that guarded the entrance to Hades.

Kerberos provides security for remote logons and can provide a single logon solution so users do not need to log on every time they access a new server. The AS stores passwords for all users in a central database. It issues credentials that clients use to access servers within the *realm* of the AS. A realm includes all the users and servers that the AS server keeps track of, as explained in a moment. The AS server is physically secured and managed by a single administrative staff. Since it authenticates users, application servers are relieved of this task. They "trust" the credentials issued by an AS for a particular client.

In any communication that requires encryption, there is always a security risk in getting the encryption key to the parties involved. The key might be compromised in transit. An important Kerberos feature is that the AS provides a way to safely distribute an encryption key to a client and a server that need to engage in secure transactions. This shared key is called a *session key*.

An AS operates within a *realm*, a security domain in which a specific security policy is set. Realms can trust other realms, meaning that if a user is authenticated by an AS in one realm, the trusting realm will not require that the user be reauthenticated to access a server in its realm. In other words, it trusts that another AS has properly identified and validated a user.

There are some important points to make before going through the step-by-step explanation of how Kerberos works:

- A client is software that acts on behalf of a user. This is only mentioned because client and server are sometimes used synonymously but are discussed separately below.

- Keep in mind that there are clients and there are servers (file servers, application servers, e-mail servers, etc.) within the realm of the AS. Before a client can access a server, it must obtain credentials from the AS.

- The credentials that a client needs in order to access a server include a *server ticket*. A server ticket has specific time parameters and only allows a specific user at a specific client computer to access a specific server. A user may hold numerous tickets at the same time to access multiple servers.

- The initial objective is to get a *TGT (ticket-granting ticket)* from the AS to the client. A TGT (not to be confused with a server ticket) is analogous to a permit or a license. With a TGT, a client has the authority to obtain server tickets from a *TGS (ticket-granting server)*. A TGS may be running on the AS computer.

- The purpose of a TGT is to eliminate the need for users to type a password every time they want to access a new server. When a TGS receives a request for a ticket that includes the TGT, it uses the information in the TGT to validate the user and does not require the user to reenter a password.

- The TGT includes the user's ID and network address, as well as the ID of the TGS. It also includes a timestamp that provides some protections from hackers. In addition, it includes the all-important session key (which is eventually distributed to the client and the target server that the user wants to access). The TGT is encrypted with a key known only to the AS and TGS. Therefore, only the TGS can decrypt the TGT after it is sent from the AS.

- The AS does not send the TGT directly to the target server. It is sent to the client where it is saved for use in all future ticket requests. When the user attempts to access a server, the TGT is sent to the TGS. The TGS decrypts the TGT and compares its contents with information provided by the user to determine authenticity, then returns a ticket to the user for the target server.

The authentication and authorization scheme is pictured in Figure K-1 and outlined here:

1. The first step is for the client to get a TGT. This step also validates the user. A simple request for a TGT is sent to the AS. The AS, which has a copy of the client's password, encrypts the TGT with a key derived from the user's password.

2. When the client receives this response, the user is prompted for a password that can decrypt the response. Only the authentic user should be able to enter a password that can decrypt the response, so the scheme effectively validates the user.

**K**

3. Once the response is decrypted, the client has a copy of the TGT. To access a server, the client sends a request to the TGS that contains the ID of the target server, the user's ID, and the TGT to prove the authenticity of the user.

4. The TGS decrypts the TGT and views its contents. If everything checks out, the TGS builds a server ticket for the target server and encrypts it with a key shared in common with the target server. The server ticket is encrypted again by the TGS with a key derived from the user's password and returned to the client.

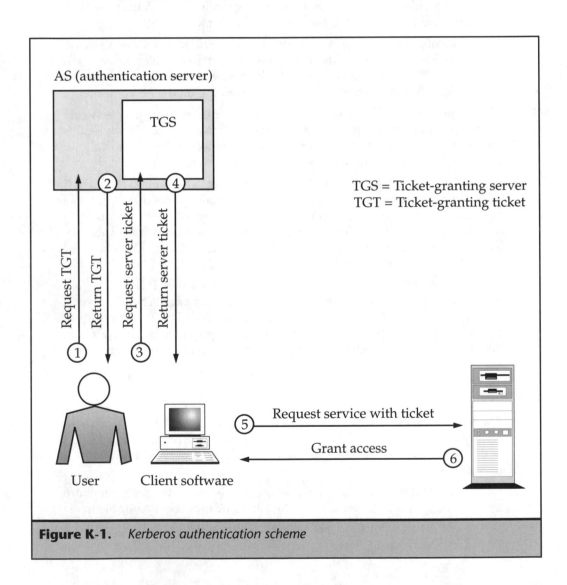

**Figure K-1.** *Kerberos authentication scheme*

5. The client decrypts the response to extract the server ticket and the session key. The ticket is then forwarded to the target server along with the user ID. Note that the ticket also contains an encrypted form of the user ID.

6. The target server decrypts the ticket and compares the user ID sent with the ticket to the user ID that was encrypted in the ticket. If they match, the user is granted access to the server.

The ticket contains the session key, which was also sent to the client. Now, both client and server have a session key they can use to encrypt and decrypt messages sent across the network, thus providing private communications.

An enhancement to the authentication process is available by requiring that users enter a token ID, which is an ID obtained from a credit-card-like device that generates tokens. Users carry the token card with them. It displays values that are synchronized with the server, and the user enters these values when logging in.

While the Kerberos scheme implements symmetric (single-key or secret-key) encryption techniques, some vendors are supporting public-key authentication schemes for the initial user authentication. Microsoft is providing this feature in its Kerberos implementation and has submitted a proposal to the IETF that recommends the technique.

**RELATED ENTRIES**   Authentication and Authorization; Certificates and Certification Systems; Digital Signatures; PKI (Public-Key Infrastructure); Public-Key Cryptography; *and* Security

**INFORMATION ON THE INTERNET**

| | |
|---|---|
| MIT's Kerberos site | http://web.mit.edu/kerberos/www |
| Kerberos FAQ (Frequently Asked Questions) | http://www.ov.com/misc/krb-faq.html |
| Kerberos links | http://www.contrib.andrew.cmu.edu/usr/ shadow/kerberos.htm |
| Kerberos document references | http://nii.isi.edu/info/kerberos |
| The Kerberos RFC | http://www.internic.net/rfc/rfc1510.txt |
| Lenny Miceli's Kerberos information and help page | http://ubvms.cc.buffalo.edu/~tkslen/ kerberos.html |

**K**

# Kernel

Kernel refers to the core components of most operating systems. It is the portion that manages memory, files, peripherals, and system resources. The kernel typically runs processes and provides interprocess communication among those processes. Some of the core functions are scheduling and synchronization of events, communication among processes (message passing), memory management, management of processes, and management of input and output routines.

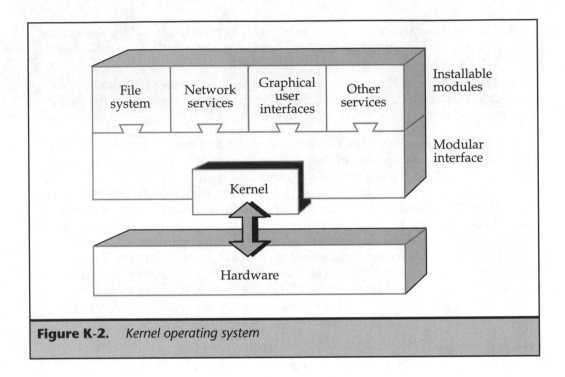

**Figure K-2.** *Kernel operating system*

A kernel-based operating system implements the layered approach shown in Figure K-2. A "generic" set of services can be installed on top of the kernel, and the kernel runs on a variety of hardware platforms. Processes interact by passing messages that run as "threads" within the microkernel. Threads provide a way to divide a single task into multiple tasks. If the system has multiple processors, threads can be distributed among the processors.

**RELATED ENTRIES**    Mach Kernel; Network Operating Systems; UNIX; *and* Windows

## Key (Security) Technologies

Key technologies are used to encrypt and and decrypt data. Refer to the related entries listed next for more information.

**RELATED ENTRIES**    Cryptography; PKI (Public-Key Infrastructure); Private-Key Cryptography; Public-Key Cryptography; *and* Security

## L2F (Layer 2 Forwarding)

*See* Virtual Dial-up Services.

## L2TP (Layer 2 Tunneling Protocol)

*See* Virtual Dial-up Services.

## Label Switching

*See* IP over ATM; IP Switching; MPLS (Multiprotocol Label Switching); *and* Tag Switching.

## LAN (Local Area Network)

A LAN is a shared communication system to which many computers are attached. A LAN, as its name implies, is limited to a local area. This has to do more with the electrical characteristics of the medium than the fact that many early LANs were designed for departments, although the latter accurately describes a LAN as well.

LANs began to appear in the early 1970s. They grew from earlier point-to-point connections where a single wire connected two systems. Often the wire was quite long. Why not let multiple computers share this same cable? This required an arbitration mechanism to ensure that only one computer transmitted at once on the cable.

Arbitration methods are called *medium access controls*. Some methods have each workstation determine whether the cable is in use. Other methods use a central controller that gives each station access in turn. See "MAC (Medium Access Control) and Medium Access Control Methods" for more information on access methods.

LANs have different topologies, the most common being the *linear bus* and the *star configuration*. In the former, a cable snakes through a building from one workstation to another. In the star configuration, each workstation is connected to a central hub with its own cable. Each has its advantages and disadvantages. Interestingly, the most popular network, Ethernet, can take advantage of both topologies. Refer to "Topology" for more details.

A LAN is a connectionless networking scheme, meaning that once a workstation is ready to transmit and has access to the shared medium, it simply puts the packets on the network and hopes that the recipient receives them. There is no connection setup phase in this scheme. See "Connection-Oriented and Connectionless Services" for more details.

Data is packaged into *frames* for transmission on the LAN. At the hardware level, each frame is transmitted as a bit stream on the wire. Even though all the computers on the network listen to the transmission, only the designated recipient actually receives the frame. A frame is usually addressed for a single computer, although a *multicast address* can be used to transmit to all workstations on the LAN. Higher-layer protocols such as IP and IPX package data into datagrams. Datagrams are in turn

*L*

divided up and put into frames for transmission on a particular LAN. See "Datagrams and Datagram Services" and "Framing in Data Transmissions" for more details.

## LAN Distance and Size Limitations

One of the reasons why LANs are considered "local" is because there are practical limitations to the distance of a shared medium and the number of workstations you can connect to it. For example, if you tried to build a single LAN for an entire organization, there might be so many workstations attempting to access the cable at the same time that no real work would get done.

The electrical characteristics of the cable also dictate LAN limitations. Network designers must find a balance among the type of cable used, the transmission rates, signal loss over distance, and the signal emanation. All of these factors must stay within physical bounds and restrictions specified by various standards and government bodies. For example, coaxial cable allows higher transmission rates over longer distances, but twisted-pair wire is inexpensive, easy to install, and supports a hierarchical wiring scheme.

Delay is another factor. On Ethernet networks, workstations on either end of a long cable may not even detect that they are transmitting at the same time, thus causing a collision that results in corrupted data. You can use the following devices to extend a LAN or improve its performance:

- **Repeaters** Extends the limitations of Ethernet cable by boosting the signal. See "Repeater" for details.

- **Bridges** Provides repeater functions along with selective filtering of traffic to reduce congestion and contention. See "Bridges and Bridging" for details.

- **Switching** Provides an overall improvement in LAN throughput and design as described under "Switched Networks."

- **Routers** Provide a way to connect multiple LANs together to create internetworks. See "Internetworking" and "IP (Internet Protocol)" for more details.

**RELATED ENTRIES** Bridges and Bridging; Broadcast Networking; Connection Technologies; Data Communication Concepts; Datagram, and Datagram Services; Data Link Protocols; Ethernet; Framing in Data Transmissions; Internetworking; LAN Emulation; MAC (Medium Access Control); Medium Access Control Methods; Network Concepts; Network Design and Construction; Network Operating Systems; Packet; Protocol Concepts; Repeater; Switched Networks; Token Ring Network; Topology; VLAN (Virtual LAN); *and* Wireless Communications

# LAN Drivers

A LAN driver is a workstation or server software module that provides an interface between a NIC (network interface card) and the upper-layer protocol software running in the computer. The driver is designed for a specific NIC. Drivers are usually

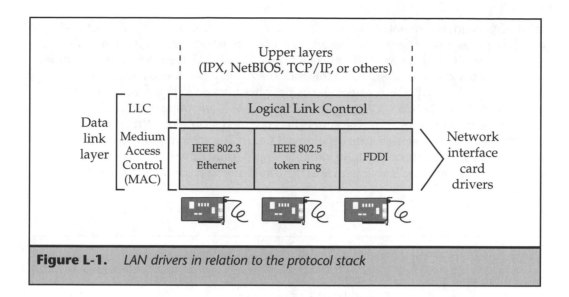

**Figure L-1.** *LAN drivers in relation to the protocol stack*

installed during the initial installation of a network-compatible client or server operating system. The setup program asks which type of NIC is installed in the system and installs the appropriate driver. If the setup program does not have a driver, you are usually asked to insert a disk from the NIC manufacturer that contains a driver. The driver is then integrated into the protocol stack (or stacks) of the computer.

Figure L-1 illustrates where in the protocol stack the IEEE LAN drivers are located. Note that they reside in the lower MAC (Medium Access Control) sublayer of the data link layer. The upper portion, called the LLC (Logical Link Control), provides a connection point for those drivers into the upper layers.

Novell and Microsoft have developed special interface support standards that let one or more interface cards work with one or more network protocols. Novell's standard is ODI (Open Data link Interface), and Microsoft's standard is NDIS (Network Driver Interface Specification). Both support multiple protocols on a single network and multiple network interface cards in a single machine.

**RELATED ENTRIES**    Data Link Protocols; LLC (Logical Link Control); MAC (Medium Access Control); NDIS (Network Driver Interface Specification); Network Concepts; *and* ODI (Open Data link Interface)

# LANE (LAN Emulation)

LANE is an ATM (Asynchronous Transfer Mode) specification that was standardized by the ATM Forum (http://www.atmforum.com) in 1995 to address ways of connecting legacy LANs such as Ethernet and token ring to an ATM backbone network. ATM provides many benefits, including a high-speed switching backbone that has the ability to deliver voice and video with a high quality of service. However, most organizations are not ready to switch their legacy LANs over to ATM networks, which requires replacing network interface cards in workstations with ATM cards.

LANE's role is to allow ATM switches to provide a backbone that can replace older and slower backbone equipment. In this role, the ATM network becomes the core network, and legacy LANs connect to it as periphery systems. This arrangement is pictured in Figure L-2. However, legacy LANs and ATM are quite different in their operating characteristics. ATM is a connection-oriented technology that sets up virtual circuits through a network before sending data. Data is transmitted in fixed-length cells. Legacy LANs transmit data in variable-length frames over a shared connectionless network. LANE provides the translation services between the two types of networks.

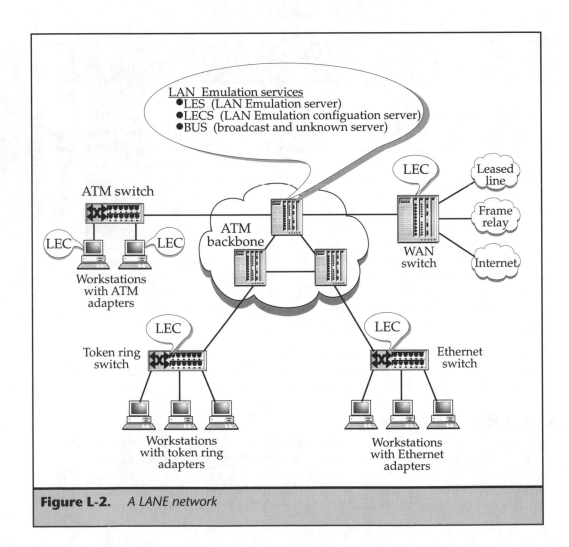

**Figure L-2.**   *A LANE network*

LANE defines a scheme for encapsulating higher-level protocol datagrams into ATM cells and delivering them across the ATM backbone as if the backbone were a LAN. The Interphase paper listed at the end of this topic under "Information on the Internet" explains this well: "the entire goal behind the LAN Emulation layer is to *lie* to the upper layer MAC interfaces and convince them that what lies below is a standard Ethernet or Token Ring network. The only discernible difference may be that the interface appears to run at speeds much higher than Ethernet or Token Ring would support." LANE provides a way to map the MAC (Medium Access Control) addresses of a workstation to an ATM address. This allows existing LAN applications to be used without alteration.

A LANE network is pictured in Figure L-2. It consists of *LECs* (*LAN Emulation clients*), devices that run LANE software to perform the translation between legacy LANs and ATM networks. LECs set up ATM connections and perform other ATM network functions that legacy systems can't handle. LECs also provide the mapping between MAC addresses and ATM virtual connections. All of this interfacing is defined by LUNI (LAN Emulation User-to-Network Interface).

There are several types of LECs. One type is the periphery switch into which legacy Ethernet or token ring workstations attach. This switch receives frames from legacy workstations and encapsulates the data in them into ATM cells. Another type of LEC is a workstation that has its own ATM network interface adapter but that runs applications that normally communicate over legacy LANs rather than ATM networks. Another type of LEC, pictured on the right in Figure L-2, is the WAN switch. It provides an interface for other types of networking technology.

A typical network consists of legacy workstations that access ATM-attached network servers. The servers are outfitted with ATM network adapters and are directly attached to the ATM network to gain performance. It is not necessary to change anything in the legacy workstations since the LANE-enabled LEC switch that they are connected to handles all the translations.

The entire network can consist of multiple *emulated LANs*, or *ELANs*. Figure L-3 illustrates how two ELANs may exist on the same network. Note that the periphery switches define two separate LECs, one for ELAN1 and one for ELAN2.

LANE consists of the legacy workstations and LECs described above, as well as LAN Emulation services. LAN Emulation services consist of the following three services, which are normally implemented within an ATM switch on the backbone network, although they might also be implemented in a special stand-alone device. Figure L-2 illustrates LAN Emulation services running in a single ATM switch.

■ **LES (LAN Emulation server)** As mentioned, the entire network can consist of multiple ELANs. Each ELAN must have a LES, which resolves legacy LAN to ATM addresses within the ELAN. It first registers all the addresses in the ELAN and then builds a table that can be used to match any MAC address with the address of the LEC that is connected to the workstation with that MAC address. Every LEC on the ELAN must maintain a connection to a LES.

*L*

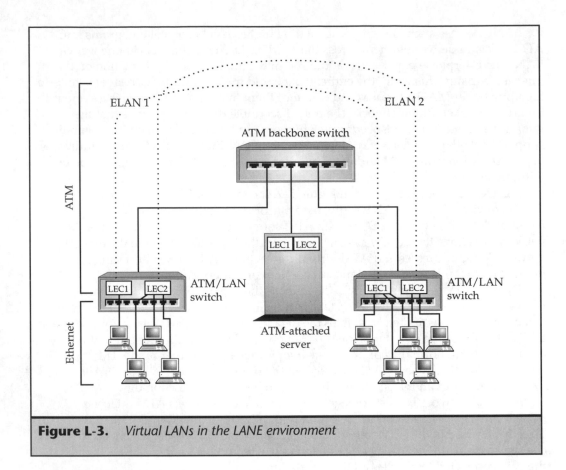

**Figure L-3.** *Virtual LANs in the LANE environment*

- **LECS (LAN Emulation configuration server)** The LECS (not to be confused with "LECs," the plural of "LEC") is required if multiple ELANs exist on the same ATM backbone network. Only one LECS is necessary, and it is responsible for assigning, managing, and tracking the membership of LECs in ELANs.

- **BUS (broadcast and unknown server)** Because ATM networks are connection-oriented in nature, the broadcast and multicast functions normally present on shared LANs must be emulated. That is the purpose of BUS. It simulates the broadcast and multicast functions by sending the messages individually to all devices in an ELAN.

To send a packet to another end system, a workstation only needs to know the MAC address of the destination station. All the other components in the LANE network handle the ATM addressing and virtual circuit connections. The local LEC requests a MAC-to-ATM address resolution from its LES, which we will assume has already built a resolution table. The LES returns the appropriate ATM connection address to the LEC, and the LEC proceeds to encapsulate the frames from the legacy workstation in cells and send them across an ATM connection to the destination.

LANE basically creates a bridged network across the ATM network. There are limitations in this design, as with any bridging solution. Routers are required to move packets from one ELAN to another, but routers are notoriously slow. The trick is to take advantage of the ATM network, which has the capability of providing a direct virtual circuit between two workstations, even if those workstations are on different ELANs. This is provided with MPOA (Multiprotocol over ATM), as discussed under a separate topic in this book.

LANE version 2.0 was under development at the time of this writing. It allows more than one LES and BUS, thus providing redundancy and minimizes the possibility of a single point of failure. The new version also improves interoperability among different vendor products.

**RELATED ENTRIES**    ATM (Asynchronous Transfer Mode); I-PNNI (Integrated-Private Network-to-Network Interface); IP over ATM; IP Switching; *and* MPOA (Multiprotocol over ATM)

**INFORMATION ON THE INTERNET**

| | |
|---|---|
| The ATM Forum | http://www.atmforum.com |
| 3Comwhite papers (search for "LANE") | http://www.3com.com |
| Interphase Corporation's LANE paper | http://www.iphase.com/Public/Products/ Technology/WP/LAN.html |

# LAN Emulation

LAN emulation is a method of emulating the characteristics of a LAN over a switched network backbone such as ATM (Asynchronous Transfer Mode). In fact, LAN emulation is synonymous with ATM-switching backbones. See "LANE (LAN Emulation)" for more information.

# LAN Management

*See* Network Management.

# LAN Manager, Microsoft

*See* Microsoft LAN Manager.

# LAN Server, IBM

*See* IBM LAN Server; OS/2 Warp Server.

L

## LANtastic

LANtastic is a peer-to-peer networking product developed and marketed by Artisoft. It was originally designed as a network that would allow small businesses to share files and resources. LANtastic version 7.0 upgrades the network operating system by improving its speed, memory management, and communication features. It now includes Internet and WAN connectivity options. LANtastic is designed to be a low-priced networking solution for small businesses. Additional features include a TCP/IP protocol stack, chat features, electronic mail, and the ability to share phone lines for remote dial-up or Internet access.

### INFORMATION ON THE INTERNET

Artisoft, Inc.        http://www.artisoft.com

## LAP (Link Access Procedure)

The LAP protocols are part of a group of data link layer protocols for framing and transmitting data across point-to-point links. LAP originates from IBM SDLC (Synchronous Data Link Control), which IBM submitted to the ISO for standardization. The ISO developed HDLC (High-level Data Link Control) from the protocol. Later, the CCITT (now referred to as the ITU) modified HDLC for use in its X.25 packet-switching network standard. It called the protocol LAP (Link Access Procedure), but later updated it and called it LAPB (LAP Balanced).

This section discusses LAPB and several derivatives of LAPB. You can also refer to "HDLC (High-level Data Link Control" and "SDLC (Synchronous Data Link Control)" for additional information.

LAPB transmissions typically take place over physical point-to-point links. It is a full-duplex protocol, meaning that each station can send and receive commands and responses over separate channels to improve throughput. The protocol is bit oriented, meaning that the data is monitored bit by bit. Bit-oriented information in the LAPB frame defines the structure for delivering data and command/response messages between communicating systems. The frame format for LAPB is similar to the frame type for HDLC. Refer to that section for more details.

As mentioned, LAPB is the data link protocol for X.25. Related LAP protocols for other data communication technologies are outlined next.

**MLP (MULTILINK PROCEDURE)**    MLP is an extension of LAPB that allows for multiple physical links, thus providing better throughput. As shown in Figure L-4(a), a device that has multiple LAPB links will implement MLP as an upper-layer management protocol to allocate frames to the links. MLP sees the multiple LAPB links as a pool of links for transmitting information from higher-layer protocols as frames. Higher-level software does not need to be aware that multiple links exist. The MLP layer handles distributing frames among the links and thus gives upper layers full access to the links.

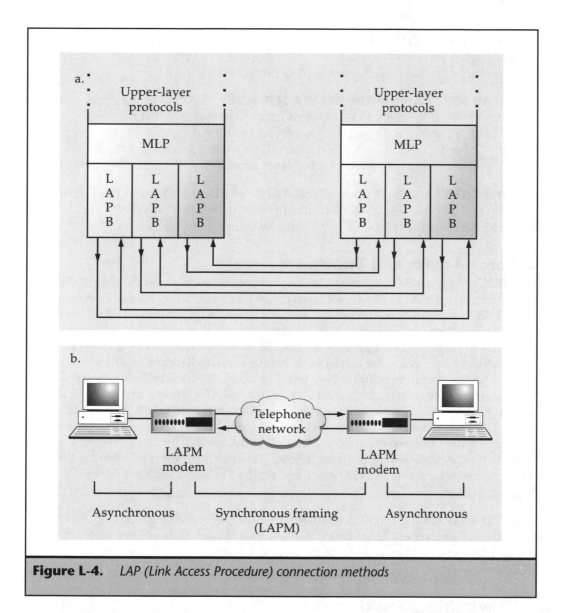

**Figure L-4.** *LAP (Link Access Procedure) connection methods*

**LAPM (LAP FOR MODEMS)** This is the data link protocol used by V.32 error-correcting modems. When two LAPM modems establish a session as pictured in Figure L-4(b), they transmit data in frames using bit-oriented synchronous techniques. An attached computer still sends data to the LAPM modems as standard asynchronous input, but the modem transmits it as synchronous frames.

*L*

**LAPD (LAP FOR D CHANNEL)**    LAPD is the protocol used on ISDN (Integrated Services Digital Network)'s D channel. Call setup and other signaling takes place on the D channel. Data transmissions take place on B channels.

**LAPF (LAP FOR FRAME-MODE BEARER SERVICES)**    LAPF is designed for use with frame relay. It is similar to LAPD in its frame format except that there is no control field in the frame. Thus, LAPF is used for carrying data only and there is no signaling at the data link layer for performing flow control and error control. End systems perform these functions in higher-layer protocols.

**RELATED ENTRIES**    Data Communication Concepts; Data Link Protocols; Frame Relay; HDLC (High-level Data Link Control); ISDN (Integrated Services Digital Network); Modems; *and* SDLC (Synchronous Data Link Control)

## LATA (Local Access and Transport Area)

The RBOCs (regional Bell operating companies) operate within specific geographical areas, which are divided into service areas called LATAs (local access and transport areas). LATAs were defined during the restructuring of AT&T in 1984, and there are close to 200 of them. *Independent telephone companies,* which are non-Bell companies, may also offer services within the LATA area. Services provided within a LATA are called *intraLATA* services. The carriers that handle services within a LATA, whether an RBOC or an independent company, are referred to as *LECs (local exchange carriers).*

Any service provided outside the LATA is an *interLATA* service, and these services are provided by *IXCs (interexchange carriers),* of which there are many, such as MCI, US Sprint, ITT, and AT&T. All LECs must provide interexchange carriers with an access point, called the *POP (point of presence),* to their LATA areas.

Note that the Telecommunications Reform Act of 1996 makes it possible for IXCs to offer services in local (intra-LATA) areas and for the LECs and RBOCs to offer long-distance services.

**RELATED ENTRIES**    Communication Services; IXC (Interexchange Carrier); LEC (Local Exchange Carrier); Local Loop; PSTN (Public-Switched Telephone Network); RBOCs (Regional Bell Operating Companies); *and* Telecommunications and Telephone Systems

## Layer 3 Switching/Routing

Layer 3 refers to the network layer (relative to the OSI protocol stack) where routing takes place. IP and IPX are layer 3 protocols. Layer 2 is the bridging/switching layer. Layer 3 switching refers to methods of combining layer 3 routing intelligence with layer 2 switching.

Routing is required to send packets on internetworks that consist of separate subnetworks. On switched networks, subnetworks are defined by creating VLANs (virtual LANs). A workstation is added to a VLAN by including its port address, MAC address, or IP address into a table that defines a particular VLAN. Then all broadcasts for that VLAN go to each workstation in the table, no matter where they are attached to the network. See "Layer 3 VLAN (Virtual LAN)" and "VLAN (Virtual LAN)" for more information on this topic.

Since multiple VLANs exist, routers are needed to move packets between VLANs. A router is used to establish paths through the network, and then packets are forwarded along the route using layer 2 switching. This allows packets that would normally be forwarded through a relatively slow routing process to be forwarded at wire speed through the switching fabric. If an ATM network constitutes the backbone switching fabric, then features such as QoS (Quality of Service) are available.

These techniques are often called *layer 3 switching*, *multilayer switching*, *shortcut routing* or *high-speed routing*. A lack of a naming convention, along with a variety of techniques from different vendors and standards bodies, has only made things more confusing. The technology was originally made popular by Ipsilon with its IP Switching technology, so the name IP switching has become a generic term. Refer to the related entries listed next for more information.

**RELATED ENTRIES**   IP over ATM; IP Switching; Layer 3 VLAN (Virtual LAN); MPOA (Multiprotocol over ATM); Switched Networks; *and* VLAN (Virtual LAN)

## Layer 3 VLAN (Virtual LAN)

Layer 3 refers to the network layer relative to the OSI protocol stack. This is the layer where routing takes place, and it resides above the data link layer (layer 2) where bridging and switching takes place. A VLAN (virtual LAN) is like a segment (subnetwork) of an internetwork, but it is defined over a switched network topology.

A switched network consists of computers attached directly to a multiport switching device. Picture the old manual telephone switching boards in which an operator connects a cable between the lines of two people that want to talk. A network switch connects two computers by temporarily bridging the ports that those computers are attached to. In an ideal switching environment, only one computer is attached to each port. When a switch connects two ports, no other computers vie for access to the line that connects the two computers. Thus, performance improves because computers do not need to take turns broadcasting on a shared cable as is the case with traditional shared LANs such as Ethernet.

One reason for segmenting networks and then joining them again with routers is that it creates smaller broadcast domains with fewer workstations contending for access. But since switched topologies also reduce contention, network administrators may be compelled to remove routers and create one large, flat, switched network.

However, removing routers has drawbacks, especially if the network is large. For example, for security reasons, an administrator may not want a computer to be able to set up a connection with some computers on the network. The administrator may also

*L*

want to retain the management and topological layout of a segmented network. That is where VLANs come into the picture.

A VLAN restores the functionality of a segmented network to an otherwise flat switched network. It allows administrators to create "pseudo-LAN segments" over the switching fabric. A unique feature of VLANs is that computers belonging to a VLAN can be anywhere on the network, not just on the same wire or switch box, in most cases. For example, a computer on port 1 of switch x can be in the same VLAN as a computer on port 6 of switch y, even though those computers may be in different departments or buildings.

Now imagine multiple VLANs that connect many groups of computers. Some computers can belong to multiple VLANs. Messages that are broadcast within a VLAN are transmitted to the computers in those VLANs and no others.

There is only one problem. Routers are still needed to transmit packets among different VLANs. So what has been solved by creating VLANs? We still need routers, which cause performance problems when a lot of traffic must travel between VLANs, as is usually the case with intranets or networks in which all the servers are at a central location.

This is where techniques such as *layer 3 switching*, also called *shortcut routing,* come into play. With layer 3 switching, a routing algorithm is used to discover paths through the switched network, but once the destination is located, a shortcut layer 2 switched path is used. This is possible because the different VLANs overlay the actual switching fabric. Even though packets would normally need to go through a router to get from one VLAN to another, the underlying network does have a direct connection. Shortcut routing just takes advantage of this direct connection after first establishing the path of the route.

Building a switched network with VLANs and shortcut routing is explored under "Network Design and Construction," with some emphasis on the issue of ATM versus Gigabit Ethernet networking.

**RELATED ENTRIES**    Broadcast Networking; IP over ATM; IP Switching; LAN (Local Area Network); LAN Emulation; Medium Access Control Methods; Network Concepts; Network Design and Construction; Routing Protocols and Algorithms; Switched Networks; *and* VLAN (Virtual LAN)

## Layered Architecture

Network communication systems adhere to layered architectures that provide a way for vendors to design software and hardware that are interoperable with other vendors' products. Without open, standardized protocols, you would need to obtain all your networking equipment from one vendor. The OSI protocol stack is the most commonly referenced layered architecture.

*Layering* is a design approach that specifies different functions and services at different levels in a "protocol stack." The lowest layer defines physical hardware specifications, while the highest layers define user-level application interfaces. Middle layers define network communication methods. Generally, each layer has a specific set of *services* that it provides to upper layers. Ideally, hardware and software developers only need to be concerned with the protocols in a specific layer related to the product they are developing, with a focus on making sure that upper-layer software can interface with it.

**RELATED ENTRIES**    Data Communication Concepts; OSI (Open Systems Interconnection) Model; *and* Protocol Concepts

# LDAP (Lightweight Directory Access Protocol)

LDAP is an IETF (Internet Engineering Task Force) directory services specification that has become widely accepted in the Internet community. A directory service provides "white page" services for an organization that helps people locate other people or services. Directory services can also be used over the Internet. A directory service is a database that can be searched and manipulated in a number of ways to display information about a network and its resources. One of the most obvious uses of a directory service is to create and manage user accounts.

LDAP can be used as a directory service on its own or it can be used to provide "lightweight" access to X.500-compatible directory services. X.500 is an ITU (International Telecommunication Union) specification for an international directory service that runs on OSI-compatible systems. LDAP is actually a subset of X.500 that operates on TCP/IP networks.

LDAP was originally designed to work as a front-end client for X.500 directory services. A protocol called DAP (Directory Access Protocol) provides the interface for accessing these services. However, DAP requires the full OSI protocol stack and more computing resources than are available in many common desktop systems. LDAP is a stripped-down version of DAP that does not consume the system resources required by DAP. The advantage of LDAP is that it runs over TCP/IP networks and still provides access to existing X.500 directories.

There are two free LDAP server implementations listed at the end of this section under "Information on the Internet." One is available from the University of Michigan and the other is available from Critical Angle. These servers are stripped down and do not require the overhead typically required by a full X.500 service.

## LDAP Directory Structure and Operation

An LDAP directory follows the X.500 inverted hierarchical tree format as shown in Figure L-5. The directory consists of *entries* that are either *containers* or *leaf objects*. A container is situated at the branches in the tree and holds other containers and leaf objects. Leaf objects represent real entities like people, computers, printers, and storage volumes, each with a CN (common name). A DN (distinguished name) is a name that defines all the containers that form a path from the top of the tree to an object. In Figure L-5, Joe's DN is

**L**

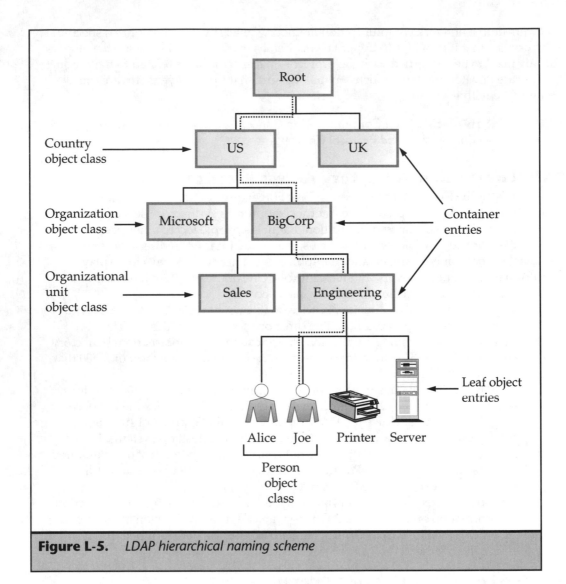

Country
object class

US   UK

Organization
object class

Microsoft   BigCorp

Container
entries

Organizational
unit
object class

Sales   Engineering

Leaf object
entries

Alice   Joe   Printer   Server

Person
object
class

**Figure L-5.**   *LDAP hierarchical naming scheme*

cn=Joe,ou=Eng,o=BigCorp,c=US

Every entry in the database (the logical directory tree) has an object class. In Figure L-5, US and UK are of object class Country, while Microsoft and BigCorp are of the object class Organization. Joe is of the object class Person.

Each object class has a specific set of *attributes* (also called properties). Attributes are basically fields in the database that can hold some value. An Organization entry will have attributes that describe a company while a Person entry will have attributes that define people. The most common attributes are Common Name, Address, Mail, Department, Phone, Fax, and so on.

Think of an object class as a predefined template. When a new entry is created, it obtains the attributes defined for the object class to which it belongs. If the attributes of the object class change, all the entries in the database that are part of that object class inherit the change. This simplifies updates and changes.

LDAP is based on a client/server model in which clients make queries to one or more LDAP directory servers. Servers respond to queries with an appropriate answer or with a pointer to another LDAP server that can handle the query. Client queries take the form of operations for adding, deleting, and modifying directory entries, or querying the directory database for information based on specific criteria.

Queries can be limited to specific branches of the tree. For example, in Figure L-5, you could execute a search for an object under the BigCorp entry in the database.

LDAP has security and authentication features to protect information in the database from unauthorized queries and edits. LDAP version 2 allows passwords to be sent as clear text or encrypted using Kerberos.

LDAP 3.0 allows interdirectory server-to-server updates between X.500 and non-X.500 directories. It can refer clients to other directory servers if necessary. It also supports replication, and has a more extensive security model that supports new Internet security standards.

At the time of this writing, the feature set for LDAP 3.0 was still being hammered out in IETF committees. Some people want to add more features, but others feel that fewer features will help move the protocol to standardization much faster. For more information, refer to the Web sites listed in the "Information on the Internet" heading in this section.

**RELATED ENTRIES**    Banyan VINES; Directory Services; LIPS (Lightweight Internet Person Schema); NDS (Novell Directory Services); Windows NT Directory Services; *and* X.500 Directory Services

## INFORMATION ON THE INTERNET

| | |
|---|---|
| LDAP (IETF RFC 1777) | http://www.internic.net/rfc/rfc1777.txt |
| University of Michigan LDAP pages | http://www.umich.edu/~dirsvcs/ldap/ldap.html |
| Critical Angle's LDAP World | http://www.critical-angle.com/ldapworld |
| Lightweight Directory Access Protocol (Version 3) | http://www.critical-angle.com/ldapworld/ldapv3.html |
| Critical Angle's LDAP FAQ | http://www.critical-angle.com/ldapworld/ldapfaq.html |
| Critical Angle Standalone LDAP v2/v3 Server | http://www.critical-angle.com/sw/slapd |

*L*

| LDAP & X.500: Road Map & FAQ | http://www-leland.stanford.edu/group/networking/directory/x500ldapfaq.html |

## Leaf Objects

Leaf objects are end nodes in a tree-structured hierarchical schema (see Figure L-5, shown previously). For example, some people talk about computers being leaf objects in a hierarchical network. A more common usage is to refer to objects at the end of hierarchical directory structures as leaf objects (i.e., files in a directory tree or objects in a directory services tree such as Novell Directory Services).

**RELATED ENTRIES**    Directory Services; LDAP (Lightweight Directory Access Protocol); *and* NDS (Novell Directory Services)

## Learning Bridges

A bridge is a device that joins networks to create a much larger network. Both networks retain the same network addressing scheme, and broadcasts on one network will propagate across the bridge if the address of a frame matches the address of a workstation on the other side of the bridge. A learning bridge, also called an *adaptive bridge*, "learns" which network addresses are on one side of the bridge and which are on the other so it knows whether or not to forward packets it receives.

**RELATED ENTRY**    Bridges and Bridging

## Leased Line

A leased line is a communication circuit that is set up on a permanent basis for an organization by a public service provider such as a LEC (local exchange carrier), a long-distance IXC (interexchange carrier), or both. Some alternate carriers, such as MCI, provide LEC bypass facilities in various metropolitan areas. Because an organization pays a fixed rate for the lines under contract, the lines are often called *leased lines*.

Note that a leased line in most cases simulates a physical circuit. In reality, the carrier guarantees an agreed-upon bandwidth through its switching system and trunk lines. For all practical purposes, we refer to a leased line as a private dedicated circuit. However, a leased line may also be established on the physical wire that runs from a customer site to the local switching office. To obtain high data rates on these lines, it is conditioned to ensure quality.

An organization uses leased lines to build *private networks* that interconnect its remote sites or the sites of business partners. The lines are called private because no one else competes for bandwidth on the line as with packet-switching networks such as frame relay (although guaranteed bandwidth is available with frame relay). They are also more secure than using open networks like the Internet for wide area connections.

Bridges and routers are set up to direct traffic across the links. Because a private network requires a dedicated leased line between each site, operating costs increase with the number of sites and the distance between them. For example, to fully interconnect four sites in different cities, you will need six leased lines (one line from each site to every other site). This is shown on the left in Figure L-6.

An alternative is to use switched network services such as frame relay, as shown on the right in Figure L-6. Then, only four leased lines are required—one from each site into the local frame relay network access point. Once frames enter the frame relay network, they follow a virtual circuit to the appropriate destination. Thus, the frame relay network handles all the interconnections with its switching capabilities, and only one leased line per site is required into the frame relay access point. This is usually a short distance, so line costs are dramatically reduced.

Leased lines can be either analog circuits or digital circuits:

■ *Analog lines* require modems at each end and typically provide the same data rates as dial-up lines except that customers contract with the carrier to keep the line available for permanent use. The carrier may provide a discount rate or a higher quality of service over dial-up lines.

■ *Digital circuits* are conditioned lines that can provide higher data transmission rates than analog lines.

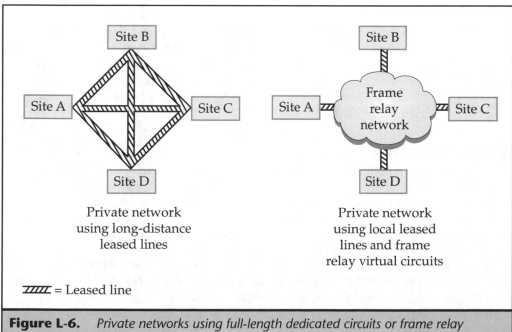

**Figure L-6.** *Private networks using full-length dedicated circuits or frame relay virtual circuits*

L

The cost of leased lines depends on the capacity of the line, the distance, and the provider. The most often used high-speed digital line service is the *T1 channel,* which provides transmission rates of 1.544 Mbits/sec. T1 lines can carry both voice and data using multiplexer devices, so they are often used to provide voice telephone connections between an organization's remote sites. A T1 line can provide 24 channels for voice or data at 64-Kbit/sec bandwidth each. Customers who don't need the full T1 bandwidth can opt for fractional T1, which provides digital services in increments of 64 Kbits/sec. Alternatively, a T3 line can provide the equivalent of 28 T1 lines for users who need a lot of bandwidth.

ISDN (Integrated Services Digital Network) also provides the equivalent of leased-line services starting in increments of 64 Kbits/sec. There are some advantages to using ISDN. For one, you can start with the bandwidth you need and work up. Various protocols are available for providing bandwidth on demand during various times of the day or when traffic levels increase. Refer to "ISDN (Integrated Services Digital Network)" for more information.

Leased lines are ordered by contacting the LEC. If the lines are long distance, you contact the LEC, the long-distance carrier, and/or a service provider that can handle all services. The Telecommunications Reform Act of 1996 makes it possible for IXCs to offer services in local (intra-LATA) areas and for the LECs and RBOCs (regional Bell operating companies) to offer long-distance services. The offerings that will become available over the next few years should be interesting. Another option is to set up virtual private networks over the Internet as discussed under "VPN (Virtual Private Network)."

**RELATED ENTRIES**   Circuit-Switching Services; Communication Service Providers; Communication Services; IXC (Interexchange Carrier); LATA (Local Access and Transport Area); LEC (Local Exchange Carrier); Packet and Cell Switching; RBOCs (Regional Bell Operating Companies); T1/T3; Telecommunications and Telephone Systems; VPN (Virtual Private Network); *and* WAN (Wide Area Network). See also "Telecommunications Companies" in Appendix A.

## LEC (Local Exchange Carrier)

A LEC is a telephone company that operates within a local area. LECs are the result of the breakup of AT&T in 1984, which created seven independent RBOCs (regional Bell operating companies) in the U.S. In addition, ITCs (independent telephone companies) were allowed to set up facilities and provide services in the local area. The RBOCs and ITOs are known as LECs. In contrast, long-distance providers such as AT&T, MCI, and US Sprint are called IXCs (interexchange carriers).

The Telecommunications Reform Act of 1996 makes it possible for IXCs to offer services in local (intra-LATA) areas and for the LECs and RBOCs to offer long-distance services. Many IXCs have signed resale agreements with the LECs to provide local services using the facilities owned by the LECs. This will allow traditional long-distance carriers to offer end-to-end services to customers. No longer will a customer need to deal with a LEC and an IXC to set up long-distance connections. At the same time, many of the LECs are getting into the long-distance business in selected high-traffic areas so they to can offer end-to-end services to their customers.

**RELATED ENTRIES**   IXC (Interexchange Carrier); LATA (Local Access and Transport Area); RBOCs (Regional Bell Operating Companies); Telecommunications and Telephone Systems; *and* WAN (Wide Area Network). See also "Telecommunications Companies" in Appendix A.

## Legacy Systems

Legacy systems are computer systems that a company already has in place and must maintain even though new computing technologies are available and being installed. There is usually a need to maintain backward compatibility with or connections to legacy systems. Originally, the term legacy system was used to refer to existing mainframe systems, but now the term is used more widely. For example, you'll often hear about legacy networks (i.e., coaxial cable Ethernet), legacy databases (i.e., databases that hold historical information), and legacy software. Legacy software must be maintained because it is often the only way to access legacy databases.

## Licensing, Electronic

*Electronic software licensing* provides automatic tracking of software usage to ensure that an organization stays within its software licensing requirements and legal boundaries for software usage.

A typical licensing package holds keys that allow users to access software applications. Each key is a license that has been purchased from the software vendor. The licensing program delivers keys to users who request the use of an application. When all the keys are in use, other users can't access applications until a key becomes available or more keys are added. Licensing programs usually include controls that prevent unauthorized users from accessing programs or prevent users from holding a key for too long.

## Line Conditioning

The local loop is the copper twisted-pair wire that runs from homes and businesses to the telephone company's switching system. From there, the telephone system is mostly all-digital. Only the local loop retains the analog signaling system that was put in place for the original phone system nearly 100 years ago. There are a number of limitations in the local loop, including a 4,000 Hz bandwidth restriction that limits data throughput to 33.3 Kbits/sec (or 56-Kbit/sec downloads with new modem technologies from Rockwell and U.S. Robotics).

To make matters worse, few modems really deliver on their full potential because they must deal with problems on the local-loop cables such as ambient line noise. Line

**L**

conditioning provides a way to gain better throughput and take full advantage of a modem's potential. A line conditioner can provide the following:

- Impedance matching, which can reduce the reflections that are generated by electrical signals as they travel across the local loop

- Balancing of the electrical current that flows between sites to reduce analog ambient line noise

- Keep signal frequencies strong to reduce circuit loss and increase line quality

Line conditioners are available from a number of manufacturers to improve the quality of modem service. The devices save you the expense of having to lease conditioning equipment from the local carrier to achieve the same results. Most work with 28.8-Kbit/sec V.34 modems. Black Box sells a V.Fast Turbo Conditioner. You can visit the company's Web site at http://www.blackbox.com.

Line conditioning is also something that the telephone company will do when you lease high-speed services such as T1. The CSU (channel service unit) installed at customer sites also provides its own line conditioning functions in the form of equalization functions and signal regeneration.

**RELATED ENTRIES**    Communication Services; DSL (Digital Subscriber Line); ISDN (Integrated Services Digital Network); LATA (Local Access and Transport Area); LEC (Local Exchange Carrier); Local Loop; Modems; RBOCs (Regional Bell Operating Companies); *and* Telecommunications and Telephone Systems

## Link Layer

*See* Data Link Protocols.

## Link State Routing

*Link state routing* provides a way to control the routing process and let routers respond faster to changes in the network, such as a broken link or the addition of a new router and network. Routes can be based on the avoidance of congested areas, the speed of a line, the cost of using a line, or various priorities. The Dijkstra algorithm is used to calculate the shortest path to a destination. The most common link-state routing method is OSPF (Open Shortest Path First).

**RELATED ENTRY**    Routing Protocols and Algorithms

## Linux

Linux is a UNIX-like 32-bit operating system that runs on a variety of platforms, including Intel, SPARC, PowerPC, and DEC Alpha processors as well as multiprocessing systems. The operating system is essentially free. You can download it from the Web or you can purchase a book that includes a CD-ROM with the entire operating system, such as *Linux: The Complete Reference*, by Richard Peterson (Berkeley, CA: Osborne/McGraw-Hill, 1996).

Linux is a "user-developed" product, meaning that many of its components and drivers have been developed by users around the world who ran the operating system for their own use. The original operating system was developed by Linux Torvalds as a college project. It is now well supported and gaining ground as a respectable operating system despite its homegrown roots.

The only problem with this approach is that drivers and fixes are only available if some user decides to develop them. Support is another issue since you can't call any particular vendor. Anyone that plans to use this operating system for production use should first make sure that applications run on the operating system and that appropriate drivers are available to support hardware and software. You can check the Linux Documentation Project's Web site at the address listed below for more information and a large list of related Web sites.

Version 2.0 of Linux provides a cross-platform, 64-bit kernel that supports SMP (symmetrical multiprocessing). It conforms to the X/Open and POSIX standards for UNIX-like operating systems, and programs intended for the SCO and SVR4 UNIX systems will run unaltered. Linux also supports standard UNIX and Internet protocols and supports Java. It can also be used as an Internet server and an Internet firewall. Documentation is provided as HOWTO files, which are written by users and developers and freely available on some of the Web sites listed in the "Information on the Internet" heading that follows.

**RELATED ENTRY**    UNIX

**INFORMATION ON THE INTERNET**

| | |
|---|---|
| Linux International | http://www.li.org/linux.int |
| Linux Documentation Project | http://sunsite.unc.edu.LDP |

# LIPS (Lightweight Internet Person Schema)

LIPS provides a way to identify people within directory services using common attributes. A group of vendors including Microsoft, IBM, Netscape, Novell, and Lotus defined the attributes and submitted them to the IETF (Internet Engineering Task Force) for consideration as a standard. LIPS follows a business card model and defines attributes for a person's name, title, phone number, e-mail address, and other information. A description of the schema and a complete list of attributes can be found at http://www2.netapps.org/netapps on the Web.

# LISTSERV

LISTSERV is the name of a mailing list product sold by L-Soft International, Inc. that has its roots in the original mailing list server product created by Eric Thomas in 1986. Refer to "Mailing List Programs," for a discussion of this topic.

**L**

# LLC (Logical Link Control)

The LLC is part of the data link layer in a protocol stack. The data link layer controls access to the network medium and defines how upper-layer data in the form of packets or datagrams is inserted into *frames* for delivery on a particular network. The underlying physical layer then transmits the framed data as a stream of bits on the network medium.

The IEEE 802.2 standard defines the LLC protocol, which is positioned in the protocol stack as pictured in Figure L-7. Note that LLC resides on the upper half of the data link layer. The MAC (Medium Access Control) sublayer is where individual shared LAN technologies such as Ethernet are defined. Early on, the data link layer contained only LLC-like protocols, but when shared LANs came along, the IEEE positioned the MAC sublayer into the lower half of the data link layer.

Basically, LLC provides a common interface and provides reliability and flow control features. It is a subclass of HDLC (High-level Data Link Control), which is used on wide area links. LLC can provide both connection-oriented and connectionless services.

When the LLC receives information from the network layer, it frames the information for an appropriate port (service access point) on the destination system.

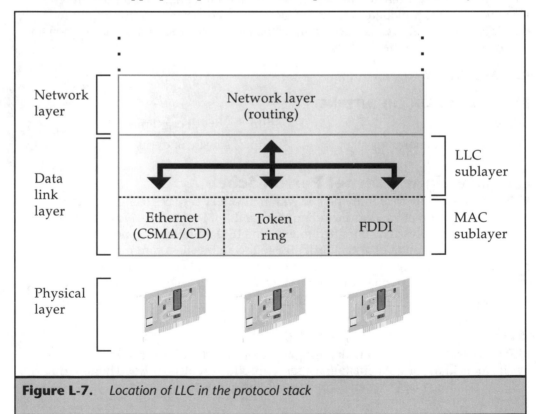

**Figure L-7.**   *Location of LLC in the protocol stack*

That port is basically the receiving point for a specific process that runs on the destination system. The MAC layer is responsible for appending the actual physical address of the destination computer to the frame. The physical address is the hardwired address on the network interface card for the destination.

**RELATED ENTRIES**    Connection-Oriented and Connectionless Services; Data Link Protocols; Framing in Data Transmissions; Protocol Concepts; *and* Virtual Circuit

## Load Balancing

Load balancing, in general, includes techniques for distributing work across multiple systems or communication channels to handle peaks in the load or traffic. Load balancing is used in a number of ways, as discussed next.

**LOAD BALANCING IN MULTIPROCESSOR SYSTEMS**    An operating system that supports multiprocessor systems can implement either asymmetric or symmetric multiprocessing. With asymmetric multiprocessing, the operating system uses one or more of the processors for its own use and runs applications on the others. An operating system that implements symmetric multiprocessing can distribute threads of operation to any processor. Thus, the operating system can balance the processing load evenly across available processors. Symmetric multiprocessing is difficult to implement but offers clear benefits over asymmetric multiprocessing.

**LOAD BALANCING ON DISK SYSTEMS**    Mirrored disks provide load balancing. Once data has been written to disk, performance gains are possible because data requests can be fulfilled from either disk in the mirrored set. In distributed file systems, similar data may be stored on systems in different locations, thus balancing the storage load and placing data closer to the user.

**LOAD BALANCING WITH CLUSTERED SYSTEMS**    A clustered system is a group of computers that share the same data stores. Requests for data or processing from users are distributed among the systems in the cluster.

**LOAD-BALANCING APPLICATION PROCESSING**    In a distributed system, many systems may be available with processing power that goes unused. Applications can be designed to seek out these systems and distribute their processing loads among them to complete a task much more quickly.

**LOAD-BALANCING BRIDGES/ROUTERS**    A load-balancing bridge/router is able to increase the bandwidth between two sites by dialing additional lines and balancing the traffic load across those lines.

**LOAD BALANCING A WEB SITE**    Many Web sites are quickly overloaded with traffic from Internet users. Additional Web servers can be installed at the same location that hold duplicate information. Web requests are then sent to any one of the

*L*

Web servers that is best able to handle the request. Web sites may also be mirrored (duplicated) in different geographic locations to handle requests close to users.

In the last case, Cisco Systems has developed load-balancing software for routers called *Distributed Director*. The software can run a routing protocol capable of sending user requests to a server that is closest to them. Basically, a single host DNS (Domain Name System) name is bound with multiple IP addresses. When a user makes a request to a Web server by its name, the router determines which one of the IP addresses can best handle the request and forwards the request to that server. Cisco's Web site is at http://www.cisco.com.

# Local Loop

The local loop is the two-wire connection between a telephone subscriber and the telephone company's central office, as shown in Figure L-8. The central office is the telephone company building seen in local neighborhoods. This connection is based on the analog signal technologies that have been used in the phone system for the past 100 years. The cable is a simple copper twisted-pair wire. Even though the telephone company's trunk lines are now mostly digital, the local loop still remains analog because the cost of upgrading it is prohibitive. The carriers use a variety of transmission systems, including fiber-optic cable and microwave transmissions systems, between its central offices and other telephone company switching systems.

The local loop has some limitations that severely restrict its data carrying capacity. First, a modem is required to convert computer digital signals to analog signals for transmission across the local loop. Signaling on the cable is limited to the 4,000 Hz bandwidth between 300 Hz and 3,100 Hz. This bandwidth can adequately handle voice but severely restricts the data-carrying capacity of the local loop. Interestingly, the telephone company converts analog voice signals into digital signals for transport over its own network. The size of the channel required to transmit digitized voice is 64 Kbits/sec, which happens to be the basic building block for digital services from the carriers.

There has been little incentive to upgrade the local loop until recently. Now, with the advent of the Internet and increased interest in digital audio and video services, nearly every household can clearly benefit from enhanced data throughput. While there is talk of extending fiber-optic cable to the home, that is unlikely in the near future. In fact, the local loop is likely the best candidate for improved digital services to the home. The CATV cabling system is another option, as discussed under "Cable (CATV) Data Networks and Modems."

Traditionally, the high-end data transfer rate was limited to 33.6 Kbits/sec, but new modem technologies from Rockwell and U.S. Robotics extend this to 56 Kbits/sec when downloading. ISDN (Integrated Services Digital Network) can provide up to 128 Kbits/sec. Even newer DSL (Digital Subscriber Line) technologies can provide throughput in the megabits-per-second range. See "DSL (Digital Subscriber Line)," "ISDN (Integrated Services Digital Network)," and "Modems" for more information.

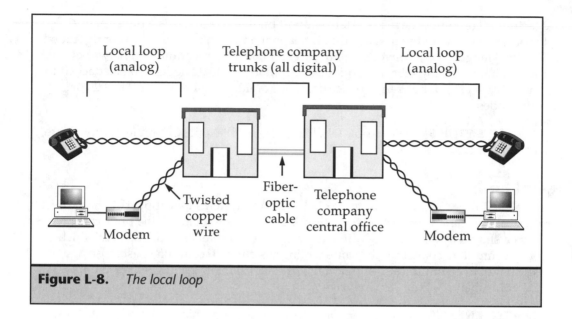

**Figure L-8.** *The local loop*

Note that the local loop can benefit from line conditioning to improve modem throughput. In most cases, line noise and other problems reduce the actual data rate that a modem can achieve over a dial-up line. See "Line Conditioning."

**RELATED ENTRIES**    Cable (CATV) Data Networks and Modems; Communication Services; DSL (Digital Subscriber Line); ISDN (Integrated Services Digital Network); LATA (Local Access and Transport Area); LEC (Local Exchange Carrier); Line Conditioning; Modems; RBOCs (Regional Bell Operating Companies); *and* Telecommunications and Telephone Systems. See also "Telecommunications Companies" in Appendix A.

## Local Procedure Calls

*See* IPC (Interprocess Communication).

## LocalTalk

LocalTalk is a LAN (local area network) protocol that defines AppleTalk packet transmission over a 230.4-Kbit/sec cabling system. LocalTalk was originally called AppleTalk, but Apple changed the name in 1989 to LocalTalk. Apple Computer's network architecture is now called AppleTalk, and it includes the protocols that operate over LocalTalk physical networks.

The original LocalTalk system was primarily designed for the attachment of a few Macintosh computers to an Apple LaserWriter printer. Transmission speeds of LocalTalk are very low (230.4 Kbits/sec), but LocalTalk is important because most

**L**

Macintosh computers have LocalTalk support built in. LocalTalk is a physical bus topology that is wired with twisted-pair telephone wire in a daisy-chain configuration. The total length of the network cannot exceed 1,000 feet, but additional networks can be attached using repeaters, bridges, or routers. Up to 32 nodes can be attached to a network segment, but performance degrades rapidly on busy networks of 20 or more nodes.

**RELATED ENTRIES**    AFP (AppleTalk Filing Protocol); Apple Computer; AppleShare; *and* Network Concepts

## Logical Links

A logical link is a communication link between two systems that appears to be a direct physical nonshared connection for transmitting data, even though the physical wire may be shared by a number of different systems. On a shared-media LAN in which many computers connect to the same cabling system, two computers establish a logical link to communicate. A logical link is established in the LLC (Logical Link Control) sublayer of the data link layer.

**RELATED ENTRIES**    Connection-Oriented and Connectionless Services; Data Link Protocols; Framing in Data Transmissions; LLC (Logical Link Control); Protocol Concepts; *and* Virtual Circuit

## Login Scripts

Login scripts are critical for setting up the environments of network users. A *login script* is a series of commands that execute when a user logs in. The commands placed in login scripts can map network drives for users, switch them to specific drives, display menus, and start applications.

In many network operating system environments, there is one login script that runs when a user logs in. In NetWare 4.x, there are up to four login scripts, any of which may execute when a user logs in. A *default login script* runs when a user first logs in and creates a number of environmental settings. However, administrators (and users to some extent) can override the default login script by creating a personal login script. Each user also has a *personal login script* that can contain commands of their choosing.

Two other login scripts are the *container login script* and the *profile login script*. A container is a branch in the NDS (Novell Directory Services) tree that relates to a department, division, or branch of the organization. When a user logs in, the login script for the container they belong to runs. This means that each department or division can have its own login script in addition to the default user login scripts. A profile login script belongs to a group of users who don't necessarily belong to the same container. For example, a profile login script can execute commands for a group of managers.

**RELATED ENTRIES**    Access Control; Account, User; Authentication and
Authorization; Challenge/Response Protocol; Logons and Logon Accounts; Rights
and Permissions; Security; *and* Users and Groups

## Logons and Logon Accounts

Logon (or login) is a procedure that a user follows to gain access to a privileged
system, such as a network, a file server, a database, a Web server, or some other
system. Logon software usually runs when the workstation is turned on or when a
user types a command such as LOGON or LOGIN. The logon procedure asks for an
account name and a password. If the user enters either of these incorrectly, the logon
procedure usually allows another chance for the user to log on. After a certain number
of repeated failures to supply the correct logon information, the system may assume
the user is an intruder and lock the account from further logon attempts.

Note that users log into accounts, not systems. The account a user logs into is
authorized to access resources on a system or network. Accounts are created by
system administrators and stored on security servers. Some systems will log users in
based on security information stored at the computer where the user is logging in. If
the user attempts to access other systems, the information collected from this logon is
automatically passed to another system or to a security server to authenticate the user
on those systems. In most cases, users log into a single security server and then obtain
an access token that can be used to access other systems.

Access to resources is based on access control lists. See "Access Control" and "ACL
(Access Control List)" for more information.

A user account may have various security restrictions applied to it. A supervisor
may apply logon restrictions to the user account that do the following:

- Restrict the time the user can log on, thus preventing the user from logging on
  after hours.

- Specify the workstation where a user logs on, preventing the user from logging
  on at unsupervised workstations.

- Require unique passwords, thus forcing the user to create a password unlike
  one the user recently used.

- A logon restriction can define an expiration date for the account, locking out
  the user after a certain period of time.

*L*

**RELATED ENTRIES** Access Control; Account, User; Authentication and Authorization; Challenge/Response Protocol; Login Scripts; Rights and Permissions; Security; *and* Users and Groups

## Long-Distance Carriers

*See* Communication Service Providers; IXC (Interexchange Carrier).

## Lotus Domino

Lotus Domino is a server technology that transforms Lotus Notes into an Internet application server that allows Web clients to interactively participate in a Notes environment and access dynamic data and applications on Notes servers. A key feature of Domino is that developers can leverage the Notes application development environment to create Web applications. Lotus is developing versions of Domino for Windows NT/Intel, Solaris/SPARC, Solaris/Intel Edition, AIX, and OS/2.

**RELATED ENTRIES** Electronic Mail; Groupware; Lotus Notes; Microsoft Exchange Server; Netscape SuiteSpot; *and* Workflow Management

**INFORMATION ON THE INTERNET**

Lotus Domino site          http://domino.lotus.com

## Lotus Notes

Lotus Notes is an enterprise-wide, client/server-based messaging system that integrates groupware, forms generation, and document flow for large network environments. It also includes full support for the Internet and the Web. It also provides a base for development of custom applications that automate business processes.

The latest release addresses the areas of integration with desktop productivity tools, including Lotus SmartSuite and Microsoft Office; Microsoft Internet Explorer integration; a new task-oriented navigation scheme to help users access the product; enhanced contact management; and POP3 support for Internet mail. Notes is an organization-wide messaging system. It uses Lotus cc:Mail and other applications as its user interface and incorporates enterprise calendaring and scheduling. It supports mobile users by using replicating techniques to keep remote users in touch and synchronized with the rest of the organization. Notes provides full security to protect the privacy of information stored on servers in databases, documents, and messages. RSA (Rivest, Shamir, Adleman) encryption and authentication systems are used.

**RELATED ENTRIES** Electronic Mail; Groupware; Lotus Domino; Microsoft Exchange Server; Netscape SuiteSpot; *and* Workflow Management

**INFORMATION ON THE INTERNET**

Lotus Development Corp.　　　http://www.lotus.com

## LU (Logical Unit) Entities

An LU is a session in an IBM SNA (Systems Network Architecture) environment, usually between a terminal and a mainframe computer. Typically, more than one LU can take place at the same time. The LU types are as follows:

- **LU Type 0**　A program-to-program data communication session that provides general purpose transport services (i.e., for file transfers)
- **LU Type 1**　Used for transmitting character strings to remote terminals
- **LU Type 2**　A communication session for IBM 3270 terminals
- **LU Type 3**　A communication session for IBM 3270 printers
- **LU Type 6.1**　A communication session for IBM databases and transaction management systems
- **LU Type 6.2**　A peer-to-peer communication session associated with IBM APPC
- **LU Type 7**　A communication session for IBM 5250 terminals

**L**

## MAC (Medium Access Control)

In the IEEE 802 protocols for shared LANs, the data link layer is divided into two sublayers, as shown in Figure M-1. The upper LLC (Logical Link Control) layer provides a way to address a station on a LAN and exchange information with it. The lower MAC layer provides the interface between the LLC and the particular network medium that is in use (Ethernet, token ring, etc.).

The MAC layer frames data for transmission over the network, then passes the frame to the physical layer interface where it is transmitted as a stream of bits. Framing is important because it packages information into distinct units that are transmitted one at a time on the network. If a frame is corrupted during transmission, only it needs to be resent, not the entire transmission.

The other job of the MAC layer is to arbitrate access to the medium that is shared by all the computers attached to the LAN. On shared networks, two stations cannot

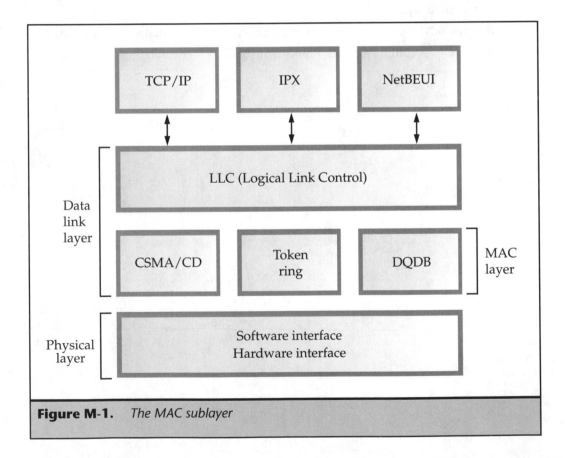

**Figure M-1.** *The MAC sublayer*

transmit on the cable at the same time; otherwise, information will be corrupted. The different access methods are described here:

- **CSMA/CD (carrier sense multiple access/collision detection)** This is a random access method that is used in Ethernet. Each station attached to the shared network contends for the medium.

- **Token bus** A distributed technology in which each station gets access to the network in round-robin fashion. A token is passed around the network and held by each station for a period of time. During that time, the station can transmit. The network topology is ring and bus. This access method is used in MAP (Manufacturing Automation Protocol), a factory floor networking scheme.

- **Token ring** This technique is similar to token bus except that the topology is ring and star. IEEE 802.5 and FDDI (Fiber Distributed Data Interface) implement this method of access.

- **DQDB (Distributed Queue Dual Bus)** This is a reservation protocol in which each station obtains a slot in a synchronous stream of slots divided by time. DQDB is used in the IEEE 802.6 MAN (metropolitan area network) standard.

- **Request priority** This is a centralized control access method in which each station is polled one by one by a central device. If a station needs to transmit, it is given access to the cable. The IEEE 802.12 standard specifies this technique, and it is used in 100VG-AnyLAN.

Finally, individual LAN addresses are assigned in the MAC layer. A network interface card such as an Ethernet adapter has a hardwired address that is assigned at the factory. This address follows an industry standard that ensures that no other adapter has a similar address. Therefore, when you connect workstations to an IEEE network, each workstation has a unique MAC address. Workstations on the same LAN use the MAC address to forward packets to one another.

Note that LANs connected by routers are internetworks and use a higher-level addressing scheme such as IP (Internet Protocol) to identify each individually connected LAN and a host computer attached to that LAN.

**RELATED ENTRIES** 100VG-AnyLAN; CSMA/CD (Carrier Sense Multiple Access/Collision Detection); DQDB (Distributed Queue Dual Bus); Ethernet; FDDI (Fiber Distributed Data Interface); MAN (Metropolitan Area Network); NDIS (Network Driver Interface Specification); ODI (Open Data link Interface); *and* Token Ring Network

## Mach Kernel

*M*

A kernel is the core component of most operating systems. It is the portion that manages memory, resources, files, peripherals, and system security. The kernel typically runs processes and provides interprocess communication among them. The *Mach* operating system was developed at Carnegie-Mellon University. It has a client/server architecture consisting of a relatively small kernel, called a *microkernel*. The microkernel architecture is designed to handle only the most critical functions of the operating system, such as thread scheduling, tasking, synchronization, timing, virtual memory management, interrupts, and system messaging.

Mach implements a modular design in which additional functions can be bound to the microkernel, such as file management, network support, graphical user interface, and others. The modules are layered on top of the Mach microkernel. A layered architecture lets the microkernel host diverse operating systems such as UNIX, and OS/2 on multiple platforms such as the Motorola PowerPC RISC processor and Intel processors. The Open Group (http://www.osf.org) implements Mach in its operating system products. However, in the early 1990s, IBM aborted its efforts to market operating systems based on the Mach kernel due to technical problems.

NeXT Software implemented Mach as the core of its OpenStep after much revision. In 1996, Apple Computer purchased NeXT and began integrating OpenStep into its operating system plans. Mach is part of the core operating system for Rhapsody, Apple's newest operating system.

## Mac OS

In 1984, Apple Computer introduced the Macintosh, one of the first widely available personal computers with a graphical user interface operating system based on a familiar metaphor, the desktop. Over the years, the Macintosh operating system evolved to provide more and more features for its users. In 1994, Apple introduced its System 7.5 operating system to provide users with greater efficiency and productivity, including the ability to use both 680x0-based Macs and Power Macintosh systems. At that time, the operating system was named *Mac OS*.

In mid-1997, Apple released Mac OS 8, a multithreaded system for executing multiple tasks simultaneously, such as launching applications and copying files. It also has an enhanced user interface and includes Internet access support in the form of TCP/IP, PPP (Point-to-Point Protocol), Netscape or Microsoft Web browsers, and the PointCast network.

Apple's current direction is to support a new and advanced operating system called Rhapsody. This new OS is based on the merging of technologies from NeXT Software, Inc. and Apple. Rhapsody joins Mac OS as an option for users and developers, although when this book was going to press, Apple was reconsidering Rhapsody's position in its product line. Rhapsody includes features such as protected memory, preemptive multitasking, and symmetrical multiprocessing. It also provides backward compatibility with most Mac OS applications and is a development platform for building media-rich applications and Java applications.

### INFORMATION ON THE INTERNET

Mac OS and Rhapsody information          http://www.macos.apple.com

## MAE (Metropolitan Area Exchange)

*See* Internet Backbone.

## Mailing List Programs

First, the industry now commonly calls mailing list programs *listservers or LISTSERV,* but the latter is a name owned by L-Soft International, Inc., which makes the LISTSERV mailing list program, originally created by Eric Thomas in 1986. This section discusses LISTSERV and Majordomo, a similar mailing list program.

A mailing list program is a program that uses Internet protocols to automate e-mail message distribution to members of a mailing list. Members subscribe to a mailing list, then receive a copy of all e-mail messages sent to the list. Any member can create a new message or respond to a message that was sent by another user. New messages and response messages are automatically forwarded to members of the list. A mailing list is usually set up to disseminate information about a particular topic, such as computers, politics, finance, stocks, or many other topics.

Mailing lists are an excellent tool for organizations to use for in-house discussions or to provide open discussions with customers or clients. For example, Microsoft uses mailing lists when beta testing its products. Beta testers receive prerelease copies of a product and participate in mailing list discussions about that product. Many problems and technical details are often hammered out in heated mailing list discussions before the product is released.

A mailing list implements a *mail list exploder.* When a message is sent to the mailing list, it is exploded, meaning that duplicates of the message are sent to everyone on the list. Recipients usually receive a message in a few minutes on the Internet. However, some recipients may choose to have messages sent in digest form, which means messages are bundled in a package and sent once per week (or some other interval).

Generally, subscriptions to a list are open to all. To subscribe, a user sends a request to the mailing list server in an e-mail message. The server then add the user to the list and returns a set of instructions for using the list. The user can send another message to unsubscribe from the list at any time. However, a list administrator or owner can screen subscribers, drop subscribers that are being rude, or perform other management functions.

As users exchange messages, they create message threads that can be archived and reviewed at any point. One message thread may spawn another message thread. Mailing list programs create logs of messages that are archived and can be reviewed at any time. Users can obtain a log file for a particular time period or use database functions to search for messages related to a specific topic or sent by a person of interest.

The two most popular mailing list programs are outlined here:

*M*

- **LISTSERV** As mentioned, the original mailing list server is LISTSERV, written in 1986 by Eric Thomas and now sold by L-Soft International. Mr. Thomas still oversees development of the product. It was originally designed for IBM mainframes but is now available on VM, VMS, Windows NT, Windows 95, Macintosh, and 13 brands of UNIX. Note that LISTSERV is always spelled in uppercase and is a trademark. Other products are often called *listserv* programs, but they are really mailing list programs.

- **Majordomo** Like LISTSERV, Majordomo is a mailing list program for automating and managing mailing lists. The product is free to download from the Great Circle Web site listed below. Its name comes from the Latin "major domus," meaning master of the house. Majordomo does not have the commercial aspect of LISTSERV nor does it have all of LISTSERV's features. Readers should visit the sites listed below to compare the features of the two products. Note that Majordomo runs on UNIX platforms and uses Sendmail, the UNIX mail agent.

**RELATED ENTRIES**    Electronic Mail; Groupware

**INFORMATION ON THE INTERNET**

| | |
|---|---|
| L-Soft's LISTSERV site | http://www.lsoft.com |
| Majordomo mailing list site | http://www.greatcircle.com/majordomo |
| L-Soft's CataList service (lists all public lists running on LISTSERV servers) | http://www.lsoft.com/lists/listref.html |

# Mail Listservers

*See* Mailing List Programs.

# Mainframe

A mainframe computer system is a high-end computing platform that has traditionally been based on the central processing model, where relatively "dumb" terminals (input and display devices) connect to a central system where all processing is done. During the 1980s, the LAN model nearly replaced the mainframe, and there were predictions that the mainframe would be a thing of the past by now. However, IBM and other mainframe vendors continue to sell these systems, although they look and operate quite a bit differently than their ancestors. Mainframes are no longer centralized processing systems that feed the displays of dumb terminals. The new breed of mainframe should be a consideration in any environment that requires a secure and reliable high-performance data server. Mainframes are being used as Web servers, client/server systems, and as systems that can provide the integrity needed to run electronic commerce applications. IBM's new System/390 operating system even hosts Windows NT applications.

The primary job of the mainframe today is to run mission-critical applications and transaction-processing databases. It's not that other systems cannot handle these tasks, but administrators trust mainframe systems that use well-established applications and procedures to handle them. In addition, mainframe systems are built from the ground up to provide performance, fail-safe operation and reliable security.

Legacy applications and data give mainframes their sticking power. IDC (International Data Corporation) estimates that nearly three fourths of all data still resides on mainframe systems. Clearly, managers have not been anxious to move this information to network servers or other platforms. The cost and risk of failure in making such a move is too high. The current trend is to build data warehouses that extract, summarize, collate, clean up, and present data from back-end production and legacy systems in a way that makes it more accessible to users. See "Data Warehousing" for more on this topic.

Web technologies are also opening mainframe systems up to the rest of the network, allowing administrators to get rid of incompatible protocols and cumbersome gateways. Software is now available from IBM and other vendors that lets Web clients access mainframe data directly using Web browsers and TCP/IP protocols. No doubt, traditional mainframe protocols such as SNA (Systems Network Architecture) will eventually be retired in favor of TCP/IP.

In fact, Web technologies are bringing back the old model of centralization in which both data and processing are handled on central computer systems. The NC (Network Computer) is an example of a system that some compare to a dumb terminal. NCs rely on other systems for data storage and much of their processing. The central systems they rely on must be powerful enough to handle all the NCs on the network. The advantage of this model is that processing systems and data are brought back under one roof where they are more easily managed and protected. NCs run Java applications, and IBM fully supports Java applications in its System/390 operating system.

*Datamation* magazine recently quoted the following figures in "Are Mainframes Cool Again?" (http://www.datamation.com, April, 1997):

- IBM System/390 shipments surged from 324,300 in 1995 to 535,000 in 1996, with 1997 shipments expected to reach over 900,000.

- Mainframe costs are plummeting due to CMOS-based systems. According to IDC, the cost per MIPS (million instructions per second) plummeted from $23,250 in 1995 to $13,780 in 1996 (although software prices are not coming down).

- A study by the International Technology Group indicates that the cost per mainframe user is $5,183 annually, while the cost per UNIX user is $7,947 annually.

- The latest operating system for the System/390 supports TCP/IP networks and runs client/server applications. UNIX applications and tools are being ported to mainframes, and software that runs Windows NT applications on a System/390 is available from Bristol Technology (http://www.bristol.com).

*M*

The article has additional statistics and information about companies that have chosen mainframes over network servers and client/server systems.

**RELATED ENTRIES**   Data Warehousing; Enterprise Networks; IBM AS/400; IBM Host Connectivity; IBM Mainframe Environment; IBM Operating Systems; IBM Servers; *and* SNA (Systems Network Architecture)

**INFORMATION ON THE INTERNET**

| | |
|---|---|
| IBM's System/390 site | http://www.s390.ibm.com |
| IBM's mainframe "catalog" (includes system specifications) | http://direct.boulder.ibm.com/us/mainframe |
| IBM's Servers site | http://www.servergroup.hosting.ibm.com |
| Aberdeen*Group*'s Mainframe Revival paper | http://www.aberdeen.com/secure/reports/mainfram.htm |

# MAN (Metropolitan Area Network)

A MAN is a backbone network that spans a metropolitan area and may be regulated by local or state authorities. The telephone company, cable services, and other suppliers provide MAN services to companies that need to build networks that span public rights-of-way in metropolitan areas. The IEEE has defined a standard for MANs called the IEEE 802.6 DQDB (Distributed Queue Dual Bus). DQDB is based on QPSX (Queued Packet Synchronous Exchange), which was developed in 1985 at the University of Western Australia. Complete information on QPSX and DQDB from the Australian point of view can be found at the University of Sydney Web site listed later.

SMDS (Switched Multimegabit Data Service) is a telephone company offering that uses the IEEE MAN standard and provides a range of service features. SMDS goes beyond the MAN standard in that it can span LANs, MANs, and WANs. What SMDS offers is switched access to MAN services, allowing customers to pay for only the service used.

An IEEE 802.6 MAN can be thought of as a large LAN that covers an entire metropolitan area. Thousands of users may share the medium using LAN-like access protocols. MANs are high-speed networks that can support data, voice, and multimedia traffic. Speeds range from 2 Mbits/sec to 300 Mbits/sec. MANs can also connect to other MANs, which allows customers to build interconnected LANs that span very large geographic areas.

Attachment to MANs is via bridges and routers over T1, ISDN (Integrated Services Digital Network), or similar links. Some companies may provide lines into MANs that bypass the local carriers. A DSU (data service unit) that can convert LAN packets into the 53-byte cells specified in the DQDB standard is required. The cell size is compatible with ATM (Asynchronous Transfer Mode) and B-ISDN (Broadband-Integrated Services Digital Network) networks. Both types of networks provide scaleable transmission rates that are possible on fiber-optic transmission media.

The DQDB physical network is pictured in Figure M-2. There are two buses that transmit data in opposite directions. The reason is that signals put on bus A by station B can only travel in one direction toward station N. Station B uses bus B to transmit to station A.

Each bus has a head end with a *slot generator* that constantly puts 53 byte cells (also called slots) on the bus so that the bus is never silent. A queue arbitration method (often called a *fair use* method) is used to ensure that stations nearest the slot generator don't grab all the available cells to use for their own transmissions. For example, assume that station B wants to transmit to station N. This transmission must occur on bus A. Station B must tell stations that are upstream from it on bus A (i.e., station A) that it needs cells. This is easily accomplished by sending a cell reservation message on bus B to all the downstream devices on bus B, which includes station A. Thus station A receives a message on its bus B connection that station B needs some cells reserved on bus A.

The MAN standard is compatible with other IEEE LAN standards and supports traffic that adheres to the 802.2 LLC (Logical Link Control) standard. MANs can support a variety of services, such as LAN-to-LAN connections, PBX connections, direct workstation attachment, and mainframe connections. In other words, the MAN

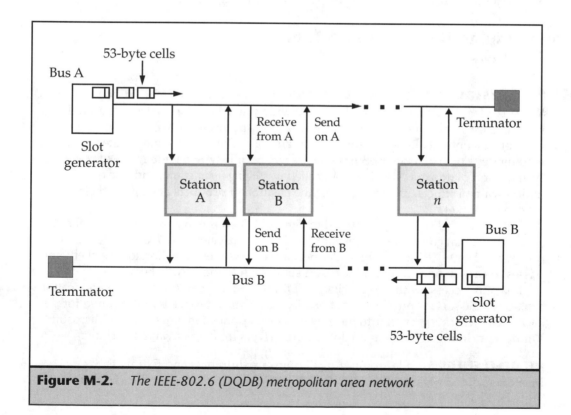

**Figure M-2.**   *The IEEE-802.6 (DQDB) metropolitan area network*

M

is an integrated voice and data network. Cells can be prioritized for isochronous data such as real-time voice and video to guarantee on-time delivery.

A typical MAN connection includes a switch that supports voice, video, and LAN data traffic. Customers maintain equipment (sometimes called a *customer network interface unit*, or *CNIU*) at their own premises and connect with a MAN service provider over leased-line links that match the data requirements. The CNIU has interfaces to support circuit-switched services for digital telephones and other isochronous services, as well as bridging modules to support a variety of LANs, including the IEEE 802 LAN standards.

**RELATED ENTRIES**    ATM (Asynchronous Transfer Mode); Network Concepts; SMDS (Switched Multimegabit Data Service); *and* WAN (Wide Area Network)

**INFORMATION ON THE INTERNET**

| | |
|---|---|
| The University of Sydney DQDB pages | http://www.arch.su.edu.au/~ng_mo/dqdb1.htm |
| Switched Multimegabit Data Service site | http://www.cerf.net/smds |
| SMDS Interest Group | http://www.smds-ig.org/home.html |

## Management Standards and Tools

*See* Network Management.

## MAPI (Messaging Application Programming Interface)

MAPI is a Microsoft API that has become a widely supported industry standard. It helps ensure system independence for messaging applications. MAPI provides a layer of functionality between applications and underlying messaging systems, helping developers create products that are compatible with a wide range of systems and platforms. MAPI is often called *messaging middleware,* and like other middleware products, it helps promote the creation of products and speed their release to market.

The MAPI architecture is pictured in Figure M-3. At the top are MAPI-compliant applications that communicate through the MAPI subsystem to MAPI service providers. The MAPI service provider performs the requested action for the client and passes the action back through the MAPI subsystem to the MAPI client.

It is only necessary to make a client application MAPI-compliant so the application can access the service provider functionality. A specific interface is not required for each provider. This is similar to the way in which applications that use the Microsoft Windows printing subsystem do not require drivers for every available printer.

**RELATED ENTRIES**    Electronic Mail; Groupware; Intranets and Extranets; Middleware and Messaging; POP (Post Office Protocol); *and* SMTP (Simple Mail Transfer Protocol)

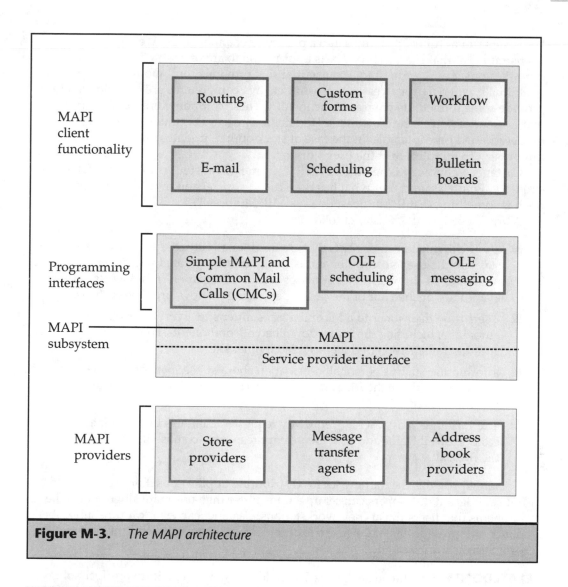

**Figure M-3.** *The MAPI architecture*

### INFORMATION ON THE INTERNET

| | |
|---|---|
| Microsoft Corporation | http://www.microsoft.com |
| Electronic Messaging Association | http://www.ema.org |
| NetLingo MAPI FAQ | http://www.netlingo.com/more/mapi.html |

*M*

## Marimba Castanet

Marimba's Castanet provides a framework for distributing Java applications and content over the Internet or an intranet. Castanet uses a broadcast metaphor in which

Web users run a "tuner" that tunes into a particular channel on the Web. A "transmitter" at that channel broadcasts information to anyone who tunes in. For example, a user might tune into a transmitter that provides continuous stock updates.

Initially, when a user accesses a transmitter, Java components are downloaded to provide some immediate program functionality. These components access information that is broadcast from the transmitter. Updates may occur continuously or at predetermined time intervals. In the case of stock quotes, updates may occur in real time, every 15 minutes, or at the user's discretion.

Castanet technology is based on HTTP (Hypertext Transfer Protocol) and Java. It is similar to PointCast and uses what has been called *push* technology. Note that true push is something that IP Multicast does (see "IP Multicast").

A brief description of Castanet follows:

- Users download components that are used for all future sessions. The software stays on the user's computer and is automatically updated whenever necessary. In contrast, a Web browser caches information from Web sites that is eventually pushed out of the cache, depending on how large the cache is.

- Users tune their tuner to a Marimba transmitter site. Everything else is automatic, including the initial download of components, component updates, and the transmission of data provided by that site.

- Information such as personal information about subscribers or the selections they have made on the interface (e.g., advertisements) can be sent back to the transmitter.

- The Castanet Proxy caches frequently requested channels to minimize cross-firewall traffic and provide prompt response to subscribers inside the firewall.

Castanet provides the framework for distributing applications. For example, in-house program developers can set up a transmitter that automatically updates the components that users run at their workstations. Castanet can also "capture subscriber feedback and provide channel personalization on a subscriber-by-subscriber basis," according to Marimba.

**RELATED ENTRIES**   Broadcast News Technology; Component Software Technology; IP Multicast; Java; Multicasting; NNTP (Network News Transport Protocol); PointCast; Push; *and* Web Technologies and Concepts

## INFORMATION ON THE INTERNET

Marimba, Inc.                http://www.marimba.com

## MARS (Multicast Address Resolution Server)

Multicasting is a technique for sending a single message inside data packets to multiple destinations. This is discussed under the heading "Multicasting." MARS provides a way to associate multicast group identifiers with the ATM (Asynchronous Transfer Mode) addresses of members of those groups. MARS is used in the MPOA (Multiprotocol over ATM) environment, which is discussed elsewhere in this book.

The MARS server is queried to resolve a layer 3 multicast address into the set of ATM addresses that make up the group. The MARS server also manages the addresses of users that are joining and leaving groups. This is similar to what IGMP (Internet Group Management Protocol) does on IP networks. You can read more about MARS in RFC 2022 at http://www.internic.net/rfc/rfc2022.txt.

**RELATED ENTRIES**    IP over ATM; IP Switching; MBone (Multicast Backbone); MPOA (Multiprotocol over ATM); *and* Multicasting

## Matrix Switch

A matrix switch (also called a crossbar switch) has a number of input ports and a number of output ports. An internal matrix of connections provides a way for any input port to connect with any output port. A 4-by-4 matrix is pictured on the left in Figure M-4, but other matrix configurations are available, such as 8 by 8 and 16 by 16. This example illustrates how a switch can provide up to four computers with a connection to a pool of four modems. Note that the switching matrix is now commonly implemented as an integrated circuit.

A multistage matrix switch is pictured on the right in Figure M-4. Note that the switch now consists of many smaller matrix switches with several switches in the middle that interconnect the input and output switches. This configuration provides more scalability. Only a few inputs are shown, but many are possible. Refer to "Packet and Cell Switching" for more information.

Matrix switches provide extremely fast any-to-any switching between connected devices. They can become quite elaborate. The principles of the matrix switch are implemented in network switching equipment, but the circuitry is more complex than the matrix switch described here. See "Switched Networks."

**RELATED ENTRIES**    ATM (Asynchronous Transfer Mode); Cell Relay; Hubs/Concentrators/MAUs; Packet and Cell Switching; Switched Networks; *and* Virtual Circuit

## MAU (Multistation Access Unit)

A MAU is a hub device in a token ring network that provides the connection point for multiple computers. It contains an internal ring that is extended to an external ring when workstations are attached, as pictured in Figure M-5.

**M**

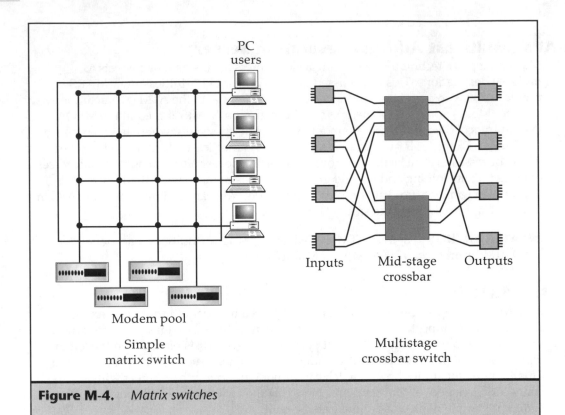

**Figure M-4.**   *Matrix switches*

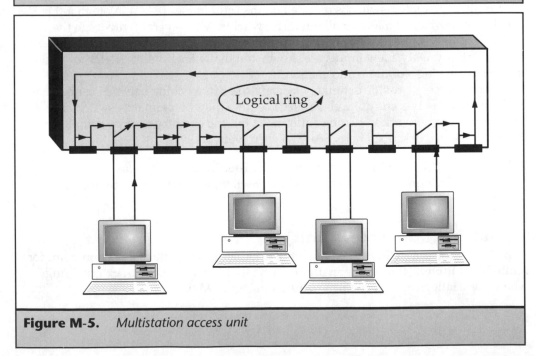

**Figure M-5.**   *Multistation access unit*

If a network card fails, the MAU automatically bypasses it to maintain the ring. To expand the network beyond the devices that can attach to the MAU, a cable is wired from a ring-out port on the first MAU to a ring-in port on the second MAU. Another cable is then wired from the ring-out port on the second MAU back to the ring-in port on the first MAU. This maintains the ring configuration while allowing it to grow.

**RELATED ENTRIES**    Hubs/Concentrators/MAUs; Token Ring Network

## MBone (Multicast Backbone)

The MBone is a multicast system for broadcasting messages and multimedia information to multiple recipients on the Internet. Unicasting is the traditional method of transmitting packets on the Internet. With unicasting, an IP packet is addressed to a single destination, whereas multicasting sends a copy of the same message to each member of a multicast group. Multicasting is more efficient than unicasting if the same message is to be sent to multiple recipients.

The MBone originated as an IETF (Internet Engineering Task Force) experiment in audiocasting, where live audio was multicast from IETF meetings to a multicast group with members located around the world. From that beginning, the MBone has grown from 40 subnets in four different countries in 1992, to more than 3,400 subnets in over 25 countries in 1997. New multicast-based services and technologies are appearing everyday.

Currently, the MBone exists on top of the physical Internet as a *virtual network* because many of the routers on the Internet do not support IP multicasting. The reason for implementing a virtual network will become apparent, but keep in mind that once all the routers on the Internet support IP multicasting, the virtual network tunneling method described in a moment will no longer be necessary.

All routers on the Internet can handle standard IP unicast packets. We will call these *urouters* for clarity. However, a growing number of computer systems on the Internet are IP multicast-enabled. These systems, usually called *mrouters*, are typically workstations that run an operating system that supports IP multicast routing software.

Currently, the Internet consists of "islands" of mrouters with urouters in between, as shown in Figure M-6. Sending an IP multicast packet from one mrouter to another may involve sending those packets across urouters, but urouters don't know how to handle IP multicast packets. To solve this problem, multicast packets are *encapsulated* in IP unicast packets. Urouters can then handle the packets.

Encapsulation is a *tunneling* technique that essentially creates a *virtual* point-to-point link between mrouters. When a packet is encapsulated, a new header is created which contains the unicast IP address of the mrouter at the other end of a tunnel. The islands (and the tunnels that connect them) form the virtual network that sits on top of the Internet as shown in Figure M-6.

The actual topology of the MBone consists of a backbone of tunnels that form a mesh topology within each country. The backbone interconnects regional networks. Regional networks implement a star topology with tunnels that fan out to connect

**M**

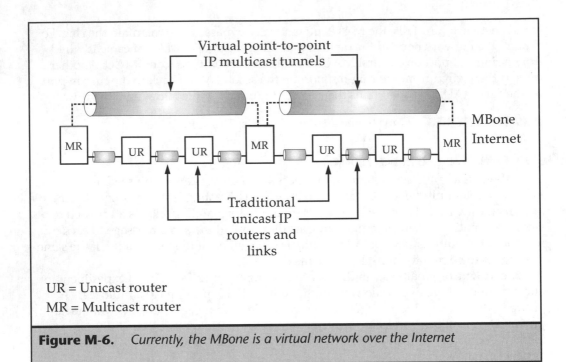

UR = Unicast router

MR = Multicast router

**Figure M-6.** *Currently, the MBone is a virtual network over the Internet*

with MBone participants in that area. There are also tunnels that interconnect countries, including tunnels that span the Atlantic and Pacific Oceans. The MBone implements a metric system that assigns a "weight" to each tunnel. This weighting system minimizes traffic congestion by keeping packets local to where they belong.

*NOTE: There are several Internet sites that provide maps and 3D visualizations of the MBone. Check the listing at the end of this section.*

The MBone is a cooperative system. When someone wants to add a new regional network, a request is made on the MBone mailing list (available at http://www.mbone.com). Other MBone participants close to the regional network then work with the new regional network to set up tunnels. If an organization wants to add its own network to the MBone, the regional MBone network operator should be contacted. This is where the MBone map comes in handy. You can view the latest version of this map at http://www.cs.berkeley.edu/~elan/mbone.html.

A typical user needs a high-speed connection to fully experience what the MBone can deliver. The usual recommendation is a 128-Kbit/sec (ISDN) or greater connection. Users also need a connection to an ISP (Internet service provider) that supports IP multicast and MBone connections. Software requirements for the user's system include multicast-aware applications and underlying multicast protocols including IGMP (Internet Group Management Protocol). IGMP talks with local multicast-aware routers and is discussed under "Multicasting." You can also refer to that topic to learn how a single multicast packet is distributed to multiple recipients on the Internet. Note that multicasting techniques can also be applied to internal intranets and used by collaborative applications to support groups of users within an organization.

**RELATED ENTRIES**    Internet; IP (Internet Protocol); Multicasting; RSVP (Resource Reservation Protocol); *and* RTP (Real-time Transport Protocol)

## INFORMATION ON THE INTERNET

| | |
|---|---|
| IETF MBone Deployment (mboned) page | http://www.ietf.org/html.charters/mboned-charter.html |
| IETF drafts (search for "mbone") | http://www.internic.net/ds/dsintdrafts.html |
| ICAST's MBone information | http://www.mbone.com |
| MBone FAQ | http://www.mbone.com/mbone/mbone.faq.html |
| MBone links | http://www.mbone.com/mbone/misc.html |
| Visualization of the MBone (3-D pictures) | http://www.nlanr.net/Viz/Mbone |
| Major MBone Routers and Links map | ftp://ftp.isi.edu/mbone/mbone-topology.gif |
| Map of the MBone | http://www.cs.berkeley.edu/~elan/mbone.html |
| Bryan O'Sullivan's Internet Multicast Backbone page | http://ganges.cs.tcd.ie/4ba2/multicast/bryan |
| University of Cambridge MBone page | http://www.cl.cam.ac.uk/mbone |
| MBone Information page | http://mojo.ots.utexas.edu/netinfo/mbone.html |
| MBONE Deployment Working Group (MBONED) | http://ns.uoregon.edu/~meyer/MBONED |

# MCI

MCI Telecommunications has an interesting history that is tied to the creation of the original Internet. In 1969, the U.S. Defense Department agency called ARPA (Advanced Research Projects Agency) created ARPANET, the first wide area, packet-switching network. Then, in 1986, the NSF (National Science Foundation) established its own network, NSFnet, which eventually assumed ARPANET's role (ARPANET was retired in 1990).

*M*

MCI, along with Merit Network Inc. and IBM, managed the NSFnet backbone until 1995, when the NSFnet was shut down and backbone services were handled on a competitive basis by a small group of commercial backbone providers, including MCI, PSINet, UUNET, ANS/AOL, and Sprint. These providers interconnected at a series of NAPs (network access points).

Currently, MCI is one of the largest global Internet backbone operators. In the United States, MCI maintains about 500 POPs (points of presence) as well as 18 major Internet backbone node sites. Concert InternetPlus, a joint effort by MCI and British Telecom, combines the existing Internet networks of the two companies into regional "superhubs" around the world.

MCI currently has a contract to develop the vBNS (Very high speed Backbone Network Service) for the National Science Foundation, which will provide massive amounts of bandwidth for voice, data, and video. The current goal is a backbone that provides up to 2 Gbits/sec of throughput.

Vint Cerf, one of the coinventors of TCP/IP and one of the pioneer developers of the ARPANET packet networks, is currently senior vice president of Internet architecture at MCI.

MCI's original network was built with microwave communication systems, but it has been switching to fiber-optic cabling systems. In fact, MCI stands for Microwave Communications, Inc., although the company has distanced itself from that name because it no longer matches the technologies used by the company. MCI's network is 100 percent digital. In 1997, MCI deployed Quad-WDM (four-wavelength wave division multiplexing) into its network, boosting transmission rates to 40 Gbits/sec. MCI's network capacity quadrupled, allowing four times the amount of traffic along existing fiber lines. In 1996, MCI quadrupled the speed of its Internet backbone to 622 Mbits/sec.

**RELATED ENTRIES**    Communication Service Providers; Internet; IXC (Interexchange Carrier); *and* Telecommunications and Telephone Systems

### INFORMATION ON THE INTERNET

MCI Telecommunications Corp.          http://www.mci.com

# Medium Access Control Methods

LANs (local area networks) are typically shared by a number of attached systems, and only one system at a time can use the network cable to transmit data. Access methods (also called medium access control, or MAC) are the rules defined within a specific network type that determine how each station accesses the cable. Simultaneous access to the cable is either prevented by using a token-passing method or a carrier sensing and collision detection method.

The primary access methods are *carrier sensing* and *token passing*. A third, *demand priority*, is implemented in 100VG-AnyLAN, a 100-Mbit/sec Ethernet standard.

- **ALOHA**  Developed in the 1970s, this technique lets users transmit on broadcast networks whenever they have data to send. Since the data is broadcast, the transmitting station can listen for its own broadcasts. If a collision occurs because another station is broadcasting, the station "hears" it and waits a random amount of time before retransmitting. See "ALOHA."

- **CSMA/CD (carrier sense multiple access/collision detection)**  Carrier sensing implies that network nodes listen for a carrier tone on the cable and send information when other devices are not transmitting. Multiple access means that many devices share the same cable. If two or more devices sense that the network is idle, they attempt to access it simultaneously (contention), causing collisions. Each station must then back off and wait a certain amount of time before attempting to retransmit. Delays caused by contention are lowered by reducing the number of workstations on the LAN. This is the standard Ethernet medium access method. See "CSMA/CD (Carrier Sense Multiple Access/Collision Detection)" for more information.

- **Demand priority access method**  This is a "round-robin" polling access method used in the Ethernet 100VG-AnyLAN (IEEE 802) networking scheme. A central hub scans all its ports in a round-robin fashion to detect stations that want to transmit. When a port is scanned on which a station needs to transmit, the hub allows the station to transmit one frame. A station can request a higher priority if it needs to transmit real-time information like video or audio. See "100VG-AnyLAN" and "Demand Priority Access Method" for more information.

- **Token passing**  ARCNET, token ring, and FDDI (Fiber Distributed Data Interface) networks use the token-passing access method. A workstation must have possession of a token before it can begin transmission. The token is passed around the network and acquired by any station that needs to transmit. See "Token and Token-Passing Access Methods."

There are other access methods such as DQDB (Distributed Queue Dual Bus) used with metropolitan area networks and CDPD (Cellular Digital Packet Data) used for wireless communications. Multiplexing is the technique for combining multiple channels of information onto a single circuit. A relatively new access protocol called WDMA (Wavelength Division Multiple Access) provides multichannel transmission capabilities on fiber-optic networks.

**RELATED ENTRIES**    ALOHA; CDPD (Cellular Digital Packet Data); DQDB (Distributed Queue Dual Bus); Ethernet; FDDI (Fiber Distributed Data Interface); MAC (Medium Access Control); Multiplexing; Token Ring Network; *and* WDMA (Wavelength Division Multiple Access)

## Merchant Services
*See* Electronic Commerce.

*M*

## Message-Oriented Middleware

*See* MOM (Message-Oriented Middleware).

## Messaging Systems

*See* Electronic Mail; MAPI (Messaging Application Programming Interface); *and* Middleware and Messaging.

## MIB (Management Information Base)

A MIB is defined as part of SNMP (Simple Network Management Protocol), a network management protocol used in TCP/IP environments. With an SNMP-compatible network management system, network administrators can monitor and manage computers and other devices (such as routers and printers) connected to the network.

A MIB is a data file that contains a complete collection of all the objects that are managed in a network. *Objects* in this case is a misleading term because it implies that an object is a physical entity. Instead, objects are variables that hold information about the state of some process running on a device or that include textual information about the device, such as a name and description. This information is strictly defined so that different management systems can access and use the information.

A particular device has many objects that describe it. An *SNMP agent* runs in each SNMP-managed device and is responsible for updating object variables. The management system then queries the SNMP agent to gain information about a system. In contrast, the agent may also alert the management system about special events on a device.

There are groups of objects, such as "system," "interface," "IP," and "TCP." System is a MIB group that contains objects that hold variables such as a device's name, its location, and other descriptive information. The interface group holds information about network adapters and tracks statistics such as bytes sent and received on the interface. The IP group has objects that track packet flow, packet fragmentation, dropped packets, and similar information. The TCP group has objects that keep track of connections.

**RELATED ENTRIES**    Network Management; SNMP (Simple Network Management Protocol)

## Microkernel

*See* Kernel.

## Microsoft

Microsoft Corporation was founded in 1975 by William H. Gates and Paul G. Allen. In 1981, Microsoft and IBM introduced MS-DOS and started the personal computer revolution. Today, Microsoft focuses on producing and marketing a broad range of products for personal computing, including development tools and languages, application software, systems software, hardware peripherals, books, and multimedia applications. Microsoft products of interest to network administrators and users are covered under the related entries given next.

**RELATED ENTRIES**   Active Platform, Microsoft; ActiveX; DCOM (Distributed Component Object Model); Microsoft BackOffice; Microsoft Exchange Server; Microsoft Transaction Server; Windows; Windows NT Directory Services; *and* Windows NT Server

### INFORMATION ON THE INTERNET

| | |
|---|---|
| Microsoft's Internet information and products | http://www.microsoft.com/internet |
| Internet developer information | http://www.microsoft.com/workshop |
| Microsoft's intranet products | http://www.microsoft.com/intranet |
| Microsoft's Developer Network (MSDN) | http://www.microsoft.com/msdn |
| Microsoft's Technical Support | http://www.microsoft.com/support |

## Microsoft BackOffice

Microsoft BackOffice is a suite of server-based business and productivity applications that run on Windows NT Server systems. These applications, described next, take full advantage of the security features of Windows NT, including directory services, user account logon, access control lists, auditing, and more.

*NOTE:  For additional information, visit Microsoft's BackOffice Web site at http://www.microsoft.com/backoffice.*

**MICROSOFT SQL SERVER**   The Microsoft SQL Server is the relational database component for managing and storing data. It provides distributed client/server RDBMS (relational database management system) components and is the foundation for an integrated set of data management products that includes development tools, system management tools, data replication processes, and open development environments. Refer to "Distributed Database" and  "SQL (Structured Query Language)" for related information.

**MICROSOFT SNA SERVER**   The Microsoft SNA Server is the host connectivity component that provides Windows, Macintosh, DOS, and OS/2 clients with access to

**M**

AS/400 and IBM mainframes. Refer to "IBM (International Business Machines)" and "SNA (Systems Network Architecture)" for more general information.

**MICROSOFT SYSTEMS MANAGEMENT SERVER** The Microsoft Systems Management Server is the network management component that reduces support and administrative costs by providing a central location for managing network hardware and software, software distribution, troubleshooting, and application management. Refer to "Network Management" for more general information.

**MICROSOFT EXCHANGE SERVER** The Microsoft Exchange Server is made up of the electronic mail and messaging components that provide a messaging infrastructure for electronic mail and collaborative computing applications. Microsoft Mail is the predecessor of Microsoft Exchange Server. For more information, see "Electronic Mail," and "Microsoft Exchange Server."

**MICROSOFT INTERNET INFORMATION SERVER** The Microsoft IIS (Internet Information Server) is the Web server component that is included with Windows NT itself without additional charge. For more information, see "Web Technologies and Concepts."

An installed Windows NT Server system is required before you can install the BackOffice components. These components take full advantage of the performance-enhancing features of the Windows NT Server as well as the administrative and client support features. The Windows NT Server and the entire BackOffice suite are modular products. You can add components and build custom applications on the BackOffice platform as your needs grow. As the core of the BackOffice platform, Windows NT provides the advantages outlined next. See "Windows NT Server" for more details.

- The Windows NT Server provides authentication services and secure data transfers, and meets C2-level security guidelines.

- Users log on once to gain access to shared resources on the SQL Server, the SNA Server, the Exchange Server, and the System Management Server. It is not necessary to maintain separate account databases on each system.

- BackOffice products make use of the networking support built into the Windows NT Server, including support for popular networks such as Ethernet and token ring, as well as popular protocols such as TCP/IP, IPX, and NetBEUI.

- Support is provided for different hardware platforms, including Intel-based PCs and servers, DEC Alpha, MIPS, and PowerPC systems. Symmetrical multiprocessing systems are also supported.

**RELATED ENTRIES** Active Platform, Microsoft; ActiveX; DCOM (Distributed Component Object Model); Microsoft; Microsoft Exchange Server; Microsoft

Transaction Server; ODBC (Open Database Connectivity), Microsoft; Windows; Windows NT Directory Services; *and* Windows NT Server

## Microsoft Exchange Server

Microsoft Exchange provides enterprise-wide information exchange by integrating electronic mail, scheduling, electronic forms, and document sharing. It also provides a basis for creating special applications that can take advantage of an enterprise-wide messaging system. With Microsoft Exchange, organizations create an enterprise-wide message system that gives everyone in the organization quick access to information. Exchange also connects with the Internet and other networks outside the organization to provide global messaging.

> **NOTE:** *Visit http://www.microsoft.com/backoffice on the Web to get more information about Microsoft Exchange.*

Exchange is a client/server product that is provided in the form of Exchange Server and Exchange clients:

- **Exchange Server**   The Exchange Server is the "engine" for exchanging information, both throughout the enterprise and outside the enterprise. It runs on top of the Windows NT Server operating system and takes full advantage of the features that the Windows NT Server provides.

- **Exchange clients**   Exchange clients run on Windows 3.1, Windows for Workgroups 3.11, Windows NT, Windows 95, Microsoft DOS, Macintosh, and UNIX computers. A client provides an environment where users can create, send, receive, view, and store messages or other types of information. Clients support features like file and object attachments (objects may be sound, video, text, or other data), address book management, and information exchange with other services like CompuServe and the Internet.

Microsoft Exchange supports *electronic forms* so that workgroups can exchange "structured" information that can be distributed throughout the enterprise. In addition, *public folders* serve as repositories for shared messages, forms, documents, applications, and databases. These folders can be replicated to other locations, placing information closer to users who need it and reducing network traffic. Exchange synchronizes replicated folders to ensure that users are working with the latest information. Shared *discussion databases,* similar to bulletin board chat sessions, are also supported in Exchange so that people can have a place to field and discuss ideas.

An example of how shared folders and information exchange can benefit an organization is best seen in the example of a customer-support organization. Problems that have been tackled by one support person can be documented in a shared database. Other support people can check this database before working on similar problems. Similarly, ideas can be shared and discussed companywide. Shared

**M**

discussion databases provide a perfect place to exchange ideas. People can read a history of a conversation and reply at any time. This eliminates the constraints of one-time meetings and phone conversations that are not documented for others to review.

Exchange provides messaging services, information services, directory services, and connectivity services. It also supports remote access, X.400 messaging standards, Internet mail standards, IBM PROFS/OfficeVision, and IBM SNADS (SNA Distributed Services) gateways. Exchange supports MAPI (Messaging Application Programming Interface) so you can create custom message-enabled applications, and ODBC (Open Database Connectivity) so you can access stored information in a variety of data formats.

**RELATED ENTRIES**    Collaborative Computing; Electronic Mail; Groupware; Lotus Notes; MAPI (Messaging Application Programming Interface); Microsoft; Microsoft BackOffice; Windows; Windows NT Directory Services; Windows NT Server; *and* Workflow Management

## Microsoft LAN Manager

Microsoft LAN Manager is a network operating system that ran on Microsoft's version of OS/2. The product was also marketed by IBM as IBM LAN Server. Both products have been superseded by new products. In the case of Microsoft, LAN Manager was replaced by Windows NT Server, a self-sufficient operating system that does not require OS/2. In the case of IBM, LAN Server was replaced with OS/2 Warp Server. See "OS/2 Warp Server" for details.

Windows NT Server maintains compatibility with servers running LAN Manager. It also includes many of the features that were in the original LAN Manager product. For example, Windows NT Server builds on the LAN Manager domain model and includes enhancements of its own. Instead of requiring a user account for each domain, users can have a single networkwide logon. In addition, Windows NT Server has much better security features.

**RELATED ENTRIES**    Microsoft; Windows NT Server

## Microsoft Transaction Server

Microsoft Transaction Server, or MTS, as it is called here, is a product for developing and deploying distributed applications that require reliable transaction-processing monitors. MTS is specifically designed to work with new categories of component-based applications that work over intranets or the Internet. In particular, MTS simplifies the development of applications that require transaction processing.

A transaction-processing system groups multiple operations into all-or-nothing transactions. In other words, all the operations are guaranteed to complete successfully, or they are backed out on each system where they were attempted so the operation can be tried again. You might imagine a musical group that is recording a song. If one of the musicians plays off key or misses a beat, everyone stops playing and the recording is started over. In a business transaction, multiple databases must coordinate write activities so that all the databases are synchronized. Imagine a bank moving money from one account to another. If those accounts are stored on different systems, communication errors can cause serious problems such as when money deducted from one account is not deposited into the other account. A transaction system monitors the transaction to make sure it completes. Refer to "Transaction Processing" for details on how this process works.

Traditionally, transaction processing has taken place among big database systems, but today millions of desktop computers are connected to the Internet and participating in electronic commerce that involves transaction processing across multiple remote systems. Coordinating these transactions is even more critical because of the unpredictable nature of the Internet.

MTS is based on traditional transaction-processing methods that have been used for many years in the computer industry. However, MTS extends these methods into the component-based software arena by providing a development environment for building transaction-enabled applications with ActiveX components. MTS provides "middleware" functionality in that it hides the complexities of transaction processing from the program developers, allowing developers to concentrate on the functionality of their applications.

Microsoft's COM (Component Object Model) provides a platform for integrating components within a single system. DCOM (Distributed COM) provides similar functionality over networks, allowing users or developers to integrate components in one system with a component in another system. DCOM is now ActiveX. What MTS brings is a framework for building integrity into component-based applications. It can ensure that concurrent transactions are atomic, consistent, and durable once committed. These features are described under "Transaction Processing."

Microsoft described MTS as an infrastructure product that can address a broad range of requirements in developing and deploying multitier applications. Multitier applications consist of client applications, application servers, and back-end database systems that store and provide access to information. The application servers reside in the middle tier and provide application logic. Clients communicate with the application server using a variety of protocols (such as HTTP or RPCs). Application servers communicate with back-end databases with SQL (Structured Query Language).

## Microsoft Transaction Server Components

The architectural elements of MTS are described here. This section provides only brief information. For more detailed information, visit the Microsoft Web site given at the end of this section. MTS-compatible applications are built with ActiveX components. Connectivity among components running in the same system is provided by Windows interprocess communication capabilities. Remote connectivity is provided by TCP/IP networking. The *Transaction Server Executive* provides run-time services and context management. *Server processes* run on server computers and host the execution of

**M**

application components. *Resource managers* are system services that ensure that committed updates to data survive failures in communication, processing, or hardware. Finally, *resource dispensers* maintain a pool of database connections and allocate those connections as they are needed to improve performance.

### Microsoft DTC (Distributed Transaction Coordinator)

MS DTC is the entity that monitors and manages transactions in Microsoft's COM architecture. It coordinates transactions between components. The basic steps performed in a DTC-controlled transaction are outlined here:

1. When a transaction begins, a *transaction object* is created by the TM (Transaction Manager) to represent the transaction.

2. The application that initiated the transaction makes calls to RMs (resource managers), which are participants in the transaction. RMs are typically tied to relational databases.

3. The TM tracks the activities of the RMs during the transaction. If a problem occurs, the TM aborts the transaction. If the application that called the transaction completes its work, the DTC can commit the transaction changes to the databases.

A two-phase commit protocol is executed upon success of the transaction. In the first phase of this commit, the RMs must signal that they are prepared to commit changes to the database. If all the RMs respond positively, then the second phase of the commit proceeds, which is to actually write the changes to the database. The RMs must signal that they wrote the changes successfully. If a response is not received from any RM during any phase of the commit, then the transaction is aborted. This procedure ensures that data is written to all the databases involved in exactly the same way, or is not written at all.

**RELATED ENTRIES**   ActiveX; COM (Component Object Model); Component Software Technology; DCOM (Distributed Component Object Model); Distributed Object Computing; Middleware and Messaging; Multitiered Architectures; Object Technologies; ORB (Object Request Broker); *and* Transaction Processing

### INFORMATION ON THE INTERNET

Microsoft's Transaction Server site        http://www.microsoft.com/transaction

## Microwave Communications

Microwaves are located in the frequency range above 1,000 MHz, i.e., above the 1.3 GHz band. A typical microwave oven has an electron tube that generates a 2.45 GHz microwave to heat leftovers. Microwave communication systems can transmit through air and open space and are the most widely used "long-haul" transmission method in the United States. Transmission frequencies are from 2 to 25 GHz, with the higher bandwidths used in short-haul private networks.

Microwave transmission is useful when cable is difficult or impractical to use and a straight line of sight is available between two points, such as:

- Satellite to ground links
- Between two buildings in a metropolitan area
- Across wide open areas where it isn't practical to lay cable, such as deserts, swamps, and large lakes

A microwave transmission system consists of two directional antennas in which beams of radio-wave energy are focused in a point-to-point configuration, as shown here:

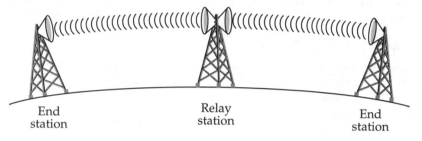

| End station | Relay station | End station |

Generally, the antennas need to be pointed at one another, but exact alignment (line of sight) is only critical as the frequency increases and the beam becomes more tightly focused. The curvature of the earth affects the distance between antennas, so the higher the tower on which the antenna is mounted, the more distance between them. An antenna mounted on a 300-foot tower can focus on an antenna 50 miles away. Of course, obstacles such as buildings and mountains must not stand between towers. Radio transceivers (*trans*mitter/re*ceivers*) are located at each tower to send and receive signals.

Unlike a radio broadcast that sends signals in all directions, microwave antennas are point-to-point communication systems. Relay stations equipped with signal amplifiers extend transmissions over much longer distances. A relay station consists of two antennas, each focused on a distant antenna in a different direction.

Higher bandwidths are susceptible to weather conditions such as rain and fog because the shorter wavelengths are more easily absorbed by water. Decreasing the distance helps. Many vendors now supply products that operate in the high microwave ranges for short-haul applications. Technical advances also reduce the problems of weather. The range has become popular because the lower frequencies are overcrowded.

Microwave is an alternative to metal or optical cable systems. Installation of a small system is often relatively simple. For example, you can establish a microwave communication link between two buildings by mounting an antenna in a window of each building and focusing the antennas together. Such systems provide considerable

**M**

savings by bypassing the local exchange carrier. In campus environments, microwave systems may be more practical than burying cable.

A typical microwave user is an organization that has offices over five miles apart in metropolitan areas. Universities are common users, as are hospitals and city/county governments. CATV service providers use microwave systems to link their networks. The telephone companies also use microwave extensively along with fiber-optic cable to replace older analog systems. As the cellular communication system expands, service providers are using microwave systems to interconnect the system. Microwave systems are also used as backup lines to provide continuous service in case other transmission systems fail.

Andrew Corporation (708) 349-3300 has a catalog of Microwave products.

**RELATED ENTRIES**    Network Concepts; Private Network; Satellite Communication Systems; Telecommunications and Telephone Systems; *and* Wireless Communications

### INFORMATION ON THE INTERNET

| | |
|---|---|
| The U.S. Department of Commerce (an interesting paper describing microwave trends, technical developments, and government spectrum allocation) | http://www.ita.doc.gov/industry/tai/telecom/microwve.txt |
| Microwave Journal | http://www.mwjournal.com |
| RF Globalnet education and information center for RF, microwave, and wireless | http://www.rfmicrowave.com |

## Middleware and Messaging

Middleware is a layer of software or functionality that sits between one system (usually a client) and another system (usually a server) and provides a way for those systems to exchange information or connect with one another even though they have different interfaces. Messaging is one of the methods that has become integral to the way that middleware is implemented.

Middleware and messaging may be employed within an organization to tie together its LAN and legacy systems, its diverse clients and back-end databases, and its local and remote systems. Middleware is also coming into widespread use on the Internet as a way to run sophisticated client/server applications with integral transaction processing, security, and management, something that is difficult to do with current Web protocols such as HTTP (Hypertext Transfer Protocol).

Here are some basic definitions of middleware:

- Middleware helps applications work together across multiple platforms or operating system environments.

- Developers write applications that interface with the middleware layer rather than recreating the functions that the middleware layer can provide.

- Middleware is used in the enterprise to make client/server applications work across the enterprise network.

- Middleware is used on the Internet to tie users together with servers at locations that are potentially worldwide.

## Types of Middleware

The following types of middleware are available for building distributed applications, heterogeneous networks, and Internet-based distributed software systems.

- **Database middleware** A layer of software that lets clients access database systems from a variety of operating systems or applications. Microsoft's ODBC (Open Database Connectivity) now fills this role in many systems. Microsoft's OLE DB provides similar services. See "Database Connectivity" for more information.

- **Web middleware** This is a relatively new category that encompasses many of the features of the above-mentioned middleware. It basically provides a way for companies to put new and legacy information systems and applications on the Web. See "Web Middleware and Database Connectivity" for more information.

- **MOM (message-oriented middleware)** Asynchronous message passing between a source or destination that does not require that the sender wait for a response. See "MOM (Message-Oriented Middleware)" for more information.

- **ORBs (object request brokers)** Sometimes referred to as a *logical bus,* an ORB provides an interface that objects can use to communicate with other objects in distributed network environments. However, not all systems are object-oriented, especially legacy systems, so ORBs may be limited in some environments. See "ORB (Object Request Broker)" for more information.

- **RPCs (remote procedure calls)** RPCs provide methods for linking clients and servers across networks. They are synchronous in that the requesting application waits for a response from the server. See "RPC (Remote Procedure Call)" for more information.

- **TP (transaction processing) monitors** Provides a high level of monitoring and control for processes occurring between objects to ensure that operations complete successfully. If even one of the operations fails, all operations are rolled back. See "Transaction Processing" for more information.

*M*

■ **E-mail middleware**  A kind of middleware that lets users of different e-mail systems exchange mail. Refer to "Electronic Mail" for more information.

Complete development environments exist which provide many of the features described above, in addition to authentication and authorization services, distribution and management services, directory services, and time services.

See "DCE (Distributed Computing Environment), The Open Group" for an example of middleware that supports building heterogeneous networks. See "Netscape ONE Development Environment" for an example of a development environment that takes advantage of Web protocols.

## Web Middleware

Using middleware for Web-based client/server development is quite a bit different than using middleware for in-house use. Instead of developing applications to tie together a variety of in-house clients and servers, applications reach out to potentially millions of global users.

Many middleware vendors have successfully made the Web transition in their products. The usual technique is to add support for HTTP and HTML (Hypertext Markup Language). However, these protocols are really only appropriate for Web publishing, not running sophisticated mission-critical applications over the Web that require transaction monitoring. A more common technique is to bypass HTTP and its limitations. Many vendors do this using proprietary calls between the client and server. Another method is to use CORBA and its industry standard IIOP (Internet Inter-ORB Protocol), which can bypass HTTP. The Web server only gets involved when the user first contacts the Web site. Components are downloaded and a connection-oriented session is initiated. In this case, the Web browser is more like an Internet program launcher that gets out of the way.

One of the primary reasons for bypassing HTTP is that it does not provide state management. That is, clients send requests to servers, but there is no session connection between the systems. If a user clicks a button on a Web page that was just received, another connection must be set up. Client/server applications, on the other hand, rely on state management. A transaction usually involves some critical operation that must be monitored to completion. A session is established so that both systems can exchange data and status information about the session. Data may be written to multiple locations, and the monitor must ensure that all those writes are completed. Products that include this state management include Microsoft Transaction Server and BEA Systems' BEA Jolt (which uses Tuxedo transaction monitoring).

Note that many middleware products are also development environments that provide middleware interface components as well as tools for building Java and ActiveX components to work with the systems. This topic is carried further under "Web Middleware and Database Connectivity."

**RELATED ENTRIES**   Client/Server Computing; Component Software Technology; CORBA (Common Object Request Broker Architecture); Database Connectivity; DCE (Distributed Computing Environment), The Open Group; DCOM (Distributed Component Object Model); Distributed Applications; Distributed Computer Networks; Distributed Database; Distributed Object Computing; IIOP (Internet Inter-ORB Protocol); Multitiered Architectures; Netscape ONE Development Environment; Object Technologies; ODBC (Open Database Connectivity), Microsoft; OLE DB; The Open Group; Oracle NCA (Network Computing Architecture); ORB (Object Request Broker); SQL (Structured Query Language); Sun Microsystems Solaris NEO; Transaction Processing; Web Middleware and Database Connectivity; *and* Web Technologies and Concepts

## INFORMATION ON THE INTERNET

| | |
|---|---|
| MOMA (Message-Oriented Middleware Association) | http://www.moma-inc.org |
| Innergy's middleware links | http://www.innergy.com/webdata.html |
| The Lewis Group's Roadmap to the Middleware Kingdom | http://www.lewisgroup.com/wpapers/mdlwre01.htm |
| AFP Technology Ltd. (search for "middleware") | http://www.afptech.com |
| Active Software's ActiveWeb | http://www.activesw.com |
| BEA Systems' Jolt | http://www.beasys.com |
| Bluestone Software's Sapphire | http://www.bluestone.com |
| Digital Equipment's ObjectBroker | http://www.digital.com |
| Expersoft's PowerBroker | http://www.expersoft.com |
| Hewlett-Packard's ORB Plus | http://www.hp.com |
| IBM's Component Broker Connector (CBConnector) | http://www.software.ibm.com |
| IONA Technologies' Orbix | http://www.iona.com |
| Microsoft's Transaction Server | http://www.microsoft.com |
| Oracle's NCA | http://www.oracle.com/nca |
| PeopleSoft, Inc. | http://www.peoplesoft.com |
| SAP | http://www.sap.com |
| Sun Microsystems' Solaris NEO | http://www.sun.com/solaris/neo |
| Visigenic's VisiBroker | http://www.visigenic.com |
| Wayfarer Communications' QuickServer | http://www.wayfarer.com |

**M**

# MIME (Multipurpose Internet Mail Extension)

MIME is an IETF (Internet Engineering Task Force) standard defined in 1992 for sending a variety of different types of information (data types) via Internet electronic mail. Traditional electronic mail messages handled text only. What MIME does is provide standard ways to encode data types for transmission in electronic mail. MIME supports binary files, non US-ASCII character sets, images, sound, video, and documents that are stored in special formats (such as compressed files). MIME also supports special fonts in the message itself.

MIME was designed to be backward compatible with the previous Internet e-mail standard (http://www.internic.net/rfc/rfc822.txt), which was strictly a text-oriented mail messaging system. While the e-mail system defined in RFC 822 worked well at the time, it clearly has limitations given today's multimedia data types.

A typical e-mail message consists of a header that include the fields Data, To, From, and Subject, followed by the text of the message. The limitations of the original RFC 822 specification include a requirement that lines cannot exceed 1,000 characters and that data must be 7-bit ASCII characters, which excludes foreign characters. To overcome these limitations, RFC 1049 (1988) added a header that could describe a particular format for the message content, although the entire content had to be the same.

MIME's contributions, as outlined in RFC 1521, are multipart attachments for messages and a way for users to choose the type of encoding they want to use. Each part of the message can hold a different data type. One way to understand MIME messages is to envision two or more separate e-mail messages, each with different data types, that are bundled together into a single message. Each part of the message is called a *body part* and can contain text, graphics, audio, or video.

MIME adds two lines to the header of an e-mail message. The first line indicates the MIME version and the second line to indicate how MIME body parts are formatted in the message. A typical header looks like this:

```
MIME-Version: 1.0
From: Tom Sheldon <tsheldon@ntresearch.com>
To: Dan Logan <dlogan@thegrid.net>
Subject: Your newsletter
Content-Type: multipart/mixed;boundary=boundary_marker
```

Note the first line indicates the MIME version number. The last line indicates that the content type is multipart (there are multiple parts to the message), and that each part is separated by a line that reads "boundary_marker." An example of a two-part message is shown here:

```
MIME-Version: 1.0
From: Tom Sheldon <tsheldon@ntresearch.com>
To: Dan Logan <dlogan@thegrid.net>
```

```
Subject: Your newsletter
Content-Type: multipart/mixed;boundary=boundary_marker

--boundary_marker
Content-Type: text/plain; charset=US-ASCII
      plain text here
--boundary_marker
 Content-Type: audio/basic
Content-Transfer-Encoding: base64
      audio data goes here
```

Note the two attached parts beginning with the text "--boundary_marker." The first contains plain text while the second contains audio. Each of the MIME headers is described here:

- **MIME-Version**   This indicates that the message conforms to MIME. This field is required.

- **Content-Type**   This header indicates the type of data as described in Table M-1. Each body part in the message can be preceded by a Content-Type. There are seven major content types and a number of subtypes.

- **Content-Transfer-Encoding**   This indicates the encoding method used on the body part. The encoding method is described in Table M-2.

- **Content-ID**   This is an optional field that uniquely identifies a body part for reference elsewhere.

- **Content-Description**   This is another optional that can be used to describe a body part.

If security and privacy are desired, users have a range of e-mail encryption techniques to choose from. S/MIME (Secure MIME) is an RSA Data Security specification for securing electronic mail. Information on S/MIME is available at the S/MIME FAQ site listed at the end of this topic. Other security schemes include Philip Zimmerman's PGP (Pretty Good Privacy), an encryption product that is available at http://www.pgp.com. See "PGP (Pretty Good Privacy)" for more information.

**MIME RFCs ON THE INTERNET**   MIME is defined in a number of different Internet RFCs, including RFC 822 (the original Internet mail definition), RFC 1049, RFC 1154, RFC 1521, RFC 1522, RFC 2045, RFC 2046, RFC 2047, RFC 2048, and RFC 2049. You can view these RFCs by entering the following address in your Web browser, replacing *nnnn* with the number of the RFC you want to view: http://www.internic.net/ rfc/rfc*nnnn*.txt.

**RELATED ENTRIES**   Electronic Mail; Groupware; IMAP (Internet Mail Access Protocol); Information Publishing; Lotus Notes; Microsoft Exchange Server;

**M**

| Content Type | Subtype | Description |
|---|---|---|
| Text | Plain | Unformatted text information |
| | Richtext | Formatted text information |
| Multipart | Mixed | Indicates multiple body parts of different data types delineated by boundaries |
| | Alternative | Indicates multiple body parts with the same data in different formats |
| | Digest | Indicates multiple body parts, all the same format |
| | Parallel | Indicates multiple body parts to be viewed simultaneously |
| Message | RFC822 | Indicates RFC 822 body part |
| | Partial | Indicates messages has been fragmented for transportation |
| | External-body | Indicates that external data should be referenced, such as data at ftp sites |
| Application | Octet-stream | Indicates uninterpreted binary data |
| | PostScript | Indicates a PostScript document |
| | SGML | Indicates SGML data |
| Image | JPEG | JPEG image data |
| | GIF | GIF image data |
| Audio | Basic | Audio data for playback on compatible hardware |
| Video | MPEG | MPEG video data for playback on compatible hardware |

**Table M-1.** *MIME Content Types*

Multmedia; PGP (Pretty Good Privacy); POP (Post Office Protocol); SMTP (Simple Mail Transfer Protocol); *and* Workflow Management

| Encoding Type | Description |
|---|---|
| 7-bit | US-ASCII characters in 1,000 character lines |
| 8-bit | Indicates 1,000 character lines US-ASCII and extended ASCII (8-bit) characters. |
| Quoted-printable | Indicates the text contains extended ASCII characters that have been encoded by replacing the character with an equal sign and the hex value for the character |
| Base64 | Indicates the data is in Base64 format, which converts 8-bit data to 7-bit data for transfer by SMTP |
| Binary | Indicates non-ASCII characters |
| X-token | Indicates a proprietary encoding scheme |

**Table M-2.**   *MIME Encoding Types*

### INFORMATION ON THE INTERNET

| | |
|---|---|
| IETF drafts (search for "mime") | http://www.internic.net/ds/dsintdrafts.html |
| Douglas W. Sauder's MIME Information page | http://www.fwb.gulf.net/~dwsauder/mime.html |
| Internet Mail Consortium | http://www.imc.org |
| Electronic Messaging Association | http://www.ema.org |
| MIME FAQ | http://www.cis.ohio-state.edu/text/faq/usenet/mail/mime-faq/top.html |
| S/MIME FAQ (Frequently Asked Questions) | http://www.rsa.com/smime/html/faq.html |
| MIME media types | http://www.isi.edu/in-notes/iana/assignments/media-types/media-types |

## MIPS (Million Instructions per Second)

Microprocessors are rated according to the number of instructions they can execute per second. The rating can be used to compare different vendors' processors if you assume they will run similar applications. The following information is provided by Intel.

| | |
|---|---|
| Intel 8088 (5 to 8 MHz) | 0.33 to 0.75 MIPS |
| Intel 80286 (8 to 12 MHz) | 1.2 to 2.66 MIPS |
| Intel386 DX CPU (16 to 33 MHz) | 5 to 11.4 MIPS |

**M**

| | |
|---|---|
| Intel486 DX CPU (25 to 100 MHz) | 20 to 70.7 MIPS |
| Intel Pentium 100 MHz | 166.3 MIPS, 3.30 SPECint95 |
| Intel Pentium 150 MHz | 4.27 SPECint95 |
| Intel Pentium 200 MHz | 5.47 SPECint95 |
| Intel Pentium MMX 200 MHz | 6.41 SPECint95 |
| Intel Pentium Pro 200 MHz | 8.09 SPECint95 |
| Intel Pentium MMX 300 MHz | 12.0 SPECint95 |

You can find more information on processor speeds at the Intel Web site (http://www.intel.com). Note that Intel is now rating its chips according SPECint95, an industry-standard workstation benchmark test developed by the Standard Performance Evaluation Corp., or SPEC (http://www.specbench.org).

Some engineers have predicted that one million MIPS processors will be available by the year 2000. Also, note that supercomputers and mainframe systems have already achieved these speeds.

## Mirroring

Mirroring is the process of duplicating stored data on a second storage device in real time so that both devices hold the same information. Mirroring is a form of fault tolerance that protects data from equipment failure. There are several different types of mirroring, as described here and pictured in Figure M-7.

- **Mirroring**  Data is copied from on-disk controller (channel) to two disk drivers. If one drive fails, the other is still operational.

- **Duplexing**  Data is duplicated over two disk channels and stored on two drives. This method extends fault tolerance to the controller.

- **Server duplexing**  This method provides fault tolerance by duplicating the entire file server. If one server fails, the other provides continuous service to users. Novell's *System Fault Tolerance Level III* provides server duplexing.

- **Replication**  A strategy of duplicating critical files and directories from a server at one location to a server at another location to make that information more accessible to users at the remote location and also to provide redundancy and backup.

- **Clustering**  A cluster is a group of servers that share access to the same resources and service clients equally. Should one of the servers go down, the others take up the processing load. Clustered servers may access the same disk systems, which may be mirrored or in a RAID configuration.

**RELATED ENTRIES**    Backup and Data Archiving; Clustering; Data Migration; Data Protection; Disaster Recovery; Fault Management; Fault Tolerance; *and* Replication

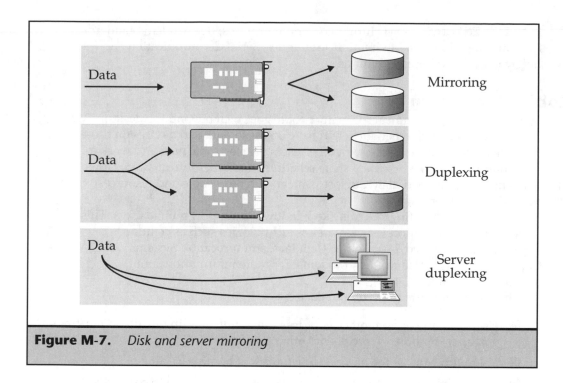

**Figure M-7.** *Disk and server mirroring*

## Mirror Site

A mirror site is a duplicate site, often associated with a busy Web site. The mirror site contains all the information contained on the master site and makes it available to users in the regional area. Mirror sites reduce traffic overloads on busy Web servers by replicating the server at other locations.

A mirror site might also be a duplicate data center meant to go into operation should a master data center site go down due to natural disasters or other problems. Companies running mission-critical applications often create mirrored sites.

## MNP (Microcom Networking Protocol)

MNP is a collection of protocols for modem data communication developed by Microcom, Inc. (http://www.microcom.com), a modem manufacturer. The protocols provide highly reliable data transmissions using error correction and data compression techniques. They are considered a de facto industry standard, and many vendors have licensed the protocols for use in their modems. Today, the CCITT (now the ITU) V series standards are commonly implemented in modems because they are accepted worldwide; however, some modem vendors use both V series and MNP.

**M**

**RELATED ENTRIES**    Asynchronous Communications; Bell Modem Standards;
Dial-up Line; Modems; Modulation Techniques; Serial Communication and Interfaces;
*and* Synchronous Communications

## Mobile Computing

The computing environment for many people goes well beyond the desktop. Most
people are connected to networks and have access to data and devices on those
networks. They communicate with other users via electronic mail and work in
collaborative groups where they share schedules and other information. However,
when users hit the road, they can lose contact with the people and resources they are
accustomed to working with.

Fortunately, operating systems like Windows 95 support mobile users. This
discussion covers support issues. Wireless technologies such as cellular
communications are covered under "Cellular Communication Systems" and "Wireless
Communications." Also refer to "Modems" for more information about
modem technologies.

There are three categories of mobile users:

- Users that move from office to office in the same building to attend meetings,
  give presentations, or work with other people

- User who work at the office and also work at home part-time

- Users who work on the road at client sites and who need to connect with the
  home office

In all cases, administrators must ensure that mobile users stay connected with
printers, fax machines, modems, and other devices that are attached to networks at the
home office and that users maintain the ability to communicate with other users via
electronic mail. Another concern is that files on mobile computers can become "out of
sync" with related files on servers. Administrators also need to set up logon servers
that can identify and authenticate remote users.

As mentioned, operating systems like Microsoft Windows have solved many of
these problems. The features outlined below first appeared in Windows 95, and many
have been extended into later versions of Windows. Note that the following
information is not meant to be Microsoft marketing hype; however, Windows does
provide the best example of a system that supports mobile users, as you can tell by
this list:

- **Dial-up networking**    Windows users can easily create dial-up connections that
  support TCP/IP, IPX, and NetBEUI network protocols over PPP (Point-to-Point
  Protocol) links. Connections into Windows NT RASs (Remote Access Servers)
  can support encrypted sessions.

- **Docking station support**  Docking and undocking of portable computers allows users to avoid shutting down their portable systems when moving them. An "Eject PC" or "Suspend" option prepares the computer for undocking and reconfigures the driver setup for the undocked configuration.

- **PC Card support**  If a user plugs in a PC Card such as a network card, modem, or disk drive, Windows automatically reconfigures itself. This is useful when plugging in network cards.

- **System policies and user profiles**  These two features allow system administrators to manage and maintain users' desktops in a consistent manner. Policies and profiles can be stored on a network server, so users always receive the same desktop regardless of their location. System policies set standard desktop configurations and profiles maintain user-definable settings.

- **File synchronization**  The Windows Briefcase helps users keep files synchronized. If a mobile user copies a file from a local system before going on the road, then makes changes to that file, the Briefcase helps the user synchronize the changes in that file with the local copy when he or she returns to the home office.

- **Deferred printing and faxing**  Mobile users often leave their printers behind, but Windows 95 lets users submit documents for printing even when they are on the road. When the user returns to the office, documents are queued up for printing. This also works for faxing.

- **Remote e-mail**  Windows fully supports electronic mail and provides performance enhancements. Users can browse message headers and download only specific messages.

- **Infrared support**  Windows 95 supports the IrDA (Infrared Data Association) standards for wireless infrared (IR) connections. With IR, users can walk up to an IR printer and print, or two IR-equipped computers can exchange files without a physical connection. See "Infrared Technologies" for more information.

- **TAPI (Telephony API)**  Windows supports TAPI, which dramatically simplifies the way that both users and application programs deal with telephone devices.

## Network Computers and Mobile Computing

The NCA (Network Computing Architecture) devised by Oracle, Sun Microsystems, and other vendors promotes a three-tier model of computing in which data resides on host computers, applications reside on servers, and users run stripped-down "thin" clients that are relatively inexpensive and store none or very little data of their own. The idea is to centralize the information resources of a company by placing information close to the administrators that manage it. NCs (Network Computers) are

**M**

specifically designed to run Java applications. See "NC (Network Computer) Devices" for more information.

This model provides a number of benefits for mobile computing, depending on the requirements of the organization that is supporting mobile users. Users can be equipped with inexpensive devices that are specifically designed to access information on an organization's servers. However, one problem with a stripped-down NC that does not have a disk drive is that mobile users can't carry information with them and must download that information from corporate servers whenever they need it. While corporate data managers may benefit by giving NCs to corporate users, most mobile users will no doubt prefer full-featured portable computers.

Microsoft's Zero Administration for Windows Initiative, or ZAWS, may be worth evaluating as a more flexible solution that delivers the best features of PCs and NCs while providing the benefits of centrally administered workstations on a corporate network. Some important features are listed below. See "Zero Administration for Windows Initiative" for more information.

- The mobile user's operating system updates itself with the latest code and drivers from a network server when booted.

- Applications located on the server are automatically installed when invoked by the user.

- A user's state information is "reflected" to servers, allowing users to roam between PCs while maintaining full access to their data, applications, and customized environment.

- A single administrator can lock down the configuration of a user's desktop to provide control, consistency, and security.

## Support and Security Issues for Mobile Users

Every day, more and more people take to the road with portable computers or move out of their corporate offices to work at home or at remote sites, and it becomes necessary to grant more and more users access to internal network resources. Increasingly, the office is just about anywhere a user happens to be, and that can lead to a lot of security problems if those users want to connect to your internal network or carry sensitive and valuable information that could get lost.

The basic idea is to let users dial in to your network and access electronic mail, sales reports, inventories, company bulletins, and other information that is vital to their job on the road or at remote locations. However, an alternative scenario that provides better security can be implemented with Web technologies. Think about how you access information on a Web server. Now think about using that same technology to provide your mobile work force with company-related information. There are several advantages to this scenario:

- Users connect with local Internet service providers, thus saving a long distance call. This is discussed further under "Virtual Dial-up Services."

- Users access a server that contains all the information they need on the outside of a firewall, thus protecting the inside network from potential intrusions. See "Firewall" for more information.

- Push technologies can be used to automatically update users with information and/or programs whenever they log on. See "Push" for more information.

- Web servers can provide a secure front-end–to–back-end database system or, with new distributed object technologies, users can be supplied with everything they need to directly connect over the Internet with back-end servers. This is discussed under "Component Software Technology" and "Distributed Object Computing."

- A number of technologies are available to provide user authentication and secure logon for users that are running Web browsers.

In general, Web technologies are discussed further under "Web Technologies and Concepts." Web protocols are very efficient at delivering information over dial-up connections; many users are already familiar with using Web browsers to access information. Web browsers have become a sort of "universal" client, so taking advantage of this technology will likely reduce training costs.

Not all remote and mobile user requirements fit into the Web server paradigm, and that is where dial-up services like Microsoft RAS (Remote Access Server) come into play. With RAS, users can gain access to your network and work as if they were using a computer directly connected to that network. To protect internal networks, Microsoft built appropriate security features into RAS. See "Remote Access" for additional information about remote access issues.

**RELATED ENTRIES**    Cellular Communication Systems; Infrared Technologies; Mobile IP; Modems; NC (Network Computer) Devices; PCS (Personal Communications Services); Remote Access; Telecommunications and Telephone Systems; Virtual Dial-up Services; VPN (Virtual Private Network); Wireless Communications; *and* Zero Administration for Windows Initiative

## INFORMATION ON THE INTERNET

| | |
|---|---|
| Mobile Computing Magazine (see mobile links at this site) | http://www.mobilecomputing.com |
| World-Wide Web Telecoms Virtual Library | http://www.analysys.com/vlib/mobile.htm |
| Mobile Management Task Force (MMTF) | http://www.epilogue.com/mmtf |
| Dataman Mobile Computing Laboratory | http://athos.rutgers.edu/dataman |
| Mobilis: the mobile computing lifestyle magazine | http://www.volksware.com/mobilis |

*M*

# Mobile IP

Traditionally, IP has assumed that a host on the Internet always connects to the same point of attachment. Any person or system that wants to send datagrams to that host addresses the datagrams to an IP address that identifies the subnetwork where the host is normally located. If the host moves, it will not receive those datagrams.

Today, a growing number of Internet users move their systems from place to place. If you normally connect to an ISP (Internet service provider) to establish an Internet connection and receive Internet mail, you'll need to dial long-distance into that ISP if you travel to another state or country. The alternative is to have a different IP address at your destination location, but this does not help if people are used to contacting you at your normal IP address.

Mobile IP, as defined in IETF RFC 2002, provides a mechanism that accommodates mobility on the Internet. It defines how nodes can change their point of attachment to the Internet without changing their IP address. The complete RFC is located at http://ds2.internic.net/rfc/rfc2002.txt.

Mobile IP assumes that a node's address remains the same as it is moved from one network location to another. It also allows a user to change from one media type to another (i.e., from Ethernet to a wireless LAN).

Mobile IP consists of the entities described in the following list. Before describing the entities, it is helpful to know about the basic operation of Mobile IP. A mobile user has a "home" network where his or her computer is normally attached. The "home" IP address is the address assigned to the user's computer on that network. When the computer moves to another network, datagrams still arrive for the user at the home network. The home network knows that the mobile user is at a different location, called the *foreign network,* and forwards the datagrams to the mobile user at that location. Datagrams are encapsulated and delivered across a tunnel from the home network to the foreign network.

- **Mobile node**   This is the mobile host computer or router that changes its point of attachment from one network or subnetwork to another without changing its "home" IP address. When the mobile node moves, it continues to communicate with other Internet nodes via its "home" IP address.

- **Home agent**   This is a router on the home network that can tunnel datagrams to a mobile node when it is away from its home network. The router maintains current location information for the mobile node.

- **Foreign agent**   When a mobile user visits another site and connects to that network, the visited network is known as the foreign network. The foreign agent resides in a router on the foreign network and is the end point of the tunnel established with the home network. The foreign agent "detunnels" and delivers datagrams to the mobile node.

Tunneling is a process of encapsulating datagrams into other datagrams for delivery across a network. Encapsulation is required because the datagrams are addressed to the network from which they are being shipped! By encapsulating the datagrams, the outer datagram can be addressed to the foreign network where the mobile user now resides. Note that the mobile node uses its home address as the source address of all IP datagrams that it sends, even when it is connected to a foreign network.

The important point is that the mobile node retains its IP address whether it is connected to the home network or some foreign network. When the mobile system is away from its home network, the home agent on the home network maintains a "care of" address that is the IP address of the foreign agent where the mobile node is located.

When a mobile node is attached to its home network, it operates without mobility services. If the mobile node is returning from a foreign network, it goes through a process that reregisters it as being attached to the home network rather than the foreign network. The details of this procedure are outlined in RFC 2002.

When a node moves to a foreign network, it obtains a "care of" address on the foreign network. The mobile node operating away from home then registers its new "care of" address with its home agent through the exchange of registration information. When datagrams arrive for the mobile node at the home network, the home agent on that network intercepts the datagrams and tunnels them to the mobile node's "care of" address, which as mentioned is usually the foreign agent router. This router then unencapsulates the datagrams and forwards them to the mobile host.

**RELATED ENTRIES**    Internet; IP (Internet Protocol); Mobile Computing; Remote Access; TCP/IP (Transmission Control Protocol/Internet Protocol); Virtual Dial-up Services; *and* Wireless Communications

**INFORMATION ON THE INTERNET**

Mobile IP (RFC 2002)                  http://www.internic.net/rfc/rfc2002.txt

IETF drafts (search for "mobile IP")  http://www.internic.net/ds/dsintdrafts.html

# Modems

Modems (*mo*dulators/*dem*odulators) are data communication devices that allow two end systems to communicate over the public-switched telephone network. A modem at the sending device converts computer digital signals into analog signals that can be transmitted over telephone lines. A modem at the other end of the link reconverts the analog signals back to digital pulses. Digital-to-analog conversion is called *mo*dulation and analog-to-digital conversion is called *dem*odulation; thus, the name *modems*.

A modem puts an AC (alternating current) *carrier* signal on the line (in the 1,000 to 2,000 Hz range) and adds digital information to this signal. A modem at the receiving end then extracts the digital information from the carrier signal. Modulation and demodulation are covered more fully under "Modulation Techniques."

*M*

There are two types of modems:

- **Consumer voice-grade modems** Most off-the-shelf modems are designed to allow PC users to communicate over the voice phone system. The modems employ compatible communication techniques that comply with several standards, most notably the ITU V series standards (previously called the CCITT standards).

- **Broadband modems** These are modems for nontelephone system connections. A company may set up its own dedicated lines or microwave towers and use broadband modems to achieve very high data rates between those sites. A fiber optic–based broadband modem can operate in the megabits-per-second range by converting electrical signals into optical signals.

A typical voice-grade modem connection is pictured in Figure M-8. The connection from the computer to the modem is typically an RS-232 serial cable. The modem connects over the *local loop* to the telephone company central office. The phone company then switches the call like any other voice call to create a point-to-point link. Serial connection methods are discussed under "Serial Communication and Interfaces."

There are some restrictions in the local loop. Long ago, the telephone company established the frequency range of 300 to 3,300 Hz as the range for voice. The telephone switching system filters out higher frequencies to eliminate noise. Unfortunately, this filtering equipment prevents using higher frequencies to boost data transmission rates. Therefore, a number of techniques, including encoding and compression, have been developed to squeeze as much digital data into the 300 to 3,300 Hz range as possible. As a side note, the digital subscriber services discussed under "DSL (Digital Subscriber Line)" allow higher frequencies (and higher data

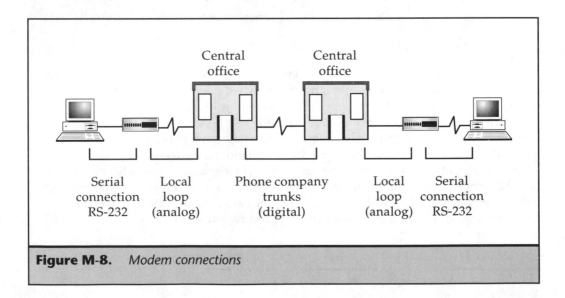

**Figure M-8.** *Modem connections*

rates) on the local loop because they bypass the telephone company's switching system filters.

Modems are asynchronous, synchronous, or both. An asynchronous transmission can be compared to the sporadic flow of cars on a highway while a synchronous transmission can be compared to a steady stream of boxcars on a train track. In asynchronous mode, data is framed and each frame is sent independently. The receiver must be able to detect when a frame starts and ends. In synchronous mode, a clock signal separates the beginning and end of each frame of data. Synchronous modems are generally more efficient and are typically used for dedicated links between two sites.

## Modem Connections

Consumer voice-grade modems for computers are available in internal or external models, or in the PC Card format for portable computers. An external modem connects to the serial port on a computer. Organizations that support a mobile work force may have racks of modems that users can dial into. In some cases, a large number of modems are shrunk down and integrated onto a single adapter or motherboard as a module for a rack system. See "Access Server," "Remote Access," and "Virtual Dial-up Services" for information about these systems.

When one modem "calls" another, the destination modem answers and a signal exchange takes place that establishes the parameters for a communication session. The negotiation process determines the maximum signaling rate available between the two modems as well as the use of compression. Negotiation and signaling are established by the modem standards discussed later.

A full-duplex modem sends signals in both directions at the same time and at the same rate. Newer, high-speed (56-Kbit/sec), voice-grade modems (such as the x2 models from U.S. Robotics) are asymmetrical, meaning that the download channel has a higher rate than the upload channel.

Most consumer modems use a single wire pair, meaning that they transmit and receive on the same channel. The modems at each end coordinate their activities and take turns transmitting. Modems may also use full-duplex mode, as shown in Figure M-9. The available bandwidth is divided into two channels at different carrier frequencies so that either modem can send and receive at the same time. Guard bands are used to separate the two duplexed channels to prevent crosstalk and corruption. This reduces transmission rates on the limited-bandwidth public telephone system.

## Modem Standards

The most recent and important ITU-T modem standards are listed in the following table. The modulation techniques described in the table are FSK (frequency-shift keying), PSK (phase-shift keying), QAM (quadrature amplitude modulation),

*M*

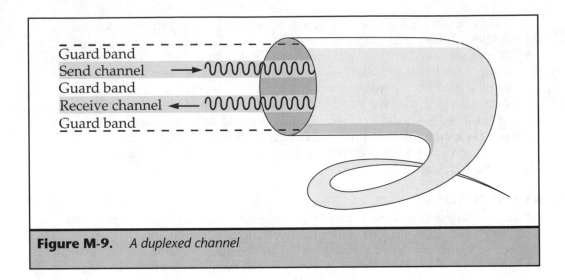

**Figure M-9.** *A duplexed channel*

and TCM (trellis-coded modulation). They are discussed in more detail under "Modulation Techniques."

| | |
|---|---|
| V.22 | 1,200 bits/sec, full-duplex, PSK encoding |
| V.22bis | 2,400 bits/sec, full-duplex, QAM encoding |
| V.32 | Asynchronous/synchronous, 4,800/9,600 bits/sec, QAM encoding |
| V.32bis | Asynchronous/synchronous, 14,400 bits/sec, TCM encoding |
| V.35 | Defines high data rates over combined circuits |
| V.42 | Defines error checking standards |
| V.42bis | Defines modem compression using the Lempel Ziv method |
| V.34 | A standard for 28 Kbits/sec using TCM encoding |
| V.34+ | Boosts V.34 to 33.6 Kbits/sec |

As most readers probably know, the line speeds quoted above are not always possible. While the standards define a top speed, line noise, distance, and the topology of the switching system between two modems can lower the actual data rate. The lines must be free of noise to achieve the top speed. Estimates are that less than 30 percent of the lines in the U.S. are clean enough to let these modems operate near top speed.

## 56K Modems

Two competing modem standards are taking advantage of a technique that can provide up to 56-Kbit/sec download speed to modem users. U.S. Robotics (now part of 3Com) calls its technology X2 and Lucent/Rockwell Semiconductor Systems calls its technology K56flex. Only the concepts, and not the differences between the technologies, are covered here. Therefore, they are collectively called 56K modems for simplicity. The following Web sites have more information:

| | |
|---|---|
| 3Com/U.S. Robotics | http://www.3com.com |
| Rockwell Semiconductor Systems | http://www.nb.rockwell.com |
| K56flex site | http://www.lucent.com/micro/K56flex |
| The Open 56K Forum | http://www.open56k.org |

56K modems have become the workhorse modems of Internet users. The reason is simple. They boost download speeds to 56 Kbits/sec when one side of the connection is digital. Most ISPs (Internet service providers) now have banks of 56-Kbit/sec modems to support high-speed access for dial-up Internet users. However, there are some restrictions and your speed may vary:

■ The other end of the connection must be digital; otherwise, the modem switches to full analog mode at 28.8 or 33.5 Kbits/sec.

■ Only downstream data is transmitted at 56 Kbits/sec. Uplink speeds are 28.8 or 33.6 Kbits/sec.

■ A compatible 56-Kbit/sec modem must be located at the other end of the link, i.e., at the Internet service provider or at the user's corporate dial-in site.

K56 modems attain their high speeds by reducing the number of analog-to-digital conversions that take place in a normal dial-up link. Analog-to-digital conversions add significant noise to a transmission, which restricts the data rate. The corruption caused by converted signals is called quantization noise. The concept behind 56K modems is to remove all digital-to-analog conversions except for the one required for outbound traffic at the user's modem. This is the only conversion that cannot be removed.

Figure M-10 illustrates a traditional connection (a) and a K56 connection (b). The traditional connection in Figure M-10(a) requires four different conversions. Quantization noise is added wherever a digital-to-analog conversion takes place. From left to right, noise occurs at 1 and 3. From right to left, noise occurs at 4 and 2.

The key to achieving higher speeds is to eliminate the analog loop at the ISP. As mentioned, most ISPs are already digitally terminated, so there is plenty of opportunity for taking advantage of this. Once the ISP's analog loop is eliminated, there are fewer conversions and less noise, allowing higher transmission speeds. However, the upstream transmission from the user remains slower to allow for higher speeds in the download channel, which is preferable to Internet users since most information is downloaded.

**RELATED ENTRIES**   Access Server; Asynchronous Communications; Bell Modem Standards; Capacity; Data Communication Concepts; Dial-up Line; DSL (Digital

*M*

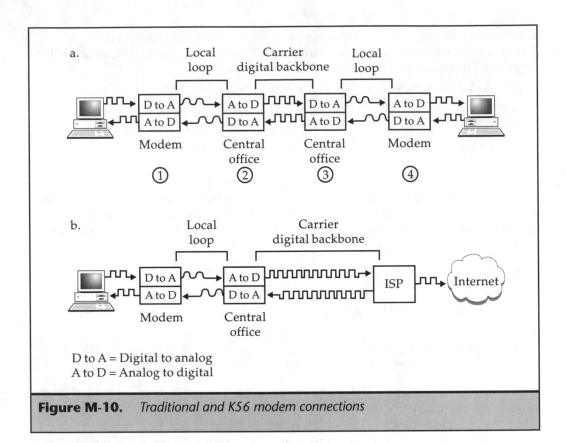

**Figure M-10.**  *Traditional and K56 modem connections*

Subscriber Line); ISDN (Integrated Services Digital Network); Local Loop; MNP (Microcom Networking Protocol); Modulation Techniques; Remote Access; Serial Communication and Interfaces; Synchronous Communications; Telecommunications and Telephone Systems; Telephony; Virtual Dial-up Services; *and* WAN (Wide Area Network)

### INFORMATION ON THE INTERNET

| | |
|---|---|
| Navas 28800-56K Modem FAQ | http://www.aimnet.com/~jnavas/modem/faq.html |
| MODEM FAQ | http://www.inetassist.com/faqs/modems.htm |
| Lynn Larrow's modems, networking and communications links | http://www.webcom.com/~llarrow/comfaqs.html |
| Curt's High Speed Modem Page | http://www.teleport.com/~curt/modems.html |
| Malcolm Hoar's Data Communications FAQ | http://www.malch.com/comfaq.html |

| Rosenet's Everything You Ever Wanted To Know About Modems page | http://www.rosenet.net/~costmo |
| Zoom Telephonics's modems page | http://www.modems.com |
| Yahoo!'s Modems page | http://www.yahoo.com/Computers_and_Internet/Hardware/Peripherals/Modems |

# Modulation Techniques

Modulation techniques are those involving the addition of information to a transmission frequency. The receiver then demodulates the signal to extract the information. Modulation is used to transmit digital data signals over telephone lines. Modems at each end of the communication link perform the digital-to-analog and analog-to-digital conversion. An analog signal with a specific frequency called the *carrier* signal is placed on the line. The transmitting modem modulates the carrier signal, and the receiving modem demodulates the signal.

Note that a baud is a pulse signal in the carrier while bits per second is the rate of information transmitted on the line. The earliest modems transmitted 1 bit per baud, meaning that a 300-baud modem actually did transmit 300 bits/sec. Modern modems use an encoding technique in which each baud can represent multiple bits of information. For example, in two-way communications, the baud limit is 1,200 pulses per second, but by encoding up to 8 bits per baud, a data rate of 9,600 bits/sec can be achieved.

The technique of encoding multiple bits into a baud is called QAM (quadrature amplitude modulation) and is discussed in a moment. Traditional modulation techniques are discussed before discussing QAM.

There are three traditional modulation techniques, as described next and pictured in Figure M-11. Note that the original digital signal is shown at the top and the modulated results are shown below it.

**AM (AMPLITUDE MODULATION)**   In AM, the height or amplitude of the wave is changed between two levels to match the digital data input. This technique was used in some of the early modems but has too many limitations for high-speed data transmissions.

**FM (FREQUENCY MODULATION)**   In FM, the frequency of a signal changes depending on the binary input. When FM is used to transmit digital signals, it is called *FSK (frequency-shift keying)* because only two frequencies are transmitted.

**PM (PHASE MODULATION)**   In this method, the period of the wave is shifted by one fourth, one half, or three fourths of its period. The shift in the waves can represent some binary value to the receiver. Note that the shift occurs in relation to the

*M*

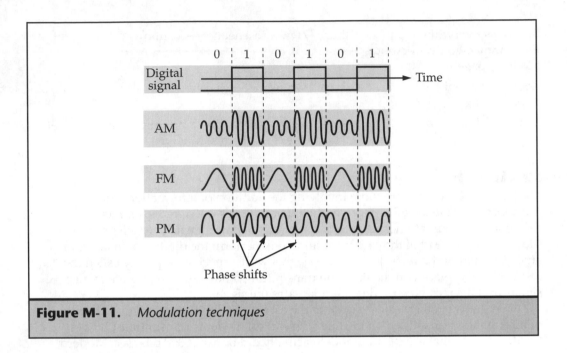

**Figure M-11.** *Modulation techniques*

preceding wave period. Since there are four different wave types, as shown here, it is possible to represent four different bit values (00, 01, 10, 11) per pulse:

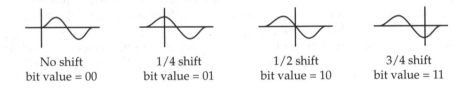

| No shift | 1/4 shift | 1/2 shift | 3/4 shift |
| bit value = 00 | bit value = 01 | bit value = 10 | bit value = 11 |

**QAM (QUADRATURE AMPLITUDE MODULATION)** This scheme extends the concept of phase modulation by using two different amplitude levels and by shifting the wave by one fourth, by one half, or by three fourths of its period. Thus, eight bit values can be represented as listed here:

| Bit Value | Phase Shift | Amplitude |
|-----------|-------------|-----------|
| 000 | None | 1 |
| 001 | None | 2 |
| 010 | ¼ | 1 |
| 011 | ¼ | 2 |

| Bit Value | Phase Shift | Amplitude |
|-----------|-------------|-----------|
| 100 | ½ | 1 |
| 101 | ½ | 2 |
| 110 | ¾ | 1 |
| 111 | ¾ | 2 |

By shifting the wave in even smaller increments, it is possible to represent even more bit values. With 16 values (4 bits in width), it is possible to transmit at 9,600 bits/sec over a 2,400-baud line. This technique can be expanded upon to achieve data rates of 28,800 bits/sec. Even higher rates are achieved by using compression and other techniques.

**RELATED ENTRIES**    Data Communication Concepts; Modems; *and* Signals

# MOM (Message-Oriented Middleware)

MOM is a middleware communication mechanism that provides applications with a way to establish a communication dialog using non-real-time, connectionless techniques. A communication dialog may consist of multiple messages going back and forth between applications, in much the same way that two people might exchange a series of e-mail messages. Messages use the store-and-forward model in which they are sent to queues and held for the recipient to pick up at a later time.

MOM can be contrasted with RPCs (remote procedure calls). RPCs provide connection-oriented links between applications in client/server environments, while MOM is generally connectionless. RPCs require tight integration between applications and the network. In contrast, MOM uses the store-and-forward model. Both RPCs and MOM have advantages and are used for different application requirements. MOM's queued message technique is appropriate when delays are acceptable.

Here are some of the most important features of MOM:

- Applications can continue processing after sending messages and do not need to wait for a connection and a reply from the recipient.

- MOM allows applications that may be running at different times to communicate.

- Messages may travel across networks and systems that are temporarily offline.

- Messages can be prioritized to ensure faster delivery.

- Delivery can be guaranteed to provide assurance that a message will make it to the destination.

- Once a system receives a message, it can return an acknowledgment at the request of the sender.

*M*

MOM is becoming more important with the growth of the Web. Connections between systems are not always possible, but many client/server applications require such connections. MOM can provide virtual connections that may support existing applications, or it can be seen as a new model for building client/server applications that work over the Internet.

In general, MOM provides peer-to-peer messaging among many different types of applications in a distributed computing environment. Unlike some middleware products, MOM is not restricted to providing front-end clients with access to back-end data. MOM works in cooperation with other types of middleware products to provide a dynamic distributed network environment. It provides more than data access by supporting interoperability among applications. For example, a message might carry a request to execute some process in another application.

According to MOMA (Message-Oriented Middleware Association), "MOM is demonstrating its ability to deliver the benefits of asynchronous messaging for applications and process-to-process interoperability, distributed transaction processing (e.g. banking, brokerage, airline reservations), distributed enterprise workflow (e.g. process manufacturing, insurance claims processing), real-time automation (e.g. utility and process control), and systems management (e.g. distributed backup, software distribution, etc.), among others."

## Messaging Products

Two message-oriented middleware products are outlined below. Other messaging products are available from the vendors listed at the end of this section. You can check the MOMA Web site listed at the end of this topic for additional vendor products information and links to vendor Web sites.

### IBM MQSeries

IBM's MQSeries is designed to allow organizations or communities of users on the Internet to run applications that communicate with store-and-forward communication technology that works over heterogeneous platforms and software environments. See "IBM Open Blueprint" for additional information on MQSeries and related IBM technologies.

MQSeries provides an environment for building mobile communications, multimedia applications, transaction-based systems, and a whole new generation of network applications. It also links with Lotus Notes to give Notes users access to transactions and data on other systems. MQSeries is supported on IBM platforms and operating systems, DEC VMS, Tandem Guardian and Himalaya, HP UX, Sun Solaris, SCO UNIX, and Microsoft Windows.

### MSMQ (Microsoft Message Queuing)

MSMQ is a fast store-and-forward service that enables applications running at different times to communicate across heterogeneous networks and systems that may be temporarily offline. Applications send messages to MSMQ, and MSMQ uses *queues of messages* to ensure that the messages eventually reach their destination. MSMQ provides guaranteed message delivery, efficient routing, security, and priority-based messaging. MSMQ allows *developers* to focus on business programming and not on networking issues, since MSMQ provides guaranteed network communication. With MSMQ, *end users* communicate across networks and systems that are occasionally offline, independent of the current state of the communicating applications and systems.

In particular, MSMQ provides support for Microsoft Transaction Server and the Microsoft Distributed Transactions Coordinator. MSMQ also provides a MAPI (Messaging Application Programming Interface) transport and supports Microsoft Exchange.

## MOMA (Message-Oriented Middleware Association)

MOMA is an international not-for-profit association of vendors, users, and consultants dedicated to promoting the use of messaging to provide multiplatform, multitier message-passing and message-queuing services for distributed computing architectures.

MOMA has developed a conceptual architecture that enables messaging and ORB technologies to interoperate and is taking on a more active role in defining how complementary technologies can be integrated.

**RELATED ENTRIES**    Client/Server Computing; Component Software Technology; CORBA (Common Object Request Broker Architecture); Database Connectivity; Distributed Computer Networks; Distributed Database; Distributed Object Computing; Middleware and Messaging; Multitiered Architectures; Object Technologies; OLE DB; ORB (Object Request Broker); Transaction Processing; *and* Web Middleware and Database Connectivity

### INFORMATION ON THE INTERNET

| | |
|---|---|
| MOMA (Message-Oriented Middleware Association) | http://www.moma-inc.org |
| Applied Communications' NET24 Middleware | http://www.tsainc.com |
| BEA Systems, Inc. | http://www.beasys.com |
| DEC's DECmessageQ InfoCenter | http://www.digital.com/info/decmessageq |
| IBM's MQSeries | http://www.hursley.ibm.com/mqseries/ |
| Momentum Software's XIPC | http://www.momsoft.com |
| NCR Corporation's Topend | http://www.ncr.com/product/topend |
| PeerLogic's PIPES Platform | http://www.peerlogic.com |
| SOFTWARE AG Americas' ENTIRE BROKER | http://www.sagus.com |
| Talarian's SmartSockets | http://www.talarian.com |

*M*

## Motif

Motif is the industry standard graphical user interface promoted by The Open Group. It is defined by the IEEE 1295 specification and is used on more than 200 hardware and software platforms. Motif provides application developers, end users, and system vendors with an environment for building applications with a standardized presentation on a wide range of platforms. Motif is the leading user interface for the UNIX-based operating system.

Motif provides application portability across a variety of platforms, allowing application developers to leverage their development work and customers to make valuable software investments. Motif is also the base graphical user interface toolkit for the CDE (Common Desktop Environment).

For more information, visit the Motif page at The Open Group's Web site. The page address is http://www.opengroup.org/tech/desktop.

## MPLS (Multiprotocol Label Switching)

The IETF MPLS Working Group is focused on developing standards that integrate a scheme for label swapping/tagging with network layer (layer 3) routing. The purpose of label swapping is to improve performance of network layer routing in the switched network environment. MPLS is not confined to any network layer or link layer technology. Initially, the MPLS Working Group will focus on IPv4 and IPv6, then it will focus on other network layer protocols such as IPX (Internetwork Packet Exchange), AppleTalk, and DECnet. A variety of media is supported, including LAN and WAN technology. MPLS was in draft form at the time of this writing, but you can read more about it at the Web sites given at the end of this topic.

MPLS forwarding must allow *aggregate forwarding* of user data, which means allowing a stream of packets to be forwarded as a unit and on a single path. MPLS must support operations, administration, and maintenance facilities at least as extensively as those supported in current IP networks. It must also support both topology-driven and traffic/request-driven label assignments, unicast and multicast streams, and multipath routing and forwarding. The protocol must be compatible with the IETF (Internet Engineering Task Force) Integrated Services Model, including RSVP (Resource Reservation Protocol).

**RELATED ENTRIES**   ARIS (Aggregate Route-based IP Switching); IP over ATM; IP Switching; Switched Networks; Tag Switching; *and* VLAN (Virtual LAN)

**INFORMATION ON THE INTERNET**

| | |
|---|---|
| IETF Multiprotocol Label Switching site | http://www.ietf.org/html.charters/mpls-charter.html |
| Colin Perkins's MPLS information | http://www.scimitar.terena.nl/standards/reports/ MERCI_ietf39/node56.html |

# MPOA (Multiprotocol over ATM)

MPOA is an ATM Forum specification for overlaying layer 3 network routing protocols like IP over an ATM switched network environment. It allows organizations to take advantage of the bandwidth and scalability of ATM while retaining legacy LANs, the ability to create VLANs (virtual LANs), and the ability to route between those VLANs. MPOA allows different subnetworks to be defined on top of the ATM switching fabric. The protocol then provides virtual routing services between the subnetworks. Once a routed path is established between two end devices, a switched virtual circuit is set directly in the ATM switching fabric to provide a direct connection between those devices.

MPOA is derived from early work done with LANE (LAN Emulation). LANE operates in layer 2 (the MAC layer) and is thus limited to creating bridged networks over the ATM switching fabric. This model does not implement layer 3 routing, so separate routers are needed to allow devices in one bridged network to communicate with a device in another bridged network. The problem with LANE is the requirement that traffic go through an external router when the underlying ATM network is fully capable of creating a direct connect between two devices connected to different VLANs. MPOA adds this capability.

LANE is still part of an MPOA network configuration. LANE defined individual VLANs while MPOA provides for routing between those VLANs. Clients use LANE to resolve addresses within the same VLAN and use MPOA for inter-VLAN addressing. MPOA uses NHRP (Next Hop Resolution Protocol) to determine routes between VLANs. NHRP was developed by the IETF (Internet Engineering Task Force) and is discussed elsewhere in this book.

MPOA also adds the ability for end systems to take advantage of ATM's QoS (Quality of Service) features. LANE does not allow end stations to tap these features. MPOA currently focuses on IP version 4 but will support other network layer protocols in the future, such as IP version 6, IPX (Internetwork Packet Exchange), DECnet, and AppleTalk. MPOA also reduces the cost of edge devices. Routing services are performed in a single MPOA routing server, so edge devices do not need to include the circuitry or software to perform those services; however some argue that routing in edge devices is more efficient.

An MPOA network consists of the following components, which are pictured in Figure M-12:

- Edge-switching devices sit at the edges of the ATM network and provide a connection point for legacy LANs. They forward packets to the ATM network at layer 2 or layer 3 and are thus multilayer switching devices. An edge device participates in routing but does not perform actual route calculations. It has only enough intelligence to participate in the NHRP routing performed by the route server.

*M*

■ *Route servers* are routers or embedded functions in ATM switches that calculate routes in the network. They map network layer addresses to ATM addresses and provide information that is used to establish a virtual circuit between two end systems. Route servers support routing protocols like RIP (Routing Information Protocol) and OSPF (Open Shortest Path First) so they can communicate routing information to other route servers and traditional routers.

■ *IASGs (Internet address summarization groups)* are groups of network addresses that define VLANs. In an IP environment, a VLAN is a set of IP addresses that equate to a subnetwork. Therefore, an IASG is a virtual subnetwork in the IP environment. A host may belong to multiple IASGs. If a host needs to forward information to another host in the same IASG, LANE methods are used and a MAC address is targeted. If a host needs to forward information to a host outside of the IASG, NHRP is used.

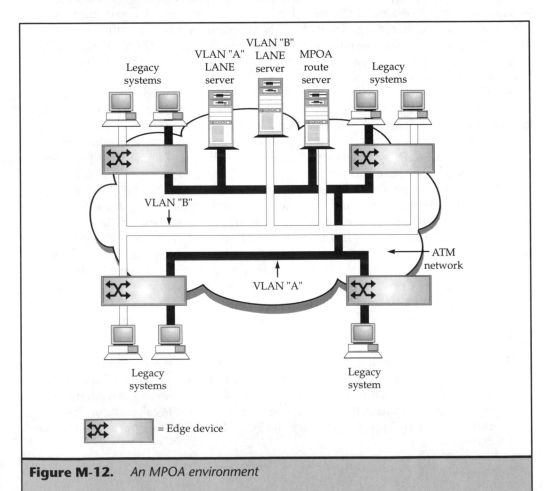

**Figure M-12.** *An MPOA environment*

The MPOA-compatible edge switches and the route servers work together to perform the functions that are normally performed by a router in a typical IP network. Edge devices do not run routing protocols—they do layer 3 forwarding, which is based on calculations performed by the route servers. Edge devices cache a certain amount of forwarding information, but if a route is not known, the edge device queries the route server. This splitting of tasks between the edge devices and route servers is called *distributed routing*.

MPOA uses a number of protocols to fully leverage ATM features, including NHRP as mentioned. It also uses the IEEE 802.1q VLAN specification. Another protocol used is MARS (Multicast Address Resolution Server), which resolves multicast addresses.

An alternative protocol also being developed by the ATM Forum is I-PNNI (Integrated-Private Network-to-Network Interface), which achieves full ATM access with a single protocol. With I-PNNI, edge devices perform their own route calculations and exchange routing information with other edge devices. A route server is not required. The advantage of this approach is that all edge devices are peers that know the network topology and can exchange information about it with other peers. One of the drawbacks of I-PNNI is that edge devices that perform routing calculations are more expensive. See "I-PNNI (Integrated-Private Network-to-Network Interface)" for more information.

Ipsilon's IP Switching techniques competes with MPOA to some extent. As mentioned, MPOA makes every attempt to leverage the ATM Forum's specification. IP Switching, on the other hand, actually bypasses many ATM features to achieve its objectives. See "Ipsilon IP Switching" for more details.

**RELATED ENTRIES**    IP over ATM; I-PNNI (Integrated-Private Network-to-Network Interface); Ipsilon IP Switching; IP Switching; *and* LANE (LAN Emulation)

### INFORMATION ON THE INTERNET

| | |
|---|---|
| The ATM Forum | http://www.atmforum.com |
| MPOA, VLANS and Distributed ROUTERS (ATM Forum paper) | http://www.atmforum.com/atmforum/library/53bytes/backissues/v4-3/article-04.html |
| Newbridge Networks Corp. (extensive information on ATM and MPOA) | http://www.vivid.newbridge.com |

# MPP (Massively Parallel Processor) Systems

Parallel processing systems are multiprocessor systems that can distribute processing tasks across the processors. The systems are especially useful for database management systems and data warehousing. They can handle multiple queries from multiple users and access vast quantities of data while doing so.

Parallel systems are implemented using three different architectural models. In the *loosely coupled model*, each processor has access to a private memory space and disk

**M**

space. A variation of this is that each processor accesses private memory and shared disks. In the SMP (symmetrical multiprocessing) model, the system is *tightly coupled*. Resources are fully shared, and all processors share the same memory and disk space.

MPP provides the advantages of clustering for large uniprocessor systems with a scaleable bus design that can handle the addition of many "processor nodes." The system is loosely coupled, and each node has its own bus, memory, and I/O (input/output) system. Each processor may also run its own operating system and applications. MPP systems perform sequential tasks well, and processing may proceed in steps as one processor passes a completed task onto another processor for further processing. A data warehouse system can summarize large amounts of data, extracting, cleaning, combining, altering, and manipulating it in a way to make the resulting data more relevant to end users. MPP systems are a good match for data warehousing operations.

NUMA (Non-Uniform Memory Access) is an architecture for building scalable systems that goes beyond clustered systems and MPPs. It defines a standard memory management scheme that allows systems to coordinate memory access. Basically, all the available memory on all the systems can be accessed by any system.

Pyramid Technology (http://www.pyramid.com) produces SMP and MPP servers. Its Reliant RM1000 can support up to 4,096 MIPS R4400 processors and run parallel databases from Oracle, Informix, and SAS Systems. IBM's RS/6000-based SP2 is a massively parallel processor computer system. Information is available at http://www.rs6000.ibm.com.

**RELATED ENTRIES**    Asymmetrical Multiprocessing; Clustering; Data Warehousing; Distributed Processing; NUMA (Non-Uniform Memory Access); Parallel Processing; Servers; Supercomputer; *and* Symmetrical Multiprocessing

# MPPP (Multilink Point-to-Point Protocol)

*See* PPP Multilink.

# MPTN (Multiprotocol Transport Networking)

MPTN is IBM software that provides a way to decouple applications from underlying transport protocols and remove the need for multiprotocol routers. With MPTN, an application written for one protocol can operate over a network that uses another MPTN-specified protocol. Basically, MPTN changes the transport header in a packet to fit an alternate protocol such as TCP/IP.

MPTN is designed around the specification found in the CTS (Common Transport Semantic) layer of the IBM Open Blueprint, which is described elsewhere in this book. MPTN is widely used to connect PCs directly to IBM AS/400 midrange systems.

**RELATED ENTRIES**    APPN (Advanced Peer-to-Peer Networking); IBM (International Business Machines); IBM Open Blueprint; *and* Routing Protocols and Algorithms

# MQSeries, IBM

*See* MOM (Message-Oriented Middleware).

# MSMQ (Microsoft Message Queuing)

*See* MOM (Message-Oriented Middleware).

# MTA (Message Transfer Agent)

In the X.400 Message Handling System developed by the CCITT (now the ITU), an MTA is like a post office through which messages are exchanged between systems. The MTA provides store-and-forward services. See "X.400 Message Handling System."

# MTP (Multicast Transport Protocol)

*See* Multicasting.

# MTU (Maximum Transmission Unit)

An MTU is a parameter that specifies how much data a frame for a particular LAN can carry. When LANs are interconnected, the MTU size becomes important. Each interconnected LAN may have a different MTU size. If a datagram arrives at a router that is connected to a LAN with an MTU that is smaller than the MTU of the source LAN, the datagram is fragmented into smaller pieces to fit within the frame size of the next-hop LAN.

There is some benefit in knowing what the smallest MTU is along an internetwork path. Once known, a host can send datagrams that do not exceed the smallest MTU along the path and thus avoid fragmentation altogether.

**RELATED ENTRY**    Fragmentation of Frames and Packets

# Multicasting

Multicasting is a way of efficiently transmitting text, audio, and video on the Internet or an internal network to a select group of people, much like a conference call includes a select group of people. Instead of sending information in individual packets to each recipient, a single message is sent to a multicast group, which includes all the people that want to participate in the multicast session. While multicasting is possible on a variety of networks, this topic concentrates on Internet multicasting.

Multicasting is a one-to-many transmission. In contrast, the traditional method of sending messages on the Internet, called *unicasting*, is a one-to-one transmission. If multicasting is comparable to a conference call, then unicasting is like a private call between two people.

Multicasting provides a way for one station to send packets to a select group of systems. A recipient can also respond to a message and the response is sent to

*M*

everyone in the multicast group. On the Internet, groups can include host systems located on different subnetworks almost anywhere. An individual user can decide whether he or she wants to be included in a multicast broadcast. Multicasting helps reduce the number of packets traversing the Internet by only sending packets to users that have requested them.

The trick is for a host to indicate to its connected router that it wants to receive a particular multicast. That router then indicates to the next router close to the source of the multicast that it wants to receive the multicast. This process continues until a path is established from the multicast source to the host that wants to receive the multicast. The result is that only routers that need multicast packets for end systems actually receive those packets. Nonparticipating routers do not receive the packets, minimizing excess traffic and making the process more efficient.

As shown in Figure M-13, you can imagine a tree of routers that branch from the multicast source and connect to end systems that want to receive the multicast. If a router has no hosts that want to receive the multicast, it excludes itself from the tree.

Multicasting on the Internet takes place on the MBone (Multicast Backbone). The current state of multicasting on the Internet is one that consists of multicast-aware routers (called mrouters) and traditional routers that only support unicast (called

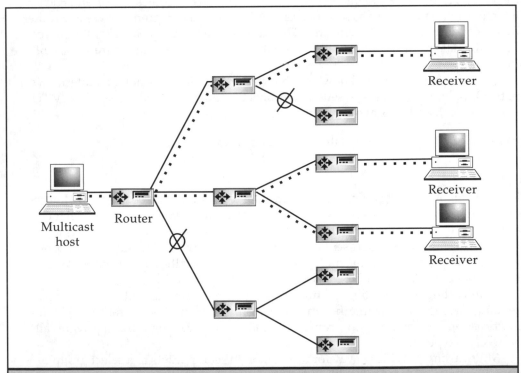

**Figure M-13.** *A multicast follows a tree of routers from the source to receivers*

urouters). This is a temporary configuration that will not be necessary once all routers are multicast enabled. The MBone exists on top of the Internet as a *virtual network* in which mrouters exist as "islands" that are surrounded by unicast routers. Mrouters must transmit IP multicast packets to other mrouters. However, they may be surrounded by urouters that do not know how to handle multicast packets. To solve this problem, tunnels are set up between mrouters that cross urouters. IP multicast packets are then encapsulated in unicast IP packets, which urouters can process. Consequently, the MBone exists as a set of mrouters connected by tunnels that overlay the Internet. This is discussed further under "MBone (Multicast Backbone)."

Anyone wanting to connect with the MBone needs a high-speed connection of 128 Kbits/sec (ISDN) or greater. Users also need a connection to an ISP (Internet service provider) that supports IP multicast and MBone connections. Software requirements for the user's system include multicast-aware applications and underlying multicast protocols including IGMP (Internet Group Management Protocol), as discussed in a moment.

RTP (Real-time Transport Protocol) is a protocol that works in conjunction with multicasting to transport real-time audio, video simulation data, and other information over multicast networks. While IP Multicast (see the next section, "IP Multicast") defines how to set up multicast groups, RTP defines how to transport real-time information to the members of the groups and monitor the quality of the information that is delivered. Refer to "RTP (Real-time Transport Protocol)" for more information.

RSVP (Resource Reservation Protocol) is a protocol that provides a way for someone to reserve a certain amount of bandwidth through the Internet for a videoconference or other real-time session. It also provides a way for ISPs to charge for the use of reserved bandwidth, which is necessary to prevent everyone from requesting such bandwidth. See "RSVP (Resource Reservation Protocol)" for more information.

## IP Multicast

IP Multicast is an open, IETF (Internet Engineering Task Force) standard for distributing data to multiple recipients. The multicast recipient group can change dynamically. A host may decide to join or leave a group at any time and a host may be a member of more than one multicast group. In addition, any host can be a multicast source by simply sending packets addressed to a particular multicast group.

Routers in this scheme must be multicast enabled. When a multicast source transmits a multicast datagram, the local router forwards the packet to other routers with attached networks that include members of the multicast group.

IP Multicast uses class D addressing, which is a special form of the IP address designed for multicasting. All hosts connected to the Internet have an IP address that is either part of the class A, class B, or class C scheme. A host can also have one or more class D multicast addresses depending on the multicast groups it wants to belong to. The class scheme for IP addresses is discussed under "IP (Internet

**M**

Protocol)." A class D address is 32 bits long. The first 4 bits are used to identify it as a class D address. The remaining 28 bits identify multicast groups.

A class D address can be compared to the channel number of a TV station. When you tune in to a particular class D address, you receive packets that are being multicast by other systems that multicast on the address.

An industry consortium called the IPMI (IP Multicast Initiative) is dedicated to advancing the deployment of IP Multicast and making information about it available. The IPMI Web site is at http://www.ipmulticast.com.

### IGMP (Internet Group Management Protocol)

Multicast receivers must indicate their desire to be included in a multicast session. This is done with IGMP, a protocol that runs between hosts and their immediately neighboring multicast routers. Hosts use the protocol to inform the local multicast router that they want to receive transmissions from a particular multicast group or that they no longer want to receive messages from a group. If the host was the only device on the local network that was receiving the packets, the multicast host will no longer need to receive the packets itself and removes itself from the receive list. This reduces network traffic.

In addition, a multicast router can use IGMP to occasionally broadcast a query on the LAN to determine if any hosts still want to receive broadcasts from the multicast transmitters that it is accepting packets from. A host responds to this broadcast by sending a *host membership report* for each group to which it belongs. If no host responds for a group, the group is dropped.

IGMP is described in RFC 1112, which is available at http://www.internic.net/rfc/rfc1112.txt.

## Routing

Like any other router-connected network, the MBone needs a routing protocol that guides packets through its mesh of tunnels. Normally, a multicast packet is sent from its source to the local mrouter. That mrouter then transmits the packet on its tunnels to other mrouters. Several routing algorithms are used or proposed to ensure that packets are delivered along the most efficient paths, as outlined here:

■ **DVMRP (Distance Vector Multicast Routing Protocol)**   In this technique, a router that receives a multicast packet wants to find out if other multicast routers it has connections to need to receive the packet (i.e., they have attached hosts that are members of the group). DVMRP sends the packet to all attached routers and waits for a reply. Routers with no group members return a "prune" message, which essentially prevents further multicast messages for that group from reaching the router.

■ **MOSPF (Multicast Open Shortest Path First)**   As the name implies, MOSPF is an Open Shortest Path First routing protocol. MOSPF routers build maps of the network topology, including the location of islands and tunnels and then determine the best path through the network to a particular multicast router. Note that MOSPF is designed for use within autonomous systems.

- **PIM (Protocol Independent Multicast)**  PIM is a new concept for routing. It uses two modes: PIM-dense and PIM-sparse. Dense mode operates like DVMRP. It floods the network with traffic, a bad thing unless the group has enough participants to warrant such an action. PIM-sparse avoids flooding (and wasted bandwidth) in cases where a group is small. Instead, a *rendezvous point* is established and all members send packets to it.

These protocols are discussed in a paper called "Introduction to IP Multicast Routing," at the IPML Web site. Connect to  http://www.ipmulticast.com/community/whitepapers/introrouting.html.

## Reliable Multicast Protocols

While IP Multicast is good at what it does, it is an unreliable connectionless mechanism. The industry believes that adding a reliable protocol on top of IP Multicast provides many benefits, just as TCP provides reliable services on top of IP. Using a reliable multicast transport protocol would help applications better deal with delivery problems. A reliable multicast protocol called MTP (Multicast Transport Protocol) is discussed under the next subheading.

IP Multicast only needs to provide best-effort delivery service. It assumes that all receivers can cope with the data being sent. Adding reliability services on top of Multicast IP is not easy, and many of the issues are still being resolved. Some of the Web sites listed at the end of this topic describe these issues. The most common issues are briefly outlined here:

- A reliable service must take steps to ensure that all the intended sites received data. Performance problems will grow as the number of receivers grows.

- A reliable service must provide flow control to prevent packets from overrunning slow receivers. In a multicast group, some receivers may be slow while others are fast. The sender must find an optimal transmission rate that accommodates all the participants.

- Lost and corrupted packets must be detected with some mechanism, usually by adding sequence numbers to packets and relying on the receiver to detect from the sequence whether a packet is missing. Perhaps only a subgroup of the multicast group has lost packets. In this case, the sender may either retransmit the packet to everyone or just the subgroup. In the latter case, a mechanism is needed to map the subgroups.

- When an error occurs, the receivers must signal the sender. If every member of the multicast group returns an error message, the sender might be swamped with messages. The transport protocol must have some mechanism of dealing with similar error messages from multiple recipients.

*M*

## MTP (Multicast Transport Protocol)

MTP (RFC 1301) describes a flow-controlled, atomic multicasting transport protocol that operates on top of any network protocol as long as the data link layer includes multicast. MTP ensures that all messages are delivered reliably, in order, and at the same time. The current standard is MTP-2, which provides some service improvements over the original standard, such as the ability to retransmit packets to a specific branch of a multicast group, thus reducing excess traffic in branches that don't need the retransmission.

MTP defines how members of a multicast group can agree on the ordering and delivery of packets for reliable delivery. A member of the group is designated as a *master* and other members of the group can be either *producer/consumers* or just *consumers*. The producer/consumer can both transmit and receive messages while consumers only receive messages. The master controls the reliability parameters of the multicast group, as well as its membership and performance.

The master controls the flow of messages from producers to consumers and can reject messages from producers that may have since dropped out of the multicast group. A producer can send messages to the group after first obtaining a token from the master. If the master approves the producer's request, it sends a token that contains a sequence number for the message the producer will send. The producer than sends messages to the multicast group that contain the sequence number and the datagram sequence number, which is incremented for each datagram in a transmission.

To reduce network traffic, MTP does not require stations to acknowledge receipt of messages. It exploits the fact that most networks today are already highly reliable. Stations receive messages "silently" without notifying the senders that they have received the information.

**RELATED ENTRIES**    IP (Internet Protocol); MARS (Multicast Address Resolution Server); MBone (Multicast Backbone); Push; Routing Protocols and Algorithms; RSVP (Resource Reservation Protocol); RTP (Real-time Transport Protocol); *and* Transport Protocols and Services

### INFORMATION ON THE INTERNET

| | |
|---|---|
| IETF Inter-Domain Multicast Routing (idmr) Working Group | http://www.ietf.org/html.charters/idmr-charter.html |
| The IP Multicast Initiative site | http://www.ipmulticast.com |
| Requirements for Multicast Protocols (RFC 1458) | http://www.internic.net/rfc/rfc1458.txt |
| Multicast Transport Protocol (RFC 1301) | http://www.internic.net/rfc/rfc1301.txt |
| Introduction to IP Multicast paper | http://ntrg.cs.tcd.ie/4ba2/multicast |
| Jon Knight's Multicast Transport Protocols links page | http://hill.lut.ac.uk/DS-Archive/MTP.html |
| IP Multicast Routing paper | http://www.ipmulticast.com/community/whitepapers/introrouting.html |

| Multicast Transport Protocol (MTP and MTP-2) page | http://www.tascnets.com/mist/doc/MTP.html |
| MTP-2 page | http://wwwwbs.cs.tu-berlin.de/~nilss/mtp/mtp.html |
| TASC's Reliable Multicast Protocols page | http://www.tascnets.com/mist/doc/mcpCompare.html |

## Multihomed Host

The basic description of a multihomed host is a computer that has multiple network connections. In some cases, this is done by installing two or more NICs (network interface cards). Alternatively, some operating systems allow a single NIC to support multiple IP addresses.

An operating system such as Windows NT Server supports multiple NICs and can route packets between the networks attached to those NICs. Alternatively, you can turn routing off and just allow traffic from the two attached networks to access the server itself. Further, you can turn routing off and then install Microsoft's Proxy Server or some similar firewall-type software that specially controls packets at the application layer (rather than the network routing layer) which are forwarded between the networks.

Another description of a multihomed host is a Web server that is connected to the Internet through multiple ISPs, thus providing redundant connections. Still another description is a Web server that supports multiple domains in the same system. When Web clients connect to one of the domains, they cannot tell they are accessing a system that is supporting other domains. UNIX systems, Windows NT Server, and other operating systems currently support multihomed features. Microsoft calls a multihomed Web server a *virtual server*.

**RELATED ENTRIES**    Routers; Servers; *and* Web Technologies and Concepts

## Multilayer Switching/Routing

*See* Layer 3 Switching/Routing.

## Multilink Point-to-Point Protocol

*See* PPP Multilink.

## Multimedia

Multimedia on private networks and the Internet consists of voice, video, and other media, such as animation, that have large bandwidth requirements. There are a number of issues to manage, including a requirement for lots of storage and network bandwidth.

*M*

Videoconferencing is a concern for networks. It must have enough bandwidth to provide real-time delivery of information across a network without causing delays that produce garbled sound and jittery video. Of course, some multimedia information is not required in real time. A training video can begin playback as soon as enough information has arrived at the end users' stations. Even short pauses in the playback may be acceptable, although irritating.

Many organizations are seeing the need to integrate their voice and data networks. Why install and support two separate cabling systems when one high-speed network will support both voice and data and support new integrated computer-telephone applications? However, in doing so, special protocols are required to ensure that real-time information gets through. One technique is to increase network bandwidth by installing switched networks and ATM or Gigabit Ethernet backbones, but this may not be enough. History has shown that bandwidth is quickly consumed. Methods for prioritizing data, reserving bandwidth, and guaranteeing on-time delivery are essential. The Internet's RSVP (Resource Reservation Protocol) and ATM QoS (Quality of Service) provide such features, as discussed in this section.

## Multimedia Applications

The demand for more performance from networks is coming from a number of areas, including videoconferencing, collaborative computing, virtual reality modeling over the network, and voice. These applications are discussed here.

### Voice and Data Networks

There is a strong movement to integrate voice and data over the same network, both private internal networks and the Internet. With a single network, organizations can do away with redundant cabling and cumbersome PBX (private branch exchange) systems. The goal of IVD (integrated voice and data) supporters is to treat voice as any other application on the network. Doing so requires that desktop computers be upgraded with voice-processing hardware such as sound cards and telephone-like equipment (i.e., a microphone and speaker combination).

MICOM (http://www.micom.com) has processors that reduce digitized voice down from 64 Kbits/sec to as little as 6 Kbits/sec. This amount of compression is necessary to reduce the traffic on networks and ensure that voice traffic does not require excess network bandwidth. In the near future, users will be dialing from their PCs and using phone headsets that are connected to multimedia adapters in the backs of their computers. More likely, a typical office user will wear a wireless headset that not only serves as a telephone headset but as a keyboard replacement by providing voice dictation services and voice command services. Within the next few years, offices will be filled with the chatter of people talking to their computers and to other people through their computers.

## Videoconferencing

Videoconferencing has become an established method for people to communicate while reducing traveling time and cost. There are two primary videoconferencing standards:

- **ITU H.320 (Videoconferencing over ISDN)** This standard is a widely adopted method for holding conferences and collaborative sessions over long distances. Systems are often called *room systems* because they are restricted to equipment that is typically set up in a single conference room. In addition, links to other conference rooms are set up over ISDN (Integrated Services Digital Network) lines.

- **ITU H.323 (Videoconferencing over LANs)** This standard supports videoconferencing over an organization's network. Each person must have the appropriate multimedia equipment, such as video camera, microphone, and speaker, but this equipment is now relatively inexpensive.

The standards are designed to ensure interoperability among products so that a user or organization can set up a videoconference with any other user or organization without the need to worry about equipment compatibility. Note that H.320 systems can work with H.323 systems through gateways that provide ISDN links.

## Other Products

Progressive Networks (http://www.realaudio.com) has been a leader in multimedia for the Internet. Its RealAudio and RealVideo were immediately popular. Most systems are proprietary, and files compressed with one system cannot be uncompressed with another system. The popularity of the RealAudio and RealVideo products ensures that a large number of people have the same software, contributing to a rise in the use of the technology.

The technology is not perfect. It is prone to distortion caused by compression algorithms that are designed to "lose" some data that is considered nonessential. Video is often limited to small windows on the screen. The problem is the massive size of the data, even when compressed, and trying to transmit data across limited-bandwidth networks. The future holds promise, however.

Collaborative applications such as Microsoft NetMeeting and NetShow demand more network bandwidth. Because they are included in Microsoft Windows, they are easily accessible to users. See "Collaborative Computing" for more information. A news service, such as the one provided by MSNBC (Microsoft and NBC), is another interesting application. The MSNBC Web site is at www.businessvideo.msnbc.com.

*M*

## Building Multimedia Networks

What makes voice and video over data networks a reality is compression, industry standards, and multimedia networks with high bandwidth and QoS. Compression reduces the amount of multimedia information that must be transmitted over network links. See "Compression Techniques" for more details.

ATM has been the great hope for multimedia networks because it supports QoS guarantees that let network administrators and users reserve network bandwidth to handle their multimedia requirements. Administrators can set up virtual circuits in advance to guarantee bandwidth for videoconferences or voice calls, but for users to specify QoS on demand will require ATM-compatible applications, ATM adapters in user workstations, or software that emulates ATM on existing network adapters. See "CIF (Cells in Frames)" and "QoS (Quality of Service)" for information about the latter.

The main issue with adding multimedia applications to the network is the traffic load. Real-time multimedia applications like videoconferencing need QoS guarantees, but that may translate to reduced bandwidth for other traffic. A multimedia network must have enough bandwidth to support all the normal data traffic and the new multimedia traffic. It is important to determine normal traffic loads and the load that will be imposed by multimedia data transfers. A videoconferencing system requires .5 to 1 Mbit/sec of bandwidth, assuming a small, low-resolution image is transmitted at a low frame rate.

A number of techniques can boost network performance. You can start building a core switched network that connects to existing departmental hubs and then eventually upgrade the department hubs to provide switched services to all users. Videoconferencing systems should be connected directly to high-performance switches. Gigabit Ethernet provides a high-performance network solution that is compatible with existing Ethernet networks. See "Gigabit Ethernet" for more information. Iso-Ethernet is a technology that incorporates voice and standard 10-Mbit/sec Ethernet on the same cable. See "Iso-Ethernet" for more information.

Protocols and techniques for obtaining quality of service over existing networks have been developed or are in the works. While QoS is built in to ATM, applications must be specifically designed to access those services (see "WinSock"). In the IP environment, the IETF (Internet Engineering Task Force) has developed RSVP, which allows an IP host to request a certain amount of bandwidth on the network. See "RSVP (Resource Reservation Protocol)" for more information.

**RELATED ENTRIES**   Collaborative Computing; Compression Techniques; Groupware; Intranets and Extranets; Iso-Ethernet; MBone (Multicast Backbone); Multicasting; Push; QoS (Quality of Service); RSVP (Resource Reservation Protocol); RTP (Real-time Transport Protocol); Videoconferencing and Desktop Video; Voice/Data Networks; VoIP (Voice over IP); *and* Web Technologies and Concepts

**INFORMATION ON THE INTERNET**

Index to Multimedia Information Sources    http://viswiz.gmd.de/MultimediaInfo

| | |
|---|---|
| W3C's Synchronized Multimedia page | http://www.w3.org/pub/WWW/ Consortium/Prospectus/RealTime.html |
| MMTA (MultiMedia Telecommunications Association) | http://www.mmta.org |
| World-Wide Web Telecoms Virtual Library on multimedia | http://www.analysys.com/vlib/ multimed.htm |
| Simon Gibbs' Multimedia Information Sources | http://fourier.dur.ac.uk:8000/mm.html |
| RTP (Real-time Transport Protocol) Overview | http://www.cs.columbia.edu/~hgs/rtp |
| VocalTec Communications Ltd. | http://www.vocaltec.com |
| Progressive Networks | http://www.realaudio.com |
| Xing Technology Corp. | http://www.xingtech.com |
| Voxware, Inc. | http://www.voxware.com |
| VOSAIC | http://www.vosaic.com |
| InterVU, Inc. | http://www.intervu.com |
| Precept Software, Inc. | http://www.precept.com |

## Multiplexing

Multiplexing combines multiple channels of information over a single circuit or transmission path. A telephone company that installs trunks between its central offices will want to get as many voice conversations on those trunks as possible. Multiplexing schemes such as T1 can handle 24 voice channels (4 kHz wide). Backbone trunks carry even more channels. A T3 trunk can carry 28 T1 lines.

There are two primary multiplexing techniques, as pictured in Figure M-14. *FDM* (*frequency division multiplexing*) divides the frequency spectrum of a circuit into bands and transmits each channel on a specific band, as shown in Figure M-14(a). *TDM* (*time division multiplexing*) divides a circuit into timeslots and assigns a channel to each slot, as shown in Figure M-14(b). FDM and TDM are discussed in the following sections.

A third technique, called *inverse multiplexing*, is the reverse of the above techniques. Inverse multiplexing is a technique of dividing a single high-speed data stream into multiple low-speed data streams for transmission over multiple low-speed connections, as shown in Figure M-14(c). This can save some expense in leasing high-speed lines and can make better use of available lines. Refer to "Inverse Multiplexing" for more information.

*M*

**NOTE:** *Cell relay like that implemented in ATM is another type of multiplexing. Cells are 53-byte packets of data that are transmitted serially across a medium.*

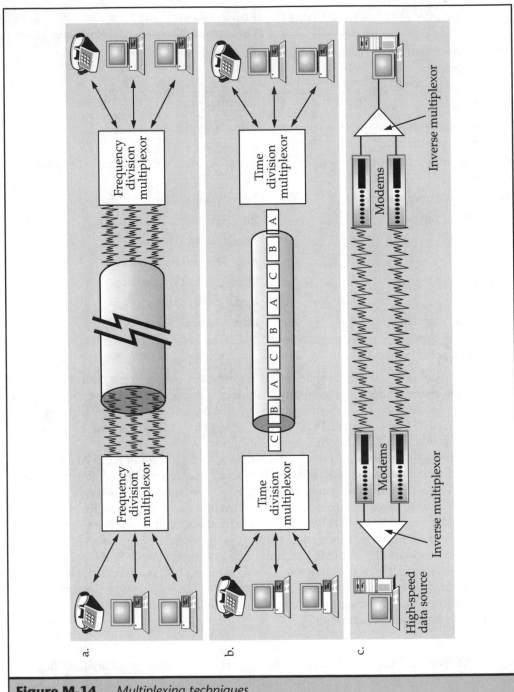

a.

b.

c.

**Figure M-14.** *Multiplexing techniques*

## FDM (Frequency Division Multiplexing)

FDM is a broadband analog transmission technique in which multiple signals are transmitted over a single cable simultaneously, as shown in Figure M-14(a). Each data or voice signal is modulated onto a carrier at different frequencies. An analogy can be found in radio broadcasting. Multiple stations transmit at the same time. To listen to a particular station, you tune your radio to the frequency that the radio station broadcasts on. The frequency range of a circuit is subdivided into narrow bands, and each band then carries a different transmission signal. Guard bands separate the subdivided transmission bands to minimize interference.

A voice conversion requires a 3,000 Hz channel, but 4,000 Hz is allocated per channel so there is adequate separation between each channel. A common frequency range used around the world is 60 to 108 kHz. The first channel occupies the 60 to 64 kHz range, the second channel occupies the 64 to 68 kHz range, and so on up to the 12$^{th}$ channel, which occupies the 104 to 108 kHz range. This is pictured here. Note the area of potential crosstalk between each channel.

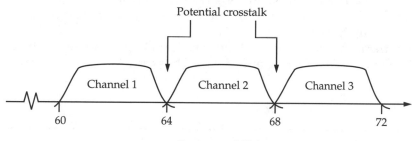

In North America, there is a hierarchical FDM scheme originally outlined by AT&T for transmitting signals on systems that have different capacities. The basic 12 channels just discussed form a *group*. The bandwidth of this group is 48 kHz and occupies the frequency range of 60 to 108 kHz. The next level in the hierarchy consists of five groups combined to carry 60 channels (called a *supergroup*) in the frequency range of 312 to 552 kHz. The hierarchy extends up into higher frequencies, with groups that contain 300, 600, 900, and so on, up to 10,800 voice channels.

## Wavelength Division Multiplexing

WDM (wavelength division multiplexing) is a variation of FDM that is used on fiber-optic cables. In this techniques two or more beams of light (rather than electrical signals) are combined by using a prism or diffraction grating. The signals are sent across a single cable. At the other end of the multiplexed cable, a prism or diffraction grating is used to separate the beams of light.

**M**

WDM is being employed to increase the capacity of the Internet backbone. The MPB (massively parallel backbone) potentially can support multiple trunks that have up to 200 WDM OC-48 circuits at 2.4 Gbits/sec each.

## TDM (Time Division Multiplexing)

TDM is a baseband technology in which individual channels of data or voice are interleaved into a single stream of bits (or framed bits) on a communication channel, as shown in Figure M-15. Analog inputs (voice) are digitized using PCM (pulse code modulation).

Each input channel gets an interleaved time segment so that all channels equally share the medium that is used for transmission. If a channel has nothing to send, the slot is still dedicated to the channel and remains empty. While this is inefficient, it guarantees that each channel has the slots its needs to deliver data on time.

The multiplexor and the transmission line must be of sufficient capacity to keep up with the sum of all the channel inputs. Consider a multilane freeway that is reduced down to a single lane due to road construction. A traffic director motions in turn to a car in each lane to proceed into the single lane. To prevent traffic congestion, the traffic director must work quickly and the cars must travel at high speed across the single lane.

The T1 carrier is the most common time division multiplexed line. As shown in Figure M-16, there are 24 repeating time slots of 8 bits each. Voice signals are digitized

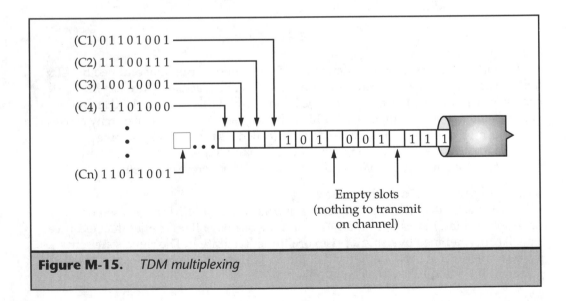

**Figure M-15.** *TDM multiplexing*

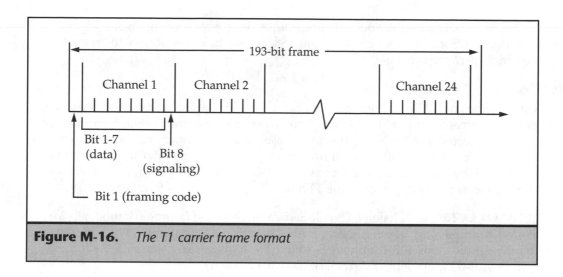

**Figure M-16.** *The T1 carrier frame format*

by codecs (*co*der-*dec*oders) and 7 bits from each channel are placed in one of the slots. The 8th bit in each slot is used for signaling. An entire frame consists of 24 8-bit slots with one extra bit used by the frame itself for synchronization. The entire frame is 193 bits in length. Each of the 24 channels has a data rate of 64 Kbits/sec, yielding a 1.544-Mbit/sec T1 line.

A T1 line can be used to send one large data stream instead of breaking the stream into slots for individual voice conversations or data transmissions. In this case, 23 channels are combined for data and the 24th channel is used to provide synchronization.

The telephone companies multiplex T1 lines on their trunks. Four T1 lines are multiplexed into a T2 line (6.312 Mbits/sec), six T2 lines are multiplexed into a T3 line (44.736 Mbits/sec), and seven T3 lines are multiplexed into a T4 (274,176 Mbits/sec).

## STDM (Statistical Time Division Multiplexing)

As mentioned, time division multiplexing allocates time slots to channels even if there is nothing to transmit on the channel. This is an inefficient use of bandwidth. One channel may be overtaxed while another is underused.

Statistical multiplexors solve this problem by dynamically allocating time slots and using the line more efficiently. Statistical multiplexors use processors and buffering techniques to allocate slots, and tend to be more expensive than standard multiplexors. Because buffering can add delays, the processors must be fast enough to keep up with the incoming data while allocating it efficiently to time slots.

*M*

There are, of course, various other techniques to improve multiplexor performance. Some of these involve compression, which is practical to do on the fly with high-performance equipment.

## Multiplexor Configurations

Multiplexors, or MUXs as they are often called, are devices that combine signals from various sources such as a PBX (private branch exchange), asynchronous terminals, or a bridge connected to a WAN and transmit those signals as a single data stream over a digital line. Figure M-17 illustrates how a multiplexor connects internal equipment to a T1 leased telephone line. Note that a CSU/DSU (channel service unit/data service unit) connects the multiplexor to the T1 line.

**RELATED ENTRIES**    Channel; Circuit-Switching Services; Communication Services; Inverse Multiplexing; Leased Line; Point-to-Point Communications; T1/T3; Telecommunications and Telephone Systems; Throughput; Transmission Media, Methods, and Equipment; *and* WAN (Wide Area Network)

**INFORMATION ON THE INTERNET**

Black Box's On-Line Catalog          http://www.blackbox.com

Jared Hall's Telecom Corner          http://www.tbi.net/~jhall

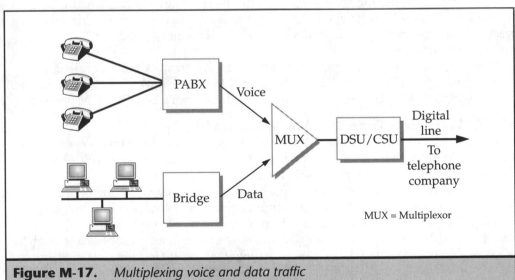

**Figure M-17.**    *Multiplexing voice and data traffic*

# Multiprocessing

A multiprocessing system is a computer that has more than one processor. Server systems and superservers are specifically designed to support multiple processors. Superservers include a high-performance bus, tens of megabytes of error-correcting memory, RAID (redundant arrays of inexpensive disks) systems, advanced system architectures that reduce bottlenecks, and redundant features such as multiple power supplies.

There are two methods for implementing an operating system on top of a multiprocessing system:

- **Asymmetrical multiprocessing system**  In asymmetrical multiprocessing systems, each processor basically stands on its own and equally shares all resources in the system. The operating system may have each processor work on a different task. For example, one processor may handle I/O (input/output) and another may handle network operating system tasks. Asymmetrical multiprocessing systems do not balance workloads. A processor handling one task can be overworked while another processor sits idle. Symmetrical multiprocessing systems distribute the workload evenly.

- **Symmetrical multiprocessing system**  In this design, system resources such as memory and disk I/O are shared by all the processors in the system. The workload is distributed evenly to available processors so that one doesn't sit idle while another is overworked with a specific task. The performance of symmetrical multiprocessing systems increases for all tasks as processors are added. Operating systems that take advantage of symmetrical multiprocessing systems are harder to design. Most high-end network operating systems, including Windows NT, now support symmetrical multiprocessing.

**RELATED ENTRIES**    Clustering; Distributed Processing; MPP (Massively Parallel Processor) Systems; NUMA (Non-Uniform Memory Access); Parallel Processing; Servers; *and* Supercomputer

# Multiprotocol Router

A multiprotocol router is designed to handle a variety of network-layer communication protocols, not just one protocol. A typical multiprotocol router can support IPX (Internetwork Packet Exchange) and IP (Internet Protocol), along with a variety of other protocols.

**RELATED ENTRIES**    Routers; Routing Protocols and Algorithms

*M*

# Multitiered Architectures

A normal client/server environment consists of clients accessing servers. In the three-tier model, most of the processing is removed from the client and placed on a middle-tier system (not the data server). In a business environment, the middle-tier system holds all the "business logic" for an organization. Business logic includes the rules, procedures, and operational sequences that provide services to data processing systems. By consolidating business logic on a shared system, all the rules are grouped onto a single server where they are easier to manage and where applications can more easily access them.

Data warehousing schemes implement a multitier model in which data from back-end servers and legacy mainframe systems is extracted, summarized, cleaned up, and consolidated onto "staging" systems where users can more easily access the information.

The Web is also built on a multitier model in which Web browsers are the client tier and Web servers are the middle tier, with back-end servers and databases being the tier where persistent data is stored. The Web server receives requests from clients and passes those requests, usually in the form of SQL (Structured Query Language) requests, to a back-end server. The Web server then receives the response, repackages it, and sends it to the client. Note that multiple Web servers may exist in this model, with clients being shunted to whichever server can best handle their requests.

As shown on the left in Figure M-18, a typical in-house system may consist of clients connecting with middle-tier systems using connection-oriented RPCs (remote procedure calls) and connectionless messaging protocols as described under "MOM (Message-Oriented Middleware)."

Web connections are slightly different, as shown on the right in Figure M-18. Initially, the user running a Web browser communicates with a Web server via standard HTTP (Hypertext Transfer Protocol). HTTP is inadequate for running advanced client/server applications, so the server updates the client with software that allows it to establish stateful connections directly with the back-end server, using protocols such as IIOP (Internet Inter-ORB Protocol). IIOP is part of the CORBA (Common Object Request Broker Architecture). IIOP allows CORBA to be implemented into Web browsers and servers. It provides services that are much better at handling mission-critical business applications over the Internet and it promotes the creation and use of distributed applications on the Web.

**RELATED ENTRIES**    Client/Server Computing; CORBA (Common Object Request Broker Architecture); Data Warehousing; DBMS (Database Management System); IIOP (Internet Inter-ORB Protocol); Middleware and Messaging; MOM (Message-Oriented

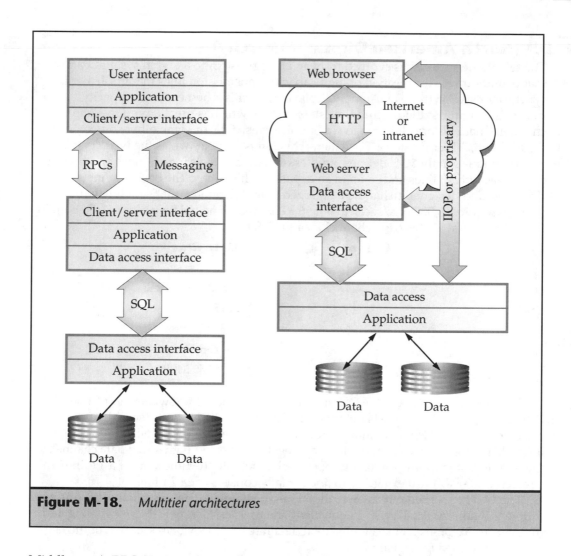

**Figure M-18.**   *Multitier architectures*

Middleware); RPC (Remote Procedure Call); SQL (Structured Query Language); Transaction Processing; *and* Web Middleware and Database Connectivity

## MVS (Multiple Virtual Storage), IBM

*See* IBM Mainframe Environment; IBM Operating Systems.

*M*

# NADH (North American Digital Hierarchy)

The telephone system has evolved from an analog system to a digital system. Part of that evolution was the creation of high-capacity transmission lines that implement synchronous TDM (time division multiplexing). In this scheme, a high-capacity transmission line is divided into time slots, each of which is preallocated to some channel. Channels are allocated to either voice calls, data, or some other source.

Early on, AT&T created a TDM hierarchy that is now known as the NADH. It is also used in Japan. NADH defines bundles of voice channels into T1 lines and bundles of T1 lines into T3 lines and so on in an expanding hierarchy. The basic channel is 64 Kbits/sec and designed to handle a digitized voice telephone call. Signaling in the channel requires 8,000 bits/sec, leaving 56 Kbits/sec for actual voice data. As shown in the following table, this basic channel is called DS-0.

| Type | Channels | Data Rate |
| --- | --- | --- |
| DS-0 | 1 | 64 Kbits/sec |
| DS-1 | 24 | 1.533 Mbits/sec |
| DS-1C | 48 | 3.152 Mbits/sec |
| DS-2 | 96 | 6.312 Mbits/sec |
| DS-3 | 672 | 44.736 Mbits/sec |
| DS-4 | 4032 | 274.176 Mbits/sec |

The next level up in the NADH hierarchy is DS-1, better known as the T1 line. It consists of 24 DS-0 channels for a total throughput of 1.544 Mbits/sec. Many organizations use T1 lines to link corporate offices. The channels can be used individually for voice telephone calls or aggregated to create a high-speed data channel. The method of mapping digital bits of each channel into the time slots of a T1 line is covered under "Multiplexing." A T3 line actually consists of 24 T1 lines.

The CCITT worked out its own digital hierarchy which, unfortunately, is slightly different than NADH. The DS-1 equivalent line uses less bandwidth for signaling and thus carries 32 DS-0 channels with a total data rate of 2.048 Mbits/sec. Two of those channels are used for signaling.

A new international standard that has the potential to integrate all the world's telephone systems and associated communication channels is SONET (Synchronous Optical Network) and the SDH (Synchronous Digital Hierarchy). SONET is the successor of NADH and SDH is the successor of the CCITT standard used outside the United States. Fortunately, in this case SONET and SDH are virtually compatible. At the same time, SONET is backward compatible with NADH. Refer to "SONET (Synchronous Optical Network)" for additional information. For more information about T1 and T3 lines and their use in wide area network connections, refer to "T1/T3" and "WAN (Wide Area Network)."

**RELATED ENTRIES**   E-1/E-3 European Digital Hierarchy; Multiplexing; SONET (Synchronous Optical Network); T1/T3; Telecommunications and Telephone Systems; *and* WAN (Wide Area Network)

**INFORMATION ON THE INTERNET**

| | |
|---|---|
| Prof. Jeffrey MacKie-Mason's Telecom page | http://www.spp.umich.edu/telecom |
| Telecom Digest | http://massis.lcs.mit.edu/telecom-archives |
| Hilary Bailey's Telecoms Virtual Library | http://www.analysys.com/vlib |
| Computer and Communication hot links | http://www.cmpcmm.com/cc/standards.html |
| Committee T1 | http://www.t1.org |

# NAK (Negative Acknowledgment)

An ACK (acknowledgment) is a confirmation of receipt. When data is transmitted between two systems, the recipient can acknowledge that it received the data. If a station receives packets that are corrupted, it can return a NAK (negative acknowledgment) to the sender. A checksum error may indicate a corrupted packet. A NAK is different than a normal acknowledgment in that it indicates that a packet was received in a corrupted state.

An alternative to sending a NAK is for the receiving station to not acknowledge that it has received packets, but this method only works on networks where the sending station expects an acknowledgment. Acknowledgments are used on unreliable networks to provide guarantees to the sending station that packets have arrived. However, most modern networks are so reliable that acknowledgments are usually disabled, so this alternative NAK method will not work.

**RELATED ENTRIES**   Acknowledgments; Connection Establishment; Connection-Oriented and Connectionless Services; Data Communication Concepts; Flow-Control Mechanisms; *and* Transport Protocols and Services

# Named Pipes

Named pipes is a high-level interface for passing data between processes that are running on separate computers connected by a network. Named pipes are the network version of IPC (interprocess communication) facilities, which provide an interface between processes running in a single, multitasking system. Named pipes were originally created as extensions of the OS/2 operating system and were implemented on Microsoft LAN Manager and IBM LAN Server network operating systems. They were modified and implemented in the Windows environment. Named pipes is connection oriented. Named pipes are based on OS/2 API calls, but in Windows NT they include additional asynchronous support and increased security.

Mail slots is a related IPC mechanism that provides store-and-forward queued messaging services. Message delivery is not guaranteed. Instead, the mechanism assumes the network is reliable and that errors will be detected by high-layer protocols. Mail slots is often used to locate or provide notification of computers and services on the network. Both named pipes and mail slots are written as file systems that share common functionality, such as caches, with other file systems.

Compared to a pipe, a named pipe is a communication process between two remote computer systems that are attached to a network. A logical connection is set up between the two remote processes and the transfer of information takes place over the physical network. Named pipes enable client/server applications in distributed computing environments.

**RELATED ENTRIES**   IPC (Interprocess Communication); MOM (Message-Oriented Middleware); NetBIOS/NetBEUI; Pipes; RPC (Remote Procedure Call); *and* SMB (Server Message Blocks)

## Name Resolution

Name resolution is the process of resolving a name into a numeric network address. Names are used to make computers more accessible to humans, but the underlying network still requires network addresses. Therefore, special name resolution software is required on workstations and/or servers to translate between the human-readable name and the network address, which may be in alphanumeric form.

In the TCP/IP environment, familiar names such as www.whitehouse.com are translated to appropriate IP addresses by DNS (Domain Name System) servers. In the Windows environment, NetBIOS names are resolved into IP addresses by WINS (Windows Internet Naming Service). DNS servers may also exist in the Windows environment if Internet naming is used.

**RELATED ENTRIES**   Directory Services; DNS (Domain Name System); IP (Internet Protocol); *and* WINS (Windows Internet Naming Service)

## Name Services

*See* Directory Services; DNS (Domain Name System); IP (Internet Protocol); *and* WINS (Windows Internet Naming Service).

## NAP (Network Access Point)

A NAP is a top-level traffic exchange point in the routing hierarchy of the Internet. It is often called an IX (Internet exchange). This topic is covered in detail under "Internet Backbone."

## NBMA (Nonbroadcast Multiple Access)

An NBMA network is the opposite of a broadcast network. On a broadcast network, multiple computers and devices are attached to a shared network cable or other medium. When one computer transmits frames, all nodes on the network "listen" to the frames but only the node to which the frames are addressed actually receives the frames. Thus, the frames are broadcast.

A nonbroadcast multiple access network is a network to which multiple computers and devices are attached, but data is transmitted directly from one computer to another over a virtual circuit or across a switching fabric. The most common examples of nonbroadcast network media include ATM (Asynchronous Transfer Mode), frame relay, SMDS (Switched Multimegabit Data Service), and X.25.

The IETF ION (Internetworking over NBMA) Working Group is focused on the creation of standards for running network layer protocols over nonbroadcast access media. See "ION (Internetworking over NBMA)."

## NC (Network Computer) Devices

NCs (as defined by Sun, Netscape, Oracle, and others) are low-cost, network-connected devices that do not have hard drives, but instead rely on network servers for their disk and storage requirements. NCs are often called *thin clients*. The NC connects to the network via TCP/IP protocols and supports terminal emulation, X Window, Java, and Web browser software. NCs can be thought of as Internet terminals. Because NCs are network-dependent devices, they can only operate when the network is up and running. The trade-off is reduced price and greater administrative control. The devices are ideal for environments where computing devices have limited tasks, such as retail counters, call centers, and kiosks.

NOTE: *An alternative "thin client" computer is the NetPC as defined by Microsoft and Intel and discussed under "NetPC."*

NCs execute Java applets that have been loaded from servers. One way to think of an NC is as just a screen and a keyboard. The major part of an application executes on a server, so the NC needs minimal resources. In the multitiered Web model, pictured in Figure N-1, the user runs a Web browser to connect with a Web server, and the Web server connects with back-end data systems.

Since the NC runs Java and Web software, virtually any processor can be used. The NC is not tied to one processor family as Microsoft Windows is largely tied to the Intel processor family. NCs are potentially very inexpensive devices. At the same time, the Microsoft and Intel NetPC design runs most existing Microsoft Windows applications.

NCs (and NetPCs) are designed to reduce the cost of client systems by centralizing control and management. Management features provide the ability to lock down the desktop, prevent users from performing some tasks, provide security (there are no disks to upload or download data), and provide centralized configuration of the system and the user's desktop. Software is stored at and runs on network servers,

**N**

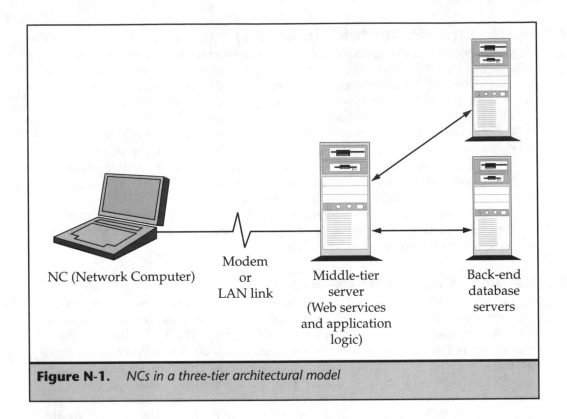

**Figure N-1.** *NCs in a three-tier architectural model*

where it is easier to manage and upgrade. However, this requires that servers in an NC environment be very powerful devices.

Typically, central servers store a desktop configuration for each NC user. Ideally, no matter where users travel, their personal desktops appear, assuming they can connect with and log onto the server where their desktops are stored. Dial-up services allow users to dial a number local to them and access remote servers over the Internet in a secure way while reducing long-distance charges. See "Virtual Dial-up Services" for more information.

The NC is more than a low-cost corporate computing device. For example, imagine logging in to your corporate network from an NC "vending machine" at an airport. You drop in a couple of quarters (or insert a credit card), connect to your home Web server, log on, then access your corporate network and e-mail. Similar devices might be mounted on the backs of airplane seats.

NCs are reintroducing the most beneficial features of the old mainframe processing model, such as centralized control and management. In addition, software updates are easier with most of the software located on central servers. Administrators don't need to worry about updating every client system individually.

Vendors of NC devices are listed at the end of this topic. The Sun Microsystems JavaStation is perhaps the most NC-like design. It runs Java applications after booting from a Solaris-based Netra-J server. Hybrid devices are also available that run X-Window applications or operate as Windows terminals, such as devices from Boundless Technologies, Neoware Systems, and Network Computing Devices. Insignia Solution's NTRIGUE Client for Java is a thin client that allows Java desktop users to run all Windows-based applications that operate under the Windows NT operating system on their Java desktops. It allows administrators to deploy Java desktops throughout the enterprise and still run legacy Windows applications.

## Initiatives and Vendor Strategies

There are several NC and NetPC management initiatives and product strategies, as outlined here:

- IBM NC products are the Network Station (IBM's NC) and NSM (Network Station Manager), a multiplatform management system that is based on HTML and JavaScript. Clients can boot from and be authenticated by network servers and access files on NFS (Network File System) servers. NSM is designed to run on LAN servers, midrange systems, and mainframes. It controls all the Network Station's applications, including access to multiple servers on the network for transaction-based applications, access to Windows applications, and also cross-platform connections to the Internet and corporate intranets. NSM is free and can be downloaded by accessing http://www.ibm.com/nc. Additional information is available at the site.

- Sun implements a complete hardware and software approach that includes a variety of products. JavaStation is a thin client desktop workstation, or *webtop*, that runs intranet software, Web protocols, and the Java language/run-time environment. JavaStation downloads Java applications on demand and executes them locally; all applications and data, however, reside on centralized servers for ease of administration. Sun Servers support zero-administration clients, deliver Java applications, and provide access to data warehouses. Sun's Netra-J provides a complete, integrated server, content-optimized to support JavaStation and other Java-enabled NCs. Finally, HotJava Views is a Java-based user environment that provides intuitive "push-button" access to Java applications across the enterprise. For more information, see the various topics under the "Sun Microsystems" headings in this book, or visit the Sun site at http://www.sun.com.

- Oracle's approach was to start up a subsidiary company called NCI (Network Computer, Inc.) and create a product called NC Network in the Box, which delivers a complete, out-of-the-box network computer system. The product requires little setup and consists of an Intel-based NC Server appliance with software for managing network computers. It also includes applications such as electronic mail and productivity software, and NC Desktop, the software for the network computer. The NC Server supports Java applications and "push"

**N**

strategies for distributing applications to clients. Visit the NCI Web site at http://nc.oracle.com.

■ Microsoft's approach to the NC is the more elaborate NetPC. Its approach to management is the Zero Administration for Windows Initiative or ZAWS. ZAWS is designed to provide desktop locking services and the ability to prevent users from performing certain operations. It also provides centralized configuration management. Refer to "NetPC" and "Zero Administration for Windows Initiative" for more details.

■ Intel has its own plan, called *Wired for Management*. It, too, is designed to reduce the cost of desktop management by providing centralized control of networked PCs. However, Intel's plan specifies the management of fully configured PCs and NetPCs. It includes support for DMI (Desktop Management Interface) and also provides support for workgroup and enterprise management. See "Wired for Management." Additional information is available on Intel's Web site at http://www.intel.com.

**RELATED ENTRIES**    Access Server; Component Software Technology; Diskless Workstation; Java; NetPC; Netscape ONE Development Environment; Network Management; Oracle NCA (Network Computing Architecture); Remote Access; Sun Microsystems Solaris NEO; Virtual Dial-up Services; Web Technologies and Concepts; WinFrame; *and* Zero Administration for Windows Initiative

## INFORMATION ON THE INTERNET

| | |
|---|---|
| Network Computer Reference Profile | http://www.nc.ihost.com |
| Network Computer News site | http://www.ncns.com |
| NC World Magazine | http://www.ncworldmag.com |
| Network Computer, Inc. (Oracle) | http://nc.oracle.com |
| Sun Microsystems' JavaStation | http://www.sun.com |
| Boundless Technologies, Inc. | http://www.boundless.com |
| Neoware Systems, Inc. | http://www.neoware.com |
| Network Computing Devices, Inc. | http://www.ncd.com |
| Wyse Technology, Inc. | http://www.wyse.com |
| Insignia NTRIGUE ICA (for running Windows applications) | http://www.insignia.com |
| Citrix Systems, Inc. | http://www.citrix.com |
| Network Computers and Push Technology article | http://www.broadband-guide.com/news/dhapr97/dh1.html |

# NCP (NetWare Core Protocol)

NCP is the principal protocol for transmitting information between a NetWare server and its clients. NCP handles login requests and many other types of requests to the file system and the printing system. IPX (Internetwork Packet Exchange) is the underlying protocol that carries NCP messages. NCP is a client/server LAN protocol. Workstations create NCP requests and use IPX to send them over the network. At the server, NCP requests are received, unpacked, and interpreted.

NCP services include file access, file locking, security, tracking of resource allocation, event notification, synchronization with other servers, connection and communication, print services and queue management, and network management.

**RELATED ENTRIES**    Novell NetWare; Novell NetWare Protocols

# NCSA (National Computer Security Association)

NCSA is an organization devoted to computer security issues in corporations, associations, and government agencies worldwide. It is dedicated to continuously improving commercial computer security through certification, sharing of knowledge, and dissemination of information. The organization was founded in 1989 and is located in Carlisle, Pennsylvania

NCSA delivers information through publications, conferences, forums, and seminars—in both traditional and electronic formats. You can obtain information at http://www.ncsa.com.

# NDIS (Network Driver Interface Specification)

The Microsoft NDIS was designed to make it easier for NIC (network interface card) vendors to market NICs that work with a variety of network protocols and operating systems. It also reduces configuration headaches for network administrators. A similar standard is Novell's ODI (Open Data link Interface). Before NDIS, NIC vendors had to create drivers that were configured for each possible configuration into which a NIC might be installed.

NDIS provides a standard software interface that upper-layer network protocols use to communicate with a network adapter card. NDIS basically hides the type of network card in use. These protocols only need to bind with the NDIS interface to work with any network adapter. System engineers only need to make sure that an NDIS-compatible driver is used for the network adapter being installed.

As shown in Figure N-2, NDIS is defined in the MAC (Medium Access Control) sublayer relative to the OSI protocol stack. The MAC sublayer is the lower half of the data link layer and interfaces directly with the physical layer. NIC drivers, which contain the software logic to transfer data between software and the NIC, are installed in the MAC sublayer.

Today, NDIS is well established, and the installation process is nearly automatic. During operating system setup, a system administrator only needs to select the type of

**N**

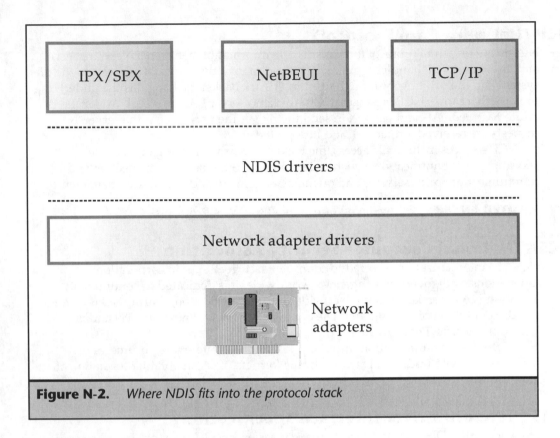

**Figure N-2.**  *Where NDIS fits into the protocol stack*

NIC in use. Operating systems like Windows 95 and Windows NT come with a large selection of NDIS-compatible MAC drivers to work with the most common NICs.

Another feature of NDIS is the ability to load multiple protocol stacks or use multiple network adapters in the same computer, as shown in Figure N-3 and as described here:

- **Single NIC/multiple protocols**  This configuration allows a system to communicate over the same network using multiple network protocols, such as IPX and TCP/IP. The NDIS layer interfaces both protocol stacks to the NIC.

- **Multiple NICs/multiple protocols**  In this configuration, shown on the right in Figure N-3, a system is attached to two different networks. NDIS handles the interface between each protocol stack and its appropriate NIC.

Support for multiple network adapters and protocols is critical in the enterprise network environment where users connected to multiple different networks may need to communicate with a server. NDIS allows servers to support multiple network protocols.

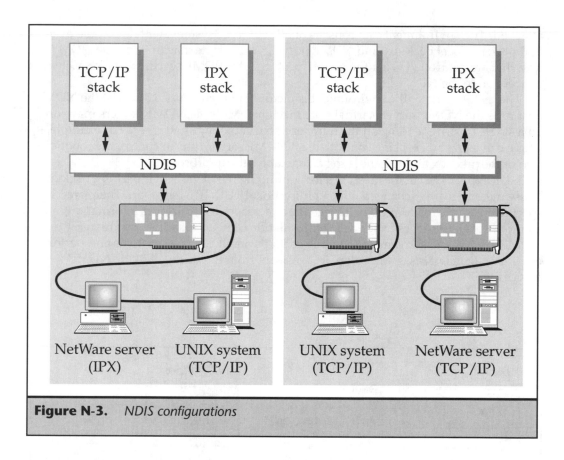

**Figure N-3.**   *NDIS configurations*

**RELATED ENTRIES**   NIC (Network Interface Card); ODI (Open Data link Interface); *and* Windows

# NDMP (Network Data Management Protocol)

NDMP is an initiative launched by the Network Data Management Protocol Task Force to create an open standard protocol for network-based backup on network-attached storage devices (specifically, tape devices, although other devices will be supported). The objective of NDMP is to provide enterprise-wide control of backup in heterogeneous environments. It also provides a standardized protocol that vendors can write to and conform with to reduce cross-platform hardware and software development efforts. With NDMP, vendors can concentrate on features and performance rather than on writing code for many different platforms and environments. They only need to be concerned with maintaining compatibility with one well-defined protocol.

An NDMP environment consists of a backup software host where the backup software, daemons, and databases exist. This host may or may not have a tape drive

**N**

attached. The environment also consists of *NDMP hosts*, systems with local tape drives that perform local backups, and *NDMP servers*, virtual state machines on the NDMP host that are controlled using the NDMP protocol. An NDMP server exists for each connection to the NDMP host.

The architecture of the environment is pictured in Figure N-4. Note that the NDMP host runs the NDMP server (virtual state machine). Multiple NDMP servers may run on a single host, depending on the number of backup devices attached. For example, if a tape drive jukebox is being controlled, an NDMP server runs to control the robotic arm of the jukebox and to handle the actual tape backup process.

NDMP provides all the messages for controlling the devices that perform backups. These messages are exchanged over a bidirectional TCP/IP connection. There are specific messages for controlling devices and messages for collecting information about the backup process, such as log information. A network administrator uses NDMP-compatible software to schedule backups on NDMP host systems and perform other management tasks. Messages are then sent from the software to the NDMP devices.

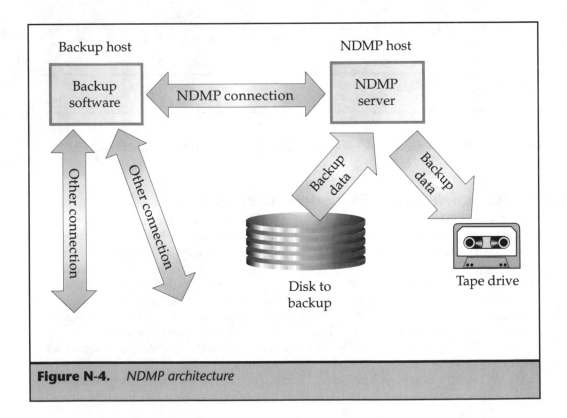

**Figure N-4.**　*NDMP architecture*

**RELATED ENTRIES**   Backup and Data Archiving; Clustering; Data Migration; Data Protection; Disaster Recovery; Fault Management; Fault Tolerance; Mirroring; Replication; Storage Management Systems; *and* Storage Systems

**INFORMATION ON THE INTERNET**

Network Data Management Protocol site            http://www.ndmp.org

# NDS (Novell Directory Services)

NDS is a distributed directory service that is similar to the ISO X.500 directory services specification. While originally developed for Novell NetWare 4.x, Novell now makes the services available for other platforms. Like most directory services, NDS keeps track of all network users, servers, and resources on enterprise networks and even global networks. This information is kept in a single database. Network administrators and network users access this database when they need to know about or access people and resources on the network.

The NDS directory tree is organized hierarchically according to an organization's structure. It is viewed and manipulated with a graphical utility called the NetWare Administrator. An example of a directory tree is pictured in Figure N-5. All network

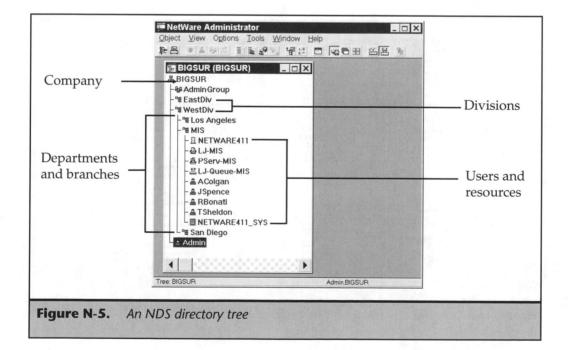

**Figure N-5.**   *An NDS directory tree*

N

users and resources are stored in NDS as objects with properties. There are three types of objects:

- The *root* object, which is the base of the directory tree and which usually has the same name as the organization
- *Container* objects, which hold other objects
- *Leaf* objects, which are either user accounts, group accounts, or resources on the network such as servers and printers.

One way to think of NDS is as a telephone book for your network, and indeed you can store information such as telephone numbers, addresses, department locations, and other identifying information for every user on your network. Then any user or network manager can find a user by searching for the name or identifying information such as ZIP code, department name, or job function. Take a look at Figure N-6. It shows a picture of how NDS user information is presented in the Windows-based management tool called NetWare Administrator.

This information is entered when the client account is created. Administrators can typically view all the information, while normal users can only see selected fields. The information is a record in the NDS database, although such a record is more properly called an *object*. The fields in the objects are its *properties*. Additional properties are available by clicking the button on the right side of the window.

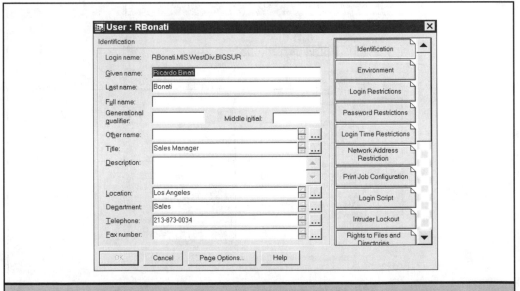

**Figure N-6.** *Information about a user in the NDS database*

An NDS directory tree is often designed around the topology of the physical network, as shown in Figure N-7. Note that the tree has container objects that represent the company name (CambrianCorp), its regional divisions (Eastern and Western), and its regional offices. Under each regional office are the *leaf objects* that represent the users and physical network entities such as servers and printers. Tree structures can be organized in different ways. An alternative method is to organize the

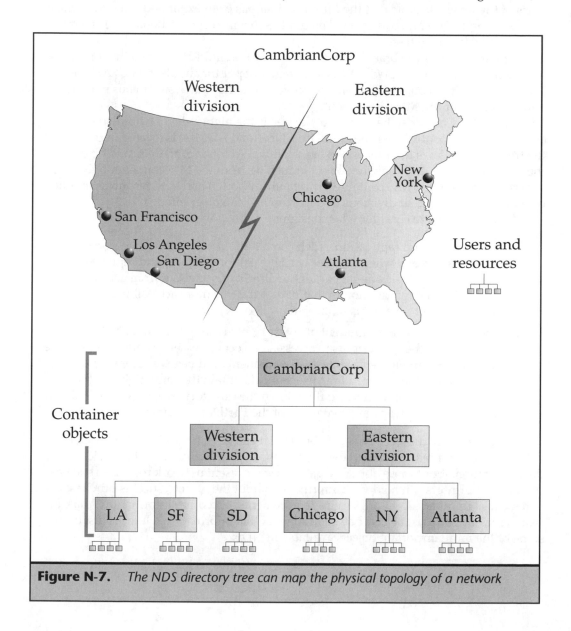

**Figure N-7.** *The NDS directory tree can map the physical topology of a network*

**N**

tree with departments such as Sales and Marketing at the highest levels and the geographic locations under those containers.

Figure N-5 illustrates how this directory tree maps into the NDS hierarchical structure and the way you see it when working with the NetWare Administrator graphical utility or other applications that access the NDS database. The tree can be expanded and collapsed so managers can view and work with objects in different parts of the network. Note that the MIS container has been expanded. The properties dialog box in Figure N-6 was opened by double-clicking on the RBonati user account object in the directory tree.

Container objects are branches in the directory that hold other container objects or leaf objects. In Figure N-5, WestDiv is a container object that holds the Los Angeles, MIS, and San Diego objects. The MIS object is a container that holds the user accounts and resources for the MIS department.

The ADMIN object at the bottom of the tree is the highest-level administrator account that has control over the entire tree. Note that ADMIN is located in the root of the tree, which allows its authority to branch down to other containers and objects in the tree. In contrast, the TSheldon object branching from the MIS container only has access to objects in the MIS container by default, although access to resources in other containers (such as other divisions or departments) can be granted.

There are things to consider when designing a directory tree:

■ **Partitioning and replication** Each container of the directory tree potentially represents a point where the tree can be partitioned (split) and replicated to other servers. Replicating a part of the directory protects it from a server failure and makes the information in that part of the tree more accessible to people near the server where it is replicated.

■ **Access rights** The assignment of access rights is simplified with NDS. A container can be given rights to access an object elsewhere in the directory tree. For example, in Figure N-5, the MIS container could be given rights to the EastDiv container. Then, all the users in MIS obtain the same rights to the EastDiv container. Rights also flow down the directory tree, so MIS will obtain the same rights in any subcontainers of the EastDiv container.

There are many different types of objects that can be defined in NDS. Objects define people and real entities all over the network. In addition, objects provide documentation about those objects. Objects that represent network resources such as servers and printers can hold vital information about the objects, such as purchase dates, serial numbers, location, service requirements, and other information. You can search for, sort, and list objects based on some of this information. Here is a list of some of the more important objects available in NDS:

■ **Country container** An organizational unit that specifies which country a branch of the tree is located in.

■ **Organization container**   A top-level container that names the company or organization.

■ **Organizational unit container**   A container for organizing units within an organization, such as departments, divisions, or geographic locations.

■ **Computer**   An object that holds information about computers on the network, along with serial numbers, node addresses, and locations.

■ **Group**   An object that defines a group of user objects.

■ **NetWare server**   This object represents a NetWare server on the network.

■ **Organizational role**   An object that is similar to the group object, but that defines a particular role in the company, such as a manager.

■ **Print server**   Defines a server that manages and queues print jobs to attached printers.

■ **Printer**   Defines a printer that is attached to a print server.

■ **User**   An object that holds information about a user, i.e., a user account.

■ **Volume**   An object that represents a physical volume of data storage.

Finally, all objects have properties, with the name being the most important. You specify the properties of an object when you create the object, and you can change them at any time by using the NetWare Administrator utility. The properties for a user are pictured in Figure N-6.

**RELATED ENTRIES**   Directory Services; Distributed Computer Networks; Novell NetWare; *and* X.500 Directory Services

# NetBIOS/NetBEUI

The NetBIOS (Network Basic Input Output System) and NetBEUI (NetBIOS Extended User Interface) protocols were designed by IBM and Microsoft to support network communication in the small- to medium-sized LAN environment. Both are implemented in the Windows environment, although Microsoft is replacing NetBEUI with TCP/IP as the network protocol of choice while still supporting NetBEUI.

Figure N-8 illustrates the protocol structure of a NetBIOS environment. Windows Sockets is another application interface that is shown for comparison. Both NetBIOS and Windows Sockets are used in the Windows environment to build distributed network applications. Both are implemented as separate DLLs (dynamic link libraries) that communicate through the TDI (Transport Driver Interface) to transport protocols.

NetBEUI is a NetBIOS-compliant transport that is called NBF (NetBEUI Frame) in the Microsoft environment. It was developed by IBM in 1985 as a network transport protocol for small- to medium-sized LANs. NetBEUI is supported by Microsoft in its networking products, including Windows 95, Windows 98, and Windows NT.

**N**

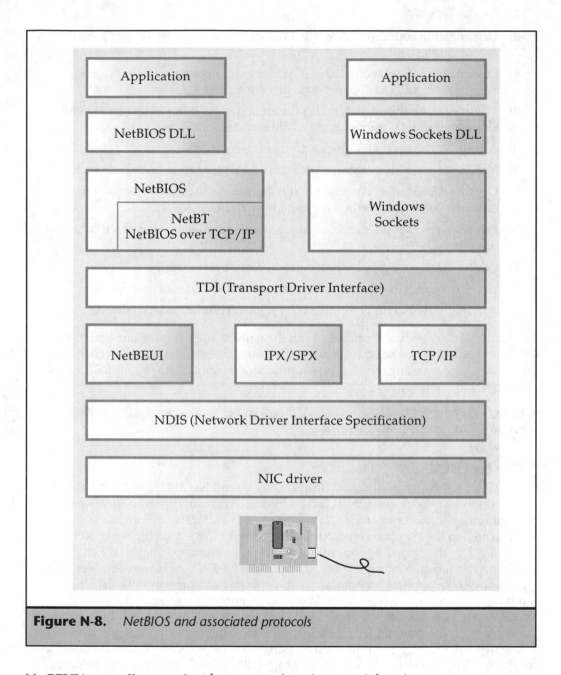

**Figure N-8.** *NetBIOS and associated protocols*

NetBEUI is a small protocol with no networking layer, and therefore no routing functions. It is suitable only for small LANs. You cannot build internetworks with NetBEUI, so it is often replaced with TCP/IP.

## More About NetBIOS

NetBIOS is an application interface that allows applications to access network services provided by network transports such as NetBEUI, SPX/IPX, and TCP/IP. NetBT (NetBIOS over TCP/IP) is a Microsoft interface for connecting NetBIOS-compatible applications to TCP/IP. Programmers traditionally used NetBIOS to create LAN applications for the IBM LAN Server, Microsoft LAN Manager, and OS/2 environments.

NetBIOS is responsible for assigning names to computers attached to a network. The name is from 1 to 15 characters long and uniquely identifies a workstation to both computers and users. Once computers are named, NetBIOS can establish logical links or *sessions* between computers and then use those links to reliably exchange data between systems. Computers can exchange data in the form of NetBIOS requests or in the form of an SMB (Server Message Blocks).

Network applications that run on NetBIOS-compliant networks use NetBIOS to locate other resources and establish connections with those resources. NetBIOS broadcasts information about the location of servers and the names of those servers. If a workstation responds to the messages, the server no longer sends it messages. If a workstation doesn't respond because it is turned off or has a defective network interface card, the server sends messages every few minutes in an attempt to get a response. This traffic can burden a network, so mechanisms are available for controlling it.

NetBIOS is well established and still supported in many environments. Newer protocols such as named pipes are available. It is also well understood, and there are many applications that use it. Windows Sockets is the alternative API and is now more commonly used.

**RELATED ENTRIES**   Named Pipes; RPC (Remote Procedure Call); Transport Protocols and Services; Windows; *and* WinSock

## Netcasting

Netcasting is an alternative to Web browsing. With Web browsing, users go out on the Web and look for information. With netcasting, information is automatically delivered to users' desktops. Netcasting is often referred to as "push" technology because content is pushed from a Web server and delivered to users who have requested receipt of the content. Content may include the latest news, weather, stock quotes, or software updates. This topic is covered further under the heading "Push."

Netcasting is also referred to as *broadcast news technology* or *webcasting*. PointCast was one of the first companies to make use of the technology and its PointCast Network has become quite popular. See "PointCast" for more details. Microsoft is using the technology in its new release of Windows. The technology is also used to update component-based software on a user's desktop with new or updated components. See "Marimba Castanet" for more information.

**N**

**RELATED ENTRIES**   Broadcast News Technology; Component Software Technology; Distributed Object Computing; Mailing List Programs; Marimba Castanet; NNTP (Network News Transport Protocol); PointCast; Push; *and* USENET

## NetDDE (Network Dynamic Data Exchange)

NetDDE is the network version of DDE (Dynamic Data Exchange) that has all the features of DDE but extends them over a network. With NetDDE, applications on two or more workstations can dynamically share information. NetDDE provides linking between workstations after a DDE share is created. A DDE share is similar to sharing a file or sharing a printer, and it includes all the security-related functions that grant remote users access to information on another computer. Newer technologies such as COM (Component Object Model), DCOM (Distributed Component Object Model), and ActiveX extend this object model. See the respective headings for information on those topics.

**RELATED ENTRIES**   ActiveX; COM (Component Object Model); Component Software Technology; DCOM (Distributed Component Object Model); OLE (Object Linking and Embedding); *and* Windows

## NetPC

Microsoft, in collaboration with Intel and major PC manufacturers, developed the NetPC Reference Platform to define an industry standard for a "sealed case" PC that runs Windows applications but prevents end users from tampering with the system. By maintaining traditional PC functionality, it lowers the cost of buying and maintaining Intel-based systems, yet still runs Windows applications. Because the NetPC is a response to the NC (Network Computer) initiatives, you should refer to "NC (Network Computer) Devices" for further reading.

The system requirements for a NetPC are outlined here:

- The system is in a lockable PC case with no end-user expansion slots. The minimum processor is an Intel Pentium 100 MHz or equivalent. The minimum memory is 16 MB. A hard disk is required for caching. The display adapter should support VGA resolutions. The system should have audio capabilities.

- Support one of the following: 10-Mbit/sec Ethernet, token ring, 28.8-Kbit/sec modems, ISDN, T1, or ATM.

- Each machine should have a unique ID, and each system device and add-on device should have a unique Plug-and-Play device ID.

- The systems should be designed to require minimal interaction from the user to install and configure devices.

Unlike the NC, the NetPC contains PC components such as a hard disk and can run applications that are stored locally. The hard disk provides a cache for startup and application settings and other information. NCs do not have local hard drives, and so must obtain this information from a server, which can reduce performance and put excess traffic on the LAN. NetPCs can boot from the local hard disk or from servers. They can also receive software and automated updates from servers. The NetPC does not contain a floppy disk or CD-ROM, so users cannot load programs and data onto hard disk or copy data to floppy disk.

Some of the advantages of centrally controlling user desktops is the ability to lock down the desktop, prevent users from performing some operation, stop users from accessing system files, and prevent users from installing unapproved applications.

A similar strategy is the Windows Terminal. It provides traditional terminal services in which Windows applications execute on a Windows NT server. The Windows Terminal accepts user input and displays results. Windows Terminal gives users access to traditional Windows applications and Java applications. Microsoft has worked closely with Citrix Systems (http://www.citrix.com) to develop WinFrame support in Windows. WinFrame is a multiuser Windows application server that shifts the processing of Windows client/server applications almost entirely to servers. The client system collects user input and displays output. See "WinFrame" for more information.

The ZAWS (Zero Administration for Windows) Initiative is a set of technologies that enable control and management of Windows-based desktops by automating tasks such as application installation and updates. ZAWS also provides tools for central administration and allows the desktop to be locked down. It also supports user roaming features that allow users to log on to different network-connected PCs and obtain their personal and familiar desktop environment. The desktop environment is stored on a central server rather than a particular workstation. See "Zero Administration for Windows Initiative" for more details.

**RELATED ENTRIES**    Access Server; Component Software Technology; Diskless Workstation; Java; NC (Network Computer) Devices; Network Management; Remote Access; Virtual Dial-up Services; VPN (Virtual Private Network); WAN (Wide Area Network); Web Technologies and Concepts; WinFrame; Wired for Management; *and* Zero Administration for Windows Initiative

## INFORMATION ON THE INTERNET

| | |
|---|---|
| Microsoft's NetPC information | http://www.microsoft.com/windows/netpc |
| Network Computer News site | http://www.ncns.com |
| NC World Magazine | http://www.ncworldmag.com |
| Citrix Systems, Inc. | http://www.citrix.com |
| Insignia NTRIGUE ICA (for running Windows applications) | http://www.insignia.com |

**N**

# Netscape

Netscape Communications was started in 1994 by Jim Clark, an investor who was involved with Silicon Graphics, Inc., and Marc Andreessen, one of the coauthors of the Mosaic Web browser. The company's first product was a spin-off of Mosaic called Netscape Navigator. It became an instant success, and when Netscape went public in August of 1994, its stock made one of the biggest one-day jumps in history—from $28 a share to $74 a share.

Netscape's entire business is based on the TCP/IP protocols, Internet, and intranet technologies. In early 1997, it announced its vision for the future, called the Networked Enterprise. This vision is based on products that are not tied to any one operating system and that take advantage of open Internet standards. Netscape is also involved in *extranet* technology, which addresses network links between the intranets of different companies. An extranet is basically a cross-business connection that allows people and businesses to engage in secure business relationships. See "Extranet" for additional information.

Here are some of the technologies that are part of Netscape's product road map:

- **Crossware**  Netscape's vision for on-demand cross-platform applications based on Internet standards, Java, and JavaScript.

- **Navigator**  Netscape's traditional Web browser software that runs on a variety of operating system platforms.

- **Communicator**  A client software suite for browsing the Web and intranets and for communicating and collaborating with others. Communicator includes Netscape Navigator 4.0 along with a variety of other components including Messenger, Composer, Conference, and Collabra, a groupware client from Collabra Software.

- **SuiteSpot**  A suite of collaborative network applications described under "Netscape SuiteSpot."

- **Constellation**  Netscape's cross-platform Internet desktop that includes netcasting (push) technologies, remote desktops (which allow users to access personal desktops no matter where they log on), and universal access to native file systems. Constellation is designed to operate on 17 different operating systems, including Microsoft Windows.

Netscape is also working on next-generation products such as Mercury, a next-generation Communicator client suite, and Apollo, a next-generation server suite.

**RELATED ENTRIES**    Collaborative Computing; EDI (Electronic Data Interchange); Electronic Commerce; Extranet; Groupware; Netscape ONE Development Environment; Netscape SuiteSpot; *and* Web Technologies and Concepts

**INFORMATION ON THE INTERNET**

| | |
|---|---|
| Netscape Communications Corp. | http://www.netscape.com |
| Actra Business Systems | http://www.actracorp.com |

# Netscape ONE Development Environment

Netscape ONE is Netscape's network-centric application development environment, based on open Internet standards. It uses HTML (Hypertext Markup Language), Java and JavaScript, the Netscape IFCs (Internet Foundation Classes) application development services, IIOP (Internet Inter-ORB Protocol), security services, and collaboration protocols that include the Internet e-mail and network news protocols.

Netscape's ONE environment is designed for platform independence and takes advantage of component software technology. This is achieved through support of the pervasive Internet protocols and standards.

The following components are part of the standard. For a complete description of Netscape ONE, refer to http://www.netscape.com/comprod/one/white_paper.html.

**HTML (HYPERTEXT MARKUP LANGUAGE)**   Netscape sees HTML and Internet/intranet Web pages as a universal desktop on which applications can execute. In particular, HTML can provide a universal container in which to place HTML text and controls, Java applets, and native code components.

**JAVA AND JAVASCRIPT**   Netscape Navigator and all future Web products fully support Java. Netscape is also adding speed to Java by integrating JIT (just-in-time) compilers that can translate Java instructions in native code that run close to the speed of optimized C++ and C code. Netscape is also working with Sun Microsystems to allow Java applets to break out of the secure virtual machine in select cases (i.e., for in-house applications). This allows the application more access to disk and other system resources. Netscape is also supporting JavaScript, an easy-to-use scripting language for controlling Java applets.

**NETSCAPE ONE PLUG-INS**   Netscape has developed client and server plug-ins that enable binary components to run as part of a currently executing application or to handle requests from Netscape enterprise servers.

**LIVECONNECT**   This component extends the platform-independent Java object model to non-Java objects, allowing Java, JavaScript, and plug-ins to share a common object and messaging model. LiveConnect includes a standard API called JRI (Java Runtime Interface). It maps platform-specific object models to the LiveConnect object model.

**LIVESITES**   LiveSites is netcasting (push) software that automatically sends information to desktops from a corporate server or an Internet site such as PointCast.

**N**

A feature called InfoStreams will display pushed information as a stream (like a ticker tape) across part of the desktop.

**IIOP (INTERNET INTER-ORB PROTOCOL) SUPPORT** IIOP brings a distributed messaging system and "component connector" system to the Netscape ONE environment. IIOP is part of CORBA (Common Object Request Broker Architecture). With IIOP, components that are distributed across the Internet can be connected to create what appear to users to be seamless applications. See "IIOP (Internet Inter-ORB Protocol)" for more information.

**NETSCAPE IFCs (INTERNET FOUNDATION CLASSES)** IFCs are services that Netscape ONE applications can access. IFC services can provide a high level of application sophistication that brings the Netscape ONE application development environment up to a level that can compete with Windows application development environments. In particular, interface controls are available, such as the following:

- Windowing environments for Java applications
- GUI (graphical user interface) application controls such as buttons, sliders, text fields, color controls, and font choosers
- Drag-and-drop features for applications
- Single-threaded concurrency framework, object persistence (to save states for later use), and support for multiple localized versions of application resources

IFCs also include a messaging service that supports SMTP (Simple Mail Transfer Protocol), POP3 (Post Office Protocol 3), and IMAP4 (Internet Mail Access Protocol, version 4). There are also security services and distributed object services.

**RELATED ENTRIES** Component Software Technology; CORBA (Common Object Request Broker Architecture); Distributed Object Computing; Java; Netscape; Netscape SuiteSpot; Object Technologies; *and* ORB (Object Request Broker)

## Netscape SuiteSpot

Netscape SuiteSpot is a set of integrated server components that provides information publishing, messaging services, groupware services, directory services, security, and replications for organizational intranets. The following components are included in the product:

- **Netscape Enterprise Server** An application for publishing and managing information, including HTML documents and documents in a variety of other formats.
- **Netscape Catalog Server** An application for finding and organizing information on the intranet using queries and browsing on user-defined categories and topics.

- **Netscape Messaging Server**  An application that supports standards-based e-mail. It includes IMAP4 and SNMP support, NT integration, message tracking, and recovery tools.

- **Netscape Collabra Server**  A collaborative application that lets users create discussion forums. It uses the NNTP (Network News Transport Protocol). Discussions can be opened to any NNTP-compliant client. Encryption and access controls are available to secure sensitive forums.

- **Netscape Calendar Server**  Provides standards-based calendaring. Users can be distributed across multiple servers, and remote calendar lookups happen in real time using a distributed search mechanism. It uses LDAP (Lightweight Directory Access Protocol) directory services and SMTP (Simple Mail Transfer Protocol) for messaging notification.

- **Netscape Media Server**  Provides a platform for distributing high-quality audio. It can embed audio in HTML documents or synchronize it with Java applets or JavaScript scripts.

- **Netscape Directory Server**  A directory server that uses LDAP. It offers X.500-based attribute storage for structured information such as names and phone numbers or unstructured information such as pictures.

- **Netscape Certificate Server**  Provides security services for the intranet. It can be used to create and sign public-key certificates. Certificates allow more secure logons, message exchange, and transactions. Includes a VGI (Verification Gateway Interface) to automate the process of verifying certificate requests and issuing certificates.

- **Netscape Proxy Server**  Provides caching of frequently accessed documents and routes network traffic according to network topology or URL. It provides centralized Internet access and enhances security. It also includes virus scanning, traffic encryption capabilities, and content filtering.

**RELATED ENTRIES**   Collaborative Computing; Electronic Commerce; Extranet; Groupware; Netscape; Netscape ONE Development Environment; *and* Web Technologies and Concepts

## NetWare, Novell

*See* Novell NetWare.

## Network Analyzers

A *network analyzer* is a monitoring, testing, and troubleshooting device. Network administrators attach a network analyzer to a network and capture network traffic. The captured frames are displayed in raw or filtered form for network technicians to evaluate. Network analyzers are generally portable devices, so technicians can move the devices to other networks.

**N**

Network analyzers operate in what is called promiscuous mode. They listen to all traffic on a network, not just traffic that has been addressed to them. The technician can choose to capture frames transmitted by a particular network computer or frames that carry information for a particular application or service. The captured information is then monitored to evaluate network performance, locate bottlenecks, or even track security breaches.

Anyone with the right components and programming skills can build a network analyzer. All that is needed is a portable computer with a network interface card that operates in promiscuous mode and a software program that can capture frames and display their contents. Products from vendors have options for selecting specific traffic and filtering out unwanted traffic. The massive amount of information that is sent on a typical LAN make this necessary. A number of vendors have very sophisticated network analyzers. They are listed under "Information on the Internet," at the end of this section.

There are low-end and high-end network analyzers. Low-end analyzers are often designed for traditional LANs such as 10-Mbit/sec Ethernet or token ring. They may even be implemented as software-only products that run in network-connected portable computers. High-end analyzers are capable of handling a variety of network types, including high-speed networks like Fast Ethernet or ATM. WAN protocol analyzers are designed to handle a diversity of link configurations and a variety of layer 2 data link protocols.

Some of the high-end network analyzers may cost tens of thousands of dollars. At the other end of the spectrum are software-based network analyzers that are available as freeware. In fact, many network analyzers are distributed on the Internet by the hacker community for the express purpose of capturing sensitive information on networks, such as passwords sent in the clear.

Here are some of things you can expect protocol analyzers to do:

- Identify excessive packet collisions and even alert you when traffic problems are occurring.

- Monitor and analyze bandwidth usage for the purpose of optimizing networks or WAN links. You may discover traffic that should not be on a link.

- Network analyzers usually accumulate statistical information as well, such as the number of packets per second or the number of packets transmitted by a particular system. More sophisticated devices provide reporting and graphing of this information.

- Many protocol analyzers may generate their own test packets under your control, which lets you test the carrying capacity of a network or test the operations of devices on the network.

- Most analyzers can only capture packets on the network segment to which they are attached. You may need to take the analyzer to other physical locations to monitor traffic. More advanced analyzers can tap other network segments, but this may generate excess traffic across network boundaries during analysis.

Buy (or rent) a protocol analyzer that works on (or has upgrades for) all the networks you will need to analyze. Some low-end models only support one type of network. Also consider the hardware platform and operating system required by the software or device, whether the device can be used remotely, the types of statistics it provides and at what layer of the protocol stack (i.e., data link, network, and application layers), the type of capturing and decoding provided (i.e., does it decode packets and provide precapture and postcapture filtering), and whether the device can generate its own traffic. Also, does the device support switched networks and VLANs (virtual LANs)?

An alternative to protocol analyzers are network management consoles that use RMON (remote monitoring). For example, a remote monitoring utility may collect statistics about a network segment and deliver it to the primary management station on a scheduled basis. Capturing actual traffic for later delivery is usually impractical. In fact, many network analyzers are incapable of monitoring switched networks, leaving RMON as the only way to capture and/or analyze traffic between switches and desktop systems.

**RELATED ENTRIES**     Distributed Management; DME (Distributed Management Environment); DMI (Desktop Management Interface); DMTF (Desktop Management Task Force); Network Management; RMON (Remote Monitoring); SNMP (Simple Network Management Protocol); *and* Testing and Diagnostic Equipment and Techniques

### INFORMATION ON THE INTERNET

| | |
|---|---|
| Digitech Industries, Inc. | http://www.digitechinc.com |
| GN Nettest | http://www.nettestca.gn.com |
| Hewlett-Packard Company | http://www.tmo.hp.com |
| Network General Corp. | http://www.ngc.com |
| RADCOM Equipment, Inc. | http://www.radcom-inc.com |
| Wandel & Goltermann, Inc. | http://www.wg.com |
| The AG Group, Inc. | http://www.aggroup.com |
| Cinco Networks, Inc. | http://www.cinco.com |
| Microtest, Inc. | http://www.microtest.com |
| Fluke Corporation | http://www.fluke.com |
| Datacom Technologies | http://www.datacomtech.com |
| En Garde Systems, Inc. | http://www.engarde.com |

## Network Applications

*See* Distributed Applications.

**N**

# Network Architecture

Network architectures define the standards and techniques for designing and building communication systems for computers and other devices. There are proprietary network architectures such as IBM's SNA (Systems Network Architecture) and DEC's DNA (Digital Network Architecture) and there are open architectures like the OSI (Open Systems Interconnection) model defined by the International Organization for Standardization.

In the past, a vendor was more concerned with making sure its own products could communicate. Third-party vendors could then build products that worked with the architecture, but there was no open discussion about the architecture itself.

If the standard is open, it provides a way for vendors to design software and hardware that is interoperable with other vendors' products. The OSI model has remained a model rather than a fully accepted international standard. Due to the wide variety of existing de facto standards, most vendors have simply decided to support many different standards rather than conform to one.

Layering specifies different functions and services at levels in a "protocol stack." The protocols define how communication takes place, such as the flow of data between systems, error detection and correction, the formatting of data, the packaging of data, and other features. Figure N-9 illustrates a simplified view. Protocols and network architectures are covered under "Protocol Concepts."

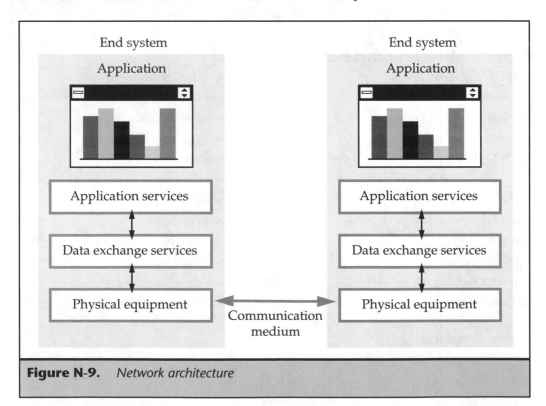

**Figure N-9.**  *Network architecture*

Protocols specify a set of rules and procedures that define how communication takes place at different levels of operation. The lowest layers define physical connections, such as the cable type, access method, and topology, and how data is sent over the network. Further up are protocols that establish connections and maintain communication sessions between systems, and still further up are protocols that provide network interfacing for applications.

As mentioned, the OSI model has become the model to which all other network architectures and protocols are compared. The purpose of the OSI model is to coordinate communication standards between vendors. Refer to "OSI (Open Systems Interconnection) Model" for additional information.

**RELATED ENTRIES**    Data Communication Concepts; Network Design and Construction; OSI (Open Systems Interconnection) Model; *and* Protocol Concepts

## Network Computer Devices

*See* NC (Network Computer) Devices.

## Network Concepts

A network is a communication system that allows users to access resources on other computers and exchange messages with other users. It allows users to share resources on their own systems with other network users and to access information on centrally located systems or systems that are located at remote offices. It may provide connections to the Internet or the networks of other organizations. Network connections allow users to operate from their home or on the road.

### The Scope of Networks

A network is a data communication system that links two or more computers and peripheral devices. As shown in Figure N-10, the network consists of a cable that attaches to NICs (network interface cards) in each of the devices. Figure N-11 illustrates the logical configuration of a network communication system. Users interact with network-enabled software applications to make a network request (such as to get a file or print on a network printer). The application communicates with the network software and the network software interacts with the network hardware. The network hardware is responsible for transmitting information to other devices attached to the network.

### LAN (Local Area Network)

A LAN is a network that is located in a relatively small area, such as a department or building. Technically, a LAN consists of a shared medium to which workstations attach and communicate with one another using broadcast methods. With broadcasting, any device on the LAN can transmit a message that all other devices on the LAN can

**N**

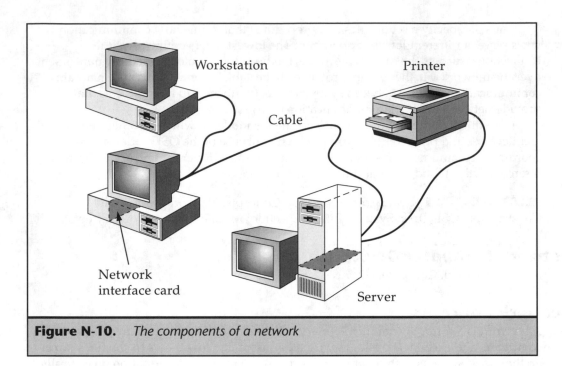

**Figure N-10.** *The components of a network*

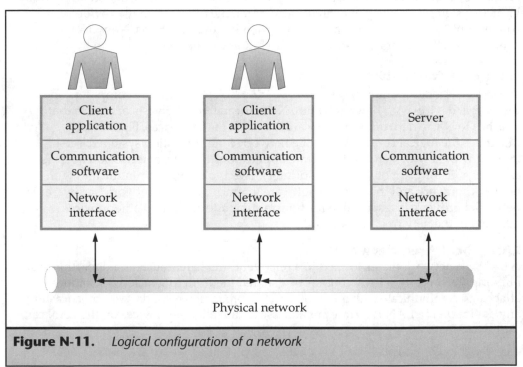

**Figure N-11.** *Logical configuration of a network*

listen to. The device to which the message is addressed actually receives the message. See "LAN (Local Area Network)" for more details.

Figure N-12 illustrates two ways to build a LAN. On the left, a relatively small LAN is built by running cable in a daisy-chain fashion from one department to the next. Each LAN segment is joined with a bridge. A bridge extends a LAN to create a much larger broadcast domain, but the bridge filters each individual segment's broadcasts by dropping frames that are not addressed to devices on connected segments. On the right, several LANs are interconnected at a centrally located hub device that handles the delivery of all inter-LAN traffic. See "Bridges and Bridging" and "Hubs/Concentrators/MAUs" for more information.

The model on the right in Figure N-13 implements a structured wiring system that is hierarchical in nature. Cables branch from a central internetwork hub to departmental hubs. This system of interconnecting cables and hub is often referred to as the backbone network. See "Backbone Networks" for more information.

The two most popular LAN technologies are Ethernet and token ring. See "Ethernet" and "Token Ring Network" for more details.

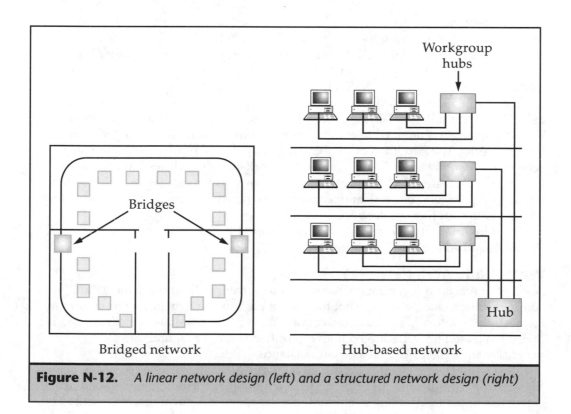

**Figure N-12.**   *A linear network design (left) and a structured network design (right)*

**N**

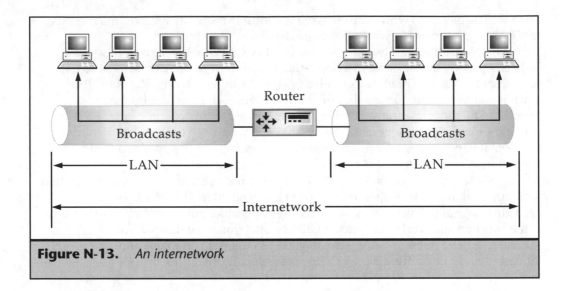

**Figure N-13.**   *An internetwork*

## Internetwork

In contrast to a LAN, an internetwork is a collection of LANs that are connected by routers. Broadcasts on one LAN do not propagate across the routers to other LANs, but routers will forward packets that are specifically addressed to devices on other interconnected LANs. Figure N-13 illustrates a simple internetwork.

Each LAN of an internetwork is called a *subnetwork*. An internetwork protocol such as TCP/IP (Transmission Control Protocol/Internet Protocol) or IPX (Internetwork Packet Exchange) is required to allow devices to communicate across router-connected internetworks. The IP portion of the TCP/IP protocol suite provides an addressing scheme for assigning each LAN in an internetwork a unique address. Routers then learn these addresses. Packets traversing the internetwork must have an address that identifies a particular network and a node on that network. Routers then forward the packets to the appropriate network.

Refer to "Internetworking," "IP (Internet Protocol)," "Routers," and "Routing Protocols and Algorithms" for more details.

## WAN (Wide Area Network)

A WAN connects an organization's remote offices over public and private data communication channels. In the not too distant past, there were only a few choices for connecting remote offices. You could connect them with slow dial-up modems or with dedicated leased lines. Dedicated lines can provide high throughput but can be expensive since the price increases with distance.

The configuration pictured on the left in Figure N-14 illustrates a scenario where four sites are completely interconnected. Six long-distance leased lines are used to create this network, resulting in an astronomical phone bill. An alternative method is shown on the right in Figure N-14. In this scenario, a short local line connects each site

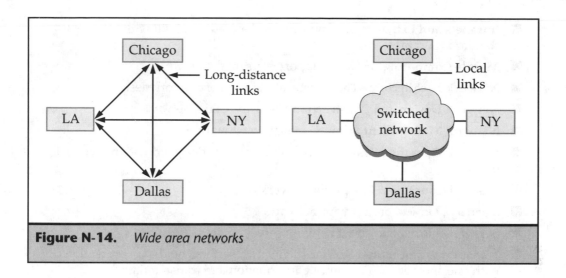

**Figure N-14.** *Wide area networks*

into a national service provider's packet-switched network. The national service provider then switches packets to appropriate locations. In this case, only four local leased lines are required. Note that the switched network could very well be the Internet.

See "Communication Service Providers," "Communication Services," "Leased Line," "Packet and Cell Switching," "VPN (Virtual Private Network)," and "WAN (Wide Area Network)" for more information.

## Other Topics of Interest

There are many other topics in this book that provide useful information for network designers and administrators, some of which are listed here:

- **Client/Server Computing** The predominant model for designing network operating systems and applications for networks

- **Data Communication Concepts** The basics of how devices communicate with networks and other links

- **Communication Services** Describes the technologies and services for building wide area networks

- **Distributed Computer Networks** Techniques for making information more accessible to users no matter where they are on the network

- **Distributed Object Computing** Describes new object-oriented technologies for intranets and the Internet

- **Enterprise Networks** Networks that span an entire organization and connect all of its information resources

**N**

- **Intranets and Extranets**   The new network paradigm, built with Internet standards and protocols
- **Mobile Computing**   How to support users on the move
- **Network Architecture**   The structural elements of network design
- **Network Design and Construction**   How to build a network
- **Network Management**   How to manage a network
- **Network Operating Systems**   Operating systems designed with networks in mind
- **Protocol Concepts**   How protocols work
- **Security**   How to protect your network
- **Servers**   Information about network server devices
- **Transport Protocols and Services**   How two systems hold a "conversation' with one another to communicate information and transmit data
- **Virtual Networks**   How to build networks that emulate other networks
- **Voice/Data Networks**   How networks can transmit both voice and data
- **VPN (Virtual Private Network)**   How to build private wide area networks over the Internet
- **WAN (Wide Area Network)**   How to build wide area networks
- **Web Technologies and Concepts**   How Internet and Web technologies are changing networks
- **Wireless Communications**   How to build networks without wires

## Network Connection Technologies

*See* Connection Technologies.

## Network Design and Construction

This section guides you through a variety of topics related to network design and construction. If you are expanding or upgrading an existing network or building a new network, it is important to be aware of new technologies that can help you build efficient and "future-proof" networks (assuming that is possible). New network designs are developed to improve bandwidth and traffic flow, something that is certainly needed as more and more users run collaborative network and Web applications that introduce large amounts of traffic to networks. This section jumps around a bit in order to cover the new network technologies, but you are encouraged to refer to the other referenced sections to continue your research.

To accommodate these users, the following should be considered as part of your network design. Note that these issues are elaborated on in this topic, as well as elsewhere in the book.

- Consider one cabling system that supports both voice, video, and data instead of maintaining separate telephone lines, data trunks, and video feeds.

- Provide bandwidth and traffic controls so real-time traffic (live voice and video) can be delivered without delay.

- Support a single protocol—TCP/IP—and support Web technologies, intranets, and extranets (business-to-business networks over the Internet).

- Upgrade from slower *shared* networks to *switched* networks that reduce contention.

- Implement VLAN (virtual LAN) schemes in which users and servers can be anywhere on the network and configured into any VLAN.

- Implement schemes that reduce the burden on routers, or implement new *router switches* that support high-speed internetworking.

- Centralize servers for better management, security, and data protection, rather than keep servers in departments.

- Support advanced services such as a global directory service and a distributed file system. See "Directory Services" and "Distributed File Systems."

## Traditional Network Architectures

This section evaluates traditional network designs. As shown in Figure N-15(a), a single Ethernet LAN provides a single broadcast domain in which multiple users share the same network topology. This scheme works well as long as the number of users remains small. Adding more users increases the number of attempts to access the shared medium. Collisions may occur, reducing network performance.

To regain performance, you split the network with a bridge or router, as shown in Figure N-15(b). Now, fewer users are contending for the shared media in each segment, but they can still communicate across the bridge or router. Broadcasts are contained within each segment, thus traffic meant for one segment does not propagate to other segments. Reducing contention and containing broadcasts are key design goals.

As networks grow, more bridges may be added, but routers are a better choice because they give administrators more control over network traffic and provide security barriers between networks. Figure N-15(c) illustrates a set of router-connected network segments. However, traffic flowing from the segment on the left crosses the intermediate network segment and adds unnecessary traffic to it.

**N**

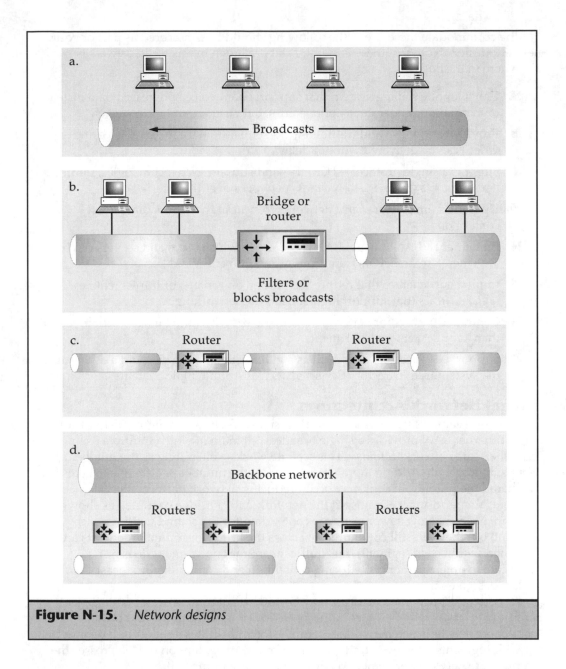

**Figure N-15.** *Network designs*

To avoid this, a high-speed backbone network is installed, as shown in Figure N-15(d). Now, traffic flowing from one network to another crosses a router to the backbone. The backbone is dedicated to handling internetwork traffic. The simplest backbones are FDDI (Fiber Distributed Data Interface) and Fast Ethernet networks running at 100 Mbits/sec.

See "Backbone Networks," "Bridges and Bridging," and "Routers" for more information.

## Hierarchical Wiring

The backbone may be either *distributed* or *collapsed*, as shown in Figure N-16. A distributed backbone is a physical cable that snakes through an entire building or across a campus. Subnetworks are attached to this cable. A collapsed backbone is a bus or a silicon-based circuit that exists on the backplane of a wiring hub. Each workgroup hub is then connected to the central hub with a dedicated cable.

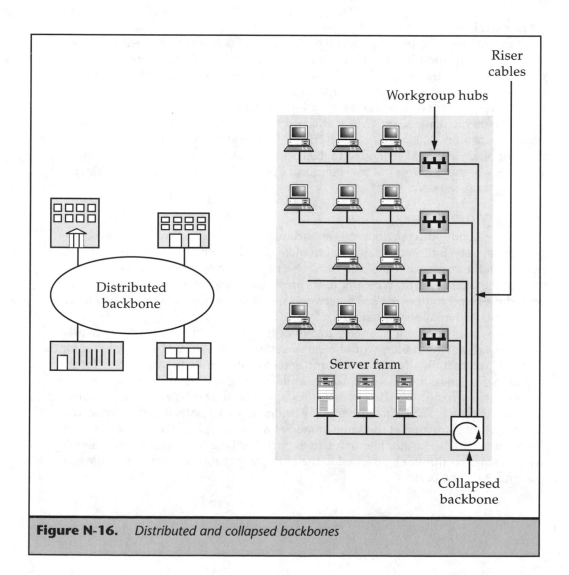

**Figure N-16.** *Distributed and collapsed backbones*

**N**

Networks with centralized cores require structured, hierarchical wiring systems. The section "TIA/EIA Structured Cabling Standards" describes such a system. It provides a standard that specifies the type of cable and the hierarchy of the cabling system.

Hierarchical cabling and network designs provide better troubleshooting and fault isolation. They also improve traffic flow and may help avoid congestion. Users in the same group can communicate with one another through the same hub without sending traffic all the way to the core hub, but the core hub provides a connection point to every other point in the network.

See also "Backbone Networks" and "Hubs/Concentrators/MAUs" for more information.

## Centralizing Services

With the introduction of a high-speed backbone, it makes sense to attach network servers and peripherals to the backbone as shown on the right in Figure N-16. Network administrators can then physically locate servers in a central location where they are easier to manage. Server centers (or *server farms*) can be staffed full time and have backup power supplies and fire-extinguishing systems.

It is better to leave some servers attached to the LAN segment of the users that access the servers. This keeps network traffic local. But if users on other subnets access a server often, it should be moved to the backbone. Otherwise, traffic for server requests will move across the backbone and into other subnets, adding additional traffic to those subnets.

## Switching Models

Increasing bandwidth requirements are driving the design and construction of networks today. Internetwork traffic has increased. The old 80/20 rule, in which 80 percent of the traffic stayed local, is now reversed. Now, 80 percent of the traffic crosses the internetwork. Typically, users are accessing servers across internetwork boundaries, and router-connected networks are failing to provide the performance requirements demanded by users.

One way to gain performance is to reduce the number of routers on a network. Normally, removing routers would mean that more users would be contending for the network and that broadcasts would propagate to more of the network. Switching technologies can reduce these problems while helping to reduce router dependence.

A switch is a multiport box in which each port on the box is essentially its own network segment. The switch can quickly bridge any two ports together so devices on those ports become part of the same broadcast network. A hub with multiple computers can also be attached to a switch port. The best performance is obtained when a single computer is attached to the port, since that computer is then the only contender for the port.

*NOTE:    Switches are often called layer 2 (data link layer) technologies while routing is a layer 3 (network layer) technology.*

Figure N-17 illustrates the progressive stages of building a switched network. Initially, as shown in Figure N-17(a), switches may be installed in workgroups to increase the performance of links between shared hubs in those workgroups or links to the internetwork routers. In Figure N-17(b), shared hubs are replaced with switches, providing better performance for individual users. In Figure N-17(c), the entire network is converted to a large switched network with the addition of a high-speed ATM or Gigabit Ethernet backbone switching hub.

By building a large switched network and eliminating routers, you create a flat network topology, as pictured in Figure N-17(c). Note that no routers exist on this network (at least not yet in this discussion). Basically, any workstation can connect with any other workstation without going through a router. This is good for access and performance, but for security reasons it may not be good that any user can reach every station.

In addition, there are practical limitations to the size of a flat network. If class C Internet addressing is used, only 255 network devices can be configured on the network. Additional networks with their own class C Internet addresses will be required to support additional stations, and these networks must be interconnected with routers.

### VLANs (Virtual LANs) and ELANs (Emulated LANs)

The advantage of LANs is that they limit network broadcasts to a specific group of workstations, but if a flat, switched network is created, this advantage is lost. Administrators can, however, create VLANs or ELANs (emulated LANs) by using hardware or software techniques to restore the functionality of LANs to the switched network. There are a number of ways to create ELANs or VLANs, as discussed under "LANE (LAN Emulation)" and "VLAN (Virtual LAN)."

Once VLANs or ELANs are created, routing is required to forward packets from one LAN to the next. A number of interesting routing solutions are being devised to handle this, as discussed in the following sections.

## Routing in the New Network

Routing is necessary with VLANs to contain broadcasts and add security. Several solutions have been proposed. The usual technique is to avoid router hops as much as possible, following the mantra "route once, switch many." Alternatively, new hardware-based router switches running on Gigabit Ethernet networks eliminate the problem altogether, as discussed later in this topic under "Router Switching."

**N**

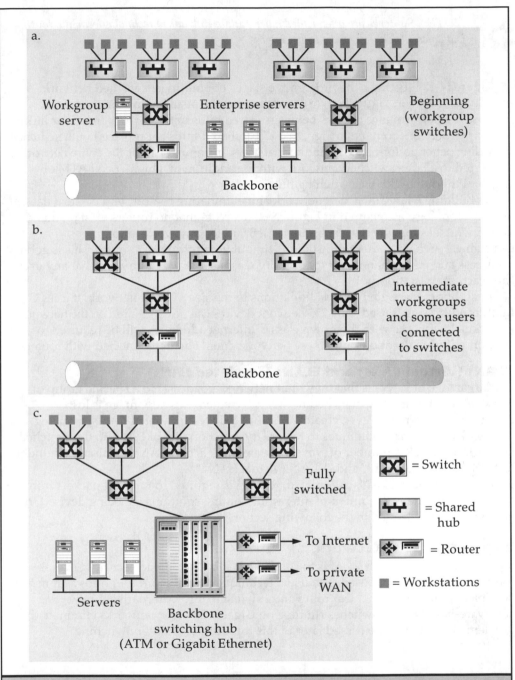

**Figure N-17.** *Progressive stages of a switched network*

## IP Routing in the ATM Environment

Since the early 1990s, ATM (Asynchronous Transfer Mode) has been considered the ultimate network architecture. It was assumed that at some point, every workstation would sport an ATM network adapter rather than an Ethernet or token ring adapter. That has not occurred, and it probably will not occur in the near future. Still, many organizations have installed ATM backbone switches because of their ability to handle network traffic at high speeds.

The only problem with this scheme is that ATM is a virtual circuit-based, connection-oriented, cell-based networking scheme while Ethernet (assuming that is the predominant LAN scheme) is a connectionless frame-based scheme. A number of overlay schemes have been developed to allow "legacy" Ethernet LANs to be connected to ATM backbones.

The usual method is to use layer 3 routing algorithms to discover paths through the network, then set up layer 2 virtual circuits through the ATM fabric that can deliver datagrams to the destination without going through a router. The technique is often called *shortcut routing*. Assuming IP is your internetwork routing protocol, you can refer to "IP over ATM" for additional information.

One of the problems with these techniques is knowing when to route and when to switch the traffic at layer 2. If a transmission is long, it makes sense to switch it. If it is short, it may be more efficient just to route it. However, traffic at layer 3 does not explicitly identify itself as a long stream that might be worth switching, so the layer 3 protocol must identify a stream, usually by inspecting the contents of datagrams. A reservation protocol may also be used. Techniques for detecting flow include 3Com FastIP, Ipsilon IP Switching, and other techniques discussed under "IP Switching."

All of these extra protocols and techniques add complexity to network construction and management. Many vendors and network administrators want to simply improve what they already have. This is what router switching is all about, as discussed under "Router Switching" on the next page.

## Gigabit Ethernet

Gigabit Ethernet has already made a name for itself as a high-speed alternative to ATM. One of its main attractions is its compatibility with legacy Ethernet networks, allowing it to avoid some of the overlay schemes required to connect legacy LANs with ATM backbones.

Gigabit Ethernet can even exceed the performance of ATM because it uses the same frame size as legacy Ethernet. ATM breaks frames up into small cells, and each cell adds overhead that reduces throughput. In addition, Gigabit Ethernet can provide some of the QoS (Quality of Service) features that ATM provides through integrated bandwidth management and the RSVP (Resource Reservation Protocol). Gigabit Ethernet allows organizations to scale up their existing Ethernet networks. Some administrators have reconsidered their ATM plans with the emergence of Gigabit Ethernet, RSVP, and IP Multicast. See "Gigabit Ethernet" for more details.

**N**

## Router Switching

Along with Gigabit Ethernet, several vendors have created router switches that can perform layer 3 routing at the same speed as layer 2 switching. These routers use new hardware-based circuitry implemented in ASICs (application-specific integrated circuits) that can perform routing at multigigabit speeds. Older routers rely on a single shared CPU (central processing unit) to inspect and forward packets. Note that router switches still implement CPUs to run normal routing protocols such as RIP (Routing Information Protocol) and OSPF (Open Shortest Path First).

Rapid City Communications (now part of Bay Networks) developed a family of router switches that provide packet-relay capabilities with the control of IP routing. The devices provide the bandwidth to accommodate increased volumes of internetwork traffic and support high-speed Gigabit Ethernet. Its f1200 has a 15-Gbit/sec shared memory switch fabric with over 7-Gbit/sec throughput. The device will forward 7 million packets/sec whether routing, switching, or doing both. A traditional router will forward 500,000 packets per second. At these speeds, most network managers can build switched networks with any routing configuration necessary.

## Other Issues

Building a network involves much more than what is discussed here. There are issues related to building intranets using TCP/IP and Web protocols, as well as WAN, wiring, and cabling issues. These are discussed under the main headings referenced in the "Related Entries" section at the end of this topic. For more conceptual information, refer to "Data Communication Concepts" and "Network Concepts."

The Internet references given at the end of the section under "Information on the Internet" also provide links to additional resources on the Internet, particularly papers related to network planning, construction, and design. You are encouraged to review these papers and other papers at vendor sites because the design of networks and what constitutes the latest technology is always changing.

**RELATED ENTRIES**    ATM (Asynchronous Transfer Mode); Backbone Networks; Data Communication Concepts; Gigabit Ethernet; Intranets and Extranets; IP (Internet Protocol); IP Switching; Network Concepts; Power and Grounding Problems and Solutions; Routers; Routing Protocols and Algorithms; Switched Networks; TIA/EIA Structured Cabling Standards; Transmission Media, Methods, and Equipment; *and* VLAN (Virtual LAN)

**INFORMATION ON THE INTERNET**

| | |
|---|---|
| Interactive Network Design Manual | http://techweb.cmp.com/nc/netdesign/series.htm |
| The Intranet Construction Site | http://www.intranet-build.com |

| | |
|---|---|
| L. David Passmore's Decisys site (architecture and design papers) | http://www.decisys.com |
| 3Com's technology papers | http://www.3com.com/technology |
| Foundry Networks' router switching papers | http://www.foundrynet.com |
| IBM's Desktop ATM versus Fast Ethernet paper | http://www.networking.ibm.com/atm/atm25fe.html |
| Bay Networks' papers on network design (see papers listed under "White Papers") | http://www.baynetworks.com/Products/Papers |
| Anixter paper on structured cabling and network design | http://www.anixter.com/techlib |
| Data Communications' Tech Tutorials site | http://www.data.com/Tutorials |
| LAN Times Online's Subject Index | http://www.lantimes.com/subject |
| Fore's ATM and the Intranet paper | http://www.fore.com/atm-edu/whitep/intranet.html |
| Cabletron's Router Reduction Techniques paper | http://www.ctron.com/white-papers/capacity |
| Xylan Corp.'s The Switching Book | http://www.xylan.com/sb |

## Network Driver Standards

*See* NDIS (Network Driver Interface Specification); ODI (Open Data link Interface).

## Network Interface Card

*See* NIC (Network Interface Card).

## Network Layer, OSI Model

The OSI (Open Systems Interconnection) model is a standard defined by the International Organization for Standardization. It is a layered architecture in which each layer defines a specific type of communication. The bottom layer, called the physical layer, is responsible for transmitting these messages as bit streams across a physical medium. The layers immediately above the physical layer define how data is

**N**

packaged for transport over the physical network. Further up the protocol stack are layers that define how computers connect and reliably exchange information. The uppermost layers define how applications interface with the network. The OSI model helps developers create interoperable products.

The network layer is the third layer of the protocol stack, just above the physical and data link layers. It is the routing layer and the layer that is responsible for network addressing. In the TCP/IP protocol suite, IP resides in the network layer. The network layer can also be called the internetwork layer because it provides the functionality that allows different types of networks to be joined and share a common addressing scheme.

**RELATED ENTRIES**   Internetworking; Layered Architecture; Network Layer Protocols; OSI (Open Systems Interconnection) Model; Protocol Concepts; *and* Routing Protocols and Algorithms

## Network Layer Protocols

In the OSI protocol stack, the network layer is layer 3, just above the physical layer and the data link layer. The physical layer is concerned with moving bits across a wire, while the data link layer is concerned with the point-to-point connection between two devices. The network layer is concerned with moving data across multiple data link connections, or put another way, moving data across multiple networks that are connected by routers.

Assume you connect three networks together as shown in Figure N-18. The three networks are interconnected with two routers. Traffic from network A must cross

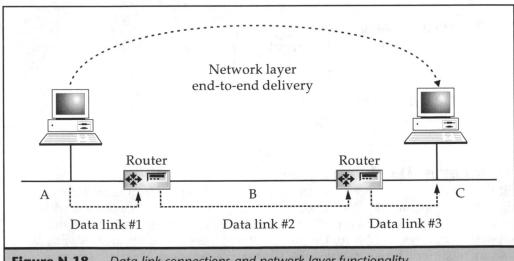

**Figure N-18.**   *Data link connections and network layer functionality*

network B to reach network C. The illustration shows that there are three separate data link layer connections to perform this task. In contrast, network layer protocols are concerned with moving packets across multiple networks and provide an addressing scheme and routing functions for doing this. The network layer is connectionless, meaning that packets are addressed to a destination but no connection negotiation is performed in advance of sending packets. Transport layer protocols provide connection-oriented sessions.

IP (Internet Protocol) is the most well-known network layer protocol. It provides an internetwork addressing scheme that allows devices to address packets to devices on other networks. Data link level addresses, which are typically the hardwired addresses on NICs (network interface cards) only work on the local LAN. To send a packet to a device on another LAN across a router, you need a higher-level addressing scheme. For example, in many small towns, it is possible for someone in the same town to address a letter to someone else in the town by putting only the street address on the envelope. However, a letter addressed to someone in another town will require the city, state, and ZIP code on the envelope. IP addresses can be compared to ZIP codes. ZIP codes provide a high-level addressing scheme that indicates a specific town in a vast web of towns across the country. See "Internetworking" and "IP (Internet Protocol)" for more information about internetworks and internetwork addressing.

The network layer is the "internetwork" layer of the protocol stack. It is involved with the topology of the internetwork and how all the subnetworks are connected together. This is the function of routers and routing protocols. A router connects two or more networks and runs a routing protocol that "discovers" the layout of the internetwork by exchanging routing information with other routers. The routers then determine which paths through the interconnected network are the best paths for sending a packet from a source to a destination. Network administrators can also get involved in specifying what these paths are because some may be preferable over others. For example, one path may be a low-speed link that is used for backup while a more preferable path provides high-speed data transmission. See "Routers" and "Routing Protocols and Algorithms" for a continuation of this topic.

**RELATED ENTRIES**    Connection-Oriented and Connectionless Services; Data Communication Concepts; Data Link Protocols; Internetworking; IP (Internet Protocol); OSI (Open Systems Interconnection) Model; Protocol Concepts; Routers; Routing Protocols and Algorithms; TCP (Transmission Control Protocol); *and* Transport Protocols and Services

# Network Layer Switching

*See*  IP over ATM; IP Switching; Layer 3 Switching/Routing; Layer 3 VLAN (Virtual LAN); *and* VLAN (Virtual LAN).

# Network Management

Network management involves active and passive monitoring of network resources for the purpose of troubleshooting, detecting potential problems, improving performance, documentation, and reporting. This section discusses management applications and protocols, but of course, there are many other management tasks that will go unmentioned here, such as backing up data, providing security, training users, setting policies, and so on. Refer to "Data Protection" for more information.

A diversity of management applications and protocols are available. Full-blown management packages use *agents* to collect information from devices all over an enterprise network and send that information back to a central *management station*. The network administrator, working at a management console, produces reports and graphs about the state of the network from this information. Agents may also provide alerts that warn of problems or performance degradations. Most management applications of this type are built around the Internet's SNMP (Simple Network Management Protocol). A newer extension to this protocol is RMON (Remote Monitoring). Both are discussed under separate sections in this book.

Management applications are also available to provide the following:

- Desktop management software to remotely manage client systems and control desktops

- Software installation, updating, and licensing to automatically install or update software over a network and ensure that an organization is within its usage license

- Network asset management to track hardware and software inventories

- Help desk management to provide user assistance over the network

- Network protocol analysis (discussed under "Network Analyzers")

- Hub and router management

- Network design, capacity planning, and simulation software

One of the problems with network management is that most enterprise networks consist of a wide variety of computer platforms, network topologies, communication protocols, operating systems, and applications. In addition, most networks are not confined to an area that is physically accessible to the network manager or technician. Therefore, the network itself is often used to extend the reach of the network administrator by using remote monitoring and control tools.

## Network Management Applications

There are a number of major network management applications on the market for managing enterprise networks. These packages are listed later. Most follow the client/server model, although the management console (which acts as a client) is called a *manager* and the servers that provide information about the network are called *agents*. Agents are deployed around the network on devices such as servers, routers, and computers. Once installed, agents settle into the task of collecting information about their host devices and reporting it back to the manager.

As mentioned, SNMP is the most common and popular network management protocol available today. The SNMP protocol defines how managers and agents communicate with one another by using request and response messaging. RMON (Remote Monitoring) is an extension that provides better management features at the location of the devices that are actually being monitored.

Devices on the network perform tasks and operations that network administrators want to monitor. For example, an administrator may wish to monitor packet throughput in a router. An *object* is created to store information about this process and given a unique name. Objects are part of a larger set of objects called the *MIB (management information base)*. As an agent gathers information, it stores it in appropriate objects in the MIB. The manager then reads information from objects in the MIB.

See "SNMP (Simple Network Management Protocol)" for more details about this management standard.

## Management Platforms

The seven major network management platforms are listed in the following table, along with the Web site addresses of the manufacturers.

| | |
|---|---|
| Cabletron's Spectrum | http://www.ctron.com/spectrum |
| Computer Associates' Unicenter | http://www.cai.com/products/uctr.htm |
| Hewlett-Packard's OpenView | http://www.hp.com/openview |
| IBM/Tivoli Systems' TME 10 | http://www.tivoli.com |
| Microsoft's Systems Management Server | http://www.microsoft.com/smsmgmt |
| Novell's ManageWise | http://www.novell.com/managewise |
| Sun Microsystems' Solstice management products | http://www.sun.com/solstice |

These products are called "platforms" because of their extensive features and ability to manage entire enterprise networks. Their features include most of those described earlier, in addition to the following:

- Autodiscovery of devices on the network.

- Network topology mapping in the form of a graphic map that can be zoomed in or out. Any device can be managed by clicking its icon on the map.

- The ability to schedule management tasks or jobs at specific times or dates.

- Wide industry support in the form of products that can be managed by the platform.

The best place to find this information is in product comparison articles published by major industry magazines. Refer to "Magazine Links" in Appendix A as a start to locating these articles on the Web.

**N**

## Desktop Management

Desktop management helps network administrators monitor and manage client workstations on a network from a central location. A standards-based approach is necessary to ensure that data from clients is in a standard format that any management system can read. A number of methods to manage desktop systems have been proposed and implemented over the years, and some operating systems include their own configuration utilities.

Refer to "Diskless Workstation," "DMI (Desktop Management Interface)," "NC (Network Computer) Devices," "NetPC," and "Zero Administration for Windows Initiative" for more information about desktop management.

## Web Management Tools

Network management tools that use Internet protocols and operate using familiar Web technologies are now common. Web-based management systems are designed for managing intranets and Internet-based networks. Managers use Web browsers as their primary network management interface. The advantage of Web-based management tools is that Web protocols and technologies are ubiquitous. In addition, the Internet can be used to communicate with and manage remote sites.

WBEM (Web-Based Enterprise Management) was developed jointly by Microsoft, Compaq, and Cisco Systems and is supported by over 60 vendors. According to the WBEM Web site, WBEM is designed to "consolidate and unify the data provided by existing management technologies," including SNMP and DMI. Administrators can use a standard Web browser for management tasks. A standard protocol called HMMP (Hypermedia Management Protocol) is used to access the data. See "WBEM (Web-Based Enterprise Management)" for more information.

SunSoft's Solstice Workshop is an environment for developing Web-based management applications with Java. The JMAPI (Java Management API) is a simple ODBC-based database for storing management information. Additional information is available at http://java.sun.com/products/JavaManagement.

## IETF Network Management Developments

The Internet Engineering Task Force has a number of working groups that are developing methods for using SNMP to access management information for a wide variety of devices on intranets and the Internet. Its work is based on managing Web servers and the HTTP MIB, but it is interested in expanding this work to include many other devices.

There are an incredible number of IETF RFCs (requests for comment) related to network management, too many to list here. One way to locate RFCs of interest is to access the Web site at http://www.internic.net/ds/dspg1intdoc.html and search for keywords such as "management," "MIB," "RMON," and "SNMP."

Information about the IETF's work on network management can be found on the Web at the Active IETF Working Groups Web page. The address for this page is http://www.ietf.org/html.charters/wg-dir.html. In particular, note the links on this page that describe MIBs.

The RFCs for SNMP and MIBs are available at the following Web addresses:

| | |
|---|---|
| Simple Network Management Protocol | http://www.internic.net/rfc/rfc1157.txt |
| Structure of Management Information | http://www.internic.net/rfc/rfc1155.txt |
| | http://www.internic.net/rfc/rfc1212.txt |
| Management Information Base | http://www.internic.net/rfc/rfc1213.txt |

**RELATED ENTRIES**    Configuration Management; Data Management; Data Protection; Distributed Management; DME (Distributed Management Environment); DMI (Desktop Management Interface); DMTF (Desktop Management Task Force); IOS (Internetwork Operating System), Cisco Systems; MIB (Management Information Base); Network Analyzers; RMON (Remote Monitoring); SNMP (Simple Network Management Protocol); Testing and Diagnostic Equipment and Techniques; WBEM (Web-Based Enterprise Management); Web-Based Network Management; Wired for Management; *and* Zero Administration for Windows Initiative

## INFORMATION ON THE INTERNET

| | |
|---|---|
| Network Management Forum | http://www.nmf.org |
| The SimpleWeb (network management information) | http://snmp.cs.utwente.nl |
| The Web Based Management Page | http://www.mindspring.com/~jlindsay/webbased.html |
| Network Management links and papers | http://netman.cit.buffalo.edu |
| Network Professionals Resource Center links | http://www.inetassist.com/url6.htm |
| University of New Hampshire's Network Management Consortium | http://www.iol.unh.edu/consortiums/netmgt |
| Network General's network management products and white papers | http://www.ngc.com |
| Nathan Muller's Web management white paper | http://www.ddx.com/webmgmt.shtml |
| Tyler Vallillee's Network Management page | http://www.concentric.net/~tkvallil/snmp.html |
| Interactive Network Design Manual | http://techweb.cmp.com/nc/netdesign/series.htm |
| Tom Nolle's network management articles | http://www.datacomm-us.com/columns/cimi/cimiweb.html |

**N**

# Network Operating Systems

Network operating systems, or NOSs, provide features for controlling LANs and/or internetworks and for serving clients. A NOS provides a set of protocols for accepting requests from clients and responding to those requests. A NOS also provides a shared file system (although that is not a strict requirement) and a set of security features and controls to control user access to network resources.

Some desktop operating systems provide peer-to-peer file- and printer-sharing services that are similar to the services offered by full-featured NOSs. However, peer-to-peer environments usually lack the security and access controls that are necessary in corporate environments. Most high-end NOSs run as dedicated servers and are strictly controlled by an administrator who manages the system, sets security policies, and controls who can access the system. Client computers run redirector software that sends requests for network service to a designated network server.

The dominant NOSs on the market today are listed in the following table, along with the Web site address where you can obtain more information. Each of these operating systems is described elsewhere in this book. Peer-to-peer network operating systems discussed elsewhere in this book include LANtastic (Artisoft), Windows (Microsoft), and Mac OS.

| | |
|---|---|
| Novell's IntranetWare | http://www.novell.com/intranetware |
| Banyan's VINES | http://www.banyan.com |
| Microsoft's Windows NT Server | http://www.microsoft.com/ntserver |
| IBM's OS/2 Warp Server | http://www.software.ibm.com/os/warp |
| Sun Microsystems' Solaris | http://www.sun.com/solaris |
| Linux and UNIX (multiple vendors) | (See "Linux" and "UNIX" in this book for links list) |

Only a few years ago, each network operating system seemed to have its own niche and provided a set of features or functions that set it apart from other network operating systems. Today, most network operating systems have similar features, use the TCP/IP protocol for internetworking, and include Web server and intranet support.

The best place to find comparative information about operating systems is at magazine sites that feature articles about network computing. Several Web sites are listed under "Information on the Internet," at the end of this section. For example, *Network Computing* magazine runs a periodic series called "State of the NOS" where it evaluates different network operating systems for the following features:

- Services provided, such as virus checking, software distribution, software and hardware inventory, and server-to-server replication
- OS features such as support for SMP (symmetrical multiprocessing), processor support, protocol support, and automatic hardware detection

- File and print service features

- Fault tolerance features such as clustering, RAID, and backup services

- Security features such as authentication, authorization, logon restrictions, and access controls

- Support for name and directory services such as X.500, LDAP, and third-party products

- Management, administration, and auditing features

- Internetworking, routing, and WAN support

- Client operating system support and support for remote dial-up users

**RELATED ENTRIES**   Access Control; Access Rights; Account, User; Accounting Services; ACL (Access Control List); Administrator Account; Auditing; Authentication and Authorization; Banyan VINES; Client/Server Computing; Directory Services; File Sharing; File Systems; LANtastic; Logons and Logon Accounts; Multiprocessing; NDS (Novell Directory Services); NFS (Network File System); Novell NetWare; Novell NetWare File System; OS/2 Warp Server; Rights and Permissions; Servers; Sun Microsystems; UNIX; UNIX File System; Users and Groups; Windows; *and* Windows NT Server

**INFORMATION ON THE INTERNET**

| | |
|---|---|
| Yahoo!'s Operating System links page | http://www.yahoo.com/Computers/ Operating_Systems |
| IDC's Network Operating System Comparison white paper | http://www.openvms.digital.com/openvms/ whitepapers/nosc/nosc.html |
| LAN Times Online's Subject Index | http://www.Online'slantimes.com/lantimes/ subject |
| Network Computing magazine | http://www.networkcomputing.com |
| TechWeb (search for "NOS" on main page) | http://www.techweb.com |
| Interesting OS information | http://www.eleves.ens.fr:8080/home/rideau/ Tunes/Review/OSes.html |
| Sven M. Paas's Operating Systems page (extensive links) | http://www.lfbs.rwth-aachen.de/~sven/OS- Projects |

# Network Troubleshooting

*See* Network Analyzers; Network Management; RMON (Remote Monitoring); SNMP (Simple Network Management Protocol); Testing and Diagnostic Equipment; *and* WBEM (Web-Based Enterprise Management).

**N**

## Newsfeed Services

*See* Broadcast News Technology; Component Software Technology; Distributed Object Computing; Mailing List Programs; Marimba Castanet; Netcasting; NNTP (Network News Transport Protocol); PointCast; *and* Push.

## News Protocols

*See* NNTP (Network News Transport Protocol); USENET.

## NFS (Network File System)

NFS is a client/server distributed file service that provides transparent file-sharing for network environments. NFS was originally designed by a small team at Sun Microsystems in the 1980s, but is now an open Internet protocol. It was defined by RFC 1094 (version 2) and updated with RFC 1813 (version 3) in 1995. NFS is now a set of X/Open specifications defined as X/Open90 and X/Open91. (X/Open is now part of The Open Group.) The AFS (Andrew File System), is related to NFS.

NFS runs on a full range of systems from PCs to mainframes in local and global environments. Multiple types of clients can access shared NFS file systems. In 1995, Dataquest estimated that NFS had an installed base of 8.5 million systems with an expected installed base of 12 million systems by 1997. While NFS is available in the public domain and from many vendors, Sun Microsystems also sells and supports the service. It includes the NIS+ enterprise naming service with its version of NFS and offers an Internet version of NFS called WebNFS, as discussed under the next subheading.

An important distinction between NFS and Internet FTP (File Transfer Protocol) is that NFS does not need to fully transfer a file to a client's system. Instead, only the blocks of the file that the client needs are transferred across the network link, thus reducing network traffic. NFS servers broadcast or advertise the directories that they share. A shared directory is often called a *published* or *exported* directory. Information about shared directories and who can access them is stored in a file that is read by the operating system when it boots.

The process of making files accessible files in a directory is called *file mounting*. An automounter process is available that automatically mounts files on demand when a user attempts to access a file. Prior knowledge of a file's location is not necessary.

NFS version 3 provides integrity features for files that may be opened by multiple users simultaneously. If several people were accessing the same file and some of those people were writing changes to the file, then other people must know about the changes that have been made. NFS solves this problem by implementing a lock manager to lock the sections of a file that are currently being accessed by different people. A status monitor works with the lock manager to ensure that people accessing and making changes to a file do not "collide."

NFS version 3 also implements a global namespace that lets users move to different network locations but still access files with the same naming scheme used at the "home site." This feature also benefits applications that are configured to access files based on specific location names.

Security features in NFS include an authentication and authorization service to check user IDs and access rights before allowing them to access a file. NFS can also be configured to use other security services such as Kerberos. Encryption services such as DES (Data Encryption Standard) can also be implemented. NFS also implements ACLs (access control lists) which hold authorization information that defines exactly how an authenticated user can access a file. See "Rights and Permissions" for information about NFS ACLs.

## WebNFS

Sun has extended NFS to operate on the Internet with WebNFS. WebNFS basically makes information on NFS servers (versions 2 and 3) available to users of Web browsers and Java applets over the Internet. It also allows users to access NFS servers through corporate firewalls. WebNFS is a complete file system for the Web, unlike FTP and HTTP. It supports in-place editing of files so users don't need to download and edit a file, then send it back in separate operations.

Files on the Internet appear as local files to users and are accessed using the NFS URL (Uniform Resource Locator) format such as nfs://*server*/*directory*/*filename*. WebNFS builds on NFS technology to bring file access and distribution to the Web. WebNFS has been designed to be much more efficient than NFS at bandwidth utilization over the Internet. This improves performance when downloading software from Web sites. Automatic error and crash recovery is also provided.

WebNFS is described in RFC 2054, at http://www.internic.net/rfc/rfc2054.txt.

**RELATED ENTRIES**   AFS (Andrew File System); CIFS (Common Internet File System); Distributed File Systems; File Systems; Rights and Permissions; *and* UNIX File System

### INFORMATION ON THE INTERNET

| | |
|---|---|
| SunSoft's NFS information | http://www.sun.com/solaris/networking/nfsindex.html |
| SunSoft's WebNFS information | http://www.sun.com/webnfs/index.html |
| Network Appliance, Inc. | http://www.netapp.com |
| RFC 1094 | http://www.internic.net/rfc/rfc1094.txt |
| RFC 1813 | http://www.internic.net/rfc/rfc1813.txt |
| Zensoft's ULTIMATE NFS Homepage | http://zensoft.com/pages/NFS.html |
| Rawn Shah's TCP/IP & NFS FAQ | http://www.rtd.com/pcnfsfaq/faq.html |

**N**

# NHRP (Next Hop Resolution Protocol)

NHRP is an IETF (Internet Engineering Task Force) protocol that is designed to assist in the routing of IP datagrams over NBMA (nonbroadcast multiple access) networks, such as ATM, frame relay, SMDS (Switched Multimegabit Data Service), and X.25. NHRP is not a routing protocol. It is an address resolution mechanism that resolves the IP address of a datagram into an NBMA (ATM, frame relay, etc.) address.

An *NBMA network* is the opposite of a *broadcast network*. On a broadcast network, multiple computers and devices are attached to a shared network cable or other medium. When one computer transmits frames, all nodes on the network "listen" to the frames, but only the node to which the frames are addressed actually receives the frames. Thus, the frames are broadcast. An NBMA network uses connection-oriented circuits to deliver frames or cells from one end of the circuit to the other. No other stations are involved in a circuit except the two endpoints. Connectionless IP datagram services are not necessarily a good fit over ATM connection-oriented networks, so a number of schemes have been cooked up to resolve the problem.

The IETF ION (Internetworking over NBMA) Working Group is focused on the creation of NBMA networking standards. It works on the NHRP protocol, as well as on IPv4 over ATM and on IPv6 over ATM. See "ION (Internetworking over NBMA)." Also see "IP over ATM" and "IP Switching" for related information.

Note that the ATM Forum has defined as a way of delivering upper-level protocols over ATM networks. LANE (LAN Emulation) and MPOA (Multiprotocol over ATM). For additional information, see "IP over ATM." As far as IP over ATM standards go, MPOA may be the best choice because the ATM Forum has designed it to work with many other standards in an attempt to provide support for all the services that might be needed to support legacy networks over ATM. The ATM Forum's MPOA supports the use of the IETF's NHRP routing protocol.

## NHRP Functionality

Consider the differences between IP routing and ATM or frame relay switching. First, routing is a layer 3 (network layer) function while switching is a layer 2 (data link layer) function. In addition, IP is a packet-switching connectionless datagram service in which packets are sent from one router to the next until they reach their destination. ATM and frame relay are connection-oriented, circuit-based networks in which traffic flows through PVCs or SVCs (permanent or switched virtual circuits).

 **NOTE:** *This section discusses NHRP in terms of ATM, although it also applies to frame relay and other NBMA networks.*

There are, of course, advantages to running IP over ATM. One is speed and the other is the possibility of taking advantage of ATM's QoS (Quality of Service) features. QoS provides a way to ship time-sensitive traffic (live voice and video) across a network and ensure that it is not held up by other traffic. Therefore, by running IP over ATM, you can access its QoS features with compatible applications.

The goal of any IP over ATM scheme is to deliver IP packets through a layer 2 virtual circuit and benefit from the circuit's speed. Part of this trick is to find a virtual circuit that can deliver IP packets from source to destination. Once an appropriate circuit is identified, packets can be delivered in the layer 2 circuit, bypassing the need to go through routers.

To understand NHRP, we must picture the topology of an ATM switched network with an overlay of IP subnetworks, as pictured in Figure N-19. Each IP subnetwork is called a *LIS (logical IP subnet)*. The ATM switching fabric may be your own organization's backbone or a carrier-based wide area network.

Assume the NHS servers in Figure N-19 already know each other's addresses. These addresses are either manually configured or discovered using an intradomain and interdomain routing protocol. Also assume the source wishes to obtain a

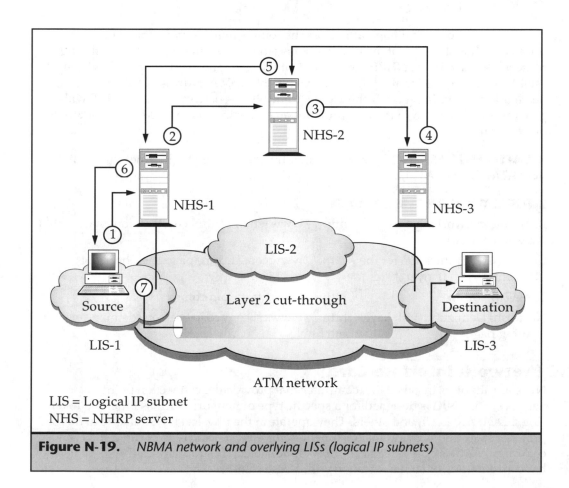

**Figure N-19.**   *NBMA network and overlying LISs (logical IP subnets)*

**N**

cut-through SVC (switched virtual circuit) across the ATM network to the destination. The following steps take place to obtain this address:

1. The source sends a request to NHS-1.

2. NHS-1 does not know the address, so it forwards the request to NHS-2.

3. NHS-2 does not know the address, so it forwards the request to NHS-3.

4. NHS-3 knows the address (because it is in the same LIS as the destination) and forwards a reply with the address back to NHS-2. NHS-2 records this information for future use.

5. NHS-2 forwards the reply to NHS-1, which also records the information.

6. NHS-1 forwards the reply to the source.

7. An SVC is built across the ATM network to provide cut-through packet transmissions.

Note that the hop-by-hop path across the routers may be preferable if the transmission is short, but if the transmission is long or requires QoS, the cut-through route is used. Basically, NHRP helps avoid all the router hops once a path has been established. Also note that NHRP will provide the NBMA address of the actual destination, assuming it is attached to the same NBMA network. If not, NHRP will give the address of the router that provides an exit point on the NBMA network to the destination.

**RELATED ENTRIES**    ATM (Asynchronous Transfer Mode); IP (Internet Protocol); IP over ATM; IP over ATM, Classical; *and* IP Switching

### INFORMATION ON THE INTERNET

| | |
|---|---|
| ION (Internetworking over NBMA) charter | http://www.ietf.org/html.charters/ion-charter.html |
| Com21 (Communication for the 21st Century) on IP over ATM | http://www.com21.com/pages/ietf.html#B4 |
| The ATM Forum | http://www.atmforum.com |
| Noritoshi Demizu's Multi Layer Routing page | http://www.csl.sony.co.jp/person/demizu/inet/mlr.html |

# NIC (Network Interface Card)

NICs are adapters installed in a computer that provide the connection point to a network. Each NIC is designed for a specific type of network, such as Ethernet, token ring, FDDI, ARCNET, and others. They operate at the physical layer relative to the OSI protocol stack and provide an attachment point for a specific type of cable such as coaxial cable, twisted-pair cable, or fiber-optic cable. NICs for wireless LANs typically have an antenna for communication with a base station.

NICs are defined by physical and data link layer protocols. Physical protocols define mechanical and electrical interface specifications such as the physical connection methods for cable. The electrical specifications define the methods for transmitting bit streams across the cable and the control signals that provide the timing of data transfers across the network. Each card implements a specific medium access method in accordance with the IEEE 802.x standards (or possibly other standards). See "Medium Access Control Methods" for more information.

> *NOTE:   Network computer publications evaluate and compare NICs on a regular basis. You can check their Web sites for these reports, which are listed under "Magazine Links" in Appendix A.*

Network interface cards are available in two categories: those that follow standard specifications, and those that follow the specifications but add enhancements to boost performance. Some of these special features are discussed later. Keep in mind that differences in hardware design among interface cards on a network can slow performance. For example, a network card with a 32-bit interface typically sends data to a 16-bit card faster than the 16-bit card can process it. To solve this bottleneck, *memory buffers* are implemented to capture and hold incoming data, preventing data overflows and allowing the 32-bit card to complete its transmission, even while the 16-bit card continues to process the information it has collected in its buffer.

Another type of bottleneck occurs between the network interface card and the memory of the computer. There are four methods for moving information from the network interface card into the computer once it has been received. With DMA (direct memory access), a DMA controller takes control of the bus and transfers data from the NIC to a memory location, thus reducing CPU load. With the shared memory option, NICs have their own memory that the system processor can access directly, or both the CPU and NIC share a block of system memory that both can directly access. With the bus mastering technique, a network adapter can transfer information directly to system memory without interrupting the system processor.

Global addressing ensures that every network interface card has a unique identifying node address. Token ring and Ethernet card addresses are hardwired on the card. The IEEE (Institute of Electrical and Electronic Engineers) is in charge of assigning addresses to token ring and Ethernet cards. Each manufacturer is given a unique code and a block of addresses. When installing a card, it is a good idea to determine the card address and write it down for future reference. You can also use a diagnostics utility supplied with the card to determine its address after you've installed the card in a system. You might also find the address on a label attached to the card.

Most network cards come with a socket for remote-boot PROM (programmable read-only memory). You use remote-boot PROMs on diskless workstations that can't boot on their own but instead boot from the network server. A diskless workstation is less expensive than a system with floppy disk and hard disk drives. It is also more secure because users can't download valuable data to floppy disk or upload viruses and unauthorized software.

**N**

**RELATED ENTRIES** Data Communication Concepts; IEEE (Institute of Electrical and Electronic Engineers); LAN (Local Area Network); MAC (Medium Access Control); Medium Access Control Methods; NDIS (Network Driver Interface Specification); Network Concepts; ODI (Open Data link Interface); *and* Protocol Concepts

### INFORMATION ON THE INTERNET

| | |
|---|---|
| Ken Yap's Network Interface Card settings info page | http://www.syd.dit.csiro.au/staff/ken/personal/NIC |
| KMJ Communications' NIC information | http://www.kmj.com/nic.html |
| City University of Hong Kong's NIC page (very interesting) | http://cctpwww.cityu.edu.hk/network/l3_nic.htm |

## NII (National Information Infrastructure)

The NII is the so-called "data superhighway" that is designed to make information available to the public in many forms, including video programming, scientific or business databases, images, sound recordings, library archives, and other media. Public databases are available at locations throughout the country, such as libraries, museums, government agencies, and research facilities. The U.S. government has vast quantities of information in the Library of Congress, the Smithsonian, and elsewhere that it will make available.

NII is promoted by NIST (National Institute of Standards and Technology) in the U.S. The High-Performance and High-Speed Networking Act of 1993 calls for federal organizations to coordinate their efforts in defining and building the NII.

The NII is also the physical network of fiber-optic lines, switches, and network software that is being put into place and maintained by communication and information service providers. According to the NIST, the NII encompasses much more than physical communication facilities. It also includes a wide range of equipment, including cameras, scanners, keyboards, telephones, fax machines, computers, switches, compact disks, video and audio tape, cable, wire, satellites, fiber-optic transmission lines, microwave nets, switches, televisions, monitors, printers, and much more.

NIST's goal is to set up a network that stimulates electronic education and makes information available in the classroom. The medical and scientific fields will also benefit from having instant access to the latest research information in databases scattered throughout the country. Increasing the available bandwidth on the network will bring big-city services to small communities.

In January of 1997, the U.S. FCC (Federal Communications Commission) announced that it would allocate 300 MHz of spectrum (from 5.15–5.35 GHz and 5.725–5.825 GHz) for unlicensed public use as a wireless component of the National Information Infrastructure called the U-NII (Unlicensed NII). Apple Computer has promoted the U-NII extensively and was responsible for many of the documents filed with the FCC to obtain this spectrum for use in education. Its efforts have been focused on obtaining adequate spectrum for local area, high-bandwidth computer applications as may be required in schools and obtaining provision for moderate-distance communications as may be required in rural and suburban areas. More information is available at the Apple address given below under "Information on the Internet."

The United States is just one of many countries pursuing national initiatives to make information freely available over communication networks. The GII (Global Information Infrastructure) is a worldwide "network of networks" that provides all the benefits of the NII on a global scale.

**RELATED ENTRIES**    GII (Global Information Infrastructure);  Internet; NIST (National Institute of Standards and Technology); *and* NREN (National Research and Education Network)

**INFORMATION ON THE INTERNET**

| | |
|---|---|
| NII site | http://nii.nist.gov/nii.html |
| NII Agenda for Action page | http://sunsite.unc.edu/nii/toc.html |
| NII Task Force test page | http://www.niit.org |
| Other NII information | http://epn.org/cme/infoactive/fall96/fall96.html |
| U-NII commentary | http://www.research.apple.com/research/niiband |
| Global Information Infrastructure Commission | http://www.gii.org |
| ITU's GII page | http://www.itu.int/Sites/wwwfiles/tel_gii.html |

# NIST (National Institute of Standards and Technology)

NIST is a U.S. government agency that was established to assist industry in the development of technology. It is an agency of the U.S. Department of Commerce's Technology Administration. NIST has consolidated the activities of the CSL (Computer Systems Laboratory) and the CAML (Computing and Applied Mathematics Laboratory) into a new information technology laboratory. The NIST Web site is at http://www.nist.gov.

# NLM (NetWare Loadable Module)

The NetWare 3.x and 4.x operating systems are modular and expandable. You add functionality to the operating system or make changes, upgrades, and additions by installing NLMs (NetWare Loadable Modules) at the server. Some of the services provided by NLMs are

- Support for storing files for operating systems other than DOS
- Communication services
- Database services

**N**

- Messaging services
- Archive and backup services
- Network management services

You can load or unload any module at any time from the server console without bringing down the server. Each module uses additional memory, so you need to make sure the server has enough memory to handle the NLMs you plan to load. Because the modules are located in the server along with the operating system, they are tightly coupled with the operating system and have instant access to services.

**RELATED ENTRY**    Novell NetWare

## NLSP (NetWare Link Services Protocol)

NLSP is a NetWare routing protocol that was developed by Novell for IPX (Internetwork Packet Exchange) internetworks and as a replacement for RIP (Routing Information Protocol). It is derived from IS-IS (Intermediate System-to- Intermediate System), the link-state routing protocol developed by the ISO (International Organization for Standardization). Routers running NLSP exchange information about network links, the cost of paths, IPX network numbers, and media types. They use this information to build routing tables.

One of the most important features of NLSP as compared to RIP is that it knows more about the entire internetwork, not just neighboring routers. This allows a router to make more intelligent decisions about how to route packets. Routers obtain information about the router from other routers and then build extensive tables that define the best way to route packets.

NLSP provides these performance benefits:

- NLSP only transmits routing information when something has changed on the network, and it uses a multicasting method for transmitting the information. With multicasting, only relevant routers bother to read the information. Other routers do not waste their processing time if they don't need the information.

- NLSP provides a more efficient service advertising method than SAP (Service Advertising Protocol). It sends out information about services that have changed on a server only when those changes occur.

- NLSP compresses the IPX header to reduce the size of the data packets. Compression helps to conserve bandwidth when IPX packets travel over low-speed WAN links.

- NLSP can forward packets through up to 127 hops and so is more scalable than RIP. It also uses hierarchical addressing of nodes, so you can deploy networks containing thousands of LANs and servers.

- NLSP can optionally split traffic across two or more equal-cost paths between two network routers so that fault-tolerant redundant links can be created.

- Administrators can manually assign costs to links so that the use of links can be controlled based on their cost. For example, traffic on overloaded links can be reduced by increasing the link's cost.

- NLSP can automatically switch to alternate links if an existing link fails. It checks for failures on a periodic basis. After switching links, the NLSP routing tables are updated in each router so that packets are sent across the new paths if necessary.

NLSP will eventually replace RIP and SAP as the default routing protocol in the NetWare IPX routing environment. Both protocols are still included in NetWare and can coexist on the same internetwork. NLSP can also be managed from SNMP (Simple Network Management Protocol) consoles.

**RELATED ENTRIES**    Novell NetWare; Novell NetWare Protocols; *and* Routing Protocols and Algorithms

**INFORMATION ON THE INTERNET**

Novell, Inc. (search for NLSP)          http://www.novell.com

# NNTP (Network News Transport Protocol)

The NNTP protocol is the delivery mechanism for the USENET newsgroup service. USENET runs on the Internet and other TCP/IP-based networks and provides a way to exchange messages, articles, and bulletins throughout the Internet. Articles are put in central databases throughout the Internet and users access the database to get the articles they need. This reduces network traffic and eliminates the need to store a copy of each article on every subscriber's system.

There are thousands of different newsgroups related to computers, social issues, science, the humanities, recreation, and other topics. See "USENET" for more information on USENET itself. This topic discusses the operation of the NNTP protocol.

USENET servers use NNTP to exchange news articles among themselves. NNTP is also used by clients who need to read news articles on USENET servers. The server-to-server and user-to-server connections are described here:

- **Server-to-server exchanges**  In the server-to-server exchange, one server either requests the latest articles from another server (*pull*) or allows the other server to *push* new articles to it. In either case, both servers engage in a conversation in which specific newsgroup information is requested and then delivered. A primary goal is to prevent the sending system from sending articles that the receiver already has. Select newsgroups and articles can be blocked.

- **User-to-server connections**  Users run news readers, which are now included with most Web browsers. The user first connects with a newsgroup server (usually located at an ISP (Internet service provider), then downloads a list of

**N**

available newsgroups. The user can then subscribe to a newsgroup and begin reading articles available in that group or post new articles.

Before NNCP, USENET servers used UUCP (UNIX-to-UNIX Copy Program) to exchange information. UUCP is a "flood broadcast" mechanism. Hosts send new news articles they receive to other hosts, which in turn forward the news on to other hosts that they feed. Usually, a host receives duplicates of articles and must discard those duplicates—a time-consuming process and waste of bandwidth.

NNTP uses an interactive command and response mechanism that lets hosts determine which articles are to be transmitted. A host acting as a client contacts a "server" host using NNTP, then inquires if any new newsgroups have been created on any of the serving host systems. An administrator can choose to create similar newsgroups on the host he or she manages.

During the same NNTP session, the client requests information about new articles that have arrived in all or some of the newsgroups. The server then sends the client a list of new articles and the client can request transmission of some or all of those articles. The client can refuse to accept articles that it already has.

Readers interested in the details of NNTP commands and responses are encouraged to read RFC 977, which is available at the Web site listed at the end of this topic.

Some organizations may prefer to set up their own USENET systems on their TCP/IP-based intranet rather than deploy groupware and collaborative applications. If you plan on setting up your own news server, you may want to consider the products listed here:

| | |
|---|---|
| InterNetNews | http://www.isc.org/isc/inn.html |
| NetWin Ltd.'s DNEWS | http://netwinsite.com |
| Netscape News Server | http://www.netscape.com |

**RELATED ENTRIES**   Broadcast News Technology; Component Software Technology; Distributed Object Computing; IRC (Internet Relay Chat); Mailing List Programs; Marimba Castanet; Netcasting; PointCast; Push; *and* USENET

## INFORMATION ON THE INTERNET

| | |
|---|---|
| Network News Transport Protocol (RFC 977) | http://www.internic.net/rfc/rfc977.txt |
| NNTP Extensions (nntpext) | http://www.ietf.org/html.charters/nntpext-charter.html |
| PSINet's Usenet News (very informative if you browse around) | http://cmc.psi.net/inet-serv/news/news-reader.html |
| Yahoo!'s NNTP links page | http://www.yahoo.com/Computers_and_Internet/Information_and_Documentation/Protocols |

# Node

A node is a network-connected device such as a workstation, a server, or a printer. Network connection devices such as bridges and routers are not usually referred to as nodes on a network even though they have network addresses.

In the IP addressing scheme, network nodes such as computers are called "hosts" while routers are sometimes called gateways, an older term that is rarely used today because gateways refer to application-layer devices that join systems or networks and provide translation services between them.

# Novell

Novell has been a major influence in the growth of the microcomputer industry. It developed Z-80-based microcomputers in the 1970s and created its first networking products in the early 1980s. Novell's main product during the emerging years of the personal computer was a file-sharing device based on the Motorola 68000 processor. In 1983, when IBM announced the IBM Personal Computer XT, which had a hard disk, Novell quickly responded with a product that converted the hard disk system into a file-sharing system. Workstations attached to the server with a star-configured cabling system known as S-Net.

As NetWare grew in popularity, its designers improved its hardware independence. Novell stopped pushing its own LAN hardware and began providing support for products from many vendors. This was one of the most important strategies in the advancement of NetWare as an industry standard. In 1986, Novell introduced Advanced NetWare, which provided even more support for LAN hardware by bridging different network types within the file server or an external workstation. For example, you could install both an Ethernet and token ring card in the server.

In 1989, Novell announced NetWare 386 version 3.0, a completely rewritten version of NetWare designed to take advantage of features built into the Intel 80386 processor. NetWare 386 was a 32-bit operating system that provided enhanced security, performance, and flexibility. Over the years, the product was improved to provide better performance and support for a wide range of clients and protocols. The current version of this product is called NetWare 3.12.

In 1993, Novell announced NetWare version 4. Its most important feature was NDS (NetWare Directory Services), which enabled network administrators to organize users and network resources such as servers and printers the way people naturally access them. NDS is discussed further under its new name, "NDS (Novell Directory Services)." Note that NetWare 3.12 is NetWare without NDS.

In 1995, Novell announced NetWare version 4.1, which provided numerous product enhancements and upgrades. Then, in 1996, it upgraded the product to NetWare 4.11 and announced Novell IntranetWare, a full-service intranet platform that implements Web technologies on top of NetWare 4.11. See "Novell IntranetWare" and "Novell NetWare" for more information about these products.

**N**

Novell's current strategy is to support corporate intranets and the creation of smart global networks. Novell's vision of a smart network is one that helps users find information relevant to their needs, automatically installs new software, handles accounting and licensing, and provides many other services. Novell sees its Novell Directory Services as a foundation that can support this type of network. Its definition of a global network is a hybrid public network such as the Internet and private intranets. The global network will help businesses connect with other businesses using extranet technologies, as discussed under "Extranet." Novell's global network scheme allows people to connect with any information source at any time in a secure way.

## Other Important Novell Products

Besides its NetWare products, Novell also sells a variety of products that expand the services of NetWare, support global internetworking, and provide groupware and collaborative computing support. The most important products are outlined here. You can check the Novell sites given under "Information on the Internet" at the end of this section for additional information.

- **NetWare 4.11 SFT III**  Provides fault tolerance and guards against downtime by integrating two physically separate servers. If one server fails, the other continues to operate and provide service to users.

- **ManageWise**  An integrated management application for managing NetWare and Windows NT servers.

- **NetWare Navigator**  An automated software distribution product for NetWare.

- **LANalyzer**  A network monitoring and analyzing tool for troubleshooting Ethernet and token ring networks.

- **NetWare Connect 2**  A server-based remote communication platform that enables remote Windows, Mac OS, and DOS users to dial in and access resources on NetWare networks.

- **NetWare Multiprotocol Router**  Software-based routing products that provide concurrent routing of IPX, TCP/IP, AppleTalk, and SNA protocols.

- **Novell Connect Services**  A collection of Novell networking products designed to simplify WAN administration that includes NetWare 4.11, NDS, ManageWise, NetWare Connect, and NetWare Multiprotocol Router.

- **GroupWise**  A fully integrated messaging system that combines e-mail, personal calendaring, group scheduling, task management, document management, rules-based message management, workflow routing, and electronic discussions.

**RELATED ENTRIES**  NDS (Novell Directory Services); Network Operating Systems; Novell NetWare; *and* Novell NetWare File System

**INFORMATION ON THE INTERNET**

Novell, Inc.                                      http://www.novell.com

Novell's IntranetWare site                        http://www.novell.com/intranetware

# Novell Directory Services

*See* NDS (Novell Directory Services).

# Novell IntranetWare

Novell IntranetWare is Novell NetWare 4.11 with intranet enhancements and Internet capabilities. It includes all the capabilities of NetWare as described under "Novell NetWare," in addition to Netscape Navigator Internet browsers, FTP Services for NetWare, Novell's IPX/IP Gateway, and a multiprotocol router for wide area network and Internet connections. Organizations that already have NetWare in place can easily upgrade to IntranetWare and add intranet and Internet capabilities.

IntranetWare includes NetWare Web Server, a set of NLMs (NetWare Loadable Modules) that provide Web services for intranet and Internet users. Like any Web server, NetWare Web Server provides a platform for publishing HTML (Hypertext Markup Language) documents and other documents that can be handled within the HTML and HTTP protocols. The Web server works in conjunction with NDS (Novell Directory Services) to help users browse for network resources and information.

NetWare Web Server takes full advantage of the security features in NetWare 4.11 to provide control over who can access Web documents. Administrators can control access based on IP address, username, host name, directories, documents, users, and groups.

IntranetWare includes a copy of Netscape Navigator for each user that is licensed to access the IntranetWare server.

NetWare Multiprotocol Router provides connection support to ISPs (Internet service providers) in the form of ISDN (Integrated Services Digital Network) support, leased lines, frame relay, and ATM. The product is entirely software-based, so no external routers are required to make the connections. Traffic over the WAN is minimized with data compression.

**RELATED ENTRIES**    Directory Services; Distributed Computer Networks; Distributed File Systems; Internet; Internet Backbone; Internet Connections; Intranets and Extranets; Multiprocessing; NDS (Novell Directory Services); Novell; Novell NetWare; Novell NetWare Protocols; Routing Protocols and Algorithms; WAN (Wide Area Network); *and* Web Technologies and Concepts

**INFORMATION ON THE INTERNET**

Novell's IntranetWare site                        http://www.novell.com/intranetware

**N**

## Novell NetWare

As of 1997, Novell has three primary network operating systems, as outlined here:

- **Novell NetWare 4.11** A high-end network operating system that includes NDS (Novell Directory Services) and SFT (System Fault Tolerance) features that guard against downtime by integrating two physically separate servers.

- **Novell IntranetWare** An intranet platform product that has all the features of NetWare 4.11.

- **Novell NetWare 3.12** Novell traditional NetWare operating system without NDS, SFT, and intranet features.

This section covers the features of Novell NetWare 4.11. See "Novell IntranetWare" for information about the intranet product.

NetWare 4.11 is an NSE (network services engine) that provides a wide range of built-in services, including directory services, security, routing, messaging, management, file and print services, and TCP/IP support. It also provides a platform for expanded services such as telephony, multimedia services, Internet and intranet browsing and publishing, and more. The following sections describe the most important features of NetWare 4.11.

**NDS (NOVELL DIRECTORY SERVICES)** Through NDS, NetWare 4.11 provides a single view of the network. NDS is a distributed database that holds information about network users and network resources everywhere on the network, even global networks. Users log in once to access resources anywhere, as opposed to having to log in every time they attempt to access a resource. See "NDS (Novell Directory Services)" for more information.

**MANAGEMENT FEATURES** NetWare 4.11 includes SNMP (Simple Network Management Protocol) support so that servers can be managed by SNMP management consoles, including Novell ManageWise. An optional product provides management information to IBM NetView management consoles. NetWare 4.11 also includes remote management utilities.

**ACCOUNTING AND LICENSING** Accounting features let administrators track user access to resources and charge users for use of those resources. The services can be used to collect real charges from users (such as students in an educational environment) or to simply collect usage information. A licensing service lets administrators monitor the use of licensed applications.

**SECURITY** NetWare uses a highly secure logon sequence that implements public-/private-key authentication schemes, and an auditing feature that monitors and records networkwide events.

**STORAGE SYSTEM FEATURES**   NetWare performs automatic file-by-file compression to increase storage capacity. Compression is performed as a background process that has minimal effect on server performance. NetWare also supports automated data migration to transfer infrequently accessed files from expensive online storage to nearline or offline storage devices such as optical disk and tape. See "Storage Management Systems" for more details.

**BACKUP**   NetWare includes SMS (Storage Management Services), a collection of software modules for backing up and restoring data on NetWare networks.

**SMP (SYMMETRICAL MULTIPROCESSING)**   NetWare 4.11 supports SMP, which enables it to run on servers with multiple processors.

There are many additional features of NetWare, too numerous to mention here. You can get additional information by visiting Novell's Web site at the address given at the end of this section or by referring to the additional Novell entries in this book.

**RELATED ENTRIES**   Client/Server Computing; Directory Services; Distributed Computer Networks; Distributed File Systems; Multiprocessing; NDS (Novell Directory Services); Network Concepts; Novell; Novell IntranetWare; Novell NetWare File System; *and* Novell NetWare Protocols

**INFORMATION ON THE INTERNET**

| | |
|---|---|
| Novell, Inc. | http://www.novell.com |
| NetWare Connection magazine | http://www.novell.com/nwc |
| NetWare FAQ | http://kawnug.oznet.ksu.edu/novell/faq/nov-faq.htm |
| Novell Resources list at Network Professionals Resource Center | http://www.inetassist.com/url15.htm |
| Novell List Archive | http://www.dfm.dtu.dk/netware/nov-lst |
| NetWare Users International | http://www.novell.com/nui |
| Yahoo!'s NetWare links page | http://www.yahoo.com/Computers_and_Internet/Communications_and_Networking/Netware |

# Novell NetWare File System

The NetWare filing system consists of servers with storage systems that have one or more volumes of information. The first volume on a server is called SYS. Additional volumes can be assigned a name of choice, such as VOL1, VOL2, and so on. Each volume has its own directory structure.

**N**

The way you reference a server, its volumes, and the directories of a volume is illustrated in Figure N-20. For example, the following refers to a file called BUDGET.XLS in the BUDGDOCS directory on the APPS volume of the ACCTG server:

ACCTG/APPS:BUDGDOCS/BUDGET.XLS

A NetWare volume is the highest level of storage in the NetWare filing system. It is a physical amount of hard disk storage space. You can expand a volume at any time by adding more physical disk space and making it a part of any existing volume. Volumes appear as objects in the NDS (Novell Directory Services) directory tree, so they are easy to locate by administrators and users from anywhere on the network. A NetWare 4.11 server supports up to 64 volumes.

The NetWare UFS (Universal File System) provides many performance-enhancing features as described here:

- **Elevator seeking** Prioritizes incoming read requests according to how they can best be accessed by the read head in relation to its current location

- **File caching** Minimizes the number of times the disk is accessed by holding commonly accessed information in memory

- **Background writes** Handles disk writes separately from disk reads so that data is written to disk when disk requests from users have minimized

- **Overlapped seeks** Improves read performance if two or more hard disks are connected to their own controller (disk channel) by allowing NetWare to access each controller simultaneously

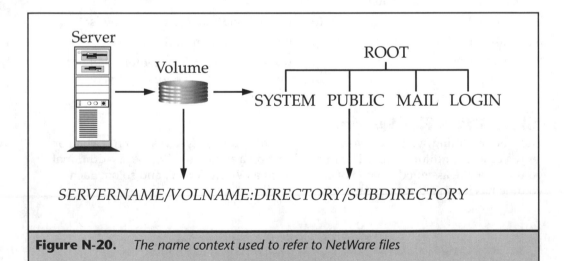

**Figure N-20.** *The name context used to refer to NetWare files*

- **Turbo FAT**   Indexes the file allocation tables of files over 2MB so that the locations of their segments are immediately available

- **File compression**   Increases disk space by up to 63 percent by compressing files as a background process

- **Block suballocation**   Maximizes disk space by allocating partial disk blocks to small files

NetWare also includes several important features that ensure the survivability and quick recovery of data on servers, as described here:

- **Read-after-write verification**   Verifies writes by reading every write after it is written.

- **Duplicate directories**   Provides a backup of the directory structure by duplicating it on disk.

- **Duplicate FAT**   Provides a backup of the file allocation table by duplicating it on disk.

- **Hot Fix**   Detects and corrects disk defects by automatically marking potentially bad sectors as unwritable.

- **TTS (Transaction Tracking System)**   Protects files from incomplete writes. If a record in a database is being altered and the server goes down, incomplete writes are backed out.

- **SFT (System Fault Tolerance)**   Provides redundancy in hardware by allowing administrators to duplicate disk controllers and mirror hard drives.

**RELATED ENTRIES**   Distributed File Systems; File Systems; NCP (NetWare Core Protocol); NDS (Novell Directory Services); Network Concepts; Network Operating Systems; Novell; Novell IntranetWare; Novell NetWare Protocols; Rights and Permissions; Storage Management Systems; *and* Volume and Partition Management

**INFORMATION ON THE INTERNET**

Novell, Inc.                                   http://www.novell.com

# Novell NetWare Protocols

The native NetWare internetworking protocol is IPX (Internetwork Packet Exchange). It was derived from the XNS (Xerox Network System) protocol, which was developed in the 1970s. Currently, a number of other network operating systems, including Windows NT, include IPX protocol stacks to provide interoperability with NetWare and NetWare-compatible applications and devices. A number of network clients also support the protocol, including Microsoft Windows.

Like IP (Internet Protocol), IPX is an internetworking protocol that provides datagram services. Internetworking protocols operate in the network layer and include routing services, as shown in Figure N-21. The other member of the Novell

**N**

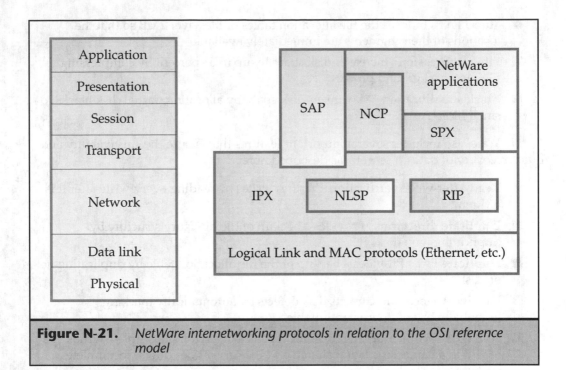

**Figure N-21.** *NetWare internetworking protocols in relation to the OSI reference model*

NetWare protocol suite is SPX (Sequenced Packet Exchange), which resides in the transport layer. When compared to the TCP/IP protocol suite, IPX provides routing and internetwork services similar to IP, and SPX provides transport layer services similar to TCP (Transmission Control Protocol). IPX and IP are connectionless datagram protocols, while SPX and TCP are connection-oriented protocols. See "Connection-Oriented and Connectionless Services" for additional information.

## IPX and SPX Details

IPX packets consist of a *data area* and a 30-byte IPX *header* that includes the network, node, and socket addresses for both the source and destination. The minimum IPX packet size is 30 bytes (the size of the header) and the maximum packet size is 65,535 bytes. In most cases, the network over which packets travel will impose a more realistic packet size of about 1,500 bytes.

Figure N-22 illustrates the structure of the IPX packet. Each field in the packet is described here:

- ■ **Checksum** Provides integrity checking
- ■ **Packet length** Length in bytes of the packet

- **Transport control**  Number of routers a packet can traverse before it is discarded
- **Packet type**  Defines the service that created the packet (either NCP, NetBIOS, NLSP, RIP, SAP, or SPX, as described later in this topic)
- **Destination network**  The network address of the destination network
- **Destination node**  MAC address of the destination node
- **Destination socket**  Address of the process running in the destination node
- **Source network**  The network address of the source network
- **Source node**  MAC address of the source node
- **Source socket**  Address of the process running in the source node

IPX addresses include a network address and a node address. Network addresses are assigned when setting up the primary server on a NetWare LAN. The node

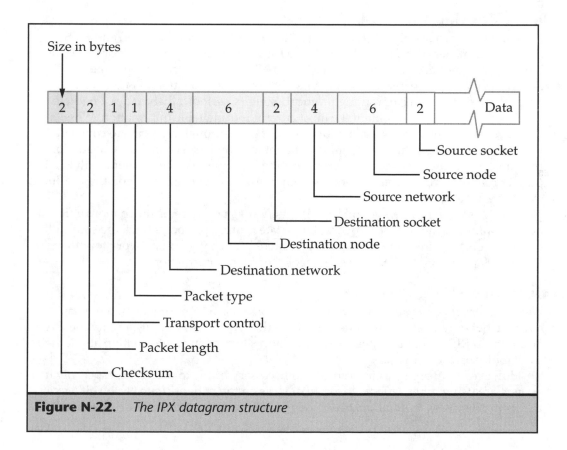

**Figure N-22.**  *The IPX datagram structure*

N

address is the hardwired address on a network interface card. A socket address is also included, which identifies a running software process in a computer. A complete IPX address is a 12-byte hexadecimal number that may look similar to the following:

> 4A87B321 14594EA221AE 0119

If this is a destination address, each of these values is placed in turn in the destination network field, the destination node field, and the socket field of the outgoing packet.

SPX is a connection-oriented protocol that operates at the transport layer. It establishes dedicated connections between nodes on an internetwork independent of the data links on the underlying router-connected LANs. When SPX is used, packets are not exchanged until a session is established between the two communicating systems. SPX uses IPX for packet delivery services and provides the data delivery guarantees that IPX cannot provide.

## NetWare Routing Protocols

NetWare uses two routing protocols: RIP (Routing Information Protocol) and NLSP (NetWare Link Services Protocol). RIP is the traditional routing protocol for NetWare, but it is being replaced by NLSP. Both RIP and NLSP can be used on the same internetwork until organizations can make the complete transition to NLSP.

RIP is a distance-vector routing protocol. Routers periodically broadcast packets to neighboring routers that contain the most current routing table information. When a router receives new routing table information, it goes through a process to consolidate this information with the routing information it already has. When the consolidation is complete, the router has the most recent routing information. The problem with RIP is that it broadcasts routing information whether updates are needed or not, thus adding excess traffic to the network.

Novell is now advocating NLSP for IPX networks because it is much more efficient at maintaining routes on the network. Link-state routing protocols track the status of other routers and links and can adapt more quickly to changes in network topology. See "NLSP (NetWare Link Services Protocol)" for more information.

## Service Advertising Protocol

NetWare servers and routers on NetWare networks use SAP to broadcast a message over the network every 60 seconds to indicate the types of services it can provide. SAP is similar to RIP in that it enables network devices to exchange information about their availability on the network.

However, SAP broadcasting can add unnecessary traffic to networks, especially if servers are using other services to locate devices on the network, such as NDS (Novell Directory Services). In addition, SAP broadcast are not important to workstations on the other side of a wide area link. To reduce SAP broadcasts, you can increase the interval at which they occur or use Novell-provided filters that reduce SAP traffic over wide area links.

## NCP (NetWare Core Protocol)

NCP is the principal protocol for handling service requests between NetWare servers and clients. NCP handles logon requests and many other types of requests to the file system and the printing system. IPX is the underlying protocol that carries the transmission. NCP is a LAN protocol that was originally designed with the assumption that servers and workstations would be relatively close. When a router gets involved and connections are made over wide area network links, NCP causes traffic congestion. It uses a request/response scheme to manage server/workstation communication. If a workstation makes a request, it must first wait for a response from the server before making another request. This required acknowledgment adds excess traffic.

**RELATED ENTRIES**    NDS (Novell Directory Services); NLSP (NetWare Link Services Protocol); Novell; Novell IntranetWare; *and* Routing Protocols and Algorithms

### INFORMATION ON THE INTERNET

| | |
|---|---|
| Novell, Inc. | http://www.novell.com |
| TCP/IP and IPX Routing Tutorial | http://www.sangoma.com/fguide.htm |
| NetWare FAQ | http://kawnug.oznet.ksu.edu/novell/faq/nov-faq.htm |
| Novell Resources list at Network Professionals Resource Center | http://www.inetassist.com/url15.htm |
| Novell List Archive | http://www.dfm.dtu.dk/netware/nov-lst |

## NREN (National Research and Education Network)

The NREN is the backbone data network of the Internet, administered by the NSF (National Science Foundation). It succeeded the NSFNET (National Science Foundation Network) as the major Internet network for research and education in the United States as of the signing of the "High-Performance Computing Act of 1991," a bill sponsored by then senator Al Gore. It calls for a high-capacity (gigabits per second) network and the coordination of networking efforts among federal organizations.

The NREN is designed to connect K–12 schools, colleges, universities, libraries, health care industries, business, and manufacturing into a national public network using the Internet. The Internet provides vast quantities of timely and useful information to these institutions over existing telecommunication links. Access is

**N**

obtained using standard desktop computer equipment and modems or by connection to networks that are connected to the Internet.

**RELATED ENTRIES**   Internet; NII (National Information Infrastructure); *and* NIST (National Institute of Standards and Technology)

# NSA (National Security Agency)

The National Security Agency/Central Security Service is responsible for protecting U.S. communications as well as for producing foreign intelligence information. It a separately organized agency within the Department of Defense. Within NSA is INFOSEC, which provides security information about information systems. The NSA site is at http://www.nsa.gov.

# NSF (National Science Foundation) and NSFNET

The NSF is a U.S. government agency that promotes and funds science research, scientific projects, and the infrastructure required for scientific research. NSF is responsible for NSFNET, a communication network that is for the most part the Internet but not completely. NSFNET is a "network of networks" that ties together local, regional, and midlevel networks with a high-speed backbone. NSF defined the structure of the current Internet, and commercial providers used that architectural design to build the Internet.

NSFNET funded the vBNS (Very high speed Backbone Network Service), which uses the same technologies as the Internet but is designed to carry government, research, and educational traffic only. MCI was awarded the contract to build vBNS in 1995. The network transmits large amounts of voice, data, and video traffic at high speeds. NSF uses the network service to link five supercomputer centers with teams of researchers in the United States. The vBNS network makes use of MCI's commercial ATM (Asynchronous Transfer Mode) service.

For more information, see "Internet Backbone" or visit the NSF Web site at http://www.nsf.gov.

# NSP (Network Service Provider)

A network service provider is a carrier or other provider that provides services to local and regional ISPs (Internet service providers). See "Internet Backbone" for more information.

# NTFS (New Technology File System)

*See* Windows NT File System.

# NTP (Network Time Protocol)

NTP is an Internet protocol that devices can use to obtain the most accurate time possible via radio or atomic clocks at various locations on the Internet. The protocol can synchronize the time of a computer client or server to another server or reference time source. Time provided by NTP servers is typically accurate within milliseconds.

## INFORMATION ON THE INTERNET

| | |
|---|---|
| Time WWW server | http://www.eecis.udel.edu/~ntp |
| Network Time Protocol, Version 3 (RFC 1305) | http://www.internic.net/rfc/rfc1305.txt |
| Yahoo!'s NTP links page | http://www.yahoo.com/Computers_and_Internet/Information_and_Documentation/Protocols |

# NUMA (Non-Uniform Memory Access)

NUMA is a parallel processing computer architecture that goes beyond SMP (symmetric multiprocessing) and MPP (massively parallel processing) in its ability to harness the power of multiprocessor systems. As discussed under "Parallel Processing," SMP systems have limited scalability (i.e., the shared bus becomes overloaded as processors are added), and MPP systems require complex programming techniques due to the distributed nature of the processing nodes.

NUMA provides the programming ease of SMP systems and the scalability of MPP systems. A NUMA system is similar to an MPP system in that it consists of *nodes*. A node can be compared to a separate computer with a set of processors and its own memory, cache, and bus. The nodes are tied together with a high-speed switching architecture. What NUMA does that MPP systems do not is combine the memory in each node into a single *virtual memory space*. This single memory space makes it easier for programmers to write programs for NUMA systems. See "Parallel Processing" for more information about this topic.

**RELATED ENTRIES**    Clustering; Data Warehousing; DBMS (Database Management System); MPP (Massively Parallel Processing) Systems; Parallel Processing; *and* Servers

## INFORMATION ON THE INTERNET

| | |
|---|---|
| Sequent's NUMA papers | http://www.sequent.com/numaq/technology/papers.html |
| Emergent Corporation's NUMA paper | http://emergent.com/epress/earticle/numa.html |

**N**

# OBI (Open Buying on the Internet)

OBI is a protocol designed by American Express and SupplyWorks, Inc. for executing real-time business transactions on the Web. The protocol is designed to reduce the cost of doing purchase transactions on the Web and to stimulate Internet commerce. Microsoft, Netscape, Oracle, Open Market, and a number of other companies back the specification. The goal is to reduce costs, improve the overall buy-pay process, and increase service levels to end users using Internet technology.

OBI will achieve some of the same results as EDI (Electronic Data Interchange), an old and established business-to-business protocol. For example, a purchasing agent at one company can create purchase orders and send them to a supplier's Web site for processing. The EDI X12-850 document standard is used for structuring and sending electronic documents. Digital certificates are required for this type of transaction so companies receiving business documents can prove their authenticity.

To get more information about OBI, send electronic mail to the OBI Consortium at OBI@supplyworks.com.

**RELATED ENTRIES**    Certificates and Certification Systems; EDI (Electronic Data Interchange); Electronic Commerce; *and* SET (Secure Electronic Transaction)

# Object Technologies

Object-oriented technology brings software development past procedural programming, into a world of reusable programming that simplifies development of applications. Operating systems and applications are created as multiple modules that are linked together to create a functional program. Any module can be replaced or updated at any time without a need to update the entire operating system or program. Modules may also be located in different places, thus supporting distributed computing and the Internet.

A Web browser can be thought of as a container into which users can add objects that provide additional functionality. For example, a user might connect with a Web server and download an object in the form of a Java applet or an ActiveX component that improves the feature set of the Web browser itself or provides some utility that runs inside the Web browser, such as a mortgage calculation program from a real estate Web site. See "Component Software Technology" and "Distributed Object Computing" for more information.

The entire Windows NT operating system is built upon an object-based architecture. Devices like printers and other peripherals are objects, as are processes and threads, shared memory segments, and access rights.

An object may be a self-contained program or package of data with external functions. An ATM (automated teller machine) is perhaps the best example of an object in the real world. You don't care about the internal workings of the machine. You request cash and the machine delivers. The machine has an external interface that you access to get something, such as cash or an account balance.

Program and database objects are the same. They are like boxes with internal code or data that perform some action when the external interface is manipulated. The external interface has *methods*, which can be compared to the buttons on the ATM that make it do things. For example, an object might display columnar data sorted on a column selected by a user. A window that displays a list of files in a graphical desktop operating system (i.e., Windows 95) is an example of an object. It is a box with data (the list of files) that has controls for manipulating the data. You can click the button at the top of any column to sort the data on that column.

Objects are combined to create complete programs. Objects interact with one another by exchanging messages. One object will act as a server and another object will act as a client. They may switch those roles at any time. If a program needs updating, only the objects that need updating are replaced.

Objects are categorized into hierarchical *classes* that define different types of objects. Parent classes have characteristics that are passed down to subclasses of the object. This is called *class inheritance*. Inheritance can be blocked if necessary. In a database, the class "people" may have the subclasses of "male" and "female." Each subclass has *generalized* features inherited from its parents, along with *specialized* features of its own.

If we consider the ATM machine at your bank as a parent class, then the much smaller credit card machines at supermarket checkout lines could be considered a subclass. They are designed with the same specifications as the larger ATM, but without some features, such as the ability to check your account balance.

Objects talk to each other by sending messages or by establishing connection-oriented links. A message usually requests that an object do something. In a network environment, objects may be located on many different computers, and they talk to each other using network protocols. An ORB (object request broker) is a sort of message-passing bus that helps objects locate one another and establish communications. See "ORB (Object Request Broker)" for more information.

**RELATED ENTRIES**    ActiveX; Client/Server Computing; COM (Component Object Model); Component Software Technology; Compound Documents; CORBA (Common Object Request Broker Architecture); DCOM (Distributed Component Object Model); Distributed Object Computing; Java; Multitiered Architectures; OLE (Object Linking and Embedding); OLE DB; OMA (Object Management Architecture); ORB (Object Request Broker); *and* UNO (Universal Networked Object)

**INFORMATION ON THE INTERNET**

| | |
|---|---|
| OMG (Object Management Group) | http://www.omg.org |
| Object Database Management Group | http://www.odmg.org |
| W3C's Object page | http://www.w3.org/pub/WWW/OOP |
| Object Magazine Online | http://www.sigs.com/omo |

| Object Basics tutorial | http://www.qds.com/people/apope/ap_object.html |
| Bob Hathaway's Object-Orientation FAQ | http://www.cyberdyne-object-sys.com/oofaq |
| Ricardo Devis's Object Oriented page | http://www.arrakis.es/~devis/oo.html |
| Terry Montlick's object technology introduction (interesting) | http://www.soft-design.com/softinfo/objects.html |
| Sysnetics (see links page) | http://www.sysnetics.com |
| Object links at Texas A&M | http://www.cs.tamu.edu/people/ganeshb/obj_tech.html |
| Object-Oriented Information Sources | http://iamwww.unibe.ch/cgi-bin/ooinfo |
| Jeff Sutherland's Object Technology page | http://web0.tiac.net/users/jsuth |

## OC (Optical Carrier)

The existing methods for carrying digitized voice signals over twisted copper wire is known as the NADH (North American Digital Hierarchy). This hierarchy defines levels of digital streams, starting with DS0, which defines a single channel for carrying a digitized voice signal. DS0 has a bit rate of 64 Kbits/sec. The next level up, DS1 (also referred to as the T1 carrier), has a bit rate of 1.544 Mbits/sec and carries 24 DS0 channels with some overhead. DS3 consists of 28 DS1 channels. The NADH is discussed elsewhere in this book.

OCs are the digital hierarchies of the SONET standard, which defines how digital signals are multiplexed on fiber-optic cable. SONET is a physical layer specification that telephone carriers use to interconnect their long-distance telephone trunks. The following table lists the various OC levels.

| OC Level | Data Rate (Mbits/sec) | Number of DS0s | Number of DS1s | Number of DS3s |
|----------|----------------------|----------------|----------------|----------------|
| OC-1 | 51.84 | 672 | 28 | 1 |
| OC-3 | 155.52 | 2,016 | 84 | 3 |
| OC-6 | 311.04 | 4,032 | 168 | 6 |
| OC-9 | 466.56 | 6,048 | 252 | 9 |
| OC-12 | 622.08 | 8,064 | 336 | 12 |
| OC-18 | 933.12 | 12,096 | 504 | 18 |
| OC-24 | 1244.16 | 16,128 | 672 | 24 |
| OC-36 | 1866.24 | 24,192 | 1008 | 36 |

| OC Level | Data Rate (Mbits/sec) | Number of DS0s | Number of DS1s | Number of DS3s |
|----------|------------------------|----------------|----------------|----------------|
| OC-48 | 2488.32 | 32,256 | 1344 | 48 |
| OC-96 | 4976.00 | 64,512 | 2688 | 96 |
| OC-192 | 9952.00 | 129,024 | 5376 | 192 |

**RELATED ENTRIES**    Fiber-Optic Cable; NADH (North American Digital Hierarchy); SONET (Synchronous Optical Network); Transmission Media, Methods, and Equipment; *and* WAN (Wide Area Network)

# ODBC (Open Database Connectivity), Microsoft

ODBC is a database connectivity architecture that provides a way for clients to access a variety of heterogeneous databases. ODBC uses a single programming interface that is open and not tied to any vendor's database. Microsoft developed ODBC and has continued to develop it as a standard.

ODBC has the following features:

- It uses SQL (Structured Query Language) for all operations that access a database.

- It contains a library of function calls for accessing DBMS (database management system) data. The function calls can be used to execute SQL statements.

- Clients do not need to know the location of a database, the type of database, or the communication method used to access it.

- ODBC applications have universal access to any database that has an ODBC driver written for it. These databases are called *data sources*.

- Data sources include everything from Oracle relational databases to Microsoft Excel spreadsheet data files.

- Because different DBMSs have widely different functions, the ODBC API was designed in a way that lets an application know what functions are available from a particular database's ODBC driver.

The ODBC environment is pictured in Figure O-1. It consists of applications that conform to ODBC and databases that have ODBC driver modules written for them.

The *application* provides an interface through which users can connect to a data source, make requests for data, and update data. The *driver manager* is the communication link between the application and the *drivers*. ODBC applications only communicate with the driver manager and not directly with drivers. The ODBC driver converts the call to a format that the *data source* can use. Once the data source processes the call, it returns the results to the ODBC driver and the ODBC driver forwards the results to the driver manager.

**O**

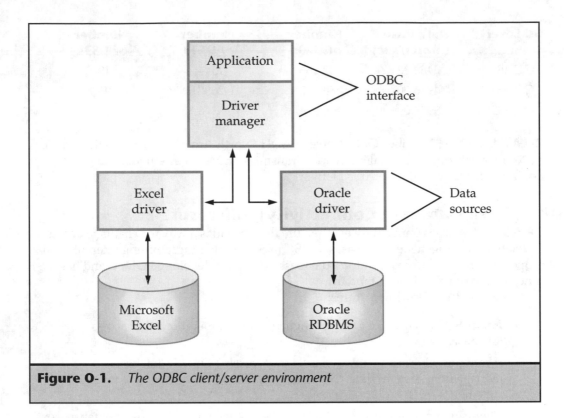

**Figure O-1.**    *The ODBC client/server environment*

In the multitiered client/server model of the Web and intranets, the middle-tier server connects with back-end databases and the client has less functionality. This means that the middle-tier server is responsible for running the different ODBC drivers that connect with back-end databases. The client only needs to run simple Web services to connect with the Web server. See "Web Middleware and Database Connectivity" for more information about enhancements that support the Web.

Microsoft has also developed OLE DB, a set of data access interfaces that allow many different types of data stores (not just SQL data stores) to work seamlessly together. Refer to "OLE DB" for more information.

**RELATED ENTRIES**    Client/Server Computing; Component Software Technology; Database Connectivity; Distributed Database; Distributed Object Computing; Interoperability; Middleware and Messaging; OLE DB; SQL (Structured Query Language); Transaction Processing; *and* Web Middleware and Database Connectivity

**INFORMATION ON THE INTERNET**
Microsoft Corp. (search for "ODBC")        http://www.microsoft.com
Roth Consulting's Win32::ODBC page        http://www.roth.net/odbc

| Roth Consulting's ODBC FAQ | http://www.roth.net/odbc/odbcfaq.htm |
| Dharma Systems, Inc. | http://www.dharmas.com |
| OpenLink Software, Inc. | http://www.openlink.co.uk |
| Simba Technologies, Inc. | http://www.simbatech.com |
| Visigenic Software | http://odbc.visigenic.com |

## ODI (Open Data link Interface)

NetWare uses a protocol-independent structure known as ODI to provide simultaneous support for different protocols on the network and the ability to install and support multiple NICs (network interface cards) in the same computer. The ODI interface resides in the data link layer (relative to the OSI protocol stack). ODI standardizes the development of network interface card drivers so that vendors don't need to write separate drivers to work with each of the different network protocols.

ODI may be implemented on servers or workstations. It allows computers to connect to the network with different communication protocols such as TCP/IP, IPX, AppleTalk, or others. ODI consists of the components discussed below.

**MLI (MULTIPLE LINK INTERFACE)**    MLI is an interface to which device drivers for the network interface card are attached. The device drivers are written by vendors of network interface cards to match the Novell specification of the Link Support Layer. Drivers are referred to as MLIDs (multiple link interface drivers).

**LSL (LINK SUPPORT LAYER)**    The LSL provides a link for drivers at the bottom and protocols at the top. It acts as a switching board, directing network traffic from MLIDs to the proper protocol, and vice versa.

**MPI (MULTIPLE PROTOCOL INTERFACE)**    MPI provides an interface for the connection of protocol stacks, such as IPX, TCP/IP, and AppleTalk. Other protocol stacks such as OSI and SNA will be available in the future.

When a packet arrives at a network interface card, it is processed by the card's MLID and passed to the LSL. The LSL determines which protocol stack the packet should go to and hands it to the protocol. The packet passes up through the protocol stack in the normal way, where it is handled by higher-level protocols.

**RELATED ENTRIES**    NDIS (Network Driver Interface Specification); NIC (Network Interface Card); *and* Novell NetWare

## OLAP (Online Analytical Processing)

OLAP defines a class of software that analyzes data (usually historical data) to find patterns and trends. A data analyst uses OLAP software to view data in a multidimensional format, rather than the two-dimensional row and column format. In the multidimensional format, the intersection of relevant data becomes much more apparent so that data is easier to group and summarize. The analyst then creates reports that are used for critical business decisions. OLAP is sometimes referred to as *data mining*.

Data comes from data warehouses and OLTP (online transaction processing) database systems. A data warehouse may contain legacy data, while an OLTP system is the actual day-to-day business system that collects and processes business data. In contrast, OLAP systems are used to read the data warehouse information and make sense of it. The data analyst may spend long periods sifting through data, or may work with summaries of that data that are more likely to reveals trends and hidden information.

**RELATED ENTRIES**    Data Warehousing; DBMS (Database Management System); *and* Transaction Processing

**INFORMATION ON THE INTERNET**

| | |
|---|---|
| OLAP Council (white papers and links) | http://www.olapcouncil.org |
| OLAP links | http://www.access.digex.net/~grimes/olap |
| Kenan Systems' FAQs about Multidimensional Database Technology | http://www.kenan.com/acumate/faq_mddb.htm |
| Pilot Software's An Introduction to OLAP | http://www.pilotsw.com/r_and_t/whtpaper/olap/olap.htm |
| The Data Warehousing Institute | http://www.dw-institute.com |
| The International Data Warehousing Association | http://www.idwa.org |

# OLE (Object Linking and Embedding)

OLE is a Microsoft Windows feature that provides a way to integrate objects from diverse applications. An *object* is a block of information from a spreadsheet, a graphic from a drawing program, or an audio clip from a sound program.

One of the main features of OLE is that it allows any OLE-compatible application to display information created in other applications. A document that displays OLE information is called a *compound document* and has the characteristics of a container that holds objects. A Web page displayed in a Web browser has these same characteristics. It may contain graphic images that are inserted on the page based on links in the HTML source code.

Objects may be *linked* or *embedded* in compound documents:

■ **Linked object**  A linked object is not part of a compound document. It is stored separately. The compound document contains a link that describes where the object file is located, and the object is displayed inside the compound document when the document is opened. This keeps the compound document size small, but if the compound document is transferred to someone else, all the linked objects must be transferred with it. If a persistent network connection remains between the links and the new compound document's location, then the links in the document may remain valid.

- **Embedded object**　Unlike linked objects, an embedded object is stored directly in the compound document. The object is carried with the document when it is transferred. The file size of the compound document increases relative to the size of the object that is embedded in it.

One of the advantages of embedding objects is that all the elements are stored in one file. If the compound document is transferred to another location, all the embedded information travels with it. In contrast, linked objects pose complications when moving a compound document. You may need to update the links in the document or move the linked objects with the document.

A linked or embedded object maintains an association with the application that created it and can be edited *in place*. In other words, it is not necessary to start the application used to create the object, make changes, and then repaste the object into the compound document. In-place editing is a feature of Microsoft Windows applications that loads the functionality of an application used to create an object into the current application.

The application where an object is created is called its *server* application. It is the server application's functions that are "brought in" when an embedded object is selected for editing. The menus, toolbars, palettes, and other controls necessary to interact with the object temporarily replace the existing menus and controls of the active window. In the case of multimedia objects, editing is a bit of a misnomer. The user interacts with such objects by *playing* them, rather than editing, although editing may be possible as well.

ActiveX, Microsoft's latest incarnation of OLE, is widely used on the Web (see "ActiveX"). As mentioned previously, Web browsers provide much of the same functionality on the Internet that OLE provides for applications that run in Windows. The Web browser is a container that displays HTML documents, which can in turn contain links to objects such as graphic images, ActiveX components, and Java applets.

Another technology similar to OLE is OpenDoc, which was developed by Apple, IBM, Novell, and other vendors. However, OpenDoc developers have moved to JavaBeans, an object container technology specifically designed for Java and the Web. See "Java" for more information. Still another object technology is CORBA (Common Object Request Broker Architecture). It is described under a separate heading in this book.

**RELATED ENTRIES**　ActiveX; COM (Component Object Model); Component Software Technology; Compound Documents; CORBA (Common Object Request Broker Architecture); DCOM (Distributed Component Object Model); Information Publishing; Java; NetDDE (Network Dynamic Data Exchange); Object Technologies; *and* Windows

**INFORMATION ON THE INTERNET**

Microsoft Corp. (search for "OLE")    http://www.microsoft.com

# OLE DB

OLE DB is a set of Microsoft data access interfaces that provides universal data integration over an enterprise's network regardless of the data type. These interfaces allow data sources to share their data through common interfaces without having to implement database functionality that is not native to the data store. OLE DB is a freely published specification designed with industrywide participation.

While Microsoft's ODBC (Open Database Connectivity) will continue to provide a unified way to access relational data. Microsoft expects OLE DB to lead to new database products that are assembled with component technology (i.e., ActiveX). OLE DB provides data access to and manipulation of both SQL (Structured Query Language) and non-SQL data sources. This provides consistency and interoperability in an enterprise's network, from the mainframe to the desktop. It also works over the Internet.

OLE DB defines interfaces for accessing and manipulating all types of data. These interfaces will be used not just by data-consuming applications but also by database providers. By splitting databases apart, the resulting components can be used in an efficient manner. For example, components called *service providers* can be invoked to expose more sophisticated data manipulation and navigation interfaces on behalf of simple data providers.

**RELATED ENTRIES**    Client/Server Computing; Component Software Technology; Database Connectivity; Distributed Database; Distributed Object Computing; Interoperability; Middleware and Messaging; ODBC (Open Database Connectivity), Microsoft; SQL (Structured Query Language); Transaction Processing; *and* Web Middleware and Database Connectivity

**INFORMATION ON THE INTERNET**

ISG white paper on OLE DB           http://www.isg-us.com/nav-whp.htm

Microsoft's OLE DB site             http://www.microsoft.com/oledb

Dave Langworthy's OLE DB page       http://www.objs.com/survey/
                                    Microsoft-OLE-DB.htm

# OLTP (Online Transaction Processing)

*See* Transaction Processing.

# OMA (Object Management Architecture)

OMA is an architecture developed by the OMG (Object Management Group) that provides an industry standard for developing object-oriented applications to run on distributed networks. The goal of the OMG is to provide a common architectural framework for object-oriented applications based on widely available interface specifications.

The OMA reference model identifies and characterizes components, interfaces, and protocols that compose the OMA. It consists of components that are grouped into application-oriented interfaces, industry-specific vertical applications, object services, and ORBs (object request brokers). The ORB defined by the OMG is part of CORBA (Common Object Request Broker Architecture).

**RELATED ENTRIES**    Component Software Technology; CORBA (Common Object Request Broker Architecture); Distributed Object Computing; IIOP (Internet Inter-ORB Protocol); Object Technologies; OMG (Object Management Group); ORB (Object Request Broker); *and* UNO (Universal Networked Object)

**INFORMATION ON THE INTERNET**

| | |
|---|---|
| OMG (Object Management Group) | http://www.omg.org |
| Thomas J. Brando's Interoperability and the CORBA Specification paper | http://www.mitre.org/research/domis/reports/UNO.html |

# OMG (Object Management Group)

OMG is an organization that represents over 700 software vendors, software developers, and end users. OMG describes its mission as developing "The Architecture for a Connected World." It was established in 1989 to promote object technologies on distributed computing systems. To this end, it has developed a common architectural framework for object-oriented applications based on an open and widely available interface specification called OMA (Object Management Architecture).

**RELATED ENTRIES**    CORBA (Common Object Request Broker Architecture); OMA (Object Management Architecture); *and* UNO (Universal Networked Object)

**INFORMATION ON THE INTERNET**

| | |
|---|---|
| OMG (Object Management Group) | http://www.omg.org |

# ONC (Open Network Computing)

ONC is a family of distributed services for Sun Microsystems' Solaris computing environment. ONC can be used to build an environment for heterogeneous distributed computing. ONC provides the building blocks for programmers to develop and implement distributed applications and the tools for administrators to manage client/server networks.

**RELATED ENTRIES**    Distributed Computer Networks; Distributed File Systems; Enterprise Networks; RPC (Remote Procedure Call); Security; Sun Microsystems; *and* Sun Microsystems Solaris NEO

**O**

**INFORMATION ON THE INTERNET**

Sun Microsystems, Inc.                          http://www.sun.com/solaris

# One-Time Password Authentication

A one-time password system is designed to reduce or eliminate security problems associated with logging on to remote systems. In the simplest type of logon, users enter a username and password and send them to the system they are trying to log on to. Someone monitoring the line could capture this information and use it to repeatedly log on in the future. The idea behind one-time passwords is to generate passwords on the fly that cannot be used for future logons.

One method is for the user to carry a *token*, a small device like a credit card that displays unique values that are time-synchronized with a security server at the site the user is trying to log on to. The value in the display changes every minute, so if it is captured, it cannot be used by someone else to log in. Another one-time password technique is the challenge/response protocol, which is discussed under a separate heading in this book.

**RELATED ENTRIES**    Authentication and Authorization; Challenge/Response Protocol; Security; *and* Token-Based Authentication

**INFORMATION ON THE INTERNET**

IETF One Time Password Authentication    http://www.ietf.org/html.charters/
(otp) Charter page                       otp-charter.html

A One-Time Password System (RFC 1938)    http://www.internic.net/rfc/rfc1938.txt

# One-Way Function

*See* Hash Function.

# OpenDoc

OpenDoc is a compound document standard that that competes with Microsoft's OLE (Object Linking and Embedding). It was developed by Apple, Borland, IBM, and other companies. Apple was the main supporter of the standard. In 1997, Component Integration Labs, a developer of OpenDoc standards announced that it was closing its site and that it accepted the strength of the component ideas within JavaBeans. At the same time, a number of other companies such as IBM decided to use JavaBeans instead of OpenDoc as well.

Those interested in OpenDoc can visit Apple's OpenDoc site listed later. For information about JavaBeans, refer to "Java."

**RELATED ENTRIES**    Component Software Technology; Compound Documents; CORBA (Common Object Request Broker Architecture); Java; Object Technologies; *and* OLE (Object Linking and Embedding)

**INFORMATION ON THE INTERNET**

Apple's OpenDoc site        http://www.opendoc.apple.com

OpenDoc eZine        http://www.componentworld.com/odz

Yahoo!'s OpenDoc links page        http://www.yahoo.com/Computers_and_Internet/ Software/Programming_Tools/Development/ OpenDoc

# The Open Group

The Open Group is an international consortium of vendors, government agencies, and educational institutions that develops standards for open systems. It was formed in 1996 as the holding company for OSF (Open Software Foundation) and X/Open Company, Ltd. Under The Open Group umbrella, the two organizations work together to deliver technology innovations and widespread adoption of open systems specifications.

**RELATED ENTRIES**     CDE (Common Desktop Environment); DCE (Distributed Computing Environment), The Open Group; Interoperability; Motif; *and* X Window

**INFORMATION ON THE INTERNET**

The Open Group        http://www.opengroup.org

# OpenVMS

OpenVMS is a DEC multiuser operating system that supports Digital's VAX and Alpha series computers. It is an open software environment that supports open standards such as OSF/Motif, POSIX, XPG3, and the OSF DCE (Distributed Computing Environment). It also includes networking support, distributed computing support, and multiprocessing.

**RELATED ENTRIES**     Alpha Microprocessors, DEC; DEC (Digital Equipment Corporation)

**INFORMATION ON THE INTERNET**

Digital Equipment Corporation        http://www.openvms.digital.com

# Optical Libraries

Optical disk library systems are designed to bring data normally stored on microfiche or paper to an online device where it is quickly accessible by network users. An optical disk library can also supplement magnetic tape backup systems or serve as an intermediate storage device for data that is "migrating" to magnetic tape in an *HMS (hierarchical management system)*.

In an HMS system, little-used files or files that have been marked for migration are moved from magnetic disk to optical disk, where they remain available to users. In this scheme, the optical disk is called *near-line storage*, as shown in Figure O-2.

**O**

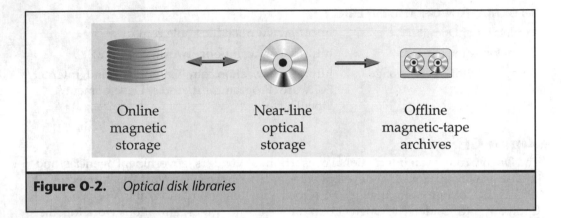

**Figure O-2.** *Optical disk libraries*

Eventually, they are moved to magnetic tape for archiving purposes. While magnetic tape offers a convenient, removable, and economical storage media, its sequential access method makes it unsuitable for online data retrieval.

Hierarchical systems will move files on optical disk to magnetic disk when requested by a user. Users are often unaware that the files are from an optical disk, except for a slight delay in accessing the files while they are moved from near-line to online storage. A hierarchical management system keeps a copy of the directory for near-line files available online to users.

**RELATED ENTRY**   Storage Management Systems

# Oracle

Oracle was founded in 1977 with the goal of developing powerful, low-cost, client/server database systems that could compete with expensive proprietary mainframe systems. It built one of the first commercial relational database systems and sold some of the first products employing SQL (Structured Query Language). It also took advantage of software portability to ensure that its products run on almost all hardware platforms. Recently, it has developed parallel software to power very large database applications such as data warehousing and information on demand. In 1996, it introduced Oracle Universal Server, a powerful software platform with the ability to integrate and consolidate all types of data for thousands of users over any network, including the World Wide Web.

**RELATED ENTRIES**   Component Software Technology; DBMS (Database Management System); Distributed Object Computing; *and* Oracle NCA (Network Computing Architecture)

**INFORMATION ON THE INTERNET**

Oracle Corporation                                    http://www.oracle.com

## Oracle NCA (Network Computing Architecture)

NCA is a set of technologies that allows all clients including PCs and network computers to access information universally on Web servers, database servers, and other systems. Its primary goal is to "transcend the Internet/object standards battle" that rages between Microsoft ActiveX/DCOM (Distributed Component Object Model) and the CORBA (Common Object Request Broker Architecture) standard, according to Oracle. NCA implements open Internet standards and special components called *cartridges* that provide a bridge between proprietary applications.

NCA is a cross-platform, object-oriented, distributed computing environment that allows any client device, whether it is a personal computer, an NC (Network Computer), or another device, to access any database or application server over any intranet or the Internet. Oracle created the architecture to ensure that its database and Web products will be viable solutions on intranets and the Web. NCA serves as a software bridge that helps component software and technologies such as Microsoft ActiveX, Java, CORBA, and IIOP (Internet Inter-ORB Protocol) work together.

Oracle has defined data cartridges as a way to expand on NCA and bridge different technologies. Data cartridges allow developers to extend Oracle database servers with user-defined data types like text, image, spatial geometry, and time series for a new generation of Web-based applications. Cartridges are basically containers for objects and component software that provide access to Oracle databases. An Inter-Cartridge Exchange service provides communication between clients and servers.

**RELATED ENTRIES** Client/Server Computing; Component Software Technology; CORBA (Common Object Request Broker Architecture); Data Warehousing; DBMS (Database Management System); Distributed Object Computing; IIOP (Internet Inter-ORB Protocol); Multitiered Architectures; Oracle; SQL (Structured Query Language); Transaction Processing; Web Middleware and Database Connectivity; *and* Web Technologies and Concepts

**INFORMATION ON THE INTERNET**

Oracle's NCA site                         http://www.oracle.com/nca

## Orange Book

The National Security Agency has outlined the requirements for secure products in a document titled "Trusted Computer System Evaluation Criteria" (TCSEC). TCSEC is more commonly called the "Orange Book." This standard defines access control methods for computer systems that computer vendors can follow to comply with Department of Defense security standards. Secure networking is defined in the "Red Book" or in "Trusted Network Interpretation." You can find TCSEC information at http://www.radium.ncsc.mil/tpep/library/rainbow/5200.28-STD.html.

**RELATED ENTRIES** C2 Security Rating; Red Book; Security; TCSEC (Trusted Computer System Evaluation Criteria); *and* TPEP (Trusted Product Evaluation Program)

**O**

# ORB (Object Request Broker)

In an object-oriented, distributed computing environment, an ORB (object request broker) can provide the key communication facility for communication among the applications, services, and facilities of the network. You can think of the ORB as a sort of software bus, or backbone, that provides a common interface through which many different kinds of objects can communicate in a peer-to-peer scheme.

An object makes a request and sends it to the ORB. The ORB then locates the requested object or an object that can provide servers and establishes communication between the client and server. The receiving object then responds to the request and returns a response to the ORB, which formats and forwards the response to the requester.

In this model, objects simply specify a task to perform. The location of the object that can satisfy the request is not important. The end user sees applications as being seamless, even though services and data may be coming from many places on the network.

The ORB process is similar to a remote procedure call with the added benefit that the ORB itself is capable of locating other objects that can service requests. Actually, an ORB is an alternative to RPCs (remote procedure calls) and message-oriented middleware.

CORBA (Common Object Request Broker Architecture) is the basic messaging technology specification defined by the OMG (Object Management Group) in its OMA (Object Management Architecture). CORBA has been implemented by a number of companies and is becoming an important standard for implementing distributed applications on the Internet. Netscape has been particularly supportive of CORBA and has incorporated it in its Web browser and server software.

A protocol called IIOP (Internet Inter-ORB Protocol) provides Internet connectivity for CORBA. In fact, IIOP may upstage HTTP (Hypertext Transfer Protocol) as the client/server protocol on the Web. It provides services that are much better at handling mission-critical business applications over the Internet. Netscape is including IIOP in its browsers. In the future, you will type iiop://www.*website*.com instead of http://www.*website*.com to access Web sites that offer business and electronic commerce services. Refer to "IIOP (Internet Inter-ORB Protocol)" for more information on this protocol.

A contrasting technology is messaging, as described under "MOM (Message-Oriented Middleware)." However, most messaging systems are proprietary, while most ORBs follow the CORBA standard.

The other major technologies that are similar to ORBs in functionality are Microsoft's DCOM (Distributed Component Object Model) and Microsoft Transaction Server. They are designed to support object transactions over in-house or Internet networks and provide connectivity to legacy systems.

**RELATED ENTRIES**   Component Software Technology; CORBA (Common Object Request Broker Architecture); DCOM (Distributed Component Object Model);

Distributed Object Computing; IIOP (Internet Inter-ORB Protocol); Middleware and Messaging; Object Technologies; OMA (Object Management Architecture); *and* UNO (Universal Networked Object)

### INFORMATION ON THE INTERNET

| | |
|---|---|
| Alan Pope's Excellent On-Line CORBA tutorial | http://www.qds.com/people/apope |
| OMG (Object Management Group) | http://www.omg.org |
| CORBA documentation | http://www.omg.org/corba/corbiiop.htm |
| CORBA information and references | http://www.acl.lanl.gov/CORBA |
| Thomas J. Brando's Interoperability and the CORBA Specification paper | http://www.mitre.org/research/domis/reports/UNO.html |

## Organizations

*See* Standards Groups, Associations, and Organizations.

## OS/2 Warp

OS/2 Warp is IBM's 32-bit desktop operating system that runs on Intel processors. A server version is called OS/2 Warp Server and is discussed in the next section. OS/2 has a long history. It was originally developed by both IBM and Microsoft, but IBM took over development of OS/2 when Microsoft developed the Windows environment. Still, OS/2 runs 16- and 32-bit DOS and Windows applications.

The current version of OS/2 Warp includes voice recognition software, Internet access, and peer-to-peer network support. Networking services include support for the TCP/IP protocols and Internet protocols such as Telnet, Gopher, and FTP.

The peer-to-peer network services in OS/2 Warp let users easily share resources such as files, printers, and modems with other OS/2 Warp users or with other network servers such as OS/2 LAN Server, Microsoft Windows for Workgroups, Microsoft Windows NT, Microsoft Windows 95, Microsoft LAN Manager 2.x, and Artisoft LANtastic 6.0.

OS/2 Warp 4 also supports Novell Directory Services, which allows OS/2 users to access resources globally across an organization without having to know exactly which NetWare server contains the information. The operating system also includes IBM Personal Communications/3270, a communication package that lets users connect with IBM SNA (Systems Network Architecture) systems over TCP/IP networks.

A remote access dial-up service feature lets telecommuters and mobile workers connect to network resources at the home office network. Dial-up users running NetBIOS, TCP/IP, or IPX protocols can connect with an office network running OS/2 Warp Server or to the Internet. A feature called Mobile File Synch detects conflicts between the client and server files and can automatically duplicate to the server any tasks performed at the client and vice versa, if the user chooses.

**O**

**RELATED ENTRIES**    IBM (International Business Machines); Network Operating Systems; *and* OS/2 Warp Server

### INFORMATION ON THE INTERNET

| | |
|---|---|
| IBM's OS/2 Warp site | http://www.software.ibm.com/os/warp |
| The OS/2 WWW Homepage at MIT | http://www.mit.edu:8001/activities/os2/os2world.html |
| OS/2 Computing Magazine | http://www.os2computing.com/magazine |
| OS/2 e-Zine | http://www.os2ezine.com |
| OS/2 FAQ | http://www.cis.ohio-state.edu/hypertext/faq/usenet/os2-faq/new-user/part1/faq.html |
| The Warped WebRing (extensive links) | http://www.geocities.com/SiliconValley/Heights/2772/warpring.html |
| Yahoo!'s OS/2 links page | http://www.yahoo.com/Computers_and_Internet/Operating_Systems/OS_2 |

## OS/2 Warp Server

IBM's server for network environments is OS/2 Warp Server. It provides network services, system management services, backup and recovery services, remote access services, and more. As a server, OS/2 Warp Server supports standard file-sharing and network print services. OS/2 Warp Server runs concurrently with Novell NetWare.

OS/2 Warp Server can also be set up as an application server that supports Microsoft Windows 95 and Windows NT applications. OS/2 Warp Server supports clients running a variety of desktop operating systems, including OS/2 Warp, DOS, Windows 3.x, Windows 95, Windows NT, AIX (Advanced Interactive Executive), and Macintosh. The operating system also supports important protocols such as TCP/IP, IPX, and NetBIOS.

OS/2 Warp Server is based on IBM's LAN Server 4.0 and includes system management tools, backup and recovery tools, remote connectivity facilities, advanced printer functionality, support for up to 1,000 users on a single server (advanced version), and secure Internet access.

IBM also provides the IBM DSS (Directory and Security Server) for OS/2 WARP, which is OS/2 Warp's implementation of The Open Group's DCE (Distributed Computing Environment), a set of distributed services for building distributed applications across multiple platforms.

IBM OS/2 Warp Server also supports SMP (symmetrical multiprocessing) for two-way and four-way SMP systems. SMP support is also available for systems equipped with up to 64 processors.

**RELATED ENTRIES**    IBM (International Business Machines); Network Operating Systems; *and* OS/2 Warp

**INFORMATION ON THE INTERNET**

IBM's OS/2 Warp Server site          http://www.software.ibm.com/os/warp-server

 *NOTE:  Additional Internet links are listed under OS/2 Warp.*

## OSF (Open Software Foundation)

*See* The Open Group.

## OSI (Open Systems Interconnection) Model

The ISO (International Organization for Standardization) is a worldwide federation that promotes international standards. In the early 1980s, it began work on a set of protocols that would promote open networking environments that would let multivendor computer systems communicate with one another using internationally accepted communication protocols. It eventually developed the OSI reference model.

The OSI model defines a layered architecture as pictured in Figure O-3. The protocols defined in each layer are responsible for the following:

■ Communicating with the same peer protocol layer running in the opposite computer.

■ Providing services to the layer above it (except for the top-level application layer).

Peer-layer communication provides a way for each layer to exchange messages or other data. For example, the transport protocol may send a "pause transmission" message to its peer protocol in the sending computer. Obviously, each layer does not have a physical wire running between it and its peer layer in the opposite system. To send a message, a protocol must put the message in a packet that passes down to the next lower layer. Thus, lower layers provide a service to higher layers by taking their messages and passing them down the protocol stack to the lowest layer, where the messages are transferred across the physical link. This process is described in more detail under "Protocol Concepts."

Note that OSI is a reference model, meaning that it defines a general description of services that should be provided at each layer, but it does not define any standard protocols. However, although the ISO has defined a set of protocols that follow the model, they are not part of the OSI definition. In addition, because OSI is a reference model, it is often used when describing other protocols such as TCP/IP. For example, IP (Internet Protocol) is said to be a network layer protocol because it performs the functions defined in the network layer of the OSI model.

Also note that while the OSI model is often used for reference, the protocols that the ISO created have not become popular for internetworking, primarily because of the popularity of the TCP/IP protocol suite. Still, the OSI model is described here because it defines how communication protocols work in general.

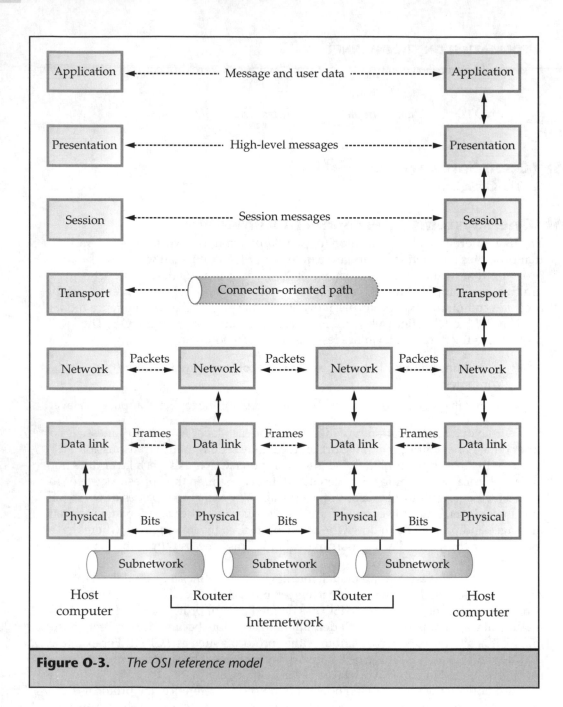

**Figure O-3.** *The OSI reference model*

Each layer of the OSI model is described here for what it defines. Remember that the ISO has defined its own protocols, but these are not widely used in the industry. The more popular TCP/IP and IPX protocols are mentioned with respect to the layers in which they reside. Note that the bottom physical layer is discussed first for clarity.

**THE PHYSICAL LAYER**   The physical layer defines the physical characteristics of the interface, such as mechanical components and connectors, electrical aspects such as voltage levels representing binary values, and functional aspects such as setting up, maintaining, and taking down the physical link. Well-known physical layer interfaces for data communication include EIA RS-232 and RS-449, the successor to RS-232. RS-449 allows longer cable distances. Well-known LAN (local area network) systems are Ethernet, token ring, and FDDI (Fiber Distributed Data Interface).

**THE DATA LINK LAYER**   The data link layer defines the rules for sending and receiving information across a physical connection between two systems. Its main purpose is to divide the data given it by the upper network layer into frames and send the frames of data across the physical link. Data is framed so it can be transmitted one frame at a time. The data link layer in the receiving system can then acknowledge receipt of a frame before the sender sends another frame. Note that the data link is a point-to-point link between two entities. The next layer up, the network layer, handles multiple point-to-point links in the case where frames are transmitted across multiple links to reach their destination. In broadcast networks such as Ethernet, a MAC (medium access control) sublayer was added to allow multiple devices to share and contend for the use of the same medium. See "Data Link Protocols."

**THE NETWORK LAYER**   While the data link layer is used to control communication between two devices that are directly connected together, the network layer provides internetwork services. These services will ensure that a packet of information reaches its destination when traveling across multiple point-to-point links, i.e., a set of interconnected networks joined by routers. The network layer basically manages multiple data link connections. On a shared LAN, packets addressed to devices on the same LAN are sent using data link protocols, but if a packet is addressed to a device on another LAN, network protocols are used. In the TCP/IP protocol suite, IP is the network layer internetworking protocol. In the IPX/SPX suite, IPX is the network layer protocol. See "Internetworking," "IP (Internet Protocol)," and "Network Layer Protocols."

**THE TRANSPORT LAYER**   The transport layer provides a high level of control for moving information between the end systems in a communication session. The end systems may be on the same network or on different subnetworks of an internetwork. Transport layer protocols set up a connection between source and destination and send data in a stream of packets, meaning that each packet is numbered sequentially and constitutes a flow that can be monitored to ensure proper delivery and identity in the flow. This flow is often called a *virtual circuit,* and the circuit may be preestablished through specific router paths in an internetwork. The protocol also regulates the flow

**O**

of packets to accommodate slow receivers and ensures that the transmission is not completely halted if a disruption in the link occurs. (In other words, it will keep trying to send until a time-out occurs.) TCP and SPX are transport layer protocols. See "TCP (Transmission Control Protocol)" and "Transport Protocols and Services" for more information.

**THE SESSION LAYER**   The session layer coordinates the exchange of information between systems by using conversational techniques, or dialogs. Dialogs can indicate where to restart the transmission of data if a connection is temporarily lost, or where to end one data set and start a new one. This layer is a remnant of mainframe/terminal communications.

**THE PRESENTATION LAYER**   Protocols at this layer are for presenting data. Information is formatted for display or printing in this layer. Codes within the data, such as tabs or special graphics sequences, are interpreted. Data encryption and the translation of other character sets are also handled in this layer. Like the session layer, this layer is a remnant of mainframe/terminal communications.

**THE APPLICATION LAYER**   Applications access the underlying network services using defined procedures in this layer. The application layer is used to define a range of applications that handle file transfers, terminal sessions, and message exchange (for example, electronic mail).

**RELATED ENTRIES**   Connection-Oriented and Connectionless Services; Data Communication Concepts; Data Link Protocols; Internet Organizations and Committees; Protocol Concepts; *and* Standards Groups, Associations, and Organizations

**INFORMATION ON THE INTERNET**

| | |
|---|---|
| ISO (International Organization for Standardization) | http://www.iso.ch |
| ISO's list of OSI standards | http://www.iso.ch/cate/3510001.html |
| Cisco Systems' OSI paper | http://www.cisco.com/univercd/data/doc/cintrnet/ito/55165.htm |

# OSPF (Open Shortest Path First) Protocol

OSPF is a link-state routing algorithm that was derived from work done with IS-IS (Intermediate System-to-Intermediate System), and OSI intradomain routing protocols. Link-state routing, as compared to distance-vector routing, requires more processing power but provides more control over the routing process and responds faster to changes. The Dijkstra algorithm is used to calculate routes. See "Routing Protocols and Algorithms" for more information.

# PACE (Priority Access Control Enabled)

PACE is a technology developed by 3Com Corporation that is designed to deliver on-time multimedia over switched Ethernet LANs that have insufficient bandwidth, nondeterministic behavior, and the inability to prioritize traffic. PACE is designed to deliver real-time traffic on existing switched Ethernet LANs. It requires a switched network made up of PACE-enabled switches, so a PACE network is largely a 3Com solution.

Real-time applications like videoconferencing require on-time delivery of data. At the same time, some traffic requires a higher priority than other traffic, such as the delivery of stock transaction information. Switched Ethernet is more capable of providing these requirements than traditional shared Ethernet. With contention reduced, time-sensitive traffic has a better chance of getting through. Still, when two switch ports are bridged together, one of the stations at either end of the bridged segment may monopolize the medium. Normally, there is no mechanism to give either station equal access to it. PACE adds this feature.

PACE's Interactive Access technology, which is implemented in hardware on Ethernet and Fast Ethernet switches, enables the switch port and end stations to take turns transmitting on the wire. Both obtain equal access to the wire. PACE produces an interleaved transmission pattern between a switch and an end station, reducing delays caused by traffic coming in the opposite direction and improving multimedia quality.

**RELATED ENTRIES**    ATM (Asynchronous Transfer Mode); Ethernet; Fast Ethernet; Gigabit Ethernet; Prioritization of Network Traffic; QoS (Quality of Service); *and* Switched Networks

**INFORMATION ON THE INTERNET**

3Com's PACE technology paper              http://www.3com.com/nsc/501316.html

# Packet

The term "packet" generally refers to a package of data exchanged between devices over a data communication link. Information in the packet may include messages and commands, such as a request for service, connection management controls, or data. Large transmissions are divided into packets instead of being transmitted as one long string. If a packet is corrupted during transmission, only that packet needs to be resent, not the entire transmission. Also, on shared networks, stations can take turns sending packets so that no computer needs to wait an excessive amount of time while another computer transmits a large amount of information.

As mentioned, *packet* loosely defines a block of data, but at the data link layer, streams of bits are grouped into *frames* and transmitted across the physical medium. In the network layer where IP operates and routing takes place, the unit of data is more appropriately called a *datagram*. Further, in the transport layer where TCP operates, the unit of data is the *segment*. Thus, people often just refer to transmitted blocks of data as packets. The significance of frames, datagrams, and segments is discussed further under the related topics listed below.

**RELATED ENTRIES**    Data Communication Concepts; Datagrams and Datagram Services; Data Link Protocols; Encapsulation; Fragmentation of Frames and Packets; Framing in Data Transmissions; IP (Internet Protocol); Network Concepts; Novell NetWare Protocols; Packet and Cell Switching; Protocol Concepts; Routing Protocols and Algorithms; TCP (Transmission Control Protocol); *and* Transport Protocols and Services

# Packet and Cell Switching

Packet switching is a technique for transmitting packets of information through multiple linked networks. A packet is defined just above under "Packet." A cell is similar to a packet, except that it is has a fixed length. ATM uses 53-byte cells. The advantage of switching fixed-length cells as opposed to variable-length packets is speed and deterministic data transmissions. This is described under "ATM (Asynchronous Transfer Mode)" and "Cell Relay." The rest of this section discusses packet switching in general, but cell switching has many of the same features.

A simple packet-switched network is shown in Figure P-1. Consider the redundant topology of this network. LANs are interconnected with routers to form a mesh topology. If the link between R1 and R2 goes down, packets from R1 can still travel through R3 and R4 to reach R2. Note that the router-connected network essentially allows any station to communicate with any other station. Packet-switched networks are often called *any-to-any* networks.

Packets make the trip through the switched network in "hops." If computer A needs to send a packet to computer Z, the packet first travels to R1. R1 uses a store-and-forward procedure, in which it receives the packet and puts it in memory long enough to read the destination address. Looking in a routing table, it determines that the port connected to R2 is the best way to forward the packet to its destination.

Routers run routing protocols to discover neighboring routers and the networks attached to them. These protocols let routers exchange information about the network topology, which may change often as devices and links go down. See "Routers" and "Routing Protocols and Algorithms."

As mentioned, the Internet is a packet-switched network that spans the globe. IP (Internet Protocol) is an internetwork protocol that defines how to put information into packets (called *datagrams*) and transmit those packets through the Internet (or your private intranet). IP provides a near-universal delivery mechanism that works on almost any underlying network. See "Datagrams and Datagram Services" and "IP (Internet Protocol)" for more information.

One interesting aspect of packet-switched networks is the ability to emulate circuits within the network. This gives the appearance of a straight-through wire from one location to another that provides faster delivery and better service. A *virtual circuit* is a permanent or switched path through a public packet-switched network that is set

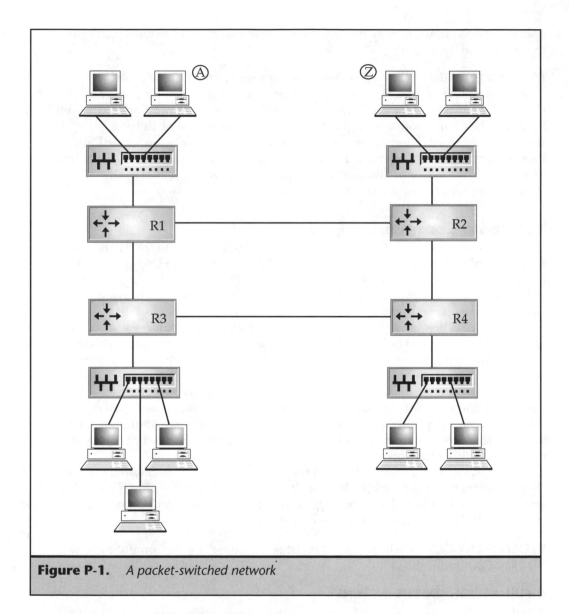

**Figure P-1.** *A packet-switched network*

up by a carrier for a customer to use. Frame relay and ATM networks provide virtual circuit services.

Virtual circuits eliminate the overhead of routing but add administrative overhead such as path setup. For example, setting up a frame relay virtual circuit may require a call to the carrier and a wait of a few minutes to a few days. Customers contract with carriers for virtual circuits that have a specific data rate, called the *CIR (committed information rate)*. The carrier will guarantee that it can supply this rate by not overbooking its network. Customers can go over this rate, but additional charges are applied and the traffic may be delayed. See "Frame Relay" and "Virtual Circuit" for more information.

**RELATED ENTRIES**    ATM (Asynchronous Transfer Mode); Cell Relay; Circuit-Switching Services; Communication Services; Connection-Oriented and Connectionless Services; Data Communication Concepts; Datagrams and Datagram Services; Data Link Protocols; Digital Circuits and Services; Frame Relay; Internetworking; IP (Internet Protocol); Network Concepts; Network Layer Protocols; Packet; Point-to-Point Communications; Routers; Routing Protocols and Algorithms; TCP (Transmission Control Protocol); Transport Protocols and Services; Virtual Circuit; WAN (Wide Area Network); *and* X.25

## Packet-Radio Communications

Packet-radio communications lets mobile users communicate with their corporate networks using computing devices such as portable computers, PDAs (personal digital assistants), pagers, and other wireless communicators. ARDIS and RAM Mobile Data are nationwide radio data communication services that provide packet-radio communications.

Packet-radio breaks a transmission into small digital packets that are sent to a radio tower or satellite and then relayed to a destination. However, transmission rates are low, typically under 19.2 Kbits/sec, and interoperability among systems can be problem.

A more common communication method used by mobile computer users is circuit-switched cellular. A modem is attached to a cellular phone, and data is transmitted on a dedicated circuit for the duration of the call instead of broken into packets. This is no different than any dial-up modem connection except that it takes place over cellular networks.

Packet switching is preferable when transmissions are short because of the way charges are incurred per packet. Cellular circuit-switched networks are preferable for transferring large files or for other lengthy transmissions where a dedicated circuit is more practical and potentially cheaper over time.

**RELATED ENTRIES**    Cellular Communication Systems; Mobile Computing; *and* Wireless Communications

**INFORMATION ON THE INTERNET**

| | |
|---|---|
| ARDIS | http://www.ardis.com |
| RAM Mobile Data | http://www.ram.co.uk |

## PAP (Password Authentication Protocol)

PAP is a security protocol that requires users to enter a password before accessing a secure system. The user's name and password are sent over the wire to a server, where they are compared with a database of user account names and passwords. This technique is vulnerable to wiretapping (eavesdropping) because the password can be captured and used by someone to log onto the system.

CHAP (Challenge Handshake Authentication Protocol) is an alternative protocol that avoids sending passwords over the wire by using a challenge/response technique as described under "Challenge/Response Protocol."

**RELATED ENTRIES**    Authentication and Authorization; Challenge/Response Protocol; Security; *and* Token-Based Authentication

**INFORMATION ON THE INTERNET**

| | |
|---|---|
| CHAP versus PAP paper | http://www.accessindy.com/herbie/linux/nag/node120.html |
| PPP Authentication Protocols (RFC 1334) | http://www.internic.net/rfc/rfc1334.txt |

# Parallel Processing

Parallel processing systems provide a way to expand the processing power of a computer system by adding additional processors. With compatible operating systems and software, processing tasks can be distributed across the processors so that none sit idle. The systems are especially useful for database management systems and data warehousing because they provide a way for a system to handle multiple queries from multiple users and access vast quantities of data while doing so. The systems are also used to process very large and complex tasks such as weather forecasting and simulated nuclear weapons testing. Parallel processing systems can be categorized as follows:

- *SMP (symmetrical multiprocessing) servers* are off-the-shelf servers sold by Dell, Compaq, IBM, and other manufacturers. A typical SMP-capable system contains four or more processors and is pictured on the left in Figure P-2. To applications, all the processors appear as a single processor and all the memory is shared, making it easy for programmers to write software for these systems. However, the systems use a shared bus that can bog down under heavy loads.

- *MPP (massively parallel processor) systems* solve the overloaded bus problem by grouping processors into nodes and interconnecting the nodes with a high-speed switch as pictured on the right in Figure P-2. Each node has its own processors, memory, cache, and interconnecting bus. While MPP systems can be scaled up to hundreds or even thousands of processors, software is difficult to write for the systems because nothing is shared among the nodes. There are multiple memory spaces instead of one contiguous memory space, and programs must be divided into segments that run in each node. In addition, nodes exchange information by sending messages to one another since they can't access a shared memory space.

- A *NUMA (Non-Uniform Memory Access) system* is a multinode system that appears as a single SMP computer to applications by using software and hardware techniques that make the memory in separate nodes appear as a

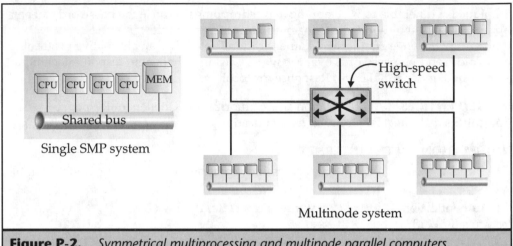

**Figure P-2.** *Symmetrical multiprocessing and multinode parallel computers*

large *virtual* block of memory. Program developers see the system as a single SMP system rather than as a multinode system. Each node stores information in its local cache that has been retrieved from other nodes. When the node needs information from another node, it looks in its local cache and retrieves it from the other node. Sequent's NUMA-Quad systems use this technique. Plug-in nodes (called *Quads* because there are four Intel Pentium Pro processors per node) can be added to scale the system. An interconnect technology called IQ-Link provides the cache coherency that makes memory appear contiguous to programs.

Note that clustered systems are similar to MPP and NUMA systems, except that each node is a separate computer system that is interconnected via a high-speed network. To programs, the systems appears as a single virtual parallel computer. See "Clustering" for more details. HPCs (high-performance computers) and supercomputers are discussed under "Supercomputer."

**RELATED ENTRIES**    Clustering; Distributed Processing; MPP (Massively Parallel Processor) Systems; Supercomputer; *and* Symmetrical Multiprocessing

**INFORMATION ON THE INTERNET**

| | |
|---|---|
| Sequent's NUMA papers | http://www.sequent.com/numaq/technology/papers.html |
| Emergent Corporation's NUMA paper | http://emergent.com/epress/earticle/numa.html |
| DIGITAL High Performance Technical Computing (HPTC) InfoCenter | http://www.digital.com/info/hpc |

| | |
|---|---|
| Jonathan Hardwick's Supercomputing and Parallel Computing Research Groups page | http://www.cs.cmu.edu/~scandal/research-groups.html |
| Jørn Amundsen's HPC links | http://hpc.ntnu.no/links |
| Nan's Parallel Computing Page | http://www.cs.rit.edu/~ncs/parallel.html |
| Yahoo!'s Supercomputing and Parallel Computing links page | http://www.yahoo.com/Computers_and_Internet/Supercomputing_and_Parallel_Computing |
| National HPCC Software Exchange | http://www.nhse.org |

## Partitions and Partition Management

*See* Replication; Volume and Partition Management.

## Passwords

A password is a secret code required to log on or access a secure system. Obviously, a malicious person who obtains a password for an account can access a computer system, with all the rights and privileges of that account. Token authentication schemes that use security cards *and* passwords are recommended for maintaining secure environments. See "Token-Based Authentication."

Always use passwords that are not real words. You can mix up characters to create passwords like Qp&yTxT8e3. That's extremely difficult to guess or even crack, but also easy to forget. A more effective method is to create a phrase and use the first letter of each word as the password. For example, the password Mbiot4oJ is derived from "My birthday is on the 4th of July."

A so-called *Trojan horse* program is a program that some unscrupulous person installs on a computer to capture passwords as they are typed in by unsuspecting users. Such programs are often installed when people leave their computers unattended. They can often be removed by simply resetting the computer.

Hackers also attempt to capture passwords that are transmitted across communication channels. Some programs and operating systems send these passwords unencrypted, which makes them easy for hackers to capture and reuse to log in to a system. Use token-based authentication schemes or challenge/response schemes, both of which avoid sending passwords across the wire.

**RELATED ENTRIES**   Authentication and Authorization; Challenge/Response Protocol; Security; *and* Token-Based Authentication

#### INFORMATION ON THE INTERNET

| | |
|---|---|
| Gateway to Information Security, Inc.'s information about passwords | http://www.securityserver.com/cgi-local/ssis.pl/category/@psword5.htm |

# PBX (Private Branch Exchange)

A PBX is a circuit-switching system that handles voice calls and data links. Traditionally, the PBX has been a telephone switching system, but it can also handle data link connections. As shown in Figure P-3, group of telephones, called extensions, connect into the PBX. The PBX is then connected to the telephone company's central office via a dedicated line, such as a digital T1 line that supports 24 voice or data channels over a single four-wire circuit (as opposed to using 24 separate circuits). Multirate ISDN (Integrated Services Digital Network) carrier connections are also common.

*NOTE: PBXs are considered important to network administrators, and they are now available for network servers and run in environments where voice calls can be carried on the data network.*

Calls coming into the organization are automatically directed to an appropriate extension. The caller may dial this extension directly (called *DID*, or *direct inward dialing*), select it in response to an automated message, or have an attendant connect

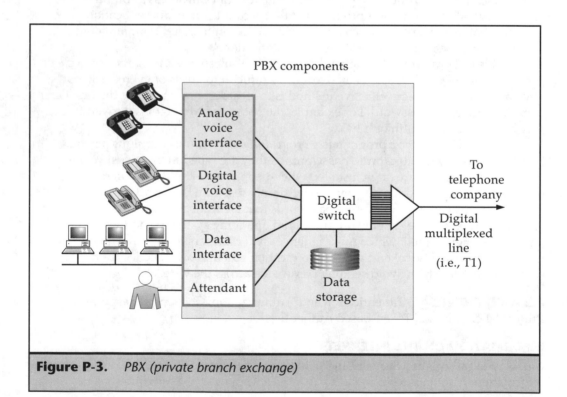

**Figure P-3.** *PBX (private branch exchange)*

the call to an extension. A PBX will also connect any internal extension with any other internal extension (station-to-station calling), or provide DOD (direct outward dialing).

*P*

> **NOTE:** Centrex *is a form of PBX that is located at the telephone company's central office. It is essentially a* virtual PBX.

Modern PBXs use digital switching and controls and support both analog and digital devices. The PBX vendor may support analog voice phones, but more likely will require that their own digital phones be used with the system. Digital phones may be single-line or multiline phones. Most PBXs also provide digital interfaces for data terminals and PCs. The latest generation of PBXs also support LAN connections.

Traditional PBX vendors include companies like Lucent Technologies (AT&T), Northern Telecom, and Siemens. These vendors have manufactured proprietary products with advanced features, such as support for ISDN and the ability to aggregate ISDN lines when more bandwidth is needed for videoconferencing or other requirements. A wireless in-building telephone system is another PBX feature that supports cordless phones for people who need to walk around the building.

A relatively new trend is the single-board PBX, which is installed in a network server to provide a relatively inexpensive PBX solution for small businesses. NetPhone's PBX-T1 has a T1 interface to provide up to 24 voice lines. Optional boards are available to increase the number of lines. The systems are a natural fit for LANs and WANs since they support desktop CTI (computer-telephony integration). Software is available for Windows clients that lets users operate phones from their PC. Users can dial a call, transfer calls, set up conference calls, or manage voice mail from the Windows desktop.

Companies involved in server PBXs include AltiGen, Dash, NetPhone, and NexPath. Their Web addresses are listed under "Information on the Internet" at the end of this section.

Other trends related to telephone systems and networks are CTI and voice over data networks. The latter refers to building a single network that supports voice and data on the same cabling system. The "Related Entries" heading, near the end of this section, lists several sections in this book that discuss how voice can be carried over ATM and IP networks.

A paper called "Connecting Your PBX to the Internet" by Pacific Telephony Design, located at the PhoneZone Web site (http://www.phonezone.com) describes a PBX connection to the Internet: "Several companies have produced software and hardware products which essentially fool a PBX into seeing the Internet as a bank of ordinary phone lines through which it can place and receive phone calls. By placing these devices in front of a PBX, you can place and receive Internet calls the same way you make ordinary phone calls, using the phone which is sitting right on your desk."

To place a call over such a system, you basically "dial" the IP address of the party you want to reach, rather than a telephone number. Low-cost voice cards and Internet telephony software is required in PCs. However, the Internet, a packet-switched network, cannot provide a dedicated end-to-end circuit for a voice call like the telephone system can. A number of techniques, one of which is compression, are used to compensate for this.

**RELATED ENTRIES**    CTI (Computer-Telephony Integration); Iso-Ethernet; Prioritization of Network Traffic; QoS (Quality of Service); TAPI (Telephony API); Telephony; Videoconferencing and Desktop Video; Voice/Data Networks; Voice over ATM; Voice over the Internet; *and* VoIP (Voice over IP)

**INFORMATION ON THE INTERNET**

| | |
|---|---|
| The PhoneZone | http://www.phonezone.com |
| AltiGen Communications, Inc. | http://www.altigen.com |
| Dash, Inc. | http://www.dashops.com |
| Diallogic Corporation | http://www.dialogic.com |
| Lucent Technologies, Inc. | http://www.lucent.com |
| NetPhone, Inc. | http://www.netphone.com |
| NexPath Corporation | http://www.nexpath.com |
| Nortel (Northern Telecom) | http://www.nortel.com |
| Siemens Nixdorf Information Systems, Inc. | http://www.sni-usa.com |
| VocalTec Communications Ltd. (Internet telephony products) | http://www.vocaltec.com |

# PCS (Personal Communications Services)

PCS is a digital wireless communications technology that includes voice, data, and video. Digital technology translates to efficient use of the radio frequency spectrums, making such services as messaging, caller ID, and voice mail possible on the same portable wireless device. PCS competes with traditional analog cellular phone services, but PCS's digital technology provides clearer voice quality, enhanced features, security through encryption, and lower user costs. In addition, PCS devices require less power and so can be smaller and lighter.

In the United States, the FCC has allocated PCS spectrum in the broadband and narrowband ranges. Broadband PCS was auctioned in 10 MHz and 30 MHz blocks. Narrowband PCS was auctioned in 1 MHz blocks. Companies bidding on 1 MHz blocks are involved in wireless messaging or paging, such as SkyTel, with its two-way paging, and PageNet, with its VoiceNow mobile answering machine.

GSM (Global System for Mobile Communications) is the international digital standard used in most PCS systems. Phones based on PCS and GSM will work in all countries where GSM is supported. A goal is to use the same phone number for a user no matter where that person travels in the world.

**RELATED ENTRIES**   Cellular Communication Systems; GSM (Global System for Mobile Communications); *and* Wireless Communications

**INFORMATION ON THE INTERNET**

| | |
|---|---|
| PCIA (Personal Communications Industry Association) | http://www.pcia.com |
| U.S. Office of Telecommunications' PCS site | http://www.ita.doc.gov/industry/tai/telecom/pcs.html |
| RF/Spread Spectrum's PCS links page | http://sss-mag.com/pcs.html |
| Pacific Bell's PCS site | http://www.pacbell.mobile.com |
| Sprint's PCS site | http://www.sprint.com/pcs |
| Cordero Consulting's PCS site | http://www.cordero2.com |
| Insight Research's PCS report | http://www.insight-corp.com/pcs.html |
| Arthur Makosinski's PCS article | http://www.volksware.com/mobilis/september.95/cellpcs1.htm |

# PCT (Private Communication Technology) Protocol

PCT is a protocol that provides secure encrypted communication between two applications (a client and server) over a TCP/IP network such as the Internet, an intranet, or an extranet. PCT was developed by Microsoft in response to security weaknesses in SSL (Secure Sockets Layer), another Web-based client/server security protocol. SSL was restricted to 40-bit key lengths by the U.S. government, so Microsoft separated the authentication and encryption functions in PCT to bypass this restriction. PCT allows applications to use 128-bit key encryption for authentication within the United States, and 40-bit key encryption as allowed by the U.S. government for export use. PCT is included with Microsoft Internet Explorer. A similar client/server security protocol is S-HTTP (Secure Hypertext Transfer Protocol).

**RELATED ENTRIES**   EDI (Electronic Data Interchange); Electronic Commerce; OBI (Open Buying on the Internet); Security; SET (Secure Electronic Transaction); S-HTTP (Secure Hypertext Transfer Protocol); *and* Web Technologies and Concepts

# Peering

ISPs (Internet service providers) establish what are called *peering agreements* with one another to exchange Internet traffic across their respective networks. See "Internet Backbone" for more information.

# PEM (Privacy-Enhanced Mail)

Electronic mail on the Internet is striving to reach several goals that can assure both sender and receiver that messages are confidential, that messages are from an authentic source, that messages have not been altered or corrupted, and that the sender cannot repudiate (disown) the message.

PEM was one of the first standards for securing the text of e-mail messages. PEM was defined by the IETF (Internet Engineering Task Force) in RFCs 1421 through 1424 as a way to encrypt 7-bit text messages. It also defined a hierarchical structure for distributing and verifying digital signatures. PEM includes a specification for a public-key infrastructure, which provides a way for users to exchange keys over large networks like the Internet. However, the specification was deficient and newer standards have been developed, as discussed under "PKI (Public-Key Infrastructure)."

PEM uses RSA (Rivest, Shamir, Adleman) public-key authentication and/or DES (Data Encryption Standard) for encryption and authentication. With PEM, the sender seals the message with a digital signature using his or her private key. The digital signature also provides the nonrepudiation feature. The recipient can verify the signature using the sender's public key. The sender can make the entire message confidential by encrypting it with the recipient's public key, and then only the recipient can read the message by opening it with his or her private key.

PGP (Pretty Good Privacy) was another early privacy protocol, although it is not an IETF standard. Phil Zimmermann designed PGP to use other encryption standards besides RSA. See "PGP (Pretty Good Privacy)" for more information.

When MIME (Multipurpose Internet Mail Extension) was introduced as a way to add binary attachments to e-mail, PEM became less important because of its support for only 7-bit text messages. PEM was then extended with MOSS (MIME Object Security Standard), a protocol with PEM compatibility and support for MIME attachments. However, MOSS is difficult to implement and use.

In 1997, the IETF was looking to standardize e-mail security specifications. RSA's S/MIME was the front runner until September, 1997, when the IETF rejected it due to RSA's licensing and royalty fee requirements. Phil Zimmermann quickly jumped in with a security specification called Open PGP and a promise to put it in the public domain. Open PGP is based on the Diffie-Hellman public-key management patents, which expired in September of 1997.

**RELATED ENTRIES**    Authentication and Authorization; Certificates and Certification Systems; Cryptography; Digital Signatures; Electronic Mail; MIME (Multipurpose Internet Mail Extension); PGP (Pretty Good Privacy); PKI (Public-Key Infrastructure); Public-Key Cryptography; RSA Data Security; Security; S/MIME (Secure Multipurpose Internet Mail Extension); *and* X.509

## INFORMATION ON THE INTERNET

| | |
|---|---|
| Internet Mail Consortium | http://www.imc.org |
| Electronic Messaging Association | http://www.ema.org |
| Peter Gutmann's Security and Encryption-related Resources and Links | http://www.cs.auckland.ac.nz/~pgut001/links.html |

*NOTE:* *To view IETF RFC 1421 through 1424, go to http://www.internic.net/ rfc/rfcxxxx.txt, replacing xxxx with the RFC number you want to view.*

## Perl

Perl stands for Practical Extraction and Report Language. It is a programming language that processes text. In this respect, it is a scripting and report tool. Recently, programmers have been using Perl to build CGI (Common Gateway Interface) scripts for Web servers. More information about Perl is available at the Web sites listed next.

### INFORMATION ON THE INTERNET

| | |
|---|---|
| Perl language site | http://www.perl.com |
| The Perl Institute | http://www.perl.org |
| Perl Resources site (everything you want to know) | http://www.progsource.com/perl.html |
| Clay Irving's Perl Reference page | http://www.panix.com/~clay/perl |
| Yahoo!'s Perl links page | http://www.yahoo.com/Computers_and _Internet/Programming_Languages/Perl |

## Permissions in Windows NT

*See* Windows NT Permissions.

## PGP (Pretty Good Privacy)

PGP is an encryption and digital signature utility for adding privacy to electronic mail and documents. PGP is an alternative to RSA's S/MIME (Secure MIME). While S/MIME uses RSA (Rivest, Shamir, Adleman) public-key algorithms, PGP uses Diffie-Hellman public-key algorithms. The results are generally the same. A similar, but older and less robust, privacy protocol is PEM (Privacy-Enhanced Mail), which is covered under its own heading.

Phil Zimmermann designed PGP on the principal that e-mail, like conversations, should be private. In addition, both sender and receiver need assurances that messages are from an authentic source, that messages have not been altered or corrupted, and that the sender cannot repudiate (disown) the message. PGP can assure privacy and nonrepudiation. It also provides a tool to encrypt information on disk.

PGP is designed to integrate into popular e-mail programs and operate on major operating systems such as Windows and Macintosh. It uses a graphical user interface to simplify the encryption process.

The package uses public-key encryption techniques in which the user generates two keys—one for distributing to the public and the other to hold privately. These keys can then be used to encrypt and digitally sign messages as discussed under "Digital Signatures" and "Public-Key Cryptography." PGP supports key servers, so users can place their public keys in a place where other people can access the keys.

PGP is packaged for corporate users and personal users. It is available for Windows and Macintosh platforms and works with common messaging programs such as Microsoft Exchange, Eudora, and Claris Emailer for Macintosh.

In late 1997, the IETF was evaluating S/MIME as an Internet standard for e-mail privacy but dropped it due to RSA's licensing and security issues. In its place, the IETF was considering Phil Zimmermann's Open PGP. The product is "open" because the Diffie-Hellman public key-management patents, which were managed by Cylink, are now publicly available due to the expiration of the 20-year patent in September of 1997.

**RELATED ENTRIES**   Authentication and Authorization; Certificates and Certification Systems; Cryptography; Digital Signatures; Electronic Mail; MIME (Multipurpose Internet Mail Extension); PEM (Privacy-Enhanced Mail); PKI (Public-Key Infrastructure); Public-Key Cryptography; RSA Data Security; Security; *and* S/MIME (Secure Multipurpose Internet Mail Extension)

**INFORMATION ON THE INTERNET**

| | |
|---|---|
| Phil Zimmermann's PGP page | http://www.pgp.com |
| PGP 5.0 freeware site | http://web.mit.edu/network/pgp.html |
| PGP information and link sites | http://thegate.gamers.org/~tony/pgp.html |
| Internet Mail Consortium | http://www.imc.org |
| Electronic Messaging Association | http://www.ema.org |

# Physical Layer, OSI Model

OSI (Open Systems Interconnection) is a layered model for defining and building communication systems. It is defined by the ISO (International Organization for Standardization). The lower layers define physical components and transmission schemes, the middle layers define communication management routines, and the upper layers define how applications connect into the model.

Well-known physical layer interfaces for data communication include EIA (Electronic Industries Association) RS-232 and RS-449, the successor to RS-232. RS-449 allows longer cable distances. Well-known local area network systems are Ethernet, token ring, and FDDI (Fiber Distributed Data Interface).

**RELATED ENTRIES**   Connection Technologies; Data Communication Concepts; OSI (Open Systems Interconnection) Model; Protocol Concepts; *and* Transmission Media, Methods, and Equipment

## PIM (Protocol Independent Multicast)

PIM is a multicast routing protocol that handles the routing of multicast data over the Internet or intranets. It is an alternative to two other multicast routing protocols: DVMRP (Distance Vector Multicast Routing Protocol) and MOSPF (Multicast Open Shortest Path First). See "Multicasting" for more information.

## Ping (Packet Internet Groper)

Ping is a utility associated with UNIX, the Internet, and TCP/IP networks. Since most network operating systems now support TCP/IP, they also include a ping utility. Ping is the equivalent to yelling in a canyon and listening for the echo. You "ping" another host on a network to see if that host is reachable from your host. The command takes the form ping *ipaddress*, where *ipaddress* is the numeric IP address of the host you want to contact.

Ping uses the ICMP (Internet Control Message Protocol) for its operation. Specifically, it sends an ICMP echo request message to the designated host. If the device is reachable before a time-out period, your host will receive an ICMP echo reply message. Ping can be used as a troubleshooting tool when communication problems occur. The first thing to do is ping the address of the machine you are working with. This ensures that your network software is working. Next, ping the destination system. If no response is heard, try pinging another system just to see if the network is reachable. If another system responds, the network is probably OK and the destination network or host may have a problem. If possible, go to the destination and ping that machine to see if its network connection is working. If not, check the configuration settings, the connection, or the network interface card itself.

**RELATED ENTRIES**    ICMP (Internet Control Message Protocol); IP (Internet Protocol)

## Pipes

Pipes are IPC (interprocess communication) features of the UNIX, Windows, and OS/2 operating systems. Pipes are like queues in which one process running in the multitasking operating system can store information it wants to pass to itself, to another process running in the computer, or to multiple processes running in the computer. The information is stored on a first-in, first-out basis and flows as a stream of bits that is not altered during transmission. A pipe is opened like a file and read to or written to in the manner of a file. They are unidirectional in that one pipe is used to read and another is used to write information.

*Named pipes* are logical structures in a server that other systems access when they need to use the resources of the server. Named pipes are a networking extension of the IPC mechanism. A named pipe is a communication channel used to transfer information among programs, processes, and devices over the network. It is the basis for the communication mechanism between the client and advanced client/server applications such as SQL (Structured Query Language) servers and communication servers.

**RELATED ENTRIES**    IPC (Interprocess Communication); RPC (Remote Procedure Call)

# PKI (Public-Key Infrastructure)

Public-key infrastructures can provide a structure for verifying and authenticating the parties involved in transactions on the Internet, intranets, or extranets. A number of Internet protocols and applications already use public-key technology to secure transactions. You can refer to "Public-Key Cryptography" and "Security" for more information about how public-key cryptosystems are used.

The purpose of a PKI is to provide a secure infrastructure for managing public keys that allows anyone to exchange private documents with anyone else without knowing those people in advance. The United States Commerce Department's NIST (National Institute of Standards and Technology) is developing a PKI in partnership with companies such as AT&T, BBN, Cylink, Motorola, Northern Telecom, VeriSign, and others.

The reason for developing a PKI is essentially to build an infrastructure of trust. If you want to send a private message to someone, you can obtain their public key, encrypt the message and send it. The recipient can then decrypt the message with his or her private key (which should never be made publicly available). In theory, public keys should be as available as phone numbers printed in a phone book. Following this analogy, it is useful (but not a strict requirement) to have some public entity maintain and publish public keys like the phone company publishes phone numbers. That is where CAs (certificate authorities) enter the picture.

In the simplest scheme, the CA provides a certificate that contains a person's public key along with information about that person. The CA signs (encrypts) the certificate with its own key. You decrypt the certificate with the CA public key to access the end user's public key inside. Thus, you are trusting that the CA will vouch for the contents of the certificate. Typically, CAs only assign certificates after first identifying the credentials of the person in much the same way that credit cards are issued. The level of this verification depends on the CA. In addition, the CA must verify the contents of the certificate. Is this really the public key of the person being represented? Are the contents of the certificate authentic, such as username, address, social security number, medical records, or whatever? When a CA creates a certificate, it basically puts its seal of approval on the certificate by signing it with its private key.

Now the inevitable question. If CAs prove the authenticity of some end user's public key, who vouches for the public key of the CA? What you need is another certificate from some other trusting entity that can prove the authenticity of the CA's public key. Then you need another trusting entity to verify that key, and so on. The purpose of PKI is to build a trust network that can provide just such a hierarchy of trust. At the top are state, federal, or international agencies.

NIST is working on the hierarchy CAs and digital certificates based on X.509 standards. X.509 defines certificate structures and methods for distributing public keys within certificates that are managed by CAs. X.509 is an ITU-T (International

Telecommunication Union-Telecommunications Sector) standard. NIST's initial work is centered around developing a root CA that can be used to examine hierarchical and nonhierarchical CA relationships, scalability, and other operational issues. In other words, it is concerned with developing a chain of legitimate CAs.

The IETF (Internet Engineering Task Force) is also working on a PKI. Its PKIX (X.509 Certificate Policy and Certification Practice) Working Group is developing Internet standards needed to support an X.509-based PKI. The group is working to implement X.509 certificates in multiple applications and to promote interoperability among X.509 implementations. The resulting PKI should provide a framework to support a range of trust/hierarchy environments and usage environments.

The IETF SPKI (Simple PKI) Working Group is developing mechanisms to support security in a wide range of Internet applications, including IPSec protocols, encrypted electronic mail and WWW documents, payment protocols, and any other application that will require the use of public-key certificates and the ability to access them. It is intended that the SPKI will support a range of trust models.

**NOTE:**  *The draft papers at the IETF SPKI site listed below are interesting, enlightening (and amusing). Anyone interested in how certificates can and will be used should visit this site. Carl Ellison's "Generalized Certificates" paper (listed below under "Information on the Internet") is similar and equally enlightening.*

**RELATED ENTRIES**   Authentication and Authorization; Certificates and Certification Systems; Cryptography; Digital Signatures; Public-Key Cryptography; Security; and X.509

## INFORMATION ON THE INTERNET

| | |
|---|---|
| IETF Public-Key Infrastructure (X.509) (pkix) charter | http://www.ietf.org/html.charters/pkix-charter.html |
| IETF Simple Public Key Infrastructure (spki) charter | http://www.ietf.org/html.charters/spki-charter.html |
| The Open Group's PKI site | http://www.rdg.opengroup.org/public/tech/security/pki |
| NIST's PKI site | http://csrc.ncsl.nist.gov/pki |
| NIST's PKI Technical Working Group | http://csrc.ncsl.nist.gov/pki/twg/twgindex.html |
| Distributed Systems Technology Centre's PKI site | http://www.dstc.qut.edu.au/MSU/projects/pki/index.html |
| Marc Branchaud's PKI references (very complete) | http://www.xcert.com/~marcnarc/PKI |
| Gateway to Information Security, Inc.'s PKI links | http://www.securityserver.com/cgi-local/ssis.pl/category/@x509.htm |

| Carl Ellison's Generalized Certificates paper | http://www.clark.net/pub/cme/html/cert.html |

## PNNI (Private Network-to-Network Interface)

PNNI is a dynamic link-state routing protocol for building ATM-based networks in campus, metropolitan, or wide area network environments. A typical large-scale ATM network may consist of groups of ATM switches from different vendors, as shown in Figure P-4. These switches are connected locally and communicate with one another using a vendor-specific NNI (Network-to-Network Interface). PNNI provides a routing protocol to communicate topology information about the network among these groups of ATM switches.

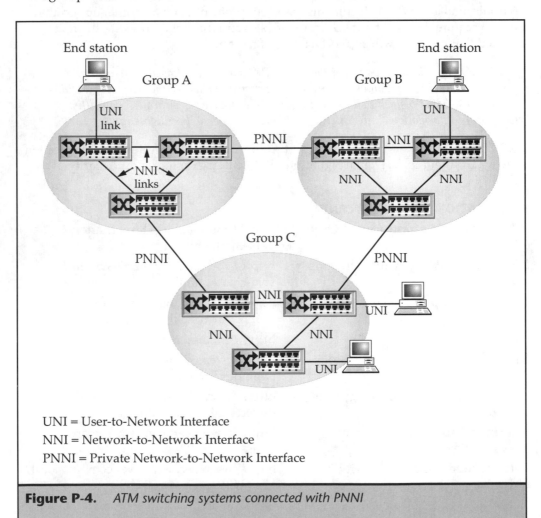

UNI = User-to-Network Interface

NNI = Network-to-Network Interface

PNNI = Private Network-to-Network Interface

**Figure P-4.** *ATM switching systems connected with PNNI*

**P**

Basically, PNNI provides a standard signaling protocol so that multivendor equipment can exchange topology information. The topology information is then used by switches to determine the best path through the network for end station-to-end station communications. Once the path is determined, an SVC (switched virtual circuit) is set up through the network. The ATM network could consist of thousands of interconnected switches from multiple vendors, so a standard protocol such as PNNI is critical to allow equipment to work together.

PNNI establishes hierarchical groupings of ATM switches that help cut down on the amount of topology information that must be exchanged throughout the network. On large ATM networks, it does not make sense to exchange information about the entire network with every node. Instead, groups of ATM switches with similar addressing structures are created. In Figure P-4, three groups (A, B, and C) exist, each representing one level of a hierarchy. These three groups may be grouped together to form a level-2 hierarchy (group ABC) that exchanges information with other level-2 groups. PNNI supports up to 100 hierarchical levels.

Groups exchanging topology information are called peer groups. Each group has a PGID (peer group identifier). At least one node within each group, called a *border node*, exchanges PGIDs and topology information with border nodes in other peer groups. Border nodes exchange information that describes the topology of its routing domain, which is the logical group of nodes that share the same PGID. This information is used to calculate routes through the network.

When a connection is being established, nodes will query other nodes about whether they have the resources to handle a particular connection. For example, streaming video will require a high amount of bandwidth. The target node will evaluate its own traffic and determine whether it can handle the new connection. If not, the requesting node will back off and seek another connection.

Obviously, there are many details not covered here, especially those related to requesting a particular QoS (quality of service). Some details of PNNI are still under development. In addition, an enhancement called I-PNNI (Integrated PNNI) will allow legacy routers to participate in the routing process at the level of the individual network. For more information, refer to the sites listed below. Bay Networks is one of the biggest supporters of PNNI and has information on the protocol.

**RELATED ENTRIES**    ATM (Asynchronous Transfer Mode); I-PNNI (Integrated-Private Network-to-Network Interface); *and* Routing Protocols and Algorithms

**INFORMATION ON THE INTERNET**

| | |
|---|---|
| The ATM Forum | http://www.atmforum.com |
| Bay Networks, Inc. | http://www.baynetworks.com |

# PointCast

PointCast is a broadcast news service that uses "push" technology to update the desktops of Internet-connected users. PointCast works in the background, updating the latest headlines, displaying weather for selected cities, or scrolling stock prices across the screen. Instead of users going to a Web site on their own to get information, they set up a PointCast client called a *ChannelViewer* to automatically retrieve information from PointCast Web server sites.

PointCast uses a computer's "idle" time to initiate information retrieval from PointCast servers. The most current information automatically replaces outdated data on the screen and in the disk cache.

Users that have a continuous connection to the Internet will receive automatic and continuous desktop updates. Users that dial into the Internet will receive updates upon connection. They can also schedule automatic dial-up sessions to update their desktop.

The PointCast network itself is a very large, scalable system that is designed for growth. It performs load balancing among many servers to accommodate the needs of many users. All hardware in the PointCast data center is fully redundant to reduce downtime and allow PointCast to guarantee continuous news coverage.

**RELATED ENTRIES**   Broadcast News Technology; Component Software Technology; Distributed Object Computing; Mailing List Programs; Marimba Castanet; Netcasting; NNTP (Network News Transport Protocol); Push; *and* USENET

**INFORMATION ON THE INTERNET**

PointCast, Inc.                http://www.pointcast.com

# Point-to-Point Communications

A point-to-point connection is a communication link between two end systems. A real point-to-point connection is a wire that directly connects two systems. However, virtual circuits through packet-switched networks, as shown in Figure P-5, simulate a single point-to-point link to the end systems that use them, even though the connections may consist of multiple *physical* point-to-point links.

A LAN also provides point-to-point connections over a shared medium. While all nodes can hear a broadcast from one station to another, only the intended recipient of the broadcast bothers to receive it, so during the time of the transmission, a point-to-point connection exists between the systems.

A point-to-multipoint connection is shown at the bottom of Figure P-5. Multiple devices, usually terminals, are connected to a single device in what is often called a *multidrop link*. The device that provides the multipoint connection is usually an intelligent controller that manages the flow of information from the multiple devices attached to it. Multicasting simulates this in packet-switched networks.

**RELATED ENTRIES**   Broadcast Networking; Data Communication Concepts; Data Link Protocols; Multicasting; Network Concepts; PPP (Point-to-Point Protocol); *and* PPP Multilink

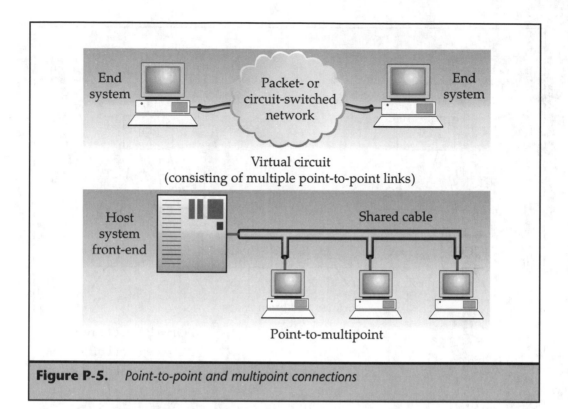

**Figure P-5.**   *Point-to-point and multipoint connections*

## POP (Point of Presence)

A POP is the point where long-distance telephone service providers (IXCs, or
interexchange carriers) connect into regional and local telephone systems. An RBOC
(regional Bell operating company) or other regional carrier must make these points
available to any long-distance carrier by law. Figure P-6 illustrates how the IXCs
establish a POP that is connected into either regional offices or central offices.

POPs are the result of the 1984 breakup of AT&T into a long-distance company and
23 RBOCs. Part of the judgment stipulated that the new RBOCs were to open their
facilities to long-distance carriers for competitive reasons and to give customers a
choice of carriers. Today, AT&T, MCI, Sprint, and many other IXCs connect with POPs
at regional facilities throughout the country. In 1996, the rules were changed again.
The RBOCs were allowed to get into the long-distance business and the long-distance
companies were allowed to build facilities in the geographic areas formerly controlled
by the regional carriers.

**RELATED ENTRIES**   AT&T (American Telephone and Telegraph); IXC
(Interexchange Carrier); LEC (Local Exchange Carrier); Local Loop; RBOCs (Regional
Bell Operating Companies); *and* Telecommunications and Telephone Systems

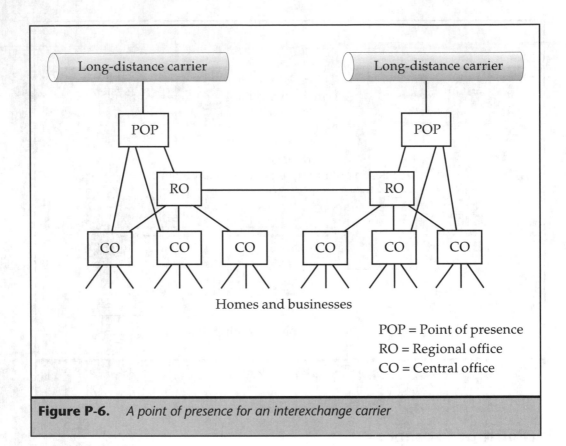

**Figure P-6.** *A point of presence for an interexchange carrier*

## POP (Post Office Protocol)

POP is an Internet mail server protocol that provides an incoming message storage system. It works in conjunction with the SMTP (Simple Mail Transfer Protocol), which provides the message transport services required to move mail from one system to another. The current version is called POP3. However, a new protocol called IMAP4 (Internet Mail Access Protocol, version 4) is replacing POP in many installations.

POP and SMTP are tightly linked. A mail server must run both protocols if it is to receive, store, and forward messages. The job of exchanging messages is handled by the SMTP protocol. Messages are routed from one mail server to another until they reach their destination. The SMTP then hands the messages to the POP server, which puts them into a mailbox. If the destination POP server is offline, the most recent POP server to receive a message will hold it until it can be forwarded to the destination POP server. The destination POP server then puts the mail in the recipient's mailbox for retrieval.

POPs centralized mailbox scheme ensures that recipients get their mail even if their computer is not on because the mail is held by the POP server until it can be picked up. The POP server screens users to make sure that only the intended recipient accesses mail in a mailbox. Users' e-mail addresses and passwords are enough to prove their identity, although more secure systems using certificates are available.

Users run an SMTP-compatible mail client to connect with a POP server and download mail from their mailbox. As soon as the user connects, the mail is downloaded. POP does not let users keep some of their mail at the POP server for later perusal, which is convenient if users are working at someone else's workstation. IMAP allows users to selectively download messages and keep unread messages at the mail server until another time.

In-house networks may consist of a single POP server that holds all the users' mailboxes. Large corporations may have individual POP servers for each department or division. The Internet has the biggest network of POP servers in the world. Schools, companies, and ISPs (Internet service providers) maintain Internet-connected POP servers that allow people all over the world to exchange mail. An ISP's POP server, for example, holds mailboxes for the customers of that ISP.

**RELATED ENTRIES**    Collaborative Computing; Electronic Mail; Groupware; IMAP (Internet Mail Access Protocol); Intranets and Extranets; SMTP (Simple Mail Transfer Protocol); *and* Workflow Management

### INFORMATION ON THE INTERNET

| | |
|---|---|
| POP version 3 (RFC 1939) | http://www.internic.net/rfc/rfc1939.txt |
| Electronic Messaging Association | http://www.ema.org |
| Internet Mail Consortium | http://www.imc.org |
| Yahoo!'s Electronic Mail links page | http://www.yahoo.com/Computers_and _Internet/Communications_and _Networking/Electronic_Mail |

## Ports, TCP

A computer on a network that offers services to users typically runs a number of different processes. In the TCP/IP network environment, these services are available at *ports*. When a computer connects with another computer to access a particular service, an end-to-end connection is established and a socket is set up at each end of the connection. The socket is created at a particular port number, depending on the application. You can think of a socket as being like the telephones at either end of a phone call and the port as being like a phone number.

The most common services are available at predefined port numbers that serve as unique identifiers for those services. The assignment of port numbers to particular services is not strictly controlled but is commonly followed throughout the industry. For example, an HTTP (Web) server uses port 80. Refer to "TCP (Transmission Control Protocol)" for more information.

## POTS (Plain Old Telephone Service)

POTS is the analog telephone service that runs over copper twisted-pair wires and is based on the original Bell telephone system. Twisted-pair wires connect homes and businesses to a neighborhood central office. This is called the local loop. The central office is connected to other central offices and long-distance facilities.

**RELATED ENTRIES**  Carrier Services; Circuit-Switching Services; CO (Central Office); Communication Service Providers; Communication Services; *and* Telecommunications and Telephone Systems

## Power and Grounding Problems and Solutions

Electrical power is rarely supplied as a smooth wave of steady energy. You can see this when lights flicker or when the TV goes haywire while you blend a milkshake. Electrical connections are polluted with surges and spikes (collectively called *noise*). You can think of these surges and spikes as shotgun blasts of energy to delicate electrical components. Here's how computer equipment may handle transient energy:

- **Data corruption**  Electrical disturbances may corrupt memory or data transmissions. A program in memory may fail or cause errors that are thought to be program bugs.

- **Equipment failure**  High-energy transients can permanently damage equipment. Small microprocessor circuitry is especially susceptible. Surge suppressors should be used at primary power supply feeds or at individual stations.

- **Slow death**  Equipment that is repeatedly subjected to low-energy surges will fail over time. The delicate circuits in a chip break down, and the equipment eventually fails for no apparent reason.

Improper grounding is also often a source of problems. In fact, surge suppressors are often a cause of grounding problems because many devices route surges to ground. The surges then find their way back into the electrical system, where they cause problems elsewhere.

Electrical environments are *noisy*. Air conditioners, elevators, refrigerators, and even laser printers cause transients when they are switched on and off. The electric company causes transients when it switches grids to balance the system. In fact, any device that uses electricity in a nonlinear way can cause transients that affect other devices. Some common electrical line problems are described here:

■ **Noise**  Often referred to as surges, spikes, or transients. Noise problems cause slow or immediate damage to sensitive electronic equipment.

■ **Sag**  When circuits become overloaded, the power drops may be below the required level, causing a sag or dropout. A sag might continue for a period of time if the building is incorrectly wired or the utility company is having a problem. A long sag can cause damage to power supplies.

■ **Swell**  A swell is the opposite of a sag and can also cause damage to power supplies.

■ **Hum**  Hum is high-order harmonics caused by neutral-to-ground connection problems. Such problems indicate a defect in one of the electrical wires to ground. Hum can cause transmission errors in data communication lines. Network performance can suffer if systems must constantly resend corrupted packets.

## Grounding Problems

Buildings are wired so that ground connections can drain electrical charges into the earth and protect people from electric shock. Without proper grounding, a charge will pass through a person to the earth. A problem in many buildings and with many computer and network installations is that sensitive electronic equipment and computers are often in the path of the shortest lead to ground. Thus, noise on the AC circuit can infiltrate sensitive electronics through the grounding circuit as well as the hot leads.

Grounding problems are especially prevalent in a network environment because the cabling system can provide a path for *ground loops*. For example, departmental LANs may normally be connected to different sources of power, which are individually grounded. When these department LANs are interconnected, the network cable can form a bridge between the two grounded systems that causes transient energy to seek equilibrium by flowing from ground to ground. In doing so, it flows through the computer systems attached to the cable and causes noise problems. To prevent these problems, equipment connected to different power sources must be electrically isolated.

On a large network, the creation of a single-point ground is usually impossible to achieve. Interconnected networks form links between close or distant points, any one of which can produce electrical problems due to poor wiring. These separate power sources might be in separate buildings or in a multistory office building that has separate power transformers on every floor or every other floor. Each transformer has its own electrical characteristics and should not be connected to equipment connected to other transformers.

One solution is to connect the entire network to one central power source and ground as shown in Figure P-7. A power conditioner and an uninterruptible power supply are used at the server. The power conditioner provides dedicated transformer isolation, a clean source of power, and a solid reference ground. Similar devices should be attached to workstations if possible. A surge suppressor is placed at the feed to the electrical panel. If the surge suppressors are placed on the branch circuits, they will divert surges to ground and back into the circuits of other systems through the ground connection.

Ensure that a single LAN segment is connected to circuits that branch from a single power source and that no point in the segment shares a ground with other power sources. An electrical contractor can perform this service.

While a single power source is beneficial, it is usually impractical on large networks. One trick is to use nonconductive fiber-optic cable to interconnect networks that are using different power supplies. Figure P-8 illustrates how electrical isolation is maintained between two LAN segments, allowing better control over ground and noise problems.

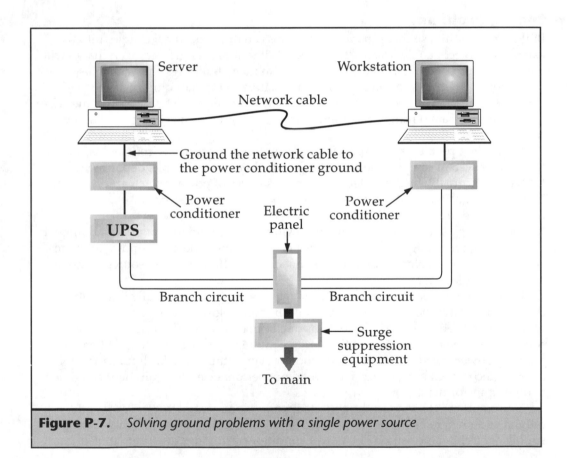

**Figure P-7.**   *Solving ground problems with a single power source*

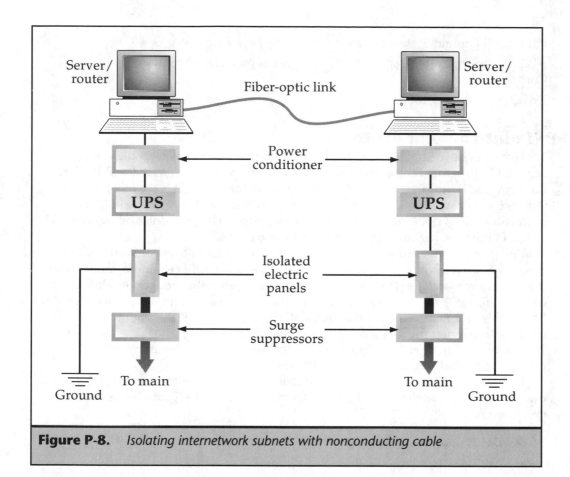

**Figure P-8.**   *Isolating internetwork subnets with nonconducting cable*

It is a good idea to buy uninterruptible power supplies and surge suppressors to protect your network equipment. An *uninterruptible power supply* is a battery backup device, generator, or other device that provides a computer with power during an outage. A *surge suppressor* is a device that protects a system against spikes in the electrical power. Most power supplies in desktop systems can handle surges of up to 800 volts. A surge suppressor is required to protect against surges above these levels.

**RELATED ENTRIES**   Fiber-Optic Cable; Network Concepts; Network Design and Construction; Testing and Diagnostic Equipment and Techniques; TIA/EIA Structured Cabling Standards; Transmission Media, Methods, and Equipment; *and* UPS (Uninterruptible Power Supply)

**INFORMATION ON THE INTERNET**
Sutton Designs, Inc.                    http://suttondesigns.com
Power Quality Assurance Online          http://www.powerquality.com/index.html

Power and Ground Systems Corporation     http://www.powerground.com

APC (American Power Conversion) Corporation     http://www.apcc.com

Excide Electronics Group, Inc.     http://www.exide.com

## PPP (Point-to-Point Protocol)

Two schemes have been adopted by the Internet community to encapsulate and transmit IP (Internet Protocol) datagrams over serial point-to-point links. SLIP (Serial Line Internet Protocol) is one, and PPP (Point-to-Point Protocol) is the other. While SLIP is the original protocol, PPP predominates because it also works with other protocols such as IPX (Internetwork Packet Exchange). The protocol is defined in IETF (Internet Engineering Task Force) RFC 1661 through 1663.

PPP provides router-to-router, host-to-router, and host-to-host connections. PPP is commonly used for Internet connections over dial-up lines. For example, home users dial into their local ISPs (Internet service providers). After the modems establish a connection, a PPP session is set up between the user's system and the service provider. Part of this setup can include a user authentication and the assignment of an IP address. In essence, the user's computer is now an extension of the ISP's IP network and the user's serial port and modem have the same functionality as a network interface card that is connected to the ISP's network.

PPP uses a framing method to encapsulate high-level protocol packets and transmit them across the link. The frame format is pictured in Figure P-9 and described here:

- **Delimiters**   Mark the beginning and ending of the frame
- **Address**   Holds the destination address
- **Control**   Holds the sequence number to ensure proper handling
- **Protocol**   Identifies the protocol contained in the frame (IP, IPX, AppleTalk, etc.)
- **Data**   Contains the data, which can vary in length
- **Frame Check Sequence**   Calculates a check sum used for error checking

The physical layer for PPP supports transmissions over asynchronous and synchronous lines using serial communication protocols such as EIA-232-E, EIA-422, EIA-423, as well as CCITT V.24 and V.35.

The data link layer is based on the frame structure of HDLC (High-level Data Link Control). An LCP (Link Control Protocol) establishes and manages links between connected stations. It establishes encapsulation methods and packet sizes, compression methods, and authentication protocols (user ID and password). The receiving system responds with other LCP packets that acknowledge receipt and verify or reject configuration options. Once a connection is made, a network control

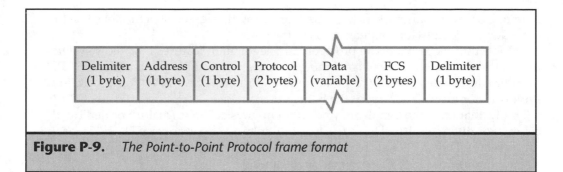

| Delimiter (1 byte) | Address (1 byte) | Control (1 byte) | Protocol (2 bytes) | Data (variable) | FCS (2 bytes) | Delimiter (1 byte) |
|---|---|---|---|---|---|---|

**Figure P-9.** *The Point-to-Point Protocol frame format*

**P**

protocol is used to negotiate the type of protocol configuration, and the two PPP hosts can begin exchanging datagrams.

**RELATED ENTRIES**    Internet Connections; IPSec (IP Security); PPTP (Point-to-Point Tunneling Protocol); Routers; Security; Serial Communication and Interfaces; SLIP (Serial Line Internet Protocol); S/WAN (Secure WAN); Tunnels; Virtual Dial-up Services; VPN (Virtual Private Network); *and* WAN (Wide Area Network)

### INFORMATION ON THE INTERNET

| | |
|---|---|
| PPP Authentication Protocols (RFC 1334) | http://www.internic.net/rfc/rfc1334.txt |
| IETF Point-to-Point Protocol Extensions (pppext) charter | http://www.ietf.org/html.charters/ pppext-charter.html |
| Yahoo!'s PPP (Point-to-Point Protocol) links page | http://www.yahoo.com/Computers_and _Internet/Information_and_Documentation /Protocols/PPP_Point_to_Point_Protocol |
| PPP FAQ | http://www.incoma.ru/protocols/ ppp.html |
| PPP FAQ Part 2 | http://usenet.umr.edu/faqs/ppp-faq/part2 |

*NOTE:  IETF RFC 1661 through 1663 cover PPP. To view the RFCs, go to http://www.internic.net/rfc/rfcxxxx.txt, replacing xxxx with the RFC number you want to view.*

## PPP Multilink

PPP Multilink is a bandwidth-on-demand protocol that can connect multiple links between two systems as needed to provide bandwidth on demand. The technique is often called *bonding*. For example, the two 64-Kbit/sec B channels of ISDN can be combined to form a single 128-Kbit/sec data channel. Another example would be to bind one or more dial-up asynchronous channels with a leased synchronous line to provide more bandwidth at peak hours of the day.

PPP Multilink provides the protocols and negotiation features that allow systems to indicate they are capable of combining multiple physical links into a "bundle." PPP Multilink is an extension to PPP (Point-to-Point Protocol). See "PPP (Point-to-Point Protocol)" for information about the basic protocol.

Links that form the bundle may be different physical links (dial-up or dedicated circuits) or different virtual links (such as multiplexed circuits over ISDN, X.25, or frame relay). The links in the bundle may also be different, such as dial-up asynchronous lines and leased synchronous lines.

When multiple lines are combined, some method is needed to divide data among the channels and recombine it at the other end. On packet networks such as IP, the obvious method is to alternate packets among each of the combined data channels. Packet 1 goes to line 1, packet 2 goes to line 2, and so on in a round-robin approach. The protocol fragments packets to ensure equal distribution across the links so that the lines are used efficiently and to ensure that packets arrive across multiple channels at approximately the same time for efficient reordering.

When two systems perform initial session negotiations, they also indicate their ability to establish multilink connections. The two systems indicate their ability to send/receive upper layer PDUs (protocol data units) in fragmented form and negotiate a packet size. Once the session is negotiated, network layer packets are encapsulated (or fragmented, then encapsulated) into data link layer frames and a multilink header is attached to the frames.

PPP Multilink started out as a way to bond two or more ISDN channels but is now capable of bonding many different types of connections. BACP (Bandwidth Allocation Control Protocol) works in conjunction with PPP Mulilink to provide dynamic channel aggregation. Two peer systems negotiate with one another to change PPP Multilink bandwidth as needed.

> **NOTE:** *A number of related PPP extensions are described at the IETF PPP extensions page listed below. These extensions are related to bandwidth allocation, compression, and other techniques for extending the functionality of PPP.*

**RELATED ENTRIES** BACP (Bandwidth Allocation Control Protocol); Bandwidth on Demand; Bandwidth Reservation; Bonding; Circuit-Switching Services; DDR (Dial-on-Demand Routing); Inverse Multiplexing; ISDN (Integrated Services Digital Network); Load Balancing; *and* PPP (Point-to-Point Protocol)

**INFORMATION ON THE INTERNET**

| | |
|---|---|
| PPP Multilink Protocol (RFC 1990) | http://www.internic.net/rfc/rfc1990.txt |
| IETF PPP extensions site | http://www.ietf.org/html.charters/pppext-charter.html |

# PPS (Packets per Second)

Packets per second (pps) is a measure of throughput for network devices such as bridges and routers. You can use the following table as a reference when evaluating network routers. Note that traditional routers are devices that rely on a single CPU for routing functions. Newer routers may use custom architectures with multiple processors to boost processing speeds. The latest router design combines switching and routing to boost routing speed even more. Some vendors claim route switching speeds of 10 million pps! Even if this is overstated, the real speed is many times higher than traditional routers. See "IP Switching" and "Routers" for more details.

| | |
|---|---|
| Traditional and legacy routers | Up to 500,000 pps |
| Traditional designs with optimized architectures | 1 million pps |
| Routing switches | 1 to 10 million pps |

# PPTP (Point-to-Point Tunneling Protocol)

PPTP is one of several services that provide what is called *virtual dial-up services*. A remote user wishing to connect with the corporate LAN from a location that would normally require a long-distance telephone call instead connects with a local ISP (Internet service provider). The user then obtains a virtual connection across the Internet to the corporate network. Thus, only a local call is made and the user obtains long-distance connections over the Internet, which is essentially free. Authentication and encryption can be added to virtual dial-up sessions to provide a private and secure connection.

PPTP is a Microsoft proposal for virtual dial-up services that was submitted to the IETF (Internet Engineering Task Force) for standardization in 1996. As of this writing, PPTP was still under IETF development. In the meantime, Cisco developed L2F (Layer 2 Forwarding), a similar protocol, and then both Microsoft and Cisco merged features in their respective protocols to create L2TP (Layer 2 Tunneling Protocol), which is also under IETF consideration as a standard. See "Virtual Dial-Up Services" for more general information on these protocols. This section covers PPTP.

PPTP is supplied with Windows NT Server as a solution to provide "tunneled" connections over the Internet between remote clients and corporate servers. Client support is available for Windows and Macintosh users.

PPTP turns the Internet into a virtual private network and removes much of the costs of expensive leased lines and long-distance calling. In addition, it removes the cost of installing and maintaining banks of modems at the corporate site. This is pictured in Figure P-10. At the top, the corporate site must maintain a bank of modems attached to an access server. Users dial in over what may be long-distance lines to

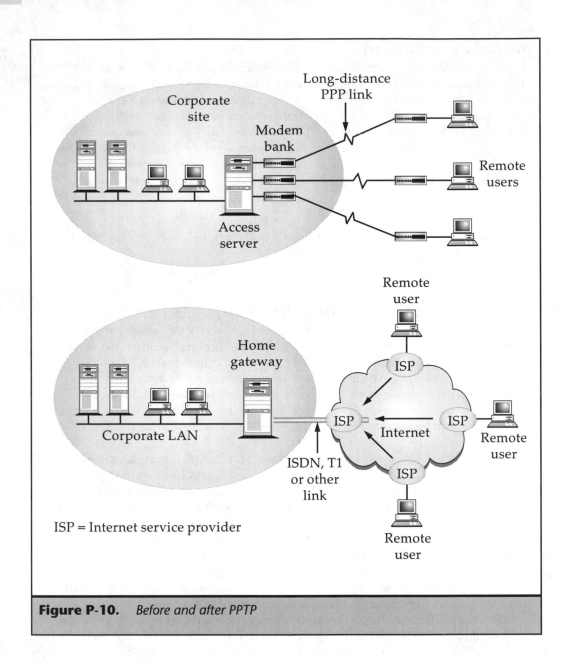

**Figure P-10.** *Before and after PPTP*

access the server. In the lower figure, the corporate site is connected to a local ISP (Internet service provider) and the Internet over a short, relatively low-cost dedicated leased line. Remote users dial into a local ISP and gain a connection directly to the home gateway over PPTP connections that cross the Internet.

PPTP *tunnels* packets across the Internet. You can think of a tunnel as a pipe through which any type of packet may be transmitted. A user's protocol packets are encapsulated in IP datagrams that can traverse the Internet on their own, so users can access the corporate network with almost any network protocol, including IPX, AppleTalk, and others. Note that PPTP is an extension of PPP. It extends PPP framing all the way to the corporate site. (Normally it extends only from the user to the ISP.)

The usual setup is a Windows client with a PPTP driver as its WAN driver. The client accesses a remote LAN by connecting to a Windows NT RAS (Remote Access Server) at the corporate site that is PPTP-enabled. During the initial session negotiation, a 40-bit key is exchanged between client and server, and this key is used to secure the session using RSA RC4 encryption.

**RELATED ENTRIES**    IPSec (IP Security); PPP (Point-to-Point Protocol); Routers; Security; S/WAN (Secure WAN); Tunnels; Virtual Dial-up Services; VPN (Virtual Private Network); *and* WAN (Wide Area Network)

**INFORMATION ON THE INTERNET**

| | |
|---|---|
| Microsoft's PPTP information (search for "PPTP") | http://www.microsoft.com |
| Ascend Communications' PPTP FAQ (go to Resource Library) | http://www.ascend.com |
| Shiva's Remote Access white paper | http://www.shiva.com/remote/prodinfo/tunnel |
| 3Com's PPTP site | http://infodeli.3com.com/infodeli/tools/remote/general/pptp/pptp.htm |
| MAS NET's VPN information | http://www.masnet.net/internet/issues/vpn.html |

# Premises Distribution System

A premises distribution system is a preplanned network of cabling within a building or campus environment designed for the transmission of voice and data. Early premises systems were proprietary, but today, most cabling systems follow *TIA/EIA 568 Commercial Building Wiring Standard,* which is covered under "TIA/EIA Structured Cabling Standards."

# Presentation Layer, OSI Model

OSI (Open Systems Interconnection) is a layered model for defining and building communication systems. It is defined by the ISO (International Organization for Standardization). The lower layers define physical components and transmission schemes; the middle layers define communication management routines; and the upper layers define how applications connect into the model.

The presentation layer is layer 6 in the protocol stack, just below the top-level application layer and above the session layer. The presentation layer provides translation of data, defines data formatting, and provides syntax. The presentation layer prepares incoming data for the application layer, where the user views the data. For outgoing data, the presentation layer translates data from the application layer into a form that is suitable for transfer over the network. There are various encoding rules built into the presentation layer protocols that handle all the data translations.

**RELATED ENTRIES**   Connection Technologies; Data Communication Concepts; OSI (Open Systems Interconnection) Model; Protocol Concepts; *and* Transmission Media, Methods, and Equipment

## Prioritization of Network Traffic

Prioritization can be explained as follows: implement some method to get important packets through a network when the network is congested and delay unimportant packets until later. Important packets are generally classified as *delay-sensitive traffic* such as that generated by live videoconferencing, voice calls, mission-critical transaction processing, remote monitoring, and collaborative computing (in which people work in real time on their computer screens across networks). Unimportant packets may include packets carrying electronic mail or packets downloaded from Internet Web sites by freeloading users.

The problem with priority schemes (also called *class of service*, or *CoS*) is that they can prevent lower-priority traffic from getting through. A high-priority transmission may hold up a midlevel priority transmission for an unacceptable period of time. One solution is to add more bandwidth (often called *over-provisioning*). Once that is done, reserving bandwidth for special needs becomes more practical.

Prioritization and bandwidth reservation are features of QoS (quality of service). QoS covers an entire range of services that provide certain guarantees that traffic will be delivered on time, in order, and either fully intact or with an acceptable level of loss if the network becomes congested.

*NOTE:*   *This section is closely related to the QoS. Refer to "QoS (Quality of Service)" for additional information.*

Prioritization has been used in multiprotocol routers to give some protocols higher priority than other protocols. For example, SNA (Systems Network Architecture) traffic will time-out and cause retransmissions that degrade network performance if it is not delivered promptly. Such protocols should be given high priority to prevent retransmissions, even through the actual data being delivered may not be that important.

There are a number of developments underway to add prioritization and QoS to LANs and the Internet. However, doing so is not an easy task because most legacy networks do not have built-in features for prioritizing traffic. Only ATM

(Asynchronous Transfer Mode) networks are designed from the ground up to support QoS, as described under "QoS (Quality of Service)." In addition, most applications are not designed to take advantage of QoS features in networks. The relatively new WinSock 2.0 API allows applications to request different level of service, but at this writing, developers are just beginning to use it.

The IETF (Internet Engineering Task Force) is promoting RSVP (Resource Reservation Protocol) as a method for providing QoS levels on intranets and the Internet. RSVP allows a host to request a QoS level from the network. RSVP then sets about establishing a reserved path through the network, going to each router in turn and requesting that it reserve bandwidth for the user's traffic. See "RSVP (Resource Reservation Protocol)" for more information.

## Vendor Initiatives

A number of vendors have developed methods that add support for prioritization and policy-based networking to existing "best-effort" datagram networks. These services allow users or their applications to request priority on the network. The services may also give prioritization to certain types of applications or rely on *flow detection*, a method that detects traffic flows and switches (rather than routes) the traffic at high speed. Two examples are given next. See "IP over ATM" and "IP Switching" for additional information.

### 3Com TranscendWare

TranscendWare is an end-to-end networking solution that adds intelligent software to network components, allowing the components to support delay-sensitive traffic. Software is added to the network core switches, edge switches, and end systems (desktop PCs and servers). The software components are

- **Network control software** This is end-system software that improves bandwidth control and end-to-end response time. It includes Fast IP and PACE (priority access control enabled). See "Fast IP" and "PACE (Priority Access Control Enabled)" for more information.

- **Global policy software** This is the software that runs on 3Com's Gigabit Ethernet products to set policies for applications and network operations.

- **Management software** This software is embedded at the core, edge, and end system to implement policies, provide bandwidth control, and monitor traffic.

In general, the software provides a way to prioritize data applications, provide delay-sensitive traffic with QoS, and prevent the LAN from being flooded with multicast data flows. The control software running in 3Com's NICs (network interface cards) identifies client application requirements, sets priorities, and initiates prioritized sessions with the network core and edge systems. Fast IP is used to speed the flow of IP by creating data paths that bypass routers through the layer 2 switching network. This is called *cut-through* routing and is discussed under "Fast IP."

3Com's class of service features allow network managers to automate the control of bandwidth utilization and priority by assigning different users lower or higher classes of services. Prioritization is achieved through standards-based tagging techniques, switches with multiple queues, and the over-provisioning of bandwidth. The software will also map Ethernet prioritization to ATM QoS features so customers can connect with carrier ATM networks.

## Cisco IOS Extensions for QoS

Cisco IOS (Internetwork Operating System) is a platform for delivering and managing network services. Cisco IOS QoS is a set of IOS extensions that provide end-to-end QoS across heterogeneous networks. Cisco IOS QoS is targeted at ISP (Internet service providers) and provides them with a way to prioritize traffic on their networks based on the customer, the application, or other factors. Most important, it provides ISPs with a way to charge users for the services they use, an important requirement if customers want to obtain any kind of guaranteed service on the Internet. Cisco IOS QoS services are discussed in more detail under "QoS (Quality of Service)."

## IEEE Prioritization Efforts for 802 Networks

The IEEE (Institute of Electrical and Electronic Engineers) has developed most of the LAN standards in use today, such as Ethernet and token ring. One of those standards is IEEE 802.1D, which defines LAN-level bridging and switching standards. The Internetworking Task Group is working on an adaptation of this standard called 802.1p, which provides a way for users to set priority bits in frames that specify different classes of traffic.

The 802.1p specification defines an extended frame format for carrying the extra bits over Ethernet, token ring, FDDI (Fiber Distributed Data Interface), or other MAC-layer media in a consistent way. The user priority bits serve as a label in the data stream that identifies priority packets. Downstream nodes can easily identify the streams associated with a label, thus avoiding the need to examine every packet in the stream in detail.

Eight different service classes can be defined, with 0 being the lowest and 7 being the highest. Switches are configured with a number of queues, with some queues getting higher priority than others. The number of queues is up to the operator. When a packet arrives at the switch, it is directed into a queue based on its priority level. The switch then forwards packets in the higher-level queues before the lower-level queues.

Information about 802.1p is available at the IEEE Web site. The IETF Integrated Services over Specific Link Layers (issll) Working Group also has information about the standard. It's Web site is at http://www.ietf.org/html.charters/issll-charter.html.

**RELATED ENTRIES**    ATM (Asynchronous Transfer Mode); Cell Relay; Fast IP; IP over ATM; IP Switching; ISA (Integrated Services Architecture); PACE (Priority Access Control Enabled) QoS (Quality of Service); RSVP (Resource Reservation Protocol); Switched Networks; Tag Switching; *and* VLAN (Virtual LAN)

**INFORMATION ON THE INTERNET**

| | |
|---|---|
| Bengt J. Olsson's IP backbone provisioning paper | http://www.communicator.se/whitepapers/IP_Backbone.HTM |
| 3Com Corporation | http://www.3com.com |
| Cisco Systems, Inc. | http://www.cisco.com |
| Decisys, Inc. (see "Directory of Published Articles" and "White Papers" sections) | http://www.decisys.com |
| IEEE (Institute of Electrical and Electronic Engineers) | http://www.ieee.org |

## Private-Key Cryptography

Private-key cryptography is often called *secret-key* or *symmetric* cryptography. A single key is used to encrypt data. If data is encrypted for storage on a hard drive, the person encrypting the data must make sure not to forget the key.

If private-key cryptography is used to send secret messages between two parties, then both the sender and receiver must have a copy of the secret key. However, the key may be compromised during transit. If you know the party you are exchanging messages with, then you can give them the key in advance. However, if you need to send an encrypted message to someone you have never met, you need to figure out a way to exchange keys in a secure way. One method is send it via another secure channel or even via overnight express, but this may be risky in cases where you suspect someone is actively trying to obtain the key.

As mentioned, private-key cryptography is often used to encrypt data on hard drives. The person encrypting the data holds the key privately and there is no problem with key distribution. Private-key cryptography is also used for communication devices like encrypting routers, where all data transmitted between two devices must be encrypted. A network administrator programs two devices with the same key, and then personally transports them to their physical locations.

*NOTE:  An alternative key scheme is discussed under "Public-Key Cryptography."*

**RELATED ENTRIES**    Cryptography; DES (Data Encryption Standard); Digital Signatures; PKI (Public-Key Infrastructure); Public-Key Cryptography; *and* Security

## Private Network

*Private network* is a term used to describe a wide area network that crosses public properties but that is controlled by an organization. Private networks are created with dial-up or dedicated lines that are leased from local and long-distance carriers. The important point is that the service provider guarantees a certain bandwidth and no one else competes for that bandwidth (unlike public packet-switching networks). The downside is that bandwidth may go unused during lulls in traffic. The related entries given below provide information about building private networks.

An alternative to the private network is the VPN (virtual private network), which is built on packet- or cell-switching networks. The carrier preprograms a path through the network, called a *virtual circuit,* and provides a contracted amount of bandwidth called *CIR (committed information rate).* The networks are shared by all of the carrier's customers, but as the network becomes busy, the carrier maintains enough bandwidth to meet customer CIRs. The advantage of packet switching as compared to leased lines is that you pay only for the bandwidth you need. You can underestimate your load but still obtain extra bandwidth to handle unexpected peaks in traffic if it is available.

VPNs over the Internet are another alternative. This technique requires encryption to protect data since it travels over public networks. See "VPN (Virtual Private Network)" for more information.

**RELATED ENTRIES**    Bandwidth on Demand; Circuit-Switching Services; Communication Service Providers; Communication Services; IXC (Interexchange Carrier); LATA (Local Access and Transport Area); Leased Line; LEC (Local Exchange Carrier); Packet and Cell Switching; T1/T3; Telecommunications and Telephone Systems; VPN (Virtual Private Network); *and* WAN (Wide Area Network). See also "Telecommunications Companies" in Appendix A.

## Promiscuous Mode

A network-connected device operating in promiscuous mode captures all frames on a network, not just frames that are addressed directly to it. A network analyzer operates in this mode to capture network traffic for evaluation and to measure traffic for statistical analysis. A hacker may also use a promiscuous mode device to capture network traffic for unscrupulous activities. Network traffic can be encrypted to protect against such eavesdropping. Refer to "Network Analyzers" for a discussion of how promiscuous mode is applied.

## Propagation Delay

Propagation delay is a delay caused by the time it takes information to be transmitted from one place to another. In the case of satellite transmissions, the delay is often noticeable, especially for voice and video transmissions.

## Protocol Analyzers

*See* Network Analyzers.

## Protocol Concepts

Network communication protocols are defined within the context of a layered architecture, usually called a *protocol stack*. The OSI (Open Systems Interconnection) protocol stack is often used as a reference to define the different types of services that are required for systems to communicate. Figure P-11 compares the OSI protocol stack to the more common protocols found today.

The lowest layers define physical interfaces and electrical transmission characteristics. The middle layers define how devices communicate, maintain a connection, check for errors, and perform flow control to ensure that one system does not receive more data than it can process. The upper layers define how applications can use the lower network layer services.

The protocol stack defines how communication hardware and software interoperate at various levels. *Layering* is a design approach that specifies different functions and services at levels in the protocol stack. Layering allows vendors to build products that interoperate with products developed by other vendors.

Each layer in a protocol stack provides services to the protocol layer just above it. The service accepts data from the higher layer, adds its own protocol information, and passes it down to the next layer. Each layer also carries on a "conversation" with its *peer* layer in the computer it is communicating with. Peers exchange information about the status of the communication session in relation to the functions that are provided by their particular layer.

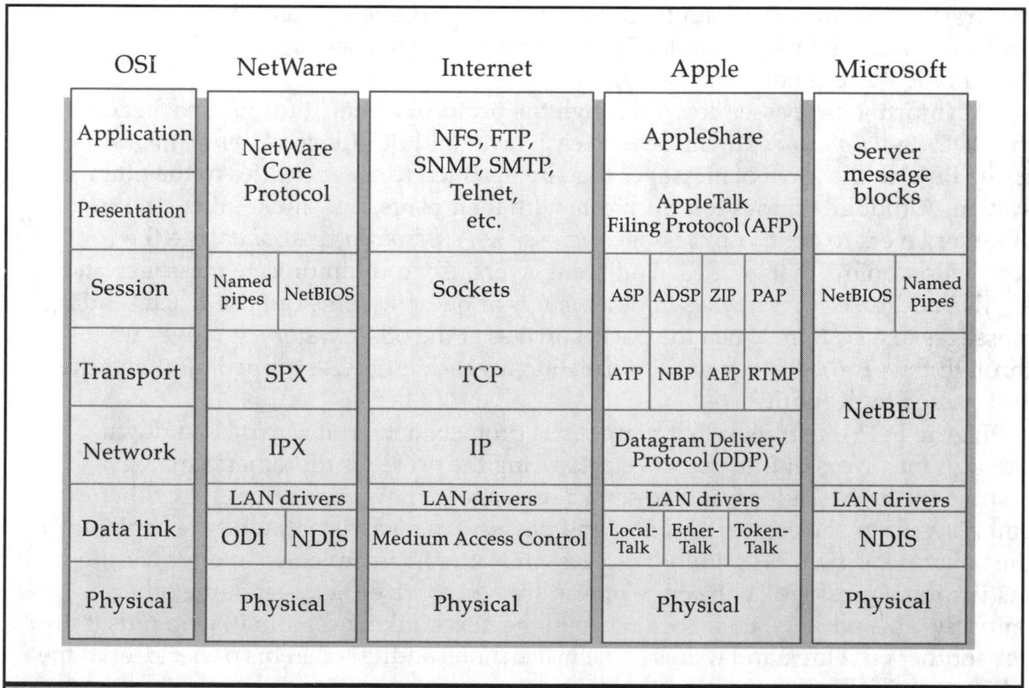

| OSI | NetWare | | Internet | Apple | | | | Microsoft | |
|---|---|---|---|---|---|---|---|---|---|
| Application | NetWare Core Protocol | | NFS, FTP, SNMP, SMTP, Telnet, etc. | AppleShare | | | | Server message blocks | |
| Presentation | | | | AppleTalk Filing Protocol (AFP) | | | | | |
| Session | Named pipes | NetBIOS | Sockets | ASP | ADSP | ZIP | PAP | NetBIOS | Named pipes |
| Transport | SPX | | TCP | ATP | NBP | AEP | RTMP | NetBEUI | |
| Network | IPX | | IP | Datagram Delivery Protocol (DDP) | | | | | |
| Data link | LAN drivers | | LAN drivers | LAN drivers | | | | LAN drivers | |
| | ODI | NDIS | Medium Access Control | Local-Talk | Ether-Talk | Token-Talk | | NDIS | |
| Physical | Physical | | Physical | Physical | | | | Physical | |

**Figure P-11.**    *Common protocol stacks*

As an analogy, imagine the creation of a formal agreement between two embassies. At the top, formal negotiations take place between ambassadors, but in the background, diplomats and officers work on documents, define procedures, and perform other activities. Diplomats have rank, and diplomats at each rank perform some service for higher-ranking diplomats. The ambassador at the highest level passes orders down to a lower-level diplomat. That diplomat provides services to the ambassador and coordinates his or her activities with a diplomat of equal rank at the other embassy. Likewise, diplomats of lower rank, who provide services to higher-level diplomats, also coordinate their activities with peer diplomats in the other embassy. Diplomats follow established diplomatic procedures based on the ranks they occupy. For example, a diplomatic officer at a particular level may provide language translation services or technical documentation. This officer communicates with a peer at the other embassy regarding translation and documentation procedures.

In the diplomatic world, a diplomat at one embassy simply picks up the phone and calls his or her peer at the other embassy. In the world of network communication, software processes called *entities* occupy layers in the protocol stack instead of diplomats of rank. However, these entities don't have a direct line of communication between one another. Instead, they use a *virtual communication path* in which messages are sent down the protocol stack, across the wire, and up the protocol stack of the other computer, where they are retrieved by the peer entity. This whole process is illustrated in Figures P-12 and P-13. Note that the terminology used here is for the OSI protocol stack. The more popular TCP/IP protocol suite uses slightly different terminology, but the process is similar.

As information passes down through the protocol layers, it forms a packet called the *PDU (protocol data unit)*. Entities in each layer add *PCI (protocol control information)* to the PDU in the form of messages that are destined for peer entities in the other system. Although entities communicate with their peers, they must utilize the services of lower layers to get those messages across. *SAPs (service access points)* are the connection points that entities in adjacent layers use to communicate messages; they are like addresses that entities in other layers or other systems can use when sending messages to a system. When the packet arrives at the other system, it moves up through the protocol stack, and information for each entity is stripped off the packet and passed to the entity.

Figure P-13 illustrates what happens as protocol data units are passed down through the layers of the protocol stack. Using the previous diplomatic analogy, assume the ambassador wants to send a message to the ambassador at the other embassy. He or she creates the letter and passes it to an assistant, who is a diplomat at the next rank down. This diplomat places the letter in an envelope and writes an instructional message on the envelope addressed to his or her peer at the other embassy. This package then goes down to the next-ranking diplomat, who puts it in yet another envelope and writes some instructions addressed to his or her peer at the other embassy. This process continues down the ranks until it reaches the "physical" level, where the package is delivered by a courier to the other embassy. At the other

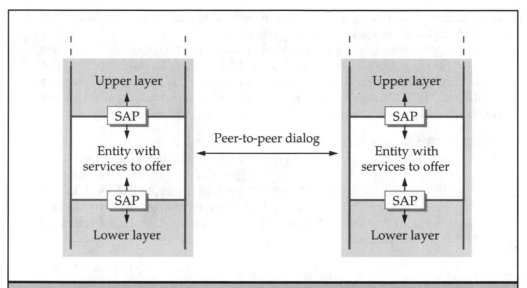

**Figure P-12.**    *Communication process between two separate protocol stacks*

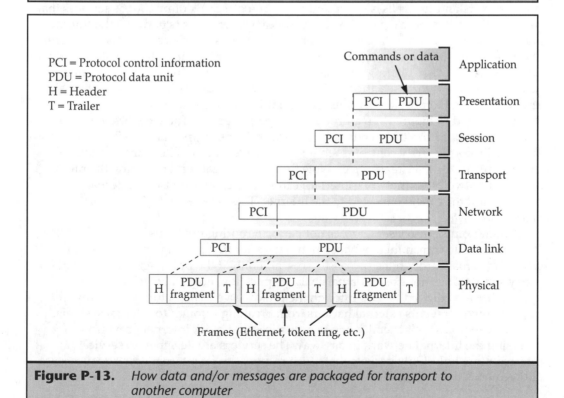

**Figure P-13.**    *How data and/or messages are packaged for transport to another computer*

embassy, each diplomat reads the message addressed to him or her and passes the enclosed envelope up to the next-ranking officer.

Each layer performs a range of services. In particular, you should refer to "Data Communication Concepts," "Data Link Protocols," "Network Layer Protocols," and "Transport Protocols and Services" for more information. The sections "IP (Internet Protocol)" and "TCP (Transmission Control Protocol)" also provide some insight into the functions of the two most important layers as related to the Internet protocol suite.

**RELATED ENTRIES**   Connection Establishment; Data Communication Concepts; Datagrams and Datagram Services; Data Link Protocols; Encapsulation; Flow-Control Mechanisms; Fragmentation of Frames and Packets; Framing in Data Transmissions; Handshake Procedures; IP (Internet Protocol); Network Concepts; Network Layer Protocols; Novell NetWare Protocols; OSI (Open Systems Interconnection) Model; Packet; Sequencing of Packets; TCP (Transmission Control Protocol); *and* Transport Protocols and Services

## Proxy Servers

A proxy server, like a firewall, is designed to protect internal resources on networks that are connected to other networks such as the Internet. The difference between proxy servers and firewalls is often confusing. You can think of proxies as services that run on a firewall, where the firewall is a physical server that sits between the Internet and the internal network. In general, a firewall provides extensive controls for filtering and monitoring both incoming and outgoing traffic. For example, a firewall may run network layer packet-filtering services to block packets that have a specific source address or that are for a specific service. Proxy services run on the firewall at the application level to provide a sophisticated traffic control system.

As pictured in Figure P-14, a firewall runs proxy services for each different type of Internet application that needs to be controlled. For example, an HTTP (Hypertext Transfer Protocol) proxy controls Web services, while an FTP (File Transfer Protocol) proxy controls file transfer services. Note that the physical server running the proxy services has two NICs (network interface cards), one connected to the internal network and the other connected to the Internet. This is called a *dual-homed* or *multihomed system*.

A dual-homed proxy server does not perform routing functions between the NICs. Packets are only transmitted between networks after first passing up the protocol stack and across through the proxy services, and only if the proxy services allow it. If a proxy service does not exist for a particular application, no packets related to the application are allowed to pass through the proxy server. This setup, when properly implemented, prevents external hackers from breaking through to internal systems.

Proxy services are generally one-way services that block Internet users from accessing the internal network in any way. The services are designed to service internal users only. Only packets that are in response to an internal user's requests are allowed back through the firewall.

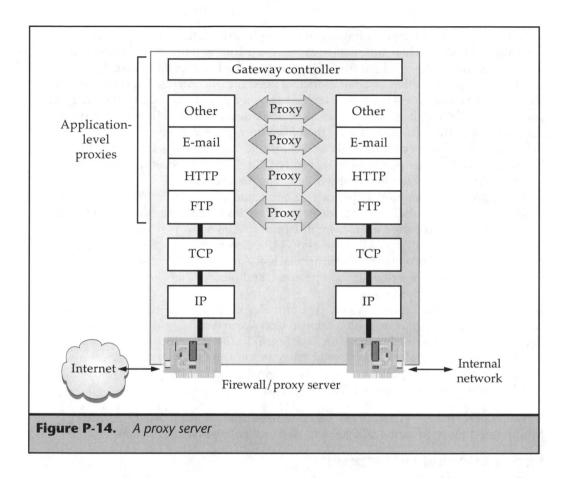

P

**Figure P-14.** *A proxy server*

For example, assume an internal client wants to access a Web server on the Internet. The HTTP proxy service running in the firewall intercepts the user's HTTP packets, repackages the requests, and forwards the repackaged request to the Web server on the Internet. The packets carry the source IP address of the proxy server, not the internal user's IP address. Externally, it looks like all packets are coming from the proxy server, which provides a level of security by hiding all internal addresses. When the Web server responds to the request, the proxy server receives the responses and forwards them to the internal client. An advantage of this approach is that internal networks don't need to conform to Internet addressing standards, something that is especially important since the Internet is running out of IP addresses.

For security reasons, incoming response packets may be inspected for viruses or possible alteration by an external hacker. The proxy server may also set up a secure encrypted session with the Web server to ensure that eavesdroppers cannot look at the packets and glean useful information.

Proxy servers also provide important *caching* functions. Since they provide a centralized location where internal users access the Internet, the proxy server can cache frequently accessed documents from sites on the Internet and make them quickly available for other internal users that need the documents. For example, thousands of users access the *Dilbert* comic site every day. If a company has a caching proxy server, the comic is cached after the first request of the day. Subsequent users get the comic from the local cache rather then from the *Dilbert* Web site.

Since a proxy server handles all packets for internal users, it is fairly easy to perform such things as virus scanning, content filtering, and access control. Packets that contain undesirable content or words can be discarded.

Most proxy servers provide proxies for applications like HTTP, FTP, Telnet, and other Internet protocols. Some include generic proxies that can be configured for other applications. In some cases, each client must run special software to access the firewall. For example, Microsoft's proxy server allows IPX (Internetwork Packet Exchange) clients to access the proxy server with special software. In addition, some proxy servers use SOCKS, an authentication protocol, and require that clients have software that can negotiate with SOCKS.

SOCKS is a generic proxy system that provides extensive security features along with auditing, management, fault tolerance, and alarm notification features. It is defined in IETF (Internet Engineering Task Force) RFC 1928, which you can read at the address listed below. Many commercial proxy servers are based on SOCKS. See "SOCKS" for more information. One of the original proxy servers was developed by CERN and is described at the CERN address given below.

**RELATED ENTRIES**    Firewall; Hacker; Internet Connections; IPSec (IP Security); Multihomed Host; Security; SOCKS; *and* Web Technologies and Concepts

## INFORMATION ON THE INTERNET

| | |
|---|---|
| SOCKS Protocol Version 5 (RFC 1928) | http://www.internic.net/rfc/rfc1928.txt |
| NEC's SOCKS site | http://www.socks.nec.com |
| Aventail Corporation's SOCKS links | http://www.aventail.com/educate/security.html |
| CERN proxy server site | http://www.w3.org/Daemon |
| Les Carleton's list of proxy servers | http://www.zeuros.co.uk/firewall/proxy.htm |
| Yahoo!'s Proxies links page | http://www.yahoo.com/Computers_and_Internet/Software/Internet/World_Wide_Web/Servers/Proxies |
| Microsoft's Proxy Server site | http://www.microsoft.com/proxy |
| Netscape's Proxy Server site | http://www.netscape.com/comprod/server_central/product/proxy/index.html |

## PSTN (Public-Switched Telephone Network)

PSTN was put into place many years ago as a voice telephone call-switching system. The system transmits voice calls as analog signals across copper twisted cables from homes and businesses to neighborhood COs (central offices); this is often called the *local loop*. The PSTN is a circuit-switched system, meaning that an end-to-end private circuit is established between caller and callee. Modems are required to transmit digital data over these lines. The COs are connected together with a variety of transmission facilities, including copper cable, fiber-optic cable, and microwave transmission towers. Voice calls are typically converted to digital data for transmission across these trunks. Only the local loop retains all the characteristics of the original telephone system.

**RELATED ENTRIES**    Circuit-Switching Services; CTI (Computer-Telephony Integration); Modems; Telecommunications and Telephone Systems; Voice/Data Networks; Voice over ATM; Voice over the Internet; *and* VoIP (Voice over IP)

## PU (Physical Unit) Entities

A PU is a data communication device in an IBM SNA (Systems Network Architecture) network. PUs handle network management functions and control telecommunication links. Common PU types are listed here:

- **PU Type 2**   Implemented in IBM cluster controllers and IBM 3174 establishment controllers

- **PU Type 4**   Implemented in front-end processors

- **PU Type 5**   Implemented in IBM VTAM (Virtual Telecommunication Access Method) and other host communication software

## Public-Key Cryptography

Assume Bob and Alice want to exchange private encrypted messages over an insecure system like the Internet. They choose an encryption method that will make the messages unreadable to any person who happens to capture the transmissions. Bob encrypts the message using an encryption key. Alice must have this key to decrypt the message. Now, the basic problem: How does Bob get the key to Alice so she can decrypt the message? Bob could call Alice on the phone, but what if the phone line is tapped? Another method is to send the key in a separate e-mail message or via courier, but what if that message is intercepted along the way? This may seem paranoid, but consider that military communications are under constant scrutiny by attackers or foreign defense agencies. The same threat extends into the competitive corporate world and the financial world.

Traditionally, both the sender and receiver have already agreed on a key and have established some trust. For example, before leaving port, the captain of a submarine is handed a decoder book that will unscramble encrypted radio messages from home port. This is *symmetric cryptography* (both parties know the same secret key), and it is often referred to as just *private-key cryptography* or *secret-key cryptography*. DES (Data Encryption Standard) is a common secret-key encryption method. See "DES (Data Encryption Standard)."

But it is not always the case that both parties in a message exchange know and/or trust each other and have exchanged any keys in advance. To resolve these problems, Whitfield Diffie and Martin Hellman developed *asymmetric public-key cryptography* in the mid 1970s. Basically, anybody who wants to encrypt and send messages to someone else generates a pair of security keys. One key is kept private and the other is put in a public place, much like the phone book is a public list of people's phone numbers. If someone wants to send you a private message, they obtain your public key, encrypt the message with it, then send you the message. Only your private key can decrypt the message. Someone who intercepts the message cannot decrypt it with the generally available public key.

> **NOTE:**   *Although Diffie and Hellman developed asymmetric public-key cryptography, it was RSA (Rivest, Shamir, Adleman) Data Systems (now part of Security Dynamics) that turned it into a workable and commercial system.*

Figure P-15 illustrates public-key cryptography in action. Sue and Joe want to exchange secure messages. Both Sue and Joe are on the same company network and so have easy access to a security server where they can store their public keys.

1. Sue and Joe, and everybody else in the company, generate a set of keys using software commonly found in Web browsers or e-mail applications.

2. Everyone places their public key on the company's public-key server. Alternatively, a public service called a CA (certificate authority) can manage public keys.

3. When Joe wants to send a secure message to Sue, he obtains Sue's public key from the security server, encrypts the message with it, and sends it to Sue.

4. Sue receives the message and decrypts it with her private key.

The public-key scheme solves the problem of passing keys to other parties who need to decrypt your messages. In fact, it allows any person to encrypt a message and send it to another person without any prior exchange or agreement. It is not even necessary that the parties know each other, be part of the same organization, or exchange anything with one another prior to exchanging private messages. All that is required is that both parties have a way to exchange public keys.

This is where *key management* comes into the picture. Key management is all about making public keys available for general use. If individuals want to send you a message, they need to obtain a copy of your public key. On a private network, they might get it in a shared directory on a key management server that holds keys for everyone in the organization. On the Internet, CAs (certificate authorities), like

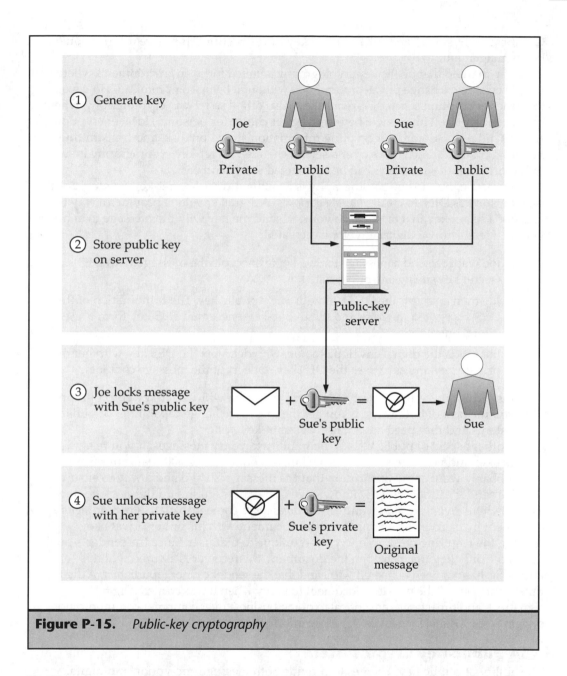

① Generate key

Joe

Sue

Private    Public    Private    Public

② Store public key
on server

Public-key
server

③ Joe locks message
with Sue's public key

Sue's public
key

Sue

④ Sue unlocks message
with her private key

Sue's private
key

Original
message

**Figure P-15.** *Public-key cryptography*

VeriSign, Commerce Net, and even the U.S. Postal Service provide key management. An important role of the CA is to guarantee to other people that your public key is authentic, just as the banking system verifies credit cards. See "Certificates and

Certification Systems" and "PKI (Public-Key Infrastructure)" for more information on key management.

Keep in mind that public-key cryptography is suited for open environments where people need to exchange private information without it being compromised. However, the other encryption scheme—private-key (also called *secret-key*) cryptography, where data is encrypted with a single key—is a better choice for personal/local encryption, such as hiding passwords, encrypting information stored on disk, and transmitting information to a branch office over a secure channel. Secret-key cryptography is suited for environments where keys can be exchanged safely and easily.

In practice, public-key cryptography is combined with a secret-key cryptography system, such as DES, to create *digital envelopes.* A digital envelope provides a way to encrypt a secret key in a message so you can send the key with the message to another person. Here's how a digital envelope is created:

1. Joe want to send a message to Sue, so he encrypts the message with DES (secret key) using an appropriate key.

2. Joe then encrypts the DES key with Sue's public key. The combination of the DES-encrypted message and the public-key-encrypted DES key form a digital envelope.

3. Joe sends the digital envelope to Sue, who decrypts the DES key with her own private key and then uses the DES key to decrypt the message contents.

This technique combines public-key cryptography with secret-key cryptography to give you the best of both worlds. You get the secure exchange capabilities of public-key systems and the speed advantages of secret-key systems.

Another aspect of public keys is their ability to verify messages. If you're a stockbroker and you receive a message from a client to buy 1,000 shares of Microsoft, you probably want some verification that the message is valid and a way to ensure that the sender cannot disavow knowledge of the message should the stock go down. This is where *digital signatures* and *digital timestamps* come into play. A person *signs* a document by encrypting all or part of the document with his or her private key, making the resulting message encryption unique to that user. Since the sender's public key is the only key that can open the document, the receiver is assured that it is authentic, has not been tampered with, and that the sender cannot repudiate it. A digital timestamp "binds" the time to a document to verify when it was created. Digital signatures and timestamps are critical to doing business over computer communication systems. See "Digital Signatures" for more information.

## The RSA Public-Key Cryptosystem

The ability of public-key schemes to provide both message encryption and digital signatures is a boon to communication over digital networks. The strength of the encryption becomes the defining factor for ensuring privacy. The size of the key ensures that encrypted information will be secure for a long time.

If you're a real crypto-head, you might be wondering how the public and the private keys are generated in the RSA cryptosystem. First, the RSA system is based on taking two large prime numbers and multiplying them to produce a key. From this, it follows that *factoring* is the process of attempting to discover the original key by finding the prime numbers that were multiplied together to create it. Factoring is mentioned because it is the technique that someone might use to discover a key and open private messages, as discussed in a moment.

The RSA paper *Frequently Asked Questions About Today's Cryptography* describes RSA public-key cryptography as follows: "Take two large primes, $p$ and $q$, and find their product $n = pq$; $n$ is called the modulus. Choose a number, $e$, less than $n$ and relatively prime to $(p-1)(q-1)$, which means that $e$ and $(p-1)(q-1)$ have no common factors except 1. Find another number, $d$, such that $(ed-1)$ is divisible by $(p-1)(q-1)$. The values $e$ and $d$ are called the public and private exponents, respectively. The public key is the pair $(n,e)$; the private key is $(n,d)$. The factors $p$ and $q$ may be kept with the private key, or destroyed. It is difficult (presumably) to obtain the private key $d$ from the public key $(n,e)$. If one could factor $n$ into $p$ and $q$, however, then one could obtain the private key $d$. Thus the security of RSA is related to the assumption that factoring is difficult. An easy factoring method or some other feasible attack would 'break' RSA."

A *cryptanalyst* is a person who analyzes and attacks a cipher. *Factoring* is the technique that cryptanalysts use to split the modulus into the original integers that were multiplied together to obtain it. Prime factorization requires splitting an integer into factors that are prime numbers. The strength of the public-key system relies on the fact that multiplying two prime integers together is easy, but factoring the product is difficult (at least to date). Factoring an RSA modulus would allow an attacker to figure out the private key and decrypt messages and forge signatures. Because factoring large numbers takes more time than factoring small numbers, the bigger the modulus, the more resistant it is to attack.

In most cases, attacks require time, money, and coordination of resources. A. M. Odlyzko showed in 1995 that a 512-bit RSA key could be factored for less than $1,000,000 with eight months of effort. Factoring has become easier because of more powerful computer hardware and because better factoring algorithms have been developed. But at the same time, hardware improvements make RSA more secure. Users can simply choose larger keys (without degrading performance) to minimize factoring threats.

**RELATED ENTRIES**    Certificates and Certification Systems; Cryptography; Digital Signatures; PKI (Public-Key Infrastructure); Private-Key Cryptography; *and* Security

## INFORMATION ON THE INTERNET

RSA Data Security, Inc.                    http://www.rsa.com

RSA's Cryptography FAQ                 http://www.rsa.com/PUBS

Ron Rivest's Links (possibly the most complete set of links on the Web)

http://theory.lcs.mit.edu/~rivest/crypto-security.html

Gateway to Information Security, Inc.

http://www.securityserver.com/cgi-local/ssis.pl/category/@rsa.htm

The Computer Virus Help Desk (a good archive of encryption software and information)

http://iw1.indyweb.net/~cvhd/crypto.html

## Public-Key Infrastructure

*See* PKI (Public-Key Infrastructure).

## Publish and Subscribe

Publish and subscribe is one way of describing "push" technologies for distributing information over the Internet or on intranets. Users subscribe to a service that publishes information on the Internet. When information content changes or new information is added, the subscriber is automatically updated. Note that current push models rely on client software to automatically check with the publisher to see if new information is available. Models that use *multicast* technology, which provides more efficient delivery systems, are just emerging on a wide scale. See "Multicasting" and "Push" for more information.

## Push

Traditionally, the term *push* defines a way for one computer to send data to another computer without the recipient specifically requesting it. It is the opposite of *pull*, where a client requests some data from another computer. But the assumption is that the computer doing the push has the network address of the recipient. Now the term "push" is associated with the Web and the techniques used by advertisers, information publishers, and news services to automatically provide subscribers with information. The technology is often called *broadcast news technology*, or *netcasting*.

In a nutshell, a user *subscribes* to some push service (such as a stock quote service), and once subscribed, information is automatically delivered to the user (the *push client*) at prescribed intervals. However, the term "push" is used loosely. What many so-called push services are doing is really pull. It's easy to think that the publisher maintains some large list of subscribers and then updates those subscribers as content changes, but this is not what happens in most cases. Most of the current services such as PointCast are really using a "pull that looks like push" model. Client software periodically "checks in" with a publishing server to see if new information is available in the areas that the user has subscribed to.

A true push model is (will be) based on *IP Multicast*, which is described under "IP Multicast" and "Multicasting." With IP Multicast, datagrams are assigned an IP class D address. Hosts that want to receive the datagrams are then assigned the same multicast address (along with their regular IP address). There are over 250 million class D multicast addresses, and thus the potential for that many "channels" of multicast information. Assigning a multicast address to a host is equivalent to subscribing that host to a multicast "channel." Any host can be assigned one or more class D multicast addresses. Multicast datagrams propagate through the Internet in an efficient way to reduce excess traffic. The datagrams only pass through routers that are connected to other routers or to end systems that are designated to receive a particular multicast.

While true IP Multicast push is being developed, we have the "pull that looks like push" model made famous by PointCast. The PointCast system includes a free desktop *ChannelViewer* that lets users select the "channels" of information they want delivered to their desktop. The ChannelViewer works in the background to retrieve information. Publishing services provide what is commonly called *channel changers*. At any time, you can click icons or choose menu options to select a content channel. For example, you could click "Sports" to see the latest sports news, or "Financial" to see the latest financial news.

One supposed advantage to the push model is that it reduces network traffic. Indeed, much of the traffic related to requesting information is eliminated. The alternative to push is traditional Web browsing: you jump from site to site, making selections as you go, all the while waiting for pages to download. Push is much more efficient. You choose the content to be delivered by filling out a subscription form. The push server then knows what you need, thus reducing Web browsing and request packets. However, network traffic will inevitably increase as users request delivery of content that may be largely unnecessary to their day-to-day activities.

Push works on the Internet and on corporate intranets. Companies can set up internal push servers to deliver the latest company news or, more importantly, to provide automatic software updates for corporate client/server programs. Software vendors can also provide automatic software updates over the Internet. But network administrators need to be concerned with the way the push technologies use network resources such as network bandwidth, disk space, and the corporate firewall gateway. If everyone in the company is having news delivered to their desktop through the corporate firewall, high-priority traffic will be impeded.

A number of techniques are used to minimize bandwidth problems, such as delivering only information that has changed, not entire pages. Another technique is to update during idle time. Compression helps as well.

In the near future, more and more people will access the Web at home using TV-like desktop viewers that implement both push and pull technologies. Home users are already used to the way that content is provided to them by TV broadcasters. With push, home users can get a constant stream of content updates and programming schedules, then use pull to make interactive selections. If the bandwidth of the Internet can be boosted to support high-end multimedia content, then the Web is a much better platform for entertaining the masses than one-way broadcast television.

## Microsoft CDF (Channel Definition Format)

Microsoft's pull model is based on a technique called *smart pull,* which is accomplished by an agent called a *crawler* that visits and examines Web sites on a scheduled basis and then either notifies users of the changes or delivers those changes to the user. Web site managers, knowing that crawling is being used, can organize their sites in a way that makes it easier for crawlers to learn the structure of the site, and then create a CDF (Channel Definition Format) file that is basically an index of the Web site. The file implements an open standard format that potentially any Web browser that implements crawling should be able to read and use.

A basic CDF file contains a list of URLs (Uniform Resource Locators) that point to pages at a site. A more useful and advanced CDF can provide users with a very elaborate description of a site and its contents. The CDF lists each page at the site in the form of its URL. The title of the page is given along with an abstract that describes what is on the page. A schedule of updates can also be included. Web site authors can personalize and customize the descriptions of their site, knowing that Web users will be looking through the descriptions as if looking through a table of contents for the site.

Microsoft worked with the W3C (World Wide Web Consortium) to create the CDF file format. It is based on XML (Extensible Markup Language), which lets authors embed rich structured information in Web pages that, while not displayed, can be used for a variety of other purposes. End users benefit from CDF by being able to choose the content they want to download or have pulled to their site. Being able to select the content eliminates the problem of downloading everything from a site.

For more information about CDF, visit the Microsoft or W3C site listed under "Information on the Internet" at the end of this section.

**RELATED ENTRIES**    Broadcast News Technology; Component Software Technology; Distributed Object Computing; Information Publishing; Mailing List Programs; Marimba Castanet; Netcasting; NNTP (Network News Transport Protocol); PointCast; *and* USENET

**INFORMATION ON THE INTERNET**

Thunder Lizard Productions (excellent set    http://www.thunderlizard.com/
of links, articles, and commentary about    wb-links.html
Web broadcasting)

| Terry Kuny's Push page (contains links) | http://www.nlc-bnc.ca/pubs/netnotes/notes41.htm |
| Lee Fleming's digital distribution paper (contains vendor list) | http://www.atvantage.com/atvhome/leaders/dg022700.htm |
| Digital Horizon's push information | http://www.broadband-guide.com/news/dhapr97/dh1.html |
| Netscape Communications' white paper about push | http://home.netscape.com/comprod/at_work/white_paper/vision/print.html |
| Microsoft's Internet Explorer site | http://www.microsoft.com/ie |
| World Wide Web Consortium | http://www.w3.org |

## PVC (Permanent Virtual Circuit)

A virtual circuit is a pathway through a packet-switched, mesh-type network that appears to be a dedicated, physically connected circuit. The virtual circuit is predefined and maintained by the end systems and nodes along the circuit, but the actual pathway through the packet-switched network may change due to routing around downed or busy connections. The important point is that packets are transferred in order over a specific path and arrive at the destination in order.

A *PVC* is a fixed circuit that is defined in advance by a public network carrier (or a network manager on an internal network). The permanence of the line removes the setup overhead and improves performance. A PVC is used on a circuit that includes routers that must maintain a constant connection in order to transfer routing information in a dynamic network environment. Carriers assign PVCs to customers to reduce overhead and improve performance on their networks.

In contrast, an *SVC (switched virtual circuit)* establishes a temporary virtual circuit between individual workstations, with sessions lasting only as long as needed. Once a communication session is complete, the virtual circuit is disabled.

**RELATED ENTRY**   Virtual Circuit

## Px64

Px64 is a set of interoperable videoconferencing standards. Refer to "Videoconferencing and Desktop Video" for more information.

## QAM (Quadrature Amplitude Modulation)

*See* Modulation Techniques.

## QoS (Quality of Service)

QoS describes what you get if you can guarantee the timely delivery of information on networks, control bandwidth, set priorities for selected traffic, and provide a good level of security. QoS is usually associated with being able to deliver delay-sensitive information such as live video and voice while still having enough bandwidth to deliver other traffic, albeit at a lower rate. Prioritization is related to tagging some traffic so that it gets through congested networks before lower-priority traffic.

**NOTE:**   *This section is closely related to the section "Prioritization of Network Traffic." Prioritization is also called* class of service, *or* CoS.

Providing QoS requires improvements in the network infrastructure. One technique is to increase bandwidth by building network backbones with ATM (Asynchronous Transfer Mode) or Gigabit Ethernet switches. It may also mean upgrading a traditional shared LAN to a switched LAN. In addition, new protocols are required that can manage traffic priorities and bandwidth on the network. The following analogy will help put QoS in perspective:

Assume you have the opportunity to redesign metropolitan area freeway systems. Current freeway systems provide no guarantees that you will arrive at your destination on time, nor do they provide priority levels for special traffic, such as emergency vehicles or people who might be willing to pay more for an uncongested lane. This situation is analogous to the "best-effort" delivery model of the Internet, where packets are treated equally and must vie for available bandwidth.

The first task is to determine how to improve the quality of service provided by the freeway. That means reducing or avoiding delays, providing more predictable traffic patterns, and providing some priority scheme so that some traffic can get through in a hurry if necessary.

One obvious solution is to add more lanes, which is equivalent to improving the bandwidth of a network by upgrading to ATM or Gigabit Ethernet. Another solution is to create more direct routes to major destinations, which is equivalent to creating a switched network environment in which dedicated circuits can be set up between any two systems.

The inevitable laws of freeways and networks dictate that new lanes or increased bandwidth will be quickly used up. In the network environment, emerging multimedia applications will eventually use up any extra bandwidth you provide. If you increase the bandwidth, you will still need to provide services that manage it. This is where new network QoS protocols come into play.

Q

In the freeway analogy, assume you set aside one lane for special use, for emergency vehicles and buses, for example. Another lane is set aside for people that qualify to use it, such as diamond lanes that can be used by vehicles with two or more passengers. On networks, we can reserve some bandwidth and only make it available to qualified users such as managers, special applications such as videoconferencing, or special protocols such as SNA (Systems Network Architecture), which must be delivered within a specific time period to prevent time-outs.

Prioritization assumes that someone is managing priorities. If more people ride-share, then even the diamond lanes become jammed, so you might want to establish some other means of controlling access, such as pay-for-use through a tollgate. Then, anyone that is willing to pay for uncongested lanes can get access to the lanes. If usage increases, so can the fee. Eventually, the system will balance, at least in theory. Some people may gain access to special lanes because of political connections, government service, or credits earned through community service. The driver is identified and authorized via a computerized system that controls such policies.

In the internal network environment, user priorities are set by network managers on *policy* servers. On the Internet, priorities and bandwidth are provided on a pay-for-use basis. This prevents anyone from hogging bandwidth, but it requires that ISPs (Internet service providers) have agreements with other ISPs to establish a user's requested QoS across the Internet and that they have accounting/billing systems in place to charge customers.

## ATM QoS

Providing QoS on ATM networks is relatively easy for a number of reasons. First, ATM uses fixed-size cells for delivering data, as opposed to the variable-size frames used in the LAN environment. The fixed size makes it easy to predict throughput and bandwidth requirements. Assume you are trying to figure out how many vehicles pass through a tunnel per hour. That's easy if all the vehicles are the same size, but if the vehicles are cars, buses, and semi trucks, the varying sizes make it difficult to determine the throughput in advance. The advantage of ATM's fixed-size cells is that service providers can allocate network bandwidth in advance and create contracts with their clients that guarantee a QoS.

ATM is also connection oriented. Cells are delivered over *virtual circuits* in order, an important requirement for real-time audio and video. Before any data can be sent, a virtual circuit must be set up. This circuit may be preestablished or set up on demand (switched). In the latter case, the network will only provide the circuit if it can fulfill the user's request. QoS for in-house networks is set up based on administrative or other policies. If the network is connected to a carrier's ATM network, the QoS parameters may be passed on to that network as well.

Applications are just emerging that can make QoS requests of ATM networks for services such as emulated circuits with a specific bandwidth. Common ATM QoS parameters include *peak cell rate* (maximum rate in cells per second required to deliver the user data), *minimum cell rate* (minimum acceptable cell rate that the ATM network must provide; if the network cannot provide this rate, the circuit request is rejected), *cell loss ratio* (cell loss that is acceptable), *cell transfer delay* (delay that is acceptable), and *cell error ratio* (cell error rate that is acceptable).

During the call setup phase, ATM performs a set of procedures called CAC (connection admission control) to determine whether it can provide the requested ATM connection. Admission is determined by calculating the bandwidth requirements that will be needed to satisfy the user's request for service. If the circuit is granted, the network monitors the circuit to ensure that the requested parameters are not exceeded. If traffic exceeds the contracted level for the circuit, the network may drop packets in that circuit rather than other circuits. However, if bandwidth is available, the network may allow traffic to exceed the contracted amount.

## Bandwidth and QoS in the Carrier Networks

Having enough bandwidth has always been a problem in the WAN environment. On fixed-rate leased lines, packets are dropped when traffic exceeds the available rate. Techniques for providing bandwidth on demand solved these problems to some extent. Upon sensing an excess load, a router would dial one or more additional lines to handle the excess load. This is discussed under "Bandwidth on Demand."

Carrier-based packet-switched networks such as frame relay and ATM are designed to handle temporary peaks in traffic. Customers contract for a specific CIR (committed information rate), and that CIR can be exceeded for an additional charge if network bandwidth is available.

Still, packet-switched networks must provide some guarantees that priority traffic can get through ahead of nonpriority traffic and that real-time traffic can make it through the network in time. That is where QoS comes in. X.25 packet-switched networks support a variety of QoS features, which were needed in order to guarantee delivery. However, data rates on X.25 were slow. In contrast, frame relay networks do not have many QoS features because the designers traded them off for speed. On the other hand, ATM was designed from the ground up for speed and for quality of service, as described earlier.

### Cisco IOS QoS Services

Cisco IOS (Internetwork Operating System) is a platform for delivering and managing network services. Cisco IOS QoS is a set of IOS extensions that provide end-to-end QoS across heterogeneous networks. ISPs can use it to provide QoS across their networks and to charge customers for bandwidth usage.

Cisco IOS QoS services can provide congestion control; preferential treatment of higher-priority traffic; sorting and classifying of packets into traffic classes or service

Q

levels; the ability to commit bandwidth and enforce the commitment; measurement and metering of traffic for billing/accounting and network performance monitoring; and resource allocation based on physical port, address, and/or application. Another important feature is support for networks built with different topologies (such as routers, frame relay, ATM, and tag switching) to cooperate in providing QoS from end system to end system. These services are provided by the following features:

- **IP Precedence**   This is used to partition traffic into up to six classes of service. Congestion handling and bandwidth allocation are then managed for each class based on extended ACLs (access control lists). Precedence can be set by customers or by defined policies. Customer applications set class of service assignments in packets by changing bits in the Type-of-Service field in the IP header. In heterogeneous environments where networks consist of different network technologies (frame relay, ATM, tag switching), precedence can be mapped into the frame or cell to provide end-to-end QoS. Thus precedence can be set without external signaling or major changes to applications.

- **CAR (Committed Access Rate)**   The network operator uses CAR to allocate bandwidth commitments and limitations and to handle traffic that exceeds bandwidth allocations. CAR thresholds are applied based on IP address, port, or application flows.

- **NetFlow Switching**   Provides a boost in performance by routing the first packet in a "flow" and caching the information required to send that packet through the network. Subsequent packets are forwarded based on the information in the cache, which reduces packet processing. NetFlow also collects data about flows for accounting/billing purposes and provides security.

- **RED (Random Early Detection)**   Allows network operators to manage traffic during periods of congestion based on policies. RED works with TCP to provide fair reductions in traffic proportional to the bandwidth being used. WRED (weighted RED) works with IP Precedence to provide preferential traffic handling for higher-priority packets.

- **WFQ (Weighted Fair Queuing)**   Provides a way to handle delay-sensitive, high-priority traffic in an expeditious way while fairly sharing the remaining bandwidth between lower-priority traffic.

Applications can request a specific QoS through the RSVP (Resource Reservation Protocol). Cisco IOS QoS services then take the RSVP requests and map them into high-priority packets that are tunneled through the ISP backbone to the far-end router where they are converted back to RSVP signals. According to Cisco, this method maintains the benefits of RSVP but avoids the overhead of using it in the backbone network.

In general, Cisco IOS QoS provides a way for ISPs to "generate revenue by defining, customizing, delivering and charging for differentiated, value-added network services," according to Cisco. It allows ISPs to offer multiple service tiers with different pricing policies based on usage, time of day, and traffic class.

## QoS on the Internet and Intranets

A number of trends are providing a network infrastructure for delivering real-time multimedia over internal networks. These are the explosive growth of Web protocols, the use of switched networks that provide dedicated Ethernet, and the use of high-speed backbones (ATM or Gigabit Ethernet). Bandwidth management protocols are needed to complete the picture.

The Internet community has come up with RSVP as a way to provide QoS on the Internet and on intranets. RSVP is mostly a router-to-router protocol in which one router requests that another router set aside (reserve) a certain bandwidth for a specific transmission. Each router along a path from the source to the destination is asked to set aside bandwidth. RSVP is discussed further under "RSVP (Resource Reservation Protocol)."

At the time of this writing, a number of IETF (Internet Engineering Task Force) working groups were working on QoS-related network protocols, as outlined here:

■ The IETF QoS Routing (qosr) Working Group is defining QoS routing techniques for the Internet. QoS routing is concerned with finding packet-forwarding paths that provide requested services. These paths may not be the traditional "shortest path," but paths that meet the class and quality of service requested by the user. New packet-handling techniques are required to find paths that provide these services. The qosr Web site is located at http://www.ietf.org/html.charters/qosr-charter.html.

■ The IETF Audio/Video Transport (avt) Working Group is developing protocols for real-time delivery of audio and video over UDP (User Datagram Protocol) and IP multicast networks. The group is responsible for RTP (Real-time Transport Protocol) and for RFCs (requests for comment) that define payload formats for JPEG, MPEG, and videoconferencing standards. The avt Web site is at http://www.ietf.org/html.charters/avt-charter.html. See also "RTP (Real-time Transport Protocol)" for more information.

■ The IETF Integrated Services (intserv) Working Group is concerned with the transport of audio, video, and other data over the Internet. The group is defining and documenting the services that will be provided by this enhanced Internet service model. It is also defining application interfaces and a new set of routing requirements that will ensure that the Internet can support the new service model. The intserv Web site is located at http://www.ietf.org/html.charters/intserv-charter.html.

■ The IETF Integrated Services over Specific Link Layers (issll) Working Group is developing extensions for the IP architecture that will allow applications to request and receive a specific level of service from the internetwork on which to transmit audio, video, and data. Several technologies have been developed, including integrated services over shared and switched LAN technology, as well as ATM networks. A number of Internet drafts are available at the issll Web site at http://www.ietf.org/html.charters/issll-charter.html.

■ The IETF Resource Reservation Setup Protocol (rsvp) Working Group is responsible for developing the RSVP specification. RSVP is discussed further under "RSVP (Resource Reservation Protocol)." The rsvp Web site is at http://www.ietf.org/html.charters/rsvp-charter.html.

## QoS from the Application Perspective

Much of the work being done to provide QoS on intranets and the Internet was still under development at the time of this writing. However, applications such as Microsoft NetMeeting provide some insight into how an application itself can optimize bandwidth usage. NetMeeting is basically a videoconferencing solution that operates over corporate networks and the Internet. It allows users to transfer files and engage in "whiteboard" sessions (displaying and editing graphics) during the videoconference.

Microsoft calls NetMeeting a "bandwidth-smart" application because it has built-in mechanisms for caching, compressing, and optimizing transmissions. Policies can be set to restrict the amount of bandwidth that the application uses for audio and video so that administrators can prevent the application from hogging bandwidth.

During normal NetMeeting operation, separate audio, video, and data streams are transmitted across the network. Data streams constitute the whiteboard sessions and control information. NetMeeting treats the audio stream with the highest priority, followed by the data stream and then the video stream. Four transmission modes can be selected: 14.4 Kbits/sec, 28.8 Kbits/sec, ISDN (Integrated Services Digital Network), and LAN speeds. NetMeeting then automatically balances the three separate streams according to their priorities and the available bandwidth. In the lowest-bandwidth configuration, the video image may appear mostly as a still image that changes only occasionally.

NetMeeting transmits a complete video frame every 15 seconds and then refreshes the image with changes as they occur. It also does some unique things to reduce the amount of data going over the line. For example, graphic information may reside in a queue temporarily before being transmitted. If part of that waiting image changes while it is still in the queue, only the new information is sent and the old information is discarded rather than being sent across the link and then immediately overlapped by the new image.

**RELATED ENTRIES**    ATM (Asynchronous Transfer Mode); Bandwidth on Demand; Cell Relay; CIF (Cells in Frames); Fast IP; IP over ATM; IP Switching; ISA (Integrated Services Architecture); Prioritization of Network Traffic; RSVP (Resource Reservation Protocol); RTP (Real-time Transport Protocol); Switched Networks; Tag Switching; *and* VLAN (Virtual LAN)

## INFORMATION ON THE INTERNET

| | |
|---|---|
| IETF Integrated Services (intserv) Working Group | http://www.ietf.org/html.charters/intserv-charter.html |
| IETF Integrated Services over Specific Link Layers (issll) Working Group | http://www.ietf.org/html.charters/issll-charter.html |
| Cisco Systems, Inc. | http://www.cisco.com |
| European Workshop for Open Systems' QoS page | http://www.ewos.be/qos/gtop.htm |
| Medhavi Bhatia's QoS over the Internet: The RSVP protocol paper | http://www.rvs.uni-hannover.de/people/neitzner/Studienarbeit/literatur/more/rsvp.html |
| Applied Research Laboratory QoS paper with links | http://www.arl.wustl.edu/arl/refpapers/gopal/os.html |
| Saurav Chatterjee's QoS-related papers and links | http://www.erg.sri.com/projects/quasar |

## Radio Communication and Networks

*See* AMPS (Advanced Mobile Phone Service); CDPD (Cellular Digital Packet Data); Cellular Communication Systems; GSM (Global System for Mobile Communications); Microwave Communications; Mobile Computing; PCS (Personal Communications Services); Satellite Communication Systems; *and* Wireless Communications.

## RADIUS (Remote Authentication Dial-In User Service)

RADIUS is a service for authenticating and authorizing dial-up users. A typical site has an access server attached to a modem pool. A RADIUS server is attached to the network as a third-party authentication service. Remote users dial into the access server, and the access server requests authentication services from the RADIUS server. The RADIUS server authenticates users and allows them to access resources. The access server is essentially a client to the RADIUS server.

As an example, Steel-Belted RADIUS from Funk Software is a full implementation of the RADIUS standard that runs on Novell NetWare or Windows NT servers. Steel-Belted RADIUS serves as a single centralized remote access authentication server that can use the user accounts, groups, passwords, and other security information already available in NetWare's Bindery and NDS (Novell Directory Services), or Windows NT Domains and Workgroups. Administrators create user profiles at the RADIUS server that determine the authorizations that are given to remote dial-up users. A challenge/response protocol is used during user logon to avoid sending passwords in clear text over the communication link. See "Challenge/Response Protocol" for more information.

**RELATED ENTRIES**    Access Server; Authentication and Authorization; Communication Server; Mobile Computing; Remote Access; Security; TACACS (Terminal Access Controller Access Control System); *and* Token-Based Authentication

### INFORMATION ON THE INTERNET

| | |
|---|---|
| IETF RFC 2058 (RADIUS) | http://www.internic.net/rfc/rfc2058.txt |
| RADIUS links at Gateway to Information Security | http://www.securityserver.com/cgi-local/ssis.pl/category/@radius.htm |
| Livingston Enterprises' RADIUS white papers and FAQs | http://www.livingston.com/Marketing/Products/radius.shtml |
| Funk Software's RADIUS page | http://www.funk.com/sbrframe.html |
| RADIUS links (under Authentication section) | http://www.spitbrook.destek.com/isp |
| Bay Networks, Inc. (choose "White Papers") | http://www.baynetworks.com/Products/Papers |

R

# RAID (Redundant Arrays of Inexpensive Disks)

RAID defines techniques for combining disk drives into arrays. Data is written across all drives, which improves performance and protects data. The alternative is to use one large drive, which does not have the performance benefits of an array and is a single point of failure.

A RAID appears as a single drive. Data is written evenly across the drives by using a technique called *striping*. Striping divides data over two or more drives, as shown by the crude example in Figure R-1. The figure shows characters for clarity, but data is usually written in blocks to sectors on each drive. A data file that might take 4 seconds to write on a single drive can be striped to four separate drives in 1 second. Likewise, disk reads are improved because there is a speed advantage in simultaneously reading data from four separate drives.

One form of RAID (level 3, as discussed in the following list) provides redundancy that protects against the failure of one disk in the array. Parity information is generated from the data written to each of the RAID drives, and that parity information is written to a backup drive. If one drive in the array fails, the parity information can be used to rebuild the information that is not available due to the failed drive. However, this parity technique does not provide protection if multiple drives fail. Therefore, some vendors have come up with their own redundancy schemes. Some examples can be found at the Advanced Computer & Network Corp. Web site given later.

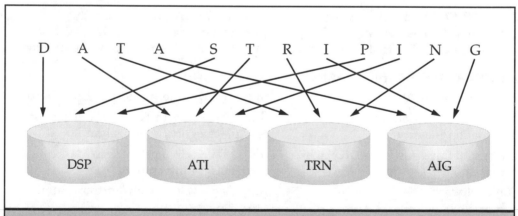

**Figure R-1.**    *RAID systems stripe data over several drives*

RAID levels 0 through 5 are outlined in the following list. As mentioned, other levels of RAID have been developed, but some are proprietary. Additional information can be found at the Web sites given later.

- **RAID level 0**  Data is striped over several drives, but there is no redundant drive.

- **RAID level 1**  Data is striped to an array of drives, and each drive is also mirrored to a backup drive for added protection.

- **RAID levels 2, 3, and 4**  Data is striped to multiple disks, and parity information is generated and written to a separate parity disk. Each level defines different ways to write data to disk.

- **RAID level 5**  Data is written in disk sector units to all drives in the drive array. Error-correction codes are also written to all drives. This level provides quicker writes because the parity information is spread over all the drives rather than being written to a single parity drive.

**RELATED ENTRIES**    Backup and Data Archiving; Clustering; Data Migration; Data Protection; Disaster Recovery; Fault Management; Fault Tolerance; Mirroring; Replication; Storage Management Systems; *and* Storage Systems

### INFORMATION ON THE INTERNET

| | |
|---|---|
| Advanced Computer & Network Corp.'s RAID technology overview | http://www.acnc.com/raid.html |
| RAID links at LAN Times Online | http://www.lantimes.com/lantimes/buyers/index/c126.html |
| DynaTek's RAID overview | http://www.dynatek.co.uk/pages/dptraid.htm |

# Rainbow Series

Rainbow Series is the name given to a set of documents published by the NCSC (National Computer Security Center). The documents describe the requirements in the TCSEC (Trusted Computer System Evaluation Criteria). TCSEC is a collection of criteria used to grade or rate the security offered by computer systems. The documents are printed with different colored covers, hence the name. TCSEC and most of the other Rainbow Series documents are available at the Web address under the subheading, "Information on the Internet."

**RELATED ENTRIES**    C2 Security Rating; Security; TCSEC (Trusted Computer System Evaluation Criteria); *and* TPEP (Trusted Product Evaluation Program)

**INFORMATION ON THE INTERNET**

Rainbow Series library     http://www.radium.ncsc.mil/tpep/library/rainbow

NCSC FAQ     http://www.radium.ncsc.mil/tpep/process/faq-sect2.html

## RAM Mobile Data

RAM Mobile Data USA Limited Partnership is a business venture between RAM Broadcasting Corporation and Bell South. It provides two-way wireless communication services for mobile users. Services cover most of the United States, with relatively low transmission speeds of 8 Kbits/sec. However, the service is inexpensive and was originally designed for the consumer market.

RAM's core technology is Mobitex, an international standard for two-way wireless data communications, currently operational in 18 countries worldwide. It covers more than 93 percent of the urban business population. RAM's market is interactive paging, computing/office automation, transportation, wireless LAN-based access, and more.

The RAM Mobile Data Web site given below under "Information on the Internet" describes how RAM's network competes with CDPD (Cellular Digital Packet Data) and the ARDIS (Advanced National Radio Data Service) network.

**RELATED ENTRIES**    ARDIS (Advanced National Radio Data Service); CDPD (Cellular Digital Packet Data); Cellular Communication Systems; Mobile Computing; Packet-Radio Communications; *and* Wireless Communications

**INFORMATION ON THE INTERNET**

RAM Mobile Data USA         http://www.ram-wireless.com

## RARP (Reverse Address Resolution Protocol)

RARP is part of the TCP/IP protocol suite. It allows a computer, particularly a diskless workstation, to obtain an IP address from a server. When a diskless TCP/IP workstation is booted on a network, it broadcasts a RARP request packet on the local network. This address packet is broadcast on the network for all to receive because the workstation does not know the IP address of the server that can supply it with an address. It includes its own physical network address (the MAC address) in the request so the server will know where to return a reply. The server that receives the request looks in a table and matches the MAC address with an IP address, and then returns the IP address to the diskless workstation. See also "ARP (Address Resolution Protocol)."

## RBOCs (Regional Bell Operating Companies)

The RBOCs were formed as a result of the breakup of AT&T and are based on a restructuring agreement that took effect in 1984. The final restructuring agreement was the United States District Court's Modification of Final Judgment (MFJ). MFJ ended the Justice Department's suit against AT&T. The RBOCs were organized into seven regional Bell holding companies called Ameritech, Bell Atlantic, Bell South, Nynex, Pacific Telesis, Southwestern Bell, and US West. Each RBOC was assigned a specific geographical area, and each geographical area was divided into service areas called LATAs (local access and transport areas).

> *NOTE:* *See "Telecommunications Companies" in Appendix A for a list of carrier Web sites.*

ITCs (independent telephone companies), which are non-Bell companies, may also offer services within the LATA area. IXCs (interexchange carriers) such as AT&T, MCI, and Sprint were allowed to operate long-distance services but not local services. The Telecommunications Act of 1996 changed the restrictions that were imposed on carriers. Long-distance carriers such as AT&T, MCI, and Sprint can now offer services in local areas, and the LECs can offer long-distance services.

**RELATED ENTRIES** AT&T (American Telephone and Telegraph); Communication Service Providers; Communication Services; IXC (Interexchange Carrier); LEC (Local Exchange Carrier); Telecommunications and Telephone Systems; *and* WAN (Wide Area Network)

## Real-Time Network Services

*See* Multimedia; Prioritization of Network Traffic; QoS (Quality of Service); RSVP (Resource Reservation Protocol); *and* RTP (Real-time Transport Protocol).

## Red Book

The Red Book is part of the Rainbow Series of documents published by the NCSC (National Computer Security Center) that describe the requirements in the TCSEC (Trusted Computer System Evaluation Criteria). TCSEC is a collection of criteria used to grade or rate the security offered by computer systems. The documents are printed with different colored covers, thus the name Rainbow Series. In particular, the Red Book, which has the official title "Trusted Network Interpretation (TNI)," describes the TCSEC in terms of computer networks.

**RELATED ENTRIES** C2 Security Rating; Orange Book; Rainbow Series; Security; TCSEC (Trusted Computer System Evaluation Criteria); *and* TPEP (Trusted Product Evaluation Program)

## Redirector

A *redirector* is a program running in a network-attached workstation that intercepts network-related requests and redirects them over the network to file servers or peer workstations. For example, if a workstation user makes a request for local files, the redirector forwards the request to the local operating system. If the request is for files on a network server, the redirector forwards the request out over the network to the appropriate server. The request is placed in a packet with the address of the server. Redirector software is individually installed at each workstation along with the driver software for the network interface adapter installed in the computer.

## Reliable Data Delivery Services

The Internet and IP networks are often called "best effort" connectionless delivery systems. Packets are sent on their way without setting up a connection to ensure that they reach their destination or arrive in order. TCP (Transmission Control Protocol) adds reliability services to the Internet and intranets by adding connection-oriented services. In the Novell NetWare environment, IPX (Internetwork Packet Exchange) provides best effort connectionless services while SPX (Sequenced Packet Exchange) provides reliable connection-oriented services. However, TCP is considered a superior protocol for large internetworks and is now used globally.

**RELATED ENTRIES**    Connection-Oriented and Connectionless Services; TCP (Transmission Control Protocol); *and* Transport Protocols and Services

## Remote Access

Remote access covers a range of techniques that let home users, mobile users, and remote office users access resources on a corporate network. The usual connection method is through a dial-up modem, although remote access may also be through permanently connected leased lines or even across the Internet. The latter option is dramatically changing the way that remote access and wide area networks are configured and used.

Remote access software should let remote users access a network as if they are directly attached to it. Limited bandwidth is usually the biggest hold-up. There are two dial-up connection techniques, as described here and pictured in Figure R-2:

- **Remote node**   In this mode, the user's remote computer becomes another node on the network. All requests and responses cross the dial-up connection.

- **Remote control**   In this mode, the dial-up user remotely controls a computer that is connected to the corporate network. Only keyboard commands and screen updates cross the dial-up connection.

The remote control method can provide better performance for the user, but a dedicated computer must be set up on the corporate LAN that the remote user controls. Access servers that emulate a number of PCs in the same box are available. Remotely controlling a computer at the corporate site cuts down on bandwidth requirements.

The remote node connection allows users to connect to the network using native protocols, such as TCP/IP or IPX, and access the corporate network much like directly

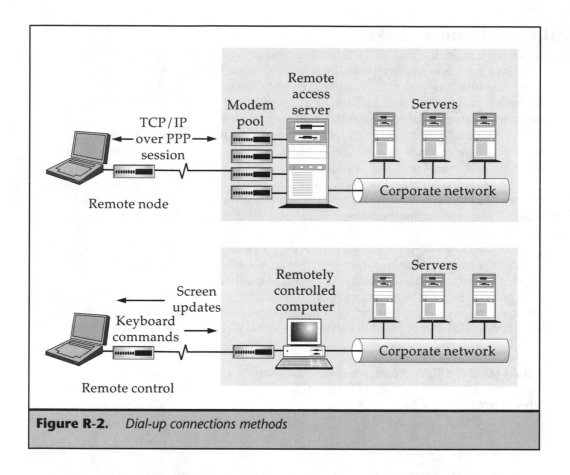

**Figure R-2.**   *Dial-up connections methods*

connected users. Anyone that has connected to the Internet by dialing an ISP (Internet service provider) uses this method. Windows NT and other network operating systems typically include remote node software. Refer to "Access Server" and "Communication Server" for more information.

Virtual dial-up services let users at remote locations dial into a local ISP and obtain a secure tunnel through the Internet to the corporate office. This techniques cuts down on long-distance charges. Refer to "Virtual Dial-up Services" for more information.

The Web provides an interesting alternative to the remote dial-up model. Consider the last time you visited any Web site. You could view information published by the company and probably make database queries into the company's database. The site might also have chat rooms and mailing lists. Companies can offer the same services to their remote users by setting up Web sites that can only be accessed by employees. Once authenticated, remote users can browse corporate Web pages and query the company database.

## LAN-to-LAN Remote Links

A dial-up connection may be sufficient for connecting small remote offices to the corporate network. At some point, the traffic levels will increase to the point where a dedicated link is required. This can be accomplished with a leased line, a connection through a packet-switched network, or a virtual circuit over the Internet. An initial solution is to use a dial-up connection that stays connected, at least during business hours. Eventually, this line may be insufficient. An ISDN (Integrated Services Digital Network) connection is the next choice because it provides circuit-switching and the ability to add more bandwidth as needed. See "Bandwidth on Demand."

The next step up is a dedicated leased line such as T1 (1.544 Mbits/sec) or packet-switched services such as frame relay. These services are discussed further under "Circuit-Switching Services," "Communication Services," and "WAN (Wide Area Network)."

A typical LAN-to-LAN remote connection is pictured in Figure R-3. A router is required at each location, assuming each site has a different network address. The routers are connected via modem, ISDN, T1, or another method.

There are some unique advantages to connecting remote offices over the Internet. The most important are that long-distance charges are reduced and that the links can supplement dedicated leased lines. Refer to "VPN (Virtual Private Network)" for more details.

**RELATED ENTRIES**    Access Server; Authentication and Authorization; Communication Server; Mobile Computing; Security; Virtual Dial-up Services; *and* VPN (Virtual Private Network)

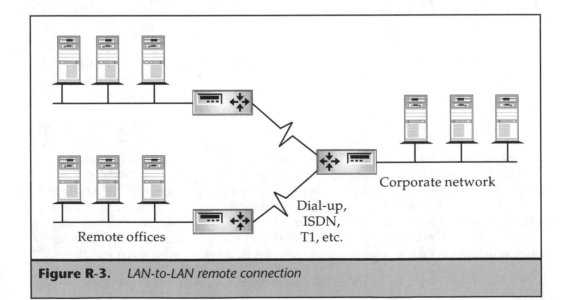

**Figure R-3.**    *LAN-to-LAN remote connection*

**INFORMATION ON THE INTERNET**

| | |
|---|---|
| Yahoo!'s Remote Access links page | http://www.yahoo.com/Computers_and_Internet/Software/Communications_and_Networking/BBS/Remote_Access |
| Bay Networks' remote access and VPN paper | http://www.baynetworks.com/Products/Papers/2746.html |
| Shiva's interesting remote access information | http://www.shiva.com/remote |
| Lantronix's Dial-up Remote Access paper | http://www.lantronix.com/htmfiles/whitepapers/lrswp.htm |
| Xylogics' remote access tutorial | http://www.xylogics.com/prod/white/pages/eliminat.htm |
| LAN Times Online's remote access links | http://www.lantimes.com/lantimes/buyers/index/c166.html |
| Mobile Computing Magazine (see mobile links at this site) | http://www.cfgworld.com/mags/mobilecomputing/index.shtml |
| Mobile Management Task Force (MMTF) | http://www.epilogue.com/mmtf |
| Mobilis: the mobile computing lifestyle magazine | http://www.volksware.com/mobilis |

## Repeater

A repeater is a simple add-on device for extending a network by boosting the cable's signal. As electrical signals are transmitted on a cable, they tend to degenerate in proportion to the length of the cable. This is called *attenuation*. A repeater helps reduce the problems of attenuation. It does not change a signal. Some repeaters also do their best to filter noise. A repeater can provide an extension to a network that reaches a distant workstation, but bridges or routers should be used to extend networks if a lot of additional workstations are involved. Bridges and routers help control traffic problems.

**RELATED ENTRIES**   Bridges and Bridging; Network Concepts; *and* Routers

## Replication

Replication is a strategy for automatically copying data to other systems for backup reasons or to make that data more accessible to people at other locations. Another reason is to distribute the data to multiple servers to spread out traffic loads. Data may be replicated by directories, by database, or by replicating an entire server. One consideration in any replication scheme is whether users are allowed to change data that has been replicated to remote locations. Administrators must take steps to ensure that replication data is kept synchronized across its multiple locations.

Replication is often used on the Internet to duplicate information from one Web site to another and thus ease traffic loads on Web servers. For example, information on a Web server in New York might be replicated to a mirror site in Los Angeles. California users can then access the Los Angeles site, thus avoiding extensive router hops over the Internet to reach the New York site.

Another interesting replication scheme is to duplicate data across a firewall from a secure internal server to a public server. The master data is stored and edited on a secure internal server. The Web server is on the outside of the corporate firewall, where it is considered less secure and potentially open to hacker attacks. If the external server is attacked, it can be rebuilt by replicating data from the internal server.

Microsoft Windows NT Server uses replication to duplicate data to other servers. In Figure R-4, the Windows NT Server computer that holds the master data is called the export server; it replicates data to import servers. An import server on the local LAN acts as a backup device. The import server at the remote location makes data more available to remote users. Users can access data locally rather than accessing the master data over the WAN link. Replication takes place automatically on a periodic basis as files are added to the master directory or as information changes.

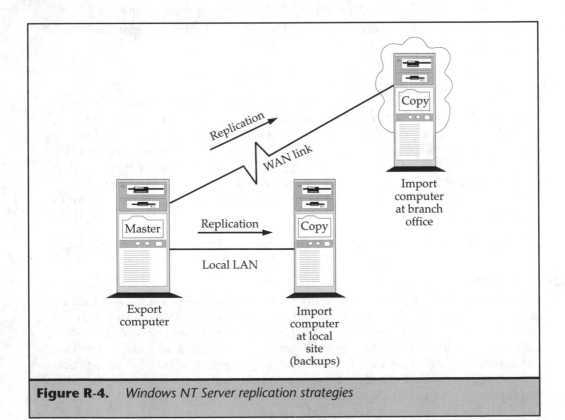

**Figure R-4.** *Windows NT Server replication strategies*

R

In the local environment, users can access either the computer holding the master data or the import computer that holds a copy. This provides *load balancing*. In the third case, replicating data to the branch office on a periodic basis uses much less bandwidth than if multiple users access the master database over the WAN link.

In the Novell NetWare environment, NDS (Novell Directory Services) uses replication to distribute all or part of the directory database to other servers. The database holds user account information and information about resources on the network. Users and administrators access this database to find other users or resources on the network. The database is tree structured, as pictured in Figure R-5, and it can be split into two or more partitions. A partition can be replicated to another location. As shown in the figure, the entire database may be managed by an administrator in the AdminGroup, but the WestDiv portion of the database is partitioned and replicated to the Los Angeles office so users at that site have more direct access to the information in that portion of the database. Refer to "NDS (Novell Directory Services)" for more information.

**RELATED ENTRIES**   Backup and Data Archiving; Data Migration; Data Protection; Directory Services; Disaster Recovery; Fault Management; Fault Tolerance; NDS (Novell Directory Services); *and* Storage Management Systems

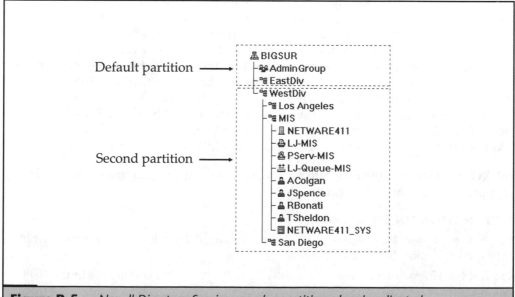

**Figure R-5.**   *Novell Directory Services can be partitioned and replicated*

## Requester Software

Requester software resides in a network-attached workstation. It provides a way for applications running in the workstation to make service requests to devices on the network, such as network servers. The requester software serves as a traffic director, diverting commands for local services to the local operating system and diverting commands for network services to the network protocols running in the workstation. The network protocols package information for delivery over the network and send it to the appropriate destination.

## Reservation of Bandwidth

*See* Prioritization of Network Traffic; QoS (Quality of Service); RSVP (Resource Reservation Protocol); *and* RTP (Real-time Transport Protocol).

## RFC (Request for Comment)

RFCs are the official publications of the Internet and have been used since 1969 to describe and get comments about protocols, procedures, programs, and concepts. They are typically listed by number, such as *RFC 1771*, or name, such as *Border Gateway Protocol 4 (BGP4)*. If you know an RFC number, you can view it in your Web browser by typing the following address and replacing *xxxx* with the RFC number:

    http://www.internic.net/rfc/rfcxxxx.txt

The "Request For Comments indexed by Glimpse" site, listed below under "Information on the Internet," displays a line of text from the RFC for every matching search word. The Nexor RFC Index Search Form site produces a list of titles with short descriptions and hyperlinks to the RFCs that match the search text.

In general, the best place to go for information about all the Internet organizations and committees, and to get a starting place for further links, is the IETF (Internet Engineering Task Force) Web site at http://www.ietf.org. Additional Web sites where you can find RFC information are listed below under the subheading, "Information on the Internet." Refer to "Internet Organizations and Committees" in this book for information about how RFCs are developed in the Internet community.

**RELATED ENTRIES**   Internet; Internet Organizations and Committees; *and* Standards Groups, Associations, and Organizations

### INFORMATION ON THE INTERNET

| | |
|---|---|
| InterNIC documentation (RFCs, FYIs, etc.) with number or text search | http://www.internic.net/ds/dspg0intdoc.html |
| Request For Comments indexed by Glimpse | http://www.pasteur.fr/other/computer/RFC |
| Nexor RFC Index Search Form | http://www.nexor.com/public/rfc/index/rfc.html |

## Rights and Permissions

Network operating systems have access rights (called *permissions* in Windows NT) that are assigned by network administrators to grant users access to file systems, directories, and other resources. For example, the Read right allows a user to open but not change a file, while the Write right lets the user change the file.

Every network operating system has a specific set of rights/permissions, as shown in the Table R-1. Note that some operating systems such as Windows NTFS (NT File System) clearly provide more security options at the directory level than other operating systems.

When a right/permission is granted to a user in a directory, the user typically *inherits* the same right/permission in subdirectories of that directory. Inherited rights are a boon to directory administration because a user or a group of users can be given access to a whole directory tree in one step. However, administrators/supervisors can block inherited rights to prevent users from accessing specific directories in a tree. They can also set custom rights as appropriate.

While most rights/permissions have the same end goal, there are slight differences in their names and usage. A description of the directory and file rights in Novell NetWare follows. You can refer to "Windows NT Permissions" for more information

**R**

| Right/ Permission | MS-DOS | NTFS | NetWare | UNIX | OS/2 | MVS | OS/400 | VAX | VM |
|---|---|---|---|---|---|---|---|---|---|
| No Access | | X | X | X | | X | X | X | X |
| List | | X | X | | | | | X | |
| Read | | X | X | X | | X | X | X | X |
| Add & Read | | X | X | | | | X | | |
| Change (Write) | X | X | X | X | X | X | X | X | X |
| Delete | | X | X | | | X | X | X | X |
| Execute | | X | X | X | | X | X | X | |
| Change Permissions | | X | X | | | X | X | X | X |
| Take Ownership | | X | | * | | | | | |

*Available in some versions

**Table R-1.**   *Rights and Permissions in Network Operating Systems (compiled by Dennis Martin of the Rocky Mountain Windows NT User Group in November, 1994)*

about rights and permissions in the Windows NT environment. Note that *rights* in Windows NT define what types of operations users can perform on servers, while *permissions* define access to objects such as files and resources. For example, there are user rights that allow local logon to a computer, logon from the network, the right to create user accounts, and the right to backup files and directories.

In the NetWare environment, users that are granted access to files, directories, or objects in NDS (Novell Directory Services) are called *trustees*. NetWare includes directory rights that control access to the directories in disk volumes and the files within them, file rights that control access to files within directories, object rights that control who can access and manage objects in the NDS system, and property rights that control who can view and change the properties of objects in the NDS system. The directory and file rights are listed here:

- **Supervisor**   All rights to the directory, its files, and its subdirectories
- **Read**   The right to run programs to open files and read their contents
- **Create**   The right to create new files and subdirectories in the directory
- **Write**   The right to open and change the contents of existing files in the directory
- **Erase**   The right to delete a directory and the files in a directory or subdirectory
- **Modify**   The right to change the attributes or names of directories and files, but not the right to change their contents
- **File Scan**   The right to see the directory and its files by using directory listing commands
- **Access Control**   The right to change the trustee assignments and inherited rights filter of the directory, its files, and its subdirectories

**RELATED ENTRIES**   Access Rights; ACL (Access Control List); File Systems; Novell NetWare File System; Rights and Permissions; Windows NT File System; *and* Windows NT Permissions

## Ring Network Topology

Ring network topology is a closed-loop topology that does not require terminators. The token ring topology forms a logical ring but has the cable layout of a star topology with a central hub. The ring is actually maintained in the hub. When a workstation attaches to the hub, the ring extends out to the workstation through the cable and back again to the hub. If another hub is attached, the ring is maintained by running cables from the ring-out connector on the first hub to the ring-in connector on the second hub, from the ring-out connector on the second hub to the ring-in connector on the first hub. See "Token Ring Network" and "Topology" for more information.

# RIP (Routing Information Protocol)

RIP is an interior or intradomain routing protocol that uses the distance-vector routing algorithms. RIP is used on the Internet and is common in the NetWare environment as a method for exchanging routing information between routers. The Internet standard OSPF (Open Shortest Path First) routing protocol is a successor to RIP. See "Routing Protocols and Algorithms" for more information.

# RISC (Reduced Instruction Set Computer)

Microprocessors have instruction sets called *microcode* that programmers use to create low-level computer programs. The instruction sets perform various tasks, such as moving values into registers or executing instructions to add the values in registers. Microcode can be either simple or complex, depending on the microprocessor manufacturer's preference and the intended use of the chip.

RISC designs, as the name implies, have a reduced set of instructions that improve the efficiency of the processor, but require more complex external programming. RISC designs are based on work performed at IBM by John Cocke. He found that about 20 percent of a computer's instructions did about 80 percent of the work. His 80/20 rule spawned the development of RISC architecture, which reduces the number of instructions to only those that are used most. The other instructions must be implemented in external software.

**RELATED ENTRY**    CISC (Complex Instruction Set Computer)

# RMI (Remote Method Invocation)

RMI is an API for the Java development environment that provides a way for Java applets to cooperate across networks. It provides some of the functionality of CORBA (Common Object Request Broker Architecture) and is similar to IIOP (Internet Inter-ORB Protocol) except that RMI is Java-only while IIOP can be used to access legacy applications.

RMI provides the tools that programmers need to create distributed Java applications (objects) that can invoke methods on other Java applications that are running on other Java virtual machines, such as remote hosts across the Internet. Invoking a method is like asking another program to do something. A Java object must first obtain a reference to another Java object before it can invoke its methods. It may obtain these references via another Java application or it may obtain them through a naming service that is built into RMI.

RMI provides service similar to an ORB (object request broker) but it does not have the functionality or the heterogeneous features of CORBA. It also operates like RPCs (remote procedure calls) in that it can call up the functions of remote objects across networks in a connection-oriented way.

*R*

In July of 1997, RMI's developer, JavaSoft, announced that RMI requests would be enabled to travel over IIOP and that RMI functionality would be built into IIOP.

**RELATED ENTRIES**   Component Software Technology; CORBA (Common Object Request Broker Architecture); Distributed Object Computing; IIOP (Internet Inter-ORB Protocol); Java; ORB (Object Request Broker); *and* Sun Microsystems Solaris NEO

### INFORMATION ON THE INTERNET

| | |
|---|---|
| Sun Microsystems' RMI page | http://www.javasoft.com/products/jdk/1.1/docs/guide/rmi |
| Java and RMI links | http://www.rhein-neckar.de/~cetus/oo_javabeans.html |
| OMG paper evaluating Java, RMI, and CORBA | http://www.omg.org/news/wpjava.htm |
| Frequently Asked Questions on RMI and object serialization | http://www.informatik.fh-wiesbaden.de/~turau/java/serialfaq.html |

# RMON (Remote Monitoring)

RMON is an IETF network monitoring and analysis standard similar to SNMP (Simple Network Management Protocol) that was developed to overcome some of the limitations of SNMP. To put these protocols in perspective, assume you are a city planner and you need to monitor traffic at various intersections throughout the city. One way to do this is to have people (called *agents*) stationed at important intersections to gather traffic information. These agents have portable phones. As they collect traffic information, they write it down. Also part of this scheme are data entry clerks at a central office. They call the agents on a continuous basis to collect the information that agents have obtained and enter it in a computer for future analysis.

The only problem with this technique is the overhead of making all those phone calls. A more efficient method would be to give the agents their own personal computers and have them enter the traffic data as it occurs, then transfer that data to the central office on a regular basis or upon the request of a manager who needs it.

Of course, the less efficient model described above is analogous to traditional SNMP data collection while the more efficient method is related to RMON. Both SNMP and RMON employ *agents*, more commonly called *probes* in RMON, which are software processes running on network devices to collect information about network traffic and store it in a local MIB (management information base). With SNMP, a network management console must continually *poll* the SNMP agents to obtain MIB information. This information is collected to monitor historical trends. Gathering this information not only increases congestion on the network, it also places a large burden on the network management console to gather the information.

With RMON, as pictured in Figure R-6, probes located in network devices such as hubs, routers, and switches collect and maintain historical information. The network management console does not need to constantly poll probes in order to ensure that this historical information is properly collected. In this scheme, the probes are the servers and the management console is the client in a client/server relationship. However, SNMP is not out of this picture. It provides the communication layer for transmitting information between RMON probes and management consoles.

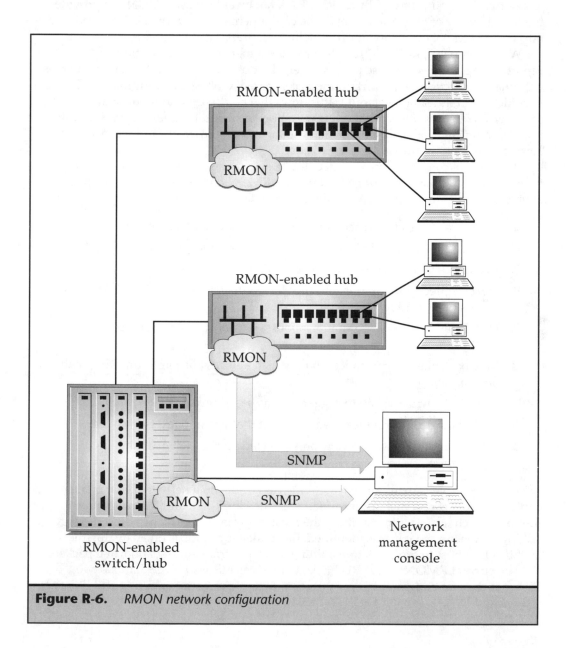

**Figure R-6.**    *RMON network configuration*

A goal of the IETF's RMON standard is to provide vendor-independent monitoring of all LANs from any network management platform. The IETF modeled RMON on the capabilities of traditional LAN analyzers. It supports packet capturing and filtering on specific LAN segments and allows network managers to remotely analyze traffic at all seven layers of the protocol stack. Managers don't need to travel to a network site and physically attach a LAN analyzer because RMON can provide the functionality of a LAN analyzer in the components of the network itself. Vendors implement RMON capability in network hubs, routers, and switches.

When compared to SNMP, RMON provides superior traffic collection and reporting capabilities. Because probes collect their own historical information, there is a dramatic reduction in network traffic as compared to SNMP. In addition, RMON can provide useful information about traffic flows that can be used to monitor and manage sessions. It collects statistics that can reveal short-term and long-term trends in traffic. It can also reveal users and systems that use the most bandwidth, and it can sound alarms when certain thresholds are exceeded.

If abnormal conditions are detected, the manager can take steps to analyze traffic in more detail with the help of RMON probes. RMON has the following groups that enable managers to obtain more detailed information about specific activities:

- **Statistics**   Collects and accumulates LAN traffic statistics and errors
- **History**   Collects statistics at defined intervals for use in historical analysis
- **Alarms**   Provides alerts when predefined thresholds are exceeded
- **Host**   Collects information and provides statistics based on MAC (Medium Access Control) addresses
- **HostTopN**   Collects information about which hosts are transmitting the most traffic
- **Matrix**   Collects information about which devices are communicating with one another
- **Events**   Provides a way to trigger actions based on alarms
- **Packet Capture**   Provides a way to select the type of packets to collect
- **Filter**   Provides a way to view only selected packets when analyzing information

As an example, a manager may detect excess traffic on a network. That manager could then collect and monitor information in the HostTopN and Matrix groups to find out which hosts are transmitting the most information and which host they are talking to. Once a busy host is identified, the manager can focus on analyzing the traffic of that host to see if it is transmitting and/or retransmitting abnormal packets.

The current RMON RFC is RFC 1757, which was released in 1995. It has two Ethernet-specific groups and seven groups that apply to both token ring and Ethernet. The second RMON standard is RFC 1513, which defines token ring extensions.

RMON 2 expands on the features of the original RMON by providing support all the way up to the application layer. In particular, it lets managers monitor the amount of traffic that is produced by individual applications running in workstations and servers. This feature is useful in client/server network environments and provides information about the actual usage of the network, not just traffic flows. RMON 2 can also provide information about end-to-end traffic flows.

One of the most complete overviews of RMON is the Bay Networks' white paper "The Future of RMON: Managing The Client/Server Network," which is available at the Web site listed under this section's subheading, "Information on the Internet."

**RELATED ENTRIES**    Distributed Management; DME (Distributed Management Environment); DMI (Desktop Management Interface); DMTF (Desktop Management Task Force); Network Analyzers; Network Management; SNMP (Simple Network Management Protocol); *and* Testing and Diagnostic Equipment and Techniques

**INFORMATION ON THE INTERNET**

| | |
|---|---|
| Bay Networks' RMON white paper | http://www.baynetworks.com/Products/Papers/rmon.html |
| Lantronix's RMON white paper | http://www.lantronix.com/htmfiles/whitepapers/rmonwp.htm |
| Cabletron's Remote Network Monitoring MIB paper | http://www.ctron.com/white-papers/spectrum/rmonmib.html |
| RMON (RFC 1757) | http://www.internic.net/rfc/rfc1757.txt |
| RMON Token Ring Extensions (RFC 1513) | http://www.internic.net/rfc/rfc1513.txt |
| RMON 2 (RFC 2012) | http://www.internic.net/rfc/rfc2012.txt |
| Traffic Flow Measurement (RFC 2063) | http://www.internic.net/rfc/rfc2063.txt |

# ROLC (Routing over Large Clouds)

*See* ION (Internetworking over NBMA).

# Routers

Routers are internetworking devices. They are used to connect similar and heterogeneous network segments into internetworks, as pictured in Figure R-7. In A, two LANs are connected across a dial-up, ISDN (Integrated Services Digital Network), or leased line via routers. In B, three separate department or divisional networks are interconnected via routers to a backbone network. C represents the hierarchical routing structure of the Internet. End users connect to local ISPs (Internet service providers), which are in turn connected via routers to regional ISPs, which are in turn connected via routers to national ISPs.

Routers allow each interconnected network to retain its subnetwork address, broadcast characteristics, and so on, but each network can still communicate through

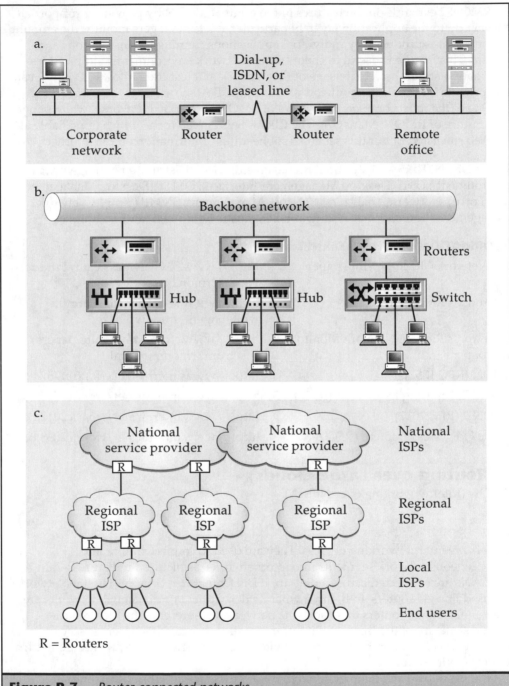

**Figure R-7.** *Router-connected networks*

the router connections with other networks. Bridges, in contrast, typically connect two LAN segments into a single logical LAN with the same network address.

Not all router-connected networks implement the organized hierarchical topology shown in B and C of Figure R-7. Figure R-8 shows a common mesh connection scheme that provides redundancy and multiple paths. In fact, the clouds representing the local, regional, and national network in C of Figure R-7 typically look more like this mesh network.

A packet traveling from A to D requires only one hop. A packet traveling from A to C requires two hops. In this example, no more than two hops are required to reach any point in the internetwork. The links provide redundancy. If link A-B goes down, a packet can still get from A to C by going through F.

A router is basically a box with an input and one or more outputs. Figure R-9 illustrates the back panel of an Ascend Pipeline 75, which can be used to connect an internal Ethernet network to an ISDN WAN link. There is a serial connector for a computer terminal/management station. In addition, there are ports for either thick Ethernet or 10Base-T Ethernet. The port on the right is the ISDN WAN connector for connecting to a remote office via ISDN. Routers may also connect two LANs within an organization. You order routers with the appropriate LAN and WAN interfaces to match your needs.

## Router Operation

Each of the networks attached to an internetwork has a specific network address. Packets are addressed to a destination network and a host on that network. Figure R-8

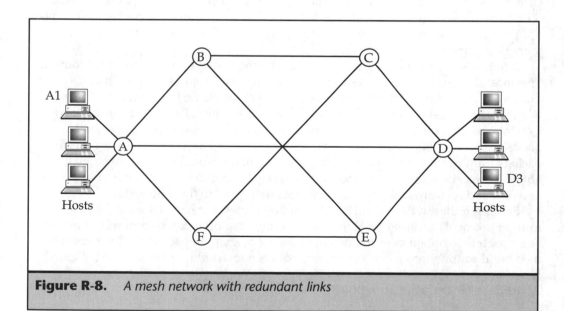

**Figure R-8.**  *A mesh network with redundant links*

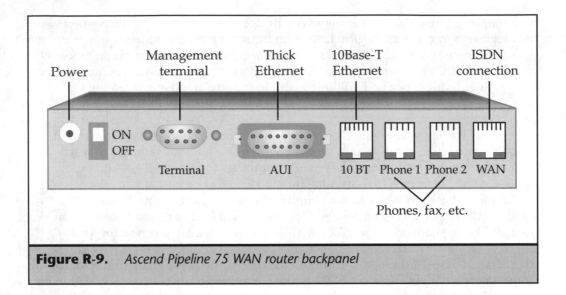

**Figure R-9.**   *Ascend Pipeline 75 WAN router backpanel*

can help illustrate a simple addressing scheme. Assume one of the hosts on network A has the address A1. Likewise, one of the hosts on network D has the address D3. The letter represents the network, and the number represents the node on that network.

Now assume host A1 wants to send a packet to D3. It puts the internetwork address D3 into the packet and forwards the packet to router A. Router A then forwards the packet to router B or F, depending on a number of conditions, such as the current network load or predefined rules. Router B or F forwards the packet to router C or E, which in turn forwards the packet to D. D then forwards the packet to D3. This is the routing scheme of the Internet, and it, as well as IP addressing, is discussed in more detail under "IP (Internet Protocol)."

A traditional router has a processor, some memory, and two or more input/output interfaces. When a router receives a packet, it temporarily stores the packet and examines its header to determine where the packet should be forwarded, to evaluate whether the packet is corrupted, and to check its hop count. Packets are only allowed a certain number of hops. Each router increments the hop count in the packet. If a packet exceeds its hop count, it is considered invalid and dropped. This prevents lost packets from circulating endlessly. If a packet is not corrupted and its hop count has not been exceeded, the router rebuilds the packet header to match the next-hop network and forwards the packet on the port connected to that network.

Finding routes in the network and avoiding routes that have failed is the job of routing protocols and routing algorithms. Routers use protocols to communicate with other routers to obtain information about the topology of the network. The routers then build routing tables that are referenced when forwarding packets. Next, a router forwards packets based on routing table information. See "Routing Protocols and Algorithms" for more information.

## High-Performance Routers

A traditional router can process about 300,000 to 500,000 packets/sec. Higher-end routers operate in the 1-million packet/sec range. New multigigabit routers operate in the millions of packets per second range. A multigigabit router is a router that has been optimized in every way to improve speed. The bus architectures of previous routing devices are replaced with switching matrices, and packet processing is handled by dedicated processors designed specifically for that purpose. The following techniques are used to improve router performance:

- **Routing switch**  A routing switch is a new class of router that uses specially designed ASICs (application-specific integrated circuits) that can perform routing at multigigabit speeds. Older routers rely on a single shared CPU to inspect and forward packets. Rapid City Communications (now part of Bay Networks) combines routing with packet-relay capabilities to achieve bandwidth levels that can accommodate new high-speed networking. Rapid City's f1200 has a 15-Gbit/sec shared memory switch fabric that can potentially forward 7 million packets/sec whether routing, switching, or doing both.

- **Layer 3 switching**  These are protocol software techniques for switching packets that would normally be routed. The techniques are used on switched networks that implement ATM backbones or other switching environments. The basic concept is to detect a "flow" of packets, route the first packet to determine where it is going, and then switch the remaining packets across a layer 2 dedicated path. For more information, refer to "IP Switching" and "Layer 3 Switching/Routing."

**RELATED ENTRIES**    Backbone Networks; Data Communication Concepts; Internet Backbone; IP Switching; Network Concepts; Network Design and Construction; Routing Protocols and Algorithms; Switched Networks; VLAN (Virtual LAN); *and* WAN (Wide Area Network)

### INFORMATION ON THE INTERNET

| | |
|---|---|
| Bay Networks | http://www.baynetworks.com |
| Foundry Networks' router switching papers | http://www.foundrynet.com |
| FORE Systems' edge routing white paper | http://www.fore.com/atm-edu/whitep/intranet.html |
| LAN Times Online's Routers page | http://www.lantimes.com/lantimes/buyers/index/c107.html |
| Yahoo!'s Routing Technology links page | http://www.yahoo.com/Computers_and_Internet/Communications_and_Networking/Routing_Technology |

*R*

# Routing Arbiter

The Routing Arbiter was a creation of Merit Network, the University of California Information Sciences Institute, and the NSF (National Science Foundation). Its purpose was to provide a central place where ISP (Internet service provider) routers could obtain routing updates, thus eliminating the need to establish separate peering sessions with other routers at each exchange point. Route servers provide routing information to ISPs and a boost in throughput that allows ISPs to deliver their customers' data more efficiently through the Internet.

The NSF stopped funding the Routing Arbiter project in December of 1996 and recommended that the route server service go commercial. Merit then launched the RSng (Route Server Next Generation), a commercial service that makes it possible for exchange point operators to purchase route server services from Merit in support of customer peering. According to Merit, the MAE-East and AADS NAPs (network access points), MAE-West, the Digital Internet Exchange in Palo Alto, and the Atlanta-NAP are offering Route Server services through RSng. Not all ISPs choose to use the routing arbiter services. Instead, many ISPs have established and maintain agreements with one another to exchange routing information and network traffic on their own.

**RELATED ENTRIES**    Internet Backbone; Routers

**INFORMATION ON THE INTERNET**

The Routing Arbiter Project (a Merit/ISI collaboration)    http://www.ra.net

Routing Arbiter Project at USC    http://www.isi.edu/div7/ra

# Routing, Multilayer

*See* Layer 3 Switching/Routing.

# Routing Protocols and Algorithms

An internetwork such as a TCP/IP-based intranet or the Internet consists of many interconnected routers and connections among those routers. The internetwork has a "topology" that must be mapped out so routers can determine what to do with packets that must be forwarded to other networks and hosts. Routers use routing protocols and algorithms to dynamically map the network topology and share that information with one another. Hence, routing protocols provide *dynamic routing configuration*. Without routing protocols, network administrators must manually configure routing tables in routers. This is called *static routing*.

Routers store the information in tables and then look it up to determine an optimal path through the network for packets. If the network gets congested or a connection fails, alternate routes can be found in the tables. Over the years, a number of routing protocols have been developed. This section concentrates on those developed for the Internet. You'll find related information under "IP (Internet Protocol)" and "Routers."

## Distance-Vector Routing Protocols

Distance-vector routing protocols base their routing decisions on the number of hops or some predefined cost to a destination. This information is provided by neighboring routers. The technique generally follows the Bellman-Ford algorithm. A common distance-vector routing protocol is RIP (Routing Information Protocol).

A router with a number of ports such as that pictured in Figure R-10 has a cost assigned to each of its ports. These costs are assigned by the network administrator as a value that can show preference for one router over another. Routers inform other routers of their cost assignments, and these neighboring routers add up the costs to come up with a figure that is used to determine the most efficient route through a network. For example:

```
Port 1 cost 10 + neighbor cost 17 = 27
Port 2 cost 20 + neighbor cost 5 = 25
Port 3 cost 30 + neighbor cost 7 = 37
```

In this case, the router would send the packet through port 2 because it represents the least cost to the destination. The neighboring router attached to port 2 will then calculate additional pathways through other routers, if necessary. Note that other routes are used during heavy traffic or for prioritized traffic.

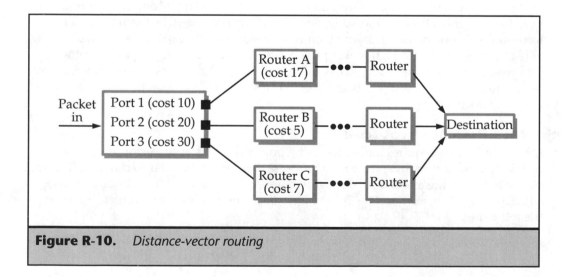

**Figure R-10.**   *Distance-vector routing*

Routing information is exchanged among routers approximately every 30 seconds. From this information, routers rebuild their tables by adding new routes or deleting old routes. Routing tables include network numbers, port numbers, cost metrics, and the address of the next hop. Note that distance-vector routing is not suitable for large networks that have hundreds of routers or networks that are constantly updated. On large networks, the table update process can take so long that tables in the farthest routers may fall out of synchronization with other tables. Link state routing protocols are preferable in these situations, as discussed below under "Link State Routing Protocols."

### RIP (Routing Information Protocol)

RIP is an interior or intradomain routing protocol that uses the distance-vector routing algorithms. RIP is used in TCP/IP and NetWare IPX/SPX (Internetwork Packet Exchange/Sequenced Packet Exchange) networks. While commonly used, OSPF is now taking its place. RIP-based routers request routing information from other routers to update their internal tables, respond to route requests from other routers, periodically broadcast their presence to make sure other routers are aware of the internetwork configuration, and broadcast changes in the internetwork configuration when they are detected.

Some characteristics of RIP are that packets are limited to 15 hops and routing tables are exchanged with other routers approximately every 30 seconds. If a router does not broadcast within 180 seconds, its paths are considered failed. Problems can occur if a router gets behind in rebuilding its routing table, which can occur if that router is connected over a slow WAN link. In addition, exchanging tables can add a lot of overhead, causing congestion and further delays.

RIP version 2 is an extension of the original RIP protocol that provides extensions to the message format which allows routers to share important additional information used for authentication, multicasting, and other features. The IETF Routing Information Protocol (rip) Working Group (Web site given later) developed this version. It feels that although newer protocols such as the link state routing protocols (discussed next) are important, RIP is still useful on small networks. It has little overhead in terms of bandwidth and is easier to set up and manage than the newer protocols.

## Link State Routing Protocols

Link state routing requires more processing power than distance-vector routing but provides more control over the routing process and responds faster to changes. Routes can be based on the avoidance of congested areas, the speed of a line, the cost of using a line, or various priorities. The *Dijkstra algorithm* is used to calculate routes, based on the following:

- Number of routers the packet must go through to get to its destination. These are called hops, and the fewer hops the better.

- The speed of transmission lines between LANs. Some routes use slow asynchronous connections, while other are high-speed digital connections.

- Delays caused by traffic congestion. If a workstation is transmitting a large file, a router might send packets along a different route to avoid congestion.

- Cost of the route, which is a metric defined by an administrator, usually based on the transmission medium. The cheapest route might not be the fastest, but is preferable for some types of traffic.

**R**

The most common link state routing protocol is the OSPF (Open Shortest Path First), but the OSI IS-IS (Intermediate System-to-Intermediate System) is similar. OSPF was originally developed by Proteon and is derived from an early version of the OSI IS-IS. OSPF is used to route IP traffic on the Internet and TCP/IP networks.

Link state routing, as compared to distance-vector routing (i.e., RIP), requires more processing power but provides more control over the routing process and responds faster to changes. OSPF routing table updates only take place when necessary, rather that at regular intervals. This significantly reduces traffic and saves network bandwidth. Paths through the network are selected based on the criteria listed above. A network administrator can program paths through the network based on the type of traffic. For example, a path that uses more hops through the network might be preferable if the lines have higher transmission rates. Alternatively, a path might be programmed for less significant traffic (e-mail) because the lines are low speed and low cost.

## Autonomous Environments

Internet routing (via TCP/IP) and OSI routing use the concept of an AS (autonomous system), or AD (administrative domain), which can simply be referred to as a domain. A *domain* is basically an organization's internal network, a collection of hosts and routers that are administered by a single authority, as pictured in Figure R-11. In other words, a domain might be an internetwork administered by a university or a company. The Internet is a set of linked autonomous systems consisting of educational institutions, government organizations, and companies.

In this environment, there are interior and exterior routing protocols. Interior protocols are used to route packets within the domain. Interior gateway protocols include RIP and OSPF. At the edges of autonomous domains are routers that exchange information with routers in other autonomous domains using exterior routing protocols. BGP (Border Gateway Protocol) is the primary exterior routing protocol for the Internet.

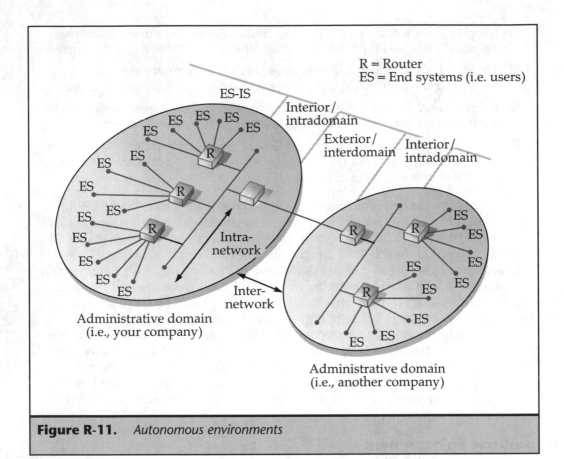

R = Router
ES = End systems (i.e. users)

**Figure R-11.** *Autonomous environments*

The reason for these different protocols and the division of domains is that on a network as large as the Internet, it is not practical for all routers to keep track of every other system in the network. There are millions of addresses on the Internet! Routing information is organized so each routing device only needs to keep enough information to guide packets to the next most important router.

The current version of BGP is version 4, which is documented in RFC 1771. It uses a distance-vector algorithm that has some of the features of link state algorithms. For example, upon initial contact, routers exchange entire routing tables, but later only exchange changes in the table to cut down on network traffic. BGP is used to tell other autonomous networks about the routes on interior networks. The BGP paper at Avi Freedman's Web site (see address at the end of this topic) puts this succinctly: "The primary purpose of BGP4 is to advertise routes to other autonomous systems. When you advertise routes to other autonomous systems, one way of thinking of those route 'advertisements' is as 'promises' to carry data to the IP space represented in the route being advertised."

**RELATED ENTRIES**    Backbone Networks; Data Communication Concepts; Internet; Internet Backbone; IP (Internet Protocol); IP Switching; Network Concepts; NHRP (Next Hop Resolution Protocol); *and* Routers

**INFORMATION ON THE INTERNET**

| | |
|---|---|
| IETF Routing Information Protocol (rip) Working Group (lists related RFPs) | http://www.ietf.org/html.charters/rip-charter.html |
| IETF Open Shortest Path First IGP (ospf) Working Group (lists related RFPs) | http://www.ietf.org/html.charters/ospf-charter.html |
| Border Gateway Protocol 4 (RFC 1771) | http://www.internic.net/rfc/rfc1771.txt |
| Avi Freedman's BGP routing paper (very informative) | http://www.netaxs.com/~freedman/bgp.html |
| Joe Lindsay's BGP page (good links) | http://www.mindspring.com/~jlindsay/bgp.html |
| IETF Inter-Domain Routing (idr) Working Group | http://www.ietf.org/html.charters/idr-charter.html |
| IETF New Internet Routing and Addressing Architecture (nimrod) Working Group | http://www.ietf.org/html.charters/nimrod-charter.html |
| The Routing Arbiter Project (a Merit/ISI collaboration) | http://www.ra.net |
| Sangoma's TCP/IP and IPX Routing Tutorial | http://www.sangoma.com/fguide.htm |
| Routing on the Internet paper | http://www.scit.wlv.ac.uk/~jphb/comms/iproute.html |
| Cisco Systems' Routing Basics | http://www.cisco.com/univercd/data/doc/cintrnet/ito/55171.htm |

# RPC (Remote Procedure Call)

A procedure call provides a way for procedures running in a computer to talk to one another. On a stand-alone computer, the procedures are running in the same memory space, and the procedure call is relatively easy. A procedure call that takes place between two different computers via some communication link is called a *remote procedure call*, or *RPC*. RPCs first appeared on Sun Microsystems and Hewlett-Packard computers running under the UNIX operating system.

Client/server applications use RPCs as an intersystem communication mechanism, as shown in Figure R-12. If you think of a client/server application as a program that has been split, a server can run the data-access portion because it is closest to the data, and the client can run the portion that presents the data to the user and interacts with the user. In this arrangement, the RPC can be viewed as the component that reintegrates the split portions of the program over the network. RPCs are sometimes called *coupling* mechanisms.

RPCs tend to operate in real time because the calling program usually waits until it receives a response from the called program. In this respect, RPCs are synchronous. RPCs are required in applications where a procedure must not continue until it receives the information it needs from the remote system. One variation is to use multithreaded operations in the calling computer so it can continue with other operations while it waits for the response from the called system.

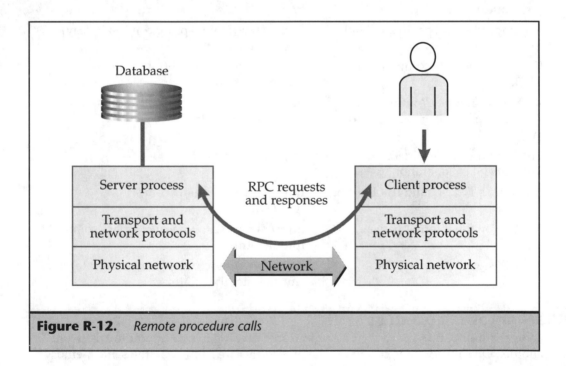

**Figure R-12.**    *Remote procedure calls*

One of the problems with using RPCs in a heterogeneous environment is that different machines represent data differently. RPCs get around this problem by tagging calls with a description of the calling machine's basic data representation. When the call is received, the receiver converts the data if the tag indicates that the two machines represent data differently.

Messaging middleware, ORBs (object request brokers) such as CORBA (Common Object Request Broker Architecture), and technologies like IIOP (Internet Inter-ORB Protocol) are alternative interprocess communication techniques. Refer to the related entries listed next for addition information.

**RELATED ENTRIES**    Client/Server Computing; Component Software Technology, CORBA (Common Object Request Broker Architecture); DCOM (Distributed Component Object Model); Distributed Applications; Distributed Computer Networks; Distributed Database; Distributed Object Computing; IIOP (Internet Inter-ORB Protocol); Middleware and Messaging; *and* ORB (Object Request Broker)

**INFORMATION ON THE INTERNET**

| | |
|---|---|
| Introduction to RPC | http://nemo.ncsl.nist.gov/nistir/5277/node1.html |
| IETF ONC Remote Procedure Call (oncrpc) charter | http://www.ietf.org/html.charters/oncrpc-charter.html |
| IETF RPC Version 2 | http://www.internic.net/rfc/rfc1831.txt |

# RSA Data Security

RSA Data Security was founded in 1982 by Rivest, Shamir, and Adleman, the inventors of the RSA public-key cryptosystem. Today, more than 75 million copies of RSA encryption and authentication technologies are installed worldwide.

RSA technologies are part of existing and proposed standards for the Internet and World Wide Web, ITU (International Telecommunication Union), ISO (International Organization for Standardization), ANSI (American National Standards Institute), IEEE (Institute of Electrical and Electronic Engineers), as well as business, financial and electronic commerce networks around the globe. The company, which was acquired by Security Dynamics in 1996, develops and markets platform-independent developers' kits and end-user products and also provides comprehensive cryptographic consulting services.

**RELATED ENTRIES**    Authentication and Authorization; Certificates and Certification Systems; Cryptography; Digital Signatures; PKI (Public-Key Infrastructure); Public-Key Cryptography; *and* Security

**INFORMATION ON THE INTERNET**

| | |
|---|---|
| RSA Data Security, Inc. | http://www.rsa.com |
| RSA Laboratories | http://www.rsa.com/rsalabs |
| Security Dynamics | http://www.securid.com |

# RSVP (Resource Reservation Protocol)

RSVP is an Internet protocol for delivering data on time and in order on TCP/IP networks. The traditional "best effort" delivery service of IP does not guarantee delivery. TCP, a connection-oriented service, can guarantee delivery but cannot guarantee on-time delivery. Guaranteed on-time delivery is essential for delay-sensitive information associated with videoconferencing, voice conversations, and virtual reality. To compensate, the IETF developed RSVP.

RSVP is an attempt to provide QoS (quality of service) to the Internet and other TCP/IP networks. What RSVP can do is reserve bandwidth across a router-connected network by asking each router to reserve some of its bandwidth for a specific traffic flow. With reserved bandwidth, TCP/IP networks can obtain some of the QoS features of ATM, as discussed further under "QoS (Quality of Service)."

At the time of this writing, QoS-related protocols for the Internet were just beginning to be provided by vendors and put to real use, so the outcome of retrofitting the Internet for QoS is still unknown. One big problem with reserving bandwidth is that it reduces the bandwidth available to other users and applications. Hopefully, the Internet's bandwidth will increase to support the use of RSVP.

RSVP's job is to establish and maintain bandwidth reservations on a network. The protocol works from router to router to set up a reservation that stretches from one end system to another. RSVP is a control and signaling protocol. It is not a routing protocol. If one router along a path cannot provide bandwidth reservation, then another path must be sought out. Router manufacturers must RSVP-enable their routers.

Applications must be able to make QoS requests as well. Fortunately, the WinSock 2.0 API provides a way for applications to do just that, as described under "WinSock."

## The Reservation Process

The process of setting up a resource reservation starts at the data source with a PATH command that travels through routers along a path to one or more destinations, as shown in Figure R-13. Note that RSVP also supports multicast transmissions, so multiple systems may receive data across the reserved path. The PATH command contains a flow ID that identifies the RSVP session that is being set up. The

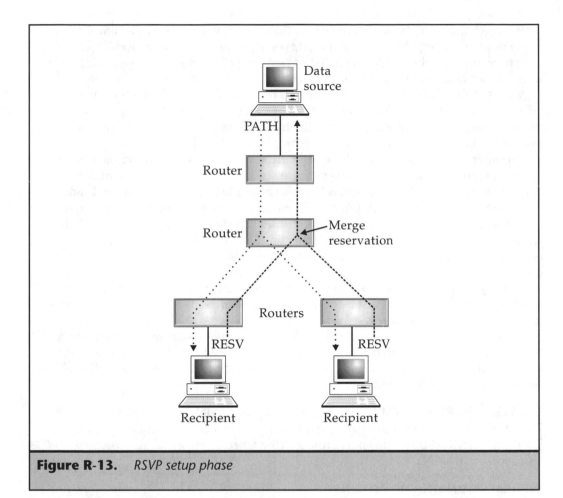

**Figure R-13.** *RSVP setup phase*

PATH command also provides information about the type of flow and its bandwidth requirements.

The PATH command travels through the potential route and each router along the way logs the information contained in the PATH command for future reference. It does not reserve the bandwidth just yet. When the recipient systems receive the PATH command, they indicate their willingness to participate in the session by returning a RESV command back across the same route. As each router receives the RESV command, it will reserve the required bandwidth. In a multicast session, some routers may receive multiple RESV commands for the same flow ID. The router simply combines the requests instead of setting up separate resource reservations.

There are a number of issues related to reserving bandwidth. One is making sure users do not attempt to greedily reserve bandwidth for their own use. On internal networks, policy servers can be installed that hold information about which users can reserve bandwidth and what priority they have on the network. Routers check this server before reserving bandwidth. On the Internet, resource reservation will be subject to billing by ISPs (Internet service providers).

Another issue is how routers handle priorities. In a case where multiple sessions require bandwidth reservations, one of those sessions will no doubt have higher priority than another. One method is to create multiple queues in routers and rank those queues from low to high priority. As packets arrive at a router, they are put in a queue based on a tag in the packet that indicates its priority value. The router then forwards packets in the highest-level queue first. A *weighted fair queuing algorithm* is used to ensure that at least some of the packets in the lower-level queues also get through.

One thing that RSVP is sure to do is reduce the performance of routers with all the additional processing that must be done. New high-performance routers as discussed under "Routers" will be necessary.

As mentioned, QoS services for the Internet were still under development at the time of this writing. The Web sites listed below provide additional information. You can also refer to "QoS (Quality of Service)." In particular, refer to the subheading, "QoS on the Internet and Intranets."

**RELATED ENTRIES**   ATM (Asynchronous Transfer Mode); Fast IP; IP Switching; ISA (Integrated Services Architecture); Prioritization of Network Traffic; QoS (Quality of Service); RTP (Real-time Transport Protocol); Switched Networks; Tag Switching; *and* VLAN (Virtual LAN)

## INFORMATION ON THE INTERNET

| | |
|---|---|
| Resource Reservation Setup Protocol (rsvp) charter | http://www.ietf.org/html.charters/rsvp-charter.html |
| USC Information Sciences Institute's RSVP ReSerVation Protocol paper | http://www.isi.edu/div7/rsvp/rsvp.html |
| Medhavi Bhatia's QoS over the Internet: The RSVP protocol paper | http://www.rvs.uni-hannover.de/people/neitzner/Studienarbeit/literatur/more/rsvp.html |

# RTP (Real-time Transport Protocol)

RTP provides a way to deliver delay-sensitive real-time data such as live audio and video from end station to end station across the Internet or intranets. The developers designed RTP for use in multimedia conferencing, where multiple participants are involved, but also recommend that RTP be used for handling any continuous data stream, interactive distributed simulations, and control and measurement applications.

The services provided by RTP include payload-type identification, sequence numbering, timestamping, and delivery monitoring. In this respect, RTP does not actively get involved in making sure that QoS (quality of service) guarantees are met. RTP will run on top of UDP (User Datagram Protocol) and uses UDP as a delivery mechanism.

**RELATED ENTRIES**    Multimedia; Prioritization of Network Traffic; QoS (Quality of Service); RSVP (Resource Reservation Protocol); *and* RTSP (Real-Time Streaming Protocol)

### INFORMATION ON THE INTERNET

| | |
|---|---|
| IETF Audio/Video Transport (avt) Working Group | http://www.ietf.org/html.charters/avt-charter.html |
| RTP: A Transport Protocol for Real-Time Applications (RFC 1889) | http://www.internic.net/rfc/rfc1889.txt |
| RTP FAQ page | http://www.cs.columbia.edu/~hgs/rtp/faq.html |

# RTSP (Real-Time Streaming Protocol)

RTSP is a protocol for streaming data across the Internet and intranets. RealNetworks developed the protocol in conjunction with Netscape and submitted it to the IETF (Internet Engineering Task Force) for standardization. RealNetworks is the development of the popular RealAudio, a streaming protocol that drastically reduces the overhead of delivering multimedia over the Internet.

The type of content that RTSP can deliver includes live audio and video and prerecorded audio and video. Additional features include bidirectional control, support for IP Multicast, low overhead, security, and more. RTSP is available on most popular computer platforms.

**RELATED ENTRIES**    Multimedia; Prioritization of Network Traffic; QoS (Quality of Service); RSVP (Resource Reservation Protocol); *and* RTP (Real-time Transport Protocol)

### INFORMATION ON THE INTERNET

| | |
|---|---|
| RealNetworks, Inc. | http://www.realaudio.com |

**R**

## SAA (Systems Application Architecture)

SAA is a set of application, communication, and user-interface specifications for IBM mainframe operating systems such as VM, MVS, midrange operating systems like OS/400 (for IBM AS/400 series), and OS/2 for desktop systems. The SAA standard defined *common applications,* which are applications that can run on any SAA platform. Thus, applications written to SAA can run on a wider range of systems. There are three main components in the architecture:

- **CPI (Common Programming Interface)**   Provides a common environment across the SAA platforms for executing programs. The APIs within a CPI provide database, communication, presentation, and other services. CPI-C (Common Programming Interface for Communications) is part of the IBM Open Blueprint.

- **CUA (Common User Access)**   Defines how information is presented to the user using an interface that is common over different platforms.

- **CCS (Common Communication Support)**   Defines the interconnection of SAA systems and the protocols used for communications and data exchange.

Some industry analysts see SAA as a failed strategy because it only linked IBM systems and did not produce enough products to make it a significant standard. The Open Blueprint is IBM's newest vision that encompasses support for multiple application interfaces, networking protocols (TCP/IP, SNA, and NetBIOS), and transmission methods such as frame relay and ATM.

**RELATED ENTRIES**   CPI-C (Common Programming Interface for Communications), IBM; IBM (International Business Machines); *and* IBM Open Blueprint

## Samba

Samba is a suite of programs that provides the same resource-sharing services as Microsoft's SMB (Server Message Blocks). SMB was originally developed for Microsoft operating system environments and is used in Windows 95, Windows 98, Windows NT, and OS/2. Samba provides compatible SMB services for UNIX, NetWare, OS/2, and VMS environments. The primary UNIX platforms are SunOS and Linux, but many other UNIX versions are supported. Samba was originally created by Andrew Tridgell, but it was expanded as a community effort by its users.

Although SMB was primarily designed to work in Microsoft Windows environments, Samba has features that let users of other operating systems use it in modes they are accustomed to. For example, UNIX users can use an FTP-like interface to access shared SMB resources on other servers. Samba includes a NetBIOS name server, which provides the naming service required to browse for shared resources with user-friendly names.

Samba is available for download from the Web site listed below. You will also find additional information at that site.

**RELATED ENTRIES**  CIFS (Common Internet File System); DFS (Distributed File System), Microsoft; Distributed File Systems; File Systems; NetBIOS/NetBEUI; Network Operating Systems; Rights and Permissions; Samba; SMB (Server Message Blocks); *and* Windows NT File System

**INFORMATION ON THE INTERNET**
Andrew Tridgell's Samba page          http://samba.anu.edu.au

## SAP (Service Advertising Protocol)

SAP is used by NetWare servers, print servers, gateways, and other service providers on a NetWare network to advertise their services. Workstations look at SAP messages to locate servers to attach to. A SAP broadcast normally occurs every 60 seconds and includes the name, network address, and type of service provided by a server.

SAP traffic is usually excessive on large networks and can flood a WAN (wide area network) with unnecessary traffic that drives up WAN costs. SAP filtering can be used to reduce the amount of network traffic generated by SAP, hide servers by filtering their SAP packets, and reduce or eliminate SAP traffic from rarely used servers.

**RELATED ENTRIES**  Novell NetWare; Novell NetWare Protocols

## Satellite Communication Systems

Satellite communication systems receive and transmit signals between earth-based stations and space satellites, as pictured in Figure S-1. There are "high-orbit" geosynchronous satellites, LEO (low earth orbit) satellites, and satellites in a variety of mid-orbits. LEOs are close to the earth and have lower-power requirements, thus supporting smaller handheld devices. Motorola's Iridium project is a constellation of LEO satellites.

Geosynchronous satellites are placed in high stationary orbits 22,300 miles above the earth, where they receive "uplink" signals from earth-based transmitters (or other satellites) and downlink those signals to earth. The downlink covers an area called the *footprint*, which may be very large or cover a focused area. The satellites are typically used for video transmissions. The geosynchronous orbit is ideal because the satellites stay synchronized above a specific location and travel at a speed that exactly counters the pull of gravity. However, there are only so many slots in this orbit, and all the slots are taken above the most important areas of the earth.

One problem with high-orbit geosynchronous satellites is that a typical back-and-forth transmission has a delay of about a half second, which causes problems in time-critical computer data transmissions, as discussed in a moment. LEOs orbit low enough to minimize this problem, but they must be in a fast orbit to keep them from falling back to earth. That means a LEO can only be used in the brief time that it crosses over a particular area. To solve the problem, multiple satellites are placed in the same orbit. As one moves out of range, the other moves into range. Calls and other transmissions are handed off from one satellite to another in this process.

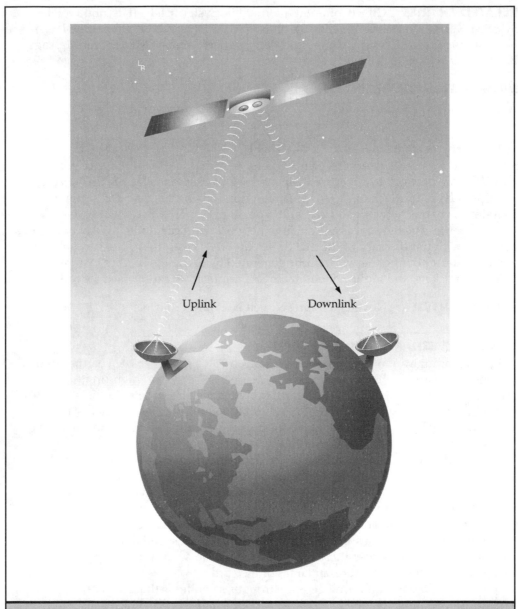

**Figure S-1.** *Satellite communication links*

Motorola's Iridium project is a constellation of 66 LEOs. The satellites follow a north/south polar orbit at an altitude of 750 km (450 miles) and together form a web around the earth to provide complete and continuous coverage. The system is basically a space-based cellular network that projects over 1,600 cells onto the planetary surface. Unlike earth-based cellular systems in which people move in and out of cells, the cells move with the satellites. Each cell has 174 full-duplex channels, and the whole system has over 283,000 channels. The system is primarily designed for voice calls, paging systems, and navigation.

There are a number of applications for using satellites in data communications, but time delays and low transmission rates must be considered. Some applications include videoconferencing, nondelay-sensitive data transmissions, and temporary backup links.

Recently, using satellites for Internet and Web traffic has gained a lot of attention. Satellites can help relieve Internet congestion and bring the Internet to countries that do not have an existing network structure. However, current TCP/IP transmission methods are not a good match for satellite transmissions. In particular, the *slow start* technique used at the beginning of a communication is inefficient over satellite links. The purpose of slow start is to avoid network congestion that can cause dropped packets. Initially, the sender may transmit as little as 200 bytes of information (called a *window*), then wait for an acknowledgment. If the receiver acknowledges, the sender commits more data by doubling the size of the transmission window. If that transmission is acknowledged, the sender doubles the window size again, and this continues until the sender is sending large amounts of data.

However, all this back-and-forth communication adds excessive delay during satellite transmissions. In addition, many Web transmissions are very short and can often be transmitted in the initial transmission. A number of proposals are in the works to increase the size of this initial window, which will reduce or eliminate the round-trip delays and improve performance.

The IETF TCP over Satellite Working Group is working on issues that affect the throughput of TCP traffic, including delays that have adverse affects on slow start and other congestion control algorithms. The group is also working on security issues related to transmitting data over satellite links. A similar group is the IETF TCP Large Windows Working Group. The Web addresses for both groups are listed below under "Information on the Internet."

**RELATED ENTRIES**    Cellular Communication Systems; Iridium System; Microwave Communications; Network Concepts; Telecommunications and Telephone Systems; Transmission Media, Methods, and Equipment; WAN (Wide Area Network); *and* Wireless Communications

## INFORMATION ON THE INTERNET

| | |
|---|---|
| ITU satellite links | http://info.itu.ch/special/wwwfiles/tel_satel.html |
| Iridium System information | http://www.iridium.com |
| Small Satellites page | http://www.ee.surrey.ac.uk/CSER/UOSAT/SSHP/index.html |
| Hugh's Satellite 101 page | http://www.hcisat.com/sat/sat.html |

| Tor E. Wisløff Big LEO (low-earth orbiting) Satellite page | http://www.idt.unit.no/~torwi/synopsis.html |
| Lloyd's satellite constellations | http://www.ee.surrey.ac.uk/Personal/L.Wood/constellations/overview.html |
| Telecoms Virtual Library Satellite listing | http://www.analysys.com/vlib/satellit.htm |
| IETF TCP over Satellite Working Group | http://www.ietf.org/html.charters/tcpsat-charter.html |
| The TCP Large Windows Working Group | http://www.ietf.org/html.charters/tcplw-charter.html |

## SCSI (Small Computer System Interface)

SCSI (pronounced "scuzzy") is a disk interface system that is focused on a host adapter. The host adapter provides a shared bus that attached peripherals use to pass data to and from the host system. You attach devices such as disk drives, CD-ROM discs, optical disks, and tape drives to the adapter. Theoretically, you can plug any SCSI device into any SCSI controller. Some of the features of the SCSI interface are described here:

■ The original SCSI standard supports up to seven devices on a single host adapter, but new standards support high-speed operation with up to 16 devices and bus lengths of up to 25 meters.

■ SCSI devices are "smart" devices with their own control circuitry. They can "disconnect" themselves from the host adapter to process tasks on their own, thus freeing up the bus for other transmissions.

■ The bus can handle simultaneous reads and writes.

SCSI has gone through three standards processes. In 1986, as the original SCSI (now called SCSI-1) was being standardized, engineers were already laying out plans for SCSI-2. Plans for SCSI-3 were started not long after that. SCSI-2 features and enhancements include the following:

■ New command sets were added. The connector is physically smaller, but uses 68 pins instead of 50.

■ New bus widths (more data lines) were devised. These enhancements are called Wide SCSI. They include bus widths of 16 bits (2 bytes) or 32 bits (4 bytes), allowing higher data transfer rates and addressing of up to 16 devices instead of the original 8.

■ Fast transfer rates are achieved by using synchronous data transfers instead of asynchronous data transfers.

Ultra SCSI (also called Fast 20) was the next advancement to this scheme. It uses new SCSI chip sets with internal clock speeds that are doubled, thus doubling the megabyte-per-second transfer rates. Basically, Ultra SCSI doubles the transfer rate independent of the bus width. Thus, the original 8-bit SCSI-1 is boosted to 10 MB/sec by applying the Fast enhancements.

Yet another enhancement to the SCSI standard is called Ultra2 SCSI (also called Fast 40). It uses a more efficient bus signaling scheme to achieve even better performance. Table S-1 outlines each of the SCSI standards. The first entry in the table is the original SCSI standard. The next seven entries are based on SCSI-2 with the Ultra enhancements, and the last two entries are based on SCSI-2 with Ultra2 enhancements.

This chart is derived from an article by the same name published for the STA (SCSI Trade Association) in the May, 1996 issue of *Computer Technology Review*. The terminology was standardized through the joint efforts of the ANSI (American National Standards Institute) X3T10 (SCSI) Committee and the SCSI Trade Association. Note that there are three bus types: single-ended, differential, and LVD (low-voltage differential). A *single-ended bus* uses a signaling scheme that has limited

| SCSI Trade Association Terms | Maximum Bus Speed (MB/sec) | Bus Width (bits) | Maximum Bus Length* | | | Maximum Device Support |
|---|---|---|---|---|---|---|
| | | | Single-Ended | Differential | LVD | |
| SCSI-1 | 5 | 8 | 6 | 25 | 12 | 8 |
| Fast SCSI | 10 | 8 | 3 | 25 | 12 | 8 |
| Fast Wide SCSI | 20 | 16 | 3 | 25 | 12 | 16 |
| Ultra SCSI | 20 | 8 | 1.5 | 25 | 12 | 8 |
| Ultra SCSI | 20 | 8 | 3 | 25 | 12 | 4 |
| Wide Ultra SCSI | 40 | 16 | | 25 | 12 | 16 |
| Wide Ultra SCSI | 40 | 16 | 1.5 | | | 8 |
| Wide Ultra SCSI | 40 | 16 | 3 | | | 4 |
| Ultra2 SCSI | 40 | 8 | ** | ** | 12 | 8 |
| Wide Ultra2 SCSI | 80 | 16 | ** | ** | 12 | 16 |

*In meters (may be exceeded in point-to-point and engineered applications).

**Single-ended and high-powered differential are not defined at Ultra2 speeds.

**Table S-1.** *STA-Endorsed Terminology for SCSI Parallel Interface Technology (source: Computer Technology Review)*

cable lengths. These lengths must be strictly adhered to if Fast enhancements are used to boost the transfer rate. The *differential bus* is part of the SCSI-2 standard. It uses a special signaling technique that improves the signal-to-noise ratio, thus allowing cable lengths of up to 25 meters. However, the differential bus pushes down the number of devices supported on the bus to as few as four devices. An *LVD (low-voltage differential) bus* uses a low-voltage termination design that supports up to 16 devices over a cable length of 12 meters.

## The Future

SCSI designers are working on faster data transfer rates (up into the 160-MB/sec range) and bus lengths beyond 25 meters. The latest SCSI standard is SCSI-3, which has features that are a major departure from the original SCSI specification. It allows different physical interfaces, including serial connections, whereas earlier SCSI standards are parallel interconnects. SCSI-3 supports a parallel interface, Fibre Channel, Firewire (IEEE 1394), SSA (Serial Storage Architecture), and a variety of packet interfaces.

Serial buses have a number of advantages over parallel buses. A serial bus transmits one bit after another over a single wire at very high speed. A parallel bus transmits data in synchronization over multiple lines, which can go out of synchronization as cable lengths increase. Basically, serial interfaces support greater distances and high data rates. The serial interfaces described above have some distinct advantages, one of which is the ability to build LAN-like configurations where multiple desktop and server systems have access to multiple devices. A common setup might support over 100 devices shared by many users and all operating at very high speed.

**RELATED ENTRIES**    Connection Technologies; Fibre Channel; Firewire; SSA (Serial Storage Architecture); *and* Storage Systems

## INFORMATION ON THE INTERNET

| | |
|---|---|
| SCSI Trade Association | http://www.scsita.org |
| T10 (information about I/O interfaces) | http://www.symbios.com/x3t10 |
| Dan Kegel's Fast Hard Drives Page | http://www.kegel.com/drives |
| Lacie's SCSI page | http://www.lacie.com/scsi.html |
| Lacie's Encyclopedia of Hard Drive Terms and Concepts | http://www.lacie.com/data.html |
| Neutron's hard drive FAQ | http://www.neutronet.com/faqinfo/hdd.htm |
| Wilko Bulte's "What is SCSI?" page | http://www.freebsd.org/handbook/scsi.html |
| Yahoo!'s SCSI links page | http://www.yahoo.com/Computers_and_Internet/Hardware/Peripherals/SCSI |

# SDH (Synchronous Digital Hierarchy)

SDH is the ITU standard for a synchronous optical network that supports multiple gigabit-per-second transmission speeds over fiber-optic cable. Long-distance and regional telecommunications companies outside of North America implement SDH on their fiber-optic trunk lines. SONET, which is basically a subset of SDH, is used in the United States. Refer to "SONET (Synchronous Optical Network)" for more information.

# SDLC (Synchronous Data Link Control)

SDLC is an IBM-defined Data Link Control protocol developed in the 1970s for communication over wide area links to IBM host systems in SNA (Systems Network Architecture) environments. SDLC is based on synchronous, bit-oriented operations as compared to byte-oriented protocols such as BISYNC (Binary Synchronous Communications).

In SDLC, a primary station controls the operation of other secondary stations. Secondary stations are polled to see if they have data to send. If a secondary station has data, it transmits when recognized by the primary station. The primary station is responsible for establishing and maintaining links. There are several connection methods, including point-to-point, multipoint, and loop. In a loop configuration, messages are passed from one station to the next.

SDLC uses a typical frame format in which information is bounded by flags to separate each frame. An *address field* contains the address of the secondary station, a *control field* specifies the type of frame, and an *FCS (frame check sequence)* contains error-checking values. A typical SDLC configuration consists of multiple 3270 dumb terminals at a remote site connected to a cluster controller such as an IBM model 3x74. The cluster controller then connects with the host system over a leased line. Companies such as Cisco Systems have improved this connection scheme.

**RELATED ENTRIES**    Data Communication Concepts; Data Link Protocols; HDLC (High-level Data Link Control); LAP (Link Access Procedure); SDLC (Synchronous Data Link Control); *and* Synchronous Communications

# Search Engines

While many desktop computer applications provide search capabilities, the term *search engines* has become synonymous with search algorithms that find information on the Web or on intranets. Search engines are especially adept at locating information on Web pages. The most popular search engines on the Internet are AltaVista, Excite, Infoseek, and Lycos.

A search engine implements a program called a *spider* or *Web crawler*, which goes out on the Web and retrieves Web documents based on predefined parameters or requests made by users. The administrator of a Web site can also submit a request to search sites such as AltaVista to have his or her site searched. The pages that are collected are then indexed, and the indexed material is added to the searchable content of the search site so that users may query it.

The most common search sites are given here:

| | |
|---|---|
| AltaVista Search (DEC) | http://www.altavista.digital.com |
| Excite | http://www.excite.com |
| HotBot | http://www.hotbot.com |
| Infoseek | http://www.infoseek.com |
| Lycos | http://www.lycos.com |
| Magellan | http://www.mckinley.com |
| Open Text Index | http://index.opentext.net |
| WebCrawler | http://www.webcrawler.com |
| World Wide Web Worm | http://wwww.cs.colorado.edu/wwww |
| Yahoo! | http://www.yahoo.com |

## Security

Security is all about protecting data and data systems. Physical security techniques are fairly straightforward—you lock things up in secure rooms. Software security includes user logon, authentication, authorization, and access controls. This section covers security controls in operating systems and security techniques for network- and Internet-connected computers. Refer to "Data Protection" for information about physical security techniques.

### Security Threats

Threats are the reason you need to be concerned about security. Internal users may try to access unauthorized data systems. Internet users may try to attack systems that are connected to the Internet. We will refer to these attackers as "hackers" (see "Hacker" for a profile) with apologies to hackers who consider themselves good citizens.

The most common security breach is unauthorized access to user accounts. The attacker *impersonates* or *masquerades* as the legitimate user. The username and password of the legitimate user is obtained in a variety of ways, such as reading them on sticky notes, watching a user type them, or monitoring network cables with network analyzers. The latter can be avoided by encrypting passwords that cross network channels or by using advanced schemes that do not send passwords.

A *password cracker* is a person that *guesses* passwords. This is easy if the password is the name of the user's child, pet, car, and so on. Another technique is called a *dictionary attack,* in which the cracker is armed with a very large dictionary of words that are commonly used for passwords. (Such dictionaries have been compiled over many years and are available on the Internet). A solution to this attack is to lock a user account after a number of failed logon attempts.

The most serious attack of this type is when someone gains access to an administrator or superuser account. Attackers may lock out the legitimate account owner and have their way with the system. They may also perform activities that go undetected, such as changing critical data values or copying proprietary information and selling it to competitors.

*Eavesdropping* involves monitoring network traffic with wiretaps or sniffers, but the attack goes beyond simply trying to obtain a username and password. The attacker may monitor the network for long periods of time and record valuable and sensitive information that can be sold to competitors or foreign governments, or that can be used for later attacks. Captured packets can even be resent in what is called a *replay attack.* An attacker could replay an authentication routine to gain illegal access to a system. Packet replays can be avoided by timestamping and sequencing packets. An eavesdropper may also capture packets, modify their contents, and reinsert them in the data stream.

Another type of threat is the denial of service attack, in which an attacker causes a server to slow or stop operations using techniques that either overwhelm it with some useless task or corrupt the operating system. A competitor or foreign agent might stage this type of attack.

## Securing Data Systems

Network security features such as access controls help protect data and other resources from unauthorized access. Every object (directory, file, or other resource) has an access control list that contains entries specifically identifying which users and groups can access the object and the permissions they have on that object. These controls allow file owners to grant specific users different levels of access such as read, write, or execute. Initially, the administrator or superuser owns all objects, but network users can control access to files in directories that have been assigned to them. See "Access Control" and "Rights and Permissions."

Most network operating systems have an auditing system designed to record network activities. The auditing records can then be reviewed on a regular basis to determine if a system is being attacked or to determine how it was attacked. An auditing system may record activities like logons, file access, and the editing of user accounts. Auditing records must be properly secured (i.e., write them to a write-once optical disk) so that an attacker cannot change records that would reveal their activities.

## Authentication Techniques

Authentication systems identify users. Once users are authenticated, they can access resources based on authorizations. For example, an authenticated user may only be authorized to log in to a specific workstation during specific hours of the day.

An authentication system is possibly the most important part of any network operating system. It requires that users supply some identity information, such as a user name and password. If a token-based authentication device is used, the user may need to supply a username and a special code generated by the token, as discussed below.

Simple password systems are relatively safe for small in-house systems that are not connected to external networks and where everyone "trusts" everyone else. If tight security is required, advanced security systems are necessary, as outlined here:

- **Kerberos** This is an advanced authentication system that allows network applications to verify the identity of clients (and other peer servers) by using a third-party security server, authenticating the user upon first logon, and then providing other servers with verification that users are who they claim to be. See "Kerberos Authentication" for more information.

- **Dial-back systems** Authorized remote users who dial in to a system are disconnected and then called back to verify that they are calling from a predefined phone number. This prevents impersonation.

- **GPS (Global Positioning System)** This system can verify the physical location of a user anywhere on the planet, thus ensuring that a call is not coming from an unauthorized location. For more information on this location authentication system, contact Peter MacDoran at International Series Research, at (303) 447-0300 (Boulder, CO).

- **Biometric devices** These scan eyes or fingerprints to verify the identity of a user for access to computer systems, data centers, and other facilities.

- **Token authentication devices** Devices such as microprocessor-controlled *smart cards* are used to implement *two-factor authentication*. The smart card generates *one-time passwords* that are good for only one logon session. Users enter this password during logon to gain access to a system. See "Token-Based Authentication."

Of course, these systems assume that the person logging in has an account on the local network. Authentication on the Internet is another matter because there is usually no previous contact between client and vendor. This requires authentication techniques that use digital certificates. With digital certificates, a vendor trusts that a third-party CA (certificate authority) has already verified a user's credentials, in much the same way that retail stores trust that a financial institution will stand behind its credit card users. Refer to "Certificates and Certification Systems" for more details.

There are other reasons why authentication is important, including a need to ensure that a message has not been altered in transit and that a message is indeed from the person who claims to have sent it. In addition, messages should be nonrevocable, i.e., the digital signing technique should prevent the sender from claiming that he or she did not send the message. These techniques are possible with digital signatures and public-key cryptography. See "Digital Signatures" and "Public-Key Cryptography" for more information.

## Cryptographic Techniques

Passwords, stored data, and transmitted data can be encrypted to obtain privacy. Encryption is handled by cryptographic algorithms that take some input called *plaintext* and a key, and then convert it to *ciphertext*. Encryption algorithms are routines that "churn" data to make it unreadable. Refer to "Cryptography" for more details.

Two primary schemes have been developed to make use of encryption algorithms. The *symmetrical (private-key) scheme* uses one key to both encrypt and decrypt data. The *asymmetrical (public-key) scheme* uses two keys—one to encrypt and one to decrypt. If encrypted data is to be exchanged, then a method is needed to safely exchange keys so the recipient can decrypt the data. The asymmetrical scheme provides the best solution because one of the keys in the pair is intended to be available for public use. To send a private message to someone, you obtain their public key and encrypt the message with it. The recipient then uses his or her private key to decrypt the message. These key schemes are covered in more detail under "Private-Key Cryptography" and "Public-Key Cryptography."

In the public-key scheme, public keys must be readily available so anyone can use them to encrypt messages. Assume you want to send a message to someone you've never met or to an Internet business you've never done business with. How do you know the public key you've obtained is authentic and not some spoofed key that will let someone else view the information you have encrypted? *Certificate authorities*, or CAs, solve this problem. They are public organizations such as the U.S. Postal Service that validate the credentials of a person and then bind that person's public key and credentials into an "electronic package" called a *digital certificate*. The CA then locks the digital certificate with its own public key.

There is an element of trust in this arrangement. You must trust that the CA's public key is authentic. If you do, then you trust the contents of the digital certificate, which it can open. But how can you trust that the CA's certificate is authentic? That is the purpose of a public-key infrastructure, which creates different levels of trust that can be traced back up to an ultimate authority, such as a government agency or a world organization. Such an infrastructure would allow people and organizations who have never met or done business to engage in trusted and secure transactions. Refer to "Certificates and Certification Systems" and "PKI (Public-Key Infrastructure)" for more information.

## Secure Session and Transaction Systems

Once keys have been exchanged, clients and servers can engage in secure sessions and transactions. A number of protocols have been developed to handle secure sessions and secure transactions, as outlined here and discussed under separate headings in the book:

- **PCT (Private Communication Technology)** A Microsoft-developed protocol for setting up secure sessions.

- **SET (Secure Electronic Transaction)** An industry standard protocol for securing credit card transactions between cardholders, merchants, and financial institutions.

- **S-HTTP (Secure Hypertext Transfer Protocol)** A version of the HTTP protocol that encrypts HTTP message exchanges between client and server.

- **SSL (Secure Sockets Layer)** Like S-HTTP, SSL secures client/server sessions, but SSL goes a step further by providing a way to encrypt everything that is exchanged, not just HTTP. This is because it works at a lower layer in the protocol stack.

There are also security protocols for exchanging secure electronic mail, including PGP (Pretty Good Privacy) and S/MIME (Secure Multipurpose Internet Mail Extension). These protocols are also covered elsewhere in this book.

## Virtual Private Networking and Firewalls

There is a growing trend for organizations to connect their remote sites via links created over the Internet. Basically, WAN (wide area network) connections are created over the public Internet rather than over private leased lines or public packet-switched networks. These Internet-based VPNs (virtual private networks) require security and, in some cases, special relationships with ISPs (Internet service providers) that can reserve bandwidth and stable site-to-site connections.

Several initiatives and standards are under development. The IETF (Internet Engineering Task Force) is working on IPSec (IP Security), which strives to provide interoperability among different vendors' tunneling products. Another is the S/WAN (Secure WAN) initiative, which is promoted by RSA Data Security. See "IPSec (IP Security)," "S/WAN (Secure WAN)," and "VPN (Virtual Private Network)" for more information. A related technology that provides secure private connections for remote dial up users is discussed under "Virtual Dial-up Services."

Organizations that connect their internal networks to the Internet provide an open door into their systems for Internet users unless secure routers and firewalls are put into place that monitor, filter, and block incoming packets. Any TCP/IP system that is connected directly to the Internet is reachable by any user on the Internet unless these devices are in place. Refer to "Firewall" for more information.

## Other Security Specifications, Initiatives, Coalitions, and APIs

The Internet community is working to resolve many security-related issues, You can learn more about these activities by visiting the IETF "Working Groups" Web site, at http://www.ietf.org/html.charters/wg-dir.html. The page provides links to IETF groups that are working on firewalls, authentication technology, IPSec (IP Security), one-time passwords, public-key infrastructure, transport layer security protocols, and Web transaction security.

A number of other security protocols, initiatives, and specifications are being developed. Some of the more important schemes are outlined here:

- **TCSEC (Trusted Computer System Evaluation Criteria)** The U.S. National Security Agency has outlined the requirements for secure products in a document titled "Trusted Computer System Evaluation Criteria" (TCSEC). TCSEC is more commonly called the "Orange Book." Refer to "TCSEC (Trusted Computer System Evaluation Criteria)" for more information.

- **CDSA (Common Data Security Architecture)** CDSA is a security reference standard that provides a way to develop applications that take advantage of software security mechanisms. CDSA has been accepted by The Open Group for evaluation, and IBM, Intel, and Netscape are refining it. It addresses the security problems of Internet and intranet applications, provides an open interoperable standard, and provides an expansion platform for future security elements. CDSA information is available at http://developer.intel.com/ial/security/cdsa.

- **CAPI (Crypto API)** CAPI is an application programming interface from Microsoft that makes it easier for developers to create applications that contain encryption and digital signatures. RSA Data Security is working with CAPI, and Intel may layer CDSA on top of it. Visit http://www.microsoft.com for more information.

- **GSS-API (Generic Security Services API)** The GSS-API (RFC 1508 and 2078) is a high-level interface that works to give applications an interface into security technologies such as private and public encryption schemes. It works above CDSA. Go to http://www.internic.net/rfc/rfc2078.txt for more information.

A more complete list of organizations, protocols, and other miscellaneous security information can be found at the following site or at the sites listed at the end of this section:

http://rs6000.e-technik.uni-rostock.de/~ploog/crypto-s.htm

**RELATED ENTRIES** Access Control; Access Rights; Auditing; Authentication and Authorization; Backup and Data Archiving; C2 Security Rating; Certificates and Certification Systems; Challenge/Response Protocol; Data Protection; Digital Signatures; Disaster Recovery; EDI (Electronic Data Interchange); Electronic Commerce; Fault Management; Fault Tolerance; Hacker; IPSec (IP Security); Orange Book; PKI (Public-Key Infrastructure); Public-Key Cryptography; Red Book; Rights and Permissions; Security; SET (Secure Electronic Transaction); S/WAN (Secure WAN); TCSEC (Trusted Computer System Evaluation Criteria); TPEP (Trusted Product Evaluation Program); Tunnels; *and* VPN (Virtual Private Network)

## INFORMATION ON THE INTERNET

| | |
|---|---|
| CERT (Computer Emergency Response Team) | http://www.cert.org |
| COAST (Computer Operations, Audit, and Security Technology) | http://www.cs.purdue.edu/coast/coast.html |
| CSI (Computer Security Institute) | http://www.gocsi.com |
| Cylink Corporation | http://www.cylink.com |
| Electronic Frontier Foundation | http://www.eff.org/pub/Privacy |
| Electronic Privacy Information Center | http://www.epic.org |
| Entrust Technologies, Inc. | http://www.entrust.com |
| Grafman Productions' Internet Security page | http://www.graphcomp.com/grafman/secure |
| Internet Privacy Coalition | http://www.crypto.org |
| James M. Atkinson, Communications Engineer ("spy vs. spy" information) | http://www.tscm.com |
| Lawrence Livermore Computer Security Technology Center | http://ciac.llnl.gov/cstc |
| National Institute of Health Computer Security Information | http://www.alw.nih.gov/Security/security.html |
| OnWatch Security Links page | http://www.public-key.com/sec.html |
| Peter Gutmann's Security and Encryption-related Resources and Links | http://www.cs.auckland.ac.nz/~pgut001/links.html |
| Quadralay's Cryptography Archive | http://www.austinlinks.com/Crypto |
| Ron Rivest's links (possibly the most complete set of links on the Web) | http://theory.lcs.mit.edu/~rivest/crypto-security.html |
| Rotherwick Firewall Resource page | http://www.zeuros.co.uk/firewall |
| RSA Data Security, Inc. | http://www.rsa.com |
| Security and Hackerscene page | http://www.geocities.com/CapeCanaveral/3498/security.htm |
| Telstra Corp.'s Security Papers and Documents | http://www.telstra.com.au/pub/docs/security |
| Terry Ritter's "Cyphers by Ritter" page | http://www.io.com/~ritter |
| The Computer Virus Help Desk (has a good archive of encryption software and information) | http://iw1.indyweb.net/~cvhd/crypto.html |
| VeriSign, Inc. (certificate authority) | http://www.verisign.com |

| W3C Security Resources page | http://www.w3.org/Security |
| World Wide Web Security FAQ | http://www-genome.wi.mit.edu/WWW/faqs/<br>www-security-faq.html |
| Yahoo!'s Security and Encryption<br>links page | http://www.yahoo.com/Computers_and<br>_Internet/Security_and_Encryption |
| Yahoo!'s Security links page | http://www.yahoo.com/Business_and<br>_Economy/Companies/Computers/Security |

## Sequencing of Packets

In the TCP/IP networking scheme, packets can be assigned sequence numbers so that when they arrive at the destination, the packets can be put back in order. Sequencing is a feature of transport layer protocols such as TCP.

**RELATED ENTRIES**   TCP (Transmission Control Protocol); Transport Protocols and Services

## Serial Communication and Interfaces

Serial communication equipment and interfaces transmit signals across point-to-point data links. Bits are sent one after another in a serial stream. Serial ports on PCs are almost always used to connect modems, although they may be used to connect monitoring equipment, remote terminals, or remote control devices. In contrast, a parallel port, which is normally used to connect a printer, has eight lines for transmitting data bits (a byte at a time) in parallel. Parallel connections have potentially higher data throughput rates, but distances are restricted to avoid bit-synchronization problems.

Serial ports on a PC are usually 9-pin (DB-9) or 25-pin (DB-25) connectors called COM1 to COM4. The computer side of the connection is called a DTE (data terminal equipment) and the connected device, usually a modem, is called the DCE (data circuit-terminating equipment). While data is sent over a wire serially, a typical connection uses several lines in the same cable. Data is transmitted on one wire and received on another. Other pins are used for sending control signals such as "request to send" and "permission to send."

The standard for serial interfacing is the EIA/TIA-232 (DB-25) and the EIA/TIA-574 (DB-9). The former was commonly called the RS-232-C serial interface, but the EIA changed the name in 1987. Only recently has it been supplanted by new high-speed serial standards called USB (Universal Serial Bus). Many PCs released in 1997 have USB ports, and the new standard will probably supplant the older serial standards on PCs in a few years. USB was developed by Intel and Microsoft, and it is now built into all new Intel-based motherboards. See "USB (Universal Serial Bus)" for more information.

Other serial technologies include Firewire (IEEE 1394), SSA (Serial Storage Architecture), and HSSI (High-Speed Serial Interface), which are discussed under separate headings in this book. Due to their high data transfer rates, these technologies are being used to connect disks or build small local networks.

**RELATED ENTRIES**    Asynchronous Communications; Connection Technologies; EIA (Electronic Industries Association); Modems; SSA (Serial Storage Architecture); *and* Synchronous Communications

## Servers

A server is a network-connected computer system that provides services to network users. Most large companies have banks of relatively inexpensive computers that operate as file servers, application servers, database servers, e-mail gateways, and communication servers. These systems run network operating systems such as Novell NetWare, Windows NT, or a version of the UNIX operating system. At the same time, many organizations still run mainframe systems, and these systems have been recast as high-end network servers. In between are so-called *superservers*, systems that run many processors in parallel and include arrays of disks and fully redundant hardware systems. This section will explore the state of the server.

The "new" server is often a scalable system into which additional processors and other components may be added at any time. Such systems are platforms for future expansion and growth. They provide centralized services to support the new class of NCs (Network Computers) and NetPCs. This model may seem similar to the old centralized mainframe computing model; however, these new systems run client/server, component-based programs that are written with Java and ActiveX and that take advantage of Web protocols. Servers do most of the processing.

In some cases, the processing load is so large that multiple servers are clustered together and processing is distributed among the servers (this is called *load balancing*), as shown on the left in Figure S-2. This is in contrast to earlier "server farms" in which some servers provided only file services while others provided e-mail services or communication services. Clustered systems protect against the loss of any one system. Data is stored in separate fully redundant arrays that any server can access. The system can be scaled by simply adding more servers. When a request comes in from a Web client, it is shuttled to any server that can immediately process the request. A single application can also be run across the cluster, and all the servers are used as a single processor. See "Clustering" and "Data Warehousing" for more information.

Placing fully capable systems at multiple sites provides redundancy and protects a company from local disasters, as shown on the right in Figure S-2. It also makes data more accessible to local users. Data that must be available at all sites can be replicated to those sites from a master site. Replication may not ensure *real-time* synchronization of data, but in many cases (such as directory services) that is not essential.

### Server Features

If you shop for a server today, you will find that multiple processor systems with large disk arrays and high-performance processors are reasonably priced. Many of these

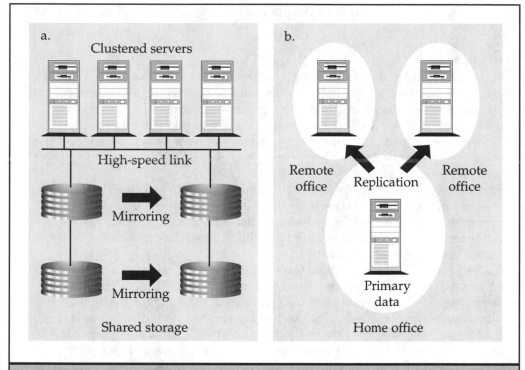

**Figure S-2.**    *Server clustering and replication techniques*

systems provide mainframe-like performance. This section discusses server-specific features. You can also refer to other sections in this book for more information about server components, such as "Parallel Processing," "RAID (Redundant Arrays of Inexpensive Disks)," and "SCSI (Small Computer System Interface)."

Assuming you have a conservative budget, the best way to gain performance at a reasonable price is with multiprocessor systems. A typical Intel-based multiprocessor system has four processors. To take advantage of this system, you'll need an operating system that supports SMP (symmetrical multiprocessing). Windows NT and Novell NetWare are examples. An SMP system breaks processing tasks into separate threads, and each thread is processed by a separate CPU. Thus, a four-processor system could theoretically complete a task four times faster than a single-processor system.

Multiprocessor servers have become commodity items and most popular PC vendors such as Compaq, DEC, Dell, Hewlett-Packard, and IBM sell them through mail-order channels.

SMP systems implement shared memory, disk storage, and other system features. A single operating system ensures that any processing task is handed off to any processor that is available to handle it. Since the processors use shared memory and disk space, all processing output can be put in a place where the other processors can easily access it if necessary.

## Superservers

Moving up the price and processing scale, we get to so-called *superservers*. While a few years ago, a four-processor system was considered a superserver, today's superservers are classified as systems with eight or more processors, memory capacity in the gigabyte range, terabyte RAID storage systems, and redundant features such as multiple power supplies. The most distinguishing feature is a custom architecture that includes a proprietary bus. Sun Microsystems and NetFRAME Systems are the most common vendors.

Sun Microsystems' Ultra Enterprise 10000 supports up to 64 UltraSPARC II processors running at 250 MHz each, up to 64GB of memory, and up to 20TB (terabytes) of online storage. The system runs Sun's UNIX-compatible Solaris operating system, which provides SMP capabilities across the processors. The system is designed as a mainframe alternative.

NetFRAME's Clustersystem 9000 takes a different approach. It uses only four Intel processors, but provides vastly improved I/O (input/output) by implementing a unique bus design. The system has three PCI buses designed to handle thousands of simultaneous network requests. One bus handles system-specific traffic, such as keyboard data, while the other two buses handle network traffic at high speeds.

MPP (massively parallel processor) systems provide yet another model for high-end servers. MPP systems can scale up to the supercomputer level with hundreds or even thousands of processors. While an SMP system consists of a group of processors that share the same memory and bus, an MPP system consists of multiple *nodes*, with each node being like a separate SMP system. See "Parallel Processing for more information. A very interesting article on Tandem's NetServer MPP system can be found at the BYTE site listed at the end of this topic under "Information on the Internet."

## Server Switching

GigaLabs and other vendors are implementing an interesting server design that specifically targets network I/O bottlenecks. GigaLabs' I/O Switching approach allows high-performance servers to pump data directly onto the backbone by extending the server's native I/O bus into the switch fabric. This direct connectivity produces ten times the normal throughput to the network and reduces the number of interrupts that network interface cards impose on a server. I/O Switching is outlined in a white paper at the GigaLabs' Web site listed at the end of this topic.

With I/O switching, a server's bus connects directly to a server switch, which is part of the network backbone. Normal protocol translation is bypassed, allowing the server to "blast" data directly from its bus to the backbone switch as bus-to-bus transactions. In addition, GigaLab's I/O Switching supports native SCSI II and III links, allowing storage devices to connect directly to the switching fabric, as shown on the right in Figure S-3. This configuration allows data transfers to bypass the server altogether and move directly to the network backbone.

Of course, if data is moving directly from disk to a server switch, the server switch must package the data into the frames or cells used by the attached networks. This is just one more activity that is off-loaded from the server. In addition, the GigaLabs server switch filters out network traffic that is not important to the server.

## I₂O Architecture

Another interesting development for servers is I₂O, which provides an I/O device driver architecture that allows the creation of device drivers that are portable across operating systems. Most important from a server performance perspective, I₂O facilitates intelligent I/O subsystems that relieve the host of interrupt-intensive I/O tasks. This improves I/O performance and allows servers to better service the high-bandwidth requirements of busy networks. Information about I₂O is available at the I₂O Special Interest Group Web site given below under "Information on the Internet."

**RELATED ENTRIES**    Clustering; Data Warehousing; DBMS (Database Management System); Distributed Processing; IBM Servers; Mainframe; MPP (Massively Parallel Processor) Systems; Multiprocessing; NUMA (Non-Uniform Memory Access); Parallel Processing; *and* Supercomputer

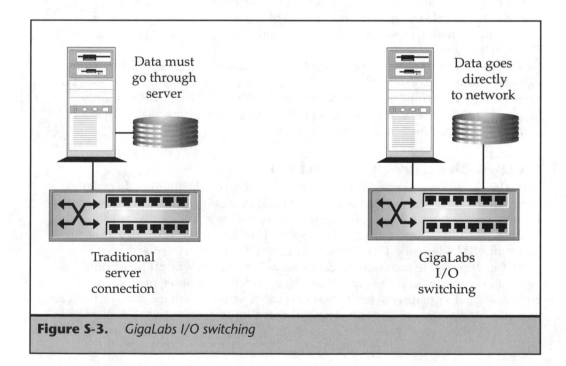

**Figure S-3.**    *GigaLabs I/O switching*

**INFORMATION ON THE INTERNET**

| | |
|---|---|
| Compaq Computer Corporation | http://www.compaq.com/products/servers |
| Digital Equipment Corporation | http://www.digital.com/alphaserver |
| Hewlett-Packard's Server Products page | http://www.hp.com/Networking/servprod.html |
| IBM's Servers page | http://www.ibm.com/Servers |
| Sun Microsystems' servers site | http://www.sun.com/servers |
| NetFRAME Systems, Inc. | http://www.netframe.com |
| GigaLabs, Inc. | http://www.gigalabs.com |
| BYTE article: "The Network in the Server," by Thom Thompson | http://www.byte.com/art/9607/sec12/art1.htm |
| I2O Special Interest Group | http://www.i2osig.org |

## Service Providers

*See* Communication Service Providers; ISPs (Internet Service Providers).

## Session Layer, OSI Model

The OSI (Open Systems Interconnection) model is a standard defined by the International Organization for Standardization that defines a layered protocol architecture for data communication. A layer of functionality in one computer communicates with its peer layer in other computers. This is discussed under "Protocol Concepts."

The session layer provides protocols that applications use to establish sessions with one another across a network or other communication system. The session layer is not used much in modern network communications because it was primarily designed to specify how sessions are set up between remote time-sharing systems. Authentication routines are defined in this layer.

## SET (Secure Electronic Transaction)

Secure transactions are critical for electronic commerce on the Internet. In order for merchants to automatically and safely collect and process payments from Internet clients, a secure protocol is required that is supported by major credit card companies, vendors, consumers, and software developers. The SET protocol was developed by Microsoft, IBM, Netscape, GTE, Visa, and MasterCard for this purpose.

SET is designed to secure credit card transactions by authenticating cardholders, merchants, and banks and by preserving the confidentiality of payment data. SET requires digital signatures to verify that the customer, the merchant, and the bank are legitimate. It also uses multiparty messages that allow information to be encrypted directly to banks. This feature prevents credit card numbers from ending up in the wrong hands. In addition, it requires integration into the credit card processing system, which is currently underway.

SET includes a negotiation layer that negotiates the type of payment method, protocols, and transports. The definition of this layer is the task of the JEPI (Joint Electronic Payment Initiative) project. Examples of payment methods include credit cards, debit cards, electronic cash, and checks. Payment protocols (for example, SET) define the message format and sequence required to complete the payment transaction. Transports include such protocols as SSL (Secure Sockets Layer) and S-HTTP (Secure Hypertext Transfer Protocol).

As mentioned, an important part of SET's success will be its overall acceptance by cardholders (who run SET-compatible computers), credit card issuers, merchants, acquirers (payment processing), and CAs (certificate authorities). CAs provide digital certificates that are critical in verifying the authenticity of cardholders and others involved in the transactions. Microsoft and Netscape have included SET support in their browsers.

**RELATED ENTRIES**    Certificates and Certification Systems; Digital Signatures; EDI (Electronic Data Interchange); Electronic Commerce; *and* OBI (Open Buying on the Internet)

**INFORMATION ON THE INTERNET**

| | |
|---|---|
| Visa's SET information | http://www.visa.com/cgi-bin/vee/nt/ecomm/set/intro.html |
| RSA's SET Central page | http://www.rsa.com/set |

## SFT (System Fault Tolerance)

SFT is the fault-tolerant system built into NetWare operating systems. *Fault tolerance* is the more general term for SFT. Fault tolerance allows you to provide redundancy for hardware in a system. With SFT, you can install two disks and then mirror the contents of the main disk to the secondary disk (see "Mirroring"). If the main disk fails, the secondary disk takes over. The disk controller can also be duplicated, or *duplexed*, to further protect the system from hardware failure. Novell SFT Level III takes redundancy a step further by duplexing entire servers. If the primary server goes down, the secondary server takes over without an interruption.

**RELATED ENTRIES**    Backup and Data Archiving; Clustering; Data Migration; Data Protection; Disaster Recovery; Fault Management; Fault Tolerance; Mirroring; *and* Replication

## SGML (Standard Generalized Markup Language)

SGML is an open standard markup language for adding tags to text documents that indicate how documents should be formatted. The term "markup" is historically based on the marks made by copy editors to pages that indicate how they should be formatted and typeset. In the early days of computer typesetting, there were many different typesetting systems, and each used its own proprietary markup language. These languages consisted of special control characters to indicate the beginning and end of a particular format. The markups were so obscure that users quickly realized a standard markup language was needed to reduce confusion.

Two organizations, the Graphics Communications Association and ANSI, went to work on the problem in the 1980s. They eventually combined their work, and in 1986 the ISO (International Organization for Standardization) introduced it as SGML (Standard Generalized Markup Language). The most important part of SGML is that files contain standard ASCII text, which means they are portable from one system to another. SGML goes beyond simple document formatting by defining document structures and relationships. Document parts are defined in a hierarchical tree, and formatting is applied based on that hierarchy. Information in documents is translated to perform actions or formatting on other systems.

An SGML document consists of the actual text file (called the *document instance*) and a separate DTD (Document Type Definition) file. The DTD specifies the rules for tagging the document. The DTD defines all the ways that the document instance can be laid out and formatted. Since the DTD defines how the associated document will look, the DTD can be changed to alter the document's appearance.

HTML (Hypertext Markup Language), the markup language used for Web pages, is related to SGML, except that everything is stored in a single document. The W3C (World Wide Web Consortium) is working to make SGML a Web standard. It feels that generic SGML will promote large-scale commercial Web publishing and make it easier to incorporate Java.

**RELATED ENTRIES**   Document Management; HTML (Hypertext Markup Language); Information Publishing; *and* Workflow Management

## INFORMATION ON THE INTERNET

| | |
|---|---|
| SGML Open Consortium | http://www.sgmlopen.org |
| World Wide Web Consortium's SGML site | http://www.w3.org/pub/WWW/MarkUp/SGML |
| Allette Systems' House of SGML | http://www.allette.com.au/allette/sgml |
| Naggum Software's SGML FAQ | http://ruff.cs.umbc.edu:1080/courses/491/html/SGML.html |
| Benoît Marchal's (PineappleSoft) Introduction to SGML | http://www.pineapplesoft.com/reports/sgml |
| Robin Cover's SGML page | http://www.sil.org/sgml/sgml.html |
| SoftQuad's SGML Primer | http://www.sq.com/sgmlinfo/primbody.html |
| SGML/HTML Resource Centre | http://www.geocities.com/Athens/2694/sgml.html |

| Yahoo!'s SGML links page | http://www.yahoo.com/Computers_and _Internet/Information_and_Documentation/ Data_Formats/SGML |

---

## S-HTTP (Secure Hypertext Transfer Protocol)

The native protocol that Web clients and servers use to communicate is HTTP (Hypertext Transfer Protocol). This protocol is ideal for open communications, but in its native form it does not provide authentication and encryption features. S-HTTP works in conjunction with HTTP to enable clients and servers to engage in private and secure transactions. S-HTTP is especially useful for encrypting forms-based information as it passes between clients and servers.

A protocol similar to S-HTTP is SSL (Secure Sockets Layer), which provides the same authentication and encryption functionality. However, SSL encrypts all data being passed between client and server at the IP socket level. S-HTTP only encrypts HTTP-level messages at the application layer.

S-HTTP provides a lot of flexibility in terms of what cryptographic algorithms and modes of operation can be used. Messages may be protected by using digital signatures, authentication, and encryption. Upon first contact, the sender and receiver establish preferences for encrypting and handling secure messages.

A number of encryption algorithms and security techniques can be used, including DES and RC2 encryption or RSA public-key signing. In addition, users can choose to use a particular type of certificate, or no certificate at all. In cases where public-key certificates are not available, it is possible for a sender and receiver to use a session key that they have exchanged in advance. A challenge/response mechanism is also available (see "Challenge/Response Protocol").

The IETF Web Transaction Security (wts) Working Group is in charge of developing S-HTTP. The Web site is listed under "Information on the Internet," along with two other IETF security-related groups.

**RELATED ENTRIES**    Certificates and Certification Systems; Digital Signatures; PKI (Public-Key Infrastructure); Public-Key Cryptography; Security; SET (Secure Electronic Transaction); *and* SSL (Secure Sockets Layer)

### INFORMATION ON THE INTERNET

| IETF Web Transaction Security (wts) Working Group | http://www.ietf.org/html.charters/ wts-charter.html |
| IETF Transport Layer Security (tls) Working Group | http://www.ietf.org/html.charters/ tls-charter.html |
| IETF Public-Key Infrastructure (X.509) (pkix) Working Group | http://www.ietf.org/html.charters/ pkix-charter.html |
| Entrust Technologies' Web Security Primer (information about SSL and S-HTTP) | http://www.entrust.com/primer.htm |

Yahoo!'s S-HTTP links page

http://www.yahoo.com/Computers_and_
Internet/Internet/World_Wide_Web/HTTP
/Security/SHTTP___Secure_Hypertext_
Transfer_Protocol

## Signals

An *analog signal* is a form of propagated energy, such as a sound wave, that vibrates
the medium it travels through. Sound waves are measured by their frequency in cycles
per second, or *hertz (Hz)*. One hertz is one cycle per second. The majority of home
telephone connections use analog signaling over copper wire.

*Digital signals* are transmitted over media by representing the binary digits as
electrical pulses in which each pulse is a signal element. The voltage of the line is
varied between a high state and a low state. Thus binary 1 is transmitted by applying a
positive, or *high*, voltage, and binary 0 is transmitted by applying a negative, or *low*,
voltage. Note that the reverse of this is also possible, where a negative voltage may
represent a 1, and a positive voltage may represent 0.

Figure S-4 depicts both analog and digital signals, with the analog signal
representing the equivalent of the digital signal.

As signals travel long distances, some degradation occurs. Analog signals are
periodically amplified, but if the signal is already distorted, that distortion is also
amplified. In contrast, digital signals are more reliable over long distances because
they can be regenerated without distortion.

As mentioned, digital information is transmitted across a medium by representing
data bits as pulses. In a one to one correspondence. a binaty 0 may be represented by

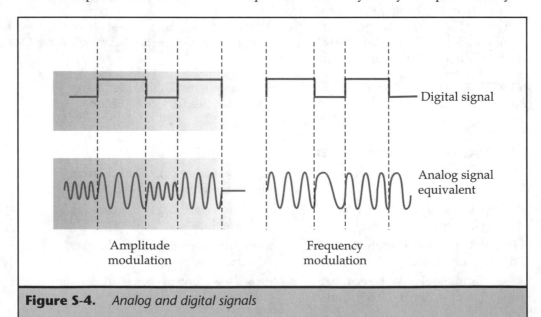

**Figure S-4.**   *Analog and digital signals*

low voltage on the line, while a binary 1 may be represented by a high voltage. However, this is very inefficient, and encoding schemes are often used to improve throughput. The throughput, or data rate, is the number of bits per second that are transmitted. See "Data Transfer Rates" for more information.

An encoding scheme modulates a signal in a way that makes it represent more bits. The modulation rate is expressed in terms of baud, or the number of signal changes per second. The data bits are then mapped onto the modulation scheme. The efficiency of the encoding scheme determining the data rate. Factors that decrease the data rate include errors and noise on the line, but data rate can be improved by increasing the bandwidth and using higher frequencies.

A receiver of a digital signal must have some way of knowing the beginning and end of each bit sequence in the data stream. One method of doing this is to set up a clocking mechanism that the sender and receiver can synchronize with. This can exist on a separate wire or be encoded directly into the signal that is transmitted. The latter is used on LANs and WANs.

Now we get to the signaling and encoding schemes, some of which are described in the following list and pictured in Figure S-5 for the bit sequence of 0100110001. Some goals are to use a small bandwidth to transmit as many signals as possible, to use low voltage levels to reduce the affects of attenuation over large distances, and to provide a synchronization mechanism directly in the signal.

- **Unipolar** In this scheme, 1s are represented by voltage and 0s by no voltage. There is no special encoding. This scheme requires high voltage levels and has a relatively high bandwidth.

- **Bipolar** In this scheme, 1s are represented by positive voltage and 0s by negative voltage. This scheme reduces power requirements and reduces the attenuation of high voltage levels, but still has a high bandwidth.

- **RZ (return-to-zero)** In this scheme, the voltage state returns to zero after a signal state. This method has a high bandwidth.

- **NRZI (nonreturn-to-zero, invert on ones)** In this scheme, a 1 bit is represented by a transition in voltage. If the previous voltage was high, the next 1 bit reduces the voltage. This technique reduces bandwidth requirements. This method is used in RS232 serial communication.

- **Manchester** In this scheme, a transition occurs in the middle of a bit period, which provides a low-error clocking mechanism. A high transition represents a 1 and a low transition represents a 0. This scheme is used on LANs and has high bandwidth requirements.

Of course, there are many other encoding schemes, and you should refer to a suitable book on data communication concepts for more information. A system designer chooses a scheme based on the physical restrictions and communication requirements of a system.

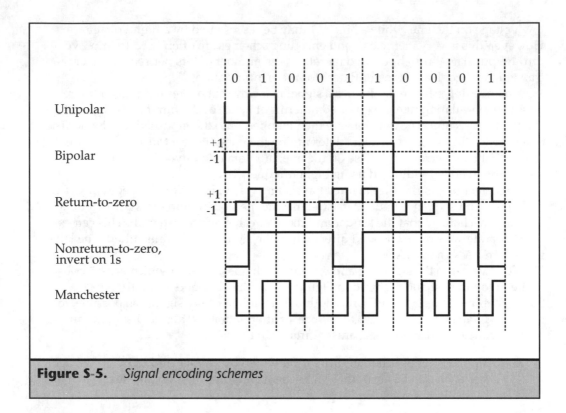

**Figure S-5.** *Signal encoding schemes*

**RELATED ENTRIES**    ADC (Analog-to-Digital Conversion); Analog Signals; Bandwidth; Capacity; Data Communication Concepts; Data Transfer Rates; *and* Transmission Media, Methods, and Equipment

## Sliding-Window Flow Control

Sliding-window flow controls are techniques used by transport layer protocols such as TCP to reduce the overhead associated with sending acknowledgments to indicate that a frame of data was successfully received. See "Flow-Control Mechanisms" for more information.

## SLIP (Serial Line Internet Protocol)

When one TCP/IP system connects with another TCP/IP system over a serial point-to-point communication line (i.e., a dial-up modem link), some way is needed to transport IP packets (a network layer activity) across the serial link (a lower-level data link layer activity). Basically, IP packets must be encapsulated into data link layer frames to make the trip across the serial link.

Two schemes have been adopted by the Internet community to provide these links: SLIP and PPP (Point-to-Point Protocol). Both protocols do similar things, but SLIP can only carry IP packets, while PPP can carry other protocol packets, including DECnet, IPX (Internetwork Packet Exchange), and AppleTalk, due to the addition of a protocol identifier field. SLIP was designed earlier than PPP.

SLIP can provide connections between hosts, routers, and workstations over communication lines that support most modem speeds, including new 56K modems. However, it supports only asynchronous transfers, not synchronous transfers. PPP supports synchronous transfers. In most cases, PPP is the preferred protocol.

**RELATED ENTRIES**    Asynchronous Communications; IP (Internet Protocol); PPP (Point-to-Point Protocol); Serial Communication and Interfaces; *and* Synchronous Communications

### INFORMATION ON THE INTERNET

| | |
|---|---|
| SLIP (RFC 1055) | http://www.internic.net/rfc/rfc1055.txt |
| Yahoo!'s SLIP links page | http://www.yahoo.com/Computers_and_Internet/ Information_and_Documentation/Protocols/ SLIP_Serial_Line_IP |

## Smart Cards

A smart card is a card about the size of a credit card that can store information and, in most cases, contains a microprocessor that can perform some activities as programmed by the card's issuer. A phone card is an example of a simple smart card. It allocates a specific amount of time for phone calls and keeps track of usage. Smart cards may also track digital cash. A more "intelligent" smart card may run a relatively sophisticated program.

Unlike *stripe cards*, which have magnetic strips on the outside of the card, smart cards hold information internally and so are much more secure. Smart cards are often used as token authentication devices that generate access codes for secure systems.

Smart cards have gained rapid industry acceptance in all sorts of applications. Microsoft and a number of other vendors are using the devices as peripherals to PCs and NCs (Network Computers). Several industry organizations have been formed to standardize and promote smart-card usage (see "Information on the Internet" below).

**RELATED ENTRIES**    Access Control; Authentication and Authorization; Security; and Token-Based Authentication

### INFORMATION ON THE INTERNET

| | |
|---|---|
| Smart Card Forum | http://www.smartcrd.com |
| AMERKORE's Smart Card Resource Center | http://www.smart-card.com |
| Global Chipcard Alliance | http://www.chipcard.org |

# SMB (Server Message Blocks)

SMB is a high-level protocol for sharing resources in the Microsoft Windows environment. It is the native file-sharing protocol in the Windows 95, Windows 98, Windows NT, and OS/2 operating system environments. It is also used in pre-Windows 95 versions of the Windows operating system for file sharing across networks. In addition, the new CIFS (Common Internet File System), which allows file sharing across the Internet, is based on SMB. SMB is also widely available in the UNIX and VMS environments in the form of Samba. See "Samba" for more information.

SMB provides redirector services that allow a client to locate files on other network computers running SMB and open, read, write to, and delete those files. NetBIOS is used to establish logical connections, or sessions, between networked computers. NetBIOS also uses a unique logical name to identify workstations on the network. Once a session is established, a two-way conversation takes place in which the following types of SMB messages are exchanged:

- **Session control** Commands that start and end a redirector connection to shared resources at a server
- **File** Messages to gain access to files at a server
- **Printer** Messages to send print jobs to shared printers or get information about print queues
- **Message** Provides a way to send messages to or receive messages from other network-attached workstations

**RELATED ENTRIES** CIFS (Common Internet File System); DFS (Distributed File System), Microsoft; Distributed File Systems; File Systems; NetBIOS/NetBEUI; Network Operating Systems; Rights and Permissions; Samba; *and* Windows NT File System

**INFORMATION ON THE INTERNET**

Microsoft's Technical Support Knowledge Base    http://www.microsoft.com

Samba site at Australian National University    http://samba.anu.edu.au

Richard Sharpe's "Just what is SMB?" paper    http://samba.anu.edu.au/cifs/docs/what-is-smb.html

# SMDS (Switched Multimegabit Data Service)

SMDS is a LEC (local exchange carrier) service for building local area networks in a city-wide area. SMDS may also be used for WAN connections, but interconnecting one carrier's SMDS systems with another carrier's system in another area has been difficult. SMDS was developed by Bellcore and is offered as a service by LECs in some metropolitan areas. Customers can extend their LANs over SMDS networks.

As a switching technology, SMDS has advantages over building private networks with dedicated digital lines such as T1. Customers set up one line (of appropriate bandwidth) into the LEC's SMDS network, rather than setting up lines between all the sites that need interconnection. It is a connectionless, cell-based transport service that can provide any-to-any connections between a variety of sites.

SMDS provides usage-based billing and some interesting network management features. It builds packets on top of the cell structure, taking advantage of both packet features and fast cell switching. Packet features include the ability to address special groups or screen packets. Customers can build a logical private network through the SMDS network, if necessary. Note that frame relay may be a better choice in some areas, depending on availability.

SIG (SMDS Interest Group) is an association of local and long-distance telecommunications carriers, SMDS product vendors, service providers, and end users. The SMDS Web address is given at the end of this topic.

**RELATED ENTRIES**   ATM (Asynchronous Transfer Mode); Carrier Services; Frame Relay; LEC (Local Exchange Carrier); *and* T1/T3

**INFORMATION ON THE INTERNET**

| | |
|---|---|
| SMDS Interest Group | http://www.smds-ig.org |
| Switched Multimegabit Data Service (SMDS) page | http://www.cerf.net/smds |

# S/MIME (Secure Multipurpose Internet Mail Extension)

S/MIME is an extension of the popular MIME (Multipurpose Internet Mail Extension) electronic mail standard that adds security to protect against interception and e-mail forgery. Basically, S/MIME is designed to secure messages from prying eyes.

Because S/MIME is an extension of MIME, it easily integrates with existing electronic messaging products. The demand for e-mail security is growing, along with a demand to validate the authenticity of messages. It is too easy for someone to post a message in a public forum that appears to be from someone else. E-mail security lets users electronically sign messages to prove their origin.

S/MIME uses the RSA (Rivest, Shamir, Adleman) public-key algorithms for key exchange, making it easy for people to exchange keys, even if they have never met. The key scheme can also be used to digitally sign e-mail messages. Encryption can be handled by DES (Data Encryption Standard), Triple-DES, or the RSA RC2 algorithm.

RSA Data Systems promotes S/MIME and VeriSign has set up a certificate hierarchy that supports S/MIME. The Web sites for these companies are listed below under "Information on the Internet."

There are other electronic mail security protocols including PGP (Pretty Good Privacy) and PEM (Privacy-Enhanced Mail), which are discussed elsewhere in this book.

The IETF (Internet Engineering Task Force) was considering S/MIME as its primary standard for securing e-mail, but in September of 1997, the IETF rejected S/MIME because RSA had not removed licensing and royalty fee requirements.

Instead, the IETF is considering a version of PGP (Pretty Good Privacy), called Open PGP.

**RELATED ENTRIES**  Certificates and Certification Systems; Digital Signatures; Electronic Mail; MIME (Multipurpose Internet Mail Extension); PEM (Privacy-Enhanced Mail); PGP (Pretty Good Privacy); Public-Key Cryptography; *and* Security

## INFORMATION ON THE INTERNET

| | |
|---|---|
| RSA's S/MIME Central page | http://www.rsa.com/smime |
| VeriSign, Inc. | http://www.verisign.com |
| S/MIME message specification | http://www.imc.org/draft-dusse-smime-msg |
| S/MIME certificate handling information | http://www.imc.org/draft-dusse-smime-cert |
| S/MIME: Anatomy of a Secure E-mail Standard | http://www.ema.org/html/pubs/mmv2n4/s-mime.htm |
| The premail page (information about e-mail security and a free S/MIME client) | http://atropos.c2.net/~raph/premail.html |
| Internet Mail Consortium | http://www.imc.org |
| Electronic Messaging Association | http://www.ema.org |

# SMTP (Simple Mail Transfer Protocol)

SMTP is the Internet mail exchange mechanism for the Internet. It is responsible for moving messages from one e-mail server to another. The e-mail servers run a message-handling protocol called POP (Post Office Protocol) or IMAP4 (Internet Mail Access Protocol, version 4). IMAP4 is a new and more flexible protocol that will eventually replace POP. SMTP is like the mail carrier, responsible for transporting mail, while POP and IMAP4 are like the post office, responsible for receiving, storing, and forwarding mail. SMTP uses the Internet mail addressing that most people are familiar with—the *username@company.com* format.

POP holds mail in user mailboxes. When users connect to the mail server, their e-mail name is used to verify who they are and give them access to their mailbox. Messages are then downloaded to their computer. IMAP4 improves this model by allowing users to keep mail in their mailboxes on the mail server, rather than have it automatically download to their computer. This is useful for remote mobile users.

SMTP uses a basic request and response mechanism to transfer mail between POP or IMAP4 computers on the Internet (or on an internal network). A few simple commands make this exchange possible. The commands are formed with ASCII (text). The simple command structure makes it easy to build mail servers and clients for any platform.

The network of mail servers on the Internet is quite elaborate. In most cases, a message sent from one user to another is routed through a number of SMTP servers before it reaches its destination.

**RELATED ENTRIES** Collaborative Computing; Electronic Mail; Groupware; Intranets and Extranets; Middleware and Messaging; POP (Post Office Protocol); *and* Workflow Management

## INFORMATION ON THE INTERNET

| | |
|---|---|
| The IMAP Connection | http://www.imap.org |
| IMAP Information Center | http://www.washington.edu/imap |
| Electronic Messaging Association | http://www.ema.org |
| Internet Mail Consortium | http://www.imc.org |
| SMTP (RFC 821) | http://www.internic.net/rfc/rfc821.txt |
| SMTP Service Extensions (RFC 1869) | http://www.internic.net/rfc/rfc1869.txt |
| SMTP Service Extension for Delivery Status Notifications (RFC 1891) | http://www.internic.net/rfc/rfc1891.txt |
| Yahoo!'s Internet Electronic Mail links page | http://www.yahoo.com/Computers_and_Internet/Software/Internet/Electronic_Mail |

# SNA (Systems Network Architecture)

SNA, first introduced in 1974, was IBM's scheme for connecting its 3270 family of products. SNA was designed in the days when large numbers of nonprogrammable terminals connected to IBM host systems. SNA provided static routing between interconnected hosts so that a user working at one of the terminals could access any of the interconnected hosts.

While SNA was designed for centralized IBM-only mainframe computing environments, it was inadequate in peer-to-peer, client/server, multivendor, and multiprotocol network environments. IBM introduced solutions such as APPC (Advanced Program-to-Program Communications) and APPN (Advanced Peer-to-Peer Networking), which altered the mainframe-centric approach and allowed large and small systems to interoperate as peers.

Starting in 1996, many IBM sites began to see the possibility of moving to TCP/IP rather than using IBM networking schemes. In fact, IBM and other vendors like Cisco Systems are developing hardware and software for integrating legacy systems into TCP/IP networks, not the other way around. These are discussed under "IBM Host Connectivity."

## SNA

The SNA protocol stack is compared to the OSI protocol stack in Figure S-6. It is interesting to note that the ISO (International Organization for Standardization) used IBM's SNA protocol stack as a starting model for its OSI stack. The protocol stack has the following layers:

- The *physical* layer allows many different types of physical connections.

- The *data Link* layer defines SDLC (Synchronous Data Link Control) and LAN protocols such as Token Ring.

- The *path control* layer controls routing and can subdivide datagrams and reassemble them to accommodate the transmission facilities.

- The *transmission* layer provides connection-oriented services that can set up a link between two endpoints to monitor data flow and guarantee delivery.

- The *data flow* layer monitors the flow of data and handles "conversations" between endpoints to prevent data overflow.

- The *presentation* layer performs data conversions and application interfacing.

- The *transaction* layer provides the interface into networking services for applications.

As discussed under the heading "IBM Mainframe Environment," an IBM SNA network consists of host systems, terminals (or PCs running emulation software) and printers, cluster controllers, communication controllers, and other components. The terminals and printers are connected to cluster controllers, which in turn connect to the host or to a communication controller if they are remote from the host. These hardware components and the software that runs in them are called *nodes,* and they are interconnected with *data links.* Nodes are endpoints or junctions in the network of various types, including Type 2 (computers, terminals, and printers), Type 4 (communication controllers), and Type 5 (host computers).

The media that interconnect nodes are copper wire, fiber-optic cable, or microwave. Data links are handled by the SDLC (Synchronous Data Link Control) protocol, the BISYNC (Binary Synchronous Communications) protocol, Token Ring, and more recently, Ethernet, Frame Relay, and FDDI (Fiber Distributed Data Interface). WAN links are achieved over X.25, Frame Relay, ATM, and, most recently, the Internet.

When a user runs an application, he or she does so through sessions. A session is a communication channel to network addressable units. The SNA network consists of logical units, or LUs (ports for accessing network resources), and physical units, or PUs, which handle network management functions and control telecommunication links. Software called SSCP (System Services Control Point) runs in the host and manages all the resources within the host's domain. Software called NCP (Network Control Program) runs in communication controllers (front-end processors) to relieve hosts of communication processes such as routing, session management, buffering of

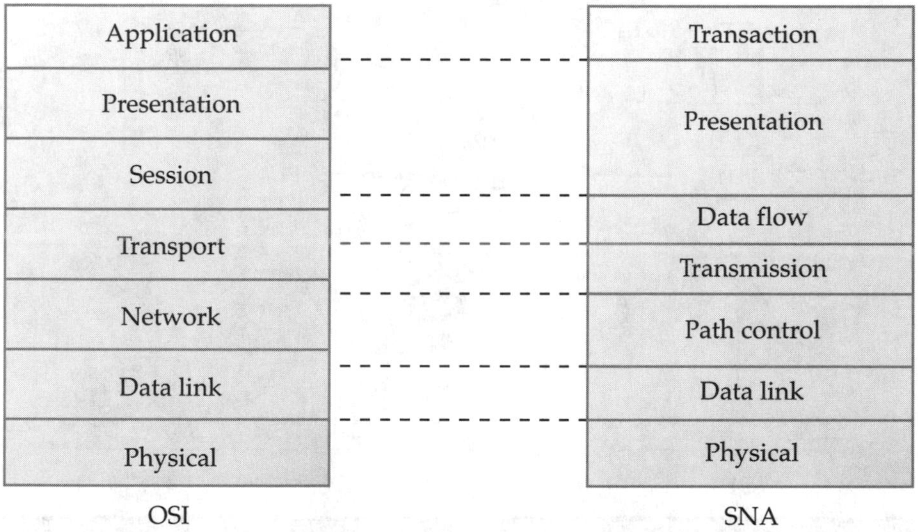

| OSI | | SNA |
|---|---|---|
| Application | | Transaction |
| Presentation | | Presentation |
| Session | | |
| Transport | | Data flow |
| | | Transmission |
| Network | | Path control |
| Data link | | Data link |
| Physical | | Physical |

**Figure S-6.**   *SNA and OSI protocol stacks compared*

incoming and outgoing data, error detection and correction in communications, and other tasks.

The different components of an SNA network are pictured in Figure S-7. An SNI (SNA network interconnect) feature provides a way to connect two separate host systems, which are located in separate areas called *subareas* or *domains*. SNI merges and maps the network resource names and addresses on the joined systems and provides alias names to avoid conflicts. SNI is sometimes used for EDI (Electronic Data Interchange) applications between suppliers and manufacturers, or when two companies merge.

## SNA in the New Network Environment

SNA is a problem in most internetwork environments. The existence of legacy systems demands that SNA support be maintained, but SNA is a nonroutable protocol, meaning that it can't traverse router-connected boundaries. Some organizations build two communication infrastructures—one for nonroutable SNA traffic and one for TCP/IP traffic. Another solution is to encapsulate SNA into the packets of a routable protocol such as IP. This is called *tunneling*. DLSw (Data Link Switching) is a standard for tunneling or encapsulating IBM SNA (Systems Network Architecture) and

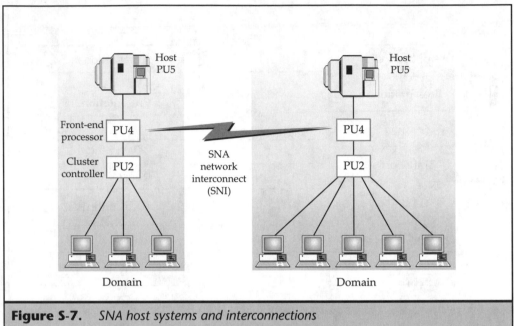

**Figure S-7.**  *SNA host systems and interconnections*

NetBIOS applications across IP (Internet Protocol) networks. See "DLSw (Data Link Switching)" for more details.

Still another solution is to install SNA gateways, which are servers that connect SNA systems to LANs and provide all the necessary translations to move traffic between those systems. Microsoft's SNA Server is such a system. Today, the trend is to extend TCP/IP networks all the way up to the mainframe system, which also runs the TCP/IP protocol. Thus, all the systems use the same protocol and no gateway is required.

Web browsers are providing a new way to get at corporate data, even when that data is stored on mainframe systems that use non-Web protocols. For example, Web browsers can provide access to SNA applications over TCP/IP-based intranets or remote connections. IBM and other vendors promote technology that provides SNA access via Web browsers.

These issues are covered further under "IBM Host Connectivity."

**RELATED ENTRIES**    AnyNet, IBM; APPC (Advanced Program-to-Program Communications); APPN (Advanced Peer-to-Peer Networking); DLSw (Data Link Switching); Enterprise Networks; HPR (High-Performance Routing), IBM; IBM (International Business Machines); IBM Host Connectivity; IBM Mainframe Environment; *and* IBM Open Blueprint

**INFORMATION ON THE INTERNET**

| | |
|---|---|
| IBM Corporation | http://www.ibm.com |
| IBM products | http://www.ibm.com/Products |
| IBM software | http://www.software.ibm.com |
| IBM networking | http://www.networking.ibm.com |
| H. Gilbert's Introduction to SNA | http://pclt.cis.yale.edu/pclt/COMM/SNA.HTM |

## Sniffer

*Sniffer* is the name of a network analyzer from Network General. See "Network Analyzers" for more information.

## SNMP (Simple Network Management Protocol)

SNMP is a popular management protocol defined by the Internet community for TCP/IP networks. It is a communication protocol for collecting information from devices on the network. Each device runs an agent that collects information and provides that information to a management console. Each piece of information to be collected about a device, such as the number of packets received, is defined by a managed object. A MIB (management information base) is a collection of managed objects. SNMP and its MIBs define the grammar and vocabulary for managing networks. It is up to vendors to build products that adhere to SNMP standards and allow devices to exchange management information.

SNMP is described in a variety of IETF (Internet Engineering Task Force) RFCs (requests for comment). You can find these RFCs at the Web sites listed at the end of this topic.

### The SNMP Environment

A typical SNMP environment is pictured in Figure S-8. The components are described here:

- **Managed devices** Network devices such as hubs, routers, and bridges running agents that collect information about their operation and provide it to the management console by way of the SNMP protocol.

- **Management systems** An administrative system that collects information from agents that run in managed devices.

- **SNMP** This is a protocol that provides the query language and transport mechanisms for querying the agents that run in managed devices. SNMP uses UDP (User Datagram Protocol), which is part of the TCP/IP suite, to carry its messages and data across the network.

- **Proxy agent** Some devices do not have the capability of running an agent. A proxy agent is a device that can run an agent for such a device and provide it with SNMP functions.

Management systems run a management application and include a database for collecting information. Most SNMP management systems can automatically discover the topology of the network and display that topology in graphic form. Administrators can "drill down" into a global view of the network to focus on segments or rings. They can then choose a device to manage and view information that has been collected about that device. Most network management systems are UNIX based, although Windows NT systems are becoming popular.

Common management console functions include network topology mapping, event trapping with alarms, traffic monitoring, network diagnostic functions, report generators, historical record management, and trend analysis.

An SNMP engine runs in the background to carry out the network tasks requested by the user. SNMP uses a request and response process to communicate with agents

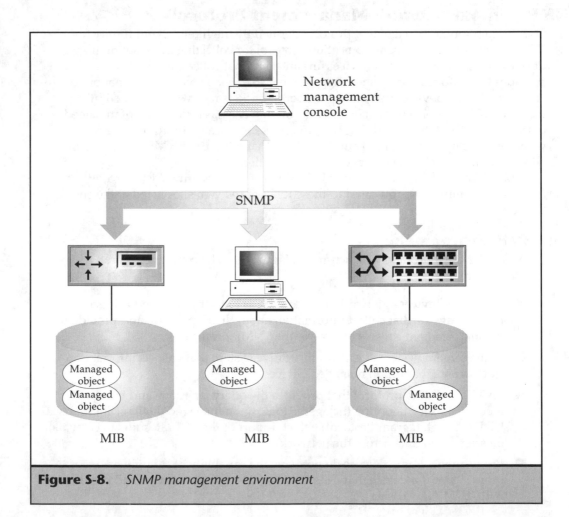

**Figure S-8.** *SNMP management environment*

and get values or change the status of network elements. It is a connectionless transport protocol with a simple command set. In this respect, SNMP is efficient and can even operate over networks that are overloaded and failing. Agents do little work of their own, except to monitor significant events that occur within the device.

Alarms can alert administrators when defined events occur on the network. Events are defined in MIB modules and are usually based on thresholds that have been exceeded, such as when traffic on a segment has exceeded a particular level. Managed devices are responsible for initiating alarms. An agent running in a device "traps" some event and sends a report to all management stations.

The key to SNMP popularity is its simplicity. It has a small command set that does a good job of collecting information from almost any network device. However, an SNMP network management console must continually *poll* the SNMP agents to obtain information and store it for historical purposes. Gathering this information not only increases network traffic, it also places a large burden on the network management console to gather the information. A MIB extension called RMON (Remote Monitoring) provides a way for agents running on network segments to collect information on their own about network segments, thus reducing network traffic caused by polling. See "RMON (Remote Monitoring)" for more information.

More important than understanding the simple SNMP command set is understanding the vocabulary of a MIB and the data that can be derived from it. The best management products know how to fully exploit this information and extract meaningful information that allows administrators to better manage their networks.

## MIB (Management Information Base)

A MIB is a database of managed objects having a hierarchical structure and is the focus of the management structure. There are generic and vendor-specific MIB objects. Over 1,000 different objects have been registered with the Internet community as managed objects. A managed object is a logical representation of a real physical entity on the network. Each object collects some information, such as the number of packets that have been received, and holds that information as a value that can be collected by the management system.

A MIB has a tree structure, and the top of the tree is defined by the ISO (International Organization for Standardization). Lower levels of the tree are defined by other organizations, and some branches define vendor-specific objects. The top of the tree contains groups of objects, including System (described equipment), Interfaces (described traffic on network interfaces), IP (IP packet statistics), ICMP (ICMP messages), TCP (TCP traffic statistics), UDP (UDP traffic statistics), EGP (Exterior Gateway Protocol statistics), and SNMP (SNMP traffic statistics). RMON is a MIB extension that collects information about entire network segments.

A MIB is defined by SMI (Structure of Management Information), which provides the tools for creating and identifying data types and data representations. Data types include integer values, network addresses, counters, gauges, time ticks, and table information. SMI also defines a hierarchical naming structure to identify each managed object. Objects are assigned names and a location in the hierarchical structure that helps identify what the object does. Objects include fields that define how the information is stored and how the information may be accessed (i.e., read-only or read/write). An object is defined via SMI and compiled to create code that can be integrated with an agent that runs on a particular device. The object then collects the defined information and makes it available to management systems.

## Enhancing SNMP

In 1992, the Internet community began working on extensions to SNMP that became known as SNMPv2. A primary goal was to improve security, add new management features, and make information retrieval more efficient. However, it was found that adding security would make the new version incompatible with the original SNMP protocol. SNMPv2 development fell into chaos, and the IETF disbanded the SNMPv2 group in 1996, although it was later reformed and in 1977 created a number of proposals that were combined into what is now called SNMPv3.

In the meantime, a new trend has emerged in which the HTTP protocol is used to transport management information. In this scheme, each managed device acts as a sort of Web server, providing information to Web browsers that have been modified to operate as management consoles. See "WBEM (Web-Based Enterprise Management)" and "Web-Based Network Management" for more information.

**RELATED ENTRIES**    Distributed Management; DME (Distributed Management Environment); DMI (Desktop Management Interface); DMTF (Desktop Management Task Force); Network Analyzers; Network Management; RMON (Remote Monitoring); Testing and Diagnostic Equipment and Techniques;  WBEM (Web-Based Enterprise Management), *and* Web-Based Network Management

**INFORMATION ON THE INTERNET**

| | |
|---|---|
| The Simple Web (network management links) | http://snmp.cs.utwente.nl |
| Cisco Systems' SNMP papers | http://www.cisco.com/univercd/data/doc/cintrnet/ito/55029.htm<br>http://www.cisco.com/warp/public/535/3.html |
| Yahoo!'s SNMP links page | http://www.yahoo.com/Computers_and_Internet/Information_and_Documentation/Protocols/SNMP__Simple_Network_Management_Protocol |
| Complete list of network management RFCs | http://www.iol.unh.edu/consortiums/netmgt/rfc-main.html |
| SNMP FAQs (contains a large list of SNMP-related RFCs) | http://www.cis.ohio-state.edu/hypertext/faq/bngusenet/comp/protocols/snmp/top.html |
| SNMP Research FAQs on SNMP | http://www.snmp.com/FAQs |

## Sockets API

Sockets are communication mechanisms used between running processes in UNIX and TCP/IP environments. Sockets defines the communication mechanisms and an application programming interface for building client/server applications. The programming interface has a set of common functions that programmers use to build applications. It was first implemented in the early 1980s as part of UNIX and the TCP/IP protocols. Sockets are now used in other environments such as Windows, as described under "WinSock."

Clients access server processes running on other network-connected computers. Server processes basically wait in a standby mode until they are requested by some client to provide a service. A network-attached computer may run several different processes, and each process is identified by a particular socket number. The socket number is appended to the IP address of the computer running the process.

Thus, clients can access specific processes running in specific computers by addressing the computer and a socket number. For example, a Web server running on a TCP/IP network such as the Internet has an IP address in this format:

*xxx.xxx.xxx.xxx/port#*

The *x* values represent the normal dotted notation IP address, while *port#* is a value that represents a particular server. Port 80 is the industry-accepted socket number for a Web server.

Sockets can provide a full-duplex communication channel between two or more systems. A local port makes a connection to a remote socket. Once a channel is opened, information is sent or received, and the circuit is then dismantled. There are stream and datagram sockets. A stream socket is a connection-oriented link that uses TCP (Transmission Control Protocol). It provides reliable data transmissions. A datagram socket is a connectionless service that uses UDP (User Datagram Protocol).

**RELATED ENTRIES**     Ports, TCP; TCP/IP (Transmission Control Protocol/Internet Protocol); UNIX; *and* WinSock

### INFORMATION ON THE INTERNET

| | |
|---|---|
| Sockets programming information | http://www.scit.wlv.ac.uk/~jphb/comms/ sockets.html |
| Stuart Sechrest's Sockets Tutorial | http://www.mcs.newpaltz.edu/~sigal/netg/ sockets.html |

## SOCKS

SOCKS is a proxy protocol that provides a secure channel between two TCP/IP systems, typically a Web client on an internal corporate network that wants to access an outside Web server (on the Internet, another company's network, or on another part of an intranet). SOCKS provides firewall services, as well as auditing, management, fault tolerance, and other features. With SOCKS in place, an internal corporate network can be connected to the Internet and provide a safe way for internal users to access servers on the Internet. NEC Corporation has been a big promoter of SOCKS.

There are several types of firewall devices, as discussed under "Firewall." SOCKS is a circuit-level proxy gateway that provides security based on connections (i.e., at the TCP layer). A SOCKS configuration is pictured in Figure S-9. It consists of SOCKS-enabled clients on the internal corporate network, a SOCKS server and a packet-filtering router acting as a firewall, and Web servers or other application servers on the Internet (or any other "foreign" network).

When a client needs to contact a Web server on the Internet, the request is intercepted by the SOCKS server. The SOCKS server relays this request to the target Web server. It may first evaluate whether the request is allowed based on company policies. When the response arrives from the Web server, the SOCKS server evaluates the packet before relaying it to the internal client. Thus the SOCKS server can collect, audit, screen, filter, and control data flowing in and out of the network. According to NEC, SOCKS is a "rich network application data warehouse." It also provides the foundation for other critical networking services such as security, management, auditing, and accounting.

As mentioned, SOCKS evaluates connection requests for internal users, sets up proxy circuits, and relays data between the client and target server. The latest version,

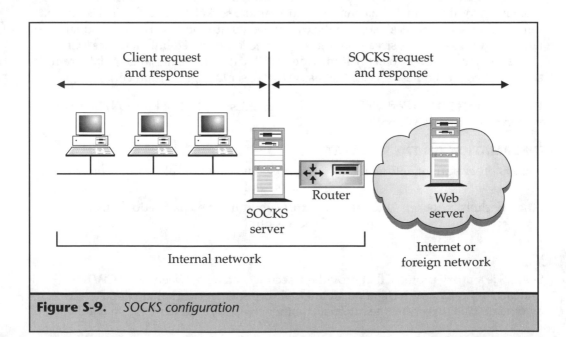

**Figure S-9.**  *SOCKS configuration*

SOCKS5, adds authentication, which allows network administrators to control user access through the SOCKS server. A variety of authentication schemes can be used, and the scheme is negotiable. SOCKS5 was created by a committee of industry supporters and submitted to the IETF (Internet Engineering Task Force) for standardization. SOCKS5 is outlined in RFC 1928, which is available at the Web site given below.

**RELATED ENTRIES**   Firewall; Proxy Server; *and* Security

**INFORMATION ON THE INTERNET**

SOCKS Protocol Version 5 (RFC 1928)   http://www.internic.net/rfc/rfc1928.txt

Aventail Corporation   http://www.aventail.com

Aventail's SOCKS links   http://www.aventail.com/educate/security.html

NEC's SOCKS page   http://www.socks.nec.com

## Software Distribution, Electronic

*See* Electronic Software Distribution and Licensing.

## Solaris, SunSoft

*See* Sun Microsystems Solaris.

## SONET (Synchronous Optical Network)

SONET is a standard that defines telecommunication transmissions over fiber-optic cables. It was first proposed by Bellcore in the mid-1980s, then standardized by the ANSI (American National Standards Institute). The ITU (formerly the CCITT) adapted SONET to create SDH (Synchronous Digital Hierarchy), a worldwide telecommunication standard. SONET is a subset of SDH that is used in North America.

Think of SONET as a means to deploy a physical network for a global commincation system in much the same way that Ethernet or token ring are used to deploy a LAN. SONET is built on fiber-optic cable, and standardized rates are used to ensure that telecommunications companies around the globe can interconnect their systems with little trouble. SONET removes the boundaries between the telephone companies of the world.

A SONET network typically implements a fully redundant multiple ring topology that is designed to survive breaks, earthquakes, backhoe accidents, or similar problems that might disrupt service. Sprint's recent SONET ring deployment provides an example of what a SONET network is like. The fiber-optic ring runs through Springfield, Massachusetts; Buffalo, New York; Montreal; and Toronto. In the event of a fiber cut or electronics failure, calls are rerouted around failure points in milliseconds. The system is a four-fiber, bidirectional, line-switched SONET ring (4 BLSR), as pictured in Figure S-10. Two fibers carry traffic, while another two are in standby, or "protect" mode, ready to take over in the event of a service disruption. In the actual network, each fiber ring follows different routes to avoid local disasters.

SONET was designed to supersede the T-carrier and E-carrier digital hierarchies that have been in use in the United States and Europe, respectively. It solves problems with incompatibilities in these digital hierarchies while providing backward compatibility. In addition, the designers made sure that SONET could be extended high up into the gigabit-per-second range. The SONET digital hierarchy is outlined in the following table, with each level having a specific OC (optical carrier) level number.

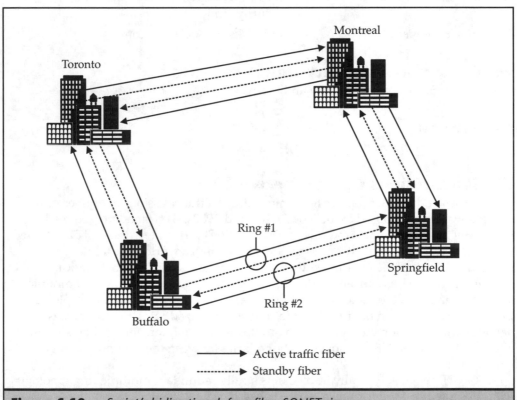

**Figure S-10.**  *Sprint's bidirectional, four-fiber SONET ring*

| Optical Carrier Level | Data rate (Mbits/sec) | Number of DS0s | Number of DS1s | Number of DS3s |
|---|---|---|---|---|
| OC-1 | 51.84 | 672 | 28 | 1 |
| OC-3 | 155.52 | 2,016 | 84 | 3 |
| OC-6 | 311.04 | 4,032 | 168 | 6 |
| OC-9 | 466.56 | 6,048 | 252 | 9 |
| OC-12 | 622.08 | 8,064 | 336 | 12 |
| OC-18 | 933.12 | 12,096 | 504 | 18 |
| OC-24 | 1,244.16 | 16,128 | 672 | 24 |
| OC-36 | 1,866.24 | 24,192 | 1,008 | 36 |
| OC-48 | 2,488.32 | 32,256 | 1,344 | 48 |
| OC-96 | 4,976.00 | 64,512 | 2,688 | 96 |
| OC-192 | 9,952.00 | 129,024 | 5,376 | 192 |

SONET implements synchronous transmissions in which individual channels are merged into a higher-level channel using time division multiplexing. In this scheme, each channel gets a specific time slot in the transmission. SONET multiplexes a variety of data streams, called *tributaries*, into higher and higher OC levels. For example, T1 and T3 streams can be multiplexed into an OC-1, and multiple OC-1s can then be multiplexed into an OC-3 and so on.

SONET carries data and control information in 810-byte frames that travel across the fiber in a synchronous stream. Control information is embedded in the frame and is referred to as the *overhead*. The overhead contains the following components:

- The *section* overhead handles frame generation and error monitoring. All devices on the line use these features.

- The *line* overhead provides a way to monitor the status of the line.

- The *path* overhead provides control signaling and error-monitoring data between the endpoints (path termination equipment) on the network.

These overhead components relate to SONET's physical layer architecture, as pictured in Figure S-11. The *photonic sublayer* is the lowest layer that specifies properties of the fiber and the light. The *section sublayer* handles a single point-to-point link, such as between the original source and a repeater. The *line sublayer* is concerned with multiplexing, and the *path sublayer* is involved with actual end-to-end connections across repeaters and multiplexors.

**S**

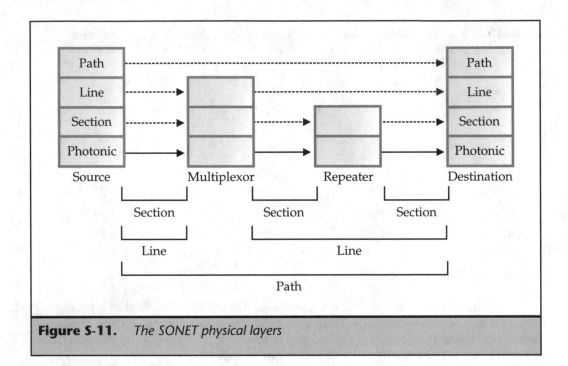

**Figure S-11.**   *The SONET physical layers*

The latest trend in SONET is WDM (wavelength division multiplexing), which provides the technology to dramatically multiply the data rate of optical cables. WDM allows a single fiber-optic line to accommodate multiple light signals at different wavelengths. For example, MCI upgraded its backbone network, which previously operated at 2.5 Gbits/sec, to Quad-WDM (four wavelengths). The backbone now operates at 10 Gbits/sec, "enough capacity to carry 129,000 simultaneous telephone calls over the hair-thin strand," according to MCI.

**RELATED ENTRIES**   E-1/E-3 European Digital Hierarchy; Fiber-Optic Cable; Multiplexing; NADH (North American Digital Hierarchy); T1/T3; Telecommunications and Telephone Systems; *and* WAN (Wide Area Network)

**INFORMATION ON THE INTERNET**

| | |
|---|---|
| SONET Interoperability Forum | http://www.atis.org/atis/sif/sifhom.htm |
| Committee T1's SONET page | http://www.t1.org/html/sonet.htm |
| SONET paper at Carnegie Mellon University | http://fedida.ini.cmu.edu/sonetdoc.html |
| SONET tutorial | http://bugs.wpi.edu:8080/EE535/hwk11cd95/dks1/dks1.html |

| Chris Trown's SONET paper | http://www.ecst.csuchico.edu/~ctrown/sonet_notes.txt |
| Sprint's SONET information | http://www.sprintbiz.com/data1/sonet/sonet1.html |

## Source Routing

Source routing is used in IP networks to specify a specific route though the network under some conditions. A network technician might use source routing to diagnose problems or time the throughput of packets along a specific path. The *strict* source-routing option is used to specify a complete path through the network from source to destination. The *loose* source-routing option is used to specify routers that the packet must cross, although intermediate routers not in the list can also be crossed.

IBM Token Ring networks use a *source-routing* routine that can provide bridges with information about where packets should go and how to get there. In source routing, the packets themselves hold the forwarding information. The bridge does not maintain forwarding tables; it sends packets to LAN segments based on the packet address information. Bridges that do source routing use a *discovery* method to determine the route a packet should take to a device. Note that although this sounds like routing, the source-routing bridge is simply a forwarding device that knows the addresses of other bridges.

**RELATED ENTRIES**    Routing Protocols and Algorithms; Token Ring Network

## Spanning Tree Algorithm

The spanning tree algorithm is used in bridged internetwork environments to detect and break circular traffic patterns by disabling certain links. The IEEE 801.2-D STP (Spanning Tree Protocol) inhibits loops in redundant bridges by maintaining the secondary bridge as a backup. If the first bridge should go down, the secondary bridge takes over. See "Bridges and Bridging" for more information.

## SPARC (Scalable Performance Architecture)

Sun Microsystems' SPARC processors are based on a RISC architecture design that provides scalability from desktop systems to supercomputer systems.

- The *microSPARC* line is designed for desktop use. It is evolving into a powerful low-voltage chip for portable systems.

- The *SuperSPARC* line is designed for high-end desktop and server usage and has a 32-bit design with clock speeds in the 40 MHz to 90 MHz range. The 50 MHz version is said to perform at 135 to 1,000 MIPS (million instructions per second).

■ The *UltraSPARC* is a line of high-end 64-bit processors that operate in the 200 MHz to 300 MHz range. UltraSPARC is the successor to SuperSPARC.

While the SPARC processor was originally designed for high-end workstations, it has evolved in two directions to support low-cost desktop systems and high-end engineering/scientific workstations and server systems. Sun's Ultra Enterprise 10000 is a mainframe-like system that runs from 16 to 64 UltraSPARC processors.

**RELATED ENTRIES**    Servers; Sun Microsystems

**INFORMATION ON THE INTERNET**

Sun Microsystems' SPARC information        http://www.sun.com/microelectronics

## Spoofing

Spoofing is a form of security breach in which a hacker masquerades as another user and manages to illegally log on to a computer system. The simplest form of spoofing is to simply obtain the username and secret password of the target user's logon account. Another method is to use a piece of equipment such as a network analyzer to monitor and capture network traffic, then insert bogus packets into the data stream.

**RELATED ENTRIES**    Hacker; Network Analyzers; *and* Security

## Spread Spectrum Signaling

Radio communication is widely used as the medium for computer networks, including in-office networks that allow users to move around the office with their portable computers. A central transmitter/receiver, or *transceiver*, is installed that broadcasts signals to workstations. One method for transmitting signals is called *spread spectrum*. Spread spectrum is also used in digital cellular communication systems. Conventional analog systems use narrowband transmission techniques.

Spread spectrum technology was first used in World War II as a way to provide jam-proof radio communication for guided torpedoes. Spread spectrum distributes a signal over a wide range of frequencies for transmission. The receiver then collects the signals based on information that has been prearranged with the sender. Spread spectrum signals are hard to detect and if detected, difficult to demodulate. This provides security. In addition, spread spectrum signals produce little if any interference with other signals. The wide signal requires less transmission power. In fact, spread spectrum signals can occupy the same band as narrowband signals.

The main characteristic of spread spectrum is that the original signal is spread out to a very wide bandwidth, often over 200 times the bandwidth of the original signal. There are a number of spread spectrum techniques, but the two methods described next are the most often used.

**DIRECT SEQUENCE SPREAD SPECTRUM**    In this scheme, the data to transmit is altered by a bit stream that is generated by the sender. The bit stream represents every bit in the original data with multiple bits in the generated stream, thus spreading the signal across a wider frequency band. If 100 bits are used to represent each bit of data, the signal is spread out to 100 times its original bandwidth. The source generates a pseudorandom bit stream to modulate the original data and the destination generates the same bit stream to demodulate what it receives. Spread spectrum broadcasts in bands where noise is prominent, but does not rise above the noise. Its radio signals are too weak to interfere with conventional radios and have fewer FCC (Federal Communications Commission) restrictions.

**FREQUENCY HOPPING SPREAD SPECTRUM**    In this technique, the original data signal is not spread out, but is instead transmitted over a wide range of frequencies that change at split-second intervals. Both the transmitter and the receiver jump frequencies in synchronization during the transmission so a jammer would have difficulty targeting the exact frequency on which the devices are communicating. The frequencies are derived from a table that both the sender and receiver follow.

The FCC has allocated spread spectrum frequency bands for commercial use in the ranges of 902 to 928 MHz, 2.4000 to 2.4835 GHz, and 5.725 to 5.850 GHz.

CDMA (Code Division Multiple Access) is a digital cellular standard that uses wideband spread spectrum techniques for signal transmission. It combines both digital voice and data into a single wireless communication network. A CDMA call at a rate of 9,600 bits/sec is spread out to over 1 Mbit/sec.

**RELATED ENTRIES**    CDMA (Code Division Multiple Access); Cellular Communication Systems; *and* Wireless Communications

**INFORMATION ON THE INTERNET**

| | |
|---|---|
| Spread Spectrum Scene Magazine (see links page) | http://sss-mag.com |
| Cylink papers (see "Wireless Tutorials" section) | http://www.cylink.com/tutorial |

# SPX (Sequenced Packet Exchange)

*See* Novell NetWare Protocols.

# SQL (Structured Query Language)

SQL, pronounced "see-quel," was originally developed by IBM in the mid-1970s as a database query language to operate on the VM/370 and MVS/370 operating systems. It was later commercialized by Oracle Corporation, after which many other companies jumped on the bandwagon. Today, SQL is viewed as an interface to access data on many different types of database systems, including mainframes, midrange systems, UNIX systems, and network servers.

In the 1980s, the process of standardizing the language was initiated by the ISO (International Organization for Standardization), the ANSI (American National Standards Institute), and X/Open (now part of The Open Group). Standardization is an ongoing process, and the latest implementation, which is called SQL3, was being standardized at the time of this writing. SQL3 includes object-oriented technology. For historical reference, SQL2 was standardized in 1992 and is commonly referred to as SQL-92. More information about ongoing standardization can be found at the SQL Standards Home Page listed at the end of this section.

In the client/server environment, the user's front-end application interfaces to a DBMS (database management system) engine running on a back-end server. The interface between the front end and the back end is a specific API (application programming interface). While SQL provided a standard for accessing databases, there were differences in the way each system was implemented. Database systems have traditionally been tied to a specific front-end interface that did not work with just any client-side application. One of the following programming interfaces is usually implemented:

- **Embedded SQL**   In this approach, SQL statements are embedded into the source code of programs that are written in a host language such as C. A typical embedded SQL program contains a number of SQL statements, but these statements cannot be directly compiled into C, so they are precompiled to make them compatible with the host language and the program is then compiled for execution. The program can then operate directly with the database because the SQL statements are embedded in it.

- **CLI (Call-Level Interface)**   With this approach, programs must call a set of external functions in an API library in order to work with the database. CLI is normally used when the client and server are on two different systems and the API is located on the client system. The client application makes a call to the API, and the API communicates with the DBMS.

The current trend is to provide so-called "middleware" products between the clients and servers to allow users to access any back-end server using a variety of front-end applications. They hide the differences between access languages and database APIs. The most common middleware today is the Microsoft-defined ODBC (Open Database Connectivity). Another is IBM's DRDA (Distributed Relational Database Architecture).

**RELATED ENTRIES**   Client/Server Computing; Database Connectivity; DBMS (Database Management System); DRDA (Distributed Relational Database Architecture); Middleware and Messaging; ODBC (Open Database Connectivity), Microsoft; *and* Web Middleware and Database Connectivity

### INFORMATION ON THE INTERNET

SQL Standards page               http://www.jcc.com/sql_stnd.html

SQL Access Group                 http://www.opengroup.org

# SS7 (Signaling System 7)

SS7 is an out-of-band signaling system used by the carriers to set up telephone calls. It is a protocol standard defined by the ITU (International Telecommunication Union). Network elements in the public-switched telephone network use SS7 to exchange information used not only to set up calls but to affect routing and control the network. SS7 is a message-based system that operates on a separate digital line from the actual phone calls. This differs from the older signaling system in which signals were transmitted as multifrequency tones in the same channels as calls.

The system consists of SSPs (service switching points) that provide the origination or termination points for calls. SSPs can send signals to other SSPs to set up and manage calls. They may also use SS7 signaling to query a database for information about how to route a call. STPs (signal transfer points) are packet switches that route SS7 messages based on the routing information obtained by an SSP.

**RELATED ENTRIES**    IXC (Interexchange Carrier); LEC (Local Exchange Carrier); Local Loop; PSTN (Public-Switched Telephone Network); *and* Telecommunications and Telephone Systems

**INFORMATION ON THE INTERNET**

| | |
|---|---|
| SS7 page at Michigan Public Service Commission | http://ermisweb.state.mi.us/mpsc/reports/jbbb/xccs7.htm |
| MicroLegend's SS7 Tutorial | http://www.microlegend.com/aboutss7.htm |
| Committee T1's SS7 page | http://www.t1.org/html/ss7.htm |

# SSA (Serial Storage Architecture)

SSA is a high-performance serial interface that is commonly used to connect peripheral devices like disk drives, optical disks, printers, and scanners to computer workstations and servers. It can handle up to two 20-MB/sec transmissions at the same time (in opposite directions) on a single port. A typical interface has two ports, so an SSA system has a total bandwidth of 80 MB/sec.

SSA was originally developed by IBM, but it is now being developed by the ANSI (American National Standards Institute) subcommittee called X3T10.1. SSA is also specified as a physical layer serial interface in the SCSI-3 standard. Although SCSI (Small Computer System Interface) designers have achieved high data rates with parallel SCSI, serial designs such as SSA are considered critical for high-data-rate performance and to boost cabling distances to devices.

An SSA connection consists of a shielded four-wire cable (two pairs). The distance between the host and a peripheral can be up to 25 meters (82 feet). At this writing, the longest SCSI cable distance was 25 meters (with 32 meters planned in the future). Devices can be configured in daisy-chain fashion or connected to switch boxes in a star configuration. A loop configuration is also available to provide a fault-tolerant cabling path that has no single point of failure.

**RELATED ENTRIES**    Connection Technologies; Fibre Channel; Firewire; SCSI (Small Computer System Interface); Serial Communication and Interfaces; *and* Storage Systems

**INFORMATION ON THE INTERNET**

## SSL (Secure Sockets Layer)

SSL is a Web protocol that sets up a secure session between a Web client and server. All data transmitted over the wire is encrypted. S-HTTP (Secure HTTP) is a similar protocol that encrypts only at the HTTP (Hypertext Transfer Protocol) level, while SSL encrypts all data being passed between client and server at the IP socket level. SSL was originally developed by Netscape, then submitted to the IETF (Internet Engineering Task Force) for standardization.

Both SSL and S-HTTP provide security benefits for electronic commerce, including protection from eavesdroppers and tampering. With SSL, browsers and servers *authenticate* one another, then *encrypt* data transmitted during a session. This procedure verifies to the client that the Web server is authentic before it submits confidential information, and it allows Web servers to verify that users are authentic before granting them access to restricted and sensitive information or letting them buy goods. Digital certificates are required in this scheme. See "Certificates and Certification Systems" for more information.

Both Web browsers and Web servers must be SSL-enabled, as is now common. Note that authentication can work both ways, but that it is not essential. Often, the client is only interested in authenticating the server before transmitting confidential information. In addition, a one-way authentication is all that is needed for both parties to obtain a key that can be used to encrypt transmitted data. When a client contacts a server, the server forwards a certificate signed by a CA (certificate authority). The client then uses the CA's public key (which it has presumably already obtained) to open the certificate and pull out the Web site's public key.

SSL consists of the SSLHP (SSL Handshake Protocol), which provides authentication services and negotiates an encryption method. SSL also consists of the SSLRP (SSL Record Protocol), which performs the job of packaging data so it can be encrypted. SSLHP operates in the application layer and SSLRP operates in the presentation layer relative to the OSI protocol stack.

The IETF Transport Layer Security (tls) Working Group is evaluating SSL and methods for providing secure and authenticated channels over the Internet. The Public-Key Infrastructure (X.509) (pkix) Working Group and the Web Transaction Security (wts) Working Group are also working on secure transaction protocols. Their Web sites are listed below. Note that Microsoft's PCT (Private Communication

Technology) protocol was developed in response to weaknesses in SSL. See "PCT (Private Communication Technology) Protocol" for more information.

**RELATED ENTRIES**    Certificates and Certification Systems; Digital Signatures; PKI (Public-Key Infrastructure); Public-Key Cryptography; Security; SET (Secure Electronic Transaction); *and* S-HTTP (Secure Hypertext Transfer Protocol)

**INFORMATION ON THE INTERNET**

| | |
|---|---|
| The SSL-Talk FAQ at Consensus Development Corp. | http://www.consensus.com/security/ssl-talk-faq.html |
| Jeremy Bradley's SSL paper (excellent; very detailed) | http://www.cs.bris.ac.uk/~bradley/publish/SSLP |
| IETF Transport Layer Security (tls) Working Group | http://www.ietf.org/html.charters/tls-charter.html |
| IETF Public-Key Infrastructure (X.509) (pkix) Working Group | http://www.ietf.org/html.charters/pkix-charter.html |
| IETF Web Transaction Security (wts) Working Group | http://www.ietf.org/html.charters/wts-charter.html |
| Entrust Technologies' Web Security Primer (information about SSL and S-HTTP) | http://www.entrust.com/primer.htm |
| Netscape's SSL document | http://www.netscape.com/newsref/std/SSL.html |
| T J Hudson's and E A Young's SSL Programmer Reference | http://scorch.doc.ic.ac.uk/~ul/ssl.html |

## Standards Groups, Associations, and Organizations

The primary standards groups and organizations related to networking and the Internet are listed in the following table. Refer to the related headings in this book for more information. A complete list of standards organizations, associations, consortiums, and other groups would fill a whole book. Therefore, this section provides links to sites on the Web that have hotlinks to standards groups, organizations, and associations. Also refer to "Internet" and "Internet Organizations and Committees" for information about Internet-related organizations and standards. Also refer to Appendix A for additional references.

| | |
|---|---|
| ANSI (American National Standards Institute) | http://www.ansi.org |
| EIA (Electronic Industries Association) | http://www.eia.org |
| IEEE (Institute of Electrical and Electronic Engineers) | http://www.ieee.org |
| ISO (International Organization for Standardization) | http://www.iso.ch |
| ITU (International Telecommunication Union) | http://www.itu.ch |

**S**

**INFORMATION ON THE INTERNET**

| | |
|---|---|
| Telecoms Virtual Library (complete subject list with subpages of links) | http://www.analysys.co.uk/vlib |
| Standards and Standardization Bodies | http://www.iso.ch/VL/Standards.html |
| Prof. Jeffrey MacKie-Mason's links to associations, nonprofits: foundations and professional, trade, and interest groups | http://www.spp.umich.edu/telecom/associations.html |
| Prof. Jeffrey MacKie-Mason's links to standards bodies | http://www.spp.umich.edu/telecom/standards.html |
| Telstra Corp.'s Telecommunications Information Sources | http://www.telstra.com.au/info/communications.html |
| Stefan Dresler's links | http://www.telematik.informatik.uni-karlsruhe.de/~dresler/communications.html |
| Cellular Networking Perspectives' telecom links | http://www.cadvision.com/cnp-wireless/pointers.html |
| Webstart Communications' standards links | http://www.cmpcmm.com/cc/standards.html |

## Stateful and Stateless Connections

A *stateful connection* in one in which some information about a connection between two systems is retained to maintain the current connection or to use for future connections. In contrast, a *stateless connection* is best described by a client/server connection on the Web. A client sends a request to the server, and the server responds with a reply and disconnects. If the Web user clicks a button on the Web page to jump to a hyperlink, a whole new connection is set up between the client and server. The server has not retained any information about the client that might be used to maintain a connection or to assist in the next request. No information is cached in expectation of the user's next request.

Stateless systems are efficient if users tend to make few and infrequent requests from servers. However, stateless systems are inefficient if the client needs to make a large number of requests from the same server. Each request requires a setup phase which requires time and the exchange of packets that add traffic to the network. Sophisticated client/server applications require connection-oriented sessions in which the server caches information about the client during the session. This is especially true in transaction processing systems where information on both the client and server systems must be written in synchronization and verified.

**RELATED ENTRIES**    Client/Server Computing; HTTP (Hypertext Transfer Protocol); IIOP (Internet Inter-ORB Protocol); Internet; IP (Internet Protocol); *and* Web Technologies and Concepts

## Static Routing

An internetwork typically consists of subnetworks connected with bridges or routers. Large internetworks typically have many different paths that packets can take to reach a destination. Routers are the switches that direct packets over one path or another based on stored information that indicates the best path to a destination.

Static routing implies that the paths are manually programmed into the router by a network administrator. If a path fails, the administrator must reprogram the router so packets follow other paths. In mission-critical environments, this is usually unacceptable, so dynamic routers are used that automatically locate and determine the best paths through the internetwork and dynamically recalculate paths when lines fail. However, most routers support both static and dynamic routing.

**RELATED ENTRIES**    Routers; Routing Protocols and Algorithms

## Storage Management Systems

Storage management systems consist of data storage devices and storage management software, which provide online and near-line access to data, as well as archival storage of data. A typical system consists of online hard disk storage, writable optical disks, and tape backup systems. As data on hard drives becomes old or falls into disuse, it is transferred to near-line optical disk storage where it is still readily available if necessary. After a certain time, near-line data that is no longer used may be transferred to tape backup systems and archived. Because data is moved to a hierarchy of devices, these systems are usually called *HSM (hierarchical storage management)* systems.

The process of moving little-used or targeted files from primary magnetic disk storage to secondary optical disk or magnetic tape storage is called *migration.* Data can be *de-migrated* back to magnetic disk if users need to view historical information or files that have been migrated. HSM systems are designed for the following circumstances:

- When gigabytes of information must be available at all times
- To operate as backup and archiving systems that require little human intervention (except to move disks or tapes off-site for safekeeping)
- To benefit document imaging applications

HSM optical devices are commonly referred to as *jukeboxes.* They read and write to rewritable optical disks and use an autochanger mechanism that mounts and dismounts disks as requested. A typical jukebox may contain four or more optical drives and a device that picks disks from a bay and inserts them into the drives at the user's request.

Figure S-12 illustrates the configuration of a typical HSM system. Files are migrated from the server's magnetic online storage to the optical disk after a period of nonuse. After more time, these files may move to tape storage. Some files can be marked for immediate migration, or migration at a specific time. You can also

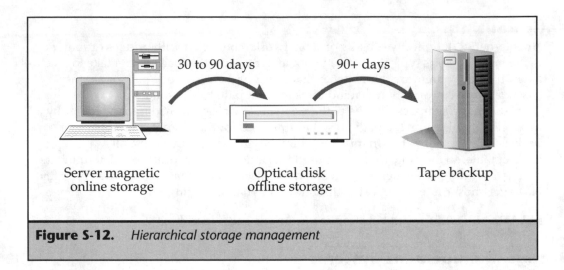

30 to 90 days    90+ days

Server magnetic
online storage

Optical disk
offline storage

Tape backup

**Figure S-12.** *Hierarchical storage management*

de-migrate files in the same way. For example, if a file is required for end-of-month reporting, you can have that file de-migrated to magnetic disk the night before running the report. De-migration times for tapes are approximately 1 to 3 minutes, and de-migration times for optical disks are about 8 to 10 seconds.

Because HSM files are essentially always online, HSM eliminates the bother associated with retrieving files from conventional data archives. For example, a user doesn't need to contact the archive operator, who then locates the tape (or other) archive, mounts it, and restores the data. Users who need migrated files access them by searching a familiar directory structure. Access to migrated files may take a little longer, but not as long as it takes to retrieve files from conventional archives.

HSM is designed for law firms, hospitals, insurance companies, and other organizations with documents that are rarely accessed. The benefits HSM provides to large, geographically diverse organizations are also important. For example, an insurance agent could call up an insurance company's central archives and access old client records without an operator's intervention.

**RELATED ENTRIES**    Backup and Data Archiving; Data Protection; Disaster Recovery; Fault Management; Fault Tolerance; Jukebox Optical Storage Devices; *and* Storage Systems

## Storage Systems

Storage systems are supposed to make data and applications available to users when they need it. That will only happen if you make sure that enough storage is available and that it is not overwhelmed with useless or unnecessary data. A storage system may include magnetic disks, optical disks, and tape storage systems. Magnetic disks and optical disks provide direct access to data, while tape systems provide slower sequential access. By arranging these systems in a hierarchical structure, it is possible to support three different data storage models:

- **Online storage** Data is stored on high-speed magnetic disk drives that can provide the highest response to user queries.
- **Near-line** Data is stored on high-volume optical disks, which have slower read and write times than magnetic disks.
- **Offline** Data is stored on tape for archival purposes.

These systems are discussed further under "Storage Management Systems." This section covers the different types of storage devices. Interface technologies used to connect storage devices are discussed elsewhere in this book. Refer to the following sections for more details:

- **Fibre Channel** Supports data transfer rates in the 100-MB/sec to 4-GB/sec range and supports very high-capacity, high-speed drives.
- **Firewire (IEEE 1394)** Supports data transfer rates of 100 MB/sec to 400 MB/sec. Devices are daisy-chained together and connected to a single port.
- **SCSI (Small Computer System Interface)** SCSI has been a standard disk drive interface since the early days of desktop computers. Storage devices are daisy-chained together and connected to a host adapter.
- **SSA (Serial Storage Architecture)** A high-speed serial interface with a total throughput of up to 80 MB/sec and relatively long cable distances.

*NOTE: A new way to connect storage devices is directly to the network, as described in the "Server Switching" section under the topic "Servers."*

## Hard Disk Technologies

Hard disks provide the performance required to support online data access. A typical server that supports hundreds of users at a time will require high-performance disk interfaces and drives. Here are features to consider when evaluating hard drives:

- **Rotation speed** This is the speed at which the disk platters spin. Spin rates are typically 5,400 rpm and 7,200 rpm. The newest and fastest drives run at 10,000 rpm.
- **Seek time** This is the amount of time it takes for the read/write head to move one-third of the way across the disk. Seek times for server drives should be between 8 and 12 milliseconds.
- **Data transfer rate** This is the amount of data transfer divided by the access time.

- **Access time** This is based on the rotation speed, seek time, and overhead of the drive system.

As mentioned, buying a disk with the fastest rotation rate is a virtual guarantee that you will get good performance, as long as you match it with a host adapter that is recommended by the manufacturer. RAID systems are a popular choice. They provide large amounts of storage, fast access, and fault tolerance at a reasonable price. Refer to "RAID (Redundant Arrays of Inexpensive Disks)" for more information. Some operating systems, such as Windows NT, let you configure your own disk array configurations.

You don't need a RAID configuration to take advantage of fault tolerance features. Most network operating systems support *mirroring* of data on one disk to another disk. Mirroring protects against disk failures by continuously duplicating data on a primary drive or set of drives to secondary drives. In the event of a drive failure, the matching secondary drive set can take its place.

## Optical Storage

Optical disks provide the next type of storage in the hierarchical storage management scheme—near-line storage. Optical disks can also provide *library storage,* in which large amounts of information that does not require high-speed access is kept online for network users to access.

Optical disks provide huge amounts of data storage and easily support the requirements of document imaging systems. A typical optical *jukebox* system with automatic disk-changing capabilities can keep hundreds of gigabytes of information online. An *autochanger* mechanism mounts and dismounts disks at the user's request.

There are two optical disk technologies: *rewritable* and *WORM (write once, read many),* as discussed in the following sections. With rewritable disks, data can be stored and erased. WORM disks can only be written to once and not overwritten. WORM technology is also called CD-R (recordable), and a CD-E (erasable) format is in the works.

### Rewritable Optical Disk Technologies

The rewritable optical disk provides a changeable data storage solution for library data, backups, and data archiving. While rewritable disks store large amounts of information, there are limitations in the number of times you can actually rewrite the disks. The three main rewritable optical disk technologies are described here:

- **MO (magnetic-optical) technology** This technology is currently used in most rewritable drives. The recording medium in the disks is a magnetic material. The write heads of the drive change the magnetic field of the material to record digital information with the assistance of a laser. The material is highly resistant to change, but when heated with a laser, a high magnetic flux can be applied to change the magnetic state of the very small area heated by the laser, thus allowing high data packing. The magnetically altered disk is read by using a laser that reflects a polarized beam of light off the magnetically aligned particles of the disk. MO disks have a long shelf life and are less susceptible to accidental erasure than other media.

■ **Phase-change technology** This technique uses a laser to change a crystalline material to an amorphous state, altering the reflectivity of the material and thus providing a way to record digital information. Disks must be retired after a certain number of changes due to limitations in the writable material.

■ **Dye polymer technology** In this technique, the heat of a laser causes a spot on a dye-tinted polymer material sandwiched between the disk's outer casing to physically change its state. The change of state can represent binary information. To erase the disk, the material is reheated with another laser and returns to its original state. Disks must be retired after a certain number of changes due to limitations in the writable material.

### CD (Compact Disc) Formats

CD-ROM (Compact Disc Read-Only Memory) is an optical data disc that is an adaptation of the audio compact disc. The disc sizes and formats are the same. In fact, computer CD-ROM drives will play audio compact discs. As the name implies, CD-ROMs are read-only, but new CD-R (recordable) technologies have become popular, and many organizations are using the medium to record and distribute catalogs, price sheets, and other information. They are also used at Web sites to provide information for Web users that is safe from corruption (i.e., hackers cannot destroy data on CD-ROMs).

The traditional CD-ROM holds up to 600MB of information, which is over 300,000 pages of information, but new optical disc formats are available such as DVD-ROM (Digital Video Disk ROM) that have seven times this capacity. A typical DVD-ROM can hold from 4.7GB to 8.5GB of data or 90 minutes of high-quality video. DVD-ROM drives are also backward compatible with CD-ROM. DVD provides all the benefits of the WORM/CD-ROM technology, but supports many times the storage capacity of any previous technology. DVD technologies consist of DVD-ROM (a high-capacity storage medium), DVD-Video, DVD-Audio, DVD-R (Recordable), and DVD-RAM (an erasable format).

## Linear Tape Technologies

Tape is the third level of a hierarchical storage management system. It provides offline storage for backing up and archiving data. Tape storage is inexpensive and provides high capacities. Automated tape devices provide a way to make archived data on tape available to network users, if necessary. A variety of tape formats and drive technologies are available as outlined in the following subsections. A comparison of tape capacities and data transfer rates is provided in Table S-2, but keep in mind that these numbers are typically high-end values and depend on the quality of the systems you buy. Also, keep in mind that tape lengths have a lot to do with capacity!

### QIC (Quarter-Inch Cartridge) and Travan

The QIC (pronounced "quick") tape was the standard backup solution up until a few years ago. It was first introduced by 3M Company in 1972 as a medium for recording continuous data streams such as backups. Conner Peripherals (now owned by Seagate

| Format | Uncompressed Capacity | Data Transfer Rate |
|---|---|---|
| QIC | 4GB | 200 KB/sec to 500 KB/sec |
| DDS-1 (DAT 4 mm) | 2GB | 200 KB/sec to 2 MB/sec |
| DDS-2 (DAT 4 mm) | 8GB | 2 MB/sec |
| DDS-3 (DAT 4 mm) | 12GB | 2 MB/sec |
| 8 mm Helical Scan | 10GB | 200 KB/sec to 3 MB/sec |
| DLT | 4 to 20GB | 1.2 MB/sec to 3 MB/sec |

**Table S-2.** *Linear tape system specifications*

Technology) upgraded the format, and potentially saved it from death, by creating a new format called Travan QIC. Travan drives will read the smaller QIC minicartridges.

With QIC, data is sequentially recorded on parallel tracks of a tape, first in one direction on one track, and in the other direction on the next track. The original tapes are 6 ∀ 4 ∀ 5/8 inches in size. QIC *minicartridges* use the same belt drive systems as QIC cartridges, but are smaller in size and have a capacity of 1GB.

Travan uses new tape formulations to increase capacity. The tape is also thinner and stronger, and thus longer, meaning that more data can be stored on a single tape. Travan improves the QIC capacities as outlined here:

| QIC Format | QIC Uncompressed Capacity | Equivalent Travan Format | Travan Capacity |
|---|---|---|---|
| QIC-80 | 120MB to 400MB | TR-1 | 400MB |
| QIC 3010 | 340MB to 800MB | TR-2 | 800MB |
| QIC-3020 | 680MB to 1.6GB | TR-3 | 1.6GB |
| | | TR-4 | 4GB |
| | | TR-5 | 10GB |

## Helical-Scan Tape Systems

In a helical-scan system, magnetic tape wraps around a moving drum that reads and writes data in parallel, diagonally adjoining paths. The combination of the moving tape and moving drum provide a high data transfer rate. The technique was first used in the television industry as a way to record television pictures on tape. The rotating read/write head (or drum) is tilted at a slight angle to the tape, which traces a repeating helix pattern on the tape and optimizes tape surface tracking. The drum is part of the recording device, and tape feeds out of the cartridge around it. One interesting feature is that tracks can overlap because data can be written into each track at different angles. Thus, when the head reads a track, it only reads data written at a specific angle. Data written at other angles has a weaker signal with respect to the head.

Two standard tape formats use helical-scan technology: DAT (Digital Audio Tape) and 8 mm tape.

**DAT (DIGITAL AUDIO TAPE)**    The DAT format was originally designed for music, but was quickly adopted for data backup because of its high transfer rates and capacities. DAT cassettes are 2.9 ∀ 2.1 ∀ 0.4 inches in size with a tape width of 4 mm. Tapes can hold 2.5GB or more of uncompressed data. DATs use the DDS (Digital Data Storage) storage format, which writes data sequentially and can append new data to existing data. The DAT format supports random reading of files.

DDS-2 is an enhancement that basically doubles the data storage density. Another enhancement called DDS-DC performs data compression. DDS-3 is the latest enhancement that provides up to 12GB of storage and backward compatibility with previous formats.

DAT vendors include Direct Connections (http://www.directdc.com), FWB (http://www.fwb.com), Microtech (http://www.microtechint.com), DynaTek (http://www.dynatek.co.uk), Hewlett-Packard (http://www.hp.com), and Dantz Development (http://www.dantz.com).

**EIGHT-MILLIMETER HELICAL-SCAN TAPES**    Eight-millimeter helical-scan tape systems use a tape that is 8 mm wide (obviously) in a cassette that measures 3.75 ∀ 2.5 inches. Since the tape is twice as big as DAT tape, it can hold twice their capacity. All 8 mm devices are manufactured by Exabyte Corporation, although Sony was the original developer. Various vendors repackage the 8 mm Exabyte devices and provide special backup software and other add-ons to go with the drives. It is possible to store up to 2.5MB to 5MB of data on a single tape without compression and up to 10MB with compression. Refer to Exabyte (http://www.exabyte.com) for information about 8 mm systems.

### DLT (Digital Linear Tape)

DLT is an open ANSI (American National Standards Institute) standard that uses a fixed head to record onto a fast-streaming tape. The tape moves at 100 to 150 inches per second. Tape capacity is in the 20GB range (40GB compressed) and data transfer rates are from 1.2 MB/sec to 3 MB/sec. Enhancements are boosting capacity to 35 GB/sec and transfer rates to 5 MB/sec. Compression can nearly double these numbers.

The DLT recording method differs quite a bit from the helical-scan techniques. Data is placed in longitudinal tracks and can accommodate multiple recording and playback heads. Multiple heads can provide performance by allowing both reads and writes at the same time.

DLT is designed for high-end server backup, unlike other tape technologies discussed here, which have traditionally been targeted for desktop computers. The price of DLT reflects this positioning. However, increases in capacity and throughput of the other formats are allowing them to compete with DLT.

Quantum (http://www.quantum.com) manufactures DLT drives and other vendors package its product. DLT vendors include Direct Connections (http://www.directdc.com) and Microtech (http://www.microtechint.com), among others.

**RELATED ENTRIES**   Backup and Data Archiving; Jukebox Optical Storage Devices; *and* Storage Management Systems

### INFORMATION ON THE INTERNET

| | |
|---|---|
| Lacie's Encyclopedia of Hard Drive Terms and Concepts | http://www.lacie.com/data.html |
| Lacie's SCSI page | http://www.lacie.com/scsi.html |
| Neutron, Inc.'s hard drive FAQ | http://www.neutronet.com/faqinfo/hdd.htm |
| Alison Chaiken's Magnetic Recording Web Sites page | http://www.wsrcc.com/alison/magrec.html |
| DISK/TREND, Inc. (general storage information and links) | http://www.disktrend.com |
| Network Buyer's Guide (links to manufacturers) | http://www.sresearch.com/search/105008.htm |
| Harddrive Related Terms and Tricks | http://www.computercraft.com/docs/evsterms.html |
| Rod Van Meter's storage FAQ | http://alumni.caltech.edu/~rdv/comp-arch-storage/FAQ-1.html |
| Nicholas Majors' Technicians' Guide to PC Hard Disk Subsystems | http://www.wi.leidenuniv.nl/ata/hdtech.html |
| Dan Kegel's Fast Hard Drives Page | http://www.kegel.com/drives |
| Yahoo!'s SCSI links page | http://www.yahoo.com/Computers_and_Internet/Hardware/Peripherals/SCSI |
| Quarter-Inch Cartridge Drive Standards, Inc. (QIC) | http://www2.qic.org/qic |
| DVD Special Interest Group (SIG) | http://www.tully.com/dvdsig |
| Exabyte Corporation | http://www.exabyte.com |

## Store-and-Forward Networking

Store-and-forward is a concept that is used often in the computer and network world. Packets are stored and forwarded through routers, as discussed under "Routers" and "Routing Protocols and Algorithms." Network applications use store-and-forward messaging when real-time connections are not essential, as discussed under "MOM

(Message-Oriented Middleware)." Finally, electronic mail systems use store-and-forward techniques to move e-mail from one user to another across messaging servers, as discussed under "Electronic Mail."

# Stream Transmission

A stream transmission is usually associated with transport layer data transmissions and sometimes also with data link layer transmissions. A stream is a long data transmission between a specific sender and receiver. Unlike network layer protocols, which simply flood the network with packets that may follow different paths and arrive unorganized at the destination, transport layer streams are sequentially numbered to overcome delivery problems. Also, if a stream is interrupted, the transmission can be restarted where it left off. See "Transport Protocols and Services."

# StreetTalk, Banyan

*See* Banyan VINES; Directory Services.

# Structured Cabling Standards

Structured wiring or cabling is a preplanned cabling system that is designed with growth and reconfiguration in mind. The EIA (Electronic Industries Association) and the TIA (Telecommunications Industry Association) developed a wiring standard for commercial buildings called the *TIA/EIA 568 Commercial Building Wiring Standard*. This standard provides a uniform wiring system and supports multivendor products and environments.

Structured wiring forms an infrastructure that is usually hierarchical in design with a high-speed backbone. The backbone must be high speed because periphery networks are connected to it. The backbone should be built with a high-speed medium or an enterprise hub that contains a high-speed collapsed backbone. Many modern designs rely on ATM or Gigabit Ethernet switches at the backbone.

**RELATED ENTRIES**   Backbone Networks; Data Communication Concepts; Hubs/Concentrators/MAUs; Network Concepts; Network Design and Construction; TIA/EIA Structured Cabling Standards; *and* Transmission Media, Methods, and Equipment

# Subnetting (IP Addresses)

Companies that want to connect their internal networks to the Internet can request an IP network number that represents their entire network. As described under "IP (Internet Protocol)," an IP address contains both a network number and a host address. A company that receives an IP network number can then assign each host on their network an IP address that includes the assigned network number plus a specific host address.

There are different classes of IP address. If a company was lucky enough to obtain a class A address (there are only 127), it could create over 16,000,000 host addresses. There are 16,382 Class B network addresses that support 65,000 hosts per address. Class C addresses allow over 2,000,000 networks with only 254 hosts per network.

Most companies are now given class C addresses. If they have more than 254 hosts, they can either obtain another class C address, which are in short supply, or use subnetting to extend the number of hosts that can be defined.

The normal IP address contains a network address and the host address. Subnetting defines a three-part addressing scheme. Basically, a company takes the two-part IP address it has been assigned and then, for its own internal use, applies a *subnet mask* that creates a three-part addressing scheme. The three-part scheme creates an *IP address*, which defines the network number assigned by the Internet authority; a *subnet address*, which can represent departments or workgroups; and a *host address*, which represents computers or other devices on a subnet. Subnetting allows an organization to create a number of internal subnetworks, which are beneficial from a security and management perspective.

Basically, a subnet mask is applied to the IP address that defines which bits in the host portion of the IP address can be used to define a subnet. The more bits used, the larger the number of subnets but the smaller the number of hosts on each subnet. This is because as bits are used to define a larger number of subnets, the number of bits available to define hosts on those subnets is reduced. A subnet numbering scheme is outlined under the topic "IP (Internet Protocol)."

Subnetting also has implications for routers. When a packet is crossing the Internet, all that matters is the network address. When the packet reaches the destination network that is using subnetting, routers on that network must be aware of the subnetting scheme so they can properly break out the three-part subnet addressing scheme from the normal two-part address.

The details of subnetting are too complex to describe in this limited space, so you are encouraged to visit the Web sites listed under "Information on the Internet" below for more information.

**RELATED ENTRIES**   CIDR (Classless Interdomain Routing); Data Communication Concepts; Internet; IP (Internet Protocol); Network Concepts; Routing Protocols and Algorithms; *and* TCP/IP (Transmission Control Protocol/Internet Protocol)

**INFORMATION ON THE INTERNET**

| | |
|---|---|
| 3Com's IP paper (excellent) | http://www.3com.com/nsc/501302s.html |
| UnixWorld Online tutorial on subnet addressing | http://www.uworld.com/uworld/archives/95/tutorial/001.html |
| NetPartners' Fast Guide to Subnets | http://www.netpart.com/news97/articles/subnet.html |

## Subnetworks

An internetwork is a collection of individual LANs and network links joined by routers. Each individual LAN or network link constitutes a *subnetwork*. In the IP addressing scheme, each subnetwork has its own network address and each node on a subnetwork has its own host address. Therefore, an IP address consists of a two-part number that identifies a network and a host on that network. If the network is attached to a much larger network such as the Internet, then each network address constitutes the address of a subnetwork.

**RELATED ENTRIES**    IP (Internet Protocol); Network Concepts; Routers; Routing Protocols and Algorithms; *and* TCP/IP (Transmission Control Protocol/Internet Protocol)

## Sun Microsystems

Sun Microsystems, located in Mountain View, California, was founded in 1982 on the premise that "the network is the computer." By the mid-1990s, the company's revenues were in the $6 billion dollar range and it provided a full range of software and hardware products, including operating systems, high-performance workstations, and network equipment. Sun Microsystem's philosophy is based on open, nonproprietary systems. Its technologies are designed to be freely adopted by any manufacturer.

Sun Microsystems consists of a number of internal divisions:

- **Sun Microsystems Computer Company**   Handles network systems business and a family of SPARC-based workstations and servers.

- **JavaSoft**   A business unit of Sun Microsystems that is dedicated to promoting the Java programming language and development environments.

- **Sun Microelectronics**   Develops SPARC technologies and products. See "SPARC (Scalable Performance Architecture)."

- **SunSoft**   A software subsidiary that develops core network computing products, including the Solaris operating environment.

- **SunExpress**   Sun's aftermarketing company.

- **Sun Microsystems Laboratories**   Sun's advanced research and development lab.

Sun Microsystems' most important products are listed here. Note that many of these products are described at the Sun Microsystems' site listed at the end of this topic or elsewhere in this book where mentioned.

- **Java**   An object-oriented development environment by Sun for building component applications that operate on the Internet and intranets. See "Java" for more information.

- **JavaChip**   A microprocessor family optimized for Java technology.

- **Java Workshop**   An integrated development environment for creating Internet applications and Web pages.

- **JavaStation Network Computer**   An inexpensive, platform-independent thin client. See "NC (Network Computer) Devices" for details.

- **Joe**   Connects Java applets running on any Java-enabled browser to business applications running on corporate networks. See "Java" for more information.

- **NEO**   A complete development, operating, and management environment for object-oriented networked applications. See "Sun Microsystems Solaris NEO" for more information.

- **Netra**   A line of Internet/intranet servers.

- **Solaris**   A leading UNIX operating environment for enterprise network computing.

- **Solstice**   A suite of system administration and network management products for enterprise networks.

- **SPARC**   A RISC (Reduced Instruction Set Computer) processor for systems ranging from laptops to supercomputers.

- **SunScreen SPF-100**   A firewall system and encryption device.

- **Ultra**   A family of workstations that implement the UltraComputing architecture, high-speed UltraSPARC processors, high-bandwidth networking, and accelerated graphics.

- **Ultra Enterprise**   A family of servers ranging from low-end systems to high-end, mainframe-like systems.

**RELATED ENTRIES**    Java; ONC (Open Network Computing); Sun Microsystems Solaris; *and* Sun Microsystems Solaris NEO

**INFORMATION ON THE INTERNET**

| | |
|---|---|
| Sun Microsystems, Inc. | http://www.sun.com |
| Sun's Java Source page | http://java.sun.com |

## Sun Microsystems Solaris

The Solaris operating environment is based on industry standard UNIX System V Release 4. It has been optimized for distributed network environments and performance enhanced for running database and Web applications. The system is also Java-enabled and includes support for the Java VM (Virtual Machine). The HotJava browser is also included. Centralized administration features allow administrators to control the operating system remotely.

The latest release includes CDE (Common Desktop Environment) as the default desktop. CDE is based on the X Window System Motif desktop and provides a consistent look and feel across UNIX platforms.

The operating system is designed for Web networking (intranets) and enterprise networking. It includes WebNFS, a version of the popular Network File System that is designed for use on the Web and intranets. Network computing features in Solaris include ONC (Open Network Computing) technology—a TCP/IP-based set of services, facilities, and APIs that include file and printer sharing, data exchange, RPC (remote procedure call), and distributed naming services. NIS+ Global Directory Services provides a secure, high-performance, distributed data repository for network and system management information. The operating system also includes DCE (Distributed Computing Environment).

Solaris runs on SPARC and Intel platforms and will be available on PowerPC platforms. Multiprocessor systems are supported, and Solaris uses symmetrical multiprocessing techniques to take full advantage of these systems. Multithreading is supported, which allows applications to be broken into segments that execute simultaneously on each processor.

**RELATED ENTRIES**    Java; ONC (Open Network Computing); Sun Microsystems; Sun Microsystems Solaris NEO; *and* WebNFS (Network File System)

### INFORMATION ON THE INTERNET

| | |
|---|---|
| Sun Microsystems' Solaris site | http://www.sun.com/solaris |
| Sven M. Paas's extensive operating system links (see links to Sun) | http://www.lfbs.rwth-aachen.de/~sven/OS-Projects |

## Sun Microsystems Solaris NEO

Solaris NEO 2.0 is Sun's distributed object environment for building and deploying component applications that run on the Internet or on corporate intranets. NEO is not an acronym. It is simply NEO.

Solaris NEO provides a run-time environment for networked objects that can be quickly and easily modified, extended, and maintained. It includes a CORBA-compliant Object Request Broker and IIOP (Internet Inter-ORB Protocol), which provides a way for Solaris NEO objects to link with objects created in other vendors' CORBA environments. It also includes Solstice NEO administration tools for managing networked object applications.

**RELATED ENTRIES**    Component Software Technology; CORBA (Common Object Request Broker Architecture); Distributed Object Computing; IIOP (Internet Inter-ORB Protocol); Intranets and Extranets; Java; Object Technologies; ONC (Open Network Computing); *and* Sun Microsystems

**INFORMATION ON THE INTERNET**

Solaris NEO site         http://www.sun.com/solaris/neo

# Supercomputer

Supercomputers are high-performance processing systems that typically consist of multiple processors processing nodes, or clustered systems running in parallel. High-performance computing is a branch of computer science that develops supercomputer and parallel processing technologies, including operating systems and software that runs on supercomputer systems. The market for supercomputers has been increasing. They are used for large data warehousing systems and to run complex tasks such as weather forecasting.

Cray was one of the original supercomputer manufacturers, but demand for supercomputer's waned in the late 1980s and early 1990s. Then, Digital Equipment Corporation managed to put the Cray supercomputer design onto a single Alpha processor. Silicon Graphics eventually bought Cray and has been reviving its supercomputer designs.

Supercomputers may be SMP (symmetrical multiprocessing) or MPP (massively parallel processing) systems. In the SMP design, all processors share the same memory and bus, which makes programs easy to develop, but shared resources can become a bottleneck as more processors are added. An MPP system consists of multiple distinct processing nodes where each node has its own processors, memory, cache, and bus. The nodes are interconnected with a high-speed switch.

MPP systems can be scaled by adding more nodes. Doing so does not bog down the system because nodes do not share the same bus or memory. But programs are difficult to write because they must be segmented to run in each node. In addition, since memory is not shared, a messaging system must be used by nodes to exchange information.

The NUMA (Non-Uniform Memory Access) architecture solves the "nothing-is-shared" problem of MPP systems. NUMA defines software and hardware that makes the separate memory spaces of each node appear to be a single virtual memory space which makes application development easier. The memory is said to be coherent, even though it is distributed in separate processing nodes. A coherent memory space simplifies programming, and the system can be scaled by adding more processing nodes without the performance degradation of typical shared-bus SMP systems.

While most supercomputers implement NUMA, Sun Microsystems has implemented the SMP architecture in its UltraHPC supercomputer system. The system supports up to 64 UltraSPARC II CPUs and provides up to 32 GFLOPs of performance. The system uses special caching techniques to route prefetched data into the cache ahead of when a processor might need it. This reduces memory latency problems.

NCSA (National Center for Supercomputing Applications) has the following systems at its site. It provides time on these systems for appropriate projects. More information on each system is available at the NCSA Web site listed under "Information on the Internet" below.

- **HP-Convex Exemplar SPP-2000 (X-Class)** A cache-coherent, NUMA supercomputer based on the HP PA-RISC 8000 processor

- **Silicon Graphics' CRAY Origin2000** A cache-coherent, NUMA supercomputer based on the MIPS R10000 processor

- **Silicon Graphics POWER CHALLENGE array** A networked array of bus-based shared-memory supercomputers based on MIPS R8000 and MIPS R10000 processors

- **HP-Convex Exemplar SPP-1200** A cache-coherent, NUMA supercomputer based on the HP PA-RISC 7200 processor

- **The Mass Storage System from UniTree** NCSA's hierarchical archival storage system that runs on a HP-Convex C3 machine (access is via the FTP interface)

**RELATED ENTRIES** Asymmetrical Multiprocessing; Clustering; Distributed Processing; MPP (Massively Parallel Processor) Systems; NUMA (Non-Uniform Memory Access); Parallel Processing; *and* Symmetrical Multiprocessing

**INFORMATION ON THE INTERNET**

| | |
|---|---|
| NCSA (National Center for Supercomputing Applications) | http://www.ncsa.uiuc.edu |
| Concurrent Supercomputing Consortium | http://www.ccsf.caltech.edu/cscc.html |
| Supercomputing and Parallel Computing Resources | http://www.cs.cmu.edu/~scandal/resources.html |
| High-performance computing links | http://hpc.ntnu.no/links |
| Internet Parallel Computing Archive | http://www.hensa.ac.uk/parallel |
| Yahoo!'s Supercomputing and Parallel Computing links page | http://www.yahoo.com/Computers_and_Internet/Supercomputing_and_Parallel_Computing |

## SVC (Switched Virtual Circuit)

A virtual circuit is basically a predefined path through a packet-switched network. Defining a virtual circuit defines the path that packets will take though the network and relieves routers of the need to make routing decisions for each packet. Virtual circuits improve performance for long transmissions but are not necessary for short transmissions. An SVC is a temporary virtual circuit that is set up on the fly, as opposed to a PVC (permanent virtual circuit) which is programmed into a network for continuous use. See "Virtual Circuit" for more information.

## S/WAN (Secure WAN)

S/WAN is an initiative of RSA Data Security, in conjunction with leading firewall and TCP/IP stack vendors. S/WAN's goal is to help companies build secure firewall-to-firewall connections over the Internet between their company sites or between business partners. All data that is transmitted between sites is encrypted to make it private, and the connection mimics a private leased line, albeit over the Internet. Basically, S/WAN creates secure VPNs (virtual private networks). S/WAN uses the IETF's IPSec specification as the basis for implementing interoperability among different firewall and TCP/IP products.

**RELATED ENTRIES**    IPSec (IP Security); Security; Tunnels; VPN (Virtual Private Network); *and* WAN (Wide Area Network)

**INFORMATION ON THE INTERNET**

| | |
|---|---|
| RSA's S/WAN page | http://www.rsa.com/rsa/SWAN |
| John Gilmore's Swan: Securing the Internet against Wiretapping paper | http://www.cygnus.com/~gnu/swan.html |
| IETF IPSec charter | http://www.ietf.org/html.charters/ipsec-charter.html |
| Security Architecture for IP (RFC 1825) | http://www.internic.net/rfc/rfc1825.txt |
| The IETF IP Security Working Group News | http://www.cs.arizona.edu/xkernel/www/ipsec/ipsec.html |

## Switched-56 Services

Switched-56 is a digital communication technology for transporting data over switched synchronous lines at 56 Kbits/sec or switched asynchronous lines at 57.6 Kbits/sec, although compression can provide four times the bandwidth. The channels are dial-up, so customers can use the service only when needed or establish a link to handle traffic overflow from another line. Switched-56 is useful for videoconferencing, LAN-to-LAN connections, Group 4 facsimile interconnections, and as a high-speed service for telecommuters.

Switched-56 lines are digital and require a CSU/DSU (channel service unit/data service unit) device to connect a network to the Switched-56 phone line. A typical Switched-56 connection between two LANs is pictured in Figure S-13. The interface between the router and CSU/DSU is typically a V.35 serial cable. Once set up, the lines operate like dial-out lines. With the proper equipment, additional Switched-56 lines can be automatically dialed to provide bandwidth on demand.

**RELATED ENTRIES**    Bandwidth on Demand; Circuit-Switching Services; Telecommunications and Telephone Systems; *and* WAN (Wide Area Network)

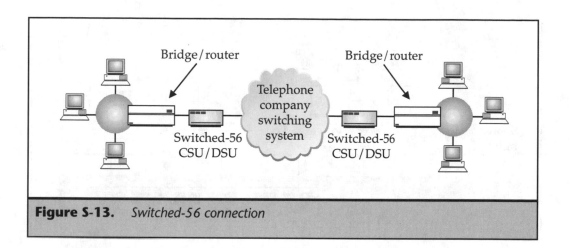

**Figure S-13.** *Switched-56 connection*

## Switched Networks

Switched networks have revolutionized the way that LANs and corporate networks are constructed. To put the switching revolution into perspective, an analogy can be drawn from the telephone system. Some of the earliest phone systems consisted of a few phones connected to the same trunk wire. Since many people shared the same trunk line, you were likely to hear another conversation taking place if you picked up the phone, at which point you would need to wait until those callers were finished before you could make your call. This is similar to shared Ethernet, in which a workstation must first check to see if the cable is busy before transmitting.

The phone system grew, and operators eventually took over the job of arbitrating phone calls. To place a call, you would ask an operator to connect you with another party. The operator would then connect a cable on a switchboard from your phone outlet to the outlet of the callee. The cable provided a direct connection between phones for the duration of the call. This is basically how switched networking schemes work.

Eventually, private cables were strung from the phone company's switchboards to every phone, thus putting an end to the so-called "party line." When you pick up the phone, no one else is on that line because it is your private line. The line goes directly to the telephone company's switching office. This required a lot more wire, but certainly made customers happy.

This structure is very similar to star-wired Ethernet, in which every workstation is connected directly to a central hub. However, the first Ethernet hubs were simple repeaters ("party line" devices), which meant that all attached stations still vied for access to a shared network. Switching hubs create a truly private-line network by directly connecting the private line from one computer to the private line of another computer for the duration of a transmission. This can be seen with the workstations on the right in Figure S-14.

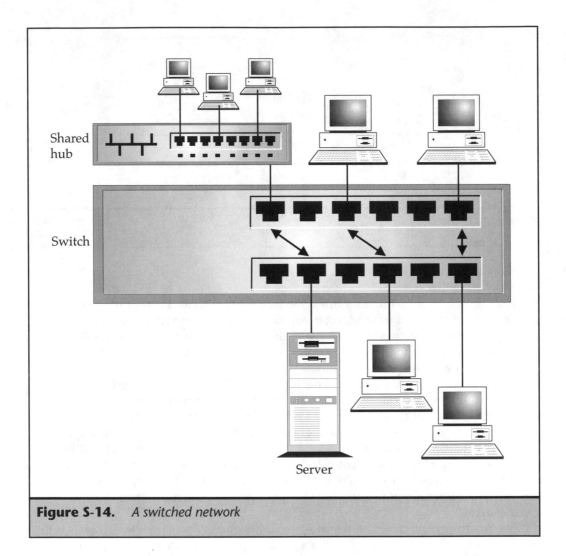

**Figure S-14.** *A switched network*

Note that switches can support shared network hubs, as shown on the left in the Figure S-14. While users on the shared hub must vie for access to their local network, once they get access they can obtain a private line to any other port on the switch. This is much like the phone system was when it was in transition from a party-line to a private-line system. Some neighborhoods still had party lines because the telephone company has not upgraded the shared trunk to private lines.

Switching is necessary for large, shared Ethernet networks. On a shared Ethernet LAN, if two stations try to transmit at the same time, collisions occur, and this results in delays. The more stations attached to the network, the more collisions and the bigger the delay problem. One solution is to divide the network up into smaller segments so there are fewer workstations vying for access. A 100-node network might be divided into two 50-node networks and joined with a bridge or router. Then only 50 stations on each segment vie for access. If problems still exist, four 25-node network segments might be created.

With switches, this segmentation process can continue until as few as one workstation is connected to a network segment. You can think of a switch as a multiport bridge device in which each port is a private network segment. A single workstation or a hub of workstations can be attached to one of the ports. A switch can create a bridge between any two ports on the fly and at a very rapid rate. A single station attached to a port has the full bandwidth of that port. The primary advantage of switching is that it eliminates the contention, collisions, and delays that are a problem with shared networks.

The other advantage of switches is that they support hierarchical network designs like that pictured in Figure S-15. At the top of the hierarchy is a high-performance switch that handles traffic from lower-level switches at the department or workgroup level. With this hierarchy, it is possible for a system anywhere on the network to set up a switched connection with any other system on the network. This architecture is especially important for corporate intranets where users need to communicate with systems and users all over the network, not just within their department. Note also that servers are attached directly to the backbone switch, where they can provide the best performance.

A typical vendors sells a range of switching devices. High-end switches are built for speed to support the backbone needs of large organizations. Low-end switches are designed for departments and workgroups. These different types of switches can be connected together to create hierarchical network schemes that utilize structured cabling designs, as discussed under "TIA/EIA Structured Cabling Standards." Also refer to "Network Design and Construction" for information on building a switched network.

Switches operate at layer 2 (the data link layer) relative to the OSI protocol stack, so in this respect, switches are very much like bridges. They provide a single-box solution for dividing networks into multiple segments. A performance boost is gained on the network without the need to upgrade existing NICs (network interface cards) in workstations.

## VLANs (Virtual LANs)

One aspect of building a switched network that spans the entire enterprise is that it creates a single flat network topology. Many administrators do not consider this advantageous for security reasons, because any user can potentially reach any system. Router-connected networks are more secure in this respect because they separate networks into individual broadcast domains that contain traffic and can be used to control traffic that passes beyond the routers.

VLANs provide a solution. A VLAN is basically an overlay of subnetworks over the flat, switched network topology. Unlike a physical subnetwork in which stations

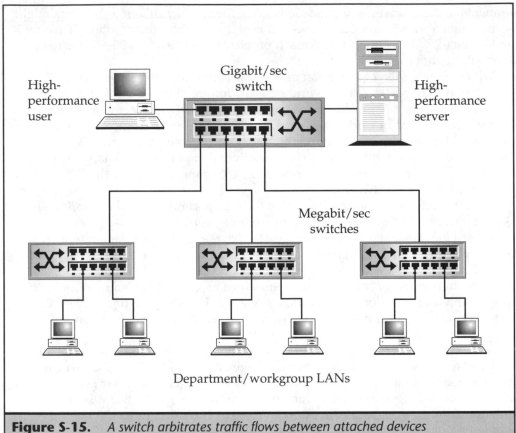

High-performance user

Gigabit/sec switch

High-performance server

Megabit/sec switches

Department/workgroup LANs

**Figure S-15.** *A switch arbitrates traffic flows between attached devices*

are connected to the same coaxial cable segment or to the same shared hub, a VLAN is created by specifying which workstations will be members. A workstation can be a member based on the port it is attached to, its MAC address, its IP address, or some other method. Once a workstation becomes a member of a VLAN, all broadcasts for that VLAN go to each member workstation, no matter where they are located on the network. VLAN configuration and other VLAN issues are discussed further under "VLAN (Virtual LAN)."

There are other issues related to VLANs that must be considered. Because each VLAN is basically a subnetwork with its own IP address (assuming that TCP/IP is the internetwork protocol in use), then routers are still needed to move packets between VLANs. One way to do this is to install traditional routers that sit outside the switched network and move packets between VLANs, but this assumes that ports are available that provide access into and out of VLANs. In some cases, a *route server* provides centralized control and routing of traffic between VLANs. These topics are explored further under a number of topics in this book, including "IP over ATM" and "IP Switching."

## Inside the Switch

In the last few years, the market has been flooded with low-cost switching devices, and this is largely due to ASIC (application-specific integrated circuit) technology. ASICs are programmable chips that, for switches, have switching code programmed into their silicon.

A typical switch may be implemented as one of the configurations pictured in Figure S-16 and described here:

- **Crossbar switch**  These switches have been around for a long time. Any input can connect with any output. An integrated circuit makes the connection at the junction of an input and a target output. An input buffer stores incoming information in the event of blocking (an output port is in use).

- **Shared-memory switch**  In this switch, incoming data is stored in a shared memory area, then forwarded to another port. Data moves directly into memory, then to an output port, so a backplane bus is not required. The only problem with this design is that storing data in memory adds considerable delay.

- **High-speed bus switch**  In this design, ASIC-enabled ports are connected to a high-speed data bus. Data arrives on one port, crosses the data bus, and exits on a destination port. The high-speed bus, which implements TDM (time division multiplexing) is fast enough to handle transmissions from all ports at the same time if necessary; therefore, it is nonblocking (i.e., produces no bottlenecks of its own).

The high-speed bus switch is most often implemented. Cisco's Catalyst 3000 switch has sixteen 10Base-T Ethernet ports and two expansion ports that can support Fast Ethernet (100 Mbits/sec), ATM, or WAN expansion modules. The switching architecture of this device is pictured in Figure S-17. It implements a 480-Mbit/sec bus (called a *switching fabric*) through which all ports (LAN modules) communicate. Each LAN module has up to 256K of memory and an LMA (LAN module ASIC) that controls buffering and I/O for the port. An arbiter ASIC with its own Intel i960 processor controls access to the bus for each port module. The high-speed expansion modules plug directly into the bus.

Additional information about switch designs can be found under "ATM (Asynchronous Transfer Mode)," "Cell Relay," "Hubs/Concentrators/MAUs," "Matrix Switch," and "Packet and Cell Switching."

## Congestion and Flow Control in Switches

Switches are susceptible to congestion, but traditional flow-control methods that prevent a workstation from further transmitting frames are not available. The problem

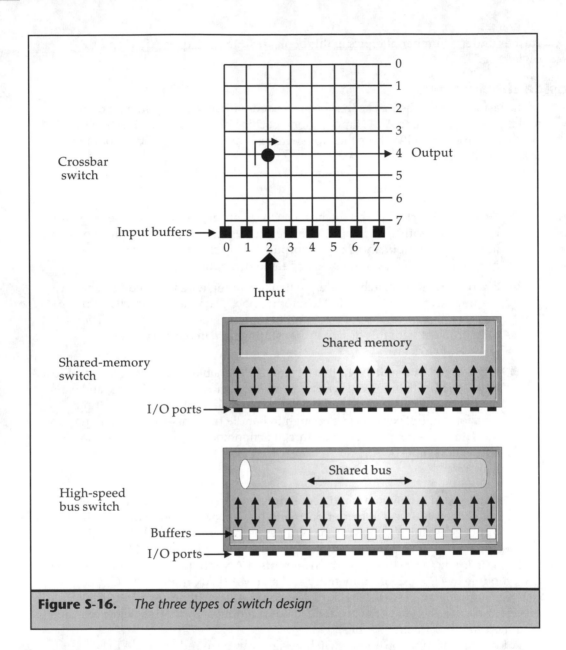

**Figure S-16.** *The three types of switch design*

is that no matter how fast a switch is, congestion will occur if a device on an output port backs up and cannot receive all the frames or cells being sent to it.

First, you should differentiate between ATM switching and LAN switching. With ATM switching, a virtual circuit (often called a *call*) must be set up between a source and a destination before cells can be sent. The ATM switch determines in advance

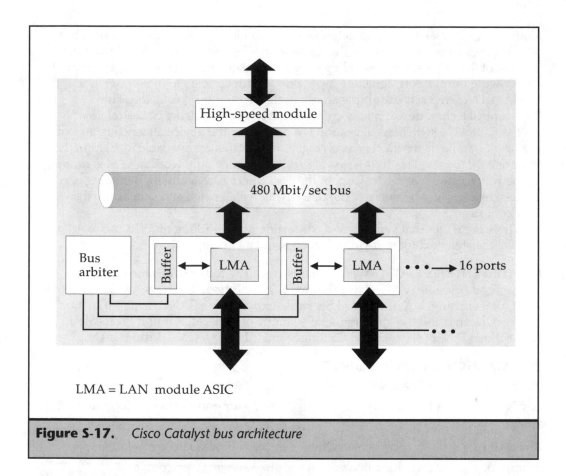

**Figure S-17.**    *Cisco Catalyst bus architecture*

whether it has the capacity to handle the data flow across this circuit. Therefore, the ATM switch has more up-front control for preventing congestion.

In contrast, LANs are connectionless environments in which frames are directed to a LAN switch without first setting up a circuit. If frames overwhelm the switch, they may be dropped. Frame switches must have input buffers to hold frames that arrive if the switch port is busy. While buffers are necessary in switches, they point out an inherent flaw. Buffers are holding data for delivery, and that means delay. The usual solution is to just make the switch very fast—faster than the aggregate throughput of all the devices attached to it—but not everyone has a budget for such fast ports, so a careful consideration of a switch's buffer design is necessary.

While input buffers can prevent lost frames on the input side, what if the device on the output port is congested? Do you need output buffers as well? Consider the case of a server attached to a high-speed port on the switch. Its port may become flooded in high-traffic conditions. Under this condition, a station may continue to send packets to an input port even though the congested server port is dropping packets. This will require retransmission and add delay. One solution is to increase the buffering, but this becomes a trade-off between the amount of delay caused by buffering and the amount of delay caused by resending dropped packets. Another method is to have the overflowing output port signal the input port, which appears to the sender as a CSMA/CD (carrier sense multiple access/collision detection) collision. This flow-control technique essentially creates what has been called a *virtual collision*.

Even on ATM switches, congestion is a problem if the device attached to an exit port can't handle the traffic it is receiving. Flow controls are available in ATM in the form of ABR (available bit rate) class of service, but they only work if ATM is running all the way to the sender's desktop. In the case where LAN emulation is being used, the desktop may not be aware of the underlying ATM switch and cannot use the flow controls.

These are issues that vendors and consortiums are working on. You can refer to the references listed next for more information about switching.

**RELATED ENTRIES**    ATM (Asynchronous Transfer Mode); Backbone Networks; Bridges and Bridging; Cell Relay; Ethernet; Gigabit Ethernet; Internetworking; IP over ATM; IP Switching; ISA (Integrated Services Architecture); LANE (LAN Emulation); Network Design and Construction; QoS (Quality of Service); Routing Protocols and Algorithms; TIA/EIA Structured Cabling Standards; *and* VLAN (Virtual LAN)

### INFORMATION ON THE INTERNET

| | |
|---|---|
| 3Com's Technology Document Center | http://www.3com.com/technology |
| Bay Networks' Online Library | http://support.baynetworks.com/Library |
| DEC's network information | http://www.networks.digital.com |
| Xylan Corp.'s white papers on switching | http://www.xylan.com/whitepaper |
| Xylan Corp.'s The Switching Book | http://www.xylan.com/sb |
| Cisco Systems' LAN Switches page | http://www.cisco.com/warp/public/729 |
| ATM links at Texas A&M | http://www.cs.tamu.edu/research/realtime/atm.html |
| The ATM Forum | http://www.atmforum.com |
| Gigabit Ethernet Alliance | http://www.gigabit-ethernet.org |

# Switched Telephone Services

A telephone call is a switched service. You can dial any phone number to establish a temporary connection. You only pay for the time the call is connected. Switched data services provide the same features. Temporary connections can be made to a variety of sites to make bulk data transfers (electronic mail and backup data) or to provide additional bandwidth when needed. In contrast, dedicated leased lines are always connected between two sites. You pay for the line whether you use it or not.

Customers using public-switched data services have two service options, as described next. There are circuit-switching services and packet-switching services. *Circuit-switched services* provide digital circuits between two points on a temporary basis, giving customers who don't need full-time dedicated services an economical option for obtaining high-speed private lines only when required. *Packet-switching services* provide any-to-any connections for simultaneous transmissions over a mesh-type packet-switched network. These services offer three important features:

- Switching services can provide any-to-any connectivity. Customers can change the endpoints of the link to accommodate changing business needs, such as an office move or the addition of a new remote office.

- Switching services can provide bandwidth on demand. The network can usually handle peaks in a customer's traffic. The customer is typically charged a different rate for any bandwidth used over the contracted rate.

- Charges are based on actual customer usage, as opposed to leased lines in which customers pay a flat rate, even if the line goes unused part of the time.

Circuit-switching services include Switched-56 and ISDN (Integrated Services Digital Network). Packet-switching services include X.25, frame relay, and the Internet. Most carriers also offer ATM cell-relay services. Refer to the related entries listed next for more information.

**RELATED ENTRIES**    ATM (Asynchronous Transfer Mode); Cell Relay; Circuit-Switching Services; Communication Service Providers; Communication Services; Frame Relay; ISDN (Integrated Services Digital Network); Packet and Cell Switching; PSTN (Public-Switched Telephone Network); Telecommunications and Telephone Systems; *and* WAN (Wide Area Network). See also "Telecommunications Companies" in Appendix A.

# Switching, Multilayer

*See* Layer 3 Switching/Routing.

# Switch Routers

*See* Routers.

# Symmetrical Multiprocessing

Multiprocessor systems have two or more processors. Operating systems and applications use two primary techniques to take advantage of these systems. With *symmetrical multiprocessing,* workloads can be distributed evenly to available processors so that one processor doesn't sit idle while another is overworked with a specific task. System resources such as memory and disk I/O are shared by all the processors in the system. The performance of symmetrical multiprocessing systems increases for all tasks as processors are added, up to about 10 processors. Then MPP (massively parallel processing) systems provide better scalability.

*Asymmetrical multiprocessing* is a multiprocessing technique in which each processor works on specific tasks, such as I/O (input/output).

**RELATED ENTRIES**   Asymmetrical Multiprocessing; Clustering; Distributed Processing; MPP (Massively Parallel Processor) Systems; NUMA (Nonuniform Memory Access); Parallel Processing; *and* Servers

# Synchronous Communications

When devices exchange data, there is a flow or stream of information between the two. In any data transmission, the sender and receiver must have a way to extract individual characters or blocks (frames) of information. Imagine standing at the end of a data pipe. Characters arrive in a continuous stream of bits, so you need a way to separate one block of bits from another. In asynchronous communications, each character is separated by the equivalent of a flag so you know exactly where characters are located. In synchronous communications, both the sender and receiver are synchronized with a clock or a signal encoded into the data stream.

In synchronous communications, the sender and receiver must synchronize with one another before data is sent. To maintain clock synchronization over long periods, a special bit-transition pattern is embedded in the digital signal that assists in maintaining the timing between sender and receiver. One method of embedding timing information is called *bipolar encoding,* as pictured in Figure S-18. In this method, the bit stream pictured at the top is meshed with the clock pulse pictured in the middle to produce the transmission signal shown at the bottom.

Synchronous communications is either character oriented or bit oriented. Character-oriented transmissions are used to send blocks of characters such as those found in ASCII (American Standard Code for Information Interchange) files. Each block must have a starting flag similar to asynchronous communications so the receiving system can initially synchronize with the bit stream and locate the beginning of the characters. Two or more control characters, known as SYN (synchronous idle) characters, are inserted at the beginning of the bit stream by the sender. These characters are used to synchronize a block of information. Once correct synchronization has been established between sender and receiver, the receiver places the block it receives as characters in a memory buffer.

Bit-oriented synchronous communication is used primarily for the transmission of binary data. It is not tied to any particular character set, and the frame contents don't need to include multiples of eight bits. A unique 8-bit pattern (01111110) is used as a flag to start the frame.

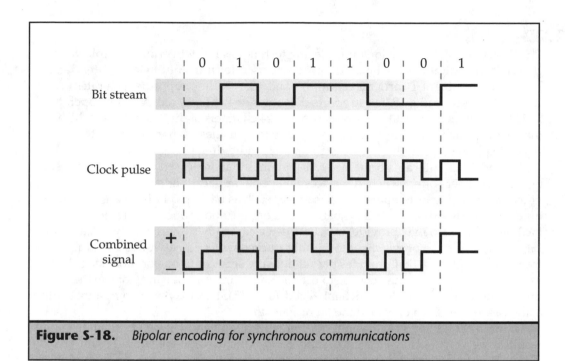

**Figure S-18.** *Bipolar encoding for synchronous communications*

**RELATED ENTRIES**  Asynchronous Communications; Data Communication Concepts; Data Link Protocols; HDLC (High-level Data Link Control); *and* SDLC (Synchronous Data Link Control)

# SystemView, IBM

SystemView is an enterprise-wide network management system that recognizes and manages systems in heterogeneous environments. It was one of IBM's first products to recognize industry-standard protocols such as TCP/IP, and not just IBM's own SNA (Systems Network Architecture) protocols. In 1996, IBM acquired Tivoli Systems, Inc., and in this process, the Tivoli division took over development of IBM's SystemView products. It also linked SystemView with its own environment, TME (Tivoli Management Environment).

**RELATED ENTRIES**  IBM (International Business Machines); Network Management

**INFORMATION ON THE INTERNET**

Tivoli Systems, Inc.                    http://www.tivoli.com

# T1/T3

The T-carrier services provide multiplexing techniques for delivering multiple voice channels over digital trunk lines. They are also used for transmitting computer data. The most prominent T-carrier levels are T1 and T3. A T1 line supports data rates of 1.544 Mbits/sec, and a T3 line supports data rates of 45 Mbits/sec. A T4 line operates at 274.176 Mbits/sec. A T1 circuit can provide 24 channels of digitized voice, which means the phone company can install one line to a business to handle up to 24 separate phone calls, rather than install up to 24 individual phone cables.

T1 and T3 circuits are normally dedicated lines that are leased on a monthly basis, but some carriers offer switched services for special applications such as videoconferencing or temporary data services such as backups. T1 lines are commonly used to provide private data links between an organization's local and remote facilities. They also may provide links between a company's internal network and an ISP (Internet service provider) or to a public packet-switched network such as a frame-relay network that provides packet delivery services to one or more sites. For example, the customer may choose to use the entire line for data and not use the time-slotted channels (called unchannelized T1 or T3). This may be incompatible with some carriers and can only be done on private lines.

When T1 lines are used to connect a company's local and remote office, the resulting network is called a *private network* and is pictured on the left in Figure T-1. These lines are considered private because the customer maintains all the endpoint equipment and gets full use of the line to deliver any type of information (data/voice/video).

While private networks built with T1 lines (or T3 lines) have many benefits, cost is not one of them if the lines are long distance. T1 leased rates increase with distance. A short distance line within a metropolitan area may cost $1,500 per month while a long-distance line across the Unites States may cost $20,000 per month. To create long-distance network connections, it is often better to lease a short-haul T1 line to create a connection into a carrier's packet-switched network, as shown on the right in Figure T-1. The short T1 line will be inexpensive, and the packet-switched network can deliver traffic on a pay-for-use basis to other sites. Refer to "Packet and Cell Switching" for more information.

T1 and T3 circuits are based on the transmission of multiple channels of digital information over a single cable using TDM (time division multiplexing). The circuit is divided into time slots, each of which is preallocated to some channel. Early on, AT&T created a TDM hierarchy that is now known as the NADH (North American Digital Hierarchy). The basic channel provides 64 Kbits/sec of throughput, which is the amount needed to transmit a digitized voice telephone call. A T1 line consists of 24 of these channels. The process of digitizing voice is discussed under "ADC (Analog-to-Digital Conversion)." Refer to "NADH (North American Digital Hierarchy)" and "Multiplexing" for more information on digital lines.

A traditional T1 line is basically a *conditioned* line, meaning that the signal is regenerated at regular intervals (every 6,000 feet, except for the first and last which are

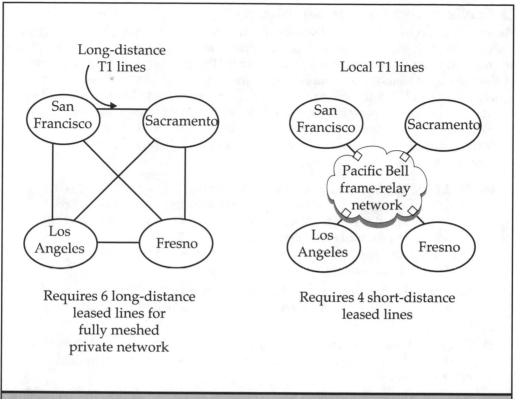

**Figure T-1.**    *Leased line private network versus packet-switched network*

3,000 feet from the endpoints) to maintain a high signal quality. Two pairs of wires are required. However, the phone companies found that installing and maintaining repeaters was costly and inefficient, so they developed a signaling scheme called HDSL (High-bit-rate Digital Subscriber Line) that provides T1 or greater transmission rates over copper wires without the need for repeaters. As customer demand for T1 rates increased, HDSL satisfied those needs with a service that could be set up in hours and that required little maintenance on the part of the provider. That resulted in cheaper T1 rates.

HDSL requires two twisted-pair lines to run at T1 rates, but will operate at up to 768 Kbits/sec over a single twisted pair. In addition, HDSL allows four times the distance of a conditioned T1 line. ADSL (Asymmetrical Digital Subscriber Line) is an extension to HDSL that can transmit at up to 6 Mbits/sec in one direction over the same copper wire. An interesting paper on HDSL technology is available at the PairGain Web site given below under "Information on the Internet."

## T1/T3 Services and Connection Methods

The three most common T-carrier services are fractional T1, T1, and T3. Fractional T1 is an offering that lets you lease a T1 line in increments of 64 Kbits/sec each. The normal setup cost is incurred, but you only pay for the channels you use. T1 provides 24 channels of 64 Kbits/sec each and a total bandwidth of 1.544 Mbits/sec. T3 is equivalent to 28 T1 circuits and provides a total bandwidth of 44.736 Mbits/sec. This service was initially employed to transmit between microwave stations. The full hierarchy is described under "NADH (North American Digital Hierarchy)."

Some common T1 connection scenarios are pictured in Figure T-2, and the equipment for these connections is described here:

- **CSU/DSU (channel service unit/data service unit)**   The CSU/DSU is the actual connection point for the T1 wires. It provides line diagnosis and keep-alive functions for the line. The T1 line connects to the unit via an RJ connector and the bridge/router connects via a V.35 interface. The CSU/DSU provides signal conversion and clocking between the two communication channels.

- **Multiplexor**   A multiplexor provides a way to direct multiple channels of voice or data onto a T1 line. Many multiplexors have built-in CSU/DSU for direct connection to T1 lines.

- **Bridge or router**   The bridge or router provides the interface that allows internal servers and networks to use the T1 link as a network extension or interconnection.

In Figure T-2(a), the entire T1 line is used for data. In Figure T-2(b), a multiplexor fills the time slots in the T1 channel with voice or data. Some of the channels can be reserved for voice, and the rest may be allocated to data. In Figure T-2(c), a T1 inverse multiplexor is used to combine multiple T1 lines into a single high-bandwidth channel between two network sites.

Leased lines are fixed point-to-point connections that provide a fixed rate. The downside of this is that companies can't easily change their lines and the data rate is inflexible. Customers pay the monthly rate whether the bandwidth is used or not. If more bandwidth is needed at irregular intervals, often the only choice is to set up dial-up lines that provide bandwidth on demand. See "Bandwidth on Demand" for more information.

Many organizations need to change their wide area network connections as markets change, as workgroups form and disband, or as mergers take place. In this case, fast packet-switching services such as frame relay can provide a more flexible solution. They provide bandwidth on demand and the ability to switch connections. In addition, they can mimic dedicated circuits through "virtual circuit" capabilities. Some alternative methods for building wide area networks include building VPNs (virtual private networks) over the Internet. See "VPN (Virtual Private Network)" for more details.

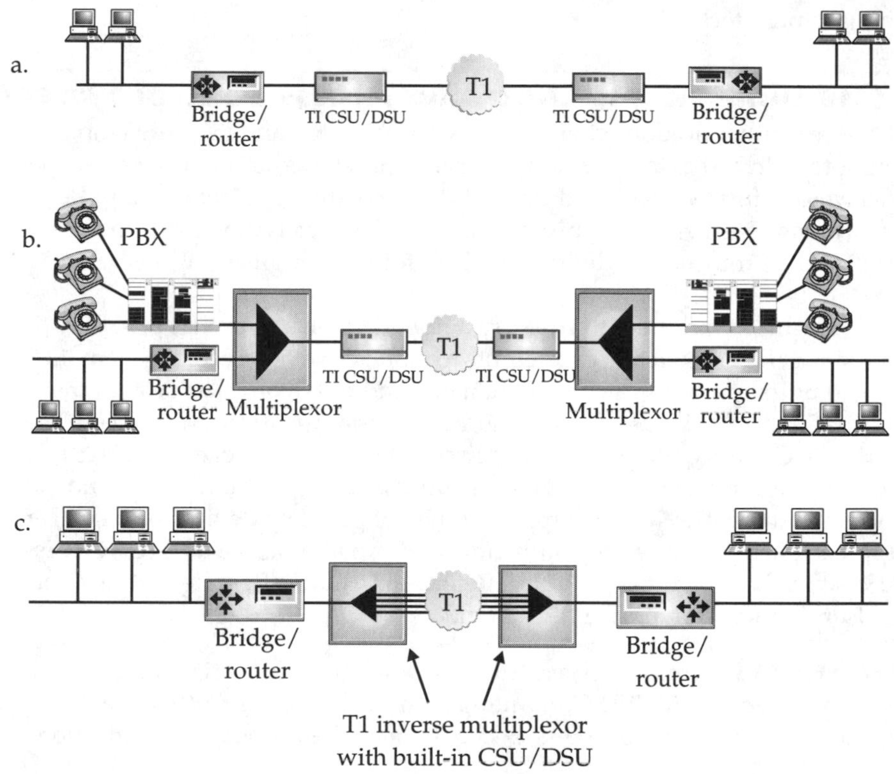

**Figure T-2.**  *T1/T3 connection methods*

**RELATED ENTRIES**    Circuit-Switching Services; Communication Service Providers; Communication Services; CSU/DSU (Channel Service Unit/Data Service Unit); DSL (Digital Subscriber Line); Leased Line; Multiplexing; NADH (North American Digital Hierarchy); Packet and Cell Switching; Point-to-Point Communications; Private Networks; Telecommunications and Telephone Systems; VPN (Virtual Private Network); *and* WAN (Wide Area Network)

**INFORMATION ON THE INTERNET**

| | |
|---|---|
| Committee T1's site | http://www.t1.org |
| Black Box's T1 page | http://www.blackbox.com/bb/refer/ remote/11000/p3.html/tigf6bd |

Teletutor T1 training course      http://www.teletutor.com/t1basics.html

PairGain's CopperOptics white paper      http://www.pairgain.com/copperop.htm
on T1 replacement technology

## TACACS (Terminal Access Controller Access Control System)

TACACS is an authentication scheme that can be used to validate users who are attempting to gain access to information servers, networks, and remote access servers. TACACS was originally developed by the U.S. Department of Defense and BBN Planet Corp. (an Internet service provider). Cisco Systems is now the primary supporter of the protocol. It is defined in IETF (Internet Engineering Task Force) RFC 927 and RFC 1492.

TACACS runs as a distinct third-party authentication server that provides verification services. When a user attempts to gain access to a secure system, the secure system first prompts the user for a name and password. The system then passes this information to the TACACS server and requests authentication services. The original TACACS was quite simple, and Cisco extended it to create TACACS+, which is modular in design and supports plug-in authentication, authorization, and accounting schemes. The system supports physical card-key devices or token cards and supports Kerberos secret-key authentication. An alternative to TACACS+ is RADIUS, which is an Internet standard. Refer to "RADIUS (Remote Authentication Dial-In User Service)" for more information.

**RELATED ENTRIES**     Access Server; Authentication and Authorization; Communication Server; Mobile Computing; RADIUS (Remote Authentication Dial-In User Service); Remote Access; Security; *and* Token-Based Authentication

### INFORMATION ON THE INTERNET

Cisco Systems' TACACS white paper      http://www.cisco.com/warp/public/
732/Security/ossec_wp.htm

IETF RFC 1492      http://www.internic.net/rfc/rfc1492.txt

Shiva's TACACS information      http://home.hkstar.com/~unet/shiva.html

## Tag Switching

Tag switching is a Cisco technology to integrate layer 2 (data link layer) switching with layer 3 (network layer) routing for large-scale network environments, i.e., the Internet. Tag switching is aimed at service providers and allows them to integrate ATM switches into the Internet core and implement routing on top of those switches. What tag switching does is add fixed-length labels of information to packets that provide switching nodes with immediate information about how to switch packets. Packet header analysis like that done by routers is not necessary. Therefore, packets that would normally be routed hop by hop through a network can instead be switched at high speed. The virtual circuit capabilities of layer 2 networks can be integrated into router-based networks such as the Internet.

An internetwork that implements tag switching consists of *tag edge routers* at the boundaries of the network, which add the tags to packets; *tag switches*, which read the tag information in packets and switch packets accordingly; and TDP (Tag Distribution Protocol), which performs functions similar to a routing protocol by distributing information about the layout of the tag-switched network among tag-switching devices.

The basic tag-switching process is to first identify routes through the network. This is done using standard routing protocols such as BGP (Border Gateway Protocol) and OSPF (Open Shortest Path First). Routing tables are created as normal. Tag routers and switches use this information to create tag-based tables that will be used to provide information about how to switch packets that have tag information. This information is distributed among tag devices by using TDP.

When a tag edge router receives a packet, it examines the packet header information in order to determine a router for the packet through the network. This is a normal routing procedure. It then adds tag information to the packet and forwards the packet to a tag switch that is associated with the first hop of the route. When the tag switch receives the packet, all it needs to do is look at the tag information in the packet and switch the packet.

Tag switching allows ATM switches to be used as tag switches. An ATM switch must implement an appropriate layer 3 routing protocol along with the tag distribution protocol. Tags are then placed in the VCI (virtual channel identifier) field of ATM cells by the tag edge routers and tag-enabled ATM switches look at the VCI field to determine how to switch the cells.

The IETF MPLS (Multiprotocol Label Switching) Working Group is focused on developing standards that integrate a label swapping/tagging scheme with network layer (layer 3) routing. Cisco's tag switching is being evaluated by the group. The working group is initially focusing on IPv4 and IPv6, but it will eventually focus on other network layer protocols such as IPX (Internetwork Packet Exchange), AppleTalk, and DECnet. The MPLS Web site is given below.

**RELATED ENTRIES**    IP over ATM; IP Switching; MPLS (Multiprotocol Label Switching); Switched Networks; *and* VLAN (Virtual LAN)

**INFORMATION ON THE INTERNET**

| | |
|---|---|
| Cisco's Tag Switching site | http://www.cisco.com/warp/public/732/tag |
| IETF Multiprotocol Label Switching site | http://www.ietf.org/html.charters/mpls-charter.html |

# Tape Backup Standards
*See* Storage Systems.

# TAPI (Telephony API)

TAPI is a Microsoft API for developing and using CTI (computer-telephony integration) applications. TAPI abstracts the hardware layer so that developers can create products that are network and device independent. TAPI applications can be used on the public-switched telephone network, ISDN (Integrated Services Digital Network), PBX (private branch exchange), and IP networks. TAPI is based on the Microsoft Windows platform and is complemented by other Microsoft APIs such as Win32, MAPI (Messaging API), SAPI (Speech API), and MCI (Media Control Interface).

Microsoft is quick to point out that Windows is the best platform for developing CTI applications. Windows is an operating system with a very large installed base and a graphical interface that is already designed to handle telephony applications. The operating system also supports network communications. TAPI consists of two interfaces. Vendors who develop CTI applications write to the API (application programming interface) on the top side. The lower part of TAPI is called the SPI (Service Provider Interface). The SPI provides connections for PBXs, key telephone systems, ISDN, the analog phone system, cellular systems, Centrex, and other types of telephone networks.

**RELATED ENTRIES** CTI (Computer-Telephony Integration); Telephony; Voice/Data Networks, Voice over ATM; *and* VoIP (Voice over IP)

**INFORMATION ON THE INTERNET**

| | |
|---|---|
| Windows Telephony API (TAPI) | http://www.microsoft.com/ntserver/communications/tapi.htm |
| Ken Persson's telephony page (very complete) | http://www.pi.se/ken/linkcti.html |

# TCP (Transmission Control Protocol)

TCP is a transport layer component of the Internet's TCP/IP protocol suite. It sits above IP (Internet Protocol) in the protocol stack and provides reliable data delivery services over connection-oriented links. To put this into perspective, assume you are writing one of the many thousands of network applications that must exchange messages and data with other network computers. Your program should be able to make a requests of lower-layer network protocols to have data delivered. At the same time, you should not need to write routines into your program that verify whether messages and data were received. This is a task that reliable protocols such as TCP perform.

TCP in turn uses IP to deliver information across a network. Interestingly, IP is a connectionless network protocol that does not guarantee reliable delivery. While IP provides an efficient data delivery mechanism, TCP makes up for its deficiencies by providing reliable services. TCP messages and data (officially called segments, as described later) are encapsulated into IP datagrams and IP delivers them across the network.

An interesting aspect of TCP is that early on, in the days when the Internet was still being defined, IP was not part of the design. During early development, Denny Cohen at USC argued that the connection-oriented features of TCP are unnecessary for some types of data transmissions and that they created excess overhead and traffic. He recommended splitting TCP to accommodate "timeliness rather than accuracy." What was needed was a way to quickly get data to another system. Thus, TCP became TCP and IP.

At that time, UDP (User Datagram Protocol) was also created to provide an alternative application interface to IP. Both TCP and UDP use IP. While UDP resides in the transport layer, it does not have any of the reliability features of TCP. What it does have are fields in the header that identify a source and destination port address, which basically identifies a particular process (an application) running in the destination computer. Thus, an application can connect with an application in another system without using the reliability features of TCP.

The original TCP was developed to interconnect many different types of computers at research institutes, universities, and government agencies. An encapsulation scheme was implemented because the designers did not want the owners of the various networks to alter their internal networking schemes to accommodate internetworking. It was assumed that every network would implement its own communication techniques. Routers (originally called *gateways*) provided this encapsulation service.

For more history of the TCP/IP protocol suite, refer to "TCP/IP (Transmission Control Protocol/Internet Protocol)." For a general history of the Internet, refer to "Internet." Also refer to "IP (Internet Protocol)" for a discussion of this component of the TCP/IP protocol suite.

TCP is described in IETF RFC 793. Some revisions are described in RFC 1122 and further extensions are described in RFC 1323. Some references are given at the end of this section.

## TCP Features

Perhaps the most important characteristic of TCP is that it sets up end-to-end connections between two computers that need to exchange data. An end-to-end connection is *virtual* because it is created in software and extends across all the point-to-point connections that make up a typical router-connected network. This is shown in Figure T-3. Note that *point-to-point connections* are between two physical systems such as a host to router or router to router, while an *end-to-end connection* is between the end systems of a communication session.

An end-to-end connection does not simply terminate at the network interface. It actually extends up into the application layer to a specific process running on a computer. Each computer creates a *socket*, and the endpoints of the connection attach to this socket. Each socket has an address, called the *port number*. You can think of a socket as being like the telephones at either end of a phone call and the port as being like a phone number. Ports have specific addresses that are "well known" throughout

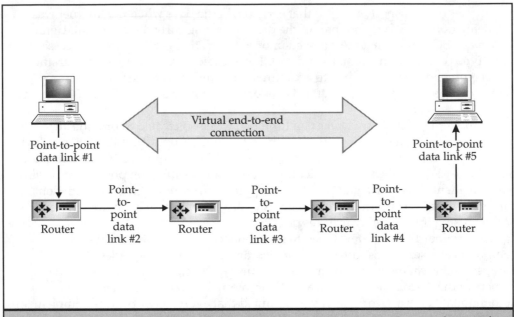

**Figure T-3.** *TCP establishes end-to-end connections over router-connected networks*

the computer industry. For example, it is "well known" that Web servers operate at port 80, so Web clients always connect with this port when accessing Web servers. The Web client and server then set up a temporary end-to-end connection at this port to exchange data. The full IP address of a Web server running in a computer has the form *x.x.x.x*:80, but it's usually not necessary to enter the port number.

A connection must first be requested by the sender and granted by the receiver. This provides the first level of reliability by ensuring that the receiver is ready to receive data. It also points out how TCP manages data delivery. If an application were to pass data directly to IP for delivery, IP would simply start sending packets to the destination. But if the destination is off-line or busy, those packets will be dropped and IP by itself has no way to inform the application that the packets were not delivered. TCP manages this by starting with a simple connection request, which IP delivers. When the recipient responds, TCP then starts passing more information to IP for delivery, making sure that IP doesn't go out of control. In this respect, one might think of TCP as a traffic controller for IP.

Some of the other features that TCP provides are outlined here:

■ TCP connections are *full-duplex*, two-way virtual channels that allow either end system to send data at any time. In this respect, a connection is really like two separate transmit and receive channels. Buffers are used to hold incoming and outgoing data so other activities are not held up by the communication process.

- The receiver can *acknowledge* receipt of datagrams to provide assurance of delivery to the sender . This acknowledgment scheme is used in a number of ways, as discussed in a moment.

- *Flow control* provides a way for two systems to actively cooperate in the transmission of data to prevent overflows and lost datagrams caused by fast senders. This feature lets transmitting systems quickly adapt to the traffic loads on the network and/or the available buffer size on the receiver.

- *Sequencing* is a technique for numbering datagrams so the receiver can put them back into the correct order and determine if datagrams are missing.

- A *checksumming* feature is used to ensure the integrity of packets.

## TCP Segments

A TCP segment is the official name for what is often loosely referred to as a packet (where a packet is some package of information). A segment is the actual entity that TCP uses to exchange data with its peers. The segment is what gets encapsulated into an IP datagram and transmitted across the network. Segments have a 20-byte header and a variable-length Data field. The fields of the TCP segment are described below and pictured in Figure T-4. Keep in mind that either station may send a segment that contains just header information and no data to provide the other system with connection information, such as an acknowledgment that a segment was received.

- **Source and destination port** Contains the port number of the sockets at the source and destination sides of the connection.

- **Sequence number** This field contains information for the receiver, which is a sequential number that identifies the data in the segment and where it belongs in the stream of data that has already been sent. The receiver can use the sequence number to reorder packets that have arrived out of order. It can also indicate that a segment is missing.

- **Acknowledgment number** This field is used by the receiver to indicate to the sender in a return message that it has received a previously sent packet. The number in this field is actually the sequence number for the next segment that the receiver expects. That number is calculated by incrementing the value in the Sequence Number field.

- **TCP header length** Specifies the length of the header.

- **Codes** This field contains the following bit codes, which serve as flags to indicate specific conditions:

  **URG (*urgent*)** This bit is set to 1 if there is information in the Urgent Pointer field of the header.

  **ACK (*acknowledgment*)** If ACK is set to 1, it indicates that the segment is part of an ongoing conversation and the number in the Acknowledgment Number field is valid. If this flag is set to 0 and SYN is set to 1, the segment is a request to establish a connection.

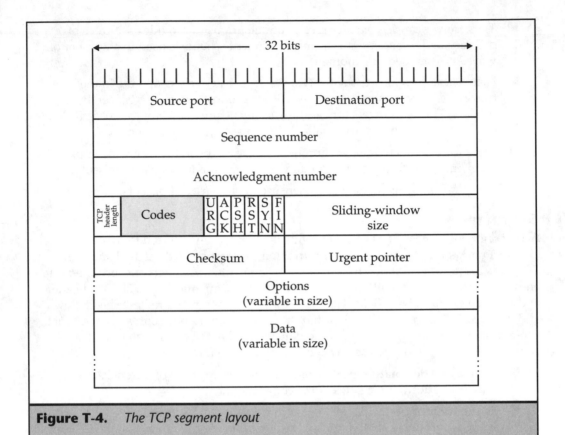

**Figure T-4.** *The TCP segment layout*

**PSH** (*push*)  A bit set by the sender to request that the receiver send data directly to the application and not buffer it.

**RST** (*reset*)  When set, the connection is invalid for a number of reasons and must be reset.

**SYN** (*synchronize*)  Used in conjunction with ACK to request a connection or accept a connection. SYN=1 and ACK=0 indicates a connection request. SYN=1 and ACK=1 indicates a connection accepted. SYN=0 and ACK=1 is an acknowledgment of the acknowledgment.

**FIN** (*finish*)  When set, this bit indicates that the connection should be terminated

■ **Sliding-window size** Transmits information about how much space is available in the receiver's buffers. This field is used by the receiver to inform the sender to slow down transmissions because the sender is sending data faster than the receiver can process it. If the receiver wants the sender to stop transmitting altogether, it can return a segment with 0 in this field. Later, when it can resume receiving data, it can send a segment with this field set to a nonzero value and an appropriate value in the Acknowledgment Number field to indicate which segment it needs.

■ **Checksum** Provides an error-checking value to ensure the integrity of the segment.

■ **Urgent pointer** This field can be used by the sender to indicate a location in the data where some urgent data is located.

■ **Options** A variable set aside for special options

■ **Data** A variable-length field that holds the messages or data from applications.

## Establishing Connections

The transport layer establishes connection-oriented sessions over which data is reliably transmitted during the period that the session is running. A connection is first established, data is transferred, and the connection is terminated.

Establishing a connection is a simple matter of sending a connection request to the target host. If it is available, it responds with a *connection acknowledgment message*. The systems may then negotiate session parameters (or some parameters may be included in the Options field of the TCP segment). For example, a station may indicate in a connection setup message that it cannot handle payloads larger than 2,000 bytes. The opposite station may indicate that it cannot handle payloads larger than 1,000 bytes. The lower value is then negotiated. There are a number of other parameters that can be negotiated to improve the efficiency of transmissions.

Connections are established using a *three-way handshake* mechanism, which takes place as follows:

1. Host A (the sender) sends a TCP segment to Host B with the SYN flag set to 1 and the ACK flag set to 0. A proposed initial sequence number is also inserted into the Sequence Number field of the header. This is the sequence number that Host A will use to send segments to Host B.

2. Host B stores the sequence number and returns a segment to Host A in which both the SYN and ACK flags are set to 1. To acknowledge that it has received Host A's sequence number, Host B increments the sequence number by 1 and inserts it into the Acknowledgment field of the segment it returns to Host A. In addition, it inserts its own sequence number into the Sequence Number field. This is the sequence number that Host B will use to send segments to Host A.

3. Host A can now acknowledge to Host B that it received its acknowledgment. It sends a segment in which ACK=1 and SYN=0. It also increments the sequence number received from Host B by 1 and inserts it into the Acknowledgment field to indicate that it accepts B's sequence numbering scheme.

After data is transmitted, the session is terminated. Host A sends a FIN=1 to Host B. Host B then responds with ACK=1 and FIN=1 and Host A responds to that with ACK=1.

TCP may have to deal with a number of connection parameters during the connection setup phase. One of these is to establish transmission delay parameters. Suppose Host A sends a segment to Host B and Host B returns an acknowledgment, but for some reason the acknowledgment does not arrive at Host A in a reasonable time. Host A must assume that Host B did not receive its transmission, so it retransmits the segment. In the meantime, the "lost" acknowledgment eventually finds its way to Host A and the retransmission arrives at Host B, which now has two of the same segment to deal with.

The amount of time that a sender should wait for an acknowledgment cannot be a fixed value because some links, such as satellites, have longer delays than others. TCP can negotiate this value by measuring the time it takes to receive responses. It then estimates a round-trip delay value and uses this value to clock transmissions and acknowledgments for a connection.

There are many other communication parameters that TCP must deal with in order to provide reliable services. For information about other transport layer connection and control mechanisms, refer to the Related Entries list below.

You are encouraged to visit the Web sites given below or refer to a specific text on TCP/IP protocols. As mentioned, Internet RFCs 1122 and 1323 provide information about fixes and extensions to TCP. Another interesting RFC is RFC 2001, which has the title "TCP Slow Start, Congestion Avoidance, Fast Retransmit, and Fast Recovery Algorithms." In addition, the IETF has a range of working groups that are developing transport layer extensions related to multimedia transport, satellite connections, and other issues. You can refer to the IETF Working Groups Web site listed below for more information.

**RELATED ENTRIES**    Acknowledgments; Congestion; Connection Establishment; Data Communication Concepts; Flow-Control Mechanisms; Fragmentation of Frames and Packets; Frame Switch; Handshake Procedures; Internet; IP (Internet Protocol); NAK (Negative Acknowledgment); Network Concepts; QoS (Quality of Service); TCP/IP (Transmission Control Protocol/Internet Protocol); *and* Web Technologies and Concepts

**INFORMATION ON THE INTERNET**

Transmission Control Protocol     http://www.internic.net/rfc/rfc793.txt
(RFC 793)—1981!

| | |
|---|---|
| TCP revisions (RFC 1122) | http://www.internic.net/rfc/rfc1122.txt |
| TCP Extensions for High Performance (RFC 1323) | http://www.internic.net/rfc/rfc1323.txt |
| A Primer On Internet and TCP/IP Tools and Utilities (RFC 2151) | http://www.internic.net/rfc/rfc2151.txt |
| TCP Slow Start, Congestion Avoidance, Fast Retransmit, and Fast Recovery Algorithms (RFC 2001) | http://www.internic.net/rfc/rfc2001.txt |
| TCP Extension for High-Speed Paths (RFC 1185) | http://www.internic.net/rfc/rfc1185.txt |
| Extending TCP for Transactions (RFC 1379) | http://www.internic.net/rfc/rfc1379.txt |
| IETF Working Groups (select "Transport Area" link) | http://www.ietf.org/html.charters/wg-dir.html |
| A User's Guide to TCP Windows | http://www.ncsa.uiuc.edu/People/vwelch/net_perf/tcp_windows.html |
| Charles Hedrick's Introduction to the Internet Protocols | http://oac3.hsc.uth.tmc.edu/staff/snewton/tcp-tutorial |
| Thomas Riemer's port numbers page | http://www.con.wesleyan.edu/~triemer/network/regports.html |
| U.C. Davis TCP/IP tutorial | gopher://gopher-chem.ucdavis.edu/11/Index/Internet_aw/Intro_the_Internet/intro.to.ip |
| H. Gilbert's Introduction to TCP/IP paper | http://pclt.cis.yale.edu/pclt/comm/tcpip.htm |
| Yahoo!'s TCP/IP links page | http://www.yahoo.com/Computers_and_Internet/Information_and_Documentation/Protocols/TCP_IP |

## TCP/IP (Transmission Control Protocol/Internet Protocol)

In the late 1960s and early 1970s, the Internet began to take shape in the form of a wide area network called ARPANET. ARPANET was funded by the DARPA (Defense Advanced Research Projects Agency). It consisted of computers that, starting in 1969, had been set up and connected using an experimental packet-switching system. At first, the systems used a client/server relationship, but it was decided that a host-to-host protocol was preferred. This protocol was called the NCP (Network Control Protocol).

> *NOTE:*  *The following historical outline is compiled from "A Brief History of the Internet," a paper available at the Internet Society's home page (http://www.isoc.org/internet-history).*

By 1972, demonstrations were taking place in which many terminals were connected to a variety of hosts over various telecommunication links. As the experiment continued, there was an increased need to simplify the process of interconnecting many different types of computers, but each computer vendor used different interconnection techniques. The goal was to develop an interconnection method that could support many different types of computers over many different types of transmission schemes, including low-speed, high-speed, and wireless connections.

Development on the TCP (Transmission Control Protocol) was started in 1973 by Bob Kahn, then with DARPA, and Vinton Cerf, then at Stanford University. Kahn started work on a detailed design for the protocol and asked Vincent Cerf for help because Cerf had done a lot of the original work on NCP. One of the objectives at this point was to gain knowledge about how the protocol would interface with existing operating systems. With Kahn's architecture and Cerf's NCP experience, TCP (not TCP/IP as explained later) was born. Its model was created before LANs and PCs were envisioned. It was meant to support a nationwide system of approximately 256 networks, but this turned out to be too small in scale when LANs started appearing in the late 1970s.

Note that the original protocol was called TCP. It attempted to provide as many services as possible, including a variety of connection-oriented features. Connection-oriented sessions require a setup phase, a take-down phase, and a lot of monitoring, which generates a lot of excess and unnecessary traffic for some data transmissions. During the development of TCP, Denny Cohen at USC recommended splitting the TCP protocol to accommodate "timeliness rather than accuracy." He argued that the reliability features were not always necessary. What was needed was a way to quickly get data to another system, then let that system handle all the error checking and sequencing on its own. Thus, TCP was reorganized into TCP and IP, with TCP handling flow control and packet recovery and IP providing basic addressing and packet-forwarding services. The UDP (User Datagram Protocol) was also created to provide a way for applications that do not need TCP's reliability features to access IP. Both TCP and UDP use IP.

The actual transition from NCP to TCP/IP took place on January 1, 1983. In one day, the majority of the connected networks made the transition. Over the years, the addressing scheme was modified to fit the growing number of networks and hosts connecting to the Internet. TCP/IP was also made to run on PCs and other small computers. DNS (Domain Name System) was invented by Paul Mockapetris so that people could use names instead of IP addresses to access computers. Routing protocols were developed to handle the creation of routing tables.

At one point in the late 1970s, there was an effort to integrate the TCP/IP protocol suite into the OSI (Open Systems Interconnection) protocol suite, but this effort failed. DARPA had already funded UC Berkeley to integrate TCP/IP into its UNIX version, and the integrated product that was created became a commercial success and helped make TCP/IP the internetworking standard of choice in the United States.

You can find out more about the TCP/IP protocols in the history paper described earlier or at the Web sites listed below. For additional historical information, see "Internet."

**RELATED ENTRIES**    ARPANET (Advanced Research Projects Agency Network); DARPA (Defense Advanced Research Projects Agency); Internet; Internet Backbone; Internet Connections; Internet Organizations and Committees; Intranets and Extranets; IP (Internet Protocol); ISPs (Internet Service Providers); NII (National Information Infrastructure); Standards Groups, Associations, and Organizations; TCP (Transmission Control Protocol); *and* Web Technologies and Concepts

### INFORMATION ON THE INTERNET

| | |
|---|---|
| The original TCP RFC (1981!) | http://www.internic.net/rfc/rfc793.txt |
| Internet Society | http://www.isoc.org |
| World Wide Web Consortium | http://www.w3.org/pub/WWW |
| IETF (Internet Engineering Task Force) | http://www.ietf.org |
| A Primer On Internet and TCP/IP Tools and Utilities | http://www.internic.net/rfc/rfc2151.txt |
| H. Gilbert's Introduction to TCP/IP  paper | http://pclt.cis.yale.edu/pclt/comm/tcpip.htm |
| Charles Hedrick's Introduction to the Internet Protocols | http://oac3.hsc.uth.tmc.edu/staff/snewton/tcp-tutorial |
| Yahoo!'s TCP/IP links page | http://www.yahoo.com/Computers_and_Internet/Information_and_Documentation/Protocols/TCP_IP |

## TCSEC (Trusted Computer System Evaluation Criteria)

TCSEC is a publication of the United States NCSC (National Computer Security Center). It is often referred to as the "Orange Book" and is part of the NSA (National Security Agency) security "Rainbow Series" of publications. TCSEC defines the criteria used to grade or rate the security of computer system products. Vendors like to claim that they have been certified to these specifications, but according the NCSC, "security-level requirements are open to interpretations that change over time. When undergoing evaluation, each vendor negotiates with the NSA about whether or not the details of its particular system implementation conform with the abstract security policy concepts in the NSA's books. The vendor must provide evidence that the requirements are being met."

**RELATED ENTRIES**   C2 Security Rating; Rainbow Series; Security; *and* TPEP (Trusted Product Evaluation Program)

**INFORMATION ON THE INTERNET**

| | |
|---|---|
| TCSEC paper | http://www.radium.ncsc.mil/tpep/library/rainbow/5200.28-STD.html |
| The Computer Security Evaluation Frequently Answered Questions | http://www.radium.ncsc.mil/tpep/process/faq-sect2.html |
| NIST document: Minimum Security Functionality Requirements For Multi-User Operating Systems | http://csrc.ncsl.nist.gov/nistgen/msfr.txt |

# TDMA (Time Division Multiple Access)

TDMA is a technique for allocating multiple channels on the same frequency in a wireless transmission system, such as a cellular phone system or a satellite communication system. For example, INTELSAT uses TDMA for its satellite communication systems. (Refer to the Web site given at the end of this topic.)

TDMA gets most of its attention for its use in cellular phone systems, where it allows many more users to access the same radiofrequency channel than older cellular systems. Each user gets a specific time slot in the channel and that time slot is fixed for the user during the call. Even if the device has nothing to transmit, the time slot is still reserved.

TDMA competes with CDMA (Code Division Multiple Access) techniques for cellular networks. CDMA uses spread spectrum technologies, which spreads the information contained in a transmission over a very large bandwidth. See the topic of the same name in this book.

GSM (Global System for Mobile Communications) uses TDMA for its access scheme. GSM frequency bands are 200 kHz wide and are divided into eight time division channels. GSM is known in the United States as PCS (Personal Communications Services). These services are discussed elsewhere in this book.

**RELATED ENTRIES**   AMPS (Advanced Mobile Phone Service); CDMA (Code Division Multiple Access); CDPD (Cellular Digital Packet Data); Cellular Communication Systems; GSM (Global System for Mobile Communications); PCS (Personal Communications Services); *and* Wireless Communications

**INFORMATION ON THE INTERNET**

| | |
|---|---|
| AT&T's Wireless site | http://www.attws.com |
| Cellular Telecommunications Industry Association | http://www.wow-com.com |

| Cellular Networking Perspectives' TDMA information | http://www.cnp-wireless.com/tdma.html |
| INTELSAT's Time Division Multiple Access (TDMA) service | http://www.intelsat.int/s-m/products/tdma.htm |

## Telecommunications and Telephone Systems

"Telecommunications" is derived from the Greek "tele" (distant) and "communicate" (sharing). In modern terms, telecommunication is the electronic transmission of sound, data, facsimiles, pictures, voice, video, and other information between systems using either analog or digital signaling techniques. Transmissions may take place over guided media (copper cables and fiber-optic cables) or unguided media (wireless radio).

Most of the telecommunication systems around the world are regulated by governments and international organizations. In the United States, regulation began in 1866 with the signing of the Post Roads Act, which gave the U.S. Postmaster General control over the telegraph industry. Today, the interstate telecommunication industry is regulated by the FCC (Federal Communications Commission), which was formed with the Communications Act of 1934. Individual state PUCs (public utility commissions) regulate communications within their jurisdictions. The FCC also regulates the use of wireless radio frequencies through a system of spectrum allocation and licensing.

AT&T (American Telephone and Telegraph) played an important part in the formation of the U.S. telecommunication system, so much so that the government brought a number of antitrust suits against it over the years. In 1913, AT&T was forced to divest itself from Western Union and allow independent carriers to use its long-distance networks. With the 1921 Graham Act, Congress created exceptions to antitrust laws for telecommunications companies that would allow them to build what were essentially monopolistic infrastructures within their service areas. To provide balance, the companies were required to provide *universal service*, which dictated that all customers be treated equally.

Eventually, AT&T assumed dominant control of this structure, and by 1984, AT&T was forced by the Justice Department to break up into seven regional holding companies called the RBOCs (regional Bell operating companies), in addition to the research division called Bellcore (now Lucent). Competition was also allowed in local markets, and about 1,200 independent LECs (local exchange carriers) now exist to compete with the RBOCs. The RBOCs and the independent LECs were limited to providing local phone service, producing yellow pages, and selling equipment, but restricted from providing long-distance service, information services, and cable TV services. Long-distance services opened up to competition, and companies like Sprint and MCI began to build radio and fiber-optic cable infrastructure.

The most recent regulation was the Telecommunication Act of 1996, which attempts to open local and long-distance markets to a plethora of alternate providers,

*T*

including cable, cellular, and broadcast companies. It allows traditional long-distance providers like AT&T and MCI to compete in local markets and allows local providers like the RBOCs to compete in long-distance markets. Alternative providers can provide services in both areas, and all companies can provide a wider range of services than was previously allowed.

The new laws allow for *end-to-end packaging* of services that is supposed to promote competition and benefit customers. Basically, local carriers are required to discount their local services so other service providers can buy them at competitive rates and rebundle them for resale to customers. Thus, customers can purchase end-to-end services from a single provider rather than creating separate contracts with local and long-distance carriers. At this writing, the RBOCs were challenging the act by claiming that it allowed unfair access to their operations by competing companies.

## Organizations Governing Telecommunication Standards

As mentioned, the FCC regulates telecommunications in the United States. On a global scale, several organizations recommend telecommunication standards and develop policies that encourage cooperation. The primary standards organizations are the ITU (International Telecommunication Union), ISO (International Organization for Standardization), and the IEC (International Electrotechnical Commission). The ITU and ISO are described elsewhere in this book.

The ITU was founded in 1865 when telegraph systems were the primary means of international communication. It is now an agency of the United Nations and is concerned with developing technical specifications, allocating electromagnetic spectrum (for global communication), and assembling world conferences and study groups. The ISO and the IEC formed the ISO/IEC JTC1 (Joint Technical Committee 1) in 1987 to study standards related to information technologies.

Committee T1 is a U.S. organization concerned with public network standards in the United States. It is supported by both ANSI (American National Standards Institute) and the FCC. In Europe, the ETSI (European Telecommunications Standards Institute) is concerned with telecommunication standards for Eastern and Western Europe.

## Structure of the Telephone Network

The public-switched telephone network (PSTN) consists of transmission components, switching components, and facilities for maintenance equipment, billing systems, and other internal components. *Transmission components (links)* define the actual media used to transmit signals. *Switching components (nodes)* include transmitters and receivers for voice and data routing using circuit-switching or packet-switching techniques.

The existing telecommunication systems in the United States consist largely of copper twisted-pair wiring in the local loop (the wiring from the phone company to homes and offices) and fiber-optic cable or radio systems for backbone trunks and long-distance lines. The local loop still uses analog transmission methods for voice calls.

Figure T-5 illustrates the service areas and facilities of the telecommunication system in the United States. LECs (local exchange carriers) operate within specific franchised service areas (basically service monopolies) called LATAs (local access and transport areas). LATAs were defined during the split-up of AT&T. The border of a LATA defines where local service ends and long-distance service begins. A LATA is generally associated with a telephone area code. LECs may be one of the RBOCs or an independent company that competes with an RBOC inside a LATA. The local carrier typically has several switching offices (called central offices, or COs) within the same LATA. Carriers such as the RBOCs are not restricted to just one LATA. Pacific Bell, for example, operates franchises in all the California LATA areas. An *IXC (interexchange carrier)* is any long-distance provider, such as AT&T, MCI, or US Sprint, that provides services between the LECs. The LECs are required to provide a point of presence (an interface) for the IXCs. Communication facilities employed by the IXCs include fiber-optic cable, ground-based microwave towers, and satellite-based microwave systems.

The telephone system consists of a hierarchy of switches that set up calls across COs, across LATAs, or across long-distance connections. This hierarchy is pictured in Figure T-6.

The hierarchy can be traced back to the first phone systems. In the late 1800s, when telephones were first introduced, people would buy pair of phones and run a wire between the phones. Soon, cities were enmeshed in telephone cables running in all directions. Savvy entrepreneurs like Alexander Graham Bell built telephone companies so customers could run their wires to a single location and let operators connect them with other phones via a manually operated switching system. At first, customers could only connect with other customers of the phone company they used, but soon, trunk lines were established between phone companies and everybody could call everybody else in the same local area. This grew into the hierarchy of switches that eventually extended to outlying areas and other cities, and then in the 1950s and 1960s exploded into an automated global switching system.

Note in Figure T-6 that calls within the same CO do not need to be switched any further up the hierarchy than the local CO. A call attached to another CO within the same LATA may go directly to that CO if a line exists or go through a tandem or toll office (toll if the link is considered long distance by the LEC). InterLATA calls are handled by IXCs such as AT&T or MCI. The calls are routed to the IXC's point of presence within the LATA, then out across the long-distance lines and back into a point of presence at the remote LATA. While this system can be explained as a hierarchical structure, today almost all switching offices are interconnected to avoid congestion. In Figure T-6, the dotted lines indicate the addition of these trunks.

The bottom of the hierarchy in Figure T-6 seems to indicate that all lines from COs terminate at a single phone. In fact, the phone company extends multichannel digital lines (T1 and T3 lines) into businesses that have multiple phones. The business sets up a PBX (private branch exchange) that essentially provides an extension of the telephone company's switching system into the local business. The telephone company can then route all calls for phones within a business to the PBX and rely on

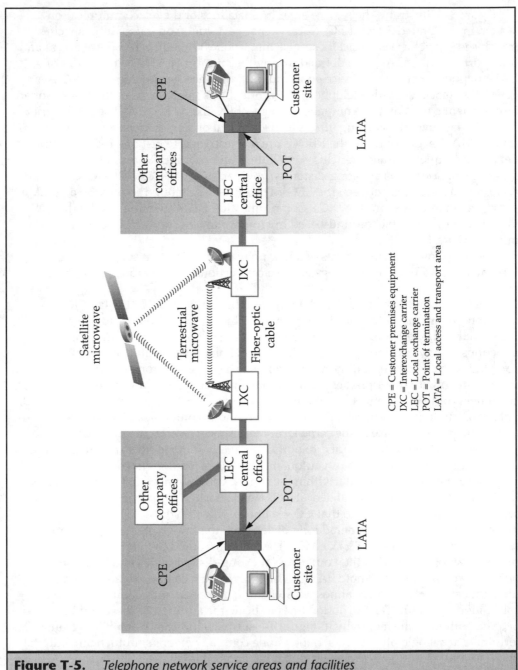

**Figure T-5.** *Telephone network service areas and facilities*

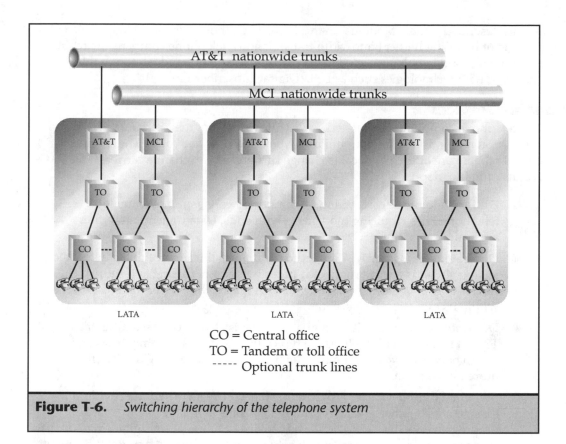

**Figure T-6.** *Switching hierarchy of the telephone system*

the PBX to distribute those calls. An interesting thing about PBX systems is that they are changing rapidly with the integration of computers and telephony, as described under "PBX (Private Branch Exchange)" and "Telephony" in this book.

## Signaling and Transmission Methods

The primary connection between most homes and businesses and the telephone company is the *local loop*, which is a pair of copper wires that transmit voice signals in the range of 300 Hz to 3,100 Hz. Frequencies above this range are filtered to avoid noise. If you call someone in your own neighborhood, chances are that the call is completely analog from end to end. If you call someone that is attached to another switching office, the call is probably converted to a digital signal for transmission from CO to CO.

While the 3,000 Hz bandwidth is fine for voice, high-speed data transmissions are severely restricted by it. Digital signals must be converted by a modem to analog signals for transmission across the local loop. The highest data rates are 33.6 Kbits/sec, or about 53 Kbits/sec in one direction when using special techniques such as X2 or

K56 as described under "Modems" in this book. Even though the local loop cable is capable of handling higher bandwidth transmissions, telephone company switching equipment is still largely restricted to operating in the voice band, although this is changing with technologies such as DSL (Digital Subscriber Line).

## Available Services

The telephone companies are related service providers that make a range of connection methods available for building voice and data networks. The services described here are offered by local exchange carriers, interexchange carriers, and VACs (value added carriers).

- **Dial-up telephone connection** A temporary connection over analog telephone lines requiring modems at both ends. Data transmission rates are limited.

- **Dedicated analog circuit** Similar to the dial-up line, except that a dedicated analog circuit is always connected (does not require dialing and setup). The carrier may provide a special rate on such lines if they cover long distances within its own area of operation.

- **Dedicated digital circuit** A digital line that is always connected, such as T1, T3, or Fractional T1. The lines are typically leased on a monthly basis and set up between two fixed points. Refer to "Leased Line" and "T1/T3" for more information.

- **Switched digital circuit** A digital line that can be switched to provide connections to other sites, but usually only sites that have been preprogrammed by a carrier. The advantage of this type of digital circuit is that you only pay for the time that you actually use the line but you get the benefits of a private leased line. The circuits are ideal for temporary connections and backup lines to supplement dedicated lines.

- **Packet-switching network** A pay-for-use service that can provide any-to-any connections, but the carrier must usually program in the connection points, which form VCs (virtual circuits). Frame relay is a common packet-switched service.

*NOTE: Any of these circuits can be used to obtain access to the Internet. The Internet then provides a global network with inexpensive access to anywhere in the world. Refer to "VPN (Virtual Private Network)" for more information.*

ISDN is another type of switched digital circuit that combines the convenience of dial-up service to anywhere with high-quality digital links. The ISDN line consists of two 64-Kbit/sec voice or data lines that can be combined to provide a 128-Kbit/sec data line. Other digital services include emerging DSL (Digital Subscriber Line) services, as described under the topic of the same name in this book.

Wide area networks benefit from fast packet-switching services such as frame relay, ATM (Asynchronous Transfer Mode), and SMDS (Switched Multimegabit Data Service). The "fast" in fast packet technologies comes from the fact that much of the error-checking, packet-sequencing, and acknowledgment services have been removed to improve the speed of the network. Refer to "Communication Services" for more information on these services.

## New Trends and Services

The Internet has had an incredible effect on the telecommunication systems. People are demanding more bandwidth and are considering a variety of alternatives, such as satellite and cable TV. In addition, voice and videoconferencing over the Internet has become an inexpensive reality. At the same time, wireless services may reduce the need for copper wire local loops. Developing countries are skipping wired systems altogether and building wireless systems at a rapid rate. The traditional monopolistic phone companies in the United States and elsewhere are scrambling to keep up.

There is little room here to predict what the telecommunication system will be like in a few years. Eventually, the public network "pyramid," in which users at the low end have limited bandwidth, will give way to a network in which everyone has access to high bandwidth. In fact, bandwidth may become so inexpensive that it will cost too much for carriers to meter it. Instead, you may just pay a monthly connection fee, much like Internet users pay today. Carriers are installing fiber-optic cable at a fast pace to meet future demand, and new transmission techniques such as WDM (wavelength division multiplexing) are already increasing bandwidth on existing lines. WDM allows a single fiber-optic line to accommodate multiple light signals at different wavelengths. MCI has already upgraded its backbone network to Quad-WDM (four-wavelength wave division multiplexing), boosting transmission rates from 2.5 Gbits/sec to 10 Gbits/sec. According to MCI, that is "enough capacity to carry 129,000 simultaneous telephone calls over the hair-thin strand."

**RELATED ENTRIES**    ATM (Asynchronous Transfer Mode); AT&T (American Telephone and Telegraph); Cell Relay; Circuit-Switching Services; Communication Service Providers; Communication Services; DSL (Digital Subscriber Line); Frame Relay; IXC (Interexchange Carrier); LATA (Local Access and Transport Area); Leased Line; LEC (Local Exchange Carrier); Local Loop; MCI; Multiplexing; Packet and Cell Switching; Point-to-Point Communications; PSTN (Public-Switched Telephone Network); RBOCs (Regional Bell Operating Companies); SMDS (Switched Multimegabit Data Service); SONET (Synchronous Optical Network); T1/T3; Telephony; Transmission Media, Methods, and Equipment; Videoconferencing and Desktop Video; Voice/Data Networks; Voice over ATM; VoIP (Voice over IP); VPN (Virtual Private Network); WAN (Wide Area Network); Wireless Communications; *and* X.25.

**INFORMATION ON THE INTERNET**

| | |
|---|---|
| ITU (International Telecommunication Union) | http://www.itu.ch |
| ITU site listing (very complete) | http://www.itu.ch/Sites |
| Committee T1 | http://www.t1.org |
| FCC (Federal Communications Commission) | http://www.fcc.gov |
| Telecommunications Act of 1996 | http://www.technologylaw.com/techlaw/act_index.html |
| ETSI (European Telecommunications Standards Institute) | http://www.etsi.fr |
| Chuck Eby's telephone history page | http://www.cybercomm.net/~chuck/phones.html |
| Advanced Telecommunications Institute (technical papers) | http://www.ati.stevens-tech.edu/directory.html |
| Telecoms Virtual Library | http://www.analysys.com/vlib |
| Prof. Jeffrey MacKie-Mason's telecommunication links | http://www.spp.umich.edu/telecom |
| Goodman's Book Marks | http://www.wp.com/goodmans |
| Telstra's {Tele}Communications Information Sources | http://www.telstra.com.au/info/communications.html |
| Yahoo!'s Telecommunications links page | http://www.yahoo.com/Business/Corporations/Telecommunications |
| Yahoo!'s Telecommunications links page (another) | http://www.yahoo.com/Science/Engineering/Electrical_Engineering/Telecommunications |
| InfoAmericas2000's telecommunication information | http://www.infoamericas.org |
| Telecommunication Magazine online | http://www.telecoms-mag.com/tcs.html |
| Telecom Digest | http://massis.lcs.mit.edu/telecom-archives |
| Lucent info | http://www.lucent.com/netsys |
| The Phone Zone | http://www.phonezone.com |

# Telecommunications Companies

*See* Appendix A for information about telecommunications companies, vendors, and other online resources.

# Teleconferencing

*See* Videoconferencing and Desktop Video.

# Telephony

Telephony is all about converting sounds such as voice for delivery over a medium, such as copper wire or radio waves. Telephony in that respect is covered under "Telecommunications and Telephone Systems." Recently, the term "telephony" has become synonymous with a variety of services such as voice mail and the integration of telephones and computers. Telephony in this respect is covered under the following headings:

- **CTI (Computer-Telephony Integration)**  Covers the integration of telephones and computers into the same box and over the same networks

- **Videoconferencing and Desktop Video**  Covers videoconferencing over intranets and the Internet

- **Voice Mail**  As defined in this book, voice mail has to do with sending voice mail messages over data networks

- **Voice/Data Networks**  Describes how companies can use their data networks for voice

- **Voice over ATM**  Discusses standards being developed to carry voice calls over ATM networks

- **Voice over Frame Relay**  Describes methods for delivering voice calls over frame-relay networks

- **Voice over the Internet**  Discusses products, standards, and techniques for carrying voice calls over the Internet

## INFORMATION ON THE INTERNET

| | |
|---|---|
| Goodman's Book Marks (telephony) | http://www.wp.com/goodmans/resfor.html |
| Andrew Sears' Telephony resource list (very complete) | http://rpcp.mit.edu/~itel/resource.html |
| Prof. Jeffrey MacKie-Mason's telecommunication links | http://www.spp.umich.edu/telecom |
| The Phone Zone | http://www.phonezone.com |
| The Internet Telephony Consortium | http://itel.mit.edu |
| Enterprise Computer Telephony Forum | http://www.ectf.org |
| International Multimedia Teleconferencing Consortium | http://www.imtc.org |
| International Teleconferencing Association | http://www.itca.org |
| Internet Telephony Magazine | http://www.internettelephony.com |

| Goodman's Book Marks (Internet telephony) | http://www.wp.com/goodmans/ipt.html |
| Ken Persson's telephony page (very complete) | http://www.pi.se/ken/linkcti.html |
| Yahoo!'s Computer Telephony links page | http://www.yahoo.com/Business_and _Economy/Companies/Computers/ Networking/Computer_Telephony |

# Telnet

Telnet is the login and terminal emulation protocol common on the Internet and in UNIX environments. It operates over TCP/IP networks. Its primary function is to allow users to log into remote host systems. Originally, Telnet was a simple terminal program that sent all user input to the remote host for processing. Newer versions perform more processing locally, thus providing better response and reducing the amount of information transferred over the link to the remote host. Administrators often use Telnet to control remote servers.

Telnet is a client/server process in which the user invokes the Telnet application on the local system and sets up a link to a Telnet process running on a remote host. The user issues requests at the keyboard that are passed to the Telnet client running in his or her system. Telnet then transmits the requests to the Telnet server on the remote host. Through this process, users can initiate programs on the remote host and run those programs from their own systems as if they were attached directly to the remote host. Most processes run on the remote host. It receives requests from the user's system and processes them in its workspace, thus reducing traffic over the link.

## INFORMATION ON THE INTERNET

| Yahoo!'s Telnet links page | http://www.yahoo.com/Computers_and_Internet/ Software/Internet/Telnet |
| Telnet protocol information | http://www.scit.wlv.ac.uk/~jphb/comms/telnet.html |

# Terminal Servers

Terminal servers can connect large numbers of terminals to mainframe or minicomputer systems over a LAN (local area network). The terminals are attached to the terminal server via RS-232 serial interfaces and the terminal server is connected to an Ethernet or token ring network. The network then serves as the link between the host system and the terminals. A terminal server is basically an asynchronous multiplexor that connects not only terminals but computers, modems, printers, and other peripherals to the host system. The terminal server has a number of serial ports and the appropriate network interface.

Terminal servers are not gateways because the attached terminal devices are using a communication protocol that is compatible with the host. When a personal computer is attached to a host through a terminal server, it runs a terminal emulation program that lets it mimic the communication protocols of a terminal. Note, however, that the terminal server does encapsulate data from terminals for transport over the network to the host system.

## Testing and Diagnostic Equipment and Techniques

This section primarily discusses the tools that technicians can carry around with them to troubleshoot network problems and make sure that network cabling has been installed to specifications. But network testing and diagnostics should also be proactive, i.e., it is extremely useful to have equipment that can monitor the condition of the network and warn you of impending problems. That is where network management systems based on SNMP (Simple Network Management Protocol) and RMON (Remote Monitoring) come in handy (see the corresponding topics in this book, as well as the topic "Network Management"). These systems gather up and display useful information about the condition of networks and provide statistical information that can help you justify your management techniques and requirements for new equipment.

Aside from these management systems, the primary tools for managing and troubleshooting networks include cable testers and network analyzers. Cable testers are used to test or certify the physical cable plant, while network analyzers can provide sophisticated information about protocol packets, traffic conditions, potential sources of bad packets, and other information. Refer to "Network Analyzers" for more information about the latter products. The remainder of this section covers cable testing equipment.

## Network Cable Testers

Network cabling is a common source of problems. Cables may be misconfigured, have faulty connectors, or be near some noise source that is distorting signals. In some cases, the wrong cable may have been installed, or it may be of inferior quality. For example, a recent shortage of *fluorinated ethylene propylene*, which is used to create fire-safe insulation for cables, forced some manufacturers to use inferior materials in their Category 5 twisted-pair cable. This caused a problem called *delay skew*, in which parallel signals propagate across a cable at different velocities. This problem is only relevant on networks that transmit signals in parallel on multiple cables at high speed, such as 100Base-T4 and 100VG-AnyLAN. Most good cable testers can now test for this problem.

Cable testers are used to certify that a cable installation meets its intended specifications or to verify that the cable is working properly. Some testers are quite affordable and should be part of any network manager's toolkit. More expensive devices can be rented, or you can rely on the services of consultants and professional cable installers.

A new breed of relatively inexpensive multifunction cable testers is now available that provides a wide range of functions. Some testers have the ability to monitor network protocols and can even run Ping and Traceroute commands over IP networks.

But these devices usually don't have all the features of high-end protocol analyzers, such as the ability to display much more sophisticated network information that savvy operators can evaluate to diagnose problems.

Here are some of the tests that a cable tester should perform:

- *Continuity* testing can determine whether a cable, either on the roll or installed, will conduct electricity as specified by the manufacturer from one end to the other. Cable testing devices include the components for measuring at one end of the cable if it is already installed.

- *Electrical noise* testing is important for cable that has been installed. Noise below 150 kHz is from electrical transmission lines and fluorescent lights. Noise above 150 kHz is from electrical equipment such as computers and copiers. Impulse noise occurs spontaneously and lasts only a short time, so measurements must be taken over time to determine if external sources are causing a continuous impulse problem on the cable plant.

- *Crosstalk* is noise emanating from the signals transmitted on adjacent wire pairs. Most testing devices can measure crosstalk by injecting a signal in a wire pair and measuring the energy induced by the signal in adjacent pairs.

- *Attenuation* is measured by sending a signal through a cable and measuring the signal strength at the other end of the cable. Attenuation is a natural characteristic of cable, but uncharacteristic attenuation may indicate excessive bends or partial breaks in the cable.

- *Capacitance* measurements can indicate whether a cable has been stretched or has kinks. Cable has a capacitance value that is measured in pF (picofarads) per foot. A test of cable, either on the spool or installed, will indicate damage.

- A *TDR (time domain reflectometer)* can locate breaks and shorts in cables. It sends a high-frequency pulse down the length of the cable and then measures the time it takes for the signal to reflect back. Reflections occur at shorts and breaks, and the time and amplitude of the reflection indicates the distance to the problem. In addition, the polarity indicates whether the problem is a short or an open connection. TDRs can provide *length measurements* to determine if cable runs are longer than allowed for proper signaling.

- *Cable tracing* is used to find the path of a cable in a wall or ceiling, or its source and destination. You attach a tone generator to a cable termination in an office, then listen for the tone either in the walls or at the punchdown block or path panel in the wiring closet. The cable tester will indicate when you are near the wire that is producing the tone.

When purchasing testers, make sure they support the type of cable you need to test. Most testers today should be "CAT5-compatible," meaning that they provide a full suite of tests for four-pair Category 5 copper cabling. Such devices should be able to test 100-Mbit/sec Ethernet and 155-Mbit/sec ATM networks. Another feature is the ability to store test results so you can download and print them later. Some devices can connect to oscilloscopes for detailed analysis of test results. Cable testers are also available for fiber-optic cable. The vendors listed below can provide you with additional information about test equipment.

**RELATED ENTRIES**    Network Analyzers; Network Management; RMON (Remote Monitoring); SNMP (Simple Network Management Protocol); *and* Transmission Media, Methods, and Equipment

### INFORMATION ON THE INTERNET

| | |
|---|---|
| Black Box Corporation | http://www.blackbox.com |
| Datacom Technologies | http://www.datacomtech.com |
| Fibronics International, Inc. | http://www.fibusa.com |
| Fluke Corporation | http://www.fluke.com |
| Fotec, Inc. | http://www.std.com/fotec |
| Microtest, Inc. | http://www.microtest.com |
| Network General Corp. | http://www.ngc.com |
| Scope Communications, Inc. | http://www.scope.com |
| Telecommunications Techniques Corp. | http://www.ttc.com |
| UNICOM Electric, Inc. | http://www.connectors.com |
| Wavetek, Inc. | http://www.wavetek.com |

## TFTP (Trivial File Transfer Protocol)

TFTP is a Internet file transfer protocol similar to FTP (File Transfer Protocol), but it is scaled back in functionality so that it requires fewer resources to run. TFTP uses the UDP (User Datagram Protocol) rather than TCP (Transmission Control Protocol), which allows TFTP to be used in environments where TCP is not available. TFTP also differs from FTP in that it only supports file transfers and does not have the user interface features that FTP has. The command set is minimized so the users cannot get directory listings. There is also no login procedure.

**RELATED ENTRIES**    File Systems; FTP (File Transfer Protocol); Internet; *and* TCP/IP (Transmission Control Protocol/Internet Protocol)

## Threads

Threads are individual processes that execute simultaneously in multitasking operating systems. Developers that create programs for multitasking operating systems can design processes that can be split up into threads and processed at the same time. The real power of a multitasking system is realized when the underlying computer has multiple processors. Then, each processor can handle different tasks or different threads of execution for a single task. More processors can be added as necessary.

If the system has only one processor, then each thread is executed in turn, one after the other. A single thread does not dominate the processor, but instead is given a small amount of time to complete some or all of its tasks. Users have the illusion that several programs are running at the same time.

Threads are useful because they eliminate the need for the operating system to constantly load and unload information to and from memory. The information required for each thread is kept in memory. This reduces overhead, not only in memory space but in the time it takes to create the information in memory. Each thread may interact with a different part of the system, such as disk systems, network I/O (input/output), or the user. Threads are scheduled for execution because some threads may need to wait for events to occur or the completion of a task by another thread.

**RELATED ENTRIES**   MPP (Massively Parallel Processor) Systems; Multiprocessing; NUMA (Non-Uniform Memory Access); Parallel Processing; *and* Servers

**INFORMATION ON THE INTERNET**

| | |
|---|---|
| Sun Microsystems' Threads site (very complete) | http://www.sun.com/software/Products/Developer-products/sig/threads |
| Bryan O'Sullivan's threads FAQ | http://www.cis.ohio-state.edu/hypertext/faq/usenet/threads-faq/part1/faq.html |

# Throughput

Throughput is a measurement of the rate at which a system can process or transmit information. Throughput is typically an overall measure of a system and its components. For example, the throughput of a server depends on its processor type, the type of network interface card, the size of the data transfer bus, the speed of the disk, memory buffer size, and the efficiency of the operating system. In a communication system, throughput is measured as the number of bits or packets that can be processed per second.

Delay may be a factor, depending on how you measure a system. For example, measuring the throughput of an Ethernet LAN with a single user will provide different results from measuring the same LAN with multiple users. When multiple users attempt to access the system at the same time, collisions, backoffs, random waits, and retransmissions occur, which throw off a "pure" measurement.

Another consideration when measuring actual throughput is the overhead introduced by the communication protocols. Data travels in frames and packets that include header information. The more header information, the less data sent. In addition, some protocols require that individual frames and packets or groups of frames and packets be acknowledged by the receiver. This creates excess traffic that is not sending real data. Finally, systems along the transmission path may impose delays. A store-and-forward router holds a packet, reads its address, and forwards it appropriately.

**RELATED ENTRIES**   Bandwidth; Capacity; Channel; Circuit; Data Communication Concepts; Data Transfer Rates; Delay; Electromagnetic Spectrum; Modulation Techniques; *and* Transmission Media, Methods, and Equipment

## TIA (Telecommunications Industry Association)

The TIA serves as the voice of the communications and information technology industry. Its members include vendors, service providers, and organizations that get involved in all aspects of modern communication networks. The TIA is involved in legislative efforts, international marketing opportunities, trade show sponsorship, and standards development. The TIA works in association with the EIA (Electronic Industries Association) and recently has become affiliated with the MultiMedia Telecommunications Association to work jointly on the convergence of computing technologies and communications. The TIA's Web site is one of its most important assets. The Web site provides information that helps manufacturers in their business decisions and provides educational material for anyone that wants to access it.

**RELATED ENTRIES**   TIA/EIA Structured Cabling Standards; Transmission Media, Methods, and Equipment

**INFORMATION ON THE INTERNET**

| | |
|---|---|
| TIA (Telecommunications Industry Association) | http://www.tiaonline.org |
| Alternative TIA site | http://www.industry.net/tia |
| EIA (Electronic Industries Association) | http://www.eia.org |
| MultiMedia Telecommunications Association | http://www.mmta.org |

## TIA/EIA Structured Cabling Standards

In the mid-1980s, the TIA (Telecommunications Industry Association) and the EIA (Electronic Industries Association) began developing methods for cabling buildings, with the intent of developing a uniform wiring system that would support multivendor products and environments. In 1991, the TIA/EIA released the TIA/EIA 568 Commercial Building Telecommunication Cabling Standard. In the following years, it released addenda to the standard, and it is now called the TIA/EIA-568-A standard.

The TIA/EIA structured cabling standards are international specifications that define how to design, build, and manage a structured cabling system. The standard defines a structured, star-topology network. This design is ideal for enterprise networks that have high-speed backbones (or hub-based collapsed backbones) and slower periphery networks. It allows users to communicate with any other system on the network while maintaining localized workgroups.

The TIA/EIA defined a range of standards related to network cabling, as outlined here:

- **TIA/EIA-568-A**   Defines a standard for building cable system for commercial buildings that support data networks, voice, and video

- **TIA/EIA-569**   Defines how to build the pathways and spaces for telecommunication media

- **TIA/EIA-606**   Defines the design guidelines for managing a telecommunication infrastructure

- **TIA/EIA-607**   Defines grounding and bonding requirements for telecommunication cabling and equipment

This section discussed the TIA/EIA-568-A standard. For more information about the other standards, refer to the TIA Web site given at the end of this section. Note that this section is related to the section called "Transmission Media, Methods, and Equipment," which discusses cabling in general and provides addition information on cable and equipment specified in the TIA/EIA-568-A standard.

According to TIA/EIA-568-A documents, the wiring standard is designed to provide the following features and functions:

- A generic telecommunication wiring system for commercial buildings

- Defined media, topology, termination and connection points, and administration

- Support for multiproduct, multivendor environments

- Direction for future design of telecommunication products for commercial enterprises

- The ability to plan and install the telecommunication wiring for a commercial building without any prior knowledge of the products that will use the wiring

The last point has benefits for users because it standardizes network cabling and installation, opening the market for competing products and services in the area of premises wiring, design, installation, and management. The standard defines the use of fiber-optic cable (single and multimode), STP (shielded twisted-pair) cable, and UTP (unshielded twisted-pair) cable (Categories 3 through 5, as outlined under "Transmission Media, Methods, and Equipment").

The layout of a TIA/EIA-568-A structured cable system is illustrated in Figure T-7. The hierarchical structure is apparent in the multifloor office building. A vertical backbone cable runs from the central hub in the main equipment room to a hub/switch in the telecommunication closet on each floor. Work areas are then

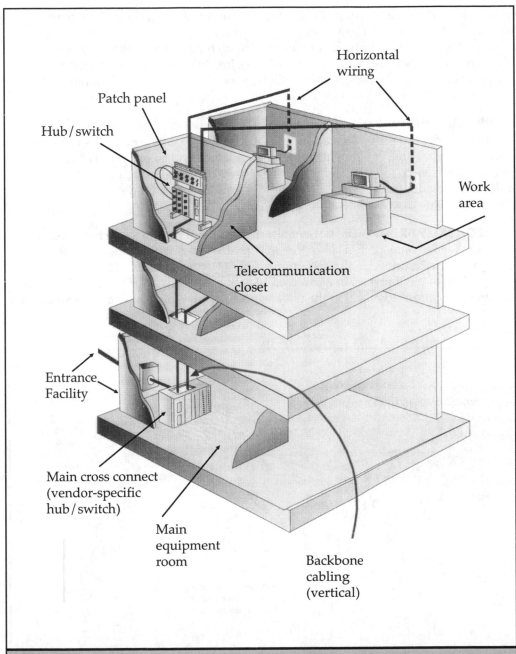

Horizontal
wiring

Patch panel

Hub/switch

Work
area

Telecommunication
closet

Entrance
Facility

Main cross connect
(vendor-specific
hub/switch)

Main
equipment
room

Backbone
cabling
(vertical)

**Figure T-7.**    *TIA/EIA-568-A structured cabling layout*

individually cabled to the equipment in the telecommunication closet. The logical hierarchy is illustrated in Figure T-8.

The TIA standard defines the parameters for each part of the cabling system, which includes work area wiring, horizontal wiring, telecommunication closets, equipment rooms and cross-connects, backbone (vertical) wiring, and entrance facilities. Each of these is described here.

**WORK AREA WIRING**   The work area wiring subsystem consists of the communication outlets (wallboxes and faceplates), wiring, and connectors needed to connect the work area equipment (computers, printers, and so on) via the horizontal wiring subsystem to the telecommunication closet. The standard requires that two outlets be provided at each wall plate—one for voice and one for data. The cabling requirements are discussed next.

**HORIZONTAL WIRING**   The horizontal wiring system runs from each workstation outlet to the *telecommunication closet*. The maximum horizontal distance from the telecommunication closet to the communication outlets is 90 meters (295 feet) independent of media type. An additional 10 meters is allowed for patch cables at the telecommunication closet and at the workstation. As mentioned above, the work area

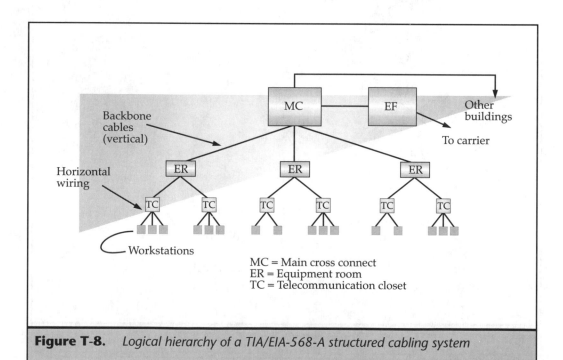

**Figure T-8.**   *Logical hierarchy of a TIA/EIA-568-A structured cabling system*

must provide two outlets. The voice outlet must use four-pair 100 ohm UTP cable (Categories 3 through 5), while the data outlet can be cabled with a choice of four-pair 100 ohm UTP cable, two-pair 150 ohm STP, or 62.5/125 mm fiber-optic cable, depending on requirements.

**TELECOMMUNICATION CLOSETS**    The telecommunication closet contains the connection equipment for workstations in the immediate area and a cross-connection to an equipment room. The telecommunication closet is a general facility that can provide horizontal wiring connections as well as entrance facility connections. There is no limit on the number of telecommunication closets allowed. Some floors in multistory office buildings may have multiple telecommunication closets, depending on the floor plan. These may be connected to an equipment room on the same floor.

**EQUIPMENT ROOMS AND MAIN CROSS-CONNECTS**    An equipment room provides a termination point for backbone cabling that is connected to one or more telecommunication closets. It may also be the main cross-connection point for the entire facility. In a campus environment, each building may have its own equipment room, to which telecommunication closet equipment is connected, and the equipment in this room may then be connected to a central campus facility that provides the main cross-connect for the entire campus.

**BACKBONE WIRING**    The backbone wiring runs up through the floors of the building (risers) or across a campus and provides the interconnection for equipment rooms and telecommunication closets. The distance limitations of this cabling depends on the type of cable and facilities it connects. Refer to Figure T-8 and the following table. Note that data transmissions over UTP are limited to 90 meters.

| Cable Type | MC to TC | ER to TC | MC to ER |
|---|---|---|---|
| Multimode fiber | 2,000 m (6,560 ft.) | 500 m (1,640 ft.) | 1,500 m (4,820 ft.) |
| Single-mode fiber | 3,000 m (9,840 ft.) | 500 m (1,640 ft.) | 1,500 m (4,820 ft.) |
| UTP (voice) | 800 m (2,624 ft.) | 500 m (1,640 ft.) | 300 m (984 ft.) |

**ENTRANCE FACILITIES**    The entrance facility contains the telecommunication service entrance to the building. This facility may also contain campus-wide backbone connections. It also contains the *network demarcation point,* which is the interconnection to the local exchange carrier's telecommunication facilities. The demarcation point is typically 12 inches from where the carrier's facilities enter the building, but the carrier may designate otherwise.

**RELATED ENTRIES**    Backbone Networks; Data Communication Concepts; Ethernet; Fast Ethernet; Fiber-Optic Cable; Gigabit Ethernet; Hubs/Concentrators/MAUs; Network Concepts; Network Design and Construction; Power and Grounding Problems and Solutions; Testing and Diagnostic Equipment and Techniques; Token Ring Network; *and* Transmission Media, Methods, and Equipment

**INFORMATION ON THE INTERNET**

| | |
|---|---|
| TIA (Telecommunications Industry Association) | http://www.tiaonline.org |
| Alternative TIA site | http://www.industry.net/tia |
| Anixter's white papers on structured cabling | http://www.anixter.com/techlib |
| Hubbell Premise's Wiring white paper | http://www.hubbell-premise.com/eia568_a.htm |

## Time Synchronization Services

Distributed network systems require time synchronization to ensure accurate timestamping and event executions. Time synchronization helps establish and maintain the order of events. A time service keeps track of time in networks and determines the accuracy associated with each clock used to synchronize time. The service provides fault-tolerant clock synchronization for systems in both local and wide area networks. The NTP (Network Time Protocol) may be used to obtain time values from outside sources. The Tymserve 2000 Network Time Server from Datum, Inc. provides NTP time service functions.

NDS (Novell Directory Services) is an example of how time synchronization services help to keep the activities of servers synchronized. NDS holds information about user accounts and network resources. Changes must be replicated (copied) to all servers where the NDS database is stored. Time synchronization helps to ensure that everything is kept synchronized.

There are two time synchronization schemes. The first uses a *single-reference time server* for relatively small, geographically close networks. The time server is the sole source of time on the network. Any time changes are set on this server, and then others synchronize with it. The other method is used for geographically distant networks and includes the following time servers:

- **Primary server** A primary server synchronizes time with other primary time servers or a reference time server, and provides the correct time to secondary time servers.

- **Reference server** A reference server gets its time from an external source (such as a radio clock) and is a contact to what the outside world says the time should be.

All other servers on the network can be *secondary time servers*, which get their time from single reference, primary, or reference time servers and do not participate in the establishment of a common time over the network. Note that the master time signal is obtained from public time servers.

**RELATED ENTRIES**   NDS (Novell Directory Services); NTP (Network Time Protocol)

**INFORMATION ON THE INTERNET**

| | |
|---|---|
| TimeSync site | http://www.eecis.udel.edu/~ntp |
| Public times server list | http://www.eecis.udel.edu/~mills/ntp/servers.html |
| Yahoo!'s NTP links page (choose NTP link) | http://www.yahoo.com/Computers_and_Internet/Information_and_Documentation/Protocols |
| Network Time Protocol, version 3 (RFC 1305) | http://www.internic.net/rfc/rfc1305.txt |
| Datum, Inc. | http://www.datum.com |

# TN3270

Clients running TN3270 software can connect to TN3270 servers running on host systems such as IBM mainframes and access those systems as if they were using an IBM 3270 terminal. TN3270 connections can be made over TCP/IP networks and the Internet. Many systems on the Internet that provide front ends to database systems and other libraries of information require the use of TN3270 client software. TN3270 is a special version of the Internet's Telnet protocol that allows users with non-3270-compatible systems to access IBM hosts.

SNA (Systems Network Architecture) gateways such as Microsoft SNA Server support TN3270 clients by allowing TN3270 users on a TCP/IP LAN to access a host mainframe through an add-on server package that runs on SNA Server. OpenConnect Systems makes the TN3270 Server software that runs on SNA Server. It is implemented as a Windows NT service. OpenConnect Systems has developed products and schemes that help Web clients access mainframe data.

**RELATED ENTRIES**    DLSw (Data Link Switching); IBM Host Connectivity; IBM Mainframe Environment; SNA (Systems Network Architecture); TCP/IP (Transmission Control Protocol/Internet Protocol); *and* Web Technologies and Concepts

**INFORMATION ON THE INTERNET**

| | |
|---|---|
| TN3270 Enhancements (RFC 1647) | http://www.internic.net/rfc/rfc1647.txt |
| OpenConnect Systems, Inc. | http://www.oc.com |

# Token and Token-Passing Access Methods

A token is a special control frame on token ring, token bus, and FDDI (Fiber Distributed Data Interface) networks that determines which stations can transmit data on a shared network. Generally, the node that has the token can transmit. Unlike contention-based networks, such as Ethernet, workstations on token-based networks do not compete for access to the network. Only the station that obtains the token can transmit. Other stations wait for the token rather than trying to access the network on their own. On Ethernet networks, "collisions" occur when two or more workstations attempt to access the network at the same time. They must back off and try again later, which reduces performance, especially as the number of workstations attached to a network segment increases.

In token ring networks, a station takes possession of a token and changes one bit, converting the token to a SFS (start-of-frame sequence). A field exists in the token in which workstations can indicate the type of priority required for the transmission. The priority setting is basically a request to other stations for future use of the token. The other stations compare a workstation's request for priority with their own priority levels. If the workstation's priority is higher, the other stations will grant the workstation access to the token for an extended period.

**RELATED ENTRIES**    FDDI (Fiber Distributed Data Interface); MAC (Medium Access Control); Medium Access Control Methods; Network Concepts; *and* Token Ring Network

# Token-Based Authentication

Token-based authentication is a security technique that authenticates users who are attempting to log in to a server, a network, or some other secure system. These devices help eliminate insecure logons, which are logons that send the user's password across the wire where they could be monitored. Someone capturing the password could use it to repeatedly masquerade as the user and log on to a secure system. Encrypting the password may not help since the logon sequence could be captured and "replayed." The solution is to avoid sending passwords in any form across insecure channels. This is the purpose of using a token.

A token is a physical device about the size of a credit card with a built-in computer that generates information for the user to enter during logon. The token provides what is often called *two-factor authentication*, in which the user supplies something that they know (their password), and something that they have (a one-time value generated by the token). Two-factor authentication helps to first *identify* a user and then *authenticate* the user. Organizations often assign tokens to remote and mobile users who need to access internal systems from outside locations.

SecurID, a token from Security Dynamics, uses a time-based technique in which the device displays a number that changes every minute in synchronization with a security server at the corporate site. When users log in, they are prompted for the value on the SecurID card. Because the value changes constantly (it is a one-time password), it cannot be reused by someone who manages to capture it on the line.

Software-based token devices are also available that provide much the same functionality as hardware tokens. They consist of software programs that run in portable computers. However, some feel that this approach is less secure than hardware tokens because the software system could be more easily compromised.

ActivCard, a manufacturer of token-based authentication devices, employs several modes of operation in its token devices:

- In the "challenge/response" mode, a user attempting to access a secure site is issued a *challenge* by the host authentication server. This alphanumeric value appears on the user's screen and the user enters it into the token device. The token device then computes a *response* (using its special algorithm) based on the random challenge and a secret key. The response appears on the token device's display and the user types this in to log on. The authentication server goes through similar steps to generate a response using the challenge and secret key. If the response matches the user's, the user is logged on. If the login fails, the server issues a new challenge with each new logon attempt.

- In ActivCard's time-plus-event challenge/response mode, the token and the authentication software calculate unique passwords based on an event counter and an internal clock. Time/event synchronous authentication uses the number of passwords already processed by both the token and the authentication server for a particular service on a sequential basis to calculate passwords. The result is an even stronger level of security when it comes to user authentication.

Kerberos, which is discussed elsewhere in this book, is a security server system that provides a software-based token and one-time password authentication scheme. Other security server systems that can implement token authentication include RADIUS (Remote Authentication Dial-In User Service) and TACACS (Terminal Access Controller Access Control System).

**RELATED ENTRIES**   Access Server; Authentication and Authorization; Challenge/Response Protocol; Digital Signatures; Mobile Computing; RADIUS (Remote Authentication Dial-In User Service); Remote Access; Security; *and* TACACS (Terminal Access Controller Access Control System)

### INFORMATION ON THE INTERNET

| | |
|---|---|
| ActivCard, Inc. | http://www.activcard.com |
| Security Dynamics, Inc. | http://www.securitydynamics.com/solutions/products/tokens.html |
| Shiva's white paper on remote access security | http://www.shiva.com/remote/prodinfo/security |
| Gateway to Information Security's token authentication site | http://www.securityserver.com/cgi-local/ssis.pl/category/@tokens.htm |
| Smart Card Forum | http://www.smartcrd.com |

| Amerkore's Smart Card Resource Center | http://www.smart-card.com |
| Global Chipcard Alliance | http://www.chipcard.org |

## Token Bus Network

A token bus network is similar to a token ring network in that a station must have possession of a token before it can transmit on the network. However, the topology and token-passing method are different. The IEEE (Institute of Electrical and Electronic Engineers) 802.4 Committee has defined token bus standards as broadband networks, as opposed to Ethernet's baseband transmission technique.

The token and frames of data are passed from one station to another following the numeric sequence of the station addresses. Thus, the token follows a logical ring rather than a physical ring. The last station in numeric order passes the token back to the first station. The token does not follow the physical ordering of workstation attachment to the cable. Station 1 might be at one end of the cable and station 2 might be at the other, with station 3 in the middle. ARCNET (Attached Resource Computing Network) is a token bus network, but it does not conform to the IEEE 802.4 standards. Refer to "ARCNET" for illustrations of token bus topologies.

## Token Ring Network

Token ring is the IEEE (Institute of Electrical and Electronic Engineers) 802.5 standard for a token-passing ring network that can be configured in a star topology. IBM promoted the standard in the mid-1980s by marketing its first 4-Mbit/sec Token Ring network products. While the network physically appears as a star configuration, internally, signals travel around the network from one station to the next in a ring. Even though each station connects to a central hub called a MAU (multistation access unit), each station is still connected to the next station in line via a point-to-point link. As shown in Figure T-9, the MAU contains a "collapsed ring."

The problem with ring topologies is that a break anywhere in the ring prevents further transmissions. However, token ring networks avoid this problem by implementing special bypass circuitry in the MAU that can quickly reestablish the ring if a station goes offline unexpectedly or if a cable to a workstation is cut.

Expanding the token ring network is a simple matter of installing additional MAUs and connecting new workstations to the MAUs. A ring-in and ring-out receptacle is provided on each MAU for this purpose. The ring formation is maintained when MAUs are connected in this way. If any of these cables are cut or inadvertently disconnected, the ring reverts back on itself. This is possible because MAU interconnect cables contain multiple wire pairs. As shown in Figure T-10, signals simply reroute in the opposite direction, creating a loopback cable configuration.

Figure T-11 illustrates how a token ring network may be configured in a large office or multistory building. The main ring connects all the MAUs in a circular formation.

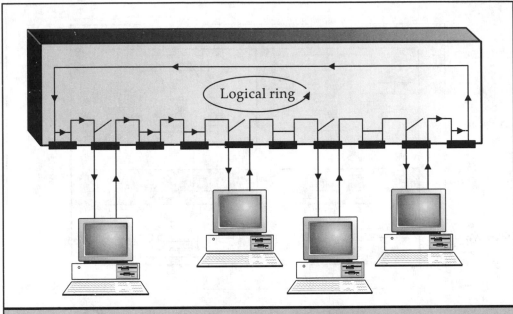

**Figure T-9.**   *The token ring MAU is a collapsed ring in a box*

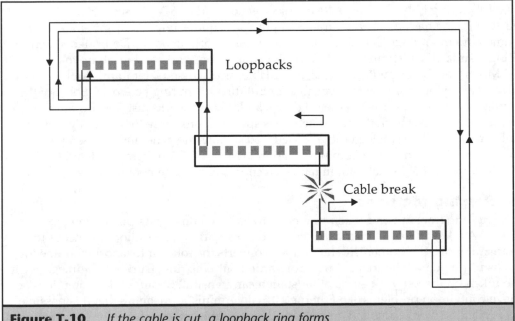

**Figure T-10.**   *If the cable is cut, a loopback ring forms*

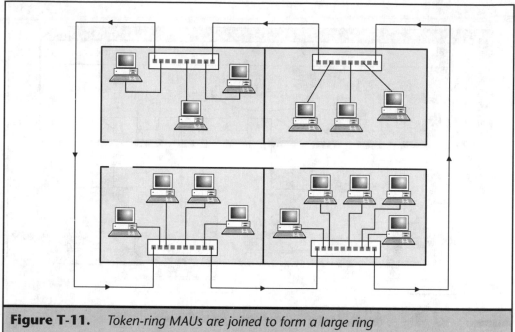

**Figure T-11.** *Token-ring MAUs are joined to form a large ring*

Token ring is available in a 4-Mbit/sec version and a 16-Mbit/sec version. The faster version has an increased frame length that requires fewer transmissions for the same amount of data. The 802.5 committee is also working on the Dedicated Token Ring standard, which provides full-duplex connections and bandwidth up to 32 Mbits/sec. Token switching is also available, as discussed later in this topic.

A variety of equipment is available for building token ring networks. Some of the equipment is not specified in the original standards but works just fine. Because of these differences, check the manufacturer's specifications for network configuration information. When shielded cable is used, 260 stations are generally allowed per ring with a maximum distance from workstation to MAU of 101 meters (330 feet). MAU devices are available that contain fault-detection and management features.

## Token-Passing Methods

The right to transmit on a token ring network is based on having possession of a token. A token is a small frame that circles the network until a station that needs to transmit grabs the frame. The station then converts the token into a normal frame for transmitting data. The frame is then forwarded onto the ring. During this time, there is no token on the network, so no other station can transmit. Because token ring does not have contention problems like Ethernet, it is deterministic, meaning that it is possible to predict delivery times and delays, which is useful when sending delay-sensitive information such as real-time audio or video.

Since token ring is a ring network made up of point-to-point connections between each station, the frame of data that a sender puts on the network goes from one station to the next until it reaches its destination. Thus, each workstation acts as a repeater. The destination reads in the frame, but the frame still continues on around the network. The sender is responsible for removing the frame from the network. Note that the returning frame can contain an acknowledgment that the destination did receive it.

A field exists in the token in which workstations can indicate the type of priority required for the transmission. The priority setting is basically a request to other stations for future use of the token. The other stations compare the workstation's request for priority with their own priority levels. If the workstation's priority is higher than theirs, they grant the workstation access to the token for an extended period. Other workstations can override the priorities, if necessary.

The role of *active monitor* is assigned to one of the workstations on the network, usually the first workstation recognized when the LAN comes up. The active monitor watches over the network and looks for problems, such as errors in the delivery of frames or the need to bypass a workstation at a MAU because it has failed. The active monitor basically makes sure the network runs efficiently and without errors. If the active monitor fails, another workstation can take its place.

## Token Ring Frames

The two token ring frame types are pictured in Figure T-12. The top frame illustrates the token while the bottom frame illustrates the frame that is used to transmit messages and data. The fields of these frames are described here:

- **Start delimiter**  Signifies the beginning of data. It has a unique code to differentiate it from data.

- **Access control**  Contains information about the priority of the frame and a need to reserve future tokens, which other stations will grant if they have a lower priority.

- **Frame control**  Defines the type of frame, either MAC (Medium Access Control) information or information for an end station. If the frame is a MAC frame, all stations on the ring read the information. If the frame contains information, it is only read by the destination station.

- **Destination address**  Contains the address of the station that is to receive the frame. The frame can be addressed to all stations on the ring.

- **Source address**  Contains the address of the station that sent the frame.

- **Data**  Contains the data "payload." If the frame is a MAC frame, this field may contain additional control information.

- **Frame check sequence**  Contains error-checking information to ensure the integrity of the frame to the recipient.

- **End delimiter**  Indicates the end of the frame.

*T*

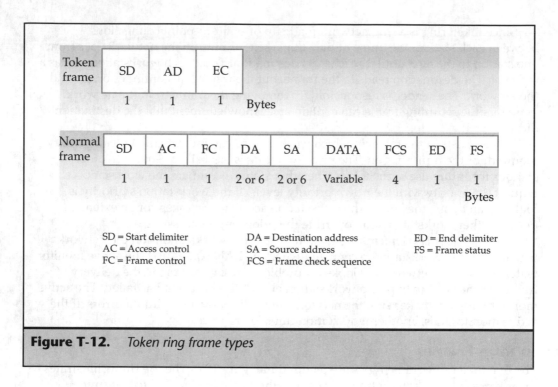

**Figure T-12.**    *Token ring frame types*

■ **Frame status**    Provides indications of whether one or more stations on the ring recognized the frame, whether the frame was copied, or whether the destination station is not available.

## Token Ring Switching

A relatively recent development for token ring has been the advent of token ring switches. Switches can solve some of the problems related to token ring, such as congestion on backbones and migration paths to higher-speed networks. Switches can also provide performance improvements that bring token ring speeds closer to high-speed Ethernet. Many administrators have been questioning their choice of token ring as Ethernet performance grows into the gigabit-per-second range.

Token ring switching basically divides a token ring network up into many smaller rings so that fewer stations are waiting to transmit on the ring. Token ring switches replace existing bridge solutions so that each port on the switch represents a ring that can communicate with rings on other ports without the need for external bridging and routing.

Switches can provide high-speed direct-connect ports for devices like printers and provide other devices on the switches much more efficient access to those devices. Switches can also be joined with other switches to expand the network without degrading performance. Many vendors are also promoting switched Ethernet as a migration path to faster network technologies such as FDDI (Fiber Distributed Data Interface) and ATM (Asynchronous Transfer Mode).

**RELATED ENTRIES**    Network Concepts; Network Design and Construction; Switched Networks; Token and Token-Passing Access Methods; Topology; *and* Transmission Media, Methods, and Equipment

**INFORMATION ON THE INTERNET**

| | |
|---|---|
| ASTRAL (Alliance for Strategic Token Ring Advancement and Leadership) | http://www.astral.org |
| ASTRAL's token ring white papers | http://www.astral.org/astralwp.html |
| Token Ring Consortium | http://www.iol.unh.edu/consortiums/tokenring |
| NetSuite's Token Ring Information site | http://www.netsuite.com/ts/tr/tring.htm |
| 3Com's Token Ring Switching paper | http://www.3com.com/nsc/500603.html |
| Network Computing Online's Interactive Token-Ring Network Troubleshooting paper | http://techweb.cmp.com/nc/netdesign/tintro.html |
| Yahoo!'s Token Ring links page | http://www.yahoo.com/Computers_and _Internet/Communications_and _Networking/LANs/Token_Ring |

# Topology

A network topology is the physical layout of a network. There are local network topologies and enterprise network, or WAN (wide area network), topologies. LAN topologies consist of the designs pictured in Figure T-13 and described here:

- **Bus**    A single trunk cable connects each workstation in a daisy-chain topology. Signals are broadcast to all stations, but packets are received only by the station to which they are addressed. Ethernet implements this topology. A break in the cable affects the entire LAN. Traditional Ethernet uses this topology.

- **Star**    Workstations attach to hubs and signals are broadcast to all stations or passed from station to station. A break in the cable affects only the attached workstation.

- **Star-configured ring**    A ring network in which signals are passed from one station to another in a circle. The physical topology is a star in which workstations branch from concentrators or hubs, but the logical topology is a hub. Token ring is an example of this topology.

- **Star/bus configuration**    A network that has groups of star-configured workstations connected with long linear bus trunks. Ethernet 10Base-T and Fast Ethernet use this topology.

*T*

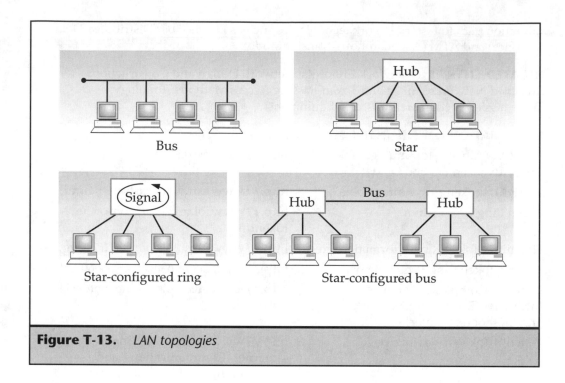

**Figure T-13.** *LAN topologies*

Enterprise networks and wide area networks expand on these topologies, as discussed here and pictured in Figure T-14:

- **Backbone network**  Typically found in office or campus environments in which departments or buildings are interconnected over the backbone cables. Bridges or routers manage traffic flow between attached subnetworks and the backbone.

- **Mesh network**  Routers are interconnected with other routers. The topology may be configured locally, but is often found in metropolitan or wide area networks. The Internet is a mesh network.

- **Interlinked star**  This is a hierarchical topology that is created when complying to structured wiring designs like the TIA/EIA (Telecommunications Industry Association/Electronic Industries Association) structured cabling standards.

**RELATED ENTRIES**  ARCNET; Backbone Networks; Ethernet; Gigabit Ethernet; Hubs/Concentrators/MAUs; Network Concepts; Network Design and Construction; Token Ring Network; *and* WAN (Wide Area Network)

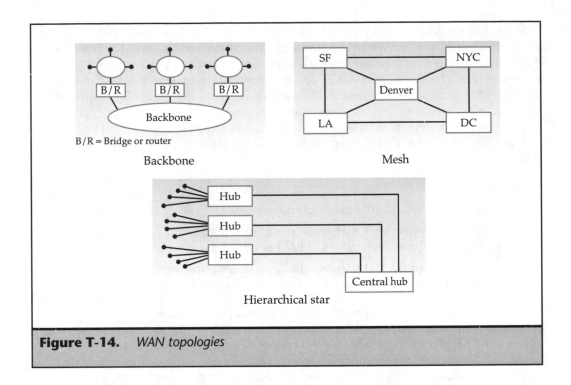

**Figure T-14.** *WAN topologies*

## TPEP (Trusted Product Evaluation Program)

TPEP is the program by which the NCSC (National Computer Security Center) evaluates computer systems against security criteria. TPEP is operated by an organization separate from the NCSC. TPEP performs computer security evaluations for, and on behalf of, the NCSC.

**RELATED ENTRIES**    C2 Security Rating; Rainbow Series; Security; *and* TCSEC (Trusted Computer System Evaluation Criteria)

### INFORMATION ON THE INTERNET

TPEP home page          http://www.radium.ncsc.mil/tpep/index.html
TPEP FAQ                http://www.radium.ncsc.mil/tpep/process/faq.html

## Transaction Processing

A transaction is a discrete unit of work that is typically part of a business process. An OLTP (online transaction processing) system operates in real time to collect and process transaction-related data and post changes to shared databases and other files.

In online transaction processing, transactions are executed immediately, as opposed to batch processing, in which a batch of transactions is stored over a period of time, then executed later. Most batch processes, such as posting to accounts, are run during evening hours. The results of an OLTP are immediately available in the database, assuming that transactions complete. The most common examples of OLTPs are airline reservation systems and banking transaction systems.

Database management systems execute transactions using statements in languages such as SQL (Structured Query Language). IBM has defined the following types of transactions:

- One statement at a time executed against one database
- A *unit of work,* which includes multiple statements executed on one database
- A *distributed unit of work* that involves multiple statements executed on multiple databases with one statement per database at a time
- A *distributed request* that involves multiple statements executed on multiple databases, with multiple statements per database at a time

Obviously, as transactions are distributed to multiple databases, safety mechanisms must be used to ensure data integrity. A feature of transaction processing is the ability to roll back a transaction that cannot be completed (due to insufficient funds or lack of credit, for example). A power failure or a failed communication link may also cause an incomplete transaction. A transaction must be either fully completed or rolled back so all the involved databases return to their pretransaction state. A *transaction monitor* is a program that monitors this process. As a user steps through a transaction, changes are made to databases. If the user needs to abort the transaction, the transaction monitor makes sure that all affected databases revert to their pretransaction states.

There are four requirements (collectively called ACID) for transaction processing in distributed environments:

- **Atomicity** Defines individual units of work. If a transaction is distributed, all the subtransactions that affect data at separate sites must execute together as a single transaction, either to completion or rolled back if incomplete. To keep data at multiple sites consistent, a *two-phase commit* procedure is used, as described in a moment.

- **Consistency** Consistency is basically a requirement that databases move from one state to another in coordination. The transaction monitor must verify that all affected data is consistent.

- **Isolation** Transactions must execute in isolation until completed, without influence from other transactions.

■ **Durability** This property has to do with the final commitment of a transaction. Once a transaction is verified to be accurate on all affected systems, it is committed and from then on cannot be rolled back.

## Two-Phase Commit

Two-phase commit separates the writing of data into two phases, each ending with a verification of completeness. In the following steps, assume that no faults occur during the transaction:

1. The database systems involved in the transaction hold the data to commit to the database in memory.

2. The transaction monitor sends a "precommit" command to the database systems.

3. The database systems reply that they are ready to commit.

4. On hearing back from every database system, the transaction monitor sends a "commit" command.

5. The database systems reply that they successfully committed the data.

6. The transaction monitor completes the transaction when it receives a response from all database systems that data was successfully committed.

If the transaction monitor fails to hear a response from every database system in steps 3 and 5, the transaction monitor alerts the systems to roll back their transactions.

## Component Software, the Web, and Transaction Processing

The Internet and new intranet environments, along with component software technology based on Java, ActiveX, and CORBA (Common Object Request Broker Architecture), are creating an environment in which transaction-processing models are greatly needed. It is now common to build modular software programs using component technology, then run the programs in an environment where components and data are stored at different locations across corporate networks or the Internet. In this respect, component software can be easily distributed and made available on a wide scale.

However, distributed components require different management strategies. Compare the difference between a component program that runs in a single computer and one that is distributed over a network. The components in the single computer are pretty much guaranteed to be available when needed. If a transaction is taking place and the system goes down, recovering from failed transactions takes place when the system restarts. If the same program is distributed, problems can occur when needed components on other computers are unavailable. Also, if a transaction fails, parts of that transaction may have already been distributed to other systems that will need to be contacted for recovery.

To solve these problems and stimulate the growth of distributed component software that can handle mission-critical tasks, many software developers are creating transaction middleware products for Internet and intranet environments. Some examples are listed here. The Web sites of these and other relevant vendors are provided at the end of this topic.

- Microsoft Transaction Server is a product for developing and deploying distributed applications that require reliable transaction-processing monitors. It is discussed further under "Microsoft Transaction Server."

- IBM's MQSeries software provides an open scalable, industrial-strength messaging and information backbone that enables organizations and entire communities to transact complex business processes across heterogeneous hardware and software platforms.

- Iona Technologies is working with Transarc, a long-time developer of transaction-processing systems, to integrate Transarc's products with its object request broker technologies.

**RELATED ENTRIES**   ActiveX; COM (Component Object Model); Component Software Technology; DCOM (Distributed Component Object Model); Distributed Object Computing; Middleware and Messaging; Multitiered Architectures; Object Technologies; ORB (Object Request Broker); Web Middleware and Database Connectivity; *and* Web Technologies and Concepts

## INFORMATION ON THE INTERNET

| | |
|---|---|
| Microsoft's Transaction Server site | http://www.microsoft.com/transaction |
| Iona Technologies | http://www.iona.com |
| BEA Systems, Inc. | http://www.beasys.com |
| Borland International, Inc. | http://www.borland.com |
| DEC's Digital TP Internet Server site | http://www.software.digital.com/tpi |
| IBM's transaction systems site | http://www.software.ibm.com/ts |
| IBM's CICS site | http://www.hursley.ibm.com/cics |
| IBM's MQSeries site | http://www.software.ibm.com/ts/mqseries |
| Transarc Corp. (Encina) | http://www.transarc.com |
| Transaction Processing Counsel | http://www.tpc.org |
| Christopher P. Avram's New paradigms for transaction processing paper | http://www.ct.monash.edu.au/~cavram/papers/tp/tr94-02h.html |

# Transmission Media, Methods, and Equipment

Managers who need to cable networks face critical decisions. Cable and cable equipment must meet current and future requirements for data transmission, electrical characteristics, and topology. Fortunately, there are a lot of choices, but that can complicate the decision process. To help managers make informed decisions and design workable cable systems, cabling standards are available such as those described under "TIA/EIA Structured Cabling Standards."

Communication in the LAN and WAN environments requires the transmission of signals through some medium. There are two types of media for data transmission:

- **Guided media** Includes metal wire (copper, aluminum, and so on) and fiber-optic cable

- **Unguided media** Refers to transmission of signals through air and space using radio signals

Figure T-15 illustrates the primary types of cable used for data transmissions. These cable types are described here:

- **Straight cable** This is the simplest type of cable. It consists of copper wires surrounded by an insulator. The wire comes in bundles or as flat "ribbon" cables and is used to connect various peripheral devices over short distances. Cables for internal disk drives are typically flat cables with multiple transmission wires running in parallel.

- **Twisted-pair cable** This cable consists of copper-core wires surrounded by an insulator. Two wires are twisted together to form a pair, and the pair form a balanced circuit. The twisting prevents interference problems. Multicore twisted-pair wire has multiple twisted pairs, each color coded to differentiate it from other pairs. UTP (unshielded twisted-pair) is common in the telephone network. STP (shielded twisted-pair) provides protection against external crosstalk.

- **Coaxial cable** This cable consists of a solid copper core surrounded by an insulator, a combination shield and ground wire, and an outer protective jacket. In the early days of LANs, coaxial cable was used for its high bit rates, but those same rates or higher rates can be achieved with twisted-pair cable. Coaxial cable also supports longer distances than twisted-pair cable, but hierarchical cabling schemes are now commonly used to construct twisted-pair networks.

- **Fiber-optic cable** This cable consists of a center glass core through which light waves propagate. This core is surrounded by a glass cladding that basically reflects the inner light of the core back into the core. A thick plastic outer jacket surrounds this assembly, along with special fibers to add strength. Fiber-optic cable is available with a metal core for strength if the cable will be hung over distances.

T

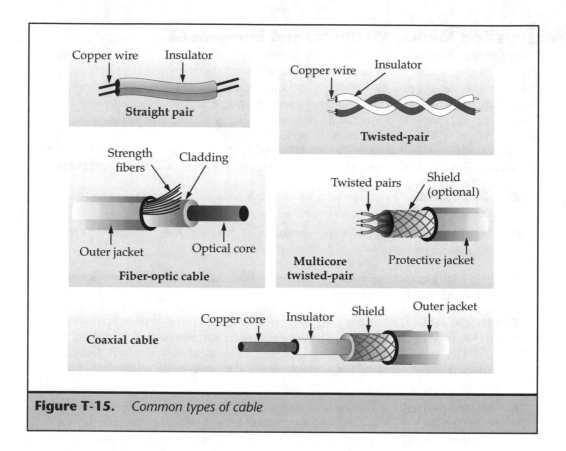

**Figure T-15.** *Common types of cable*

*Copper cable* is a relatively inexpensive, well-understood technology. However, it has various electrical characteristics that impose restrictions on its use. For example, copper resists the flow of electrons, which limits the distance of cables. It also radiates energy in the form of signals that can be monitored. It is also susceptible to external radiation that can distort transmissions. In contrast, *fiber-optic cable* transmits light signals (photons) through a core of pure silicon dioxide that is so clear, a three-mile thick window of it would not distort the view. Thus, fiber cable has high transmission rates and is preferred where distance is a factor. Photonic transmissions produce no emissions outside the cable and are not affected by external radiation. Thus, fiber cable is preferred where security is an issue.

A characteristic of cable that must not be overlooked is its fire rating. In order to comply with the NEC (National Electrical Code), all cable installed in the plenum space, which is the airspace between the ceiling and the next floor or roof, must be installed in metal conduit, or must meet local fire codes. It must not produce noxious or hazardous gases in a fire that would be pumped to other parts of a structure through the plenum. Normal cables have PVC (polyvinyl chloride) jackets, while plenum-rated cables have jackets made with fluoropolymers such as Du Pont's Teflon.

The remainder of this topic primarily discusses copper cabling. See "Fiber-Optic Cable" for a discussion of optical cable types. For a discussion of unguided media, see "Wireless Communications."

## Copper Cable Characteristics

Binary data is transmitted over copper cable by applying a voltage at one end and reading it at the other. Digital 1 can be represented by a high voltage on the line, while digital 0 can be represented by a low voltage. Copper cable is subject to attenuation, capacitance, delay distortion, and noise. The measure of these effects depends on the material used to construct the cable and can be diminished with various cable designs. The longer a cable, the more likely you will find signal distortion. In addition, increasing the frequency of the signal to boost data transfer rates will require a reduction in cable lengths to avoid signal distortion.

**ATTENUATION**    Signal transmissions over long distances are subject to *attenuation*, a loss of signal strength or amplitude. Attenuation is also caused by broken or damaged cables. Attenuation is the main reason networks have various cable-length restrictions. If a signal becomes too weak, the receiving equipment will interpret it incorrectly or not at all. This causes errors that require retransmission and loss of performance. Attenuation is measured in dB (decibels) of signal loss. For every 3dB of signal loss, a signal loses 50 percent of its remaining strength. Repeater or amplifier devices are used to extend the distance of a network beyond the distance limitation of its cable type. Attenuation is measured by devices that inject signals with a known power level at one end of the line and measure the power level at the other end of the line. The following shows the effect of signal loss caused by attenuation:

Original signal        Received signal

+V
-V

**CAPACITANCE**    Capacitance is the ability of some material to store a charge. Copper cables have capacitance that can distort signals by storing some of the energy of a previous signal bit. Capacitance is a measure of the energy that a cable and its insulator can store. Adjoining wires in wire bundles also contribute to the capacitance of a wire. Cable testers can check capacitance values to determine if a cable has kinks or has been stretched. All cable has known capacitance values that are measured in pF (picofarads). Twisted-pair wire used for network cabling is rated at 17 to 20 pF.

**IMPEDANCE AND DELAY DISTORTION**    A signal made up of various frequencies is prone to delay distortion caused by *impedance*, resistance that changes at different frequencies. It can cause the different-frequency components within a signal to arrive out of step at the receiver. If the frequency is increased to boost data throughput, the effect worsens and the receiver may not be able to interpret data signals correctly. Decreasing the cable length and/or lowering the transmission frequency can solve the problem. Note that the impedance value of a cable can be measured to detect breaks or faulty connections. Data-grade cable should have an impedance value of 100 ohms at the frequency used to transmit data.

**NOISE**    Transmission lines will have some amount of background noise that is generated by external sources, the transmitter, or adjacent lines. This noise combines with and distorts a transmitted signal. While noise may be minor, attenuation can enhance its effects. As shown here, the signal is higher than the noise level at the transmitter but is equal to the noise level at the receiver due to attenuation:

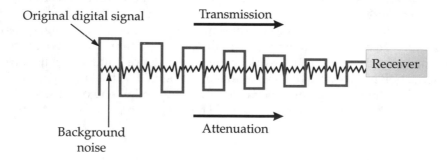

Ambient noise on digital circuits is caused by fluorescent lights, motors, microwave ovens, and office equipment such as computers, phones, and copiers. Technicians can certify wire by testing for noise levels and crosstalk. To test crosstalk levels, the technician injects a known signal into a wire and measures crosstalk on adjacent wires. If noise is a persistent problem is some areas, it can be avoided by running wire away from sources of noise, by using shielded cable, or by using fiber-optic cable.

**INDUCTANCE**    Inductance occurs when current flows on two adjacent metallic conductors. Electromagnetic fields created by the current flows can create signal distortions in adjoining wires. The biggest problem this creates is *near-end cross talk*, or *NEXT*, which occurs near the transmitter and creates distortions that typically affect signals on an adjacent receive line, as shown here:

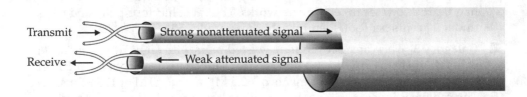

Twisting wire pairs is the primary method for reducing the effects of inductance, but the type of conductor and insulation also play a role. Twisting wire pairs cancels the positive and negative energy on the cable. Cable designed for high data rates has the most twists per length of cable.

## Twisted-Pair Cable

Twisted-pair cable has been used for decades to transmit both analog and digital information. The existing telephone system is mostly wired with voice-grade twisted-pair wires. Twisted-pair wire is now the preferred wire for network cabling. The twisting of pairs, the quality of the conductive material, the type of insulator, and the shielding largely determine the rate at which data can be transmitted over twisted-pair cable. Twisted-pair cable constitutes the primary medium in the TIA/EIA-568-A Commercial Building Wiring Standard, which spells out the different types of cables and provides a general design for building a cabling system that is likely to be compatible with future network designs. Refer to "TIA/EIA Structured Cabling Standards" for more information.

The following categories of cable are most often used, but the TIA/EIA-568-A specification only recognizes Category 3, Category 4, and Category 5 cable:

- **Category 1** Traditional unshielded twisted-pair telephone cable that is suited for voice. Most telephone cable installed before 1983 is Category 1 cable. Not recommended for network use.

- **Category 2** Unshielded twisted-pair cable certified for data transmissions up to 4 Mbits/sec. This cable has four twisted pairs. Not recommended for network use.

- **Category 3** This category is rated for signals up to 16 MHz and supports 10-Mbit/sec Ethernet, 4-Mbit/sec token ring, and 100VG-AnyLAN networks. The cable has four pairs and three twists per foot (although the number of twists is not specified). Costs are around 10 cents per foot. Plenum cable costs about 40 cents per foot. This cable is installed as telephone cabling at many sites.

- **Category 4**  This category is rated for signals up to 20 MHz and is certified to handle 16-Mbit/sec token ring networks. The cable has four pairs and costs under 20 cents per foot. Plenum cable costs under 50 cents per foot.

- **Category 5**  This category has four twisted pairs with eight twists per foot and is rated for signals up to 100 MHz, which is adequate to support Fast Ethernet (which has frequency requirements of 62.5 MHz) and ATM at 155 Mbits/sec. The cable has low capacitance and exhibits low crosstalk due to the high number of twists per foot. It costs under 30 cents per foot. Plenum cable costs under 60 cents per foot. In the mid-1990s, this cable was installed in over 60 percent of existing buildings.

Even though Category 5 is widely used, there are many things that can prevent a cabling system from delivering the intended data rate. Cable runs should not exceed 100 meters (300 feet). The TIA/EIA specification calls for 90-meter maximum runs from the wiring closet to the wall outlet. An extra 10 meters is allowed to connect computers to the wall outlet and to connect the cable runs to patch panels. Category 5 installations must use Category 5 connectors, patch panels, wall plates, and other components. In addition, proper twisting must be maintained all the way up to connectors. Note that Scope Communications has some interesting white papers detailing problems with ATM on Category 5 cable. Scope's Web site is at http://www.scope.com/whitepap.htm.

*NOTE:*  *Cable installers should implement grounding schemes that prevent ground loops, as discussed under "Power and Grounding Problems and Solutions." The TIA/EIA-607 Grounding and Bonding specification also covers this topic.*

Some network managers have recently discovered that all Category 5 cable is not created equal. Due to recent material shortages, some manufacturers use low-quality composite insulation in their cable. This cable is subject to *delay skew*, which occurs during high-speed transmissions on networks that split the data signal across two pairs, such as 100Base-T4 and 100VG-AnyLAN. What happens is that signals arrive out of step with one another. Delay skew is not a problem on networks that transmit on a single pair. According to a paper available from Anixter ("Category 5: How Did We Get Here and Where Do We Go Next?"), buyers should obtain product specifications from manufacturers at the time of purchase. The paper outlines the delay skew problem in more detail and what to look for in cable specifications.

Even though Category 5 was considered future-proof, new gigabit-per-second networking schemes are not supported. However, compression and signaling schemes are being developed to boost data rates to above Category 5 levels, but these schemes require additional processing power in network devices. For those who are rewiring or installing new wire, two new cabling categories are available:

- **Enhanced Category 5**  This cable has all the characteristics of Category 5, but is manufactured using higher-quality processes that minimize crosstalk by twisting the cable even more than is done in traditional Category 5. It can carry data at frequencies up to 200 MHz, which is double the transmission capability of traditional Category 5. Some vendors claim bandwidth up to 350 MHz, but these claims should be questioned. The cable costs under 40 cents per foot.

- **Category 6**   This is a four-pair cable in which each pair is wrapped with a foil insulation. The four-pair bundle is then wrapped in another foil insulation and the whole bundle is wrapped in a fire-retardant polymer jacket. The foil helps reduce crosstalk and the cable is rated at six or more times the transmission rate of traditional Category 5.

The TIA and ISO (International Organization for Standardization) were in the process of standardizing Category 6 at the time of this writing, and one of their intentions was to create a standard that supports Gigabit Ethernet. The intention was to divide the data signal among all four pairs in the cable and transmit in full-duplex parallel mode. Instead of separate pairs to transmit and receive, each wire pair does both and is connected to a transceiver (transmitter/receiver) at each end of the connection. The transceiver uses special circuitry to handle both transmit and receive signals. This scheme provides a bandwidth of 400 MHz (100 MHz per each of the four pairs).

## Components of a Structured Cabling System

In the 1980s, vendors and standards organizations saw a need to standardize cabling schemes and eventually created the TIA/EIA-568 structured cabling standard. The TIA/EIA standard defines a star-wired hierarchical topology in which computers are attached to wall plates, wall plates lead to wiring closets, and wiring closets lead to central equipment rooms that service an entire enterprise. A campus network may follow this same scheme, but wires lead across the campus to a central administrative area.

The typical components of a Category 5 wiring scheme are illustrated in Figure T-16. The patch panel provides a place to terminate the horizontal wiring that fans out to work areas. The twisted pairs in the cable are directly attached to the back of the patch panel. The front of the patch panel then provides a place to attach patch cables that connect to network hubs and switches. This arrangement makes moves and changes easy. When someone must be moved to another workgroup or subnetwork, the patch cable on the port leading to that individual's computer is moved to another port on the network hub or switch. Note that other techniques exist for configuring workgroups, as discussed under "VLAN (Virtual LAN)."

The TIA/EIA standard calls for two cables to each workstation. Therefore, wall plates will normally have two jacks—one for data and one for voice—although this arrangement is flexible. The wire-pair and pin-wiring configuration for T568A 8-pin jacks and connectors is pictured in Figure T-17 and outlined here:

- **Pair 1**   White-blue stripe/solid blue
- **Pair 2**   White-orange stripe/solid orange

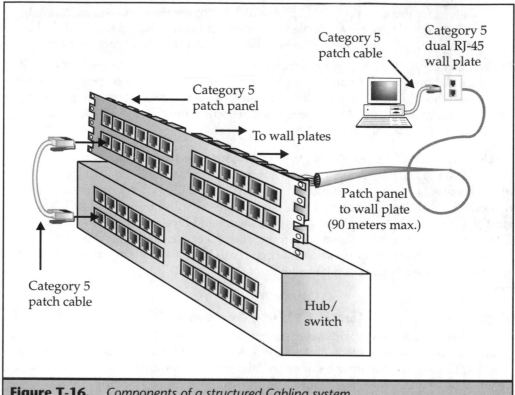

**Figure T-16.** *Components of a structured Cabling system*

- ■ **Pair 3** White-green stripe / solid green
- ■ **Pair 4** White-brown stripe / solid brown

Note that all the components in this configuration must be Category 5-compliant. This ensures that signal quality is retained and allows high data rates. Special care must be taken when pulling the cable runs between wiring closets and work area wall plates. The physical shape of the cable cannot be drastically altered, meaning that it should not be stretched, twisted, or bent beyond a radius that is 10 times the outside diameter of the cable. Figure T-18 illustrates what can happen to wires that are bent beyond compliance. The twisted pairs are pushed closer together, which can cause crosstalk. When attaching Category 5 cable to patch panels and wall plates, it should not be untwisted more than one half inch from the end of the cable to avoid crosstalk and other problems.

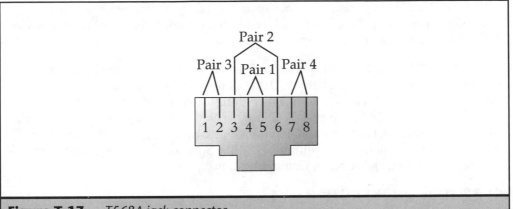

**Figure T-17.**   *T568A jack connector*

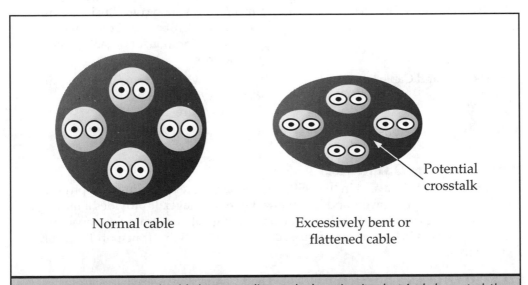

Normal cable

Excessively bent or
flattened cable

Potential
crosstalk

**Figure T-18.**   *Stressed cable becomes distorted, changing its electrical characteristics*

The TIA/EIA-568-A standard defines specific cabling requirements which are discussed further under "TIA/EIA Structured Cabling Standards." The illustrations in that section also elaborate on the layout of the cable.

**RELATED ENTRIES** ATM (Asynchronous Transfer Mode); Backbone Networks; Bandwidth; Capacity; Channel; Circuit; Data Communication Concepts; Data Transfer Rates; Ethernet; Fast Ethernet; Fiber-Optic Cable; Gigabit Ethernet; Hubs/Concentrators/MAUs; Network Concepts; Network Design and Construction; Power and Grounding Problems and Solutions; Signals; Testing and Diagnostic Equipment and Techniques; Throughput; TIA/EIA Structured Cabling Standards; Token Ring Network; *and* Wireless Communications

### INFORMATION ON THE INTERNET

| | |
|---|---|
| Peter Macaulay's Cabling FAQ | http://www.cis.ohio-state.edu/hypertext/faq/usenet/LANs/cabling-faq/faq.html |
| Cabling Contractors Directory | http://www.cabling-contractors.com |
| TIA (Telecommunications Industry Association) | http://www.tiaonline.org |
| Yahoo!'s Cables and Connectors links page | http://www.yahoo.com/Business_and_Economy/Companies/Computers/Hardware/Components/Cables_and_Connectors |
| Yahoo!'s Wire and Cable links page | http://www.yahoo.com/Business_and_Economy/Companies/Industrial_Supplies/Wire_and_Cable |
| Anixster, Inc. (numerous white papers) | http://www.anixter.com |

## Transport Layer, OSI Model

The transport layer is layer 4 in the OSI protocol stack. It resides above the physical, data link, and network layers and just below the session layer. It provides a messaging service for the session layer and hides the underlying network from the upper layers. Transport services in general are discussed in the next section, "Transport Protocols and Services."

**RELATED ENTRIES** Connection-Oriented and Connectionless Services; Data Communication Concepts; OSI (Open Systems Interconnection) Model; Protocol Concepts; TCP (Transmission Control Protocol); *and* Transport Protocols and Services

# Transport Protocols and Services

In the OSI protocol stack, transport protocols occupy layer 4, which is just above the network layer. Of all the layers, it could be said that that the transport layer is the most important because it provides network applications with reliable data delivery services. In the TCP/IP protocol suite, TCP provides transport services while IP provides network services. In the Novell SPX/IPX protocol suite, SPX (Sequenced Packet Exchange) provides transport services while IPX (Internetwork Packet Exchange) provides network services.

As pictured in Figure T-19, the simplest model of a network consists of three layers, with an application layer at the top, a transport layer in the middle, and a network layer at the bottom. In this model, an application running in one computer communicates with an application running in another computer. The source application relies on the lower two layers to move messages, files, and other information to the application running in the other computer. Top-level applications are built by relying on the underlying services.

The network layer is involved with actually transmitting information from one system to another. It deals with physical interfaces, cabling schemes, putting data in frames, and delivery of data across a series of point-to-point links (i.e., frames, router-connected internetworks). To use an analogy, if network layer protocols were airline systems, the transport layer protocols would be the air traffic controllers. While airplane pilots obviously have the ability to fly from one airport to another on their own, doing so on a busy flying day would be unsafe without the traffic controllers.

Figure T-19 illustrates a phone connection between transport service providers. This analogy is appropriate because the two layers engage in a conversation to make sure that data is reliably delivered. However, the "connection" is virtual because the messages that make up the conversation are not exchanged directly between the two layers but are put in packets and delivered as frames across the physical layer.

The transport layer establishes connection-oriented sessions over which data is reliably transmitted during the period that the session is open. The following events take place during such a session:

1. Establish connections

2. Negotiate session parameters

3. Manage the transfer of data

4. Terminate the connection

Establishing a connection is a simple matter of sending a connection request to the target host. If it is available, it responds with a *connection acknowledgment message*.

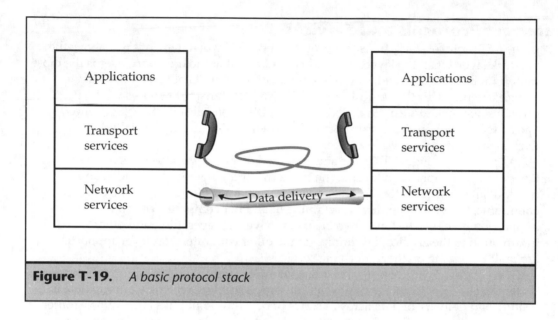

**Figure T-19.** *A basic protocol stack*

The systems then negotiate session parameters such as timing, packet size, and syntax. A virtual circuit may also be established through a routed network so that each router along the way does not need to make a decision about how to route packets to the destination.

The services provided by transport protocols are outlined here. In general, these topics are described in more detail where mentioned, or you can refer to "TCP (Transmission Control Protocol)" for a description of how transport layer services are implemented in the Internet environment.

**RELIABILITY SERVICES**   These provide error-recovery and retransmission mechanisms to ensure that data is delivered to the destination. If a packet is lost along the way, either the sender or the receiver must detect the loss and recover from it. If a sender is responsible for error recovery, then the receiver can send an ACK (acknowledgment) back to the sender when it receives packets. If the sender does not receive an ACK within a period of time, it may assume the receiver never received the packet and send another one. If the receiver is responsible for detecting lost packets, it reads the sequence numbers in packets to determine if a packet is missing. TCP uses a combination of these techniques, as described in "TCP (Transmission Control Protocol)."

**SEQUENCING** As mentioned above, adding sequence numbers to packets allows the receiver to detect missing packets. Sequence numbers are also used to reorder packets that arrive out of sequence. Packets may arrive out of order if they take different routes through an internetwork, where some routes cross slow links or links that are experiencing problems. See "Sequencing of Packets" for more information.

**FLOW CONTROL** Senders and receivers will not always have the same ability to revive and process packets. A sender can overflow a receiver with too many packets and still continue to send packets if it does not know about the overflow. Packets are dropped in this condition that will eventually need to be retransmitted. If the receiver can signal to the sender and it is overflowing, the sender can slow down or stop its transmissions and thus reduce the need to retransmit at a later time. See "Flow-Control Mechanisms" for more details.

**FRAGMENTATION/REASSEMBLY** When packets travel across internetworks, they may encounter networks that cannot handle large packet sizes. The router leading into such networks must fragment such packets and insert information in the fragmented packets that helps the receiver to reassemble them. See "Fragmentation of Frames and Packets" for more details.

Some related topics are provided next. Many of these topics are related to the way that the TCP transport mechanisms work.

**RELATED ENTRIES** Acknowledgments; Congestion; Connection Establishment; Data Communication Concepts; Flow-Control Mechanisms; Fragmentation of Frames and Packets; Frame Switch; Handshake Procedures; IP (Internet Protocol); NAK (Negative Acknowledgment); Network Concepts; Packet; Packet and Cell Switching; Protocol Concepts; QoS (Quality of Service); Sequencing of Packets; TCP (Transmission Control Protocol); TCP/IP (Transmission Control Protocol/Internet Protocol); *and* Virtual Circuit

# Trust Relationships

Trust is generally a good thing, even among computers, but when one computer trusts another, that relationship can be exploited by a malicious user, or *hacker*. Networked computers have trust relationships so they can exchange information without needing some administrator to authorize each and every transaction. For example, a client may log in to a network and be authenticated by a security server. Other servers on that same network "trust" that the security server has properly authenticated the user.

Trust relationships may also be set up between the departments or divisions of a company. For example, the accounting or auditing department may require periodic access to information on computers in other departments. A trust relationship allows the accountants or auditors, or the computers within their departments, to access systems in other departments. In this case, the trust relationship is one-way, meaning that accountants can access some computers in the sales department but salespeople can't access computers in the accounting department.

As mentioned, hackers may exploit trust relationships. If they are unsuccessful at attacking a system, they may target a system that has a trust relationship with the original target. This second target may be easier to break into, and once successfully attacked, it may provide a link to the original target that can be exploited.

Trust relationships are common when setting up electronic commerce relationships with other companies and business partners. This has become even easier with Internet/intranet protocols and so-called extranet technologies, which help companies build secure private networks across the Internet with one another. However, business partners need to be especially careful when setting up such relationships because they may be exploited by internal employees that have special access to systems that make hacking easy.

**RELATED ENTRIES**   Electronic Commerce; Extranet; Hacker; *and* Security

## Tunnels

Tunnels are used to deliver data packets across networks that use different protocols than the source and destination network. The tunnel is a virtual path that extends across the intermediate network. The best analogy is a ferry that carries cars across a river or channel. An example of a tunnel is pictured in Figure T-20. The tunneling process involves encapsulating a packet from the source network into a packet of the intermediate network. When the packet arrives at the destination network, it is removed from the packet and forwarded on the network.

An organization that has two IPX networks that are separated by a large TCP/IP network can join the two IPX networks by encapsulating IPX packets into IP packets for delivery across the TCP/IP network. Tunneling is also often used to deliver nonroutable protocols such as SNA (Systems Network Architecture) or NetBEUI (NetBIOS Extended User Interface) across a routed network.

More recently, tunneling has become popular as a way to build secure private networks over the Internet. A company installs an encrypting router at one site and

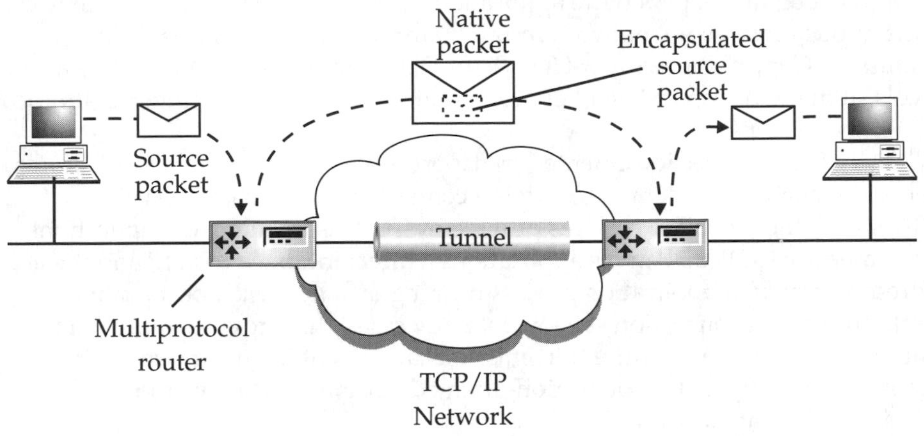

**Figure T-20.**   *A tunnel delivers packets across an intermediate network*

another encrypting router at another site. All data traffic sent between the sites, no matter what protocol is used, can be placed in IP packets that are routed to the other site. The data in the packets is encrypted to keep it private, but the headers of the packets are not encrypted so that they may traverse the Internet in the normal way. A similar technique is used to allow remote and mobile users to connect into corporate networks by going through the Internet. These techniques are covered further under "Virtual Dial-up Services" and "VPN (Virtual Private Network)."

## Two-Factor Authentication

*See* Token-Based Authentication.

## Two-Phase Commit

*See* Transaction Processing.

# UDP (User Datagram Protocol)

When application developers write applications that use TCP/IP networks, they can have the applications access network resources through two interfaces: TCP (Transmission Control Protocol) or UDP (User Datagram Protocol). Both of these protocols sit in the transport layer between applications and the IP (Internet Protocol) in the network layer.

While TCP is a connection-oriented transport service with a number of features that provide reliable data delivery, UDP is a connectionless transport service that dispenses with the reliability services provide by TCP. As mentioned, applications need an interface to IP. UDP gives applications a direct interface with IP and the ability to address a particular application process running on a host via a port number without setting up a connection session. In many cases, this provides more efficient communication because an entire transmission can be sent in one or two UDP datagrams. Setting up a TCP connection-oriented session would take too much time in proportion to the data to send.

A port is the address where an application makes itself available on a particular host. Incoming datagrams find their way to a host via the IP address, but when they arrive at the host, a port address is required to shuttle the contents of the datagram to the appropriate process running on the host. If the host is a server, multiple processes may be running such as HTTP (port 80), FTP (port 21), and Gopher (port 70). With UDP, an application can send a datagram to a service without establishing a connection, as is required with TCP.

The UDP header, pictured here, illustrates how port addressing is the primary function of UDP. The header is mostly port-addressing fields. A checksum is used to detect corruption of transmitted data, but if corruption is detected, the data is discarded and no other action is taken. If an application requires more reliability services than this, TCP should be used.

| Source port | Destination port |
|:---:|:---:|
| Length | Checksum |

Multicast applications, the Internet MBone, RTP (Real-time Transport Protocol), and other protocols use UDP as their delivery mechanism. They are designed to deliver delay-sensitive real-time data such as live audio and video from end station to end station across the Internet or an intranet. Because the content is live, the services offered by TCP (such as acknowledgment and retransmission) are not necessary and add too much overhead. If a packet of voice or video is lost, retransmitting it is usually not practical since the retransmitted information would be out of synchronization with the current audio and video being received by the destination.

**RELATED ENTRIES**    Internet; IP (Internet Protocol); Network Concepts; TCP (Transmission Control Protocol); TCP/IP (Transmission Control Protocol/Internet Protocol); *and* Transport Protocols and Services

**INFORMATION ON THE INTERNET**

| | |
|---|---|
| User Datagram Protocol (RFC 768) | http://www.internic.net/rfc/rfc768.txt |
| Requirements for Internet Hosts (RFC 1122) | http://www.internic.net/rfc/rfc1122.txt |

# UNI (User Network Interface)

UNI defines physical and protocol interfacing specifications for devices that are connected at the edges of ATM networks. This includes user systems that are connected to a private ATM switch or a private ATM switch connected to an ATM switch owned by a public carrier. Note that interface connections between two ATM switches in a backbone network are defined by NNI (Network-to-Network Interface). However, the interface between a private ATM switch and a public ATM switch uses UNI, or more precisely public UNI. This is because the public-to-private switch connection does not need to exchange the NNI protocol, which has different cell formats and carries different information.

**RELATED ENTRY**    ATM (Asynchronous Transfer Mode)

# UNIX

The UNIX operating system was developed at AT&T Bell Laboratories by Ken Thompson and Dennis Ritchie in 1969 and the early 1970s. The original versions were designed to run on DEC PDP-11 16-bit computers and VAX 32-bit computers. The name UNIX comes from UNICS (UNiplexed Information and Computer System), a tongue-in-cheek play on words derived from Multics. Multics was an early time-sharing (allows many tasks to be automatically interspersed) operating system created as a test platform in 1964 by General Electric, Massachusetts Institute of Technology, and AT&T, although AT&T eventually dropped out of the collaborative effort. Multics is historically recognized as the first operating system to implement most of the multitasking features now common in most operating systems.

In 1973, Bell Labs completely rewrote UNIX in the C programming language. This made UNIX highly portable, and it now contains system components written in a common, well-known programming language that are easily recompiled to work on a variety of systems. About the same time, *pipes* were introduced into the operating system, which provided a way to combine data from different programs.

Around 1975, AT&T made the operating system available on an open basis to universities and colleges for use in research projects and computer science programs. This was a major step in the popularization of UNIX, and from this many variants were created (the releases originating from AT&T's original work are now called the System V release or SRV). The University of California at Berkeley produced some of the most important work on UNIX outside Bell Labs. The versions it created became known as the *Berkeley Software Distributions, or BSDs*. U.C. Berkeley added TCP/IP networking and ported UNIX to the DEC VAX. AT&T eventually merged its UNIX development under a single unit called UNIX System Laboratories, or USL. In 1991, Novell and AT&T joined forces to create Univell, a company with the goal of developing UnixWare, a desktop UNIX system with built-in Novell NetWare support. Then, in 1993, Novell purchased USL and formed the USG (UNIX Systems Group) to manage UnixWare.

With the purchase of USL, Novell gained control of UNIX SVR4, to the dismay of other UNIX vendors. In an attempt to consolidate the industry on a common UNIX operating system, Novell gave the UNIX trademark to the X/Open organization (described below). But the UNIX and NetWare engineers could not build an operating system that leveraged the best features of both UNIX and NetWare. Novell began to see UNIX as a threat to its long-standing NetWare product and sold UNIX off to the Santa Cruz Operation in December of 1995.

The X/Open group was founded in 1984 by Bull, Nixdorf, Philips, Siemens, and other companies to promote open UNIX standards by testing for conformity among products. X/Open now grants the UNIX trademark to UNIX implementations that are compatible with a set of specifications that promote the portability of applications between operating systems. In 1996, The Open Group was created with the merger of X/Open and OSF (Open Software Foundation). The Open Group manages UNIX standards such as the CDE (Common Desktop Environment) and Motif graphical user interfaces. Information about The Open Group can be found under "The Open Group."

Another effort to promote portability of applications across UNIX environments was the creation of POSIX (Portable Operating System Interface for UNIX) by the IEEE community in the early 1980s. However, POSIX is not just a standard for UNIX. It has been implemented on other operating system platforms such as DEC VMS.

All of this standardization has caused vendors to explain their products in wording that resembles the following (this taken from DEC's Web site): "Digital UNIX Operating System is a 64-bit advanced kernel architecture based on Carnegie-Mellon University's Mach V2.5 kernel design with components from BSD (Berkeley Software Distribution) 4.3 and 4.4, UNIX System V, and other sources. Digital UNIX is Digital Equipment Corporation's implementation of the OSF's OSF/1 R1.0, R1.1, and R1.2 technology, and the Motif graphical user interface and programming environment. Under the X/Open UNIX branding program, Digital has received the UNIX 95 brand for the Digital UNIX operating system, and is licensed to use the UNIX trademark in conjunction with the Digital UNIX product."

Sun Microsystems' Solaris is perhaps the most popular UNIX system. It is a BSD UNIX with many of the features of the SVR releases. Refer to "Sun Microsystems

Solaris" for more information. Still another interesting variant is FreeBSD, a version of UNIX that is based on the Berkeley BSD releases and that runs on Intel processors. The FreeBSD operating system is free and can be obtained at the Web site listed below under "Information on the Internet." It is an advanced BSD UNIX operating system for "PC-compatible" computers.

Linux is another free UNIX-like operating system that runs on a variety of platforms, including Intel, SPARC, PowerPC, and DEC Alpha processors as well as multiprocessing systems. Linux is a "user-developed" product, meaning that many of its components and drivers have been developed by users around the world who ran the operating system for their own use. The original operating system was developed by Linux Torvalds as a college project. It is now well supported and gaining ground as a respectable operating system despite its homegrown roots. Refer to "Linux" for more information.

## General Features of UNIX

UNIX is a multiuser system that supports networking and distributed file systems such as Sun Microsystems' NFS (Network File System) or the Open Software Foundation's implementation of the AFS (Andrew File System). The traditional operating system consists of a small kernel that runs processes such as user applications and services. The UNIX kernel is a solid core that changes little from system to system, while processes are added at the user's discretion. This design approach makes it easy for the user to add new services or remove unnecessary services. It also makes upgrades easier since the entire operating system does not need to be recompiled.

Users interact with the operating system through a *shell*, which is also a process that accepts user input and performs various tasks. Because the shell is a replaceable process, there are many variations, such as the Bourne shell, the C shell, and the Korn shell. Graphical user interfaces such as Motif have been developed as replacements for text-based shells.

The file system is hierarchical. There is a root directory and branching subdirectories, and each subdirectory can have its own set of subdirectories. Devices such as displays and printers have device names that are handled in the same way as files. For example, a user could direct the output of a process or file listing to the display or a printer by using the display or printer name in a command. The piping feature provides a way to direct the output of one command, such as a sort, into another command.

UNIX and the TCP/IP protocols are closely linked. Every UNIX implementation now includes TCP/IP and support for Ethernet. In addition, Sun Microsystems' NFS is the common distributed file-sharing system included with UNIX, although the AFS is also used. Thus, UNIX provides in one package the ability to install a powerful operating system on a computer that lets users share files and run programs on other users' computers through one of the most common and powerful networking protocols in the industry.

**U**

**RELATED ENTRIES** CDE (Common Desktop Environment); DCE (Distributed Computing Environment), The Open Group; Motif; Multiprocessing; Network Operating Systems; NFS (Network File System); The Open Group; Rights and Permissions; Sun Microsystems Solaris; UNIX File System; *and* X Window

## INFORMATION ON THE INTERNET

| | |
|---|---|
| The Open Group | http://www.opengroup.org |
| UNIX.ORG (UNIX resources) | http://www.unix.org |
| UnixWorld Magazine | http://www.unixworld.com/unixworld |
| DEC's UNIX site | http://www.unix.digital.com |
| SCO (Santa Cruz Operation) | http://www.sco.com |
| FreeBSD site | http://www.freebsd.org |
| Jennifer Myers's UNIX Reference Desk | http://www.geek-girl.com/unix.html |
| Indiana University's Unix System Administration Independent Learning | http://www.uwsg.indiana.edu/usail |
| UNIX FAQs | http://www.cis.ohio-state.edu/hypertext/faq/usenet/unix-faq/faq/top.html |
| Yahoo!'s Unix links page | http://www.yahoo.com/Computers_and_Internet/Operating_Systems/Unix |
| Hans Kuhn's UNIX System Administration Tools | http://darkwing.uoregon.edu/~hak/unix.html |
| ISC UNIX Security Library | http://www.att.com/isc/lib/unix.html |
| Sven M. Paas's extensive operating system links (see Linux links) | http://www.lfbs.rwth-aachen.de/~sven/OS-Projects |

## UNIX File System

The UNIX file system is a hierarchical, tree-structured namespace that is designed to help users organize and access files. The namespace consists of directories that hold files. The UNIX file system consists of the following:

- *Disk-based file systems* store files on magnetic media, CD-ROMs, and other media. Sun Microsystems Solaris uses three formats, including ufs (UNIX file system), which is based on the BSD file allocation table file system; hsfs (High Sierra and ISO 9660 file system), a CD-ROM file system; and pcfs (PC file system), which provides access to data on DOS-formatted disks.

- *Network file systems* provide network-wide file sharing and file access. NFS (Network File System) and rfs (remote file sharing) file systems are commonly used.

■ *Pseudo file systems* are virtual file systems that exist in temporary memory and provide a place to store files or directory entries for fast access.

File systems can be mounted and unmounted at any time. A mounted file system is available for use. If it is a network file system, it is available for remote users on the network to access.

As mentioned, the UNIX file system is hierarchical in structure and starts with a root directory (called /) from which all other directories branch. The root directory and subdirectories hold other files and other subdirectories. UNIX includes some unique subdirectories where system files are stored, including **/bin, /etc,** and **/dev.** A typical UNIX directory structure is pictured here:

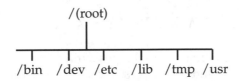

UNIX has three access file permissions—read, write, and execute—and these are issued to three categories of users: owner, group, and others. Each of these is described here:

■ **read (r)**  Allows the user to read a file or list the contents of a directory
■ **write (w)**  Allows the user to write to (change) a file or do a number of things in a directory, including create, rename, and delete a file
■ **execute (x)**  Allows the user to run a program or search a directory

The three categories of users are described here:

■ **owner (u)**  The owner of a file
■ **group (g)**  A group of users to which the owner of a file belongs
■ **others (o)**  All other users

Commands in the UNIX environment such as **ls** (list), **cat** (catalog), and the **ftp** utility display file permissions in a format similar to the following:

```
-rw-r--r--    1    Tom    Research    1009 Nov 11  1996     stars.gif

drwxrwxr-x    2    DC     Research     512 Sep 16 02:03     stats
```

The first column of the file listing displays the permissions, and the remaining columns define the following in order: number of links, owner, group, file size, date, and filename. The permissions are listed as shown here:

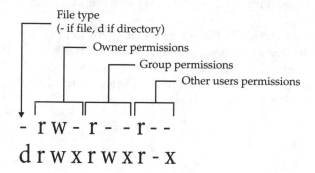

The UNIX system also defines special types of files that represent physical devices such as printers, terminals, and tape drives. Because devices are defined in this way, it is possible to direct the output of a command to the devices as if you were storing information in a file. If the device is a printer, it will print the output. Special device files are stored in the **/dev** directory. UNIX *pipes* are temporary files that store information that is being directed from one place to another.

**RELATED ENTRIES**    Access Rights; ACL (Access Control List); AFS (Andrew File System); Distributed File Systems; File Systems; Network Operating Systems; NFS (Network File System); Rights and Permissions; Sun Microsystems Solaris; *and* UNIX

## UNO (Universal Networked Object)

UNO is a specification developed by the OMG (Object Management Group) that supports interoperability among different ORBs (object request brokers). It allows a client using one ORB to invoke an operation on an object in another ORB. UNO is described in detail in Thomas J. Brando's paper called "Interoperability and the CORBA Specification" referred to at the end of this topic. The paper describes the following UNO components and extensions:

- An *ORB Interoperability Architecture* provides a framework for interoperability among ORB components.

- A *GIOP (General Inter-ORB Protocol)* consisting of the following, which can be mapped onto multiple transport layers:

    - A CDR (common data representation) for all data types

    - An IOR (interoperable object reference) format

    - Interoperable *TypeCodes* for all data types

- IOP (Inter-ORB Protocol) message contents, formats, and semantics, independent of the method of message conveyance

- The IIOP (Internet Inter-ORB Protocol), which is the first transport mapping for the GIOP. The Internet IOP maps the GIOP to TCP/IP. It will be mandatory for CORBA (Common Object Request Broker Architecture) 2.0 networked ORBs and guarantees out-of-the-box interoperability among them.

- Extensions to CORBA for building bridges between different ORBs.

- An ESIOP (Environment-Specific Inter-ORB Protocol), such as DCE-CIOP (Distributed Computing Environment Common Inter-ORB Protocol), that supports out-of-the-box interoperability at sites where a particular networking or distributed computing infrastructure is already in general use.

### INFORMATION ON THE INTERNET

Thomas J. Brando's Interoperability and the CORBA Specification paper

http://www.mitre.org/research/domis/reports/UNO.html

## UPS (Uninterruptible Power Supply)

A UPS provides electrical power to computers or other devices during a power outage and can be one of the following:

- A battery system

- A rotary UPS that uses the inertia of a large flywheel to carry the computer system through brief outages

- Internal combustion motors that run AC generators

UPS devices come in two forms: online and standby. A *standby* device kicks in only when the power goes down. It must therefore contain special circuitry that can switch to backup power in less than five milliseconds. An *online* device constantly provides the source of power to the computer. Because of this, it doesn't need to kick in. If the outside source of power dies, the batteries within the unit continue to supply the computer with power. Although online units are the best choice, they are more expensive than standby units. But because online units supply all the power to a computer, that power is always clean and smooth.

When purchasing a battery backup system, you need to know the following about the devices:

- The amount of time the UPS battery supplies power

- Whether the UPS provides a warning system to the server when the UPS is operating on standby power

- Whether the UPS includes power-conditioning features that can clip incoming transient noise

- The life span of the battery and how it degrades over time
- Whether the device warns you when the batteries can no longer provide backup power
- When the batteries need to be replaced

You also need to know the power requirements of the devices you'll hook to the UPS. For a server installation, this might include the CPU (and any added devices), the monitor, external routers, concentrator units, and wiring centers. You can find out the power requirements of these devices by looking at the backs of the equipment. Labels on the equipment list the power drawn by the units. UPSs have a VA (volt-ampere) rating, which is the line voltage multiplied by the current (amperes). You'll need to add up the power requirements of the equipment you plan to attach to the UPS, then purchase a UPS that can handle the load. Start by obtaining the amp rating on the back of each device you plan to hook up and multiply that rating by the voltage (usually 120 volts), then add the values obtained for each device and select an UPS that can handle at least 20 percent over that load.

A UPS attached to a file server usually requires an additional cable that alerts the file server when the UPS is running on standby power. The server will then proceed with shutdown procedures. Check with the UPS vendor to make sure this feature is available for the operating systems you have in mind.

Some vendors have developed advanced features for their power protection equipment. American Power Conversion's Smart-UPS series provides network managers with diagnostic information via a software control program called PowerChute. The software is installed on the server and communicates with the UPS over a cable. Managers can then track power quality, UPS operating temperature, line frequency, UPS output voltage, maximum and minimum line power, battery strength, line voltage, and UPS load.

**RELATED ENTRIES**    Data Protection; Disaster Recovery; Fault Management; Fault Tolerance; *and* Power and Grounding Problems and Solutions

## INFORMATION ON THE INTERNET

| | |
|---|---|
| The UPS Warehouse | http://www.the-ups-warehouse.co.uk |
| American Power Conversion Corp. | http://www.apcc.com |
| JT Packard & Associates' power supplies | http://www.jtpackard.com |
| LAN Times Online's power management buyers guide | http://www.lantimes.com/lantimes/buyers/index/s124.html |
| Battery Wholesale Distributors' battery FAQ | http://www.mywebplace.com/batterywholesale/batinfo.html |

| IETF Uninterruptible Power Supply (upsmib) Working Group | http://www.ietf.org/html.charters/upsmib-charter.html |
| Yahoo!'s Power Supplies links page | http://www.yahoo.com/Business_and _Economy/Companies/Computers/ Hardware/Components/Power_Supplies |

## URL (Uniform Resource Locator)

A resource is an object on the Internet or an intranet that resides on a host system. Objects include directories and an assortment of file types, including text files, graphics, video, and audio. A URL is the address of an object that is normally typed in the Address field of a Web browser. The URL is basically a pointer to the location of an object. This book is filled with URLs that point you to Web sites that provide more information about each of the topics. According to IETF RFC 1738, the syntax for a URL is

*<scheme>:<scheme-dependent-information>*

It is best to discuss this in terms that are more understandable. *scheme* is any one of the Internet protocols, including HTTP, FTP, Gopher, News (USENET news), NNTP (Network News Transport Protocol), Telnet, and WAIS (Wide Area Information Servers), among others. The following address uses an http scheme:

http://www.ntresearch.com/papers/security.html

First, http indicates that the HTTP protocol is to be used to access the site. The double slash indicates that the host name follows and the first single slash indicates that either a directory or a filename follows. In this case, "papers" is a directory, and "security.html" is a file in that directory that is displayed when this URL is entered in a Web browser as an address.

**RELATED ENTRIES**    Internet; IP (Internet Protocol); *and* Web Technologies and Concepts

### INFORMATION ON THE INTERNET

| Uniform Resource Locators (RFC 1738) | http://www.internic.net/rfc/rfc1738.txt |
| Relative Uniform Resource Locators (RFC 1808) | http://www.internic.net/rfc/rfc1808.txt |
| Guide to URLs | http://www.netspace.org/users/dwb/ url-guide.html |
| W3C's URL guide | http://www.w3.org/Addressing/ Addressing.html |

U

# USB (Universal Serial Bus)

USB is a data communication standard for a peripheral bus that was developed by Intel and Microsoft. It is a replacement for the plethora of connectors and ports on the back of desktop PCs and provides an interface for computer-telephony devices. Instead of having separate connections for keyboard, mouse, printer, modem, joystick, audio devices, CD-ROMs, digital cameras, and other devices, USB provides a single port for connecting all of the devices. USB eliminates many of the problems associated with the PC, such as the need to open the computer to install adapter cards, change dip switches, and configure IRQs (interrupt requests).

USB defines the ports and the bus topology with data transfer rates up to 12 Mbits/sec. A single cable up to 5 meters in length is used to daisy-chain devices to a single port. Up to 63 devices can be added to the port at any time without rebooting the system. The topology is a tiered star, which allows peripherals to be connected to repeater hubs that provide multiple port connectors. In some cases, hubs may need power. USB also supplies power to some devices so they will not need power cords or batteries. USB even allows devices to communicate their power requirement needs with the USB host controller.

**RELATED ENTRIES**    Connection Technologies; CTI (Computer-Telephony Integration)

**INFORMATION ON THE INTERNET**

| | |
|---|---|
| Universal Serial Bus Implementers Forum Home Page | http://www.usb.org |
| Microsoft Corporation (search for USB) | http://www.microsoft.com |
| Intel's USB site | http://www.intel.com/design/usb |
| Newnex's USB site | http://www.newnex.com/usb.html |

# USENET

USENET is a newsgroup service for implementing discussion groups on the Internet and other TCP/IP-based networks. Originally, USENET relied on a message exchange system called UUCP (UNIX-to-UNIX Copy Program). Today, message delivery is primarily handled by an Internet protocol called NNTP (Network News Transport Protocol).

Discussion groups are based on the exchange of news articles, bulletins, and messages. The process is an extension of the e-mail process, but much more efficient at delivering information to large groups of people. Basically, USENET automates information exchange and provides an alternative to sending e-mail to everyone that needs to read an article or bulletin. Articles and messages are put in a central database, and users access the database to get at the information. This reduces network traffic and eliminates the need to store a copy of each article/message on every subscriber's system. On the Internet, there are thousands of different newsgroups related to computers, social issues, science, the humanities, recreation, and other topics. News servers can also be set up for private use on internal TCP/IP networks (intranets).

There are three activities related to newsgroups:

- Subscribe to newsgroups and unsubscribe from newsgroups. This is done by users with no need to contact a central administrator.

- Use a newsgroup reader to read messages that have been posted to the newsgroup. Most Web browsers now include a newsgroup reader.

- Post messages to the newsgroup. Messages are posted in a very short time for others to read.

The process of signing up to a newsgroup is to first connect with a newsgroup server. If you connect to the Internet through an ISP (Internet service provider), your ISP will supply you with the Internet address of their news server. You enter this address in the configuration fields for your news reader which, as mentioned, is probably included with your Web browser. Once you connect with the server, the news reader will download a list of groups available on the news server and you can choose which one you want to subscribe to. The ISP's news server exchanges information with other news servers around the world in order to keep up with the latest newsgroup information. Note that some newsgroup servers are restricted and require a login.

Newsgroups are grouped into a hierarchy with top-level groups having names such as Comp (computers), Humanities, Misc (miscellaneous), News, Rec (recreation), Sci (science), Soc (social), Talk, and Alt (alternative). Under these main groups are subgroups such as comp.unix.admin and comp.unix.solarix. Most groups are rather formal in that new groups are formed after they have been evaluated and voted on by USENET users. The Alt group, on the other hand, is very informal. People start their own groups at will, and the category contains such groups as alt.society.revolution and alt.tasteless.jokes.

A USENET site gets its information from other USENET sites through newsfeeds in which USENET sites exchange information. A site may actively *pull* information from another site or the other site may *push* the information to it. A USENET site does not need to store every USENET topic. In some cases, an administrator may choose to block some topics, such as those with dubious content.

**U**

The workings of the transport protocol and methods for information exchange are covered further under "NNTP (Network News Transport Protocol)."

**RELATED ENTRIES**   Broadcast News Technology; Component Software Technology; Distributed Object Computing; IRC (Internet Relay Chat); Mailing List Programs; Marimba Castanet; Netcasting; ; NNTP (Network News Transport Protocol); PointCast; *and* Push

## INFORMATION ON THE INTERNET

| | |
|---|---|
| Network News Transport Protocol (RFC 977) | http://www.internic.net/rfc/rfc977.txt |
| USENET message format (RFC 1036) | http://www.internic.net/rfc/rfc1036.txt |
| PSInet's USENET information (very informative if you browse around) | http://cmc.psi.net/inet-serv/news/news-reader.html |
| Lee Ratzan's Mining nuggets from Usenet paper (techniques for finding information) | http://www.sun.com/sunworldonline/swol-10-1996/swol-10-usenet.html |
| General USENET info, including history | http://sunsite.nus.sg/pub/zen/zen-1.0_6.html |
| USENET FAQs | http://www.sci.muni.cz/~haring/sub/usenet_general.html |

# Users and Groups

Network operating systems provide security by requiring that all users log on by typing their user account name and a password. Once a user is verified or authenticated (see "Authentication and Authorization"), the user can access the network based on the rights they have been granted throughout the network. Some network operating systems require users to log on every time they access a resource at a different location on the network. The latest trend is to incorporate user authentication features that verify the authenticity of a user one time for all resources on a network. Trust relationships are established so that one server "trusts" that another server has properly authenticated a user.

User accounts hold information about the user, including any restrictions they have on a network. For example, a user might be restricted to logging on at a specific workstation or during a specific time. Groups are collections of users that network administrators create to simplify user management. It is far easier to include users in a group, then assign network access rights to the group, than it is to assign those rights individually to each user. Groups also simplify messaging. For example, it's easier to send an electronic mail message to a group called Managers than to each person in that group individually. Managers should create groups for users, projects, and management purposes when planning and setting up the network, then add user accounts to groups as users are added to the network.

A user account is granted certain rights and permissions to network resources. These accounts may have the following restrictions (from NetWare):

- **Account balance restrictions** You can restrict a user's access to the system and its resources by specifying a credit limit. A credit limit is a balance in an account that depletes as time and resources are used. Once depleted, the user can't log in to the system until given more credit.

- **Expiration restrictions** You can set an expiration date and time for a user account. The account is closed at the time specified. You might use this restriction for temporary employees.

- **Password restrictions** The administrator or a supervisor can specify the length and uniqueness of login passwords. You can force users to change their passwords at regular intervals and to use passwords that they haven't used recently.

- **Disk space restrictions** Disk space restrictions help administrators control how much disk space users can use.

- **Connection restrictions** Connection restrictions can limit the number of stations a user can log in to simultaneously.

- **Time restrictions** Time restrictions specify the times, in half-hour blocks, when users can log in to the system.

- **Station restrictions** Station restrictions prevent a user from logging in at any station other than the specified workstation. This prevents users from logging in at unsupervised workstations where their activities cannot be monitored. In NetWare, these restrictions can be assigned individually to each account or assigned as default settings that are applied when new accounts are created.

**RELATED ENTRIES**    Access Control; Access Rights; Groups; Novell NetWare File System; Rights and Permissions; UNIX File System; Windows NT Permissions; *and* Workgroups

# UTP (Unshielded Twisted-Pair) Cable

*See* Transmission Media, Methods, and Equipment.

**U**

# VAN (Value Added Network)

VANs have created data networks that they make available to organizations at leased-line rates (monthly charge) or at dial-up rates (per-use charge). A typical VAN has a web of national and/or global connections. Circuits consist of the VAN's own private lines or lines leased from major carriers such as AT&T. Dial-up or dedicated lines are used to connect with a VAN at access points that are available in most metropolitan areas. Services provided typically include X.25, frame relay, and ATM (Asynchronous Transfer Mode). Some of the major VANs are listed here:

- CompuServe Information Services offers access points in hundreds of locations throughout the United States with a variety of VAN services. Visit http://www.compuserve.com.

- GE Information Services provides packet-switching and high-speed services, as well as asynchronous and synchronous services. Visit http://www.geis.com.

- Infonet Services Corp. provides an array of international services. Visit http://www.infonet.com.

Using a PDN (public data network) saves you the trouble of contracting for the lines and setting up your own switching equipment. The service provider handles any problems with the network itself and can guarantee data delivery through a vast mesh of switched lines.

**RELATED ENTRIES**   Communication Service Providers; Communication Services; Extranet; Private Network; Telecommunications and Telephone Systems; Tunnels; VPN (Virtual Private Network); *and* WAN (Wide Area Network). See also "Telecommunications Companies" in Appendix A.

**INFORMATION ON THE INTERNET**

| | |
|---|---|
| The World Wide Web Virtual Library Telecommunication Links | http://www.analysys.com/vlib |
| PTC Telecom Resources Links | http://alex.ptc.org/links |

# VAX (Virtual Address Extension), DEC

The VAX line of computer systems was first introduced in 1977. The first system, the VAX 11/780, competed with IBM systems and provided an upgrade path for existing customers of DEC (Digital Equipment Corporation). The VAX 11/780 had a compatibility mode in which it could run software written for DEC's PDP-11 minicomputer systems. The VMS (Virtual Memory System) 32-bit operating system was announced with the VAX line to provide a true multitasking/multiuser environment. Also announced with the VAX was DECnet, a networking system that took advantage of the newly emerging Ethernet standard.

# vBNS (Very high speed Backbone Network Service)

The NSF (National Science Foundation) has played an important role in the development of the Internet. Today, it is involved in the evolution of both the NREN (National Research and Education Network) and the NII (National Information Infrastructure) program. But its early role was critical in defining the structure of the Internet. In the mid 1980s, it funded the NSFnet, and in 1990, the NSFnet took over the role of ARPANET (Advanced Research Projects Agency Network). The NSFnet connected five supercomputer centers in the United States.

In 1995, the NSFnet was shut down because the NSF felt that the growing Internet would be better off if backbone services were provided by commercial providers such as MCI, PSINet, UUNET, ANS/AOL, Sprint, and others. At that time, all the providers interconnected their own backbones with one another at NAPs (network access points). Today, many more providers are involved, and interconnections are handled at NAPs, MAEs (metropolitan area exchanges), and other points as discussed under "Internet Backbone."

When NSF shut down the NSFnet, it also awarded MCI a five-year contract to develop the vBNS, a high-speed next generation backbone network designed for delivering massive amounts of voice, data, and video at speeds nearly four times faster than current technology. The vBNS is built with MCI's commercial ATM (Asynchronous Transfer Mode) service, and the goal is to create a network with data rates in the 2-Gbit/sec range. At this writing, the backbone runs at 622 Mbits/sec and links the same supercomputer centers that were connected with the original NSFNET.

**RELATED ENTRIES**    GII (Global Information Infrastructure); Internet; Internet Backbone; Internet Organizations and Committees; NII (National Information Infrastructure); NIST (National Institute of Standards and Technology); *and* NREN (National Research and Education Network)

## INFORMATION ON THE INTERNET

| | |
|---|---|
| MCI's vBNS site | http://www.vbns.net |
| NLANR (National Laboratory for Applied Network Research) | http://www.nlanr.net |
| NLANR's vBNS site | http://www.nlanr.net/VBNS/vBNS.html |

# Videoconferencing and Desktop Video

Network videoconferencing is a tool for communicating via audio, video, and data in real time. Until recently it was a pricey tool, but low-priced components (such as cameras), multimedia PCs, and an increasing demand for collaboration over the Internet and intranets has pushed the development of the technology. Operating systems such as Microsoft Windows now include voice and videoconferencing tools, making the technology even more accessible to users. Even low-end videoconferencing systems offer interesting features such as document/application sharing and a whiteboard that can be used simultaneously. With these applications, users can collaborate almost as if they were in the same room.

Other factors contributing to the growing interest in videoconferencing include better compression techniques, maturing standards that encourage interoperability, high-speed LANs and WANs that support the data requirements of video, and high-performance multimedia computers. New uses for videoconferencing are also helping to drive development. In work environments, it is being used for tech support, distance learning, telemedicine, job recruiting interviews, direct sales, legal work, telecommuting, and manufacturing. It can also cut travel costs.

When it comes to choosing videoconferencing systems, buyers should have a clear idea of how the system will be used because there are many trade-offs between price and functionality. Bandwidth limitations also influence the buying decision. There is no point buying the best system if the network and/or telecommunication link cannot deliver high-quality video due to bandwidth limitations. If packets are lost or dropped due to insufficient bandwidth and congestion, the video will appear jerky. Television operates at about 30 fps (frames per second), and the image shows no jerkiness or blurring. The fastest room systems operate at 24 to 30 fps. Anything below 10 fps appears as a series of still pictures. An acceptable rate for low-bandwidth networks is 15 fps, but the video still has an unnatural appearance.

ISDN (Integrated Services Digital Network) has been the medium of choice for videoconferencing, though at $1,000 to $2,000 per station it is still too expensive to be put in general use. And ISDN is still a compromise between cost and image quality. To achieve frame rates of 20 to 22 fps, 384 to 512 Kbits/sec of bandwidth are needed. A 128-Kbit/sec basic rate ISDN line may not have enough bandwidth to provide the quality of video desired. Note that it is common for organizations to plan ahead for videoconferences and reserve a temporary high-speed link such as a switched T1 line for a specific time and date. This requires a T1 line and T1 equipment, but the equipment may be cost-justified if the system is used often.

The most recent development in the videoconferencing field are the modem-based videoconferencing systems found in multimedia PCs. Like any videoconferencing system, these systems require a camera, a microphone, and software. These low-cost videoconferencing systems operate over standard telephone lines at 28.8 to 33.6 Kbits/sec. Some systems aggregate multiple phone connections to boost bandwidth. The systems operate at 3 to 10 fps, but fast motion momentarily defeats them, causing blurred, slowed, or stopped motion. However, if both parties are sitting at their desks and not moving much, the slow frame rate won't have much impact, and low-cost videoconferencing is fine for these "talking head" meetings. Often it is only necessary to see people pointing out parts of a picture or object. In fact, audio is often the major consideration in videoconferencing. If the audio is good, users will tolerate video that is not up to television standards.

In the arena of low-end videoconferencing systems, CU-SeeMe was developed at Cornell University in 1992, signaling the start of the dial-up videoconferencing industry. Bundled with the inexpensive Connectix QuickCam, CU-SeeMe has established a large user base. The commercial version, called Enhanced CU-SeeMe and put out by White Pine Software, supports the H.323 interoperability standard when it is used with White Pine's MeetingPoint conference server. Enhanced CU-SeeMe supports 24-bit, true-color videoconferencing, and it can be run over dial-up modems or ISDN on PCs. See "CU-SeeMe" for more information.

## Standards

New videoconferencing standards have moved manufacturers away from proprietary systems and in the direction of interoperability. The ITU H.320 standard (1990) is an umbrella standard that established the means for making different vendors' videoconferencing equipment interoperate over switched digital phone lines. Under H.320, the H.261 standard defines video image compression. H.221, H.230, and H.242 define communications and control, while the G.711, G.722, and G.728 standards address audio signals.

The newer H.323 standard (1996) is a videoconferencing standard that builds on the H.320 standard. H.323 promotes multimedia videoconferencing from desktops over LANs, intranets, and the Internet. It supports a variety of performance levels and an H.323/H.320 gateway will link H.320 ISDN and H.323 videoconferencing systems. For more information on H.323, see "VoIP (Voice over IP)." On LANs, H.323 allows managers tighter control over how videoconferencing uses network resources. H.323 is still so new that vendors haven't yet taken full advantage of it, but the industry is changing rapidly.

Another new standard promises to improve dial-up videoconferencing. The H.324 standard allows H.324-compliant devices to connect over standard telephone lines (and the V.80 standard found in newer modems will keep the audio and video synchronized). However, like H.323, the standard H.324 is still new enough that interoperability among vendors' products isn't assured.

The T.120 series of standards for "audiographic teleconferencing" were ratified by the ITU in late 1996. These standards define protocols for transporting, controlling, and displaying multimedia conferencing information. The IMTC and DataBeam sites given below under "Information on the Internet" have additional information.

**RELATED ENTRIES**    Collaborative Computing; CTI (Computer-Telephony Integration); CU-SeeMe; Groupware; ISDN (Integrated Services Digital Network); Iso-Ethernet; Multimedia; Prioritization of Network Traffic; QoS (Quality of Service); Voice/Data Networks; Voice over the Internet; *and* VoIP (Voice over IP)

**INFORMATION ON THE INTERNET**

| | |
|---|---|
| IMTC (International Multimedia Teleconferencing Consortium) | http://www.imtc.org |
| International Teleconferencing Association | http://www.itca.org |

| | |
|---|---|
| HEI Glossary of Audioconferencing, Videoconferencing, Telecommunications, Video Compression, ITU-T Standards | http://www.hei.ca/hei/glossary.html |
| DataBeam Primer on the T.120 Collaboration Standards | http://www.databeam.com/Products/CCTS/t120primer/index.html |
| Goodman's Book Marks | http://www.wp.com/goodmans/resfor.html |
| Dan Kegel's ISDN Home Page | http://alumni.caltech.edu/~dank/isdn |
| Ken's CTI, IVR and Call Center Page | http://www.pi.se/ken/linkcti.html |
| Telecom Information Resources on the Internet | http://www.spp.umich.edu/telecom/internet-telephony.html |
| Versit's H.320 page | http://www.versit.com/h320.html |
| White Pine Software | http://www.wpine.com |

## VIM (Vendor Independent Messaging)

VIM is an electronic mail API (application programming interface) developed by Lotus and supported by Apple, Borland, IBM, MCI, Novell, Oracle, WordPerfect, and other electronic mail developers and vendors. Vendors use electronic mail APIs to add connectivity to network operating systems. Competing standards include Novell's NetWare Global Messaging and SMF (Standard Message Format) and Microsoft's MAPI (Messaging Application Programming Interface). MAPI is now the most commonly used messaging API and is discussed under "MAPI (Messaging Application Programming Interface)."

## VINES, Banyan

*See* Banyan VINES.

## Virtual Circuit

A virtual circuit is a dedicated point-to-point communication line between two end stations on a packet-switched or cell-relay network. It provides a temporary or dedicated *connection-oriented* link or path through a router- or switch-connected network. Devices along the circuit are programmed with a circuit number so that when packets arrive, the switch knows exactly how to forward them without the need to examine the packet header in detail. This predefined path improves performance and reduces the header size of frames and packets, thus improving throughput as well. Technically, the underlying physical paths through the packet-switching network may change to avoid congestion or downed lines, but the two end stations maintain a connection and update the path specification as necessary.

There are permanent and switched virtual circuits, as described next:

- **PVC (permanent virtual circuit)** A connection between end stations that is defined in advance, usually with a predefined and guaranteed bandwidth. In public-switched carrier services such as ATM (Asynchronous Transfer Mode) or frame relay, customers negotiate the endpoints of PVCs in advance with the carrier. For internal networks, administrators create PVCs in advance to direct traffic through specific parts of the network or to reserve bandwidth for special applications such as in-house videoconferencing. Reserving bandwidth by setting up a virtual circuit that is used for a specific purpose is a form of prioritization. Refer to "Prioritization of Network Traffic" for more information.

- **SVC (switched virtual circuit)** An "on-demand" temporary connection between end stations, much like a voice phone call is a temporary connection. Connections last only as long as necessary and are taken down when complete. Carriers may let customers define SVC "on the fly" or a carrier may set up a number of predefined SVCs for the connections that a customer requires most often. The carriers have recently started to offer SVC services in their networks. For example, SVCs on frame relay networks can be used to make voice calls across the network. AT&T now offers SVC services over ATM. Pricing is on a per-minute basis, with pricing as low as 1 cent per minute. The connection speed determines the actual price.

Note that PVCs are best when large amounts of traffic are anticipated between two locations on a regular basis. SVCs are more appropriate for temporary or recurring connections, such as voice and video conferences. Also note that carriers are most comfortable with connection-oriented PVCs because they allow them to manage bandwidth and easily bill customers. A PVC may have a monthly rate or a per-packet charge. For frame-relay networks, the carrier and the customer negotiate *CBS (committed burst size)*, the maximum amount of data that the network provider agrees to transfer; *CIR (committed information rate)*, the rate at which the network provider agrees to transfer CBS data; and *EBS (excess burst size)*, the amount of data that can be sent over the CBS rate assuming extra bandwidth is available.

In the ATM environment, there are *VPs (virtual paths)* and *VCs (virtual circuits)*. A VP is a defined *path* that one or more VCs follow through the ATM network to reach the same destination. Think of a VP as a cable that contains a bundle of wires as pictured in Figure V-1. In this analogy, the VP acts as a sort of multiwire cable that connects two points and the individual circuits within the cable connect to individual systems or processes at the ends of the VP. For example, you might contract for a single VP between the home office and a remote office that contains multiple VCs. Each VC within the VP can have different data rates, priorities, and so on. In addition, since multiple VCs share the same path through the network, they can take advantage of the same management functions. If a VP is already set up, adding new VCs is easy since the work of defining paths through the network is already done. In addition, if the network needs to change a path to avoid congestion or downed lines, all the VCs set up for a VP are directed along the new path.

**V**

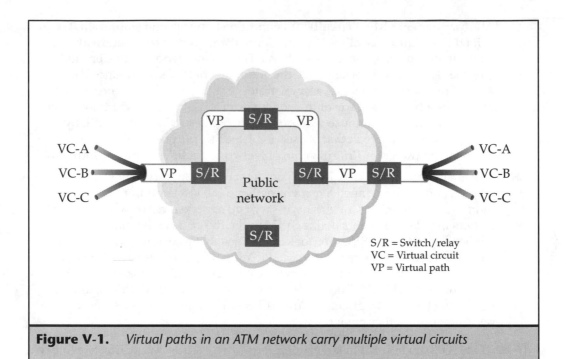

**Figure V-1.** *Virtual paths in an ATM network carry multiple virtual circuits*

One of the important features of VCs is that they provide a certain guaranteed data rate and path through a network that is useful for delivering real-time information such as videoconferencing and voice calls. Refer to "Prioritization of Network Traffic" and "QoS (Quality of Service)" for additional information.

**RELATED ENTRIES** ATM (Asynchronous Transfer Mode); Bandwidth on Demand; Bandwidth Reservation; Cell Relay; Circuit-Switching Services; Connection-Oriented and Connectionless Services; Data Communication Concepts; Frame Relay; IP over ATM; IP Switching; Packet and Cell Switching; Prioritization of Network Traffic; QoS (Quality of Service); RSVP (Resource Reservation Protocol); Telecommunications and Telephone Systems; *and* WAN (Wide Area Network)

# Virtual Dial-up Services

This section describes ways to reduce the cost and complexity of remote dial-up networking by taking advantage of ISP (Internet service provider) facilities and the Internet. The primary protocol discussed here is the IETF L2TP (Layer 2 Tunneling Protocol), which is derived from Cisco's L2F (Layer 2 Forwarding) protocol. L2TP also includes features from Microsoft's PPTP (Point-to-Point Tunneling Protocol), which is described elsewhere in this book.

As an aside, Microsoft and Cisco Systems developed similar protocols with different objectives in mind. Both technologies let organizations move their remote access services to ISPs, but since Cisco is a hardware company, its L2F protocol ended up requiring that hardware at the ISP and corporate site be upgraded to L2F-compatible equipment. PPTP is a software solution that requires little in the way of costly upgrades. L2F also supports a variety of layer 3 protocols, while PPTP is an IP-only solution. L2TP improves on L2F. It does not require special hardware support, and it supports a variety of protocols. Flow control is the major feature that was added.

A typical Internet connection for a dial-up user involves the PPP (Point-to-Point Protocol). PPP is a layer 2 protocol that frames data so it can be sent across a dial-up connection. The protocol allows users to run TCP/IP software such as Web browsers as if they were directly connected to the Internet. In fact, user TCP/IP packets are put into PPP frames for transport across the dial-up link to an ISP (Internet service provider). The ISP then extracts the TCP/IP packets and forwards them on the Internet.

L2TP enhances PPP by providing a way for a remote user to extend a PPP link across the Internet all the way to a corporate site. Basically, a tunnel is established across the Internet from the ISP to a corporate site and frames are transmitted through the tunnel. Once the tunnel is set up, the ISP is basically out of the picture and the user communicates to the corporate network over what appears to be a direct dial-up connection.

There are several motivations for doing this:

- Users can take advantage of the low cost of the Internet. Instead of making a long-distance call to connect directly with the corporate site's remote access server, remote users dial in to a local ISP and use the Internet to handle all long-distance connections.

- The protocol provides *virtual dial-up* because the user doesn't really dial in to the corporate network, but when the connection is complete, it appears that way.

- Because PPP framing is used, remote users can access corporate sites using a variety of protocols such as IP, IPX, SNA, and so on.

- The corporate site assigns an IP address to a remote client instead of the ISP. This alleviates the address shortage problem with ISPs and the Internet.

- L2TP provides end-system transparency, meaning that the remote client and the corporate site do not require any special software to use the service in a secure way.

- An organization can use an authentication scheme that operates independently of the ISP. Authentication can be provided by CHAP (Challenge Handshake Authentication Protocol), PAP (Password Authentication Protocol), TACACS+ (Terminal Access Controller Access Control System Plus), RADIUS (Remote Authentication Dial-In User Service), token access cards, and one-time password schemes.

**V**

*Tunneling* is the key to L2TP (and other virtual dial-up services). With tunneling, protocol packets of one type of network are put inside or *encapsulated* in the protocol packets of another network for transport across that network. Think of a ferry that shuttles cars across a river. A tunnel has an entry point and an exit point that are essentially interfaces between two different types of networks, although they are defined in software.

## Implementation

Figure V-2 illustrates a typical L2TP setup. The remote client dials in to a NAS (network access server) located at an ISP. A tunnel is then set up across the Internet to a corporate gateway server. Once the tunnel is set up, remote clients access the corporate network as if they had dialed directly into that network.

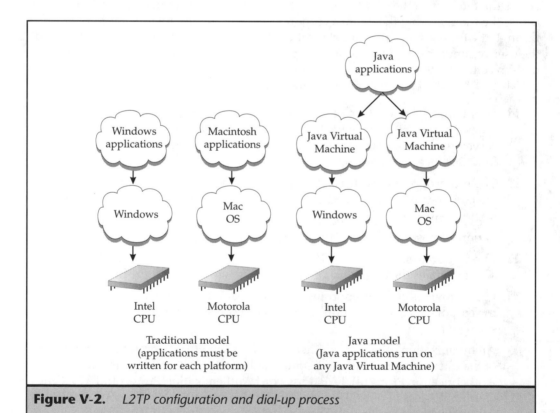

**Figure V-2.**   *L2TP configuration and dial-up process*

The dial-up and connection process for an Internet-based tunnel proceeds as follows:

1. The remote client dials the ISP's NAS and the NAS collects logon information from the client. A PPP (analog modem) or native ISDN connection is established between the client and the ISP.

2. The NAS inspects the username in the logon information and determines whether a virtual dial-up service is required. The ISP maintains a database for a corporation that associates the username with a specific endpoint (i.e., the corporate gateway).

3. A tunnel is now established (assuming that one has not already been set up). The NAS contacts the corporate gateway and assigns a MID (multiplex ID) to the new tunnel. The MID identifies a particular connection within the tunnel. Note that other remote client connections may use this same tunnel but are assigned a specific MID.

4. Now the remote client is authenticated by the corporate security server to ensure that this is a legitimate user. The authentication information that was initially collected from the client in Step 1 is forwarded to the corporate gateway.

5. If the user is authenticated, a new tunnel is set up or an existing tunnel is used to create a connection across the Internet. Many links can be multiplexed over the same tunnel.

6. Now the user has an end-to-end PPP link and the NAS may log call information for accounting purposes.

At this point, the connection between the remote client and the corporate network is like any PPP connection. All the normal mechanisms for managing user sessions can proceed as normal. When the ISP's NAS receives frames from the remote client over the PPP link, they are stripped of any link framing or transparency bytes, encapsulated in L2TP, and forwarded over the tunnel. The corporate gateway receives these frames, strips L2TP, and processes them as normal incoming frames.

L2TP provides authentication but does not encrypt data as it travels across the Internet. The IETF's IPSec protocol operates at layer 3 (network layer) to provide encryption for various tunneling protocols. It also provides mechanisms for securely exchanging keys between encrypting devices.

**RELATED ENTRIES**    Access Server; Communication Server; Encapsulation; IPSec (IP Security); Mobile Computing; Mobile IP; NC (Network Computer) Devices; NetPC; PPTP (Point-to-Point Tunneling Protocol); Remote Access; Routers; Security; S/WAN (Secure WAN); Tunnels; VPN (Virtual Private Network); *and* WAN (Wide Area Network)

**INFORMATION ON THE INTERNET**

| | |
|---|---|
| IETF Point-to-Point Protocol Extensions (pppext) Charter | http://www.ietf.org/html.charters/pppext-charter.html |
| Bay Networks' remote access and VPN paper (very complete!) | http://www.baynetworks.com/Products/Papers/2746.html |
| Shiva's remote access white paper | http://www.shiva.com/remote |
| MASNET's VPN information | http://www.masnet.net/internet/issues/vpn.html |
| John Wobus's Remote Access Technology paper | http://web.syr.edu/~jmwobus/comfaqs/serial-technology.html |
| Cisco Systems' virtual dial-up information | http://www.cisco.com/warp/public/728/General/vpdn_wp.htm |
| Ascend Communications' PPTP FAQ (go to resource Library) | http://www.ascend.com |
| 3Com's PPTP site | http://infodeli.3com.com/infodeli/tools/remote/general/pptp/pptp.htm |

## Virtual Directory

A virtual directory is basically a directory that appears to a user as being located on the service they are accessing, but may be located on a linked server. Virtual directories are commonly used in the Web server environment. They often appear as subdirectories of the home directory but in fact may be directories on entirely different servers. For example, a company's home page might have a "product information" option. When you click this option, information is pulled from a server in the Marketing department. However, the URL in the browser gives no indication that you have changed servers, only that the information appears to located in a subdirectory of the home server.

Virtual directories can distribute the load of a server farm. For example, the content of a Web site can be distributed over several servers but still give users a single directory view of information. By distributing the contents, you also distribute the processing and I/O (input/output) load. With directories distributed to multiple servers and hard drives, information can be retrieved much faster because a single system is not doing all the work.

## Virtual Machine, Java

Java is a programming language and development environment created by Sun Microsystems that is discussed fully in the "Java" section of this book. Java programmers create Java applets that run inside what is called a Java VM (Virtual Machine). One way to think about the VM is as a CPU that runs in software—a software CPU that can run on almost any computing platform and provide the same interface to applications. In the past, applications were designed to run on platforms that were based on a CPU family, such as Intel processors. With Java running on top of the hardware CPU as a software process, applications written to run on any computer platform where the Java VM is running, no matter what hardware CPU is in place.

The significance of this can be seen in Figure V-3. On the left, traditional computing platforms require that applications be written to specifically work on those platforms. On the right, Java applications run on any computing platform for which a Java Virtual Machine is available. That includes almost every computing platform in the world, all the way from small handheld devices to IBM mainframe systems.

The advantage of this approach is that programmers can write one application that works on many different computer platforms rather than different versions of an application to run on different computing platforms.

The Java VM is so much modeled after a CPU that it even converts Java code into a language that is very similar to the CPU-level machine language. The machine-like language it creates is specific to the particular CPU that the VM runs on. In this way, the VM has an upper layer and a lower layer. The upper layer is compatible with all Java applications and the lower layer is compatible with a specific computing platform, such as the Intel family. Refer to Figure J-1 in the "Java" section of this book for a diagram of the Java model.

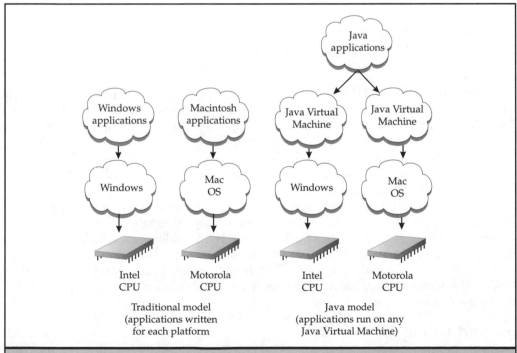

**Figure V-3.** *Java applications run on any computer with a Java Virtual Machine*

The VM makes hardware calls to the processor of the machine that it is running on. These calls perform standard CPU operations just like any other program that is designed for the platform it is running on. But the VM hides the platform specifics from Java applications. These applications only need to make calls to the Java VM, which then converts the application calls to calls that are specific to the platform for which the VM was designed. Thus, Java applications are portable to any VM because they only need to interface with the top level of the VM.

**RELATED ENTRIES**    Java; Sun Microsystems

**INFORMATION ON THE INTERNET**

Sun Microsystems' Java Computing site      http://www.sun.com/java

# Virtual Network

Virtual networks are networks that are defined in software or through configuration switching on top of other networks. In the public carrier networks, virtual networks are defined by virtual circuits. In internal networks, virtual networks are defined as subnetworks or VLANs (virtual LANs). See "Virtual Circuit," "VLAN (Virtual LAN)," and "VPN (Virtual Private Network)" for a discussion of two different types of virtual networks.

# Virtual Reality Modeling

*See* VRML (Virtual Reality Modeling Language).

# Virus and Antivirus Issues

A *virus* is a computer program that infects other programs with copies of itself. It clones itself from disk to disk or from one system to the next over computer networks. A virus executes and does its damage when the program it has infected executes. Only code that executes can be infected with viruses. Previously, only executable files were at risk, but new viruses attack macros in programs like Microsoft Word and do their damage when the macro is executed.

The damage caused by viruses may be harmless, such as displaying a happy birthday message for the creator on the appropriate day. Alternatively, the virus may do considerable damage by destroying boot records, file tables, and valuable data on disk. To maintain a protective stance against virus threats, you must stay in contact with the organizations and vendors listed at the end of this section. Most of the Web sites have extensive information on viruses, including databases, recent activities, and even virus hoaxes.

## Viruses and Other Threats

Now let's examine just a few of the virus classifications outlined by organizations such as NCSA (National Computer Security Association) and CSI (Computer Security Institute).

- **Boot Sector Virus** This type of virus infects the master boot record of a computer by overwriting the original boot code and replacing it with infected boot code. A boot virus is spread to the hard disk when the system is booted with an infected floppy disk.

- **File-infecting Virus** This virus infects files on disk—usually executable files with the extension COM, EXE, or OVL. Operating system files are also targeted. Differences in file size usually indicate an infection. In some cases, the original program is often replaced with an infected program.

- **Polymorphic Virus** This type of virus changes its appearance to avoid detection by antivirus software. The virus encrypts itself with a special algorithm that changes every time an infection occurs. To find polymorphic viruses, antivirus software must use special scanning techniques.

- **Stealth Virus** This is a virus that attempts to hide itself from the operating system and antivirus software. Stealth viruses stay in memory to intercept attempts to use the operating system and hide changes made to file sizes. These viruses must be detected while they are in memory.

- **Multipart Virus** This type of virus infects boot sectors as well as executable files. Multipart viruses are a real problem because they use stealth and polymorphism to prevent detection.

- **Macro Virus** This is the newest breed of virus. Macro viruses are executable programs that attach themselves to documents created in Microsoft Word and Excel. When an unsuspecting user receives the document and executes a macro, the virus executes and does its damage.

Besides viruses, your systems are also vulnerable to other types of destructive programs that are not classified as viruses. These include *worms*, *Trojan horses*, and *logic bombs*.

- **Worm** A worm is often mistaken for a virus. It is a single destructive program on a single system often planted by someone who has direct access to the system. Worms do not replicate themselves like viruses.

- **Trojan horse** This is a program that may appear to be another program, waiting for an unsuspecting user to execute and unleash it. A Trojan horse may infect other files on the system or on other network computers. In some cases, a Trojan horse is not destructive. Instead, it collects information, such as logon passwords, or copies sensitive files to another system on a network without the host user knowing what is happening. Often, you don't know a Trojan horse program is running. The program may be sending your private files to a coworker's computer!

- **Logic bomb** A logic bomb is basically a Trojan horse with a timing device. It goes off at a certain time and does its damage, which might be to destroy data on a local hard drive or to release a virus. A disgruntled employee may create a bomb to go off long after leaving the company so as to avoid suspicion.

**V**

## Virus Infections and How to Avoid Them

A system becomes contaminated with a virus through file system activity. A contaminated file is either copied from a disk or downloaded from an online service, bulletin board, or the Internet. Employees may bring viruses into an organization on their portable computers or disks that they have brought from home.

When files are contaminated, they may increase in size, so it is relatively easy for a virus detection program to report such problems. However, so-called *stealth viruses* are able to spoof the preinfected file size of a document so it appears that nothing has changed. Worse, *active stealth viruses* can actually fight back against virus detection programs by disabling their detection functions. Still worse is the *polymorphic* or *mutation* virus, which changes its unique features upon replication. Virus detection programs rely on these unique features to quickly locate "known" viruses.

In almost all cases, it is easy to avoid viruses if one is careful to never copy files from unknown or untrusted sources. That is a particularly difficult strategy to maintain, however.

The Internet and World Wide Web have created a whole new way to spread viruses. It is now possible to execute programs while browsing the Web without actually copying a file to your system's disk. Java and Microsoft ActiveX modules are automatically copied to your system while browsing the Web. Although a number of precautions have been taken to prevent these components from causing damage, recent incidents have shown that we are not safe.

Trojan horse programs and worms are typically installed by people inside the company with specific intentions to capture data or do some damage to a system. The best protection is to lock up systems and carefully monitor the activities of employees, especially people who might be leaving the company or who are suspected of being malicious for some reason.

Even after detecting and cleaning up a virus infection, there is still a good chance that the virus is lurking somewhere in your organization, ready to reinfect systems. If the virus is detectable, you need to check all workstations for its existence. You might need to check all floppy disks and other data sources for infections and, in some cases, destroy floppy disks or use them only on "quarantined" systems.

Here are some general policies for controlling viruses:

- Create education programs and post regular bulletins about virus problems.

- Never transfer files from unknown or untrusted sources unless an antivirus utility is available to scan the files.

- Set up "quarantine computers" that are isolated from other computers. Test new programs or open unknown documents on this system.

- Lock down computers to prevent malicious people from infecting systems or installing Trojan horse programs.

- Use the Windows NT operating system because of its secure logon and authentication.

■ Do not use dual-boot partitions. A virus in one partition may infect the other.

Administrators should keep up with the latest virus information by reading weekly computer journals or joining organizations like the NCSA. Check the NCSA and CSI Web sites on a regular basis to get late-breaking news about new viruses.

There are a number of virus protection programs for desktop computers and for networks. Virus detectors attempt to detect known viruses that have infected files or memory locations. On workstations, interrupts can be monitored to detect and stop system calls that may indicate virus activity. Another technique is to look for unique identifiers that indicate a virus. These methods are called *signature scanning*. In order for an antivirus program to detect the latest viruses, it must be periodically updated with the latest identifiers by the vendor. The down side is that signature scanning is only as good as the most recent signature file.

**RELATED ENTRIES**    Data Protection; Hacker; *and* Security

**INFORMATION ON THE INTERNET**

| | |
|---|---|
| NCSA (National Computer Security Association) | http://www.ncsa.com |
| CSI (Computer Security Institute) | http://www.csi.com |
| Data Fellows's Computer Virus Information page | http://www.datafellows.fi/vir-info |
| Data Rescue's virus encyclopedia | http://www.datarescue.com/avpbase |
| Trend Micro (see Virus Alert section) | http://www.antivirus.com |
| Symantec Corporation | http://www.symantec.com |
| McAfee | http://www.mcafee.com |

# VLAN (Virtual LAN)

Many companies have moved toward the switched network paradigm, in which computers are connected to dedicated ports on Ethernet switches, Gigabit Ethernet switches, ATM switches, or other types of switches. Departmental switches are connected to enterprise switches so the entire organization is essentially interconnected. The network can be constructed as one big flat network in which there are no subnetworks or routers, and where any computer can potentially link with any other computer. However, many administrators prefer the physical division of networks that routers provide. They contain broadcasts within their boundaries and add security.

The techniques described in this section explain how network administrators can create VLANs (virtual LANs) to gain the advantages of router-connected subnetworks in a flat switched network environment. The first goal is to organize computers and users into separate VLANs based on computer hardware address, port connector address, IP address, or other techniques. Once VLANs are created, routers are required to forward packets among them, as shown on the left in Figure V-4. Note that the underlying network is a flat switched network, and that VLANs are defined as overlays onto this network. The router interconnects the VLANs.

The illustration on the right in Figure V-4 shows an important concept that must be kept in mind. While routing adds the advantages of subnetworking back into the flat switched network topology, routing packets is slower than switching them. Even though a network may be subdivided into VLANs, the underlying network is still capable of switching packets to any computer at high speed. So, what network designers are striving to do through various protocol standards is a technique called "route first, then switch." A router (or a server that provides router-like functions) is initially used to establish a route between two systems in different VLANs and to provide security aspects of verifying that the two systems can set up a connection. Once the route is established and security is checked, packets are switched using the layer 2 switching fabric. This basically avoids moving all but the first few packet through the slow router once it has done its job.

The technique for doing this is often called *layer 3 switching* or *layer 2 routing*, depending on your point of view and the vendor you are talking with. If IP is the primary protocol, the term *IP switching* is used. You can get additional information by referring to "IP over ATM," "IP Switching," "NHRP (Next Hop Resolution Protocol)," and "Switched Networks."

Figure V-5 illustrates how VLANs are configured. The bottom of the illustration shows the structure of the physical LAN. Backbone switches and local area switches

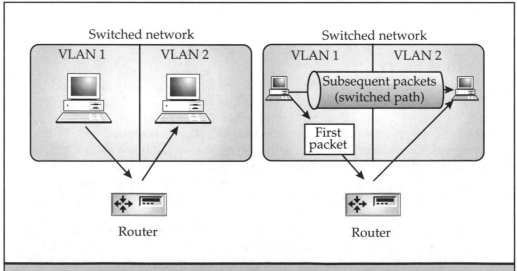

**Figure V-4.** *VLANs logical subnetworks that overlay the physical network*

provide VLAN configuration functions. Note that *work area switches* are switches located in wiring closets for connecting computers in the general vicinity.

The network administrator adds a computer (or user) to a VLAN based on a switch port address, a computer hardware address (the MAC or medium access control address of a network interface card), an IP address, or some other method. In Figure V-5, the VLANs are pictured above the physical network. When computer B transmits, it sends a message that is broadcast to all the computers in the Marketing VLAN, which includes computers E, G, H, and J. If computer B needs to send a message to a user in the Research VLAN, the message must be routed. This is handled by a routing function in the backbone switch or by a separate router.

VLANs are essential in organizations where users move from one group to another or the structure of the organization is such that members of the same workgroup are located in different physical locations. VLANs let scattered group members share common resources such as storage devices and be part of the same broadcast domain. In other words, traffic generated by users in a group should stay

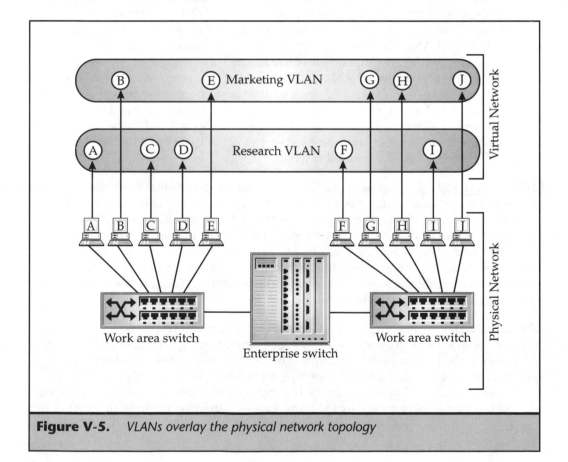

**Figure V-5.** *VLANs overlay the physical network topology*

confined to their group. If users are highly mobile and move from one office to another as part of their job, the network administrator can use VLAN techniques to keep the user within a broadcast group no matter where they plug in to the network.

## VLAN Configuration Methods

Switching architectures are ideal for the creation of VLANs. The first VLANs were configured manually. Then, as the technology became better understood and more popular, more advanced techniques were employed. The following sections describe the various techniques that can be used to build VLANs. Many vendors are implementing some or all of these techniques. For example, the more advanced methods rely on IP protocols, but networks that use both IP and nonroutable protocols such as NetBIOS may need to use the MAC-based method described next in addition to the IP methods.

**PORT CONFIGURATION METHODS** The port configuration method is really a way to configure separate LANs within the same box. The resulting LANs are technically not VLANs because they are configured as distinct wiring configurations. The network administrator ties together specific ports on hub or switching devices to create individual LANs. For example, ports 2, 4, 5, and 8 are grouped as LAN #1 and ports 1, 3, 6, 7, 9, and 10 are grouped into LAN #2. Two backplane designs are used in hub or switch devices to allow LAN configuration: *multibus backplanes* or *TDM (time division multiplexing)* backplanes. With the multibus design, each bus represents a LAN and ports are linked to a specific bus. In the TDM design, specific time slots on a single bus are owned by a specific LAN. Because LANs are configured within the hub or switch itself, it is not possible with some hubs or switches to bridge a LAN configured in one device with a LAN configured in another device.

**MAC-BASED VLANS** The MAC address is the hardwired address built into network interface cards. The network administrator essentially creates a table that defines which MAC addresses belong with what VLAN. Compared to port configuration methods, this method provides true VLAN capabilities because membership in a VLAN is not directly tied to a specific port. Configuration is done in software and, in some cases, a computer can belong to two or more VLANs. In addition, if a computer is moved to another location, it still belongs to the same VLAN because its MAC address moves with it.

**LAYER 3 VLANS** This type of VLAN uses layer 3 information to build VLANs based on internetwork protocol addresses. For example, in Figure V-5, all the computers in the Marketing VLAN might have IP address 100.200.1.x (where x is a specific number for each workstation) while computers in the Research VLAN have the IP address 100.200.2.x. A layer 3 switch is capable of looking at the network address in a frame and forwarding the frame based on information in a table that matches the network address with membership in a particular VLAN. However, looking at the layer 3 address can cause performance problems. Like the MAC-based VLANs, moves are easy because the port of the workstation does not determine VLAN membership. The layer 3 approach can be extended to include more routing functionality right in the switch, and that is what many vendors have done with their high-end switches. You can refer to "Switched Networks" to learn about the architectural details of these high-end switches.

**IP MULTICAST VLANS**    In this approach, a VLAN is defined by membership in an IP multicast group. IP multicasting is a way for one workstation to transmit to some but not all workstations on a network. The workstations that receive the transmissions are known as the multicast group. Multicasting is one-to-many communication supported by Internet standards. Multicasting is set up by using IP class D addresses. Routers must be multicast enabled to use this feature. Multicasting is a two-way process. Routers set up multicasting among themselves, but a router only does multicasting if some host on its attached network has requested to be a member of a multicast group. Routers without any need to be part of a particular multicast do not get involved, in order to avoid unnecessary traffic. Multicasting is dynamic in that workstations can join and drop out of a multicast group at any time. Using this feature to create VLANs is useful and flexible. Multicasting also allows the VLAN to span WAN-based routers. The IEEE 802.1p standard called "Standard for Traffic Class and Dynamic Multicast Filtering Services in Bridged Local Area Networks" defines building VLANs with multicast protocols.

**RULES-BASED VLANS**    Some vendors have implemented so-called rules-based VLAN configuration techniques, which allows administrators to create VLANs based on information contained in packets that switches look at and evaluate. This method involves creating rules in software that are followed to determine VLAN membership. While this technique adds a lot of flexibility, setup and maintenance can be complex. For example, a VLAN might be described with these rules:

> All stations with subnet address 200.100.10.$x$
> > excluding these IP addresses: 200.100.10.5, 200.100.10.6
> > excluding these MAC addresses: 06-1A-0A-05-3C-02-04

*NOTE:   The IEEE 802.1q is a VLAN specification that allows switches to exchange information among themselves about VLANs. It will help vendors build interoperable VLAN-enabled switches. The standard defines how frames can be tagged to identify which VLAN they belong to. Switches use this information to forward frames.*

## Routing and VLANs

Routing is an essential component in a VLAN environment. They provide a way for each VLAN to maintain its autonomy and broadcast nature while forwarding packets between VLANs when necessary. Routing allows administrators to put security policies in place as well, such as packet-filtering techniques as discussed under "Firewall." An optimally designed network will have VLANs configured to reduce as much inter-VLAN routing as possible.

VLAN configurations that use layer 2 exclusively (port configuration and MAC-based VLANs) require that at least one port in each VLAN be set aside to provide a VLAN-to-router connection. Using stand-alone routers is often not acceptable in new switched environments due to the inherent delay caused by their store-and-forward operation.

VLANs built on switched networks have a lot more flexibility. In particular, switches often have the intelligence to switch packets at high speed between VLANs once a path has been defined by a router or a special route server device that relays routing information to switches. In some cases, the switch itself checks a local routing table to determine what to do with a packet. This routing table may be constructed by some external router or a route server.

A number of interesting routing techniques have been developed in the ATM environment. A more complete discussion is found under "IP over ATM" and "IP Switching." The ATM Forum has developed MPOA (Multiprotocol over ATM), which moves routing to a special server called the *route server*. Frames in the same VLAN are switched at layer 2. To transmit frames to other VLANs, a routing path is obtained from a *route server*, which first creates a logical path through the network. The path is converted to a virtual circuit on which data is transmitted. Refer to "MPOA (Multiprotocol over ATM)" for more information.

The IEEE is working to simplify VLAN configuration and management with the 802.1q standard, which specifies a way to define and set up VLANs in frame-based networks such as Ethernet and token ring. The standard expands the frame format by adding fields that associate frames with a specific VLAN. The standard is basically a tagging scheme.

**RELATED ENTRIES**    ATM (Asynchronous Transfer Mode); Backbone Networks; Bridges and Bridging; Ethernet; Gigabit Ethernet; Internetworking; IP over ATM; IP Switching; ISA (Integrated Services Architecture); LANE (LAN Emulation); Network Design and Construction; QoS (Quality of Service); *and* Routing Protocols and Algorithms

**INFORMATION ON THE INTERNET**

| | |
|---|---|
| Xylan Corp.'s white papers on switching | http://www.xylan.com/whitepaper |
| Xylan Corp.'s The Switching Book | http://www.xylan.com/sb |
| 3Com papers (choose "Switching and Virtual LAN" option) | http://www.3com.com/technology |
| Bay Networks' Online Library | http://support.baynetworks.com/Library |
| The ATM Forum | http://www.atmforum.com |

| The ATM Forum's MPOA, VLANS and Distributed ROUTER paper | http://www.atmforum.com/atmforum/library/53bytes/backissues/v4-3/article-04.html |
| Cisco Systems' VLAN Roadmap site | http://www.cisco.com/warp/public/538/7.html |
| Newbridge Networks (extensive information on ATM and MPOA) | http://www.vivid.newbridge.com |
| Gigabit Ethernet Alliance | http://www.gigabit-ethernet.org |
| Yahoo!'s VLAN links page | http://www.yahoo.com/Computers_and_Internet/Communications_and_Networking/LANs/Virtual_LAN__VLAN |

## VMS (Virtual Memory System)

*See* OpenVMS.

## Voice/Data Networks

A voice/data network is a network that supports both voice and data and that does away with the need to maintain a separate telephone wiring system. As of this writing, most network managers are interested in the concept but are in a wait-and-see mode. Certainly, a complete conversion to a single voice/data network is a long way off for many organizations. Still, making telephone calls over the Internet has become quite popular as more and more computers sport multimedia features that can convert voice into compressed digital data. Faxing is also a viable option. Managers may have good reasons to support voice over data networks, if only for a few special users. For example, the Internet eliminates long-distance charges. If some employees make recurring calls to employees at foreign offices, it may be worthwhile to support those users with a new breed of voice over IP products. Refer to "VoIP (Voice over IP)" for additional information.

The terms *CTI (computer-telephony integration)* and *IVD (integrated voice and data)* are used to describe the consolidation of voice and data. The difference between CTI and IVD is that IVD is seen as a more sophisticated approach, a single-wire solution for carrying voice and data, whereas CTI currently suggests schemes such as Novell's TSAPI (Telephony Services API) and Microsoft's TAPI (Telephony API) where computers are used to control telephony devices that are connected to plain old analog telephone lines. Note that telephony generally refers to a mix of services such as voice messaging, conferencing, and advanced call routing, not just voice telephone calls. See "CTI (Computer-Telephony Integration)" and "IVD (Integrated Voice and Data)" for more information.

Note that while CTI has been very successful and is popular among desktop users, IVD is a technology with a hazy future. No one is quite sure how successful it will be. Many things are required for its success, including the upgrade of existing networks to high-speed networks that can support voice calls and maintain quality. Still, MICOM has created compression algorithms that reduce the digital data requirements of a voice call from 64 Kbits/sec to as little as 8 Kbits/sec (or 6 Kbits/sec if silence reduction circuitry is used).

In order for networks to support large numbers of voice calls, networks with high data rates are required. ATM and Gigabit Ethernet can fulfill that role. In addition, schemes for prioritizing traffic, such as 3Com's PACE (priority access control enabled), are also helpful. With prioritization, traffic from specific users (the CEO) or specific systems (a videoconferencing system) is assigned a high level of priority, while other traffic, such as e-mail, is assigned a low priority. For more information on PACE, see "PACE (Priority Access Control Enabled)."

Still, prioritization doesn't guarantee that enough bandwidth will be reserved to ensure high quality. It just delivers some traffic ahead of other traffic. ATM networks provide QoS (Quality of Service), which goes a lot further in guaranteeing high-quality delivery of voice calls (and real-time video). ATM's fixed-size cells allow predictable delivery of network traffic so that bandwidth can be reserved in advance and high-priority users (such as the CEO) can be guaranteed the bandwidth they need, while remaining bandwidth is allocated to other users on an "as available" basis. See "Prioritization of Network Traffic" and "QoS (Quality of Service)" for more information.

While ATM was built from the ground up to provide QoS, the IETF (Internet Engineering Task Force) is working to develop protocols that can provide the same QoS features over IP networks and the Internet. RSVP (Resource Reservation Protocol) is a signaling protocol that attempts to reserve bandwidth from router to router in an RSVP-enabled network. See "RSVP (Resource Reservation Protocol)" for more information.

Some other interesting work has been done by the IEEE (Institute of Electrical and Electronic Engineers) 802.1p Task Force, which provides a way for users to set priority bits in frames that specify different classes of traffic. This is discussed under "Prioritization of Network Traffic." Iso-Ethernet (isochronous Ethernet) is an IEEE standard that supports voice and video over data networks, but it has not gained much support due to its low data rate. It basically combines Ethernet and ISDN (Integrated Services Digital Network) on the same cable. Refer to "Iso-Ethernet" for more information.

One last thing worth discussing is how applications can take advantage of prioritization and QoS if it is available. A telephony application must be able to signal to the network that it needs prioritization. The new WinSock 2.0 has hooks that allow applications to do just that. Refer to "WinSock" for more information.

**RELATED ENTRIES**    ATM (Asynchronous Transfer Mode); Collaborative Computing; CTI (Computer-Telephony Integration); Ethernet; Fast Ethernet; Gigabit Ethernet; Iso-Ethernet; IVD (Integrated Voice and Data); Multimedia; PACE (Priority Access Control Enabled); Prioritization of Network Traffic; QoS (Quality of Service); RSVP (Resource Reservation Protocol); TAPI (Telephony API); Videoconferencing and

Desktop Video; Voice over ATM; Voice over the Internet; VoIP (Voice over IP); *and* WinSock

**INFORMATION ON THE INTERNET**

For Web site listings, refer to the appropriate related entry listed above.

# Voice Mail

Voice mail has found its way into network communication technologies as users seek to unify all types of messaging, including e-mail and fax, in one place. This will involve CTI (computer-telephony integration) technologies and standards for packaging and transmitting voice messages for delivery across computer networks.

The EMA (Electronic Messaging Association) is working on a specification called *VPIM (Voice Profile for Internet Mail)* that will define how voice-mail systems can link over IP networks and the Internet. VPIM defines how SMTP (Simple Mail Transfer Protocol) can become a common protocol for transporting messages between different voice-mail systems. It will also help voice messaging products from different vendors exchange messages with one another. (VPIM was still on its way to becoming an IETF standard at the time of this writing.)

The basic concept is simple: someone records a voice-mail message in the normal way and enters the phone number or other information that identifies the recipient. The voice-mail system identifies the recipient's Internet e-mail address from the phone number or other information and creates a digital message that can be delivered across the Internet. The voice-mail message is attached to the Internet e-mail message and forwarded to the recipient.

Voice-mail messages are attached to e-mail messages like any other MIME (Multipurpose Internet Mail Extension) attachment. This allows the recipient to listen to the message using a phone or on his or her own computer, assuming software and hardware exist for interpreting the format, which is relatively simple. Computer-telephony products for handling such messages are already available. Most products that work on end-user systems convert voice messages to files that can be played like any other digitized sound file. Alternatively, the voice-mail message may be routed to a voice-mail system, where the recipient could retrieve the message like any other voice-mail message.

The EMA is involved in the integration of voice messaging and computer telephony. EMA's Web site, listed below under "Information on the Internet," has further information. Lucent and Octel (recently acquired by Lucent) are major providers of voice-mail systems. Octel's Unified Messenger lets users retrieve both voice and e-mail messages from a unified mailbox that is accessible from either a telephone or personal computer. The product also does text-to-speech conversions, so e-mail messages can be listened to over the phone.

**RELATED ENTRIES**   CTI (Computer-Telephony Integration); Electronic Mail; Multimedia; Voice/Data Networks; *and* Voice over the Internet

| | |
|---|---|
| Electronic Messaging Association VPIM workgroup | http://www.ema.org/vpimdir |
| MacroVoice Corporation | http://www.macrovoice.com |
| Lucent Technologies' Intuity messaging platform | http://www.lucent.com |
| Octel Communications' Universal Messenger | http://www.octel.com |
| Centigram Communication | http://www.centigram.com |

# Voice over ATM

The goal of many network managers is to consolidate both voice and data traffic on a single network. ATM (Asynchronous Transfer Mode) is the best networking technology to provide this because it was designed from the ground up to provide the QoS (Quality of Service) features that are necessary to deliver real-time voice (and video) traffic over data networks.

The ATM Forum is working to develop voice over ATM standards so that organizations can consolidate networks for voice, data, video, and multimedia. It sees three potential users of voice over ATM solutions: enterprise or large business users, carriers offering ATM-based virtual private voice and data networks and services, and carriers offering traditional voice and telephony services (voice messaging, conferencing, and advanced call routing). Carriers and service providers see ATM as an underlying technology for voice trunking and switching.

**RELATED ENTRIES**    ATM (Asynchronous Transfer Mode); CTI (Computer-Telephony Integration); Multimedia; Prioritization of Network Traffic; QoS (Quality of Service); Videoconferencing and Desktop Video; Voice/Data Networks; *and* VoIP (Voice over IP)

**INFORMATION ON THE INTERNET**

| | |
|---|---|
| The ATM Forum (search for "Voice over ATM") | http://www.atmforum.com |

# Voice over Frame Relay

Voice over frame relay is all about transporting voice over frame relay networks. The idea is to use frame-relay networks for the equivalent of phone calls. That allows companies to build single private networks over public packet-switched networks to transport both voice and data. The current method of running voice over frame relay requires proprietary time division multiplexors that are not always interoperable with other vendors' devices.

The Frame Relay Forum is working on the Voice over Frame Relay Implementation Agreement that defines how to transport compressed voice data over a frame relay network. The standard assumes that voice has been subjected to extensive compression and uses less than 8 Kbits/sec of bandwidth (compared to 64 Kbits/sec for uncompressed digitized voice).

**RELATED ENTRIES**    Communication Services; Data Communication Concepts; Frame Relay; Virtual Circuit; Voice/Data Networks; *and* WAN (Wide Area Network)

**INFORMATION ON THE INTERNET**

| | |
|---|---|
| Frame Relay Forum | http://www.frforum.com |
| Motorola's Frame Relay Resources site (very extensive) | http://www.mot.com/MIMS/ISG/tech/ frame-relay/resources.html |
| High Bandwidth Frame Relay page | http://www.specialty.com/hiband/ frame_index.html |

# Voice over the Internet

Despite a number of technological issues still to be worked out, the potential of real-time voice transmission over the Internet is being widely recognized. Advanced compression techniques have reduced voice data transfer rates from 64 Kbits/sec to as little as 6 Kbits/sec. *Voice over the Internet*, or *VON*, allows users to call worldwide for the cost of a local call. A user's IP address basically becomes a phone number. Additionally, computer-based phone systems can be linked to servers that run a variety of interesting telephony applications, including PBX services and voice messaging. Internet telephony is breaking down the distinctions between telecommunications services and the Internet, sparking re-evaluations of the entire industry from technical, economic, and regulatory points of view. The government is taking a hands-off attitude regarding growth of the Internet telephony industry. At the 1997 Voice on the Net conference in Boston, a Federal Communications attorney said the FCC wants to encourage growth of Internet telephony and had no plans to regulate it soon.

The development of standards for Internet telephony is giving further impetus to industry growth. The International Telecommunication Union's H.323 protocol allows Internet telephone apparatus from different vendors to communicate on WANs, LANs, and the Internet. Though H.323 doesn't guarantee that different vendors' products will communicate, more vendors are aiming for interoperability, and within a year or two, interoperability should be common. Refer to "Videoconferencing and Desktop Video" for more information about these standards.

To send and receive voice over the Internet, one needs a PC equipped with at least 16MB of memory, a sound card, speakers, a microphone, and software—which is currently a standard multimedia PC configuration. And new technologies starting to appear in the marketplace will simplify VON and enhance its performance on PCs. Windows users can take advantage of USB (Universal Serial Bus), a peripheral bus standard enabling a 12-Mbit/sec data transfer rate. USB devices, including computer-telephony devices, will automatically configure when they are attached to the system. Intel and Microsoft designed USB with telephony devices in mind. Refer to "USB (Universal Serial Bus)" for more information.

**V**

Other IP technologies are being introduced to minimize voice traffic's drain on network resources. MICOM's V/IP (Voice over IP) phone/fax IP gateway uses G.729 voice compression technology to compress a call to 8 Kbits/sec. Silence suppression allows the gateway to reduce the call to about 6 Kbits/sec. Information on V/IP can be found at the MICOM site given later.

Also being introduced are Internet telephony gateways that link PBXs to the Web. Pacific Telephony offers an interesting design tutorial entitled "How To Build an Internet PBX" at its Web site (refer to http://www.phonezone.com/ip-phone.htm). Lucent Technologies, MICOM Communications, VocalTec Communications, and other manufacturers are already scaling up to systems that can support thousands of concurrent users. For additional information, see "PBX (Private Branch Exchange)."

The quality of a connection using Internet telephony depends largely on two elements: latency and distortion. *Latency* refers to the gap from when the words are spoken to when the listener can hear the words. While users can adjust to this latency period, distortion is just plain annoying. *Distortion* results when packets containing the speaker's words are lost and the Internet telephony software fills in the gaps. The more packets lost, the greater the distortion. And with real-time voice data, it doesn't do any good to retransmit a packet because the listener will have already heard the part of the speech where the data belongs.

While phone calls on the Internet rarely achieve the level of quality of circuit-switched calls, the quality is improving; the connection is often as good as or better than cellular, which is prone to packet errors and distortion due to its wireless nature. The market has found that many customers will tolerate a small decrease in the quality of the call for the significantly reduced cost of making a call, particularly an international call, where savings can run to 50 percent or more. Savings on fax calls may be even greater. In fact, transmitting fax over the Internet is very practical because real-time delivery is not required. Missing and corrupted packets can be retransmitted.

Dedicated resources improve VON quality. The IETF (Internet Engineering Task Force) is looking at RSVP (Resource Reservation Protocol) to guarantee delivery of time-sensitive traffic and provide high-quality service. See "RSVP (Resource Reservation Protocol)" for more information.

Such organizations as the ECTF (Enterprise Computer Telephony Forum) and the ITC (Internet Telephony-interoperability Consortium) are helping to create a competitive market for standards-based computer-telephony services. Also, a number of IETF Working Groups are developing standards for delivering multimedia (including voice) over the Internet. You can access these working groups by going to the IETF Working Groups Web site (http://www.ietf.org/html.charters/wg-dir.html). Groups of interest at the site include "Integrated Services (intserv)," "Multiparty Multimedia Session Control (mmusic)," and "Audio/Video Transport (avt)."

**RELATED ENTRIES**    Collaborative Computing; CTI (Computer-Telephony Integration); IVD (Integrated Voice and Data); Multimedia; Prioritization of Network Traffic; QoS (Quality of Service); RSVP (Resource Reservation Protocol); TAPI

(Telephony API); USB (Universal Serial Bus); Videoconferencing and Desktop Video; Voice/Data Networks; *and* VoIP (Voice over IP)

**INFORMATION ON THE INTERNET**

| | |
|---|---|
| Enterprise Computer Telephony Forum | http://www.ectf.org |
| IETF Working Groups | http://www.ietf.org/html.charters/ wg-dir.html |
| IMTC (International Multimedia Teleconferencing Consortium) | http://www.imtc.org |
| International Teleconferencing Association | http://www.itca.org |
| The Internet Telephony Consortium | http://itel.mit.edu |
| VON (Voice over the Internet) Coalition | http://www.von.org |
| The Phone Zone (a wealth of information!) | http://www.phonezone.com |
| Internet Telephony Magazine | http://www.internettelephony.com |
| Telegate's A gateway to virtually free long-distance calling paper | http://www.telecom.array.ca |
| Ken Persson's telephony page (very complete) | http://www.pi.se/ken/linkcti.html |
| Prof. Jeffrey MacKie-Mason's telecommunication links (in particular, see the "Internet Telephony" section) | http://www.spp.umich.edu/telecom |
| Andrew Sears's Telephony resource list (very complete) | http://rpcp.mit.edu/~itel/resource.html |
| Goodman's Book Marks on Internet Telephony | http://www.wp.com/goodmans/ipt.html |
| Lucent Technologies, Inc. | http://www.lucent.com |
| MICOM Communications Corp. | http://www.micom.com |
| Virtual Voice Internet Telephony | http://www.virtual-voice.com/index.html |
| VocalTec Communications, Ltd. | http://www.vocaltec.com |
| Yahoo!'s Computer Telephony links page | http://www.yahoo.com/Business_and _Economy/Companies/Computers/ Networking/Computer_Telephony |

# VoIP (Voice over IP)

VoIP is the name of a group of Internet telephony vendors that is defining the details for delivering real-time voice communication over the Internet and other IP networks. The group is part of the IMTC (International Multimedia Teleconferencing Consortium). The IMTC's Web site is at http://www.imtc.org.

In 1996, the VoIP Forum recommended that members standardize on the ITU's G.723.1 audio codec, thus providing a path toward interoperable Internet telephony equipment from multiple vendors. The G.723.1 codec is also included in the ITU's H.323 standard, an umbrella standard that establishes how audio, video, and data communications take place on IP networks.

While these standards will help to ensure that systems will communicate with one another, they don't provide any quality of service guarantees. Because latency and congestion problems can be more easily dealt with on intranets, intranet users are likely to be the first to establish VoIP networks. The second generation of VoIP gateway products will appear in 1998. Many second-generation VoIP products will include bandwidth reservation for voice sessions, though the use of the RSVP (Resource Reservation Protocol) will also require infrastructure upgrades.

**RELATED ENTRY**    Voice over the Internet

## Volume and Partition Management

Volumes are collections of directories, subdirectories, and files. The term "volumes" is primarily used in the NetWare environment, but is applied to other environments as well. This section will define volumes in NetWare.

The first default volume on a NetWare server is called SYS and is automatically created in the free space of the first disk drive. It exists in what is called *logical partition #1*, which assumes that a small DOS partition used for startup is *logical partition #0*. While a server can have one large volume called SYS, additional volumes can be created as necessary with a name of choice. Different volumes are usually created to store different types of files.

Volumes can range in size from small to large. The illustration on the top in Figure V-6 shows how multiple volumes can fit on a single disk. The illustration on the bottom shows how a volume can span multiple disks.

With volume spanning, the size of a volume is not limited by the storage capabilities of a disk drive. Volumes can span multiple drives and provide many megabytes of storage. This is essential for some database files.

In network operating systems such as Novell NetWare, volumes are the primary unit of storage. Spanning a volume over several disks provides some performance enhancements, and it can be done with one controller and multiple drives or with several controllers and multiple drives. Volumes can be increased in size by simply adding another drive and making part of that drive available as a volume attachment. It is not necessary to reformat the original volume because NetWare simply adds the new volume attachment to it.

Although spanning can improve performance, it can also be risky unless precautions are taken. If one drive in a spanned volume fails, NetWare cannot use the entire volume. Fault-tolerance features such as disk mirroring and duplexing should be used in this configuration.

**RELATED ENTRIES**    Storage Systems; Volume and Partition Management

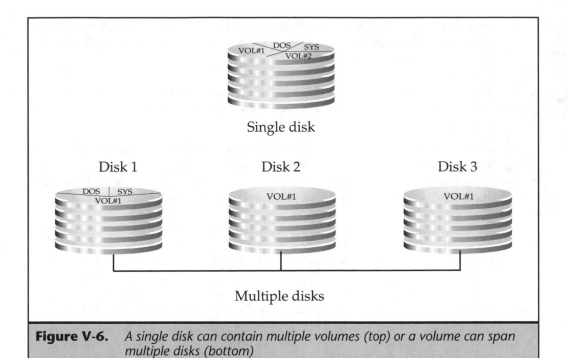

**Figure V-6.** *A single disk can contain multiple volumes (top) or a volume can span multiple disks (bottom)*

# VPN (Virtual Private Network)

The industry is currently confused about what a VPN is, but as you will see, the confusion has more to do with what to call VPNs as they *evolve* into new networking technologies. Traditionally, a VPN has been defined as a private network for voice and data built with carrier services. More recently, however, VPN has come to describe private, encrypted tunnels through the Internet for transporting both voice and data between an organization's different sites. The different definitions of a VPN are as follows:

- **Voice VPN** In this scheme, a single carrier handles all your voice call switching. The "virtual" in VPN implies that the carrier creates a virtual voice-switching network for you within its switching equipment. See the next heading, "Traditional Carrier-Based Voice VPN," in this topic for more details.

- **Carrier-based voice/data VPN** Packet-, frame-, and cell-switching networks carry information in discrete bundles (herein called *packets* for simplicity) that are routed through a mesh network of switches to a destination. Many users share the network. Carriers program virtual circuits into the network that simulate dedicated connections between a company's sites. A web of these virtual circuits form a virtual private network over the carrier's packet-switched network. For more details, see the heading "Carrier-Based Voice/Data VPN" in this topic.

- **Internet VPN** An Internet VPN is similar to the VPN just described, except that the IP-based Internet is the underlying network. See the heading "Internet VPN" in this section for more details.

> *NOTE: A VPN should be contrasted with a* private network, *which is built by linking corporate sites with dedicated leased lines. See "Private Network" for more details.*

While carrier-based VPNs can provide service guarantees with virtual circuits, setting up and using Internet VPNs is a lot easier and cheaper although getting service and bandwidth guarantees is a problem. But those guarantees may not be an issue. An important aspect of Internet VPNs is that they can be used to supplement carrier-based VPNs or even leased lines and to carry low-priority traffic.

*Data Communication Magazine* (http://www.datacomm.com) created a hypothetical network that fully linked sites in Los Angeles, Houston, and Boston to come up with the numbers shown in Table V-1. See the article "Secure VPNs, Lock the Data, Unlock the Savings" by Andrew Cray (5-21-97, p. 49) available at the magazine's Web site.

Unlike private networks or carrier-based VPNs, which have traditionally connected a company's different sites, Internet VPNs can include everyone in the company, including mobile users and home workers. Users anywhere simply dial in to a local Internet service provider, rather than in to the corporate network, using 800 numbers, modem pools, and remote access servers. In addition, users and sites can connect using a variety of connections methods, including 28.8-Kbit/sec modem dial-up lines or high-speed dedicated leased lines into the Internet. An Internet VPN can replace all the on-site equipment associated with remote access services, essentially moving all that functionality to an ISP.

## Traditional Carrier-Based Voice VPN

As mentioned, a voice VPN is a carrier offering in which voice-switching services for an organization are performed by a service provider such as AT&T or MCI.

|  | **Leased Lines** | **Frame Relay VPN** | **Internet VPN** |
|---|---|---|---|
| Annual charges | $133,272 | $89,998 | $38,400 |
| Installation | $2,700 | $5,760 | N/A |
| Four VPN encrypting devices | N/A | $16,000 | $16,000 |
| Total first year cost | $135,972 | $111,758 | $54,400 |

**Table V-1.** *Comparison of leased line and VPN rates (source: Data Communication Magazine)*

Long-distance leased lines for voice between company sites are replaced with short lines into a carrier's switching system.

The best example is AT&T's SDN (Software-Defined Network), which is discussed here, but readers are encouraged to check offerings from other providers, such as MCI's Vnet (http://www.mci.com). Refer to the list of providers under the "Telecommunications Companies" heading in Appendix A.

SDN allows customers to use portions of AT&T's switched network in concert with their dedicated private line networks to get the wide area network access they need. The service is a good choice for businesses that have many geographically dispersed offices. An optional component called SDDN (Software-Defined Data Network) allows users to negotiate additional bandwidth for data transmissions (bandwidth on demand) within AT&T's switched network.

The SDN service can provide bandwidth on demand at rates of 64 Kbits/sec, 384 Kbits/sec, and 1.5 Kbits/sec. It is compatible with existing private networks and PBXs and is often used to provide backups for dedicated private lines in the event of disasters. Call costs are based on duration and distance, with discounts available based on time of day, day of week, and various other options. The service is available in most of the United States and for international calling.

SDN is quite extensive and readers are encouraged to visit AT&T's Web site (http://www.att.com) for additional information.

## Carrier-Based Voice/Data VPN

*V*

Virtual circuits can simulate the qualities of leased lines while providing more flexibility and cost savings. A virtual circuit is created within a packet (X.25), frame (frame relay), or cell-switching (ATM) network. It follows a path that is programmed through the switches and relays of the switching network. Frame relay is now the most common switching service, although ATM is growing.

There are PVCs (permanent virtual circuits) and SVCs (switched virtual circuits). A PVC is a preprogrammed circuit between two defined points, while an SVC is a circuit that can be set up on the fly between any other points in the network. PVCs are most common, while SVCs are not even offered by some carriers.

Contracts with service providers are negotiated for PVCs and/or SVCs, depending on needs. Both are defined only within the carrier's packet-switched network. You still need a data pipe into the network from each of your offices, as shown in Figure V-7. These can be dial-up or dedicated lines with a data capacity to meet the needs of the site.

There are many advantages to using a carrier-based VPN. One is the ability to handle surges in data traffic. Since the network is shared, some users may not be using the bandwidth they have been allocated. This bandwidth can be used by others, if necessary, at an extra charge. In contrast, a dedicated circuit such as a T1 line has a fixed capacity (1.544 Mbits/sec). If your traffic needs are under that rate, you are paying for unused bandwidth. If they go over, you may lose packets.

When you negotiate a virtual circuit from a carrier, you specify a CIR (committed information rate), which is basically the average data rate requirement for the virtual

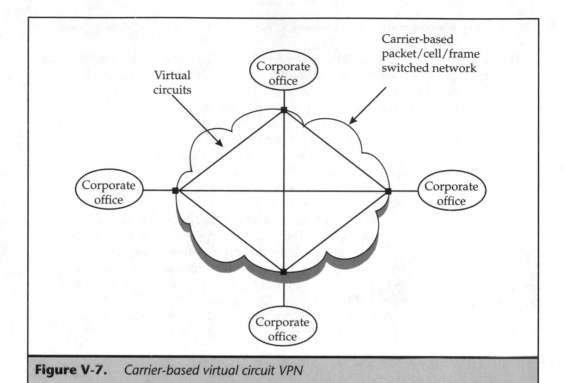

**Figure V-7.** *Carrier-based virtual circuit VPN*

circuit. The carrier then attempts to guarantee that service level by managing the network infrastructure. If the carrier cannot meet the guarantees, it may offer various levels of free service.

To handle surges in traffic, you negotiate a burst rate, which is what you pay for traffic over the CIR. This formula provides great flexibility and cost savings because most of the time you are only paying for what you use, but you can go over if necessary. Note that bursts can only occur if the network has unused bandwidth. The advantage of sharing the network with others is that some users might be underusing their share. The disadvantage is that the network may become overloaded.

Even though the packet-switched network has a lot of flexibility, the leased line into that network from your site can be a choke point. You must install a line that meets the requirements of the site being connected.

## Internet VPN

An Internet VPN can provide a secure way to move packets across the Internet with the right equipment. There are two methods for doing this:

- **Transport mode**   Describes the techniques of encrypting only the payload portion of an IP packet for transport across the Internet. The header information is left intact and readable so that routers can forward the packet as it traverses the Internet. This is an IP-only technique.

- **Tunnel mode**   With this technique, IP, IPX, SNA, and other packets are encrypted, then encapsulated into new IP packets for transport across the Internet. This technique has the advantage of hiding the source and destination addresses of the original packet and improves security.

In either case, Internet VPNs trade off the guaranteed capacity and predictability available on frame relay or ATM virtual circuits for the low cost of creating VPNs over the Internet. In addition, they are much cheaper than leased lines, as outlined earlier in Table V-1.

While inexpensive, extending a private network across the public Internet has security and privacy implications. However, vendors of Internet VPN products have gone to great lengths to ensure security and privacy. Encryption provides security, but authentication is also required to ensure that people or devices at the other end of the link are authentic and authorized to use the link.

There are two types of connections in the Internet VPN scenario, as pictured in Figure V-8 and discussed here:

- **Site-to-site connections**   A connection that tunnels large amounts of traffic between two network sites

- **Virtual dial-up services**   A tunnel for an individual user into a corporate site

Both schemes take advantage of local connections to an ISP and the wide area connections provided by the Internet. Each is discussed further in the following sections.

## Site-to-Site Connections
A site-to-site connection is the most common way to set up an Internet VPN between two network sites. Two encrypting routers are required, and an *SA (security association)* is set up between them. An SA is a symmetrical (single key) connection in which the same security techniques (encryption, decryption, and authentication) are used by the transmitter and receiver. In the simplest setup, an administrator creates two separate private keys to handle encryption and decryption in each direction. One key is used to encrypt data as it leaves one router and decrypt it as it arrives at the destination. The other key is used to encrypt and decrypt data in the reverse direction. The administrator typically programs the keys into the devices and personally delivers them to the intended sites to avoid compromise.

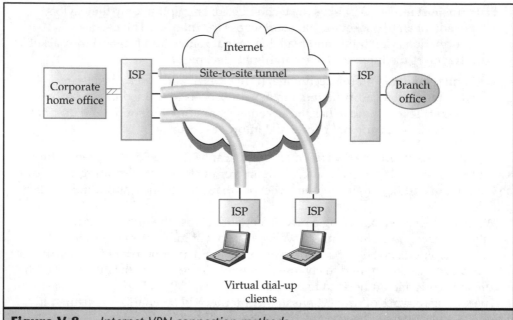

**Figure V-8.** *Internet VPN connection methods*

Once the routers are set up and the link is established into the Internet, all data traffic across the link is encrypted to hide it from anyone that might manage to tap the line (most likely near the ISP facility).

Several initiatives and standards are under development for this type of connection. The IETF is working on IPSec (IP Security), which strives to provide interoperability among different vendors' tunneling products. RSA Data Security helped establish the S/WAN initiative in 1995 to provide an industry forum for interoperability and standardized implementation of IPSec. These protocols are designed to operate in layer 3 (the network layer) of the protocol stack and encrypt all data that crosses the link. See "IPSec (IP Security)" and "S/WAN (Secure WAN)."

## Virtual Dial-up Services

Virtual dial-up protocols are designed to support remote user access into the corporate network with what might be called *personal tunnels*. If you consider Internet VPNs to be the highways that connect an organization's branch offices with tunnels, then personal tunnels are like the side roads that connect individual users into the Internet VPN.

Virtual dial-up protocols help organizations better manage their remote access capabilities and reduce connect charges by taking advantage of the Internet. Instead of dialing in to a corporate remote access server, users dial in to a local ISP or carrier access point. A tunnel is then created between the remote client and the corporate site through the ISP and across the Internet. These protocols are discussed further under "Virtual Dial-up Services."

**RELATED ENTRIES**    ATM (Asynchronous Transfer Mode); Firewall; Frame Relay; IPSec (IP Security); PPP (Point-to-Point Protocol); PPTP (Point-to-Point Tunneling Protocol); Private Network; Routers; Security; S/WAN (Secure WAN); Telecommunications and Telephone Systems; Tunnels; Virtual Dial-up Services; *and* WAN (Wide Area Network)

**INFORMATION ON THE INTERNET**

| | |
|---|---|
| MAS NET's VPN paper | http://www.masnet.net/internet/issues/vpn.html |
| Goodman's Telecom Bookmarks (very complete) | http://www.wp.com/goodmans |
| Yahoo!'s Telecommunication links page | http://www.yahoo.com/Science/Engineering/Electrical_Engineering/Telecommunications |
| ITU's Telecom Links | http://www.itu.int/Sites/web-sites.html |
| Prof. Jeffrey MacKie-Mason's telecommunication links | http://www.spp.umich.edu/telecom/technical-info.html |
| Pacific Telephony Design's PhoneZone | http://www.phonezone.com |
| IETF IPSec charter | http://www.ietf.cnri.reston.va.us/html.charters/ipsec-charter.html |

| | |
|---|---|
| IETF Point-to-Point Protocol Extensions (pppext) charter | http://www.ietf.org/html.charters/pppext-charter.html |
| AT&T Corporation | http://www.att.com |
| Aventail Corporation | http://www.aventail.com/simpresnet/sld022.htm |
| Cylink Corporation | http://www.cylink.com |
| Data Fellows, Inc. | http://www.datafellows.com |
| DEC's Internet Tunnel Products site | http://www.digital.com/info/internet/whitepapers/tunnelprod_abstract.html |
| IntraShield Corporation | http://www.intrashield.com |
| Signal 9 Solutions, Inc. | http://www.signal9.com |
| Timestep Corporation | http://www.timestep.com |
| VPNet, Inc. | http://www.vpnet.com |

## VRML (Virtual Reality Modeling Language)

VRML provides an interface that delivers virtual graphical three-dimensional worlds to users of Web browsers without consuming an exorbitant amount of bandwidth. VRML is based on an ASCII file format and three-dimensional modeling environments originally developed at Silicon Graphics. The key to VRML is that the description of objects in the three-dimensional world (not the actual graphics) are transmitted to the user. This reduces the bandwidth requirements and makes virtual reality practical on the Web. Another key feature is *scaling*, which allows the user to move toward an object and watch that object grow in size. VRML provides information that describes three-dimensional objects that can be rotated and viewed from varying distances.

Although VRML is a coding language, you won't need to do much coding to create virtual worlds. Instead, you create virtual worlds using tools that are essentially three-dimensional painting and modeling packages. VRML files have the extension .wrl (world) and their own MIME type.

**RELATED ENTRY**    Web Technologies and Concepts

**INFORMATION ON THE INTERNET**

| | |
|---|---|
| VRML Repository | http://www.sdsc.edu/vrml |

## VSAT (Very Small Aperture Terminal)

*See* Satellite Communication Systems.

## W3C (World Wide Web Consortium)

The W3C is an international industry consortium that was founded in 1994 to develop common protocols for the evolution of the World Wide Web. The W3C works with the global community to produce specifications and references that are vendor neutral and freely available throughout the world.

The consortium is led by Tim Berners-Lee, original creator of the World Wide Web technologies. Initially, the W3C was established in collaboration with CERN, where the Web originated, with support from DARPA (Defense Advanced Research Projects Agency) and the European Commission. The consortium is jointly hosted by the MIT/LCS (Massachusetts Institute of Technology Laboratory for Computer Science) in the United States; INRIA (Institut National de Recherche en Informatique et en Automatique) in Europe; and the Keio University Shonan Fujisawa campus in Asia.

The W3C Web site has a wealth of information about the Internet and emerging protocols and standards. You will find information related to the history of the Web, user interface specifications such as HTML (Hypertext Markup Language) and HTML extensions, electronic commerce, security and privacy issues, and Web architecture standards such as HTTP (Hypertext Transfer Protocol) and object technologies. The W3C Web site is at http://www.w3.org.

## WAN (Wide Area Network)

The traditional enterprise network has been defined with a hierarchy of network topologies. Internal networks are constructed with LANs (local area networks), while local and regional networks are constructed with campus backbones and MANs (metropolitan area networks). WANs link geographically dispersed offices in other cities or around the globe. Just about any long-distance communication medium can serve as a WAN link, including switched and permanent telephone circuits, terrestrial radio systems, and satellite systems.

However, WANs are notorious for their high cost and slow data rates, especially if long-distance leased lines are required. The slow data rate is due to the nature of the lines that must be used to create WANs and the fact that costs can get exorbitant as data rates increase. A T1 leased line (1.544 Mbits/sec) between two remote offices may cost many thousands of dollars per month, depending on distance. One alternative to a long-distance leased line is a satellite link, although the costs and data rates must be compared.

Today, a diversity of connections are used to create WANs, as shown in Figure W-1. Remote offices are interconnected with virtual circuits through packet-switched, frame-relay, or cell-relay (ATM) networks that are more economical than private leased-line networks. In addition, the Internet can provide inexpensive long-distance connections between remote offices, or between remote or mobile users at the cost of monthly fees paid to ISPs (Internet service providers). See "Virtual Dial-up Services" and "VPN (Virtual Private Network)" for more information.

Business-to-business relationships are set up over *extranets*, extensions over the Internet of one company's internal network to another company's internal network.

W

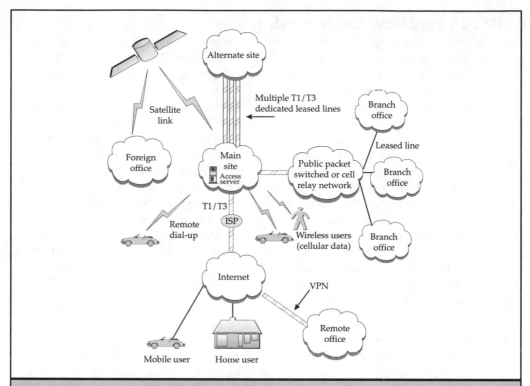

**Figure W-1.**   *There are many ways to build WANs*

Such connections require authentication and encryption. The inside network must be secured against attacks from the outside with firewalls and other protective measures. Refer to "Authentication and Authorization," "Firewall," and "Security" for more information.

## WAN Technologies

At its basic level, a WAN is meant to simultaneously transport the traffic of many users across a transmission medium. Unlike shared LANs, in which access to the network is mediated so that only one transmission can take place at a time, WAN links must accommodate all the users that need to use it in a fair way, although prioritization of some traffic can also be done. That means some technique such as TDM (time division multiplexing), packet switching, or cell relay is required to transport data from many users at the same time.

Routers are also an essential part of the WAN interconnection. They ensure that only WAN traffic is delivered across WAN connections. Routers provide the traffic control that delivers packets to the right destination.

The technologies for building WANs are listed here and pictured in Figure W-1:

- Dial-up private networks
- Switched digital services
- Leased-line private networks
- Packet-switching and frame relay services
- Cell relay (i.e., ATM)
- SMDS (Switched Multimegabit Data Service)
- Internet (a public packet-switched network)

These communication techniques are briefly outlined in the following subsections with references to appropriate sections in this book that provide more detail. General discussions of telecommunication technologies are outlined in "Circuit-Switching Services," "Communication Service Providers," "Communication Services," and "Telecommunications and Telephone Systems."

### Dial-up Lines and Modems

A dial-up line can provide an economical WAN connection in a number of scenarios. For example, a dial-up line can be used to provide additional bandwidth when an existing dedicated leased-line WAN link becomes overburdened. A dial-up line may also be used to handle on-again, off-again traffic between corporate sites where little traffic is exchanged. The modem may connect and disconnect continuously throughout the day to handle fluctuations in network traffic, such as e-mail delivery or an occasional user connection. In some cases, it may be more economical to leave a dial-up line on all the time rather than lease a dedicated line from a carrier.

For additional information, refer to "Bandwidth on Demand," "Circuit-Switching Services," "Modems," "Modulation Techniques," "Point-to-Point Communications," "Telecommunications and Telephone Systems," and "WAN (Wide Area Network)."

### Dedicated (Private Leased Line) Services

A leased line is a communication circuit that is set up on a permanent basis for an organization by a public service provider such as a LEC (local exchange carrier), a long-distance IXC (interexchange carrier), or both. Because an organization pays a fixed rate for the lines under contract, the lines are often called *leased lines*.

An organization uses leased lines to build *private networks* that interconnect its remote sites or the sites of business partners. The lines are called private because the organization controls transmissions on the line and no one else competes for bandwidth on the line as with packet-switching networks such as frame relay (although guaranteed bandwidth is available with frame relay). They are also more secure than using open networks like the Internet for wide area connections.

Bridges or routers are set up to direct traffic across the links. Because a fully meshed private network requires a dedicated leased line between each site, operating costs increase with the number of sites and the distance between them. For example, to fully interconnect four sites in different cities, you will need six leased lines (one line from each site to every other site).

**W**

For additional information, refer to "CSU/DSU (Channel Service Unit/Data Service Unit)," "Dedicated Circuits," "Inverse Multiplexing," "Leased Line," "Multiplexing," "Point-to-Point Communications," and "T1/T3."

### DSL Services

DSL (Digital Subscriber Line) services are the new kids on the block. The carriers are just starting to make these services available, although they are based on technology that the carriers have used for T1 circuits. They provide very efficient throughput on existing lines and customers can use the services in the same way that dedicated leased lines are used, or they can use them to make short-haul connections into packet-switched networks. There are actually seven types of DSL service, ranging in speeds from 16 Kbits/sec to 52 Mbits/sec. The most important thing is that DSL services operate over the twisted-pair wiring that exists in the *local loop*, the phone network that is wired to homes and offices throughout the country. Refer to "DSL (Digital Subscriber Line)" for more information.

### Switched Digital Services (Including ISDN)

Switched digital services provide many of the same benefits as do dedicated digital lines, including expandable bandwidth. You only pay when the service is connected. ISDN (Integrated Services Digital Network) is the most obvious service. Basic-rate ISDN starts out as two 64-Kbit/sec lines that can be combined to create a 128-Kbit/sec line. Primary-rate ISDN is for companies that need switchable bandwidth in increments of 64 Kbits/sec all the way up to multimegabit rates. As bandwidth is required, additional circuits are added and bonded together if necessary.

For additional information, refer to "BACP (Bandwidth Allocation Control Protocol)," "Bandwidth on Demand," "Circuit-Switching Services," "ISDN (Integrated Services Digital Network)," and "Switched-56 Services."

### Packet-Switching, Frame Relay, and Cell Relay Services

These services are grouped together because they provide similar end results, which are any-to-any connections over shared mesh networks that allow variable data rates. The services put data to be delivered into packets (X.25 and the Internet), cells (ATM), or frames (frame relay) that are delivered across a network composed of many point-to-point links. The network has many endpoints and potentially many paths that lead to endpoints, thus providing redundancy and load balancing.

Bandwidth is shared by packets/cells/frames (herein called packets) from all of the carrier's customers, and assuming the bandwidth is not overbooked, customers can go over the allotted bandwidth requirements to accommodate surges in traffic at an additional charge from the carrier. The carrier usually defines virtual circuits through the network that provide the same guaranteed bandwidth and efficient delivery as a dedicated leased line.

Frame relay is one of the most cost-effective WAN technologies available. It allows great flexibility in designing a WAN with a variety of endpoints over wide areas and allows managers to easily change the topology as the organization changes.

Carrier-based ATM networks provide the same benefits with the added features of QoS (Quality of Service), which is useful for prioritizing network traffic such as real-time audio and video. Another service in this category offered by carriers is SMDS (Switched Multimegabit Data Service).

For additional information, refer to "ATM (Asynchronous Transfer Mode)," "Cell Relay," "Connection-Oriented and Connectionless Services," "Datagrams and Datagram Services," "Frame Relay," "Internetworking," "IP (Internet Protocol)," "Network Layer Protocols," "Packet," "Packet and Cell Switching," "PSTN (Public-Switched Telephone Network)," "Virtual Circuit," and "X.25."

### Remote Access and Wireless Connections

Remote access covers a range of techniques that let home users, mobile users, and remote-office users access resources on a corporate network. The usual connection method is through a dial-up modem, although remote access may also be through permanently connected leased lines or even across the Internet. The latter option is discussed next.

For more information on remote connections, refer to "Access Server," "Cellular Communication Systems," "Communication Server," "Mobile IP," "Modems," "NC (Network Computer) Devices," "NetPC," "PCS (Personal Communications Services)," "Remote Access," and "Wireless Communications."

### The Internet

The Internet is providing a new basis for building wide area networks that span the globe and that reduce telecommunication cost. A flat monthly fee to an ISP (Internet service provider) pays for connection to a network that lets you deliver data to any location in the world at no extra charge. The only problem is that the Internet is a shared public network with little security and no way to guarantee bandwidth. If you need guaranteed service, then look into leased lines or carrier-based services such as frame relay. Also, any time you connect an internal network to the Internet, you are essentially opening your network up wide to attack, so firewalls are needed.

Still, the Internet provides a low-cost way for mobile and remote users to dial in to corporate networks, as discussed under "Virtual Dial-up Services." Companies can also build VPNs (virtual private networks) over the Internet, which are basically encrypted tunnels through the Internet for delivering packets from one site to another. See "VPN (Virtual Private Network)" for more details.

Additional information about using the Internet for WAN services can be found under "Firewall," "IPSec (IP Security)," "PPP (Point-to-Point Protocol)," "PPTP (Point-to-Point Tunneling Protocol)," "Private Network," "Remote Access," "S/WAN (Secure WAN)," and "Virtual Dial-up Services."

**RELATED ENTRIES**   Cable (CATV) Data Networks and Modems; LATA (Local Access and Transport Area); LEC (Local Exchange Carrier); Line Conditioning; Local Loop; RBOCs (Regional Bell Operating Companies); *and* Wireless Communications

**W**

## Wavelength Division Multiplexing

*See* WDM (Wavelength Division Multiplexing).

## Wavelength Division Multiple Access

*See* WDMA (Wavelength Division Multiple Access).

## WBEM (Web-Based Enterprise Management)

Network management tools that use Internet protocols and operate using familiar Web technologies are now common. Web-based management systems are designed for managing intranets and Internet-based networks. Web browsers are becoming the primary network management interface. The advantage of Web-based management tools is that Web protocols and technologies are ubiquitous for internal networks (intranets) and the Internet. Managers can use Web-based management tools to manage systems at remote sites.

However, Web-based management tools are straying from the traditional SNMP (Simple Network Management Protocol) management protocols. WBEM was developed jointly by Microsoft, Compaq, and Cisco Systems, and is supported by over 60 vendors. According to the WBEM Web site, WBEM is designed to complement existing management standards such as SNMP and DMI (Desktop Management Interface) while helping to "consolidate and unify the data provided by existing management technologies." WBEM allows data from a variety of sources to be "described, instantiated and accessed, regardless of the source."

A standard protocol called HMMP (Hypermedia Management Protocol) is used to publish and access data, and to exchange management and control messages between HMMP entities. Also part of WBEM is CIM (Common Information Model), a schema that provides a formal representation of data. HMMP is used to access and manipulate the schemas held by HMMP management entities. The CIM scheme is a set of published and standardized classes that represent hardware devices and other manageable objects in the network environment.

The HMMP protocol is similar to HTTP (Hypertext Transfer Protocol) in its client/server operation. HMMP clients make requests of HMMP servers. The clients in this case can be management processes running in standard Web browsers. The client may also be a dedicated process that runs on a continuous basis to monitor and manage systems. Servers accept requests from clients and try to satisfy those requests. A server may need to pass a request on to another server, in which case it becomes a client to the server receiving the request. This scheme relieves clients of the need to find and directly manage a device on the network. The client can instead make request to a server that manages a group of devices. The devices it manages may use other protocols' vendor-specific management mechanisms, but the server provides information to the client using HMMP protocols.

WBEM was still under development at the time of this writing. Refer to the WBEM Web site listed at the end of this topic for up-to-date information.

**RELATED ENTRIES**    Distributed Management; DME (Distributed Management Environment); DMI (Desktop Management Interface); DMTF (Desktop Management Task Force); Network Management; RMON (Remote Monitoring); SNMP (Simple Network Management Protocol); Web-Based Network Management; *and* Web Technologies and Concepts

**INFORMATION ON THE INTERNET**

WBEM Initiative site                               http://wbem.freerange.com

Web-based Management paper                 http://www.compaq.com/products/servers/
(at Compaq's Web site)                             strategy/wbem-eo.html

## WDM (Wavelength Division Multiplexing)

WDM is a FDM (frequency division multiplexing) technique for fiber-optic cable. It allows a single fiber cable to accommodate multiple light signals instead of a single light signal. Each light signal occupies a different frequency. WDM is employed by carriers such as MCI to dramatically boost the data rates of their networks. MCI recently incorporated Quad-WDM (four-wavelength WDM) in its backbone, quadrupling the network capacity by adding additional fiber-optic cable. The backbone operated at 2.5 Gbits/sec before Quad-WDM and at 10 Gbits/sec after installing Quad-WDM multiplexor devices.

WDM sends multiple signals through a single cable at different frequencies. Note that a single fiber cable has a very wide bandwidth (25,000 GHz), but only a very small portion of this bandwidth is used by a single channel. Optical channels have a narrow bandwidth because it is difficult to perform fast conversions from electrical signals to optical signals. However, multiple channels operating at different frequencies can be multiplexed onto a fiber cable to make more efficient use of the cable. This is pictured in Figure W-2.

A typical WDM configuration consists of a multiplexor that accepts input from multiple fiber-optic sources (up to 32 in some systems) and modulates each signal at a different frequency for transmission over a single fiber-optic trunk. A multiplexor at the other end demultiplexes the signals.

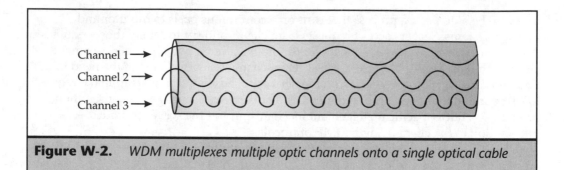

**Figure W-2.**   *WDM multiplexes multiple optic channels onto a single optical cable*

WDM is not just for carrier backbones. IBM's Muxmaster uses WDM to handle up to 20 Gbits/sec of digital data over fiber-optic links that can span 50 kilometers. It supports 10 full-duplex 2-Gbit/sec channels. Interface cards are available for IBM Escon, FDDI (Fiber Distributed Data Interface), Fibre Channel, and OC (optical carrier) rates of 155 Mbits/sec (OC3) and 622 Mbits/sec (OC12).

The All Optical Networking Consortium was formed by AT&T Bell Laboratories, Digital Equipment Corporation, and the Massachusetts Institute of Technology to investigate architectures for, and build prototypes of, all optical networks. The work is funded by the DARPA (Defense Advanced Research Projects Agency). Refer to the first Web site given in the "Information on the Internet" section.

**RELATED ENTRIES**   Fiber-Optic Cable; MCI; *and* Multiplexing

**INFORMATION ON THE INTERNET**

| | |
|---|---|
| All Optical Networking Consortium | http://www.ll.mit.edu/aon |
| MCI's Quad-WDM information (search for "WDM") | http://www.mci.com/technology |
| International Society for Optical Engineering | http://www.spie.org |
| Lightwave Research Centre | http://www.ollrc.on.ca |
| Photonics Resource Centre | http://www.optics.org |

# WDMA (Wavelength Division Multiple Access)

WDMA defines how multiple transmissions can be put on a fiber-optic cable system that is doing WDM (wavelength division multiplexing), as described under the preceding topic. WDM allows multiple channels of data to be transmitted at different frequencies on the same cable. WDMA divides each channel into a series of time slots (time division multiplexing), and data from different sources can be assigned to a repeating set of time slots.

# Web

The *World Wide Web* is often referred to as simply "the Web." Refer to "Web Technologies and Concepts" for more information.

# Webcasting

*See* Broadcast News Technology; Push.

# Web-Based Network Management

Web-based network management is all about monitoring and managing networks using Web technologies such as Web browsers and Web protocols. It allows administrators to remotely monitor systems in real time, gather information about systems for later evaluation, troubleshoot systems, and produce reports about network problems or network activities in general. Web-based network management takes advantage of the ubiquity of TCP/IP protocols, both on the intranet and the Internet. Network administrators can use the same tools to manage a server in the same room or anywhere on the worldwide Internet. Many vendors of network management systems have already added Web browser interfaces to their systems.

To take advantage of this universal interface and the power of Web protocols, five companies (BMC Software, Cisco Systems, Compaq Computer, Intel, and Microsoft) formed the Web-Based Enterprise Management Consortium in July of 1996. The WBEM consortium has the goal of integrating disparate management protocols, management information, and management systems. Currently, the Internet's SNMP (Simple Network Management Protocol) is the most popular protocol for managing systems. Another standard is DMI (Desktop Management Interface). However, the data created with systems that use these protocols is not always easily accessible.

The WBEM initiative is promoting new Internet standards such as HMMP (Hypermedia Management Protocol) that allow network management system vendors to create systems that use the same protocols and that can be accessed with the same user interface. Another important strategy is to create a common data structure for storing management information that is more easily accessible. Refer to "WBEM (Web-Based Enterprise Management)" for more information. WBEM is oriented toward Microsoft Windows platforms.

An alternative strategy called JMAPI (Java Management API) has been put forth by Sun Microsystems and 15 other companies. JMAPI is an environment for developing Web-based management applications around the Java programming language. A simple ODBC-based database is used to store management information. Developers write applets that run on any system that has a Java-enabled operating system. A Java-enabled browser can then access the management information. SNMP is supported, allowing JMAPI applications to obtain management information collected by SNMP agents.

SNMP Research International, a well-respected developer of SNMP products, has stated that the goals of WBEM and JMAPI are too lofty and will not result in timely

**W**

products. Similar grandiose efforts have failed in the past, it claims. The company has its own solution in the form of DR-Web, a product that makes it easy to view SNMP management information by mapping SNMP data into HTML (Hypertext Markup Language), which is the document description language for Web browsers. DR-Web also includes agents that essentially turn managed devices into Web servers that "publish" management information just like a Web server publishes HTML pages. DR-Web also lets administrators execute SNMP commands from Web browsers. The product will support HMMP interfaces and JMAPI products as they become available. Because DR-Web takes a more modest approach to Web-based management, developers can bring products to market more quickly.

**RELATED ENTRIES**   Distributed Management; DME (Distributed Management Environment); DMI (Desktop Management Interface); DMTF (Desktop Management Task Force); Network Management; RMON (Remote Monitoring); SNMP (Simple Network Management Protocol); *and* Web Technologies and Concepts

**INFORMATION ON THE INTERNET**

| | |
|---|---|
| WBEM Initiative site | http://wbem.freerange.com |
| Web-based Management paper (at Compaq's Web site) | http://www.compaq.com/products/servers/strategy/wbem-eo.html |
| SunSoft's Solstice Workshop | http://www.sun.com/workshop |
| Java Management API | http://java.sun.com/products/JavaManagement |
| SNMP Research International | http://www.snmp.com |

# Web Middleware and Database Connectivity

The original Web model was simple: create static HTML (Hypertext Markup Language) documents, store them on a single Web server, and then let Web users access them using HTTP (Hypertext Transfer Protocol) protocols. Because the documents were created and stored on the server, every Web user had access to the same document.

Then CGI (Common Gateway Interface) came along. It allowed users to request *dynamic documents* from a Web server by filling out a form that specified the type of information they wanted. The Web server would create the dynamic document on the fly and send it to the user. However, this approach is slow and somewhat limited in functionality. In many cases, it also restricts operations to a single Web server that can quickly become overloaded.

The Web has become a very sophisticated environment, and users are demanding access to data that is traditionally stored on back-end servers and mainframe systems. Web users must have more direct access to back-end data. That is were Web-based middleware and database connectivity products come into the picture.

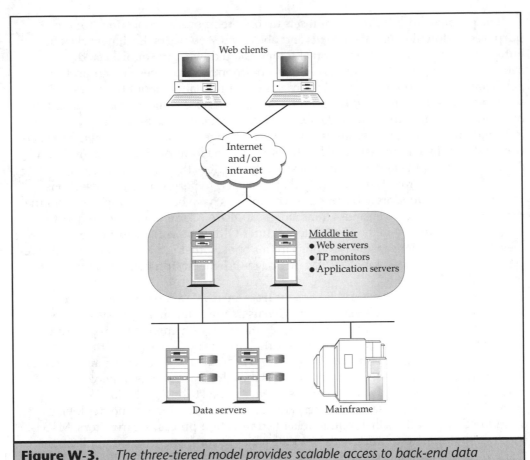

**Figure W-3.** *The three-tiered model provides scalable access to back-end data*

The Web database connectivity architecture has the form of the three-tiered model shown in Figure W-3. The three-tiered model consists of the presentation tier (Web browser), the business logic tier (Web server), and the data tier (back-end databases and mainframe systems). This model fully supports component software designs and a highly dynamic Web page construction. It is also scalable—additional servers can be added to the middle tier and the database tier to handle increased Web user access.

In the three-tiered model, the middle tier does more than respond to HTTP requests and deliver static or dynamic Web pages. It also provides application services, TP (transaction processing) monitoring functions, and host component software created with Java, ActiveX and other technologies. For more information about component software, refer to "Component Software Technology," "CORBA (Common Object Request Broker Architecture)," and "Distributed Object Computing."

The problem with HTTP is that it sets up only temporary connections for the purposes of downloading Web pages and objects on Web pages. Each new click of a button is set up as a new connection and then taken down, but sophisticated client/server applications cannot run in an environment that does not support some persistence in the connections and the caching of information about the current session by both the client and the server. For example, electronic business transactions can involve changes to multiple databases at different locations as well as changes to information on the client's systems. All of these changes must occur in a synchronized way and be fully committed in all locations. If any one location does not complete a transaction, all of the systems must back out the changes they have made.

HTTP cannot provide the integrity that is needed to perform such transactions. Therefore, many vendors and standards committees have been working to extend the Web for safe and secure business transactions. CORBA (Common Object Request Broker Architecture) and the IIOP (Internet Inter-ORB Protocol) are examples, and are they discussed under separate headings in this book. Other sections related to this are "Middleware and Messaging," "MOM (Message-Oriented Middleware)," and "Transaction Processing."

Tuxedo by BEA Systems and Encina by Transarc (IBM) are transaction processing systems that now provide Web support. Web users make normal requests to Web servers, but these requests are handled by TP monitors, which pass them on to an appropriate server for processing. An important aspect of TP systems is that they offload work from the Web server. Initially, users contact the Web server, and requests are then distributed to other servers. This has the added advantage of allowing requests to be distributed among many servers, thus distributing the load.

MTS (Microsoft Transaction Server) is a product for developing and deploying distributed applications that require reliable transaction-processing monitors. MTS is specifically designed to work with new categories of component-based applications that work over intranets or the Internet. In particular, MTS simplifies the development of applications that require transaction processing. See "Microsoft Transaction Server" for more details.

## Database Development Tools for the Web

An incredible number of tools are now available to make database information on legacy mainframe systems and network servers available to Web users over the Internet or corporate intranets. One objective of these tools is to help Web servers access information on back-end databases and build dynamic Web pages based on information requested by users. Another objective of Web development tools is to give Internet and intranet users the tools they need to directly access database systems after initially connecting with a Web site.

A few examples of the standards and tools now available for developing Web database connectivity are outlined here:

- **ODBC (Open Database Connectivity)** This is an open standard architecture that defines how clients can access data on a variety of heterogeneous databases. It was originally defined by Microsoft but is now used almost universally. See "ODBC (Open Database Connectivity), Microsoft" for more information.

- **Microsoft OLE DB** This is an extension of ODBC that defines access to universal data types (i.e., multimedia data, including pictures, sound, and video). See "OLE DB" for more information.

- **Microsoft ADO (ActiveX Data Objects)** This is an ODBC-compliant set of interfaces that exposes all of the functionality in modern databases through accessible objects. ADO can be used with virtually any scripting language, such as JavaScript, VB Script, and Perl.

- **Microsoft dbWeb** This product assists Web servers in connecting with ODBC drivers.

- **JDBC (Java Database Connectivity)** JDBC provides much of the same functionality as ODBC but provides support from programs written in Java and JavaScript. See "Java" for more information.

- **J/SQL** This is an Oracle standard for creating Java applications that can access relational databases. Oracle promotes J/SQL as an open standard.

- **Oracle NCA (Network Computing Architecture)** NCA is a set of technologies that allows all clients, including PCs and network computers, to universally access information on Web servers, database servers, and other systems. See "Oracle NCA (Network Computing Architecture)."

**W**

## Universal Databases

With the Web, database vendors were forced to finally deal with a plethora of data types, not just structured data. When a Web user accesses a Web site, the server at the site must build dynamic pages, based on the user's request, that include not only text, but images, sound, and even video. Database vendors have introduced so-called *universal databases* to deal with this. Each vendor has its own way of providing universal database functionality. Oracle implements plug-in software *cartridges,* while Informix employs *datablades*. Both add support for new data types and functions. Sybase relies on its OmniConnect middleware. Refer to the IBM, Informix, Oracle, and Sybase sites listed below for more information.

**RELATED ENTRIES** Component Software Technology; Database Connectivity; DBMS (Database Management System); Distributed Applications; Distributed Computer Networks; Distributed Database; Distributed Object Computing; IBM Host Connectivity; IIOP (Internet Inter-ORB Protocol); Middleware and Messaging;

Multitiered Architectures; Object Technologies; ODBC (Open Database Connectivity), Microsoft; NCA (Network Computing Architecture); OLE DB; Oracle ORB (Object Request Broker); SQL (Structured Query Language); Transaction Processing; *and* Web Technologies and Concepts

### INFORMATION ON THE INTERNET

| | |
|---|---|
| Database Magazine | http://www.onlineinc.com/database |
| DBMS Magazine | http://www.dbmsmag.com |
| Object Magazine (extensive links) | http://www.sigs.com/omo |
| BEA Systems, Inc. | http://www.beasys.com |
| Bluestone Software's Sapphire | http://www.bluestone.com |
| Expersoft's PowerBroker | http://www.expersoft.com |
| IBM's DB2 Universal Database | http://www.software.ibm.com |
| Informix's Universal Database | http://www.informix.com |
| Innergy's Gateways to Data, A Web-to-Database Tool Sampler | http://www.innergy.com/webdata.html |
| IONA Technologies' Orbix | http://www.iona.com |
| Microsoft Corporation | http://www.microsoft.com |
| Oracle's Universal Server | http://www.oracle.com |
| Sybase's Adaptive Server | http://www.sybase.com |
| Transarc's Encina | http://www.transarc.com |
| Visigenic's VisiBroker | http://www.visigenic.com |
| AFP Technology Ltd. (search for "middleware") | http://www.afptech.com |

**NOTE:** *Refer to "DBMS (Database Management System)" for additional Web resources related to databases.*

## WebNFS (Network File System)

WebNFS is Sun Microsystem's attempt to bring a file system to the Internet. It is based on the popular NFS (Network File System) that is the primary file system in UNIX and other environments. WebNFS makes file access across the Internet as easy as accessing files on local systems. It is specifically designed to handle the unique problems associated with accessing files across the Internet. It provides enhanced download performance and reliability through automatic error and crash recovery. If a connection is broken in the middle of a file download, the download continues when the connection is restored.

Perhaps the most important feature is that file systems at other locations on the Internet can appear to a user as a file system that is local. WebNFS works through firewalls and implements features such as read-ahead and write-behind to improve data access over the Internet. A file can be referenced with a URL format similar to the following:

nfs://*servername*/*directory*/*filename*

Another important feature of WebNFS is that it can provide from five to ten times the performance of HTTP (Hypertext Transfer Protocol) when displaying graphics and animation. This is because WebNFS is optimized to use bandwidth efficiently. In addition, files can be edited in place without being downloaded to the user's computer. Because the files are edited in place where other users access them, file integrity is maintained. With other systems, a user may download a file, edit it, then copy it back—overwriting the original copy of the file, which may have just been changed by another user.

Like NFS, administrators specify which directories or files are to be exported. These are the files that will be available to network users, either on intranets or the Internet. WebNFS handles the task of locating these files, negotiating file access privileges, and locally mounting the files so users at remote locations can access them.

Sun is promoting WebNFS as the best file system for NCs (Network Computers), computers that have reduced local file systems and that rely on network-based file systems.

Netscape Communications, Oracle, Spyglass, IBM, Apple Computer, and Novell support WebNFS in their product lines. Another file system that has been refined for use on the Internet is Microsoft's CIFS (Common Internet File System), which is an enhanced version of Microsoft's SMB (Server Message Blocks) protocol, the native file-sharing protocol for Windows.

**RELATED ENTRIES**   CIFS (Common Internet File System); DFS (Distributed File System), Microsoft; File Sharing; File Systems; Internet; NC (Network Computer) Devices; NFS (Network File System); Sun Microsystems; *and* Web Technologies and Concepts

**INFORMATION ON THE INTERNET**

| | |
|---|---|
| Sun Microsystems' WebNFS site | http://www.sun.com/webnfs |
| Rawn Shah's "What WebNFS means to you" paper | http://www.sun.com/sunworldonline/swol-08-1996/swol-08-connectivity.html |

# Web Technologies and Concepts

The World Wide Web (or "Web") is built on top of the Internet, which itself is made possible by the TCP/IP protocols. Web clients and Web servers communicate with one

**W**

another using a protocol called HTTP (Hypertext Transfer Protocol). Web servers provide information that is formatted with HTML (Hypertext Markup Language), which is basically a page description language. Public Web servers provide information on the Internet to anyone with a Web browser. At the same time, Web technology can be used to build private in-house information systems, called *intranets*, over TCP/IP networks.

Web browsers provide a unique tool for accessing information on any network, whether it is an internal intranet or the Internet. They remove the mystery of the Internet and eliminate the need for users to understand arcane commands. Most people begin accessing resources the first time they use a browser. Little training is necessary, and most browser software is free. Browsers do most of the work of accessing and displaying the documents, making the process almost transparent to the user.

Much of the World Wide Web's impact has come from its making the public aware of hypertext and hypermedia. Hypertext and hypermedia are interactive navigation tools; mouse clicking on a hypertext or hypermedia link takes the user directly to the desired Web document. Hypertext refers to documents containing only text. Hypermedia refers to documents with text, audio, video, images, graphics, animation, or other active content.

The traditional role of a Web browser has been to contact a Web site and obtain information from the site in the form of an HTML page. Today, even this is changing. So-called "push" technology makes the Web browser and/or desktop a place where dynamic information can automatically appear from sites on the Internet. For example, weather information may appear in the right-hand corner of your desktop while stock quotes may banner across the bottom portion. This information is "pushed" to you on a real-time basis, so the concept of starting up a Web browser and actively searching for information is only one way to access the Web. The new paradigm is multicasting, which provides true broadcasting on the Internet. Refer to "Multicasting" and "Push" for more information.

Despite the impact of new technologies that are changing the way content is delivered, browsers can also work with other, older Internet services such as e-mail, FTP, and Gopher.

## How the Web Works

HTTP is a fast and efficient communication protocol that controls many different operations that take place between the Web browser client and the server. HTTP uses the TCP (Transmission Control Protocol) to transport all of its control and data messages from one computer to another.

Web pages are typically grouped at a Web site, where the main page is referred to as the *home page*. The user navigates by mouse clicking on hyperlinks displayed as text, buttons, or images. These hyperlinks reference other information. When you click a hyperlink, you jump to another part of the same page, a new page at the same Web site, or to another Web site. You might also execute a program, display a picture, or download a file. All of this hyperlinking is done with HTML, which works in concert with HTTP. HTTP is the command and control protocol that sets up communication between a client and a server and passes commands between the two systems. HTML provides the document with formatting instructions that control how a Web page displays on a browser. See "Hypermedia and Hypertext" and "HTML (Hypertext Markup Language)" for more information.

To connect with a Web site, you type the URL (Uniform Resource Locator) for the site into the Address field of a Web browser. Here is an example of the URL that retrieves a document called INFO.HTM in the public directory of a Web site called www.tec-ref.com:

http://www.tec-ref.com/public/info.html

When you type this request, the Web browser first gets the IP address of www.tec-ref.com from a DNS (Domain Name System) server, and then it connects with the target server. The server responds to the client and the tail end of the URL (public/info.html) is processed. In this case, the info.html file in the /public directory has been requested, so the Web server transfers this HTML-coded document to your Web browser. Your Web browser then translates and displays the HTML information.

The browser can also handle much of the processing in this relationship. It formats and displays the HTML information, which is transferred as a simple, relatively small file from the Web server. The browser can also include add-ons that allow it to display video, sound, and 3-D images. These add-ons do most of the processing based on a relatively small set of commands or data transferred from the Web server, thus reducing excessive dialog between the Web client and server.

The Web client/server relationship is stateless, meaning that the server does not retain any information about the client, and the connection between Web browser and Web server is terminated as soon as the requested information is sent. While this is efficient for activities such as downloading a single Web document, it produces a lot of overhead if the client keeps requesting additional information from the server. Each new connection requires a negotiation phase, which takes time and requires that packets be exchanged between client and server. In addition, each object on a Web page, such as a graphic image, is sent using a separate connection. The inefficiency of this process has prompted the development of new Web protocols and component applications that are more efficient at transmitting information.

## Component Software

The latest trend is component technology in the form of Java applets and Microsoft ActiveX controls. These self-contained programs follow object-oriented program design methods. They download to a Web browser and either run as separate programs or attach themselves to existing components to enhance the features of those components. When a Web user visits a Java-enabled or ActiveX-enabled Web site, the appropriate components download to the user's computer.

**W**

There are three types of Web documents:

- Static documents written once by the Web author and distributed to anyone that can access the URL for the document. Each document must be manually updated.

- Dynamic documents created on the fly, based on information requests made by users. For example, sports scores, stock prices, or news updates are put on the page by the Web server software based on the latest information it has available. It may obtain this information from a variety of servers.

- Active documents contain components that run on a user's browser. The components are downloaded to a user's browser and remain available to the browser for future use. The next time the user connects to the Web site where the components were obtained, the components may interact with the server at the site to obtain additional information or perform some other task. For example, a stock portfolio management utility automatically updates itself with information from a Web site. Java and ActiveX are part of this technology.

With regard to business transactions over the Internet, the Web protocols leave a lot to be desired. The stateless operation of the HTTP protocols is not a good match for client/server applications, which require continuous connections and, in some cases, transaction-processing monitors to ensure that writes to databases are handled correctly. Refer to "Web Middleware and Database Connectivity" for more information.

## Security

HTTP sets up the connection between the client and the server, and in many cases that connection must be secure. For example, assume your company sets up an Internet Web server to provide sensitive documents to its mobile work force. These documents should not be accessible to anyone else (since the site is connected to the Internet, anyone could attempt to access them). To prevent unauthorized access, you set up private directories and require logon authentication. You can also do the following:

- Use digital certificates to authenticate the Web client. See "Certificates and Certification Systems."

- Encrypt all the data that passes between client and server with an SSL (Secure Sockets Layer) connection or use Microsoft's similar PCT (Private Communication Technology) protocol. See "PCT (Private Communication Technology) Protocol" and "SSL (Secure Sockets Layer)."

- Use the SET (Secure Electronic Transaction) protocol to secure credit card transactions. See "SET (Secure Electronic Transaction)."

## Related Topics of Interest

See "Internet" for related information and links to other sections in this book about the Web. The following list also provides useful links:

■ **Internet and Web organizations**  See "Internet Organizations and Committees" and "W3C (World Wide Web Consortium)."

■ **The protocols and standards of the Internet**  See "Internet," "Internet Organizations and Committees," "IP (Internet Protocol)," "TCP (Transmission Control Protocol)," and "TCP/IP (Transmission Control Protocol/Internet Protocol)."

■ **The structure of the Internet**  See "Internet," "Internet Backbone," "IP (Internet Protocol)," and "NII (National Information Infrastructure)."

■ **Getting on the Web**  See "Internet Connections."

■ **Putting up a Web site**  See "Firewall," "Internet Backbone," "Internet Connections," "Intranets and Extranets," and "Security."

■ **Using the Internet as a private WAN**  See "Virtual Dial-up Services" and "VPN (Virtual Private Network)."

■ **Finding information**  See "Search Engines" and references under "Internet."

■ **Electronic commerce on the Web**  See "EDI (Electronic Data Interchange)," "Electronic Commerce," "Extranet," and "Mailing List Programs."

■ **Collaborative computing and workflow**  See "Groupware," "Multimedia," "Videoconferencing and Desktop Video," "Voice over the Internet," and "Workflow Management.

■ **Electronic mail**  See "Electronic Mail," "IMAP (Internet Mail Access Protocol)," "Mailing List Programs," "POP (Post Office Protocol)," "SMTP (Simple Mail Transfer Protocol)," and "Workflow Management."

■ **Multimedia and broadcasting**  See "Broadcast News Technology," "MBone (Multicast Backbone)," "Multicasting," "Multimedia," "Push," "RSVP (Resource Reservation Protocol)," "RTP (Real-time Transport Protocol)," "Videoconferencing and Desktop Video," and "Voice over the Internet."

### RELATED ENTRIES

**Web content development, data access, and application development:**  ActiveX; COM (Component Object Model); Component Software Technology; Compound Documents; CORBA (Common Object Request Broker Architecture); Database Connectivity; DBMS (Database Management System); DCOM (Distributed Component Object Model); Distributed Applications; Distributed Object Computing; IIOP (Internet Inter-ORB Protocol); Java; Middleware and Messaging; Multitiered

**W**

Architectures; Netscape ONE Development Environment; Object Technologies; OLE DB; OMA (Object Management Architecture); Oracle NCA (Network Computing Architecture); ORB (Object Request Broker); Sun Microsystems Solaris NEO; Transaction Processing; *and* Web Middleware and Database Connectivity

**Security for internal networks and the Internet:** Authentication and Authorization; Certificates and Certification Systems; Digital Signatures; Hacker; IPSec (IP Security); PKI (Public-Key Infrastructure); Public-Key Cryptography; *and* Token-Based Authentication

### INFORMATION ON THE INTERNET

| | |
|---|---|
| World Wide Web Consortium | http://www.w3.org |
| Yahoo!'s WWW links page | http://www.yahoo.com/Computers/Internet/World_Wide_Web |

 *NOTE:* *See additional links under "Internet."*

## WinFrame

WinFrame is a product of Citrix Systems. It adds multiuser functionality to the Windows environment. In this arrangement, Windows NT "thin clients" remotely access their desktops on a Windows NT server. WinFrame allows the Windows NT server to host multiple, simultaneous client sessions. Users still see the familiar Windows desktop and interface, but the server does most of the processing.

Winframe is based on Citrix's ICA (Independent Computing Architecture), a general-purpose presentation services protocol for Microsoft Windows. It is similar to X Window in the UNIX environment and allows applications to execute on a WinFrame multiuser Windows application server. Only the user interface, keystrokes, and mouse movements are transferred between the server and the client device over any network or communications protocol, minimizing the resources used by the client. ICA runs over TCP/IP, NetBEUI, IPX/SPX, and PPP, as well as remote communication protocols such as ISDN, frame relay, and ATM.

By distributing the Windows architecture, Windows applications can perform at very high speeds over low-bandwidth connections. It also allows 16- and 32-bit applications to run on legacy PCs as well as the new generation of "thin clients" such as the NetPC. In fact, WinFrame is getting so much attention because of the move to "thin clients."

Citrix obtained a license from Microsoft to add this multiuser capability to the Windows NT kernel, but the last version of NT that Citrix modified on its own was Windows NT 3.51. Then Microsoft got in on the act and made Windows NT 4.0 multiuser-capable with the help of Citrix. At the same time, Microsoft began developing its own multiuser technology for Windows NT 5.0, partly with work obtained from Citrix and a French company called Prologue.

Microsoft has code-named the NT 5.0 version "Hydra Server," and it will be capable of hosting a variety of desktops that are Windows-based and those that are not Windows-based, either directly or via third-party add-on products. Hydra delivers 32-bit Windows applications to "thin clients," NetPCs, and any legacy desktop, including UNIX, Macintosh, or older Windows-based PCs that cannot be upgraded to 32-bit Windows due to hardware limitations. Hydra also includes a remote protocol that allows a Windows NT "Hydra" client to connect to the server. This protocol is based on T.SHARE/T.120, an ITU (International Telecommunication Union) standard multichannel conferencing protocol tuned for high-bandwidth enterprise environments. These same standards are used in Microsoft's NetMeeting videoconferencing software.

Since Microsoft now has control over multiuser capabilities in Windows, Citrix has begun to develop other market opportunities. It will continue to provide value-added products for multiuser NT, but will focus primarily on promoting its ICA. It's goal is to make ICA a general-purpose architecture for thin client/network computer environments. The company formed the Open ICA Forum to work toward that goal, with IBM and Motorola participating in the forum.

**RELATED ENTRIES**   Diskless Workstation; NC (Network Computer) Devices; NetPC; Remote Access; Virtual Dial-up Services; Web Technologies and Concepts; Windows; Windows NT Server; WinFrame; Wired for Management; X Window; *and* Zero Administration for Windows Initiative

### INFORMATION ON THE INTERNET

| | |
|---|---|
| Citrix Systems | http://www.citrix.com |
| Microsoft's NetPC information | http://www.microsoft.com/windows/netpc |
| Microsoft's Hydra information | http://www.microsoft.com/ntserver |

## Windows

The Microsoft Windows family of products began as a graphical user interface that ran on top of the DOS operating system. The first versions of Windows were important because of their multitasking capabilities, which allowed them to run multiple applications at the same time. Today, the operating system has grown into a full-featured operating system for desktop users and network server applications. The product lineup as of this writing is described here:

- **Windows CE**   A "small footprint" operating system designed for specialized computing devices such as hand-held PCs, telephones, and consumer devices such as television sets.

- **Windows 95**   A 32-bit desktop operating system that can preemptively multitask 32-bit applications. The platform is scalable and performance improves when memory is increased. It includes built-in networking, fax, electronic messaging, Internet access software, mobile computing support, and support for DOS applications. Literally thousands of applications are available to run on Windows 95.

- **Windows 98**   This latest desktop operating system is an evolutionary upgrade to Windows 95. It is fully integrated with Internet/Web technologies and supports new multimedia hardware technologies and entertainment platforms. The user interface and desktop have changed somewhat with the integration of Microsoft's Internet Explorer Web browser software.

- **Windows NT Workstation 4.0**   Microsoft's high-end desktop operating system that provides the most powerful 32-bit and high-end performance. Most important, the operating system is designed to provide very high levels of security, reliability, manageability, networking, and performance.

- **Windows NT Server 4.0**   Microsoft's high-end network server operating system. Refer to "Windows NT Server" for more information.

- **Windows NT Workstation 5.0 and Windows NT Server 5.0**   These are the latest versions of the Windows NT operating system and they should be available in 1998.

Microsoft, in collaboration with Intel and major PC manufacturers, developed the NetPC Reference Platform to define an industry standard for a "sealed case" PC that runs Windows applications but prevents end users from tampering with the system. By maintaining traditional PC functionality, it lowers the cost of buying and maintaining Intel-based systems, yet still runs Windows applications. Because the NetPC is a response to the NC (Network Computer) initiatives, you should refer to "NC (Network Computer) Devices" for further reading.

Microsoft's Hydra Server will provide multiuser capabilities directly in the operating system so that Windows-based terminals or so-called "thin clients" can replace traditional "dumb terminals" in many environments. WinFrame developed this technology in earlier versions of Windows NT, as discussed under "WinFrame."

**RELATED ENTRIES**   Microsoft; Microsoft BackOffice; Microsoft Exchange Server; Microsoft Transaction Server; NetPC; Windows NT Directory Services; Windows NT File System; Windows NT Permissions; *and* Windows NT Server

### INFORMATION ON THE INTERNET

| | |
|---|---|
| Microsoft's Windows site | http://www.microsoft.com/windows |
| Microsoft's Windows NT site | http://www.microsoft.com/ntserver |
| Microsoft's Windows 98 site | http://www.microsoft.com/windows98 |

# Windows NT Directory Services

A directory service can provide white page and yellow page services in distributed computing environments. It allows people and applications to look up other people or services in a hierarchical database. Microsoft's directory service runs on Windows NT

Server version 4.0 and version 5.0 and combines features of the Internet's DNS (Domain Name System) locator service and X.500 naming. With it, administrators can unify and manage multiple namespaces over heterogeneous systems.

The core protocol for the service is LDAP (Lightweight Directory Access Protocol), which allows the service to work across operating system boundaries and integrate multiple namespaces. Because of this cross-platform capability, administrators can manage other vendors' directory services from Windows NT Directory Services and reduce administrative workload.

The service goes beyond simple name lookup. Administrators can locate and manage resources throughout the organization—computers, filing systems, peripheral devices, connection devices, database systems, and Internet connections, as well as user and group accounts.

Directory services also include the following features:

- Supports multimaster replication, which allows updates to occur at servers that are closest to the operator rather than at a master server

- Supports short-life-span services such as Internet telephony, videoconferencing, and chat services

- Interoperable with NetWare environments and backward compatible with Windows NT domain services

- Programmable via a wide range of scripting languages

- Goes beyond providing simple white page and yellow page services by providing a wide variety of query, administrative, registration, and resolution needs, as shown in Figure W-4

Windows NT Directory Services supports Internet and OSI naming formats. For example, Internet e-mail addresses such as *name@company.com* are supported. Windows NT Directory Services combines DNS locator services and X.500 standards. DNS is the location service of the Internet, and it can also be used for intranets. In addition, a Web browser can be used to access directory services via the HTTP (Hypertext Transfer Protocol) protocol using a URL (Uniform Resource Locator) name such as http://*server.company.com/service*. LDAP URLs and X.500 names are also supported, which have a form similar to the following:

LDAP://*server.company.com*/CN=*user*,OU=*department*,OU=*division*,O=*company*,C=*country*

The Windows NT Directory Services domain tree could be compared to Novell's NDS (Novell Directory Services) tree, except that Microsoft has retained its domain model, which was available in previous versions of Windows NT. Domains are represented by partitions of the directory tree and domains can be subdivided into OU (organizational unit) containers. Each OU can become an administrative unit that is managed by a person delegated by some higher-level administrator.

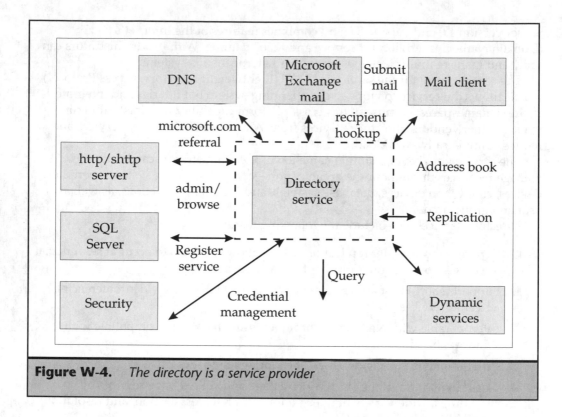

**Figure W-4.** *The directory is a service provider*

The "container" concept allows administrators to build a hierarchy of containers as shown in Figure W-5. This type of hierarchical structure allows administrators and users to "drill down" through the hierarchy to locate people and resources. A global catalog also exists that allows users to easily find an object no matter where it is in the tree.

The hierarchical structure allows for decentralized administration while maintaining security. In previous versions of Windows NT, the domain was the scope of administration and security. With Windows NT Directory Services, security can be administered independently within each domain, within a subtree of OUs that are part of a domain, or within a single OU.

**RELATED ENTRIES**    Active Platform, Microsoft; Directory Services; LDAP (Lightweight Directory Access Protocol); Microsoft; Microsoft BackOffice; Microsoft Exchange Server; Microsoft Transaction Server; NetPC; Windows; Windows NT Directory Services; Windows NT File System; Windows NT Permissions; Windows NT Server; *and* X.500 Directory Services

**INFORMATION ON THE INTERNET**

Microsoft's Windows NT site                http://www.microsoft.com/ntserver

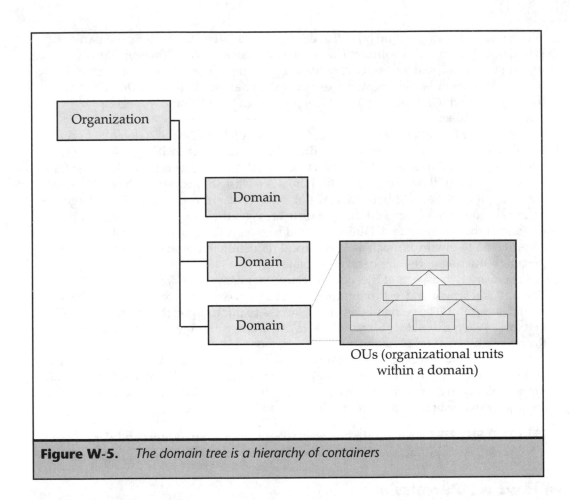

**Figure W-5.**   *The domain tree is a hierarchy of containers*

W

## Windows NT File System

NTFS (NT File System) is the file system for Microsoft's Windows NT Workstation and Windows NT Server operating systems. NTFS provides more security than file systems such as the FAT (file allocation table) system used in DOS and other versions of Windows. During Windows NT installation, you can choose to install either NTFS or FAT, but NTFS should always be selected if you want to take advantage of its sophisticated security and permission features (see "Windows NT Permissions").

Like Windows 95, Windows NT does not rely on DOS system services in any way. It boots on its own and uses its own services. All low-level disk access functions are performed by Windows NT-specific software drivers, not by lower-level disk drivers. This provides performance and security. If you run a DOS program from within Windows NT, NT does not allow the program to directly write to hard drives.

NTFS is designed for quick file operations on very large hard drives. It includes a file recovery system and built-in attributes to handle security and access control.

When you format a partition on a disk drive with the NTFS file system, the partition is initialized as an NTFS volume. This volume contains the MFT (master file table), which holds information about every file in the volume. The information is stored in 2,048-byte records and operates like a relational database. Files are identified by a number, which depends on the file's position in the MFT and a special sequence number.

The *cluster* is the fundamental unit of disk allocation for NTFS. A default cluster size is selected based on the size of the drive, but a 512-, 1,024-, 2,048-, or 4,096-byte allocation size can be selected. Using a large allocation unit size is better for large files, but storing small files in large allocation units is a waste of disk space. Note that small files may fit into the 2,048-byte data area of the MFT file record, but if a file is large, an entry is made in the file record that points to areas on the disk where the cluster or clusters of the file are stored. Directories and files on NTFS partitions can be compressed to obtain as much as a 50 percent reduction in the size of a text file or a 40 percent reduction in the size of an executable file.

There are two aspects of file-system security for computers connected to networks. The first is restricting access to information on a local computer to people who log on to that computer. The second is restricting access to information that is shared over the network. When a directory is shared, users can access it from workstations attached to the network, based on permissions.

To make information on a Windows system available to other users on a network, you share a folder (or an individual file). When you share a folder, all the files and all the subfolders in it are shared as well. You can then change the access permissions on any file or folder in the shared folder if you need to block access.

**RELATED ENTRIES**    Microsoft; Novell NetWare File System; Rights and Permissions; UNIX File System; Windows; Windows NT Permissions; *and* Windows NT Server

# Windows NT Permissions

In the Windows NTFS (NT File System), access to folders and files is controlled by permissions, and permissions are set by administrators or the owners of a resource. There are *standard permissions* and *individual permissions*. The individual permissions in the following list are used in combination to make up standard permissions, which will be described in a moment.

- **Read (R)**   Open and view the contents of a file
- **Write (W)**   Change the contents of a file or create a new file
- **Execute (X)**   Run a program or executable file
- **Delete (D)**   Delete files
- **Change Permission (P)**   Alter the permissions of an existing file or directory
- **Take Ownership (O)**   Make oneself the owner of a file or directory

The standard permissions are a combination of these individual permissions and are designed to provide a set of permissions appropriate for the most common user requirements. The standard permissions for folders are listed in Table W-1. The second column lists the individual permissions that make up the standard permissions, and the third column indicates the permissions that new files obtain when they are added to the folder.

Table W-2 lists the individual permissions that make up the standard permissions for files. Of course, you can create your own "special access permissions" at any time to fit a custom need.

Users may get permission to access folders or files from a number of sources. For example, they might have Read permissions through their user account and Change permissions because they are members of a group. Permission assignments from different sources are combined, and the highest-level permission applies. However, a No Access permission from any source denies access to the file or directory, no matter what other permissions are granted.

While NTFS provides a high level of security through its permission system, it is important to understand that this security is available only when the Windows NT operating system is up and running. Someone who steals your system or hard drive could use a low-level byte editor to scan the drive and read or change its contents. NTFS provides a way to control access to files and directories with permissions, but those permissions do no good if the operating system is not available to control access. Your security must include physical security measures, and you might want to install encryption utilities to protect stored data.

**RELATED ENTRIES**    Microsoft; Novell NetWare File System; Rights and Permissions; UNIX File System; Windows; Windows NT File System; *and* Windows NT Server

**W**

| Standard Folder Permission | Individual Permissions | Permissions for New Files |
|---|---|---|
| No Access | None | None |
| List | Read, Execute | Not specified |
| Read | Read, Execute | Read, Execute |
| Add | Write, Execute | Not specified |
| Add and Read | Read, Write, Execute | Read, Execute |
| Change | Read, Write, Execute, Delete | Read, Write, Execute, Delete |
| Full Control | All | All |

**Table W-1.**    *Permissions for Folders*

| Standard File Permission | Individual Permissions |
|---|---|
| No Access | None |
| Read | Read, Execute |
| Change | Read, Write, Execute, Delete |
| Full Control | All |

**Table W-2.** *Permissions for Files*

## Windows NT Server

Windows NT is Microsoft's advanced operating system that provides full 32-bit operations on high-performance single-processor and multiprocessor systems. It includes built-in security that meets government ratings and networking support that is optimized to run back-end applications for a large number of clients. The Windows NT operating system was designed specifically to serve the needs of network users and to provide high levels of performance and security. A few of Windows NT's most important features are outlined here:

- **32-bit modular architecture** Data is transferred in 32-bit blocks, which provides better performance than 16-bit applications provide.

- **Flat address space** Windows NT accesses all of a system's memory as a linear block of memory, rather than the segmented memory architecture that was common in previous operating systems. This enables larger and more efficient applications.

- **Processor support** Windows NT runs on Intel, MIPS, DEC Alpha, and PowerPC processors. The retail version of Windows NT Server supports up to four processors, but it has the capability of supporting up to 32 processors when modified by system vendors.

- **Preemptive multitasking** Windows NT uses *preemptive multitasking,* a scheme in which the operating system is in charge of allocating processing time to applications so no single application can overuse the processor.

- **Multithreading** Windows NT is a *multithreading* operating system, which means that more than one process can execute at the same time. This is especially beneficial on multiprocessor systems.

- **Network and distributed computing support**   The Windows environment supports workgroup (peer-to-peer) networking and domain networking (which provides centralized storage of user account information). All Windows environments support the TCP/IP, IPX/SPX, and NetBEUI protocols, as well as popular interprocess communication protocols for distributed computing, including Windows Sockets and RPCs (remote procedure calls).

- **Internet and Web support**   The latest versions of Windows NT include Web server software, DNS Server, and multiprotocol routing support.

- **Future enhancements**   Microsoft is enhancing Windows NT version 5.0 with features such as Windows NT Directory Services. You can find out about these new features at http://www.microsoft.com/windowsnt.

## Security Features

Windows NT supports C2-level security, which is the U.S. Department of Defense's criteria for a secure system. The C2 rating is required for systems that are installed at many U.S. government installations. The characteristics of C2 are described under "C2 Security Rating." Note that no operating system is ever C2 certified. Certification applies to a particular installation, including hardware, software, and the environment that the system is in. But Microsoft designed Windows NT to meet the C2 ratings as closely as possible.

All resources in Windows NT are treated as individual objects and only the Windows NT operating system can provide access to those objects. Examples of objects are files, which can be opened, read, written, and closed, as well as windows, which can be opened, resized, painted, scrolled, minimized, maximized, and closed. No program can directly access an object. Therefore, the operating system can check and verify every access to objects that programs want to make.

Because Windows NT provides a consistent interface, it can also provide a consistent security mechanism to control access, making the Windows NT security system very robust. While Windows NT controls access to objects, it also tracks accesses and attempted accesses and produces audit records that are useful for tracing security problems. Windows NT also sets quotas for accessing objects to make sure that a single user does not overuse resources.

### User Logon and Access Security

All current Windows operating systems, including Windows 95, Windows 98, and Windows NT, support both workgroup and domain network models. How workgroups and domains apply to Windows NT is outlined here:

**W**

- **Workgroups**  In this arrangement, Windows users share files and resources with a local group of other computer users. Users are in charge of sharing resources on their systems, but if a Windows NT system is part of the network, it can provide a central place to create and store user accounts that other users can access when they want to define who can access the resources on their computer.

- **Domains**  Domains provide a way for administrators to implement high levels of security, but require that at least one Windows NT Server system be available. A domain is a logical grouping of systems and users within a department, division, or other organizational structure that is centrally managed by some authority. User account information is stored in a database on a central Windows NT Server that is shared by all the Windows NT Servers in the domain. Refer to "Domains in Windows NT" for more information.

Windows NT Server has sophisticated security features that are discussed further under "Windows NT File System" and "Windows NT Permissions."

## Fault Tolerance and System Protection Features

Fault-tolerant systems are designed to withstand hardware failures and software errors. For example, a fault-tolerant feature called *disk mirroring* writes data to two disks at the same time. If one disk in the pair fails, the other disk remains accessible to users. Windows NT Server supports the use of UPSs (uninterruptible power supplies) and RAID (redundant arrays of inexpensive disks) configurations.

A UPS is designed to protect against power failures by providing battery power to the system. If power fails, a UPS automatically supplies power and sends a signal to Windows NT Server to inform it that it is running on battery power. The server then performs an orderly shutdown of applications, services, and the file system before battery power is depleted.

Windows NT Server supports disk mirroring and disk striping. With disk striping, data is divided and written to multiple disk drives to improve performance and protect against disk failure. Should one of the drives in the array fail, the data can be reconstructed with parity information that is stored on the drives.

**RELATED ENTRIES**    Microsoft; Microsoft BackOffice; Microsoft Exchange Server; Microsoft Transaction Server; NetPC; Windows; Windows NT Directory Services; Windows NT File System; Windows NT Permissions; *and* X.500 Directory Services

**INFORMATION ON THE INTERNET**

Microsoft's Windows NT site                http://www.microsoft.com/ntserver

# Windows Sockets

*See* WinSock.

## WINS (Windows Internet Naming Service)

WINS runs on Windows NT Server-based networks. It is a service that keeps a database of computer name-to-IP address mappings so that the NetBIOS computer names used in Windows network environments can be mapped to IP addresses when the underlying network is IP-based. When a user needs to access some computer, the NetBIOS name is referenced, and this name is handed to the nearest WINS server, which then returns an IP address. WINS is almost completely automatic from an administrative point of view. It builds its own database over time and automatically updates itself.

## WinSock

Windows Sockets, or "WinSock" as it is commonly called, is the interface that allows Microsoft Windows programs to interface with TCP/IP (Transmission Control Protocol/Internet Protocol) networks. The standard is now pervasive, and all Windows applications, as well as IBM OS/2 applications, are developed to the standard. The standard was first discussed in 1991 and has been under continuous development since. The latest version, WinSock 2.0, has some interesting features, as discussed later.

WinSock was originally developed because many different vendors had developed TCP/IP protocol stacks that had their own application interfaces. With many different TCP/IP stacks available, product developers often had to choose one stack over another or support all the available APIs at great expense. Windows Sockets was developed by a group of vendors as a standard that could tie together the inconsistencies in PC-based TCP/IP products on the market. The specification is also called Windows Network Transit Protocol. It allows Windows applications to communicate regardless of underlying protocols. The specification was released in June 1992 and is available free to developers.

WinSock is designed to provide the same types of services that Berkeley Sockets provide in the UNIX environment. Programmers and developers who are familiar with either standard can easily make the transition to working in the other standard. In the Windows environment, WinSock is implemented as a DLL (dynamic link library) that sits above the TCP/IP protocol stack and below applications that need to access that protocol stack. The DLL has a top layer that applications interface with and a bottom layer that interfaces with TCP/IP. Program developers simply write applications to work with the top layer of WinSock. WinSock then converts commands and messages from applications to work with the underlying TCP/IP protocol stack.

**NOTE:** *The WinSock Group is a loose industry coalition involved in the creation of WinSock specifications. The WinSock Lab is a group of vendors organized by Stardust Technologies that performs WinSock interoperability testing.*

## WinSock 2

WinSock 2 is the latest version of the Windows Sockets interface. It is available for Windows 95 in a redistributable package and shipped with Windows NT version 4.0 and later versions. The Intel Web site given at the end of this topic has complete information on WinSock 2, along with a developer's kit.

The new interface maintains backward compatibility with previous versions of WinSock while extending support beyond TCP/IP networks by supporting multiple communication protocols. In particular, WinSock 2 now supports real-time multimedia communications across a variety of communication infrastructures. It provides "hooks" to access QoS (quality of service) features and prioritization features in ATM networks and networks that support such protocols as 3Com's PACE (priority access control enabled).

**NOTE:** *Prioritization refers to tagging packets with priority levels so that high-priority traffic is delivered ahead of low-priority traffic. QoS refers to setting priority levels, guaranteeing delivery, and reserving bandwidth on a network.*

With these hooks, software developers can finally create applications that can request a particular priority or QoS feature from underlying networks that offer these features. This will allow an application to request the kind of service level it needs from a network in order to deliver real-time voice and video without delays that cause distortion.

Note that IP (Internet Protocol) does not natively support QoS features, but the IETF (Internet Engineering Task Force) is developing the RSVP (Resource Reservation Protocol) to provide some semblance of QoS. The WinSock 2 specification defines how applications can request bandwidth reservations from RSVP-enabled networks. The specification is called WinSock 2 GQoS (Generic QoS) Mapping.

**RELATED ENTRIES**    Sockets API; TCP/IP (Transmission Control Protocol/Internet Protocol); *and* UNIX

### INFORMATION ON THE INTERNET

| | |
|---|---|
| WinSock 2 Developer Resource Center | http://www.stardust.com/wsresource |
| Sockets WinSock Development Information (a wealth of information and links!) | http://www.sockets.com |
| Winsock Archives, FAQs, and Related URLs | http://webcom.com/~llarrow/winsock.html |
| The alt.winsock FAQ | http://www.well.com/user/nac/alt-winsock-faq.html |

Intel Winsock 2 information (including    http://www.intel.com/IAL/winsock2
developer kit)

Stroud's Consummate Winsock    http://cws.internet.com
Applications

## Wired for Management

Intel's WfM (Wired for Management) initiative seeks to raise the level of management
capabilities for mobile, desktop, and server platforms. It complements Microsoft's
ZAWS (Zero Administration for Windows) initiative, which helps administrators
manage operating systems and applications. Together, WfM and ZAWS are designed
to provide an environment for planning, deploying, and managing distributed
computing environments.

According to Intel, WfM defines a baseline set of requirements for managing
hardware, including requirements for instrumentation, remote wake-up, power
management, and service boot capability. It enables centralized system management,
including inventory, fix/repair, configuration, and diagnostics, and provides for
off-hours maintenance to minimize downtime. WfM includes support for DMI, as
described under "DMI (Desktop Management Interface)." WfM would allow a
technician to diagnose and upgrade a remote system while the user of that system
continues working on other tasks. It also allows software upgrades in the background
or during scheduled hours.

Both Intel and Microsoft are working together to develop the Network PC (NetPC)
specification. The companies are also working on the PC 98 System Design Guideline
and the WHIIG (Windows Hardware Instrumentation Implementation Guide),
expected to be available in late 1997 or early 1998. Information about these works is
available at the Intel and Microsoft Web sites.

**RELATED ENTRIES**    Configuration Management; DMI (Desktop Management
Interface); DMTF (Desktop Management Task Force); NetPC; Network Management;
*and* Zero Administration for Windows Initiative

### INFORMATION ON THE INTERNET

Intel's Wired for Management site    http://www.intel.com/ManagedPC/index.htm

Microsoft's Zero Administration    http://www.microsoft.com/windows/zaw
for Windows site

## Wireless Communications

Wireless communications is all about transmitting signals through air and space
using radio, microwave, and infrared frequencies in the megacycle/second and

W

kilomegacycle/second range. Other wireless transmission techniques are also possible, such as direct point-to-point laser systems, but these systems are not as common as the radio, microwave, and infrared systems discussed in this section. The three wireless communication categories that are discussed are

- **Wireless mobile communications** Radio communications over public carrier facilities using packet-radio, cellular networks, and satellite stations for users who are "out of the office" and "on the road."
- **Wireless LAN communications** Radio communications within a company's premises over privately owned equipment. This usually involves connecting PCs within a single office or floor of a building.
- **Wireless bridging and internetworking** Radio communications used to connect buildings and other facilities in campus areas, metropolitan areas, or offices at other locations on the planet (using satellites).

Each of these technologies is discussed in the following sections.

## Wireless Mobile Communications

Mobile communication is used to keep in touch with roving salespeople, delivery trucks, field technicians, and other personnel. Mobile computer users use wireless communication to connect with corporate networks, query corporate databases, exchange electronic mail, transfer files, and even participate in collaborative computing. This is all being done with portable computers, PDAs (personal digital assistants), and a variety of small wireless communication devices. Users are also connecting to the Internet over these devices, and a special language called HDML (Hand-held Device Markup Language) has been devised just for this purpose. See "HDML (Hand-held Device Markup Language)" for more information.

Operating system vendors are taking mobile users into consideration by building new features that keep track of mobile user locations and maintain environments from one session to another. For example, as a mobile user travels from site to site, he or she disconnects and reconnects to remote systems on a regular basis. The operating system can restore connections and the desktop of the previous session automatically. If a user was accessing a database, previous queries to that database are waiting for the user the next time he or she connects. PDAs use interfaces that are often foreign to most network operating systems and applications. However, vendors are working to integrate these systems as the number of mobile computer users increases.

Mobile computing naturally involves telephone carriers or other service providers. Users must be concerned with the level of access (range and signal penetration), potential data transfer rates, and store-and-forward capabilities that allow users to pick up messages when they come back into range. For example, data transfer rates to and from mobile devices using the communication systems described later are low, from 8 Kbits/sec to 19.2 Kbits/sec. Error-correction requirements can drastically reduce transmission rates.

The following topics in this book describe wireless communications for mobile users:

- **AMPS (Advanced Mobile Phone Service)** Describes the oldest original analog circuit-switched cellular phone systems

- **CDPD (Cellular Digital Packet Data)** Describes how to package data and carry it over existing analog cellular radio systems such as AMPS

- **Cellular Communication Systems** Discusses the differences between analog and digital cellular systems

- **GSM (Global System for Mobile Communications)** Describes the all-digital cellular system being deployed around the world

- **Mobile Computing** Describes mobile computing technologies

- **Packet-Radio Communications** Describes services offered by nationwide radio data communication services such as ARDIS (Advanced National Radio Data Service) and RAM Mobile Data

- **PCS (Personal Communications Services)** Describes how GSM services are being deployed in the United States

Digital systems use a specific transport mechanism to move information between the mobile user and the base station. The following are two primary transport mechanisms, which are described in more detail under their own headings in this book:

- **CDMA (Code Division Multiple Access)** CDMA uses spread spectrum techniques in which data bits in each conversation are coded and transmitted simultaneously with other conversations. The code helps each receiver access the bits that are meant for it. The coded data is spread out in a very wide band signal, which is hard for eavesdroppers to listen in on.

- **TDMA (Time Division Multiple Access)** This is a time-slot technique in which each device on the network is given a specific time slot in which to transmit. The time allocation for a device is fixed. Even if the device has nothing to transmit, the time slot is still reserved.

*NOTE: Refer to the above sections in this book for Web links related to wireless mobile communications.*

## Wireless LAN Communications

As mentioned, wireless LANs are typically located within an office environment. For example, products from RadioLAN can transmit up to 120 feet in semi-open offices and over 800 feet in open air offices. Most wireless LAN designs employ a fixed-position wireless transceiver (transmitter/receiver) that occupies a central location within an office. Users with portable computers are allowed some mobility, typically within the immediate area of the transceiver. Wireless LANs can eliminate the need to run cable, especially if the LAN site is a temporary installation or serves a workgroup that might disband in the near future.

A typical wireless LAN configuration consists of a transceiver unit connected to servers and other equipment using standard Ethernet cable. The transceiver broadcasts and receives signals from workstations around it, as shown in Figure W-6.

There are several techniques for wireless data transmission, as described here:

- **Infrared light**  This method offers a wide bandwidth that transmits signals at extremely high rates. Infrared light transmissions operate by line of sight, so the source and receiver must be aimed at or focused on each other, similar to a television remote control. Obstructions in the office environment must be considered, but mirrors can be used to bend infrared light if necessary. Because infrared light transmissions are susceptible to strong light from windows or other sources, systems that produce stronger beams might be necessary. Note that infrared light is not regulated by the government and there are no restrictions on transmission rates. Typical transmission speeds range up to 10 Mbits/sec. Refer to "Infrared Technologies" for more information.

- **Spread spectrum radio**  This technique broadcasts signals in two frequency bands: 900 MHz and 2.4 GHz. Neither of these bands requires FCC licensing. Spread spectrum radio does not interfere with conventional radio because its energy levels are too weak. Transmission speeds are typically in the 2-Mbit/sec range, and signaling distance is below 1,000 feet, but these speeds and ranges are being improved. Refer to "Spread Spectrum Signaling" for more information.

- **Narrowband (or single-frequency) radio**  This technique is similar to a broadcast from a radio station. You tune in to a "tight" frequency band on both the transmitter and receiver. The signal can penetrate walls and is spread over a wide area, so focusing is not required. However, narrowband radio transmissions have problems with radio reflections (ghosting) and certain frequencies are regulated by the FCC.

A wireless LAN has a number of advantages. It does not require cabling and is relatively cheap to maintain. However, the wireless LAN market has been weak because data rates were below 2 Mbits/sec for most products. But in early 1997, the

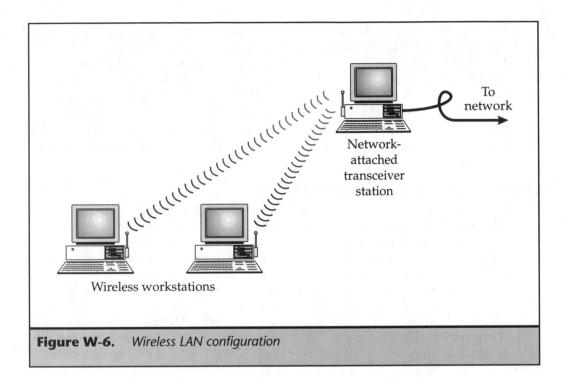

**Figure W-6.**   *Wireless LAN configuration*

FCC opened up 300 MHz of spectrum for unlicensed wireless local area networking. The spectrum is from 5.15 to 5.35 GHz and 5.725 to 5.825 GHz, which is a high enough frequency that data rates can go as high as 20 Mbits/sec. The spectrum is free to use, just like cordless telephone spectrum. Many emerging high-speed wireless LAN products use this new frequency. Apple Computer is mainly responsible for pushing the FCC (Federal Communications Commission) to unlicense the spectrum. It intends to develop products for use in schools, where rewiring is often not cost justified. The spectrum is commonly called the U-NII (Unlicensed National Information Infrastructure) and is discussed under "NII (National Information Infrastructure)."

RadioLAN introduced the first wireless LAN to operate in the unlicensed 5.8 GHz radiofrequency band. The system combines narrowband, single frequency transmission with low power and achieves data rates of 10 Mbits/sec. The frequency band is not crowded by competing devices (cordless phones, microwave ovens, etc.). The products operate at low power, which results in less electromagnetic radiation than other wireless technologies.

**W**

In June of 1997, the IEEE (Institute of Electrical and Electronic Engineers) approved the 802.11 wireless LAN specification, which spells out interoperability standards for 1-Mbit/sec to 2-Mbit/sec wireless LAN devices. The standard also promotes wireless bridging between networks. However, many feel that the technology is "too little, too late." In fact, the IEEE is already working on a 10-Mbit/sec enhancement. The current standard specifies operation in the 2.4 GHz frequency range using spread spectrum, infrared, and other techniques. Aironet Wireless Digital Ocean and Lucent Technologies were developing a common access point protocol to ensure interoperability at the time of this writing.

## Wireless Bridging and Internetworking

Connecting two separate networks is usually an easy task. You install a pair of bridges or routers and connect cable between the two devices, or use a dial-up or dedicated telephone line. But such connections are not always practical or cost effective. In campus environments or metropolitan areas, it may be more practical to use wireless systems to connect networks. Once again, data transfer rates are the most important consideration, but equipment costs and the eventual savings over dial-up lines or private cabling are another important consideration.

Wireless bridging issues are less complex than wireless LAN communications because connections are usually point-to-point and don't need to deal with issues such as walls and reflections. The bridge must perform filtering to keep unnecessary traffic from crossing the link, or a router can be used to control traffic between networks. Wireless bridging can also be used to back up other types of data connections.

Most wireless bridges use frequency-hopping spread spectrum radio techniques, which are not susceptible to interference and have a high level of security. Refer to "Spread Spectrum Signaling." Most products operate in the range of 3 to 6 miles, but some products have a range of 25 miles. Data rates are typically in the range of 2 Mbits/sec, but newer products operate in the 10-Mbit/sec range.

Raytheon Wireless Solutions is one vendor of wireless bridges. Its Raylink Access Point is a wireless LAN-to-Ethernet bridge that conforms to the IEEE 802.11 wireless LAN networking standard. Other vendors include Digital Ocean, OTC Telecom, Aironet Wireless Communication, Breeze Wireless Communications, C-SPEC, Proxim, and Windata. Web sites for these vendors are listed below under "Information on the Internet."

Other wireless solutions include terrestrial microwave systems and satellite communication systems. See "Microwave Communications" and "Satellite Communication Systems" for more details.

**RELATED ENTRIES**  AMPS (Advanced Mobile Phone Service); CDPD (Cellular Digital Packet Data); Cellular Communication Systems; GSM (Global System for Mobile Communications); HDML (Hand-held Device Markup Language); Microwave Communications; Mobile Computing; Mobile IP; PCS (Personal Communications Services); Remote Access; *and* Satellite Communication Systems

**INFORMATION ON THE INTERNET**

| | |
|---|---|
| RF Globalnet education and information center for RF, Microwave, and Wireless | http://www.rfmicrowave.com |
| IEEE P802.11 Working Group for Wireless Local Area Networks | http://stdsbbs.ieee.org/groups/802/11 |
| Wireless LAN Alliance | http://www.wlana.com |
| Cellular Network Perspective, Inc. (wireless publications) | http://www.cadvision.com/cnp-wireless |
| PCIA (Personal Communications Industry Association) | http://www.pcia.com |
| SRS Technologies' RF Products site | http://www.srs-rf.com |
| George Gilder's The New Rule of the Wireless article | http://homepage.seas.upenn.edu/~gaj1/wireless.html |
| International Trade Administration's communication industry information | http://www.ita.doc.gov/industry/tai/telecom/industry.html |
| CTIA (Cellular Telecommunications Industry Association) | http://www.wow-com.com |
| AT&T's Wireless site | http://www.attws.com |
| Aironet Wireless Communications, Inc. | http://www.aironet.com |
| ARDIS | http://www.ardis.com |
| Breeze Wireless Communications, Inc. | http://www.breezecom.com |
| C-SPEC Corporation | http://www.c-spec.com |
| Digital Ocean | http://www.digitalocean.com |
| OTC Telecom, Inc. | http://www.ezylink.com |
| Proxim | http://www.proxim.com |
| RadioLAN | http://www.radiolan.com |
| Raytheon Wireless Solutions | http://www.raytheon.com/re/adc/raylink.html |
| Windata, Inc. | http://www.windata.com |

## Wiring and Wiring Standards

*See* Cable and Cable Installation; TIA/EIA Structured Cabling Standards; Topology; *and* Transmission Media, Methods, and Equipment.

## Workflow Management

The purpose of workflow software is to automate document procedures in an organization by replacing paper systems with electronic documents. A network provides the routing system that moves documents to and from storage, and among users who need to view and make changes to the documents or sign the documents and validate their authenticity. Workflow software encourages workgroup collaboration by automating processes and eliminating footwork.

A typical workflow application combines document imaging with electronic messaging and advanced security features such as digital signatures, which can provide proof that documents are from the specified source and that they have been validated by the person indicated in the form.

In accounting environments, documents typically move from clerks to supervisors in various stages of processing and validation. A workflow package can display the forms used by an organization for a clerk to fill out. Some fields in the form are automatically filled out by the software, based on the job or the clerk manipulating the form. It's possible to assign predefined routing schemes to forms and eliminate some of the management headaches associated with manual paper flow. Forms are sent directly to the person who is supposed to handle the next step in the procedure. Automated features prevent hang-ups in forms processing. For example, users can be alerted when a form must be dealt with to prevent overdue charges or other problems caused by late processing. Publishing is another example of a collaborative environment that can benefit from workflow software. Documents are transferred from writer to editor to production in stages, using the network and its resources to store and eventually print the completed work.

These are some of the key features of workflow software:

- Documents contain routing information that serves to distribute the document to predefined users or devices.

- Documents can have simultaneous access.

- A document is viewed as "under construction" until it exits the workflow process.

- The software has a filing system, queue, and workflow manager that keep the system running.

- Authorized users sign off at various stages, locking parts or all of the document from further editing.

Most workflow software provides some sort of security mechanism, usually in the form of authentication and digital signatures. With this security, the recipient is sure of the sender's authenticity, that the document is authentic, and that it hasn't been altered in the transmission. Likewise, the sender is assured that any alterations to the document by the recipient can be detected.

From a management point of view, workflow software can help an organization track how information is flowing and how to better manage that flow. Workflow software can eliminate many time-consuming and often expensive activities such as meetings, phone calls, and express mail deliveries. But as users take to the new software, bandwidth requirements will increase. Workflow software allows users to view large image files, graphics, sound, and even video. This type of traffic can saturate the network.

**RELATED ENTRIES**    Collaborative Computing; Compound Documents; Document Management; Electronic Mail; Groupware; Information Publishing; Lotus Notes; Microsoft Exchange Server; *and* Netscape SuiteSpot

### INFORMATION ON THE INTERNET

| | |
|---|---|
| Workflow Management Coalition (see links page) | http://www.aiai.ed.ac.uk/project/wfmc |
| Association for Information and Image Management International | http://www.aiim.org |
| Anaxagoras | http://www.anaxagoras.com |
| Workflow tutorial at George Mason University | http://cne.gmu.edu/modules/workflow |
| Ensemble, from Filenet | http://www.filenet.com |
| InConcert, from InConcert | http://www.inconcert.com |
| OPEN/workflow, from Wang | http://www.wang.com |
| PaperClip Workflow, from PaperClip Software | http://www.paperclip.com |

**W**

RouteOne, from Syrius Research          http://www.routeone.com

Workman, from Reach Software          http://www.reachsoft.com

WorkPoint, from WorkPoint Systems     http://www.workpoint.com

# World Wide Web

*See* Internet; Web Technologies and Concepts.

# World Wide Web Consortium

*See* W3C (World Wide Web Consortium).

# WOSA (Windows Open Services Architecture)

WOSA is an architecture that promotes the easy integration of Windows and Windows-based applications within enterprise environments. It provides three categories of information resource services:

- **Common application services**   Includes ODBC (Open Database Connectivity), MAPI (Messaging API), and TAPI (Telephony API), all of which are covered under separate headings in this book. LSAPI (License Service API) is an API that helps automate software licensing.

- **Communication services**   These services include Windows SNA API (provides open access to existing IBM SNA APIs), Windows Sockets API (provides programs with an interface to networking protocols), and Microsoft RPC (Remote Procedure Call). Refer to "WinSock" and "RPC (Remote Procedure Call)" for more information.

- **WOSA extensions for vertical markets**   Includes extensions for financial services and extensions for real-time market data.

**RELATED ENTRIES**   Microsoft; Windows; *and* Windows NT Server

**INFORMATION ON THE INTERNET**

Microsoft Corporation          http://www.microsoft.com

## X12 Accredited Standards Committee

X12 is an EDI (Electronic Data Interchange) standard that provides a uniform way for businesses to exchange electronic documents and business transactions. The DISA (Data Interchange Standards Association) was chartered by ANSI (American National Standards Institute) to provide the X12 committee with administrative support. DISA is a not-for-profit organization that supports the development and use of electronic data interchange standards in electronic commerce.

**RELATED ENTRIES**    EDI (Electronic Data Interchange); Electronic Commerce; *and* Extranet

**INFORMATION ON THE INTERNET**

DISA (Data Interchange Standards          http://www.disa.org/x12
Association)

## X2

*See* Modems.

## X.25

The X.25 protocol is a CCITT (ITU) recommendation that defines connections of terminals and computers to packet-switching networks. Packet-switching networks route packets of data through a network to destination nodes. Companies have used X.25 in place of dial-up or leased-line circuits as a way to set up links to remote offices or remote users.

X.25 is a well-established (and now somewhat dated) packet-switching service traditionally used to connect remote terminals to host systems. The service provides any-to-any connections for simultaneous users. Signals from multiple users on a network can be multiplexed through the X.25 interface into the packet-switched network and delivered to different remote sites. The X.25 interface supports line speeds up to 64 Kbits/sec. The protocol was standardized in 1976 and revised a number of times. The CCITT revised the standard in 1992 and boosted the speed to 2 Mbits/sec.

The packet-switching architecture of X.25 has advantages and disadvantages. Packets of information are routed through a mesh network based on destination address information in the packet header. Users can connect with many different sites, unlike circuit-oriented networks in which a dedicated path exists between only two points. However, because the network is shared, users may experience delays during heavy traffic loads.

Frame relay offers many of the same connection-oriented, packet-switched network services as X.25, but with better performance. X.25 was designed in the days when the physical network was prone to errors. Acknowledgments must be returned for every point-to-point link through the network that a packet takes. This produces

*XYZ*

unnecessary and excessive overhead on modern networks. Frame relay avoids excessive acknowledgments. Frame relay nodes simply look at the packet header destination information and immediately forward the packet, in some cases even before it is completely received. Frame relay does not require the state tables used in X.25 at each intermediate node to deal with management, flow control, and error checking. Nodes only need to detect missing frames and request a retransmission.

X.25 may be the only reliable way to set up international network links to countries with unreliable phone systems. Almost every country has X.25 services. In contrast, obtaining reliable dedicated circuits in some countries is next to impossible. In the United States, X.25 is available from most of the telecommunication carriers and VACs (value-added carriers). X.25 predates the OSI (Open Systems Interconnection) protocol model, so some of the terminology used to explain X.25 is different. The standard defines protocols in three layers, which closely correspond to the lower three layers of the OSI protocol stack:

- The *physical layer*, called the X.21 interface, defines the physical/electrical interface from the computer/terminal (data terminal equipment, or DTE) to the node of attachment in the X.25 packet-switching network. RS-232-C is often substituted for the X.21 interface.

- The *link access layer* defines data transmission as a sequence of frames. The protocol used is LAPB (Link Access Procedure Balanced), which is designed for point-to-point connections. It provides the frame structure, error, and flow-control mechanism for an asynchronous balanced-mode session. LAPB provides a way to acknowledge that a packet has reached each link in the network.

- The *packet layer* defines reliable virtual circuits through the packet-switched network. Thus, X.25 provides point-to-point data delivery rather than point-to-multipoint delivery.

X.25 supports switched and permanent virtual circuits. A virtual circuit is a "logical" communication channel between two endpoints across the packet-switched network. The use of a circuit guarantees that packets arrive in sequence because they follow the same path. It also provides reliable transport of data through the network. A switched circuit is a temporary, call-based circuit that is set up and dismantled once the data transfer is complete. A permanent virtual circuit is set up in advance by the carrier and provides continuous service. X.25 is a connection-oriented service, so packets do not require source and destination addresses. They follow the virtual circuit's path through the network.

X.25 networks are easy to install and maintain. Charges are based on the number of packets sent and, in some cases, the time connected. But other services such as frame relay are much more practical and provide better data rates. Still, X.25 is often the only choice available in some areas of the world.

**RELATED ENTRIES**   Carrier Services; Connection-Oriented and Connectionless Protocols; Frame Relay; Network Concepts; Packet and Cell Switching; Virtual Circuit; *and* WAN (Wide Area Network)

**INFORMATION ON THE INTERNET**

# X.400 Message Handling System

The CCITT (Consultative Committee for International Telephony and Telegraphy) which is part of the ITU (International Telecommunication Union), defined the X.400 MHS standard, an electronic system for exchanging messages among store-and-forward mail systems running on a wide variety of platforms. In the terminology of the ISO (International Organization for Standardization), X.400 is called the MOTIS (Message-Oriented Text Interchange System). The goal of the standard is to provide compatibility among multivendor products and interfaces as well as public and private message services.

X.400 was first introduced in 1984 and has been through several enhancements. It outlines the protocols, procedures, components, terminology, and testing methods required to build interoperable e-mail systems. X.400 is based on a distributed client/server model that includes the components described here and pictured in Figure X-1.

*XYZ*

- **UA (user agent)**   The UA is a software component that runs in the computer of every user attached to the X.400 system. It provides the functions that let users create e-mail messages, read received messages, or browse message lists. UAs communicate with one another through the messaging system, and each UA has a unique name. Users can look up these unique names by accessing a directory service such as the one defined by the X.500 standard, which is described under the next topic, "X.500 Directory Services."

- **MTA (message transfer agent)**   An MTA accepts messages from UAs and routes them to other MTAs. The MTA must translate the address information in the message and determine how to route the message. The MTA contains an agent of the X.500 directory services system for doing this. Address translation is required because of the many different types of networks possible within the enterprise. The MTA packages the message and addresses it with the address it has translated. It then sends the message to the MTA of the recipient.

- **MS (message store)** The MS is a storage area for messages that can't be delivered directly to a user because the user's system is offline or unavailable. Users can access their messages in the MS at any time.

- **AU (access unit)** An AU provides access to the mail system for other entities, such as fax, teletex, and telex users.

- **DS (directory system)** The DS contains a complete list of the names and addresses of other X.400 users. It usually follows the X.500 standard.

The X.400 message structure is the same for all systems. An *envelope header* contains a message ID, source and destination address, content type information, and encryption information. This information is in a form used by MTAs to route messages. Following the envelope header is the contents header, which contains To:, From:, cc:, Subject:, and other information that the recipient can read. Below this header is the body of the message.

Other services defined in X.400 include distribution lists, management domains, and security features:

- *Distribution lists* are groups of users. Mail sent to a distribution list is automatically sent to all users in the list. A user manages the list, and only specified users can submit mail to the list.

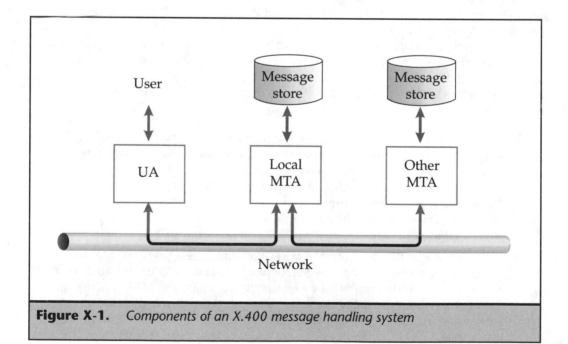

**Figure X-1.**   *Components of an X.400 message handling system*

- *Management domains* include the local PRMD (private management domain) and public X.400 service providers, called ADMDs (administrative management domains). ADMDs can provide delivery of messages to remote sites on a global scale.

- *Security* features specified in X.400 include source authentication, proof of correct delivery and receipt, detection of unauthorized users, protection against message alteration during transit, and other features.

At one time, many thought that X.400 would provide a global mail system, but with the rise of the Internet and Internet electronic mail protocols, X.400 has faded. While it is probably a better system than the Internet mail protocols, it is difficult to manage and use. In contrast, Internet mail is an open and pervasive standard that is easy to use.

**RELATED ENTRIES**  Electronic Mail; Groupware; *and* X.500 Directory Services

**INFORMATION ON THE INTERNET**

| | |
|---|---|
| Index to X.400 sites | http://domen.uninett.no/~hta/x400 |
| X.400 Message Handling Systems | http://www.ewos.be/mhs/gmhs.htm |
| Electronic Messaging Association | http://www.ema.org |
| Mapping between X.400 (RFC 1327) | http://www.internic.net/rfc/rfc1327.txt |
| Equivalences between 1988 X.400 and RFC 822 Message Bodies (RFC 1494) | http://www.internic.net/rfc/rfc1494.txt |
| Mapping between X.400 and RFC 822 Message Bodies (RFC 1495) | http://www.internic.net/rfc/rfc1495.txt |
| IETF MIME - X.400 Gateway (mixer) | http://www.ietf.org/html.charters/mixer-charter.html |

*XYZ*

# X.500 Directory Services

X.500 is a CCITT (ITU) recommendation for a "white pages" directory services system that can provide a global "look-up" service for people and objects everywhere. The standard defines a hierarchical tree-structured directory in which countries form the top level of the directory and organizations or organizational units branch from this tree as shown in Figure X-2. The original intent was to define an international authority at the root of the tree that would manage the global structure. X.500 can also be installed within an organization as a private directory service and can then be connected to the global X.500 directory service.

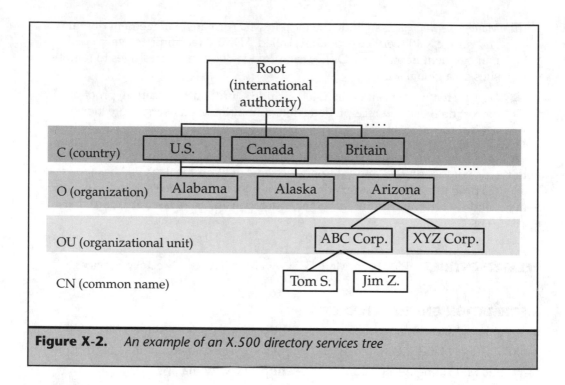

**Figure X-2.** *An example of an X.500 directory services tree*

X.500 defines how an organization can share names and the objects associated with them over a global network. A complete X.500 system is called a "directory." The X.400 electronic mail standard uses X.500 as its "white pages" directory service. X.500 is hierarchical in that there are administrative domains (organizations, divisions, departments, and workgroups) that provide information about the users and resources in those domains. X.500 is considered the best way to implement a directory service, but it costs more to implement and is slower than other methods.

X.500 directory services can provide information to electronic mail systems, applications that need to access resources elsewhere on the network, or management systems that need to know the name and location of entities on the network. The directory is a database, or DIB (directory information base) as it is called in the X.500 lexicon. Entries in the database are *objects*. For example, there are user account objects, resource objects (such as printers), and directory/file objects.

X.500 has proven to be more a complex system than most organizations need. In addition, it assumes that organizations want to open their directory structures for the world to see. Headhunters from competing organizations like this idea. In the meantime, the Internet has become the global internetwork of choice, not some network based on OSI standards. So X.500 has not become a popular standard. No international authority ever took charge of the top of the tree and few applications were ever offered that directly used the standard. However, some network operating system vendors such as Novell based their own directory services on X.500. See "Directory Services" and "NDS (Novell Directory Services)" for more information.

The LDAP (Lightweight Directory Access Protocol), now widely accepted in the Internet community, is actually a subset of X.500. LDAP was originally designed to work as a front-end client for X.500 directory services. A protocol called DAP (Directory Access Protocol) provides the interface for accessing these services. However, DAP requires the full OSI protocol stack and more computing resources than are available in many common desktop systems. LDAP is a stripped-down version of DAP that does not consume the system resources required by DAP, and most important, it has been adapted to run on TCP/IP networks.

**RELATED ENTRIES**   Directory Services; LDAP (Lightweight Directory Access Protocol); LIPS (Lightweight Internet Person Schema); NDS (Novell Directory Services); *and* Windows NT Server

### INFORMATION ON THE INTERNET

| | |
|---|---|
| LDAP & X.500: Road Map & FAQ | http://www-leland.stanford.edu/group/networking/directory/x500ldapfaq.html |
| X.500 Pointers | http://www.nexor.com/public/directory.html |
| Barbara Shuh's Introduction to directories and X.500 | http://www.nlc-bnc.ca/pubs/netnotes/notes45.htm |
| Colin Robbins's (NEXOR) X.500 page | http://www.nexor.co.uk/public/directory.html |
| Executive Introduction to Directory Services Using the X.500 Protocol (RFC 1308) | http://www.internic.net/rfc/rfc1308.txt |
| Technical Overview of Directory Services Using the X.500 Protocol (RFC 1309) | http://www.internic.net/rfc/rfc1309.txt |
| Introduction to White Pages Services based on X.500 (RFC 1684) | http://www.internic.net/rfc/rfc1684.txt |

*XYZ*

# X.509

X.509 is an ITU (International Telecommunication Union) recommendation that defines a framework for authentication (i.e., services). It is based on X.500, which itself is not yet completely defined. As a result, the X.509 standard is being interpreted in a number of ways, depending on the vendor that decides to use it. X.509 was first published in 1988, and subsequent revisions have been published to address security problems that have cropped up since the initial publication.

X.509 supports both secret-key (single-key) cryptography and public-key cryptography. X.509 defines the field contents of a certificate, which include version number, serial number, signature algorithm ID, issuer name, validity period, subject (user) name, subject public-key information, issuer unique identifier, subject unique identifier, extensions, and signature on the above fields.

A certificate authority basically puts the public key of some person that it has identified into the certificate and then signs the certificate with its private key. This "binds" the key to the certificate. Anyone that needs to use the subject's public key can open the certificate with the certificate authority's public key (it was signed or locked down with the certificate authority's private key). Thus, the user must trust that the certificate authority has validated the owner of the public key and that the public key used to open the certificate is indeed the public key of the certificate authority. This is where PKIs (public-key infrastructures) come into play. A PKI is a hierarchy of certificate authorities that verify each other's public keys, as discussed under "PKI (Public-Key Infrastructure)."

**RELATED ENTRIES**   Authentication and Authorization; Certificates and Certification Systems; Cryptography; Digital Signatures; PKI (Public-Key Infrastructure); Public-Key Cryptography; *and* Security

## INFORMATION ON THE INTERNET

| | |
|---|---|
| Public Key Infrastructure References | http://www.xcert.com/~marcnarc/PKI |
| E. Gerck and MCG's Overview of Certification Systems: X.509, CA, PGP and SKIP | http://novaware.cps.softex.br/mcg/cert.htm |
| Gateway to Information Security X.509 site | http://www.securityserver.com/cgi-local/ssis.pl/category/@x509.htm |
| IETF Simple Public Key Infrastructure (spki) charter | http://www.ietf.org/html.charters/spki-charter.html |
| IETF Public-Key Infrastructure (X.509) (pkix) Working Group | http://www.ietf.org/html.charters/pkix-charter.html |

| | |
|---|---|
| NIST's PKI site | http://csrc.ncsl.nist.gov/pki |
| NIST's PKI Technical Working Group | http://csrc.ncsl.nist.gov/pki/twg/twgindex.html |
| Carl Ellison's Generalized Certificates paper | http://www.clark.net/pub/cme/html/cert.html |

## XML (Extensible Markup Language)

XML is a subset of the SGML (Standard Generalized Markup Language) that has been defined by the W3C (World Wide Web Consortium). XML is designed to make data stored and published on Web sites not only easier to manage, but much richer in presentation. XML allows Web developers to define the content of documents by creating custom tags, unlike HTML (Hypertext Markup Language), which is locked into a set of industry-standard tags (although Microsoft and Netscape have been known to create their own). XML borrows many features from SGML, including the need to create a document type declaration, which defines what the customer tags are supposed to do when a user receives the document. You can refer to "SGML (Standard Generalized Markup Language)" or refer to W3C's Web site, at http://www.w3.org.

## X/Open

X/Open Company Ltd. was established to provide standards for the UNIX environment. Its main goal is to promote open systems protocols for UNIX languages, interfaces, networks, and applications. It also promotes portability of applications between the different UNIX environments and supports the IEEE (Institute of Electrical and Electronic Engineers) POSIX (Portable Operating System Interface for UNIX) specifications.

In 1996, The Open Group was formed by merging the OSF (Open Software Foundation) and X/Open Company Ltd. Refer to The Open Group's Web site at http://www.opengroup.org for more information.

**XYZ**

## X Window

The X Window System, or "X" as it is sometimes called, can be thought of as a terminal for UNIX environments in one respect. X was developed in the early 1990s as a basic client/server system, except that the terminology is reversed from the way people think of client/server today. In X terminology, the X server is the client terminal that provides display output and keyboard input functions. A host is typically a powerful machine that runs applications for multiple X terminals. The X terminal may be a basic terminal device or a desktop computer.

An interesting aspect of X is that it is the model for newer NC (Network Computer) systems, which are "thin client," small-footprint computers that run Java applications, relying heavily on centralized servers to do much of the work.

X was designed from the beginning as a client/server platform for building remote applications. Users interact with a GUI (graphical user interface) that sends instructions back to the application running on the host. X provides an environment for developing graphical user interfaces, and a developer can use a GUI development toolkit such as Motif to create the applications.

The latest version of The X Window System is System 11 Release 6.3 (X11R6.3). The most significant feature of this version is the ability to use X to create and access interactive applications on the Web. According to The Open Group, which manages the X specification, "any application linked to the Web using X11R6.3 can be located, accessed, and executed with the same tools used for accessing static HTML documents today—Web browsers. X11R6.3 provides seamless access to remotely hosted programs over the Internet and World Wide Web."

The significance of this is that existing shrink-wrapped or custom applications can be seamlessly accessed from within an X11R6.3-enabled Web browser. No changes are required to application programs. The browser can invoke remote applications, and its integration with HTTP (Hypertext Transfer Protocol) protocols makes access to applications platform independent, allowing "universal access" to any application. Optimization techniques are used to improve performance over WANs and serial lines by using caching, compression, and other techniques.

**RELATED ENTRIES**    CDE (Common Desktop Environment); Motif; The Open Group; *and* UNIX

### INFORMATION ON THE INTERNET

| | |
|---|---|
| X and Motif information page | http://www.cen.com/mw3 |
| The Open Group's X information | http://www.opengroup.org/tech/desktop/x |
| The XFree86 Project | http://www.xfree86.org |
| Jennifer Myers's Web page (see "X-Window System" section for links) | http://www.geek-girl.com/unix.html |

## Zero Administration for Windows Initiative

The Zero Administration for Windows, or ZAWS, initiative is a Microsoft scheme for managing Windows-based network clients. It automates the task of operating system updates, application installation, desktop configuration, and user access. It allows users to "roam" from location to location while maintaining the same desktop because personal desktop preferences and application information is stored on central servers.

The ZAWS initiative is designed to support "thin client," small-footprint computers such as the NetPC (see "NetPC") as well as other desktop systems.

Key capabilities enabled by the Zero Administration for Windows initiative are as follows:

- Centralized administration and control of desktop computers, with the ability to lock down desktop configurations
- Automatic operating system updates and application installations from a central location
- Stateless desktop computing, with persistent central data storage
- Side-by-side machine replacement in case of desktop hardware failure
- Client-side ability to cache data, thus improving performance, reducing network traffic, and enabling work to continue if the network fails

All of these features allow users to run applications and access data from anywhere without the need to transfer files and applications between computers. ZAWS also helps to reduce help desk and support calls because users operate with a familiar desktop wherever they go and the desktop information is stored in a central location that support staff can configure and troubleshoot. The desktop configuration can also be locked down to prevent users from changing it in a way that would make the desktop appear confusing the next time they log on.

Microsoft Windows NT 5.0 includes Hydra Server components, which provide multiuser capabilities as well as the capability to host a variety of desktops. Hydra delivers 32-bit Windows applications to "thin" clients, NetPCs, and legacy desktops, including UNIX, Macintosh, and older Windows-based PCs. The significance of multiuser capabilities is discussed under "WinFrame." WinFrame is a product from Citrix, a company that pioneered multiuser systems in the Windows NT network server environment. ZAWS is part of Microsoft's scheme to manage the desktops for these systems on centralized servers.

Intel's WfM (Wired for Management) initiative complements Microsoft's ZAWS initiative. While ZAWS is primarily software based, WfM is hardware based. Together, WfM and ZAWS are designed to provide an environment for planning, deploying, and managing distributed computing environments. According to Intel, WfM defines a baseline set of requirements for managing hardware, including requirements for instrumentation, remote wake-up, power management, and service boot capability. It enables centralized system management, including inventory, fix/repair, configuration, and diagnostics, and provides for off-hours maintenance to minimize downtime.

*XYZ*

**RELATED ENTRIES**   Configuration Management; DMI (Desktop Management Interface); DMTF (Desktop Management Task Force); Microsoft; NetPC; Network Management; Windows; Windows NT Server; *and* Wired for Management

### INFORMATION ON THE INTERNET

| | |
|---|---|
| Microsoft's Zero Administration for Windows site | http://www.microsoft.com/windows/zaw |
| Microsoft's management site | http://www.microsoft.com/management |
| Intel's Wired for Management site | http://www.intel.com/ManagedPC/index.htm |

# Appendix A

# Links for Finding Companies and Products

There are a number of exceptional Web sites that provide extensive links to companies, products, and technical information. Most sites categorize links so you can "drill down" and get a list of just what you are looking for. Here are the sites, listed in the order of my personal preference.

| | |
|---|---|
| Analysys Telecoms Virtual Library | http://www.analysys.com/vlib |
| Prof. Jeff MacKie-Mason's Telecom Information Resources on the Internet | http://www.spp.umich.edu/telecom |
| Webstart's Computer and Communication Hot Links | http://www.cmpcmm.com/cc |
| LAN Times Buyers Directory (sorted by companies or categories of products) | http://www.lantimes.com/lantimes/buyers |
| The ITU's list of Web sites | http://www.itu.int/Sites |
| Goodman's Book Marks | http://www.wp.com/goodmans |
| High Bandwidth Web page | http://www.specialty.com/hiband |
| Matt Noah's Technical Links | http://www.west.net/~noah/tech |

## Magazine Links

Computer-related magazines and journals often have Web sites that contain incredible amounts of information presented in articles, product reviews, lab test reports, and other documents. One of the best sources for magazine links is the Computer Information Center, which is listed below, along with some important magazine sites.

| | |
|---|---|
| Computer Information Center | http://www.compinfo.co.uk/itmag.htm |
| Analysys Telecoms Virtual Library, Journals and Other Electronic Media | http://www.analysys.com/vlib/journal.htm |
| Yahoo!'s Magazines links page | http://www.yahoo.com/Computers_and_Internet/Magazines |
| Prof. Jeffrey MacKie-Mason's Mailing Lists and On-line Publications | http://www.spp.umich.edu/telecom/online-pubs.html |
| LAN Times Online | http://www.lantimes.com |
| Data Communications Magazine | http://www.data.com |
| CMPnet TechWeb site | http://www.techweb.com |

## Telecommunications Companies

A complete list of telecommunications companies and operators around the globe can be found at the Analysys Telecoms Virtual Library Web site listed below. An alternate list is also provided:

| Analysys Telecoms Virtual Library operators list | http://www.analysys.com/vlib/operator.htm |
| Analysys Telecoms Virtual Library service providers list | http://www.analysys.com/vlib/service.htm |
| Prof. Jeffrey MacKie-Mason's Telecom Operating Companies list | http://www.spp.umich.edu/telecom/ telecom-operating.html |
| Prof. Jeffrey MacKie-Mason's Internet Service Providers list | http://www.spp.umich.edu/telecom/isp.html |

> **NOTE:** *Refer to "ISPs (Internet Service Providers)" for an additional list of Web sites that provide listings and information about ISPs.*

**LECS (LOCAL EXCHANGE CARRIERS)**   The following companies provide local carrier services in their respective regions of the United States.

| Ameritech, Inc. | http://www.ameritech.com |
| Bell Atlantic Corp. | http://www.bell-atl.com |
| Bell South | http://www.bell.bellsouth.com |
| GTE Service Corp. | http://www.gte.com |
| NYNEX Corp. | http://www.nynex.com |
| Pacific Bell | http://www.pacbell.com |
| Southwestern Bell (SBC Communications, Inc.) | http://www.sbc.com |
| US West Communications Group | http://www.uswest.com |

**INTEREXCHANGE CARRIERS**   The following carriers provide long-distance services between the areas covered by the local exchange carriers.

| AT&T Corp. | http://www.att.com |
| LDDS WorldCom, Inc. | http://www.wcom.com |
| GTE Service Corp. | http://www.gte.com |
| MCI Telecommunications Corp. | http://www.mci.com |
| Sprint Communications Co., L.P. | http://www.sprintbiz.com |
| MFS Communications Co., Inc. | http://www.mfsdatanet.com |
| Norlight Telecommunications, Inc. | http://www.norlight.com |

# Index

## A

## D

## E

## J

# O

## P

## Q

## R

# X

# Z

# About the CD

**How to Use the *Encyclopedia of Networking* CD-ROM:** The CD that accompanies this book contains a special electronic edition of the *Encyclopedia of Networking* by Modern Age Books. Now with this electronic version, you can easily store all of the valuable information contained in the book on your PC while the print version of the book remains in your office or home.

## System Requirements

The *Encyclopedia of Networking* CD will run on a Windows 95 computer (8MB RAM). You can install the entire book on your hard drive for best performance or run it from the CD to conserve hard drive space.

## Installation

To use the CD, you must first install it on your system. To start the installation program, please follow this procedure:

1. Click the Start button and choose Run.

2. Type d:\ (or the appropriate drive letter for running a CD on your system), and click the Browse button.

3. Choose either the Setup16 folder (for Win 3.1) or the Setup32 folder (for Win 95 or Win NT).

4. Click the setup.exe file, click OK, and follow the onscreen instructions.

*NOTE: If you are using or plan to use the Microsoft IntelliMouse, you will have difficulty running the electronic document on the enclosed CD-ROM. Please contact George Friedman at Modern Age Books (gfreidman@mabooks.com) to receive the latest edoc16.exe or edoc32.exe file and instructions for upgrading the engine for this book.*

## Getting Started

**Windows 3.1 Users:** Go into the Program Manager and double-click on the book icon.

**Windows 95 and NT Users:** Click the Start button and then point to Programs. Point to Modern Age Books and click on the book icon to start the book.

**Special Features Search Button:** The Search button invokes a dialog box that allows you to search for information anywhere in the electronic book using words and phrases. An assisted search gives you additional help in finding what you are looking for.

**Automatic History:** Keep a record of the last 40 pages referenced during searches.

**Go Back:** The Go Back button brings the user to the point from which the last hypertext jump was made.

**Pop-ups:** Notes and warnings trigger pop-up dialog boxes that appear when a user drags the mouse over or clicks an icon.

**Electronic Books:** To see more electronic books, come to the Modern Age Books marketplace Web site:

http//www.mabooks.com